READINGS IN SOCIOLOGY

Edgar A. Schuler • Thomas F. Hoult
MICHIGAN STATE UNIVERSITY ARIZONA STATE UNIVERSITY

°99

READINGS IN SOCIOLOGY

FOURTH EDITION

Duane L. Gibson • Wilbur B. Brookover
MICHIGAN STATE UNIVERSITY MICHIGAN STATE UNIVERSITY

THOMAS Y. CROWELL COMPANY • NEW YORK • ESTABLISHED 1834

Published in Canada by Fitzhenry and Whiteside Limited, Toronto.

3 4 5 6 7 8 9 10
L. C. Card 79-146068
ISBN 0-690-68478-9
Manufactured in the United States of America

PREFACE

TO THE FOURTH EDITION

With this, the fourth edition of *Readings in Sociology,* our book is completing its second decade of use in colleges and universities. As the editors, we are pleased with its wide acceptance and continued adoption, and like its predecessors, this edition attempts to portray and illuminate the concepts and principles of sociology rather than to analyze them in depth, leaving to text and instructor the latter critical function.

This purpose and approach of our book has continuously forced us to recognize that the changing nature of the world and of sociology requires substantial changes in the selections for each edition. In a sense, then, this book seems always to have been "in-process." Though we have permitted it to grow and change through inclusion of new selections reflecting the temper of the times, we have sought at the same time to retain the truly classic items whose utility clearly persists.

We had occasion, as we were preparing this 1971 version of our book, to review the state of the world during the period we were developing the first edition, and we were struck not only by many of the drastic changes that had occurred in the intervening years, but also by the similarity of others to the current condition. For example, major events during the twelve months prior to the appearance of the first edition in the spring of 1952 included the following:

A nationwide railroad strike that paralyzed rail transportation in this country.

A complaint by Prime Minister Nehru of India that Pakistan was violating the cease-fire agreement in Kashmir.

An accusation by Chinese Communists and the Soviet Union that the United States was engaging in germ warfare in the fighting in North Korea.

A rebellion against French rule in Indochina led by Ho Chi Minh and focusing heavily on guerrilla tactics.

Bombing by the Israeli Air Force of Syrian military positions in retaliation for an alleged violation of the Israeli frontier (finally brought to a halt by a cease-fire order of the United Nations Security Council).

A Russian proposal of joint disarmament and a ban on atomic weapons which was rejected by the United States with an accompanying demand that the USSR honor its already existing obligations.

It leaves one feeling almost as though the more things change, the more they stay the same. Or perhaps one might better say that the capacity (and willingness) to resolve human problems has not kept pace with the increase in knowledge and the developments in technology. In any event, this book aims to illustrate the concerns of sociologists within the context of the current scene, whether those concerns are new or abiding in character.

Our approach has made it possible, in each edition, to draw illustrative materials from some of the best writings of sociologists as well as from specialists in other disciplines and from journalists, essayists, and novelists, for our criteria for inclusion consisted basically of two elements: (a) does the article effectively *illustrate* a central concept, principle, theory, or problem, and (b) is it *readable?* Moreover, we have systematically sought to include selections from sources other than the American scene, in order to provide cross-cultural perspectives for the reader.

As to our social science objectives in preparing this readings book, our statement in the first edition still stands: "Believing in the possibility of genuine *liberal education,* [we] have sought to provide an orientation that will expand the reader's horizon and human concerns beyond his own immediate place and time; to inculcate a truly scientific humility in the face of diverse peoples, customs, and beliefs; and to affirm [our] own belief in the values of a maturing social science for our own democratic society, and for an increasingly rich and humane life for all peoples everywhere."

We are indeed pleased that the earlier editions have been used by a wide range of people, including high school students, college students and the general adult population. Although the selections have been chosen primarily because we felt they would contribute to sociological understanding in introductory college and university courses, we hope this edition also will prove useful and interesting to both younger and older audiences.

A manual containing objective questions based on each of the readings has been prepared by Carleton W. Smith for the convenience of teachers who use this book.

We wish to thank here all authors and publishers who made their work available for inclusion, though individual acknowledgments appear in footnotes at the beginning of each of the selections. As in the earlier editions, brief biographical information is also presented about each author.

The cooperation and assistance of numerous librarians and library staff members at Michigan State University and the Hayden Library at Arizona State University are gratefully acknowledged. Marcia Ditchie prepared the new and the updated biographical notes and, in addition, accurately and conscientiously prepared the manuscript for submission to the publisher. Georgia Ishikawa assisted in preparing the correlations table. To them, and to our able and dependable secretarial colleagues—at Michigan State University, Almeda Ritter and Laura Johnston and, at Arizona State University, the Department of Sociology office staff—we wish to express our deep appreciation.

We also acknowledge a debt to our students and professional colleagues who by their frank reactions to the earlier editions helped to shape our decisions regarding selections to be used, and by their continued use of the earlier editions encouraged us to undertake the preparation of this fourth edition.

Finally, we wish to express to the members of our respective families our gratitude for their much and prized assistance, and especially for their patient tolerance during the long period required to complete once more this demanding venture.

E.A.S. D.L.G.
T.F.H. W.B.B.

CONTENTS

III. PERSON AND GROUP

IV. SOCIAL ORGANIZATION: TYPES OF GROUP RELATIONSHIPS

V. SOCIAL ORGANIZATION: COLLECTIVE BEHAVIOR

VI. SOCIAL ORGANIZATION: STRATIFICATION AND MOBILITY

VII. SOCIAL ORGANIZATION: INSTITUTIONS AND ASSOCIATIONS

VIII. SOCIAL ORGANIZATION: COMMUNITY AND ECOLOGY

IX. SOCIAL PROCESSES

X. SOCIAL AND CULTURAL CHANGE: DISORGANIZATION, PLANNING, AND VALUES

EPILOGUE
SOCIOLOGY AND EDUCATION FOR ACTION

APPENDIXES: SOCIOLOGISTS AT WORK

PROLOGUE

SOCIAL SCIENCE IN LIBERAL EDUCATION

PERSPECTIVES OF STUART CHASE, PETER BERGER, ROBERT REDFIELD, AND ROBERT BIERSTEDT

Now that the practical usefulness of the social sciences in general, and sociology in particular, has become more widely accepted, many will study sociology because it will help them to earn a living. But acquaintance with sociology can have far more than economic value. Properly approached, the study of sociology can help us to improve the quality of our lives and realize our capabilities as human beings—in other words, it will help us to become liberally educated. In this prologue, the editors have assembled the ideas of four well-known writers and scholars, which they believe provide justification of sociology as a humanistic study. It is hoped that many of the subsequent selections, chosen with great care, will exemplify the position of Bierstedt, which is that "Sociology has an honorable place in the realm of humane letters and it belongs with the liberal arts as well as with the sciences."

MR. CHASE

. . . . .

To cope with the tough problems ahead of us we should be able to see all the way around them. Experts and specialists are invaluable, but, as specialists, they see only the trees, sometimes only the twigs under the trees. We need power to see the woods. We need generalists who do not get lost in the trees. This does not mean two kinds of people, for everyone is a specialist in some degree, perhaps as a typist, perhaps as a nuclear physicist. It means more room in our minds for the over-all view, especially for relationships and balancing of alternatives.

. . . The competence of the specialist today has overawed the intelligent layman until he says: "It's way over my head; I'll leave it to the experts." How often do we all say or think something like that? Yet it is a dangerous attitude in this day and age. It tends to create an oligarchy of knowledge, which can become a monopoly of power, a series of tight little principalities with no minds left to survey the whole country.

I know a generalist who is also a learned specialist. He has written me that he would like to tell his specialist confreres: "Wake up! Live at the level of your time! Crawl out of that talent-trap which you refer to as your 'field' and look around. You may learn something about the only era you will ever live in, and about the only species you will ever be a

SOURCE: Stuart Chase, *Some Things Worth Knowing*. • Stuart Chase is the author of many interpretive works in social science, especially in economics and communications. He has been an investigator for the Federal Trade Commission and has acted as a consultant for many organizations, among which are the United States Treasury, SEC, and UNESCO. His books include *The Proper Study of Mankind, The Tyranny of Words,* and *The Economy of Abundance.*

member of. You will certainly learn something about yourself!"

To leave learning exclusively to specialists is not only dangerous but weak. It deprives civilized people of an essential part of their life on earth, something that many primitive peoples have naturally exercised—the full expression of curiosity, honestly confronting the mystery of existence, trying to understand their world and themselves. It is pitiful to retreat from this facing of life, especially at a time when so much new knowledge is coming in. Even if the astrophysicists have shown the universe to be far grander and more complex than we used to think, shall we say: "It's all beyond me," and turn our backs and go indoors? Or shall we look up with new wonder and delight, trying to imagine the vast recesses of the whirling sky? Similarly for the marvels unfolding before the electronic microscope, and for new aspects of human behavior now being revealed.

• • • • •

A mature mind combines reliable information with good judgment, and one definition of good judgment is appreciation of relationships between fields of information. . . .

The intelligent layman . . . also wants to know what knowledge is available to promote negotiation and accommodation between the great powers. This is a question in the area of the behavioral sciences.

He wants to understand too what can be done to lessen tension between the races, and between worker and employer, and how to improve community relations. He would especially like to understand himself better, and why he often has so much trouble doing what he thinks he ought to do, and how he can get on more happily with his family, and in his personal relations generally.

Aside from these rather practical motives a good generalist possesses a healthy curiosity. . . . How and where [Homo sapiens] originally developed, how he survived as a hunter for many thousands of years, as a farmer and city dweller for a few more thousands; the purpose of his excess brain capacity even beyond what he needs for the intricate skills of language—these are some of the mysteries. The study of various cultures (where indeed the behavioral sciences begin) answers some questions but raises others: for example, which traits are common to man of every age and place, which are unique in a given society or even individual; why can the same complex customs arise independently in widely separate cultures?

• • • • •

. . . Specialists have distorted the environment of the world today and pulled human behavior out of scale. Generalists are needed in great numbers to offset what the specialists are doing to us. To put it in another way, we need more specialists equipped with wide perspective, to exert critical judgment on what they are doing as specialists. This, I take it, was Robert Oppenheimer's motive when he demurred about working on the hydrogen bomb: his general philosophy came in conflict with his expert knowledge. Almost everyone, as I said earlier, is both specialist and generalist; but the latter function has grown more and more neglected as specialties become more complex and demanding.

In *Fables for Our Time*, James Thurber imagines a conference of ostriches concerned with the loss of their ability to fly. One of them named Oliver complains that men can fly sitting down, while ostriches cannot fly at all. "The old ostrich glared at Oliver severely, first with one eye and then with the other. 'Man is flying too fast for a world that is round,' he said. 'Soon he will catch up with himself, in a great rear-end collision, and man will never know that what hit Man from behind was Man.' "

MR. BERGER

Any intellectual activity derives excitement from the moment it becomes a trail of discovery. In some fields of learning this is the discovery of worlds previously unthought and unthinkable. This is the excitement of the astronomer or of the nuclear physicist on the antipodal boundaries of the realities that man is capable of conceiving. But it can also be the excitement of bacteriology or geology. In a different way it can be the excitement of the linguist discovering new realms of human expression or of the anthropologist exploring human customs in faraway countries. In such discovery, when undertaken with passion, a widening of awareness, sometimes a veritable transformation of consciousness, occurs. The universe turns out to be much more wonder-full than one had ever dreamed. The excitement of sociology is usually of a different sort. Sometimes, it is true, the sociologist penetrates into worlds that had previously been quite unknown to him—for instance, the world of crime, or the world of some bizarre religious sect, or the world fashioned by the exclusive concerns of some group such as medical specialists or military leaders or advertising executives. However, much of the time the sociologist moves in sectors of experience that are familiar to him and to most people in his society. He investigates communities, institutions and activities that one can read about every day in the newspapers. Yet there is another excitement of discovery beckoning in his investigations. It is not the excitement of coming upon the totally unfamiliar, but rather the excitement of finding the familiar becoming transformed in its meaning. The fascination of sociology lies in the fact that its perspective makes us see in a new light the very world in which we have lived all our lives. This also constitutes a transformation of consciousness. Moreover, this transformation is more relevant existentially than that of many other intellectual disciplines, because it is more difficult to segregate in some special compartment of the mind. The astronomer does not live in the remote galaxies, and the nuclear physicist can, outside his laboratory, eat and laugh and marry and vote without thinking about the insides of the atom. The geologist looks at rocks only at appropriate times, and the linguist speaks English with his wife. The sociologist lives in society, on the job and off it. His own life, inevitably, is part of his subject matter. Men being what they are, sociologists too manage to segregate their professional insights from their everyday affairs. But it is a rather difficult feat to perform in good faith.

The sociologist moves in the common world of men, close to what most of them would call real. The categories he employs in his analyses are only refinements of the categories by which other men live—power, class, status, race, ethnicity. As a result, there is a deceptive simplicity and obviousness about some sociological investigations. One reads them, nods at the familiar scene, remarks that one has heard all this before and don't people have better things to do than to waste their time on truisms—until one is sud-

SOURCE: Peter L. Berger, *Invitation to Sociology*, pp. 20–24, 175. • Peter L. Berger is a member of the graduate faculty at the New School for Social Research, New York. His special interests include the sociology of religion, the sociology of knowledge, the sociology of politics, and sociological theory. In addition to *Invitation to Sociology*, he has written *Noise of Solemn Assemblies and Precarious Vision* and *The Sacred Canopy*.

denly brought up against an insight that radically questions everything one had previously assumed about this familiar scene. This is the point at which one begins to sense the excitement of sociology.

Let us take a specific example. Imagine a sociology class in a Southern college where almost all the students are white Southerners. Imagine a lecture on the subject of the racial system of the South. The lecturer is talking here of matters that have been familiar to his students from the time of their infancy. Indeed, it may be that they are much more familiar with the minutiae of this system than he is. They are quite bored as a result. It seems to them that he is only using more pretentious words to describe what they already know. Thus he may use the term "caste," one commonly used now by American sociologists to describe the Southern racial system. But in explaining the term he shifts to traditional Hindu society, to make it clearer. He then goes on to analyze the magical beliefs inherent in caste tabus, the social dynamics of commensalism and connubium, the economic interests concealed within the system, the way in which religious beliefs relate to the tabus, the effects of the caste system upon the industrial development of the society and vice versa—all in India. But suddenly India is not very far away at all. The lecture then goes back to its Southern theme. The familiar now seems not quite so familiar any more. Questions are raised that are new, perhaps raised angrily, but raised all the same. And at least some of the students have begun to understand that there are functions involved in this business of race that they have not read about in the newspapers (at least not those in their hometowns) and that their parents have not told them —partly, at least, because neither the newspapers nor the parents knew about them.

It can be said that the first wisdom of sociology is this—things are not what they seem. This too is a deceptively simple statement. It ceases to be simple after a while. Social reality turns out to have many layers of meaning. The discovery of each new layer changes the perception of the whole.

Anthropologists use the term "culture shock" to describe the impact of a totally new culture upon a newcomer. . . .

. . . The first encounters with polygamy or with puberty rites or even with the way some nations drive their automobiles can be quite a shock to an American visitor. With the shock may go not only disapproval or disgust but a sense of excitement that things can *really* be that different from what they are at home. To some extent, at least, this is the excitement of any first travel abroad. The experience of sociological discovery could be described as "culture shock" minus geographical displacement. In other words, the sociologist travels at home—with shocking results.

. . . The discovery, for instance, that his own church has considerable money invested in the missile industry or that a few blocks from his home there are people who engage in cultic orgies may not be drastically different in emotional impact. Yet we would not want to imply that sociological discoveries are always or even usually outrageous to moral sentiment. Not at all. What they have in common with exploration in distant lands, however, is the sudden illumination of new and unsuspected facets of human existence in society. This is the excitement and the humanistic justification of sociology.

People who like to avoid shocking discoveries, who prefer to believe that society is just what they were taught in Sunday School, who like the safety of the rules and the maxims of what Alfred

Schuetz has called the "world-taken-for-granted," should stay away from sociology. People who feel no temptation before closed doors, who have no curiosity about human beings, who are content to admire scenery without wondering about the people who live in those houses on the other side of that river, should probably also stay away from sociology. They will find it unpleasant or, at any rate, unrewarding. People who are interested in human beings only if they can change, convert or reform them should also be warned, for they will find sociology much less useful than they hoped. And people whose interest is mainly in their own conceptual constructions will do just as well to turn to the study of little white mice. Sociology will be satisfying, in the long run, only to those who can think of nothing more entrancing than to watch men and to understand things human.

. . . . .

We maintain that the teaching of sociology is justified insofar as a liberal education is assumed to have a more than etymological connection with intellectual liberation. Where this assumption does not exist, where education is understood in purely technical or professional terms, let sociology be eliminated from the curriculum. It will only interfere with the smooth operation of the latter, provided, of course, that sociology has not also been emasculated in accordance with the educational ethos prevailing in such situations. Where, however, the assumption still holds, sociology is justified by the belief that it is better to be conscious than unconscious and that consciousness is a condition of freedom. To attain a greater measure of awareness, and with it of freedom, entails a certain amount of suffering and even risk. An educational process that would avoid this becomes simple technical training and ceases to have any relationship to the civilizing of the mind. We contend that it is part of a civilized mind in our age to have come in touch with the peculiarly modern, peculiarly timely form of critical thought that we call sociology.

SOURCES: Robert Redfield, "Research in the Social Science: Its Significance for General Education," *Social Education* (December 1941). Reprinted by permission. Robert Redfield, "The Art of Social Science," *American Journal of Sociology*, LIX, 3 (November 1948), 189–90. Copyright 1948 by The University of Chicago. Reprinted by permission of The University of Chicago Press. • For biographical data on Robert Redfield see selection 5.

MR. REDFIELD

. . . . .

It is part of a general education to understand, in the first place, that there is a social science, as distinct from commonsense knowledge about society and as distinct from social reform. Every educated person should know that to a great extent society can be studied objectively and systematically, as can starfish or the action of glaciers. One can get impersonal, organized, verifiable knowledge about housing, crime, and race relations, as one can get such knowledge about any other phenomena of nature. An educated person will know how to distinguish the scientific way of attacking a social problem from those ways of attacking it which are more generally practiced around him. He will understand that in a great many instances people do something about a social problem because they feel badly about it rather than because they understand it and that what they do corresponds with their feelings rather than with the facts underlying the problem. He will understand that this is true, whether the action taken be to write a letter to the newspapers, to pass a law, or to demand changes in the school curriculum. It is a part of general education to understand that scientific knowledge is different from feeling strongly about something and from common-sense knowledge and that it is a more secure basis for social action than either.

The successful teacher of the social studies will make clear that there is a difference between the analysis of processes, which are matters of efficiency, and other objective judgments. The citizen must know what are his values, and he should understand how to act so as to protect or realize them. The uneducated person confuses values and processes, ends and means; a good education in social science will help to keep them distinct.

As a part of this understanding, the educated man or woman will have been taught that a social problem is not a simple thing. Social problems are closely intermeshed with one another. If one makes a beginning with the problem of housing, one finds that it is only one aspect of the larger problem of national insecurity. It is also related to the problem of the national income and to that of the national health. The solutions given in the form of new housing projects or in zoning laws encounter the problems of racial intolerance. It follows from this that a social problem does not mean the same thing to everybody.

. . . The problem of housing looks very differently to laymen, landowners, builders, tax officials, and city planners, and . . . full understanding of the problem depends upon special scientific knowledge of economists, sociologists, and students of government. The contribution of social-science research to a general education is not made use of when a social problem is presented to young people as if it existed with simple reference to some social ideal. It is not made use of if the problem is presented as if all one had to do was to take note of the social injustice attending the present state of things. That is not functional education; it does not prepare the young person for life.

A further contribution which social-science research can make to general education is the understanding that although social science is like physical or biological science in that it is objective, systematic description of the world around us, it differs from physical and biological science in that all the facts and all the problems are controversial. The social scientist is studying, chiefly, to put it strongly, himself, and one cannot help feeling and caring about one's self. We, as human beings, care about the institutions and social problems which the social scientist studies. Therefore it is harder for the social scientist to maintain objectivity than it is for the physicist, and it is harder for Society, with a capital "S," to keep from interfering with the social scientist than with the physicist. This is one of the elements of understanding of social-science research which belongs in a general education. If social problems are presented . . . so as to communicate this general knowledge of the nature of social science it will be made clear to the learner that the mere facts of social science lie within a realm of controversy and prejudice. As Professor Wirth has pointed out even the number of people living in a given city of the United States is a controversial matter in the sense that if the city has been losing population the Chamber of Commerce will not want the fact to get abroad. The number of people unemployed in this country is a controversial fact, first, in the sense that various interest groups care as to what criterion is selected for determining who is unemployed, and, second, because even if it is decided who are unemployed, various groups will interpret the fact according to their interests. For some employers there will be just enough unemployed to assure a labor reserve, while for other of our citizens these same unemployed constitute a problem of providing relief.

At the same time the educated man or woman will understand that this special difficulty under which the social scientist labors has its compensation in a special advantage enjoyed by the social scientist and understanding of the nature of social-science research is not complete until another general characteristic of it is recognized. It is a peculiarity of the scientific method as applied to man in society that the investigator can get a more intimate knowledge of his subject matter than can the physicist of his, just because he is part of it. The physical scientist learns of his subject matter only as caliper and scales can tell him about it. The social scientist can ask questions of his subject matter and get answers, and he can project his own humanity imaginatively into the subject matter and so increase his understanding of it. The contribution of social-science research to a general education is provided in part by an understanding of the advantages and the dangers of this essential characteristic of social-science research. The social scientist does not abolish his own prejudices any more than he abolishes his own human nature. But he controls prejudice by making it explicit. So, too, he develops controlled use of his human insights. It is more important to a general education that the individual knows that there is a problem of using and controlling the human faculty of insight as a scientific instrument than that he know the latest facts with regard to any problem studied by that method.

* * *

The humanistic aspect of social science is the aspect of it that is today not well appreciated. Social science is essentially scientific in that its propositions describe, in general terms, natural phenomena; in that it returns again and again to special experience to verify and to modify these propositions. It tells what is, not what ought to be. It investigates nature. It strives for objectivity, accuracy, competency. It employs hypotheses and formal evidence; it values negative cases; and, when it finds a hypothesis to be unsupported by the facts, it drops it for some other which is. But these are all aspects of social science so well known that it is tedious to list them again. What is less familiar, but equally true, is that to create the hypothesis, to reach the conclusion, to get, often, the very first real datum as to what are A's motives or what is the meaning of this odd custom or that too-familiar institution, requires on the part of one who studies persons and societies, and not rocks or proteins, a truly humanistic and freely imaginative insight into people, their conventions and interests and motives, and that this requirement in the social scientist calls for gifts and for a kind of education different from that required of any physicist and very similar to what is called for in a creative artist.

If this be seen, it may also be seen that the function of social science in our society is a double function. Social science is customarily explained and justified by reason of what social science contributes to the solution of particular problems that arise in the management of our society, as a help in getting particular things done. As social scientists we take satisfaction in the fact that today, as compared with thirty years ago, social scientists are employed because their employers think that their social science is applicable to some practical necessity. Some knowledge of techniques developed in social science may be used: to select taxicab drivers that are not likely to have accidents; to give vocational guidance; to discover why one business enterprise has labor troubles while a similar enterprise does not; to make more effective some governmental program carried into farming communities. . . .

All these contributions to efficiency and adjustment may be claimed with justice by social scientists. What is also to be claimed, and is less commonly stressed, is that social science contributes to that general understanding of the world around us which, as we say, "liberalizes," or "enriches." The relation of social science to humanistic learning is reciprocal. Social scientists need humanistic learning the better to be social scientists. And the understanding of society, personality, and human nature which is achieved by scientific methods returns to enrich that humanistic understanding without which none can become human and with which some few may become wise. Because its subject matter is humanity, the contribution of social science to general, liberal education is greater than is the contribution of those sciences with subject matter that is physical. In this respect also, creative artist and social scientist find themselves side by side. The artist may reveal something of universal human or social nature. So too may the social scientist. No one has ever applied, as a key to a lock, Sumner's *Folkways* or Tawney's *Religion and the Rise of Capitalism* or James's *The Varieties of Religious Experience*. These are not the works of social science that can be directly consulted and applied when a government office or a business concern has an immediate problem. But they are the books of lasting influence. Besides what influence they have upon those social scientists who come to work in the government office, or the business concern, in so far as they are read and understood and thought about by men and women who are not social scientists, or even as they are communicated indirectly by those who have read them to others, they are part of humanistic education, in the broad sense. Releasing us from our imprisonment in the particular, we are freed by seeing how we are exemplifications of the general. For how many young people has not Sumner's book, or Veblen's book, or some work by Freud, come as a swift widening of the doors of vision, truly a liberation, a seeing of one's self, perhaps for the first time, as sharing the experiences, the nature, of many other men and women? So I say that social science, as practiced, is something of an art and that, as its best works are communicated, it has something of the personal and social values of all the arts.

MR. BIERSTEDT

. . . . .

Sociology has an honorable place in the realm of humane letters and it belongs with the liberal arts as well as with the sciences. We have seldom been able to escape the public belief that it is the principal business of sociology to solve social problems; and the identification of our discipline with such problems is too well known to require comment. That sociology might also have something to do with culture in the narrower and nonsociological sense of intellectual cultivation seems seldom to have occurred to anyone, including sociologists.

I invite your attention, therefore, to the fact that sociology, like the other arts, is

SOURCE: Robert Bierstedt, "Sociology and Humane Learning," *American Sociological Review*, vol. 25 (February 1960), 8–9. Reprinted by permission of the American Sociological Association. • Robert Bierstedt is professor of sociology and anthropology at New York University. He is an advisory editor for Dodd, Mead & Company, Inc., and has served in an editorial capacity on the *American Sociological Review* and the *American Journal of Sociology*. In 1960–61 he was executive officer of the American Sociological Association. He is chiefly interested in sociological theory and is the author of *The Social Order*, *The Making of Society*, and *Emile Durkheim*.

one of the ornaments of the human mind, that its literature extending from Plato to our contemporaries is in a great and humane tradition, that sociology—like all of the liberal arts—liberates us from the provincialisms of time and place and circumstance, that the social order is a study worthy of a free man, and that society itself, like every other thing that has ever agitated the restless and inquisitive mind of man, is a fit and dignified subject of inquiry.

CHAPTER I

SOCIOLOGY AND SOCIETY

1 The Transition to Science in Human Relations

GEORGE A. LUNDBERG

Sociology consists of the scientific study of human groups and human interaction. To consider sociology a science *means that we stand ready to observe human behavior as scientists would observe any* natural *phenomenon and to look for systematic regularities in this human behavior. In this selection Lundberg, long an exponent of the rigorous application of the natural science approach to the study of human behavior, describes some of the practical results of this approach and presents the steps that he felt must be taken if the social sciences are to help achieve a more rational "management of social relations."*

I. CONSENSUS ON METHODS

I have expressed the view that the best hope for man in his present social predicament lies in a type of social science strictly comparable to the other natural sciences. We have reviewed some of the objections that have been urged both by physical and social scientists to this proposal. I am not under the illusion that my argument can be established conclusively in so brief a compass. Actually, of course, only time and future scientific development can finally demonstrate the validity of the position which I have outlined.

In the meantime, we are confronted with the necessity of proceeding on *some* hypothesis as to the way out of our difficulties. It is generally agreed, even by those who differ most radically as to the proper approach, that our first need is a unified, coherent theory on which to proceed. A society cannot achieve its adjustments by mutually incompatible or contradictory behavior, any more than can an individual organism. However we may differ on details and on ends, we must agree on certain broad means, certain principles of action toward whatever ends we do agree upon.

In short, we all apparently agree with Comte's appraisal of the situation as he saw it a hundred years ago. Speaking of the theological, the metaphysical, and the

SOURCE: George A. Lundberg, *Can Science Save Us?* (New York: David McKay Company, Inc., 1961), 42–51. Reprinted by permission. • The author (1895–1966) was professor emeritus of sociology, University of Washington. He was the editor of *Sociometry*, 1941–1945, and served as consultant to the National Resources Planning Board for many years. Among his publications are *Foundations of Sociology, Social Research,* and *Sociology,* of which he was the coauthor. He was a past president of the American Sociological Association.

positive scientific approaches, he said: "Any one of these might alone secure some sort of social order: but, while the three co-exist, it is impossible for us to understand one another upon any essential point whatever."

Of course there are some who find in our present predicament merely further evidence of the futility of the scientific approach in human affairs. They overlook the fact that, actually, science has as yet not been tried on social problems. Consequently, they advocate a return to theology, or "the" classics, either in their historic forms or in new versions in which the advocates of these approaches personally can play the role of major prophets. If I could see any chance of bringing about a return to theology or "the" classics, I might give it serious consideration, because any one unified approach might be better than two or more contradictory ones. But I see no such possibility in the long run. The commitments we have already made to science, chiefly in our technological culture, are of such character that we can neither go back nor stand still.

Our technological developments and our methods of communication have resulted in a fundamental interdependence which dominates our lives. This state of affairs requires, as we shall see, that we bring our social arrangements into line with this basic technological pattern, rather than vice versa. This basic technological pattern unquestionably rests upon natural science. On this ground, rather than on any assumption of absolute or intrinsic superiority of science as a philosophy of life, I think the following conclusion is inescapable: *In our time and for some centuries to come, for better or for worse, the sciences, physical and social, will be to an increasing degree the accepted point of reference with respect to which the validity (Truth) of all knowledge is gauged.*

II. WHAT CAN BE DONE—SOME EXAMPLES

What are some examples of types of work by social scientists that are of vast importance in managing human relations?

When we speak of *types* of work by social scientists, we are obviously announcing an undertaking so large as to prevent even a summary within the confines of this book. There are at least five well-recognized social sciences, and if we use the larger category of "behavioral science," the number rises to twelve or more. The social sciences are well-recognized in the sense that they are firmly established as departments in nearly all leading universities and colleges as well as in professional, industrial, and governmental circles. Over a hundred journals publish every year hundreds of research reports of studies large and small, designed to yield new knowledge or to test and refine previous conclusions and to predict behavior under stipulated conditions. We shall confine ourselves to a few illustrations selected chiefly because they are individually of interest to more than one of the social sciences. Readers interested in more comprehensive accounts, including methodological details, will find a large literature readily available.

For our present purpose we shall not here become involved in the question of the degree of scientific refinement attained in the different sciences. My argument has been based in large part on what appears to me to be warranted anticipations regarding *future developments* of the social sciences. Here I shall rather take the view that, *even with their present shortcomings*, the social sciences must be taken seriously. The recent

(1960) elevation of the Office of Social Sciences to full divisional status in the National Science Foundation is an indication of this growing recognition.

The work of such agencies at the Census Bureau is known to all and is more or less taken for granted. Without the data and the analyses which it provides, the administration of public affairs would certainly dissolve in chaos and perhaps in civil war. It is equally certain that no international organization can function without an elaborate organization of this kind to provide the essential facts regarding people and their characteristics and activities. Perhaps the most permanently valuable contribution of the ill-fated League of Nations was its establishment of an international statistical bureau which managed to survive until taken over by the larger information agencies of the United Nations. The Office of Population Research at Princeton University has engaged in detailed studies of local and international population trends in various parts of the world and has predicted the future areas of population pressure. This knowledge is of the utmost practical importance in the administration of national and international organizations of any kind. The Scripps Foundation, the Milbank Memorial Fund, and many others are engaged in similar or related work of a character that measures up very well to the standards of the physical sciences.

Social scientists have also been prominent in pointing out one of the most serious of the world's *problems*, namely, the problem of overpopulation. As a result of the drastic decline in the death rate resulting from the application of medical science, world population is increasing at an unprecedented rate. For example, although it took thousands of years for the human species to reach the number of one billion of living people (about 1830) it required only one century to add the second billion. It is now taking less than thirty-five years for the world population to add a third billion—probably before 1965. The United Nations' population experts estimate that it will take only fifteen years to add a fourth billion, and another ten years to add the fifth billion if present rates should continue. The idea that any expansion of the food supply could do more than temporarily alleviate the starvation of people under such rates of population increase is merely a confusion of wishful thinking with stern realities.

However, just as the application of science to health and sanitation has produced this situation, science has provided the means for its control. Further improvements in the latter are highly likely and imminent. The distinctively social problem of securing the widespread adoption of known methods of control involves a number of problems of a type not yet fully solved, but under extensive inquiry by social scientists. In the meantime we have an example of successful population control in the case of postwar Japan. We are not here concerned with these problems in themselves, but with the role of scientifically gathered and analyzed human social data in the prediction of future population, and the solution of a problem which some regard as more dangerous than nuclear war. Also in other ways, statistics of individual countries, and the data collected by the United Nations organization, are of fundamental importance to the work of many scientists engaged in a wide variety of particular projects. Human ecology, which cuts across the conventional boundaries of demography, geography, sociology, economics, political science (and perhaps others), has produced very impressive work both of applied and theoretical significance.

Reliable and objective knowledge of other peoples and cultures constitutes another field in which social scientists have made distinguished contributions. This knowledge has thrown a flood of light on our own civilization and permits the formulation and test of hypotheses regarding human behavior patterns in general. The Human Relations Area Files contain, systematically filed and indexed, virtually all present reliable knowledge regarding some two hundred cultures. To make a long story short, if a researcher happens to be interested in some subject as, for example, divorce, crime, education, law (and about a thousand other topics), in other cultures, he can go to one of the twenty or more libraries which subscribe to the File, and find all the known information on any or all of these subjects for each of about two hundred cultures. The information is neatly filed away in a separate drawer for each subject. Information which it might take years to locate as scattered in hundreds of books in a library can be secured in a few hours from the File. The importance of this kind of knowledge and its ready availability in facilitating our contacts with people of other lands and cultures became very evident during and after World War II.

We [have recognized] the importance of instruments and methods of observation and measurement in the social as well as in the physical sciences. Social scientists have produced revolutionary developments in this field in the last thirty years. Thousands of such instruments have been invented by means of which vocational aptitudes, success in college and other undertakings, and social behavior of great variety can be accurately measured and predicted. Instruments and scales for the measurement of attitudes have opened vast new fields for investigation.

Perhaps the best known, but by no means the only one, of these devices is the public opinion poll. We have in this technique an illustration of how a development in the social sciences may be as significant for the future of social organization as many physical inventions have been in our industrial development. The mechanisms by which the "public will" can make itself reliably felt in government and community action has always been in the foreground of political discussion. With the expansion of the areas in which public opinion must operate, many students of the problem have despaired of the capacity of the town meeting technique adequately to make operative the "public will." In the face of this situation, the scientific public opinion poll constitutes an instrument which cheaply and accurately permits us to learn the beliefs, the attitudes, and the wishes of the rank and file of the population. Public opinion polls are at present frequently thought of as interesting devices mainly for predicting the outcome of elections. They do permit such prediction, but this is a very minor aspect of their full possible importance. Polls were extensively used in the armed forces in World War II as a guide to the administration of the invaded areas, the return of the armed forces after the war, and in many other ways.

Public opinion polling may be a device through which can be resolved one of the principal impasses of our time, namely, the apparent irreconcilability of authoritarian control on the one hand and the "public will" on the other. It may be that through properly administered public opinion polls professionalized public officials can give us all the efficiency now claimed for authoritarian centralized administration and yet have that administration at all times subject to the dictates of a more delicate barometer of the peoples' wills than is provided by all the technologically obsolete paraphernalia of traditional democratic processes. In short, it is not impossible that as the advancing technology in the physical adjustments of our lives leads to a threatened breakdown of democracy, so an improved social research instrument may restore and even increase the dominance of the people's voice in the control of human society.

The time may come when the reliable polling of public opinion will be a science comparable to meteorology. Charts of all kinds of social weather, its movements and trends, whether it be anti-Semitism, anti-Negro sentiment, or mob-mindedness will be at the disposal of the administrators of the people's will in every land. A barometer of international tension has been designed to detect reliably and early the tensions that lead to war. It is true that mere knowledge of these tensions does not necessarily operate to alleviate them. But it is also true that a reliable diagnosis of the tension and an understanding of the feelings and sentiments that underlie tensions is essential for an effective approach to the problem. "Statesmen" will doubtless continue for some time to value their intuitions more highly than scientific prediction. Pious platitudes doubtless will continue to be heard about the "unpredictability" of human behavior. It remains a fact that social scientists predicted within a fraction of 1 per cent the actual voting behavior of sixty-eight million voters in the U.S.A. in the presidential election of 1960. The pollsters have been doing so regularly since 1936 with a maximum error of 6 per cent. Nor are such results limited to voting behaviors. The late Professor Stouffer of Harvard predicted, also within a fraction of 1 per cent, the number of discharged soldiers after World War II who would take advantage of the educational privileges of the G.I. Bill of Rights. Hundreds of other cases could be reported from a great variety of fields of human social behavior, including the vast areas of market research.

To those who constantly have their minds on quick and dramatic solutions to the world's troubles this type of research is likely to seem offensively trivial—a kind of fiddling while Rome burns. "Writers" are fond of referring contemptuously to basic scientific work as an "ivory tower" and as "lecturing on navigation while the ship sinks." Navigation today is what it is because some people were willing to study the *principles* of their subject while their individual ships went down, instead of rushing about with half-baked advice as to how to save ships that could not be saved, or were not worth saving anyway. As A. J. Carlson has recently said: "The failure of bacteria to survive in close proximity to certain moulds looked trivial at first, but few informed people would label the discovery of that initial fact *trivial* today."

So much, then, for a few illustrations, rather than a summary, of the type of work that is being done and that needs to be done in the social sciences. Is there enough of it being done? Clearly not, or we would not need to flounder as we are in national and international affairs, pursuing diametrically opposite courses within the same decade. Can the social sciences ever hope to catch up with the other sciences, the increasingly rapid advance of which constantly creates new social problems? Certainly we can, if we devote ourselves to the business with something like the seriousness, the money, and the equipment that we have devoted to physical research. Consider how the physical scientists are today given vast resources to concentrate on the invention of a new submarine detector or a new bomb, not to mention the peacetime occupations of these scientists with penicillin and sulpha drugs. Obviously, I am not criticizing this action. On the contrary, it is the way to proceed if you want results. Is there anything like that going on regarding the world organization and its numerous subsidiary problems, all of them important to peace and prosperity?

Comparatively speaking, there is almost nothing that could be called fundamental research into the basic nature of human relations. To be sure, there are endless petty projects, surveys, conferences, oratory, and arguments by representatives of pressure groups, as if argument ever settled any scientific questions. Of basic social research there is very little. Why isn't there more? It is not yet realized that scientific knowledge is relevant to successful world organization. We still think that common sense, good will, eloquent leaders, and pious hopes are sufficient when it comes to management of social relations.

2 Population Studies: Fertility in Taiwan

JAMES E. HANEY

People often ask, "What good is sociological knowledge? Does it have practical value?" Answers to such questions are suggested by this selection, which examines a successful attempt to teach family planning in Taiwan. On the basis of the experiment described here, one may infer that even though favorable social changes may occur without systematic planning, sociological knowledge can be used to influence social change in a desired direction. The selection also illustrates the rigor that characterizes high quality experimental research in the social sciences.

The Population Studies Center has been engaged in fertility studies in Taiwan since 1962 in programs sponsored by the provincial health department of Taiwan and supported by the Population Council, a private U.S. foundation. The Taiwan Population Studies Center, established with the assistance of the U–M Center, has set basic policies and conducted the field work. The U–M group has provided training assistance and consultation, and has participated in joint work on research analyses. The principal object of the research has been to understand the population changes underway and to test the efficacy of various means of accelerating a slow decline in fertility that began in 1958. Taiwan has become increasingly urbanized and industrialized recently, with fairly widespread education and literacy, transportation, commu-

SOURCE: *Research News,* vol. 19, no. 10 (Ann Arbor: University of Michigan, Office of Research Administration, April 1969). A book-length treatment of this study is found in Ronald Freedman and John Y. Takeshita, *Family Planning in Taiwan* (Princeton: Princeton University Press, 1969). Reprinted by permission of the publisher. • James Haney is Associate Editor, Office of Research Administration, the University of Michigan. Among the numerous articles he has written for the *Research News* are "The Modern Discipline of Geography," "The Scholarly Editing of Matthew Arnold's Works," "Perception and Social Change," "International Relations and Chinese Affairs," and "The Use of Games in Research and Teaching." • EDITORS' NOTE: This selection was written by Haney in consultation with Professor Ronald Freedman, professor of sociology and director of the Population Studies Center, University of Michigan.

nications, and medical facilities. Its population also has few religious or cultural objections to contraception; less than 5 percent of the women in any age group believe that the number of children they bear is up to "fate" or "providence." The island has thus been suitable for an experimental program designed to study various means of accelerating what is known as the "demographic transition"—a trend in which birth rates decline following a decline in death rates. In various Western countries this transition required, on the average, about 50 years.

In 1962, Taichung, a city of about 325,000, was selected for a sample-survey and two small pilot-projects designed to measure contraceptive knowledge, attitudes, and practices. The pilot-projects explored the acceptability of modern contraceptives, the pill and the intrauterine device (IUD), in relation to older means of contraception, abortion, and sterilization. (Although abortion is illegal in Taiwan, the law is not strictly enforced.) An experimental program covering all of Taichung was then set up to test a number of important questions concerning the diffusion of contraceptive knowledge and practices. Although other large-scale family planning programs have possessed some of the features of this program, they have had few provisions for analyzing their own effectiveness. The Taiwan program is one of the largest social science studies ever conducted under some approximation of experimental conditions.

The pre-program survey indicated that Taichung's married couples were having more children than they wanted. A significant minority of them were attempting family planning, but they were not well informed, and their efforts were too ineffective to achieve their goals. Based on this situation the Taiwanese designed an action-study program to answer the following questions:

1. How much can the practice of family planning be increased by a massive information and service campaign of short duration? This was perhaps the single most important question to be answered by the study. In 1962 there was no example anywhere in the world of a program for a large population that was successful in substantially changing the proportion of people practicing contraception.

2. Must both husbands and wives be approached in an education program, or is it enough to approach the wife alone? Most programs had concentrated on reaching wives. The failure of many of them to achieve significant results was often attributed to the hostility or indifference of husbands, but this view had rarely been tested. It was important to know whether the additional effort is worthwhile, because reaching husbands as well as wives is difficult and expensive.

3. Can family planning ideas be spread cheaply and simply by mail? Most programs involve expensive person-to-person contacts by field workers. Given sufficient literacy among a population, mail campaigns could have great potential. Within a given budget, the number of acceptors might be much greater, even though the proportion of people influenced to accept might be much smaller than through personal contacts.

4. Can direct communication to systematically spaced subgroups of a population indirectly affect a much larger population by a diffusion of information from the points of direct contact? What are the dynamics of "circulation" effects? Will the population itself spread the desired innovation, and, if so, how large an initial effort is required to prime this process? To communicate directly with each couple of childbearing age is expensive. Word-of-mouth diffusion probably was

mainly responsible for spreading ideas about family planning in Western countries and in Japan over long periods of time and without organized programs. To what extent can centers of direct communication speed up this process?

5. Does a new innovation in contraception, the IUD, influence diffusion and acceptances? Significant numbers of women were beginning to use the IUD at the outset of the Taichung study. It was necessary to test its relative acceptability, whether it would diffuse rapidly, and whether some potential disadvantages would create special problems.

6. Would a significant adoption of family planning actually accelerate the decline in fertility already evident in Taichung and Taiwan? The recognition that child mortality had greatly declined was already influencing couples to want less children and to think of adopting contraception. Could the program effects be separated from a fertility decline that might be expected to accelerate even in the absence of any program?

7. What demographic and social characteristics of the couples are most important in determining whether they accept family planning in an organized program? Which is more important: the pressures of growing family size, or education and other signs of modernization? How do the characteristics of acceptors in the program compare with those of couples who had adopted family limitation prior to the program? Are the younger women readier than others to adopt family planning?

8. What are the characteristics of couples who express an intention to accept family planning but do not do so? Who express an intention not to, but do? It was important to learn how the demographic and social characteristics of the couples affect their intentions, whether the intentions predict behavior, and whether the reasons given to explain intentions help to discriminate between acceptors and non-acceptors.

9. Is the recent fertility of those accepting family planning high enough so that their use of contraception will produce a distinct reduction in birth rates? If the couples who accept family planning via the program are above average in their fecundability, the program is potentially more effective.

10. Which characteristics of the couples are related to persistence in effective use of contraception once it is adopted? High acceptance rates in a program mean little unless the acceptors continue to use contraception.

11. How does the discussion and perception of what others are doing affect acceptances? This question relates to the diffusion of information through informal contacts. Studies elsewhere have since shown diffusion to be an important factor (in Chicago, Kentucky, Korea, Puerto Rico, Thailand, and Japan).

Providing a data base to attempt to answer these questions required a rather sophisticated action program designed to reach 36,000 married couples of Taichung with wives 20–39 years old. For statistical purposes, however, Taichung was already organized into about 2,400 *lin*'s—neighborhood units containing an average of about 20 households, each including about 12 married women aged 20–39. For purposes of the experiment, the city was divided into three wedge-shaped sectors, placing about one-third of the lins in each sector. The sectors were roughly equated initially on fertility, rural-urban distribution, occupational composition, and educational levels.

Four different "treatments" were devised for application to individual lins:

1. *Everything—husband and wife.* These lins received all of the stimuli of

the program: personal visits to both husbands and wives by trained health workers, mailings of information to newlyweds and couples with at least two children, and neighborhood meetings that mixed entertainment with information about family planning, including slides, film strips, flip charts, etc.

2. *Everything–wife only.* This treatment included all of the major stimuli except the personal visit to the husband.

3. *Mailings.* This treatment involved no personal visits or neighborhood meetings, but a series of mailings of letters and pamphlets to newlyweds and couples with at least two children. The mailings provided general information on methods, rationale, location of clinics, etc., and included a return-post device for requesting more information or a personal visit from a field worker.

4. *Nothing.* In this treatment, no effort was made to reach the couples directly. There were, however, posters in these areas, because posters had been distributed throughout the city. Also, some meetings were held at the *li* level (a neighborhood unit of about 350 households).

The three sectors of about 800 lins each were differentiated in terms of the proportion of lins within each sector that received a given "treatment." The sectors were designated as heavy-, medium-, or light-density, according to the percentage of their lins to receive the "Everything" treatment. In the heavy-density sector, half of the lins received an Everything treatment; in the medium-density sector, one-third of them; and in the light-density sector, one-fifth of them. The remaining lins in each sector were divided equally between "Mail" and "Nothing" treatments. Once these percentages of lin treatments were assigned, the lin treatments within each sector were randomly distributed throughout the sector.

All of the couples in the lins receiving a particular treatment supposedly received the same set of prescribed stimuli (or none) regardless of the density sector in which they were located. The difference lay only in the percentage of surrounding lins receiving the same or another treatment. That is, Nothing lins in the heavy-density sector bordered many more lins that were receiving an Everything treatment than did Nothing lins in the light-density sector.

In addition to the specific treatments, posters were placed throughout the city; some city-wide mass media messages were broadcast; and meetings were held with such occupational groups as the farmers' association and the pedicab drivers' association. In the course of the program, some 12,000 initial home visits were made and 500 neighborhood meetings were held. More than 20,000 follow-up home visits of various kinds were made. Family planning services and supplies were offered at ten clinics located throughout the city. Information, services, and supplies were offered with respect to the diaphragm, jelly, foam tablets, condom, withdrawal, rhythm, oral pills, and the IUD, although no effort was made to set up procedures that would test the attractiveness of different methods. Except for the oral pills and the IUD, which were available only at the clinics, supplies were available on request from field workers during home visits or group meetings. There was a nominal charge, except for indigents, for any kind of contraceptive device or chemicals accepted. A charge of $.75 was made for an IUD insertion or for a set of 20 oral pills.

How were all of the data obtained? The data base was compiled from three sources: (1) an Intensive Survey of 2,443 women interviewed prior to and following the experimental program. This was a probability, cross-section sample of all wives of childbearing age in the city; (2) a Household Survey interview of the more than 11,000 women in the Everything lins; and (3) the clinic records of all women who were acceptors, regardless of where they came from. These clinic records also included answers to the Household Survey questions. Clinic records were linked to the Household Survey records for those acceptors who were interviewed in either the Household Survey sample or the Intensive Survey sample. It was therefore possible to relate the characteristics of the respondent on a survey to whether she later became an acceptor.

The survey instruments and clinical records established an extensive data base of demographic and social characteristics, including detailed information on marriage, births, pregnancies, household composition, fecundity, family size, attitudes and practices relating to family planning, reading skills and habits, wife's background, husband's background, occupation, and income, and household facilities. Questions on household facilities included some relating to the social and economic status of the household in terms of conveniences associated with economic and technological "modernity"—whether or not the couple had a bicycle, motorcycle, clock or watch, newspaper subscription, radio, record player, electric fan, electric rice cooker, or sewing machine. Ownership of these objects is an indication of economic modernization, of a transition to a market economy. The number of these objects owned was found to be much more closely related to the educational level of the couple than to their household income. Modernization is broadly defined as a shift from dependence on relatively self-contained local institutions to participation in larger social, economic, and political units. Such a shift implies a change in the division of labor: Family and village units give up many functions to larger units not based on kinship ties. Education and literacy are relevant to this process. It was not surprising to find that several indicators of modernization were linked to the pre-program practice of birth control. A more significant finding was that, once the program began, these indicators of modernization were no longer indicative of who accepted family planning in the program. This is important, because most of the population in developing countries is in less modern categories.

• • • • •

What were the major results of the study? As of the end of 1962, when the program began, 36 percent of all married couples in Taichung had practiced some form of birth control. By July of 1965 this figure had risen to 51.2 percent, and it is now estimated to be about 60 percent. Much of this rise is believed to be directly attributable to the program, but it is difficult to separate these program effects from social and economic influences outside the program. The experiment did establish, however, that demographic variables are much more important than social and economic variables in determining who becomes an acceptor. Demographic variables indicate in various ways the stages of the family life-cycle, and their relation to the desired number and sex of children. The acceptance rate increased markedly with increasing numbers of children, with increasing numbers of sons, and with increasing age or years of marriage. It was also high among couples who had already tried to limit their family's size. On the other hand, nine social and economic variables, including wife's education and husband's occupation, were only weakly correlated with acceptances.

By July of 1965 the vast majority of

acceptors (86 percent) had chosen the new IUD. The Taichung program was the first to have introduced the IUD on a large scale in a developing country; its educational material stressed the IUD and traditional methods, rather than the pill. Yet a similar mass campaign based on the pills might have had equal or greater success in such a population. The Taichung experiment did not definitively answer the question of which method of contraception is the most suitable in such a population. A substantial minority of acceptors removed the IUD after a time, for various reasons. A three-year follow-up did indicate, however, that the great majority of couples who accepted an IUD had reduced their birth rates sharply. Even if they gave up the IUD, they found other ways to limit further family growth.

What conclusions can be drawn from results of the variation in densities and treatments in Taichung? Four stand out:

1. Contacting the husband as well as the wife in home visits was not discernibly more effective than contacting only the wife. The principal method chosen (the IUD) is pertinent here. Moreover, the probability of a high incidence of agreement between the spouses about the need for family planning would often make contacts with the husband redundant.

2. The direct personal contacts in the Everything lins produced more acceptances, but this is less remarkable than the substantial acceptance rates obtained in neighborhoods in which the influence was almost entirely by diffusion.

3. The use of letters was not effective in Taichung. The acceptance rate in the Mail lins was no higher than in the Nothing lins. The letters mentioned only that family planning information could be obtained from a field worker upon request, or from the nearest health station. Possibly they might have been more effective if they had been keyed specifically to the IUD. In Seoul, Korea, however, in a similar experiment, mailings keyed to the IUD failed to produce any significant effects. Since the Taichung experiment, mass mailings keyed to the IUD and addressed to couples with a very recent birth have been highly effective in Taiwan.

4. The heavy-density sector yielded acceptance rates distinctly higher than the medium- and light-density sectors. Contrary to expectation, results in these other two sectors did not differ in any consistent, meaningful way. These results led to the conclusion that for most purposes the 12-fold experimental design could be collapsed into four cells by reducing the four treatments to a dichotomy—Everything and Nothing—and reducing the three density sectors to another dichotomy—heavy and light.

In the heavy-density sector there was relatively little difference in IUD acceptances between the Everything and the Nothing lins, after sufficient time had passed. In relation to the three major subperiods of the study, a small advantage in the Everything lins during the first period was neutralized in the second period and reversed in the third, indicating an extremely effective diffusion process. During the second period, when free insertion of the IUD was offered, the rate of acceptances in Nothing lins in the heavy-density sector was actually higher than in the Everything lins. These heavy-density Nothing lins also had a higher IUD acceptance rate than the Nothing lins in the light-density sector. The intensive treatment made a significant difference initially, but as time progressed the IUD diffused so widely throughout the city as to minimize the initial differences in treatment. It is significant also that diffusion did not stop at the city's border.

As much as 26 percent of all of the acceptances in the experimental period came from outside Taichung, where no formal effort had been made to recruit them. By July, 1965, 30 percent of all acceptances were from outside the city, and 97 percent of these acceptors had chosen the IUD.

About one-half of the acceptors within the city reported having heard of the program through a neighbor, friend, or relative, and 67 percent of the acceptors from outside the city gave this as their source of information. Other important sources of information were the regular health station personnel, who had good rapport with the public in their routine health service activities. Some of the health station nurses in outlying areas brought in groups of women for IUD insertions. Finally, the program's home visitors, who apparently talked to people outside of the Everything lins in addition to making their scheduled home visits, helped to circulate information.

One of the consequences of the diffusion process was the increased perception of support from relatives, friends, and neighbors. Wives interviewed before and after the intensive program were asked whether some or many of their relatives, friends, and neighbors were using family limitation methods. When the "before" and "after" responses were compared, results indicated a significant drop in the "don't know" answers, and definite shifts toward perception of more use of contraception among relatives, friends, and neighbors. The greatest changes in awareness occurred in Everything lins, but there were also significant changes in the Mail and Nothing lins. The increase in the perceptions that significant "others" were practicing contraception related positively to acceptance in the program. "Before" and "after" responses indicated that acceptance rates were related less to increased *discussion* about family limitation than to increased *perception* of its use by others; whether more discussion with significant "others" took place was evidently less important than whether people believed that more of their primary contacts were actually adopting family limitation.

Although 854 neighborhood group meetings were originally planned, only about 500 were held, owing to a shortage of personnel and unexpected difficulties in assembling a group in some areas. But this situation inadvertently provided an opportunity for an independent test of the influence of group meetings. The meetings were rated as "effective," "somewhat effective," or "ineffective" by the field workers who conducted them, immediately after they were held and before the workers could know what the response in acceptances would be. Results indicated that a higher proportion of meetings were rated as effective in the high-density sector than in the other two sectors. Yet, despite the relatively high acceptance rates in the Everything lins taken as a whole, almost one-third of the Everything lins had no acceptances by the end of the first period. But this phenomenon was much less common in lins that had had effective or somewhat effective meetings.

An examination of the reliability of expressed intentions indicated that they were a useful but not very reliable predictor of later actions. Women had been asked whether they intended to adopt birth control "soon" or "later" or not at all. Of all women interviewed, 15 percent said they would act "soon" and 38 percent said "later." Yet by July of 1965, thirty months after the program began, only 19 percent of all home-visited cases had accepted. Stated intentions to adopt family planning were, however, more predictive than demographic and social characteristics considered alone.

Many of the program acceptors in Taichung and elsewhere were women over 30 and of relatively high parity (number of live births). Because women over 30 have a much lower average fertility than younger women, some observers are pessimistic about the capacity of such programs for reducing fertility. The Taichung acceptors were, however, whatever their age, a selected high-fertility group. Acceptors in their 30's had recent fertility rates not much below the average fertility levels of women in their 20's. It is therefore unsafe to assume that such acceptances can have little impact on the birth rate.

When the Taichung experiment was begun, almost all family planning programs were concentrating on influencing large numbers of couples to begin using contraception. Little attention was given to problems of continuation and termination. An assumption concerning the IUD, only sometimes made explicit, was that continuation rates would be high. Theoretically, the IUD could remain in place for years and would require no recurrent decisions concerning its use. It soon became apparent that, in Taiwan and elsewhere, despite the many advantages of the IUD, many couples were terminating its use. Most terminations resulted from voluntary removal of the device for medical or other reasons. In some cases the IUD produced side effects such as bleeding, headaches, backaches, etc. Although these side effects were diagnosed as not serious from a medical point of view, and were believed to be psychological in origin in a substantial proportion of the cases, nevertheless the symptoms were very real to the women involved.

In Taichung, 34 percent of IUD acceptors had terminated the use of the first device within one year after the initial insertion, and 51 percent had done so within two years. The results were disappointing to those who expected the IUD to be the perfect contraceptive. Yet, so far as is known, no other contraceptive has even as good a record for continuation over a period of a year or two in a mass program in a developing country. Preliminary reports of experiments underway with the pill in Taiwan and Korea indicate lower continuation rates than for the IUD. Moreover, the rate of termination of first insertions is less significant when reinsertions are considered; 29 percent of those who terminated had at least one subsequent reinsertion. A comparison of continuation rates for IUD acceptors and for women who accepted traditional methods of contraception indicates that IUD acceptors had much higher rates of continuation and much lower pregnancy rates.

Without careful study, termination rates for the IUD cannot be extrapolated from one population to another. Even within a single society, it is risky to extrapolate from a particular stratum to the whole society. The frequent practice of basing IUD studies on special clinic samples or on the population of experimental health areas is especially suspect as a basis for generalizing to a whole population. These special populations frequently receive a quality of medical care and attention not generally available elsewhere, and this can affect termination rates considerably. It is even more risky to attempt to develop some universal coefficient that will translate the number of IUD insertions into the "number of births averted," as is so often done. The number of births averted will depend, first, upon the termination rate, which is not a constant. Secondly, it will depend upon a number of other non-constant factors: the fertility of the couples prior to the insertion, on what they would do if there were no insertion, and on what they do about alternative methods after the use of an IUD is terminated. Administrators who demand a fixed universal number that translates acceptances into births averted, without research on the local situation, can be given an answer based on an arbitrary set of assumptions. But actual results may prove to be far different.

What are the implications of the Taichung experience for population planning programs in other countries? There is a natural tendency to reject out of hand the experience of Taiwan or Korea for programs in such places as India, Pakistan, Indonesia, or Egypt. The argument is that Taiwan and Korea are so much more developed and so much farther along the road of demographic transition that they are not comparable with countries in which literacy, per-capita income, availability of medical personnel, evidence of pre-existing birth control practice, etc., is much less. The basic premise of this argument is that birth control practice and declining birth rates occur only when a society has passed a minimal threshold of economic and social change. A counter-argument is that no one knows what specific changes in mortality or in social structure are necessary preconditions for specific changes in birth control practice and fertility. Recent studies of the history of demographic transition in Europe have challenged some premises of theories relating to the European fertility decline—premises central to much theorizing and prediction concerning the future fertility of developing countries. Many of the generalizations about developing countries seem to be based on the dubious assumption that these countries stand socially where Europe was before its fertility began to decline—that developing countries are no different today than they were 25 or 50 or 100 years ago, when their mortality levels and kinship-centered social structures were probably strongly supportive of high-fertility norms and behavior. They have, in fact, changed in several ways. Lower mortality is profoundly affecting internal demographic pressures. The elite, as well as increasing numbers of the non-elite, have been linked to other countries through the mass media and the market place. There are rapidly changing levels of aspirations for consumer goods, education, better health, etc. These changes have proceeded further in urban and educated strata than in the mass of these populations, but even remote villages of India show evidence of linkage to a wider national and world community, of an incongruous juxtaposition of new and traditional ideas and objects. Even though it may be true that population programs cannot be completely successful without profound social changes with respect to the role of women, industrialization, social security outside the family, etc., it can still be argued that family planning programs are justified in conjunction with the pursuit of more general social and economic transformations.

One argument for the idea that India, for example, is "not ready" for a Taiwan-type program is that the Indian program of many years has not been very successful. For years, however, the Indian program was poorly staffed and inadequately organized. Recently there has been considerable increase in efforts, expenditures, and acceptance rates. The test of what would happen with an "all-out" program in India has not yet been made; no systematic program has been conducted in any large unit of the country over a reasonable period of years. The point is not that such a program would be greatly successful, but that it needs to be tested.

It is possible to assume that the past

failure of a country like India to carry out a systematic program is an endemic symptom of the lack of development. This may be true, but, again, this argument has not really been tested. India and Pakistan are unevenly developed. The most advanced parts of the population would presumably respond most readily to a program effort. This is an argument for concentrating effort in some areas and strata more than others. For various reasons, quite a different policy is being followed in many important programs. Resources and efforts are spread rather thinly and uniformly throughout the country. This would appear to ignore some motivational aspects, including the provision of social support for actions that millions view with considerable ambivalence.

An argument commonly advanced against current programs is that even if they are successful in helping to reduce the average number of children per family from seven to four, the "population problem" will not be solved. There are several answers to this: If the ideal goal for some countries may be an average of two children per family, it is still necessary to move through the average size of four to attain the ultimate goal of two. Programs that legitimate the idea that birth control can limit family growth at three or four children also spread the idea that birth control can be used to achieve any desired family size. The emphasis in current programs on reaching those who want no more children (rather than trying to change values about desired family size) is ethically justifiable, politically practical, and pedagogically sound.

The power of diffusion demonstrated in Taichung (and, later, throughout Taiwan) may very well indicate that programs should concentrate their efforts at a number of focal points, rather than spreading them thinly over an entire population. Everything possible, consistent with truth, should be done to increase awareness in the population that birth control is accepted by trusted members of their primary group. This reduces "pluralistic ignorance"—the situation in which many people accept an idea but believe that everyone else is against it. In line with this idea, ten acceptors in each of ten villages may be much more effective than one acceptor in each of 100 villages. While respondents in a survey may say "yes" or "no" to the question of "do you want more children" or "do you want birth control," the Taiwan experience indicates that what most people mean is "maybe."

Primary attention should be given to couples who feel themselves to be under demographic pressure. This includes couples who say they want no more children, and also those who have had the moderate number of children and sons that they want. The goal of reaching younger or lower-parity women is much more difficult to attain.

Programs should also be organized so that primary attention is given to the continuing practice of birth control by acceptors, rather than to the continued use of any particular method in the program. Evidence from Taichung, from Taiwan, and from Korea is that high termination rates for the IUD, for example, do not mean the end of birth control practice.

Every major family planning program should include means of evaluating itself. Although the evaluation activities in Taichung and Taiwan had many inadequacies, they provided several advantages: The initial surveys helped to alleviate doubts about the feasibility of such a program, and led to a program larger than was originally planned. The quick reporting of results from the Taichung experience helped to provide a basis for rapid expansion to an island-wide program. When anecdotal reports of IUD terminations worried administrators, follow-up surveys helped to define the magnitude of the problem. Information indicating that IUD-terminated cases were finding other means of limiting their birth rates was relevant to questions about whether it was important to invest in programs designed to reduce termination rates. Information about the fact that older and higher-parity acceptors still had high fecundability provided reassurance that the program was reaching women whose actions could make a difference, for both their families and for the general population.

The Taichung study was the first step toward an island-wide program that by the end of 1968 had provided services to 500,000 couples. Social changes throughout Taiwan are now under joint study by the Taiwan and Michigan research groups. Although this larger program is reaching the less modern strata of the population, it is still evident that the practice of birth control is strongly associated with modernization and development. It is still an open question whether organized family planning programs will be successful in reaching the rural, illiterate, tradition-directed masses in countries that lack an elite strata or centers of influence of the kind found in Taiwan. This question has been decided neither by historical evidence nor recent experience. Certain developmental changes are very likely important to reducing fertility: more education, particularly for women; involvement in markets that transcend the local economy; links with other societies through such mass media as the newspaper, radio, television, etc. Such changes have profound effects on population growth rates, but family planning programs can also make an important contribution. The types of programs suitable for particular populations must, however, be selected with care. In assessing proposed programs, several factors must be considered: their ethical acceptability, presumed effectiveness, and technical, political, economic, and administrative feasibility. A weakness in any of these six aspects can limit a beautiful paper plan to little more than that—paper. And if such a plan is put into operation, it can become very expensive paper.

3 What Do Attitude Surveys Tell Us?

PAUL F. LAZARSFELD

Sociologists are not infrequently accused by laymen of "elaborating the obvious"—of investing time, energy, and dollars in surveys which, in the end, only reveal "what everybody already knows." But there are dangers inherent in too-heavy dependence on common-sense generalizations about attitudes and behavior, as Paul Lazarsfeld demonstrates dramatically here. He makes his point as a part of a review of two publications which set forth the findings of extensive attitude surveys conducted by the Army during World War II—the results of which were used in a new and wholly unprecedented fashion to improve the selection, training, assignment, and morale of American soldiers.

It will be helpful to consider the special role played by attitude surveys in contemporary social science. Although surveys are only one of the many techniques available, at the moment they undoubtedly constitute the most important and promising step forward that has been made in recent years.

The limitations of survey methods are obvious. They do not use experimental techniques; they rely primarily on what people say, and rarely include objective observations; they deal with aggregates of individuals rather than with integrated communities; they are restricted to contemporary problems—history can be studied only by the use of documents remaining from earlier periods.

In spite of these limitations survey methods provide one of the foundations upon which social science is being built. The finding of regularities is the beginning of any science, and surveys can make an important contribution in this respect. For it is necessary that we know what people usually do under many and different circumstances if we are to develop theories explaining their behavior. Furthermore, before we can devise an experiment we must know what problems are worthwhile; which should be investigated in greater detail. Here again surveys can be of service.

Finding regularities and determining criteria of significance are concerns the social sciences have in common with the natural sciences. But there are crucial differences between the two fields of inquiry. The world of social events is much less "visible" than the realm of nature. That bodies fall to the ground, that things are hot or cold, that iron becomes rusty, are all immediately obvious. It is much more difficult to realize that ideas of right and wrong vary in different cultures; that customs may serve a different function from the one which the people practising them believe they are serving; that the same person may show marked contrasts in his behavior as a member of a family and as a member of an occupational

SOURCE: Paul F. Lazarsfeld, "The American Soldier—An Expository Review," *The Public Opinion Quarterly*, vol. 13, no. 3 (Fall 1949), 378–80. Reprinted by permission. • The author is professor emeritus at Columbia University and was formerly director of the Bureau of Applied Social Research. He has acted as a consultant for agencies concerned with problems of communication by radio, newspaper, or magazine. He is a former president of the American Sociological Association and the coauthor of *The People's Choice, Continuities in Social Research,* and *Language of Social Research.*

group. The mere description of human behavior, of its variation from group to group and of its changes in different situations, is a vast and difficult undertaking. It is this task of describing, sifting and ferreting out interrelationships which surveys perform for us. And yet this very function often leads to serious misunderstandings. For it is hard to find a form of human behavior that has not already been observed somewhere. Consequently, if a study reports a prevailing regularity, many readers respond to it by thinking "of course that is the way things are." Thus, from time to time, the argument is advanced that surveys only put into complicated form observations which are already obvious to everyone.

Understanding the origin of this point of view is of importance far beyond the limits of the present discussion. The reader may be helped in recognizing this attitude if he looks over a few statements which are typical of many survey findings and carefully observes his own reaction. A short list of these, with brief interpretive comments, will be given here in order to bring into sharper focus probable reactions of many readers.

1. Better educated men showed more psychoneurotic symptoms than those with less education. (The mental instability of the intellectual as compared to the more impassive psychology of the-man-in-the-street has often been commented on.)
2. Men from rural backgrounds were usually in better spirits during their Army life than soldiers from city backgrounds. (After all, they are more accustomed to hardships.)
3. Southern soldiers were better able to stand the climate in the hot South Sea Islands than Northern soldiers. (Of course, Southerners are more accustomed to hot weather.)
4. White privates were more eager to become non-coms than Negroes. (The lack of ambition among Negroes is almost proverbial.)
5. Southern Negroes preferred Southern to Northern white officers. (Isn't it well known that Southern whites have a more fatherly attitude toward their "darkies"?)
6. As long as the fighting continued, men were more eager to be returned to the States than they were after the German surrender. (You cannot blame people for not wanting to be killed.)

We have in these examples a sample list of the simplest type of interrelationships which provide the "bricks" from which our empirical social science is being built. But why, since they are so obvious, is so much money and energy given to establish such findings? Would it not be wiser to take them for granted and proceed directly to a more sophisticated type of analysis? This might be so except for one interesting point about the list. *Every one of these statements is the direct opposite of what actually was found.* Poorly educated soldiers were more neurotic than those with high education; Southerners showed no greater ability than Northerners to adjust to a tropical climate; Negroes were more eager for promotion than whites; and so on.

If we had mentioned the actual results of the investigation first, the reader would have labelled these "obvious" also. Obviously something is wrong with the entire argument of "obviousness." It should really be turned on its head. Since every kind of human reaction is conceivable, it is of great importance to know which reactions actually occur most frequently and under what conditions; only then will a more advanced social science develop.

4 Manifest and Latent Functions

ROBERT K. MERTON

Most social scientists are "functionalists." That is, they are more concerned with the functions of various phenomena than with trying to ascertain the "real nature" of the phenomena. Stated in another way, modern social science is more concerned with what things do *than with what things allegedly* are. *As one investigator has expressed it, the usefulness of electricity was limited as long as physicists concerned themselves with the vain attempt to find out what electricity is; progress came only when men turned to the task of finding what electricity could do and contented themselves with defining electricity as "that which does such and such." In this article, Robert K. Merton applies the functionalist approach to political machines, by concentrating on what they do, rather than what they are. In using this approach, he illustrates that a function may be manifest (obvious or intended) or latent (hidden or unintended), and points up the utility of these theoretical ideas for would-be "social engineers."*

SOME FUNCTIONS OF THE POLITICAL MACHINE

Without presuming to enter into the variations of detail marking different political machines—a Tweed, Vare, Crump, Flynn, Hague are by no means identical types of bosses—we can briefly examine the functions more or less common to the political machine, as a generic type of social organization. We neither attempt to itemize all the diverse functions of the political machine nor imply that all these functions are similarly fulfilled by each and every machine.

The key structural function of the Boss is to organize, centralize and maintain in good working condition "the scattered fragments of power" which are at present dispersed through our political organization. By this centralized organization of political power, the Boss and his apparatus can satisfy the needs of diverse subgroups in the larger community which are not adequately satisfied by legally devised and culturally approved social structures.

To understand the role of bossism and the machine, therefore, we must look at two types of sociological variables: (1) the *structural context* which makes it difficult, if not impossible, for morally approved structures to fulfill essential social functions, thus leaving the door open for political machines (or their structural equivalents) to fulfill these functions and (2) the subgroups whose distinctive needs are left unsatisfied, except for the latent functions which the machine in fact fulfills.

Structural Context

The constitutional framework of American political organization specifically

SOURCE: Reprinted from *Social Theory and Social Structure,* pp. 71–81, by permission of The Free Press, Glencoe, Illinois. Copyright 1949. • The author is Giddings Professor of Sociology, Columbia University, and associate director of the Bureau of Applied Social Research. He is a past president of the American Sociological Association. His main interests include the sociology of professions, the sociology of science, sociological theory, and mass communications. He is the author of *On Theoretical Sociology* and *On The Shoulders of Giants,* and the coeditor of *Sociology Today* and *Reader in Bureaucracy.*

precludes the legal possibility of highly centralized power and, it has been noted, thus "discourages the growth of effective and responsible leadership. The framers of the Constitution, as Woodrow Wilson observed, set up the check and balance system 'to keep government at a sort of mechanical equipoise by means of a standing amicable contest among its several organic parts.' They distrusted power as dangerous to liberty: and therefore they spread it thin and erected barriers against its concentration." This dispersion of power is found not only at the national level but in local areas as well. "As a consequence," Sait goes on to observe, "when *the people or particular groups* among them demanded positive action, no one had adequate authority to act. The machine provided an antidote."

The constitutional dispersion of power not only makes for difficulty of effective decision and action but when action does occur it is defined and hemmed in by legalistic considerations. In consequence, there develops "a much *more human system* of partisan government, whose chief object soon became the circumvention of government by law. . . . The lawlessness of the extra-official democracy was merely the counterpoise of the legalism of the official democracy. The lawyer having been permitted to subordinate democracy to the Law, the Boss had to be called in to extricate the victim, which he did after a fashion and for a consideration."

Officially, political power is dispersed. Various well-known expedients were devised for this manifest objective. Not only was there the familiar separation of powers among the several branches of the government but, in some measure, tenure in each office was limited, rotation in office approved. And the scope of power inherent in each office was severely circumscribed. Yet, observes Sait in rigorously functional terms, "Leadership is necessary; and *since* it does not develop readily within the constitutional framework, the Boss provides it in a crude and irresponsible form from the outside."

Put in more generalized terms, *the functional deficiencies of the official structure generate an alternative (unofficial) structure to fulfill existing needs somewhat more effectively.* Whatever its specific historical origins, the political machine persists as an apparatus for satisfying otherwise unfulfilled needs of diverse groups in the population. By turning to a few of these subgroups and their characteristic needs, we shall be led at once to a range of latent functions of the political machine.

FUNCTIONS OF THE POLITICAL MACHINE FOR DIVERSE SUBGROUPS

It is well known that one source of strength of the political machine derives from its roots in the local community and the neighborhood. The political machine does not regard the electorate as a vague, undifferentiated mass of voters. With a keen sociological intuition, the machine recognizes that the voter is primarily a man living in the specific neighborhood, with specific personal problems and personal wants. Public issues are abstract and remote; private problems are extremely concrete and immediate. It is not through the generalized appeal to large public concerns that the machine operates, but through the direct, quasi-feudal relationships between local representatives of the machine and voters in their neighborhood. Elections are won in the precinct.

The machine welds its link with ordinary men and women by elaborate networks of personal relations. Politics is transformed into personal ties. The precinct captain "must be a friend to every man, assuming, if he does not feel, sympathy with the unfortunate, and utilizing in his good works the resources which the boss puts at his disposal." The precinct captain is forever a friend in need. In our prevailingly impersonal society, the machine, through its local agents, fulfills the important social *function of humanizing and personalizing all manner of assistance* to those in need. Food-baskets and jobs, legal and extra-legal advice, setting to rights minor scrapes with the law, helping the bright poor boy to a political scholarship in a local college, looking after the bereaved—the whole range of crises when a feller needs a friend, and, above all, a friend who knows the score and who can do something about it—all these find the ever-helpful precinct captain available in the pinch.

To assess this function of the political machine adequately, it is important to note not only the fact that aid *is* provided but *the manner in which it is provided.* After all, other agencies do exist for dispensing such assistance. Welfare agencies, settlement houses, legal aid clinics, medical aid in free hospitals, public relief departments, immigration authorities—these and a multitude of other organizations are available to provide the most varied types of assistance. But in contrast to the professional techniques of the welfare worker which may typically represent in the mind of the recipient the cold, bureaucratic dispensation of limited aid following upon detailed investigation of *legal* claims to aid of the "client," are the unprofessional techniques of the precinct captain who asks no questions, exacts no compliance with legal rules of eligibility and does not "snoop" into private affairs.

For many, the loss of "self-respect" is too high a price for legalized assistance. In contrast to the gulf between the settlement house workers who so often come from a different social class, educational background and ethnic group, the precinct worker is "just one of us," who understands what it's all about. The condescending lady bountiful can hardly compete with the understanding friend in need. In *this struggle between alternative structures for fulfilling the nominally same function* of providing aid and support to those who need it, it is clearly the machine politician who is better integrated with the groups which he serves than the impersonal, professionalized, socially distant and legally constrained welfare worker. And since the politician can at times influence and manipulate the official organizations for the dispensation of assistance, whereas the welfare worker has practically no influence on the political machine, this only adds to his greater effectiveness. More colloquially and also, perhaps, more incisively, it was the Boston ward-leader, Martin Lomasny, who described this essential function to the curious Lincoln Steffens: "I think," said Lomasny, "that there's got to be in every ward somebody that any bloke can come to—no matter what he's done—and get help. *Help, you understand; none of your law and justice, but help.*"

The "deprived classes," then, constitute one subgroup for whom the political machine clearly satisfies wants not adequately satisfied in the same fashion by the legitimate social structure.

For a second subgroup, that of business (primarily "big" business but also "small"), the political boss serves the function of providing those political privileges which entail immediate economic gains. Business corporations, among which the public utilities (railroads, local transportation companies, communications corporations, electric light) are simply the most conspicuous in this regard, seek special political dispensations which will enable them to stabilize their situation and to near their objective of maximizing profits. Interestingly enough, corporations often want to avoid a chaos of uncontrolled competition. They want the greater security of an economic czar who controls, regulates and organizes competition, providing this czar is not a public official with his decisions subject to public scrutiny and public control. (The latter would be "government control," and hence taboo.) The political boss fulfills these requirements admirably.

Examined for a moment apart from any "moral" considerations, the political apparatus of the Boss is effectively designed to perform these functions with a minimum of inefficiency. Holding the strings of diverse governmental divisions, bureaus and agencies in his competent hands, the Boss rationalizes the relations between public and private business. He serves as the business community's ambassador in the otherwise alien (and sometimes unfriendly) realm of government. And, in strict business-like terms, he is well-paid for his economic services to his respectable business clients. In an article entitled, "An Apology to Graft," Steffens suggested that "Our economic system, which held up riches, power and acclaim as prizes to men bold enough and able enough to buy corruptly timber, mines, oil fields and franchises and 'get away with it,' was at fault." And, in a conference with a hundred or so of Los Angeles business leaders, he described a fact well known to all of them: the Boss and his machine were an *integral part* of the organization of the economy. "You cannot build or operate a railroad, or a street railway, gas, water, or power company, develop and operate a mine, or get forests and cut timber on a large scale, or run any privileged business, without corrupting or joining in the corruption of the government. You tell me privately that you must, and here I am telling you semi-publicly that you must. And that is so all over the country. And that means that we have an organization of society in which, *for some reason,* you and your kind, the ablest, most intelligent, most imaginative, daring, and resourceful leaders of society, are and must be against society and its laws and its all-around growth."

Since the demand for the services of special privileges are built into the structure of the society, the Boss fulfills diverse functions for this second subgroup of business-seeking-privilege. These "needs" of business, as presently constituted, are not adequately provided for by "conventional" and "culturally approved" social structures; consequently, the extra-legal but more-or-less efficient organization of the political machine comes to provide these services. To adopt an *exclusively* moral attitude toward the "corrupt political machine" is to lose sight of the very structural conditions which generate the "evil" that is so bitterly attacked. To adopt a functional outlook on the political machine is not to provide an apologia, but a more solid base for modifying or eliminating the machine, *providing* specific structural arrangements are introduced either for eliminating these effective demands of the business community or, if that is the objective, of satisfying these demands through alternative means.

A third set of distinctive functions fulfilled by the political machine for a special subgroup is that of providing alternative channels of social mobility for those otherwise excluded from the more conventional avenues for personal "advancement." Both the sources of this special "need" (for social mobility) and the respect in which the political machine comes to help satisfy this need can be understood by examining the structure of the larger culture and society. As is well known, the American culture lays enormous emphasis on money and power as a "success" goal legitimate for all members of the society. By no means alone in our inventory of cultural goals, it still remains among the most heavily endowed with positive affect and value. However, certain subgroups and certain ecological areas are notable for the relative absence of opportunity for achieving these (monetary and power) types of success. They constitute, in short, subpopulations where "the cultural emphasis upon pecuniary success has been absorbed, but where there is *little access to conventional and legitimate* means for attaining such success. The conventional occupational opportunities of persons in (such areas) are almost completely limited to manual labor. Given our cultural stigmatization of manual labor, and its correlate, the prestige of white-collar work," it is clear that the result is a tendency to achieve these culturally approved objectives *through whatever means are possible*. These people are on the one hand, "asked to orient their conduct toward the prospect of accumulating wealth [and power] and, on the other, they are largely denied effective opportunities to do so institutionally."

It is within this context of social structure that the political machine fulfills the basic function of providing avenues of social mobility for the otherwise disadvantaged. Within this context, even the corrupt political machine and the racket "represent the triumph of amoral intelligence over morally prescribed 'failure' when the channels of vertical mobility are closed or narrowed *in a society which places a high premium on economic affluence [power], and social ascent for all its members*." As one sociologist has noted on the basis of several years of close observation in a "slum area":

> The sociologist who dismisses racket and political organizations as deviations from desirable standards thereby neglects some of the major elements of slum life. . . . *He does not discover the functions they perform for the members* [of the groupings in the slum]. The Irish and later immigrant peoples have had the greatest difficulty in finding places for themselves in our urban social and economic structure. Does anyone believe that the immigrants and their children could have achieved their present degree of social mobility without gaining control of the political organization of some of our largest cities? The same is true of the racket organization. *Politics and the rackets have furnished an important means of social mobility for individuals, who, because of ethnic background and low class position,* are blocked from advancement in the "respectable" channels.

This, then, represents a third type of function performed for a distinctive subgroup. This function, it may be noted in passing, is fulfilled by the *sheer* existence and operation of the political machine, for it is in the machine itself that these individuals and subgroups find their culturally induced needs more or less satisfied. It refers to the services which the political apparatus provides for its own personnel. But seen in the wider social context we have set forth, it no longer appears as *merely* a means of self-aggrandizement for profit-hungry and power-hungry *individuals*, but as an organized provision for *subgroups* otherwise excluded or restricted from the race for "getting ahead."

Just as the political machine performs services for "legitimate" business, so it operates to perform not dissimilar services for "illegitimate" business: vice, crime and rackets. Once again, the basic sociological role of the machine in this respect can be more fully appreciated only if one temporarily abandons attitudes of moral indignation, to examine with all moral innocence the actual workings of the organization. In this light, it at once appears that the subgroup of the professional criminal, racketeer, gambler, has basic similarities of organization, demands and operation to the subgroup of the industrialist, man of business, speculator. If there is a Lumber King or an Oil King, there is also a Vice King or a Racket King. If expansive legitimate business organizes administrative and financial syndicates to "rationalize" and to "integrate" diverse areas of production and business enterprise, so expansive rackets and crime organize syndicates to bring order to the otherwise chaotic areas of production of illicit goods and services. If legitimate business regards the proliferation of small business enterprises as wasteful and inefficient, substituting, for example the giant chain stores for the hundreds of corner groceries, so illegitimate business adopts the same businesslike attitude, and syndicates crime and vice.

Finally, and in many respects, most important, is the basic similarity, if not near-identity, of the economic role of "legitimate" business and "illegitimate" business. *Both are in some degree concerned with the provision of goods and services for which there is an economic demand.* Morals aside, they are both business, industrial and professional enterprises, dispensing goods and services which some people want, for which there is a market in which goods and services are transformed into commodities. And, in a prevalently market society, we should expect appropriate enterprises to arise whenever there is a market demand for given goods or services.

As is well known, vice, crime and the rackets *are* "big business." Consider only that there have been estimated to be about 500,000 professional prostitutes in the United States, and compare this with the approximately 200,000 physicians and 200,000 nurses. It is difficult to estimate which have the larger clientele: the professional men and women of medicine or the professional men and women of vice. It is, of course, difficult to estimate the economic assets, income, profits and dividends of illicit gambling in this country and to compare it with the economic assets, income, profits and dividends of, say, the shoe industry, but it is altogether possible that the two industries are about on a par. No precise figures exist on the annual expenditures on illicit narcotics, and it is probable that these are less than the expenditures on candy, but it is also probable that they are larger than the expenditure on books.

It takes but a moment's thought to recognize that, *in strictly economic terms,* there is no relevant difference between the provision of licit and illicit goods and services. The liquor traffic illustrates this perfectly. It would be peculiar to argue that prior to 1920 (when the 18th amendment became effective), the provision of liquor constituted an economic service, that from 1920 to 1933, its production and sale no longer constituted an economic service dispensed in a market, and that from 1934 to the present, it once again took on a serviceable aspect. Or, it would be *economically* (not morally) absurd to suggest that the sale of bootlegged liquor in the dry state of Kansas is less a response to a market demand than the sale of publicly manufactured liquor in the neighboring wet state of Missouri. Examples of this sort can of course be multiplied many times over. Can it be held that in European countries, with registered and legalized prostitution, the prostitute contributes an economic service, whereas in this country, lacking legal sanction, the prostitute provides no such service? Or that the professional abortionist is in the economic market where he has approved legal status and that he is out of the economic market where he is legally taboo? Or that gambling satisfies a specific demand for entertainment in Nevada, where it is one of the largest business enterprises of the largest city in the state, but that it differs essentially in this respect from movie houses in the neighboring state of California?

The failure to recognize that these businesses are only *morally* and not *economically* distinguishable from "legitimate" businesses has led to badly scrambled analysis. Once the economic identity of the two is recognized, we may anticipate that if the political machine performs functions for "legitimate big business" it will be all the more likely to perform not dissimilar functions for "illegitimate big business." And, of course, such is often the case.

The distinctive function of the political machine for their criminal, vice and racket clientele is to enable them to operate in satisfying the economic demands of a large market without due interference from the government. Just as big business may contribute funds to the political party war-chest to ensure a minimum of governmental interference, so with big rackets and big crime. In both instances, the political machine can, in varying degrees, provide "protection." In both instances, many features of the structural context are identical: (1) market demands for goods and services; (2) the operators' concern with maximizing gains from their enterprises; (3) the need for partial control of government which might otherwise interfere with these activities of businessmen; (4) the need for an efficient, powerful and centralized agency to provide an effective liaison of "business" with government.

Without assuming that the foregoing pages exhaust either the range of functions or the range of subgroups served by the political machine, we can at least see that *it presently fulfills some functions for these diverse subgroups which are not adequately fulfilled by culturally approved or more conventional structures.*

Several additional implications of the functional analysis of the political machine can be mentioned here only in passing, although they obviously require to be developed at length. First, the foregoing analysis has direct implications for *social engineering.* It helps explain why the periodic efforts at "political reform," "turning the rascals out" and "cleaning political house" are typically short-lived and ineffectual. It exemplifies a basic theorem: *any attempt to eliminate an existing social structure without providing adequate alternative structures for fulfilling the functions previously fulfilled by the abolished organization is doomed to failure.* (Needless to say, this theorem has much wider bearing than the one instance of the political machine.) When "political reform" confines itself to the manifest task of "turning the rascals out," it is engaging in little more than sociological magic. The reform may for a time bring new figures into the political limelight; it may serve the casual social function of reassuring the electorate that the moral virtues remain intact and will ultimately triumph; it may actually effect a turnover in the personnel of the political machine; it may even, for a time, so curb the activities of the machine as to leave unsatisfied the many needs it has previously fulfilled. But, inevitably, unless the reform also involves a "re-forming" of the social and political structure such that the existing needs are satisfied by alternative structures or unless it involves a change which eliminates these needs altogether, the political machine will return to its integral place in the social scheme of things. *To seek social change, without due recognition of the manifest and latent functions performed by the social organization undergoing change, is to indulge in social ritual rather than social engineer-*

ing. The concepts of manifest and latent functions (or their equivalents) are indispensable elements in the theoretic repertoire of the social engineer. In this crucial sense, these concepts are not "merely" theoretical (in the abusive sense of the term), but are eminently practical. In the deliberate enactment of social change, they can be ignored only at the price of considerably heightening the risk of failure.

A second implication of our analysis of the political machine also has a bearing upon areas wider than the one we have considered. The "paradox" has often been noted that the supporters of the political machine include both the "respectable" business class elements who are, of course, opposed to the criminal or racketeer and the distinctly "unrespectable" elements of the underworld. And, at first appearance, this is cited as an instance of very strange bedfellows. The learned judge is not infrequently called upon to sentence the very racketeer beside whom he sat the night before at an informal dinner of the political bigwigs. The district attorney jostles the exonerated convict on his way to the back room where the Boss has called a meeting. The big business man may complain almost as bitterly as the big racketeer about the "extortionate" contributions to the party fund demanded by the Boss. Social opposites meet—in the smoke-filled room of the successful politician.

In the light of a functional analysis all this of course no longer seems paradoxical. Since the machine serves both the business man and the criminal man, the two seemingly antipodal groups intersect. This points to a more general theorem: *the social functions of an organization help determine the structure (including the recruitment of personnel involved in the structure), just as the structure helps determine the effectiveness with which the functions are fulfilled.* In terms of social status, the business group and the criminal group are indeed poles apart. But status does not fully determine behavior and the inter-relations between groups. Functions modify these relations. Given their distinctive needs, the several subgroups in the large society are "integrated," whatever their personal desires or intentions, by the centralizing structure which serves these several needs. In a phrase with many implications which require further study, *structure affects function and function affects structure.*

5 A Critique of Cultural Relativism

ROBERT REDFIELD

In this discussion of the basic theoretical viewpoint known as "cultural relativity," Robert Redfield does not argue against the obvious fact that truths may be regarded as relative to time, place, and a particular culture. But he does assert that acceptance of relativity does not necessitate rejection of all value commitments. Redfield's assertion has immense practical significance because he points to the dangers, as well as to the logical fallacies, of those who would say, for example, "since everything is right in terms of its own logic, I cannot condemn the excesses of totalitarianism." As Redfield shows, science itself would cease to exist if such an attitude were carried to its logical extreme.

I will consider some of the questions that arise when we look at the primitive or the precivilized cultures with a view to the goodness or the badness of them. . . . My own behavior, as an anthropologist, is relevant to the subject now to be discussed, for I am interested here in the way anthropologists do or do not place values on the things they see in prehistoric or in contemporary nonliterate or illiterate societies, and what comes of it if they do. I shall venture to anthropologize the anthropologists, and shall not leave myself out of their number.

. . . Writing of Petalesharoo, the Pawnee Indian who in the face of the customs of his tribe rescued a woman prisoner about to be put to death ceremonially and strove to end human sacrifice among his people, I called him "a hint of human goodness." Plainly I placed a value on his conduct. Looking back twenty-five years, I recall when as a student I first heard the story of Petalesharoo from Professor Fay-Cooper Cole, anthropologist. He told the story with great human warmth, and I know that then I responded sympathetically. Now I begin to wonder if he or I *could* tell the tale barely, neutrally, without implying admiration of the deed.

In my writings, I have not infrequently indicated my admiration for some act, my approval of some turn in human events. The long story of human affairs which I have been sketchily recounting is a story in which I have not pretended to be disinterested. It is the human biography; it is your story and mine; how can we help but care? I have not tried to conceal a certain sense of satisfaction that in the childhood of our race, before there were cities, precivilized men, like the preliterates of today, recognized moral obligations, even if the moral rules were not my rules. I think this better than the unrestrained selfishness which Hobbes imagined wrongly to characterize the behavior of men before political society developed. So when in the course of these discussions I have encountered in some uncivilized

SOURCE: Robert Redfield, *The Primitive World and Its Transformations* (Ithaca, N.Y.: Cornell University Press, 1953), 139–64, passim. • Robert Redfield (1897–1958) was chairman of the Department of Anthropology and Distinguished Service Professor at the University of Chicago. His chief interests lay in ethnological studies. From 1930 to 1947 he directed ethnological field work in Yucatan and Guatemala. Among his books are *The Folk Culture of Yucatan, The Primitive World and Its Transformations, The Little Community,* and *The Social Uses of Science.*

society a custom which I liked or disliked, I think I have in many cases shown how I felt about it. I regret that the Siriono in the Bolivian forest abandon their dying kinsmen without a word, while I come to understand the rigors of their life that make such conduct excusable. I am pleased that the Yagua in their big communal houses respect even a child's desire to be alone, and refrain from speaking to him when he turns his face to the wall. . . .

This is, perhaps, a shocking admission. What right have I, who admit to caring about the human career, to speak as an anthropologist? For are not anthropologists enjoined to adopt in their work a rigid objectivity? Professor Kroeber has written that "there is no room in anthropology for a shred of ethnocentricity, of homino-centricity." My ethnocentricity appears in the positive valuations I have placed on the increase and widening of humane standards, for are not such standards a special pride of Euro-American civilization? And my homini-centricity is patent: I have placed myself squarely on the side of mankind, and have not shamed to wish mankind well.

My predicament stimulates an examination of some of the problems of objectivity and value judgment that arise in anthropology. There are a good many of these problems, and I shall try to sort them out and to reach at least the first points of understanding as to what is involved in some of them.

. . . . .

Since Westermarck wrote two books to show that it is not possible to establish one way of thought or action as better than another, if not before that time, anthropologists have taken this position. It has come to have a name: cultural relativism. Most anthropologists would, I think, accept the term as naming their position, or would take the position without perhaps accepting the name. Cultural relativism means that the values expressed in any culture are to be both understood and themselves valued only according to the way the people who carry that culture see things. In looking at a polygamous society and a monogamous society, we have no valid way to assert that the one is better than the other. Both systems provide for human needs; each has values discoverable only when we look at marriage from the point of view of the man who lives under the one system or the other. This is, necessarily then, also to be said in comparing cultures which practice torture, infanticide, in-group sorcery, and homosexuality with those that do not. The gist of cultural relativism as stated by Professor Herskovits, who has discussed the concept at length, is that "judgments are based on experience, and experience is interpreted by each individual in terms of his own enculturation."

With this proposition I do not disagree. I fail to see that having accepted it one finds it necessary to accept everything else that Professor Herskovits says about cultural relativism. . . .

. . . I am persuaded that cultural relativism is in for some difficult times. Anthropologists are likely to find the doctrine a hard one to maintain. The criticisms of philosophers will be directed more sharply against it. Moreover, the experiences of anthropologists are changing, and these changed experiences will work changes in their judgments as to the relativity of values. (It occurs to me that this proposition is itself an application of the principle!) It was easy to look with equal benevolence upon all sorts of value systems so long as the values were those of unimportant little people remote from our own concerns. But the equal benevolence is harder to maintain when one is asked to anthropologize the Nazis, or to help a Point Four administrator decide what to do for those people he is committed to help. The Point Four man is committed to do something to change that people, for he cannot help them without changing them, and what is the anthropologist to say when the Point Four man asks him just what he ought to do? Perhaps the anthropologist can keep on saying: "Do A, and X will result, but Y will result from doing B—*you* choose which to do." But I doubt that if the anthropologist says only this, he and the administrator will get on very well together. And perhaps the anthropologist, if he continues this neutrality, and yet sees a smash coming, will be just a little restless at night.

At any rate, I should like to point out that the doctrine of cultural relativism does enjoin the benevolence. It is a doctrine of ethical neutralism, but it is not a doctrine of ethical indifference. Ruth Benedict's *Patterns of Culture* is an exemplification of cultural relativism. She wrote in large part to tell us that all cultures are "equally valid." But this meant, for her, not that we are to value none of them, but that we are to value all of them. The book is a call to positive sympathetic valuation of other ways of life than our own. Malinowski has gone so far as to write of "the respect due even to savages." And Herskovits states the positive element in the doctrine very clearly. He is not confused into supposing that cultural relativism is a mere scientific method, a procedure instrumental in reaching statements as to fact. No, he says, "cultural relativism is a *philosophy* which, in recognizing the values set up by every society to guide its own life, lays stress on the dignity inherent in every body of custom, and on the need for tolerance of conventions though they may differ from one's own." And again: "Emphasis on the worth of many ways of life, not one, is an affirmation of the values of each culture."

However, the two parts of this doctrine are not logically or necessarily interdependent. The first part says that people are brought up to see the value in things that their local experience has suggested. The second part says that we should respect all cultures. But there is no true "therefore" between these two parts. It cannot be proved, from the proposition that values are relative, that we ought to respect all systems of values. We might just as well hate them all. . . . It is Professor Herskovits who has intruded upon the objectivity of science a moral judgment, which I personally admire, but for which he can show no demonstration of proof.

The anthropologist is, then, ethically neutral, but unlike him of whom the partisan demanded, "Just who are you neutral *for?*," the anthropologist is neutral for everybody. This, at least, is the way anthropologists represent their position. It seems to me that their success in living up to their doctrine may be questioned.

The difficulties of doing so were remarked by not a few of the anthropologists themselves when in 1947 the Executive Board of their American professional association submitted a statement to the Commission on Human Rights of the United Nations. The statement urged the Commission to recognize that, not only should the personality of the individual be accorded respect, but that "respect for the cultures of differing human groups is equally important." It declared the principle of cultural relativity and told the UN Commission that therefore any attempt it might make to write something about human rights ("formulate postulates") "that grow out of the beliefs or moral codes of one culture must to that extent detract from the applicability of any declaration of Human Rights to mankind as a whole." So the Commission was advised to incorporate in the Declaration of Human Rights a statement of the right of men to live in terms of their own traditions.

I understand that the UN Commission did not follow this advice. I imagine that some anthropologists are rather relieved that they did not. Such a declaration might seem to authorize the head-hunting peoples to continue head hunting, for would they not, by continuing head hunting, be living in terms of their own traditions? Of course the anthropologists who drafted this statement were not thinking of the head hunters. They knew, as well as you or I, that the head hunters and the cannibals will not be permitted to live in terms of these particular traditions if it is our heads and bodies they go for. They were thinking of the great and influential world civilizations—Indonesian, Indian, Chinese, African, Euro-American. But even here it is not clear just what the writers of the declaration expected to guarantee to these traditional ways of life—the right of a Mississippi human group to maintain its traditional white supremacy, of Russia to maintain a dehumanizing, fear-ridden way of life? At the time the anthropologists wrote their statement it was perhaps nazism that presented to their minds most plainly the difficulties with their statement, for they wrote in the following sentence: "Even where political systems exist that deny citizens the right of participation in their government, or seek to conquer weaker peoples, underlying cultural values may be called on to bring the peoples of such states to a realization of the consequences of the acts of their governments." If we call upon underlying values to save us, it is we, on the outside of the culture, who are making them effective. And what if the underlying approved values are not there? The sentence is, to put it bluntly, a weasel; by including it, the declaration was made self-contradictory. You either respect all values or you do not. If the Nazis had come to have values approving the subjugation of everybody else, we, or the United Nations, would have either to respect this traditional way of life or not respect it. . . .

. . . . .

As soon as the anthropologist puts his attention on the particular human individuals in a primitive society, it becomes difficult to avoid the suggestion if not the fact that he is valuing one culture, or cultural situation, as better than another. It is not uncommon for an anthropologist, now studying a primitive culture disorganized by its contact with civilization, to see that the people he is studying are less comfortable than they were. Some of them, indeed, as those Oceanic natives whom Rivers described, appear now on their way to extinction just because they do not find life worth living any more. The anthropologist can hardly convince us—or himself—that so far as he is concerned a disorganized culture that fails to provide a desire to live is as valid as any other. Equal validity can be safely attributed only to cultures that arrange it so people do what they want to do and are convinced that it is the right thing to do.

But even among such cultures, the well-integrated and the motive-providing, it is not always possible for the anthropologist to avoid at least the suggestion that he is preferring one of them to another. Ruth Benedict was a cultural relativist who told us that cultures are equally valid. Nevertheless, in reading some of her pages, one doubts that she found them equally good. In the seventh chapter of *Patterns of Culture* she introduces the concept of "social waste." Here she leads the reader to see a resemblance between the values of Kwakiutl society and those of his own (Middletown); both emphasize rivalry. But rivalry, wrote Benedict, is "notoriously wasteful. It ranks low in the scale of human values." One asks, Whose scale? Is there a universal scale of values which ranks rivalry low? She goes on to point out not only that "Kwakiutl rivalry produces a waste of material goods," but also that "the social waste is obvious." In Middletown, also, rivalry is "obsessive." Thus she is led to the conclusion that "it is possible to scrutinize different institutions and cast up their cost in terms of social capital, in terms of the less desirable behavior traits they stimulate, and in terms of human suffering and frustration." . . .

• • • • •

It is that disturbing fellow, the living human individual, who makes trouble for the scientist's stern principle of perfect objectivity. Whenever the anthropologist looks at him, something human inside the anthropologist stirs and responds. It is easy enough to be objective toward objects; but the human individual refuses to be only an object. When he is there before you, he insists on being judged as human beings are judged in life, if not in science. While the anthropologist is looking at the bones of the dead, at flint implements, or at institutions formally conceived and named—the Omaha kinship system or the tribal ideology—he is not much distracted by these claims upon his own human nature. But when the anthropologist meets and talks with some particular Indian or Oceanic islander, then he is apt to feel for that native while he is trying to describe him objectively. If the society is one that is running along the traditional ways of life, the field ethnologist is apt to respond with sympathy and indeed with favor toward the culture that keeps men's lives going in directions that they find good. If the ethnologist is himself gifted in communicating the human warmth of an exotic scene, as was Malinowski, an account results which communicates not only the humanity of the life described, but something of the enjoyment and satisfactions which the ethnologist himself experienced in coming to know that life. If the culture is one which puts the people who live by it into constant and fearful anxieties, the anthropologist is apt to show the disfavor he feels toward such a life. Reo Fortune's Dobuans are familiar; so I mention here instead the Tzeltal Indians of Chiapas, where Alfonso Villa Rojas found a people often sick, always believing that each sickness was the result of some moral transgression committed by the sufferer or, more terribly, by some one of his near kinsmen, and who are continually ridden by anxiety and compulsions to confess sins. Villa has described this people objectively, in the sense that his report is well documented and obviously trustworthy. But it would be untrue to assert that he has not shown, strongly in conversation and of course much more reservedly in his written description, his own unfavorable view of such a life. Furthermore, if one reads such an account of people whose traditional ways of life have been disrupted, as, for example, McGregor's account of a reservation community of Sioux Indians, one finds oneself making value judgments that seem to reflect those of the writer, as to the somewhat unhappy predicament in which these people find themselves.

I think that the objectivity claimed by the anthropologist must admit of difficulties and qualifications. Professor Herskovits declares that "a basic necessity of ethnographic research . . . calls for a rigid exclusion of value judgments." This seems a little too strongly put. Rather, I should say, ethnographic research calls for as much objectivity as can be combined with the necessity to come to know the values of the people one is studying. The exception to allow the ethnographer to respect—i.e., value positively—all cultures has already been noted. Professor R. H. Tawney is then expressing an opinion with which we may suppose that Professor Herskovits would agree when he writes that the student of a society must bring to his study "respect and affection." The necessity to understand the values of the people one is studying requires, I should say, the projection into unfamiliar words and actions of human qualities—sympathy, pride, wish to be appreciated, and so on. Otherwise the ethnologist will not find out what the people he is studying are proud about or what, for them, deserves appreciation. My own opinion is that it is not possible to make use of these human qualities in field work, as I think one must, without also valuing what one sees. In the very necessity to describe the native, one must feel for him—or perhaps against him. The feelings are mixed with valuations. In Indian communities in which I have worked, I have found myself constantly liking and disliking some people as compared with others, some customs as compared with others, and some aspects of the total culture as compared with others. I remember, after having spent a good deal of time in Chan Kom, Yucatan, how I had come to admire a certain quality of decency and dignity about the people, and how bored I had become with their—to me—overemphasis on the prudent and the practical. If they would only once admire a sunset or report a mystic experience, I used to hear myself thinking. I would not know how to find out about a culture without this sort of valuing. Objectivity requires that I hold in suspense each formulation I make about the native life. It requires me to become aware of the values I have that may lead me in one direction rather than another. It demands that I subject my descriptions to the tests of documentation, internal consistency, and if possible the evidence and judgments of other observers. But I do not think that it asks of me that I divest myself of the human qualities, including valuing. I could not do my work without them.

. . . . .

. . . Perhaps we should ask of the field ethnologist, not that he divest himself of values, for that is impossible, nor that he emphasize in every case values predominating in his own times with regard to applied science, increased production, and adjusted personalities, but that he make plain what he does find that is good or bad about the people he reports. And then, also, perhaps he can help to bring it about that he is followed in the same community to be studied by an ethnologist with a contrasting value emphasis! It was the *New Yorker* that suggested that we do not want balanced textbooks; we want balanced libraries. We do not want ethnologists so balanced that they have no humanity. We want a balanced profession, a varied lot of anthropologists.

. . . . .

My praise of Petalesharoo here receives explanation, if not justification. Petalesharoo acted against the customary practice of his people. It is a little easier to do that after civilization than before; in precivilized societies it was harder. So Petalesharoo gets my praise on that count. And when he acted, he acted in conformity with the trend of the human career of which he was ignorant, but which I know about, being some thousands of years older in civilization than was he. So it is not remarkable that I praise him. Perhaps also you, my reader, do too.

If you do, and you are not an anthropologist, no one will scold. But I am an anthropologist, and have taken the oath of objectivity. Somehow the broken pledge—if it is broken—sits lightly on my conscience. In me, man and anthropologist do not separate themselves sharply. I used to think I could bring about that separation in scientific work about humanity. Now I have come to confess that I have not effected it, and indeed to think that it is not possible to do so. All the rules of objectivity I should maintain: the marshaling of evidence that may be confirmed by others, the persistent doubting and testing of all important descriptive formulations that I make, the humility before the facts, and the willingness tc confess oneself wrong and begin over. I hope I may always strive to obey these rules. But I think now that what I see men do, and understand as something that human beings do, is seen often with a valuing of it. I like or dislike as I go. This is how I reach understanding of it. The double standard of ethical judgment toward primitive peoples is a part of my version of cultural relativity. It is because I am a product of civilization that I value as I do. It is because I am a product of civilization that I have both a range of experience within which to do my understanding-valuing and the scientific disciplines that help me to describe what I value so that others will accept it, or recognizing it as not near enough the truth, to correct it. And if, in this too I am wrong, those others will correct me here also.

6 Is Freedom Dying in America?

HENRY STEELE COMMAGER

Only an irresponsible sociologist would claim to be unaccountable for the consequences of his actions in society. The extent to which today's educated Americans hold social scientists, including sociologists, responsible for helping to solve the problems of our society is evidence both of the maturing of sociology and public identification of the social sciences with science generally. The professional historian who performs his role responsibly combines the philosophy and methods of the social scientist and the humanist in a unique fashion. In this troubled world Henry Steele Commager performs the historian's unique role magnificently by both raising and answering the question, "Is Freedom Dying in America?"

For 2,500 years, civilized men have yearned and struggled for freedom from tyranny—the tyranny of despotic government and superstition and ignorance. What explains this long devotion to the idea and practice of freedom? How does it happen that all Western societies so exalt freedom that they have come to equate it with civilization itself?

Freedom has won its exalted place in philosophy and policy quite simply because, over the centuries, we have come to see that it is a necessity; a necessity

SOURCE: *Look,* vol. 34, no. 14 (July 14, 1970), 16–21. • The author is Sperenze Lecturer and professor of history at Amherst College. He is author of *Majority Rule and Minority Rights, The American Mind, Living Ideas in America,* and *Freedom, Loyalty, Dissent.*

for justice, a necessity for progress, a necessity for survival.

How familiar the argument that we must learn to reconcile the rival claims of freedom and order. But they do not really need to be reconciled; they were never at odds. They are not alternatives, they are two sides to the same coin, indissolubly welded together. The community—society or nation—has an interest in the rights of the individual because without the exercise of those rights, the community itself will decay and collapse. The individual has an interest in the stability of the community of which he is a part because without security, his rights are useless. No community can long prosper without nourishing the exercise of individual liberties for, as John Stuart Mill wrote a century ago, "A State which dwarfs its men, in order that they may be more docile instruments in its hands . . . will find that with small men no great thing can really be accomplished." And no individual can fulfill his genius without supporting the just authority of the state, for in a condition of anarchy, neither dignity nor freedom can prosper.

The function of freedom is not merely to protect and exalt the individual, vital as that is to the health of society. Put quite simply, we foster freedom in order to avoid error and discover truth; so far, we have found no other way to achieve this objective. So, too, with dissent. We do not indulge dissent for sentimental reasons; we encourage it because we have learned that we cannot live without it. A nation that silences dissent, whether by force, intimidation, the withholding of information or a foggy intellectual climate, invites disaster. A nation that penalizes criticism is left with passive acquiescence in error. A nation that discourages originality is left with minds that are unimaginative and dull. And with stunted minds, as with stunted men, no great thing can be accomplished.

It is for this reason that history celebrates not the victors who successfully silenced dissent but their victims who fought to speak the truth as they saw it. It is the bust of Socrates that stands in the schoolroom, not the busts of those who condemned him to death for "corrupting the youth." It is Savonarola we honor, not the Pope who had him burned there in the great Piazza in Florence. It is Tom Paine we honor, not the English judge who outlawed him for writing *The Rights of Man.*

Our own history, too, is one of rebellion against authority. We remember Roger Williams, who championed toleration, not John Cotton, who drove him from the Bay Colony; we celebrate Thomas Jefferson, whose motto was "Rebellion to tyrants is obedience to God," not Lord North; we read Henry Thoreau on civil disobedience, rather than those messages of President Polk that earned him the title "Polk the Mendacious"; it is John Brown's soul that goes marching on, not that of the judge who condemned him to death at Charles Town.

Why is this? It is not merely because of the nobility of character of these martyrs. Some were not particularly noble. It is because we can see now that they gave their lives to defend the interests of humanity, and that they, not those who punished them, were the true benefactors of humanity.

But it is not just the past that needed freedom for critics, nonconformists and dissenters. We, too, are assailed by problems that seem insoluble; we, too, need new ideas. Happily, ours is not a closed system—not yet, anyway. We have a long history of experimentation in politics, social relations and science. We experiment in astrophysics because we want to land on the moon; we experiment in biology because we want to find the secret of life; we experiment in medicine because we want to cure cancer; and in all of these areas, and a hundred others, we make progress. If we are to survive and flourish, we must approach politics, law and social institutions in the same spirit that we approach science. We know that we have not found final truth in physics or biology. Why do we suppose that we have found final truth in politics or law? And just as scientists welcome new truth wherever they find it, even in the most disreputable places, so statesmen, jurists and educators must be prepared to welcome new ideas and new truths from whatever sources they come, however alien their appearance, however revolutionary their implications.

"There can *be* no difference anywhere," said the philosopher William James, "that doesn't make a difference elsewhere—no difference in abstract truth that doesn't express itself in a difference in concrete fact. . . ."

Let us turn then to practical and particular issues and ask, in each case, what are and will be the consequences of policies that repress freedom, discourage independence and impair justice in American society, and what are, and will be, the consequences of applying to politics and society those standards and habits of free inquiry that we apply as a matter of course to scientific inquiry?

Consider the erosion of due process of law—that complex of rules and safeguards built up over the centuries to make sure that every man will have a fair trial. Remember that it is designed not only for the protection of desperate characters charged with monstrous crimes; it is designed for every litigant. Nor is due process merely for the benefit of the accused. As Justice Robert H. Jackson said, "It is the best insurance for the Government itself against those blunders which leave lasting stains on a system of justice. . . ."

And why is it necessary to guarantee a free trial for all—for those accused of treason, for those who champion unpopular causes in a disorderly fashion, for those who assert their social and political rights against community prejudices, as well as for corporations, labor unions and churches? It is, of course, necessary so that justice will be done. Justice is the end, the aim, of government. It is implicitly the end of all governments; it is quite explicitly the end of the United States Government, for it was "in order to . . . establish justice" that the Constitution was ordained.

Trials are held not in order to obtain convictions; they are held to find justice. And over the centuries, we have learned by experience that unless we conduct trials by rule and suffuse them with the spirit of fair play, justice will not be done. The argument that the scrupulous observance of technicalities of due process slows up or frustrates speedy convictions is, of course, correct, if all you want is convictions. But why not go all the way and restore the use of torture? That got confessions and convictions! Every argument in favor of abating due process in order to get convictions applies with equal force to the use of the third degree and the restoration of torture. It is important to remember that nation after nation abandoned torture (the Americans never had it), not merely because it was barbarous, but because, though it wrung confessions from its victims, it did not get justice. It implicated the innocent with the guilty, it outraged the moral sense of the community. Due process proved both more humane and infinitely more efficient.

Or consider the problem of wiretapping. That in many cases wiretapping "works" is clear enough, but so do other things prohibited by civilized society, such as torture or the invasion of the home. But "electronic surveillance," said Justice William J. Brennan, Jr., "strikes deeper than at the ancient feeling that a man's home is his castle; it strikes at freedom of communication, a postulate of our kind of society. . . . Freedom of speech is undermined where people fear to speak unconstrainedly in what they suppose to be the privacy of home or office."

Perhaps the most odious violation of justice is the maintenance of a double standard: one justice for blacks and another for whites, one for the rich and another for the poor, one for those who hold "radical" ideas and another for those who are conservative and respectable. Yet we have daily before our eyes just such a double standard of justice. The "Chicago Seven," who crossed state lines with "intent" to stir up a riot, have received heavy jail sentences, but no convictions have been returned against the Chicago police who participated in that riot. Black Panthers are on trial for their lives for alleged murders, but policemen involved in wantonly attacking a Black Panther headquarters and killing two blacks have been punished by demotion.

Turn to the role and function of freedom in our society—freedom of speech and of the press—and the consequences of laying restrictions upon these freedoms. The consequence is, of course, that society will be deprived of the inestimable advantage of inquiry, criticism, exposure and dissent. If the press is not permitted to perform its traditional function of presenting the whole news, the American people will go uninformed. If television is dissuaded from showing controversial films, the people will be denied the opportunity to know what is going on. If teachers and scholars are discouraged from inquiring into the truth of history or politics or anthropology, future generations may never acquire those habits of intellectual independence essential to the working of democracy. An enlightened citizenry is necessary for self-government. If facts are withheld, or distorted, how can the people be enlightened, how can self-government work?

The real question in all this is what kind of society do we want? Do we want a police society where none are free of surveillance by their government? Or do we want a society where ordinary people can go about their business without the eye of Big Brother upon them?

The Founding Fathers feared secrecy in government not merely because it was a vote of no-confidence in the intelligence and virtue of the people but on the practical ground that all governments conceal their mistakes behind the shield of secrecy; that if they are permitted to get away with this in little things, they will do it in big things—like the Bay of Pigs or the invasion of Cambodia.

And if you interfere with academic freedom in order to silence criticism, or critics, you do not rid the university of subversion. It is not ideas that are subversive, it is the lack of ideas. What you do is to silence or get rid of those men who have ideas, leaving the institution to those who have no ideas, or have not the courage to express those that they have. Are such men as these what we want to direct the education of the young and advance the cause of learning?

The conclusive argument against secrecy in scientific research is that it will in the end give us bad science. First-rate scientists will not so gravely violate their integrity as to confine their findings to one government or one society, for the first loyalty of science is to scientific truth. "The Sciences," said Edward Jenner of smallpox fame, "are never at war." We have only to consider the implications of secrecy in the realm of medicine: What would we think of doctors favoring secrecy in cancer research on the grounds of "national interest"?

The argument against proscribing books, which might normally be in our overseas libraries, because they are critical of Administration policies is not that it will hurt authors or publishers. No. It is quite simply that if the kind of people who believe in proscription are allowed to control our libraries, these will cease to be centers of learning and become the instruments of party. The argument against withholding visas from foreign scholars whose ideas may be considered subversive is not that this will inconvenience them. It is that we deny ourselves the benefit of what they have to say. Suppose President Andrew Jackson had denied entry to Alexis de Tocqueville on the ground that he was an aristocrat and might therefore be a subversive influence on our democracy? We would have lost the greatest book ever written about America.

There is one final consideration. Government, as Justice Louis D. Brandeis observed half a century ago, "is the potent, the omnipresent teacher. For good or for ill, it teaches the whole people by its example." If government tries to solve its problems by resort to large-scale violence, its citizens will assume that violence is the normal way to solve problems. If government itself violates the law, it brings the law into contempt, and breeds anarchy. If government masks its operations, foreign and domestic, in a cloak of secrecy, it encourages the creation of a closed, not an open, society. If government shows itself impatient with due process, it must expect that its people will come to scorn the slow procedures of orderly debate and negotiation and turn to the easy solutions of force. If government embraces the principle that the end justifies the means, it radiates approval of a doctrine so odious that it will in the end destroy the whole of society. If government shows, by its habitual conduct, that it rejects the claims of freedom and of justice, freedom and justice will cease to be the ends of our society.

Eighty years ago, Lord Bryce wrote of the American people that "the masses of the people are wiser, fairer and more temperate in any matter to which they can be induced to bend their minds, than most European philosophers have believed possible for the masses of the people to be."

Is this still true? If the American people can indeed be persuaded to "bend their minds" to the great questions of the preservation of freedom, it may still prove true. If they cannot, we may be witnessing, even now, a dissolution of the fabric of freedom that may portend the dissolution of the Republic.

7 The Juke Myth

SAMUEL HOPKINS ADAMS

In this amusing account, Samuel Hopkins Adams illustrates the importance, to science in general and to social science in particular, of carefully gathered data. It has been fortunate for the valid development of sociology that today's standards of data collection and interpretation are radically different from those that prevailed when the Juke study was considered sound research. Another important change has occurred in our basic theory of human behavior. Early in this century, as the popularity of the Juke study illustrates, most people were convinced that the behavior of humans is largely inborn. Now, as Selection 9 and some of the selections in Chapter II suggest, the great majority of professional students of human behavior are agreed that the most important factors in human action are learned. The controversy has been renewed recently with claims of inherited differences in ability among races. "Innate Intelligence: An Insidious Myth?" by William H. Boyer and Paul Walsh, presents the opposite position.

No other family in American annals is so well and unfavorably known as the Jukes. The name is a synonym for depravity. What the Rothschilds embody in finance the Jukes represent in misdemeanor. If there were an International Hall of Ill Fame they would get top billing.

And they never existed otherwhere than in the brain of an amateur criminologist. Richard L. Dugdale did not precisely invent them; rather, he compiled them from an assortment of human derelicts whom he collected after a method peculiarly his own, for the purpose of bolstering his theory of criminal heredity. He passed on his findings to posterity in his *magnum opus, The Jukes: A Study in Crime, Pauperism, Disease, and Insanity.*

This classic has permeated the sociology of nations. Geneticists like Giddings, East, and Walter have swallowed it whole. The New York State Prison Association sponsored it. Putnam's brought out three large editions, which were accepted as sociological gospel. Dugdale became the recognized authority on crime. His qualifications as an expert are peculiar. When the Dugdale family came to this country from England in 1851 Richard was ten years old. It was intended that he should go to college. After three years of schooling in New York something went awry in his education. He left school and became assistant to a sculptor. In the evenings he attended classes at Cooper Union, where he won something of a reputation as a debater on social topics.

His career, if such it were, was interrupted by the departure of the family to try farming in the Middle-west. The venture was unsuccessful. The Dugdales returned to New York and Richard turned his hands to manufacturing. He was then twenty-three. The business failed. Richard had a nervous breakdown and with-

SOURCE: "The Juke Myth," by Samuel Hopkins Adams. First published in the *Saturday Review*, vol. 38, no. 14 (April 2, 1955), 13, 48–49. • The author (1871–1958) was a distinguished essayist and a former staff member of *McClure's Magazine*. Among his works are *The Santa Fe Trail, Erie Canal,* and *Grandfather Stories.*

drew from active endeavor. "For four years I could neither earn nor learn," he records. Such was his technical equipment as a sociologist.

The Jukes came into his life quite by chance. He happened to be in a Kingston, N.Y., police court in 1873, where a youth was on trial for receiving stolen goods. Five relatives were present as witnesses. They came of a breed, to quote the incipient investigator, "so despised that their family name had come to be used generically as a term of reproach." They were alleged to live like haggards of the rock, in the caves of a nearby lake region. "Crime-cradles," our author calls the locality. He was a neat hand at a phrase.

He invented the name Juke for the clan.

The fact that the Juke at the bar of justice was acquitted in no wise discouraged young Dugdale. He made inquiries about the others present. An uncle of the accused is set down as a burglar. No proof is adduced. Two male cousins had been charged with pushing a boy over a cliff, one of whom was convicted. The remaining witnesses, two girls, he lists as harlots. By the Dugdale method "under the heading of harlots are included all women who have made lapses, however seldom." This is fairly indicative of his standards of investigation and attribution.

With this auspicious start he canvassed the neighborhood for further specimens.

> With comparatively little inquiry [he writes], it was found that out of twenty-nine male adults, the immediate blood relations of the six, seventeen were criminals and fifteen others convicted of some degree of offense.

Impressed by this suggestive ratio—as who would not be by thirty-two out of a possible twenty-nine?—Dugdale went sleuthing back through the generations until he came upon an old Dutch reprobate who kept a turnpike hostelry in Orange County about the middle of the eighteenth century. Old Max appears to have been a sporting character. Several illegitimate children were imputed to him. He enjoyed a local reputation for drinking, gaming, and wenching, divertissements fairly general in those lusty pioneer days. He became Exhibit A in the Dugdale rogues' gallery, though nothing criminal appears in his record.

Max had two legitimate sons who married into a family of six sisters. With the discovery of the sisterhood Dugdale really hits his stride. The family line of the six is obscure; it "has not been absolutely ascertained," he admits. "One, if not all, of them were illegitimate," he surmises, on what grounds he does not explain. Delia is recorded as a "harlot before marriage," and Bell as a "harlot after marriage." Clara, he notes (presumptively with reluctance), was "reputed chaste." She did, however, marry a man who shot a neighbor. Effie's reputation was unknown to author Dugdale, which was certainly a break for Effie.

Another sister *circa* 1760 is Dugdale's prize specimen. "Margaret, Mother of Criminals," he calls her, although her name was Ada. Apt alliteration's artful aid again! To her goes the credit for "the distinctly criminal line of the family." But, what family? For all that he reveals Margaret-Ada, of unascertained parentage, may have been a Van Rensselaer, a Livingston, a Saltonstall, a Biddle, or the granddaughter of the original Joe Doakes. To be sure, he later characterizes the whole lot as "belonging to the Juke blood." Pure assumption. As their derivation was unknown and they were suspectedly illegitimate anyway, how could Dugdale or anybody else know anything of their ancestry?

As a "Mother of Criminals" Margaret (or Ada) hardly lives up to her name. Her daughter is designated as a harlot, but, by way of palliation perhaps, our author adds, "not industrious." One son was a laborer, "somewhat industrious." The other, a farmer, is stigmatized as having been "indolent" and "licentious in youth." The same might be said of some eminent non-Jukes, including Robert Burns and the Apostle Paul.

Margaret-Ada was married to one of Old Max's sons. She had a son of her own, whom Dugdale holds to be co-responsible for the evil Juke inheritance. But this son was a Juke only in name. He was illegitimate. Dugdale says so.

Thus, the notorious criminal-Juke strain derives on one side from a progenitor who was not criminal (Old Max) and on the other from a line which was not Juke except by Dugdale fiat. (Margaret-Ada through her illegitimate son.)

It sufficed Dugdale. He had his theory; now he set out after supporting facts. He made a year's tour of prisons, almshouses, and asylums, collecting Jukes. The result he published in 1875. It is still regarded by those who have not read it, and even some who have, as an authoritative document. It established the Jukes as the type-family of degeneration.

Dugdale invented a terminology to go with his Jukes. His thesis is based, so he states, upon "Positive Statistics and Conjectural Statistics . . . Conjectural Statistics consists in Political Arithmetic and the Theory of Probabilities." This recondite process "reduces the method of study to one of historico-biographical synthesis united to statistical analysis," which sounds as if it might have come out of Lewis Carroll.

Applying this yardstick, Dugdale lists 709 alleged Jukes of whom 507 were social detrimentals. Such conventional crimes as murder, arson, rape, and robbery, quite lacking in proof for the most part, are cited. But there were not enough of them to support satisfactorily the Dugdale political arithmetic and theory of probabilities. So he fattens up the record with entries like the following:

Reputed sheep-stealer, but never caught.
Thief, but never caught.
Petty thief, though never convicted.
Guilty of murder, but escapes punishment.
Unpunished and cautious thief.
Bastardy prosecution.
Supposed to have attempted rape.
Cruelty to animals.
Habitual criminal.
Impossible to get any reliable information, but it is evident that at nineteen he was a leader in crime.

And such scattered attributions as "pauper," "harlot," "brothel-keeper," "vagrant," "lazy," "intemperate," "drunkard," "immoral," "lecherous," etc., etc., etc. There was also a "contriver of crime," and a hardened character who, in addition to frequenting a saloon, was accused of breaking a deaf man's ear-trumpet. Like the Juke who started it all, he was acquitted. It did not matter to our investigator; the non-breaker of the ear trumpet comes down the ages, embalmed in criminal history.

All this might seem rather attenuated evidence on which to indict an entire family. It sufficed Dugdale. He followed the long and proliferating branches of the clan through the generations and worked out a diagram as framework for the composite portrait. This he calls "Leading Facts."

Consanguinity

		F		
C	Prostitution	O	Illegitimacy	P
		R		A
R		N		U
		I		P
I	Exhaustion	C	Intemperance	E
		A		R
M		T		I
		I		S
E	Disease	O	Extinction	M
		N		

Not Consanguineous

In other words, *fornication* [the italics are his], either consanguineous or not, is the backbone of their habits, flanked on the one side by *pauperism*, on the other by *crime*. The secondary features are *prostitution*, with its complement of *bastardy*, and its resultant of miseducated childhood; *exhaustion*, with its complement, *intemperance*, and its resultant, unbalanced minds; and *disease*, with its complement, *extinction*.

Dugdale's investigations into hygiene and morality are on a par with his criminological efforts. Insanity, epilepsy, deformity, impotency, and tuberculosis appear to have been as typical Juke phenomena as thievery, bastardy, and general lawlessness. Some of the evidence cited is calculated to astonish students of heredity. For example, it is recorded that the original Max went blind and transmitted the affliction to his posterity. As he lost his sight late in life, after his children were born, it is difficult to see how he can be held responsible for their blindness unless he poked them in the eye with a burnt stick.

Our author's figures on tuberculosis are confident, but where he found them is left a mystery. Nobody bothered to keep statistics in those days. Still more difficult would it have been to gather reliable data on venereal disease. Yet our conjectural statistician specifies, in one branch of the Jukes, forty harlots who contaminated 440 men, presumably eleven per harlot. In another genealogical line he states that 23½ per cent of the females were immoral. That ½ percent is fairly awe-inspiring.

Not until long after the author's death did anyone rise to challenge his thesis. The late Thomas Mott Osborne, of prison-reform fame and at one time president of that same prison association which certified the Dugdale revelations, studied the Juke records with growing skepticism. Himself a practised investigator, he raised questions about the Dugdale methods which that author might have found awkward to answer.

Whence, Mr. Osborne wished to know, did Dugdale derive those cocksure figures on disease, insanity, and death? Vital statistics at the time of his inquiry were practically non-existent. How did he acquire his data on criminality when court records for the period were notoriously unreliable, if, indeed, they were available at all? What genealogical method did he use in tracing back the Juke line through the mazes of its prevalent bastardy, for a century and a quarter? Legitimate family lines, Mr. Osborne pointed out, were difficult enough to trace; illegitimate were flatly impossible, beyond a generation or two. Further, the objector indicated, a specially trained sociological investigator would have required at least three years to do the work which Dugdale completed in one.

Analyzing the indicated method of investigation, Mr. Osborne suggested that Dugdale based it on a formula of retroactive hypothesis as follows:

That every criminal was a putative Juke.

That every Juke was a presumptive criminal.

By the system which Dugdale employed in tracing down his Jukes, Mr. Osborne concluded, it would be possible to asperse the morality, sanity, and legitimacy of any family in America. As for the Jukes, they were "pure folklore."

Another dissident raised objections in *The Clinical Review* for April 1902. Was it credible, Edmund Andrews asked, that Old Max possessed "such a miraculous energy of vicious propagation that, by his sole vital force, he begat and transmitted the degeneracy of all the Jukes for five generations?" Each descendant in the fifth generation, the critic pointed out, had fifteen other progenitors. Why assign his or her lawless, shiftless, or bawdy habits to Max any more than to any other of the uncharted Jukes or Jakes or Jeeks or Jenkins? A sturdy breeder like Max might well be the ancestor of a couple of thousand great-great-grandchildren, 1,500 of whom, for all that Dugdale knew to the contrary, might have been missionaries.

"It is sheer nonsense," Mr. Andrews contends "to suppose that he (a fifth-generation Juke degenerate) got them all (his vicious proclivities) from that one lazy, but jovial old Rip Van Winkle, the original Juke."

These were but voices crying in a wilderness. To scotch a good, sturdy historical fake, once it has got its growth, is impossible. Nine-tenths of America devoutly believes that Robert Fulton invented the steamboat and that Abner Doubleday was the founder of baseball. So the Jukes will doubtless continue to furnish texts to trusting sociologists, and no great harm done.

But they are in the wrong category. The proper place of a Juke is not in criminology. It is in mythology.

8 A Witness at the Scopes Trial

FAY-COOPER COLE

Facts never speak for themselves. For the scientist they speak in terms of theoretical assumptions. For the layman they are interpreted to fit his basic beliefs. If, for example, one assumed the earth was flat, then data that suggested that the world has a spherical shape could be discounted as optical illusions. Action would likewise be affected; sailors who believed the world was flat would hesitate to sail far from land. Similarly, if one believed that man was created just as he exists today—a conception that was widely accepted for centuries—then one would hardly be motivated to search for data tracing the development of man through the ages. This is the significance of the Scopes trial as discussed by Fay-Cooper Cole. It represented the most famous dramatic public test of the traditional belief about the nature of man. By 1925, almost all respected scientists and other learned people had accepted the theory that man and his works were products of evolutionary forces that extended back countless thousands of years. This theory has had a profound effect upon teaching and research in social science and religion. It should be noted, however, that the theory does not and cannot say anything about man's ultimate beginnings.

"This is Clarence Darrow," said the voice at the other end of the wire, "I suppose you have been reading the papers, so you know Bryan and his outfit are prosecuting that young fellow Scopes. Well, Malone, Colby and I have put ourselves in a mess by offering to defend. We don't know much about evolution. We don't know whom to call as witnesses. But we do know we are fighting your battle for academic freedom. We need the help of you fellows at the University, so I am asking three of you to come to my office to help lay plans."

That afternoon in Darrow's office three

SOURCE: *Scientific American,* vol. 200, no. 1 (January 1959), 121–30. Reprinted by permission. • The author (1881–1961) was professor emeritus of anthropology at the University of Chicago. He had done archaeological work in the United States and abroad. His books include *Peoples of Malaysia, Kincaid—A Prehistoric Illinois Metropolis,* and *The Bukidnon of Mindanao.*

of us from the University of Chicago—Horatio Hackett Newman, professor of biology; Shailer Mathews, dean of the Divinity School; and I—met to outline the strategy for what turned out to be one of the most publicized trials of the century. The Scopes trial proved also to be a historic occasion in the cause of popular understanding of science. A century ago the educated world was shaken by the discoveries of Charles Darwin and Alfred Russel Wallace, and the evidence they presented for the evolution of life on this planet. In 1959, as we celebrate the centenary of the *Origin of Species,* few informed persons, if any, question the theory of evolution. However, the century has witnessed several attempts to stifle investigation and outlaw the teaching of the theory. The best known of these was the Scopes trial, held in Dayton, Tenn., in 1925. The trial resulted in an immense revival of public interest in Darwin and in evolution; there has been no comparable effort since then to suppress this advance in man's understanding of himself and the world he lives in.

To understand the trial and what lay back of it, one must recall the climate of the 1920s. It was a time of uncertainty, unrest and repression. We had just emerged from a world war. Old standards were badly shaken; the young were labeled "the lost generation"; intolerance was rampant. The Ku Klux Klan was on the march, not only in the South but in the North as well. In many towns in Illinois, Indiana and other parts of the Midwest, staid business men—even members of the clergy—put on "white nighties" and burned fiery crosses to put the Negro, the Jew, the Catholic and the immigrant "in their places." The Fundamentalists, under the leadership of William Jennings Bryan, had organized in some 20 states and were putting pressure on all institutions of learning to curb the teaching of science, particularly evolution, which they considered in contradiction to the Bible. Prohibitive bills had been passed in Tennessee and Mississippi and were pending in six other states.

Then came the great opportunity. In the little town of Dayton the high-school science teacher and football coach, 24-year-old John Thomas Scopes, found himself engaged in a discussion of the new law with George W. Rappelyea, a young mining engineer and superintendent of the local coal mines. Scopes expressed bewilderment that the state should supply him with a textbook that presented the theory of evolution, yet make him a lawbreaker if he taught the theory. Rappelyea agreed that it was a crazy law and clearly unconstitutional. Then suddenly he asked: "Why don't I have you arrested for teaching evolution from that text and bring the whole thing to an end?" Scopes replied: "Fair enough."

Scopes was duly arrested. But neither of the principals had any idea of what they were starting. Within a few hours the Chattanooga papers carried the story. Soon it was spread across the nation. The Fundamentalists were quick to realize the opportunity to dramatize their battle against evolution. Bryan and his associates offered their services to the Prosecution. They were accepted. Here was big news.

At this point, it happened, three lawyers met in New York City for a conference on some business matters. They were Clarence Darrow, controversialist and defender of unpopular causes; Bainbridge Colby, an eminent corporation lawyer and, like Bryan, a former Secretary of State; and Dudley Field Malone, a leading Catholic layman and a fashionable barrister. Their conversation turned to the Tennessee situation. One said: "It is a shame. That poor teacher, who probably doesn't know what it is all about, is to be sacrificed by the Fundamentalists." Another said: "Someone ought to do something about it." The third replied: "Why don't we?" Through the American Civil Liberties Union they offered to defend young Scopes. Their offer was accepted.

This was real news! Bryan, three times candidate for the presidency of the U.S., the great Fundamentalist leader and orator, on one side. On the other, three of the nation's most famous lawyers, including Darrow, master jury-pleader. The papers were full of the story.

This was the background of Darrow's call to me and of our meeting at his office in Chicago early in the summer of 1925. By telephone, wire and letter we proceeded to assemble a panel of expert witnesses: scientists to testify on the theory of evolution and theologians to give evidence on the history and interpretation of the Bible. In addition to Newman, Mathews and myself, our panel finally included Kirtley Mather, professor of geology at Harvard; Jacob G. Lipman, director of the New Jersey Agricultural Experiment Station at Rutgers University; W. C. Curtis, professor of zoology at the University of Missouri; Wilbur Nelson, state geologist of Tennessee; Maynard Metcalf, professor of zoology at Johns Hopkins University; Charles Judd, head of the University of Chicago School of Education; and Rabbi Herman Rosenwasser of San Francisco, a noted Hebrew scholar. All of us, along with our counsel, undertook to go to Dayton at our own expense and to serve without fee.

The trial was scheduled for Friday, July 10. But long before that date the town was crowded with newspapermen, Fundamentalist supporters and others who were just curious. No one was willing to house "the heretics," that is, the scientific witnesses and defense attorneys. So an old "haunted house" on a hill overlooking the town was fitted out as a dormitory.

When I reached town, I took care not to associate myself at once with the Defense group, and was able to wander about for a time listening to the talk of the local people. For the most part they were extremely partisan to the Fundamentalist cause. But they were apprehensive of the famous Darrow, and they were not yet aware of his plan to present expert testimony on evolution and the scriptures.

That evening I joined the group at the "haunted house" and there met young Scopes for the first time. He was a fine, clean-cut young man, a little shy and apparently overwhelmed by the controversy he had stirred up. He expressed amazement that famous lawyers like Darrow, Colby, Malone and Arthur Garfield Hays (counsel to the American Civil Liberties Union) should come to his defense, and that a group of well-known scientists should join them.

Little happened on the first day of the trial beyond the selection of the jury. A panel was offered, and Darrow accepted it without change after a casual examination. But he did bring out the fact that 11 jurors were Fundamentalist church members. All admitted that they knew little about science or evolution. One said that the only Darwin he had ever heard about ran a local notion store. One could not read or write.

The events of Sunday provided us with an interesting insight into the local climate of opinion. Charles Francis Potter, a liberal Unitarian minister and writer who had been invited to conduct services at the Methodist-Episcopal church, was barred from the pulpit by the parishioners. Meanwhile Bryan addressed an overflow house at the Southern Methodist church. That afternoon, in an open courtyard in the center of town, Bryan talked to an immense audience. He said he welcomed the opportunity to bring "this slimy thing, evolution, out of the darkness. . . . Now the facts of religion and evolution would meet at last in a duel to the death." It was a fine example of Bryan's oratory, and it swept the crowd.

The court opened on Monday with a prayer in which a local clergyman urged God to preserve his sacred word against attack. It was a scarcely veiled plea to the jury.

The Defense filed a motion to quash the indictment on the ground that the act violated the Constitution of the State of Tennessee and Section 1 of the Fourteenth Amendment of the Constitution of the United States, which extends the Bill of Rights to limit action by the governments of the states. The Defense argued further that the indictment was contrary to a U.S. Supreme Court decision which says: "The law knows no heresy, and is committed to the support of no dogma, nor to the establishment of any sect." In support of this attack on the indictment, the Defense declared that it wished to offer the testimony of scientists and biblical scholars. These expert witnesses, the Defense contended, would show that there was no necessary conflict between evolution and Christianity.

Though the Defense asked that judgment on its motion to dismiss should be reserved until its witnesses had been heard, Judge John T. Raulston ordered the argument to proceed. On motion of the Prosecution, he sent the jury from the courtroom. Apparently the introduction of scientific witnesses had taken Bryan and his associates by surprise. Their ultimate response to our efforts to argue the underlying issues of the case was to lose them the trial in the minds of the American people.

That afternoon Darrow pressed for dismissal with an eloquent attack on ignorance and bigotry. Coatless in the sweltering courtroom, tugging at his suspenders, he paced up and down, firing shot after shot at the Prosecution. He stressed the danger to freedom of press, church and school if men like Bryan could impose their opinions and interpretations on the law of the land. "The fires of bigotry and hate are being lighted," he said. "This is as bold an attempt to destroy learning as was ever made in the Middle Ages. . . . The statute says you cannot teach anything in conflict with the Bible." He argued that in the U.S. there are over 500 churches and sects which differ over certain passages in the Bible. If the law were to prevail, Scopes would have to be familiar with the whole Bible and all its interpretations; among all the warring sects, he would have to know which one was right in order not to commit a crime.

Darrow said: "Your Honor, my client is here because ignorance and bigotry are rampant, and that is a mighty strong combination. . . . If today you can make teaching of evolution in the public schools a crime, tomorrow you can make it a crime to teach it in the private schools. At the next session of the Legislature you can ban books and newspapers. You can set Catholic against Protestant, and Protestant against Protestant, when you try to foist your own religion upon the minds of men. If you can do the one, you can do the other. After a while, Your Honor, we will find ourselves marching backward to the glorious days of the 16th century when bigots lighted the fagots to burn men who dared to bring any intelligence and enlightenment to the human mind."

The speech made a profound impression. Townspeople agreed that anything might happen with that man Darrow around. Judge Raulston adjourned court until Wednesday in order that he might consider the motion to quash.

That night, as we gathered in our

haunted house for a conference, a terrific storm swept the town. When a brilliant flash of lightning struck nearby, Darrow said: "Boys, if lightning strikes this house tonight . . . !"

Tuesday was a quiet day. At Rappelyea's office, where he had been invited to take advantage of the secretarial facilities, Potter found that the stenographer would not take dictation from any Unitarian minister. Rappelyea himself was arrested three times for speeding in the course of his service to us as guide and chauffeur. We were besieged by Holy Rollers, who came in from the hills to convert us. We also had to protect ourselves from a supporter. H. L. Mencken had come to town. His vitriolic articles so antagonized the people we wanted most to reach that we had to persuade him to leave the scene.

After the jury was sworn in on Wednesday, the Court ruled against the Defense motion to quash the indictment. The law, said Judge Raulston, did not deprive anyone of speech, thought or opinion, for no one need accept employment in Tennessee. He ruled the law constitutional, saying that the public has the right to say, by legislative act or referendum, whether Latin, chemistry or astronomy might be taught in its schools.

The Prosecution then called the county superintendent of schools, the heads of the school board and seven students. All testified to what Scopes had taught. Darrow limited his cross-examination to establishing simply that the State had furnished the textbook. After offering the King James version of the Bible as an exhibit, the Prosecution rested.

The first witness for the Defense was Maynard Metcalf. A recognized scientist, he was also an eminent Congregational layman and teacher of one of the largest Bible classes in the country. Darrow established his competence as a witness, then asked a question on evolution. The Prosecution at once challenged the testimony as irrelevant; according to them the only question was: Did Scopes violate the law?

The judge agreed to hear arguments on this point the next day. Meanwhile he excused the jury, with instructions not to enter the courtroom or to remain within hearing of the loudspeakers. A lot of angry jurors filed out. They had not only lost their reserved seats, but also were barred from the proceedings entirely.

The trial reached its high point on Thursday. After an impassioned plea by the State's Attorney against the admission of expert testimony, Bryan took over for the Prosecution. Instead of making good on his challenge of "a duel to the death," he argued against the presentation of scientific evidence. He said that the jury did not need the help of scientists or Bible experts to decide the facts and to interpret the law: "The law is what the people decided." He then presented an enlargement of the picture of the evolutionary tree from the textbook Scopes had used; it showed man in a circle with other mammals. Bryan shouted: "Talk about putting Daniel in the lions' den. How dare these scientists put man in a little ring with lions and tigers and everything that smells of the jungle. . . . One does not need to be an expert to know what the Bible says. . . . Expert testimony is not needed!"

With that speech Bryan lost the argument with the press and with the radio audience. When Malone had finished his reply, Bryan had also lost the argument, for a time, with most of his Dayton followers.

Malone was a Patrick Henry that day. He asked whether our children are to know nothing of science beyond that permitted by certain sects. "I have never seen greater need for learning," he declared, "than is exhibited by the Prosecution, which refuses information offered by expert witnesses. . . . Why this fear of meeting the issue? Mr. Bryan has said this is to be a duel to the death. I know little about dueling, Your Honor, but does it mean that our only weapon, the witnesses, is to be taken away while the Prosecution alone carries the sword? This is not my idea of a duel. . . . We do not fear all the truth they can present as facts. We are ready. We stand with progress. We stand with science. We stand with intelligence. We feel that we stand with the fundamental freedoms in America. We are not afraid. Where is the fear? We defy it." Then, turning toward Bryan and pointing his finger, he cried: "There is the fear!"

The crowd went out of control—cheering, stamping, pounding on desks—until it was necessary to adjourn court for 15 minutes to restore order.

I was sitting next to the aisle. Beside me was a Chattanooga policeman, one of the squad brought in to protect us from the Ku Klux Klan. As Malone finished, my guard beat the desk in front of me so hard with his club that a corner of the desk broke off. His chief came up and asked: "Why didn't you cheer when Malone made that speech?" My guard replied: "Hell. What did you think I was doing? Rapping for order?"

We had won for the day. Even the hostile crowd was with us.

That night Darrow said: "Today we have won, but by tomorrow the judge will have recovered and will rule against us. I want each one of you to go to the stenographer's room the first thing in the morning and prepare a statement for the press, saying what you would have said if allowed to testify in court."

As we were preparing our statements next morning, Judge Raulston looked in. I was nearest to the door. He asked what we were doing. When I told him, he asked the others in turn. Then he went to Darrow and told him he must not release the testimony: "It might reach the jury." Darrow replied: "Your Honor, you can do what you please with that jury. You can lock it up, but you cannot lock up the American people. The testimony will be released."

When court resumed, the judge ruled against us on all points. Rising and pushing his long hair from his forehead, Darrow spoke slowly and clearly. "The outcome is plain. We expect to protect our rights in some other court. Is that plain?" The judge replied: "I hope, Colonel Darrow, you don't attempt to reflect upon the Court." To which Darrow drawled: "Your Honor has the right to hope." The insult was deliberate. For an instant there was complete silence; then the judge mumbled that he had the right to do something else. A moment later he adjourned court until Monday.

Public reaction to the ruling was emphatic, and Bryan's prestige was shaken. Townspeople admitted to me, one of the "heretics," that they could not understand why Bryan had backed down. They asked: "What can you do now, if you can't talk?"

On Monday Darrow apologized to the Court, momentarily relieving the tension. Then, in order to secure the foundation for appeal, Hays read into the record the prepared statements of the scientific and other scholarly witnesses, and concluded by placing in evidence three versions of the Bible that differed from one another and from the King James version submitted by the Prosecution. Suddenly Hays electrified the crowd with the announcement that the Defense wished to call Bryan to the stand "as a biblical witness."

Darrow submitted Bryan to grueling

examination. In reply to Darrow's questions Bryan stated that he accepted the Bible literally as God's revealed word. What he didn't understand he accepted on simple faith. He believed that Eve was the first woman, created from Adam's rib; that God had sent childbirth pains to all women because of her transgression; that the snake must crawl on its belly because it tempted Eve; that everything outside the Ark, except fish, perished in the flood; that all existing animals had descended from the pairs saved by Noah; that all men spoke one language until the Tower of Babel; and that present languages had developed since then. Only once did he falter, when he admitted that the seven days of creation might mean seven epochs. He conceded that he was not familiar with the work of archaeologists, who had uncovered civilizations more than 5,000 years old, but he declared that he had never had much interest in those scientists who disputed the Bible. Repeatedly the State's Attorney tried to stop the questioning, but always Bryan replied: "No. Let it go on. I am not afraid to defend my religion."

Finally Malone intervened, saying he would have asked the same questions, but only to challenge Bryan's literal interpretation of the King James version. As a churchman and a Christian, however, he objected to any effort by counsel for the State to pin Darrow's views of religion on the defense. "I don't want this case to be changed by Mr. Darrow's agnosticism or Mr. Bryan's brand of religion." Malone further observed that this was supposed to be a trial by jury, yet the jury had not been permitted in the court for more than 15 minutes since being sworn in.

On Tuesday Judge Raulston struck the examination of Bryan from the record. The only question remaining, he said, was: What did Scopes teach? To this ruling Darrow replied: "Your Honor, we are wasting time. You should call the jury and instruct it to bring in a verdict of guilty." The Court did so, and Scopes was fined $100.

Scopes had come on to graduate study in geology at the University of Chicago when the Tennessee Supreme Court heard Darrow's appeal and at last handed down its decision in January, 1927. The court narrowly affirmed the anti-evolution statute, but threw out the $100 fine on a technicality. It brought an end to the formal proceedings by advising the State to desist from further prosecution: "We see nothing to be gained by prolonging the life of this bizarre case."

The Defense was also content to accept the Court's advice. No attempt at repression has ever backfired so impressively. Where one person had been interested in evolution before the trial, scores were reading and inquiring at its close. Within a year the prohibitive bills which had been pending in other states were dropped or killed. Tennessee had been made to appear so ridiculous in the eyes of the nation that other states did not care to follow its lead.

At the University of Chicago I had been teaching modest-sized classes. When the University resumed in the autumn my lecture hall was filled. Students were standing along the walls and sitting in the windows. I thought I was in the wrong room. When I asked a boy at the door what class was meeting, he replied: "Anthropology. The prof who teaches it defended that fellow Scopes." From that time on Introductory Anthropology had to be limited to lecture-hall capacity. My mail, mostly hostile, increased until the University gave up trying to put it in my box, but tied it in bundles and sent it to my office.

Some time after the trial I was summoned to the office of Frederick Woodward, acting president of the University. He handed me a long document, a series of resolutions from a Southern Baptist conference. They took the University to task for the part members of its faculty had taken in the trial, taking note of the University's strong Baptist origins. They voiced objections to Professors Judd, Newman and Mathews, but reserved the real condemnation for me—the witness on human evolution. I was "a snake in the grass corrupting the youth of a nation," and so on, concluding with "and we have been investigating Professor Cole still further, and we find that he is not even a Baptist."

I began to laugh, but the president said: "This is no laughing matter. You are a rather new man here, but already we have more demands for your removal than any other man who has been on our faculty. These resolutions are typical and were considered of such importance that they were read yesterday at the meeting of the Board of Trustees." "Yes," I replied. "And what did they do?" He reached across his desk and handed me a piece of paper. They had raised my salary.

CHAPTER II

ENVIRONMENTAL FACTORS

9 Innate Intelligence: An Insidious Myth?

WILLIAM H. BOYER AND
PAUL WALSH

A long-standing controversy in American social science concerns the relative importance of heredity and environment in the development of human behavior, especially school achievement. This controversy has recently been rekindled by the claim that lower-class and black children are unable to learn in school as other children do. The basis for this claim is the presumed genetic differences in children. In this selection Boyer and Walsh examine the evidence of such genetic individual differences and the possibility that such differences are the result of environmental forces. They also demonstrate how our educational system is based upon the model of unequal innate abilities. The resulting public policy and educational practice tend to reinforce the differences that are observed.

In societies where power and privilege are not equally distributed, it has always been consoling to those with favored positions to assume that nature has caused the disparity. When man himself creates unequal opportunity, he can be obliged or even forced to change his social system. But if nature creates inequality, man need only bow to supreme forces beyond his control, and the less fortunate must resign themselves to their inevitable disadvantage.

SOURCE: William H. Boyer and Paul Walsh, "Are Children Born Unequal," *Saturday Review*, vol. 51, no. 42 (October 19, 1968), 61–63, 77–79. • William H. Boyer is professor emeritus of psychology at the University of Idaho and a member of the Department of Education at the University of Hawaii. His major interests include learning and psychometrics. • Paul Walsh is assistant professor in the Department of Education at the University of Hawaii.

The metaphysics of natural inequality has served aristocracies well. The Greeks had wealth and leisure as a result of the labor of slaves. Plato expressed the wisdom of the established order with the claim that nature produces a hierarchy of superiority in which philosophers, such as himself, emerge at the top. Aristotle's belief that all men possess a rational faculty had more heretical potential, but it was not difficult to believe that some men are more rational than others.

In later periods, nations that possessed economic superiority explained their advantages on the basis of innate superiority. Sir Francis Galton was convinced that the English were superior and that the propertied classes were even more superior than the general population. They were the repository of what was the most biologically precious in mankind.

The democracies of the new world shattered many elements of the old order, and brought a new, radical, equalitarian outlook. In principle, if not always in practice, man became equal before the law, and the idea of "the worth of the individual" established a principle of moral equality. Yet legal and moral equalitarianism did not necessarily mean that men were intellectually equal. So the assumption upon which American schools and the American market place developed was that democracy should mean *equal opportunity for competition among people who are genetically unequal.* This creed has satisfied the requirements of modern wisdom even for the more liberal founding fathers such as Thomas Jefferson, and it equally fit into the social Darwinism of an emerging industrial society.

In contemporary American education many of these assumptions remain. People are usually assumed to be not only different in appearance, but also innately unequal in intellectual capacity and therefore unequal in capacity to learn. The contemporary creed urges that schools do all they can to develop *individual* capacities, but it is usually assumed that such capacities vary among individuals. Ability grouping is standard practice and begins in the earliest grades. Intelligence tests and the burgeoning armory of psychometric techniques increasingly facilitate ability tracking, and therefore the potentially prosperous American can usually be identified at an early age. If it is true that people have inherently unequal capacities to learn, the American educational system is built on theoretical bedrock, and it helps construct a social order based on natural superiority. But if people actually have inherently equal capacities, the system is grounded in quicksand and reinforces a system of arbitrary privilege.

Four types of evidence are typically offered to prove that people are innately different in their capacity to learn. The first is self-evidential, the second is observational, the third is logical-theoretical, and the fourth is statistical.

The self-evidential position is based on high levels of certainty which include a strong belief in the obviousness of a conclusion. Many people are very certain that there is an innate difference between people in intellectual capacity. However, such tenacity of feeling is not itself a sufficient basis for evidence, for it offers no method of cross-verification. The mere certainty of a point of view regarding the nature of intelligence must be discounted as an adequate basis for verification.

The observation of individual differences in learning capacity cannot be dismissed as a basis for evidence; useful information for hypotheses requiring further verification can be obtained in this way. For instance, parents may notice different rates of learning among their children. People from different social classes learn and perform at different levels. The city child may learn particular skills more rapidly than the rural child. Observations require some care if they are to produce reliable evidence, but it is possible to observe carefully, and such observation can be cross-verified by other careful observers.

But if people learn particular tasks at different rates, does it follow that people must therefore be *innately* different in their learning capacity? It does *not* necessarily follow. Increasingly, as we know more about the role of environment, we see that there are not only differences between cultures, but also differences within cultures. Even within families, no child has the same environment as the others. Being born first, for instance, makes that child different; he is always the oldest sibling. A whole host of variables operates so that the environment as perceived by an individual child has elements of uniqueness (and similarity) with other children raised in proximity.

Observational evidence can be a useful part of the process of understanding when it raises questions that can be subjected to more conclusive evidence, but it is often used as a way of selectively verifying preconceived notions which are endemic in the culture. Western culture is strongly rooted in the belief in a natural intellectual hierarchy. Few observers have been taught to make observations based on assumptions of natural intellectual equality. Observational evidence must be carefully questioned, for it is often based on a metaphysic of differential capacity which encourages selective perception and a priori categories of explanation. Yet these preconceptions are rarely admitted as an interpretive bias of the observer.

Theories based on carefully obtained data provide a more adequate basis for reaching a defensible position on the nature-nurture controversy than either of the previous procedures. A general theory in the field of genetics or psychology which fits available information would be a relevant instrument for making a deduction about the nature of intelligence. If a logical deduction could be made from a more general theory about heredity and environment to the more specific question of innate intellectual capacity, the conclusion would be as strong as the theory. Such deduction is a commonly used procedure.

Both genetic and psychological theories have often been used to support the belief in inherited intelligence. Genetic connections between physical characteristics such as eye color, hair color, and bodily stature are now clearly established. Certain disease propensity has a genetic basis, yet the best established research is now between single genes and specific physical traits. It is commonplace to assume that if a hereditary basis for differential physical traits has been established, there is a similar connection between genes and intelligence. The conclusion, however, does *not* necessarily follow. Intelligence defined as the capacity to profit by experience or as the ability to solve problems is not a function of a single gene. Whatever the particular polygenetic basis for learning, it does not follow that intellectual capacity is variable because physical traits are variable. Current genetic theory does not provide an adequate basis for deducing a theory of abilities.

Similarly, the Darwinian theory of natural selection is often used to ascribe superiority to those in the upper strata of a hierarchical society. Yet a system of individual economic competition for survival is actually a very recent phenomenon in human history, characteristic of only a few societies, primarily in the eighteenth, nineteenth, and early twentieth centuries. It is very likely that it is irrelevant to genetic natural selection because of its recent origin. American immigration came largely from the lower classes, a fact which could condemn America to national inferiority if the Darwinian theory were used. In the long span of human history, most societies have relied mainly on cooperative systems or autocratic systems for their survival, and individual competition is an untypical example drawn largely from the unique conditions of Western, particularly American experience.

Psychological theories which emphasize individual difference have often assumed that the descriptive differences in physical characteristics, personality, and demonstrated ability are all due largely to heredity. Psychology has had strong historical roots in physiology, but as social psychologists and students of culture have provided new understanding of the role of experience, hereditarian explanation has shifted toward environmentalism. Even the chemical and anatomical characteristics of the brain are now known to be modifiable by experience. Psychologists such as Ann Anastasi point out that, "In view of available genetic knowledge, it appears improbable that social differentiation in physical traits was accompanied by differentiation with regard to genes affecting intellectual or personality development."

Anthropologists, with their awareness of the effects of culture, are the least likely to place credence in the genetic hypothesis. Claude Levi-Strauss, a social anthropologist, claims that all men have equal intellectual potentiality, and have been equal for about a million years. Whether or not this is true, it is clear that the best-supported general genetic or psychological theory does not validate the conclusion that individual intellectual capacity is innately unequal.

Statistical studies under controlled conditions, on the other hand, can provide some of the most reliable information. For instance, when animals are genetically the same, there is the possibility of inferring genetic characteristics through experimental studies. Identical twins develop from the separation of a single egg and have identical genetic inheritance. If human twins could be raised under controlled experimental conditions, much could be learned about the respective role of heredity and environment. Many studies have been made of twins, but none under sufficiently controlled experimental conditions. The results, therefore, permit only speculative conclusions. Most twins are so similar that unless they are separated they are likely to be treated alike. When they are separated, in most cases, one twin is moved to a family of the same social class as the other twin. And people of similar appearance tend to be treated similarly—a large, handsome child is not usually treated the same as a short, unattractive child. The resultant similarity of IQ scores of separate twins has not been surprising.

Even if particular identical twins were to show marked differences in ability when they live in substantially different environments, as they occasionally do, the evidence does not prove the *environmentalist* thesis unless a significantly large number of random cases is compared with a similarly random selection of non-identical twins. In a small sample, difference could be due to the experience deprivation of one twin. It is possible to stultify any type of development, and so the variation between identical twins, identified in some studies up to forty points, by no means disproves the hereditarian position. Consequently, current studies do not provide conclusive statistical evidence to support either position over the other.

The second most commonly used statistical evidence to show the hereditary basis of intelligence is the constancy of IQ scores at different age periods. Usually, IQ scores do not change appreciably, but occasionally the changes are dramatic. It is now understood that a standard IQ test is culturally loaded toward middle-class values, and so the general constancy of most IQ scores can be explained as the expected result of limited mobility between social class and the resultant constancy of subcultural experiences. So even the statistical "evidence," so often used to support a belief in innate intelligence, is really not conclusive.

Studies of innate intelligence, then,

have not produced conclusive evidence to justify the claim for an innate difference in individual intellectual capacity. Equally, there has not been conclusive evidence that the innate potential between people is equal. The research is heavily marked by the self-serving beliefs of the researchers. Psychologists have usually created "intelligence" tests which reflect their own values, predetermining that their own scores will be high. When they have discovered they are high, they have often proclaimed such tests to be indicators of innate superiority.

Many studies are built on simple-minded assumptions about the nature of environment. Psychological environment is related to the subject. A researcher who says that two children live in the "same" environment is quite wrong, for the environment that each child perceives may be quite different from that perceived by the researcher.

Also, it is often assumed that environment is only postnatal, but evidence is now available on the role of prenatal environment, both psychologically and nutritionally. Malnutrition of a pregnant mother can, and often does, have permanent debilitating psychological and physiological effects on her child. Certain diseases contracted by the mother (measles, for example) and certain drugs (thalidomide, for instance) can produce destructive "environmental" effects which limit intellectual capacities. Clearly, people do demonstrate varying capacities to learn, but they have had varying prenatal and postnatal opportunities. If they are female, they are generally treated differently than if they are male. Negroes are treated different from whites—one social class is treated different from another. The *kind* of employment people engage in has a profound effect on what they become. They probably become different through different treatment and different experience, yet our institutions, reflecting our culture, usually operate on the assumption that such differences in ability are innate.

There are at least three ability models which can be supported by current evidence. Each is based on different assumptions about human nature and therefore provides a basis for different social philosophies and different conceptions of government and education.

The first model assumes a great variety of innate ability and a high level of intellectual demand on the average person. In this model, there are hereditary geniuses and idiots, while most people have an intellectual capacity about equal to the demands of their society.

The second model assumes that the innate ability potential of everyone (who has not been injured pre- or postnatally) is equal and far exceeds the normal demand level. (The actual opportunities a person has may produce differential *performance* similar to model No. 1.)

The third model assumes the possibility of some variation, but since all of the ability potential is well beyond the normal demand level, the variation makes virtually no operational difference.

In an economic or educational system, model No. 1 would justify the usual culling, sorting, and excluding through screening devices to create a "natural" hierarchy of ability. It would also justify the common belief in "equal opportunity for competition between unequals," where sorting is achieved through competition.

Both models two and three would justify maximum social effort to develop the abilities of all people, and the failure to achieve high levels of ability in all people would constitute social failure rather than individual failure. American society, with its considerable disparity of

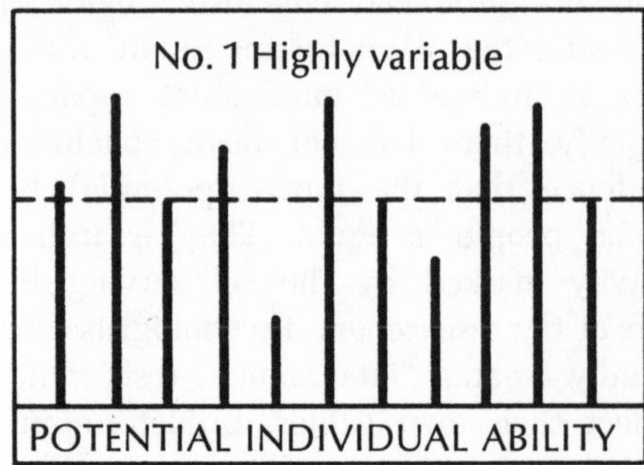

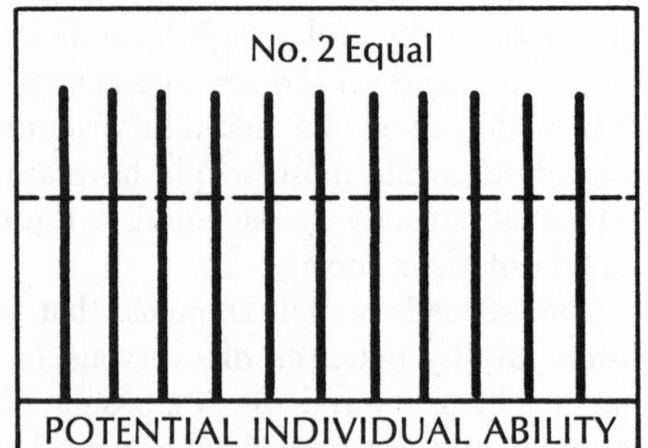

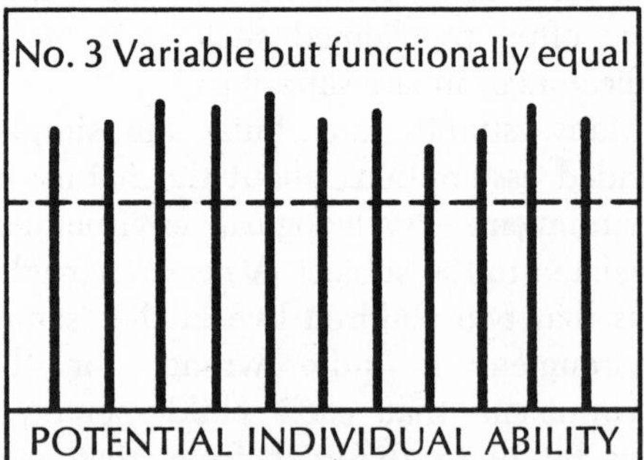

Ability Models Each model is based on different assumptions about the nature of potential human ability. The dotted line indicates the intellectual level at which individuals must function to meet the requirements of society.

wealth and power, is largely a success based on the inequality assumed in the first of the three models. It is largely a failure based on the equality assumed in the second and third models.

Schools make little effort to develop the kind of equal ability assumed in models two and three. IQ tests are widely used to identify presumed differences in innate ability so that culling and grouping can make the management of the school easier and more efficient. The disastrous effects of the schools on lower-class children are now finally becoming known. The "compensatory" concept has gained some headway, but most educators are so overloaded with work and so traditional in outlook that the schools have become partners with the economic system in reinforcing a system of privilege that usually panders to the children of those in power and finds metaphysical excuses to make only minor gestures toward the less fortunate. The "special programs for the gifted" would be more accurately labeled "special programs for the privileged," for the gifted are primarily the children from socio-economic classes which provide the most opportunities. The less fortunate (usually lower class children) are ordinarily neglected or convinced that they are innately inferior. Once they become convinced, the prophesy is soon realized.

Part of the problem is the way "intelligence" is defined. It can be defined in many different ways, each leading to a somewhat different educational direction. We can view it as environmental adaptation, as ability to solve problems, as ability to use logical convergent thinking, or it can emphasize divergent thinking and the creation of ideas and problems. When intelligence is defined as abstract verbal-conceptual ability drawing on the modal experiences of middle class environment, as it is in most IQ tests, a selection has been made which excludes many other plausible and often more useful definitions.

The capacity to become intelligent does, of course, have a genetic basis. A cat is not capable of becoming a psychologist. But this does not mean that demonstrated differences in intelligence among psychologists are innate. What is particularly important is whether intelligence is defined primarily as the input or the output. The input is not subject to control, but the output depends on experience; so it is intelligence as output that should be the central concern of the educator.

Until the particular beliefs, which are endemic in many cultures, including American culture, are seen to be part of the heritage of an ancient, anachronistic, elitist tradition, there is little likelihood that the official liberal and equalitarian goals of many modern nations are likely to be realized, even though the wealth of modern technology gives every promise that they are capable of being achieved. Government, industry, education, and virtually all other institutions are now part of the problem, hobbled by a metaphysics of innate inequality. Elitist assumptions about the meaning of ability permeate all fields of education. When teachers of music, mathematics, art, or physical education find that a student doesn't demonstrate the requisite ability, they often reject him (low grades can be a form of rejection). Then counselors shuttle the student to courses where he shows "ability." All this assumes that the school should not develop abilities, but only grant them opportunity to be expressed. The Rousseauian belief in the pre-existing self is widespread.

The environmental hypothesis may be wrong, but if it is, it should be shown to be wrong only after a society has done everything possible to develop the abilities of people. We should begin with prenatal care, and should eliminate the experience of economic deprivation, ghettoized living, and elitist schools and businesses. *Lacking definitive scientific evidence about human potentialities, social policy should be based on moral considerations.* We should base our policy on the most generous and promising assumptions about human nature rather than the most niggardly and pessimistic. Men will do their best only when they assume they are capable. Liberal assumptions and conservative assumptions about human nature create their own self-fulfilling prophesies. We now create millions of people who think of themselves as failures—as social rejects. Their sense of frustration and despair is a travesty on the potentialities of an affluent nation.

Poor teaching is protected in the American educational system through the assumption that the child doesn't have the ability. An American environmentalist commitment (toward liberal rather than totalitarian goals) would aim at *creating* ability, at *increasing* intelligence, at *developing* interests. The meaning of "education" would need to be broader than merely institutional schooling. It should also include community responsibility, especially for business and the mass media, which must supplement the work of the school if Americans are to receive more equal educational opportunity. This requires more social planning and more public responsibility than Americans have previously been willing to undertake.

Most American institutions, including the schools, still base their policy largely on the old conservative ideology. This outlook resists change and condemns many to inferiority. Ideological rigidity is not exclusive to the United States; in fact, many other nations are even more rigid. Yet the expanding wealth produced by modern technology is beginning to encourage the have-nots within the United States and throughout the world to demand their share by force and violence if necessary. Violence is likely to be an increasingly common road to social change unless a new public morality based on new assumptions about human potentiality is translated into both foreign and domestic policy. It is not merely racism which bogs down American progress, but also the more pervasive belief in intellectual inequality. The failure to develop the abilities of people was useful to the early American aristocracy and to the power elite of an industrial-scarcity economy. But modern economies of abundance flourish through the maximum development of the abilities of people. There is potentially plenty for all. More widespread development of the capabilities of people would not only add greatly to the wealth of nations, but it can also permit people to participate in a social and cultural renaissance.

Aside from the compelling moral obligation to create equal opportunities within nations and even between nations, the excluded millions in the world are starting to force the changes which should have occurred long ago. Some of them don't believe they are inferior, and they are understandably impatient about changing the old processes of exclusion. All institutions, including the schools, will either need to re-examine their self-consoling elitist beliefs and create real and equal opportunity, or else risk that violence and revolution will increasingly become the dominant instruments of social change.

10 A Study of Values

EVON Z. VOGT AND
JOHN M. ROBERTS

If it can be shown that the inborn characteristics of people in communities do not differ significantly, and at the same time one observes that such groups solve similar problems quite differently, then the differences must be ascribed to the learned factors which sociologists and anthropologists call "culture." This point is illustrated by Evon Z. Vogt and John M. Roberts as they demonstrate that persons basically similar biologically, but having different cultures, may settle in the same general geographical area and yet develop markedly different modes of life.

"No tenet of intellectual folklore has been so damaging to our life and times as the cliché that 'science has nothing to do with values.' If the consideration of values is to be the exclusive property of religion and the humanities, a scientific understanding of human experience is impossible."

In these words the anthropologist Clyde Kluckhohn recently defined a major challenge and frontier of social research. The forming and choosing of values is a central concern of all men and societies. Conceptions of the desirable, the fitting and the good vary widely among the world's 3,000 or so cultures. They strongly influence the selection of the modes, the means and the ends of human behavior. The social scientist cannot view "man in culture" as conditioned only by economic forces and biological impulses. People see the world through cultural lenses compounded of particular combinations of values; they respond in different ways in accordance with their differing values. We must recognize that people are not just "driven" by situational pressures: they are also "pulled" by the ideals and goals of their cultures.

As we advance the frontiers of the social sciences it becomes increasingly clear that values must be studied as a part of our actual subject matter and not left entirely to the humanists and philosophers. Values are, in fact, the subject of an increasing number of investigations today. But how can values be brought under the same kind of objective study as linguistic systems and the techniques of salmon fishing?

The apparent difficulty is reduced if we recall that the object of such study is not to make an ethical judgment of goodness or badness. We want to know, rather, how values function in organizing behavior. Since it is virtually impossible to experiment with human cultures, the social scientist must find his laboratory situation ready-made. Preferably he should be able to observe and compare the role of

SOURCE: *Scientific American*, vol. 195, no. 1 (July 1956), 25–30. Reprinted by permission. • Evon Z. Vogt is professor of anthropology at Harvard University. His interests include social anthropology, cultural change, primitive religion, and American ethnology. Among his books are *Modern Homesteaders; The Life of a Twentieth-Century Frontier Family; Navaho Veterans;* and *Water Witching, U.S.A.* • John M. Roberts is professor of sociology and anthropology at Cornell University. His fields of study are southwestern ethnology, small group cultures, codes and models, values, highway studies, and primitive law and government. He has written *Three Navaho Households, Zuni Law,* and *Zuni Daily Life* as well as coauthored *Language of Experience.*

values in one or two cultures other than his own. Ideally he will find a situation where he can observe variations in values against a background in which other variables are relatively constant.

This article is concerned with . . . the region south of Gallup, N.M., where communities of five different cultural traditions—Zuñi and Navaho Indians, Mormons, Catholic Spanish-Americans and Protestant-American homesteaders from Texas—all contend with the same high-altitude semi-arid environment. Since our research has not yet reached the phase of synthesis and final theory construction, it is still too early to summarize the project's over-all results. At this stage, however, we are able to report that the Gallup region has given us a practically ideal laboratory for investigation of the manifold questions presented by the role of values in human life.

The value study . . . has engaged the collaboration of 30 investigators from the disciplines of anthropology, sociology, psychology, philosophy, history, government and law. They have approached their common concern with values through a wide variety of topical interests, such as religion, cultural change, politics, land use, child rearing, adult personality, mythology, music and graphic arts. The full battery of research techniques—direct observation, participant observation, personal interviews, group discussions, interaction analysis, psychological tests and questionnaires—is represented in the immense documentation now assembled. Since the populations of the five communities are small (3,000 Zuñis, 650 Navahos, 700 Spanish-Americans, 250 Mormons, 250 Texans) it has been possible to emphasize intensive methods and reduce the problems of sampling and statistical analysis which attend so much social research. The extensive existing literatures on some of the cultures have helped to give the study historical depth.

In all its undertakings the values study has been faced with the delicate problem of rapport and public relations in the five communities. No research could be conducted that might endanger future investigations. Among the Zuñi, for example, it has so far not been politic to study prayers, ceremonials and other religious matters at close range. Because we have had to be careful to protect individuals and groups in every way, this is the first over-all account of the project to be published outside a few specialized professional journals and monographs.

The geography of the Gallup region establishes some much-needed constants for a study that is otherwise bedeviled by a multiplicity of uncontrolled variables. Each of the peoples of the five cultures see the same plateau and mesa country, sparsely covered with gramagrass, sagebrush, pinyon and juniper and with stands of ponderosa pines at the higher elevations. All of the people must contend with the same fluctuation in rainfall, averaging only 12 to 15 inches per year, and with the short, changeable growing season typical of the American Southwest at this 7,000-foot altitude. There are permanent springs in the region, but the small Zuñi River, a tributary of the Little Colorado, is the only year-round stream. Soils, however, are fertile and productive when watered.

To meet the problems of making a living in this landscape, each of the five communities has essentially the same technology available to it. In face-to-face contact with one another for a generation or more, all have been subjected to markedly similar historical pressures. These pressures have mounted during the last 10 years, as hard-surfaced roads, telephone lines and public power have spread through their country. The five communities remain distinct, however, and present significant contrasts.

Each of the cultures, for example, has worked out its own solution for the problem of physical survival. The Zuñis, oldest of the peoples in the region, conduct a long-established irrigation agriculture supplemented by stock-raising and by crafts, notably the making of silver jewelry. The Navahos were originally roving hunters and gatherers and came into the region only a century ago; they have become dry farmers and sheepherders with wage work providing an increasing percentage of their income as contact with our American culture becomes more extensive. Livestock ranching and wage work provide the principal income for the three Spanish-American villages, which were settled about 75 years ago. The Mormons, also established in this region since the 1880's, have been conspicuously successful at irrigation farming; they also engage in livestock ranching and wage work. The Texans staked out the last Homestead Act lands in the region during the 1930's, as refugees from the dust bowl to the east; they raise cattle and carry on a commercial and largely mechanized dry-land farming, with pinto beans as their principal crop.

The five cultures present corresponding contrasts in their community organization and family life. The sedentary Zuñis spend their winters in the stone houses of their large central pueblo, moving in the agricultural season to three farming villages. Their social structure is based on the matrilocal household (with the husband living with his wife's kinfolk), matrilineal clans, and various priesthoods and other religious groupings. The Navahos also have matrilocal extended families and matrilineal clans. They are less tightly organized, however, and families dwell in widely scattered hogans: hexagonal log houses with dirt roofs. As compared to the other two non-Indian cultures, the Mormons resemble the Zuñis in having a strong sense of identity with their community. Their life centers around the single village of Ramah, where the values study maintains its field headquarters. For the Spanish-Americans the family and the Catholic church are paramount institutions. The Texan homesteads are scattered over several townships; their identity is loosely maintained by competing Protestant churches and cliques.

The values study seeks answers to a number of questions that are suggested by the differences among these five cultures. It has set out to define, first of all, the value system of each of them and to establish the role that values play in making these cultures different from one another. The changes in values that are occurring in each culture represent another important line of inquiry. Of equal challenge is the question of why their different value systems persist, despite their contact with each other and their exposure to the same environmental pressures.

One of the most promising areas of investigation is the connection between the values and the social structures of the various communities. For example, the Spanish-Americans lay strong emphasis upon "lineality"—the view that social relations are desirable when they are consistent with the hierarchy of their society. In their communities younger relatives are subordinate to older kinsmen, females to males, and the *peón* to his *patrón*. The secular structure gears into the hierarchically arranged Catholic church with its offices extending from the parish priest through the bishops, archbishops, cardinals and on up to the Pope. Much the same type of hierarchy is found in the sacred world of the Spanish-Americans, from the local images of the saints up to the Deity.

The Texan homesteaders, in marked contrast, place a strong American-frontier stress upon individualistic social relations in which each man is expected to be self-reliant and to be "his own boss." The social order of the community is composed of relatively isolated families, each living on its own farm and competing with other families for position and prestige. Instead of the single, hierarchically arranged church, the homesteaders subscribe to no less than 10 competing Christian denominations, each distinguished by a slightly different doctrine and type of service.

The Texan homesteaders fail to understand why "anybody wants to live all bunched up in a little village and take orders from the big landholders and the priests." The Spanish-Americans say of the Texans that "everybody tries to be his own *patrón*."

The Mormons present still another picture. The formal structure of the Mormon church has hierarchical aspects with lines of authority running upward from the local ward bishops through the state presidents to the 12 apostles and church president in Salt Lake City, Utah. But within this framework the local community enjoys much autonomy to work out its own affairs, and great value is placed upon collateral, cooperative economic and social relationships. Around the village and the large cohesive family system there is a proliferation of cooperatives in economic affairs. The little village of Ramah boasts a mutual irrigation company, a cooperative land and cattle company and a cooperative dairy. The spirit of individualistic competition which pervades the Texan community is consciously suppressed in favor of the values of cooperation in the Mormon village.

These values have deep roots in Mormon history. Joseph Smith, the founder of the church, proposed the "law of consecration" which required that all who had surplus wealth must impart it through the church to the poor. Although this "law" was abandoned as early as 1838, the values it expressed lent a strong cooperative bias to much of later Mormon activity. The compact village settlement was a social invention of the Mormons, motivated by a sense of urgent need to prepare a dwelling place for the "Savior" at "His second coming." Through the years cooperation became a strong defense against "persecution" by the "gentiles," first in the Middle West and later in the Far West, when the political and legal movements to stamp out Mormon polygamy came to a head. The cooperative spirit was also strongly reinforced in the arid West by the requirements of irrigation agriculture—the construction of storage reservoirs, the building and maintaining of networks of ditches, and the necessity of organized arrangements for the distribution of scarce water supplies among the various farms within a village.

The Spanish-Americans, Texans and Mormons, different as they are, belong to a single major historical tradition which contrasts with that of the Zuñis and Navahos. In former times Zuñi was ruled by a theocracy. Today personal relationships among the Zuñis are organized in a complicated series of interlocking religious, kinship and secular units, in which the individual strikes a delicate balance with external authority. No true Zuñi wishes to live away from Zuñi, particularly in the wintertime. The Zuñis have been characterized as having a kind of "middle of the road," "avoidance of excess" approach to life, in the manner of the ancient Greeks. Although this characterization must be qualified, it still symbolizes the Zuñi ideal.

While both Mormons and Zuñis can be characterized as "cooperative" and both societies manifest important linkages between their cooperative value systems and the requirements of irrigation agriculture, there are some interesting differences between them. In the Mormon community the values of cooperation are propounded by a single organized church which embraces the entire community. The Zuñi spirit of cooperation is expressed and institutionalized in the activities of a whole series of priesthoods, dancing groups and curing societies, in which the individual Zuñi may hold two or more memberships. Cooperation is stressed also as a matter of Zuñi kinship obligation. Kinship is important to the Mormons, but sustained kinship-based activity seldom goes beyond the closest relatives. In Zuñi there are large groups of near and distant relatives to whom one owes duties and from whom one derives benefits and position.

The Navahos, with their scattered hogans are more like the Texans in their settlement pattern. Except near agencies and railroad towns, they have no villages. From the core of the extended matrilineal family the Navaho views his relationships as reaching outward to include an ever-widening circle of kinsmen, some of whom he may rarely, if ever, see during the course of a year or more. Until recent times the Navahos have had no organized political leadership, the "tribe" consisting merely of a series of local bands which shared the same language and customs.

Although the Texans and Navahos can be characterized as being less communally inclined and more "individualistic" than the Mormons and Zuñis, there are, again, interesting differences in pattern and emphasis. The Texan focus is upon the individual farmer and his immediate family engaged in a competitive struggle with others for economic wealth and social prestige within the community. The Navaho sense of kinship involves no idea of striving and competing. Navahos cooperate easily with kinsmen and neighbors when the occasion arises, such as the work of putting on the larger ceremonials. But there are no organized and regular cooperative activities on a community-wide basis, unless these are actively promoted by Indian Service officials or other whites.

Differences in culture can thus be related to differences in values. The relationship comes into sharper focus when we consider the varying cultures in the context of their adjustment to their relatively unvarying natural environment, the constant in our laboratory situation. First we shall describe the general orientations of the five groups toward nature and time. Then we shall see how the values thus expressed relate to the way each of the groups reacts to the environmental problem of drought.

The Spanish-Americans have what might be called a "normal curve" view of the workings of nature. Out of so many children born, so many die before maturity; from every row of seeds, only so many plants come up; and out of every 10 or so summers, two or three are bound to be without rain. One can do little but accept what comes. Corresponding to this view of nature is an orientation in time that lays stress upon the present, as opposed to the past, which slowly recedes into obscurity, or to the even more elusive future. Life flows secure in the traditional familial mold; the important thing is the present, with its immediate drama, color and spontaneity. It is foolish to work too hard, and to worry about the future is even more ridiculous. About the mysteries of the world neither curiosity nor knowledge extend much beyond a shrug of the shoulders and a "*Quién sabe?*" These Spanish-American values find concrete expression in the traditional fiesta, a combined religious and recreational affair which is conducted each year in honor of the patron saint of the village. Catholic Masses and processions, combined with drinking, dancing, singing and visiting, express at once the solemn traditionalism and the love of present excitement and drama in the life of the small Spanish-American village.

By contrast the Texan frontier homesteaders manifest a drive for mastery over the workings of nature. Nature is defined as something to be controlled and exploited by man for his own ends and material comfort. The homesteader therefore equips himself with the most modern type of tractor, practices modern farming methods and attempts to extend even further his control over nature in the face of great odds in this semi-arid environment. The past can be forgotten, even rejected, and the present is merely a step along the road to the future. If the crops fail, there is always the hope that "next year we'll make it." There is strong perennial optimism that "progress" will continue and that their crossroads will eventually grow into a modern city. While the homesteaders feel that their Spanish-American neighbors are lazy and "not getting any place," the latter feel just as strongly that the homesteaders are senselessly working themselves to death in a life in which one should live fully in the present.

The Mormon villagers share with the Texan homesteaders the view that mastery over nature is desirable. Indeed, in some respects they carry this idea much farther, for they hold the theological view that the Mormon people have "put on the uniform of the flesh" and live out this earthly life in order to learn about and attain mastery over gross matter. "The Latter-Day Saints," as the Mormons call themselves, have developed a work-health-education-recreation value complex to guide their activities: work to gain mastery over the world; health to keep man effective in the struggle for continuing progress; education to accelerate his progress; and recreation to strengthen both man's body and the community he lives in. Like the Texans, they emphasize the future, but not so much for the purpose of economic development as for participation in the eternal progress of the universe in which man himself progresses toward godhood.

To the Zuñi the universe looks very different. He neither feels that he is a master of nature nor that he is its victim. In his colorful and beautiful religion he has developed techniques of cooperating with nature. This attitude is of course sustained by a body of realistic information on ways to make a living in a difficult environment. The Zuñi equivalent of the Spanish-American fiesta has an important place in his life, but he is less taken with its recreational aspects. He lives in the present, but in many things, much more than any of his neighbors, he looks back to the past. It is a glorious past, an ancient mythological time when Zuñis came up from the "wombs" of the earth, wandered around, and finally settled at "the middle place," where their descendants to this day still maintain a shrine to mark the center of the universe.

The Navahos resemble the Spanish-Americans and the Zuñis in their orientation to nature and time. Like the Zuñis, the Navahos view man as having an integral part to play in a general cosmic scheme. But they see the universe as more powerful than man and profoundly threatening. In dealing with nature circumspection is the best guide to action, and fear is the dominant emotional theme. Yet the Navaho is not completely fatalistic. There are small things one can do to maintain and restore harmony in the scheme. Thus individual curing ceremonials, performed with care, can keep matters from becoming worse. The present is the important time-dimension, but the Navahos also recall a "holy people" who came up from the underworld, created four sacred mountains and the "earth surface people" and then departed for their permanent homes in the six directions: east, south, west, north, zenith and nadir.

For all five cultures the annual drought is a serious common concern. Each group responds differently to this problem in terms of its distinctive value-orientation. The Zuñis increase the intensity and tempo of their ceremonial activity; they give more attention to the planting of prayer feathers and to the fasting and prayers of the rain priests. This is in line with their view of the ultimate harmony of nature; man need only do his part and the gods will do the rest. With centuries of summer rains to testify to the soundness of this view, Zuñi is deeply opposed to rainmaking with airplanes and silver iodide.

The Navahos also tend to respond to drought by increasing ceremonial activity. But they are not so certain of the efficacy of their rainmaking ceremonies. They direct less ritual to that purpose and are more humble in the face of a more threatening universe.

The Spanish-Americans, on the other hand, seem to do little or nothing about drought beyond collecting in small groups on the plaza to talk about it. In their view, to attempt to alter the course of natural events by ceremonial is as useless as trying to alter it by rainmaking.

Against the ceremonial response of the Zuñis and Navahos and the fatalistic response of the Spanish-Americans, the behavior of the Mormons and Texans draws a dramatic contrast. They actively support the artificial rainmaking projects, they reduce their livestock herds and crop acreages, and they organize to enlist government aid in meeting the drought conditions. The Navahos and Zuñis, in contrast, have to be forced by the government to practice acreage restriction in bad years.

Ceremonial and ritual responses are not entirely lacking, however, in the Mormon and Texan communities. Mormons occasionally say prayers in church for rain. The Texans have held special prayer meetings during droughts; indeed, the governor of Texas set aside a special day for such meetings during the recent severe southwestern drought. A minority within each community also feels that seeding the clouds is "interfering with the work of the Lord." But the majority responds in the vein expressed by one of the more articulate farmers in the Texan community, who declared: "The Lord will look down and say, 'Look at those poor ignorant people. I gave them the clouds, the airplanes and the silver iodide, and they didn't have the sense to put them together.' "

Thus systems of values may promote and justify radically different modes of behavior among people confronted with the same objective problem. Why do such different values persist in the same tiny region among peoples living so close to one another? There appear to be at least two basic aspects to this question. First, we know that the values are intricately related to the total structure of each culture. Accordingly, unless the structure breaks down completely, values will tend to persist as functional parts of the whole. Second, we have also discovered that face-to-face contacts between the five cultural groups have not always encouraged the easy communication and interaction which might eventually level the differences between them. In fact, some of the intercultural contacts appear to have reinforced, rather than changed, the original value systems. There is, for example, good evidence that Navahos and Zuñis cling tenaciously to certain of their aboriginal values precisely because missionaries and other agents of white culture bring strong pressure upon them to change.

11 The Concept of Culture

CLYDE KLUCKHOHN

Among the environmental factors that have the most significant effect on man's behavior are those that man himself has created. The term that social scientists use to describe this social heritage is "culture," but that word has a variety of popular meanings with which it may be confused. A close reading of the following statement by Clyde Kluckhohn should help in understanding the special meaning given to "culture" by social scientists. Additional light can be shed on this concept by examining some patterns of culture from different societies, such as may be found in the next two selections.

Why do the Chinese dislike milk and milk products? Why would the Japanese die willingly in a Banzai charge that seemed senseless to Americans? Why do some nations trace descent through the father, others through the mother, still others through both parents? Not because different peoples have different instincts, not because they were destined by God or Fate to different habits, not because the weather is different in China and Japan and the United States. Sometimes shrewd common sense has an answer that is close to that of the anthropologist: "because they were brought up that way." By "culture" anthropology means the total life way of a people, the social legacy the individual acquires from his group. Or culture can be regarded as that part of the environment that is the creation of man.

This technical term has a wider meaning than the "culture" of history and literature. A humble cooking pot is as much a cultural product as is a Beethoven sonata. In ordinary speech a man of culture is a man who can speak languages other than his own, who is familiar with history, literature, philosophy, or the fine arts. In some cliques that definition is still narrower. The cultured person is one who can talk about James Joyce, Scarlatti, and Picasso. To the anthropologist, however, to be human is to be cultured. There is culture in general, and then there are the specific cultures such as Russian, American, British, Hottentot, Inca. The general abstract notion serves to remind us that we cannot explain acts solely in terms of the biological properties of the people concerned, their individual past experience, and the immediate situation. The past experience of other men in the form of culture enters into almost every event.

SOURCE: Clyde Kluckhohn, *Mirror for Man* (New York: McGraw-Hill Book Company, Inc., 1949), 17–36. Reprinted by permission. • Clyde Kluckhohn (1905–1960) was professor of anthropology and director of the Russian Research Center at Harvard University. He was the author of *To the Foot of the Rainbow,* the coauthor of *Navaho Means People* and *How the Soviet System Works,* and the coeditor of *Personality in Nature, Society and Culture.*

Each specific culture constitutes a kind of blueprint for all of life's activities.

One of the interesting things about human beings is that they try to understand themselves and their own behavior. While this has been particularly true of Europeans in recent times, there is no group which has not developed a scheme or schemes to explain man's actions. To the insistent human query "why?" the most exciting illumination anthropology has to offer is that of the concept of culture. Its explanatory importance is comparable to categories such as evolution in biology, gravity in physics, disease in medicine. A good deal of human behavior can be understood, and indeed predicted, if we know a people's design for living. Many acts are neither accidental nor due to personal peculiarities nor caused by supernatural forces nor simply mysterious. Even those of us who pride ourselves on our individualism follow most of the time a pattern not of our own making. We brush our teeth on arising. We put on pants—not a loincloth or a grass skirt. We eat three meals a day—not four or five or two. We sleep in a bed—not in a hammock or on a sheep pelt. I do not have to know the individual and his life history to be able to predict these and countless other regularities, including many in the thinking process, of all Americans who are not incarcerated in jails or hospitals for the insane.

To the American woman a system of plural wives seems "instinctively" abhorrent. She cannot understand how any woman can fail to be jealous and uncomfortable if she must share her husband with other women. She feels it "unnatural" to accept such a situation. On the other hand, a Koryak woman of Siberia, for example, would find it hard to understand how a woman could be so selfish and so undesirous of feminine companionship in the home as to wish to restrict her husband to one mate.

Some years ago I met in New York City a young man who did not speak a word of English and was obviously bewildered by American ways. By "blood" he was as American as you or I, for his parents had gone from Indiana to China as missionaries. Orphaned in infancy, he was reared by a Chinese family in a remote village. All who met him found him more Chinese than American. The facts of his blue eyes and light hair were less impressive than a Chinese style of gait, Chinese arm and hand movements, Chinese facial expression, and Chinese modes of thought. The biological heritage was American, but the cultural training had been Chinese. He returned to China. Another example of another kind: I once knew a trader's wife in Arizona who took a somewhat devilish interest in producing a cultural reaction. Guests who came her way were often served delicious sandwiches filled with a meat that seemed to be neither chicken nor tuna fish yet was reminiscent of both. To queries she gave no reply until each had eaten his fill. She then explained that what they had eaten was not chicken, not tuna fish, but the rich, white flesh of freshly killed rattlesnakes. The response was instantaneous—vomiting, often violent vomiting. A biological process is caught in a cultural web.

A highly intelligent teacher with long and successful experience in the public schools of Chicago was finishing her first year in an Indian school. When asked how her Navaho pupils compared in intelligence with Chicago youngsters, she replied, "Well, I just don't know. Sometimes the Indians seem just as bright. At other times they just act like dumb animals. The other night we had a dance in the high school. I saw a boy who is one of the best students in my English class standing off by himself. So I took him over to a pretty girl and told them to dance. But they just stood there with their heads down. They wouldn't even say anything." I inquired if she knew whether or not they were members of the same clan. "What difference would that make?"

"How would you feel about getting into bed with your brother?" The teacher walked off in a huff, but, actually, the two cases were quite comparable in principle. To the Indian the type of bodily contact involved in our social dancing has a directly sexual connotation. The incest taboos between members of the same clan are as severe as between true brothers and sisters. The shame of the Indians at the suggestion that a clan brother and sister should dance and the indignation of the white teacher at the idea that she should share a bed with an adult brother represent equally nonrational responses, culturally standardized unreason.

All this does not mean that there is no such thing as raw human nature. The very fact that certain of the same institutions are found in all known societies indicates that at bottom all human beings are very much alike. The files of the Cross-Cultural Survey at Yale University are organized according to categories such as "marriage ceremonies," "life crisis rites," "incest taboos." At least seventy-five of these categories are represented in every single one of the hundreds of cultures analyzed. This is hardly surprising. The members of all human groups have about the same biological equipment. All men undergo the same poignant life experiences such as birth, helplessness, illness, old age, and death. The biological potentialities of the species are the blocks with which cultures are built. Some patterns of every culture crystallize around focuses provided by the inevitables of biology: the difference between the sexes, the presence of persons of different ages, the varying physical strength and skill of individuals. The facts of nature also limit culture forms. No culture provides patterns for jumping over trees or for eating iron ore.

There is thus no "either-or" between nature and that special form of nurture called culture. Culture determinism is as one-sided as biological determinism. The two factors are interdependent. Culture arises out of human nature, and its forms are restricted both by man's biology and by natural laws. It is equally true that culture channels biological processes—vomiting, weeping, fainting, sneezing, the daily habits of food intake and waste elimination. When a man eats, he is reacting to an internal "drive," namely, hunger contractions consequent upon the lowering of blood sugar, but his precise reaction to these internal stimuli cannot be predicted by physiological knowledge alone. Whether a healthy adult feels hungry twice, three times, or four times a day and the hours at which this feeling recurs is a question of culture. *What* he eats is of course limited by availability, but is also partly regulated by culture. It is a biological fact that some types of berries are poisonous; it is a cultural fact that, a few generations ago, most Americans considered tomatoes to be poisonous and refused to eat them. Such selective, discriminative use of the environment is characteristically cultural. In a still more general sense, too, the process of eating is channeled by culture. Whether a man eats to live, lives to eat, or merely eats and lives is only in part an individual matter, for there are also cultural trends. Emotions are physiological events. Certain situations will evoke fear in people from any culture. But sensations of pleasure, anger, and lust may be stimulated by cultural cues that would leave unmoved someone who has been reared in a different social tradition.

Except in the case of newborn babies and of individuals born with clear-cut structural or functional abnormalities we can observe innate endowments only as modified by cultural training. In a hospital in New Mexico where Zuñi Indian, Navaho Indian, and white American babies are born, it is possible to classify the newly arrived infants as unusually active, average, and quiet. Some babies from each "racial" group will fall into each category, though a higher proportion of the white babies will fall into the unusually active class. But if a Navaho baby, a Zuñi baby, and a white baby—all classified as unusually active at birth—are again observed at the age of two years, the Zuñi baby will no longer seem given to quick and restless activity—*as compared with the white child*—though he may seem so as compared with the other Zuñis of the same age. The Navaho child is likely to fall in between as contrasted with the Zuñi and the white, though he will probably still seem more active than the average Navaho youngster.

It was remarked by many observers in the Japanese relocation centers that Japanese who were born and brought up in this country, especially those who were reared apart from any large colony of Japanese, resemble in behavior their white neighbors much more closely than they do their own parents who were educated in Japan.

I have said "culture channels biological processes." It is more accurate to say "the biological functioning of individuals is modified if they have been trained in certain ways and not in others." Culture is not a disembodied force. It is created and transmitted by people. However, culture, like well-known concepts of the physical sciences, is a convenient abstraction. One never sees gravity. One sees bodies falling in regular ways. One never sees an electromagnetic field. Yet certain happenings that can be seen may be given a neat abstract formulation by assuming that the electromagnetic field exists. Similarly, one never sees culture as such. What is seen are regularities in the behavior or artifacts of a group that has adhered to a common tradition. The regularities in style and technique of ancient Inca tapestries or stone axes from Melanesian islands are due to the existence of mental blueprints for the group.

Culture is a way of thinking, feeling, believing. It is the group's knowledge stored up (in memories of men; in books and objects) for future use. We study the products of this "mental" activity: the overt behavior, the speech and gestures and activities of people, and the tangible results of these things such as tools, houses, cornfields, and what not. It has been customary in lists of "culture traits" to include such things as watches or lawbooks. This is a convenient way of thinking about them, but in the solution of any important problem we must remember that they, in themselves, are nothing but metals, paper, and ink. What is important is that some men know how to make them, others set a value on them, are unhappy without them, direct their activities in relation to them, or disregard them.

It is only a helpful shorthand when we say "The cultural patterns of the Zulu were resistant to Christianization." In the directly observable world of course, it was individual Zulus who resisted. Nevertheless, if we do not forget that we are speaking at a high level of abstraction, it is justifiable to speak of culture as a cause. One may compare the practice of saying "syphilis caused the extinction of the native population of the island." Was it "syphilis" or "syphilis germs" or "human beings who were carriers of syphilis"?

"Culture," then, is "a theory." But if a theory is not contradicted by any relevant fact and if it helps us to understand a mass of otherwise chaotic facts, it is useful. Darwin's contribution was much less the accumulation of new knowledge than the creation of a theory which put in order data already known. An accumulation of facts, however large, is no more a science than a pile of bricks is a house. Anthropology's demonstration that the most weird set of customs has a consistency and an order is comparable to modern psychiatry's showing that there is meaning and purpose in the apparently incoherent talk of the insane. In fact, the inability of the older psychologies and philosophies to account for the strange behavior of madmen and heathens was the principal factor that forced psychiatry and anthropology to develop theories of the unconscious and of culture.

Since culture is an abstraction, it is important not to confuse culture with society. A "society" refers to a group of people who interact more with each other than they do with other individuals —who cooperate with each other for the attainment of certain ends. You can see and indeed count the individuals who make up a society. A "culture" refers to the distinctive ways of life of such a group of people. Not all social events are culturally patterned. New types of circumstances arise for which no cultural solutions have as yet been devised.

A culture constitutes a storehouse of the pooled learning of the group. A rabbit starts life with some innate responses. He can learn from his own experience and perhaps from observing other rabbits. A human infant is born with fewer instincts and greater plasticity. His main task is to learn the answers that persons he will never see, persons long dead, have worked out. Once he has learned the formulas supplied by the culture of his group, most of his behavior becomes almost as automatic and unthinking as if it were instinctive. There is a tremendous amount of intelligence behind the making of a radio, but not much is required to learn to turn it on.

The members of all human societies face some of the same unavoidable dilemmas posed by biology and other facts of the human situation. This is why the basic categories of all cultures are so similar. Human culture without language is unthinkable. No culture fails to provide for aesthetic expression and aesthetic delight. Every culture supplies standardized orientations toward the deeper problems, such as death. Every culture is designed to perpetuate the group and its solidarity, to meet the demands of individuals for an orderly way of life and for satisfaction of biological needs.

However, the variations on these basic themes are numberless. Some languages are built up out of twenty basic sounds, others out of forty. Nose plugs were considered beautiful by the predynastic Egyptians but are not by the modern French. Puberty is a biological fact. But one culture ignores it, another prescribes informal instructions about sex but no ceremony, a third has impressive rites for girls only, a fourth for boys and girls. In this culture, the first menstruation is welcomed as a happy, natural event; in that culture the atmosphere is full of dread and supernatural threat. Each culture dissects nature according to its own system of categories. The Navaho Indians apply the same word to the color of a robin's egg and to that of grass. A psychologist once assumed that this meant a difference in the sense organs, that Navahos didn't have the physiological equipment to distinguish "green" from "blue." However, when he showed them objects of the two colors and asked them if they were exactly the same colors, they looked at him with astonishment. His dream of discovering a new type of color blindness was shattered.

Every culture must deal with the sexual instinct. Some, however, seek to deny all sexual expression before marriage, whereas a Polynesian adolescent who was not promiscuous would be distinctly abnormal. Some cultures enforce lifelong monogamy, others, like our own, tolerate serial monogamy; in still other cultures, two or more women may be joined to one man or several men to a single woman. Homosexuality has been a permitted pattern in the Greco-Roman world, in parts of Islam, and in various primitive tribes. Large portions of the population of Tibet, and of Christendom at some places and periods, have practiced complete celibacy. To us marriage is first and foremost an arrangement between two individuals. In many more societies marriage is merely one facet of a complicated set of reciprocities, economic and otherwise, between two families or two clans.

The essence of the cultural process is selectivity. The selection is only exceptionally conscious and rational. Cultures are like Topsy. They just grew. Once, however, a way of handling a situation becomes institutionalized, there is ordinarily great resistance to change or deviation. When we speak of "our sacred beliefs," we mean of course that they are beyond criticism and that the person who suggests modification or abandonment must be punished. No person is emotionally indifferent to his culture. Certain cultural premises may become totally out of accord with a new factual situation. Leaders may recognize this and reject the old ways in theory. Yet their emotional loyalty continues in the face of reason because of the intimate conditionings of early childhood.

A culture is learned by individuals as the result of belonging to some particular group, and it constitutes that part of learned behavior which is shared with others. It is our social legacy, as contrasted with our organic heredity. It is one of the important factors which permits us to live together in an organized society, giving us ready-made solutions to our problems, helping us to predict the behavior of others, and permitting others to know what to expect of us.

Culture regulates our lives at every turn. From the moment we are born until we die there is, whether we are conscious of it or not, constant pressure upon us to follow certain types of behavior that other men have created for us. Some paths we follow willingly, others we follow because we know no other way, still others we deviate from or go back to most unwillingly. Mothers of small children know how unnaturally most of this comes to us—how little regard we have, until we are "culturalized," for the "proper" place, time, and manner for certain acts such as eating, excreting, sleeping, getting dirty, and making loud noises. But by more or less adhering to a system of related designs for carrying out all the acts of living, a group of men and women feel themselves linked together by a powerful chain of sentiments. Ruth Benedict gave an almost complete definition of the concept when she said, "Culture is that which binds men together."

It is true any culture is a set of techniques for adjusting both to the external environment and to other men. However, cultures create problems as well as solve them. If the lore of a people states that frogs are dangerous creatures, or that it is not safe to go about at night because of witches or ghosts, threats are posed which do not arise out of the inexorable facts of the external world. Cultures produce needs as well as provide a means of fulfilling them. There exist for every group culturally defined, acquired drives that may be more powerful in ordinary daily life than the biologically inborn drives. Many Americans, for example, will work harder for "success" than they will for sexual satisfaction.

Most groups elaborate certain aspects of their culture far beyond maximum utility or survival value. In other words, not all culture promotes physical survival. At times, indeed, it does exactly the opposite. Aspects of culture which once were adaptive may persist long after they have ceased to be useful. An analysis of any culture will disclose many features which cannot possibly be construed as adaptations to the total environment in which the group now finds itself. However, it is altogether likely that these apparently useless features represent survivals, with modifications through time, of cultural forms which were adaptive in one or another previous situation.

Any cultural practice must be functional or it will disappear before long. That is, it must somehow contribute to the survival of the society or to the adjustment of the individual. However, many cultural functions are not manifest but latent. A cowboy will walk three miles to catch a horse which he then rides one mile to the store. From the point of view of manifest function this is positively irrational. But the act has the latent function of maintaining the cowboy's prestige in the terms of his own subculture. One can instance the buttons on the sleeve of a man's coat, our absurd English spelling, the use of capital letters, and a host of other apparently nonfunctional customs. They serve mainly the latent function of assisting individuals to maintain their security by preserving continuity with the past and by making certain sectors of life familiar and predictable.

Every culture is a precipitate of history. In more than one sense history is a sieve. Each culture embraces those aspects of the past, which, usually in altered form and with altered meanings, live on in the present. Discoveries and inventions, both material and ideological, are constantly being made available to a group through its historical contacts with other peoples or being created by its own members. However, only those that fit the total immediate situation in meeting the group's needs for survival or in promoting the psychological adjustment of individuals will become part of the culture. The process of culture building may be regarded as an addition to man's innate biological capacities, an addition providing instruments which enlarge, or may even substitute for, biological functions, and to a degree compensating for biological limitations—as in ensuring that death does not always result in the loss to humanity of what the deceased has learned.

Culture is like a map. Just as a map isn't the territory but an abstract representation of a particular area, so also a culture is an abstract description of trends toward uniformity in the words, deeds, and artifacts of a human group. If a map is accurate and you can read it, you won't get lost; if you know a culture, you will know your way around in the life of a society.

Many educated people have the notion that culture applies only to exotic ways of life or to societies where relative simplicity and relative homogeneity prevail. Some sophisticated missionaries, for example, will use the anthropological conception in discussing the special modes of living of South Sea Islanders, but seem amazed at the idea that it could be applied equally to inhabitants of New York City. And social workers in Boston will talk about the culture of a colorful and well-knit immigrant group but boggle at applying it to the behavior of staff members in the social-service agency itself.

In the primitive society the correspondence between the habits of individuals and the customs of the community is ordinarily greater. There is probably some truth in what an old Indian once said, "In the old days there was no law; everybody did what was right." The primitive tends to find happiness in the fulfillment of intricately involuted cultural patterns; the modern more often tends to feel the pattern as repressive to his individuality. It is also true that in a complex stratified society there are numerous exceptions to generalizations made about the culture as a whole. It is necessary to study regional, class, and occupational subcultures. Primitive cultures have greater stability than modern cultures; they change—but less rapidly.

However, modern men also are creators and carriers of culture. Only in some respects are they influenced differently from primitives by culture. Moreover, there are such wide variations in primitive cultures that any black-and-white contrast between the primitive and the civilized is altogether fictitious. The distinction which is most generally true lies in the field of conscious philosophy.

The publication of Paul Radin's *Primitive Man as a Philosopher* did much toward destroying the myth that an abstract analysis of experience was a peculiarity of literate societies. Speculation and reflection upon the nature of the universe and of man's place in the total scheme of things have been carried out in every known culture. Every people has its characteristic set of "primitive postulates." It remains true that critical examination of basic premises and fully explicit systematization of philosophical concepts are seldom found at the nonliterate level. The written word is an almost essential condition for free and extended discussion of fundamental philosophic issues. Where dependence on memory exists, there seems to be an inevitable tendency to emphasize the correct perpetuation of the precious oral tradition. Similarly, while it is all too easy to underestimate the extent to which ideas spread without books, it is in general true that tribal or folk societies do not possess competing philosophical systems. The major exception to this statement is, of course, the case where part of the tribe becomes converted to one of the great proselytizing religions such as Christianity or Mohammedanism. Before contact with rich and powerful civilizations, primitive peoples seem to have absorbed new ideas piecemeal, slowly integrating them with the previously existing ideology. The abstract thought of nonliterate societies is ordinarily less self-critical, less systematic, nor so intricately elaborated in purely logical dimensions. Primitive thinking is more concrete, more implicit—perhaps more completely coherent than the philosophy of most individuals in larger societies which have been influenced over long periods by disparate intellectual currents.

No participant in any culture knows all the details of the cultural map. The statement frequently heard that St. Thomas Aquinas was the last man to master all the knowledge of his society is intrinsically absurd. St. Thomas would have been hard put to make a pane of cathedral glass or to act as a midwife. In every culture there are what Ralph Linton has called "universals, alternatives, and specialties." Every Christian in the thirteenth century knew that it was necessary to attend mass, to go to confession, to ask the Mother of God to intercede with her Son. There were many other universals in the Christian culture of Western Europe. However, there were also alternative cultural patterns even in the realm of religion. Each individual had his own patron saint, and different towns developed the cults of different saints. The thirteenth-century anthropologist could have discovered the rudiments of Christian practice by questioning and observing whomever he happened to meet in Germany, France, Italy, or England. But to find out the details of the ceremonials honoring St. Hubert or St. Bridget he would have had to seek out certain individuals or special localities where these alternative patterns were practiced. Similarly, he could not learn about weaving from a professional soldier or about canon law from a farmer. Such cultural knowledge belongs in the realm of the specialties, voluntarily chosen by the individual or ascribed to him by birth. Thus, part of a culture must be learned by everyone, part may be selected from alternative patterns, part applies only to those who perform the roles in the society for which these patterns are designed.

Many aspects of a culture are explicit. The explicit culture consists in those regularities in word and deed that may be generalized straight from the evidence of the ear and the eye. The recognition of these is like the recognition of style in the art of a particular place and epoch. If we have examined twenty specimens of the wooden saints' images made in the Taos valley of New Mexico in the late eighteenth century, we can predict that any new images from the same locality and period will in most respects exhibit the same techniques of carving, about the same use of colors and choice of woods, a similar quality of artistic conception. Similarly, if, in a society of 2,000 members, we record 100 marriages at random and find that in 30 cases a man has married the sister of his brother's wife, we can anticipate that an additional sample of 100 marriages will show roughly the same number of cases of this pattern.

The above is an instance of what anthropologists call a behavioral pattern, the practices as opposed to the rules of the culture. There are also, however, regularities in what people say they do or should do. They do tend in fact to prefer to marry into a family already connected with their own by marriage but this is not necessarily part of the official code of conduct. No disapproval whatsoever is attached to those who make another sort of marriage. On the other hand, it is explicitly forbidden to marry a member of one's own clan even though no biological relationship is traceable. This is a regulatory pattern—a Thou Shalt or a Thou Shalt Not. Such patterns may be violated often, but their existence is nevertheless important. A people's standards for conduct and belief define the socially approved aims and the acceptable means of attaining them. When the discrepancy between the theory and the practice of a culture is exceptionally great, this indicates that the culture is undergoing rapid change. It does not prove that ideals are unimportant, for ideals are but one of a number of factors determining action.

Cultures do not manifest themselves solely in observable customs and artifacts. No amount of questioning of any save the most articulate in the most self-conscious cultures will bring out some of the basic attitudes common to the members of the group. This is because these basic assumptions are taken so for granted that they normally do not enter into consciousness. This part of the cultural map must be inferred by the observer on the basis of consistencies in thought and action. Missionaries in various societies are often disturbed or puzzled because the natives do not regard "morals" and "sex code" as almost synonymous. The natives seem to feel that morals are concerned with sex just about as much as with eating—no less and no more. No society fails to have some restrictions on sexual behavior, but sex activity outside of marriage need not necessarily be furtive or attended with guilt. The Christian tradition has tended to assume that sex is inherently nasty as well as dangerous. Other cultures assume that sex in itself is not only natural but one of the good things of life, even though sex acts with certain persons under certain circumstances are forbidden. This is implicit culture, for the natives do not announce their premises. The missionaries would get further if they said, in effect, "Look, our morality starts from different assumptions. Let's talk about those assumptions," rather than ranting about "immorality."

A factor implicit in a variety of diverse phenomena may be generalized as an underlying cultural principle. For example, the Navaho Indians always leave part of the design in a pot, a basket, or a blanket unfinished. When a medicine man instructs an apprentice he always leaves a little bit of the story untold. This "fear of closure" is a recurrent theme in Navaho culture. Its influence may be detected in many contexts that have no explicit connection.

If the observed cultural behavior is to be correctly understood, the categories and presuppositions constituting the implicit culture must be worked out. The "strain toward consistency" which Sumner noted in the folkways and mores of all groups cannot be accounted for unless one grants a set of systematically interrelated implicit themes. For example, in American culture the themes of "effort and optimism," "the common man," "technology," and "virtuous materialism" have a functional interdependence, the origin of which is historically known. The relationship between themes may be that of conflict. One may instance the competition between Jefferson's theory of democracy and Hamilton's "government by the rich, the wellborn, and the able." In other cases most themes may be integrated under a single dominant theme. In Negro cultures of West Africa the mainspring of social life is religion; in East Africa almost all cultural behavior seems to be oriented toward certain premises and categories centered on the cattle economy. If there be one master principle in the implicit culture, this is often called the "ethos" or *Zeitgeist*.

Every culture has organization as well as content. There is nothing mystical about this statement. One may compare ordinary experience. If I know that Smith, working alone, can shovel 10 cubic yards of dirt a day, Jones 12, and Brown 14, I would be foolish to predict that the three working together would move 36. The total might well be considerably more; it might be less. A whole is different from the sum of its parts. The same principle is familiar in athletic teams. A brilliant pitcher added to a nine may mean a pennant or may mean the cellar; it depends on how he fits in.

And so it is with cultures. A mere list of the behavioral and regulatory patterns and of the implicit themes and categories would be like a map on which all mountains, lakes, and rivers were included—but not in their actual relationship to one another. Two cultures could have almost identical inventories and still be extremely different. The full significance of any single element in a culture design will be seen only when that element is viewed in the total matrix of its relationship to other elements. Naturally, this includes accent or emphasis, as well as position. Accent is manifested sometimes through frequency, sometimes through intensity.

The indispensable importance of these questions of arrangement and emphasis may be driven home by an analogy. Consider a musical sequence made up of three notes. If we are told that the three notes in question are *A*, *B*, and *G*, we receive information which is fundamental. But it will not enable us to predict the type of sensation which the playing of this sequence is likely to evoke. We need many different sorts of relationship data. Are the notes to be played in that or some other order? What duration will each receive? How will the emphasis, if any, be distributed? We also need, of course, to know whether the instrument used is to be a piano or an accordion.

Cultures vary greatly in their degree of integration. Synthesis is achieved partly through the overt statement of the dominant conceptions, assumptions, and aspirations of the group in its religious lore, secular thought, and ethical code; partly through habitual but unconscious ways of looking at the stream of events, ways of begging certain questions. To the naïve participant in the culture these modes of categorizing, of dissecting experience along these planes and not others, are as much "given" as the regular sequence of daylight and darkness or the necessity of air, water, and food for life. Had Americans not thought in terms of money and the market system during the depression they would have distributed unsalable goods rather than destroyed them.

Every group's way of life, then, is a structure—not a haphazard collection of all the different physically possible and functionally effective patterns of belief and action. A culture is an interdependent system based upon linked premises and categories whose influence is greater, rather than less, because they are seldom put in words. Some degree of internal coherence which is felt rather than rationally constructed seems to be demanded by most of the participants in any culture. As Whitehead has remarked, "Human life is driven forward by its dim apprehension of notions too general for its existing language."

In sum, the distinctive way of life that is handed down as the social heritage of a people does more than supply a set of skills for making a living and a set of blueprints for human relations. Each different way of life makes its own assumptions about the ends and purposes of human existence, about what human beings have a right to expect from each other and the gods, about what constitutes fulfillment or frustration. Some of these assumptions are made explicit in the lore of the folks; others are tacit premises which the observer must infer by finding consistent trends in word and deed.

12 The Amish: A Cultural Island

JOHN HOSTETLER

One way of learning the meaning of the culture is to examine a cultural island within one's own society. Another is to compare the codes of proper behavior in different societies. This selection presents the former. Hostetler's examination of strongly traditional Amish codes of behavior and the symbols associated with these codes helps us to understand not only the concept of culture, but also the means by which groups such as the Amish resist assimilation into the larger society. In the next selection, Levy illustrates the meaning of culture using a sharply different pattern from another society.

THE AMISH CHARTER

We turn now to the moral principles of the contemporary Amish community. By moral we mean that which is considered right and wrong, and the principles for which life is worth living. The fundamentals of right and wrong are made relevant in the life of the society. Behavior in the Amish community is oriented to absolute values, involving a conscious belief in religious and ethical ends, entirely for their own sake, and quite independent of any external rewards. This orientation to *Wert-rational*, or absolute values, requires of the individual certain unconditional demands. Regardless of any possible cost to themselves, the members are required to put into practice what is required by duty, honor, personal loyalty, and religious calling. The fundamental values and common ends of the group, recognized by the people and accepted by them, have been designated as the charter. A charter need not be reduced to writing to be effective in the little community; it may be thought of as the common purpose of the community, corresponding to a desire or a set of motives embodied in tradition. Although Amish life is oriented to absolute values, there is an almost automatic reaction to habitual stimuli that guides behavior in a course which has been repeatedly followed. Behavior is traditionally oriented by belief and the habit of long experience.

The Amish view of reality is conditioned by a dualistic world view. They believe, as have many other ascetic brotherhoods, that light and truth coexist with the powers of darkness and falsehood. Purity and goodness are in conflict with impurity and evil. The rejection of the world is based upon this dualistic conception of reality and is manifest in specific life situations. While the Amish

SOURCE: John A. Hostetler, *Amish Society* (Baltimore: The Johns Hopkins Press, 1963). Reprinted by permission. • John A. Hostetler is professor of sociology and anthropology at Temple University. He was born in Mifflin County, Pennsylvania, and was reared as an Amishman, but he left his Plain Folk community to pursue an education. His special interests include social change, problems of the marginal man, and cultural anthropology. His research and numerous publications have focused on the Amish, Mennonites, and Hutterites. He is the author of *Annotated Bibliography on the Amish*, which was awarded the International Folklore Prize, University of Chicago; *The Sociology of Mennonite Evangelism; Education and Marginality in the Communal Society of the Hutterites;* and *The Hutterites in North America.*

share this fundamental doctrine of the two worlds with other believers, it becomes a reality to the Amish, while to many Christian people it is greatly modified.

Separation from the World

To the Amish there is a divine spiritual reality, the Kingdom of God, and a Satanic Kingdom that dominates the present world. It is the duty of a Christian to keep himself "unspotted from the world" and separate from the desires, intent, and goals of the worldly person. Amish preaching and teaching draws upon passages from the Bible which emphasize the necessity of separation from the world. Two passages, perhaps the most often quoted, epitomize for the Amishman the message of the Bible. The first is: "Be not conformed to this world, but be ye transformed by the renewing of your mind that ye may prove what is that good and acceptable and perfect will of God." This to the Amishman means among other things that one should not dress and behave like the world. The second is: "Be ye not unequally yoked together with unbelievers; for what fellowship hath righteousness with unrighteousness? and what communion hath light with darkness?" This doctrine forbids the Amishman from marrying a non-Amish person or from being in business partnership with an outsider. It is applied generally to all social contacts that would involve intimate connections with persons outside the ceremonial community. This emphasis upon literalness and separateness is compatible with the Amish view of themselves as a "chosen people" or "peculiar people."

The principle of separation conditions and controls the Amishman's contact with the outside world; it colors his entire view of reality and being. Bible teaching is conditioned by the totality of the traditional way of life. Compatible with the doctrine of separation is the doctrine of non-resistance. By the precepts of Christ, the Amish are forbidden to take part in violence and war. In time of war they are conscientious objectors, basing their stand on biblical texts, such as "My kingdom is not of this world: if my kingdom were of this world, then would my servant fight." The Amish have no rationale for self-defense or for defending their possessions. Like many early Anabaptists they are "defenseless Christians." Problems of hostility are met without retaliation. The Amish farmer, in difficulty with the hostile world around him, is admonished by his bishop to follow the example of Isaac: after the warring Philistines had stopped up all the wells of his father Abraham, Isaac moved to new lands and dug new wells. This advice is taken literally, so that in the face of hostility, the Amish move to new locations without defending their rights.

The Amish share with the Mennonites the principles of Anabaptism as evidenced by their common endorsement of the Dortrecht Confession. Both practice adult rather than infant baptism, non-resistance and refusal to bear arms, and refusal to swear an oath, and both refrain from holding public office. Religion tends to be pervasive and associated with a total way of life, not a specialized activity. The Amish today differ from the Mennonites mainly in the extent to which external changes have affected the groups. The Amish are more literal in the observance of certain practices such as fasting and shunning, in practical informal mutual aid, and in keeping the young on the farm. The Mennonites have been readier to accept changes and to incorporate them into their religious values. Mennonites are technologically modern, and they generally accept higher education. Furthermore, during the nineteenth century they founded institutions of higher education to train missionaries. Mennonites developed along the lines of modern Protestantism, while the Amish have retained literalism, limited education, and agrarianism.

The Amish are "otherworldly" minded, in contrast to the many Christian churches that are concerned with making the world a better place in which to live. The Amish show little interest in improving the world or their environment. They profess to be "strangers and pilgrims" in the present world.

• • • • •

Amish preaching and moral instruction emphasize self-denial and obedience to the teaching of the Word of God, which is equated with the rules of the church. All ministers constantly warn their members to beware of worldliness. Long passages from the Old Testament are retold, giving prominence to crucial events in the lives of Abraham, Isaac, Jacob, Joseph, and Moses. The escape of the Israelites from Egyptian bondage and Moses's giving of the law are sermon themes; punishments meted out to the lawbreakers are emphasized. The themes: "Offenders were executed for breaking the law," and "we are not better than they," are emphatically stressed. The choice put before the congregation is to obey or die. To disobey the church is to die. To obey the church and strive for "full fellowship," that is, complete harmony with the order of the church, is to have *lebendige Hoffnung,* a living hope of salvation. An Amish person simply puts faith in God, obeys the order of the church, and patiently hopes for the best.

Separation from the world is a basic tenet of the Amish charter; yet the Amish are not highly ethnocentric in their relationships with the outside world. They accept as a matter of course other people as they are, without attempting to convert them to the Amish way of life. But for those who are born into the Amish society, the sanctions for belonging are deeply rooted in the belief in separatism.

The people of the little community have an "inside view" as well as a contrasting "outside view" of things. The doctrine of separation shapes the "outside view," and in discussing further aspects of the Amish charter we turn now to the "inside view."

The Vow of Obedience

The ceremony of baptism may be viewed as a rite of passage from youth to adulthood, but it also reveals the "inside view" of things. The meaning of baptism to the individual and the community reflects ethos. Taking the baptismal vow admits one to full fellowship in the church. When young people reach late adolescence, they are urged to become members of the church. In their sermons, ministers challenge young people to join the church. The parents are concerned that young people take this step. In most cases no overt urging by the parents is necessary, since it is normal for young people to follow the role expectation and be baptized. No young person could be married in the Amish church without first being baptized in the faith.

After the spring communion, a class of instructions is held for all those who wish to join the church. This is known as *die Gemee nooch geh,* or literally, "to follow the church." The applicants meet with the ministers on Sunday morning at worship service in the *Kämmerli,* the consultation room where the ordained customarily meet. The ministers very simply acquaint the applicants for baptism with the incidents in the Bible that suggest the right relationship with God. At the same time the *Regel und Ordnung* (rules and order) of the Amish church are explained. After six or eight periods of instruction, roughly from May to August, a day is set for the baptismal service. The consent of the members is obtained to receive the applicants into fellowship. Baptism occurs prior to the fall *Ordnungsgemee* (preparatory service), which is followed by *Grossgemee* (communion). Great emphasis is placed upon the difficulty of walking the "straight and narrow way." The applicants are told that it is better not to make a vow than to vow and later break it; on a Saturday prior to baptism they are asked to meet with the ministers where they are given opportunity to "turn back" if they so desire. The young men are asked to promise that they will accept the duties of a minister should the lot ever fall on them.

• • • • •

The Rules for Living

Once the individual has been baptized, he is committed to keep the *Ordnung* or the rules of the church. For a single person this means keeping one's behavior more in line with the rules than before. With marriage the individual assumes responsibility for keeping the rules as well as for "building the church," which means taking an active part in promoting the rules. The little Amish community is distinctive from other church groups in that the rules governing life are traditional ways not specified in writing. These rules can be known only by being a participant. The rules for living tend to form a body of sentiments that are essentially a list of taboos within the environment of the small Amish community.

All Amish members know the *Ordnung* of their church district and these generally remain oral and unwritten. Perhaps most rules are taken for granted and it is usually those questionable or borderline issues which are specified in the *Ordnung*. These rules are repeated at the *Ordnungsgemee* just preceding communion Sunday. They must have been unanimously endorsed by the ordained body. At the members' meeting following the regular service they are presented orally, after which members are asked to give assent. If there is any change from previous practice, allowing a new innovation or adaptation, this change is not announced. The former taboo is simply not mentioned. A unanimous expression of unity and "peace" with the *Ordnung* makes possible the communion. But without unity there can be no communion.

The following *Ordnung* of a contemporary group, published in English, appears to be representative of the Old Order Amish, except for those portions indicated by brackets. That it appears in print at all is evidence of change from the traditional practice of keeping it oral. This *Ordnung* allows a few practices not typically sanctioned by the Old Order: the giving of tithes, distribution of tracts, belief in assurance of salvation, and limited missionary activity.

ORDNUNG OF A CHRISTIAN CHURCH

Since it is the duty of the church, especially in this day and age, to decide what is fitting and proper and also what is not fitting and proper for a Christian to do (in points that are not clearly stated in the Bible), we have considered it needful to publish this booklet listing some rules and ordinances of a Christian Church.

We hereby confess to be of one faith with the 18 articles of Faith adopted at Dortrecht, 1632, also with nearly all if not all articles in booklet entitled "Article und Ordnung der Christlichen Gemeinde."

No ornamental bright, showy form-fitting, immodest or silk-like clothing of any kind. Colors such as bright red, orange, yellow and pink not allowed. Amish form of clothing to be followed as a general rule. Costly Sunday clothing to be discouraged. Dresses not shorter than half-way between knees and floor, nor over eight inches from floor. Longer advisable. Clothing in every way modest, serviceable and as simple as scripturally possible. Only outside pockets allowed are on work eberhem or vomas and pockets on large overcoats. Dress shoes, if any, to be plain and black only. No high heels and pump slippers, dress socks, if any, to be black except white for foot hygiene for both sexes. A plain, unshowy suspender without buckles.

Hat to be black with no less than 3-inch rim and not extremely high in crown. No stylish impression in any hat. No pressed trousers. No sweaters.

Prayer covering to be simple, and made to fit head. Should cover all the hair as nearly as possible and is to be worn wherever possible. [Pleating of caps to be discouraged.] No silk ribbons. Young children to dress according to the Word as well as parents. No pink or fancy baby blankets or caps.

Women to wear shawls, bonnets, and capes in public. Aprons to be worn at all times. No adorning of hair among either sex such as parting of hair among men and curling or waving among women.

A full beard should be worn among men and boys after baptism if possible. No shingled hair. Length at least half-way below tops of ears.

No decorations of any kind in buildings inside or out. No fancy yard fences. Linoleum, oilcloth, shelf and wall paper to be plain and unshowy. Overstuffed furniture or any luxury items forbidden. No doilies or napkins. No large mirrors (fancy glassware), statues or wall pictures for decorations.

[No embroidery work of any kind.] Curtains either dark green rollers or black cloth. No boughten dolls.

No bottle gas or high line electrical appliances.

Stoves should be black if bought new.

Weddings should be simple and without decorations. [Names not attached to gifts.]

No ornaments on buggies or harness.

Tractors to be used only for such things that can hardly be done with horses. Only either stationary engines or tractors with steel tires allowed. No airfilled rubber tires.

Farming and related occupations to be encouraged. Working in cities or factories not permissible. Boys and girls working out away from home for worldly people forbidden except in emergencies.

Worldly amusements as radios, card playing [party games], movies, fairs, etc., forbidden. [Reading, singing, tract distribution, Bible games, relief work, giving of tithes, etc., are encouraged.]

Musical instruments or different voice singing not permissible. No dirty, silly talking or sex teasing of children.

Usury forbidden in most instances. No government benefit payments or partnership in harmful associations. No insurance. No photographs.

No buying or selling of anything on Sunday. It should be kept according to the principles of the Sabbath. [Worship of some kind every Sunday.]

[Women should spend time doing good or reading God's Word instead of taking care of canaries, goldfish or house flowers.]

Church confession is to be made if practical where transgression was made. If not, a written request of forgiveness should be made to said church. All manifest sins to be openly confessed before church before being allowed to commune. I Tim. 5, 20. A period of time required before taking new members into full fellowship.

Because of great falling away from sound doctrine, we do not care to fellowship, that is hold communion, with any churches that allow or uphold any unfruitful works of darkness such as worldliness, fashionable attire [bed-courtship, habitual smoking or drinking, old wives fables, non-assurance of salvation, anti-missionary zeal] or anything contrary to sound doctrine.

The rules of the Amish church cover the whole range of human experience. In a society where the goal is directed toward keeping the world out, there are many taboos, and customs become symbolic. There are variations in what is allowed from one community to another in the United States and Canada. Custom is regional and therefore not strictly uniform. The most universal of all Amish norms across the United States and Canada are the following: no electricity, telephones, central-heating systems, automobiles, or tractors with pneumatic tires; required are beards but not moustaches for all married men, long hair (which must be parted in the center, if allowed at all), hooks-and-eyes on dresscoats, and the use of horses for farming and travel. No formal education beyond the elementary grades is a rule of life.

The *Ordnung* is an essential part of the Amish charter. It is the way in which the moral postulates of society are expressed and carried out in life. The charter is constantly subjected to forces of change, a source of conflict to be discussed later.

The Punishment of the Disobedient

A moral principle in the little Amish community is the practice of *Bann und Meidung*. These words rendered in English mean excommunication and shunning. *Meidung* was the crucial question in the controversy that gave rise to the Amish as a sect movement in their secession from the Swiss Brethren. This doctrine was intrinsic in the Anabaptist movement from its very beginning and appeared in the earliest confession of faith. The Anabaptist concept of the church was that it should be a pure church of believers only; persons who fall into sin must be first excommunicated, then shunned. Menno Simons taught that the ban applies to "all—great and small, rich and poor, without any respect of persons, who once passed under the Word but have now fallen back, those living or teaching offensively in the house of the Lord—until they repent." The method of dealing with a backslider is that given by Christ in Matthew 18:15–17, and "If he neglect to hear the church, let him be unto thee as a heathen man and a publican." In other words, a person who has broken his vow and will not mend his ways must be expelled just as the human body casts off an ulcer or infectious growth. Through the years the *Meidung* has been applied in different ways. The doctrine among the Mennonites of Holland and Switzerland was of a mild character, in which the offender was excluded from communion. But a stricter conception of the ban was advanced by Jakob Ammann. The strict interpretation requires shunning of all (1) members who leave the Amish church to join another and (2) members who marry outside the brotherhood. *Meidung* requires that members receive no favors from the excommunicated person, that they do not buy from or sell to an excommunicated person, that no member shall eat at the same table with an excommunicated person, and if the case involves husband or wife, they are to suspend their usual marital relations.

The Amish make no effort to evangelize or proselyte the outsider, nor are they concerned with the redemption of the outside society to the extent that they wish to draw members from the outer society into the brotherhood. It is their primary concern to keep their own baptized members from slipping into the outer world, or into other religious groups. With greater mobility and ease of travel and communication, isolation is breaking down, and Amish solidarity is threatened by more and more of their members wanting to become like outsiders. The Amish leaders meet this threat with the ban. Members who wish to have automobiles, radios, or the usual comforts of modern living, face the threat of being excommunicated and shunned. Thus the ban is used as an instrument of discipline, not only for the drunkard or the adulterer, but for the person who transgresses the order of the church. It is a powerful instrument for keeping the church intact and for preventing members from involvement in the wider society.

The meaning of *Bann und Meidung* is made clearer if we understand how it works in life situations. Let us take the case of a young man whom we shall fictitiously name Joseph. Joseph grew up in a very strict Amish home, under the guidance of parents who were known for their orthodoxy. He was baptized at the age of twenty. Three years after his baptism Joseph was excommunicated and shunned. Charges laid against him included the following: he had attended a revival meeting, began to chum with excommunicated persons, bought an automobile, and began to attend a Mennonite church.

Joseph was excommunicated with the counsel of the assembly and was informed in their presence. After being asked to leave the service he thought to himself: "It is strange to think that I am now to be 'mited.' I don't feel very comfortable." At home, the young man was shunned: he could no longer eat at the family table. He ate at a separate table, with the younger children, or after the baptized persons finished eating. Joseph was urged to mend his ways, to make good his broken promise. His normal work relations and conversational pattern were strained. Several times he attended preaching services with his family. Since members may not accept services, goods, or favors from excommunicated members, he could not take his sisters to church, even if he used a buggy instead of his offensive automobile, but they could drive a buggy and take him along. It was not long until Joseph accepted employment with a non-Amish person and began using his automobile for transportation to and from home. When shunned friends came to his home for conversation, Joseph's parents met them at the gate and turned them away. It was not long until father and mother asked him to leave home. He explained: "I had to move away from home or my parents could not take communion. My parents were afraid that younger persons in the family would be led astray. They didn't exactly chase me off the place, but I was no longer welcome at home."

One of the purposes of excommunication is to restore the erring member by showing him his lost condition so that he will turn to repentance. The excommunication service itself is a painful and sober procedure. John Umble's description is fitting: "The excommunication of members was an awful and solemn procedure. The members to be expelled had been notified in advance and were present. An air of tenseness filled the house. Sad-faced women wept quietly; stern men sat with faces drawn. The bishop arose; with trembling voice and with tears on his cheek he announced that the guilty parties had confessed their sin, that they were cast off from the fellowship of the church and committed to the devil and all his angels (*dem Teufel und allen seinen Engeln übergeben*). He cautioned all the members to exercise 'shunning rigorously.' "

Once an individual is in a state of *Bann* (or *Bond* as the Amish call it), members are to receive no favors from him. In a very real sense he is "an outcast, rejected of God and man. His only hope is not to die before he should be reinstated, lest he should be an outcast also in the world to come."

Among the Amish communities today there are numerous divisions as a result of differing opinions on shunning. The moderate interpretation of the ban, taken by most of the midwestern groups, holds that moral transgressors should be excommunicated and shunned, but if the offender is restored to another Christian church of the non-resistant faith then shunning should no longer be applied. But this, according to the adherents of the strict ban, is a departure from Jakob Ammann. In speaking of a former Amish member who joined the Mennonites a bishop told the writer: "The only way for us to lift the ban is for him to make peace with the Old Order church, going back to one of them and living his promise he made in his baptismal vow on his knees before God and the church. It does not need to be here but in any of the churches that are in peace with us." According to this view, an excommunicated person must be shunned for life unless he restores his previous relationship with the group. The ban becomes an effective means of dispensing with the offender. By shunning him in all social relations, he is given a status that minimizes the threat to other members of the community. This perpetuation of the controversy undoubtedly aids the Old Order group to remain distinct and socially isolated.

Closeness to Nature

The little Amish community has a strong affinity for the soil and for nature. Unlike science, which is occupied with the theoretical reconstruction of the order of the world, the Amish view comes from direct contact with nature by the reality of work. The physical world is good, and in itself not corrupting or evil. The beautiful is apprehended in the universe, by the orderliness of the seasons, the heavens, the world of growing plants as well as the many species of animals, and by the forces of living and dying. While it is wrong to attend a show in a theater, it is not uncommon for an Amish family to visit the zoo or the circus to see the animals God has made.

The Amishman feels contact with the world through the working of his muscles and the aching of his limbs. In the little Amish community toil is proper and good, religion provides meaning, and the bonds of family and church provide human satisfaction and love.

The charter of Amish life requires members to limit their occupation to farming or closely associated activity such as operating a saw mill, carpentry, or mason work. In Europe the Amish lived in rural areas, always having close association with the soil, so that the community was entirely agrarian in character. It is only in America that the Amish have found it necessary to make occupational regulations for protection from the influence of urbanism.

The preference for rural living is reflected in attitudes and in the informal relations of group life, rather than in an explicit dogma. For the Amish, God is manifest more in closeness to nature, in the soil and in the weather, and among plants and animals, than he is in the man-made city. Hard work, thrift, and mutual aid find sanction in the Bible. The city by contrast is held to be the center of leisure, of non-productive spending, and often of wickedness. The Christian life, they contend, is best maintained away from the cities. God created Adam and Eve to "replenish the earth, and subdue it; and have dominion over the fish of the sea, and over the fowl of the air, and over every living thing that moveth upon the earth." In the same way, man's highest place in the universe today is to care for the things of creation. One Amishman said, "The Lord told Adam to replenish the earth and to rule over the animals and the land—you can't do that in cities." Another said, "While the Lord's blessings were given to the people who remained in the country, sickness and ruination befell Sodom. Shows, dances, parties, and other temptations ruin even the good people who now live in cities. Families are small in cities; in the city you never know where your wife is, and city women can't cook. People go hungry in the cities but you will never starve if you work hard in the country."

The Amish have generally prospered on the land more often than their neighbors. Lancaster County, Pennsylvania, which is the center of Amish life, has long been distinguished as the garden spot of the nation, representing an intensive kind of farming on relatively small holdings. Their success is based upon long experience with agricultural practices in the

Old World and upon a philosophy of work and thrift.

. . . . .

. . . The Amish attribute their material success in farming to divine blessing.

The main objective of their farming, as Walter Kollmorgen has pointed out, "is to accumulate sufficient means to buy enough land to keep all the children on farms. To this end the Amish work hard, produce abundantly, and save extensively."

. . . . .

There are other moral directives in the little community but these form the essential core of what is viewed as right and wrong. The view of life and of man's place in the total scheme of things are determined by the sacred guides to life. These guides are: a biblical view of separation from the world, the vow of obedience, observance of the *Ordnung*, upholding the true doctrine of shunning, and living close to the God-created environment. In all of these tradition plays an important part. The people of the little Amish community tend to regard the ways of their ancestors as sacred and to believe that these time-hallowed practices should be carefully guarded.

THE SYMBOLIC COMMUNITY

The Amish community is a multibonded community. The members are held together not by a single interest but by many symbolic ties which they have in common. The ecologic and ceremonial functions are bounded by the limits of horse-and-buggy travel. But there exists also a symbolic community made up of many social rules for living and a culture that has set definite boundaries. A member of the Amish faith is bound to the norms and practices of his social group. He is a member of the in-group or *unser Satt Leit* (our sort of people) and is marked by certain symbols. The out-group is *anner Satt Leit* (other sorts of people), who are distinguished by their symbols. This sharp line of distinction gives rise to a general principle by which in-groups tend to stereotype out-groups, and any threat from an out-group tends to intensify the cohesion of the in-group.

Before observing in detail the intimately shared activities which make the Amish community a multibonded one, it is well to note the over-all complexity of these ties. Language provides a guide to a social reality that is different from that of other people. All new members with rare exceptions are offspring and they are assimilated gradually by a majority of the old members. Physical property, including farms that were the abodes of the forefathers, and preference for certain soils and topography come to have sentimental attachment. Common traditions and ideals which have been revered by the whole community from generation to generation embody the expectations of all. All relatives are Amish or of Amish descent. There are formal church rules that guide the members in their conduct with each other and with outsiders. The specialists, the lifetime ordained persons, carry on the functions of the church and enable it to act as a unit in maintaining separation from the world. The size of each church district is kept to a minimum, enabling it to function as a small, intimate, and informally controlled group, whereas largeness would make consensus more difficult. There are special means to resist shock such as mutual aid in times of fire, death, and sickness. The life of the community is prolonged because the basic needs of the individual are met from the cradle to the grave. The Amish baby grows up strongly attached to those of his kind and remains indifferent to contacts outside his culture. The tendency to symbolize all of life provides a basis for action in meeting the future. It assures internal unity and community longevity.

Symbols, Convention, and Tradition

Symbols form an important maintenance function in everyday life. The symbols are different from the non-Amish or "English" symbols. In the world around them, the Amish see the symbols of worldly civilization. They are such objects as the cathedral, the skyscraper, the modernistically designed automobile and house, the television set, the missile, and modern ways of clothing the body. To the Amishman these symbols represent the world. They are a reminder of danger to him and are to be avoided.

The Amish have their own symbolism which provides a basis for common consciousness and a common course of action. We may hypothesize that in a simple society like the Amish the people themselves become symbolic, and not their achievements as in world civilization. The horse and buggy, the beard of the married man, and the styles of dress—all take on symbolic meaning. All Amish know that this is the accepted way of doing things, and symbolism becomes an effective means of social control as the nonconformist can quickly be detected from the conformist. Symbols which are universal in all Amish communities include the following: hooks-and-eyes on the Sunday coat and vest of all men, trouser styles that have no fly-closing but a flap that buttons along the waist, wide-brimmed black-felt hats for men, white organdy caps for women, plain rather than patterned or striped dresses for women, uncut hair for women, and long hair cut in bangs for men. All these symbols together constitute a world of social reality, a way of life that teaches how people should live and what they should imitate.

An illustration of convention which is symbolic is the way courtesy is expressed among the Amish. Acts rather than words perform this function. In a small society where convention is understood few words are needed between actor and alter to make meanings precise. Words of courtesy, as expressed by the English-speaking world, are conspicuously absent among members of the Amish family and community. The dialect contains few if any words of endearment between husband and wife, but young people of courting age frequently employ English words of endearment. Amish parents who hear "English" couples exchange words like "honey" and "sweetheart" have remarked that such a relationship is probably anything but "sweet." There are no words in the Amish spoken language that correspond to "pardon me" or "excuse me." Children might use such English terms in their play but persistence in using them in family relationships would not be approved. They would be accused of trying to be "society" persons. "Oops" is sometimes used to indicate that a certain act was not intentional. "Please" and "thank you" are not a part of table manners nor a part of everyday conversation, but children are taught to say *Denki* (thank you) and *Wilkomm* (you are welcome) when giving or receiving gifts on special occasions.

Acts of politeness are much more characteristic than words. The wife may brush the husband's hat on Sunday morning before he gets around to it. The act requires no "thank you." If the husband is thoughtful he will carry the toddler, help his wife into the carriage, and tuck the blankets around her. Belching is a normal occurrence around the dinner table and conceived as a sign of good appetite with no thought of discourtesy. A boy who was chewing his food vigorously at the breakfast table was greeted by his older brother with the words: "Fer was machst so wiescht?" (Why do you make so ugly?) The boy did not reply but modified his behavior. However, in the presence of English people the Amish will adopt the polite language of the outsider. An Amish woman walking along a village sidewalk who approached a woman washing her sidewalk said "pardon me" as she stepped over the washed part of the sidewalk.

Symbolism in Amish life performs the functions of communication. When much of life is governed by symbols, fewer words are needed for communication. The conspicuous absence of words of courtesy in the Amish dialect would appear to be a function of the importance of symbols, making such words unnecessary. Like dress patterns, the speech habits have also been preserved in the New World. Polite language in Medieval Europe was characteristic of the nobility and not of the peasant groups. Actions among the Amish speak louder than words of courtesy. Acts and intentions are understood, while words of courtesy which might be adopted from the English language would not be understood. The large number of symbols which function within the Amish society aid the growing Amish child to find his place within the family, the community, and within the world of the Amish people.

The Language of Dress

Anything that can be perceived through the senses can be symbolized, and in Amish society styles of dressing become very important as symbols of group identity. The garb not only admits the individual to full fellowship but also clarifies his role and status within his society.

The hat, for example, distinguishes the Amishman from the outsider and also symbolizes his role within his social structure. When the two-year-old boy discards a dress and begins wearing trousers for the first time, he also receives a stiff jet-black hat with three or more inches of brim. Hat manufacturers produce at least twenty-eight different sizes and a dozen different styles of Amish hats. The bridegroom in Pennsylvania gets a telescopic hat that is worn during the early married years. The hat is distinguished by a permanent crease around the top of the crown. Grandfather's hat has a four-inch crown and a four-inch brim. The bishop's hat has a four- and one-half-inch crown, slightly rounded, and a wide seam around the brim. A hat which has a flatter crown is worn by the rank and file of Amish fathers. The outsider may never notice these differences, or if he does he may regard them as accidental. But to the Amish these symbols indicate whether people are fulfilling the expectations of the group. A young man who wears a hat with a brim that is too narrow is liable for sanction. The very strict Amish congregations can be distinguished from the more progressive ones by the width of the brim and the band around the crown. Thus when the writer's family moved from Pennsylvania to Iowa, one of the first adaptations to make was to take out the scissors and cut off some of the brim. This made my brothers and myself more acceptable to the new community of Amish. At the same time the act symbolized other adaptations that had to be made to adjust to a more "westernized" group of Old Order Amish.

. . . . .

One of the most highly symbolic of all garments among the women is the *Kapp* or head cap worn by every woman and even by infants. Girls from about age twelve to marriage wear a black cap for Sunday dress and a white cap at home. After marriage a white cap is always worn. The size, style, and color of caps varies slightly with regions and with degrees of orthodoxy in a single community. The fine pleats ironed into some of these caps requires hours of tedious work. The specific way in which they are made, including the width of the *fedderdeel* (front part) and the *hinnerdeel* (back part), and the width of the pleats and seams are sacred symbols of the community. Though this headpiece has undergone some changes in detail, the present Amish cap is essentially the same as that worn by the Palatine women of earlier centuries. Among most American Mennonites of Swiss-German origin the cap has become a "prayer cap" or "veiling" required of women "when praying or prophesying." (I Corinthians 11:5)

These few illustrations of Amish dress could be supported with still many others. But this is sufficient to indicate how dress styles serve as symbols for a group. The symbols function very effectively in maintaining separatism and continuity. The language of dress forms a common understanding and mutual appreciation among those who share the same traditions and expectations. Dress keeps the insider separate from the world and also keeps the outsider out. These shared conventions are given sacred sanction and biblical justification: *unser Satt Leit* (our sort of people) are distinguishable from *englische Leit* (English people) or *anner Satt Leit* (other people). The attempts by theatricals to reproduce the dress of the Amish never quite measure up to the authentic. They appear ludicrous if not hilarious to the Amish.

The Language of Speech

The Amish community is also a speech community. Language provides familiarity in which individuals find common grounds for understanding. Although the Amish came from Switzerland, from Alsace and Lorraine in France, and from the Rhineland of Germany, yet their conversational speech is remarkably uniform. The reason for this is that they came from the same (Allemanic) dialect-speaking area. Some of the Alsatian Amish could speak French when they arrived in America and a few French words have been incorporated into their dialect which is Pennsylvania Dutch (or German). Dutch in this instance is a usage from "Deutsch" meaning German, and not the language of the Netherlands. The four districts of Amish in Adams County, Indiana, around Berne, speak a Swiss dialect, but it poses no real barrier for interaction with other Amish. An Amish person traveling from Pennsylvania through the midwestern states on a kinship visit can speak his own familiar dialect and be understood.

Linguists have observed that the Amish are trilingual, that is, they can speak three somewhat distinctive yet intermixed tongues. These are: Pennsylvania Dutch, High German, and English. The usage of three distinctive tongues, rather than one or two languages, lends itself to social isolation in that there are speech groupings within the community. Roles and functions tend to organize around each language; thus when speaking English the Amishman tends to think and behave like the English-speaking person.

Pennsylvania Dutch is the familiar tongue of children at home and in informal conversation. It is the mother tongue of children born to Amish parents. Professor Albert Buffington has made it clear that this speech is not a "garbled English" or "corrupted German in the mouths of ignorant people who speak with a heavy accent," but a distinct dialect of the German language. The dialect resembles the Palatine German folk speech. It is, of course, spoken by many

Pennsylvania Dutch people who are not Amish.

The second language of the growing Amish child is English. A child is introduced to English when he attends school; as he learns it he also learns that his non-Amish playmates are "English" or *Englisher* in the dialect. They are *anner Satt Leit* (the other sort of people). Amish children learn to speak the two languages without difficulty and without noticeable accent. Upon entering school the child frequently has no English vocabulary, but he readily learns his second language.

English is used when speaking with non-Amish persons in town, at school, or when talking to an "English" visitor or salesman. Thus Amishmen employ the English language on "forced" occasions. An Amish person may shift his conversation from the dialect to English, or from English to the dialect, whichever he finds most convenient for the situation. An outsider as a guest at an Amish table may find that dialect chatter prevails at one end of the table, while one or two members of the family keep the general conversation in English for the benefit of the guest. Frey has described the Amish use of English as "American English built on a framework of Pennsylvania Dutch language patterns and interjected continually with whole or part loan-translations from the dialect." The Amish generally experience little difficulty in speaking correct English.

High German, or more precisely "Amish High German," is used exclusively for the preaching service and at formal ceremonial occasions.

. . . . .

The Amish nomenclature denoting an outsider as an *Englischer* has symbolic meaning. Such a general term means that he may be Methodist, Baptist, Lutheran, or anything but Amish. The Mennonites are not classed as English. Since the Mennonites are only a step removed from the Amish they are *Mennischte* and not really as "English" as other people. On the other hand a person of Catholic affiliation is called a *Gedolischer* (from the German word *Katholischer*). Outsiders who are neighbors of the Amish people often refer to the Amish as "The Dutch."

Conversation in the dialect becomes an especially important function of community life as the Amish are very sociable and hospitable people. The Amish devote more space to the subject of visiting in their weekly newspaper than to any other topic. Visits to the homes, preaching services, particularly before and after the service, funerals, weddings, sales, quiltings, barn-raisings, frolics of various kinds, sewings, singings, and Sunday visiting are all occasions for conversing at length.

Controlled and Limited Education

Limiting education to the elementary grades prevents exposure to many areas of scientific knowledge and vocational training. It functions also as a form of boundary maintenance. New inventions and knowledge find their way into the little Amish community by many diffuse and delayed means. As soon as the law will allow, Amish children are taken out of school for work at home. The Amish viewpoint is that "Our people are engaged in some form of agriculture and we feel positive that as farmers we are better off with only a common school education. Education does not build muscle like tilling the soil in the open field and sunshine with lots of hard work. If a boy does little hard work before he is twenty-one, he probably never gets to like it afterward. In other words, he will not amount to much as a farmer."

Conflict over the school question arose

in Pennsylvania, a few years later in Ohio, and continues in some areas. Pennsylvania law requires that children attend school until their seventeenth birthday but that children engaged in farm work may be excused through permits when they reach the age of fifteen. The conflict arose when it became clear that some Amish children completed grade eight more than once because their parents were opposed to sending them to high schools. When the parents were summoned to court and refused to pay their fines on grounds that this would admit to being guilty, they were sent to jail. Friends and businessmen paid the fines to release the parents. Some were arrested as many as ten times. The Amish took the position that compulsory attendance beyond the elementary grades interferes with the exercise of their religious liberty. Meanwhile a compromise plan has been worked out in Pennsylvania where pupils who have completed grade eight report to special "Saturday" schools conducted by the Amish themselves. Some of the more progressive Amish groups have allowed their children to enter the high school believing that it is not wrong to comply with the law. The Old Order Amish state that their children are needed for agricultural labor at home and that farming does not require higher education. The Amish leaders believe that exposure to the consolidated high school would constitute a real danger to their future community life. An Amishman who was called to court for challenging the school attendance law said: "We teach our children not to smoke or use profane language and do such things as that. I know most of the high school pupils smoke cigarettes and many girls I guess too. . . . It is better to have them at home. . . ."

The Amish strategy is merely one of withdrawal from the world. In some areas school boards have been able to keep the one-room school open in deference to the Amish, and in other areas where consolidation has occurred the Amish have built their own schools. The establishment of their own schools in recent times is an attempt to avoid participation in the centralized school and to bypass its whole socializing influence, rather than for the purpose of religious indoctrination. However, there seems to be a tendency after several years of experience for some schools to take over from the home the function of teaching religion.

The Old Order Amish are firm in their stand against formal education in the American high school. It is an effective means of maintenance, especially when linked to the doctrine of shunning. With set limits to the amount of knowledge a young person can acquire on one hand, and with the dread of censure (and of excommunication) on the other, one can scarcely find a more effective way of bounding the little community. A person who receives knowledge outside of the Amish bounds equips himself for capable living outside of the Amish community but makes himself liable to the severe sanctions of the ban and shunning. Limited knowledge preserves the existing order of things; it reinforces traditional values by keeping alternate courses of action to a minimum. Traditional values and stereotypes are thus maintained by unfamiliarity with alternate courses of action. Furthermore, questions about ingroup practices are kept to a minimum.

13 Chinese Footbinding

HOWARD S. LEVY

This selection, like the preceding one about the Amish, is intended to illuminate the concept of culture. Unlike the preceding article, however, in which there is an exploration of a wide range of cultural elements in a segment of American society, this selection focuses upon footbinding as it was once practiced in China—a limited feature of the culture of a society relatively "foreign" to Western readers. Westerners have always viewed footbinding as a bizarre and repugnant practice but, as can be seen here, at one time in China footbinding was not only considered to be acceptable but the practice was highly valued. In fact, Chinese men were typically aroused by the "lotus blossom" resulting from footbinding. Culture, it thus appears, can make anything "right" or "wrong" for the members of a particular society. This selection also demonstrates that cultural patterns can and do change, sometimes drastically and with painful consequences for the members of the society.

There are aged Chinese gentlemen today who still consider bound feet more attractive than natural ones, but they are usually reticent on the subject, hesitant to express opinions which seem inconsonant with the present age. They may also be embarrassed to try to justify footbinding to an unsympathetic and hostile Western audience.

. . . . .

The tiny foot was a popular theme in poetry, fiction, and essay as late as the first third of the twentieth century. The lotus enthusiast generally avoided foreign confrontation, but presented an eloquent defense of footbinding to the domestic audience:

> There are many good points about tiny feet, but I will talk only about the best ones. A tiny foot is proof of feminine goodness. Women who don't bind their feet look like men, for the tiny foot serves to show the differentiation. It is also an instrument for secretly conveying love feelings. The tiny foot is soft and when rubbed, leads to great excitement. If it is touched under the coverlet, love feelings of the woman are immediately aroused. The graceful walk gives the beholder a mixed feeling of compassion and pity. Natural feet are heavy and ponderous as they get into bed, but tiny feet lightly steal under the coverlets. The large-footed woman is careless about adornment, but the tinyfooted frequently wash and apply a variety of perfumed fragrances, enchanting all who come into their presence. The tiny shoe is inexpensive and uses much less material, while the large foot by way of contrast is called a lotus boat. The really tiny foot is easy to walk on, but the large tiny foot is painful and inconvenient. The natural foot looks much less aesthetic in walking. Everyone welcomes the tiny foot, regarding its smallness as precious. Men formerly so craved it that its possessor achieved harmonious matrimony. Because of

SOURCE: Howard S. Levy, *Chinese Footbinding: The History of a Curious Erotic Custom* (New York: Walton H. Rawls, 1966; distributed by Twayne Publishers), pp. 181–227. Reprinted by permission of Walton H. Rawls. • Howard S. Levy is Director of the United States Department of State Foreign Service Institute Japanese Language School, Tokyo, Japan. He is author of *Biography of Huang Ch'ao, Harem Favorites of an Illustrious Celestial,* and is the editor of *Warm-Soft Village,* and Twayne's "Chinese Literature" Series.

its diminutiveness, it gives rise to a variety of sensual pleasures and love feelings.

. . . . .

There were also stories about smelling the tiny foot, generally favorable in tone. Whether the odor pleased or offended depended on whether the individual was an impartial observer or a lotus enthusiast. A Japanese visitor to Shanghai in 1919, for example, said that bound feet, usually washed only once every two weeks, smelled most unpleasant. But he admitted that the Chinese male was pleased rather than offended by the aroma. During his student days in Kwangtung, a Chinese writer made a similar observation. He met a studious scholar there named Kuan, who lived with his wife in perfect harmony. When they slept together, Kuan placed his head by his wife's feet, so that the couple resembled two steamed and salted fish. Kuan slept this way in order to smell the aroma of his wife's bound feet, for only then was he able to sleep soundly.

. . . . .

Chinese storytellers commonly created fiction from a basis of fact by building their plots around famous historical figures. They depicted charms of the tiny foot by conjuring up suggestive and mildly erotic bedroom scenes. Nan-kung Po, a master of this technique, is a well-known contemporary Chinese historical novelist. He once wrote a fictional adaptation of Sung dynastic episodes called *The Lady of An County* and included incidental remarks about the sensual delights of footbinding. A few of these passages have been translated below because of their relevance to our study, as they indicate how the attractions of the tiny foot were described in widely-read popular works. The plot centered about the love affair of Han Shih-chung, a Southern Sung general, and a courtesan with the art-name of Carmine Jade. The first scene describes how they met:

It was an early hour, with few guests present. More than ten courtesans were seated at tables, idly chatting. Shih-chung's army friend nudged him with his elbow:

"Look how tiny their feet are! They must be only an inch long!"

"An inch? You silly fool, the smallest golden lotus is three inches; I've never heard of one an inch long."

"I was really referring to their width."

While the courtesans couldn't hear what was being said, they seemed to have guessed the topic of conversation. They displayed their tiny feet, forming a sort of Bound Foot Exhibition.

"Look," said Shih-chung in embarrassment, "they seem to know what we're talking about."

"They're all purchasable, so why shouldn't we first look over the goods?"

Shih-chung failed to reply, for he was staring at a pair of tiny feet in startled appreciation. They were the most beautiful he had ever seen. Though the shoes were not pretty, being an ordinary black color and lacking ornamentation, the foot itself was slightly over four inches long and about three fingers in width. Viewed in its over-all dimensions, the foot was unusually lovable. It narrowed from heel to toe, and about halfway towards the tip narrowed so suddenly that it was as slender as a long pepper. The tip curled upwards slightly.

A foot that long was a common sight in the capital, but it was rare to see one which narrowed as this one did. Most feet were unavoidably puffed up at the ankle, with the instep shaped like a dumpling, looking very much like a horse's hoof. Such tvpes, no matter how small, were not aesthetic in the slightest.

Only this pair of bound feet led the viewer to think of rubbing them in his palms. Han Shih-chung imagined that her feet must be as soft as a ball of flour; otherwise, how could they be so delicate and tender? Shih-chung suddenly resolved to take them in the palms of his hands and knead them furiously with his fingers.

"Ouch!" The lovable pair of bound feet suddenly jumped up. Shih-chung was startled, thinking that he must have hurt her by the very thought of kneading her feet. This of course was not true, but "lovely feet" had cried out in actual pain. There had been a glass of boiling water at her table. When she turned to look at Shih-chung, the courtesan beside her deliberately spilled it over her and accused her of having done it herself. The women quarreled, spurred on by the words of the other courtesans, who were envious of "lovely feet," and began fighting furiously. This alarmed Shih-chung, who realized the tiny feet of the courtesan whom he admired were the object of widespread jealousy. A ponderous five-inch foot suddenly stamped down on "lovely feet." Shih-chung bellowed out in rage and rushed to her side, causing her adversaries to flee in panic.

"It must be very painful; I hope that you did not suffer serious injury."

"They tried to break my feet," she murmured, pressing her tiny feet with both hands."

"What is your name?"

"Carmine Jade . . . and your name, sir?"

For the general and the courtesan, it was love at first sight. In the bedroom scenes which follow, the ways in which the tiny foot enhanced sensation are clearly suggested:

Carmine Jade's bed was spotless; Shih-chung threw himself on it, stretched out, and beckoned to her:

"Why don't you come closer?"

She blushed, but slowly approached the bed and sat down, leaning on the bedpost. Shih-chung looked her over greedily, from tip to toe, until he felt satiated. He finally fixed his glance upon her thighs and raised her skirt in order to inspect her tiny feet.

Carmine Jade felt giddy; she reclined, extending her feet. Shih-chung, who was very strong, placed her foot in his palm, where it fitted perfectly. He pressed the foot with his fingers, causing her to cry out involuntarily.

"You press my foot till it hurts, without feeling tenderly towards me," complained Carmine Jade, struggling to free herself . . .

A pair of tiny feet, encased in red sleeping slippers, was outlined by the bedcovers. Her legs were crossed and entangled under a single coverlet, with the curve of her thighs enticingly revealed. Shih-chung was amazed that her thighs were so voluptuous and large. He stared at them thinking: "How hard it must be for tiny feet to support those thighs!" He couldn't help feeling compassion for her lower extremities. Compressing the feet in order to thicken the thighs must have been the invention of a genius. And of course the inventor must have been a woman. . . .

She felt at ease with him and, without thinking, extended her feet across his stomach. Shih-chung was just then reflecting on other matters, but when she placed her feet there he conveniently grasped them and rubbed them in his palms. He had very powerful hands and grasped and rubbed her feet so that she became more excited with each passing moment. For her it was a mixture of suffering and pleasure. The more it hurt, the more intense became her feelings of delight; she moaned, unable to bear the excitement any longer . . .

She usually felt pain in her little feet, bound so tightly, whenever she walked around. But when her feet were held in Shih-chung's palms and powerfully rubbed, though she cried out, this pain was really delightful. Not only was she unafraid, but she hoped that he would apply even greater pressure . . .

He rubbed her feet as usual; she cried out as usual. She thought: "If I hadn't made my feet so tiny through binding, perhaps Shih-chung couldn't enclose them in his palms so tightly." . . . Shih-chung had previously doubted that women's bound feet were of any use. Now he understood for the first time that they were for the convenience of a man to knead, and in addition made the flesh of the thighs especially sensual. "This was certainly the invention of an unknown genius!"

. . . . .

Footbinding achieved its greatest popularity towards the end of the Ch'ing dynasty, but the seeds of destruction were already evident. The frequent dynastic prohibitions against it increased awareness of its shortcomings, and an abolition movement came to be supported by liberal Chinese critics and Western missionaries. These diverse elements worked together closely as time went on; after the Revolution, the attack gathered increasing momentum and wider scope.

. . . . .

Wives who had formerly bound their

feet now found themselves deserted or divorced. They had been forced into binding by their mothers to enhance their marital prospects, but the result was the reverse. When women heard of wives being rejected because of tiny feet, they tried everything to make the foot revert to normal size. To accelerate the process they would soak their feet in cold water nightly, suffering as much as in early childhood. No matter how hard they tried, there was really no way to keep up with the changing times. Women who had let out their feet in middle age could be seen plodding through the streets in visible discomfort. Footbinding was dictated by male preference and submitted to because the male view of aesthetics demanded it. Women who were born in the traditional age but reached maturity during or after the Revolution were the tragic figures of the period. Some recorded their experiences in the nineteen-thirties, at a time when memories were still fresh and events were vividly recalled. The motive may have been to further the cause of emancipation; whatever it was, the accounts have a ring of truth to them and obviously were the result of firsthand experience.

. . . . .

[For example:]

THE TWIN-HOOKED MAID

by Lotus-Loving Scholar

Two years ago, my wife hired a maid servant named Chang. She had twin hooks under her skirt, slender and not enough to grasp in one's hand. This is what *Tun-fang yu-chi* meant in saying that they could be placed in a glass; such words were true. Though the maid was middle-aged, she still had an air of elegance about her. But she walked in a rather forlorn manner and could barely fulfill household tasks. My wife encouraged her to let her feet out, but this so increased her pain that she decided against it. She was of a gentle nature, and our family greatly enjoyed conversing with her. My wife was especially fond of her and always rendered a helping hand. One day, the maid unexpectedly spoke in great detail about footbinding experiences:

I was born in a certain district in western Honan Province, at the end of the Manchu dynasty. In accordance with custom, at the age of seven I began binding. I had witnessed the pain of my cousins, and in the year it was to begin was very much frightened. That autumn, distress befell me. One day prior my mother told me: "You are now seven, just at the right age for binding. If we wait, your foot will harden, increasing the pain. You should have started in the spring, but because you were weak we waited till now. Girls in other families have already completed the process. We start tomorrow. I will do this for you lightly and so that it won't hurt; what daughter doesn't go through this difficulty?" She then gave me fruit to eat, showed me a new pair of phoenix-tip shoes, and beguiled me with these words: "Only with bound feet can you wear such beautiful shoes. Otherwise, you'll become a large-footed barbarian and everyone will laugh at and feel ashamed of you." I felt moved by a desire to be beautiful and became steadfast in determination, staying awake all night.

I got up early the next morning. Everything had already been prepared. Mother had me sit on a stool by the bed. She threaded a needle and placed it in my hair, cut off a piece of alum and put it alongside the binding cloth and the flowered shoes. She then turned and closed the bedroom door. She first soaked my feet in a pan of hot water, then wiped them, and cut the toenails with a small scissors. She then took my right foot in her hands and repeatedly massaged it in the direction of the plantar. She also sprinkled alum between my toes. She gave me a pen point to hold in my hands because of the belief that my feet might then become as pointed as it was. Later she took a cloth three feet long and two inches wide, grasped my right foot, and pressed down the four smaller toes in the direction of the plantar. She joined them together, bound them once, and passed the binding from the heel to the foot surface and then to the plantar. She did this five times and then sewed the binding together with thread. To prevent it from getting loosened, she tied a slender cotton thread from the tip of the foot to its center.

She did the same thing with the left foot and forced my feet into flowered shoes which were slightly smaller than the feet were. The tips of the shoes were adorned with threads in the shape of grain. There was a ribbon affixed to the mouth of the shoe and fastened on the heel. She ordered me to get down from the bed and walk, saying that if I didn't the crooked-shaped foot would be seriously injured. When I first touched the ground, I felt complete loss of movement; after a few trials, only the toes hurt greatly. Both feet became feverish at night and hurt from the swelling. Except for walking, I sat by the *k'ang.* Mother rebound my feet weekly, each time more tightly than the last. I became more and more afraid. I tried to avoid the binding by hiding in a neighbor's house. If I loosened the bandage, mother would scold me for not wanting to look nice. After half a year, the tightly bound toes began to uniformly face the plantar. The foot became more pointed daily; after a year, the toes began to putrefy. Corns began to appear and thicken, and for a long time no improvement was visible. Mother would remove the bindings and lance the corns with a needle to get rid of the hard core. I feared this, but mother grasped my legs so that I couldn't move. Father betrothed me at the age of nine to a neighbor named Chao, and I went to their house to serve as a daughter-in-law in the home of my future husband. My mother-in-law bound my feet much more tightly than mother ever had, saying that I still hadn't achieved the standard. She beat me severely if I cried; if I unloosened the binding, I was beaten until my body was covered with bruises. Also, because my feet were somewhat fleshy, my mother-in-law insisted that the foot must become inflamed to get the proper results. Day and night, my feet were washed in a medicinal water; within a few washings I felt special pain. Looking down, I saw that every toe but the big one was inflamed and deteriorated. Mother-in-law said that this was all to the good. I had to be beaten with fists before I could bear to remove the bindings, which were congealed with pus and blood. To get them loose, such force had to be used that the skin often peeled off, causing further bleeding. The stench was hard to bear, while I felt the pain in my very insides. My body trembled with agitation. Mother-in-law was not only unmoved but she placed tiles inside the binding in order to hasten the inflammation process. She was deaf to my childish cries. Every other day, the binding was made tighter and sewn up, and each time slightly smaller shoes had to be worn. The sides of the shoes were hard, and I could only get into them by using force. I was compelled to walk on them in the courtyard; they were called distance-walking shoes. I strove to cling to life, suffering indescribable pain. Being in an average family, I had to go to the well and pound the mortar unaided. Faulty blood circulation caused my feet to become insensible in winter. At night, I tried to warm them by the *k'ang,* but this caused extreme pain. The alternation between frost and thawing caused me to lose one toe on my right foot. Deterioration of the flesh was such that within a year my feet had become as pointed as new bamboo shoots, pointing upwards like a red chestnut. The foot surface was slightly convex, while the four bean-sized toes were deeply imbedded in the plantar like a string of cowry shells. They were only a slight distance from the heel of the foot. The plantar was so deep that several coins could be placed in it without difficulty. The large toes faced upwards, while the place on the right foot where the little toe had deteriorated away pained at irregular intervals. It left an ineffacable scar.

My feet were only three inches long, at the most. Relatives and friends praised them, little realizing the cisterns of tears and blood which they had caused. My husband was delighted with them, but two years ago he departed this world. The family wealth was dissipated, and I had to wander about looking for work. That was how I came down to my present circumstances. I envy the modern woman. If I too had been born just a decade or so later, all of this pain could have been avoided. The lot of the natural-footed woman and mine is like that of heaven and hell.

Love of the lotus disappeared when I heard her words; my wife was also similarly affected. I have recorded this in order to warn the young girls of today against binding their feet.

14 Sexual Codes in Teen-Age Culture

IRA L. REISS

Some contemporary sociologists maintain that the adolescent age group develops a subculture somewhat divergent from the main stream of adult culture. Others suggest that the adolescent differences we observe are only imperfect reflections of the dominant group behavior. Regardless of the position one takes, it is important to recognize that adolescents spend much of their time in association with their own age group. Thus the teen-age codes will greatly affect behavior within this age group, although adult, particularly parental, norms will remain significant. This selection analyzes the modern code in an important realm of adolescent behavior.

Teen-age sexual codes reflect quite clearly the bold outlines of adult sexual codes. The high degree of conformity in teen-age culture increases the observability of teen-age beliefs and adds to our understanding of adult beliefs. The teenager exists in a world somewhere between youthful idealism and adult realism, and his sexual codes reflect this state of being. In a very real sense, he is a marginal man with one foot in the world of the child and the other foot in the world of the adult.

The teen-ager is at the stage at which it is vitally important for him to learn how to exist in society independent of his parents. For this reason, he transfers his dependence to his peers and strives to learn from them the secrets of entrance into the adult world. One would think that this vaguely defined status of "almost adult" would lead to confusion and weak statements of belief. To a large extent, this is the case, but, nevertheless, it is equally true that it leads to dogmatic statements of belief and a search for conviction through conformity. Teen-agers translate and adapt the sexual codes of adults to fit their particular circumstance and state of mind.

SOURCE: *The Annals of the American Academy of Political & Social Science,* vol. 338 (November 1961), 53–62. Reprinted by permission. • The author is professor and the director of the Family Study Center of the Department of Sociology at the University of Minnesota. His chief interests include the sociology of the family, and sociological theory, and methodology. He is the author of *Premarital Sexual Standards in America* and *The Social Context of Premarital Sexual Permissiveness.*

GOING STEADY

When unchaperoned dating gained prevalence in the early part of this century, it involved a much more rapid change of dating partners than occurs today. Nevertheless, by the time of World War II, going steady had taken root, and, today, it seems that slightly more than half of the high school students have some going-steady experience. Even among the early teen-agers, possibly one quarter go steady.

Class differences are important in examining the going-steady complex. It seems that those high school people who go steady and plan to go to college are not likely to marry their high school steadies, and those who are from lower economic classes and who do not plan to go to college are much more likely to marry their high school steadies. Thus, in looking at the custom of going steady, one must realize that there are different subtypes and that the consequences differ for each type.

Although a psychologist may point to the security of going steady as its chief reason for being, as a sociologist, I would point out how Western society has, for centuries, been developing an association of sexual behavior with mutual affection. This association is hard to achieve in casual dating; but, in steady dating, sex and affection can quite easily be combined, and, in this way, a potential strain in the social system is reduced. Another area of strain which is reduced by going steady is the conflict a girl may feel between her desire for sexual experience and her desire to maintain her reputation. For many, sexual behavior is made respectable by going steady. In these ways, one may say that no other dating custom is quite as central to the understanding of teen-age sexual codes as going steady.

GIRLS' SEXUAL CODES

One of the most popular sexual codes among teen-age girls is petting-with-affection. This code is a modern day subtype of our formal abstinence standard. This subtype of abstinence seems extremely popular among high school couples who are going steady. Such couples feel it is proper to engage in heavy petting if they are going steady, the justification being that they are in love or at least extremely fond of each other. The petting-with-affection sex code probably grew along with the going-steady custom; they both illustrate adaptations of our dating institution to the newer unchaperoned dating circumstances.

What evidence do we have for such petting behavior among teen-agers? Though surely not perfect, the most extensive study of sexual behavior is that done by the Institute for Sex Research, formerly headed by Alfred C. Kinsey and now run by Paul H. Gebhard. It should be noted that the Kinsey studies are most valid for urban, white, northeastern, college-educated people, and, thus, great care must be taken when applying the results to other groups. The reader should keep in mind the tenuousness of any such generalizations made in this paper.

Kinsey's data show that, of the females who were twenty years old or older when interviewed, about one-fifth to one-fourth admitted they had petted to orgasm while still in their teens. Most of this behavior occurred between the ages of sixteen and twenty. About three-quarters of all the girls twenty years old or more admitted being aroused by some form of petting or kissing in their teens, and approximately 90 per cent stated they had at least been kissed during their teens.

Those girls who marry in their teens start their petting and kissing behavior earlier than those who marry later. In general, the few years previous to marriage are by far the most sexually active for girls. Lower class females marry earlier, and, thus, they are more active in their teens and more likely to marry their teen-age steadies.

The above rates are averages for Kinsey's entire sample of several thousand females; were we to take only the females born in more recent decades, the rates would be considerably higher. For example, of those females born before 1900, only 10 per cent ever petted to orgasm in their teens, whereas, of those girls born in the 1920's, almost 30 per cent, or three times the proportion, petted to orgasm in their teens.

It seems clear that we have developed not only new dating forms such as going steady but also, as we have seen, new sexual codes to go with them. These new codes allow females much more freedom in heavy petting, provided affection is involved. Of course, other girls, particularly in the early teens, adhere to standards which only permit kissing, and a few others adhere to standards which allow full sexual relations, but, by and large, petting-with-affection seems the increasingly popular sex code for high school girls.

The most recent evidence of the nature of teen-age sex codes also supports these contentions. This evidence comes from research which the author is engaged in at present. Some preliminary reports on this study were made in the author's book *Premarital Sexual Standards in America.* The study involves 1,000 high school and college students, most of whom are teenagers. Although final analysis of the study has not been completed, it is clear that petting-with-affection is an extremely popular code with teen-age girls, particularly with the teen-agers who are high school juniors and seniors.

Finally, one should note that, in my own study and in the Kinsey study, religion was another key factor affecting girls' sexual beliefs and behaviors. Those girls who were devout in their religion were much more conservative in their sexual behavior and belief. Religion was not as strong a factor for boys and did not control their behavior as much. As we shall see, amount of education was the key determinant for male sexual behavior.

BOYS' SEXUAL CODES

Among the teen-age boys, we find a different code dominant. Abstinence is given some form of lip service, particularly among the more highly educated classes, but, by and large, it is not an operational code; it is not adhered to in the behavior of the majority of the teen-age boys. Even among the males destined for college, about half have coitus in their teens; among those who stop their education in high school, about three-quarters have coitus in their teens, and, among those whose education stops before high school, about eight-tenths have coitus in their teens. Thus, it is clear that the majority of all males, in this sample of Kinsey's at least, experienced full sexual relations before reaching twenty years of age.

For teen-age girls, the rate of nonvirginity appears to be considerably lower. Kinsey reports approximately 20 per cent nonvirginity for females by age twenty. Of course, the greater liberality of the boys does not involve a single standard; that is, they are predominantly adherents of the double standard which allows boys to have coitus but condemns girls for the same thing. This is an ancient standard reaching back many thousands of years in Western culture. It is by no means a universal standard, however, for we do find many cultures where the sexes are treated equally.

Although in recent generations, due to our greater equalitarianism and the evolving nature of the dating institution, the double standard seems to have been weakened sharply, it is still quite dominant among teen-age boys. The greater freedom allowed the male child in almost all areas of life constantly buttresses this standard and makes it seem obvious to teen-agers. Teen-agers are not sufficiently objective or sophisticated to be bothered by the contradictions in this or any other sexual code. For example, if all women abided fully by the double standard, then no men could, for the men would have no partners! Thus, this code operates only to the extent that someone violates it.

Some of these double standard teen-age boys will condemn a girl who accepts petting-with-affection, for they believe petting is improper for girls. However, my own data indicate that most of these teen-age males will accept heavy petting in a going-steady relationship. They, of course, allow themselves to go further and may try to have coitus with a steady in order to see if she is a "good" girl. It is not unusual to find a relationship either broken up or its affectionate nature altered if a girl gives in to her double standard steady. Such condemnatory behavior on the part of double standard males keeps many girls from going as far sexually as they might want to. Thus, the double standard male eliminates many potential sex partners because of the attitude he takes toward such sex partners.

Teen-age double standard males are often stricter than their older brothers who accept coitus for a girl when she is in love and/or engaged. These teen-age males are supported in this rigidity by the conformity of their peer group. Double standard males typically view the act of coitus as a conquest, as a source of peer group prestige. Thus, they are quite prone to tell their friends all of the details of any affair. This characteristic tends further to discourage females from yielding to double standard males. Instead, the girl is encouraged to be, in part at least, a tease, that is, to show just enough sexual activity to keep the male interested but not enough to arouse his condemnation. Sexual behavior in this sense involves a great deal of the aspect of a game. Sex comes to be used as a power leverage to control the relationship. Under such circumstances, sexual desire is developed so sharply in the male and so differently in the female that the male wants the female to be both sexually active and sexually pure. Under such conditions, sexual behavior can only with great difficulty relate directly to feelings of affection. This is particularly true for the act of coitus. In fact, one finds very often an inverse relation, in that boys prefer to have coitus with girls they do not care for, because they regard the girls they do care for as "too good" for such behavior. Girls, too, may control their sexual reactions, particularly with someone they care for, until they are sure they will not be condemned for their sexual response.

Thus, in the area of coitus among teen-agers, the double standard does seem to block the association of sex and affection. However, one should quickly add that, on the level of petting, sex and affection can more easily be combined, for this behavior is much more likely to be accepted for both sexes by both males and females.

MINOR STANDARDS

There are minor teen-age standards which are more permissive than petting-with-affection or the double standard. For the older teen-ager, the most popular minor standard is what I shall call permissiveness-with-affection. This standard accepts full sexual intercourse for both boys and girls, provided they are involved in a stable, affectionate relationship. The degree of stability and affection required varies among adherents from feeling strong affection to being in love and engaged. Some teen-age couples who are going steady have coitus in accord with this standard. The situation here is quite different from that of the double standard boy and his girl friend, for, in permissiveness-with-affection, both the boy and girl accept for each other what they are doing. They combine sex with affection and use affection as one of the key justifications of the sexual act.

There is a class difference in sexual standards among boys. My evidence indicates that the lower classes are more likely to be strong supporters of the double standard, while the upper classes, though still mostly double standard, contain a large proportion of boys who are not so dogmatic in their beliefs and a minority who accept permissiveness-with-affection. In general, the upper classes seem to stress equality of the sexes and the importance of affection more than the lower classes. A permissiveness-without-affection code seems more widespread at the lower levels.

Age is a crucial factor among teen-agers. Teen-agers under sixteen are much more likely to accept only kissing than are older teen-agers, who may accept petting or coitus. As noted earlier, religion does not restrict sexual behavior as much among boys as it does among girls. Education is a more important factor, with the more highly educated groups being the most conservative.

PROMISCUITY

The newspapers from time to time pick up stories of high school "sex clubs" and other forms of promiscuous teen-age sexual behavior. The available evidence indicates that promiscuous coitus is common predominantly for double standard males and a few females. Promiscuous coitus is not common on an equalitarian basis, that is, where both male and female accept the behavior as right for each other. Our culture has stressed the association of sex-with-affection to such an extent that it is difficult, at least for many females, to violate this association in coitus. In the case of petting, one finds more likelihood of violation of this norm by both men and women, but, in the case of coitus, it is much more often violated by males. Ehrmann's study of 1,000 college students supports this difference between male and female sexual activity and attitudes. Females, in addition to associating love with sexual behavior more than males, also have more nonsexual motives for sexual behavior, such as the desire to please the boy or to cement a relationship.

During the teens, the sexual outlets of boys and girls differ considerably. The chief outlet for girls seems to be masturbation and petting, whereas for boys the chief outlets include coitus at the fore. In Kinsey's sample, about one-third of the girls masturbated to orgasm in their teens, while over 90 per cent of the boys have so masturbated in their teens. Despite their high rate of masturbation, males also have a high rate of coitus. The lower class boys rely less on masturbation and petting and more on coitus for their sexual outlets than do those boys who go to college.

The teen-age girl today is still typically the much more conservative partner and the guardian of sexual limits. However, she appears increasingly to be a half-willing guardian who more and more seeks her self-satisfaction and strives to achieve sexual equality.

There is a general trend in American society toward more equalitarian and more permissive sexual codes in all areas. This is true for teen-age sexual codes, too. The growth within abstinence of petting-with-affection is one sign of this increasing equalitarian and permissive force. Also, within the double standard, one finds increased willingness by males to accept some coitus on the part of females, especially if it occurs when the girl is in love and/or engaged. Finally, in the minor standard of permissiveness-with-affection, one sees this trend in the increased strength of this standard among teen-agers, particularly among older, college teen-agers. And these trends toward equalitarianism and permissiveness seem even stronger among older dating couples in their twenties. The teen-agers are relatively new at sexual behavior, and they, at first, grab the basic outlines of the older couples' codes. With the passage of time, they come to behave in a somewhat more equalitarian and permissive manner.

In my current research, there is evidence that the real change-over in a teen-ager's sexual code is more one of integrating attitudes and changing overt behavior than of changing basic attitudes. In short, it seems that a person holds his basic sexual attitudes in rudimentary form in his teens, but he is not fully ready to act upon them and has not fully learned how to combine these values into a coherent code of living. As he learns to do this, his behavior changes and so does his awareness of his beliefs and their unity, but his basic beliefs may well remain the same. This entire area of how our sexual beliefs are formed and how they change is in need of more careful study. My own research is aimed at probing some aspects of this problem.

Parents are prone to be most aware of what they consider excessive sexual behavior, for they are concerned about the consequences of such behavior as they may affect their children. Thus, parents complain about sexual acts of which they become aware, and they often believe teen-agers are sexually promiscuous. Actually, according to our best estimates, the real increases in teen-age sexual behavior over the last generation are not in the area of sexual intercourse but rather in the area of petting and in the public nature of some petting behavior. Thus, these parents of today have probably had similar rates of coitus but perhaps lower rates of petting. In addition, one should note that the petting behavior today very often is not promiscuous but occurs in a stable affectionate relationship.

YOUTH CULTURE: TAME OR WILD?

About twenty years ago, Kingsley Davis and Talcott Parsons wrote of a youth culture and of a parent-youth conflict and, in doing so, implied in part that youth culture was largely irresponsible, impulsive, and antiadult. Many people have come to share this view and to expect rather extreme sexual behavior from teen-agers. I myself formerly accepted this view of the teen-ager as valid. However, after examining the evidence in the key areas of teen-age sexual behavior, I must admit that I can no longer accept such a conception of youth culture without serious modification and qualification. I would submit that the vast majority of our approximately twenty million teen-agers are not only not extreme but are quite conservative and restrained in the area of premarital sexual codes and behavior when we compare them to their older brothers and sisters.

There is evidence to show that teen-agers are unsure of how far to go sexually, that they feel ill at ease on dates, and that they are concerned with such "tame" issues as whether one should kiss good night on a first date. A recent study showed that teen-agers rate themselves lower in comparison to adults than adults rate them. Teen-agers in this study rated adults considerably higher than themselves on most all "good" qualities. These are hardly the attitudes of an arrogant or antiadult youth. They seem more those of a group desirous of becoming like adults and striving toward that goal.

Further, when we look at the rates of female petting to orgasm in the Kinsey studies, we find considerably more of this behavior among girls in their twenties than among girls in their teens. The coitus rate for females doubles between the ages of twenty and twenty-five. Masturbation rates also increase considerably after the teens. In all these ways, the teen-agers seem more conservative than those individuals who are in their twenties.

August Hollingshead's excellent study of a midwest community also gives evidence on the conservatism of youth. He found a very close correspondence between social class of parents and social class of teen-agers' dating partners. In this study, too, we are given a picture of youth culture that is very much like adult culture in its status consciousness. Hollingshead and others have also noted the fact that a large proportion of the teen-age population is virtually not involved in any dating. A good estimate for the high school age group would be that about one-third of the boys and one-fifth of the girls are not involved in dating.

VENEREAL DISEASE AND PREGNANCY

Let us now examine two key indices, venereal disease and pregnancy, which should give us additional insights into the behavior of teen-agers. Teen-agers do have significant rates of venereal disease and illegitimacy. However, the press has largely exaggerated such rates. The teen-age rate of venereal disease for ages fifteen to nineteen is only about a third of the rate for the twenty to twenty-four age group and is also lower than that of the twenty-five to twenty-nine age group.

There has been a slight rise in the number of teen-age venereal disease cases in recent years, and this has received much publicity. It is quite likely that the actual rates for teen-agers are not higher and that this slight increase is due to the greater number of teen-agers today. More than 80 per cent of the venereal disease reported is from older groups of people. Finally, the rate of venereal disease among teen-agers is not evenly distributed in the teen-age group. As far as we can tell from reported cases, it is highly concentrated in the lower social classes.

When one examines the national figures for unwed mothers, one finds that 40 per cent are teen-agers. Here, too, several qualifications are needed. First, most of these reported cases are Negro, and class status in general is low. The upper classes, according to Paul Gebhard's recent study, are much more willing to resort to abortion. The upper classes, also, have a greater ability to stay out of public statistics and may, thus, show lower rates. According to Clark Vincent's study, when upper class females become pregnant before marriage, it is more likely to be the result of a love affair, whereas, when lower class females become pregnant, it is more likely to be a result of a casual affair. Thus, there are important class differences here, too.

When we compare teen-age unwed motherhood with that for girls in their twenties, we find that the older girls have about the same proportion of the illegitimate children. We also find that the teen-age rates are not increasing as much as the rates for older groups. For example, in 1940 teen-age mothers were 46 per cent of the total; in 1957 they were 40 per cent.

Thus, from the evidence of national figures, it seems reasonable to conclude that it is a small and specific segment of the teen-age population that becomes involved with venereal disease or premarital pregnancy. Furthermore, the people in their twenties seem somewhat more likely to be involved in such circumstances. Also, these older couples are much more involved in adult culture in terms of their occupations and their nearness to marriage, and yet their sexual behavior is less conservative.

A warning must be added at this point concerning the venereal disease rates and unwed motherhood rates. They are far from perfect indices and, as mentioned, many higher class people manage to be excluded from them because they can afford more private means of coping with their problems. However, to the extent that we use these rates, we fail to find support for the charges made about teen-agers. It is no doubt true that teen-agers are irresponsible in the sense that they seek "to have a good time," but I would suggest that, in the area of sexual codes and behavior, the evidence shows more conservatism and responsibility than one might otherwise suspect. It may be well to avoid the over-all impressions given by a general use of the term "youth culture" as described by Parsons. Here, as elsewhere, qualification and specific research is a step toward better theoretical formulation and better understanding.

A FINAL OVERVIEW

What has occurred in teen-age sexual codes in recent generations is a working out of sexual practices acceptable to teen-agers. Many of these practices are at the level of petting. In short, as unchaperoned dating came into vogue and as adolescence became more prolonged due to our specialized industrial culture, young people worked out additional sexual codes to supplement and modify the older codes of abstinence and the double standard. There always were people who engaged in coitus; today there are more, but, for girls in their teens, it is still a minor activity. When we look at petting, we note something different, for here we see a much more continuous and current change among teen-agers—it is here in this middle ground that teen-agers have come to accept a petting-with-affection standard. The equalitarian and permissive aspects of this standard in many cases lead at later ages to acceptance of the more radical permissiveness-with-affection standard. However, during the teens, petting-with-affection is probably the major standard involved in stable affectionate relationships at middle and upper class levels.

At the present time, it is impossible to predict precise changes in sexual codes. This is especially true because, as we have seen, there are differences according to social class, religion, educational level, and so forth. But one can say that all the signs indicate a continued trend toward equalitarian and permissive codes. The trend seems to be toward that which now obtains in the Scandinavian countries, with the inclusion of sex education in the schools and with permissive attitudes on the formal as well as covert levels. This does not forebode the end of the double standard, for the double standard is still deeply rooted in our male dominant culture, but it does mean a continued weakening of the double standard and more qualifications of its mandates.

Teen-agers are a paradoxical group. They are not as wild as their parents or they themselves sometimes think. Teen-agers do want independence. But, judging by their sexual codes, they want independence from their parents, not from the total adult culture.

15 Fundamental Notions of the Folkways and of the Mores

WILLIAM GRAHAM SUMNER

The manners, usages, folkways, mores, and institutions of every society tend to be regarded by the members of that society as the only right and proper ones. Perhaps Sumner's famous book, Folkways, *published in 1906, did more than any other to demonstrate the great variety of human behavior patterns thus regarded. As a result, it has induced many people to pause before they say—or even to refrain from thinking—"My ways—our ways—are the only civilized ways of behaving." The terms* "folkways" *and* "mores," *first given currency as sociological terms by Sumner, are now a part of our everyday language.*

DEFINITION AND MODE OF ORIGIN OF THE FOLKWAYS

If we put together all that we have learned from anthropology and ethnography about primitive men and primitive society, we perceive that the first task of life is to live. Men begin with acts, not with thoughts. Every moment brings necessities which must be satisfied at once. Need was the first experience, and it was followed at once by a blundering effort to satisfy it. It is generally taken for granted that men inherited some guiding instincts from their beast ancestry, and it may be true, although it has never been proved. If there were such inheritances, they controlled and aided the first efforts to satisfy needs. Analogy makes it easy to assume that the ways of beasts had produced channels of habit and predisposition along which dexterities and other psychophysical activities would run easily. Experiments with newborn animals show that in the absence of any experience of the relation of means to ends, efforts to satisfy needs are clumsy and blundering. The method is that of trial and failure, which produces repeated pain, loss, and disappointments. Nevertheless, it is a method of rude experiment and selection. The earliest efforts of men were of this kind. Need was the impelling force. Pleasure and pain, on the one side and the other, were the rude constraints which defined the line on which efforts must proceed. The ability to distinguish between pleasure and pain is the only psychical power which is to be assumed. Thus ways of doing things were selected, which were expedient. They answered the purpose better than other ways, or with less toil and pain. Along the course on which efforts were compelled to go, habit, routine, and skill were developed. The struggle to maintain existence was carried on, not individually, but in groups. Each profited by the other's experience; hence there was concurrence towards that which proved to be most

SOURCE: William Graham Sumner, *Folkways* (Ginn and Company, 1940, Centennial Edition), sect. 1–3, 28–29, 31–32, 34–35, 66–68. Reprinted by permission. • The author (1840–1910) was one of the pioneer American sociologists with Ward, Giddings, Small, Cooley, and Ross. He was also an economist and a rector. In 1872 he became professor of political and social science at Yale University. He was the second president of the American Sociological Association. He wrote *A History of American Currency* and *What Social Classes Owe to Each Other* and was the coauthor of *The Science of Society.*

expedient. All at last adopted the same way for the same purpose; hence the ways turned into customs and became mass phenomena. Instincts were developed in connection with them. In this way folkways arise. The young learn them by tradition, imitation, and authority. The folkways, at a time, provide for all the needs of life then and there. They are uniform, universal in the group, imperative, and invariable. As time goes on, the folkways become more and more arbitrary, positive, and imperative. If asked why they act in a certain way in certain cases, primitive people always answer that it is because they and their ancestors always have done so. A sanction also arises from ghost fear. The ghosts of ancestors would be angry if the living should change the ancient folkways.

THE FOLKWAYS ARE A SOCIETAL FORCE

The operation by which folkways are produced consists in the frequent repetition of petty acts, often by great numbers acting in concert or, at least, acting in the same way when face to face with the same need. The immediate motive is interest. It produces habit in the individual and custom in the group. It is, therefore, in the highest degree original and primitive. By habit and custom it exerts a strain on every individual within its range; therefore it rises to a societal force to which great classes of societal phenomena are due. Its earliest stages, its course, and laws may be studied; also its influence on individuals and their reaction on it. It is our present purpose so to study it. We have to recognize it as one of the chief forces by which a society is made to be what it is. Out of the unconscious experiment which every repetition of the ways includes, there issues pleasure or pain, and then, so far as the men are capable of reflection, convictions that the ways are conducive to societal welfare. These two experiences are not the same. The most uncivilized men, both in the food quest and in war, do things which are painful, but which have been found to be expedient. Perhaps these cases teach the sense of social welfare better than those which are pleasurable and favorable to welfare. The former cases call for some intelligent reflection on experience. When this conviction as to the relation to welfare is added to the folkways they are converted into mores, and, by virtue of the philosophical and ethical element added to them, they win utility and importance and become the source of the science and the art of living.

FOLKWAYS ARE MADE UNCONSCIOUSLY

It is of the first importance to notice that, from the first acts by which men try to satisfy needs, each act stands by itself, and looks no further than the immediate satisfaction. From recurrent needs arise habits for the individual and customs for the group, but these results are consequences which were never conscious, and never foreseen or intended. They are not noticed until they have long existed, and it is still longer before they are appreciated. Another long time must pass, and a higher stage of mental development must be reached, before they can be used as a basis from which to deduce rules for meeting, in the future, problems whose pressure can be foreseen. The folkways, therefore, are not creations of human purpose and wit. They are like products of natural forces which men unconsciously set in operation, or they are like the instinctive ways of animals, which are developed out of experience, which reach a final form of maximum adaptation to an interest, which are handed down by tradition and admit of no exception or variation, yet change to meet new conditions, still within the same limited methods, and without rational reflection or purpose. From this it results that all the life of human beings, in all ages and stages of culture, is primarily controlled by a vast mass of folkways handed down from the earliest existence of the race, having the nature of the ways of other animals, only the topmost layers of which are subject to change and control, and have been somewhat modified by human philosophy, ethics, and religion, or by other acts of intelligent reflection. We are told of savages that "It is difficult to exhaust the customs and small ceremonial usages of a savage people. Custom regulates the whole of a man's actions,—his bathing, washing, cutting his hair, eating, drinking, and fasting. From his cradle to his grave he is the slave of ancient usage. In his life there is nothing free, nothing original, nothing spontaneous, no progress towards a higher and better life, and no attempt to improve his condition, mentally, morally, or spiritually." All men act in this way with only a little wider margin of voluntary variation.

. . . . .

FOLKWAYS DUE TO FALSE INFERENCE

Folkways have been formed by accident, that is, by irrational and incongruous action, based on pseudo-knowledge. In Molembo a pestilence broke out soon after a Portuguese had died there. After that the natives took all possible measures not to allow any white man to die in their country. On the Nicobar islands some natives who had just begun to make pottery died. The art was given up and never again attempted. White men gave to one Bushman in a kraal a stick ornamented with buttons as a symbol of authority. The recipient died leaving the stick to his son. The son soon died. Then the Bushmen brought back the stick lest all should die. Until recently no building of incombustible materials could be built in any big town of the central province of Madagascar, on account of some ancient prejudice. A party of Eskimos met with no game. One of them returned to their sledges and got the ham of a dog to eat. As he returned with the ham bone in his hand he met and killed a seal. Ever afterwards he carried a ham bone in his hand when hunting. The Belenda women (peninsula of Malacca) stay as near to the house as possible during the period. Many keep the door closed. They know no reason for this custom. "It must be due to some now forgotten superstition." Soon after the Yakuts saw a camel for the first time smallpox broke out amongst them. They thought the camel to be the agent of the disease. A woman amongst the same people contracted an endogamous marriage. She soon afterwards became blind. This was thought to be on account of the violation of ancient customs. A very great number of such cases could be collected. In fact they represent the current mode of reasoning of nature people. It is their custom to reason that, if one thing follows another, it is due to it. A great number of customs are traceable to the notion of the evil eye, many more to ritual notions of uncleanness. No scientific investigation could discover the origin of the folkways mentioned, if the origin had not chanced to become known to civilized men. We must believe that the known cases illustrate the irrational and incongruous origin of many folkways. In civilized history also we know that customs have owed their origin to "historical accident,"—the vanity of a princess, the deformity of a king, the whim of a democracy, the love intrigue of a statesman or prelate. By the institutions of another age it may be provided that no one of these things can affect decisions, acts, or interests, but then the power to decide the ways may have passed to clubs, trades unions, trusts, commercial rivals, wire-pullers, politicians, and political fanatics. In these cases also the causes and origins may escape investigation.

HARMFUL FOLKWAYS

There are folkways which are positively harmful. Very often these are just the ones for which a definite reason can be given. The destruction of a man's goods at his death is a direct deduction from other-worldliness; the dead man is supposed to want in the other world just what he wanted here. The destruction of a man's goods at his death was a great waste of capital, and it must have had a disastrous effect on the interests of the living, and must have very seriously hindered the development of civilization. With this custom we must class all the expenditure of labor and capital on graves, temples, pyramids, rites, sacrifices, and support of priests, so far as these were supposed to benefit the dead. The faith in goblinism produced other-worldly interests which overruled ordinary worldly interests. Foods have often been forbidden which were plentiful, the prohibition of which injuriously lessened the food supply. There is a tribe of Bushmen who will eat no goat's flesh, although goats are the most numerous domestic animals in the district. Where totemism exists it is regularly accompanied by a taboo on eating the totem animal. Whatever may be the real principle in totemism, it overrules the interest in an abundant food supply. "The origin of the sacred regard paid to the cow must be sought in the primitive nomadic life of the Indo-European race," because it is common to Iranians and Indians of Hindostan. The Libyans ate oxen but not cows. The same was true of the Phœnicians and Egyptians. In some cases the sense of a food taboo is not to be learned. It may have been entirely capricious. Mohammed would not eat lizards, because he thought them the offspring of a metamorphosed clan of Israelites. On the other hand, the protective taboo which forbade killing crocodiles, pythons, cobras, and other animal enemies of man was harmful to his interests, whatever the motive. "It seems to be a fixed article of belief throughout southern India, that all who have willfully or accidentally killed a snake, especially a cobra, will certainly be punished, either in this life or the next, in one of three ways: either by childlessness, or by leprosy, or by ophthalmia." Where this faith exists man has a greater interest to spare a cobra than to kill it. India furnishes a great number of cases of harmful mores. "In India every tendency of humanity seems intensified and exaggerated. No country in the world is so conservative in its traditions, yet no country has undergone so many religious changes and vicissitudes." "Every year thousands perish of disease that might recover if they would take proper nourishment, and drink the medicine that science prescribes, but which they imagine that their religion forbids them to touch." "Men who can scarcely count beyond twenty, and know not the letters of the alphabet, would rather die than eat food which had been prepared by men of lower caste, unless it had been sanctified by being offered to an idol; and would kill their daughters rather than endure the disgrace of having unmarried girls at home beyond twelve or thirteen years of age." In the last case the rule of obligation and duty is set by the mores. The interest comes under vanity. The sanction of the caste rules is in a boycott by all members of the caste. The rules are often very harmful. "The authority of caste rests partly on written laws, partly on legendary fables or narratives, partly on the injunctions of instructors and priests, partly on custom and usage, and partly on the caprice and convenience of its votaries." The harm of caste rules is so great that of late they have been broken in some cases, especially in regard to travel over sea, which is a great advantage to Hindoos. The Hindoo folkways in regard to widows and child marriages must also be recognized as socially harmful.

. . . . .

THE FOLKWAYS ARE "RIGHT"

The folkways are the "right" ways to satisfy all interests, because they are traditional, and exist in fact. They extend over the whole of life. There is a right way to catch game, to win a wife, to make one's self appear, to cure disease, to honor ghosts, to treat comrades or strangers, to behave when a child is born, on the warpath, in council, and soon in all cases which can arise. The ways are defined on the negative side, that is, by taboos. The "right" way is the way which the ancestors used and which has been handed down. The tradition is its own warrant. It is not held subject to verification by experience. The notion of right is in the folkways. It is not outside of them, of independent origin, and brought to them to test them. In the folkways, whatever is, is right. This is because they are traditional, and therefore contain in themselves the authority of the ancestral ghosts. When we come to the folkways we are at the end of our analysis. The notion of right and ought is the same in regard to all the folkways, but the degree of it varies with the importance of the interest at stake. The obligation of conformable and coöperative action is far greater under ghost fear and war than in other matters, and the social sanctions are severer, because group interests are supposed to be at stake. Some usages contain only a slight element of right and ought. It may well be believed that notions of right and duty, and of social welfare, were first developed in connection with ghost fear and other-worldliness, and therefore that, in that field also, folkways were first raised to mores. "Rights" are the rules of mutual give and take in the competition of life which are imposed on comrades in the in-group, in order that the peace may prevail there which is essential to the group strength. Therefore rights can never be "natural" or "God-given," or absolute in any sense. The morality of a group at a time is the sum of the taboos and prescriptions in the folkways by which right conduct is defined. Therefore morals can never be intuitive. They are historical, institutional, and empirical.

World philosophy, life policy, right, rights, and morality are all products of the folkways. They are reflections on, and generalizations from, the experience of pleasure and pain which is won in efforts to carry on the struggle for existence under actual life conditions. The generalizations are very crude and vague in their germinal forms. They are all embodied in folklore, and all our philosophy and science have been developed out of them.

THE FOLKWAYS ARE "TRUE"

The folkways are necessarily "true" with respect to some world philosophy. Pain forced men to think. The ills of life imposed reflection and taught forethought. Mental processes were irksome and were not undertaken until painful experience made them unavoidable. With great unanimity all over the globe primitive men followed the same line of thought. The dead were believed to live on as ghosts in another world just like this one. The ghosts had just the same needs, tastes, passions, etc., as the living men had had. These transcendental notions were the beginning of the mental outfit of mankind. They are articles of faith, not rational convictions. The living had duties to the ghosts, and the ghosts had rights; they also had power to enforce their rights. It behooved the living therefore to learn how to deal with ghosts. Here we have a complete world philosophy and a life policy deduced from it. When pain, loss, and ill were experienced and the question was provoked, Who did this to us? the world philosophy furnished the answer. When the painful experience forced the question, Why are the ghosts angry and what must we do to appease them? the "right" answer was the one which fitted into the philosophy of ghost fear. All acts were therefore constrained and trained into the forms of the world philosophy by ghost fear, ancestral authority, taboos, and habit. The habits and customs created a practical philosophy of welfare, and they confirmed and developed the religious theories of goblinism.

• • • • •

DEFINITION OF THE MORES

When the elements of truth and right are developed into doctrines of welfare, the folkways are raised to another plane. They then become capable of producing inferences, developing into new forms, and extending their constructive influence over men and society. Then we call them the mores. The mores are the folkways, including the philosophical and ethical generalizations as to societal welfare which are suggested by them, and inherent in them, as they grow.

TABOOS

The mores necessarily consist, in a large part, of taboos, which indicate the things which must not be done. In part these are dictated by mystic dread of ghosts who might be offended by certain acts, but they also include such acts as have been found by experience to produce unwelcome results, especially in the food quest, in war, in health, or in increase or decrease of population. These taboos always contain a greater element of philosophy than the positive rules, because the taboos contain reference to a reason, as, for instance, that the act would displease the ghosts. The primitive taboos correspond to the fact that the life of man is environed by perils. His food quest must be limited by shunning poisonous plants. His appetite must be restrained from excess. His physical strength and health must be guarded from dangers. The taboos carry on the accumulated wisdom of generations, which has almost always been purchased by pain, loss, disease, and death. Other taboos contain inhibitions of what will be injurious to the group. The laws about sexes, about property, about war, and about ghosts, have this character. They always include some social philosophy. They are both mystic and utilitarian, or compounded of the two.

Taboos may be divided into two classes, (1) protective and (2) destructive. Some of them aim to protect and secure, while others aim to repress or exterminate. Women are subject to some taboos which are directed against them as sources of possible harm or danger to men, and they are subject to other taboos which put them outside of the duties or risks of men. On account of this difference in taboos, taboos act selectively, and thus affect the course of civilization. They contain judgments as to societal welfare.

• • • • •

MORE EXACT DEFINITION OF THE MORES

We may now formulate a more complete definition of the mores. They are the ways of doing things which are current in a society to satisfy human needs and desires, together with the faiths, notions, codes, and standards of well living which inhere in those ways, having a genetic connection with them. By virtue of the latter element the mores are traits in the specific character (ethos) of a society or a period. They pervade and control the ways of thinking in all the exigencies of life, returning from the world of abstractions to the world of action, to give guidance and to win revivification. "The mores [*Sitten*] are, before any beginning of reflection, the regulators of the political, social, and religious behavior of the individual. Conscious reflection is the worst enemy of the mores, because mores begin unconsciously and pursue unconscious purposes, which are recognized by reflection often only after long and circuitous processes, and because their expediency often depends on the assumption that they will have general acceptance and currency, uninterfered with by reflection." "The mores are usage in any group, insofar as it, on the one hand, is not the expression or fulfillment of an absolute natural necessity [e.g. eating or sleeping], and, on the other hand, is independent of the arbitrary will of the individual, and is generally accepted as worthy."

RITUAL

The process by which mores are developed and established is ritual. Ritual is so foreign to our mores that we do not recognize its power. In primitive society it is the prevailing method of activity, and primitive religion is entirely a matter of ritual. Ritual is the perfect form of drill and of the regulated habit which comes from drill. Acts which are ordained by authority and are repeated mechanically without intelligence run into ritual. If infants and children are subjected to ritual they never escape from its effects through life. Galton says that he was, in early youth, in contact with the Mohammedan ritual idea that the left hand is less worthy than the right, and that he never overcame it. We see the effect of ritual in breeding, courtesy, politeness, and all forms of prescribed behavior. Etiquette is social ritual. Ritual is not easy compliance with usage; it is strict compliance with detailed and punctilious rule. It admits of no exception or deviation. The stricter the discipline, the greater the power of ritual over action and character. In the training of animals and the education of children it is the perfection, inevitableness, invariableness, and relentlessness of routine which tells. They should never experience any exception or irregularity. Ritual is connected with words, gestures, symbols, and signs. Associations result, and, upon a repetition of the signal, the act is repeated, whether the will assents or not. Association and habit account for the phenomena. Ritual gains further strength when it is rhythmical, and is connected with music, verse, or other rhythmical acts. Acts are ritually repeated at the recurrence of the rhythmical points. The alternation of night and day produces rhythms of waking and sleeping, of labor and rest, for great numbers at the same time, in their struggle for existence. The seasons also produce rhythms in work. Ritual may embody an idea of utility, expediency, or welfare, but it always tends to become perfunctory, and the idea is only subconscious. There is ritual in primitive therapeutics, and it was not eliminated until very recent times. The patient was directed, not only to apply remedies, but also to perform rites. The rites introduced mystic elements. This illustrates the connection of ritual with notions of magical effects produced by rites. All ritual is ceremonious and solemn. It tends to become sacred, or to make sacred the subject-matter with which it is connected. Therefore, in primitive society, it is by ritual that sentiments of awe, deference to authority, submission to tradition, and disciplinary coöperation are inculcated. Ritual operates a constant suggestion, and the suggestion is at once put in operation in acts. Ritual is strongest when it is most perfunctory and excites no thought. By familiarity with ritual any doctrinal reference which it once had is lost by familiarity, but the habits persist. Primitive religion is ritualistic, not because religion makes ritual, but because ritual makes religion. Ritual is something to be done, not something to be thought or felt. Men can always perform the prescribed act, although they cannot always think or feel prescribed thoughts or emotions. The acts may bring up again, by association, states of the mind and sentiments which have been connected with them, especially in childhood, when the fantasy was easily affected by rites, music, singing, dramas, etc. No creed, no moral code, and no scientific demonstration can ever win the same hold upon men and women as habits of action, with associated sentiments and states of mind, drilled in from childhood. Mohammedanism shows the power of ritual. Any occupation is interrupted for the prayers and prescribed genuflections. The Brahmins also observe an elaborate daily ritual. They devote to it two hours in the morning, two in the evening, and one at midday. Monks and nuns have won the extreme satisfaction of religious sentiment from the unbroken habit of repeated ritual, with undisturbed opportunity to develop emotional effects of it.

THE RITUAL OF THE MORES

The mores are social ritual in which we all participate unconsciously. The current habits as to hours of labor, meal hours, family life, the social intercourse of the sexes, propriety, amusements, travel, holidays, education, the use of periodicals and libraries, and innumerable other details of life fall under this ritual. Each does as everybody does. For the great mass of mankind as to all things, and for all of us for a great many things, the rule to do as all do suffices. We are led by suggestion and association to believe that there must be wisdom and utility in what all do. The great mass of the folkways give us discipline and the support of routine and habit. If we had to form judgments as to all these cases before we could act in them, and were forced always to act rationally, the burden would be unendurable. Beneficent use and wont save us this trouble.

16 Catastrophe by the Numbers

CHARLTON OGBURN, JR.

For a number of years, competent students of population trends and natural resources have contended that the present rate of population growth in the world is almost certain to continue unabated and, if it does, before very long mankind will exhaust the resources necessary to maintain even our present standard of living. In this selection Ogburn, supporting the position that population growth will surely continue unabated, examines the dire consequences that will result and assesses alternative means of resolving the problem as well as the likelihood of implementing the solutions. For a more optimistic view of this question, see Selection 17, "The End of the Population Explosion," by Donald J. Bogue.

The poet, who a century and a quarter ago, "dipt into the future, far as human eye could see" and "saw the Vision of the world, and all the wonder that would be," would, if he dipt into it today, find disaster for the human race squarely ahead down the road our species is travelling with gathering speed. Even in 1842, however, when Tennyson's paean of optimism and affirmation was published, there was no need to have been unprepared for the fate mankind now appears bent on bringing on itself. More than forty years earlier, the professor of history and political economy at East India College in Haileybury, England, the Reverend Thomas Malthus, had called attention to the fact that the power of the human race to reproduce itself is infinite, while the capacity of the earth to support its numbers is finite. By 1842 birth rates and death rates in England, which had been in a rough balance a century before, showed a wide disparity. Owing to a fall in the death rate, the annual excess of births over deaths had reached thirteen per thousand persons, which meant that in another fifty years the population would double.

Death rates for the human race as a whole have been tumbling ever since, as science has been bringing the big killers of mankind under control and extending its beneficent sway from the advanced parts of the world to the less favored. The paradoxical result has been that human existence is threatened. Scientists concerned with the world's future have for a decade and more been urging mankind to grasp and be guided by the ominous statistics—so far with little response. The figures cannot be too often rehearsed.

The population of the world, from an estimated 5 million 8,000 years ago, reached 500 million about 300 years ago, having doubled about every 1,000 years. It reached one billion before 1850, having doubled in less than 200 years. Two billion was reached about 1930,—the doubling period having been reduced to about eighty years. The population of the world is now over 3.5 billion, and

SOURCE: *American Heritage,* vol. 21, no. 1 (December 1969), 116–17. Reprinted by permission of the publisher. • Charlton Ogburn, Jr., is a free-lance writer. He has served as chief of the Division of Research in the Near East, South Asia, and Africa, and served with the Division on Southeast Asian Affairs, Department of State. He is a trustee of the National Parks Association. Among his books are *The White Falcon; The Bridge; The Gold of the River Sea; The Winter Beach,* which won the 1967 John Burroughs Award for nature writing; and *The Forging of Our Continent.*

the doubling period is now down to about thirty-five years. *Every day* the population goes up by 190,000,—the equivalent of a fair-sized city.

The joker in the population pack, the terrible, cruel joker,—is that with a rate of population increase that is constant, or even somewhat declining, the population will not only continue to grow, but the amount by which it grows will *every year become greater*. The principle is that of compound interest. If the present rate of population increase were to continue, at the end of only 650 years there would be one person for every square foot of the earth's surface. Such a horror could not, of course, actually come to pass. If birth rates had not long since been sufficiently reduced to bring them back into balance with death rates, nature would have achieved the same end by scourging mankind with one of the traditional mass killers—war, famine, and plague or with a more modern agent, crippling psychic ills.

The rate of population increase is highest in the poorer countries. What most of us have failed to grasp, however, is that the rate of increase is menacing in the United States—menacing to ourselves and, because of our disproportionate demands on the world environment, menacing to everyone else. As in other technologically advanced countries, though less so than in some others, the birth rate in the United States has markedly declined in the past century. Nevertheless, our population, having passed 100 million in 1917, passed 200 million in 1967. Even at the present low fertility rate (the birth rate for women of childbearing age), which is the lowest since the 1930's, it will reach 400 million before a child born today is seventy years old (by which time the population of the world will have reached fifteen billion). When the Republic is as old again as it is now, in 2162, the number of Americans will be getting on toward 1.5 billion, while many children born that year may live to see the equivalent of the entire population of the world today jammed into the United States.

To picture what is in store for us as the population mounts we do not have to peer into the future far as human eye can see. We need only apply a little imagination to the effects of population pressure that we are already enduring. Nearly all of the problems we are wrestling with today are being rendered far more difficult of solution by the addition of nearly 5,500 lodgers to the national boardinghouse every day—such problems as providing adequate education and job training, housing, medical services, parks, playgrounds, sports fields and swimming pools, highways, airports and rapid mass-transit, and the wherewithal to relieve the plight of the poor in slums and rural backwaters. If we are finding urban problems today almost more than we can manage, how are we going to handle them as the cities are swelled by ever more millions? Our streams and lakes are already so befouled with human, industrial, and agricultural wastes and to clean them up will cost one hundred billion dollars, we are told. Our garbage is piling up around us: a million tons more every day, according to specialists at the Massachusetts Institute of Technology. Noise, taking a toll in health and efficiency and generally adding to the strain of life, has been doubling in volume every ten years. The cost of maintaining a nation of 200 million in the ever more expansive style to which we are accustomed comes high, and it bears not on the American people alone. With one seventeenth of the world's population, we consume two-fifths of its production of raw materials, and, even with allowance made for the finished products we return, the disparity is enormous. Into the common atmosphere of the earth we Americans annually pour 140 million tons of pollutants, of which some ninety million come from transport (we burn more gasoline in motorcars than the rest of the world put together) and more than fifteen million from electric-power generation (of which our share of the world's total is a third). Our contribution to the carbon-dioxide content of the atmosphere, which has gone up by over 10 per cent in the past century (and which by creating a "greenhouse effect" could result in the melting of the polar ice caps and the inundation of all the world's ports and coastal plains) is comparable to our share of the world's fossil fuel combustion —34 per cent.

Within thirty or thirty-five years we may expect to have 100 million more Americans generating refuse, water pollutants, and toxic gases; demanding their share of the world's resources and of our own—forests and minerals, soil, and water. We shall have the same 100 million more taxing those services which already the nation is supplying with difficulty—where, indeed, it is not already woefully in arrears. As the population continues to soar, the costs of providing for its needs will far outpace it. For example, to supply water-deficient areas of the western part of the continent there is already being proposed a North American Water and Power Alliance to redirect southward the flow of several large Canadian rivers now emptying in the north, at a price of one hundred billion dollars, just to have water come out of the faucets.

And that will be only part of it. The inflation of any commodity results in its devaluation, and so must it be with human life. Humanity, from having been an object to be loved and cherished, will become one to be escaped, which will scarcely be possible as the teeming hordes press in on the resorts of privacy, convert the cities into the psychological equivalent of concentration camps, and necessitate a regimentation and computerization of life in order to manage the packed masses. Human inflation must also strike at the individual's estimate of his importance. The average American, from having been one hundredth or one thousandth part of a rural community or town two centuries ago, has become one two-hundred-thousandth part of a city today; if he is on the young side of middle age, he can expect to be reduced to one thirty-millionth part of a megalopolis. As the individual is overwhelmed by and lost in a society of ever more monstrous and inhuman forms, we must anticipate a progressive multiplication of the symptoms of anomie and alienation, which range from apathy and despondency to aggression and violence.

We shall also witness the desolation of what remains of the natural world around us and the closing of avenues of escape from the mounting tensions of an increasingly overwrought, high-pressure civilization. Beaches, lakes, mountains—the green kingdoms that have always stood for the living world in our eyes and have been the matrix of every human culture—will be overrun, debased, and obliterated by the products of that civilization, human and material. The process accelerates rapidly today. The cottages crowd rank on rank along the shores and lakesides. The suburbs spread like a skin eruption ever farther into farm land, and with them come the shopping centers and industrial plants, converting fields and forests to asphalt, masonry, and neon lights in eighty- and hundred-acre swoops. To the rear, even as they spread outward, the cities are cut to pieces by freeways on which, beneath thickening palls of smog, swelling streams of motorcars race eight abreast.

Of course, events in the world at large may preclude the climax of this spoilage. Despite our poor, the average American can purchase nine times as much in the way of goods and services as the average Latin American, and more than twenty times as much as the average Asian or African. And the have-not peoples are ill content with this dispensation. There has been let loose in the world a so-called "revolution of rising expectations." Actually, those expectations only *aim* at revolution. They amount to a demand, affecting billions, for the health and comforts the West has shown to be attainable. We might ask ourselves what course those billions are likely to take as they see the disparity between what they have and what we have grow wider—as it is doing—and if they see no prospect of substantial relief from their poverty under the institutions they are accustomed to. At the same time we might ask ourselves what the consequences would be if their expectations of the more abundant life were met: what overwhelming demands would be made on the resources of the globe, and what damage done to the environment of life if the incomes of the disadvantaged billions should approach our own and all peoples began to live on the American model—felling forests for paper as we do, burning fuels and pouring pollutants into the air and the rivers and the sea as we do, and consuming an equivalent share of the earth's minerals. "The ecology of the earth," says Harvard nutritional expert Jean Mayer, "—its streams, woods, animals—can accommodate itself better to a rising *poor* population than to a rising *rich* population."

What remains clear is that the higher the rate of population growth among the economically laggard peoples, and, to repeat, it is now the highest in the world —the slower any improvement in their lot is likely to be, and the more costly to the earth and its ecology would be the dramatic improvement we have taught them to expect. Year by year the alternatives ahead grow more dangerous. With a continuation of present rates of world population growth, either progress or lack of progress in satisfying the wants of the multiplying billions will alike become ever more hazardous, ever more certain to be destructive of world order.

How vast a human multitude the planet can feed is moot. Fanatic agriculturalists speak of 50 billion and more and present us a graphic picture of the world's forests being "sheared off at ground level" by " a huge steel blade . . . pushed by a heavy crawler-type tractor" to provide farm land. That forests are indispensable in preserving watersheds and water tables and tempering climates, that the need will be for more forests in the future to provide lumber and pulp, does not seem to concern them. But at least they point up the insanity of devoting our energies, not to creating conditions in which man's potentialities may be realized, but to converting this splendid earth into a dreary food-factory to provide a mere subsistence for overflowing billions with whom no one in his right mind could wish to see the planet burdened.

. . . . .

In the face of all warnings, we Americans brought over 3.5 million new human beings into the world last year, to send the population of the United States up by 1.5 million. And with each of these added lives representing a burden on the earth equal to a half dozen or more Asians or

Africans, we should perhaps not expect those unenlightened folk to be much moved by our exhortations to them to reproduce less. A Gallup poll in November a year ago showed that 41 per cent of Americans considered *four or more* children ideal for a family, the percentage being 50 among Roman Catholics, 56 among Negroes, and higher than average among the poor—47.

Admittedly, there were once good reasons for large families. At the time of the American Revolution, only half of the children born lived to sixteen. Most of us were farmers, and on the farm children were an asset. In any case, land and resources appeared inexhaustible. Let it be acknowledged too that while times have changed drastically, asking couples to limit the number of their children is asking a great deal. Watching a human personality gradually take shape, one that you have helped bring out of nothing, is an incomparable satisfaction. Children lend a kind of charm to life that nothing else can.

That the traditional indulgent view of large families should die hard is not surprising. The fact remains—and it is a fact of which there is no excuse for ignorance—that those who reproduce as if they were living in the past are preparing for the children of the future a world in which life will scarcely be worth living. Yet evidently little stigma attaches to their doing so. If suburban mothers hesitate to traipse across the shopping center with a train of offspring, nothing in their bearing betrays it. A father of ten grins with self-satisfaction out of the television tube on "Generation Gap," while another parent beside him apologizes for being, by comparison, an underachiever. A prominent clergyman of the nation's capital and his wife are evidently unembarrassed at having brought nine children into the world. Newspapers regularly report the plight—and complaints—of parents of twelve on relief, without any suggestion that society has rights in the matter, rights which have been grossly violated. Public figures who have become known partly because of their concern with the nation's future, like columnist Jack Anderson and entertainer Dick Gregory, can have nine and seven children, respectively, and not feel that they owe the public an apology any more than John Wayne, who also has seven children. The governor of New Jersey, Richard J. Hughes, had three children by one wife, acquired three more with a second wife, and by her had an additional three. Presumably his career has not been impaired as a result—or Governor Nelson Rockefeller's by his having six children, or ex-Congressman Hugh L. Carey's by his having had fourteen.

The crucial test of public opinion on the issue came last year when a strong bid for the presidential nomination was made by a dynamic and appealing young politician whose ten children (with an eleventh on the way) marked him as entirely disqualified to address himself to the problem that Dwight Eisenhower had called one of the most critical of our time. During his campaign for a Senate seat Robert Kennedy had indeed lightheartedly confessed to this disqualification. The next year he had gone further. Speaking in a country in which one of the world's most rapidly growing populations had for two decades been outstripping an already inadequate food production by 10 per cent—Peru—he gaily challenged his audience to outbreed him. ("Deadly dangerous," the Washington *Post* termed the ploy, and with reason. If all the speaker's eleven children and their descendants reproduced as he had, there would be over 214 million descendants of the Robert Kennedys in the ninth generation, and seven times as many as there are people in the entire world today in the eleventh.) Not only, however, did Senator Kennedy's exemplification of the procreative irresponsibility that is pushing the world toward catastrophe create no bar to his political ambitions; no public figure, editorialist, or columnist that I know of deemed it important enough to mention as bearing on his eligibility for the supreme office.

In a statement hailed by family-planning groups, the heads of thirty governments in the United Nations have announced "that the opportunity to decide the number and spacing of children is a basic human right." Not to *limit* but to *decide* the number. What this "right" is, of course, is the "right" of any part of the human race to make the planet uninhabitable for the whole. It is the "right" of any passenger in a lifeboat to help himself to as much of the provisions as he wants, regardless of the consequences to his fellows.

Just as early humanoids were probably unaware of any connection between sexual intercourse and its subsequent issue, so their descendants today, one could almost believe, are unaware of any between the number of children individual couples have and the growth of the population as a whole. That would explain how the *Reader's Digest* can run an excellent article hammering home the implications of the problem, and in an advertisement a few months later, beam upon John and Mary Ann Forristal of Houston and their nine children as a representative *Digest* family. It would explain the report issued in November, 1968, by a committee of highly qualified citizens set up by the President to recommend steps to deal with population pressure. On one page the report tells us that the current rate of growth of the American population "cannot be maintained indefinitely," on the opposite that the national objective is "a society in which all parents can have the number of children they want when they want them." What we do if the number of children parents want must produce a rate of population growth impossible to maintain, which is the case at present, the committee does not say. Last July, in the strongest public statement on population yet made by an American President, Mr. Nixon detailed the enormous scope of the problem and proposed the creation by Congress of a "Commission on Population Growth and the American Future"; then he went on to vitiate all he had been urging with the pious pronouncement that the government's pursuit of the goal of population control would "in no circumstances . . . be allowed to infringe upon the religious convictions or personal wishes and freedom of any individual, nor . . . to impair the absolute right of all individuals to have such matters of conscience respected by public authorities." One wonders how close to final debacle we shall have to come before a President summons up the nerve to do what is clearly imperative now and gives the American people to understand that if they care anything for posterity, for their country, and for the handiwork of the Creator that has made North America so hospitable and inspiring to human habitation, they are going to have to accept a ceiling on the number of children per couple, and that the national interest will be best served if that ceiling for the present is no more than two.

Even if such a national policy were enunciated, however—as sooner or later it will have to be—there will remain the question of how individual couples are to be brought to conform to it. What results could be expected from a mere appeal to conscience?

Harmful ones, Garrett Hardin of the

University of California argues persuasively. The person whose conscience is appealed to, says Professor Hardin, is caught in a "double bind" of a kind that can induce schizophrenia. For he is damned if he does and damned if he doesn't. If he ignores the appeal and has three or four children, he stands to be publicly condemned as selfish, irresponsible, and antisocial. If he obeys it while others ignore it, he can only feel he has been had—one whom others "secretly condemn . . . for a simpleton."

Of course, we should not have to fear these consequences if an appeal to conscience were *uniformly* acceded to. But one thing that experience of this world should teach us is the futility of expecting human beings in the aggregate to curb their instincts or desires for any length of time just for the general good. Were it otherwise, we could have government by exhortation instead of by laws—laws with teeth in them. Can it be imagined that wartime rationing that depended on voluntary compliance would be of any effect? And rationing is what we are talking about.

To move human beings to what is uncongenial and unnatural to them requires the carrot and/or the stick. For the great majority of us, over the long run, nothing else will serve. The question is, what sort of carrot and what sort of stick would be most likely to prove effective in preventing the earth from being swamped by people and at the same time provide an equitable apportionment of the right to bear children? That is the question to which those most concerned with the future of life on earth should address themselves—or show how these ends may otherwise be achieved.

Professor Hardin favors coercion—but "mutual coercion, mutually agreed upon by the majority of the people affected." Social sanctions could perhaps meet the need. If anyone with three or four children automatically brought obloquy and ostracism on himself as an antipatriot and an offender against the Deity (who presumably would have some interest in the preservation of his magnificent creation, the earth), we might have the answer. But the world might be close to irreversible disaster, or over the line, before such an effective consensus could form, even in the United States.

Meanwhile, economic levers are available. Federal and state income-tax exemptions now authorized for every minor child could be denied in the case of children over the number of two, born nine months or more after the enactment of the legislation. Annual payments could be made to sexually mature females who refrain from bearing children, and in lesser amounts to those who stop with two. Fines, proportionate to the offender's capacity to pay, could be levied against parents for each child they produce in excess of two; beyond a certain limit the offenders could be deprived of the right to vote. (Why should those indifferent to society's future be given a voice in it?) At the same time, of course, anti-abortion laws—which in any case represent a tyrannical denial by the state of the rights of an individual—should be repealed; contraceptives should be made freely available to all, and every effort should be made to devise simpler, surer, safer methods of contraception.

Obviously strong opposition to any program equal to arresting the population explosion is to be expected, especially on the part of the Roman Catholic hierarchy. But public opinion can be swayed. The Vatican has changed its mind in the past, and can and must change it again. The more public discussion there is, the sooner the public will become accustomed to and will accept measures to deal effectively with a crisis that four thousand scientists at a recent meeting of the American Association for the Advancement of Science termed—along with the related crisis of pollution—the most serious facing mankind. Too-long delay in meeting it can result only in having the issue taken out of our hands, for under the strains to which the population explosion must increasingly subject civilization, the institutions of representative self-government will be among the surest to give way.

17 The End of the Population Explosion

DONALD J. BOGUE

Though most demographers agree with the pessimistic view regarding population growth represented by the preceding selection, some are convinced that the situation is not nearly so bleak. This selection by the eminent demographer Donald Bogue examines some of the reasons for greater optimism. It is Bogue's hope that his arguments will not cause a relaxation of efforts but will, rather, provide encouragement for redoubled activity among family planning workers whose morale has been "sapped" for a long time by "the Malthusian pessimism . . . radiated by many demographic reports." The reader is left to choose or to strike his own balance between the optimism of this selection and the pessimism of the preceding one.

Recent developments in the worldwide movement to bring runaway birth rates under control are such that it now is possible to assert with considerable confidence that the prospects for success are excellent. In fact, it is quite reasonable to assume that *the world population crisis is a phenomenon of the 20th century, and will be largely if not entirely a matter of history when humanity moves into the 21st century.* No doubt there will still be problematic areas in the year 2000, but they will be confined to a few nations that were too prejudiced, too bureaucratic, or too disorganized to take action sooner, or will be confined to small regions within some nations where particular ethnic, economic, or religious groups will not yet have received adequate fertility control services and information. With the exception of such isolated remnants (which may be neutralized by other areas of growth-at-less-than-replacement), it is probable that by the year 2000 each of the major world regions will have a population growth rate that either is zero or is easily within the capacity of its expanding economy to support.

The implications of these assertions for the feeding of the human race are obvious. Given the present capacity of the earth for food production, and the potential for additional food production if modern technology were more fully employed, mankind clearly has within its

SOURCE: *The Public Interest,* no. 7 (Spring 1967), 11–20. • The author is professor of sociology and the director of the Community and Family Study Center at the University of Chicago. He is a former president of the Population Association of America and is editor of the *Journal of Demography.* His major interests include methodology and statistics, social psychology, population, and urban sociology. He is author of *Economic Areas of the United States, Skid Row in American Cities,* and *Principles of Demography.*

grasp the capacity to abolish hunger—within a matter of a decade or two. Furthermore, it is doubtful whether a total net food shortage for the entire earth will ever develop. If such a deficit does develop, it will be mild and only of short duration. The really critical problem will continue to be one of maldistribution of food among the world's regions.

These optimistic assertions are not intended to detract from the seriousness of the present population situation. Some years of acute crisis lie immediately ahead for India, China, the Philippines, Indonesia, Pakistan, Mexico, Brazil, Egypt, and other nations. Severe famines quite probably will develop within local areas of some of these nations unless emergency international measures are taken. My purpose here is to emphasize that the engineers and the agricultural technicians striving to increase the output of material goods in these nations are not working alone. Paralleling their activity is a very ambitious international fertility control program which is just starting to "pay off."

These remarks are certainly not intended to cause the participants in this international fertility control program to relax their efforts and be lulled into complacency. The successful outcome anticipated above is not one that will come automatically, but only as a result of a continued all-out "crash program" to make the widest and most intensive use of the medical, sociological, and psychological knowledge now available, and of the practical experience that has recently emerged from experimental family planning programs. It also anticipates a continued flow of new research findings and enriched practical experience that is promptly fed back into programs of fertility reduction.

This view is at variance with the established view of many population experts. For more than a century, demographers have terrorized themselves, each other, and the public at large with the essential hopelessness and inevitability of the "population explosion." Their prophecies have all been dependent upon one premise: "If recent trends continue. . . ." It is an ancient statistical fallacy to perform extrapolations upon this premise when in fact the premise is invalid. It is my major point that *recent trends have not continued, nor will they be likely to do so.* Instead, there have been some new and recent developments that make it plausible to expect a much more rapid pace in fertility control. These developments are so new and so novel that *population trends before 1960 are largely irrelevant in predicting what will happen in the future.*

In times of social revolution, it often is fruitless to forecast the future on the basis of past experience. Instead, it is better to abandon time series analysis and study the phenomenon of change itself, seeking to understand it and to learn in which direction and how rapidly it is moving. If enough can be learned about the social movement that is bringing about the change, there is a hope that its eventual outcome can be roughly predicted. This procedure is followed here. The result is subjective and crude, but I believe it to be nearer the future course of demographic history than the official population projections now on record.

II

Limitations of space permit only a listing of major social developments which, in my view, justify the relatively optimistic prospect I have set forth.

1. Grass roots approval. All over the world, wherever surveys of the attitudes of the public with respect to fertility have been taken, it has uniformly been found that a majority of couples with three

living children wish to have no more. Of these, a very large proportion approve of family planning in principle and declare they would like to have more information about it. They also approve of nationwide health service that includes family planning. In other words, active objections among the masses on cultural, moral, or religious grounds are minor rather than major obstacles. This is true both in Asia and Latin America, and seems to be developing rapidly in Africa. Thus, at the "grass roots" level, the attitudinal and cultural conditions are highly favorable. Previously, it had been feared that traditionalism and religious attitudes would prove to be almost insuperable blocks to rapid fertility control. But the more sociologists study the situation, the more they accept as correct the generalization that, in most places where there is a population problem, the attitude toward family planning among the mass of the people is strongly positive.

2. Aroused political leadership. Whereas fertility control was regarded as a subversive, immoral, and sinful program during the 150 years of fertility decline in Europe and the United States, in the nations with a population problem today the national political leadership openly accepts family planning as a moral and rational solution. Heads of state in India, Pakistan, Korea, China, Egypt, Chile, Turkey, and Colombia, for example, have made fertility control an integral part of the national plan for economic development. In this, they have followed the lead of Japan. The national ministers of health and welfare not only are permitted but are expected to provide family planning services. National health services are adding family planning to their clinic services, financed by public tax funds. The mass media are increasingly carrying official endorsements, public encouragements, and specific information.

3. Accelerated professional and research activity. Professional groups in the developing countries (as well as in the rest of the world) are rapidly losing whatever antipathy or prejudice against family planning they may have had. Everywhere, the medical profession is rapidly giving it a solid endorsement—even in nations where there have been problems of religious objection. Within religious groups where there formerly was a hard inflexible prohibition against the use of chemical or mechanical contraceptive appliances, there is now a great deal of difference of opinion. Gradually, the laity is reaching the belief that the control of natality is a matter for the individual conscience, or a medical matter to be discussed with a physician—but not with the priest. Physicians and priests alike tend to accept this interpretation without forthright challenge.

Universities, both in the United States and abroad, have undertaken large-scale and sustained research activities in the fields of family planning. Their activities cover the entire range of topics—medical, sociological, and psychological. Most of the nations with a national family planning program are sponsoring research into the problem. This includes not only projects to discover new and improved ways of promoting fertility control, but also the evaluation of present programs. These activities are not amorphous, but within a remarkably short time have been coordinated. The process of integration was greatly facilitated by the holding in Geneva in 1965 of an International Conference on Family Planning Programs.

Much of the credit for the development described above is due to the activities of not-for-profit organizations that have taken population control as a focus of their activities: the Ford Foundation, Rockefeller Foundation, Population Council, and International Planned Parenthood are the leaders. The Swedish Government, the Milbank Memorial Fund, the Planned Parenthood Association of America, and the Pathfinder Fund have also been highly important sponsors of these activities. These organizations have provided unprecedented financial and technical support.

4. The slackening of progress in death control. Immediately after World War II, the industrialized nations of the world realized that there was a series of public health and medical programs that could be accomplished quickly and cheaply to bring about a reduction in mortality. These have now been largely carried out—there have been campaigns against malaria, smallpox, cholera, yellow fever, and other diseases that can be brought under control with an injection, a semiannual house spraying, etc. The results have been dramatic, and death rates have tumbled. However, further progress in death control will be slower, because the remaining problems are those for which a solution is more difficult or is as yet unknown. For example, the death rate in Latin America stands at about 14 per thousand now. Modern medicine could bring it, at best, only to about 8 per thousand—a fall of 6 points. But a very much greater investment must be made, and over a considerably longer span of time, to achieve these 6 points than was required to obtain the preceding 6 points. In Asia the death rate still stands at about 20, even after the advent of the "miracle drugs" and the mass-innoculation and mass-treatment programs. It may be expected to drift lower, but at a slower pace than before.

This slackening of death control has a most important implication—a decline in the birth rate would be more directly reflected in a decline in the rate of population growth. During the past two decades, even if birth rates were declining, death rates were declining still faster, so that the population growth rate increased. That trend now appears to be reaching the end of a cycle: the cycle appears to be on the verge of reversing itself.

5. A variety of sociological and psychological phenomena, previously unknown or underappreciated, are promoting the rapid adoption of family planning by the mass of the people. Here we can only list them, without explanation:

a. Privation is itself a powerful motivating force for fertility control.

b. Private communciation about family planning is far greater than had been thought, and can easily be stimulated to attain flood proportions.

c. "Opinion leaders"—indigenous men and women who are knowledgeable about birth control and freely undertake to influence others to adopt it—can be mass-produced cheaply and very rapidly by means of mass media and other action programs. Thus, in this area just as in economic development, there is a "multiplier effect" which, if capitalized upon, can greatly hasten "takeoff" into rapidly declining fertility.

d. It is becoming evident that fathers are very nearly equally as interested and responsible in controlling fertility as are wives. Programs aimed at couples, instead of at females, are highly effective.

e. We are discovering that illiterate rural populations will make use of the traditional methods of family planning—condom, suppositories, etc.—very nearly as readily as urban populations, after a brief period of information and trial. They will also adopt the newer methods as—or even more—readily.

6. Improved technology in contraception promotes massive adoption by uneducated people at a rapid pace. Oral contraceptives and the intra-uterine devices have both proved to be highly acceptable after only short periods of instruction and familiarity. Even illiterate rural villagers make sustained use of these methods where they have been given unprejudiced trial. These developments are

only half-a-decade old, but they already have had a profound impact upon fertility control programs and plans. As yet there is still a great deal of prejudice against the oral compounds in Asia, so that the advantages of a two-method assault have not been fully realized there. In Latin American experiments, where the "pills" and intra-uterine devices were used side-by-side as alternative methods, the results are highly impressive.

We are repeatedly being told by the physiologists, however, that our so-called "modern" methods of contraception are crude and barbarous—each with unpleasant side-effects and unsuitable for as much as one-quarter of the population. They insist that much superior methods are on the horizon—that soon there will be dramatic improvements, that costs will be cheaper, and that the need for "sustained motivation" to practice contraception will be greatly reduced. Millions of dollars are being poured into experimental research on this front each year. This activity is taking place both in the public and the private sector. The giants of the drug industry know that huge markets can be gained by improving upon present contraceptive technology—and that huge markets will be lost if a competitor discovers and markets a superior product. As a result, all of the leading motives that bring about frenzied activity for progress among scientists have been harnessed and are at work in behalf of improving contraceptive technology—prestige, economic gain, anxiety, compassion.

III

In order to illustrate the above points, let us take as an example the recent experience of Korea. In 1962, the Republic of Korea formally adopted family planning as one of its national policies. In 1965, a National Survey of Family Planning was conducted. Following are some points from that survey.

1. Eighty-nine percent of the wives and 79 percent of the husbands approved of family planning.
2. The rate of approval was only slightly lower in the rural than in the urban areas (88 percent for rural women and 77 percent for rural men).
3. Of the minority who disapproved, only 8 percent mentioned religion or morals. Traditional resistance was as low in rural as in urban areas.
4. Inability to read was no barrier; 81 percent of those unable to read nevertheless approved of family planning.
5. On the verbal level, the population declared itself willing to practice family planning if given services. Seventy-seven percent of the urban women and 71 percent of the rural women made such a declaration. Among husbands, 71 percent of the urban and 65 percent of the rural made such a declaration.
6. Unwillingness to practice family planning was concentrated primarily among young couples who had not yet had the number of children they desired and older couples (past 40 years of age) who were approaching the end of their childbearing. Couples in the years of prime importance for birth control, 25–40, were most positive in their attitudes. Moreover, the greater the number of living children, the greater the willingness to practice
7. As a result of the national information program, 85 percent of the urban and 83 percent of the rural population had heard of family planning. Moreover, 67 percent of the urban and 64 percent of the rural population had knowledge of at least one contraceptive method. Even among the illiterate, 51 percent knew of one method or more. Knowledge of the more reliable methods—oral pill, IUCD, condom—was only very slightly less widespread in rural than in urban areas.
8. At the time of the interview, 21 percent of the urban and 14 percent of the rural couples were practicing family planning. Even among the illiterate population, 10 percent were currently practicing family planning. Although small, these percentages very obviously have sprung from a condition of near-zero within a span of

three years. If only 2 percent are added each year, within 35 years population growth would be near zero.

9. The methods used by rural families were equal to or superior to those of the urban population in terms of reliability:

Method	*Percent of those using a method* *Rural*	*Urban*
Condom	51.1	61.1
I.U.C.D.	18.4	27.0
Oral Pill	8.5	3.5
Foam tablet	34.5	42.2

Note: Figures add to more than 100 because some couples employed more than one contraceptive.

10. In April of 1965 there were 2,207 field workers in the national family planning service, stationed in the health centers or in local offices. This is only the first wave of a rapid build-up to a point where there will be one field worker for each 10,000 population. The medical and social science departments of Seoul National University are actively engaged in research, evaluation, and participation in the national program. A private organization, Planned Parenthood Federation of Korea, has a branch in each province and is providing service and information through its office. Yonsel Medical College is conducting special experiments in rural areas, with assistance from the Population Council.

11. The progress of the national program in giving planning services is most impressive. The progress that results when a well-designed family planning program is carried out in a population of low education is illustrated by the Sungdong Gu Action-Research Project on Family Planning, Conducted by Seoul National University School of Public Health under the sponsorship of the Population Council. This program started in July, 1964. It included the use of mass media (T.V., radio, newspaper, posters, pamphlets, leaflets), group meetings, and home visiting. During the first 15 months of the program, of a total of 44,900 eligible (married women in the ages 20–44), 9,809 visited the family planning station for family planning information. About 85 percent of these visitors (19 percent of all the eligible women) accepted a method of family planning. Acceptance was divided roughly equally between condoms and other traditional methods and the IUCD's. Within the period, a total of 5,722 insertions (13 percent of the eligible women) were made. Even when allowance is made for the fact that the first year's experience would "skim off" the accumulated group of already-motivated people, the fact that one-fifth of the fertile population could be induced to adopt family planning within such short time is most impressive. It suggests the potential progress that can be made when a well-balanced program of information and service is provided, making use both of the mass media and personal contact.

The above brief notes on the progress of fertility control in Korea are not isolated instances. A recent report from the Pakistan Family Planning Programme suggests that more than one million families in that nation of 100 million (about 5 percent of the eligible population) now are currently contracepted through this program alone. In India, more than a million insertions of IUCD's are being made annually—in addition, the use of other methods of contraception is rising. In Colombia in Latin America, the oral pills and the IUCD both are being accepted at phenomenal rates; it is estimated that more than 120,000 couples in this nation of 18 million persons are using the oral pills alone; this is roughly 3 percent of the eligible population. In addition, large quantities of other methods are known to be used. In Santiago, Chile, the IUCD is so well known and widely used that it is a part of the medical service throughout the metropolitan area.

To summarize: wherever one looks in the underdeveloped segments of the world, one finds evidence of firmly established and flourishing family planning activity. By whatever crude estimates it is possible to make, it is quite clear that a sufficiently large share of the population already is making use of modern contraceptives to have a depressing effect upon the birth rate. Even conservative evaluation of the prospects suggests that *instead of a "population explosion" the world is on the threshold of a "contraceptive adoption explosion."* Because of lack of adequate vital statistics, the effects of this new "explosion" will not be readily measurable for a few years, but they will start to manifest themselves in the censuses of 1970 and will be most unmistakable in 1980.

IV

Given the situation that has just been described, what can be said concerning the future population of the world? If we insist on extrapolating past trends, we are making the unrealistic assertion that conditions have remained and will continue to remain unchanged. If we predict a slow change of the type that was typical of Europe and Northern America before 1960, we are implicitly asserting that the current programs are having zero effect: this assertion is contrary to fact. The course taken here has been to try to comprehend the nature of the change that is taking place, and to predict its probable course and speed, so that its impact may be guessed. As crude and subjective as this procedure is, it appears to offer more valid predictions than conventional population projections.

Looking at the developments listed above, realizing that they are only 5 years old or less, knowing that accomplishments in this area are cumulative and grow by exponential curves, and appreciating that new discoveries and improvements will accrue promptly along all fronts—medical, social, and psychological—both from basic research and from accumulating experience and evaluation —the following generalizations appear to be justified:

The trend of the worldwide movement toward fertility control has already reached a state where declines in death rates are being surpassed by declines in birthrates. Because progress in death control is slackening and progress in birth control is accelerating, the world has already entered a situation where the pace of population growth has begun to slacken. The exact time at which this "switch-over" took place cannot be known exactly, but we estimate it to have occurred about 1965. From 1965 onward, therefore, the rate of world population growth may be expected to decline with each passing year. The rate of growth will slacken at such a pace that it will be zero or near zero at about the year 2000, so that population growth will not be regarded as a major social problem except in isolated and small "retarded" areas.

In evaluating these conclusions, it must be kept in mind that the topic is a deadly serious one, and the penalties for misjudgment may be very great. There is one set of penalties that results from over-optimism. But there is another set of penalties that results from over-pessimism. It is quite possible that nothing has sapped the morale of family planning workers in the developing countries more than the Malthusian pessimism that has been radiated by many demographic reports. It is like assuring soldiers going into battle that they are almost certain to be defeated. If the comments made here should be so fortunate as to fall into the hands of these same family planning workers, it is hoped that those who read them will appreciate just how close they actually are to success. They have it within their grasp to improve dramatically their countries' fortunes. Coupled with the companion programs of industrialization and modernization, the effects could appear almost miraculous as they unfold in the 1970's and 1980's.

18 Man Adapting: His Limitations and Potentialities

RENÉ JULES DUBOS

W. D. Wallis once said, "Geographical environment is the cradle in which man's genius awaits the prompting of motives which give him mastery over his fate." But Wallis would seem by this statement to deny a role to environment in affecting man's behavior. Nor does Wallis tell us what it is that prompts man's motives to attempt "mastery over his fate," which still leaves unanswered many questions regarding the interrelationship of environment, culture, and society. In this selection Dubos examines the extent to which man really "masters" his environment and discusses the manner in which environmental factors (including the man-made ones) condition many aspects of human life.

Admittedly, the fact that modern man is constantly moving into new environments seems to indicate that he has enlarged the range of his biological adaptability and is escaping from the bondage of his past. But this is only an appearance. Wherever he goes, and whatever he does, man is successful only to the extent that he functions under environmental conditions not drastically different from the ones under which he evolved. He can climb Mount Everest and fly at high altitudes only because he has learned to protect himself against cold and to carry an adequate oxygen supply. He moves in outer space and at the bottom of the sea only if he remains within enclosures that duplicate certain physicochemical characteristics of the terrestrial environment. Even the Eskimos, who appear so well adapted to the Arctic winter, in reality cannot long resist intense cold. Sheltered in their igloos or clothed in their parkas, they live almost a tropical life!

Thus man does not really "master" the environment. What he does is to create sheltered environments within which he controls local conditions. Such control has been achieved for temperature, food, water, and oxygen tension, and a few other obvious physicochemical requirements. But human life is affected by many other factors that are poorly understood, and often not controllable at all. For example, the biological cycles mentioned earlier became inextricably woven in the human fabric during evolutionary times, and they still link modern man to cosmic events. The dissociation of modern life from these natural cycles is likely to exert some deleterious effects on the human organism. In fact, man is likely to suffer from many of the new environmental forces he has set in motion because he has not encountered them in his evolutionary past. He may develop some tolerance against environmental pollution, severe

SOURCE: William R. Ewald, Jr., ed., *Environment for Man: The Next Fifty Years* (Bloomington, Ind.: The Indiana University Press, 1967), pp. 15–22. • The author is professor of pathology at Rockefeller University. He has received the Howard Taylor Ricketts Award and the Science Achievement Award from the American Medical Association. His major interests include oxidations and reductions in bacterial cultures, bacteriology, tuberculosis, nutrition, and infection. He is author of *The White Plague–Tuberculosis, Man and Society; The Dreams of Reason; The Touch of Life;* and *Man Adapting.*

crowding, constant exposure to intense sensory stimuli, and the regimentation of life in a completely mechanized world. But one can anticipate that this tolerance will have deleterious consequences for the human race in the long run.

In brief, the genetic endowment of *Homo sapiens* has changed only in minor details since the Stone Age, and there is no chance that it can be significantly or usefully modified in the foreseeable future. This genetic stability defines the potentialities and requirements of man's nature. It also determines the physiological limits beyond which human life cannot be safely altered by social and technological innovations. The frontiers of technology are in final analysis less significant for the life of man than his own frontiers, which are determined by the genetic constitution he acquired during his evolutionary past.

THE POTENTIALITIES OF MAN

While the fundamental traits of *Homo sapiens* are permanent and universal, man's ways of life and the structures of his societies differ from one area to another and change endlessly with time. The biological evolution of man's body and mind almost came to a standstill some 50,000 years ago, but his sociocultural evolution now transforms human life at an accelerated rate.

Civilizations have their primary origin in the various responses to environmental stimuli. This versatility of response, in turn, is a consequence of the wide range of differences that exist among human beings. Except for identical twins, no two individual persons are genetically alike. Furthermore, the physical and psychic character of each person is profoundly influenced by environmental forces. From nutrition to education, from the topography of the land to urban design, countless influences play a role in determining the expression of the genetic endowment and thus in shaping the body and the mind of man.

Sociocultural forces are ultimately derived of course from man's biological nature, but through a feedback process they continuously alter his body, his mind, and his social patterns. This feedback accounts for the paradox that experiential man and his ways of life are continuously changing even though his genetic make-up is so remarkably stable.

Contrary to popular belief, genes do not determine the traits of a person; they merely govern his responses to the physical and social environment. Furthermore, not all the genes of a person are active at all times. Through complex mechanisms that are only now being recognized, environmental stimuli determine which parts of the genetic equipment are repressed and which parts are activated. Thus each individual person is as much the product of the environment as of his genetic endowment. Human beings perceive the world, and respond to it, not through the whole spectrum of their potentialities, but only through the areas of this spectrum that have been made functional by environmental stimulation. The life experiences determine what parts of the genetic endowment are converted into functional attributes.

The conditioning of the physical and mental personality by the environment has of course long been recognized. Winston Churchill was aware of its importance for human life when he urged that the House of Commons, damaged by German bombs during the war, be rebuilt as exactly as possible in its original form instead of being replaced by a modern and more efficient building. He feared that changing the physical appearance and organization of the House might alter the character of parliamentary debates and therefore of English democracy. In his words, "We shape our buildings and then they shape us."

The environment and ways of life determine in fact not only the conditions under which men function, but also the kind of persons their descendants will become. In fact, environmental factors have their most profound and most lasting effects when they impinge on the young organism during the formative phases of its development. Suffice it to mention as an example the acceleration in growth and in sexual development that is occurring at present in the Western world as well as in the Oriental countries that have become Westernized. Japanese teenagers are now very much taller than their parents not as a result of genetic changes, but probably because they are better protected against malnutrition and childhood infections.

The experiences of early life are of particular importance because the human body and especially the brain are incompletely differentiated at the time of birth. The infant develops his physical and mental individuality as he responds to the stimuli that impinge on him during growth. To a very large extent, the physical appearance and mental characteristics of the adult are thus the products of the responses made to the total environment during the formative years. In other words, anatomic structures and physical performance, as well as behavioral patterns, are molded by the surroundings and conditions of life during childhood; furthermore, the effects of such early influences commonly persist throughout the whole life span. For example, a child brought up in Florence is constantly exposed to the sights, sounds, and smells characteristic of this beautiful city; his development is conditioned by the stimuli derived from palaces, churches, and parks. He may not be aware of the responses aroused in him by these repeated experiences. But they become part of his biological make-up and render him lastingly different from what he would have become had he developed in London, Paris, or New York.

From all points of view, the child is truly the father of the man. Most aspects of human life are governed by a kind of biological Freudianism, because socially and individually, the responses of human beings to the conditions of the present are always conditioned by the biological remembrance of things past.

ENVIRONMENT FOR MAN

Each person has a wide range of innate potentialities that remain untapped. Whether physical or mental, these potentialities can become expressed only to the extent that circumstances are favorable to their existential manifestation. Society thus plays a large rule in the unfolding and development of man's nature.

One can take it for granted that the latent potentialities of human beings have a better chance to become actualized when the social environment is sufficiently diversified to provide a variety of stimulating experiences, especially for the young. As more persons find the opportunity to express their biological endowment under diversified conditions, society becomes richer in experiences and civilizations continue to unfold. In contrast, if the surroundings and ways of life are highly stereotyped, the only components of man's nature that flourish are those adapted to the narrow range of prevailing conditions.

The lesson to be derived from the story of biological evolution is that man has been so successful because he is the least specialized creature on earth; he is indeed the most adaptable. He can hunt or farm, be a meat eater or a vegetarian, live in the mountains or by the seashore, be a loner or engaged in teamwork, function in a free democracy or in a totalitarian state.

History shows, however, that societies which were once efficient because they were highly specialized rapidly collapsed when conditions changed. A highly specialized society is rarely adaptable. Adaptability is essential for social as well as for biological success. Therein lies the danger of the standardization and regimentation so prevalent in modern life. We must shun uniformity of environment as much as absolute conformity in behavior.

At the present time, unfortunately, the creeping monotony of our technological culture goes hand in hand with the monotony of our behavior, taste, patterns of education and of mass communication. And yet it is certain that we can exploit the richness of man's nature only if we make a deliberate effort to create as many diversified environments as possible. This may result in some loss of efficiency, but the more important goal is to provide the many kinds of soil that will permit the germination of the seeds now dormant in man's nature. Diversity of social environment constitutes in fact a crucial aspect of functionalism, whether in the planning of cities, the design of dwellings, or the management of life. So far as possible, the duplication of uniformity must yield to the organization of diversity.

Irrespective of genetic endowment, a child who grows in a city slum will differ as an adult from one who has spent most of his life within the sheltering cocoon of a modern apartment house, or from one who has participated in the chores of a family farm. Unfortunately, awareness of the fact that surroundings exert a profound effect on human life is based largely on untutored observations and has not yet been converted into scientific knowledge.

Environmental factors obviously condition all aspects of human life, but nobody really knows which factors are influential or how they work. The problem, however, is not hopeless. Experiments have revealed that in animals, also, early influences condition growth, longevity, behavior, resistance to stress, and learning ability. The effects exerted on human life by early influences can therefore be studied through the use of experimental models, much as is being done for other types of biological problem. The knowledge thus acquired will certainly help in the rational management of society.

The population avalanche and the universal trend toward urbanization will, needless to say, affect all aspects of future life. By the end of this century, most human beings will be born, will live, and will reproduce within the confines of megalopolis. Until now, cities have constantly grown and renewed themselves through the influx of people originating from rural areas or from primitive countries. Very soon, however, and for the first time in history, this transfusion of new blood will come to an end; the human race will reproduce itself almost exclusively out of persons city-born and city-bred. To a very large extent, the future will therefore depend upon our ability to create urban environments having the proper biological qualities.

• • • • •

. . . Human beings can become adapted to almost anything—polluted air, treeless avenues, starless skies, aggressive behavior, the rat-race of overcompetitive societies, even life in concentration camps. But in one way or another, we have to pay later for the adjustment we make to undesirable conditions. The cost includes for example increase in chronic diseases and decadence of human values. Congested environments, even though polluted, ugly, and heartless, are compatible with economic growth and with political power. But they damage the physical and spiritual aspects of human life.

The adaptability of human beings to environments that are compatible with organic life, but destructive of human values, creates difficult problems for community planning. We have to determine simultaneously on the one hand the kind and intensity of stimulation required for individual and social development; on the other hand, the levels of stimulation and adaptation that are potentially dangerous for the future.

In brief, it is obvious that the technological factors, such as supplies of food, power, or natural resources, that are required for the operation of the body machine and of the industrial establishment are not the only factors to be considered in determining optimum population size. Just as important for maintaining *human* life is an environment in which it is possible to satisfy the longing for quiet, privacy, independence, initiative, and open space. These are not frills or luxuries but constitute real biological necessities. They will be in short supply long before there is a critical shortage of the sources of energy and materials that keep the human machine going and industry expanding.

19 Murder in Eden or the New Dogma of Man's Origin

ROBERT ASCHER

The contemporary concern over man's cruelty and over war has led to a renewed interest in man's origin as a possible explanation for his behavior. Several writers have postulated that belligerence as well as similar human behavior is a direct result of genetic forces continuing from the earlier evolutionary stages in man's origin. In the following selection, Ascher examines the validity of these postulations as presented by Ardrey and Lorenz. His examination presents alternate explanations that cast doubt on the easier generalizations, which derive from the hypothesis that man is like other animals and that his behavior is thus genetically determined.

In the opening episode of the film 2001–A Space Odyssey, the emergence of man is depicted in cineomatic splendor. We first see a band of very hairy, glassy-eyed primates scrounging in a bone bed. Next, a member of the band turns his head as if to announce an idea. After some intermediary grunting, the entire band, now all armed with bones, is seen attacking a neighboring band. The neighbors have no implements and are quickly routed. It is made clear to the moviegoer that through these acts proto-man becomes man.

SOURCE: *The Cornell Plantations,* vol. 26, no. 1 (Spring 1970), 7–11. Reprinted by permission of the publisher. • Robert Ascher is professor of anthropology and archaeology at Cornell University. His major interests include anthropological and archaeological theory and method and biocultural evolution. He has written articles for *Science, The American Anthropologist,* and *The American Scientist.*

Can this be passed off as just a Hollywood version of how man got started? I think not. Prior to the showing of 2001, increasing numbers of people conceived of man's origin in a way realized in the movie. Moreover, many believed that there was strong evidence to support the Hollywood version, or something like it. Although details vary, the crucial act is ever present: man is born in violence as one primate (or group of primates) armed with implements attacks another primate (or group of primates).

After hearing this gory tale told several times, I probed for its sources. I was most often directed to Ardrey's *African Genesis*, and to *On Aggression* by Konrad Lorenz. I examined these sources: here are examples of what I found. First, from Ardrey: "Far from the truth lay the antique assumption that man had fathered the weapon. The weapon, instead, had fathered man." Turning to Lorenz, we read: "There is evidence that the first inventors of pebble tools, the African Australopithecines promptly used their new weapon to kill not only game, but fellow members of their own species as well." In short, I found that the theme for the human origins episode in 2001 could have been taken from notions in these books.

Nowadays many people write freely about human origins. Everyone knows this was not always the case. Before Darwin, the bible set the outer boundaries for the discussion. Man is more than a hundred years older now, and those upsetting issues about science and religion are supposedly resolved. Why then should one be concerned with a certain twist in the story of human origins? Mainly because the newer version seeks to account for mankind's present behavior in an unacceptable manner. In this essay, I concentrate on crucial evidence for the thesis, namely the nature and use of man's first artifacts.

To begin, suppose we uncritically go along with those who are convinced that man was born in violence. Taking this path, where does it end up? We recall the statement from Ardrey cited above and follow it to the end of the paragraph. "Far from the truth lay the antique assumption that man had fathered the weapon. The weapon, instead, had fathered man." And Ardrey immediately adds: "The mightiest predators had come about as the logical conclusion to an evolutionary transition. With his big brain and his stone handaxes, man annihilated a predecessor who fought only with bones. And if all human history from that date has turned on the development of superior weapons, then it is for very sound reason. It is for genetic necessity." Violent episodes, together with such diverse happenings as the present armaments race and the rise of Hitler youth can be accounted for by what Ardrey variably calls "genetic necessity," or "animal instincts," or "drive." Ardrey clearly means to say that today we act violently toward one another in the sense that we cannot elect to do otherwise. All is determined by our animal ancestry in general, and in particular by "the legacy bequeathed us by those killer apes, our immediate forebears."

One might unfairly dismiss *African Genesis* as the work of a man without proper scientific credentials. Few would dispute the credentials of Konrad Lorenz. Referring to recent events, Lorenz hopes to explain events such as the dropping of bombs ". . . on sleeping cities, thereby committing hundreds and thousands of children to a horrible death in the flame" by "perfectly good-natured men who would not even smack a naughty child." Incidents like these are "amazing paradoxes," says Lorenz. But, he explains, they fall into place ". . . like the pieces of a jigsaw puzzle, if one assumes that human behavior, and particularly social behavior, far from being determined by reason and cultural tradition alone, is still subject to all the laws prevailing in all phylogenetically adapted instinctive behavior." Our problem started, according to Lorenz, when our vegetable-loving ancestors first used tools. Immediately, as evolutionary time goes, they began to hunt and eat meat. Having none of the natural inhibitions of meat eaters, they became unnaturally aggressive, and killed and even ate one another. There are differences between Ardrey and Lorenz, but on these two essentials they agree (a) man originated in violence, and (b) since we are tied to our origins, we are necessarily violent.

I am not of course the first to discuss *On Aggression* and *African Genesis*. Some reviews imply that the books are appealing because the ideas expressed in them are useful. Let us consider just how the ideas may be used according to those who write in this vein.

There is much aggression in the world, the argument goes, and we do not understand why this should be so. Ardrey and Lorenz have an answer that is direct and requires nothing from us. "It is easy," writes one reviewer, "to accept the idea of an instinctive cause for man's aggression for that explains everything." The answer of Ardrey and Lorenz is not only useful for explaining everything; it works equally well on particular things. Specifically, it has been applied to the Vietnam war, as follows:

"A line of argument like that of Ardrey's, therefore, seems to legitimate our present morality, in regarding the threat system as dominant at all costs, by reference to our biological ancestors. If the names of both antiquity and science can be drawn upon to legitimate our behavior, the moral uneasiness about napalm and the massacre of the innocent in Vietnam may be assuaged." Neither you, nor I, nor the commentators cited above really know how anyone uses the ideas found in these books. The alleged wide readership may reside more in literary merit than in ideology. It may be, as another commentator says, that the works of Ardrey and Lorenz are popular because many people enjoy reading about animals. In any case, if the scientific foundation is difficult to accept, so will be any application dangled from it. It is from two disciplines—ethology and anthropology—that the scientific argument of Ardrey and Lorenz is drawn.

The contribution from ethology is based upon an operation I call *beastomorphizing*. This word is not in the dictionary, so I will describe it by reference to a word that is in the dictionary, namely anthropomorphizing. When one attributes human characteristics to a non-human animal, he is anthropomorphizing. Doing the same thing in the opposite direction, that is, attributing animal characteristics to humans, is beastomorphizing.

The scientific vocabulary of Ardrey and Lorenz includes the term anthropomorphize. I counted five appearances of it in *On Aggression*, and it occurs at least four times in *African Genesis*. It is usually accompanied with the statement that the author knows better than to do this wrong-headed kind of thing. Beastomorphizing is an entirely different matter: it is advanced as a pathway to truth. So much is this the case that one need only describe some particular behavior pattern such as of wild geese. The similarities to human patterns are then clear, and further argument would be, to use Lorenz's term, "superfluous." In this same mode, Ardrey tells us that the ". . . animal foundation for that form of human misconduct known as war, is so obvious as to demand small attention."

This marks an unusual departure in

scientific method. The connection between a caged rat, an aquarium fish, and me is not self-evident. It is no easy matter to show that the three of us need oxygen to live, or that we are more closely related to each other than any one of us is related to an ant. To establish the connection between behaviors, one must specifically demonstrate the connection, not simply place them side by side. Those who see a man in the face of a dog are no worse off than those who see a dog in the face of a man. That is to say, beastomorphizing is as suspect as anthropomorphizing.

In the literature, the ethology of Ardrey and Lorenz is picked apart rather fully; by contrast, their anthropology is neglected. The best guess as to why this is so is that few commentators know the available hard evidence concerning man's origin. Instead of confronting the Ardrey-Lorenz origin story point-for-point, I offer a background to help the reader formulate an independent judgment.

A familiar, if minimal, portrait of early man contains four elements: a cave, an artifact, a man, and a source of food. Usually the man is shown peering off into the distance in search of game. This portrait is, first of all, historically significant. The evidence that led to the fall of the literal interpretation of the bible consisted of finding in the same geological deposit, in close association, three kinds of things: the bones of extinct animals, the bones of men, and materials shaped by men. All of the elements could be found, in association as far back as forty thousand years ago, thus extending man's presence on earth ten times that allowed under the biblical model. However, the association is not as common as is often supposed. It is therefore fortunate that enough examples of it were discovered to convince nineteenth-century man of the antiquity of his descent.

The portrait also serves to illustrate how evidence changes with time. The first substantial evidence for the use of caves by man occurs half a million years ago. If we want a portrait prior to that time, we remove the cave. As we move backwards to about one-half million years ago, we pass three species of the genus *Homo*. The man at the cave entrance continuously changes in detail. For example, moving backwards at first he has a chin and then he has none. Toward the two million years mark, we need to choose some form of our ancestor to represent our closest relative. Interpretation of much of the fossil evidence in the last decade is confused; whatever the choice, there will be a clatter of dissent. How much of the man to draw in independent of the kind of man drawn. The bone is the same, whether it be a femur of *Homo erectus* or *Homo sapiens*. The rule is simple: the further back in time, the less there is likely to be. The food source in the portrait is subject to the same rule of decay, and if the source were not attached to a bony skeleton, the chance of its survival as evidence would be close to zero. We can now redraw a portrait that more closely approximates earliest man: this second version consists of a few scraps of animal and human bone and an artifact. Let us focus down on the artifact.

An early man made many things in his lifetime and he dropped them over a wide area. By contrast, one man has one skeleton and this he deposits in one place. The things men made were often fashioned from durable material and they outlasted their maker's bones. The abundance, distribution, and material of man's workmanship should make artifacts the best source for reconstructing behavior. Yet, as we approach our expected origin, it becomes increasingly difficult to tell whether something is or is not an artifact. This is particularly the case if questionable specimens are found in places where auxiliary clues are hard or impossible to find. For example, on an open plain the bones of men and animals are often absent, and the materials shaped by men are mixed with materials altered by natural agencies alone. If artifacts occur in such a setting, they will be outnumbered by hundreds of thousands of similar-looking objects. The expectation is that the earlier the artifact, the simpler it will be. The simpler it is, the more like naturally broken materials it will be. There should be verifiable ways to distinguish a bone or a rock fractured by a man from one that has been changed by other means such as rolling in a rapid stream. Right now, authoritative pronouncement decides the issue, although the first steps away from this have been taken. What if we decide that something was made by man? The next question is: what was it used for? The means for deciding this issue are slightly better than those employed to determine whether something was made by man, but any as-to-use inference is only one of many possibilities. We redraw the portrait of earliest man once again, this time adding something. In the third and final version, there are a few scraps of bone and a broken rock with a question mark on it. It is from evidence such as this that stories about man's origin are woven.

The foregoing provides minimal critical equipment for examining notions about man's origin, violent or otherwise. Let us finally consider a few alternate ways of thinking about the evidence, in particular the cultural evidence. Coda: another piece of critical equipment.

For generations, people thought that simply shaped stones were made in heaven. Michel Mercatus, physician to Pope Clement VIII wrote: "Some people carry them as a protection against lightning, and believe that this power derives from the fact that they are hurled down by the lightning. But it is the place *where* they fall that receives such immunity, and this is a matter of pure chance." This view was recorded sometime before 1590. Modern men call these same rocks artifacts and say that they were made on earth. However, it is still possible to look at the same thing and see different things. J. B. S. Haldane looked at the first one hundred thousand years of stone tools and thought that they might have been made by instinct in the same way, to use his analogy, as spiders weave webs. V. G. Childe looked at somewhat later specimens and thought they showed an implicit knowledge of cause and effect. Childe discovered the origins of scientific thought in stone tools. Robert Ardrey looked at the same things Mercatus, Haldane, and Childe looked at before him, and Ardrey says that ". . . they reveal the continuity of developments in man's cultural efforts is not truly that of the tool; it is that of the weapon."

In her lectures on Stonehenge, Jacquette Hawkes shows sketches of that famous and complex artifact done at different times. In the romantic era, the stones are jagged; in classical times, stones were drawn with smooth lines. "Every age," concludes Miss Hawkes, "has the Stonehenge it deserves—or desires."

A case could be made for the idea that man's early artifacts are more related to aesthetics than to aggression. Early workmanship shows a scarcity in design that compares favorably with many modern concepts of the beautiful. Later artifacts show elaboration that reached beyond any practical functions. These specimens fit yet another concept of the beautiful. Were these shaped stones really weapons that led to the irresistible built-in need to kill members of our own species? Answered directly, thoughts about earliest man and his way of life are mostly reflections of our particular vision of man.

CHAPTER III

PERSON AND GROUP

20 Final Note on a Case of Extreme Isolation

KINGSLEY DAVIS

For centuries there have been reports of children who were raised by animals or in some other way managed to live in complete isolation from human beings. If such feral men could be found, they would have great significance for social science, since they would provide a crucial means of determining the nature and extent of sociocultural influence on human behavior. Investigation of all reported cases has, however, shown them to have little validity and to be heavily laden with myth and rumor. It is highly doubtful if any child ever lived without at least some *human association. In recent years, however, a few verified instances have been found in which extremely limited association with humans has occurred. Kingsley Davis gives here his final report on such a case and makes some comparisons between the child, Anna, and another child, Isabelle, who lived under similar circumstances. One cannot be sure to what extent Anna's failure to achieve the level of socialization of a normal ten-year-old was due to organic deficiency. Clearly, however, a tremendous change took place in her behavior after the isolation was ended. It seems certain that many typically human behavior patterns were not achieved until Anna was able to associate with other humans from whom she could learn such behavior.*

Early in 1940 there appeared . . . an account of a girl called Anna.[1] She had been deprived of normal contact and had received a minimum of human care for almost the whole of her first six years of life. At that time observations were not complete and the report had a tentative character. Now, however, the girl is dead, and, with more information available, it is possible to give a fuller and more definitive description of the case from a sociological point of view.

Anna's death, caused by hemorrhagic jaundice, occurred on August 6, 1942. Having been born on March 1 or 6, 1932, she was approximately ten and a half years of age when she died. The previous report covered her development up to the

[1] Kingsley Davis, "Extreme Social Isolation of a Child," *American Journal of Sociology,* XLV (January 1940), 554–65.

SOURCE: *The American Journal of Sociology,* vol. 52, no. 5 (March 1947), 432–37. Reprinted by permission of the University of Chicago Press and the author. • The author is professor of sociology and Director of International Population and Urban Research at the University of California, Berkeley, and chairman of the National Research Council's Behavioral Science Division. He is past president of the American Sociological Association and has served as United States representative to the Population Commission of the United Nations. His main interests are population, urbanization, and family. Among his books are *Youth in Depression, Human Society,* and *The Pattern of World Urbanization.*

age of almost eight years; the present one recapitulates the earlier period on the basis of new evidence and then covers the last two and a half years of her life.

EARLY HISTORY

The first few days and weeks of Anna's life were complicated by frequent changes of domicile. It will be recalled that she was an illegitimate child, the second such child born to her mother, and that her grandfather, a widowed farmer in whose house her mother lived, strongly disapproved of this new evidence of the mother's indiscretion. This fact led to the baby's being shifted about.

Two weeks after being born in a nurse's private home, Anna was brought to the family farm, but the grandfather's antagonism was so great that she was shortly taken to the house of one of her mother's friends. At this time a local minister became interested in her and took her to his house with an idea of possible adoption. He decided against adoption, however, when he discovered that she had vaginitis. The infant was then taken to a children's home in the nearest large city. This agency found that at the age of only three weeks she was already in a miserable condition, being "terribly galled and otherwise in very bad shape." It did not regard her as a likely subject for adoption but took her in for a while anyway, hoping to benefit her. After Anna had spent nearly eight weeks in this place, the agency notified her mother to come to get her. The mother responded by sending a man and his wife to the children's home with a view to their adopting Anna, but they made such a poor impression on the agency that permission was refused. Later the mother came herself and took the child out of the home and then gave her to this couple. It was in the home of this pair that a social worker found the girl a short time thereafter. The social worker went to the mother's home and pleaded with Anna's grandfather to allow the mother to bring the child home. In spite of threats, he refused. The child, by then more than four months old, was next taken to another children's home in a near-by town. A medical examination at this time revealed that she had impetigo, vaginitis, umbilical hernia, and a skin rash.

Anna remained in this second children's home for nearly three weeks, at the end of which time she was transferred to a private foster-home. Since, however, the grandfather would not, and the mother could not, pay for the child's care, she was finally taken back as a last resort to the grandfather's house (at the age of five and a half months). There she remained, kept on the second floor in an attic-like room because her mother hesitated to incur the grandfather's wrath by bringing her downstairs.

The mother, a sturdy woman weighing about 180 pounds, did a man's work on the farm. She engaged in heavy work such as milking cows and tending hogs and had little time for her children. Sometimes she went out at night, in which case Anna was left entirely without attention. Ordinarily, it seems, Anna received only enough care to keep her barely alive. She appears to have been seldom moved from one position to another. Her clothing and bedding were filthy. She apparently had no instruction, no friendly attention.

It is little wonder that, when finally found and removed from the room in the grandfather's house at the age of nearly six years, the child could not talk, walk, or do anything that showed intelligence. She was in an extremely emaciated and undernourished condition, with skeleton-like legs and a bloated abdomen. She had been fed on virtually nothing except cow's milk during the years under her mother's care.

Anna's condition when found, and her subsequent improvement, have been described in the previous report. It now remains to say what happened to her after that.

LATER HISTORY

In 1939, nearly two years after being discovered, Anna had progressed, as previously reported, to the point where she could walk, understand simple commands, feed herself, achieve some neatness, remember people, etc. But she still did not speak, and, though she was much more like a normal infant of something over one year of age in mentality, she was far from normal for her age.

On August 30, 1939, she was taken to a private home for retarded children, leaving the county home where she had been for more than a year and a half. In her new setting she made some further progress, but not a great deal. In a report of an examination made November 6 of the same year, the head of the institution pictured the child as follows:

> Anna walks about aimlessly, makes periodic rhythmic motions of her hands, and, at intervals, makes guttural and sucking noises. She regards her hands as if she had seen them for the first time. It was impossible to hold her attention for more than a few seconds at a time—not because of distraction due to external stimuli but because of her inability to concentrate. She ignored the task in hand to gaze vacantly about the room. Speech is entirely lacking. Numerous unsuccessful attempts have been made with her in the hope of developing initial sounds. I do not believe that this failure is due to negativism or deafness but that she is not sufficiently developed to accept speech at this time. . . . The prognosis is not favorable. . . .

More than five months later, on April 25, 1940, a clinical psychologist, the late Professor Francis N. Maxfield, examined Anna and reported the following: large for her age; hearing "entirely normal"; vision apparently normal; able to climb stairs; speech in the "babbling stage" and "promise for developing intelligible speech later seems to be good." He said further that "on the Merrill-Palmer scale she made a mental score of 19 months. On the Vineland social maturity scale she made a score of 23 months."

Professor Maxfield very sensibly pointed out that prognosis is difficult in such case of isolation. "It is very difficult to take scores on tests standardized under average conditions of environment and experience," he wrote, "and interpret them in a case where environment and experience have been so unusual." With this warning he gave it as his opinion at that time that Anna would eventually "attain an adult mental level of six or seven years."

The school for retarded children, on July 1, 1941, reported that Anna had reached 46 inches in height and weighed 60 pounds. She could bounce and catch a ball and was said to conform to group socialization, though as a follower rather than a leader. Toilet habits were firmly established. Food habits were normal, except that she still used a spoon as her sole implement. She could dress herself except for fastening her clothes. Most remarkable of all, she had finally begun to develop speech. She was characterized as being at about the two-year level in this regard. She could call attendants by name and bring in one when she was asked to. She had a few complete sentences to express her wants. The report concluded that there was nothing peculiar about her, except that she was feeble-minded—"probably congenital in type."

A final report from the school, made on June 22, 1942, and evidently the last report before the girl's death, pictured only a slight advance over that given above. It said that Anna could follow directions, string beads, identify a few colors, build with blocks, and differentiate between attractive and unattractive pictures. She had a good sense of rhythm and loved a doll. She talked mainly in phrases but would repeat words and try to carry on a conversation. She was clean about clothing. She habitually washed her hands and brushed her teeth. She would try to help other children. She walked well and could run fairly well, though clumsily. Although easily excited, she had a pleasant disposition.

INTERPRETATION

Such was Anna's condition just before her death. It may seem as if she had not made much progress, but one must remember the condition in which she had been found. One must recall that she had no glimmering of speech, absolutely no ability to walk, no sense of gesture, not the least capacity to feed herself even when the food was put in front of her, and no comprehension of cleanliness. She was so apathetic that it was hard to tell whether or not she could hear. And all this at the age of nearly six years. Compared with this condition, her capacities at the time of her death seem striking indeed, though they do not amount to much more than a two-and-a-half-year mental level. One conclusion therefore seems safe, namely, that her isolation prevented a considerable amount of mental development that was undoubtedly part of her capacity. Just what her original capacity was, of course, is hard to say; but her development after her period of confinement (including the ability to walk and run, to play, dress, fit into a social situation, and, above all, to speak) shows that she had at least this much capacity—capacity that never could have been realized in her original condition of isolation.

A further question is this: What would she have been like if she had received a normal upbringing from the moment of birth? A definitive answer would have been impossible in any case, but even an approximate answer is made difficult by her early death. If one assumes, as was tentatively surmised in the previous report, that it is "almost impossible for any child to learn to speak, think, and act like a normal person after a long period of early isolation," it seems likely that Anna might have had a normal or near-normal capacity, genetically speaking. On the other hand, it was pointed out that Anna represented "a marginal case, [because] she was discovered before she had reached six years of age," an age "young enough to allow for some plasticity." While admitting, then, that Anna's isolation *may* have been the major cause (and was certainly a minor cause) of her lack of rapid mental progress during the four and a half years following her rescue from neglect, it is necessary to entertain the hypothesis that she was congenitally deficient.

In connection with this hypothesis, one suggestive though by no means conclusive circumstance needs consideration, namely, the mentality of Anna's forebears. Information on this subject is easier to obtain, as one might guess, on the mother's than on the father's side. Anna's maternal grandmother, for example, is said to have been college educated and wished to have her children receive a good education, but her husband, Anna's stern grandfather, apparently a shrewd, hard-driving, calculating farmowner, was so penurious that her ambitions in this direction were thwarted. Under the circumstances her daughter (Anna's mother) managed, despite having to do hard work on the farm, to complete the eighth grade in a country school. Even so, however, the daughter was evidently not very smart. "A schoolmate of [Anna's mother] stated that she was retarded in school work; was very gullible at this age; and that her morals even at this time were discussed by other students." Two tests administered to her on March 4, 1938, when she was thirty-two years of age, showed that she was mentally deficient. On the Stanford Revision of the Binet-Simon Scale her performance was equivalent to that of a child of eight years, giving her an I.Q. of 50 and indicating mental deficiency of "middle-grade moron type."

As to the identity of Anna's father, the most persistent theory holds that he was an old man about seventy-four years of age at the time of the girl's birth. If he was the one, there is no indication of mental or other biological deficiency, whatever one may think of his morals. However, someone else may actually have been the father.

To sum up: Anna's heredity is the kind that *might* have given rise to innate mental deficiency, though not necessarily.

COMPARISON WITH ANOTHER CASE

Perhaps more to the point than speculations about Anna's ancestry would be a case for comparison. If a child could be discovered who had been isolated about the same length of time as Anna but had achieved a much quicker recovery and a greater mental development, it would be a stronger indication that Anna was deficient to start with.

Such a case does exist. It is the case of a girl found at about the same time as Anna and under strikingly similar circumstances. A full description of the details of this case has not been published, but, in addition to newspaper reports, an excellent preliminary account by a speech specialist, Dr. Marie K. Mason, who played an important role in the handling of the child, has appeared. Also the late Dr. Francis N. Maxfield, clinical psychologist at Ohio State University, as was Dr. Mason, has written an as yet unpublished but penetrating analysis of the case. Some of his observations have been included in Professor Zingg's book on feral man. The following discussion is drawn mainly from these enlightening materials. The writer, through the kindness of Professors Mason and Maxfield, did have a chance to observe the girl in April, 1940, and to discuss the features of her case with them.

Born apparently one month later than Anna, the girl in question, who has been given the pseudonym Isabelle, was discovered in November, 1938, nine months after the discovery of Anna. At the time she was found she was approximately six and a half years of age. Like Anna, she was an illegitimate child and had been kept in seclusion for that reason. Her mother was a deaf-mute, having become so at the age of two, and it appears that she and Isabelle had spent most of their time together in a dark room shut off from the rest of the mother's family. As a result Isabelle had no chance to develop speech; when she communicated with her mother, it was by means of gestures. Lack of sunshine and inadequacy of diet had caused Isabelle to become rachitic. Her legs in particular were affected; they "were so bowed that as she stood erect the soles of her shoes came nearly flat together, and she got about with a skittering gait." Her behavior toward strangers, especially men, was almost that of a wild animal, manifesting much fear and hostility. In lieu of speech she made only a strange croaking sound. In many ways she acted like an infant. "She was apparently utterly unaware of relationships of any kind. When presented with a ball for the first time, she held it in the palm of her hand, then reached out and stroked my face with it. Such behavior is comparable to that of a child of six months." At first it was even hard to tell whether or not she could hear, so unused were her senses. Many of her actions resembled those of deaf children.

It is small wonder that, once it was established that she could hear, specialists working with her believed her to be feeble-minded. Even on nonverbal tests her performance was so low as to promise little for the future. Her first score on the Stanford-Binet was 19 months, practically at the zero point of the scale. On the Vineland social maturity scale her first score was 39, representing an age level of two and a half years. "The general impression was that she was wholly uneducable and that any attempt to teach her to speak, after so long a period of silence, would meet with failure."

In spite of this interpretation, the individuals in charge of Isabelle launched a systematic and skillful program of training. It seemed hopeless at first. The approach had to be through pantomime and dramatization, suitable to an infant. It required one week of intensive effort before she even made her first attempt at vocalization. Gradually she began to respond, however, and, after the first hurdles had at last been overcome, a curious thing happened. She went through the usual stages of learning characteristic of the years from one to six not only in proper succession but far more rapidly than normal. In a little over two months after her first vocalization she was putting sentences together. Nine months after that she could identify words and sentences on the printed page, could write well, could add to ten, and could retell a story after hearing it. Seven months beyond this point she had a vocabulary of 1,500–2,000 words and was asking complicated questions. Starting from an educational level of between one and three years (depending on what aspect one considers), she had reached a normal level by the time she was eight and a half years old. In short, she covered in two years the stages of learning that ordinarily require six. Or, to put it another way, her I.Q. trebled in a year and a half. The speed with which she reached the normal level of mental development seems analogous to the recovery of body weight in a growing child after an illness, the recovery being achieved by an extra fast rate of growth for a period after the illness until normal weight for the given age is again attained.

When the writer saw Isabelle a year and a half after her discovery, she gave him the impression of being a very bright, cheerful, energetic little girl. She spoke well, walked and ran without trouble, and sang with gusto and accuracy. Today she is over fourteen years old and has passed the sixth grade in a public school. Her teachers say that she participates in all school activities as normally as other children. Though older than her classmates, she has fortunately not physically matured too far beyond their level.

Clearly the history of Isabelle's development is different from that of Anna's. In both cases there was an exceedingly low, or rather blank, intellectual level to begin with. In both cases it seemed that the girl might be congenitally feeble-minded. In both a considerably higher level was reached later on. But the Ohio girl achieved a normal mentality within two years, whereas Anna was still markedly inadequate at the end of four and a half years. This difference in achievement may suggest that Anna had less initial capacity. But an alternative hypothesis is possible.

One should remember that Anna never received the prolonged and expert attention that Isabelle received. The result of such attention, in the case of the Ohio girl, was to give her speech at an early stage, and her subsequent rapid development seems to have been a consequence of that. "Until Isabelle's speech and language development, she had all the characteristics of a feeble-minded child." Had Anna, who, from the standpoint of psychometric tests and early history, closely resembled this girl at the start, been given a mastery of speech at an earlier point by intensive training, her subsequent development might have been much more rapid.

The hypothesis that Anna began with a sharply inferior mental capacity is therefore not established. Even if she were deficient to start with, we have no way of knowing how much so. Under ordinary conditions she might have been a dull normal or, like her mother, a moron. Even after the blight of her isolation, if she had lived to maturity, she might have finally reached virtually the full level of her capacity, whatever it may have been. That her isolation did have a profound effect upon her mentality, there can be no doubt. This is proved by the substantial degree of change during the four and a half years following her rescue.

Consideration of Isabelle's case serves to show, as Anna's case does not clearly show, that isolation up to the age of six, with failure to acquire any form of speech and hence failure to grasp nearly the whole world of cultural meaning, does not preclude the subsequent acquisition of these. Indeed, there seems to be a process of accelerated recovery in which the child goes through the mental stages at a more rapid rate than would be the case in normal development. Just what would be the maximum age at which a person could remain isolated and still retain the capacity for full cultural acquisition is hard to say. Almost certainly it would not be as high as age fifteen; it might possibly be as low as age ten. Undoubtedly various individuals would differ considerably as to the exact age.

Anna's is not an ideal case for showing the effects of extreme isolation, partly because she was possibly deficient to begin with, partly because she did not receive the best training available, and partly because she did not live long enough. Nevertheless, her case is instructive when placed in the record with numerous other cases of extreme isolation. This and the previous article about her are meant to place her in the record. It is to be hoped that other cases will be described in the scientific literature as they are discovered (as unfortunately they will be), for only in these rare cases of extreme isolation is it possible "to observe *concretely separated* two factors in the development of human personality which are always otherwise only analytically separated, the biogenic and the sociogenic factors."

21 Killers of the Dream: When I Was a Child

LILLIAN SMITH

The previous selection illustrates the importance of association with other human beings in the development of human personality. Since the transmission to children of human habits, attitudes, and beliefs begins very early, and goes on constantly in every family, school, and other groups, we are often not keenly aware of this pervasive social process. In this selection Lillian Smith reveals, with sensitivity and candor, how she was taught a particular pattern of behavior and attitudes considered appropriate for white southern Christian girls of her generation.

Even its children knew that the South was in trouble. No one had to tell them; no words said aloud. To them, it was a vague thing weaving in and out of their play, like a ghost haunting an old graveyard or whispers after the household sleeps—fleeting mystery, vague menace to which each responded in his own way. Some learned to screen out all except the soft and the soothing; others denied even as they saw plainly, and heard. But all knew that under quiet words and warmth and laughter, under the slow ease and tender concern about small matters, there was a heavy burden on all of us and as heavy a refusal to confess it. The children knew this "trouble" was bigger than they, bigger than their family, bigger than their church, so big that people turned away from its size. They had seen it flash out and shatter a town's peace, had felt it tear up all they believed in. They had measured its giant strength and felt weak when they remembered.

SOURCE: Reprinted from *Killers of the Dream* (revised and enlarged), 15–28 passim, by Lillian Smith. By permission of W. W. Norton & Company, Inc. • The author (1897–1966), a novelist, held honorary doctorate degrees from Oberlin College and Howard University. During her early career, she was principal of a two-teacher mountain school and later spent three years in China teaching music at a private school. For ten years she was editor and publisher of *South Today.* In 1950 she was granted the Southern Author's Award and also a Special Citation for Distinguished Contribution to American Letters by the National Book Award Committee. Her books include *Strange Fruit, One Hour, The Journey,* and *Now Is the Time.*

This haunted childhood belongs to every southerner of my age. We ran away from it but we came back like a hurt animal to its wound, or a murderer to the scene of his sin. The human heart dares not stay away too long from that which hurt it most. There is a return journey to anguish that few of us are released from making.

. . . . .

The mother who taught me what I know of tenderness and love and compassion taught me also the bleak rituals of keeping Negroes in their "place." The father who rebuked me for an air of superiority toward schoolmates from the mill and rounded out his rebuke by gravely reminding me that "all men are brothers," trained me in the steel-rigid decorums I must demand of every colored male. They who so gravely taught me to split my body from my mind and both from my "soul," taught me also to split my conscience from my acts and Christianity from southern tradition.

Neither the Negro nor sex was often

discussed at length in our home. We were given no formal instruction in these difficult matters but we learned our lessons well. We learned the intricate system of taboos, of renunciations and compensations, of manners, voice modulations, words, feelings, along with our prayers, our toilet habits, and our games. I do not remember how or when, but by the time I had learned that God is love, that Jesus is His Son and came to give us more abundant life, that all men are brothers with a common Father, I also knew that I was better than a Negro, that all black folks have their place and must be kept in it, that sex has its place and must be kept in it, that a terrifying disaster would befall the South if ever I treated a Negro as my social equal and as terrifying a disaster would befall my family if ever I were to have a baby outside of marrriage. I had learned that God so loved the world that He gave His only begotten Son so that we might have segregated churches in which it was my duty to worship each Sunday and on Wednesday at evening prayers. I had learned that while southerners are a hospitable, courteous, tactful people who treat those of their own group with consideration and who as carefully segregate from all the richness of life "for their own good and welfare" thirteen million people whose skin is colored a little differently from my own.

I knew by the time I was twelve that a member of my family would always shake hands with old Negro friends, would speak graciously to members of the Negro race unless they forgot their place, in which event icy peremptory tones would draw lines beyond which only the desperate would dare take one step. I knew that to use the word "nigger" was unpardonable and no well-bred southerner was quite so crude as to do so; nor would a well-bred southerner call a Negro "mister" or invite him into the living room or eat with him or sit by him in public places.

I knew that my old nurse who had cared for me through long months of illness, who had given me refuge when a little sister took my place as the baby of the family, who soothed, fed me, delighted me with her stories and games, let me fall asleep on her deep warm breast, was not worthy of the passionate love I felt for her but must be given instead a half-smiled-at affection similar to that which one feels for one's dog. I knew but I never believed it, that the deep respect I felt for her, the tenderness, the love, was a childish thing which every normal child outgrows, that such love begins with one's toys and is discarded with them, and that somehow—though it seemed impossible to my agonized heart—I too, must outgrow these feelings. I learned to use a soft voice to oil my words of superiority. I learned to cheapen with tears and sentimental talk of "my old mammy" one of the profound relationships of my life. I learned the bitterest thing a child can learn: that the human relations I valued most were held cheap by the world I lived in.

From the day I was born, I began to learn my lessons. I was put in a rigid frame too intricate, too twisting to describe here so briefly, but I learned to conform to its slide-rule measurements. I learned it is possible to be a Christian and a white southerner simultaneously; to be a gentlewoman and an arrogant callous creature in the same moment; to pray at night and ride a Jim Crow car the next morning and to feel comfortable in doing both. I learned to believe in freedom, to glow when the word *democracy* was used, and to practice slavery from morning to night. I learned it the way all my southern people learn it: by closing door after door until one's mind and heart and conscience are blocked off from each other and from reality.

I closed the doors. Or perhaps they were closed for me. One day they began to open again. Why I had the desire or the strength to open them, or what strange accident or circumstance opened them for me would require in the answering an account too long, too particular, too stark to make here. And perhaps I should not have the wisdom that such an analysis would demand of me, nor the will to make it. I know only that the doors opened, a little; that somewhere along that iron corridor we travel from babyhood to maturity, doors swinging inward began to swing outward, showing glimpses of the world beyond, of that bright thing we call "reality."

I believe there is one experience which pushed these doors open, a little. And I am going to tell it here, although I know well that to excerpt from a life and family background one incident and name it as a "cause" of a change in one's life direction is a distortion and often an irrelevance. The hungers of a child and how they are filled have too much to do with the way in which experiences are assimilated to tear an incident out of life and look at it in isolation. Yet, with these reservations, I shall tell it, not because it was in itself a severe trauma, but because it became a symbol of buried experiences that I did not have access to. It is an incident that has rarely happened to other southern children. In a sense, unique. But it was an acting-out, a private production of a little script that is written on the lives of most southern children before they know the words. Though they may not have seen it staged this way, each southerner has had his own private showing.

I should like to preface the account by giving a brief glimpse of my family, hoping the reader, entering my home with me, will be able to blend the edges of this isolated experience into a more full life picture and in doing so will see that it is, in a sense, everybody's story.

I was born and reared in a small Deep South town whose population was about equally Negro and white. There were nine of us who grew up freely in a rambling house of many rooms, surrounded by big lawn, back yard, gardens, fields, and barn. It was the kind of home that gathers memories like dust, a place filled with laughter and play and pain and hurt and ghosts and games. We were given such advantages of schooling, music, and art as were available in the South, and our world was not limited to the South, for travel to far places seemed a natural thing to us, and usually one of the family was in a remote part of the earth.

We knew we were a respected and important family of this small town but beyond this we gave little thought to status. Our father made money in lumber and naval stores for the excitement of making and losing it—not for what money can buy nor the security which it sometimes gives. I do not remember at any time wanting "to be rich" nor do I remember that thrift and saving were ideals which our parents considered important enough to urge upon us. In the family there was acceptance of risk, a mild delight in burning bridges, an expectant "What next?" We were not irresponsible; living according to the pleasure principle was by no means our way of life. On the contrary we were trained to think that each of us should do something of genuine usefulness, and the family thought it right to make sacrifices if necessary, to give each child preparation for such work. We were also trained to think learning important, and books; but "bad" books our mother burned. We valued music and art and craftsmanship but it was people and their welfare and religion that were the foci around which our lives seemed naturally to move. Above all else, the important thing was what we "planned to do." That each of us must do something was as inevitable as breathing for we owed a "debt to society which must be paid." This was a family commandment.

While many neighbors spent their energies in counting limbs on the family tree and grafting some on now and then to give symmetry to it, or in licking scars to cure their vague malaise, or in fighting each battle and turn of battle of the Civil War which has haunted the southern conscience so long, my father was pushing his nine children straight into the future. "You have your heritage," he used to say, "some of it good, some not so good; and as far as I know you had the usual number of grandmothers and grandfathers. Yes, there were slaves, too many of them in the family, but that was your grandfather's mistake, not yours. The past has been lived. It is gone. The future is yours. What are you going to do with it? He asked this question often and sometimes one knew it was but an echo of a question he had spent his life trying to answer for himself. For the future held my father's dreams; always there, not in the past, did he expect to find what he had spent his life searching for.

We lived the same segregated life as did other southerners but our parents talked in excessively Christian and democratic terms. We were told ten thousand times that status and money are unimportant (though we were well supplied with both); we were told that "all men are brothers," that we are a part of a democracy and must act like democrats. We were told that the teachings of Jesus are important and could be practiced if we tried. We were told that to be "radical" is bad, silly too; and that one must always conform to the "best behavior" of one's community and make it better if one can. We were taught that we were superior to hate and resentment, and that no member of the Smith family could stoop so low as to have an enemy. No matter what injury was done us, we must not injure ourselves further by retaliating. That was a family commandment.

We had family prayers once each day. All of us as children read the Bible in its entirety each year. We memorized hundreds of Bible verses and repeated them at breakfast, and said "sentence prayers" around the family table. God was not someone we met on Sunday but a permanent member of our household. It never occurred to me until I was fourteen or fifteen years old that He did not chalk up the daily score on eternity's tablets.

Despite the strain of living so intimately with God, the nine of us were strong, healthy, energetic youngsters who filled days with play and sports and music and books and managed to live most of the time on the careless level at which young lives should be lived. We had our times of anxiety of course, for there were hard lessons to be learned about the soul and "bad things" to be learned about sex. Sometimes I have wondered how we learned them with a mother so shy with words.

She was a wistful creature who loved beautiful things like lace and sunsets and flowers in a vague inarticulate way, and took good care of her children. We always knew this was not her world but one she accepted under duress. Her private world we rarely entered, though the shadow of it lay heavily on our hearts.

Our father owned large business interests, employed hundreds of colored and white laborers, paid them the prevailing low wages, worked them the prevailing long hours, built for them mill towns (Negro and white), built for each group a church, saw to it that religion was supplied free, saw to it that a commissary supplied commodities at a high price, and in general managed his affairs much as ten thousand other southern businessmen managed theirs.

. . . . .

Against this backdrop the drama of the South was played out one day in my life:

A little white girl was found in the colored section of our town, living with a Negro family in a broken-down shack. This family had moved in a few weeks before and little was known of them. One of the ladies in my mother's club, while driving over to her washerwoman's, saw the child swinging on a gate. The shack, as she said, was hardly more than a pigsty and this white child was living with dirty and sick-looking colored folks. "They must have kidnapped her," she told her friends. Genuinely shocked, the clubwomen busied themselves in an attempt to do something, for the child was very white indeed. The strange Negroes were subjected to a grueling questioning and finally grew evasive and refused to talk at all. This only increased the suspicion of the white group. The next day the clubwomen, escorted by the town marshal, took the child from her adopted family despite their tears.

She was brought to our home. I do not know why my mother consented to this plan. Perhaps because she loved children and always showed concern for them. It was easy for one more to fit into our ample household and Janie was soon at home there. She roomed with me, sat next to me at the table; I found Bible verses for her to say at breakfast; she wore my clothes, played with my dolls, and followed me around from morning to night. She was dazed by her new comforts and by the interesting activities of this big lively family; and I was as happily dazed, for her adoration was a new thing to me; and as time passed a quick, childish, and deeply felt bond grew up between us.

But a day came when a telephone message was received from a colored orphanage. There was a meeting at our home. Many whispers. All afternoon the ladies went in and out of our house talking to Mother in tones too low for children to hear. As they passed us at play, they looked at Janie and quickly looked away again, though a few stopped and stared at her as if they could not tear their eyes from her face. When my father came home Mother closed her door against our young ears and talked a long time with him. I heard him laugh, heard Mother say, "But Papa, this is no laughing matter!" And then they were back in the living room with us and my mother was pale and my father was saying, "Well, work it out, Mame, as best you can. After all, now that you know, it is pretty simple."

In a little while my mother called my sister and me into her bedroom and told us that in the morning Janie would return to Colored Town. She said Janie was to have the dresses the ladies had given her and a few of my own, and the toys we had shared with her. She asked me if I would like to give Janie one of my dolls. She seemed hurried, though Janie was not to leave until next day. She said "Why not select it now?" And in dreamlike stiffness I brought in my dolls and chose one for Janie. And then I found it possible to say, "Why is she leaving? She likes us, she hardly knows them. She told me she had been with them only a month."

"Because," Mother said gently, "Janie is a little colored girl."

"But she's white!"

"We were mistaken. She is colored."

"But she looks—"

"She is colored. Please don't argue!"

"What does it mean?" I whispered.

"It means," Mother said slowly, "that she has to live in Colored Town with colored people."

"But why? She lived here three weeks and she doesn't belong to them, she told me so."

"She is a little colored girl."

"But you said yourself she has nice manners. You said that," I persisted.

"Yes, she is a nice child. But a colored child cannot live in our home."

"Why?"

"You know, dear! You have always known that white and colored people do not live together."

"Can she come to play?"

"No."

"I don't understand."

"I don't either," my young sister quavered.

"You're too young to understand. And don't ask me again, ever again, about this!" Mother's voice was sharp but her face was sad and there was no certainty left there. She hurried out and busied herself in the kitchen and I wandered through that room where I had been born, touching the old familiar things in it, looking at them, trying to find the answer to a question that moaned like a hurt thing. . . .

And then I went out to Janie, who was waiting, knowing things were happening that concerned her but waiting until they were spoken aloud.

I do not know quite how the words were said but I told her she was to return in the morning to the little place where she had lived because she was colored and colored children could not live with white children.

"Are you white?" she said.

"I'm white," I replied, "and my sister is white. And you're colored. And white and colored can't live together because my mother says so."

"Why?" Janie whispered.

"Because they can't," I said. But I knew, though I said it firmly, that something was wrong. I knew my mother and father whom I passionately admired had betrayed something which they held dear. And they could not help doing it. And I was shamed by their failure and frightened, for I felt they were no longer as powerful as I had thought. There was something Out There that was stronger than they and I could not bear to believe it. I could not confess that my father, who always solved the family dilemmas easily and with laughter, could not solve this. I knew that my mother who was so good to children did not believe in her heart that she was being good to this child. There was not a word in my mind that said it but my body knew and my glands, and I was filled with anxiety.

But I felt compelled to believe they were right. It was the only way my world could be held together. And, slowly, it began to seep through me: *I was white. She was colored. We must not be together. It was bad to be together. Though you ate with your nurse when you were little, it was bad to eat with any colored person after that. It was bad just as other things were bad that your mother had told you. It was bad that she was to sleep in the room with me that night. It was bad. . . .*

I was overcome with guilt. For three weeks I had done things that white children were not supposed to do. And now I knew these things had been wrong.

I went to the piano and began to play, as I had always done when I was in trouble. I tried to play my next lesson and as I stumbled through it, the little girl came over and sat on the bench with me. Feeling lost in the deep currents sweeping through our house that night, she crept closer and put her arms around me and I shrank away as if my body had been uncovered. I had not said a word, I did not say one, but she knew, and tears slowly rolled down her little white face. . . .

And then I forgot it. For more than thirty years the experience was wiped out of my memory. But that night, and the weeks it was tied to, worked its way like a splinter, bit by bit, down to the hurt places in my memory and festered there. And as I grew older, as more experiences collected around that faithless time, as memories of earlier, more profound hurts crept closer, drawn to that night as if to a magnet, I began to know that people who talked of love and children did not mean it. That is a hard thing for a child to learn. I still admired my parents, there was so much that was strong and vital and sane and good about them and I never forgot this; I stubbornly believed in their sincerity, as I do to this day, and I loved them. Yet in my heart they were under suspicion. Something was wrong.

Something was wrong with a world that tells you that love is good and people are important and then forces you to deny love and to humiliate people. I knew, though I would not for years confess it aloud, that in trying to shut the Negro race away from us, we have shut ourselves away from so many good, creative, honest, deeply human things in life. I began to understand slowly at first but more clearly as the years passed, that the warped, distorted frame we have put around every Negro child from birth is around every white child also. Each is on a different side of the frame but each is pinioned there. And I knew that what cruelly shapes and cripples the personality of one is as cruelly shaping and crippling the personality of the other. I began to see that though we may, as we acquire new knowledge, live through new experiences, examine old memories, gain the strength to tear the frame from us, yet we are stunted and warped and in our lifetime cannot grow straight again any more than can a tree, put in a steel-like twisting frame when young, grow tall and straight when the frame is torn away at maturity.

As I sit here writing, I can almost touch that little town, so close is the memory of it. There it lies, its main street lined with great oaks, heavy with matted moss that swings softly even now as I remember. A little white town rimmed with Negroes, making a deep shadow on the whiteness. There it lies, broken in two by one strange idea. Minds broken. Hearts broken. Conscience torn from acts. A culture split in a thousand pieces. That is segregation. I am remembering: a woman in a mental hospital walking four steps out, four steps in, unable to go further because she has drawn an invisible line around her small world and is terrified to take one step beyond it. . . . A man in a Disturbed Ward assigning "places" to the other patients and violently insisting that each stay in his place. . . . A Negro woman saying to me so quietly, "We cannot ride together on the bus, you know. It is not legal to be human down here."

Memory, walking the streets of one's childhood . . . of the town where one was born.

22 Status and Role

RALPH LINTON

Through their behavior in various groups people come to perform certain roles and acquire statuses. Ralph Linton's discussion of these two concepts has become a classic. He examines the theory of status and role with illustrations from both nonliterate and complex societies.

The term *status,* like the term *culture,* has come to be used with a double significance. A *status,* in the abstract, is a position in a particular pattern. It is thus quite correct to speak of each individual as having many statuses, since each individual participates in the expression of a number of patterns. However, unless the term is qualified in some way, *the status* of any individual means the sum total of all the statuses which he occupies. It represents his position with relation to the total society. Thus the status of Mr. Jones as a member of his community derives from a combination of all the statuses which he holds as a citizen, as an attorney, as a Mason, as a Methodist, as Mrs. Jones's husband, and so on.

A status, as distinct from the individual who may occupy it, is simply a collection of rights and duties. Since these rights and duties can find expression only through the medium of individuals, it is extremely hard for us to maintain a distinction in our thinking between statuses and the people who hold them and exercise the rights and duties which constitute them. The relation between any individual and any status he holds is somewhat like that between the driver of an automobile and the driver's place in the machine. The driver's seat with its steering wheel, accelerator, and other controls is a constant with ever-present potentialities for action and control, while the driver may be any member of the family and may exercise these potentialities very well or very badly.

A *rôle* represents the dynamic aspect of a status. The individual is socially assigned to a status and occupies it with relation to other statuses. When he puts the rights and duties which constitute the status into effect, he is performing a rôle. Rôle and status are quite inseparable, and the distinction between them is of only academic interest. There are no rôles without statuses or statuses without rôles. Just as in the case of *status,* the term *rôle* is used with a double significance. Every individual has a series of rôles deriving from the various patterns in which he participates and at the same time a *rôle,* general, which represents the sum total of these rôles and determines what he does for his society and what he can expect from it.

Although all statuses and rôles derive from social patterns and are integral parts

SOURCE: *The Study of Man* by Ralph Linton, 113–21. Copyright 1936, by D. Appleton-Century Company, Inc. Reprinted by permission of Appleton-Century-Crofts. • The author (1893–1953) was Sterling Professor of Anthropology at Yale University. He was Assistant Curator of North American Ethnology, Field Museum of Natural History. He has been described as one of the greatest anthropologists of the present era. Among his works are *Acculturation in Seven American Indian Tribes; The Cultural Background of Personality; Most of the World: The Peoples of Africa, Latin America, and the East Today;* and *The Tree of Culture.*

of patterns, they have an independent function with relation to the individuals who occupy particular statuses and exercise their rôles. To such individuals the combined status and rôle represent the minimum of attitudes and behavior which he must assume if he is to participate in the overt expression of the pattern. Status and rôle serve to reduce the ideal patterns for social life to individual terms. They become models for organizing the attitudes and behavior of the individual so that these will be congruous with those of the other individuals participating in the expression of the pattern. Thus if we are studying football teams in the abstract, the position of quarterback is meaningless except in relation to the other positions. From the point of view of the quarterback himself it is a distinct and important entity. It determines where he shall take his place in the line-up and what he shall do in various plays. His assignment to this position at once limits and defines his activities and establishes a minimum of things which he must learn. Similarly, in a social pattern such as that for the employer-employee relationship the statuses of employer and employee define what each has to know and do to put the pattern into operation. The employer does not need to know the techniques involved in the employee's labor, and the employee does not need to know the techniques for marketing or accounting.

It is obvious that, as long as there is no interference from external sources, the more perfectly the members of any society are adjusted to their statuses and rôles the more smoothly the society will function. In its attempts to bring about such adjustments every society finds itself caught on the horns of a dilemma. The individual's formation of habits and attitudes begins at birth, and, other things being equal, the earlier his training for a status can begin the more successful it is likely to be. At the same time, no two individuals are alike, and a status which will be congenial to one may be quite uncongenial to another. Also, there are in all social systems certain rôles which require more than training for their successful performance. Perfect technique does not make a great violinist, nor a thorough book knowledge of tactics an efficient general. The utilization of the special gifts of individuals may be highly important to society, as in the case of the general, yet these gifts usually show themselves rather late, and to wait upon their manifestation for the assignment of statuses would be to forfeit the advantages to be derived from commencing training early.

Fortunately, human beings are so mutable that almost any normal individual can be trained to the adequate performance of almost any rôle. Most of the business of living can be conducted on a basis of habit, with little need for intelligence and none for special gifts. Societies have met the dilemma by developing two types of statuses, the *ascribed* and the *achieved*. Ascribed statuses are those which are assigned to individuals without reference to their innate differences or abilities. They can be predicted and trained for from the moment of birth. The *achieved* statuses are, as a minimum, those requiring special qualities, although they are not necessarily limited to these. They are not assigned to individuals from birth but are left open to be filled through competition and individual effort. The majority of the statuses in all social systems are of the ascribed type and those which take care of the ordinary day-to-day business of living are practically always of this type.

In all societies certain things are selected as reference points for the ascription of status. The things chosen for this purpose are always of such a nature that they are ascertainable at birth, making it possible to begin the training of the individual for his potential statuses and rôles at once. The simplest and most universally used of these reference points is sex. Age is used with nearly equal frequency, since all individuals pass through the same cycle of growth, maturity, and decline, and the statuses whose occupation will be determined by age can be forecast and trained for with accuracy. Family relationships, the simplest and most obvious being that of the child to its mother, are also used in all societies as reference points for the establishment of a whole series of statuses. Lastly, there is the matter of birth into a particular socially established group, such as a class or caste. The use of this type of reference is common but not universal. In all societies the actual ascription of statuses to the individual is controlled by a series of these reference points which together serve to delimit the field of his future participation in the life of the group.

The division and ascription of statuses with relation to sex seems to be basic in all social systems. All societies prescribe different attitudes and activities to men and to women. Most of them try to rationalize these prescriptions in terms of the physiological differences between the sexes or their different roles in reproduction. However, a comparative study of the statuses ascribed to women and men in different cultures seems to show that while such factors may have served as a starting point for the development of a division the actual ascriptions are almost entirely determined by culture. Even the psychological characteristics ascribed to men and women in different societies vary so much that they can have little physiological basis. Our own idea of women as ministering angels contrasts sharply with the ingenuity of women as torturers among the Iroquois and the sadistic delight they took in the process. Even the last two generations have seen a sharp change in the psychological patterns for women in our own society. The delicate, fainting lady of the middle eighteen-hundreds is as extinct as the dodo.

When it comes to the ascription of occupations, which is after all an integral part of status, we find the differences in various societies even more marked. Arapesh women regularly carry heavier loads than men "because their heads are so much harder and stronger." In some societies women do most of the manual labor; in others, as in the Marquesas, even cooking, housekeeping, and baby-tending are proper male occupations, and women spend most of their time primping. Even the general rule that women's handicap through pregnancy and nursing indicates the more active occupations as male and the less active ones as female has many exceptions. Thus among the Tasmanians seal-hunting was women's work. They swam out to the seal rocks, stalked the animals, and clubbed them. Tasmanian women also hunted opossums, which required the climbing of large trees.

Although the actual ascription of occupations along sex lines is highly variable, the pattern of sex division is constant. There are very few societies in which every important activity has not been definitely assigned to men or to women. Even when the two sexes coöperate in a particular occupation, the field of each is usually clearly delimited. Thus in Madagascar rice culture the men make the seed beds and terraces and prepare the fields for transplanting. The women do the work of transplanting, which is hard and back-breaking. The women weed the crop, but the men harvest it. The women then carry it to the threshing floors, where the men thresh it while the women winnow it. Lastly, the women pound the grain in mortars and cook it.

When a society takes over a new industry, there is often a period of uncertainty during which the work may be done by either sex, but it soon falls into the province of one or the other. In Madagascar, pottery is made by men in some tribes and by women in others. The only tribe in which it is made by both men and women is one into which the art has been introduced within the last sixty years. I was told that during the fifteen years preceding my visit there had been a marked decrease in the number of male potters, many men who had once practised the art having given it up. The factor of lowered wages, usually advanced as the reason for men leaving one of our own occupations when women enter it in force, certainly was not operative here. The field was not overcrowded, and the prices for men's and women's products were the same. Most of the men who had given up the trade were vague as to their reasons, but a few said frankly that they did not like to compete with women. Apparently the entry of women into the occupation had robbed it of a certain amount of prestige. It was no longer quite the thing for a man to be a potter, even though he was a very good one.

The use of age as a reference point for establishing status is as universal as the use of sex. All societies recognize three age groupings as a minimum: child, adult, and old. Certain societies have emphasized age as a basis for assigning status and have greatly amplified the divisions. Thus in certain African tribes the whole male population is divided into units composed of those born in the same years or within two- or three-year intervals. However, such extreme attention to age is unusual, and we need not discuss it here.

The physical differences between child and adult are easily recognizable, and the passage from childhood to maturity is marked by physiological events which make it possible to date it exactly for girls and within a few weeks or months for boys. However, the physical passage from childhood to maturity does not necessarily coincide with the social transfer of the individual from one category to the other. Thus in our own society both men and women remain legally children until long after they are physically adult. In most societies this difference between the physical and social transfer is more clearly marked than in our own. The child becomes a man not when he is physically mature but when he is formally recognized as a man by his society. This recognition is almost always given ceremonial expression in what are technically known as puberty rites. The most important element in these rites is not the determination of physical maturity but that of social maturity. Whether a boy is able to breed is less vital to his society than whether he is able to do a man's work and has a man's knowledge. Actually, most puberty ceremonies include tests of the boy's learning and fortitude, and if the aspirants are unable to pass these they are left in the child status until they can. For those who pass the tests, the ceremonies usually culminate in the transfer to them of certain secrets which the men guard from women and children.

The passage of individuals from adult to aged is harder to perceive. There is no clear physiological line for men, while even women may retain their full physical vigor and their ability to carry on all the activities of the adult status for several years after the menopause. The social transfer of men from adult to the aged group is given ceremonial recognition in a few cultures, as when a father normally surrenders his official position and titles to his son, but such recognition is rare. As for women, there appears to be no society in which the menopause is given ceremonial recognition, although there are a few societies in which it does alter the individual's status. Thus Comanche women, after the menopause, were released from their disabilities with regard to the supernatural. They could handle sacred objects, obtain power through dreams and practise as shamans, all things forbidden to women of bearing age.

The general tendency for societies to emphasize the individual's first change in age status and largely ignore the second is no doubt due in part to the difficulty of determining the onset of old age. However, there are also psychological factors involved. The boy or girl is usually anxious to grow up, and this eagerness is heightened by the exclusion of children from certain activities and knowledge. Also, society welcomes new additions to the most active division of the group, that which contributes most to its perpetuation and well-being. Conversely, the individual who enjoys the thought of growing old is atypical in all societies. Even when age brings respect and a new measure of influence, it means the relinquishment of much that is pleasant. We can see among ourselves that the aging usually refuse to recognize the change until long after it has happened.

In the case of age, as in that of sex, the biological factors involved appear to be secondary to the cultural ones in determining the content of status. There are certain activities which cannot be ascribed to children because children either lack the necessary strength or have not had time to acquire the necessary technical skills. However, the attitudes between parent and child and the importance given to the child in the family structure vary enormously from one culture to another. The status of the child among our Puritan ancestors, where he was seen and not heard and ate at the second table, represents one extreme. At the other might be placed the status of the eldest son of a Polynesian chief. All the *mana* (supernatural power) of the royal line converged upon such a child. He was socially superior to his own father and mother, and any attempt to discipline him would have been little short of sacrilege. I once visited the hereditary chief of a Marquesan tribe and found the whole family camping uncomfortably in their own front yard, although they had a good house built on European lines. Their eldest son, aged nine, had had a dispute with his father a few days before and had tabooed the house by naming it after his head. The family had thus been compelled to move out and could not use it again until he relented and lifted the taboo. As he could use the house himself and eat anywhere in the village, he was getting along quite well and seemed to enjoy the situation thoroughly.

The statuses ascribed to the old in various societies vary even more than those ascribed to children. In some cases they are relieved of all heavy labor and can settle back comfortably to live off their children. In others they perform most of the hard and monotonous tasks which do not require great physical strength, such as the gathering of firewood. In many societies the old women, in particular, take over most of the care of the younger children, leaving the younger women free to enjoy themselves. In some places the old are treated with consideration and respect; in others they are considered a useless incumbrance and removed as soon as they are incapable of heavy labor. In most societies their advice is sought even when little attention is paid to their wishes. This custom has a sound practical basis, for the individual who contrives to live to old age in an uncivilized group has usually been a person of ability and his memory constitutes a sort of reference library to which one can turn for help under all sorts of circumstances.

In certain societies the change from the adult to the old status is made more difficult for the individual by the fact that the patterns for these statuses ascribe different types of personality to each. This was the case among the Comanche, as it seems to have been among most of the Plains tribes. The adult male was a warrior, vigorous, self-reliant, and pushing. Most of his social relationships were phrased in terms of competition. He took what he could get and held what he had without regard to any abstract rights of those weaker then himself. Any willingness to arbitrate differences or to ignore slights was a sign of weakness resulting in loss of prestige. The old man, on the other hand, was expected to be wise and gentle, willing to overlook slights and, if need be, to endure abuse. It was his task to work for the welfare of the tribe, giving sound advice, settling feuds between the warriors, and even preventing his tribe from making new enemies. Young men strove for war and honor, old men strove for peace and tranquility. There is abundant evidence that among the Comanche the transition was often a difficult one for the individual. Warriors did not prepare for old age, thinking it a better fate to be killed in action. When waning physical powers forced them to assume the new rôle, many of them did so grudgingly, and those who had strong magic would go on trying to enforce the rights which belonged to the younger status. Such bad old men were a peril to young ones beginning their careers, for they were jealous of them simply because they were young and strong and admired by the women. The medicine power of these young men was still weak, and the old men could and did kill them by malevolent magic. It is significant that although benevolent medicine men might be of any age in Comanche folklore, malevolent ones were always old.

23 The New Feminism

LUCY KOMISAR

As is implied by the preceding article, difficulties arise both for those who have conflicting statuses and for those who seek to redefine the statuses ascribed to them. Both problems, and especially the latter, appear to be increasingly recognized by women in our society. This selection by Lucy Komisar examines the restricted and often demeaning role into which women are cast in our society, and describes some of the recent social movements that have developed to confront and alter the situation.

A dozen women are variously seated in straight-backed chairs, settled on a couch, or sprawled on the floor of a comfortable apartment on Manhattan's West Side. They range in age from twenty-five to thirty-five, and include a magazine researcher, a lawyer, a housewife, an architect, a teacher, a secretary, and a graduate student in sociology.

They are white, middle-class, attractive. All but one have college degrees; several are married; a few are active in social causes. At first, they are hesitant. They don't really know what to talk about, and so they begin with why they came.

"I wanted to explore my feelings as a woman and find out what others think about the things that bother me." Slowly, they open up, trust growing. "I always felt so negative about being a woman; now I'm beginning to feel good about it."

They become more personal and revealing. "My mother never asked me what I was going to be when I grew up." "I never used to like to talk to girls. I always thought women were inferior—I never *liked* women." "I've been a secretary for three years; after that, you begin to think that's all you're good for." "I felt so trapped when my baby was born. I wanted to leave my husband and the child."

Repeated a hundred times in as many different rooms, these are the voices of women's liberation, a movement that encompasses high school students and grandmothers, and that is destined to eclipse the black civil rights struggle in the force of its resentment and the consequence of its demands.

Some of us have become feminists out of anger and frustration over job discrimination. When we left college, male students got aptitude tests, we got typing tests. In spite of federal law, most women still are trapped in low-paying, dead-end jobs and commonly earn less than men for the same work—sometimes on the theory that we are only "helping out," though 42 per cent of us support ourselves or families.

Others have discovered that the humanistic precepts of the radical movement do not always apply to women. At a peace rally in Washington last year, feminists were hooted and jeered off the speakers' platform, and white women working in civil rights or anti-poverty programs are expected to defer to the black male ego. Many of us got out to

SOURCE: *Saturday Review*, vol. 53, no. 8 (February 21, 1970), 27–30, 55. Reprinted by permission of the author and the publisher. • The author is a free-lance writer and a board member of the New York chapter of The National Organization for Women. She is currently writing a book on feminism.

salvage our own buffeted egos. However, most of the new feminists express only a general malaise they were never able to identify.

Nanette Rainone is twenty-seven, the wife of a newspaperman, the mother of a seven-month-old child, and a graduate of Queens College, where she studied English literature. She married while in graduate school, then quit before the year was out to become an office clerk at *Life* magazine. "I could have known the first day that I wasn't going to be promoted, but it took me eight months to find it out."

She spent the next five months idly at home, began doing volunteer public affairs interviews for WBAI radio, and now produces *Womankind,* a weekly program on the feminist movement.

"I always felt as though I was on a treadmill, an emotional treadmill. I thought it was neurotic, but it always focused on being a woman. Then I met another woman, who had two children. We talked about my pregnancy—my confusion about my pregnancy—and the problems she was having in caring for her children now that she was separated from her husband and wanted to work."

One evening Nanette Rainone's friend took her to a feminist meeting, and immediately she became part of the movement. "The child had been an escape. I was seeking a role I couldn't find on the outside," she says. "Then I became afraid my life would be overwhelmed, that I would never get out from under and do the things I had hoped to do.

"You struggle for several years after getting out of college. You know—what are you going to do with yourself? There's always the external discrimination, but somehow you feel you are talented and you should be able to project yourself. But you don't get a good job, you get a terrible job.

"I think I was typical of the average woman who is in the movement now, because the contradictions, in the system existed in my life. My parents were interested in my education. I had more room to develop my potential than was required for the role I eventually was to assume.

"I don't put down the care of children. I just put down the fixated relationship that the mother has, the never-ending association, her urge that the child be something so that *she* can be something. People need objective projects. We all feel the need to actively participate in society, in something outside ourselves where we can learn and develop.

"The closest I've been able to come to what's wrong is that men have a greater sense of self than women have. Marriage is an aspect of men's lives, whereas it is the very center of most women's lives, the whole of their lives. It seemed to me that women felt they couldn't exist except in the eyes of men—that if a man wasn't looking at them or attending to them, then they just weren't there."

If women need more evidence, history books stand ready to assure us that we have seldom existed except as shadows of men. We have rarely been leaders of nations or industry or the great contributors to art and science, yet very few sociologists, political leaders, historians, and moral critics have ever stopped to ask why. Now, all around the country, women are meeting in apartments and conference rooms and coffee shops to search out the answers.

The sessions begin with accounts of personal problems and incidents. For years, we women have believed that our anger and frustration and unhappiness were "our problems." Suddenly, we discover that we are telling *the same story!* Our complaints are not only common, they are practically universal.

It is an exhilarating experience. Women's doubts begin to disappear and are replaced by new strength and self-respect. We stop focusing on men, and begin to identify with other women and to analyze the roots of our oppression. The conclusions that are drawn challenge the legitimacy of the sex role system upon which our civilization is based.

At the center of the feminist critique is the recognition that women have been forced to accept the inferior role in society, and that we have come to believe in our own inferiority. Women are taught to be passive, dependent, submissive, not to pursue careers but to be taken care of and protected. Even those who seek outside work lack confidence and self-esteem. Most of us are forced into menial and unsatisfying jobs: More than three-quarters of us are clerks, sales personnel, or factory and service workers, and a fifth of the women with B.A. degrees are secretaries.

Self-hatred is endemic. Women—especially those who have "made it"—identify with men and mirror their contempt for women. The approval of women does not mean very much. We don't want to work for women or vote for them. We laugh, although with vague uneasiness, at jokes about women drivers, mothers-in-law, and dumb blondes.

We depend on our relationships with men for our very identities. Our husbands win us social status and determine how we will be regarded by the world. Failure for a woman is not being selected by a man.

We are trained in the interests of men to defer to them and serve them and entertain them. If we are educated and gracious, it is so we can please men and educate their children. That is the thread that runs through the life of the geisha, the party girl, the business executive's wife, and the First Lady of the United States.

Men define women, and until now most of us have accepted their definition without question. If we challenge men in the world outside the home, we are all too frequently derided as "aggressive" and "unfeminine"—by women as readily as by men.

A woman is expected to subordinate her job to the interests of her husband's work. She'll move to another city so he can take a promotion—but it rarely works the other way around. Men don't take women's work very seriously, and, as a result, neither do most women. We spend a lot of time worrying about men, while they devote most of theirs to worrying about their careers.

We are taught that getting and keeping a man is a woman's most important job; marriage, therefore, becomes our most important achievement. One suburban housewife says her father started giving her bridal pictures cut from newspapers when she was six. "He said that was what I would be when I grew up."

Most feminists do not object to marriage per se, but to the corollary that it is creative and fulfilling for an adult human being to spend her life doing housework, caring for children, and using her husband as a vicarious link to the outside world.

Most people would prefer just about any kind of work to that of a domestic servant; yet the mindless, endless, repetitious drudgery of housekeeping is the central occupation of more than fifty million women. People who would oppose institutions that portion out menial work on the basis of race see nothing wrong in a system that does the same thing on the basis of sex. (Should black and white roommates automatically assume the Negro best suited for housekeeping chores?)

Even when they work at full-time jobs, wives must come home to "their" dusting and "their" laundry.

Some insist that housework is not much worse than the meaningless jobs most people have today, but there is a difference. Housewives are not paid for their work, and money is the mark of value in this society. It is also the key to independence and to the feeling of self-reliance that marks a free human being.

The justification for being a housewife is having children, and the justification for children is—well, a woman has a uterus, what else would it be for? Perhaps not all feminists agree that the uterus is a vestigial organ, but we are adamant and passionate in our denial of the old canard that biology is destiny.

Men have never been bound by their animal natures. They think and dream and create—and fly, clearly something nature had not intended, or it would have given men wings. However, we women are told that our chief function is to reproduce the species, prepare food, and sweep out the cave—er, house.

Psychologist Bruno Bettelheim states woman's functions succinctly: "We must start with the realization that, as much as women want to be good scientists or engineers, they want first and foremost to be womanly companions of men and to be mothers."

He gets no argument from Dr. Spock: "Biologically and temperamentally, I believe women were made to be concerned first and foremost with child care, husband care, and home care." Spock says some women have been "confused" by their education. (Freud was equally reactionary on the woman question, but he at least has the excuse of his Central European background.)

The species must reproduce, but this need not be the sole purpose of a woman's life. Men want children, too, yet no one expects them to choose between families and work. Children are in no way a substitute for personal development and creativity. If a talented man is forced into a senseless, menial job, it is deplored as a waste and a personal misfortune; yet, a woman's special skills, education, and interests are all too often deemed incidental and irrelevant, simply a focus for hobbies or volunteer work.

Women who say that raising a family is a fulfilling experience are rather like the peasant who never leaves his village. They have never had the opportunity to do anything else.

As a result, women are forced to live through their children and husbands, and they feel cheated and resentful when they realize that is not enough. When a woman says she gave her children everything, she is telling the truth—and that is the tragedy. Often when she reaches her late thirties, her children have grown up, gone to work or college, and left her in a bleak and premature old age. Middle-aged women who feel empty and useless are the mainstay of America's psychiatrists—who generally respond by telling them to "accept their role."

The freedom to choose whether or not to have children has always been illusory. A wife who is deliberately "barren"—a word that reinforces the worn-out metaphor of woman as Mother Earth—is considered neurotic or unnatural. Not only is motherhood not central to a woman's life, it may not be necessary or desirable. For the first time, some of us are admitting openly and without guilt that we do not want children. And the population crisis is making it even clearer that as a symbol for Americans motherhood ought to defer to apple pie.

The other half of the reproduction question is sex. The sexual revolution didn't liberate women at all; it only created a bear market for men. One of the most talked-about tracts in the movement is a pamphlet by Ann Koedt called "The Myth of the Vaginal Orgasm," which says most women don't have orgasms because most men won't accept the fact that the female orgasm is clitoral.

We are so used to putting men's needs first that we don't know how to ask for what *we* want, or else we share the common ignorance about our own physiology and think there is something wrong with us when we don't have orgasms "the right way." Freudian analysts contribute to the problem. The realization that past guilt and frustration have been unnecessary is not the least of the sentiments that draws women to women's liberation.

Feminists also protest the general male proclivity to regard us as decorative, amusing sex objects even in the world outside bed. We resent the sexual sell in advertising, the catcalls we get on the street, girlie magazines and pornography, bars that refuse to serve unescorted women on the assumption they are prostitutes, the not very subtle brainwashing by cosmetic companies, and the attitude of men who praise our knees in mini-skirts, but refuse to act as if we had brains.

Even the supposedly humanistic worlds of rock music and radical politics are not very different. Young girls who join "the scene" or "the movement" are labeled "groupies" and are sexually exploited; the flashy pornosheets such as *Screw* and *Kiss* are published by the self-appointed advocates of the new "free," anti-Establishment life-style. "*Plus ça change. . . .*"

We are angry about the powers men wield over us. The physical power—women who study karate do so as a defense against muggers, not lovers. And the social power—we resent the fact that men take the initiative with women, that women cannot ask for dates but must sit home waiting for the phone to ring.

The social conditioning began in childhood when fathers went out to work and mothers stayed home, images perpetuated in schoolbooks and games and on television. If we were bright students, we were told, "You're smart—for a girl," and then warned not to appear *too* smart in front of boys—"Or you won't have dates."

Those of us who persisted in reaching for a career were encouraged to be teachers or nurses so we would have "something to fall back on." My mother told me: "You're so bright, it's a pity you're not a boy. You could become president of a bank—or anything you wanted."

Ironically, and to our dismay, we discovered that playing the assigned role is precisely what elicits masculine contempt for our inferiority and narrow interests. *Tooth and Nail* a newsletter published by women's liberation groups in the San Francisco area, acidly points out a few of the contradictions: "A smart women never shows her brains; she allows the man to think himself clever. . . . Women's talk is all chatter; they don't understand things men are interested in."

Or: "Don't worry your pretty little head about such matters. . . . A woman's brain is between her legs. . . . Women like to be protected and treated like little girls. . . . Women can't make decisions."

The feminist answer is to throw out the whole simplistic division of human characteristics into masculine and feminine, and to insist that there are no real differences between men and women other than those enforced by culture.

Men say women are not inferior, we are just different; yet somehow they have appropriated most of the qualities that society admires and have left us with the same distinctive features that were attributed to black people before the civil rights revolution.

Men, for example, are said to be strong, assertive, courageous, logical, constructive, creative, and independent. Women are weak, passive, irrational, overemotional, empty-headed, and lacking in strong superegos. (Thank Freud for the last.) Both blacks and women are contented, have their place, and know how to use wiles—flattery, and wide-eyed, openmouthed ignorance—to get around "the man." It is obviously natural that men should be dominant and women submissive. Shuffle, baby, shuffle.

Our "sexist" system has hurt men as well as women, forcing them into molds that deny the value of sensitivity, tenderness, and sentiment. Men who are not aggressive worry about their virility just as strong women are frightened by talk about their being castrating females. The elimination of rigid sex-role definitions would liberate everyone. And that is the goal of the women's liberation movement.

Women's liberation groups, which have sprung up everywhere across the country, are taking names like Radical Women or the Women's Liberation Front or the Feminists. Most start as groups of ten or twelve; many, when they get too large for discussion, split in a form of mitosis. Sometimes they are tied to central organizations set up for action, or they maintain communications with each other or cosponsor newsletters with similar groups in their area.

Some are concerned with efforts to abolish abortion laws; a few have set up cooperative day-care centers, others challenge the stereotypes of woman's image, and many are organized for "consciousness-raising"—a kind of group therapy or encounter session that starts with the premise that there is something wrong with the system, not the women in the group.

The amorphousness and lack of central communication in the movement make it virtually impossible to catalogue the established groups, let alone the new ones that regularly appear; many of the "leaders" who have been quoted in newspapers or interviewed on television have been anointed only by the press.

The one organization with a constitution, board members, and chapters (some thirty-five) throughout the country is the National Organization for Women. Its founding in 1966 was precipitated by the ridicule that greeted the inclusion of sex in the prohibitions against job discrimination in the 1964 Civil Rights Act. (A staff member in the federal Equal Employment Opportunity Commission, which enforces the act, said it took pressure from NOW to get the EEOC to take that part of the law seriously.)

NOW members are not very different from women in other feminist groups, though they tend to include more professionals and older women. In general, they eschew "consciousness-raising" in favor of political action, and they are more likely to demonstrate for job equality and child-care centers than for the abolition of marriage or the traditional family unit.

NOW's president is Betty Friedan, who in 1963 published *The Feminine Mystique,* a challenge to the myth that a woman's place is either in a boudoir in a pink, frilly nightgown, on her hands and knees scrubbing the kitchen floor, or in a late model station wagon taking the kids to music lessons and Cub Scout meetings. (An article that previewed the theme of the book was turned down by every major women's magazine. "One was horrified and said I was obviously talking to and for a few neurotic women." When the book came out, two of these magazines published excerpts and several now have commissioned articles about the movement.)

Today, Betty Friedan says, the movement must gain political power by mobilizing the 51 per cent of the electorate who are women, as well as seeking elected offices for themselves. "We have to break down the actual barriers that prevent women from being full people in society, and not only end explicit discrimination but build new institutions. Most women will continue to bear children, and unless we create child-care centers on a mass basis, it's all talk."

Women are beginning to read a good deal about their own place in history, about the determined struggles of the suffragettes, the isolation of Virginia Woolf, and the heroism of Rosa Luxemburg. The Congress to Unite Women, which drew some 500 participants from cities in the Northeast, called for women's studies in high schools and colleges.

Present are all the accouterments of any social movement—feminist magazines such as *No More Fun and Games* in Boston, *Up From Under* in New York, and *Aphra,* a literary magazine published in Baltimore. (Anne Sexton wrote in the dedication, "As long as it can be said about a woman writer, 'She writes like a man' and that woman takes it as a compliment, we are in trouble.")

There are feminist theaters in at least New York and Boston, buttons that read "Uppity Women Unite," feminist poems and songs, a feminist symbol (the biological sign for woman with an equal sign in the center), and, to denounce specific advertisements, gum stickers that state, "This ad insults women."

With a rising feminist consciousness, everything takes on a new significance—films, advertisements, offhand comments, little things that never seemed important before. A few women conclude that chivalry and flirting reduce women to mere sex objects for men. We stop feeling guilty about opening doors, and some of us experiment with paying our own way on dates.

Personal acts are matched by political ones. The National Organization for Women went to court to get a federal ruling barring segregated helpwanted ads in newspapers, and it regularly helps women file complaints before the EEOC and local human rights commissions.

A women's rights platform was adopted last year by the State Committee of the California Democratic Party, and the Women's Rights Committee of the New Democratic Coalition plans to make feminist demands an issue in New York politics. A women's caucus exists in the Democratic Policy Council, headed by Senator Fred Harris.

At Grinnell College in Iowa, students protested the appearance of a representative from *Playboy* magazine, and women from sixteen cities converged on Atlantic City to make it clear what they think of the Miss America Pageant. In New York, a group protested advertisements by toymakers that said "boys were born to build and learn" and "girls were born to be dancers."

Women's caucuses have been organized in the American Political Science, Psychological, and Sociological associations. At New York University, a group of law students won their fight to make women eligible for a series of coveted $10,000 scholarships.

Pro-abortion groups have organized around the country to repeal anti-abortion laws, challenge them in the courts, or openly defy them. In Bloomington, Indiana, New York City, and elsewhere, women's liberation groups have set up cooperative day-care centers, which are illegal under strict state rules that regulate child-care facilities.

Free child care is likely to become the most significant demand made by the movement, and one calculated to draw the support of millions of woman who may not be interested in other feminist issues. About four million working mothers have children under six years of age, and only 2 per cent of these are in day-care centers.

Even Establishment Institutions appear to reflect the new attitudes. Princeton, Williams, and Yale have begun to admit women students, though on an unequal quota basis—and not to the hallowed pine-paneled halls of their alumni clubhouses.

Nevertheless, most people have only a vague idea of the significance of the new movement. News commentators on year-end analysis shows ignored the question or sloughed it off uncomfortably. One said the whole idea frightened him.

Yet, the women's movement promises to affect radically the life of virtually everyone in America. Only a small part of the population suffers because it is black, and most people have little contact with minorities. Women are 51 per cent of the population, and chances are that every adult American either is one, is married to one, or has close social or business relations with many.

The feminist revolution will overturn the basic premises upon which these relations are built—stereotyped notions about the family and the roles of men and women, fallacies concerning masculinity and femininity, and the economic division of labor into paid work and homemaking.

If the 1960's belonged to the blacks, the next ten years are ours.

24 Continuities and Discontinuities in Cultural Conditioning

RUTH BENEDICT

This article has been widely reprinted because it so effectively demonstrates how a particular aspect of culture, "continuities and discontinuities," affects personality development. As used by Ruth Benedict, the term "continuity" refers primarily to types of child-rearing which gradually prepare a child for his adult roles and thus help to prevent maladjustment. An example of cultural discontinuity is the fact that in our society unmarried young adults are expected to have no sexual experience, yet are supposed to become, "overnight" so-to-speak, adequate husbands and wives.

All cultures must deal in one way or another with the cycle of growth from infancy to adulthood. Nature has posed the situation dramatically: on the one hand, the newborn baby, physiologically vulnerable, unable to fend for itself, or to participate of its own initiative in the life of the group, and, on the other, the adult man or woman. Every man who rounds out his human potentialities must have been a son first and a father later, and the two roles are physiologically in great contrast; he must first have been dependent upon others for his very existence, and later he must provide such security for others. This discontinuity in the life cycle is a fact of nature and is inescapable. Facts of nature, however, in any discussion of human problems, are ordinarily read off not at their bare minimal but surrounded by all the local accretions of behavior to which the student of human affairs has become accustomed in his own culture. For that reason, it is illuminating to examine comparative material from other societies in order to get a wider perspective on our own special accretions. The anthropologist's role is not to question the facts of nature, but to insist upon the interposition of a middle term between "nature" and "human behavior"; his role is to analyze that term, to document local man-made doctorings of nature, and to insist that these doctorings should not be read off in any one culture as nature itself. Although it is a fact of nature that the child becomes a man, the way in which this transition is effected varies from one society to another, and no one of these particular cultural bridges should be regarded as the "natural" path to maturity.

From a comparative point of view, our culture goes to great extremes in emphasizing contrasts between the child and the adult. The child is sexless, the adult estimates his virility by his sexual activities; the child must be protected

SOURCE: Copyright Patrick Mullahy. Published by Thomas Nelson & Sons, New York. Originally published in *Psychiatry*, Vol. 1 (1938), 167–67. • The author (1887–1948) was an anthropologist, educator, and poet (under the name Ann Singleton). She was a member of the staff of the Department of Anthropology at Columbia University. Her researches helped to guide Allied propaganda in World War II. She studied Mission, Blackfoot, Apache, Pueblo, and Pima Indians on location and made special studies of mythology, folklore, and primitive religions. Among her books are *Patterns of Culture; Race, Science and Politics;* and *The Chrysanthemum and the Sword.*

from the ugly facts of life, the adult must meet them without psychic catastrophe; the child must obey, the adult must command this obedience. These are all dogmas of our culture, dogmas which, in spite of the facts of nature, other cultures commonly do not share. In spite of the physiological contrasts between child and adult, these are cultural accretions.

It will make the point clearer if we consider one habit in our own culture in regard to which there is not this discontinuity of conditioning. With the greatest clarity of purpose and economy of training, we achieve our goal of conditioning everyone to eat three meals a day. The baby's training in regular food periods begins at birth, and no crying of the child and no inconvenience to the mother is allowed to interfere. We gauge the child's physiological make-up and at first allow it food oftener than adults, but, because our goal is firmly set and our training consistent, before the child is two years old it has achieved the adult schedule. From the point of view of other cultures, this is as startling as the fact of three-year-old babies perfectly at home in deep water is to us. Modesty is another sphere in which our child training is consistent and economical; we waste no time in clothing the baby, and, in contrast to many societies where the child runs naked till it is ceremonially given its skirt or its public sheath at adolescence, the child's training fits it precisely for adult conventions.

In neither of these aspects of behavior is there need for an individual in our culture to embark before puberty, at puberty, or at some later date upon a course of action which all his previous training has tabooed. He is spared the unsureness inevitable in such a transition.

The illustration I have chosen may appear trivial, but, in larger and more important aspects of behavior, our methods are obviously different. Because of the great variety of child training in different families in our society, I might illustrate continuity of conditioning from individual life histories in our culture, but even these, from a comparative point of view, stop far short of consistency; and I shall, therefore, confine myself to describing arrangements in other cultures in which training, which with us is idiosyncratic is accepted and traditional and does not, therefore, involve the same possibility of conflict. I shall choose childhood rather than infant and nursing situations, not because the latter do not vary strikingly in different cultures but because they are nevertheless more circumscribed by the baby's physiological needs than is its later training. Childhood situations provide an excellent field in which to illustrate the range of cultural adjustments which are possible within a universally given, but not so drastic, set of physiological facts.

The major discontinuity in the life cycle is of course that the child who is at one point a son must later be a father. These roles in our society are strongly differentiated; a good son is tractable, and does not assume adult responsibilities; a good father provides for his children and should not allow his authority to be flouted. In addition the child must be sexless so far as his family is concerned, whereas the father's sexual role is primary in the family. The individual in one role must revise his behavior from almost all points of view when he assumes the second role.

I shall select for discussion three such contrasts that occur in our culture between the individual's role as child and as father: (1) responsible-nonresponsible status role; (2) dominance-submission; (3) contrasted sexual role. It is largely upon our cultural commitments to these three contrasts that the discontinuity in the life cycle of an individual in our culture depends.

1. RESPONSIBLE-NONRESPONSIBLE STATUS ROLE

The techniques adopted by societies which achieve continuity during the life cycle in this sphere in no way differ from those we employ in our uniform conditioning to three meals a day. They are merely applied to other areas of life. We think of a child as wanting to play and the adult as having to work, but in many societies the mother takes the baby daily in her shawl or carrying net to the garden or to gather roots, and adult labor is seen even in infancy from the pleasant security of its position in close contact with its mother. When the child can run about, it accompanies its parents still, doing tasks which are essential and yet suited to its powers, and its dichotomy between work and play is not different from that [which] its parents recognize, namely, the distinction between the busy day and the free evening. The tasks it is asked to perform are graded to its powers, and its elders wait quietly by, not offering to do the task in the child's place. Everyone who is familiar with such societies has been struck by the contrast with our child training. Dr. Ruth Underhill tells me of sitting with a group of Papago elders in Arizona when the man of the house turned to his little three-year-old grand-daughter and asked her to close the door. The door was heavy and hard to shut. The child tried, but it did not move. Several times the grandfather repeated: "Yes, close the door." No one jumped to the child's assistance. No one took the responsibility away from her. On the other hand there was no impatience, for after all the child was small. They sat gravely waiting until the child succeeded and her grandfather gravely thanked her. It was assumed that the task would not be asked of her unless she could perform it, and, having been asked, the responsibility was hers alone just as if she were a grown woman.

The essential point of such child training is that the child is from infancy continuously conditioned to responsible social participation, while at the same time the tasks that are expected of it are adapted to its capacity. The contrast with our society is very great. A child does not make any labor contribution to our industrial society except as it competes with an adult; its work is not measured against its own strength and skill but against high-geared industrial requirements. Even when we praise a child's achievement in the home, we are outraged if such praise is interpreted as being of the same order as praise of adults. The child is praised because the parent feels well disposed, regardless of whether the task is well done by adult standards, and the child acquires no sensible standard by which to measure its achievement. The gravity of a Cheyenne Indian family ceremoniously making a feast out of the little boy's first snowbird is at the furthest remove from our behavior. At birth the little boy was presented with a toy bow, and from the time he could run about serviceable bows suited to his stature were specially made for him by the man of the family. Animals and birds were taught him in a graded series beginning with those most easily taken, and as he brought in his first of each species his family duly made feast of it, accepting his contribution as gravely as the buffalo his father brought. When he finally killed a buffalo, it was only the final step of his childhood conditioning, not a new adult role with which his childhood experience had been at variance.

The Canadian Ojibwa show clearly what results can be achieved. This tribe gains its livelihood by winter trapping, and the small family of father, mother, and children live during the long winter alone on their great frozen hunting grounds. The boy accompanies his father and brings in his catch to his sister as his father does to his mother; the girl prepares the meat and skins for him as his mother does for her husband. By the time the boy is 12, he may have set his own line of traps on a hunting territory of his own and return to his parents' house only once in several months—still bringing the meat and skins to his sister. The young child is taught consistently that it has only itself to rely upon in life, and this is as true in the dealings it will have with the supernatural as in the business of getting a livelihood. This attitude he will accept as a successful adult just as he accepted it as a child.

2. DOMINANCE-SUBMISSION

Dominance-submission is the most striking of those categories of behavior where like does not respond to like, but where one type of behavior stimulates the opposite response. It is one of the most prominent ways in which behavior is patterned in our culture. When it obtains between classes, it may be nourished by continuous experience; the difficulty in its use between children and adults lies in the fact that an individual conditioned to one set of behavior in childhood must adopt the opposite as an adult. Its opposite is a pattern of approximately identical reciprocal behavior; the societies which rely upon continuous conditioning characteristically invoke this pattern. In some primitive cultures the very terminology of address between father and son, and, more commonly, between grandfather and grandson or uncle and nephew, reflects this attitude. In such kinship terminologies, one reciprocal expresses each of these relationships so that son and father, for instance, exchange the same term with one another, just as we exchange the same term with a cousin. The child later will exchange it with his son. "Father-son," therefore, is a continuous relationship he enjoys throughout life. The same continuity, backed up by verbal reciprocity, occurs far oftener in the grandfather-grandson relationship or that of mother's brother-sister's son. When these are "joking" relationships, as they often are, travellers report wonderingly upon the liberties and pretensions of tiny toddlers in their dealing with these family elders. In place of our dogma of respect to elders, such societies employ in these cases a reciprocity as nearly identical as may be. The teasing and practical joking the grandfather visits upon his grandchild, the grandchild returns in like coin; he would be led to believe that he failed in propriety if he did not give like for like. If the sister's son has right of access without leave to his mother's brother's possessions, the mother's brother has such rights also to the child's possessions. They share reciprocal privileges and obligations which in our society can develop only between age mates.

From the point of view of our present discussion, such kinship conventions allow the child to put in practice from infancy the same forms of behavior which it will rely upon as an adult; behavior is not polarized into a general requirement of submission for the child and dominance for the adult.

It is clear from the techniques described above, by which the child is conditioned to a responsible status role, that these depend chiefly upon arousing in the child the desire to share responsibility in adult life. To achieve this, little stress is laid upon obedience but much stress upon approval and praise. Punishment is very commonly regarded as quite outside the realm of possibility, and natives in many parts of the world have drawn the conclusion from our usual disciplinary methods that white parents do not love their children. If the child is not required to be submissive, however, many occasions for punishment melt away; a variety of situations which call for it do not occur. Many American Indian tribes are especially explicit in rejecting the ideal of a child's submissive or obedient behavior. Prince Maximilian von Wied, who visited the Crow Indians over a hundred years ago, describes a father's boasting about his young son's intractability even when it was the father himself who was flouted; "He will be a man," his father said. He would have been baffled at the idea that his child should show behavior which would obviously make him appear a poor creature in the eyes of his fellows if he used it as an adult. Dr. George Devereux tells me of a special case of such an attitude among the Mohave at the present time. The child's mother was white and protested to its father that he must take action when the child disobeyed and struck him. "But why?" the father said, "he is little. He cannot possibly injure me." He did not know of any dichotomy according to which an adult expects obedience and a child must accord it. If his child had been docile he would simply have judged that it would become a docile adult—an eventuality of which he would not have approved.

Child training which brings about the same results is common also in other areas of life than that of reciprocal kinship obligations between child and adult. There is a tendency in our culture to regard every situation as having in it the seeds of a dominance-submission relationship. Even where dominance-submission is patently irrelevant we read in the dichotomy, assuming that in every situation there must be one person dominating another. On the other hand some cultures, even when the situation calls for leadership do not see it in terms of dominance-submission. To do justice to this attitude, it would be necessary to describe their political and especially their economic arrangements, for such an attitude to persist must certainly be supported by economic mechanisms that are congruent with it. But it must also be supported by—or what comes to the same thing, express itself in—child training and familial situations.

3. CONTRASTED SEXUAL ROLE

Continuity of conditioning in training the child to assume responsibility and to behave no more submissively than adults is quite possible in terms of the child's physiological endowment if his participation is suited to his strength. Because of the late development of the child's reproductive organs, continuity of conditioning in sex experience presents a difficult problem. So far as their belief that the child is anything but a sexless being is concerned, they are probably more nearly right than we are with an opposite dogma. But the great break is presented by the universally sterile unions before puberty and the presumably fertile ones after maturation. This physiological fact no amount of cultural manipulation can minimize or alter, and societies, therefore, which stress continuous conditioning most strongly sometimes do not expect children to be interested in sex experience until they have matured physically. This is striking among American Indian tribes like the Dakota; adults observe great privacy in sex acts and in no way stimulate children's sexual activity. There need be no discontinuity, in the sense in which I have used the term, in such a program if the child is taught nothing it does not have to unlearn later. In such cultures, adults view children's experimentation as in no way wicked or dangerous, but merely as innocuous play which can have no serious consequences. In some societies such play is minimal and the children manifest little interest in it. But the same attitude may be taken by adults in societies where such play is encouraged and forms a major activity among small children. This is true among most of the Melanesian cultures of Southeast New Guinea; adults go as far as to laugh off sexual affairs within the prohibited class, if the children are not mature, saying that since they cannot marry there can be no harm done.

It is this physiological fact of the difference between children's sterile unions and adults' presumably fertile sex relations which must be kept in mind in order to understand the different mores which almost always govern sex expression in children and in adults in the same culture. A great many cultures with preadolescent sexual license require marital fidelity, and a great many which value premarital virginity in either male or female arrange their marital life with great license. Continuity in sex experience is complicated by factors which it was unnecessary to consider in the problems previously discussed. The essential problem is not whether or not the child's sexuality is consistently exploited—for even where such exploitation is favored, in the majority of cases the child must seriously modify his behavior at puberty or at marriage. Continuity in sex expression means rather that the child is taught nothing it must unlearn later. If the cultural emphasis is upon sexual pleasure, the child who is continuously conditioned will be encouraged to experiment freely and pleasurably, as among the Marquesans; if emphasis is upon reproduction, as among the Zuni of New Mexico, childish sex proclivities will not be exploited, for the only important use which sex is thought to serve in his culture is not yet possible to him. The important contrast with our child training is that, although a Zuni child is impressed with the wickedness of premature sex experimentation, he does not run the risk as in our culture of associating this wickedness with sex itself rather than with sex at his age. The adult in our culture has often failed to unlearn the wickedness or the dangerousness of sex, a lesson which was impressed upon him strongly in his most formative years.

4. DISCONTINUITY IN CONDITIONING

Even from this very summary statement of continuous conditioning, the economy of such mores is evident. In spite of the obvious advantages, however, there are difficulties in its way. Many primitive societies expect as different behavior from an individual as child and as adult as we do, and such discontinuity involves a presumption of strain.

Many societies of this type, however, minimize strain by the techniques they employ; and some techniques are more successful than others in ensuring the individual's functioning without conflict. It is from this point of view that age-grade societies reveal their fundamental significance. Age-graded cultures characteristically demand different behavior of the individual at different times of his life and persons of a like age-grade are grouped into a society whose activities are all oriented toward the behavior desired at that age. Individuals "graduate" publicly and with honor from one of these groups to another. Where age society members are enjoined to loyalty and mutual support, and are drawn not only from the local group but from the whole tribe, as among the Arapaho, or even from other tribes as among the Wagawaga of Southeast New Guinea, such an institution has many advantages in eliminating conflicts among local groups and fostering intratribal peace. This seems to be also a factor in the tribal military solidarity of the similarly organized Masai of East Africa. The point that is of chief interest for our present discussion, however, is that by this means an individual who at any time takes on a new set of duties and virtues is supported not only by a solid phalanx of age mates but by the traditional prestige of the organized "secret" society into which he has now graduated. Fortified in this way, individuals in such cultures often swing between remarkable extremes of opposite behavior without apparent psychic threat. For example, the great majority exhibit prideful and nonconflicted behavior at each stage in the life cycle, even when a prime of life devoted to passionate and aggressive head hunting must be followed by a later life dedicated to ritual and to mild and peaceable civic virtues.

Our chief interest here, however, is in discontinuity which primarily affects the child. In many primitive societies, such discontinuity has been fostered not because of economic or political necessity or because such discontinuity provides for a socially valuable division of labor, but because of some conceptual dogma. The most striking of these are the Australian and Papuan cultures where the ceremony of the "Making of Man" flourishes. In such societies it is believed that men and women have opposite and conflicting powers, and male children, who are of undefined status, must be initiated into the male role. In Central Australia the boy child is of the woman's side, and women are taboo in the final adult stages of tribal ritual. The elaborate and protracted initiation ceremonies of the Arunta, therefore, snatch the boy from the mother, dramatize his gradual repudiation of her. In a final ceremony he is reborn as a man out of the men's ceremonial "baby pouch." The men's ceremonies are ritual statements of a masculine solidarity, carried out by fondling one another's *churingas,* the material symbol of each man's life, and by letting out over one another blood drawn from their veins. After this warm bond among men has been established through the ceremonies, the boy joins the men in the men's house and participates in tribal rites. The enjoined discontinuity has been tribally bridged.

West of the Fly River in southern New Guinea, there is a striking development of the Making of Men cult which involves a childhood period of passive homosexuality. Among the Keraki it is thought that no boy can grow to full stature without playing the role for some years. Men slightly older take the active role, and the older man is a jealous partner. The life cycle of the Keraki Indians includes, therefore, in succession, passive homosexuality, active homosexuality, and heterosexuality. The Keraki believe that pregnancy will result from post-pubertal passive homosexuality and see evidences of such practices in any fat man, whom, even as an old man, they may kill or drive out of the tribe because of their fear. The ceremony that is of interest in connection with the present discussion takes place at the end of the period of passive homosexuality. This ceremony consists in burning out the possibility of pregnancy from the boy by pouring lye down his throat, after which he has no further protection if he gives way to the practice. There is no technique for ending active homosexuality, but this is not explicitly taboo for older men; heterosexuality and children, however, are highly valued. Unlike the neighboring Marindanim who share their homosexual practices, Keraki husband and wife share the same house and work together in the gardens.

I have chosen illustrations of discontinuous conditioning where it is not too much to say that the cultural institutions furnish adequate support to the individual as he progresses from role to role or interdicts the previous behavior in a summary fashion. The contrast with arrangements in our culture is very striking, and against this background of social arrangements in other cultures the adolescent period of *Sturm und Drang* with which we are so familiar becomes intelligible in terms of our discontinuous cultural institutions and dogmas rather than in terms of physiological necessity. It is even more pertinent to consider these comparative facts in relation to maladjusted persons in our culture who are said to be fixated at one or another pre-adult level. It is clear that if we were to look at our social arrangements as an outsider, we should infer directly from our family institutions and habits of child training that many individuals would not "put off childish things"; we should have to say that our adult activity demands traits that are interdicted in children, and that, far from redoubling efforts to help children bridge this gap, adults in our culture put all the blame on the child when he fails to manifest spontaneously the new behavior or, overstepping the mark, manifests it with untoward belligerence. It is not surprising that in such a society many individuals fear to use behavior which has up to that time been under a ban and trust instead, though at great psychic cost, to attitudes that have been exercised with approval during their formative years. Insofar as we invoke a physiological scheme to account for these neurotic adjustments we are led to overlook the possibility of developing social institutions which would lessen the social cost we now pay; instead, we elaborate a set of dogmas which prove inapplicable under other social conditions.

25 G. H. Mead's Theory of Individual and Society

CHARLES W. MORRIS

G. H. Mead's great contribution to sociology was his theoretical analysis of the basic relationship between the person and the group. His "social behaviorism" emphasized the crucial function of language and social interaction in the development of human behavior and stressed that the human mind is a social phenomenon. This selection, taken from Charles Morris' introduction to a compilation of Mead's lectures entitled Mind, Self, and Society, *presents some of the concepts central to his theory. Mead's formulation has come to be known as the "symbolic interaction" theory of behavior.*

The transformation of the biologic individual to the minded organism or self takes place, on Mead's account, through the agency of language, while language in turn presupposes the existence of a certain kind of society and certain physiological capacities in the individual organisms.

The minimal society must be composed of biologic individuals participating in a social act and using the early stages of each other's actions as gestures, that is, as guides to the completion of the act. In the "conversation of gestures" of the dog fight each dog determines his behavior in terms of what the other dog is beginning to do; and the same holds for the boxer, the fencer, and the chick which runs to the hen at the hen's cluck. Such action is a type of communication; in one sense the gestures are symbols, since they indicate, stand for, and cause action appropriate to the later stages of the act of which they are early fragments, and secondarily to the objects implicated in such acts. In the same sense, the gestures may be said to have meaning, namely, they mean the later stages of the oncoming act, and secondarily, the objects implicated: the clenched fist means the blow, the outstretched hand means the object being reached for. Such meanings are not subjective, not private, not mental, but are objectively there in the social situation.

Nevertheless, this type of communication is not language proper; the meanings are not yet "in mind"; the biologic individuals are not yet consciously communicating selves. For these results to transpire the symbols or gestures must become significant symbols or gestures. The individual must know what he is about; he himself, and not merely those who respond to him, must be able to interpret the meaning of his own gesture. Behavioristically, this is to say that the biologic individual must be able to call out in himself the response his gesture calls out in the

SOURCE: George Herbert Mead, *Mind, Self, and Society, from the Standpoint of a Social Behaviorist* (Chicago: The University of Chicago Press, 1934), pp. xx–xxvi. Edited, with introduction by Charles W. Morris. Reprinted by permission of the publisher. • Charles W. Morris is Research Professor of Philosophy at the University of Florida. During the year 1956–57 he was a Fellow at the Center for Advanced Study in the Behavioral Sciences, Palo Alto, Calif. He is the editor of *Works of George H. Mead* and the author of *Six Theories of Mind; Logical Positivism, Pragmatism and Scientific Empiricism;* and *Signs, Language and Behavior.*

other, and then utilize this response of the other for the control of his own further conduct. Such gestures are significant symbols. Through their use the individual is "taking the rôle of the other" in the regulation of his own conduct. Man is essentially the rôle-taking animal. The calling out of the same response in both the self and the other gives the common content necessary for community of meaning.

As an example of the significant symbol Mead uses the tendency to call out "Fire!" when smoke is seen in a crowded theater. The immediate utterance of the sound would simply be part of the initiated act, and would be at the best a non-significant symbol. But when the tendency to call out "Fire!" affects the individual as it affects others, and is itself controlled in terms of these effects, the vocal gesture has become a significant symbol; the individual is conscious of what he is about; he has reached the stage of genuine language instead of unconscious communications; he may now be said to use symbols and not merely respond to signs; he has now acquired a mind.

In looking for gestures capable of becoming significant symbols, and so of transforming the biologic individual into a minded organism, Mead comes upon the vocal gesture. No other gesture affects the individual himself so similarly as it affects others. We hear ourselves talk as others do, but we do not see our facial expressions, nor normally watch our own actions. For Mead, the vocal gesture is the actual fountainhead of language proper and all derivative forms of symbolism; and so of mind.

Mind is the presence in behavior of significant symbols. It is the internalization within the individual of the social process of communication in which meaning emerges. It is the ability to indicate to one's self the response (and implicated objects) that one's gesture indicates to others, and to control the response itself in these terms. The significant gesture, itself a part of a social process, internalizes and makes available to the component biologic individuals the meanings which have themselves emerged in the earlier, non-significant stages of gestural communication. Instead of beginning with individual minds and working out to society, Mead starts with an objective social process and works inward through the importation of the social process of communication into the individual by the medium of the vocal gesture. The individual has then taken the social act into himself. Mind remains social; even in the inner forum so developed thought goes on by one's assuming the rôles of others and controlling one's behavior in terms of such rôle-taking. Since the isolation of the physical thing is for Mead dependent upon the ability to take the rôle of the other, and since thought about such objects involves taking their rôles, even the scientist's reflection about physical nature is a social process, though the objects thought about are no longer social.

• • • • •

It is the same agency of language which on this theory makes possible the appearance of the self. Indeed, the self, mind, "consciousness of," and the significant symbol are in a sense precipitated together. Mead finds the distinguishing trait of selfhood to reside in the capacity of the minded organism to be an object to itself. The mechanism by which this is possible on a behavioristic approach is found in the rôle-taking which is involved in the language symbol. Insofar as one can take the rôle of the other, he can, as it were, look back at himself from (respond to himself from) that perspective, and so become an object to himself. Thus again, it is only in a social process that selves, as distinct from biological organisms, can arise—selves as beings that have become conscious of themselves.

Nor is it merely the process of being aware of one's self that is social: the self that one becomes conscious of in this manner is itself social in form, though not always in content. Mead stresses two stages in the development of the self: the stages of play and the game. In play the child simply assumes one rôle after another of persons and animals that have in some way or other entered into its life. One here sees, writ large as it were, the assumption of the attitudes of others through the self-stimulation of the vocal gesture, whereas later in life such attitudes are more abbreviated and harder to detect. In the game, however, one has become, as it were, all of the others implicated in the common activity—must have within one's self the whole organized activity in order to successfully play one's own part. The person here has not merely assumed the rôle of a specific other, but of any other participating in the common activity; he has generalized the attitude of rôle-taking. In one of Mead's happiest terms and most fertile concepts he has taken the attitude or rôle of the "generalized other."

• • • • •

Through a social process, then, the biologic individual of proper organic stuff gets a mind and a self. Through society the impulsive animal becomes a rational animal, a man. In virtue of the internalization or importation of the social process of communication, the individual gains the mechanism of reflective thought (the ability to direct his action in terms of the foreseen consequences of alternative courses of action); acquires the ability to make himself an object to himself and to live in a common moral and scientific world; becomes a moral individual with impulsive ends transformed into the conscious pursuit of ends-in-view.

Because of the emergence of such an individual, society is in turn transformed. It receives through the reflective social self the organization distinctive of human society; instead of playing his social part through physiological differentiation (as in the case of the insect) or through the bare influence of gestures upon others, the human individual regulates his part in the social act through having within himself the rôles of the others implicated in the common activity. In attaining a new principle of social organization, society has gained a new technique of control, since it has now implanted itself within its component parts, and so regulates, to the degree that this is successfully done, the behavior of the individual in terms of the effect on others of his contemplated action.

26 Riesman on Society and Character

DAVID RIESMAN, WITH
NATHAN GLAZER AND
REUEL DENNEY

The book titled The Lonely Crowd *by David Riesman and his coworkers created a sensation outside as well as inside the "sociological fraternity." The reason for this is the contention of the authors regarding the basic nature of modern Western society. Our society, they assert, has gradually become one in which people are decreasingly "inner-directed" and increasingly "other-directed." To Riesman* et al., *the inner-directed person is one who makes decisions with little regard for their current social acceptability; the other-directed individual is one who tends to commit himself to values or programs only after he has assessed their general social acceptability. These definitions are developed more fully in the following extracts from* The Lonely Crowd. *It should be noted parenthetically (in the selection by Bell, for example) that the trend from inner- to other-direction (if there is such a trend) means that ours is becoming a "mass" society.*

In western history the society that emerged with the Renaissance and Reformation and that is only now vanishing serves to illustrate the type of society in which inner-direction is the principal mode of securing conformity. Such a society is characterized by increased personal mobility, by a rapid accumulation of capital (teamed with devastating technological shifts), and by an almost constant *expansion:* intensive expansion in the production of goods and people, and extensive expansion in exploration, colonization, and imperialism. The greater choices this society gives—and the greater initiatives it demands in order to cope with its novel problems—are handled by character types who can manage to live socially without strict and self-evident tradition-direction. These are the inner-directed types.

The concept of inner-direction is intended to cover a very wide range of types. Thus, while it is essential for the study of certain problems to differentiate between Protestant and Catholic countries and their character types, between the effects of the Reformation and the effects of the Renaissance, between the puritan ethic of the European north and west, and the somewhat more hedonistic ethic of the European east and south, while all these are valid and, for certain purposes, important distinctions, the concentration of this study on the development of modes of conformity permits

SOURCE: *The Lonely Crowd* (1953) by David Riesman, pp. 25–40 passim, permission granted by Yale University Press. • David Riesman is the Henry Ford II Professor of Social Sciences at Harvard University. He was trained as a lawyer and served as a law clerk to Justice Brandeis. In addition to *The Lonely Crowd,* he is the author of *Thorstein Veblen, Individualism Reconsidered and Other Essays, Constraint and Variety in American Education,* and is the coauthor of *The Academic Revolution.* • Nathan Glazer is professor of sociology and of social science at the University of California, Berkeley. His chief interests are race relations in the United States and problems of large cities. He is the author of *American Judaism* and *Social Basis of American Communism,* and the coauthor of *Beyond the Melting Pot.* • Reuel Denney is professor of American studies at the the University of Hawaii. He is the author of *Connecticut River* and *Astonished Muse.*

their neglect. It allows the grouping together of these otherwise distinct developments because they have one thing in common: *the source of direction for the individual is "inner" in the sense that it is implanted early in life by the elders and directed toward generalized but nonetheless inescapably destined goals.*

We can see what this means when we realize that, in societies in which tradition-direction is the dominant mode of insuring conformity, attention is focused on securing external *behavioral* conformity. While behavior is minutely prescribed, individuality of character need not be highly developed to meet prescriptions that are objectified in ritual and etiquette —though to be sure, a social character *capable* of such behavioral attention and obedience is requisite. By contrast, societies in which inner-direction becomes important, though they also are concerned with behavioral conformity, cannot be satisfied with behavioral conformity alone. Too many novel situations are presented, situations which a code cannot encompass in advance. Consequently the problem of personal choice, solved in . . . [a tradition-directed period] by channeling choice through rigid social organization, in the period of . . . [inner-direction] is solved by channeling choice through a rigid though highly individualized character.

This rigidity is a complex matter. While any society dependent on inner-direction seems to present people with a wide choice of aims—such as money, possessions, power, knowledge, fame, goodness —these aims are ideologically interrelated, and the selection made by any one individual remains relatively unalterable throughout his life. Moreover, the means to those ends, though not fitted into as tight a social frame of reference as in the society dependent on tradition-direction, are nevertheless limited by the new voluntary associations—for instance, the Quakers, the Masons, the Mechanics' Associations—to which people tie themselves. Indeed, the term "tradition-direction" could be misleading if the reader were to conclude that the force of tradition has no weight for the inner-directed character. On the contrary, he is very considerably bound by traditions: they limit his ends and inhibit his choice of means. The point is rather that a splintering of tradition takes place, connected in part with the increasing division of labor and stratification of society. Even if the individual's choice of tradition is largely determined for him by his family, as it is in most cases, he cannot help becoming aware of the existence of competing traditions—hence of tradition as such. As a result he possesses a somewhat greater degree of flexibility in adapting himself to ever changing requirements and in return requires more from his environment.

• • • • •

A DEFINITION OF OTHER-DIRECTION

The type of character I shall describe as other-directed seems to be emerging in very recent years in the upper middle class of our larger cities: more prominently in New York than in Boston, in Los Angeles than in Spokane, in Cincinnati than in Chillicothe. Yet in some respects this type is strikingly similar to *the* American, whom Tocqueville and other curious and astonished visitors from Europe, even before the Revolution, thought to be a new kind of man. Indeed, travelers' reports on America impress us with their unanimity. The American is said to be shallower, freer with his money, friendlier, more uncertain of himself and his values, more demanding of approval than the European. It all adds up to a pattern which, without stretching matters too far, resembles the kind of character that a number of social scientists have seen as developing in contemporary, highly industrialized, and bureaucratic America: Fromm's "marketer," Mills's "fixer," Arnold Green's "middle class male child."

It is my impression that the middle-class American of today is decisively different from those Americans of de Tocqueville's writings who nevertheless strike us as so contemporary, and much of this book will be devoted to discussing these differences. It is also my impression that the conditions I believe to be responsible for other-direction are affecting increasing numbers of people in the metropolitan centers of the advanced industrial countries. My analysis of the other-directed character is thus at once an analysis of the American and of contemporary man. Much of the time I find it hard or impossible to say where one ends and the other begins. Tentatively, I am inclined to think that the other-directed type does find itself most at home in America, due to certain unique elements in American society, such as its recruitment from Europe and its lack of any feudal past. As against this, I am also inclined to put more weight on capitalism, industrialism, and urbanization—these being international tendencies—than on any character-forming peculiarities of the American scene.

Bearing these qualifications in mind, it seems appropriate to treat contemporary metropolitan America as our illustration of a society—so far, perhaps, the only illustration—in which other-direction is the dominant mode of insuring conformity. It would be premature, however, to say that it is already the dominant mode in America as a whole. But since the other-directed types are to be found among the young, in the larger cities, and among the upper income groups, we may assume that, unless present trends are reversed, the hegemony of other-direction lies not far off.

If we wanted to cast our social character types into social class molds, we could say that inner-direction is the typical character of the "old" middle class—the banker, the tradesman, the small entrepreneur, the technically oriented engineer, etc.—while other-direction is becoming the typical character of the "new" middle class—the bureaucrat, the salaried employee in business, etc. Many of the economic factors associated with the recent growth of the "new" middle class are well known. They have been discussed by James Burnham, Colin Clark, Peter Drucker, and others. There is a decline in the numbers and in the proportion of the working population engaged in production and extraction—agriculture, heavy industry, heavy transport—and an increase in the numbers and the proportion engaged in white-collar work and the service trades. People who are literate, educated, and provided with the necessities of life by an ever more efficient machine industry and agriculture, turn increasingly to the "tertiary" economic realm. The service industries prosper among the people as a whole and no longer only in court circles.

. . . . .

These developments lead, for large numbers of people, to changes in paths to success and to requirement of more "socialized" behavior both for success and for marital and personal adaptation. Connected with such changes are changes in the family and in child-rearing practices. In the smaller families of urban life, and with the spread of "permissive" child care to ever wider strata of the population, there is a relaxation of older patterns of discipline. Under these newer patterns the peer-group (the group of one's associates of the same age and class) becomes much more important to the child, while the parents make him feel guilty not so much about violation of inner standards as about failure to be popular or otherwise to manage his relations with these other children. Moreover, the pressures of the school and the peer-group are reinforced and continued—in a manner whose inner paradoxes I shall discuss later—by the mass media: movies, radio, comics, and popular culture media generally. Under these conditions types of character emerge that we shall here term other-directed. . . . *What is common to all the other-directed people is that their contemporaries are the source of direction for the individual—either those known to him or those with whom he is indirectly acquainted, through friends and through the mass media. This source is of course "internalized" in the sense that dependence on it for guidance in life is implanted early. The goals toward which the other-directed person strives shift with that guidance: it is only the process of striving itself and the process of paying close attention to the signals from others that remain unaltered throughout life.* This mode of keeping in touch with others permits a close behavioral conformity, not through drill in behavior itself, as in the tradition-directed character, but rather through an exceptional sensitivity to the actions and wishes of others.

Of course, it matters very much who these "others" are: whether they are the individual's immediate circle or a "higher" circle or the anonymous voices of the mass media; whether the individual fears the hostility of chance acquaintances or only of those who "count." But his need for approval and direction from others—and contemporary others rather than ancestors—goes beyond the reasons that lead most people in any era to care very much what others think of them. While all people want and need to be liked by some of the people some of the time, it is only the modern other-directed types who make this their chief source of direction and chief area of sensitivity.

. . . . .

. . . We must differentiate the nineteenth-century American—gregarious and subservient to public opinion though he was found to be by Tocqueville, Bryce, and others—from the other-directed American as he emerges today, an American who in his character is more capable of and more interested in maintaining responsive contact with others both at work and at play. This point needs to be emphasized, since the distinction is easily misunderstood. The inner-directed person, though he often sought and sometimes achieved a relative independence of public opinion and of what the neighbors thought of him, was in most cases very much concerned with his good repute and, at least in America, with "keeping up with the Joneses." These conformities, however, were primarily external, typified in such details as clothes, curtains, and bank credit. For, indeed, the conformities were to a standard, evidence of which was provided by the "best people" in one's milieu. In contrast with this pattern, the other-directed person, though he has his eye very much on the Joneses, aims to keep up with them not so much in external details as in the quality of his inner experience. That is, his great sensitivity keeps him in touch with others on many more levels than the externals of appearance and propriety. Nor does any ideal of independence or of reliance on God alone modify his desire to look to the others—and the "good guys" as well as the best people—for guidance in what experiences to seek and in how to interpret them.

27 The Organization Man

WILLIAM H. WHYTE, JR.

Like the previous selection, this one is taken from a book that has attracted much attention. Whyte's popular treatment has helped to define and clarify the concept of "The Organization Man" and thereby to add a distinctive term to our evolving language. This excerpt from the book bearing the same title briefly analyzes several typical aspects of human behavior in American bureaucratic organizations. It shows how the changing structure of American society, particularly in business, has produced dramatic changes in human behavior and ideology. But the "worship" of organization, decried by Whyte at the end of this selection (note that it dates from the mid-fifties), has probably contributed to the sociological phenomena known as the "youth rebellion" and the "generation gap." The emergence and dynamic quality of these developments suggest that organizational idolatry, having spawned its antithesis, is currently on the decline in American society.

This . . . is about the organization man. If the term is vague, it is because I can think of no other way to describe the people I am talking about. They are not the workers, nor are they the white-collar people in the usual, clerk sense of the word. These people only work for The Organization. The ones I am talking about *belong* to it as well. They are the ones of our middle class who have left home, spiritually as well as physically, to take the vows of organization life, and it is they who are the mind and soul of our great self-perpetuating institutions. Only a few are top managers or ever will be. In a system that makes such hazy terminology as "junior executive" psychologically necessary, they are of the staff as much as the line, and most are destined to live poised in a middle area that still awaits a satisfactory euphemism. But they are the dominant members of our society nonetheless. They have not joined together into a recognizable elite—our country does not stand still long enough for that—but it is from their ranks that are coming most of the first and second echelons of our leadership, and it is their values which will set the American temper.

The corporation man is the most conspicuous example, but he is only one, for the collectivization so visible in the corporation has affected almost every field of work. Blood brother to the business trainee off to join Du Pont is the seminary student who will end up in the church hierarchy, the doctor headed for the corporate clinic, the physics Ph.D. in a government laboratory, the intellectual on the foundation-sponsored team project, the engineering graduate in the huge drafting room at Lockheed, the young apprentice in a Wall Street law factory.

They are all, as they so often put it, in the same boat. Listen to them talk to each other over the front lawns of their suburbia and you cannot help but be

SOURCE: William H. Whyte, Jr., *The Organization Man*, pp. 3–15. • The author was Assistant Managing Editor of *Fortune*. In 1953, he received the Benjamin Franklin Magazine writing award and the Liberty and Justice book award. In addition to *The Organization Man*, his works include *Is Anybody Listening?*, *Open Space*, and *Cluster Development*.

struck by how well they grasp the common denominators which bind them. Whatever the differences in their organization ties, it is the common problems of collective work that dominate their attentions, and when the Du Pont man talks to the research chemist or the chemist to the army man, it is these problems that are uppermost. The word *collective* most of them can't bring themselves to use—except to describe foreign countries or organizations they don't work for—but they are keenly aware of how much more deeply beholden they are to organization than were their elders. They are wry about it, to be sure; they talk of the "treadmill," the "rat race," of the inability to control one's direction. But they have no great sense of plight; between themselves and organization they believe they see an ultimate harmony and, more than most elders recognize, they are building an ideology that will vouchsafe this trust.

. . . America has paid much attention to the economic and political consequences of big organization—the concentration of power in large corporations, for example, the political power of the civil-service bureaucracies, the possible emergence of a managerial hierarchy that might dominate the rest of us. These are proper concerns, but no less important is the personal impact that organization life has had on the individuals within it. A collision has been taking place—indeed, hundreds of thousands of them, and in the aggregate they have been producing what I believe is a major shift in American ideology.

Officially, we are a people who hold to the Protestant Ethic. Because of the denominational implications of the term many would deny its relevance to them, but let them eulogize the American Dream, however, and they virtually define the Protestant Ethic. Whatever the embroidery, there is almost always the thought that pursuit of individual salvation through hard work, thrift, and competitive struggle is the heart of the American achievement.

But the harsh facts of organization life simply do not jibe with these precepts. This conflict is certainly not a peculiarly American development. In their own countries such Europeans as Max Weber and Durkheim many years ago foretold the change, and though Europeans now like to see their troubles as an American export, the problems they speak of stem from a bureaucratization of society that has affected every Western country.

It is in America, however, that the contrast between the old ethic and current reality has been most apparent—and most poignant. Of all peoples it is we who have led in the public worship of individualism. One hundred years ago de Tocqueville was noting that though our special genius—and failing—lay in cooperative action, we talked more than others of personal independence and freedom. We kept on, and as late as the twenties, when big organization was long since a fact, affirmed the old faith as if nothing had really changed at all.

Today many still try, and it is the members of the kind of organization most responsible for the change, the corporation, who try the hardest. It is the corporation man whose institutional ads protest so much that Americans speak up in town meeting, that Americans are the best inventors because Americans don't care that other people scoff, that Americans are the best soldiers because they have so much initiative and native ingenuity, that the boy selling papers on the street corner is the prototype of our business society. Collectivism? He abhors it, and when he makes his ritualistic attack on Welfare Statism, it is in terms of a Protestant Ethic undefiled by change—the sacredness of property, the enervating effect of security, the virtues of thrift, of hard work and independence. Thanks be, he says, that there are some people left—e.g., businessmen—to defend the American Dream.

He is not being hypocritical, only compulsive. He honestly wants to believe he follows the tenets he extols, and if he extols them so frequently it is, perhaps, to shut out a nagging suspicion that he, too, the last defender of the faith, is no longer pure. Only by using the language of individualism to describe the collective can he stave off the thought that he himself is in a collective as pervading as any ever dreamed of by the reformers, the intellectuals, and the utopian visionaries he so regularly warns against.

The older generation may still convince themselves; the younger generation does not. When a young man says that to make a living these days you must do what somebody else wants you to do, he states it not only as a fact of life that must be accepted but as an inherently good proposition. If the American Dream deprecates this for him, it is the American Dream that is going to have to give, whatever its more elderly guardians may think. People grow restive with a mythology that is too distant from the way things actually are, and as more and more lives have been encompassed by the organization way of life, the pressures for an accompanying ideological shift have been mounting. The pressures of the group, the frustrations of individual creativity, the anonymity of achievement: are these defects to struggle against—or are they virtues in disguise? The organization man seeks a redefinition of his place on earth—a faith that will satisfy him that what he must endure has a deeper meaning than appears on the surface. He needs, in short, something that will do for him what the Protestant Ethic did once. And slowly, almost imperceptibly, a body of thought has been coalescing that does that.

I am going to call it a Social Ethic. With reason it could be called an organization ethic, or a bureaucratic ethic; more than anything else it rationalizes the organization's demands for fealty and gives those who offer it wholeheartedly a sense of dedication in doing so—*in extremis,* you might say, it converts what would seem in other times a bill of no rights into a restatement of individualism.

But there is a real moral imperative behind it, and whether one inclines to its beliefs or not he must acknowledge that this moral basis, not mere expediency, is the source of its power. Nor is it simply an opiate for those who must work in big organizations. The search for a secular faith that it represents can be found throughout our society—and among those who swear they would never set foot in a corporation or a government bureau. Though it has its greatest applicability to the organization man, its ideological underpinnings have been provided not by the organization man but by intellectuals he knows little of and toward whom, indeed, he tends to be rather suspicious.

Any groove of abstraction, Whitehead once remarked, is bound to be an inadequate way of describing reality, and so with the concept of the Social Ethic. It is an attempt to illustrate an underlying consistency in what in actuality is by no means an orderly system of thought. No one says, "I believe in the social ethic," and though many would subscribe wholeheartedly to the separate ideas that make it up, these ideas have yet to be put together in the final, harmonious synthesis. But the unity is there.

In looking at what might seem dissimilar aspects of organization society, it is this unity I wish to underscore. The "professionalization" of the manager, for example, and the drive for a more practical education are parts of the same phenomenon; just as the student now feels technique more vital than content, so the trainee believes managing an end in itself, an *expertise* relatively independent of the content of what is being managed. And the reasons are the same. So too in other sectors of our society; for all the differences in particulars, dominant is a growing accommodation to the needs of society—and a growing urge to justify it.

Let me now define my terms. By social ethic I mean that contemporary body of thought which makes morally legitimate the pressures of society against the individual. Its major propositions are three: a belief in the group as the source of creativity; a belief in "belongingness" as the ultimate need of the individual; and a belief in the application of science to achieve the belongingness.

. . . The gist can be paraphrased thus: Man exists as a unit of society. Of himself, he is isolated, meaningless; only as he collaborates with others does he become worthwhile, for by sublimating himself in the group, he helps produce a whole that is greater than the sum of its parts. There should be, then, no conflict between man and society. What we think are conflicts are misunderstandings, breakdowns in communication. By applying the methods of science to human relations we can eliminate these obstacles to consensus and create an equilibrium in which society's needs and the needs of the individual are one and the same.

Essentially, it is a utopian faith. Superficially, it seems dedicated to the practical problems of organization life, and its proponents often use the word *hard* (versus *soft*) to describe their approach. But it is the long-range promise that animates its followers, for it relates techniques to the vision of a finite, achievable harmony. . . .

Like the utopian communities, it interprets society in a fairly narrow, immediate sense. One can believe man has a social obligation and that the individual must ultimately contribute to the community without believing that group harmony is the test of it. In the Social Ethic I am describing, however, man's obligation is in the here and now; his duty is not so much to the community in a broad sense but to the actual, physical one about him, and the idea that in isolation from it—or active rebellion against it—he might eventually discharge the greater service is little considered. In practice, those who most eagerly subscribe to the Social Ethic worry very little over the long-range problems of society. It is not that they don't care but rather that they tend to assume that the ends of organization and morality coincide, and on such matters as social welfare they give their proxy to the organization.

It is possible that I am attaching too much weight to what, after all, is something of a mythology. Those more sanguine than I have argued that this faith is betrayed by reality in some key respects and that because it cannot long hide from organization man that life is still essentially competitive the faith must fall of its own weight. They also maintain that the Social Ethic is only one trend in a society which is a prolific breeder of counter-trends. The farther the pendulum swings, they believe, the more it must eventually swing back.

I am not persuaded. We are indeed a flexible people, but society is not a clock and to stake so much on counter-trends is to put a rather heavy burden on providence. . . .

. . . No one can say whether these trends will continue to outpace the counter-trends, but neither can we trust that an equilibrium-minded providence will see to it that excesses will cancel each other out. Counter-trends there are.

There always have been, and in the sweep of ideas ineffectual many have proved to be.

It is also true that the Social Ethic is something of a mythology, and there is a great difference between mythology and practice. An individualism as stringent, as selfish as that often preached in the name of the Protestant Ethic would never have been tolerated, and in reality our predecessors co-operated with one another far more skillfully than nineteenth-century oratory would suggest. Something of the obverse is true of the Social Ethic; so complete a denial of individual will won't work either, and even the most willing believers in the group harbor some secret misgivings, some latent antagonism toward the pressures they seek to deify.

But the Social Ethic is no less powerful for that, and though it can never produce the peace of mind it seems to offer, it will help shape the nature of the quest in the years to come. The old dogma of individualism betrayed reality too, yet few would argue, I dare say, that it was not an immensely powerful influence in the time of its dominance. So I argue of the Social Ethic; call it mythology, if you will, but it is becoming the dominant one.

• • • • •

This . . . is not a plea for nonconformity. Such pleas have an occasional therapeutic value, but as an abstraction, nonconformity is an empty goal, and rebellion against prevailing opinion merely because it is prevailing should no more be praised than acquiescence to it. Indeed, it is often a mask for cowardice, and few are more pathetic than those who flaunt outer differences to expiate their inner surrender.

I am not, accordingly, addressing myself to the surface uniformities of U.S. life. There will be no strictures . . . against "Mass Man"—a person the author has never met—nor will there be any strictures against ranch wagons, or television sets, or gray flannel suits. They are irrelevant to the main problem, and, furthermore, there's no harm in them. I would not wish to go to the other extreme and suggest that these uniformities per se are good, but the spectacle of people following current custom for lack of will or imagination to do anything else is hardly a new failing, and I am not convinced that there has been any significant change in this respect except in the nature of the things we conform to. Unless one believes poverty ennobling, it is difficult to see the three-button suit as more of a straitjacket than overalls, or the ranch-type house than old law tenements.

And how important, really, are these uniformities to the central issue of individualism? We must not let the outward forms deceive us. If individualism involves following one's destiny as one's own conscience directs, it must for most of us be a realizable destiny, and a sensible awareness of the rules of the game can be a condition of individualism as well as a constraint upon it. The man who drives a Buick Special and lives in a ranch-type house just like hundreds of other ranch-type houses can assert himself as effectively and courageously against his particular society as the bohemian against his particular society. He usually does not, it is true, but if he does, the surface uniformities can serve quite well as protective coloration. The organization people who are best able to control their environment rather than be controlled by it are well aware that they are not too easily distinguishable from the others in the outward obeisances paid to the good opinions of others. And that is one of the reasons they do control. They disarm society.

I do not equate the Social Ethic with

conformity, nor do I believe those who urge it wish it to be, for most of them believe deeply that their work will help, rather than harm, the individual. I think their ideas are out of joint with the needs of the times they invoke, but it is their ideas, and not their good will, I wish to question. As for the lackeys of organization and the charlatans, they are not worth talking about.

Neither do I intend . . . a censure of the fact of organization society. We have quite enough problems today without muddying the issue with misplaced nostalgia, and in contrasting the old ideology with the new I mean no contrast of paradise with paradise lost, an idyllic eighteenth century with a dehumanized twentieth. Whether or not our own era is worse than former ones in the climate of freedom is a matter that can be left to later historians, but . . . I write with the optimistic promise that individualism is as possible in our times as in others.

I speak of individualism *within* organization life. This is not the only kind, and someday it may be that the mystics and philosophers more distant from it may prove the crucial figures. But they are affected too by the center of society, and they can be of no help unless they grasp the nature of the main stream. Intellectual scoldings based on an impossibly lofty ideal may be of some service in upbraiding organization man with his failures, but they can give him no guidance. The organization man may agree that industrialism has destroyed the moral fabric of society and that we need to return to the agrarian virtues, or that business needs to be broken up into a series of smaller organizations, or that it's government that needs to be broken up, and so on. But he will go his way with his own dilemmas left untouched.

I . . . argue that he should fight the organization. But not self-destructively. He may tell the boss to go to hell, but he is going to have another boss, and, unlike the heroes of popular fiction, he cannot find surcease by leaving the arena to be a husbandman. If he chafes at the pressures of his particular organization, either he must succumb, resist them, try to change them, or move to yet another organization.

Every decision he faces on the problem of the individual versus authority is something of a dilemma. It is not a case of whether he should fight against black tyranny or blaze a new trail against patent stupidity. That would be easy—intellectually, at least. The real issue is far more subtle. For it is not the evils of organization life that puzzle him, *but its very beneficence.* He is imprisoned in brotherhood. Because his area of maneuver seems so small and because the trapping so mundane, his fight lacks the heroic cast, but it is for all this as tough a fight as ever his predecessors had to fight.

Thus to my thesis, I believe the emphasis of the Social Ethic is wrong for him. People do have to work with others, yes; the well-functioning team is a whole greater than the sum of its parts, yes—all this is indeed true. But is it the truth that now needs belaboring? Precisely because it *is* an age of organization, it is the other side of the coin that needs emphasis. We do need to know how to co-operate with The Organization but, more than ever, so do we need to know how to resist it. Out of context this would be an irresponsible statement. Time and place are critical, and history has taught us that a philosophical individualism can venerate conflict too much and co-operation too little. But what is the context today? The tide has swung far enough the other way, I submit, that we need not worry that a counteremphasis will stimulate people to an excess of individualism.

The energies Americans have devoted to the co-operative, to the social, are not to be demeaned; we would not, after all, have such a problem to discuss unless we had learned to adapt ourselves to an increasingly collective society as well as we have. An ideal of individualism which denies the obligations of man to others is manifestly impossible in a society such as ours, and it is a credit to our wisdom that while we preached it, we never fully practiced it.

But in searching for that elusive middle of the road, we have gone very far afield, and in our attention to making organization work we have come close to deifying it. We are describing its defects as virtues and denying that there is—or should be—a conflict between the individual and organization. This denial is bad for the organization. It is worse for the individual. What it does, in soothing him, is to rob him of the intellectual armor he so badly needs. For the more power organization has over him, the more he needs to recognize the area where he must assert himself against it. And this, almost because we have made organization life so equable, has become excruciatingly difficult.

To say that we must recognize the dilemmas of organization society is not to be inconsistent with the hopeful premise that organization society can be as compatible for the individual as any previous society. We are not hapless beings caught in the grip of forces we can do little about, and wholesale damnations of our society only lend a further mystique to organization. Organization has been made by man; it can be changed by man. It has not been the immutable course of history that has produced such constrictions on the individual as personality tests. It is organization man who has brought them to pass and it is he who can stop them.

The fault is not in organization, in short; it is in our worship of it. It is in our vain quest for a utopian equilibrium, which would be horrible if it ever did come to pass; it is in the soft-minded denial that there is a conflict between the individual and society. There must always be, and it is the price of being an individual that he must face these conflicts. He cannot evade them, and in seeking an ethic that offers a spurious peace of mind, thus does he tyrannize himself.

There are only a few times in organization life when he can wrench his destiny into his own hands—and if he does not fight then, he will make a surrender that will later mock him. But when is that time? Will he know the time when he sees it? By what standards is he to judge? He does feel an obligation to the group; he does sense moral constraints on his free will. If he goes against the group, is he being courageous—or just stubborn? Helpful—or selfish? Is he, as he so often wonders, right after all? It is in the resolution of a multitude of such dilemmas, I submit, that the real issue of individualism lies today.

28 The Theory of Mass Society

DANIEL BELL

This selection provides another perspective on the ideas contained in the two preceding articles. It is Bell's contention that there is no really substantial evidence to show that our Western world is becoming increasingly a "mass society"—stifling and preventing the expression of individual interest. He feels that "the theory of the mass society no longer serves as a description of Western society, but as an ideology of romantic protest against contemporary society." In developing this thesis, Bell examines and refutes some basic assumptions widely held by many popular writers and social scientists.

The sense of a radical dehumanization of life which has accompanied events of the past several decades has given rise to the theory of "mass society." One can say that, Marxism apart, it is probably the most influential social therapy in the Western world today. While no single individual has stamped his name on it—to the extent that Marx is associated with the transformation of personal relations under capitalism into commodity values, or Freud with the role of the irrational and unconscious in behavior—the theory is central to the thinking of the principal aristocratic, Catholic, or Existentialist critics of bourgeois society today. These critics—Ortega y Gasset, Karl Mannheim, Karl Jaspers, Paul Tillich, Gabriel Marcel, Emil Lederer, and others—have been concerned, less with the general conditions of freedom, than with the freedom of the *person,* and with the possibility for some *few* persons of achieving a sense of individual self in our mechanized society.

The conception of "mass society" can be summarized as follows: The revolutions in transport and communications have brought men into closer contact with each other and bound them in new ways; the division of labor has made them more interdependent; tremors in one part of society affect all others. Despite this greater interdependence, however, individuals have grown more estranged from one another. The old primary group ties of family and local community have been shattered; ancient parochial faiths are questioned; few unifying values have taken their place. Most important, the critical standards of an educated elite no longer shape opinion or taste. As a result, mores and morals are in constant flux, relations between individuals are tangential or compartmentalized rather than organic. At the same time greater mobility, spatial and social, intensifies concern over status. Instead of a fixed or known status symbolized by dress or title, each person assumes a multiplicity of roles and constantly has to prove himself in a succession of new situations. Because of all this, the individual loses a coherent sense of self. His anxieties increase. There ensues

SOURCE: Reprinted from *Commentary,* vol. 22, no. 1 (July 1956), 75–83. Copyright by the American Jewish Committee. The essay also appears, in revised form, in Daniel Bell, *The End of Ideology* (Glencoe, Ill.: The Free Press, 1950).
• The author is professor of sociology at Harvard University and coeditor of *The Public Interest.* His chief interests are industrial relations and industrial sociology. He is the author of *American Marxist Parties, Work in the Life of an American, Work and Its Discontents,* and *The Reforming of General Education.*

a search for new faiths. The stage is thus set for the charismatic leader, the secular messiah, who, by bestowing upon each person the semblance of necessary grace, and of fullness of personality, supplies a substitute for the older unifying belief that the mass society has destroyed.

In a world of lonely crowds seeking individual distinction, where values are constantly translated into economic calculabilities, where in extreme situations shame and conscience can no longer restrain the most dreadful excesses of terror, the theory of the mass society seems a forceful, realistic description of contemporary society, an accurate reflection of the *quality* and *feeling* of modern life. But when one seeks to apply the theory of mass society analytically, it becomes very slippery. Ideal types, like the shadows in Plato's cave, generally never give us more than a silhouette. So, too, with the theory of "mass society." Each of the statements making up the theory, as set forth in the second paragraph above, might be true, but they do not follow necessarily from one another. Nor can we say that all conditions described are present at any one time or place. More than that, there is no organizing principle—other than the general concept of a "breakdown of values"—which puts the individual elements of theory together in a logical, meaningful—let alone historical—manner. And when we examine the way the "theory" is used by those who employ it, we find ourselves even more at a loss.

As commonly used in the term "mass media," "mass" implies that standardized material is transmitted to "all groups of the population uniformly." As understood generally by sociologists, a *mass* is a heterogeneous and undifferentiated audience as opposed to a *class*, or any parochial and relatively homogeneous segment. Some sociologists have been tempted to go further and make "mass" a rather pejorative term. Because the mass media subject a diverse audience to a common set of cultural materials, it is argued that these experiences must necessarily lie outside the personal—and therefore meaningful—experiences to which the individual responds directly. A movie audience, for example, is a "mass" because the individuals looking at the screen are, in the words of the American sociologist Herbert Blumer, "separate, detached, and anonymous." The "mass" divorces—or "alienates"—the individual from himself.

. . . . .

Presumably a large number of individuals, because they have been subjected to similar experiences, now share some common psychological reality in which the differences between individual and individual become blurred; and accordingly we get the sociological assumption that each person is now of "equal weight," and therefore a sampling of what such disparate individuals say they think constitutes "*mass* opinion." But is this so? Individuals are not *tabulae rasae.* They bring varying social conceptions to the same experience, and go away with dissimilar responses. They may be silent, separate, detached, and anonymous while watching the movie, but afterward they talk about it with friends and exchange opinions and judgments. They are once again members of particular social groups. Would one say that several hundred or a thousand individuals home alone at night, but all reading the same book, constitutes a "mass"?

One could argue, of course, that reading a book is a qualitatively different experience from going to a movie. But this leads precisely to the first damaging ambiguity in the theory of the mass society. Two things are mixed up in that theory;

a judgment as to the *quality* of modern experience—with much of which any sensitive individual would agree—and a presumed scientific statement concerning the disorganization of society created by industrialization and by the demand of the masses for equality. It is the second of these statements with which this essay quarrels, not the first.

Behind the theory of social disorganization lies a romantic notion of the past that sees society as having once been made up of small "organic," close-knit communities (called *Gemeinschaften* in the terminology of the sociologists) that were shattered by industrialism and modern life, and replaced by a large impersonal "atomistic" society (called *Gesellschaft*) which is unable to provide the basic gratifications and call forth the loyalties that the older communities knew.

• • • • •

It is asserted that the United States is an "atomized" society composed of lonely, isolated individuals. One forgets the truism, expressed sometimes as a jeer, that Americans are a nation of joiners. There are in the United States today at least 200,000 voluntary organizations, associations, clubs, societies, lodges, and fraternities with an aggregate (but obviously overlapping) membership of close to eighty million men and women. In no other country in the world, probably, is there such a high degree of voluntary communal activity, expressed sometimes in absurd rituals, yet often providing real satisfactions for real needs.

"It is natural for the ordinary American," wrote Gunnar Myrdal, "when he sees something that is wrong to feel not only that there should be a law against it, but also that an organization should be formed to combat it." Some of these voluntary organizations are pressure groups—business, farm, labor, veterans, trade associations, the aged, etc., etc.—but thousands more are like the National Association for the Advancement of Colored People, the American Civil Liberties Union, the League of Women Voters, the American Jewish Committee, the Parent-Teachers Associations, local community-improvement groups, and so on, each of which affords hundreds of individuals concrete, emotionally shared activities.

Equally astonishing are the number of ethnic group organizations in this country carrying on varied cultural, social, and political activities. The number of Irish, Italian, Jewish, Polish, Czech, Finnish, Bulgarian, Bessarabian, and other national groups, their hundreds of fraternal, communal, and political groups, each playing a role in the life of America, is staggering. In December 1954, for example, when the issue of Cyprus was first placed before the United Nations, the Justice for Cyprus Committee, "an organization of American citizens," according to its statement, took a full-page advertisement in the New York *Times* to plead the right of that small island to self-determination. Among the groups listed in the Justice for Cyprus Committee were: the Order of Ahepa, the Daughters of Penelope, the Pan-Laconian Federation, the Cretan Federation, the Pan-Messian Federation, the Pan-Icarian Federation, the Pan-Epirotic Federation of America, the Pan-Thracian Association, the Pan-Elian Federation of America, the Dodecanesian League of America, the Pan-Macedonian Association of America, the Pan-Samian Association, the Federation of Sterea Ellas, the Cyprus Federation of America, the Pan-Arcadian Federation, the GAPA, and the Federation of Hellenic Organizations.

We can be sure that if, in a free world, the question of the territorial affiliation of Ruthenia were to come up before the

United Nations, dozens of Hungarian, Rumanian, Ukrainian, Slovakian, and Czech "organizations of American citizens" would rush eagerly into print to plead the justice of the claims of their respective homelands to Ruthenia.

Even in urban neighborhoods, where anonymity is presumed to flourish, the extent of local ties is astounding. Within the city limits of Chicago, for example, there are eighty-two community newspapers with a total weekly circulation of almost 1,000,000; within Chicago's larger metropolitan area, there are 181. According to standard sociological theory, these local papers providing news and gossip about neighbors should slowly decline under the pressure of the national media. Yet the reverse is true. In Chicago, the number of such newspapers has increased 165 per cent since 1910; in those forty years circulation has jumped 770 per cent. As sociologist Morris Janowitz, who studied these community newspapers, observed: "If society were as impersonal, as self-centered and barren as described by some who are preoccupied with the one-way trend from '*Gemeinschaft*' to '*Gesellschaft*' seem to believe, the levels of criminality, social disorganization and psychopathology which social science seeks to account for would have to be viewed as very low rather than (as viewed now) alarmingly high."

It may be argued that the existence of such a large network of voluntary associations says little about the cultural level of the country concerned. It may well be, as Ortega maintains, that cultural standards throughout the world have declined (in everything—architecture, dress, design?), but nonetheless a greater proportion of the population today participates in worth-while cultural activities. This has been almost an inevitable concomitant of the doubling—*literally*—of the American standard of living over the last fifty years. The rising levels of education have meant rising appreciation of culture. In the United States more dollars are spent on concerts of classical music than on baseball. Sales of books have doubled in a decade. There are over a thousand symphony orchestras, and several hundred museums, institutes, and colleges purchasing art in the United States today. Various other indices can be cited to show the growth of a vast middlebrow society. And in coming years, with steadily increasing productivity and leisure, the United States will become even more actively a "consumer" of culture. . . .

It has been argued that the American mass society imposes an excessive conformity upon its members. But it is hard to discern who is conforming to what. The *New Republic* cries that "hucksters are sugar-coating the culture." The *National Review*, organ of the "radical right," raises the banner of iconoclasm against the liberal domination of opinion-formation in our society. *Fortune* decries the growth of "organization man." Each of these tendencies exists, yet in historical perspective, there is probably less conformity to an over-all mode of conduct today than at any time within the last half-century in America. True, there is less bohemianism than in the twenties (though increased sexual tolerance), and less political radicalism than in the thirties (though the New Deal enacted sweeping reforms). But does the arrival at a political dead-center mean the establishment, too, of a dead norm? I do not think so. One would be hard put to it to find today the "conformity" *Main Street* exacted of Carol Kennicott thirty years ago. With rising educational levels, more individuals are able to indulge a wider variety of interests. ("Twenty years ago you couldn't sell Beethoven out of New York," reports a record salesman. "Today we sell Palestrina, Monteverdi, Gabrielli, and

Renaissance and Baroque music in large quantities.")

One hears, too, the complaint that divorce, crime, and violence demonstrate a widespread social disorganization in the country. But the rising number of divorces . . . indicates not the disruption of the family, but a freer, more individualistic basis of choice, and the emergence of the "companionship" marriage. And as regards crime . . . , there is actually much *less* crime and violence (though more vicarious violence through movies and TV, and more "windows" onto crime, through the press) than was the case twenty-five and fifty years ago. Certainly, Chicago, San Francisco, and New York were much rougher and tougher cities in those years. But violent crime, which is usually a lower-class phenomenon, was then contained within the ecological boundaries of the slum; hence one can recall quiet, tree-lined, crime-free areas and feel that the tenor of life was more even in the past. But a cursory look at the accounts of those days—the descriptions of the gang wars, bordellos, and street-fighting in San Francisco's Barbary Coast, New York's Five Points, or Chicago's First Ward—would show how much more violent in the past the actual life of those cities was.

At this point it becomes quite apparent that such large-scale abstractions as "the mass society" with the implicit diagnoses of social disorganization and decay that derive from them, are rather meaningless without standards of comparison. Social and cultural change is probably greater and more rapid today in the United States than in any other country, but the assumption that social disorder and *anomie* inevitably attend such change is not borne out in this case.

This may be owing to the singular fact that the United States is probably the first large society in history to have change and innovation "built into" its culture. Almost all human societies, traditionalist and habit-ridden as they have been and still are, tend to resist change. The great efforts to industrialize underdeveloped countries, increase worker mobility in Europe, and broaden markets—so necessary to the raising of productivity and standards of living—are again and again frustrated by ingrained resistance to change. Thus in the Soviet Union change has been introduced only by dint of wholesale coercion. In the United States—a culture with no feudal tradition; with a pragmatic ethos, as expressed by Jefferson, that regards God as a "workman"; with a boundless optimism and a restless eagerness for the new that has been bred out of the original conditions of a huge, richly endowed land—change, and the readiness to change, have become the norm. This indeed may be why those consequences of change predicted by theorists basing themselves on European precedent find small confirmation.

The mass society is the product of change—and is itself change. But the *theory* of the mass society affords us no view of the relations of the parts of the society to each other that would enable us to locate the sources of change. We may not have enough data on which to sketch an alternative theory, but I would argue that certain key factors, in this country at least, deserve to be much more closely examined than they have been.

The change from a society once geared to frugal saving and now impelled to spend dizzily; the break-up of family capitalism, with the consequent impact on corporate structure and political power; the centralization of decision-making, politically, in the state and, economically, in a group of large corporate bodies; the rise of status and symbol groups replacing specific interest groups—indicate that new social forms are in the making, and with them still greater changes in the complexion of life under mass society. With these may well come new status anxieties—aggravated by the threats of war—changed character structures, and new moral tempers.

The moralist may have his reservations or give approval—as some see in the break-up of the family the loss of a source of essential values, while others see in the new, freer marriages a healthier form of companionship—but the singular fact is that these changes emerge in a society that is now providing one answer to the great challenge posed to Western—and now world—society over the last two hundred years: how, within the framework of freedom, to increase the living standards of the majority of people, and at the same time maintain or raise cultural levels. American society, for all its shortcomings, its speed, its commercialism, its corruption, still, I believe, shows us the most humane way.

The theory of the mass society no longer serves as a description of Western society, but as an ideology of romantic protest against contemporary society. This is a time when other areas of the globe are beginning to follow in the paths of the West, which may be all to the good as far as material things are concerned; but many of the economically underdeveloped countries, especially in Asia, have caught up the shopworn self-critical Western ideologies of the 19th century and are using them against the West, to whose "materialism" they oppose their "spirituality." What these Asian and our own intellectuals fail to realize, perhaps, is that one may be a thoroughgoing critic of one's own society without being an enemy of its promises.

CHAPTER IV

SOCIAL ORGANIZATION

TYPES OF GROUP RELATIONSHIPS

29 Primary Groups

CHARLES HORTON COOLEY

Professor Cooley, the author of this selection, is recognized as a pioneer in the field of social psychology. One of his very fruitful contributions to sociology is the concept of primary groups as the "nursery of human nature." Here he explains the universality of primary groups and contrasts their characteristics with what we now designate as secondary groups. He carefully defines "human nature," which he declares to be fundamentally the same the world over. Although more recent discoveries have revealed certain limitations in his data, such as his statement in this selection about differences in racial capacities, in most essentials his thinking is sound and illuminating. Since 1909, when the book in which this selection appears was published, much progress has been made in developing the scientific research methods of both psychology and sociology; but many of Cooley's ideas, of which the primary-group concept is one, have a timeless quality.

By primary groups I mean those characterized by intimate face-to-face association and coöperation. They are primary in several senses, but chiefly in that they are fundamental in forming the social nature and ideals of the individual. The result of intimate association, psychologically, is a certain fusion of individualities in a common whole, so that one's very self, for many purposes at least, is the common life and purpose of the group. Perhaps the simplest way of describing this wholeness is by saying that it is a "we"; it involves the sort of sympathy and mutual identification for which "we" is the natural expression. One lives in the feeling of the whole and finds the chief aims of his will in that feeling.

It is not to be supposed that the unity of the primary group is one of mere harmony and love. It is always a differentiated and usually a competitive unity, admitting of self-assertion and various appropriative passions; but these passions are socialized by sympathy, and come, or tend to come, under the discipline of a common spirit. The individual will be ambitious, but the chief object of his ambition will be some desired place in the thought of the others, and he will

SOURCE: Reprinted with the permission of Charles Scribner's Sons from *Social Organization* by Charles Horton Cooley. Copyright 1909 Charles Scribner's Sons; renewal copyright 1937 Elsie Jones. • The author (1864–1929), an American social philosopher, was professor of sociology at the University of Michigan and a president of the American Sociological Association. He made contributions of great range and depth to the field of sociology. Among his important works are *Personal Competition, Human Nature and the Social Order, Social Organization,* and *Social Process.*

feel allegiance to common standards of service and fair play. So the boy will dispute with his fellows a place on the team, but above such disputes will place the common glory of his class and school.

The most important spheres of this intimate association and coöperation—though by no means the only ones—are the family, the play-group of children, and the neighborhood or community group of elders. These are practically universal, belonging to all times and all stages of development; and are accordingly a chief basis of what is universal in human nature and human ideals. The best comparative studies of the family, such as those of Westermarck or Howard, show it to us as not only a universal institution, but as more alike the world over than the exaggeration of exceptional customs by an earlier school had led us to suppose. Nor can any one doubt the general prevalence of play-groups among children or of informal assemblies of various kinds among their elders. Such association is clearly the nursery of human nature in the world about us, and there is no apparent reason to suppose that the case has anywhere or at any time been essentially different.

As regards play, I might, were it not a matter of common observation, multiply illustrations of the universality and spontaneity of the group discussion and coöperation to which it gives rise. The general fact is that children, especially boys after about their twelfth year, live in fellowships in which their sympathy, ambition and honor are engaged even more often than they are in the family. Most of us can recall examples of the endurance by boys of injustice and even cruelty, rather than appeal from their fellows to parents or teachers—as, for instance, in the hazing so prevalent at schools, and so difficult, for this very reason, to repress. And how elaborate the discussion, how cogent the public opinion, how hot the ambitions in these fellowships.

Nor is this facility of juvenile association, as is sometimes supposed, a trait peculiar to English and American boys; since experience among our immigrant population seems to show that the offspring of the more restrictive civilizations of the continent of Europe form self-governing play-groups with almost equal readiness. Thus Miss Jane Addams, after pointing out that the "gang" is almost universal, speaks of the interminable discussion which every detail of the gang's activity receives, remarking that "in these social folk-motes, so to speak, the young citizen learns to act upon his own determination."

Of the neighborhood group it may be said, in general, that from the time men formed permanent settlements upon the land, down, at least, to the rise of modern industrial cities, it has played a main part in the primary, heart-to-heart life of the people. Among our Teutonic forefathers the village community was apparently the chief sphere of sympathy and mutual aid for the commons all through the "dark" and middle ages, and for many purposes it remains so in rural districts at the present day. In some countries we still find it with all its ancient vitality, notably in Russia, where the mir, or self-governing village group, is the main theatre of life, along with the family, for perhaps fifty millions of peasants.

In our own life the intimacy of the neighborhood has been broken up by the growth of an intricate mesh of wider contacts which leaves us strangers to people who live in the same house. And even in the country the same principle is at work, though less obviously, diminishing our economic and spiritual community with our neighbors. How far this change is a healthy development, and how far a disease, is perhaps still uncertain.

Besides these almost universal kinds of primary association, there are many others whose form depends upon the particular state of civilization; the only essential thing, as I have said, being a certain intimacy and fusion of personalities. In our own society, being little bound by place, people easily form clubs, fraternal societies and the like, based on congeniality, which may give rise to real intimacy. Many such relations are formed at school and college, and among men and women brought together in the first instance by their occupations—as workmen in the same trade, or the like. Where there is a little common interest and activity, kindness grows like weeds by the roadside.

But the fact that the family and neighborhood groups are ascendant in the open and plastic time of childhood makes them even now incomparably more influential than all the rest.

Primary groups are primary in the sense that they give the individual his earliest and completest experience of social unity, and also in the sense that they do not change in the same degree as more elaborate relations, but form a comparatively permanent source out of which the latter are ever springing. Of course they are not independent of the larger society, but to some extent reflect its spirit; as the German family and the German school bear somewhat distinctly the print of German militarism. But this, after all, is like the tide setting back into creeks, and does not commonly go very far. Among the German, and still more among the Russian, peasantry are found habits of free coöperation and discussion almost uninfluenced by the character of the state; and it is a familiar and well-supported view that the village commune, self-governing as regards local affairs and habituated to discussion, is a very widespread institution in settled communities, and the continuator of a similar autonomy previously existing in the clan. "It is man who makes monarchies and establishes republics, but the commune seems to come directly from the hand of God."

In our own cities the crowded tenements and the general economic and social confusion have sorely wounded the family and the neighborhood, but it is remarkable, in view of these conditions, what vitality they show; and there is nothing upon which the conscience of the time is more determined than upon restoring them to health.

These groups, then, are springs of life, not only for the individual but for social institutions. They are only in part moulded by special traditions, and, in larger degree, express a universal nature. The religion or government of other civilizations may seem alien to us, but the children or the family group wear the common life, and with them we can always make ourselves at home.

By human nature, I suppose, we may understand those sentiments and impulses that are human in being superior to those of lower animals, and also in the sense that they belong to mankind at large, and not to any particular race or time. It means, particularly, sympathy and the innumerable sentiments into which sympathy enters, such as love, resentment, ambition, vanity, hero-worship, and the feeling of social right and wrong.

Human nature in this sense is justly regarded as a comparatively permanent element in society. Always and everywhere men seek honor and dread ridicule, defer to public opinion, cherish their goods and their children, and admire courage, generosity, and success. It is always safe to assume that people are and have been human.

It is true, no doubt, that there are differences of race capacity, so great that a large part of mankind are possibly incapable of any high kind of social organization. But these differences, like those among individuals of the same race, are subtle, depending upon some obscure intellectual deficiency, some want of vigor, or slackness of moral fibre, and do not involve unlikeness in the generic impulses of human nature. In these all races are very much alike. The more insight one gets into the life of savages, even those that are reckoned the lowest, the more human, the more like ourselves, they appear. Take for instance the natives of Central Australia, as described by Spencer and Gillen, tribes having no definite government or worship and scarcely able to count to five. They are generous to one another, emulous of virtue as they understand it, kind to their children and to the aged, and by no means harsh to women. Their faces . . . are wholly human and many of them attractive.

And when we come to a comparison between different stages in the development of the same race, between ourselves, for instance, and the Teutonic tribes of the time of Caesar, the difference is neither in human nature nor in capacity, but in organization, in the range and complexity of relations, in the diverse expression of powers and passions essentially much the same.

There is no better proof of this generic likeness of human nature than in the ease and joy with which the modern man makes himself at home in literature depicting the most remote and varied phases of life—in Homer, in the Nibelung tales, in the Hebrew Scriptures, in the legends of the American Indians, in stories of frontier life, of soldiers and sailors, of criminals and tramps, and so on. The more penetratingly any phase of human life is studied the more an essential likeness to ourselves is revealed.

To return to primary groups: the view here maintained is that human nature is not something existing separately in the individual, but a *group-nature or primary phase of society,* a relatively simple and general condition of the social mind. It is something more, on the one hand, than the mere instinct that is born in us—though that enters into it—and something less, on the other, than the more elaborate development of ideas and sentiments that makes up institutions. It is the nature which is developed and expressed in those simple, face-to-face groups that are somewhat alike in all societies; groups of the family, the playground, and the neighborhood. In the essential similarity of these is to be found the basis, in experience, for similar ideas and sentiments in the human mind. In these, everywhere, human nature comes into existence. Man does not have it at birth; he cannot acquire it except through fellowship, and it decays in isolation.

If this view does not recommend itself to common-sense I do not know that elaboration will be of much avail. It simply means the application at this point of the idea that society and individuals are inseparable phases of a common whole, so that wherever we find an individual fact we may look for a social fact to go with it. If there is a universal nature in persons there must be something universal in association to correspond to it.

What else can human nature be than a trait of primary groups? Surely not an attribute of the separate individual—supposing there were any such thing—since its typical characteristics, such as affection, ambition, vanity, and resentment, are inconceivable apart from society. If it belongs, then, to man in association, what kind or degree of association is required to develop it? Evidently nothing elaborate, because elaborate phases of society are transient and diverse, while human nature is comparatively stable and universal. In short the family and neighborhood life is essential to its genesis and nothing more is.

Here as everywhere in the study of society we must learn to see mankind in psychical wholes, rather than in artificial separation. We must see and feel the communal life of family and local groups as immediate facts, not as combinations of something else. And perhaps we shall do this best by recalling our own experience and extending it through sympathetic observation. What, in our life, is the family and the fellowship; what do we know of the we-feeling? Thought of this kind may help us to get a concrete perception of that primary group-nature of which everything social is the outgrowth.

30 Contrasting Types of Group Relationships

JOHN B. HOLLAND

Sociologists have introduced a number of terms to characterize types of social relationships. The primary group concept described in the previous selection, the contrasting secondary group concept, and the Gemeinschaft *and* Gesellschaft *concepts developed by Ferdinand Tönnies are probably most widely used to identify differing patterns of social interaction. In this selection John Holland defines* Gemeinschaft *and* Gesellschaft *and illustrates their usefulness in social analysis.*

The individual lives in a world made up of many groups of people. While we think of ourselves as individuals, separate and distinct from all other individuals, we do not, nor can we live without others. We are not only individuals, we are at the same time group members. We participate in many kinds of social groups. More than that we find ourselves at times, both as individuals and as group members, in conflict with other groups. And in a complex modern world we find ourselves affected by still other groups about whom we may be unaware.

The nature of these many associations that we as individuals have with other people is complex, varied, and often difficult to determine. Some progress may be made toward clarifying these relations, however, if we will distinguish between two quite different kinds of human relations. We shall use the classification of Tönnies, a German sociologist, and explore the meaning of the terms Gemeinschaft and Gesellschaft.

Before doing so it is necessary to be critical of any attempt to classify all human relations into only two general categories. Further, rather than thinking of Gemeinschaft and Gesellschaft as two separate and distinct kinds of human relations, it would seem more nearly correct to think of them as occupying the extreme ends of a straight line.

The extreme ends of such a scale represent pure types or polar extremes. Our own concrete and real experiences with other people usually fall somewhere along this scale rather than at one end or the other. Our relations with others are generally in terms of more or less rather

SOURCE: Leo A. Haak, ed., *Source Book for Effective Living* (East Lansing: Michigan State University, 1950), 196–99, reprinted by permission. • Professor Holland (1910–1953) was a member of the Department of Sociology and Anthropology and of the Social Science Department at Michigan State University. He was the coauthor of *Community Involvement.*

than all or none, for usually these relations involve both Gemeinschaft and Gesellschaft. Nevertheless, by clearly defining the polar extremes we may classify many of our relations as an individual in the group, for generally one or the other kind of relationship is predominant. The scale furnishes us with a convenient device to measure many of the kinds of associations we have as group members, though we need not assume that all human relations can be made to fit into one or the other of these categories.

This way of classifying our relations with others is not new. The ideas we are to explore here have been most explicitly developed by Tönnies, but they are really a refinement of the thinking of many others who have gone before. Confucius and Plato, Aristotle and Cicero, St. Augustine and Thomas Aquinas, to mention only a few, have attempted to understand and account for the different kinds of human relationships which they observed. Their classifications are similar to that of Tönnies. This way of looking at people, therefore, is not new, it has been useful to many of the great thinkers of the ages, and it is useful to us because it gives us a new pair of glasses with which we may look at facts which are familiar to all of us.

GESELLSCHAFT RELATIONS

First, let us define Gesellschaft, not because it comes first, but because it is the easiest to explain. A brief definition may be given as "Rational relations based on calculation of individual self-interest." Like all brief statements there are many points covered in that definition. What are some of them?

• • • • •

First of all, our Gesellschaft relations with others are based upon reason and not feeling. Second, we are concerned with our individual self-interest. Third, our obligations are limited to whatever specific contract is stated or implied. Fourth, our relationship with others covers only a specific and clearly-defined area of interest. Fifth, it is not necessary, in fact it is entirely irrelevant whether or not we have any interests in common other than these specific, individual interests which we hope to further by our relationship.

In terms of concrete, flesh and blood people what does this mean? What kind of relations do we have with other people which serve our immediate interests and are largely Gesellschaft in character?

Take an inventory of your daily activities. Whom do you see and what do you do when you are with other people? When you buy a loaf of bread is it primarily an intimate and friendly exchange, or is it a contract between buyer and seller? If you get a check from Veterans Administration do you have a warm personal feeling for the man who signed the check, or do you look to see if it is made out correctly and delivered on time? If you have a part-time job, do you usually prop your feet upon the boss's desk for an hour of friendly conversation, or do you have specific, well-defined duties which you are expected to perform? When you registered at this college, although the cashier may have been very friendly, was this principally Gesellschaft or otherwise? The illustrations could be multiplied indefinitely in terms of your own experiences, but these serve to point out the fact that you and I, living as we do in a complex society, spend a great deal of time busily engaged with the pursuit of our own self-interests. And we have many contacts with other human beings who are likewise concerned with their own interests. In this pursuit of self-interest, people have little reality for us as human beings, as personalities who think, feel, and act, and have personal problems even as we. Because so many of our relations with others are largely Gesellschaft in character it is not surprising that we sometimes fail to recognize the reality of groups and the effect on us and our personalities of our many associations with others.

GEMEINSCHAFT RELATIONS

Just as Gesellschaft is a polar type which characterizes one kind of human relations, so Gemeinschaft is the other. Broadly stated Gemeinschaft is everything that Gesellschaft is not. Gemeinschaft comes logically first in human relations.

Gemeinschaft is easier to define but harder to explain. A brief definition is: "Intimate relations based on sentiment." That is, Gemeinschaft relations are based on the way we feel about people. They are intimate relations. In such contacts with others people are real. Our concern is not with rational calculations and limited obligations but with flesh and blood people and our felt obligations to them.

We may make further contrasts. Whereas in Gesellschaft we enter into a relationship because of rational consideration of individual self-interest, in Gemeinschaft our motives are general and indefinite in character. This is so because they are not carefully calculated but are a part of our feelings. Gemeinschaft relations cover a multitude of interests not well defined at all. For example, if you are married why did you marry? There are many answers, not one or two single, specific reasons. You married for love, to have a home, to raise children, to obtain what we may call psychic security—that is, emotional security and approval. If I ask you why you entered the college bookstore you can tell me exactly. But if I ask you why you married this particular person, why you like certain friends, why you have a friendly feeling for the old home town, it is difficult to explain. This is natural since sentiments and feelings, being nonrational, are hard to explain by rational means. Frequently, however, we feel called upon to justify our feelings and in so doing we depend upon rationalizations which we offer as "good reasons" to explain our behavior.

A second contrast with Gesellschaft relations is that in Gemeinschaft obligations are unspecified and unlimited. There is no specific contract. The burden of proof is on him who would evade an obligation arising out of a Gemeinschaft relation. Let us examine the obligations in marriage. In a general sense a marriage between two people involves a ceremony in which certain obligations are stated. But these are blanket obligations which in the final analysis mean an obligation on each of the marriage partners to help in whatever contingencies arise in their common life together. A married veteran is going to school. There is nothing in the marriage contract which says that his wife will take a full or part-time job to help him in that process. And yet many veterans' wives are doing just that. If a friend of yours is down and out and needs ten dollars there is no written obligation on your part to meet his need. But if you've got the money and if he is a real friend of yours, one for whom you have an intimate and deep-seated liking, you loan him the money, even though you do not expect to get it back.

A third point that may be made about Gemeinschaft relations is that not only are obligations unlimited but they can be ignored only because of the prior obligations of another Gemeinschaft relationship. To illustrate, if you are a doctor you would not, as a husband, ordinarily leave your wife's bridge party. But if it were necessary for you to make an emergency call you would do so. Or again if you were about to meet with a friend who was in a tough spot and needed you to help him regain his bearings, you would cancel the engagement if your child were to be injured or suddenly taken ill. But it should be noted that you are relieved of one Gemeinschaft obligation only because another and higher Gemeinschaft obligation supercedes. You do not customarily ignore Gemeinschaft obligations for Gesellschaft obligations, or if you do we may safely say that there was no deep Gemeinschaft feeling on your part in the first place.

Finally, Gemeinschaft obligations are both moral and ethical in character. I mean by that that individuals in a Gemeinschaft relationship have individual interests but these interests are integrated and a part of the ultimate values of the group. It is safe to say that as a member of a family, insofar as you have intimate feelings for that family, you share in common certain beliefs and ideals. There are certain moral responsibilities that you feel and these moral responsibilities are a part of your individual codes of ethics, your standards, your values. Gemeinschaft relations are shared relations. They extend beyond individual self-interest. In Gemeinschaft relations your individual purposes and ends are integrated and a part of the purposes and ends of the group.

These are the principal characteristics of Gemeinschaft. Relations are intimate and based on feelings or sentiment, not upon reason or calculation. In Gemeinschaft there is what we might call a bond or feeling of belonging. Thus we speak of the bond that unites man and wife or friends or a group of neighbors who are intimately acquainted with each other.

We can illustrate Gemeinschaft concretely for ourselves again in terms of the groups of people with whom we associate in a day. Whom did you see today? How intimately are you concerned with their welfare? Not abstract persons, but real people about whose welfare you are genuinely and personally concerned? What bonds do you have with others and what would it take to break them?

In summary, then, Gemeinschaft relations are intimate relations based on sentiment; Gesellschaft relations are rational relations based on calculation of individual interest. These two types of relations are polar extremes and our actual relations with others vary from extreme, intimate, personal relations with others to extreme, rational calculation of people as means to serve our own immediate ends. It is useful to make this classification because it enables us to analyze more clearly our relations with others and to see in proper perspective our actions as they affect and are affected by others. But even beyond that we need to appraise what is involved in gaining and losing Gemeinschaft relations because we live in a world which is based increasingly upon Gesellschaft. How well each of us personally can survive by rational concern with limited and specific interests alone is a problem which confronts us both as individuals and as group members.

31 The Social "World" of the Transients' Camp

JOHN STEINBECK

The talented novelist often describes aspects of social reality more clearly and more vividly than the usually restrained accounts of social scientists. This skill is well illustrated in The Grapes of Wrath, *the classic story of the migrant farm family "tractored out" of Oklahoma but hopeful of finding a better life in California. The following selection from the novel shows how quickly human relationships can develop regularities and become "organized," even in so transitory a situation as the overnight camp of the westward-moving migrant farm families.*

The cars of the migrant people crawled out of the side roads onto the great cross-country highway, and they took the migrant way to the West. In the daylight they scuttled like bugs to the westward; and as the dark caught them, they clustered like bugs near to shelter and to water. And because they were lonely and perplexed, because they had all come from a place of sadness and worry and defeat, and because they were all going to a new mysterious place, they huddled together; they talked together; they shared their lives, their food, and the things they hoped for in the new country. Thus it might be that one family camped near a spring, and another camped for the spring and for company, and a third because two families had pioneered the place and found it good. And when the sun went down, perhaps twenty families and twenty cars were there.

In the evening a strange thing happened: the twenty families became one family, the children were the children of all. The loss of home became one loss, and the golden time in the West was one dream. And it might be that a sick child threw despair into the hearts of twenty families, of a hundred people; that a birth there in a tent kept a hundred people quiet and awestruck through the night and filled a hundred people with the birth-joy in the morning. A family which the night before had been lost and fearful might search its goods to find a present for a new baby. In the evening, sitting about the fires, the twenty were one. They grew to be units of the camps, units of the evenings and the nights. A guitar unwrapped from a blanket and tuned—and the songs, which were all of the people, were sung in the nights. Men sang the words, and women hummed the tunes.

Every night a world created, complete with furniture—friends made and enemies established; a world complete with braggarts and with cowards, with quiet men, with humble men, with kindly men. Every

SOURCE: *The Grapes of Wrath* by John Steinbeck. Copyright 1939, copyright © renewed 1967 by John Steinbeck. Reprinted by permission of the Viking Press, Inc. • John Steinbeck (1902-1968) was a renowned American novelist who received the Pulitzer Prive in 1940 and was awarded the Nobel Prize for literature in 1962. He was also awarded the Presidential Medal of Freedom in 1964. Among his many books are *Tortilla Flat, Of Mice and Men, Winter of Our Discontent, America and Americans,* and *Travels with Charley.*

night relationships that make a world, established; and every morning the world torn down like a circus.

At first the families were timid in the building and tumbling worlds, but gradually the technique of building worlds became their technique. Then leaders emerged, then laws were made, then codes came into being. And as the worlds moved westward they were more complete and better furnished, for their builders were more experienced in building them.

The families learned what rights must be observed—the right of privacy in the tent; the right to keep the past black hidden in the heart; the right to talk and to listen; the right to refuse help or to accept, to offer help or to decline it; the right of son to court and daughter to be courted; the right of the hungry to be fed; the rights of the pregnant and the sick to transcend all other rights.

And the families learned, although no one told them, what rights are monstrous and must be destroyed: the right to intrude upon privacy, the right to be noisy while the camp slept, the right of seduction or rape, the right of adultery and theft and murder. These rights were crushed, because the little worlds could not exist for even a night with such rights alive.

And as the worlds moved westward, rules became laws, although no one told the families. It is unlawful to foul near the camp; it is unlawful in any way to foul the drinking water; it is unlawful to eat good rich food near one who is hungry, unless he is asked to share.

And with the laws, the punishments—and there were only two—a quick and murderous fight or ostracism; and ostracism was the worst. For if one broke the laws his name and face went with him, and he had no place in any world, no matter where created.

In the worlds, social conduct became fixed and rigid, so that a man must say "Good morning" when asked for it, so that a man might have a willing girl if he stayed with her, if he fathered her children and protected them. But a man might not have one girl one night and another the next, for this would endanger the worlds.

The families moved westward, and the technique of building the worlds improved so that the people could be safe in their worlds; and the form was so fixed that a family acting in the rules knew it was safe in the rules.

There grew up government in the worlds, with leaders, with elders. A man who was wise found that his wisdom was needed in every camp; a man who was a fool could not change his folly with his world. And a kind of insurance developed in these nights. A man with food fed a hungry man, and thus insured himself against hunger. And when a baby died a pile of silver coins grew at the door flap, for a baby must be well buried, since it has had nothing else of life. An old man may be left in a potter's field, but not a baby.

A certain physical pattern is needed for the building of a world—water, a river bank, a stream, a spring, or even a faucet unguarded. And there is needed enough flat land to pitch the tents, a little brush or wood to build the fires. If there is a garbage dump not too far off, all the better; for there can be found equipment—stove tops, a curved fender to shelter the fire, and cans to cook in and to eat from.

And the worlds were built in the evening. The people, moving in from the highways, made them with their tents and their hearts and their brains.

In the morning the tents came down, the canvas was folded, the tent poles tied along the running board, the beds put in place on the cars, the pots in their places. And as the families moved westward, the technique of building up a home in the evening and tearing it down with the morning light became fixed; so that the folded tent was packed in one place, the cooking pots counted in their box. And as the cars moved westward, each member of the family grew into his proper place, grew into his duties; so that each member, old and young, had his place in the car; so that in the weary, hot evenings, when the cars pulled into the camping places, each member had his duty and went to it without instruction: children to gather wood, to carry water; men to pitch the tents and bring down the beds; women to cook the supper and to watch while the family fed. And this was done without command. The families, which had been units of which the boundaries were a house at night, a farm by day, changed their boundaries. In the long hot light, they were silent in the cars moving slowly westward; but at night they integrated with any group they found.

Thus they changed their social life—changed as in the whole universe only man can change. They were not farm men any more, but migrant men. And the thought, the planning, the long staring silence that had gone out to the fields, went now to the roads, to the distance, to the West. That man whose mind had been bound with acres lived with narrow concrete miles. And his thought and his worry were not any more with rainfall, with wind and dust, with the thrust of the crops. Eyes watched the tires, ears listened to the clattering motors, and minds struggled with oil, with gasoline, with the thinning rubber between air and road. Then a broken gear was tragedy. Then water in the evening was the yearning, and food over the fire. Then health to go on was the need and strength to go on, and spirit to go on. The wills thrust westward ahead of them, and fears that had once apprehended drought or flood now lingered with anything that might stop the westward crawling.

The camps became fixed—each a short day's journey from the last.

And on the road the panic overcame some of the families, so that they drove night and day, stopped to sleep in the cars, and drove on to the West, flying from the road, flying from movement. And these lusted so greatly to be settled that they set their faces into the West and drove toward it, forcing the clashing engines over the roads.

But most of the families changed and grew quickly into the new life. And when the sun went down——

Time to look out for a place to stop.

And—there's some tents ahead.

The car pulled off the road and stopped, and because others were there first, certain courtesies were necessary. And the man, the leader of the family, leaned from the car.

Can we pull up here an' sleep?

Why, sure, be proud to have you. What State you from?

Come all the way from Arkansas.

They's Arkansas people down that fourth tent.

That *so?*

And the great question, How's the water?

Well, she don't taste so good, but they's plenty.

Well, thank ya.

No thanks to me.

But the courtesies had to be. The car lumbered over the ground to the end tent, and stopped. Then down from the car the weary people climbed, and stretched stiff bodies. Then the new tent sprang up; the children went for water and the older boys cut brush or wood. The fires started and supper was put on to boil or to fry. Early comers moved over, and States were exchanged, and friends and sometimes relatives discovered.

Oklahoma, huh? What county?

Cherokee.

Why, I got folks there. Know the Allens? They's Allens all over Cherokee. Know the Willises?

Why, sure.

And a new unit was formed. The dusk came, but before the dark was down the new family was of the camp. A word had been passed with every family. They were known people—good people.

32 Social Relations in a Bureaucracy

GEORGE C. HOMANS

To the uninitiated, a bureaucracy, with its many rules of operation and its highly organized and formalized structure, has little room for any informal interaction, either in relation to the job or in a purely social sense. Actually, however, the work of large and complex organizations is mediated through a network of many small, interrelated groups. This selection, written by George Homans but based upon case material from Peter Blau's The Dynamics of Bureaucracy, *examines the interpersonal processes which develop in the work situation and explores the reasons for the behavior which takes place. After reading this article, the student will find it instructive to observe, utilizing Homans' approach, some small group with which he is acquainted.*

A FEDERAL AGENCY: CONSULTATION AMONG COLLEAGUES

The group consisted of a supervisor, sixteen agents, and one clerk, who formed in 1949 a department in a local branch of a Federal agency that had its headquarters in Washington, D.C. In order to protect the anonymity of the group, the investigator does not tell us what the precise job of the agency was. Broadly it was concerned with the enforcement of a certain set of Federal laws. Since we are not interested in formal organization, and since he was hardly a member of the group, we shall not have much to say about the supervisor; nor was the clerk a member. Our business is with the sixteen agents.

The members of the department were fairly experienced in their work: only one had been with the agency for less than five years. Two held the civil-service grade 9, which was the highest represented among the agents; two were in grade 7; and the rest, the great majority, were in the middle with grade 8. But regardless of their different grades, all did much the same kind of work. Only three were women, and only one was a Negro. On the average an agent spent about 40 per cent of his time in the home office, where he had a desk of his own along with the other agents. But because their

SOURCE: Abridged from *Social Behavior: Its Elementary Forms* by George C. Homans, © 1961, by Harcourt, Brace & World, Inc., and reprinted with their permission. • The author is professor of sociology at Harvard University. His major interests include industrial relations and sociological theory. In addition to *Social Behavior: Its Elementary Forms,* his writings include *The Human Group, English Villagers of the Thirteenth Century,* and *The Nature of Social Science.* He is a former president of the American Sociological Association.

duties took them often into the field, not all the agents were together in the office at any one time.

An agent's main duty was investigation. On assignment by the supervisor, he went to the office of a business firm, obtained from it a wide variety of information, then came back to the agency where, from the information he had collected, he wrote a report stating whether or not and in what way the firm had violated Federal law. In order to determine whether a violation had occurred, an agent had to know how a large and complex body of legal rulings applied to the circumstances of a particular case. And since his report might become the basis of legal action against the firm, an agent had to be sure of his facts, his argument, and the clarity of his presentation.

The quality of the reports an agent turned in to the supervisor determined more than anything else the kind of efficiency rating the latter gave him, and this in turn affected his chances for promotion to a higher grade in the civil service. Thus an agent had to do a job difficult in itself, and his success in doing it made a difference to his future. Moreover, unlike the members of many industrial groups, the agents believed strongly in the value of the work the agency was doing, and so were doubly motivated to do it right.

Yet in spite of his long experience, an agent was often in doubt which legal rules might be applicable to the case under consideration and what decision he ought to reach about it. An agent was left free to make his own decision, the only formal rule being that if he had any doubt or question, he was to bring it to the supervisor without consulting any of his colleagues. But like many formal rules, this one was disregarded. Not unnaturally the agents believed that to take a question to the supervisor was to confess one's incompetence and so to prejudice one's efficiency rating; accordingly they did go to their colleagues for help and advice, and the supervisor seems to have winked at the practice.

Although the agents all had much experience, they still recognized that some of their number were better than others at solving the problems that came up over writing reports. Blau's first job was to ask every agent to put all the others in order of their competence as he saw it. The individual rankings were highly in agreement with one another, and they agreed also with the supervisor's ranking of the competence of the different agents.

The investigator next tried to relate the perceived competence of the different agents to the number of times other agents went to them for help and advice. In the course of his observations of behavior in the department, the investigator kept a record of every contact between agents, however brief it might have been, such as a word spoken in passing. He discovered that an agent, while he was in the office, had an average of five contacts per hour with colleagues. Some of these were casual and social conversations, but many were discussions of technical problems. The investigator decided that the latter were probably the longer, and so in studying the distribution of technical consultations he included only contacts that lasted more than three minutes. The investigator also asked every agent to name the other agents whom he consulted when he ran into difficulties with his work.

The results showed a rather marked pattern. As we should expect, the more competent an agent, the more contacts he was apt to receive, and the higher was the esteem in which he was held. But the correlation was not perfect. Two of the agents who their colleagues believed were competent seem to have discouraged people that came to them for help and so to have choked off further advances. As Blau says, "The two experts who were considered uncooperative by their colleagues were generally disliked and received only few contacts. To become accepted, an expert had to share the advantages of his superior skill with his co-workers."

But most agents were ready to help. A few of them, and these among the most competent of all, were consulted by a large number of others, but did not themselves go regularly for advice to any one agent. Thus four agents had no regular partners, but all four were highly competent. Three of them were also very popular as consultants. "These three were by no means isolated from the exchange of advice. On the contrary, they participated so widely in it that they did not spend much time with any single coworker." The fourth agent had only recently been assigned to the department and had not yet been brought into much use as a consultant. The rest of the agents, on the other hand, were apt to take regular partners. Each one of them, though occasionally consulting the few highly competent men, was apt to be especially closely linked with one or two others whose competence was more nearly equal to his own. On any occasion when he needed help, he felt free to consult his partner, as long as he was ready to allow the latter the same kind of privilege in return.

REWARDS AND COSTS OF CONSULTATION

Now let us see what the investigator has to say about the social economics of consultation:

> A consultation can be considered an exchange of values; both participants gain something, and both have to pay a price. The questioning agent is enabled to perform better than he could otherwise have done, without exposing his difficulties to the supervisor. By asking for advice, he implicitly pays his respect to the superior proficiency of his colleague. This acknowledgment of inferiority is the cost of receiving assistance. The consultant gains prestige, in return for which he is willing to devote some time to the consultation and permit it to disrupt his own work. The following remark of an agent illustrates this: "I like giving advice. It's flattering, I suppose, if you feel that the others come to you for advice."

The expert who was willing to give advice got various advantages incidental to his rise in esteem. From the consultation he drew renewed confidence in his own capacity to solve technical problems. He might, indeed, pick up ideas useful to him in doing his own work without paying the price of an admission of inferiority. Each of the three most popular consultants, whom many others asked for help, could, moreover, when he needed help in return, scatter his requests among these many and did not need to concentrate them on any single agent, which would have made more conspicuous the fact that it was help he was asking for. As the investigator puts it: "Besides, to refrain from asking any particular individual too many questions helped to maintain his reputation as an expert. Consequently, three of the most popular consultants had no regular partners."

The cost that an expert incurred in getting his prestige is obvious: he had to take time from his own work. "All agents liked being consulted, but the value of any one of very many consultations became deflated for experts, and the price they paid in frequent interruptions became inflated. . . . Being approached for help was too valuable an experience to be refused, but popular consultants were not inclined to encourage further questions."

The investigator is quite explicit that asking a colleague for help incurred an agent costs: "Asking a colleague for guidance was less threatening than asking the supervisor, but the repeated admission of his inability to solve his own problems also undermined the self-confidence of an agent and his standing in the group. The cost of advice became prohibitive, if the consultant, after the questioner had subordinated himself by asking for help, was in the least discouraging—by postponing a discussion or by revealing his impatience during one."

The cost in inferiority of asking a colleague for help was rendered greater in this group than it would have been in some others by the fact that, formally, the agents were not greatly unequal: all held the same job-title, all did the same kind of work, and most of them held the same civil-service grade. A man who is already another's inferior has much less to lose in asking a service of him than one who began as his equal.

That asking for help did indeed incur a man costs is shown by the practice some agents adopted of asking for help while elaborately pretending that they were doing nothing of the sort. Such an agent would bring his problem to a colleague as if it were a case presenting special points of interest well worthy of dispassionate analysis between two discriminating judges. As one of the agents said, "Casey asks me sometimes, too, but he does it with a lot of finesse. He will just seem to ask what my opinion is, not as if he were worried about the question." And the investigator makes the comment: "Such manipulative attempts to obtain advice without reciprocating by acknowledging the need for the other's help were resented. . . . If his advice was needed, the agent demanded that the respect due him be paid by *asking* for his assistance. An official whose deliberate disguise of a consultation was discovered created resentment without averting loss of esteem." In short, this maneuver broke the rules of fair exchange: it attempted to get help without conceding superiority in return. . . .

As we have seen, three of the most competent agents did not enter into partnerships, did not regularly exchange help and advice with particular other agents. Two highly competent agents did take regular partners, but upon the whole partnerships were confined to people of middle and low competence. The investigator implies that it was precisely the costs a man incurred in asking the most competent agents for advice that led the rest to seek out partners among people more nearly of their own rank, with whom they could exchange help without losing status; for the essence of partnership was that if one man asked his partner for help on one occasion, the partner might ask the same favor back on the next. Speaking of the fact that an agent who tried to consult one of his more competent colleagues might meet with a refusal, Blau says:

> To avoid such rejections, agents usually consulted a colleague with whom they were friendly, even if he was not an expert. . . . The establishment of partnerships of mutual consultation virtually eliminated the danger of rejections as well as the status threat implicit in asking for help, since the roles of questioner and consultant were intermittently reversed. These partnerships also enabled agents to reserve their consultations with an expert whom they did not know too well for their most complicated problems.

That is, the advice a man got from his partner might not be of the highest value, but it was purchased at low cost since a partner was apt to be his social equal. And thus he was enabled to save his really difficult problems for the most competent agents, whose advice, since it did come high in confessed inferiority, he did not want to ask often. . . .

. . . Social behavior is an exchange of more or less valuable rewards. The expert agents provided for the others a service that these others found valuable and rare. In return, the experts received much interaction and were able to command from the rest a high degree of esteem, thus establishing a social ranking in the group. But in getting these rewards both parties to the exchange incurred costs—the experts in time taken away from their own work, the others in implicit admissions of inferiority. The costs, moreover, increased and the rewards declined with the number of exchanges, thus tending to cut off further exchange. The experts began to rebuff new requests, and the rest began to hesitate before approaching the experts. Indeed the rest began to look for sources of help they could exploit at lower cost. In the nature of the case, these sources could only be agents more nearly of their own rank than the experts. With such people they could both give and take advice without net loss in esteem.

Finally, most agents met the conditions of distributive justice. For instance, the experts who were ready to give help got much esteem but incurred heavy costs in time taken away from their own work: their costs were proportional to their rewards. Therefore the other agents not only respected but liked them. To win esteem it was not enough to *be* expert: a man had to devote his expert knowledge to the service of others. Thus a couple of agents, known to be competent, who repelled others approaching them with requests for help, were much disliked and left much alone. In failing to enter into exchange at all they had deprived the others of services that the others had come to expect of people with so much to give.

"SOCIAL" INTERACTION

The investigator next turned to the relations between the agents' competence and their more purely "social" behavior. Of the latter he made two different kinds of observations. In his period of watching the group he had kept a record of all the contacts (interactions) an agent received from others, but in mapping out the pattern of consultations he had included only the relatively long contacts—three minutes or more—on the ground that long contacts were more likely than short ones to have to do with the official business of the agency. Now, in mapping out "social" behavior—passing the time of day, gossiping, telling jokes—he included all the contacts an agent received, long or short, and called this a measure of *contacts received.* The investigator also asked each agent to keep a record every day of the colleagues he lunched with. "If a luncheon engagement is defined as eating with one colleague once, the total number of engagements reported (which often included several colleagues on the same day, and the same colleague on repeated days), divided by the number of days on which the respondent went out to lunch from the office, defines the value of this index,"—which the investigator called a measure of an agent's *informal relations.*

He then proceeded to study the interrelations of these three variables: competence, contacts received, and informal relations. For this purpose, he divided the rank-order of the agents on each variable into two parts, but the division did not necessarily come at the mid-point of the distribution. Thus seven agents were rated as high in competence and eight low, but six were rated as high in contacts received and nine low. (One agent transferred out of the department in the course of the study, reducing the total number of the agents considered for the present purpose to fifteen.)

Agents high in competence were statistically likely to be high also in contacts received. Not all were: the two highly competent agents who were unwilling to give the others the benefit of their competence and who were accordingly disliked received few social contacts; but the tendency was in this direction. By the same token, the less competent agents tended statistically to get few contacts.

Perhaps this finding tells us little more than we know already. An expert who was willing to share his knowledge with others was much sought after by the others for consultation, and we know that many of the contacts an expert received were of this sort. But not all were: some were more purely "social." Once a man has won esteem by providing others with rare and valuable services, another reason for their seeking him out comes into play: he is now able to offer a new kind of service. . . .

. . . Some members of a group, those not unduly troubled about their self-respect, seek out social interaction with a member of high status for reasons other than getting the service that first won him the status. But how will a member of high status receive their advances? If he is in any doubt about his status, social contacts with his inferiors will tend to bring him down to their level, and he is apt to rebuff them; but if his status is so firmly established that he need not worry about it, his willingness to allow them social access to him provides them with a new and valuable service and enhances the esteem in which they hold him.

"Contacts received" was measured by the number of interactions a man received in the office, and this might include "business" contacts as well as "social" ones. The best index of purely "social" contacts was "informal relations," which was measured by luncheons. The investigator found that, statistically speaking, agents of high competence were apt to have few informal relations and agents of low competence to have many. Some of the competent agents did not use their competence to help others; therefore they did not enjoy high status, and the others were not much interested in getting their company for lunch. Some enjoyed a status both high and secure, and could afford to wait until others approached them. And some may not have been quite sure of their high status, which may have led them to rebuff the advances of their inferiors. All of these effects tended to reduce the informal relations of the more competent people. But the less competent people, who on the average were less secure in their status than the more competent ones, tended actively to seek others out for luncheon dates. They sought out the agents of high status if they could get them, but if they could not, they found lunching with somebody better than lunching alone. No doubt man is a gregarious animal and enjoys lunching with his fellows regardless of what it does to his status. Our only point is that differences in status provide additional reasons for (or against) social contacts. By lunching with any one of his fellows an agent of low status could at least make good the fact that he was the other's equal, that he was at least an accepted member of the group. At any rate, the less competent agents "lunched in larger groups than experts and made greater efforts to arrange their work so that they would have to eat alone as rarely as possible." By eating in large groups they necessarily rolled up a high score in informal relations, since each person present at the table added to the score.

Though the competent agents tended to have fewer informal relations than the less competent, lunching more often alone or with fewer companions, the relationship was statistical and did not hold good of all of them. One agent of whom it did not hold good was the one who, in the office, was most encouraging to people who came and asked him for help.

He was better liked than any other agent, and became, as we shall soon see, the informal leader of the group. In short, his status was both high and secure. "His great willingness to assist others," the investigator comments, "was his price for maintaining this position." But this was not the only service he did for them: he was also willing to provide them with the secondary reward of lunching with him. "He was particularly hospitable to colleagues who consulted him, and he deliberately fostered informal relations with them. 'If anyone asks me for lunch,' he told the observer, 'I never say, "I have a date with another fellow; I can't." I always say, "Of course, come along."' In contrast to most experts, this agent had very extensive informal relations."

The investigator finally turned to the third of the possible relations between the three variables, the relation between informal relations and contacts received, and he found that agents who had many informal relations (luncheons) were statistically likely to receive many contacts.

• • • • •

It is interesting to reconstruct from the investigator's data what the actual pattern of social engagements among the agents must have been. We shall not give here the tedious reasoning that leads to the reconstruction but only its conclusions. The less competent agents must have lunched with one another a great deal, and in large groups, without the more competent agents' being present—indeed the investigator implies as much. The competent agents must also have lunched with one another a good deal without the less competent agents' being present—but in small groups. This suggests that they may have rebuffed some of the social advances made to them by the less competent agents. And, finally, some of the less competent managed to get some of the more competent to lunch with them fairly often, in large groups. In fact the investigator tells us that the informal leader was one of the competent men who thus allowed himself to be lunched with by his social inferiors. Equals, then, tended in general to lunch with equals, but some inferiors made successful advances to their superiors in status.

We have here further evidence of the complex interplay of two tendencies we have encountered again and again: a tendency for a man to interact with his superiors in status, and a tendency for him to interact with his equals. A man establishes superior status by providing superior services for others. By the same token, accepting the superior services becomes a cost to a man, since he thereby recognizes his inferiority. Sooner or later he will turn to others who can provide him with services that no doubt reward him less but that also cost him less in inferiority. In the nature of the case, these others can only be his equals. As the partnerships in the Federal agency show, he will turn to his equals for services at work that he can return in kind; but he is particularly apt to turn to them in the "social" field of activity, just because it is *not* the field in which his superiors win their high esteem—and he his low. A secondary development then builds on this primary one. The rest of mankind can "see" the equations of elementary social behavior just as clearly in their way as we social scientists can, and once the relation between social interaction and equality of status is established, it provides new rewards for interaction. By interacting with his fellows a man can then provide evidence for himself and for them that he is at least their equal. Still better, if he can get his superior to interact with him he may do something to raise his apparent status.

ESTEEM AND AUTHORITY

As we have just seen, people of high status tend to receive much interaction. Indeed to maneuver a man into coming to you is to establish the presumption that you are his superior. But people of high status also give much interaction, especially in the sense of originating activity. They tell a relatively large number of others what they ought to do, and the others often do it. The higher the esteem, the higher the authority, is a proposition for which the Federal agency provided much evidence.

Let us consider particularly the agent who the investigator believes was the top informal leader in the department. (The supervisor was of course the formal leader.) He was highly competent at his job, and recognized as being so both by the supervisor and by the other agents. Of the more competent agents, he was also the one most receptive and least discouraging to requests for help from others. That is, he was the most willing to incur the cost of taking time off from his own work. And he was highly popular. . . .

. . . He received high rewards in esteem from the group, but in so doing he incurred, as they saw it, high costs too.

He rewarded the others not only in the business side of their life but in the social one too. He was always ready to accept an invitation to lunch with his social inferiors, and in this he was unlike most of the other competent agents. But the very liberality with which he distributed his favors prevented his becoming identified with any one of the cliques whose members met regularly for lunch. He was in touch with everybody and not exclusively in touch with any single person or subgroup. . . .

. . . The more competent agents tended to take the lead in any undertaking in which several members of the group were engaged. They made most suggestions, and their suggestions were most often followed, whether the question was where to go for lunch or what to do about a project on which a number of agents were working together. And of all the competent agents, the one held in highest esteem was the one who also held highest authority. When a committee was appointed to draft a change in one of the regulations, he dominated the discussion, and his opinion was the one finally adopted. Above all he stood up for the other agents against the supervisor. In this connection the investigator says of him:

> This agent became the informal leader of the group, whose suggestions the others often followed and who acted as their spokesman. For example, in a departmental meeting the supervisor criticized certain deficiencies in the performance of most agents, clearly exempting experts from his criticism. Nevertheless, this official spoke up on behalf of the group and explained that agents could not be blamed for these deficiencies, since a legal regulation that restricted their operations was responsible for them. Generally, the high regard in which this agent was held made his advice and opinion influential among colleagues, and even among superiors.

A man to whom many others come singly for valuable services, in this case advice on how to do their work, and who in rendering the services incurs costs visibly proportional to the esteem they have given him, earns the right to tell them jointly what to do in new conditions that may affect the welfare of many of them, himself among the rest. By serving he becomes a leader. We must always remember that the services he provides need not be ones that you or I should find rewarding or even approve of. Leaders get to be where they are by doing some of the strangest things, and the rest of us are always asking ourselves, "What's he got that I haven't got?" The answer is that what he has got does actually reward some other men, whether or not it ought to do so, and what he has got is rare in the actual circumstances, whether or not it would be rare in others.

Nor should we lay too much stress on the difference between the followers' coming to him singly and his telling them jointly what to do. In both cases, whether he gives them advice they take or orders they obey, the important point is that he controls their behavior; and the fact that a new occasion may call for his advising them jointly is a nonessential detail. His past behavior has won him the capability of doing so, should the occasion present itself, but it may not. The advice he has given them singly they have in the past rewarded with approval, and so he is more likely to give advice again on a new occasion. He has, as we say, acquired confidence in his ability to give them advice. Nor is it just that he has more confidence but that the others have less: persons whose status is less than his own are persons whose advice has less often won approval in the past, and who are therefore less apt to have the gall to speak up now: what wise ideas they have do them no good if they lack the confidence to come out with them.

The relation between past behavior and present that holds good for the leader holds good also for the followers. Having taken his advice singly and found it rewarding, they are more ready to take it jointly—to obey him when he tells them what to do for their welfare and his own. In doing so, he puts his social capital at hazard, since if they obey and fail to find the outcome rewarding, he has done injury to his esteem and their future willingness to obey. But he has much capital to risk, and if they do find the outcome to their satisfaction, he has replaced his capital and more. Finally, though the leader may lay himself open to the social advances of his followers, he cannot allow himself to get too close to any one of them or any single clique; for frequent social interaction implies equality, and equality between people tends to be incongruent with the fact that one of their number gives orders to the rest. But the best guarantee that he shall not be too close to anyone lies in the very profusion with which he scatters his favors abroad.

NONCONFORMITY AND ISOLATION

A member of a group acquires high esteem by providing rare and valuable services for the other members. But these are obviously not the only services a member can perform: he can also perform services that, without being rare, nevertheless have their value. Prominent among them is conformity to the norms of the group—a norm being a statement of what behavior ought to be, to which at least some members of the group find it valuable that their own actual behavior and that of other members should conform. Since a norm envisages that a relatively large number of members will behave similarly in some respect, conformity to a norm cannot be a rare service: any fool can conform if he will only take the trouble; and therefore if all a man did was conform, he would never get much esteem, though he would always get some. But it does not follow that if conformity will not win a man much esteem, nonconformity will not lose him much—if he has any to lose. For his failure to conform, when the other members see no just reason why he should not, deprives them unfairly of a valuable service, and so earns him their positive hostility.

Among themselves the agents had, over time, worked out several unofficial norms. They felt that no agent, as a maximum, should complete more than the eight cases a month that the supervisor expected of every agent as a minimum. And they felt that no agent should take a report home from the office in order to work on it in the evening. Agents who showed any sign of doing these things were kidded until they stopped. Violation of these norms was an injury to the members of the group, and conformity a value to them, because an agent who finished more than eight cases a month or worked on cases at home might have gotten an advantage over the others in the race for promotion; and if everyone had started to violate the norms, they would all have found themselves, through competition, working harder than they ever had before—not that the supervisor was at all discouraged with the quantity and quality of their present work: the agents were devoted civil servants. In practice, these output norms conspired to perpetuate existing differences in competence, since they prevented slower agents from catching up with their superiors by working harder.

The agents laid an even more severe taboo against reporting to the supervisor that firms had offered them bribes, though by the official rules of the agency they were bound to report such offers. It was not that the agents accepted bribes and wanted to prevent a colleague who was puritanical about such matters from spoiling their game. Far from it: when they suspected that an officer of a firm was working up to offering a bribe, they did their best to cut him off before he could commit himself openly. In the agents' view, it was inevitable that businessmen, given the pressures they worked under, should think of bribery; therefore it ought not to be held against them, and an agent reporting them and so making them subject to legal action was a "squealer." The agents also had a more practical interest in the norm against reporting bribes. If possible an agent was expected to induce the firm he was investigating to obey the law voluntarily and not under the compulsion of legal action expensive to both parties. An offer of a bribe, however tactfully it was made, put into an agent's hand a lever by which he might without legal action get the firm to comply with the law. But it was a lever that became worse than useless once the proffered bribe was officially reported. Indeed the report might make the company all the more ready to fight it out with the government in the courts. Accordingly, agents discouraged all tendencies in their colleagues to "get tough with" and "crack down on" companies, except as a last resort. Should the agency get the reputation of behaving this way, their work would become much more difficult: all companies would meet every agent with automatic hostility, and the chances of persuading them instead of compelling them to compliance would be gone forever. For these reasons most agents felt they had a direct personal interest in seeing that all their colleagues conformed to this norm.

With these norms in mind, let us look at one of the isolates in the department. When we call him an isolate, we mean that he received few social contacts and often lunched alone. Although he appears to have been considered fairly competent, he not only was not ready to use his competence for the benefit of others but spent his time instead turning out more work than the others considered right. Already held in low esteem for behavior of this sort, he proceeded to take a "get tough" attitude toward the firms he investigated; indeed this was generally more apt to be true of the less popular agents than of the more popular ones. And he was the only agent who violated the strongest taboo of all and reported to the supervisor that a bribe had been offered him. The investigator tells us little or nothing about the social background of any of the agents, including this one, and so we cannot tell what features of his past history may have predisposed him to behave as he did. He himself admitted he had made a mistake: though he had violated the norm, he was ready to say it was a good one.

For his action the group had for a time deliberately ostracized him. Cutting off interaction with a member and thus depriving him of any social reward whatever is the most severe punishment a group can inflict on him; in fact he ceases to be a member. But once a man has stood that, he can, so to speak, stand anything; and the group has lost control of him, for it has left him with nothing more to lose. Certainly the department had pretty well lost control of this agent. Though he reported no more bribes, he did much as he pleased in other ways. For instance, the agents felt that he wasted their time by talking a great deal too much in department meetings, where the agents of higher esteem usually took the largest part in the discussion. But in spite of the laughter his remarks provoked, he kept at it and could not be cowed. In a better cause he might have been a hero. The investigator believes that this agent provided only the most conspicuous example of a general tendency: that agents of established low status conformed least closely to the norms of the group, while those of middle status—particularly those, like newcomers, whose esteem was least well established—were the greatest conformers of all.

Social behavior, in a group as elsewhere, is a continuous process of members influencing other members, and the success of influence in the past changes the probability of its success in the future. One result of the process of influence is that the members of a group become differentiated in a more or less stable way—stable so long as external circumstances do not change much. As some members, for instance, succeed in providing, under the influence of requests from others, more valuable services for these others than they can provide for themselves, the members become differentiated in esteem. This fairly stable differentiation in some pattern other than a random one is what we mean by the structure or organization of the group. But the structure is never so stable that it does not itself sow the seeds of further change, and we have been studying a particular example of this. The process of influence that has landed a man at the bottom of the ladder of esteem may render any future influence, so far as it comes from other members, still less likely to succeed with him. Suppose he would ordinarily lose esteem by doing something other than what they want, but he happens as a result of his past behavior to be left without any esteem to lose. If there is any other way in which he finds the action rewarding—and it may be rewarding just because it vexes *them*—the fact that its costs have been reduced to zero raises the odds in favor of his taking it.

A group controls its members by creating rewards for them which it can then threaten to withdraw. If the group has to make good the threat too often, it may wind up with nothing left to withdraw. Its control is always precarious as long as the members have any alternative to accepting the control, such as the alternative offered by another group they can make their escape to. We have been speaking of the low-status member who is going lower. But very high status may have something of the same effect as very low. A man who has so much status to lose that he will not mind if he loses a little of it can afford to try something new and take the risk that it may not turn out to be acceptable to the membership. He too, in his way, is exempt from the control of the group. There are deviates and deviates, some from the point of view of the group are bad deviates, some are good ones. But both are innovators; and if one looked only at the innovations they propose, it would often be hard to tell which is which.

We try to describe what happens in human behavior without taking any moral stand about it—unless laughter is a moral stand. Or rather we take only one stand out of the many open to us. We have nothing to say in favor of conformity or against it. All we have done is point out that a man who does not conform takes certain risks. But a man is born to take risks. Morally we cannot object to him unless he wants his nonconformity made easy, unless he wants to kick the group in the teeth and have it like him too. For then he is being unfair to the rest of us by asking that an exception to the human condition be made in his favor.

CHAPTER V

SOCIAL ORGANIZATION

COLLECTIVE BEHAVIOR

33 The Men from Mars

JOHN HOUSEMAN

Collective behavior depends upon some form of communication functioning within the framework of a shared culture. Under these conditions any enlargement in the available means of communication, such as radio, television, and the communication satellites, increases the potential size of the audience whose attention may be attracted and whose behavior may be influenced for either desirable or undesirable ends through control of the content transmitted. In the selection which follows, John Houseman gives a graphic account of a startling and rather disquieting episode precipitated by a radio program designed only for entertainment. Realism was necessary to ensure the full dramatic effect in its presentation. So skillful was the technique used, however, that thousands believed an actual invasion from Mars was taking place. The panic, the irrational behavior of many people who chanced to tune in, is an interesting example of the propaganda power of radio and television. Houseman rejects the idea that the incident can be dismissed as an example of the "incredible stupidity and gullibility of the American public." Instead, he indicates many other important factors that must be considered in any explanation of the effects stimulated by the broadcast.

RADIO WAR TERRORIZES U.S.—*N.Y. Daily News, October 31, 1938*

Everybody was excited I felt as if I was going crazy and kept on saying what can we do what difference does it make whether we die sooner or later? We were holding each other. Everything seemed unimportant in the face of death. I was afraid to die, just kept on listening.—*A listener*

Nothing about the broadcast was in the least credible.—*Dorothy Thompson*

The show came off. There is no doubt about that. It set out to dramatize, in terms of popular apprehension, an attempted invasion of our world by hostile forces from the planet Mars. It succeeded. Of the several million American citizens who, on the evening of October 30, 1938, milled about the streets, clung sobbing to one another or drove wildly in all directions to avoid asphyxiation and flaming death, approximately one-half

SOURCE: *Harper's Magazine,* vol. 197, no. 1183 (December 1948), 74–82. Reprinted by permission of the author and the publisher. • The author is the director of the drama division at the Julliard School of Performing Arts at Lincoln Center, New York, and was cofounder of the Mercury Theater, New York, in the 1930s. He supervised Voice of America programs during World War II for the Radio Program Bureau, Office of War Information.

were in terror of Martians—not of Germans, Japanese, or unknown enemies—but, specifically, of Martians. Later, when the excitement was over and the shadow of the gallows had lifted, some of us were inclined to take credit for more deliberate and premeditated villainy than we deserved. The truth is that at the time, nobody was more surprised than we were. In fact, one of the most remarkable things about the broadcast was the quite haphazard nature of its birth.

In October 1938, the Mercury Theater, of which Orson Welles and I were the founding partners, had been in existence for less than a year. Our first Broadway season had been shatteringly successful—"Julius Caesar," "The Cradle Will Rock," "Shoemaker's Holiday," and "Heartbreak House" in the order of their appearance. In April, Orson, in a straggly white beard, made the cover of *Time* Magazine. In June, the Columbia Broadcasting System offered him a radio show—"The Mercury Theater on the Air," a series of classic dramatizations in the first person singular with Orson as master of ceremonies, star, narrator, writer, director, and producer. He accepted. So, now, in addition to an empty theater, a movie in progress, two plays in rehearsal, and all seven of the chronicle plays of William Shakespeare in preparation, we had a radio show.

We opened on July 11. Among our first thirteen shows were "Treasure Island," "39 Steps," "Abraham Lincoln," "Three Short Stories" (by Saki, Sherwood Anderson, and Carl Ewald), "Jane Eyre," "Julius Caesar" (with running commentary by Kaltenborn out of Plutarch), and "The Man Who Was Thursday." Our second series, in the fall, began with Booth Tarkington's "Seventeen," "Around the World in Eighty Days," and "Oliver Twist." Our fifth show was to be "Life with Father." Our fourth was "The War of the Worlds."

No one, as I remember, was very enthusiastic about it. But it seemed good programming, between the terrors of Dickens' London slums, and the charm of Clarence Day's New York in the nineties, to throw in something of a contrasting and pseudo-scientific nature. We thought of Shiel's *Purple Cloud,* Conan Doyle's *Lost World,* and several others before we settled on H. G. Wells' twenty-year-old novel, which neither of us, as it turned out later, remembered at all clearly. It is just possible that neither of us had ever read it.

II

Those were our golden days of unsponsored radio. We had no advertising agency to harass us, no client to cut our withers. Partly because we were perpetually overworked and partly because that was the way we did things at the Mercury, we never seemed to get more than a single jump ahead of ourselves. Shows were created week after week under conditions of soul- and health-destroying pressure. On the whole they were good shows. And we *did* develop a system—of sorts.

It worked as follows: I was editor of the series. With Welles, I chose the shows and then laid them out. The writing, most of it, was done by Howard Koch—earnest, spindly, six-foot-two—a Westchester lawyer turned playwright. To write the first draft of an hour's radio script took him about five days, working about fifteen hours a day. Our associate producer was Paul Stewart, a Broadway actor turned director. His function was to put the broadcast through its first paces and preliminary rehearsals. Every Thursday, musicless and with rudimentary sound effects, a wax record of the show was cut. From this record, played back later that night, Orson would give us his reactions and revisions. In the next thirty-six hours the script would be reshaped and rewritten, sometimes drastically. Saturday afternoon there was another rehearsal, with sound—with or without Welles. It was not until the last day that Orson really took over.

Sundays, at eight, we went on the air. Beginning in the early afternoon—when Bernard Herrmann arrived with his orchestra of twenty-seven high-grade symphony players—two simultaneous dramas were regularly unfolded in the stale, tense air of Studio Number One: the minor drama of the current show and the major drama of Orson's gargantuan struggle to get it on. Sweating, howling, disheveled, and single-handed he wrestled with Chaos and Time—always conveying an effect of being alone, traduced by his collaborators, surrounded by treachery, ignorance, sloth, indifference, incompetence and—more often than not—downright sabotage! Every Sunday it was touch and go. As the hands of the clock moved relentlessly toward air time the crisis grew more extreme, the peril more desperate. Often violence broke out. Scripts flew through the air, doors were slammed, batons smashed. Scheduled for six—but usually nearer seven—there was a dress rehearsal, a thing of wild improvisations and irrevocable disaster. (One show was found to be twenty-one minutes overlength, another fourteen and one-half minutes short.)

After that, with only a few minutes to go, there was a final frenzy of correction and reparation, of utter confusion and absolute horror, aggravated by the gobbling of sandwiches and the bolting of oversized milkshakes. By now it was less than a minute to air time. . . .

At that instant, quite regularly week after week—with not one second to spare . . . the titanic buffoonery stopped. Suddenly out of chaos, the show emerged—delicately poised, meticulously executed, precise as clockwork, and smooth as satin. And above us all, like a rainbow over storm clouds, stood Orson on his podium, sonorous and heroic, a leader of men surrounded by his band of loyal followers; a giant in action, serene and radiant with the joy of a hard battle bravely fought—a great victory snatched from the jaws of disaster.

In later years, when the Men from Mars had passed into history, there was some bickering among members of the Mercury as to who, exactly, had contributed precisely what, to that particular evening's entertainment. The truth is that a number of us made a number of essential and incalculable contributions to the broadcast. (Who can accurately assess, for instance, the part played by Johnny Dietz's perfect engineering, in keeping unbroken the shifting illusion of imperfect reality? How much did the original old H. G. Wells, who noisily repudiated us, have to do with it? Or the second assistant sound man? Or individual actors? Or Dr. Goebbels? Or Charlie McCarthy?) Orson Welles had virtually nothing to do with the writing of the script and less than usual to do with its preliminary rehearsals. Yet first and last it was his creation. If there had been a lynching that night, it is Welles the outraged populace would have strung up—and rightly so. Orson was the Mercury. "The War of the Worlds," like everything we did, was his show.

Actually, it was a narrow squeak. Those Men from Mars barely escaped being stillborn. Tuesday afternoon—five days before the show—Howard Koch telephoned. He was in deep distress. After three days of slaving on H. G. Wells' scientific fantasy he was ready to give up. Under no circumstances, he declared, could it be made interesting or in any way credible to modern American ears. Koch was not given to habitual alarmism.

To confirm his fears, Annie, our secretary, came to the phone. She was an acid and emphatic girl from Smith College with fine blond hair, who smelled of fading spring flowers. "You can't do it!" she whined. "Those old Martians are just a lot of nonsense. It's all too silly! We're going to make fools of ourselves! Absolute fools!"

For some reason which I do not clearly remember our only possible alternative for that week was a dreary one—"Lorna Doone." I tried to reach Welles. He was at the theater and wouldn't come to the phone.

The reason he wouldn't come to the phone was that he was in his thirty-sixth successive hour of dress-rehearsing "Danton's Death," a beautiful, fragmentary play by Georg Buechner out of which Max Reinhardt, in an augmented form, had made a successful mass-spectacle in the twenties. Not to be outdone, Orson had glued seventeen hundred masks on to the back wall of the Mercury Theater, and ripped out the entire stage. Day after day actors fell headlong into the rat-ridden basement, leaped on and off erratically moving elevators, and chanted the "Carmagnole" in chorus under the supervision of Marc Blitzstein.

Unable to reach Welles, I called Koch back. I was severe. I taxed him with defeatism. I gave him false comfort. I promised to come up and help. When I finally got there—around two the next morning—things were better. He was beginning to have fun laying waste the State of New Jersey. Annie had stopped grinding her teeth. We worked all night and through the next day. Wednesday at sunset the script was finished.

Thursday, as usual, Paul Stewart rehearsed the show, then made a record. We listened to it rather gloomily, long after midnight in Orson's room at the St. Regis, sitting on the floor because all the chairs were covered with coils of unrolled and unedited film. We agreed it was a dull show. We all felt its only chance of coming off lay in emphasizing its newscast style—its simultaneous, eyewitness quality.

All night we sat up, spicing the script with circumstantial allusions and authentic detail. Friday afternoon it went over to CBS to be passed by the network censor. Certain name alterations were requested. Under protest and with a deep sense of grievance we changed the Hotel Biltmore to a non-existent Park Plaza, Trans-America to Intercontinent, the Columbia Broadcasting Building to Broadcasting Building. Then the script went over to mimeograph and we went to bed. We had done our best and, after all, a show is just a show. . . .

Saturday afternoon Paul Stewart rehearsed with sound effects but without Welles. He worked for a long time on the crowd scenes, the roar of cannon echoing in the Watchung Hills and the sound of New York Harbor as the ships with the last remaining survivors put out to sea.

Around six we left the studio. Orson, phoning from the theater a few minutes later to find out how things were going, was told by one of the CBS sound men, who had stayed behind to pack up his equipment, that it was not one of our better shows. Confidentially, the man opined, it just didn't come off. Twenty-seven hours later, quite a few of his employers would have found themselves a good deal happier if he had turned out to be right.

III

On Sunday, October 30, at 8:00 P.M., E.S.T., in a studio littered with coffee cartons and sandwich paper, Orson swallowed a second container of pineapple juice, put on his earphones, raised his long white fingers and threw the cue for the Mercury theme—the Tchaikovsky Piano Concerto in B Flat Minor #1. After the music dipped, there were routine introductions—then the announcement that a dramatization of H. G. Wells' famous novel, *The War of the Worlds,* was about to be performed. Around 8:01 Orson began to speak, as follows:

WELLES

We know now that in the early years of the twentieth century this world was being watched closely by intelligences greater than man's and yet as mortal as his own. We know now that as human beings busied themselves about their various concerns they were scrutinized and studied, perhaps almost as narrowly as a man with a microscope might scrutinize the transient creatures that swarm and multiply in a drop of water. With infinite complacence people went to and fro over the earth about their little affairs, serene in the assurance of their dominion over this small spinning fragment of solar driftwood which by chance or design man has inherited out of the dark mystery of Time and Space. Yet across an immense ethereal gulf minds that are to our minds as ours are to the beasts in the jungle, intellects vast, cool, and unsympathetic regarded this earth with envious eyes and slowly and surely drew their plans against us. In the thirty-ninth year of the twentieth century came the great disillusionment.

It was near the end of October. Business was better. The war scare was over. More men were back at work. Sales were picking up. On this particular evening, October 30, the Crossley service estimated that thirty-two million people were listening in on their radios. . . .

Neatly, without perceptible transition, he was followed on the air by an anonymous announcer caught in a routine bulletin:

ANNOUNCER

. . . for the next twenty-four hours not much change in temperature. A slight atmospheric disturbance of undetermined origin is reported over Nova Scotia, causing a low pressure area to move down rather rapidly over the northeastern states, bringing a forecast of rain, accompanied by winds of light gale force. Maximum temperature 66; minimum 48. This weather report comes to you from the Government Weather Bureau. . . . We now take you to Meridian Room in the Hotel Park Plaza in downtown New York, where you will be entertained by the music of Ramon Raquello and his orchestra.

At which cue, Bernard Herrmann led the massed men of the CBS house orchestra in a thunderous rendition of "La Cumparsita." The entire hoax might well have exploded there and then—but for the fact that hardly anyone was listening. They were being entertained by Charlie McCarthy—then at the height of his success.

The Crossley census, taken about a week before the broadcast, had given us 3.6 per cent of the listening audience to Edgar Bergen's 34.7 per cent. What the Crossley Institute (that hireling of the advertising agencies) deliberately ignored was the healthy American habit of dial-twisting. On that particular evening, Edgar Bergen in the person of Charlie McCarthy temporarily left the air about 8:12 P.M., E.S.T., yielding place to a new and not very popular singer. At that point, and during the following minutes, a large number of listeners started twisting their dials in search of other entertainment. Many of them turned to us—and when they did, they stayed put! For by this time the mysterious meteorite had fallen at Grovers Mill in New Jersey, the Martians had begun to show their foul leathery heads above the ground, and the New Jersey State Police were racing to the spot. Within a few minutes people all over the United States were praying, crying, fleeing frantically to escape death from the Martians. Some remembered to rescue loved ones, others telephoned farewells or warnings, hurried to inform neighbors, sought information from newspapers or radio stations, summoned ambulances and police cars.

The reaction was strongest at points nearest the tragedy—in Newark, New Jersey, in a single block, more than twenty families rushed out of their houses with wet handkerchiefs and towels over their faces. Some began moving household furniture. Police switchboards were flooded with calls inquiring, "Shall I close my windows?" "Have the police any extra gas masks?" Police found one family waiting in the yard with wet cloths on faces contorted with hysteria. As one woman reported later:

> I was terribly frightened. I wanted to pack and take my child in my arms, gather up my friend and get in the car and just go north as far as we could. But what I did was just sit by one window, praying, listening, and scared stiff, and my husband by the other sniffling and looking to see if people were running. . . .

In New York hundreds of people on Riverside Drive left their homes ready for flight. Bus terminals were crowded. A woman calling up the Dixie Bus Terminal for information said impatiently, "Hurry please, the world is coming to an end and I have a lot to do."

In the parlor churches of Harlem evening service became "end of the world" prayer meetings. Many turned to God in that moment:

> I held a crucifix in my hand and prayed while looking out of my open window for falling meteors. . . . When the monsters were wading across the Hudson River and coming into New York, I wanted to run up on my roof to see what they looked like, but I couldn't leave my radio while it was telling me of their whereabouts.
>
> Aunt Grace began to pray with Uncle Henry. Lily got sick to her stomach. I don't know what I did exactly but I know I prayed harder and more earnestly than ever before. Just as soon as we were convinced that this thing was real, how petty all things on this earth seemed; how soon we put our trust in God!

The panic moved upstate. One man called up the Mt. Vernon Police Headquarters to find out "where the forty policemen were killed." Another took time out to philosophize:

> I thought the whole human race was going to be wiped out—that seemed more important than the fact that we were going to die. It seemed awful that everything that had been worked on for years was going to be lost forever.

In Rhode Island weeping and hysterical women swamped the switchboard of the Providence *Journal* for details of the massacre, and officials of the electric light company received a score of calls urging them to turn off all lights so that the city would be safe from the enemy. The Boston *Globe* received a call from one woman "who could see the fire." A man in Pittsburgh hurried home in the midst of the broadcast and found his wife in the bathroom, a bottle of poison in her hand, screaming, "I'd rather die this way than that." In Minneapolis a woman ran into church screaming, "New York destroyed this is the end of the world. You might as well go home to die I just heard it on the radio."

The Kansas City Bureau of the AP received inquiries about the "meteors" from Los Angeles; Salt Lake City; Beaumont, Texas; and St. Joseph, Missouri. In San Francisco the general impression of listeners seemed to be that an overwhelming force had invaded the United States from the air—was in process of destroying New York and threatening to move westward. "My God," roared an inquirer into a telephone, "where can I volunteer my services, we've got to stop this awful thing!"

As far south as Birmingham, Alabama, people gathered in churches and prayed. On the campus of a Southeastern college——

> The girls in the sorority houses and dormitories huddled around their radios trembling and weeping in each other's arms. They separated themselves from their friends only

to take their turn at the telephones to make long distance calls to their parents, saying goodbye for what they thought might be the last time. . . .

There are hundreds of such bits of testimony, gathered from coast to coast.

IV

At least one book [1] and quite a pile of sociological literature has appeared on the subject of "The Invasion from Mars." Many theories have been put forward to explain the "tidal wave" of panic that swept the nation. I know of two factors that largely contributed to the broadcast's extraordinarily violent effect. First, its historical timing. It came within thirty-five days of the Munich crisis. For weeks, the American people had been hanging on their radios, getting most of their news no longer from the press, but over the air. A new technique of "on-the-spot" reporting had been developed and eagerly accepted by an anxious and news-hungry world. The Mercury Theater on the Air by faithfully copying every detail of the new technique—including its imperfections—found an already enervated audience ready to accept its wildest fantasies. The second factor was the show's sheer technical brilliance. To this day it is impossible to sit in a room and hear the scratched, worn, off-the-air recording of the broadcast, without feeling in the back of your neck some slight draft left over from that great wind of terror that swept the nation. Even with the element of credibility totally removed it remains a surprisingly frightening show.

Radio drama was taken seriously in the thirties—before the Quiz and the Giveaway became the lords of the air. In the work of such directors as Reis, Corwin, Fickett, Welles, Robson, Spier, and Oboler there was an eager, excited drive to get the most out of this new, all too rapidly freezing medium. But what happened that Sunday, up on the twentieth floor of the CBS building was something quite special. Beginning around two, when the show started to take shape under Orson's hands, a strange fever seemed to invade the studio—part childish mischief, part professional zeal.

First to feel it were the actors. I remember Frank Readick (who played the part of Carl Phillips, the network's special reporter) going down to the record library and digging up the Morrison recording of the explosion of the Hindenburg at Lakehurst. This is a classic reportage—one of those wonderful, unpredictable accidents of eyewitness description. The broadcaster is casually describing a routine landing of the giant gasbag. Suddenly he sees something. A flash of flame! An instant later the whole thing explodes. It takes him time—a full second—to react at all. Then seconds more of sputtering ejaculations before he can make the adjustment between brain and tongue. He starts to describe the terrible things he sees—the writhing human figures twisting and squirming as they fall from the white burning wreckage. He stops, fumbles, vomits, then quickly continues. Readick played the record to himself, over and over. Then, recreating the emotion in his own terms, he described the Martian meteorite as he saw it lying inert and harmless in a field at Grovers Mill, lit up by the headlights of a hundred cars—the coppery cylinder suddenly opening, revealing the leathery tentacles and the terrible pale-eyed faces of the Martians within. As they begin to emerge he freezes, unable to translate his vision into words; he fumbles, retches—and then after a second continues.

[1] *The Invasion from Mars* by Hadley Cantril, Princeton University Press, from which many of the above quotations were taken.

A few moments later Carl Phillips lay dead, tumbling over the microphone in his fall—one of the first victims of the Martian Ray. There followed a moment of absolute silence—an eternity of waiting. Then, without warning, the network's emergency fill-in was heard—somewhere in a quiet studio, a piano, close on mike, playing "Clair de Lune," soft and sweet as honey, for many seconds, while the fate of the universe hung in the balance. Finally it was interrupted by the manly reassuring voice of Brigadier General Montgomery Smith, Commander of the New Jersey State Militia, speaking from Trenton, and placing "the counties of Mercer and Middlesex as far west as Princeton and east to Jamesburg" under Martial Law! Tension—release—then renewed tension. For soon after that came an eyewitness account of the fatal battle of the Watchung Hills; and then, once again, that lone piano was heard—now a symbol of terror, shattering the dead air with its ominous tinkle. As it played, on and on, its effect became increasingly sinister—a thin band of suspense stretched almost beyond endurance.

That piano was the neatest trick of the show—a fine specimen of the theatrical "retard," boldly conceived and exploited to the full. It was one of the many devices with which Welles succeeded in compelling, not merely the attention, but also the belief of his invisible audience. "The War of the Worlds" was a magic act, one of the world's greatest, and Orson was just the man to bring it off.

For Welles is at heart a magician whose particular talent lies not so much in his creative imagination (which is considerable) as in his proven ability to stretch the familiar elements of theatrical effect far beyond their normal point of tension. For this reason his productions require more elaborate preparation and more perfect execution than most. At that—like all complicated magic tricks—they remain, till the last moment, in a state of precarious balance. When they come off, they give—by virtue of their unusually high intensity—an impression of great brilliance and power; when they fail—when something in their balance goes wrong or the original structure proves to have been unsound—they provoke, among their audience, a particularly violent reaction of unease and revulsion. Welles' flops are louder than other men's. The Mars broadcast was one of his unqualified successes.

Among the columnists and public figures who discussed the affair during the next few days (some praising us for the public service we had rendered, some condemning us as sinister scoundrels) the most general reaction was one of amazement at the "incredible stupidity" and "gullibility" of the American public, who had accepted as real, in this single broadcast, incidents which in actual fact would have taken days or even weeks to occur. "Nothing about the broadcast," wrote Dorothy Thompson with her usual aplomb, "was in the least credible." She was wrong. The first few minutes of our broadcast were, in point of fact, strictly realistic in time and perfectly credible, though somewhat boring, in content. Herein lay the great tensile strength of the show; it was the structural device that made the whole illusion possible. And it could have been carried off in no other medium than radio.

Our actual broadcasting time, from the first mention of the meteorites to the fall of New York City, was less than forty minutes. During that time men traveled long distances, large bodies of troops were mobilized, cabinet meetings were held, savage battles fought on land and in the air. And millions of people accepted it—emotionally if not logically.

There is nothing so very strange about that. Most of us do the same thing, to some degree, most days of our lives—every time we look at a movie or listen to a broadcast. Not even the realistic theater observes the literal unities; motion pictures and, particularly, radio (where neither place nor time exists save in the imagination of the listener) have no difficulty in getting their audiences to accept the telescoped reality of dramatic time. Our special hazard lay in the fact that we purported to be, not a play, but reality. In order to take advantage of the accepted convention, we had to slide swiftly and imperceptibly out of the "real" time of a news report into the "dramatic" time of a fictional broadcast. Once that was achieved—without losing the audience's attention or arousing their skepticism, if they could be sufficiently absorbed and bewitched not to notice the transition—then, we felt, there was no extreme of fantasy through which they would not follow us. We were keenly aware of our problem; we found what we believed was the key to its solution. And if, that night, the American public proved "gullible," it was because enormous pains and a great deal of thought had been spent to make it so.

In the script, "The War of the Worlds" started extremely slowly—dull meteorological and astronomical bulletins alternating with musical interludes. These were followed by a colorless scientific interview and still another stretch of dance music. These first few minutes of routine broadcasting "within the existing standards of judgment of the listener" were intended to lull (or maybe bore) the audience into a false security and to furnish a solid base of realistic time from which to accelerate later. Orson, in making over the show, extended this slow movement far beyond our original conception. "La Cumparsita," rendered by "Ramon Raquello, from the Meridian Room of the Hotel Park Plaza in downtown New York," had been thought of as running only a few seconds; "Bobby Millette playing 'Stardust' from the Hotel Martinet in Brooklyn," even less. At rehearsal Orson stretched both these numbers to what seemed to us, in the control room, an almost unbearable length. We objected. The interview in the Princeton Observatory—the clock-work ticking monotonously overhead, the woolly-minded professor mumbling vague replies to the reporters' uninformed questions—this, too, he dragged out to a point of tedium. Over our protests, lines were restored that had been cut at earlier rehearsals. We cried there would not be a listener left. Welles stretched them out even longer.

He was right. His sense of tempo, that night, was infallible. When the flashed news of the cylinder's landing finally came—almost fifteen minutes after the beginning of a fairly dull show—he was able suddenly to spiral his action to a speed as wild and reckless as its base was solid. The appearance of the Martians; their first treacherous act; the death of Carl Phillips; the arrival of the militia; the battle of the Watchung Hills; the destruction of New Jersey—all these were telescoped into a space of twelve minutes without overstretching the listeners' emotional credulity. The broadcast, by then, had its own reality, the reality of emotionally felt time and space.

V

At the height of the crisis, around 8:31, the Secretary of the Interior came on the air with an exhortation to the American people. His words, as you read them now, ten years later, have a Voltairean ring.

(They were admirably spoken—in a voice just faintly reminiscent of the President's—by a young man named Kenneth Delmar, who has since grown rich and famous as Senator Claghorn.)

THE SECRETARY

Citizens of the nation: I shall not try to conceal the gravity of the situation that confronts the country, nor the concern of your Government in protecting the lives and property of its people. However, I wish to impress upon you—private citizens and public officials, all of you—the urgent need of calm and resourceful action. Fortunately, this formidable enemy is still confined to a comparatively small area, and we may place our faith in the military forces to keep them there. In the meantime placing our trust in God, we must continue the performance of our duties, each and every one of us, so that we may confront this destructive adversary with a nation united, courageous, and consecrated to the preservation of human supremacy on this earth. I thank you.

Toward the end of this speech (*circa* 8:22 E.S.T.), Davidson Taylor, supervisor of the broadcast for the Columbia Broadcasting System, received a phone call in the control room, creased his lips, and hurriedly left the studio. By the time he returned, a few moments later—pale as death—clouds of heavy smoke were rising from Newark, New Jersey, and the Martians, tall as skyscrapers, were astride the Pulaski Highway preparatory to wading the Hudson River. To us in the studio the show seemed to be progressing splendidly—how splendidly Davidson Taylor had just learned outside. For several minutes now, a kind of madness had seemed to be sweeping the continent—somehow connected with our show. The CBS switchboards had been swamped into uselessness, but from outside sources vague rumors were coming in of deaths and suicides and panic injuries.

Taylor had requests to interrupt the show immediately with an explanatory station-announcement. By now the Martians were across the Hudson and gas was blanketing the city. The end was near. We were less than a minute from the Station Break. The organ was allowed to swirl out under the slackening fingers of its failing organist and Ray Collins, superb as the "last announcer," choked heroically to death on the roof of Broadcasting Building. The boats were all whistling for a while as the last of the refugees perished in New York Harbor. Finally, as they died away, an amateur shortwave operator was heard from heaven knows where, weakly reaching out for human companionship across the empty world:

2X2L Calling CQ
2X2L Calling CQ
2X2L Calling CQ
Isn't there anyone on the air?
Isn't there anyone?

Five seconds of absolute silence. Then, shattering the reality of World's End—the Announcer's voice was heard, suave and bright:

ANNOUNCER

You are listening to the CBS presentation of Orson Welles and the Mercury Theater on the Air in an original dramatization of *The War of the Worlds*, by H. G. Wells. The performance will continue after a brief intermission.

The second part of the show was extremely well written and most sensitively played—but nobody heard it. It recounted the adventures of a lone survivor, with interesting observations on the nature of human society; it described the eventual death of the Martian Invaders, slain—"after all man's defenses had failed by the humblest thing that God in his wisdom had put upon this earth"—by bacteriological action; it told of the rebuilding of a brave new world. After a stirring musical finale, Welles, in his own person, delivered a charming informal little speech about Halloween, which it happened to be.

I remember, during the playing of the final theme, the phone starting to ring in the control room and a shrill voice through the receiver announcing itself as belonging to the mayor of some Midwestern city, one of the big ones. He is screaming for Welles. Choking with fury, he reports mobs in the streets of his city, women and children huddled in the churches, violence and looting. If, as he now learns, the whole thing is nothing but a crummy joke—then he, personally, is coming up to New York to punch the author of it on the nose! Orson hangs up quickly. For we are off the air now and the studio door bursts open. The following hours are a nightmare. The building is suddenly full of people and dark blue uniforms. We are hurried out of the studio, downstairs, into a back office. Here we sit incommunicado while network employees are busily collecting, destroying, or locking up all scripts and records of the broadcast. Then the press is let loose upon us, ravening for horror. How many deaths have we heard of? (Implying they know of thousands.) What do we know of the fatal stampede in a Jersey hall? (Implying it is one of many.) What traffic deaths? (The ditches must be choked with corpses.) The suicides? (Haven't you heard about the one on Riverside Drive?) It is all quite vague in my memory and quite terrible.

Hours later, instead of arresting us, they let us out a back way. We scurry down to the theater like hunted animals to their hole. It is surprising to see life going on as usual in the midnight streets, cars stopping for traffic, people walking. At the Mercury the company is still stoically rehearsing—falling downstairs and singing the "Carmagnole." Welles goes up on stage, where photographers, lying in wait, catch him with his eyes raised up to heaven, his arms outstretched in an attitude of crucifixion. Thus he appeared in a tabloid that morning over the caption, "I Didn't Know What I Was Doing!" The *New York Times* quoted him as saying, "I don't think we will choose anything like this again."

We were on the front page for two days. Having had to bow to radio as a news source during the Munich crisis, the press was now only too eager to expose the perilous irresponsibilities of the new medium. Orson was their whipping boy. They quizzed and badgered him. Condemnatory editorials were delivered by our press-clipping bureau in bushel baskets. There was talk, for a while, of criminal action.

Then gradually, after about two weeks, the excitement subsided. By then it had been discovered that the casualties were not as numerous or as serious as had at first been supposed. One young woman had fallen and broken her arm running downstairs. Later the Federal Communications Commission held some hearings and passed some regulations. The Columbia Broadcasting System made a public apology. With that the official aspects of the incident were closed.

As to the Mercury—our new play, "Danton's Death," finally opened after five postponements. Not even our fantastic publicity was able to offset its generally unfavorable notices. On the other hand, that same week the Mercury Theater on the Air was signed up by Campbell Soups at a most lavish figure.

Of the suits that were brought against us—amounting to over three quarters of a million dollars for damages, injuries, miscarriages, and distresses of various kinds—none was substantiated or legally proved. We did settle one claim however, against the advice of our lawyers. It was the particularly affecting case of a man in Massachusetts, who wrote:

"I thought the best thing to do was to go away. So I took three dollars twenty-five cents out of my savings and bought a ticket. After I had gone sixty miles I knew it was a play. Now I don't have money left for the shoes that I was saving up for. Will you please have someone send me a pair of black shoes size 9B!"

We did.

34 Where Violence Begins

NORMAN COUSINS

The preceding selection illustrates how easily the "veneer" of rational behavior can be stripped from people, even in a society as advanced as our own. This selection shows how rapidly another veneer—that of civilized behavior—can be peeled away, divesting people of common decency, respect for their fellow man, and trust in others. The function of rumor, fear, and mass suspicion in quickly turning mutual trust and confidence into distrust, hostility, and open violence is clearly evident in this article. If inhuman behavior is so near the surface, even between friends, it becomes understandable how the army can "socialize" men to kill an "enemy" and, having learned this, how they can quickly extend their killing to persons not in uniform—including men, women, and children who may only vaguely seem like "the enemy." Thus throughout recorded history, especially during our own recent engagement in Southeast Asia, charges of atrocities against civilians, many of them verified, are made against both sides. One is tempted to paraphrase Abraham Flexner and assert that "the world is not wealthy enough to afford both war and civilization."

This is about Kamilal Deridas of India, who killed his friend. The killing occurred about seven years ago. All his life Deridas had followed the non-violence teachings of Mahatma Gandhi. He kept his thoughts free of fear and hate. And then one day, suddenly, he reached for a knife and slew his friend. Up until now that killing has had no direct connection with the American people; but it now becomes important for us to think about it as hard and carefully as we have thought about anything in our lives.

I met Deridas at a refugee camp on the outskirts of Delhi in February 1951. When I returned to India recently I tried to find him and learned that he had made himself a new home somewhere to the north of Delhi; no one knew exactly where. But, though I was unable to locate him, I shall never forget the things he told me about his experiences during India's ordeal in the summer of 1947, when the country was partitioned into three units—India proper, Pakistan West, and Pakistan East. The two sections of

SOURCE: *Saturday Review,* vol. 37, no. 3 (January 16, 1954), 22–24, 33. • Norman Cousins is editor of *Saturday Review* and vice-president and director of the McCall Corporation. He is also vice-chairman of the board of directors of National Educational Television. He received the Thomas Jefferson Award for Advancement of Democracy in Journalism in 1948 and in 1956 he received the Benjamin Franklin citation in magazine journalism. Among his many books are *Who Speaks for Man?, Present Tense, Modern Man Is Obsolete,* and *In God We Trust: The Religious Beliefs of the Founding Fathers.*

the new Pakistan were united politically, but they were separated by the geographical expanse of India at its widest. If you can imagine that Mexico, instead of being situated south of the United States, were to be split in half, with one part in Southern California and the other in New England, then you may have a fair idea of the geographic relationship of Pakistan to India, as well as the difficulties surmounted so heroically by the Pakistani leaders in operating a unified and free government.

The background of partition is long and involved. It was the culmination of more than a century of dual struggle—the struggle for national independence against England, and the struggle for power inside India between Hindu and Moslem. Centuries ago the Moslems ruled the northern part of India. When the British quit India in 1947 there were perhaps 100,000,000 Moslems in all of India, as against more than 325,000,000 Hindus. With partition some sixty-five million Moslems formed the population of the new Pakistan, the balance remaining in India. Today the population of Pakistan is more than seventy-five million, with close to forty million Moslems still in India proper.

Partition and national independence were part of the same historical event. Neither was then possible without the other. But the sudden rupture of a great nation caused it to bleed hideously. The struggle for national independence had been waged for centuries but it came virtually overnight and no one was prepared for it. The new Free India had only a bare governmental skeleton with which to administer the affairs of the second most populous nation in the world. Pakistan started absolutely from scratch, having to use empty crates for government desks.

And in those early days of uncertainty and confusion people became panicky. Whatever the animosity had been between Hindu and Moslem before Independence, the people had managed to live side by side. There had been recurrent violent flare-ups, to be sure, but they were not too serious. With partition, however, millions of people suddenly became jittery and insecure. A Hindu who lived in a city near the border like Lahore wondered what was to happen to him now that Lahore was to become part of Pakistan. A Moslem who lived on the outskirts of Calcutta wondered what was to happen now that there would be a separate Moslem Government in Pakistan that did not include him. The insecurity and confusion became multiplied as millions of people decided to move in order to be governed by their own group.

Then came violence. At first there were only sporadic incidents. A Moslem in Dacca, for example, would smash the shopwindows of a clothing store owned by a Hindu, claiming he had heard that Hindus were looting Moslem shops in Calcutta or Delhi. A Hindu in Calcutta would set fire to a Moslem home, in open view of a crowd, yelling that he had heard that Moslems were burning homes of Hindus who remained behind in Dacca or Karachi. Some Hindus or Moslems would try to take advantage of the national turmoil by seizing business properties or homes.

Each incident, of course, fed on rumors and begat even greater rumors. Outrages were carried out in the name of retaliation. Soon a civil war without battle-lines or armies raged throughout the subcontinent. People rushed through the streets with sticks or torches or whatever could be used to kill a man.

Kamilal Deridas was one of those who used a knife. When he spoke to me about it, four years later, he found it difficult to believe that it was his own arm that swung the knife over the shoulder and into the chest of a man who had been his friend.

Like millions of others who lived through the dark days of 1947, Deridas doesn't like to talk about what happened or his own part in it. It was only after we had spent many hours together, discussing the event in a general way, that he began to speak in terms of his individual experiences. I had told him that I found it difficult to understand how people who achieved so much through their belief in non-violence could suddenly abandon that belief at the very moment of its fulfillment. It was inexplicable that a non-violent victory should produce such volcanic violence within the nation itself. And what about the people, I asked. How could they allow themselves to become something they had never been? The Hindus and Moslems I knew were gentle people, peaceable people. I couldn't imagine them as killers. And Deridas's reply to my question was simple and vivid.

"I can answer you because I know how it was. I was part of it. From the very beginning I was part of it all. I was twenty-six at the time. My wife, my two little boys, and I lived with my parents in a nice house on the edge of Lahore. My father operated an arts-and-crafts shop. Lahore was something of a world convention city. The weather is clear and good almost the entire year and there were generally meetings that brought many people to the city.

"I had gone to college, studying law, but had deferred setting up an office of my own because my father was ailing and it was necessary for me to look after the business, which had prospered over the years. I had many friends in Lahore—among both Hindus and Moslems. Those of us who had gone to college thought all the old antagonisms were foolish, and we were bored by the traditional hostilities of the older people. Two of my closest friends were Moslems and they were as indifferent to the old religious and cultural rivalries as I was. The name of one was Faiz; the other Ahmed.

"After plans for the partition were made in 1947 Faiz came to me and said that he was worried about talk he had heard in town. He had heard that certain Hindu homes would be requisitioned after Pakistan came into being in order to make room for the many Moslems who could be coming to the city. And our home was on one of the lists.

"My father dismissed this talk as nonsense. He said that the new Pakistan would not tolerate such outrages because there were more Moslems in India than Hindus in what was to be the new Pakistan. He said the new Government would know only too well how much worse it would fare than India in any contest of seizure of private property. He told me to forget about it.

"But as the time for partition neared, and as reports reached Lahore of local riots in sections where there were mixed populations, I became very alarmed. One night Faiz came to my home through the back door and begged me to get my belongings together as quickly as I could, take my family, and flee Lahore.

"He said that there had been a secret meeting a few hours earlier in town and that reports were read which told of Hindu looting of Moslem shops in Delhi and Bombay and also that in several places Moslem women had been violated by Hindus and put on public exhibition. He said there were also reports that many, many thousands of Moslem homes had been seized by Hindu crowds throughout India. The men at the meeting were hysterical with rage and called for immediate retaliatory action.

"There were some at the meeting who cautioned against anything that might start a riot. They pointed out that they had lived side by side with their Hindu neighbors for many years and that these people were not responsible for the outrages that happened to Moslems many hundreds of miles away. But most of the others turned on these cautious few and shouted them down, saying they were traitors, and then the cautious few spoke no more. My friend said he knew terrible things were going to happen, and that the police would be powerless to do anything.

"I made up my mind that we would have to leave within a week at most and began to plan a way out and also to plan some way of getting the most valuable items in our store to a place of safety. I sought the help of Ahmed, who agreed to keep the most valuable items in the cellar of his home. That night and the next night, between one A.M. and four A.M., we transported the valuables in Ahmed's car from our store to his home. It was a courageous thing for him to do. It would have meant his death if he had been discovered.

"Then Ahmed and Faiz and I met in order to make plans for us to get out of Lahore until some measure of stability returned to the city. My father was difficult to persuade about this but something terrible that happened to us two days after Faiz came to warn me changed his mind. Our store was located in the resort section, which is the far side of the city. Early in the morning, shortly after I had opened the shop, I heard the sounds of a great commotion coming from afar. I locked the store, then rushed towards the center of the town. As I approached I saw the looting and the burning had already begun. There was smashed glass all over the streets. Not far away I could see smoke rising from the heart of the city.

"I ran back to the store. My father and my brother-in-law were waiting when I got there. They were very agitated. My twenty-one-year-old sister had been missing since eight A.M. It was now ten A.M. We barricaded the store to the best of our ability, then rushed home. We never saw my sister again. That night my brother-in-law learned that she had been abducted, along with sixty or seventy young Hindu wives. We could only pray for her life and her integrity of physical self, but I feared the worst.

"That night, in accordance with our plan, we left the house one by one, dressed in Moslem style, and were picked up by Faiz and Ahmed in their cars and brought to Ahmed's house, where we were to stay secretly until we completed arrangements for getting out of Lahore. It was lucky we had left our house when we did. Part of it was wrecked the very next day and the part that remained was occupied.

"Our plan for leaving Lahore was a simple one. We would travel in three pony carts. My wife, my two sons, and I would be in one cart. My father and mother would be in another. My brother-in-law and his little boy in the third. After a day's travel from Lahore we would slip over the border at night and then get a train to Delhi, 250 or 300 miles distance. At Delhi, we would try to find a place to live.

"But much was to happen to us before we left Lahore. In no time at all the riots had swept all through the city. We heard incredible stories of what was happening not only in Lahore but throughout India and Pakistan. Thousands of women and young girls on both sides were being abducted and violated. Mobs were rushing through streets, seizing people and tearing them apart. It was unbelievable—but it was happening.

"Then one night—it was after midnight—Ahmed came to the small room in his house where we were all hiding. I could see that there was something wrong. He was almost hysterical. He had just been told that his parents had been burned to death the night before in their beds. They lived in Batala, just over the border. My father tried to calm him by saying it could not be so, that Hindus would not do such a thing; and Ahmed said that there was no doubt about it. He said he knew that there were outrages on both sides; he had wanted to stay free of them, and had risked his life and the lives of his immediate family to help Hindus, and that this was now his reward—a mother and father burned in their beds by Hindus.

"My father again insisted that it was not so, and that someone had lied to Ahmed, and before I knew what was happening my father and Ahmed were quarreling and shouting at each other. I begged them to be quiet, for they were certain to rouse the entire neighborhood. But those were no days of calm tempers; we had all been without sleep and were on edge and had been infected by the ugly passions that were sweeping over the two countries. My father and Ahmed continued to shout at each other, accusing each other; then my father in a moment of rage said that he was certain that all Ahmed was after was our valuables which we had stored with him. And Ahmed, insane with grief over the killing of his parents, went into a blind fury, reached for a knife, and started after my father.

"Right then something happened to me. I don't remember it clearly; in fact, I don't remember it at all, but my wife told me about it later. The sight of the knife after everything that had happened in the past few days—the burning and the lootings and the killings and the attacks on women and having to be huddled together secretly wondering what would happen to us—all this made me lose my senses when I saw Ahmed going at my father with a knife. I took a knife that Ahmed had given me earlier for my own safety. I killed him. I reached over his shoulder with my knife and I killed him.

"Right after that we left the house, taking Ahmed's car, even though it had been decided earlier, that we would not use an automobile because cars on the road going to the border attracted too much suspicion. We knew the pony carts were small enough for the back roads. But now we had no choice. How we finally made the border is almost too incredible to tell. But we made it. Anyway, that is not what you wanted to know about. You wanted to know how peaceable men could forget all their convictions, forget everything, and kill. I have tried to tell you.

"There are many, many thousands of people like me. No one knows how many people became killers, during those dark days. What we know is that maybe 300,000 were killed; maybe half a million; maybe a million. No one stopped to count. But we do know that twelve million people lost their homes and fled in terror. Seven or eight million Hindus. Four or five million Moslems. Maybe more.

"I have talked about my part in the dark days to a very few people. But one man to whom I spoke had known Gandhiji, and you know that Gandhi himself was killed in that terrible period during partition. And this man, who would know what Gandhiji would say if he knew what I had done, told me that what had happened was not my sin alone but the sin of all the people of India and Pakistan. Gandhiji made no distinction in his life between Hindu and Moslem; he loved us all. And his friend told me that Gandhi would have said that I had temporarily lost my sanity with all the others but that I should work for friendship between Hindu and Moslem as the only way of paying for my crime.

"What he said helps. It also helps to remember that when men are soldiers they kill because they are caught up in something larger than themselves. I hope I have answered your question."

I said that he had; but I could see there was something more he had to say.

"Perhaps you are wondering," he resumed after a minute or two, "whether these terrible things happened here in India and Pakistan only because—well, because there is something perhaps primitive or uncivilized about these people; and that this could never happen to people like yourselves who are educated and refined. One thing I surely learned during that time was that everything is swept aside in panic. I was a college man; Ahmed was a college man. College men were in the crowds that set fire to the shops and the homes. And in the Western world a high literacy rate didn't keep the German people from going in for mass murder. And there were many outrages in your own Civil War. I'm afraid I would have to say that what happened to us could happen to anyone when suddenly the structure of law and order is removed and the people are governed only by their fears. It is then that the worst elements in the society can set the pattern for society itself."

35 Gary, Indiana

MARSHALL FRADY

Social movements as well as various other types of collective behavior are frequently associated with certain social forces. This selection, which describes the relevant social forces in a contemporary American city, illustrates how racial and socioeconomic strata are entwined with political power and the development of potentially violent collective action. The polarization in Gary, Indiana, is not unique among American communities. The rising power of black populations concentrated in such cities, and the resistance of groups satisfied with the status quo, provides the arena for confronting social movements. The election of Mayor Hatcher, a black, is the central incident in this dramatic social struggle.

With the beginning of the twentieth century, around 1906, U.S. Steel found itself cramped in Pittsburgh and Chicago and staked out here the site for the biggest steel mill in the world, and, along with it, a town to be manufactured whole by the company. The town, it was eventually determined, would be called Gary, after the chairman of U.S. Steel's board of directors, Judge Elbert H. Gary—a flinty Methodist who, in his portrait now hanging in city hall, is a balding moustachioed man, in a tuxedo, with small scrupulous eyes. Until this moment the area had remained largely a neglected wilderness of muck and marsh and dunes, humming with hornets and yellow jackets, through which bears and deer still wandered and ducks and geese flurried endlessly into dull autumn skies. U.S. Steel negotiated the land, for the most part, discreetly, one transaction taking place with someone carrying $1,300,000 through the streets of New

SOURCE: *Harper's*, vol. 239, no. 1431 (August 1969), 35–45. • Marshall Frady is a free-lance writer and has worked on several Southern newspapers and for *Newsweek* Magazine. He has contributed articles to *Atlantic Monthly, Mademoiselle,* and *The Saturday Evening Post.* He is author of the book *Wallace.*

York in a handbag. As late as 1907, after the carpentry had already begun on Gary, a solitary timber wolf was seen crossing a central thoroughfare as it was being paved. Finally, on May 30 in 1908, the first electric lights blinked on down Gary's main street.

• • • • •

Technically, Gary was released and left to its own devices by U.S. Steel only a few years after it was created, but inevitably it has continued to exist as the mill's civic appendage. Its population over the past sixty years has accumulated almost exclusively through great migrations that attended the mill's boom times, so that now it is made up of a kind of global tumbleweed: Poles, Czechs, Irish, Swedes, Lithuanians, Greeks, Armenians, Assyrians, Mexicans. More recently, there was a surge of Negroes from the South, who were shortly followed by the New Oakies: Appalachian whites, wandering up from the gullies and honeysuckle into the clashing steel and treeless asphalt, lank and quiet with a certain blasted look after a while in their pale blue eyes. One Gary citizen, a plant executive who was himself raised in the South, says, "They are the goddam sorriest white people I ever saw. If they're not lookin' up a mule's ass, they don't know where they are. Just goddam sorry—you know what I mean?" They have not seemed able to adapt themselves to the furnaces yet; instead, most of them have become ironworkers, their element the remote windy spaces among high girders.

But in the most profound sense, the city breathes with the mill. Shifts of workers, like its inhalations and exhalations, mingle back and forth across the bleak ground between the mill and city hall, returning again and again to a grassless landscape of smoking lagoons and slag heaps: 2,500 acres of gargantuan cranes and conduits and bins and ore ships. The sheds themselves are like the caves of Vulcan, filled with the rumbling intercourse of equipment too titanic to have been devised by human hands. Colossal vats of brimstone tip with a great fan of sparks into three-story kettles below, and diminished figures stir along high ledges and platforms like dwarves who have been left to attend somehow to the impossible constructions of giants—scurrying around the vats, they appear, against the sunflares of flames, as blank silhouettes, without sound or identity.

Finally at the gate they materialize again, reassume shape and proportion as they file out with their lunch pails before the inspector in the guardhouse, returning then briefly to the suburbs—the streets of meager brick and stucco houses on postage-stamp lots, ranked one after another down sidewalks littered with tricycles and baseball bats, small evergreens like miniature Christmas trees on the front lawns. In the small living rooms, with furniture reminiscent of frumpish hotels and boardinghouses, satin head-pillows with embroidered scenes of the Eiffel Tower and Mt. Fujiyama scattered over couches, the sunlight slants for a moment across the screen of a TV set, and fades at last against a far wall.

For these—the children and grandchildren of the Poles and Armenians and Greeks who were most of all escaping something behind them—this is what it is all for now: the neighborhoods; their own children, many adolescents, who themselves have already in their hearts renounced and abandoned it as they prime themselves for college; the corner taverns on Saturday afternoon where they may roost along the bar with beers watching the Chicago Cubs on the mounted TV. It is, in a way, a stranded population, accidentally collected here with no deep blood memory of the earth, the weathers, the past—and no way now for there ever to gather such a memory through successive generations, since any sense of earth, past, place had already been aborted here even when the first ones began to arrive.

When George Corley Wallace, during his first venture into national politics, entered the 1964 Democratic Presidential primary in Indiana, he carried Lake County decisively. Gary, with some 180,000 citizens, is the principal city in that county. In 1968, the county, which is compulsively Democratic, tipped to Humphrey, and that only because, a local newspaperman says, "the union leadership finally managed to get it across to their members that Wallace in the end just wasn't their kind of man, he was anti-union."

During those early forays beyond the South, Wallace, of course, was generally dismissed as merely an odious curiosity, a sullen political orphan on a mission of ill-tempered mischief. But Wallace himself had long been convinced that, as the Second Reconstruction amplified over the rest of the nation and became a national crisis, there would be the same kind of backfire in white communities—"then you gonna see the common folks all over the rest of this country Southernized." But despite his uncanny 1964 showings in Wisconsin, Indiana, and Maryland, the custodians of the conventional national sophistication still could not bring themselves to take him, and his potential, seriously—until, as the 1968 campaign gathered and he began to assert himself again, polls indicated he would be answered by a vote formidable enough to put the decision into the House of Representatives.

There has never really been any question that his campaign, despite its peculiar coyness on the issue, was a tacit corroboration of racism in all its varieties, from blatant to furtive, from malevolent to amicable. That this bizarre political outrider managed to figure seriously at all in the calculations of that election confirmed the suspicion of many that the nation, in its heart of hearts, is irredeemably, though elusively, racist. But his advent also suggested that, in the enormous tensions and complications of the late Sixties in America, the country might indeed be moving toward two societies in more than racial terms.

To be sure, Wallace represented an exasperated longing for the old village simplicities about life, and a retrenchment against sociologists, intellectuals, the entire national intelligentsia who have sought to impose on the nation a conscience which the harried common man has difficulty comprehending. Not the least of the dynamics at work in the Wallace phenomenon was a kind of surly class assertion: people could identify with Wallace as a class as they couldn't with Goldwater—he talked like them, he angered like them, he even dressed like them. And in an almost mystical way, he answered the vague sense of dread and inadequacy among those uncounted submerged souls in America leading what are mostly lives of quiet scrabbling desperation—who now, through the immediacy of television, feel menaced by confrontations and figures remote from their existences, which in another time would have remained quite abstract to them.

This was the unsuspected constituency disclosed by Wallace's candidacy. His campaign acted as a litmus for this reality about the nation at this time, and it may be that this discovery will be his real and lasting importance.

The white population of Gary, actually, is a relentlessly middle-class community. "There's really no elite in this town," one city-hall administrator declares. "There's no old families, no gentry. Sure—bankers, department-store owners, we've got a kind of establishment, but it's pretty small and insular, and for all practical purposes irrelevant. There's the mill, but what you have there is an absentee ownership." Almost exclusively, then, Gary is made up of what another civic figure describes as "the blue-collar middle class. Comparatively, they're better paid than elsewhere, they're a bit more affluent than most blue-collar workers." The city's preoccupations are primarily private. At a recent meeting of the civic-affairs committee of the Chamber of Commerce there was considerable fretting over a midsummer culture jubilee ("It looked like maybe eventually we'd be able to compete with Michigan City for the Miss Indiana Pageant; artistically last year we had one of the greatest parades we ever had—but these schools say they just don't have the money to send the bands this year") and some anxiety about fireworks for a Fourth of July commemoration ("It's been going on four years now since we've had any display of Americanism on the Fourth. Definitely, this is something we should go ahead with . . .").

What incipient activists can be found in Gary, primarily Jewish professional families, are mostly collected out in a northeast suburb called Miller, and are referred to around town as The Miller Mafia. "Fact is," one local political figure says, "they tend to be pseudo-liberals who meet over coffee or drinks to engage in liberal responses to things. Aside from that, they really haven't counted for much yet." Indeed, after a while in the city, one gets the sense that affairs in the rest of the country, not to mention the world, exist only as some distant half-dream.

But there are also in Gary, generally in a warren of glum streets southward from the center of the city, some 100,000 Negroes—about 60 per cent of the population. As in most other American cities, Gary's crisis begins here—a rage and desperation light-years removed from white experience. This crisis becomes a kind of impasse with the bitterness in the white suburbs. "You have to remember," one spokesman says, "that their ambitions in life out in the suburbs are really pretty modest: to get their kids in college, and to own a home of their own—their own castle. Of course, these are also the ambitions of the people in the ghetto. But when the whites out there see Negroes moving toward them, they see their castles diminishing in value, and many of them can't afford to move, they have to sit and watch their own ruin. What it is basically, though, is a psychological fear —a fear of the unknown."

At the weekly meeting of the Exchange Club in the Gary Hotel, the outgoing president, a pudgy little hamster of a man in a beetle-green suit, was presented with a gavel—"Isn't that nice! Joe, baby doll, you're too much. Oh, that's groovy, that's groovy. Let's hear it for Joe Sargent, everybody!" He then introduced the guests—three members of the Gary common council—and added, "When they're through speaking, will you please confine your questions to questions, not editorial opinions?"

There were two whites and one Negro, the president of the council—Quentin Smith, a high-school principal, a bulky man with a subterranean, booming voice. The younger white councilman stood first, inexpensively dressed in a checkered sport coat, unremittingly serious, with pale drab eyes: "Anyone who does not admit there is a problem in Gary with gangs, groups, associations—whatever you want to call them—well, all you have to do is ask your wives, your daughters, your sisters. When's the last time you allowed your daughter to walk to the Dairy Queen, when's the last time your wife went downtown to shop or to the library? The problem is a lack of respect. I may be a little old-fashioned, but this is the way I was raised. I believe the father's the head of the household, and he's got to hit you on the head early to let you know he's boss. You've got to do it in school, the coach has to hit you on the head to let you know, and when you get out, the policeman has to hit you on the head to let you know who's boss."

Smith stood up. "Well, the first thing is, whether you're an outsider or an insider, you have to know what questions to ask about a city's troubles. For all these years, there've been these lack of services in the black neighborhoods—neglect of the schools, broken-up streets, garbage, and all that. Now, many of you *knew* this was going on, we came to you and asked for your help, but what were you saying then? 'I'd like to do something, but you know, I'd lose my position here where I work, I'd have the neighbors after me. . . .' Now we've got this question of gangs. No question, there are gangs in Gary, more gangs than ever before. They feel like they got to shock you here in this town, they can't do it any other way—they say, what you're doin' is nuthin', and they *got* to do this to get you to hear them. But now, when we come to you asking you to help in dealing with these groups, in meeting their problems, you're saying, 'Why, somebody'll shoot a BB at me, I'll get attacked.' What you do, what you're still doing, is just letting things go."

Finally, a gangling black clergyman sitting in the center of the room—the Reverend Fred Lowrey, a former Chicago street-gang member himself and now pastor of the St. Timothy Community Church, who was introduced earlier as a prospective member of the club—blurted, "The problem is, we're lazy, indifferent, and irresponsible." Encircled by the other white members, his head snapped stiffly about him as he spoke from his seat, dipped and darted tautly with his hand swiping back in a kind of stifled savage distress over his hair, one long arm flailing abruptly and then clumping back down onto the table. "You say, 'Isn't this all terrible, my! I'm gonna go home and have my schnapps and cool it.' All the middle-class people do this, it's your hang-up. That's why they all look on the middle class with disdain. Now, don't tell me about the ghetto, man, I'm from there, I've lived it. Don't nobody care when you're in the ghetto, they just want you to behave. Another thing that bugs me about this town, you can't do a good thing without somebody sayin' you tryin' to play God. I'm sorry, gentlemen, I'll never get *in* this way, but I had to put this on you. You can just know too much and get upset." He ducked his head, crossed his legs with a sudden dangerous lashing, and gave his hair a few more furious swipes.

The room was soundless for a moment. Someone coughed softly. And then the outgoing club president said, "Just want to point out, you notice how he confined himself to questions instead of opinions . . ." and as the room was bombarded with laughter, Lowrey glanced around, his head still hung, in a glower of private hurt.

In November of 1967, a black man, running outside the city's normal political circuits, was elected Mayor of Gary. It was largely a matter of brute statistics—he collected over 90 per cent of the Negro vote while losing one white suburb by about the same margin. Inevitably, from the moment he assumed office, Gary became a kind of crucible, an image of the American travail.

This was particularly so because Richard Hatcher—raised in nearby Michigan City—a slight, sober bachelor of thirty-five with a rather boyish and guileless look behind his horn-rim glasses, has remained a part of the black movement. He is a shy man, with a manner soft and somewhat remote. "I mean," one of his aides says, "he's just not the kind of guy you can go up to and say, 'Why, hello, Dick, you ole sonovvabitch, how are you?' and slap him on the back. People are always asking me why he's so cold—it's not that he's cold, he's just cautious." Usually inserted neatly into a trim sedate suit with his coat buttoned snug and flat all the way up, he refrains from alcohol and tobacco and usually even profanity. But he derives directly from the past decade of the civil-rights movement, was involved in marches and confrontations in the more guttural years of the struggle, spending one summer in Mississippi as a test-case attorney.

When he assumed office, a sudden great windfall of funds came his way, from foundations and government grants, which he immediately and almost totally applied to Gary's black community. This rendered him instantly suspect to the white suburbs. What's more, he declined to repudiate certain black militants regarded with suspicion by the white community, and evidenced a patience with Gary's black street gangs, who constitute for much of the white community the ultimate black peril.

Not long ago, one city councilman—a Mexican allied with Gary's old political guard—made a proposal which would have taken nine appointments to the city's Human Relations Commission away from the Mayor and distributed them among the council. The evening when the councilmen—three whites, the Mexican, and five Negroes—gathered to consider this idea, they were greeted by a roomful of blacks. "If you're gonna take this thing and checkmate it and play a chess game with it," one speaker notified them, "then you'd better think twice. . . . Today, tonight, please, for God's sake, let it be heard here, let it be heard through the country that we're gonna back Mayor Hatcher from here to hell and eternity." There was an explosion of whoops and applause, which was briskly gaveled down. Then there was a stricken stillness as a glowering black youth stood before them in African regalia and announced his name as Elemi Olorunfummi—as one of Hatcher's Negro aides remarked later, "When that cat stood up in that dashiki and gave them that Orumfummi business, man, their minds were all messed up from then on." Olorunfummi asked, "What you want us to have? Nuthin'? . . . You crawin' with us. And we tired. Tired of playin'. The game is over. . . . We make this clear, this is not a threat. This a promise." Finally, when the time came to vote on the motion, one white councilman allowed, "I'll have to confess, sitting here tonight at this performance, that I'm in no mental condition to vote intelligently on legislation. . . . We are anxious and glad to hear personal opinion, but when we hear personal attack and threats of personal violence, under these kinds of conditions . . . frankly, I'm in no condition to vote on this myself mentally tonight either way." He accordingly abstained, while two other councilmen voted for the motion and six voted against.

Such encounters have only deepened the alienations. Not long after that evening, some 150 demonstrators, about half of them women and children, ambushed a Republican fund-raising dinner at the Gary armory for Indiana Governor Whitcomb, who had resolutely ignored their appeals to discuss welfare legislation after vetoing a welfare-reform bill passed by the legislature. Just as the guests were beginning to gather, the demonstrators flowed in, with some of the children settling themselves at the head table and dispatching salads and platters of pie that had already been set out.

When Hatcher was notified, he persuaded the demonstrators to withdraw, and Whitcomb finally arrived, about an hour late, and the dinner proceeded. But on Sunday, Indiana's attorney-general Theodore Sendak declared that the armory incident confirmed "a reign of terror" was loose on Gary. At the following city-council meeting, one Republican member described the event, somewhat ambitiously, as "a new day of infamy" which had destroyed "our image through the United States, and the world." Hatcher insisted, "Somehow, children eating pie do not call up an image of terror." Later, in private, he said, "Most of that noise is coming from the bigots, and I'm not going to occupy myself forever pacifying them. Anyway, they wouldn't be pacified if I walked down Broadway on my hands."

In the early mornings, out in the subdivisions like Glen Park and Miller, they huddle along the counters of steamy diners—self-employed businessmen in dull black suits and plastic raincoats, filling station attendants, ironworkers in plaid cotton shirts and khakis rolled twice above their brogans—humped forward as they sip from blunt mugs of coffee with a thin maroon stripe around the top, forking down flat yellow flaps of scrambled eggs, their faces still dull and waxy with sleep.

"I been here all my life," says one of them at the counter. "I got me a house I paid $35,000 for, but I'm leavin' it. My daughter graduates from school this year, that's the only thing I been waitin' for. It's not that I hate the colored or anything, but I'm dumpin' it all. Who the hell wants to live this way, I ask you. Bein' scared somebody'll hit you on the head all the time, you can't go out of the house after dark. You work all your life for something, and then they start movin' in, and suddenly you don't have anything—it's not yours anymore. First person that makes me any kind of half-ass offer on that house now, it's his, and I'm gone. With one exception—I'm not sellin' to no goddam colored, I'd put a torch to it first."

In a booth, an elderly man is sitting with a youth over coffee. "You wanna know how I feel?" the old man says quietly. His eyes squint under a bristling tangle of eyebrows. "For the first time in my life, I feel like an outsider in my own country. But listen, let me tell you something—the white man isn't about to give up this country: he took care of the Indians, he took care of the French, he took care of the English, you think he's gonna turn it over to these Nairobans now? Jesus, what do they want? I ask you, what do they want? We've passed every law under the sun we could think of for them, they've got their welfare, they even got themselves a Mayor now, but they're still raisin' hell. Listen, I'll tell you something—if the coloreds keep on, they gonna find themselves on reservations one of these days, just like the Indians. I even predict that. It has about come to that."

He lifted a hand with two fingers extended, a cigarette smoldering between them and pointed. "My eldest daughter, I bought her a .38 to keep with her not long ago, and about a week later she's out drivin' at night and this guy jumps against the fender of her car. She waves that .38 at him a few times, and he runs—but she would have put a bullet right through that windshield, right through his head, you better believe me. And now they want to move out here. Listen, I don't want no trouble, I only want for me and my wife and my family to be able to live our life in peace. But the way things are goin' now, there's gonna be warfare—

there's *got* to be. Nobody else is tryin' to stop them, not the government, not our so-called leaders. And I'll tell you the worst ones—" he placed his spread fingertips lightly for a moment on his chest, "—my own chuch. The Catholic Church. They seem to have just completely joined 'em. These young priests, some bishops I could name, in my opinion they oughtta be defrocked. There's nobody left but the workin' man, and he just can't put up with it anymore. Here, I'll show you something . . ." He picked up a crinkled brown paper bag, wrapped around something, that had been resting at his elbow on the tabletop beside the nickel-capped, fluted-glass sugar dispenser, slowly withdrawing from it a .25 Colt automatic, his other hand then lifting out two boxes of ammunition. "I got another one for my younger daughter just a while ago this morning. Now, they're both ready."

Not surprisingly, Hatcher's election had a traumatic effect on Gary's now somewhat rickety Democratic political establishment, whose main dependable asset up until then had been the city's Negro vote. While the county as a whole has tended to be instinctively Democratic, the party organization, according to one seasoned political hand, "has no more awareness of the ideals of FDR than the man in the moon—it's strictly a commercial undertaking." Indeed, the business seemed to flourish in a community which, while belonging to the middle-class ethic of thrift and discipline and duty, has nevertheless shown a certain indulgence toward the pettier and more tawdry mortal vices. It was only natural then that politics in the county would be somewhat slatternly in nature.

• • • • •

Not long after the incident at the Governor's dinner at the Gary armory, when the Negro children raided the pies and salads, the chairman of the Lake County Democratic organization, John Krupa—a grizzled political broker, his face like a portly chicken hawk's—volunteered, in a brief glow of bipartisanship, that what that affront to the Republican Governor meant was Gary could use a spell as a "police state." One spring afternoon recently, he sat in his office in the courthouse (he also happens to be county clerk) clad in a dizzy assortment of patterns, a green plaid coat with a crimson pinstripe shirt, a small tin American flag fastened to his lapel. The room itself was a cluttered nest of political memorabilia, most conspicuously featuring a large blown-up photograph, labeled "John C. Krupa and Friend," showing himself and John Kennedy caught in a momentary tilt toward each other when Kennedy passed through Indiana during the 1960 primary.

"The press has depicted this guy Hatcher as a godsend," Krupa said, "which as a matter of fact he isn't. He's such an advocate of black power, that a lot of white leadership is afraid of association with one who may be proven someday to be of the Far Left," his voice a bit reedy, his face having assumed a studiously grave and formal expression. "I doubt very much if he could get a security clearance, myself. At least Stokes, over there in Cleveland, he denounces the student demonstrators and the likes of Rap Brown and Stokely Carmichael. But I have yet to hear Hatcher speak up once and defend his country, right and wrong.

"My job as county chairman is to call attention to the fact that this guy Hatcher is of the wrong breed, whattamean is, how can a man whose allegiance to this country is secondary as can be demonstrated to anybody's satisfaction sit in defense of this city? We gotta get somebody back in there who doesn't hate white people. For your incidental information, you might be surprised to know, there's a Negro councilman here by the name of

Dozier Allen who runs a gas station out here and who was opposing Hatcher in the primary until one day Mr. Allen found himself very mysteriously engulfed in flames. He was putting gas into a can, and all of a sudden the whole thing blew up. He damn near checked out. He was incapacitated for the rest of the campaign due to this so-called accident . . ."

He paused, blinking, when asked about his recommendation that Gary be converted into a police state. "No. No, I didn't mean just Gary, I was talking about the whole thing, the campuses and towns all over this country. The only way to combat all this is as a form of police-state action."

Several days after the armory incident, Hatcher appeared for a regular morning radio show in which he answers phoned questions from the community. Sitting across the table from the moderator, hunched forward on his elbows toward the mike, he would sip coffee as he listened to the questions. "I know you are a man in your middle thirties and your mother is deceased," one woman's voice began. "What I want to know is, if when you were growing up, you had done something like those kids over at the armory, wouldn't your father have turned you over his knee and paddled you good?"

Hatcher seemed to hang for just a moment uncertainly, and then relaxed, broke into a broad grin, bouncing lightly in his chair as he bent close to the mike and confided, "Yes, well, if you had known my father, you wouldn't even have to ask that question." The voice was silent and then struck in a rapid hurrying bark of words, "Well, I'm sure when you get married, you'd never let your children act like that, I mean there was no reason those children had to act like a bunch of cannibals—" Hatcher's grin paled for just an instant, then vanished, his face emptying and his eyes going a bit dull. After a moment he murmured, "Fine. Okay, fine."

He gets a steady trickle of letters, written in a spidery hand on blue-lined notebook paper with a ballpoint pen, which will begin,

Mr. Hatcher, We are a big group of women, who would like a few answers. . . . We have nothing against colored people but we would not like to have them live next door to us. Yet it seems that the colored people are always pushing. . . . Please can you explain to us why the black people want to be near us when we don't want them deep from our hearts & never will. . . . God give them strength & let each one of the colored realize that we have nothing against them or ever to do them any harm. We just don't want them to try to mingle with us. . . . Again please answer our questions. Thank you. God Bless You. . . .

Riding in the back of his limousine one glaring May morning, slumped low with his hands tucked like a schoolboy in his trouser pockets, he admitted, "I used to have this feeling about people who were bigots, I'd think they were terrible people. I'd get letters and feel angry—I'd say, What am I doing this for? Why bother? But with time, I think I've come to understand them better, how really threatened and frightened these people feel. The sad thing—the tragic thing—is that most white people simply don't understand how truly desperate the situation is, they have no idea how close we're drawing to a real civil war."

Actually, since Hatcher became Mayor, chasmic distances have been disclosed in Gary, and if the town is an image of the American crisis, it hints profound alienations that may be withdrawing beyond the reach of even the truest voices. Hatcher's basic struggle right now is to keep Gary from disintegrating altogether. In particular, in one Gary suburb—Glen Park, a modest neighborhood where many fugitives from the inner city have reestablished themselves—there has been circulating a petition calling for secession from the city, promoted more or less overtly by the area's councilman, Eugene Kirtland, a fiftyish, chunky, bespectacled real-estate broker who once owned a twenty-four-hour supermarket. It will be a difficult play to pull off: after collecting signatures from 51 per cent of the property owners in Glen Park, Kirtland must then submit the petition to the Gary Board of Works, which is sure to shove it right back at him since its three members are appointed by Hatcher—after that would come a long and ragged passage through the courts. Whatever, Kirtland is persevering.

His secession movement, which he prefers to call dis-annexation, has actually earned for him some notice from the national press, not to mention the local papers and radio stations, and he has become somewhat conspicuous around town these days, clattering from morning diners to civic-club luncheons to city-hall hearings in a red pickup truck. At a recent meeting of the Glen Park Rotary Club—men in golf sweaters and tieless rayon shirts buttoned up to their neck gathering for lunch in a new vocational school—Kirtland arrived with a small transistor radio on a strap which he kept beside his plate, listening to local news programs and phone-in discussions throughout the meal. At one point, there suddenly issued from somewhere on his person a high thin electrical beep, somewhat startling those around him, and, blinking only once, his face impassive and slightly lifted, he quickly fumbled inside his coat to press a small black leather packet fastened to his belt—a device which signaled him whenever he had a call. He disappeared for a few minutes, and then returned: "Radio station way out in San Francisco—they want to talk to me four-twenty this afternoon."

. . . . .

"The small, middle-class property owners out here look on dis-annexation as a defense for their investments," he languidly explained. "Oh, there are many reasons—people feel we would have better economic development under our own government, for one thing. Gary's like every other middle-class community, I suppose: the good people don't say anything until it's almost too late—but then, watch out! The great thing about this country is that most of its people are in the middle class. This particular group, now, is slower to anger, but once they pick up the sword, they don't quit until it's done." He lowered his head with a musing smile, his eyes flicked slyly from side to side with his fingertips furiously diddling his Lark cigarette just a few inches from his murmuring lips while his head bobbled momentously. "When Americans get pressed too hard, they blow—and when they blow, they *blow!*" His voice ended on a kind of high emphatic falsetto.

"Now," he resumed, briefly sipping his cigarette. "Sure, what you've got now is a revolt among these people. I have great trust in the common sense of the average Joe—most people are able to size up a situation right away. I think they just generally feel institutions are getting too big, too remote and impersonal and unresponsive to individuals—that goes for business and government too. And now you've got all these taxes to finance social change, and it's the average Joe in the middle of the block who's having to pay them, but for what? He doesn't really know how they're spent, why they're spent, or how much is spent—he just knows it's a lot, and he's paying it. You better believe there's a revolt. Right here in Gary, we're being used by federal funds and tax-free foundations as a lab for social change. But it's not the super-rich who's footing the bill—*we're* footing the bill so the super-rich can protect their tomato cans. That's right. If there's a revolution, the super-rich would be right in there with the Lefties. They're the ones sponsoring all this legislation, starting with Old Man Roosevelt. The Kennedys—Jack was killed, and then Bobby came along, what would he want to go out and get killed too for? Now Teddy—why do they keep wanting to get elected President even though two of them have been killed already? Those brothers are protecting the family fortune—that's all. Now, I don't necessarily blame them for that. Everybody belongs to the same party—M.O.R.E. Sure, that might be a pretty base view of man's motivations, but really, what else is there? Altruism isn't real. It can change any moment, nobody ever knows where anybody is with altruism. But you can always count on self-interest—it explains it all. The New Left to me are simply way-out revolutionaries who want what we've got. The difference is, they want to take it away by hitting people on the head."

The afternoon was waning in the windowpanes. He snicked on a lamp beside him, turning with a violent grunting wrench with his cigarette held out carefully from him. "Now, the Negroes," he solemnly elaborated, "they're no different from anybody else in that respect, I suppose. They want more. And what the people out here in Glen Park foresee now is a tendency for Negroes to invade this area in unmanageable numbers. But of course, everywhere, ever since man has been on this earth, he has instinctively collected himself together with his own kind for protection. The Croatians, the Poles, the Slavs here in town, they all have their own way of life, all have their taverns. Their tribal habits are different, they have different objectives and different methods for getting them. But some can live together, in close proximity, better than others—for instance, the Poles and Italians and so on have never had much trouble living with your so-called Wasps and Anglo-Saxons. But I think history demonstrates the hardest two groups to have living together peacefully are black and white.

. . . . . .

There can *never* exist successfully two sets of standards in one community—the revolutionaries are going to have to accept that. Even some of your more middle-class blacks are beginning to say total integration isn't gonna work. But it seems like we have to go through this thing every generation, we have to learn it all over again. Maybe if we can put it into focus here now, it'll help people in a lot of other communities when they face the same thing. Right after the Civil War, of course, they went through this down there in the South for twenty years—blacks were running everything until the revolt of the white middle class down there. The Klan, then, you know, was made up of the better elements in the white communities, not the trash. But this is not to say I countenance any kind of physical damage. It's just, if we dis-annex out here, it will discourage them from moving in—of course, we'll still have the same old laws and everything, but they'd know they wouldn't have the protection of Hatcher."

When asked about Hatcher's description of dis-annexation as a new "apartheid," Kirtland's eyes slid askance again, he mustered a mild smile, and daintily waggled his cigarette. "Hatcher, you know, he's really cleaned up his speech. He's taken the burr out of it, he doesn't sound Negro anymore. But as far as that comment goes—well, I heard somebody from South Africa talking the other day, and he said there just isn't the kind of hard feeling between blacks and whites over there as there is here." He briefly raised his eyebrows, his eyes flaring meaningfully for a moment behind the lens of his glasses, and took a tiny tight dainty pull on his cigarette. "Anyway," he added, "it's obvious, isn't it, that down through recorded history, for whatever reason it may be—biological, physiological, I don't know—but it just seems the white man, no matter how outnumbered, has always taken the throttle all over the world. That's just been history, and I don't really see any reason that might be changing, at least for the next several centuries. . . ."

Kirtland was interrupted then by a phone call, and after a moment, his quiet voice came from the dining room—he had disappeared around a corner, and all one could see as he talked was a dinette table with a dreary litter of Pepsi-Cola bottles and paper plates and envelopes and unfolded mimeographed form-mailings in the wintry light from the window: "Well, we have some nice places I'm thinking about where a lot of newly married couples are moving in. I have two places in particular in mind right now. Uh—both he and she white? Yes. Well, I'll be happy to show them these places I'm thinking about, so why don't we set up an appointment. . . ." When he returned, he stooped briefly to scoop up a handful of nuts from a tray on the lamp table, and then, one hand in his trouser pocket, his legs spraddled manfully, his head lowered somewhat bullishly, began jauntily flipping them in his mouth from his cupped hand. "Those blockbusters, you know they'll call you a lot of times like that. I always try to be careful. . . ."

Perhaps the most thoroughly integrated suburb in Gary is the Northwest Side community, a neighborhood which looks much like Glen Park but where virtually the entire racial spectrum of Gary can be found in significant numbers: Irish, Anglo-Saxons, Poles, Puerto Ricans, Italians, and Negroes. It would seem, at least statistically, to invoke some optimism for the eventual closing of the distances in Gary.

It was a rare sunny day, just after noon, and the opening ceremonies for the Northwest Side Little League season had just concluded. The slopes down to the field were still scattered with mothers in turquoise slacks with strollers and poodles, grandmothers with kerchiefs around their heads and fathers in Hawaiian shirts sitting in the grass with their arms wrapped around their knees.

A group of parents, surrounded by a constant shrilling of children, made their way up the street to a home only a few blocks away, plopping there in couches and easy chairs in a carpeted living room, full of daylight and potted plants. They received with weary jubilation the first round of martinis and Black Labels while gusts of small boys still in their Little League uniforms clapped in and out the front screen door. These people were all members of the newly organized Northwest Side Civic Association, which, in one of its leaflets, presents a "RECIPE FOR STABILIZATION: OR, HOW TO DISCOURAGE PANIC SELLING INDUCED BY REAL ESTATE AGENTS," citing a section, emphasized with their underlining, of the 1968 civil-rights law which holds it "unlawful . . . to *induce* or *attempt to induce* any person to *sell or rent* any dwelling by *representations* regarding the entry or *prospective entry* into the neighborhood of a person or persons of a particular race . . ." and advising anyone approached by an agent who "states or *even implies that the neighborhood is changing*" that the agent "can be prosecuted *if there is a witness.*"

A small tubby man in sideburns and horn-rim glasses—the somewhat beleaguered sire of eight children and one of the officials at the Little League ceremonies down on the field, still wearing his blue official shirt with a tiny kerchief fastened around his neck—explained to a visitor, "I saw you with Kirtland the other day, and I thought, My God, if *that's* the impression he gets of everybody here—look, as a Republican myself, I think people like Kirtland are bigots."

That detail out of the way, he made a quick dip into his beer. "What we're trying to do with this civic association, now, we're just trying to stabilize the community, we have our biggest problem out here with block-busting and panic-peddling, and, hell, we just looked around and realized we had to do *something*, or it was gonna be too late. I mean, you go out to work on your lawn one evening, you happen to look over and—holy cow! you got a new neighbor, black right next door—Guess who's comin' to dinner, momma! So far, the caliber of blacks who're moving in now, everybody's been awfully surprised at how well they've kept their lawns and everything—"

"Yeah. But just a minute—" The host, a lean, leathery man in a liquid-fabric chartreuse golf shirt and Hushpuppies, leaned forward and pointed to the windows at the back of the living-room. "See that house right over there. No, the second one—see?" He leaned back in his chair again. "Well, the Hiltons moved out of there, and this Negro family just moved in the other day—seemed respectable, she's a schoolteacher, I think. Okay, a nice family, but pretty soon, we looked out and there was this *second* car parked in front of the house all the time. All right, but then a little later, we look out, and here's this *third* car parked there. Pretty soon, we start seeing all these strange people going in and out all hours of the day and night. You follow me? I mean, who the hell *are* all these strange people? But that's what happens, pretty soon there's fifteen, twenty others stuffed in the house. We called the police chief, but he said there was nothing he could do about it."

The Little League official's wife, even smaller and more harried than he, chirped, "Well, that's it! I mean, *this* is the neighborhood where they'll be coming. Where the hell else they gonna want to buy a house—in the ghetto? Glen Park? Not Glen Park—they wanna get shot?"

The color TV was clicked on to the Wide World of Sports, a boxing match from Springfield, Massachusetts, and the second round of drinks was brought in. "You wanna know where Hatcher blows it?" blurted the Little League official, poised in a frog's crouch on the very edge of the sofa with his beer glass cradled in both hands between his knees. "He just doesn't care about what white people think. If he *really* wants to have a national image, he should be trying to get everybody together. If he can pull that off, he might get elected President—in which case, though, we oughtta go ahead and give it to Brezhnev. I heard some guy say Hatcher'd never pass a security check, but I don't know. Lot of us on the Right—don't get me wrong, I'm not out there on the Far Right with those guys, and there's lots of Negroes in town feel the same way I do—but a lot of us feel he listens directly to Moscow. He got elected this last time because of a lot of fear votes—they said, let's vote for a black man and maybe the town won't burn down. Well, that's so gutless it makes me sick. But I can tell you he's finished. Unless he gets out his black guard at the polls next time around, he's done for in this city."

A nurse, who'd just gotten off work, dropped in for awhile, still in uniform and gauzy stockings, a certain bitten prettiness in her lean face. She took a chair along the wall, lit a cigarette, accepted the scotch-and-soda handed her, and then delivered, through thin taut lips, her latest tidings of old women beaten by street gangs.

"You know," said the Little League official's wife, "there's one thing that *really* gets me. I heard one of them, a woman, say the other day that all white people owed something to the blacks because of all these years they've had to suffer. Well, she's a damn fool. I was raised in a little town in Ohio where I didn't even *see* a Negro until I was a grown girl. *I* didn't make all those people suffer—why am I supposed to make up for that?"

His home sits out in the southwest section of town, in a scruffy area of sandbanks tufted with weeds. Directly across the street is the rear parking lot of a supermarket. He returned there at sunset, ate a solitary dinner of Colonel Sanders fried chicken in his den downstairs, changed into another suit, and left again, climbing into the back seat of his limousine. It was night now, a damp and musky evening. His driver carried him through the streets of the Negro neighborhood, low tunnels lit by the glare of successive streetlights.

The back room was already full of people—sitting in metal folding chairs, leaning in the entrance from the kitchen —with one door opened to the May night outside. He stood against a garish yellow wooden wall before them under the low ceiling, dressed in a black double-breasted Continental suit with a deep-blue shirt and dull-red tie, his dark face glittering, an intense dramatic figure somehow evocative of Tom Mboya or Julius Nyerere. He began talking about the armory incident—a peculiar exposition for this group, but one in which he seemed to feel he had to engage anyway. "I know a lot of folks say everybody who's on welfare are on there just because they're too lazy to work. But I can tell you, that's not so. Now, those people Saturday night, they were down there because we're *required* in this state to pay people only forty per cent of what it takes to survive. . . . Now, of course, we've taken a lot about that this week. But you know, you could spend the whole four years as Mayor just responding to attacks."

A general murmur answered, "That's right. That's right." Hatcher continued, "Now, I'm not suggesting they're just after me because I'm a black Mayor—" A crackle of calls: "They are, though. They are." His two hands now, in small compact gestures, sliced downward together to one side and then the other: "I was willing and prepared to accept whatever came two years ago, I knew it wouldn't be any bed of roses. But what concerns me now is that you'll start believing what these people are saying in the newspapers and over the radio—" And finally his voice rose above the clamor: "All right, I know. But in Reconstruction, now, blacks were in positions of political power in the South, and the only reason they were able to hold those political offices was, they were reinforced by the United States Army. But you know how the South was able to get that Army out of there? They said these blacks were incompetent, the place was going to the dogs. Pretty soon, people started believing it. You have to remember that to understand what's happening in Gary now. They trying to do the same thing. But let me tell you something—they underestimate the ability of the people to understand, they underestimate their sophistication now. . . ."

In the back, an old and heavy man finally rose and, nervously running his fingers along the top of the chair in front of him, began, "Mr. Mayor—uh, we got a problem." He began reporting incidents of gang terrorism along his street, wreckage and intimidation, his voice hesitant and labored, breathing heavily and almost panting his words—an old man afraid—finally descending again to his chair. Hatcher told him, "We not in Mississippi, we not in Nazi Germany. There is no reason anybody ought to be intimidated by anybody in this country. It's a free country. But it means some men have got to stand up and be men and make a complaint. We'll back you one hundred per cent, I want everybody here to understand that."

A tall Negro in a sport coat and open-collared shirt stood up beside Hatcher. "If you want to know the truth," he snapped, "I know there's trouble with gangs, but the way white people are carryin' on about them—well, as far as some of the things the juveniles are doin', I don't necessarily blame them. 'Cause when they look around at the so-called upstandin' leaders of this nation, who do they see? This Abe Fortas and this Judge Douglas, and that Senator sometime back, Dodd. They see men like that. Right here in our own community, we have a lot of disc jockeys who aren't the kind of men they oughtta be, lot of so-called preachers not really preachers but entertainers. I know things are bad, you even see ten-year-olds drinkin' wine. But kids are just thinkin' bad of grownups these days, period."

A man leaning in a doorway answered, "That's right, we're gonna have to start doin' something beside settin' the wrong example. We got to exercise our manhood —be real fathers to our families, real husbands to our wives. Our women can't go downtown without some white man comin' up to her and botherin' her. How many women in this room had a horn blown at 'em around a corner by a car of whites, things said out the window? Not a woman in here hadn't had that experience. Well, this has got to stop, and it'll stop when we start bein' men ourselves and lookin' out after our wives. My son must see in me the kind of man who can afford him self-respect and manhood, my wife must see in me the kind of man who can afford her security. . . ."

Hatcher took the floor one last time. "Let me say this. Despite Mr. Sendak, Mr. Krupa, Mr. Kirtland, despite all the others, I'm hoping—but you know I sort of hate to hope, I've hoped so often in my life, and I'm getting tired of disappointments. You get to where you don't want to even stand a chance of being disappointed, so you don't even hope. But I'm still hoping that maybe these people will realize—just stop and realize for a moment—the kind of hysteria they're causing. Because the only way for anybody to survive is for everybody to survive. What I'm trying to do is to pull people back together, because there's no other choice but to try."

On the sidewalk outside were several members of one of Gary's street gangs. Hatcher gathered them together briefly off in the shadows under a tree, talking to them softly as his car waited. There was, even here, a tinge of the mill in the air. "Look, you guys have *got* to help me now. If you hear about anybody fixin' to do something, you gotta stop him. We *can't* have any incidents, that's all they're waitin' for, the Kirtlands and Krupas." They listened to him with only a muttered question now and then. "Now you don't have to be an informer, you don't have to tell me anything—*you* handle it. Because I'm telling you, if we have anything this summer, another thing like that armory, we'll be washed up. Will you help me now?" They chorused thickly, "We will, Mr. Mayor, thank you, good night, Mr. Mayor," and he went on to his car.

His house is quiet, the only sound a dim hum. Down in his den, there are pictures of King and the Kennedys, along with the framed ad which appeared in the *New York Times:* "For God's Sake, Let's Get Ourselves Together. . . ." A number of blown-up photographs of moonscapes lean against the wall. The room, with its Moroccan couches and suspended globes of lights, has an amber hue. He selects a tape, clicks it into the console with its multiple dials, and a moment later the music begins, a classical score. He sits there listening to it late into the night.

36 The Relevance of Nonviolent Action

HERBERT C. KELMAN

Every social scientist must somehow reconcile his role as scientist with his role as citizen. In the selection that follows, a distinguished social psychologist illustrates his solution to this problem—playing the role of "observing participant." Following many years of personal involvement in direct action campaigns, he recommends nonviolent action as "an effective instrument of social change in Negro Americans' current struggle for justice." *Writing shortly after the martyrdom of America's greatest exemplar of nonviolent action, Martin Luther King, Jr., Kelman advocates nonviolence because it is* "consistent with . . . [his] basic values about human relationships and social change" *and because he is* "convinced that nonviolent action represents a potentially effective way of producing social change based on principles that are social-psychologically sound."

The early 1960s were a period of excitement and exhilaration in the history of social protest in the United States. The country was emerging from the long winter of the Joseph McCarthy years. A new generation of young people, who had not learned the habit of caution, rediscovered the meaning of personal commitment and social action. The civil rights movement captured the imagination of Negro and white students who, in turn, gave courage to their elders and brought them back into the struggle.

SOURCE: Herbert C. Kelman, *A Time to Speak: On Human Values and Social Research* (San Francisco: Jossey-Bass, 1968), pp. 231–44, 255–60. Reprinted by permission of the publisher. • The author is Cabot Professor in the Department of Social Relations at Harvard University. His main interests include social psychology, psychotherapy, intergroup conflict, social movements, and political ideology. He is the author of *A Time to Speak: On Human Values and Social Research* and is editor and coauthor of *International Behavior: A Socio-Psychological Analysis.*

Perhaps the most exciting feature of the civil rights movement during these years was the pattern of social action that it pursued. Though activist and militant, it was firmly committed to nonviolence; though dedicated to creating a new pride and a new image for Negro Americans, it was built on collaboration between the races. Organized nonviolent and interracial struggle against segregation and discrimination was not, of course, invented in 1960. It goes back to the formation of the Congress of Racial Equality in Chicago in 1942. By 1960, CORE chapters had almost two decades of experience in breaking down segregation through the use of the techniques of nonviolent direct action, with many local successes to their credit, mostly in Northern and border states. Nonviolent action became a major force in the South in 1956 with the Montgomery bus boycott, under the leadership of Martin Luther King, Jr., and the formation of the Southern Christian Leadership Conference. It was in the early 1960s, however, that nonviolent civil rights action began to take on the character of a national mass movement, mobilizing support throughout the country and exerting major influence on official policy.

PRINCIPLES OF NONVIOLENT ACTION

What is nonviolent action? One thing that surely ought to be clear is that nonviolence does not refer to the mere absence of violence—though it seems that both militants, who castigate nonviolence as a counterrevolutionary strategy, and establishmentarians, who embrace it as part of the process of orderly change, are not always aware of that fact. Nonviolence is not to be equated with passive yielding to superior force or with working only through established channels. It is a positive, active, and in fact militant strategy, designed to produce thoroughgoing changes in social patterns.

Though it respects the adversary as a human being and attempts to mobilize his conscience, nonviolent action is not just a moral appeal and a petition to the other that he do the right thing. It is very definitely and deliberately an exercise of power. Barbara Deming puts it very well:

> To resort to power one need not be violent, and to speak to conscience one need not be meek. The most effective action *both* resorts to power *and* engages conscience. Nonviolent action does not have to beg others to "be nice." It can in effect force them to consult their consciences—or to pretend to have them. . . . One brings what economic weight one has to bear, what political, social, psychological, what physical weight. There is a good deal more involved here than a moral appeal. It should be acknowledged both by those who argue against nonviolence and those who argue for it that we, too, rely upon force.

Indeed, a nonviolent confrontation presents real threats to the adversary. By dramatically exposing his unjust practices, by refusing continued cooperation with them, and by replacing them with new patterns, it may threaten him with embarrassment and adverse publicity, with reduction in his economic or political power, and with disruption of the orderly processes he cherishes. It does not, however, threaten to destroy him, and thus leaves open the way for reappraisal, for negotiation, and for rebuilding.

Nonviolent campaigns are most readily identified by the use of techniques of direct action. Various other techniques, however, have always been important parts of the repertoire of nonviolent action, even though they may not be unique to that strategy. Thus, nonviolent action programs overlap with and utilize protest demonstrations, educational campaigns, legislative lobbying, judicial suits, community organization, and negotiations with employers or unions. Typically, they rely on a combination of methods, which vary in dominance, depending on the nature of the problem under attack, the stage in which the campaign finds itself, and the opportunities for action that are available. What defines nonviolent action is not the specific array of techniques that have evolved, but the effort to utilize and develop appropriate techniques that are consistent with a set of basic action principles.

If we view nonviolence as a pragmatic strategy for intergroup conflict, rooted in a Gandhian philosophy of action we can describe these principles as follows:

(1) Nonviolent strategy is built on an active effort to empathize with one's opponent and to understand the perspectives, goals, fears, expectations, and preconceptions that he brings to the situation. To understand the adversary's point of view does not mean to accept it or to

compromise with injustice. Rather, it avoids the type of escalation of conflict that is caused by misperception, and permits actions that are informed by the facts, that are not unnecessarily threatening, and that are conducive to a resolution of conflict in which both sides benefit.

(2) Nonviolent strategy includes continuing efforts to maintain and broaden channels of communication, to step up the level and depth of communication, and to discuss and negotiate all disagreements directly. Even when the conflict has reached a stage of sharp confrontation, there is a readiness to enter into negotiation and to explore mutual interests and possibilities for cooperation.

(3) Nonviolent strategy calls for the deliberate initiation of steps that help to decrease tension, hostility, and reliance on violent means. Janis and Katz stress, in this connection, the importance of "adopting a consistent attitude of *trust* toward the rival group and taking overt actions which demonstrate that one is, in fact, willing to act upon this attitude." By exhibiting trust toward the adversary, by refusing to treat him as an enemy, and by dealing with him in a straightforward and above-board manner, one can often induce a reciprocal response on his part.

(4) Nonviolent strategy is committed to eschewing violence in response to hostile moves initiated by the opponent. This commitment is clearly formulated and publicly pronounced. It means refraining from acts of physical or verbal violence against members of the other group and from acts that have the effect of humiliating them, even in the face of clear provocation. It does not, however, mean a passive yielding to coercion on their part. Typically, the strategy involves disciplined nonviolent resistance, marked by a readiness to make personal sacrifices in defense of one's cause.

(5) When it becomes necessary to initiate conflict moves and to engage the opponent in a direct confrontation, nonviolent strategy continues to rely on nonviolent techniques. These techniques are aimed not at defeating the adversary, but at trying to "convert" him, while working for the achievement of concrete, positive objectives.

(6) Wherever possible, nonviolent action confronts a specific practice or law or institutional pattern that is unjust, and consists in a direct or symbolic enactment of an alternative pattern that corresponds to the desired state of affairs. This effort to give concrete expression to the desired state of affairs—to bring into reality, even if only in symbolic and rudimentary fashion, a pattern consistent with social justice—represents the most characteristic and most dramatic feature of the "classical" nonviolent action campaign. Thus, participants in lunch-counter sit-ins or in Freedom Rides refused to accept the established pattern of segregation and—by sitting where they were not supposed to sit—acted out the new pattern with which they hoped to replace it.[1]

A fundamental feature of these six principles is that they combine firmness and

[1] Such direct action techniques, however, are usually preceded and always accompanied by a variety of other activities. For example, in Baltimore CORE's campaign against segregated lunch counters in the early 1950s, we went through a series of other steps—including tests to determine existing practices, leaflet distribution, efforts to mobilize the support of various community agencies, and repeated discussions and negotiations with store managers—before mounting a sit-in campaign. Even after sit-ins began, we continued to utilize various other techniques, such as attempts to initiate negotiations between store management and some established community agencies, and attempts to put pressure on the national headquarters of a local store by picketing branches in other cities and by raising the issue at stockholders' meetings. The existence of a direct action campaign, of course, served as an important lever for the other approaches, but it was the convergence of different approaches that finally produced the desired change.

militancy with a conciliatory and open attitude. Participants in nonviolent action try to capitalize on the opponent's strengths rather than his weaknesses, to mobilize his sense of justice and self-interest in support of change rather than resistance to it, to win him over rather than to win over him. At the same time, they are utterly clear about their goals, they are firm in their commitment to a new social pattern, they insist on the opponent's responsibility to accept and promote change, and they leave no doubt that they themselves are prepared to follow through even at great personal cost. They express their militancy not by the suffering that they are prepared to inflict on the opponent, but by the suffering to which they are willing to subject themselves in order to achieve justice. In short, theirs is a militancy that is not confounded with violence and hatred. Their strategy for social change relies on power directed to two tactical purposes: (1) to confront the adversary with the fact that he can no longer rely on their willing cooperation with existing practices and that, at least in symbolic and rudimentary fashion, a new state of affairs has been instituted; and (2) to force the adversary to take active steps in reciprocating the respect, trust, openness, and objectivity that they have shown toward him.

These principles have been applied most readily and effectively in the area of public accommodations, the context in which nonviolent action was originally tailored to the struggle for racial equality in the United States. In campaigns designed to integrate public facilities it is relatively easy to define the specific practice that needs to be changed, to identify a specific adversary, and to find a dramatic and yet self-evident way of symbolically enacting the alternative desired pattern. Other areas, such as discrimination in employment or segregated housing, are not as ideally suited for a classical nonviolent action campaign. In particular, it is difficult to find a focus for direct action and confrontation that has a clear and intrinsic relevance to the old pattern under attack and to the new pattern designed to replace it. An open housing march, for example, is a mechanism of nonviolent confrontation that is only indirectly linked to the housing pattern itself; by marching through a hostile neighborhood the participants are symbolically insisting on their right to be there. If they actually erected houses on vacant lots, or moved into abandoned buildings, the link between action and issue would be as obvious as it was in the case of sit-ins and Freedom Rides. Opportunities for such actions, however, are not readily available.

The challenge to those of us who believe in the efficacy of nonviolent strategy is to develop creative new techniques, embodying the principles of nonviolent action, that are suited to the central problems and the new realities of today—that address themselves to the issues of poverty, of economic and political participation, of the improvement of ghetto life, of the upgrading of educational facilities. Efforts in that direction are under way. The Poor People's Campaign, planned by Martin Luther King before his assassination and now led by Ralph Abernathy, is the major example of such efforts. Proponents of nonviolent action have also suggested "constructive programs"—that is, ways of instituting new states of affairs—that can accompany the Washington campaign. Various self-reliance projects, such as cooperative businesses and services, and community organization efforts in the black ghettoes, though not conceived as components of a nonviolent action campaign, are in fact governed by or at least compatible with the principles of nonviolent action. The question is,

Are such efforts relevant to the current situation? Is there still a place for creative innovation in nonviolent action or is nonviolence dead?

THE RELEVANCE OF NONVIOLENCE TODAY

By now almost everyone who is willing and able to listen realizes that, despite the dedication and sacrifices of the civil rights movement, justice and equality for Negro Americans are nowhere in sight. This does not mean that the civil rights movement has failed. Rather, it means that the task is far more difficult and the changes required are far more fundamental than most of us realized. The exclusion of Negroes from American society is so systematic and racism is so thoroughly built into public attitudes and institutional arrangements that a meaningful solution requires a restructuring of the system.

This newly recognized wisdom and the new rhetoric that accompanies it, however, often blind us to the tremendous changes, both in law and social pattern, that have in fact taken place during the past ten years. In his last book, Martin Luther King summed up the important contributions that nonviolent action had made to these changes in the following words:

> It is not overlooking the limitations of nonviolence and the distance we have yet to go to point out the remarkable record of achievements that have already come through nonviolent action. The 1960 sit-ins desegregated lunch counters in more than 150 cities within a year. The 1961 Freedom Rides put an end to segregation in interstate travel. The 1956 bus boycott in Montgomery, Alabama, ended segregation on the buses not only of that city but in practically every city of the South. The 1963 Birmingham movement and the climactic March on Washington won passage of the most powerful civil rights law in a century. The 1965 Selma movement brought enactment of the Voting Rights Law. . . .

The civil rights movement not only has a series of concrete accomplishments to its credit, but it also revolutionized social action in this country by militantly working toward social changes without resort to violence and hatred. King and other Negro Americans have thus taken the lead in reshaping and revitalizing the whole of American society. White America could hardly expect nonviolence in return for the systematic violence to which Negroes had been subjected over the centuries; it surely could not expect the leadership of Negroes in giving new vitality to a society that had excluded them from its benefits. This was indeed an unanticipated blessing, perhaps grounded in part in the very suffering to which the Negro community has been subjected and which prepared it for this unique role in experimenting with radically new and more human forms of social action.

It is not surprising, at least in retrospect, that, as the struggle progresses, its emphasis has moved away from the principles of nonviolence and interracial collaboration as the central pillars of the movement. This development can be traced to the dynamics of the struggle itself, as well as to the new realities that it has created or revealed. Despite many successes, and in large part because of the hopes that these very successes engendered, there came a growing realization of the painful and costly process by which every small change had to be hammered out, of the dependence of the Negro community on white support and good will, of the profound hatred and violence that the movement elicited among some elements of the white community, of the limits beyond which even the "white liberal" was unprepared to go, of the divergencies in interest—and yet communalities in fate—between the Negro middle and lower class and between the Negro populations in the rural South and the urban North, of the irrelevance of civil rights advances to the Negro ghetto dwellers in Watts and in the large cities throughout the country, and of the desperation and isolation of the vast Negro underclass. These conditions ushered in a nationalistic phase of the struggle, in which black unity, black pride, black self-determination, and black leadership have become the central instruments. This nationalistic phase was perhaps inevitable, but its advent was hastened and intensified by the impact of the Vietnam war on our domestic programs.

The current phase is marked by the emergence of a new group of militants, committed to a transformation of the movement and bidding for its leadership by an appeal to nationalist sentiments. As is so often true in nationalist movements, some of these appeals take on an aggressively ethnocentric character. They express contempt and hatred for the white man and are often phrased in the idiom of violence and surrounded with the mystique of guerrilla warfare. The strength and influence of militants of this school are easily exaggerated, in part because they are so vocal and colorful. They represent only one branch of the nationalist revival in the Negro community, and their interpretation of Black Power is certainly not typical of all those who use the term. Charles Hamilton and Nathan Wright, for example, have something quite different in mind when they speak of Black Power. Yet the militant separatists have shifted the center of gravity in the movement and have laid down a powerful challenge to the doctrine of nonviolence. They have contributed to a widespread feeling, particularly in the younger generation, that nonviolent action is irrelevant to the current realities, a relic of the past that only "Uncle Toms," "counterrevolutionaries," and "white liberals" would think of unearthing.[2]

The assassination of Martin Luther King, the most eloquent spokesman for nonviolence and the most beautiful human being in American public life, has added a new poignancy to questions about the relevance of the philosophy for which he lived and died. Again and again we are told that this act of total violence demonstrates the futility of nonviolence and marks the end of the nonviolent phase of the struggle. This is a natural reaction to the anger, to the bitter hurt, to the sense of meaninglessness and despair evoked by the assassination. But once we turn from grief to analysis, can this reaction really be maintained?

Certainly the assassination of Martin Luther King does not provide proof of the ineffectiveness of nonviolence as a strategy, any more than did the assassination of Mohandas Gandhi twenty years ago. It is true that a nonviolent strategy is designed to call forth reciprocal behavior in the adversary, and that proponents of nonviolent action expect the number of casualties to be far lower than those suffered in a violent confrontation. Nonviolence, however, as Gandhi knew, and as King knew and repeatedly said, offers no guarantee against injury and violent death. Nonviolent action is a form of struggle, often carried out in areas in which tensions are high and emotions deep. Proponents of such action are cognizant of the fact that it may activate efforts of ruthless suppression and bring into the open blind hatreds and fears. It

[2] Barbara Deming quotes a man who said to her: "You can't turn the clock back now to nonviolence!" She comments, wistfully: "Turn the clock back? The clock has been turned to violence all down through history. Resort to violence hardly marks a move forward. It is nonviolence which is in the process of invention, if only people would not stop short in that experiment."

is quite possible, therefore, that the level of violence on the part of the adversary may at first increase after a nonviolent action campaign has been initiated, although certainly not to the same extent that it increases after rioting or other forms of violent action.

Although violent responses by the adversary are by no means necessary to the success of a nonviolent action campaign, they may in fact further it. They may mobilize widespread support for the campaign among those who were previously neutral or inactive, as they did in Birmingham and Selma. They may also bring about a gradual change in the adversary himself, as he finds that his own violence continues to be met with nonviolence and with increasing disapproval on the part of bystanders. But whether or not it furthers the campaign, a violent response is an eventuality for which nonviolent actionists must be and have been prepared.

To cite the assassination as evidence for the failure of nonviolence reveals a lack of understanding of what nonviolence means and what Martin Luther King stood for. It is similar to the lack of understanding betrayed by a number of publicists, who, in discussing King's assassination, referred to the "irony" that this nonviolent man met with such a violent death. Nonviolence for King meant active participation in controversy and struggle; he was not dedicated to keeping things calm, smooth, and orderly, but to a militant pursuit of change. As activists, practitioners of nonviolence like Martin Luther King are unique in that they refuse to inflict violence on others but are prepared for the possibility that they may bring it upon themselves. Thus, there was neither irony, nor proof of the inefficacy of nonviolence, in the fact that King met with violent death; it was consistent with his profound commitment and indicative of his extraordinary courage.

Granting, however, that the assassination did not prove the failure of nonviolence, did it not at least demonstrate that the conditions for nonviolent action do not exist today? The assassination, it can be argued, brought out dramatically the profound violence of white America and its determination to crush every effort of the Negro population to achieve a measure of justice. An atmosphere in which the internationally acknowledged spokesman for nonviolence, the man who more than any other refused to abandon faith in America, becomes a prime target for assassination may not be suited to the practice of nonviolence. In this view, then, the assassination as such does not constitute a reason or justification for abandoning nonviolence, but it serves as a symbolic reminder that such a strategy is irrelevant.

I find this a compelling position because I too reacted to the assassination of Martin Luther King with a sense of despair at the relentless violence of American society, both in its internal and external affairs. Yet, on closer reflection, I cannot accept as valid the conclusion that nonviolence is irrelevant to the present situation of our society. In fact, I shall try to show why militant nonviolent action is specifically relevant to our present dilemma, given the changes that need to be achieved and the available means that are capable of achieving them. I am convinced that nonviolent means are far more likely to be effective in producing real changes than the violence now being elevated into a positive value in the romantic mystique and the revolutionary rhetoric of some black militants and their white supporters and provokers. What is wrong with the cult of violence is not that it is too radical, but that it is not radical enough. It relies on the slogans, the methods, and the ways of thinking that have characterized all of the old nationalisms, and, in advocating violence, it is—to use King's words—"imitating the worst, the most brutal and the most uncivilized values of American life." The advocacy of violence may be radical in the sense of using an aggressive style and calling for "extreme" actions. The advocacy of nonviolence, however, is truly radical in its insistence on an analysis that goes to the roots, on a redefinition of ends and means, and on a search for innovative approaches.

Black militants are, understandably, suspicious and resentful of calls for nonviolence that come from—or are seen as coming from—representatives of the establishment. It is indeed hypocritical to demand of Negroes, in a moralizing tone of voice, that they renounce violence when the rest of the society is so saturated with it, particularly at a time when the very men who make these demands are responsible for the brutal and systematic uses of violence in Vietnam. Clearly, these demands derive from a vested interest in maintaining the status quo, which the black militant certainly does not share. It is from the same perspective that some political figures have declared in recent months that "no one has a right to riot." They reveal their complete lack of comprehension of the meaning of the riots by appealing to the legitimacy of the system, when the essential message of the riots is precisely that the system—being unjust—is illegitimate.

My own questioning of the mystique and rhetoric of violence derives, of course, from a very different perspective, formed by a concern with fundamental social change. Nevertheless, as a white man, I hesitate to urge Negroes to commit themselves to nonviolence because of its moral superiority, or even because of its pragmatic advantages. I feel that only Negroes can decide whether they prefer the risks of armed self-defense to the risks of going unarmed, whether they prefer erring in the direction of undue trust of the white society to erring in the direction of undue suspicion, or even whether they prefer expressing their anger to being effective. White men, no matter how deeply involved they may be in the struggles of the Negro community, are not exposed to the same provocations, nor subject to the same consequences, and they have a freedom to withdraw from the struggle that is not available to their Negro comrades. They must be wary, therefore, of any attempt to impose their own moral or strategic preferences on Negroes, for whom these questions represent basic existential choices.[3] But, just as it would be presumptuous for white men to pass moral judgment on the actions of black nationalists, so would it be patronizing to withhold criticism of the premises on which these actions are based, if that criticism derives from an honest and thoughtful analysis of the issues and options.

My analysis has convinced me that violence is self-defeating in Negro Americans' struggle to achieve justice and that nonviolence is ultimately more conducive to genuine change. This analysis is based on the following considerations: (1) The current phase of the struggle calls for tactics of confrontation directed to a realignment of power relationships within the society; (2) Such confrontations, however, can create meaningful and lasting changes only if they induce white Amer-

[3] By the same token, white "revolutionaries" ought to think twice before urging the Negro to adopt a strategy of violence and to form the vanguard of their revolution. In their often self-righteous conviction that they are the only true spokesmen for the oppressed, they may fail to notice that they are imposing their *own* revolution on the Negro rather than supporting *his* struggle.

icans to re-examine their attitudes and to open up the system to full Negro participation; (3) We face, therefore, a real dilemma in that confrontations and demands for changes in power relationships—particularly if they use the postures and rhetoric of violence—tend to alienate white Americans from the Negro population and its cause and to strengthen the barriers to Negro participation through repression and separation; and (4) Nonviolent action offers the most promising resolution to this dilemma, and is thus singularly relevant to the current situation, because it provides confrontations without unduly alienating the white population and challenges to existing power relationships without unduly threatening the integrity of the system.

• • • • •

THE UNIQUE POTENTIAL OF NONVIOLENT ACTION

It would be unrealistic to maintain that nonviolent confrontations completely avoid alienating the adversary. They do, after all, contain a degree of force and threat; they are often disruptive and inevitably contribute to an atmosphere of tension. Relative to violent confrontations, however, they are far more likely to create the conditions for lasting attitude changes, as well as for a restructuring of social institutions and a realignment of power relationships. What is particularly important is that the effectiveness of nonviolent tactics in generating change is likely to increase with time, whereas, as I have pointed out, the opposite is likely to occur when violent tactics are used.

What are the characteristics of nonviolent action that account for its unique potential in producing durable and cumulative changes, both at the level of individual attitudes and at the level of institutional patterns? Let me suggest some possibilities, looking first at mechanisms of attitude change and then at sources of institutional change.

Attitude change Two features of nonviolent action contribute to its unique capacity for producing lasting changes in attitude. It provides important new information about the nonviolent actor to the adversary and to relevant bystanders. At the same time, it induces them to take some form of reciprocal positive action toward him (or, in the case of bystanders, to engage in some supportive behavior). Both of these conditions facilitate change, but it is their combination that makes nonviolent action especially powerful.

When Negroes confront white America nonviolently, they provide new information, not only about their concerns and intentions, but also about their underlying character. Their militancy, because it is combined with an open and conciliatory attitude, communicates a serious commitment to changing their situation, rather than a desire to threaten or destroy whites. Their nonviolence, because it is combined with a strong determination and an obvious willingness to make sacrifices, communicates a readiness to work out mutually satisfactory resolutions, rather than a posture of weakness and a passive acceptance of white oppression. Militant nonviolence, moreover, enhances Negroes' own self-respect and thus communicates their expectation of respect from the white community. Because of the generally reduced level of tension and threat perception in a nonviolent (as compared to a violent) confrontation, whites are more likely to be attentive to these new items of information transmitted by Negroes. The information, in turn, if properly perceived, may lead whites to re-examine their image of Negroes, and to perceive them in a new light.

Nonviolent actions, however, affect not only the antagonist's perceptions, but also his own actions. What the nonviolent actor does makes certain responses by the adversary possible or necessary, and others impossible or unnecessary. Nonviolent action tends to tie the adversary's hands. He cannot respond to it as violently and as ruthlessly as he would to violent action. Instead, a nonviolent strategy often forces the adversary to reciprocate with nonviolence, just as a violent strategy invites a violent rejoinder. There are various reasons for this. Some are related to the existence of a norm of reciprocity; even if the adversary himself is prepared to violate that norm, he often has to take account of the reactions of third parties. There is also a tendency, in much of social interaction, for B's actions to come to resemble A's expectations—that is, for B to enact the role into which A casts him. Thus, if Negroes, pursuing a nonviolent strategy, treat whites as if they were friendly, trustworthy, and honorable, then they may force them actually to become friendly, trustworthy, and honorable. Finally, internal processes within the opposing group, set into motion by the nonviolent confrontation, may bring about reciprocal action. That is, the nonviolent action may challenge some elements within the white community—notably the white liberals—in terms of their own value system and mobilize supportive action on their part. It may move them from a neutral or indifferent posture into an active alliance with Negroes, with efforts to pressure the white leadership to reciprocate the nonviolent action. This is particularly likely to happen if the initial white response to the nonviolence was one of violent suppression.

As the adversary reciprocates by engaging in positive, supporting, and conciliatory actions toward those who initiated nonviolent moves, strong forces toward attitude change are likely to be mobilized in him. Positive actions by the adversary commit him to an increasingly friendly relationship with the nonviolent actors, which tends to generalize to his underlying attitudes toward them. What is crucial here is that B's observation of his own friendly actions toward A produces attitude change in a favorable direction. It is often true that our observations of our own treatment of an object exert a greater influence on our attitudes than do the characteristics of the object itself. There are various reasons why one would expect attitudes to fall into line with the actions that one has taken. One, which has been explored in a number of social-psychological studies, is the need to justify our actions to ourselves. Another and perhaps more basic one is our tendency to define people and things largely in terms of our own actions toward them (a tendency that is nicely captured in the book of children's definitions entitled *A Hole Is To Dig*). In fine, to the extent to which nonviolent action can force the adversary to reciprocate in kind, it is likely to lead to increasingly friendly attitudes, just as the reciprocation of violent action is likely to lead to increasing hostility.

The unique power of a nonviolent strategy is that it provides for the *joint occurrence* of genuinely new information about those who undertake the action and friendly behavior toward them on the part of the antagonist. New information itself may be an insufficient basis for attitude change because the recipient may lack the motivation to consider it actively and seriously. Thus, for example, an educational campaign designed to communicate the mood of the Negro population may not have much impact because whites, even if forced to expose themselves to it, may choose not to listen.

Involvement in positive action toward the other group does create the motivation for re-examining one's attitudes, but it too may fail to produce relevant attitude change if it provides no truly new information to be taken into account. Thus, for example, white assistance to poor Negroes may generate friendly feeling toward the recipients, but would provide no new inputs about the actual mood of the Negro population. (As a result, those who give such assistance are often shocked to find that the recipients are not "grateful" for it.) Someone's attitudes are most likely to be restructured when he is dramatically confronted with challenging new information about another group, in a context in which he is open and receptive to it, that is, when he himself is engaged in friendly actions (or actions that imply friendliness) toward that group.

Nonviolent confrontation has the potential of communicating relevant new information dramatically and, at the same time, forcing representatives of white society into negotiation, discussion, and reciprocal action. As whites engage in these positive interactions, forces toward re-examining their attitudes are set into motion. They become more open to the new information about the Negro and his condition, more inclined to examine the issue and its implications for their own values, and more willing to look into themselves and their society. In short, their own inner forces are mobilized toward change. Change is more likely to occur, therefore, and to be sustained.

Institutional change Nonviolent action has a unique capacity for producing changes in social patterns that are thoroughly built into institutional structures because it makes maximum use of the potential for change present *within* the system. It challenges forcefully the ways in which power is allocated and used, while at the same time expressing a firm commitment to the underlying values and procedures of the system.

Nonviolent action is directed at practices that are considered illegitimate, in the sense that they deny or fail to uphold the rights of a segment of the population and thus violate some of the system's basic assumptions. These may be laws or social patterns that have the effect of excluding that group, of discriminating against it, and of putting it at a disadvantage; or they may be policies that fail to provide some of the group's vital needs or to assure the representation, the protection, the benefits, and the opportunities to which its members are entitled. Nonviolent action does not hesitate to challenge "law and order," when they are used as a cover for practices that are unjust and hence illegitimate. It involves agitation and encourages controversy. At times it calls for civil disobedience, to test a law that is unjust or even to dramatize a protest action. Nevertheless, all of these activities, unlike those involved in violent action, uphold and in fact enhance the integrity of the system, even as they present challenges to it.

Two features of nonviolent action account for this phenomenon. First, nonviolent action is disciplined and restrained. Its purpose is never to create disorder or disruption per se, but to make a specific point and produce a specific effect. In refraining from violence, even under provocation, participants make very evident both their restraint and their commitment to those values on which any decent society is built. Violations of law are always of a very specific nature and usually based on the belief, often tested in court, that the law in question is invalid or unconstitutional. Those who break laws do so openly and are prepared to pay the price for their actions. In short, though nonviolent action involves a departure from normal politics and established channels (because these have failed to offer relief), it demonstrates a profound respect for law, for orderly processes, for the welfare of others, and for the basic human purposes that societies are designed to serve. It not only upholds the system, but actually strengthens it by attempting to restore to law and order the functions for which they were intended and thus their legitimacy.

Secondly, through the direct or symbolic enactment of an alternative pattern that corresponds to the desired state of affairs, nonviolent action provides a model of how the system might ideally work. The action is not designed to destroy the system, so that a new one can be built in its place, but to push to the limits its potential for change. Participants in sit-ins and Freedom Rides acted *as if* facilities were integrated. Participants in voter registration drives acted *as if* the Constitution applied to them. Participants in the Poor People's Campaign are acting *as if* they had access to the seats of power. Insofar as these assumptions do not hold, the action presents a challenge to the system and may even be technically illegal—as it was in the Freedom Rides and may become in the Poor People's Campaign if participants push their assumption to the point of sitting-in at Congressional offices. But the challenge is one that affirms the integrity of the system by forcing it to live up to its basic values.

In affirming the integrity of the system, nonviolent action strengthens those forces within the system that are supportive of the desired changes and, at the same time, reduces the forces of repression. Thus it becomes easier not only to introduce new patterns, but also to institutionalize them, to embed them in the societal structure. Since the new patterns are, in significant ways, continuous with the existing structure, they are more readily absorbed and maintained. Continuity is further enhanced by the fact that nonviolent efforts toward change themselves anticipate the new patterns they are designed to produce, so that new institutional arrangements can be built directly upon them.

In sum, nonviolent action mobilizes internal forces within the social system, as well as within individual antagonists and bystanders, toward the acceptance and support of change. Moreover, it sets into motion psychological and societal processes that facilitate the integration of new patterns, making changes both lasting and cumulative. By its use of tactics that emphasize concern for the adversary as a human being and by its choice of actions that exemplify the desired state of affairs, nonviolence manifests here and now the social conditions that it hopes to create for the future and thus avoids the usual split between means and ends. The continuity between means and ends, between present and future, makes possible the kinds of changes that our current racial crisis calls for: changes that are built into the structure of individual attitudes and of institutional arrangements.

37 How to Avoid Riots

DICK GREGORY

As stated by Kelman in the preceding selection, nonviolent action typically requires "a readiness to make personal sacrifices in defense of one's cause." Few feel compelled, like Martin Luther King, Jr., and his model Gandhi, to make the ultimate sacrifice of giving up one's life for his beliefs. Also important are men like Dick Gregory who are able effectively to combine social activism with humor.

During the summer of 1965, I was Peck's Bad Boy in Chicago, according to the press. For a solid month I led nonviolent marches in the city of Chicago. For thirty-one days straight, I boarded a plane each morning in San Francisco, where I was playing a nightclub engagement at the hungry i, and flew to Chicago to lead afternoon marches. Then I flew back to San Francisco each evening to go to work. Why did I commute four thousand miles each day for thirty-one days? Because I knew that if the city was being hit by nonviolent demonstrations, there was less chance of rioting in the streets. The nonviolent demonstration gives the ghetto dweller a ray of hope that perhaps the power structure will hear his just demands and do something to alleviate the problems.

It was a real struggle to keep the demonstration alive. If I had not known that this was the only way to avoid violence, I might have been discouraged. I saw my four- and six-year-old daughters get arrested that summer. Think about that. When demonstrators are arrested, the men are taken one place, the women another, and the children still another. My children had never been away from their home and their mother overnight.

But if I ever had any question about being able to justify involving my kids in demonstrations they were answered by my little four-year-old daughter Lynne. When we were being placed in the wagon to go to jail, Lynne said to me, "We're in trouble, aren't we, Daddy?" That night, I cried because of what she said. Tears of anger, really. I was angry that my momma and daddy had not taught me I was in trouble at the age of four. I didn't find out until I was twenty-nine. And here my little four-year-old daughter had a twenty-five-year head start on her father.

We all know of times when kids have been used for wrong. In election frauds in the city of Chicago, kids have voted. And if I read my Bible right, little David was only a boy when he went out to fight Goliath with a slingshot. I was not asking my kids to kill anybody, only to stand up for what was right. And there is no age limit on that.

My wife had a baby that summer on June 16. Since we were running out of demonstrators, I called her on June 18 and said, "Come on out of the hospital,

SOURCE: Dick Gregory, *The Shadow that Scares Me* (New York: Doubleday, 1968), pp. 116–19. • Dick Gregory is an author, entertainer, and lecturer who has made numerous television and college appearances. During the last decade he has wielded the cutting edge of social criticism in the contemporary black struggle for equal human rights. He is author of *From the Back of the Bus, Nigger, What's Happening,* and *Write Me In.*

baby, because we are running out of demonstrators and we can't stop this thing now." As long as we held nonviolent demonstrations, there were no riots in the city of Chicago. Even when we were arrested en masse, in acts of civil disobedience halting downtown traffic, there was no violence. Only when the demonstrations stopped did violence erupt on the West Side of Chicago.

Violence results when the power structure fails to respond to the peaceful, nonviolent demonstration. Not only does the power structure fail to consider the just demands of nonviolent demonstrators, it will try to defame and ridicule nonviolent leaders. I was arrested that summer and accused of biting a cop. I stood trial and lost my case. The story of how I lost my case is a study in governmental mockery.

The woman who actually bit the cop came to me and offered to testify on my behalf. I knew she bit the cop; the cop knew she bit him. The trouble came when city hall found out she bit him. The woman was given a job with the poverty program, paying $175 per week, with the stipulation that she not testify in court. The biter is now making more money than the bitten!

There is a pattern of governmental refusal to listen to just demands. The summer riot season in Chicago in 1966 began in the Puerto Rican neighborhood. Many people in Chicago have always wondered why there were no Puerto Rican cops. The official answer from city hall has been, "We don't have anything against Puerto Ricans, but the official height standard for Chicago policemen is five feet, ten inches. Puerto Ricans are just too short."

If Puerto Rican leaders go to city hall and ask that the height requirements be lowered three inches to allow more Puerto Ricans to become policemen, they will be politely but firmly refused. After the Puerto Ricans threw bricks in their neighborhood for three days, the height requirement *was* lowered three inches—an inch per day of rioting. If the riots had lasted a month, there would be job openings on the Chicago police force for Spanish-speaking midgets!

It is a shame that it should take rioting to get Puerto Rican policemen in Chicago. The need for Spanish-speaking policemen in Puerto Rican neighborhoods is crucial. Imagine the problem of communication which is created when the cop on the beat does not understand your language. A man whose wife has just been scalded and seriously burned comes running out of his apartment, grabs the cop, and yells excitedly at him in Spanish. The cop reacts by grabbing his nightstick because he doesn't understand what the excitement is all about.

After the rioting in the Puerto Rican neighborhoods settled down during the summer of 1966, the West Side of Chicago blew up. It is ironic that the rioting in the colored neighborhood started over some water. Negro leaders had been politely asking city hall for some swimming pools. And city hall turned a deaf ear to them. So the residents of the ghetto decided to create their own swimming pools by turning on the fire hydrants. When the cops came to shut the hydrants off, the trouble started. It seems strange to me that white folks should want to cut off the water in a colored neighborhood. They have been trying to run away from hot nigger stink for a hundred years. Instead of turning off the water, they should have brought in some soap.

Since the bricks were thrown all over the West Side of Chicago, it is hard now to walk in that section without stepping into a swimming pool. The government conveniently found forty million dollars after the rioting which did not seem to be available before. It was the same pattern in Los Angeles. Before the rioting, few people had ever heard of the Watts section of Los Angeles. After the bricks were thrown, some two hundred million dollars were poured into that community in emergency funds. As nonviolent demonstrations help to avoid violence in the streets, the refusal of government to respond to the just demands of such demonstrations creates an atmosphere of anger, frustration, and desperation which assures a violent reaction.

38 Student Rebellions

EDWARD SHILS

Student rebellions are collective efforts to initiate or to aid selective social change. Among the numerous types of such behavior today, probably none has more potential for change than student radicalism. In the selection that follows, Shils offers his ideas, based on a global and historical review, about the distinctive nature of the student rebellions in Western Europe and North America in the late 1960s, and why they differ from those of an earlier period.

At the beginning of the 1930's, there was no student movement to speak of in the United States. The young people's branches of the socialist and Communist parties—the Young Communist League (YCL), the League for Industrial Democracy, and the Young People's Socialist League (YPSL)—and tiny sects of anti-Stalinists existed as national organizations and as small isolated bodies at the major universities (at, for example, Harvard, Chicago, Berkeley). They were a little stronger in Wisconsin where they were attracted and supported by a strong local tradition; their main activity was at the City College of New York. Although the motives for their radicalism might have been personal and private or abstract and universal, all of them were attached to national organizations under the umbrella of which young persons—not students as such—stood.

In the United Kingdom, some students became Communists; pacifism and anti-fascism became moderately widespread at the London School of Economics and in Oxford by the mid-thirties. Despite the notoriety of the refusal, at the Oxford Union, to defend king and country, radical undergraduates at British universities were few, and those few were conventionally radical in their affiliation to the adult "left-wing" political parties.

In Germany, many students supported the National Socialists and the *Deutschnationale;* many fewer supported the Social Democrats or Communists. Many students expressed their hostility toward Jewish and socialist teachers by unruliness and rudeness in lectures; much more visible were their frequent altercations with socialist and Communist students, their disruption of the latter's meetings and their physical assaults on

SOURCE: Edward Shils, "Dreams of Plenitude, Nightmares of Scarcity," in *Students in Revolt,* eds. Seymour Lipset and Phillip Altbach (Boston: Houghton Mifflin, 1969). Reprinted by permission of the author and the American Academy of Arts and Sciences. • Edward Shils is professor of sociology and a member of the Committee of Social Thought at the University of Chicago. He is a Fellow at King's College, Cambridge, and is editor of the quarterly review, *Minerva,* as well as being a contributing author to *Encounter.*

their members. Whatever they did, they did to express their affiliation with and to promote the progress toward power of their non-university elders. With all their brutality, they were extremely submissive to their masters; they espoused the program of the NSDAP in all things; they denounced Jewish science and those teachers whom, by reason of their humanity, liberality and lack of xenophobia, they regarded as traitors to the German people; they stood by gleefully when their ringleaders realized the eternal dream of delinquent pupils and burned a pile of books; they marched in parades under the auspices of their adult patrons.

In Eastern Europe, nationalist student organizations created disturbances in lectures of Jewish and liberal teachers and assaulted physically Jewish and socialist students. There, too, youthful delinquency and brutality were coordinated into the movement of adults who carried on the tradition of Polish anti-Semitism. In France, students were members of the *Camelot du Roi,* which was not exclusively for students; steeped in an old tradition of the youthful upper-class brawler, they joined in the public disorders attendant on the Stavisky scandal. They were youthful ruffians at the disposal of their elders.

There were no university students in black Africa, except for the handful of pious, well-behaved students at the Fourah Bay College. In the Middle East, students were few and, their political activities being radically nationalist, anti-imperialist, and Arabophile, were kept in check by the political elites of that period who lived under French and British influence and who tried at least publicly to conciliate the foreigner. Such public manifestations as they made were a part of a larger nationalistic or ethnic movement of sentiment; students did not act on their own.

In India, at the beginning of the 1930's, the student movement was beginning to rise to the plateau of the decisive years of the independence movement. It had ostensibly one main aim: to bring about the departure of the British so that India could become independent. This entailed the organized truancy called strikes and boycotts; it involved processions and demonstrations and assorted "Jimmy Higgins" services. The political activities of students were practically always under the guidance of the Congress; when students began to become socialists, they did so under Congress patronage; when they became violent, they did so under the leadership of Congress socialists. In China, students were active politically, denouncing the Japanese invaders, the Kuomintang government and the European imperialists; there, too, students struck, boycotted classes, and demonstrated, but they always did so in close association with adult politicians. Iu Burma, the small number of students were beginning to be markedly anti-British. Later in the decade they conducted important strikes and published occasionally-appearing and short-lived periodicals. Since they were practically the first generation of nationalists, they had relatively little adult collaboration and guidance, but in this they were exceptional.

The varyingly small proportion of students who engaged in the demonstrative, expressive, and always aggressive actions of student politics were always against the existing regime—that is, where they were free to do so and could do so with impunity. (The situation was different in the Soviet Union and in Fascist Italy, where student activities were closely controlled by the government.) Where they were free to act, they always went beyond the existing regime. Where the regime was anti-Semitic, for example, they went further in their anti-Semitism. In most cases, they did not just go further, they actually went against the existing regime. Their beliefs made them oppositional; the urgency and passion of their espousal made them into extremists. They were not just against the incumbent party; they were against "the system as a whole"—either against the "Weimar system," against the entire secularist tolerant culture of the Third Republic, or against the "capitalist system." They were ideologically radical in that sense. Yet although their actions were usually directed against the prevailing system ruled by adults, they practically always had the support and encouragement, guidance and discipline brought by adults. Their organizations were almost always parts of or affiliated to oppositional organizations in which adults were in control. They were, of course, not simply creatures, instruments, and copies of the adults to whom they were affiliated; they added something of their own—resiliency, verve, dramatic actions, and an element of carnival. They were often violent, and they were sometimes courageous in their violent actions —and frequently they were only brutes and bullies. They usually enjoyed engagement in acts of violence, and they sometimes suffered injuries. They could act with more spontaneity than the adults; they had more enthusiasm than their elders; and they enjoyed the excitement of antagonistic encounters with the ruling authorities, who were usually restrained in their treatment of them, and with their antagonists and victims who in Central and Eastern Europe were often weaker than themselves. They acted from a privileged position that radicals of the lower classes did not enjoy, and they had the great advantage of more freely adaptable time-schedules. Universities have always been freer than factories and offices, and they could absent themselves from their postponable university duties as the spirit moved them.

Actively and aggressively anti-authoritarian though the relatively small student movements of those days were, their activities were sponsored and legitimated by the authority of elders. They had a tradition that sustained them, but their tradition was not theirs alone; nor was it of their own finding. It was exemplified and embodied in the corporate organizations of their elders, to which their own were affiliated. They accepted the anti-authoritarian authority of adults in the wider movements of which the student movements formed a part. They also accepted in general the authorities of the university system. Although their rebellious activities were often planned and sometimes took place in university buildings or on university grounds, they were seldom concerned with university matters. The university was not the home of their heart; that lay outside. They aimed at the world outside the university although this sometimes involved action within the university, such as the beating of Jewish classmates or the disruption of the lectures of Jewish or socialist or expatriate teachers.

Student rebellions in the present decade are more comprehensively and more fundamentally hostile toward authority than they were three and four decades ago. They are hostile, in principle, toward authority whereas their predecessors were hostile only to particular authorities and submitted enthusiastically to others. They act now without the sponsorship of external adult organizations, and they feel little sympathy with most of them. The innovators in the present generation of student radicals are antinomian; the rejection of authority by their predecessors of more than a third of a century ago was sustained and limited by a legitimating authority.

They did not venture so far or so daringly from authority as the most advanced student radicals do nowadays. The present-day student radicals act without the legitimating authority of older figures; their middle-aged courtiers who offer their legitimatory services are offering something that is neither wanted nor needed. Paul Goodman and Sartre provide agreeable but unsought applause. When the student radicals group themselves around an older figure he is of their own creation, as was the case of Senator Eugene McCarthy—who is not a charismatic person but was made into one by the student radicals' need for one. The adults most closely associated with the student radicals are usually young teachers little older than themselves, and they function more to affirm than to guide and legitimate. The "big names" of present day student radicalism—Mao Tse-tung, Fidel Castro, Ché Guevara, Frantz Fanon—are remote in space or dead; they have no commanding power over them, and they all share in the eyes of the student radicals a quasi-bohemian, free-floating, anti-institutional aroma. Even though they govern tyrannically, it is their anarchic element that appeals to the radical students. Castro's period in Oriente province, his conduct of the affairs of his high office in cafés at 3 A.M., and the generally impromptu air of his tyranny attract just as the image of Mao Tse-tung owes much to the period in the caves and the "long march." Neither of these two living amulets is in charge of an organization that the student radicals must obey.

How are these major differences to be accounted for?

The turbulence of student radicalism now has the appearance of being worldwide. Alongside the formal international federations of students that appear to be of scant significance for the more dramatic activities of the student radicals, there is a spontaneous and unorganized, or at best an informal, unity of sympathy of the student movement which forms a bridge across national boundaries. In 1968, student radical movements seemed to be synchronized among different countries and uniform in content and technique to an extent reminiscent of the monolithic phase of the Communist International and its subsidiary organizations.

Student radicalism is no longer the possession of small, relatively closed sects within larger student bodies; on the contrary, it can reach out toward the sympathy of a large minority, occasionally even the majority of students, at particular places and for limited times. Its organizations within each country, despite numerous ups and downs, are more persistent in their action and have a larger following than they used to have. They show a self-confidence reaching to arrogance in their dealings with hostile authority, and they are aware of the transnational scale of their undertaking. Nonetheless, the movement is not unified, either nationally or internationally. Synchronization is a function of a generally identical mood, not of concerted organized action.

Nor is the movement uniform internationally. There are major differences between countries and continents. In India, for example, where until the outbursts in Western countries since 1964 the university student population was the most turbulent in the world, the student radicals do not as a rule make the structures of the larger society and of the university objects of a general critique. Indian student radicals declare no fundamental criticism of their society; they have no schemes for the reconstruction of their universities. They do take stands on public issues—for example, on behalf of the construction of a steel mill in Andhra Pradesh or on behalf of or in opposition to the use of English as the medium of instruction in higher education, the nearest they come to espousing a general policy for higher education. The Indian student agitation is "occasionalist"; it responds to particular stimuli, local, regional, or national, but grievances do not become generalized and are therefore not persistent. India, however, is exceptional in its relatively apolitical agitation. In Indonesia, student radicalism is, contrarily to India's, wholly and over the past few years continuously, political. Internal university conditions, terrible though they are, scarcely engage its attention; its interest is in the public realm, where in collaboration with but not under the dominion of the army it was important in the ultimate undoing of former President Sukarno.

Elsewhere in Asia—omitting mainland China—in North Africa, and, to a lesser extent, in black Africa, Latin America, and Spain, student agitation follows the conventional nineteenth-century pattern of nationalist agitation against the repressive character of the incumbent government and its insufficient devotion to the national cause (even though the foreign rulers have departed, in some cases very long ago). Their actions are larger, more vehement, and more frequently recurrent than they were in the earlier period, but, except for the magnitude and intensity of the manifestations, they have not changed. They agitate against restrictions on freedom of organization and propaganda and against their government's moral corruption and its alleged subservience to foreign powers—in most cases nowadays the United States. The creed that declares "neo-colonialism" to be the chief enemy is to a large extent a student creed. It is a shoddier version of the Marxist-Leninist analysis of colonialism and imperialism which was a fairly common possession of the nationalistic student movements in Asia during the 1930's or of the African student movements in France and England during the 1940's and 1950's.

Nonetheless, despite these similarities with their earlier outlook, the student movements in most of the countries of the Third World, like those in the advanced Western countries, have broken away from the pattern of their antecedents by becoming independent of adult organizations. They have practically no significant older political figures to whom they look for guidance or inspiration. The leaders of an earlier generation are in power or apolitical, dead or in exile. They are, whether dead or alien, out of the question as the leaders of an effective opposition. Despite some exceptions, aggressive student radicalism is forced to stand alone, to the extent that it stands at all. In India where public opposition is still permitted, the Indian student agitation, too, has by and large lost its connection with a dominant organization of adult politicians. Although in many particular instances, party politicians are able to exploit some of the disruptive capacities of Indian students, the organizational links are loose or nonexistent. In India, too, there is no larger adult political movement of which the students regard their own movement as a part, and this is one of the main reasons why most Indian student agitation voices have no general political demands.

In Eastern Europe, particularly in Poland and Czechoslovakia, courageous students have agitated against tyranny in the larger society and on behalf of the traditional freedoms of thought, expression, and assembly, and for the rule of law—with some of the same nationalist, anti-Russian accompaniment that was characteristic of their nineteenth-century antecedents. And they do these things alone, except for the patronage of a few literary men and professors. Even in the brief periods of liberalization in Poland and Czechoslovakia, the students acted independently with the "liberalizers," not under them. The administration and functions of the university do not worry them, except insofar as party tyranny and favoritism manifest themselves there.

In Western Europe and North America, the situation is both similar and different from the other parts of the world. In their relationship to adult oppositional organizations, Western student radicalism resembles that of the Third World. In Britain, the Labour Party is ingloriously in power; in Western Germany, the Social Democratic Party is part of the Grand Coalition. In France, the socialists are futile and the Communists in their odd way, and despite what General de Gaulle claimed, are pillars of the existing order in the face of student "provocation" and "adventurism." In Italy the socialists share government responsibility, and the Communist Party has no sympathy with the student radicals whom it regards as Maoist provocateurs. In the United States, the major parties are abhorrent to the student radicals and the only adult opposition to the major parties is a racist know-nothingism. In North America, the bourgeois parties have never concerned themselves with student support, the socialist parties have always been negligible, and the Communist parties have dwindled in size and in moral standing. Official Marxism is unaccredited or discredited. There is no ideology ready to hand for student radicalism.

The student radicals have, therefore, no adult political masters; they act on their own. Those sections that maintain organizational relations with adult parties or groups are either in a state of conflict with their elders or are relegated to positions of despised insignificance by their radical contemporaries. The discrediting of the Communist parties, the moderation of the Social Democratic parties, and the eclipse or disappearance of Fascist and Nazi parties in Western Europe have left the students without either a parent organization of elders or an authoritatively promulgated doctrine to which they can give their loyalty or adherence. A "natural" Castroism, amorphous, passionately hostile to organization forms a powerful, profound undercurrent of sentiment and of vaguely formulated belief.

In most of the countries in which there is much radical student agitation, there has been nothing commensurate to it on the intellectual side. In Eastern Europe, liberalism, admirable and courageous though it has been, is no intellectual innovation. In India, *hic et nunc* protests against very particular features of university and college administration and against very particular deprivations represent a retreat from the variety of nationalist, Marxist, and Gandhian creeds and ideologies of the early depression decade. For the rest, the student movements in Africa, Japan, Indonesia, and Latin America have added nothing fundamentally new to the intellectual repertoire of the student movements.

Technologically, there are innovations; students commandeer lorries; they use "bull-roarers"; they confront the police armed in helmets and bearing shields; they have adopted Molotov cocktails from the Russians they despise and the "sit-in" from the American automobile workers' union with which their sympathies are minimal. Nor have they been original organizationally; even the spectre of a worldwide movement—which has been created for them and from which they profit through the heightening of their self-consciousness and confidence—is the work of the bourgeois press and television.

All this being said, the differences between student radicalism at the beginning of the 1930's and in 1968 are greater than the mere differences of organizational independence from adult parties or the criticism of the universities. Far more important are the differences in fundamental beliefs about the self, about authority, about institutions, and about what is "given" by the past and the present. These differences are of the greatest importance and merit close analysis since they refer to serious matters.

• • • • •

The great innovation in student radicalism that has occurred in Northwestern Europe and the United States is a moral mood. In a certain sense, the radicals among the students of France, Western Germany, Great Britain, and the United States—and increasingly of Italy and Spain—testify to a moral revolution.

The moral revolution consists in a demand for a total transformation—a transformation from a totality of undifferentiated evil to a totality of undifferentiated perfection. Evil consists in the deadening of sentiment through institutions and more particularly through the exercise of and subordination to authority. Perfection consists in the freedom of feeling and the fulfillment of desires. "Participation" is a situation in which the individual's desires and "demands" are fully realized through complete self-determination of the individual and the institutions which such freely feeling, self-determining individuals form. A good community is like Rousseau's; the common will harmonizes individual wills. But the contemporary proponents of participation do not think of the individual will as anything but the concrete empirical will of actual and immediate sentiments, impulses, and desires. The common will is not the resultant of the rationally arrived at assent of its members; it is not actually a *shared* decision-making; it is certainly not the outcome of consent to a compromise arrived at by bargaining and exchange. It is not acceptance of anything less than what one initially desired. It is the transformation of sentiment and desire into reality in a community in which all realize their wills simultaneously. Anything less is repressive.

This is why the advance guard of student radicalism is so resolute in its reaction against repression. It is resolute not just against the violent and often brutal repression by the police, but just as much against the moderate repression that is entailed by the application of the principle of *in loco parentis*. It is against the "repressiveness" of the rules of the game of parliamentary politics and of distributions of rewards in accordance with a criterion of merit. It is against "institutional repression" or "individual violence" by which is usually meant the discipline of a practicable consensus in a regime of scarcity. Whatever hampers the fulfillment of whatever happens to be desired at the moment—whether it is a student housing arrangement which stipulates the hours of visiting in halls of residence or an examination or a convention regarding dress or sexual behaviour in public places—is repressive. And, as such, it is part of an undifferentiatedly repressive system.

The conception of a life in which desires cannot be completely realized at the moment they are experienced is part of a larger view of existence as a realm of scarcity. It is a tradition with the longest history in the moral repertoire of mankind. The acceptance of the fact of scarcity has been an essential element in the outlook of most of mankind over most of its history. Poverty and injustice, illness and the brevity of life, the limitations on the possibility of gratifying desires and impulses have been regarded as inexpungible elements of the situation of mankind, and ethical patterns and theodicies have been constructed to justify or to censure—and to integrate—this ostensibly inevitable condition. The opening of the self and its elevation was confined to festivities, carnivals, and rites, but everyday life was marked by constriction imposed by nature, society, and the moral powers of the personality. It consisted in limits on experience, the suppression of experienced impulse, the "avoidance of temptation" to impulses not yet experienced to come forward into consciousness or conduct. Poverty, ignorance, oppression took care of most of the preconditions for the constriction of individuality. A few great personalities transcended these limitations and made their lives into "works of art."

Christianity, particularly in its dissenting Protestant form, the growth of wealth, the spread of literacy, and the gradual recession of the primordial categories and criteria of assessing the meaning and worth of a human being have in the course of centuries worn away some of these individuality-suppressing and -constricting conditions. A profound revolution was worked by romanticism, which spread more widely in intellectual circles the conception of genius that need not regard the laws of society and its authorities and that aimed only to be guided by the inner necessities of the expansion of the self—to embrace new experiences, to enrich itself by the opening of its sensibilities. World War I and the Great Depression were the watershed. The erosion of the bourgeois ethic and the puritanism of diligence, respectability, and self-restraint on behalf of results which rendered one respectable were greatly aided by the Great Depression. The vanity of self-restraint was made evident, saving and striving were discredited; sexual self-restraint had been undermined by psychoanalysis and its literary popularization in the period between the wars. More or less liberal, tolerant, and constitutional political elites had been shown to be incompetent by the prolonged slaughter of World War I and by their failures in dealing with unemployment during the Great Depression. The regime of scarcity with which they were associated was discredited when their own legitimacy diminished. The same happened to the virtues of abstinence and self-discipline preached from the pulpits. Ecclesiastical authority had been under a steady pressure of rational disbelief and indifference; its legitimacy was further undermined in intellectual circles because of the association of the churches with the earthly regimes of external constriction and internal restraint under assault from other sources.

World War II was followed by an efflorescence of material well-being in the advanced countries on a scale never previously experienced. Particularly for the educated classes, there seemed to exist a relatively unbounded vista of opportunity for interesting employment, for travel, and for freedom from the restraints of impecuniousness, boring toil, and confinement. Full employment, the welfare services, and inflation made unrealistic the conception of a rainy day for which to save. At the outermost reaches was the perpetual awful threat of extinction in a war fought with nuclear weapons. The anxiety about the latter accentuated the attachment to pleasures of the moment. The heir of these developments was the generation born after the end of World War II.

In a variety of ways, this was a uniquely indulged generation. Parents who were in a state of unprecedented prosperity were persuaded of the merits of hedonism and were capable of giving some reality to its precepts in the raising of their children. They were convinced of the beneficence of a life free of repression and inhibition, and they treated their offspring with a concern and affection which seemed to confirm the prediction made by Ellen Key at the beginning of the twentieth century that this was the "century of the child." Expanding incomes and unceasing freedom from the threat of unemployment—for the middle classes at least—made for a readiness to believe that scarcity had been expelled from human existence. A life beyond the dreams of avarice seemed to have become accessible to those whom the fortunes of birth—in time and status—had favored. They were an increasingly larger proportion of the population.

The postwar generation has grown up, too, in a society in which authority has lost its sacredness. As the center of society expanded, those in positions of authority acquired a new conception of their obligations. Democratic elections moreover—and a populistic outlook even where there were no democratic elections—have made rulers believe that they have to justify themselves to realizing the desires of their citizenry. The expansion of individuality and the appreciation of the self, intricately related to enhanced self-esteem throughout much of Western societies, have diminished to some extent the arrogance of authority. The range of dispersion between the highest and the quite low has narrowed. It is certainly true that all Western—and all other—societies are far from the fulfillment of an ideal of equality. Power is unequally distributed; wealth is unequally distributed; income is unequally distributed; but the deference-system of modern societies strains toward egalitarianism. Of course, this "moral equality" is far from being realized; the strength of inherited beliefs and the presence of such tremendous concentrations of authority in the state and in great economic organizations—public and private—stand in the way of its realization. Nonetheless, the younger generation—living in the midst of the culturally juvenocentric society which Johan Huizinga discerned already in the 1930's—is experiencing this moral egalitarianism to a far-reaching degree. New methods of pedagogy and exclusion from the labor market—as far as middle-class young persons are concerned—have reduced the amount of experience with severely hierarchical and repressive institutions. But as much as the arrogance of authority has diminished, it has still not disappeared. Its diminution, moreover, has been more than balanced by the increased intolerability of what it seeks to impose. Sensitivity to the impositions of authority has greatly increased, and almost every impingement on it from the outside—unless voluntarily chosen as part of the expansion of individuality—is painful to the point of unsupportability.

Basic in all this is the view that every human being simply by virtue of his humanity is an essence of unquestionable, undiscriminatable value with the fullest right to the realization of what is essential in him. What is essential is his sensibility, his experienced sensations, the contents of his imagination, and the gratification of his desires. Not only has man become the measure of all things; his sentiments have become the measure of man. The growth of the capacity for unconfined sensation is the measure of the value of an institution. The goodness of a life consists in its continuous enlargement of these sensations and of the experiences that give rise to them. Institutions—with their specialized and prescribed roles, their restrictions on individual willfulness, the crystallization of traditions and their commitments that bind the future by the past—are repugnant to this aspiration toward an individuality that creates its boundaries only in response to its internal needs. Authority is repugnant, too, and so is tradition and all that it brings down and imposes from the past.

All this is old stuff. This is what the romantics taught us. But romanticism was only a literary and more or less philosophical movement; it did not become a widely pervasive outlook and style of life for many persons. Writers, artists, and bohemians espoused and embodied it, but its consistent following was small. The desacralization of authority, the productivity of the economy, the growth of moral equality, and the spread of enlightenment and educational opportunity have resulted in the diffusion of a much more consequent romanticism throughout a much broader section of each Western society. The more prosperous classes are the recipients of its diffusion; the offspring of these classes are their purest products.

University students in Western countries, despite an increased recruitment from among the offspring of the working classes, still come largely from middle- and upper-middle-class families. Many of those who have not come from these classes live in a cultural atmosphere of hedonistic expectations for the present and the future as much as do those who have come from families in which such expectations are to some extent realized. Many are supported from the public treasury at the expense of taxpayers. The availability of opportunity to attend university is still interpreted by many students, as it was in the past, as a first step into a less constricted future. Attendance at university, which was once regarded as a stroke of the good fortune of birth or the result of exertion and which offered its beneficiaries a chance to diminish to some extent the rigors of the regime of scarcity, is now, however, regarded by student radicals as itself part of an actual realm of plenitude. Anyone should have it for the asking.

University students, in the view of forty years ago, appeared to be on a straight road into a future which, in the light of the standards of the Enlightenment and in view of the immemorial fate of human beings, seemed to be extraordinarily rich in the possibilities of a better life—at least for themselves, if not for all the other members of their own societies. The student radicals of today have a quite different view of the matter: They do not wish to live in a society in which "the danger of death by starvation is replaced by the danger of death by boredom." The denunciation of the "consumers' society" is the common slogan of the French and West German student radicals; less explicitly but no less pervasively, the same view obtains among the American and British student radicals. They do not wish to be part of a "repressively tolerant society" that seduces by its favors. They wish their universities to be "restructured" to become the microcosms of a total revolution from which, in moments of exhilaration, they think the rest of the society can be no less totally transformed. The universities must become "participatory," and from there outward their "societies" must become "participatory." They criticize their universities for having become "integrated" into their respective societies, but it is only evil integration which they oppose. They do not believe in the possibility of dispassionately acquired knowledge; they insist that "objectivity" and "neutrality" are simply masks that conceal the intention to serve the "system." They do not wish their universities to become "ivory towers"; they refuse to acknowledge the differentiation of tasks, a division of labor among institutions. There is no task that they would not have their institutions undertake in the transformation of society; only the transmission of knowledge and discovery are left unmentioned by them.

. . . . .

The radical students are opposed to competition and the scarcity which necessitates it. Their ethos is the ethos of a regime of plenitude, but they know, too, that their societies are regimes of scarcity. They know, too, that if they do not accept the rules of the regime of scarcity, they will go to the wall. Dean Marc Zamansky said to the striking students of the faculty of sciences in Paris when they were debating the boycott of examinations that even "a socialist society must be selective." How much more so a bourgeois society! Honors are scarce, first places are scarce, research grants and stipends are scarce, professorships are scarce. They are, of course, all more available than they used to be, but the student rebels do not know the past any more than most other young persons, and they do not take seriously what little they do know of it. They are entranced by a vision of plenitude of which they disapprove when they conceive of it as the "affluent society" or *société des comsommateurs* or the *Konsumentengesellschaft*, but which has nonetheless become an essential part of their construction of reality. Nonetheless they also know that they live in a world of scarcity run by adults whose legitimacy they do not acknowledge and whose ascendancy they hate; they deny the inevitability of the realm of scarcity and at the same time they know that they will not be able to avoid it. The examination system is the focal point of the repugnance for the regime of scarcity, particularly in the European universities where they are so concentrated in comparison with the dispersion of the American examination system; but in the United States, as if to compensate for the attenuation of strain from the concentrations of examinations, there is the other strain of having to obtain marks high enough to qualify for admission to an eminent graduate school—and the radicals among undergraduates are also those disposed to go on to graduate school for no other reason than that it is less obnoxious than the bourgeois world outside.

. . . . .

We are far from living in a single world community, but the rudiments of a world society do exist. The international scientific community is the most international of all the elements of this rudimentary world society. Learned and scientific periodicals, international scientific societies, and the universities are the most elaborated and most internationally coherent parts of this rudimentary worldwide network of institutions. They do, at least at their peaks, have common standards, common heroes, and a unifying sense of affinity. Students, through their membership in universities, share in some of this, and their sense of sharing is accentuated among a fluctuatingly small group by an acute sense of generational identity. Although international student organizations are of little significance in the concert of action of 1968, and although students have nothing like a major scientific or scholarly press which creates a common focus of attention and a common awareness of leading accomplishments and personalities, it has an effective surrogate in the mass media—the newspaper press, wireless, and television. Information flows rapidly without a student international, without the use of a cumbersome system of couriers and coded messages such as international revolutionary organizations once had to use. The radical students have not created this organ of their movement, but they have been responsive to it and indeed, being aware of its value, direct their actions to it. They value television publicity as much as do the figures of the entertainment world or politics.

The international society is no more egalitarian in fact than are the various national societies. This is as true of scientific distinction as it is of wealth and political power. The scientific world has its centers and its peripheries just as any national society has and so does the sphere of student radicalism. What happens in the periphery does not radiate to the center; the movement is in the contrary direction. When the Indian students erupt as they have been doing quite continuously for about twenty years, student radicals do not attend to that. They attend to it even less than their teachers in biochemistry or sociology attend to what is being done in biochemistry or sociology by their colleagues in the Indian universities. Even a more powerful country like Japan produces little demonstration effect. When the *Zengakuren* went on a rampage to prevent President Eisenhower from visiting their country, the facts become known, but they did not become exemplary. When the Indonesian KAMI's helped to bring down the unspoken coalition of Sukarno and the PKI, what they did was admired, but not attended to. When the gallant students of the *Po Prostu* circle helped to bring about the short-lived and now dead Polish October, the students of Berkeley and London found no inspiration there. But when the Berkeley students and then after them students in many other American universities began their "revolution," the radiation from the center outward began. It was like the radiation of the revolution of February from Paris in 1848, when all of Europe felt the repercussions.

. . . . .

This transience of initial issues does not testify to the forgetfulness of the student radicals and the unseriousness of their original complaints. The transience of many of the issues is a function of the more important fact that they are the occasions for confrontations with authority.

It is authority that the radical students wish to confront and affront—and almost any stick will do for the camel. This brings us back not only to the general predisposition with which we dealt earlier, but also to the immediate precipitation of this year's outbreaks. In Western Germany, Great Britain, and the United States, this has been a poor year for governments. In the United States, in particular, the image of the ineptitude of President Johnson—exemplified in the faltering and failing conduct of the war in Vietnam, the inability to bring the disturbances in Negro districts of the big cities to an end, the enfeeblement of urban public order in other respects, and the lack of spectacular results from the poverty program—has made government authority an easy target. The possibility that he could be succeeded by Senator McCarthy made for an even greater aggressiveness against incumbent authority. In Great Britain, the recurrence of the crisis of sterling and the devaluation, the failure to compel admission into the Common Market and powerlessness in the face of the Smith regime in Rhodesia, as well as the flagrant impropriety of the government's treatment of the East African Asians who held British passports have darkened the visage of the Labour government. For different reasons, the federal German government is in the same position. In France the mounting criticism of General de Gaulle from the ineffective opposition parties and the immobilism of the General's government as well as the small majority by which he was returned in the general election which preceded the crisis had similar consequences—which were aggravated, too, by the absence of the two most powerful figures in the government (General de Gaulle in Rumania and M. Pompidou in Afghanistan) when events were cascading—have all replaced the image of a strong and effective authority by one of feebleness and abdication. Where authority abdicates through failure, ineptitude, and weakened self-confidence, it invites aggression against itself. That is what happened this past spring [1968].

. . . . .

39 Community in Disaster

WILLIAM H. FORM AND
SIGMUND NOSOW

Perhaps the most dramatic form of collective behavior is that occasioned by a widespread community disaster. This selection describes the reaction of two groups to a tornado which swept a suburb near Flint, Michigan, in June, 1954. The authors examine the effect of the disaster on the way the members of the two groups—one, a family and the other, a small group of adolescent boys—analyze the problem of determining appropriate roles to play and establishing a division of labor among themselves.

After the impact of the tornado, the community was turned into chaos, but rescue behavior was immediately instituted. This postimpact stage (the *emergency stage* of community relations) was marked by three different periods: the first, during which rescue was performed by the victims and persons from the impact and contiguous areas; the second, during which help was supplemented by local organizations; and the third, during which help was supplemented by external agencies. Those periods provide an overall structural view of the disaster process, the relationships among the victims, rescuers, and organizations.

However, from the point of view of the victims and rescuers, the postimpact period was one during which their own patterns of behavior followed given forms, some activities persisting and others changing. It is possible to discern patterns of *personal behavior* and to classify these in terms of different phases. . . .

The *first phase* for an individual was concerned with action immediately after the impact. During this phase dominant activities were checking on the safety of

SOURCE: William H. Form and Sigmund Nosow, with Gregory P. Stone and Charles M. Westie, *Community in Disaster* (New York: Harper & Brothers, 1958), 33–46. William H. Form is a professor in the Department of Sociology and a research associate in the School of Labor and Industrial Relations, Michigan State University. His chief interests are industrial and occupational sociological research. He is the author of *Industry, Labor and Community* and the coauthor of *Industrial Sociology.* • Sigmund Nosow is a professor in the School of Labor and Industrial Relations, Michigan State University. His major interests are in areas involving both economics and sociology. In addition to *Community in Disaster* he is the coeditor (with William H. Form) of *Man, Work and Society.*

one's family and oneself, appraising the immediate damage, and making decisions as to the appropriate ensuing behavior. This was followed by *phase two*, which reflected a change in the patterns of activity, or a change in the site of such activity, or a change in the social orientation of the activities. *Phase three* was also characterized by a shift in activities and social orientations. This was reflected in increased mobility, sporadic activity, and finally, a general withdrawal from the scene of rescue.

The meaningfulness of this classification is best illustrated by . . . contrasting cases of personal behavior in the Flint-Beecher disaster. These case studies are of groups that were more or less enduring, more or less effective, and more or less "spontaneous."

Of the two cases presented, the first dealing with the "Rudenko" family is perhaps the most representative of the types of activities that occurred during the emergency stage. This family is described because most of its members were interviewed and because their case histories contain detailed descriptions of their activities. The second case study of adolescents provides some insights into the types of behavior that might be expected from such a group during an emergency. . . .

I. A CASE STUDY OF A FAMILY'S RESCUE ACTIVITIES

The family may be considered the basic rescue group within neighborhoods or communities in cases of disaster. Its internal integration is such that the obligations of the members to one another are clearly defined. Its integration into the neighborhood makes it an ideal rescue unit because its members are usually identified with the neighborhood and because they know the physical layout of the homes and the area. This case study of the Rudenko family describes a group consisting of six functioning adult members. The Rudenko house was the only house in its immediate vicinity that survived the tornado.

The active members of the Rudenko family included a 63-year-old grandfather and his 58-year-old wife. Living with them in the same household were their youngest son (25) and his wife (22) and a child. When the tornado struck (8:29 P.M.), the son was at work (did not return until 11 P.M.), but his wife and daughter were at home. Visiting their parents at this time were the oldest son (35), his wife (32), and their three sons (the oldest being 9). The family group, then, was composed of six adults and four children.

The father and son were working in the garden. When it started to rain the father said to his son, "You'd better put that tractor back in the garage—I don't like the looks of that cloud." In the basement of the house, the two daughters were ironing clothes. With them were the two older children, while the grandmother was upstairs with the two babies.

After the rain began, the two men went down to the basement to look at the water pump. The grandmother, upstairs, saw the tornado coming and began to pray. Describing the situation, she said, "I couldn't decide whether to run to the cellar with one baby or go in the dining room for the other baby. People yelled, 'Get the baby and come down here.' I finally went down with one baby."

Fortunately, the house escaped major damage and the second baby was found unharmed upstairs after the tornado had struck.

Not so fortunate was the nearest neighbor, living across the street, whose immediate plight mobilized this rescue group. His account of what happened to him is among the most lucid and complete obtained.

I ran for the house. As I ran, I saw the tornado pick up a car on Clio Road. As I put my foot on the front door steps, it came down the driveway and took me. It didn't seem to come from the west because it carried me north. It threw me into a tree first, then slid me along the grass. . . . I was conscious all the time. It threw me against the basement wall of my house on my head. I just laid there, then looked up and saw the house raising on the foundation. I got up on my hands, raising up; the wind grabbed me again and took me up in the air. While I was going up, something swatted me on top of my head, and I landed right in my basement (the house was gone by then). Incidentally, while I was laying against the basement wall the porch fell on my leg.

Members of the Rudenko family emerged from their house and saw that three of the immediate neighbors' houses were gone or partially destroyed. The father ran to one house and his son to another. The father found his best friend's wife (Mrs. Able) badly injured, but was unable to locate his friend. He ran for aid and located the State Police, who were trying to get into the area. With their aid and that of others, Mrs. Able was placed in a private car and taken to the hospital.

Meanwhile, the son went to Mr. Corn's house, found him and his injured children, and helped them into an automobile, which took them to the hospital. They were careful to withhold from Mr. Corn the information that his wife was dead. Her body had been found by the son 800 feet away from their home. The Rudenko father and son then searched the area and found the body of Mr. Able, who was Rudenko Sr.'s good friend and neighbor. After this, they went to the aid of other victims. Those who were not badly injured were taken to the Rudenko home to be cared for, or given first aid.

The women in the family group remained at home, and for the most part cared for the injured and homeless members of the two families whose other members had been taken to the hospital. In the words of one of the daughters:

"We just tried to calm the Riveras. The Riveras were crying and carrying on. We tried to calm them. . . . We then bandaged them up and took a piece of wood from the Rivera woman's leg."

The above description covers the first phase of activities for most members of this rescue group. This family appears to have followed a rather strict division of labor along sex lines. The women stayed at home, and cared for the children and the injured people whom the men sent to the house. The men remained in the field, performing immediate rescue functions, especially looking for those who they knew were in the area and whose homes were destroyed or damaged.

After the immediate emergency, the father appears to have stayed near the house, while his son worked with others. When the son was asked who helped him, he replied, "I guess I worked with 25 or 30 fellows—Dad, my brother, Mr. Pennel, Fred at the gas station, the man in the white house at the corner of Clio and Coldwater, and Mr. Harris the dairyman. Those are all I knew."

The influx of volunteers from the surrounding area appears to have swelled the membership of rescue groups that started out with a few people in the area working together. Almost no respondent could identify by name more than a half-dozen people with whom he worked during the course of the night.

The Rudenko family rescue group changed its character when most of the rescue work in the immediate neighborhood was finished about 11:00 P.M. After this, the father stayed close to home, while the two sons (one having just returned from work) ranged farther from home. This marked the end of the second phase for most of the Rudenko family.

Later, the eldest son went to inspect his own home some distance away. The parents of the older daughter-in-law arrived about 3:00 A.M. to take their daughter and grandchild to their home.

To summarize, this family rescued, gave first aid to and generally cared for three families of neighbors involving some fifteen to eighteen persons. They located other dead and injured, and looked for and ascertained the welfare and whereabouts of other neighbors who might have been trapped in their homes. They rapidly worked out an effective division of labor according to age and sex role patterns. It was possible for them to devote full energy to the rescue task because all members were aware of the facts that none of the family was injured, that the house was not severely damaged, and that the children were being adequately cared for. Their knowledge of the neighborhood and the family composition of victim groups enabled them to find or account for all potential or actual victims.

When asked whether their group could have done a better job, the oldest son reported: "There wasn't anything else we could do. I did wish I knew how to stop the Rivera kids from crying—you can't stop kids from crying." And the father's reply was, "There wasn't anything else we could do."

Although the Rudenko family constituted perhaps a most highly integrated and most enduring rescue unit, it cannot be conceived of as a team having a high amount of internal cohesion, permanence, and leadership. Rather, these family members set for themselves certain tasks (search, rescue, transportation, calming, first aid, care of children, and checking property). At times they worked with each other, at times with neighbors or friends, and at times with strangers, State Police, ambulance drivers, or others. There was no leadership or authority in the field or in the home. Verbal communication among members apparently was slight, because they were unable to report what functions other members of the family had performed.

The emergent division of labor enabled the Rudenkos to function effectively as individuals because they played appropriate and complementary social roles. Despite the fact that they lived in a marginal area of Beecher that was socially and economically heterogeneous, they had sufficient information about the neighbors to enable an efficient and effective rescue effort to be launched.

II. A CASE STUDY OF ADOLESCENT BEHAVIOR IN DISASTER

It is commonly observed that adolescents in contemporary society are denied adult prerogatives that they feel capable of assuming. Some sociologists and anthropologists have challenged the alleged discontinuity between adolescent and adult roles. Disaster conditions, with concomitant relaxation of social controls, initially create a situation that may permit adolescents to assume adult responsibilities. In order to test whether the adolescents in fact can assume adult roles under disaster conditions a sample of 12 boys and girls, ages 15 to 19, were interviewed intensively.

The following case presents materials gathered on the behavior of a group of adolescent boys, ages 14 to 17 years, during the postimpact period. None of the boys resided in the stricken area; all lived in the periphery. However, initially, two of them did not know whether or not their families had been injured. While the activities of five adolescents are described, at no time were there more than three boys in continuous interaction. Two of them very soon dropped out of the group and either went home or worked with adults. The nucleus of this group consisted of Jim Wilson, Lou Olesky, and Ted Braden.

8:25 P.M.

Marty Johnson (age 14) was helping his father and a neighbor (Mr. Blake) repair the door on their house when the siren from the Beecher fire station sounded. Mr. Johnson immediately left for the fire station, since he was a volunteer. As the wind and noise increased in severity, the boy, his mother, and Mr. Blake went into the basement for protection.

Meanwhile Jim Wilson and Ted Braden were driving around Flint just south of Beecher.

Lou Olesky (age 16) was puttering around the drug store where he worked part time. There were no customers in the store. As he looked outside, he saw the trees waving, and thought there was a bad storm brewing.

Hal McNaughton (age 16) was at his next-door neighbor's house when the wind started to blow. He didn't think much about it. About five minutes later, Hal went home. His father, also a volunteer with the Beecher Fire Department, was getting his gear together to join other volunteers at the station. Hal decided to go to the station with his father.

8:32 P.M. (PHASE ONE)

Marty Johnson's father returned from the station to check on his family, and then took Mr. Blake back with him to assist in the rescue activities. Marty remained at home with his mother.

Ted and Jim had driven to an auto parts store and heard over the radio that a tornado had struck the Beecher area. They got into the car and drove toward the stricken area.

Lou was still in the drug store. The lights had gone out, and he saw and heard ambulances going by. He also saw obviously injured people in cars.

8:55 P.M. (PHASE TWO)

Marty was still at home with his mother. Jim and Ted drove their car to where they lived and assured their mothers that they were all right. They then picked up a flashlight at Jim's house and went toward the impact area. On the way they picked up Marty and all three then went toward the fire station.

Lou, who had been joined by his younger brother, was still at the drug store. They saw some injured people being transported in cars toward Flint, and decided to go to the stricken area. They took a flashlight and started off. They wanted to see what had happened and did not particularly anticipate participating in any rescue activity.

9:00 P.M.

While the three boys—Marty, Jim, and Ted—were working their way through the debris toward the fire station Marty became separated from the other two. He was shocked and nearly overcome with nausea at the sight of the dead, the injured, and the damage. He wandered around in this state until he finally went home. He maintained that he went to various parts of the stricken area and its periphery looking for relatives.

Jim and Ted worked their way closer to the fire station. Ted became separated from Jim and never did get to the fire station. He said he worked alone and with different individuals. Meanwhile, Lou Olesky, on his way from the drug store, became separated from his younger brother. When Lou arrived at the fire station he saw Jim and Hal there. From this point on, these three boys—Jim, Hal, and Lou—constituted a group and were together until about 2:00 A.M.

The following is a log of their activities:

The fire station, although partially damaged, was overrun with activity. Not only were there firemen coming and going, but other persons (victims, volunteers, and residents) crowded the station. The boys were asked whether they had or could locate any flashlights and batteries. Since they could not find either in the storeroom of the fire station, they thought they should try to find some at nearby hardware stores.

As they left the fire station they noticed a panel truck belonging to one of the local hardware dealers. Finding the keys in it, Hal decided that they should take the truck and see what they could do to help in the rescue activities. So they loaded some old stretchers, sheets, and blankets in the back of the truck. They then got in and drove off. Later on, the boys revealed that they had had no specific plan in mind, but they had all agreed on the idea of taking the truck anyway. Two of them claimed that they had obtained permission from Mr. Cumberland, the owner, but the other boy denied this.

They drove the truck around the area and into the heart of the damaged sections where a bulldozer had cleared the way. They stopped where they saw a group of firemen digging out bodies, and they let the firemen load the bodies into the truck.

After picking up the first load of victims, they proceeded through the area and stopped at the baseball diamond of the school where some men were working. The workers piled two more victims into the truck. The boys still did not know what to do with the victims. Someone suggested they go to the State Police post. They did, and were told to take the victims to Hurley Hospital.

When they arrived at the hospital, the workers there told them to leave. When the boys informed them that there were victims in the truck, they were let in and the truck was unloaded. The boys then asked if anyone wanted to go back to Beecher with them. They gave one man a ride part of the way back. Then they drove to the area but had to wait in line to get in because the roads were blocked. Since they saw they could not get into the heart of the damaged area, they drove the truck back to the fire department. At the fire station, Jim and Lou got out of the truck.

Hal decided to take the truck to see if he could get water from the dairy back to the fire department. He did not succeed. When he came back he picked up Lou and took him home so that Lou could tell his mother that he was all right. They then went back to the fire station, where Hal dropped Lou off.

At this point, the group of three adolescents had broken up. Jim left the area and could not get back in because the police denied him access. Lou met his father, and went with him to check on some relatives. Hal kept the truck and drove it around performing errands, such as driving a fireman to City Hall to get batteries. He drove the truck around, visited here and there, went back home at 7:00 A.M., and then returned to the area with the truck. He did not return the truck to the owner until noon.

Unlike many of the others involved in rescue the adolescent group did not have injured or threatened family members to hamper their operations. How they would have performed under this kind of stress is, of course, unknown. However, it is clear that they did not behave like adult males. In general, their activity was regulated by others, and they showed only little initiative. At no time did they handle any of the injured, nor did they indicate any desire to do so. The three members of the group did not work out a plan for a division of labor. Any opportunity to utilize their skills was largely dissipated, because they remained together and did essentially what was a one-person job, namely, driving a truck. The fact that they remained together all this time suggests that they needed one another for moral support. Apparently they shunned the opportunities to do different tasks. Thus they neither loaded nor unloaded bodies, searched for victims in any systematic way, nor assumed any systematic liaison function. The implication gained from this case study is that adolescents may perform useful functions in an emergency if they are given task direction by adult members of the community.

The lack of a social definition of useful, responsible roles for adolescents in modern American society is strikingly documented by the behavior of these boys and by the adult attitudes expressed toward them. However, the ability of adolescents to imitate adult activity, assume responsibility, and make decisions was evident in other situations where there was serious doubt about the safety of their own families. At such times they seemed adequate to meet some of the needs of the disaster situation. Without such specific types of social definitions of behavior for *family members* guiding them, the adolescents described in the case study devolved into either errand boys, random wanderers, or emotionally dependent children who could not cope with the terror of the aftermath of the tornado.

This analysis of adolescent behavior underscores the general point that the knowledge, skills, and creativity of any group may just as well not exist if no social definition allows them to be brought into play. . . .

CHAPTER VI

SOCIAL ORGANIZATION

STRATIFICATION AND MOBILITY

40 The New Majority

PETER F. DRUCKER

One of the basic tenets of the Marxian creed has been that capitalistic, industrialized societies inevitably produce increasingly large numbers of exploited "blue-collar" workers. Recent research, however, indicates that, in the United States at least, the proportion of manual industrial workers in the total working population is declining sharply. As Peter Drucker here indicates, the largest single American socioeconomic category today is the salaried middle class. He suggests it will soon be realistic, statistically as well as ideologically, to speak of the United States as a middle-class society. The consequences of this development are profound. But one should not conclude from Drucker's analysis that America is becoming either a one-class society or a "classless" society. Differences in level and quality of education, and in command of knowledge and skills acquired, are contributing new criteria for status and creating new groupings varying in power and prestige. These new groupings may well be the social classes of our future American society.

During the past two or three years, professional, technical, and managerial people have become the largest group in the American working population. "Professional, technical, and managerial" is a statistical term. But it is not just a pompous circumlocution for "white-collar employees." "Professional, technical, and managerial" does not include clerical people, or the sales-girl in the shop. It does not even include foremen in the factories. "Professional, technical, and managerial" people, according to our definition in the United States, either determine the work of other people, or apply specialized knowledge in their own work. I know only one short term for these groups: it would be the "salaried middle class."

It is this salaried middle class that has now become our largest working group, larger in fact than the blue-collar people, the machine operators. This signals drastic changes in social structure, in the American economy, and in American politics. Thirteen years ago, when we came out of the second world war, the industrial workers were clearly still the largest

SOURCE: *The Listener* (British Broadcasting Corporation publication), October 23, 30, 1958. Two lectures broadcast on the Third Programme of the BBC. • The author is professor of management at the Graduate School of Business Administration, New York University. Methodology and institutional history are his main interests. Among his books are *Landmarks of Tomorrow*, *Managing for Results*, and *The Effective Executive*.

single group in the American working population—almost one out of every four belonged to it. This was the end of a long historical process that went back to the early years of the 19th century when manufacturing industries were first started on American soil, a process that began to gather momentum in the early years of our century, and that brought about the great changes within the last generation: the change in domestic politics that expressed itself in the New Deal, and the change internationally that led to the emergence of the United States as the greatest industrial and military power in the West. At the end of the war, the professional, technical, and managerial group was already a sizeable group; and it had been growing fast for some time. But it was still one of the smaller groups in the working population, not much more than half the size of the blue-collar workers, that is of industrial labor, and smaller even than office and service employees or farmers. In those thirteen years industrial production in the United States has almost doubled. Both total and working population have been growing fast. But the manual labor needed for this output of goods has remained the same. The number of salaried middle-class people, however, which the economy now requires and which now are employed has almost doubled: it has grown by two-thirds and is growing much faster than either total or working population. By now, one out of every five people at work in the United States works as a professional man, as a technician, or in some managerial capacity—some 13 million of them altogether.

More important than numbers is the direction of the development. All signs point to a further growth of this group, perhaps even a faster growth. By 1975—only seventeen years away—we expect our total production in the United States to be about twice what it is now. Our working population should be one-third larger than it is today. But the only group of employees which will have to grow much faster—a great deal faster than either total population or working population—will again be the salaried middle class. Seventeen years from now, when the boys and girls who are starting their first years in school will have finished their education, in 1975, we should have twice as many people in the salaried middle class as we have today. By then they should be almost two-fifths of the total working force. While there will be a real and continuing need for more highly skilled manual workers, we shall not be needing many more of the "typical" industrial workers, the semi-skilled machine operators, the men who work on the assembly lines or in the steel mills. Indeed, the three industries in the American economy where employment is likely to grow the fastest are education, electronics, and chemistry—and all three employ primarily highly educated middle-class people rather than machine operators.

Already the machine operators represent the past rather than the future. Twenty-five years ago they were by and large the youngest group in our working population. Perhaps the only exception were office personnel where there are so many young unmarried women. Shop stewards in the plants, for instance, in those days, during the great wave of unionization in the 'thirties, tended to be ten or fifteen years younger on average than the management people they dealt with. Today the industrial worker in the United States tends to be older than the population in general. Union leaders today are almost without exception older by ten years or so than their negotiating partners in management. The typical industrial worker, the machine operator, belongs to what is both a stagnant and an ageing group. Growth and youth are in the professional, technical, and managerial ranks.

. . . . .

An important question is what this shift in the structure of our work population might do to the direction in which the economy in the United States will develop. The large expansion since the end of the war has been in goods for the consumer—such things as houses, washing machines, television or furniture. As people's jobs and income improved, they bought things, that is, material objects. Is this likely to continue as the salaried middle class becomes the biggest group, and the one that is growing the most rapidly? Certainly, these salaried, middle-class people will not go without these consumer goods, without houses or without appliances. But our manufacturers are finding out that it is the industrial worker who is more likely to buy a second television set or to trade in an old but still serviceable washing machine for a new one. The status symbols of the salaried middle class are much more likely to be different. For instance, more education both for themselves and for their children. Travel is another high priority of this group. Also, its members—for whatever reason—use the telephone much more, especially for toll calls.

Already there are signs of such a shift. The real "growth" industry in the United States in the last ten years was, for instance, not television, though it was certainly the most visible one. It was probably the publishing of paper-back books; and there has been a great shift in their public and their market and their content: history, foreign affairs, art, and religion are rapidly becoming paper-back staples. In other words, a paper-back is becoming one of the chief consumer goods of the new middle classes. Schools, travel, paper-backs, or telephone service, require other things. A shift in economic preferences would not necessarily lessen the demand for material production. But in requiring different things, the shift in the structure of our working population raises real questions regarding the direction of American economic growth.

It is not only the American economy which is being transformed; the emergence of the salaried middle class is also affecting our social life—our politics, culture, values, our society as a whole. The new salaried middle class is already the leading group in our society. Take, for instance, the pleasant suburb outside New York City where I live. The people who were the "big men" in the town then, the people who headed the community activities—the hospital board, the vestries of the churches, or the school board, the golf club committee, and the Boy Scouts, and all the thousand-and-one activities for civil and personal improvement which are the real living body of American social life—these people, only thirty years ago, were either respected professional men such as a leading lawyer or owners of businesses. Today, almost all these activities are headed by managerial or professional employees, the chief engineer of this company, the sales manager of another, or the personnel director of a third.

In politics these people are much less likely to form permanent party affiliations than either the industrial worker or the business owner. They tend to be independent in their vote, or, to the pained surprise of the politician, to split their vote. But they also tend increasingly to be impatient with traditional party organization, traditional party slogans, traditional issues.

Both our chief parties, the Republicans

and the Democrats, are trying desperately to restore and to maintain their traditional alliances and allegiances, the allegiances of Theodore Roosevelt's or of Franklin Roosevelt's times respectively. Both attempts seem doomed to failure. But the new alignments, which will draw the new salaried middle classes into active politics, are still obscure, the new issues still hidden.

The greatest question, however, may be what the shift in structure of our working population means for our society. There have been many studies of the new salaried middle class of professional, technical, and managerial employees—in England as much as in our country. But we still know little about them. We know even less about a society in which this group predominates and in which it leads. They are "professional people," at least in their own eyes; but they are employed. They are subordinates, as a rule; but they consider themselves part of "management." They are managers or hope to become managers; but they are not "capitalists" any more than they are "proletarians."

The last great theory of society in the Western world was that of Karl Marx: it is now a century old. It was based on the vision—then extremely bold—of the emergence of the industrial worker or the machine operator, as the dynamic, growing class in society. For seventy-five years the machine operators were indeed the most rapidly growing group. Though they never became the majority in any industrial country, they became in every one of these countries the largest single group. This made Marxism such a powerful creed and philosophy despite its many obvious weaknesses. Today—and not only in the United States—an entirely new class is growing and is rapidly becoming the largest single group: the professional, technical, and managerial employees who are neither "capitalists" nor "proletarians," neither "exploiter" nor "exploited." But as yet we have no social theory, no social philosophy, not even adequate facts and knowledge, about the new middle-class society and the new pace-setters within it.

• • • • •

The United States has become, within a short thirty years, an educated society; that is, a society in which almost everybody is expected to have the advanced, long, formal schooling which a generation ago was still confined to a small élite group. It is worth noting that there is only one other country in which something comparable has happened during the same period: the Soviet Union. . . .

Our word "school" and all its synonyms in other European tongues comes from a Greek word meaning "leisure." Thus language still testifies to mankind's old conviction and experience that education unfits man for productive work. Only too obviously the man of education, however limited it may be, will shun the heavy toil, will forsake plough and potter's wheel. Throughout history, therefore, society has never been able to afford more than a small minority of educated people. In fact, ever since systematic education first began, educators themselves have always been haunted by the spectre of the "educated proletariat," by the danger of an unemployable and decaying surplus of educated parasites, too numerous for the few available job-opportunities for educated people, and too highly educated for honest work.

Today, however, we cannot get enough educated people. The job market in the United States last summer [1958] is a good example. With a recession, and with unemployment of six to seven per cent of the total labor force, one would have expected that jobs would be scarce for the newcomers leaving school. So it was indeed for those who had no more education than secondary school—that is no more than twelve years or so of formal schooling. College graduates, who had four more additional years of schooling, usually with some degree of specialization in a major area, all got jobs, though for the first time in five years they had to hunt for them unless they were trained in such highly specialized and still scarce areas as engineering or teaching. But there was no recession for the holders of advanced degrees: indeed, the starting salaries offered them were considerably higher last summer than they had been in 1957 or even in the overemployment of 1956.

Today, in other words, we realize that our economic progress, our defense strength and our political position in the world depend more and more on constantly increasing the supply of highly educated people both in quantity and in quality. This has long been a slogan; Jefferson preached it in the late seventeen-hundreds; Macaulay in the early years of the last century. But now, for the first time, it is fast becoming social reality. Knowledge—rather than "labor" or "capital"—is fast becoming the central and the most productive resource of our society.

In the past the question has always been: How many educated people can a society afford? Today it is increasingly: How many people who are *not* highly schooled can a society afford? For anyone, we are now beginning to realize, who is not educated to the limit of his abilities (and some of us—I belong to them—would greatly prefer to say: who is not educated quite a bit beyond the limit of his abilities) is a social weakness and a productive loss. The knowledge which the educated person brings to work is also a very different resource from either "labor" or "capital." It demands different jobs, different ways of organizing the work, different opportunities, and different rewards. This is true not just for those who hold, or will hold, jobs in management or research or who work in a profession. It is true for the great majority—for they all increasingly have the background and expectations of the highly schooled person.

"Automation" is largely a first impact of this shift in the educational status of the population. Automation is not the replacement of human work by machine. The essence of automation is the replacement of manual labor, whether skilled or unskilled, by knowledge. It is not "saving of labor": automation usually does not mean fewer people at work; often it means more people at work. But it means different people doing different work. It requires such knowledge as is brought to work by the logician, the mathematician, the psychologist, the chemist, the engineer, the economist—a whole host of highly educated people where formerly we employed manual workers.

That we are moving fast to automation in the United States, much faster than anyone thought possible only a few years ago, is precisely because of the changed educational structure of the country. The young people who became available for work today have been sitting on school benches for twelve to sixteen years or more. They may not have learned much—I am not trying to judge the quality of the education they have received, and having four of my own children in school I am sceptical—but they certainly do not look forward to manual work, even to highly skilled manual work, and even to very well paid manual work. They are not looking for jobs, in other words, in the pre-automated factories or the pre-automated office. They expect jobs in which they will put knowledge and theory to work, jobs in which they apply what they have learned rather than jobs in which they apply skill gained through experience. It is no exaggeration to say that the assembly line which only a short time ago was considered really advanced productive technology is, in the United States, already obsolete, socially at least, if not yet technically.

But this raises a big question: just what do these people with their advanced formal schooling expect from work and jobs, from incentives and opportunities, from careers and working conditions? Most of them will stay in modest jobs all their lives. Yet these jobs, too, will be knowledge jobs requiring high-grade theoretical training and considerable judgment. All these people have received an education which, in their fathers' time, was reserved for small, essentially upper and upper-middle class groups.

We have perhaps no idea how one really manages this kind of people. Our personnel management ideas, our personnel management policies, are based largely on experience with rank-and-file manual labor, especially in metal-working industries: essentially this is experience of the first world war. We all know that our ideas were never really effective or successful even for manual workers with a limited degree of formal education and with limited expectations in respect of opportunities. It is unlikely that they have even much relevance to these highly educated people who now come to work in industry and government and the armed forces. It is likely that we face brand-new problems which we do not even understand at all yet.

• • • • •

The greatest impact, however, which the educational revolution in the United States is likely to have is on social values and social structures. It is at one and the same time the fulfilment of the American dream of social equality, and a threat of a new class-structure, of a system of privilege based not on money or birth but on education. As higher education becomes general, access to opportunities becomes increasingly open to all. But at the same time—and the process is going on at high speed—opportunities are increasingly being restricted to the highly educated. It is no longer uncommon for employers to demand a college degree even for salesgirls or secretaries; and without a secondary-school degree even an unskilled factory job may today be hard to get. This is not necessarily absurd. In hiring a salesgirl the employer may hire a future department-head; in hiring a machine operator he may hire a future foreman or works-manager. But the fact remains that the higher degree is rapidly becoming what it never was before in the United States: the passport to opportunities.

I have tried to present two basic changes in American social structure: the emergence of the salaried middle class of professional, technical, and managerial people as the largest and fastest growing group in the United States; and the rapid, almost sudden conversion of the majority of the American people into people of higher, if not of advanced, education. I have tried to report rather than to appraise, and I certainly have not tried to judge.

But, in conclusion, I would like to raise the question whether these two developments have not fundamentally changed the character of American society. For almost 100 years it has been fashionable on both sides of the Atlantic to believe that American social developments follow, with a time-lag, those of Europe; Marx was the first to assert this, and it became almost an article of the faith for people on the left, Americans and Europeans, especially in the 'twenties and 'thirties.

This was always a debatable proposition. But there was some merit to it. It did, in some measure, explain to Europeans what was happening in this complicated, confused, complex country that is America. Thirty years ago, for instance, we in the United States were still much more of an agricultural society than Britain or Germany; and it made sense then to expect that the continuing shift to an industrial economy would produce in the United States such results as the growth of labor unions, of social welfare and state control; in other words, things that paralleled earlier developments in Europe. Thirty years ago we ourselves thought that it was our job to catch up educationally with Europe: the development of the modern American university was one result of this belief.

Today, however, it is the professional, technical, and managerial group that is our leading group; and in education, certainly in respect of quantity and length of schooling, ours is rapidly becoming a society of universal advanced education. These developments may be good or they may be bad. They may be specifically American or they may indicate the roads which Britain and western Europe will travel too. But what is certain is that, for better or worse, we are developing something distinct. What is certain is that to understand this society of ours one will increasingly have to understand these developments. What is certain, finally, is that increasingly the success or failure of this American society of tomorrow will depend on its success or failure as an industrial economy, in which knowledge is the truly scarce and truly productive resource, and as a middle-class society of managerial and professional highly educated people.

41 Portrait of a Striver

JOHN P. MARQUAND

Here in the colorful fiction of J. P. Marquand is a picture of a young man "trying to get ahead." The interpersonal relations and the private feelings of an upwardly mobile middle-class man are sharply portrayed—the tensions, the insecurities, the necessity to watch every step, and the satisfactions. Vividly illustrated is the importance, if one is to achieve social-financial success in this type of setting, of having many skills other than those required for the mere accurate and rapid performance of one's assigned work.

Shortly before the outbreak of the European war, Charles had begun taking the eight-thirty. This was a privilege that had raised him above the ruck of younger men and of shopworn older ones who had to take the eight-two. It indicated to everyone that his business life had finally permitted him a certain margin of leisure. It meant that he was no longer one of the salaried class who had to be at his desk at nine.

The eight-thirty train was designed for the executive aristocracy, and once Mr. Guthrie Mayhew, not one of the Mayhews who lived on South Street, not George Mayhew, but Guthrie Mayhew, who was president of the Hawthorn Hill Club and also president of Mayhew Brothers at 86 Broadway, had even spoken of getting an eight-thirty crowd together who would agree to occupy one of those club cars with wicker chairs and card tables and a porter, to be attached to the eight-thirty in the morning and again to the five-thirty in the afternoon.

. . . . .

Charles remembered Mr. Mayhew's idea vividly, if only because it had come up at the same time that Mr. Burton had suggested that Charles call him Tony.

Charles could still recall the glow he had felt on this occasion and the sudden moment of elation. Mr. Burton had been shy about it in a very nice way, as an older man is sometimes shy. Charles remembered that Mr. Burton had fidgeted with his onyx pen stand and that first Mr. Burton had called him "feller." It had all happened one evening when they had stayed late talking over the Catlin estate, which was one of the largest accounts in the trust department.

. . . . .

"Now you may remember," Mr. Burton had said, "that Mrs. Burton and I took a little trip in 1933. You hadn't been with us long then, but I don't believe that you or anyone else will forget how tense things were in 1933, and now and then I found I was getting a little taut, so when things eased up I decided to go away somewhere to get a sense of perspective.

SOURCE: *Point of No Return*, by John P. Marquand, by permission of Little, Brown & Company. • John P. Marquand (1893–1960) was a well-known American novelist. He also wrote detective stories, short stories, and a play. Among his many works are *The Late George Apley* (awarded a Pulitzer Prize, 1938), *So Little Time, Stopover Tokyo,* and *Thank You Mr. Moto.*

That was when Mrs. Burton and I went to Bagdad. You ought to go there sometime."

. . . . .

The first morning he and Mrs. Burton had gone to the museum to see the treasure from Ur, parts of which looked like something in a case at Cartier's. You got a lot out of travel if you kept your eyes open. There had been a man in the museum, a queer sort of British archaeologist, who showed him some mud bricks that were actually parts of an account book. When you got used to them, you could see how they balanced their figures; and on one brick, believe it or not, there was even an error in addition, preserved there through the centuries. This had meant a great deal to Mr. Burton.

That clerical error in mud had given him an idea for one of the best speeches he had ever written, his speech before the American Bankers' Association in 1936 at the Waldorf-Astoria. Mr. Burton had opened a drawer and had pulled out a deckle-edged pamphlet.

"Take it home and read it if you have the time," he said, "I dashed it off rather hurriedly but it has a few ideas. It starts with that mistake in addition."

The pamphlet was entitled *The Ancient Art of Banking, by Anthony Burton, President, the Stuyvesant Bank, Delivered before the American Bankers' Association, May 1936.*

"Why, thanks very much, sir," Charles had said, "I certainly will read it." It was not the time to say that he had read the speech already or that for years he had made a point of reading all Mr. Burton's speeches.

"Look here, feller," Mr. Burton said, and he had blushed when he said "feller," "why not cut out this sir business? Why not just call me Tony?"

That was in 1941 but Charles still remembered his great joy and relief, with the relief uppermost, and that he could hardly wait to hear what Nancy would say.

"You know, Charles," Mr. Burton had continued, "Guthrie Mayhew and I have quite an idea. We're going to get hold of Tommy Mapes on the New Haven and see if he can't get us a special car on the eight-thirty. How about getting aboard? My idea is to call it the Crackerbarrel."

"Why, thanks," Charles had said. "I'd like to very much, Tony."

He had worked late that night and he could not remember what train he had taken home, but Nancy had been asleep when he got there.

"Nance," he said, "wake up. I've got something to tell you. Burton's asked me to call him Tony." And Nancy had sat bolt upright in her twin bed.

"Start at the beginning," Nancy had said. "Exactly how did it happen, and don't leave out anything."

They must have talked for a long while, there in the middle of the night. Nancy had known what it meant because she had worked downtown herself.

"Now wait," she had said. "Let's not get too excited. Who else calls him Tony?"

"I don't think anyone else does," Charles had told her, "except the officers, and old Jake when he speaks of him."

"Who's old Jake?" Nancy asked.

It surprised him that Nancy did not know, for she usually kept everything straight, but when he told her that old Jake was a day watchman in the vault who had been there when Mr. Burton had first started at the bank, Nancy had remembered.

"Darling, we ought to have a drink of something, shouldn't we?" she said, but it was pretty late for a drink. "Darling, I knew it would happen sometime. I'm pretty proud of you, Charley."

It was only a week later that they found out that Mr. Burton had also asked Roger Blakesley to call him Tony and they never could find out whom Mr. Burton had asked first.

• • • • •

Though you seldom talked of salaries at the Stuyvesant, your social status was obvious from the position of your desk. Charles occupied one of the two flat mahogany desks that stood in a sort of no man's land between the roll-top desks of the officers and the smaller flat-tops of lesser executives and secretaries crowding the floor of the bank outside the cages. A green rug extended from the officers' desks, forming a neat and restricted zone that just included Charles's desk and the one beside it which was occupied by Roger Blakesley. Charles could see both their names, Mr. Blakesley and Mr. Gray, in silver letters, and he was pleased to see that he had got there first from the eight-thirty, a minute or two ahead of Roger and Mr. Burton and ahead of everyone else near the windows.

Mr. Burton's desk, which had the best light, was opened already and so was that of Mr. Stephen Merry, the oldest vice-president, and so were all the others except one. This was the desk of Arthur Slade, the youngest vice-president of the Stuyvesant, who had died in a plane accident when returning from the West Coast six months before. The closed desk still gave Charles a curious feeling of incompleteness and a mixed sense of personal gain and loss because he had been more friendly with Arthur Slade than with anyone else in the Stuyvesant—but then you had to die sometime. Once Arthur Slade had sat at Charles's own place but that was before Mr. Walter Harry, who had been president when Charles had first come to the bank, had died of an embolism and everyone had moved like players on bases—Burton to Harry, Merry to Burton, Slade to the vacant roll-top—and so on down to Charles himself. The Stuyvesant was decorously accustomed to accident and death and now it was moving time again and it was so plain where one of two persons might be moving next that it was embarrassing. Any observing depositor and certainly everyone employed in the bank, right up to the third floor, must have known that either Mr. Blakesley or Mr. Gray would move to Arthur Slade's desk by the window. Undoubtedly they were making side bets out in back as Charles used to himself when he had first come there from Boston. Undoubtedly the clerks and the secretaries and the watchmen had started some sort of pool.

• • • • •

Tony Burton looked very fit, in spite of his white hair and his roll-top desk which both conspired to place him in another generation. For years Charles had accepted him as a model willingly, even though he realized that everyone else above a certain salary rating also used Tony Burton as a perfect sartorial example, and he was pretty sure that Tony himself was conscious of it. Charles never rebelled against this convention because Tony had everything one should expect to find in a president of a first-rate bank. It was amusing but not ridiculous to observe that all the minor executives in the Stuyvesant, as well as the more ambitious clerks, wore conservative double-breasted suits like Tony Burton's at the same time allowing undue rigidity to break out into pin stripes and herringbones, just like Tony Burton's. They all visited the barber once a week. They all had taken up golf, whether they liked it or not, and most of them wore the same square type of wrist watch and the same stainless steel strap. They had adopted Tony Burton's posture and his brisk, quick step and even the gently vibrant inflection of his voice. In fact once at one of those annual dinners for officers and junior executives when everyone said a few words and got off a few local jokes about the bank, Charles had brought the matter up when he had been called upon to speak. Speaking was always an unpleasant ordeal with which he had finally learned to cope successfully largely from imitating Tony. He remembered standing up and waiting for silence, just as Tony waited, with the same faint smile and the same deliberate gaze.

"I should like to drink a toast," he had said, "not to our president but to everyone who tries to look like him. When I walk, I always walk like Tony, because Tony knows just how to walk; and when I talk, I always talk like Tony, because Tony knows just how to talk; and when I dress, I always dress like Tony, in a double-breasted suit. But no matter how I try, I cannot be like Tony. I can never make myself sufficiently astute."

It was the one time in the year, at that annual dinner, when you could let yourself go, within certain limits, and Tony Burton had loved it. He had stood up and waited for the laughter to die down and then he had spoken easily, with just the right pause and cadence. He had said that there were always little surprises at these dinners. He had never realized, for instance, that there could be a poet in the trust department, but poetry had its place. Poetry could teach lessons that transcended pedestrian prose.

"And I'm not too old to learn," Tony Burton had said, "and I'm humbly glad to learn. Sometimes on a starlit night I've wondered what my function was in the Stuyvesant. I'm very glad to know it is that of a clothing dummy. It's a patriotic duty. It's what they want us to be, in Washington."

That was back in 1941, but Tony Burton still had the same spring to his step, the same unlined, almost youthful face, and the same florid complexion; and he had the same three pictures on his desk, the first of Mrs. Burton in their garden, the second of their three girls standing in profile, like a flight of stairs, and the third of his sixty-foot schooner, the *Wanderlust* (the boat you were invited on once every summer), with Tony Burton in his yachting cap standing at the wheel. Time had marched on. All of the girls had come out and all were married, and the *Wanderlust* had been returned by the navy in deplorable condition, but Tony Burton had no superficial scars.

No matter how well Charles might know him, in that half-intimate, half-formal business relationship, he still had a slight feeling of diffidence and constraint. It was the same feeling that one had toward generals in wartime or perhaps toward anyone with power over one. There was always a vestige of a subservient desire to please and to be careful. You had to know how far to go, how long to laugh, and how to measure every speech.

• • • • •

Sycamore Park had been developed in 1938 on the forty-acre grounds of an old estate and the subdivision had been excellently managed by the local real estate firm of Merton and Pease. As Mr. Merton had said, it was a natural, and he had never understood why someone had not dreamed it up long ago—not too far from the shopping center and the trains, and yet in the neighborhood of other larger places. Every place had its own acre, and no house was to be constructed for a cost of less than thirty thousand dollars. It would have been wiser, perhaps, never to have gone there but to have bought a smaller place.

It would have been wiser, easier, and much safer. He had not at that time been moved up in the trust department and in 1939 all he had was twenty thousand dollars in savings, part of which was in paid-up life insurance. He could never analyze all the urges that made him lay everything on the line in order to live on a scale he could not immediately afford, discounting the possibilities of illness or accident and relying on possibilities of promotion. He only remembered having had an irrational idea that time was of the essence, that he would always stay on a certain business level if he did not take some sort of action, and Nancy too, had shared that feeling.

• • • • •

Not since he had left Clyde had Charles ever felt as identified with any community as he had since he had been asked to join the Oak Knoll Country Club. They were in a brave new world involving all sorts of things, of which he had scarcely dreamed after they had moved to Sycamore Park. This cleavage between past and present, Charles realized, was a part of a chain reaction that started, of course, with one of those shake-ups in the bank. Charles had known that he had been doing well. He had known for a year or so, from the way Mr. Merry and Mr. Burton and particularly Mr. Slade had been giving him little jobs to do, that something was moving him out of the crowd of nonentities around him. He was aware also that Walter Gibbs in the trust department was growing restless. There had been a premonition of impending change, just like the present tension. One day Walter Gibbs has asked him out to lunch and had told him, confidentially, that he was going to move to the Bankers' Trust and that he was recommending Charles for his place. Charles was not surprised, because he had been a good assistant to Walter Gibbs, and he was glad to remember that he had been loyal to his chief, ever since the old days in the statistical department.

"Charley," Walter Gibbs had said, "a lot of people around here have been out to knife me. You could have and you never did, and I appreciate it, Charley."

He had known, of course, for some time that Walter Gibbs was not infallible, that he was fumbling more and more over his decisions and depending more and more on Charles's support, but Walter had taught him a lot.

"Slade keeps butting in," Walter had said, and then he went on to tell the old story which Charles had often heard of conflicting personalities and suspicions. Walter had felt that frankly he was more eligible for a vice-presidency than Slade, and the truth was he had never been the same after Arthur Slade had been selected. "If they don't like you enough to move you up," Walter had said, "it's time to get out, Charley."

God only knew where Walter Gibbs was now. He was gone like others with whom you worked closely once and from whom you were separated. Walter Gibbs was gone with his little jokes and his bifocal glasses and the stooping shoulders that had given him a deceptively sloppy appearance. He was gone with his personality that would never have permitted him to be a vice-president of anything.

Charles was ready, not surprised, when Tony Burton, though of course he did not call him Tony then, had called him downstairs and had asked him if he knew what was coming, that he had been with them for quite a while and that they had all had an eye on him ever since he had done that analysis on chain stores. Even if you were prepared for such a change there was still an unforgettable afterglow, and an illuminating sense of unrealized potentiality. It was a time to be more careful than ever, to measure the new balance of power, and not to antagonize the crowd that you were leaving. One day, it seemed to Charles, though of course it was not one day, he was living in a two-family house in Larchmont that smelled of cauliflower in the evenings, stumbling over the children's roller-skates and tricycles, taking the eight-three in the morning, keeping the budget on a salary of six thousand a year. Then in a day, though of course it was not a day, they were building at Sycamore Park. The children were going to the Country Day School. They were seeing their old friends, but not so often. Instead they were spending Sundays with Arthur Slade. There was a maid to do the work. He was earning eleven thousand instead of six, and he was an executive with a future. New people were coming to call; all sorts of men he had hardly known were calling him Charley. It was a great crowd in Sycamore Park and he was asked to join the Oak Knoll Country Club. They were a great crowd in Sycamore Park.

It would have made quite a story—if it could have been written down—how all those families had come to Sycamore Park. They had all risen from a ferment of unidentifiable individuals whom you might see in any office. They had all once been clerks or salesmen or assistants, digits of what was known as the white-collar class. They had come from different parts of the country and yet they all had the same intellectual reactions because they had all been through much the same sorts of adventures on their way to Sycamore Park. They all bore the same calluses from the competitive struggle, and it was still too early for most of them to look back on that struggle with complacency. They were all in the position of being insecurely poised in Sycamore Park—high enough above the average to have gained the envy of those below them, and yet not high enough so that those above them might not easily push them down. It was still necessary to balance and sometimes even to push a little in Sycamore Park, and there was always the possibility that something might go wrong—for example, in the recession that everyone was saying was due to crop up in the next six or eight months. It was consoling to think that they were no longer in the group that would catch it first, or they would not have been at Sycamore Park—but then they were not so far above it. They were not quite indispensable. Their own turn might come if the recession were too deep. Then no more Sycamore Park, and no more dreams of leaving it for something bigger—only memories of having been there once. It was something to think about as you went over your checkbook on clear, cold winter nights, but it was nothing ever to discuss. It was never wise or lucky to envisage failure. It was better to turn on the phonograph—and someday you would get one that would change the records automatically. It was better to get out the ice cubes and have some friends in and to talk broad-mindedly about the misfortunes of others. It was better to go to the club on Tuesday evenings and to talk about something else—and that was where Charles Gray was going.

42 The Peter Principle

RAYMOND HULL

In American society, the pattern of striving for higher status positions may sometimes lead to unfortunate and inefficient results. There is no assurance that the fictional Charles in the previous selection is the best man for the position of vice-president of the bank. Neither is there certainty that Charles would find happiness in that position for which he had striven. In the following selection, the author presents a satirical essay in which he maintains that increased striving results in increased inefficiency. The Peter Principle holds that in American organizations an employee is commonly promoted to his level of incompetence and kept there. Although this is a humorous analysis of American organization, there is sufficient validity in the Peter Principle to cause us to question the basis for promotion in American social systems.

Bunglers are always with us and always have been. Winston Churchill tells us, in his history of World War II, that in August, 1940, he had to take charge personally of the Armed Forces' Joint Planning Committee because, after almost twelve months of war, the Committee had not originated a single plan.

In the 1948 Presidential election, the advance public-opinion polls awarded an easy victory to Thomas E. Dewey. In the Fifties, there was the Edsel bungle. In 1965, Houston's domed baseball stadium opened and was so ill-suited to baseball that, on sunny days, fielders could not see fly balls against the blinding glare from the skylights.

We have come to expect incompetence as a necessary feature of civilization. We may be irked, but we are no longer amazed, when our bosses make idiotic decisions, when automobile makers take back thousands of new cars for repairs, when store clerks are insolent, when law reforms fail to check crime, when moon rockets can't get off the ground, when widely used medicines are found to be poisons, when universities must teach freshmen to read, or when a hundred-ton airliner is brought down by a duck.

We see these malpractices and mishaps as unconnected accidents, inevitable results of human fallibility.

But one man says, "These occurrences are not accidents; they are simply the fruits of a system which, as I have shown, *develops, perpetuates and rewards incompetence.*"

The Newton of incompetence theory is a burly, black-haired, slow-spoken Canadian philosopher and iconoclast, Dr. Laurence J. Peter, who made his living as Assistant Professor of Education at the University of British Columbia until recently, when he moved down the coast to become a Professor of Education at the University of Southern California.

There is nothing incompetent about Dr. Peter. He is a successful author: his *Prescriptive Teaching* is a widely used text on the education of problem children. He built a house with his own hands, makes his own wine, is an expert

SOURCE: *Esquire* (January 1967), pp. 76–77. • Raymond Hull is a free-lance writer and has had thirty television and stage plays produced. He is coauthor, with Dr. Laurence J. Peter, of *The Peter Principle* and is a contributing author to *Punch, Macleans,* and *Esquire.*

cook, a skilled woodcarver, and an inventor. (He created a new tool rack for school woodwork shops and perfected an apparatus for marking fifty exam papers at once.) Yet his chief claim to fame may be his founding of the science of hierarchiology.

"Hierarchiology," he says, "is the study of hierarchies. 'Hierarchy' originally meant 'church government by clergy graded into ranks.' The term now includes any organization whose members or employees are arranged by rank or grade.

"Early in life, I faced the problem of occupational incompetence. As a young schoolteacher I was shocked, baffled, to see so many knotheads as principals, inspectors and superintendents.

"I questioned older teachers. All I could find was that the knotheads, earlier in their careers, had been capable, and that was why they had been promoted.

"Eventually I realized that the same phenomenon occurs in all trades and professions, because the same basic rule governs the climb through every hierarchy. A competent employee is eligible for promotion, but incompetence is a bar to promotion. So an employee's final position must be one for which he is incompetent!

"Suppose you own a drug-manufacturing firm, Perfect Pill Incorporated. Your foreman pill-roller dies of a perforated ulcer; you seek a replacement among the rank-and-file pill-rollers. Miss Cylinder, Mrs. Ellipse and Mr. Cube are variously incompetent and so don't qualify. You pick the best pill-roller, Mr. Sphere, and promote him to foreman.

"Suppose Sphere proves highly competent in this new job: later, when deputy-works-manager Legree moves up one step, Sphere will take his place.

"But if Sphere is incompetent as foreman, he won't be promoted again. He has reached what I call his *level of incompetence* and there he will stay till he retires."

An employee may, like Mr. Cube, reach his level of incompetence at the lowest rank: he is never promoted. It may take one promotion to place him at his level of incompetence; it may take a dozen. But, sooner or later, he does attain it.

Dr. Peter cites the case of the late General A. Jacks. "His hearty manner, informal dress, scorn for petty regulations and disregard for personal safety made him the idol of his men. He led them from victory to victory.

"Had the war ended sooner, Jacks might have retired, covered in glory. But he was promoted to the rank of field marshal. Now he had to deal, not with fighting men, but with politicians of his own country, and with two punctilious Allied field marshals.

"He quarreled with them all and took to spending whole days drunk, sulking in his trailer. The conduct of the war slipped out of his hands and into those of his subordinates.

"The final promotion had brought him from doing what he *could* do, to attempting what he could not do. He had reached his level of incompetence."

The Jacks case exemplifies the Peter Principle, the basic theorem of hierarchiology. *In a hierarchy each employee tends to rise to his level of incompetence: every post tends to be occupied by an employee incompetent to execute its duties.*

How is it, then, that any work is done at all? Peter says, "Work is done by people who have not yet attained final placement at their level of incompetence."

And how is it that we occasionally see a competent person at the very top of a hierarchy? "Simply because there are not enough ranks for him to have reached his level of incompetence: in other words, *in that hierarchy* there is no task beyond his abilities.

"As a rule, such a prodigy of competence eventually sidesteps into another hierarchy—say from the Armed Forces into industry, from law to politics, from business to government—and there finds his level of incompetence. A well-known example is Macbeth, a successful general, but an incompetent king."

In an unpublished monograph, *The Pathology of Success: Morbidity and Mortality at the Level of Incompetence,* Peter expands his theory to take in matters of health.

"Certain physical conditions are associated with final placement: peptic ulcers, high blood pressure, nervous disorders, migraine headaches, alcoholism, insomnia, obesity and cardiovascular complaints. Obviously such symptoms indicate the patient's constitutional incompetence for his level of responsibility.

"Edgar Allan Poe, a highly competent writer, proved incompetent when raised to the rank of editor. He became 'nervous in a very unusual degree,' took to drink and then to drugs in a vain search for relief."

Such ailments, usually appearing two or more together, constitute the Final Placement Syndrome.

"Medication and surgery are often prescribed for F.P.S. patients, but they miss the root cause of the condition. Psychoanalysis fails for the same reason. The analyst is probing into the patient's subconscious for Oedipus complex, castration-complex, penis-envy or whatnot, when the trouble really lies outside, in the patient's hierarchal placement."

Is there no escape? Must every worker reach his level of incompetence, suffer the miseries of Final Placement Syndrome and become a laughingstock for his behavioral or temperamental symptoms?

Peter describes two escape routes. The first is for a man who realizes that he has reached his level of incompetence, yet still wants to preserve health, self-respect and sanity.

"Many an employee adjusts to final placement by the process of Substitution. Instead of executing his proper duties, he substitutes a set of irrelevant duties, and these self-imposed tasks he carries out to perfection.

"A. L. Tredwell, assistant principal of a secondary school, was intellectually competent and maintained good relationships with teachers, students and parents. He was promoted to principal. Soon it became clear that he lacked the finesse to deal with newspaper reporters, school-board members and the district superintendent. He fell out of favor with the officials, and his school lost community support. Realizing consciously or subconsciously—it doesn't matter which—that he was incompetent for the proper duties of a principal, Tredwell *Substituted.* He developed an obsessive concern with the movement of students and staff about the school.

"He drew complex plans of traffic-flow, had white lines painted on floors and arrows on walls, spent hours prowling the building looking for violations of his rules, and bombarded professional journals with articles about his scheme.

"Tredwell's Substitution is a great success. He is active and contented now, and shows no sign of the Final Placement Syndrome."

Peter's alternate escape route is for the employee who is capably and happily doing his work and who wants to avoid ever reaching his level of incompetence.

Merely to *refuse* promotion seldom leads

to happiness. It annoys one's superiors, rouses suspicion among one's peers, and shames one's wife and children. Few people can endure all that. So one must contrive never to be *offered* promotion.

The first step is to avoid asking, or seeming to ask, for it. The oft-heard complaint, "My job lacks challenge," is usually understood as showing desire for promotion. So don't give voice to such complaints!

The second step is described by Peter in his lecture, Creative Incompetence: "I have found some employees who are contented in their work, and who seem to be using effective means of maintaining their position.

"Adam Greenaway, a gardener, happily tends the landscaped grounds of the Ideal Trivet Company. He is competent in all aspects of his work but one: He keeps losing delivery slips for goods received. He gives vague explanations such as 'I must have planted the papers with the shrubs.' Most important, he concealed the fact that he wanted to avoid promotion.

"Lack of delivery slips so upsets the accounting department that, when a new maintenance foreman was needed, Greenaway was not considered for the post.

"Thus he could stay indefinitely at a level of competence and enjoy the keen personal satisfaction of regularly accomplishing useful work. Surely this offers as great a challenge as the traditional drive for higher rank!"

By his Darwinian Extension Theorem, Peter applies his Principle to the whole human race. Man may go the way of the dinosaur and the sabre-tooth tiger. Those beasts were destroyed by excessive development of the qualities—bulk and fangs—that had originally favored their survival. Man's cleverness was originally a survival characteristic, but now he has become clever enough to destroy himself. If he takes that step, he will achieve his ultimate level of incompetence, in proving himself unfit to live.

"Man's one hope," says Peter, "lies in hierarchiology. I feel that it will soon be recognized as the supreme science. Earlier sociological studies have insufficiently recognized man's hierarchal nature.

"A knowledge of the Peter Principle becomes more and more important as hierarchal systems become stronger. Government and education are prime examples. Both already swollen, both expanding their demands for money and manpower, both extending their influence as more people stay longer in school, and as government controls more functions of life. Even industry, once a stronghold of individualism, is largely an aggregation of hierarchies. My point is that man ought to be using the hierarchal system for his benefit. But he can't possibly use it unless he understands it, and to do that he must understand the Peter Principle. Failing such understanding, the system will destroy the individuals who comprise it."

Many people accept the Peter Principle on first hearing. It sounds so obvious, so like common sense; it explains so aptly a group of hitherto mystifying phenomena.

In academic circles, however, the Principle has made little impression. A few of Peter's subordinates when he was at the University of British Columbia grasped it, but none of his superiors. Some of them saw it as a humorous trifle, others as sociological heresy. Said Peter at the time: "I'm neither primarily funny nor unfunny. I study society scientifically because I must live in it. I present my findings to you because they describe the world you live in.

"Anyway, I'm too busy to worry much

about what others think of me. I teach future schoolteachers how to work with handicapped and disturbed children. I'm pursuing two fascinating lines of research: into autism, a profound emotional disorder in which children have no sense of self, and no ability to learn by experience; and into developmental dyslexia, an inability to recognize printed words that often, tragically, pins a 'mentally retarded' label on a genuinely intelligent child. It's all deeply satisfying: I'm about as happy in my work as anyone I know."

The thought then occurred that Peter's hierarchiology might, just might, be *his* form of Creative Incompetence—a means of making himself slightly suspect, and so avoiding an unwanted academic promotion.

"No, no! Of course not!" said the doctor. "But even if it were, of course I wouldn't admit it!"

43 The Culture of Poverty

OSCAR LEWIS

Because so many of us in the United States have middle-class origins, and because middle-class ways of living tend to set the standards for our whole society, it is easy for us to assume that these ways of living permeate all strata from top to bottom. Studies show, however, that even in our "affluent society" there are still millions of people who live meager lives, with no ties to the past, with no present resources, and with no hope for the future. In this selection Oscar Lewis shows that those in these bottom strata—the poverty-ridden—are not simply persons who think and act like everyone else except that they don't happen to have as much money. In actuality, as Lewis demonstrates, their outlook on life is different, and they live in a different culture—a "culture of poverty." Moreover, this culture of poverty is a worldwide phenomenon and, perhaps most significant from a social science point of view, he claims it "has some universal characteristics which transcend regional, rural-urban, and even national differences." That is, among poverty-stricken people in a variety of settings as different as "London, Glasgow, Paris, Harlem and Mexico City," there tend to develop remarkably similar traits of this culture of poverty.

• • • • •

It is the anthropologists, traditionally the spokesmen for primitive people in the remote corners of the world, who are increasingly turning their energies to the great peasant and urban masses of the less-developed countries. These masses are still desperately poor in spite of the social and economic progress of the world in the past century. Over a billion people in seventy-five nations of Asia, Africa, Latin America, and the Near East have an average per capita income of less than $200 a year as compared with over $2,000 a year for the United States. The anthropologist who studies the way of life in these countries has become, in effect, the student and spokesman of what I call the culture of poverty.

SOURCE: Oscar Lewis, *Introduction to the Children of Sanchez.* • Oscar Lewis (1914–1970) was professor of anthropology at the University of Illinois. He was a propaganda analyst for the United States Department of Justice and a consulting anthropologist for the Ford Foundation in India. His special interests were comparative analysis of peasant societies, cultural change, and applied anthropology. In addition to *The Children of Sanchez,* Dr. Lewis wrote *Life in a Mexican Village: Tepoztlan Restudied, Five Families: Mexican Case Studies in the Culture of Poverty,* and *La Vida, A Puerto Rican Family in the Culture of Poverty: San Juan and New York.*

To those who think that the poor have no culture, the concept of a culture of poverty may seem like a contradiction in terms. It would also seem to give to poverty a certain dignity and status. This is not my intention. In anthropological usage the term culture implies, essentially, a design for living which is passed down from generation to generation. In applying this concept of culture to the understanding of poverty, I want to draw attention to the fact that poverty in modern nations is not only a state of economic deprivation, of disorganization, or of the absence of something. It is also something positive in the sense that it has a structure, a rationale, and defense mechanisms without which the poor could hardly carry on. In short, it is a way of life, remarkably stable and persistent, passed down from generation to generation along family lines. The culture of poverty has its own modalities and distinctive social and psychological consequences for its members. It is a dynamic factor which affects participation in the larger national culture and becomes a subculture of its own.

The culture of poverty, as here defined, does not include primitive peoples whose backwardness is the result of their isolation and undeveloped technology and whose society for the most part is not class stratified. Such peoples have a relatively integrated, satisfying, and self-sufficient culture. Nor is the culture of poverty synonymous with the working class, the proletariat, or the peasantry, all three of which vary a good deal in economic status throughout the world. In the United States, for example, the working class lives like an elite compared to the lower class of the less developed countries. The culture of poverty would apply only to those people who are at the very bottom of the socio-economic scale, the poorest workers, the poorest peasants, plantation laborers, and that large heterogeneous mass of small artisans and tradesmen usually referred to as the lumpen proletariat.

The culture or subculture of poverty comes into being in a variety of historical contexts. Most commonly it develops when a stratified social and economic system is breaking down or is being replaced by another, as in the case of the transition from feudalism to capitalism or during the industrial revolution. Sometimes it results from imperial conquest in which the conquered are maintained in a servile status which may continue for many generations. It can also occur in the process of detribalization such as is now going on in Africa where, for example, the tribal migrants to the cities are developing "courtyard cultures" remarkably similar to the Mexico City *vecindades*. We are prone to view such slum conditions as transitional or temporary phases of drastic culture change. But this is not necessarily the case, for the culture of poverty is often a persisting condition even in stable social systems. Certainly in Mexico it has been a more or less permanent phenomenon since the Spanish conquest of 1519, when the process of detribalization and the movement of peasants to the cities began. Only the size, location, and composition of the slums have been in flux. I suspect that similar processes have been going on in many other countries of the world.

It seems to me that the culture of poverty has some universal characteristics which transcend regional, rural-urban, and even national differences. In my book, *Five Families* (Basic Books, 1959), I suggested that there were remarkable similarities in family structure, interpersonal relations, time orientations, value systems, spending patterns, and the sense of community in lower-class settlements in London, Glasgow, Paris, Harlem, and Mexico City. Although this is not the place for an extensive comparative analysis of the culture of poverty, I should like to elaborate upon some of these and other traits in order to present a provisional conceptual model of this culture based mainly upon my Mexican materials.

In Mexico, the culture of poverty includes at least the lower third of the rural and urban population. This population is characterized by a relatively higher death rate, a lower life expectancy, a higher proportion of individuals in the younger age groups, and, because of child labor and working women, a higher proportion of gainfully employed. Some of these indices are higher in the poor *colonias* or sections of Mexico City than in rural Mexico as a whole.

The culture of poverty in Mexico is a provincial and locally oriented culture. Its members are only partially integrated into national institutions and are marginal people even when they live in the heart of a great city. In Mexico City, for example, most of the poor have a very low level of education and literacy, do not belong to labor unions, are not members of a political party, do not participate in the medical care, maternity, and old-age benefits of the national welfare agency known as *Seguro Social*, and make very little use of the city's banks, hospitals, department stores, museums, art galleries, and airports.

The economic traits which are most characteristic of the culture of poverty include the constant struggle for survival, unemployment and underemployment, low wages, a miscellany of unskilled occupations, child labor, the absence of savings, a chronic shortage of cash, the absence of food reserves in the home, the pattern of frequent buying of small quantities of food many times a day as the need arises, the pawning of personal goods, borrowing from the local money lenders at usurious rates of interest, spontaneous informal credit devices (*tandas*) organized by neighbors, and the use of second-hand clothing and furniture.

Some of the social and psychological characteristics include living in crowded quarters, a lack of privacy, gregariousness, a high incidence of alcoholism, frequent resort to violence in the settlement of quarrels, frequent use of physical violence in the training of children, wife beating, early initiation into sex, free unions or consensual marriages, a relatively high incidence of the abandonment of mothers and children, a trend toward mother-centered families and a much greater knowledge of maternal relatives, the predominance of the nuclear family, a strong predisposition to authoritarianism, and a great emphasis upon family solidarity—an ideal only rarely achieved. Other traits include a strong present time orientation with relatively little ability to defer gratification and plan for the future, a sense of resignation and fatalism based upon the realities of their difficult life situation, a belief in male superiority which reaches its crystallization in *machismo* or the cult of masculinity, a corresponding martyr complex among women, and finally, a high tolerance for psychological pathology of all sorts.

Some of the above traits are not limited to the culture of poverty in Mexico but are also found in the middle and upper classes. However, it is the peculiar patterning of these traits which defines the culture of poverty. For example, in the middle class, *machismo* is expressed in terms of sexual exploits and the Don Juan complex whereas in the lower class it is expressed in terms of heroism and lack of physical fear. Similarly, drinking in the middle class is a social amenity whereas in the lower class getting drunk has different and multiple functions—to forget one's troubles, to prove one's ability to drink, and to build up sufficient confidence to meet difficult life situations.

Many of the traits of the subculture of poverty can be viewed as attempts at local solutions for problems not met by existing institutions and agencies because the people are not eligible for them, cannot afford them, or are suspicious of them. For example, unable to obtain credit devices without interest. Unable to afford doctors, who are used only in dire emergencies, and suspicious of hospitals "where one goes only to die," they rely upon herbs or other home remedies and upon local curers and midwives. Critical of priests "who are human and therefore sinners like all of us," they rarely go to confession or Mass and rely upon prayer to the images of saints in their own homes and upon pilgrimages to popular shrines.

A critical attitude toward some of the values and institutions of the dominant classes, hatred of the police, mistrust of government and those in high position, and a cynicism which extends even to the church gives the culture of poverty a counter quality and a potential for being used in political movements aimed against the existing social order. Finally, the sub-culture of poverty also has a residual quality in the sense that its members are attempting to utilize and integrate into a workable way of life the remnants of beliefs and customs of diverse origins.

44 The Other America

MICHAEL HARRINGTON

Michael Harrington's book, The Other America, *has become a classic of social commentary, a well-deserved recognition. For just as we were beginning to think of America as the first truly affluent society, Harrington awakened us to the fact that we have not yet created the economic component of a perfect society. Even before the eruptions in Watts, Detroit, Newark, and elsewhere, his book helped to make known to the complacent members of the middle class the plight of the lower one-third of the population, the faceless and voiceless American poor. His vivid descriptions have convinced many people that a society can never maintain stability when large segments of that society fail to share in its economic benefits. By bringing these ideas out into the open, Harrington played a significant part in mobilizing public support for the still continuing "war on poverty."*

I

The millions who are poor in the United States tend to become increasingly invisible. Here is a great mass of people, yet it takes an effort of the intellect and will even to see them.

I discovered this personally in a curious way. After I wrote my first article on poverty in America, I had all the statistics down on paper. I had proved to my satisfaction that there were around 50,000,000 poor in this country. Yet, I realized I did not believe my own figures. The poor existed in the Government reports; they were percentages and numbers in long, close columns, but they were not part of my experience. I could prove that the other America existed, but I had never been there.

SOURCE: Reprinted with permission of the Macmillan Co. from *The Other America*, by Michael Harrington. Copyright © Michael Harrington 1962. • Michael Harrington is a free-lance writer. He has been an editor of the *Catholic Worker* and has worked on various projects of the Fund for the Republic. He is a contributing editor to *Dissent* and has written numerous articles for *Commentary, Commonweal,* and *Partisan Review*. He is the author of *The Accidental Century* and coeditor of *Labor in a Free Society*.

My response was not accidental. It was typical of what is happening to an entire society, and it reflects profound social changes in this nation. The other America, the America of poverty, is hidden today in a way that it never was before. Its millions are socially invisible to the rest of us. No wonder that so many misinterpreted Galbraith's title and assumed that "the affluent society" meant that everyone had a decent standard of life. The misinterpretation was true as far as the actual day-to-day lives of two-thirds of the nation were concerned. Thus, one must begin a description of the other America by understanding why we do not see it.

There are perennial reasons that make the other America an invisible land.

Poverty is often off the beaten track. It always has been. The ordinary tourist never left the main highway, and today he rides interstate turnpikes. He does not go into the valleys of Pennsylvania where the towns look like the movie sets of Wales in the thirties. He does not see the company houses in rows, the rutted roads (the poor always have bad roads whether they live in the city, in towns, or on farms), and everything is black and dirty. And even if he were to pass through such a place by accident, the tourist would not meet the unemployed men in the bar or the women coming home from a runaway sweatshop.

. . . . .

These are normal and obvious causes of the invisibility of the poor. They operated a generation ago; they will be functioning a generation hence. It is more important to understand that the very development of American society is creating a new kind of blindness about poverty. The poor are increasingly slipping out of the very experience and consciousness of the nation.

If the middle class never did like ugliness and poverty, it was at least aware of them. "Across the tracks" was not a very long way to go. There were forays into the slums at Christmas time; there were charitable organizations that brought contact with the poor. Occasionally, almost everyone passed through the Negro ghetto or the blocks of tenements, if only to get downtown to work or to entertainment.

Now the American city has been transformed. The poor still inhabit the miserable housing in the central area, but they are increasingly isolated from contact with, or sight of, anybody else. Middle-class women coming in from Suburbia on a rare trip may catch the merest glimpse of the other America on the way to an evening at the theater, but their children are segregated in suburban schools. The business or professional man may drive along the fringes of slums in a car or bus, but it is not an important experience to him. The failures, the unskilled, the disabled, the aged, and the minorities are right there, across the tracks, where they have always been. But hardly anyone else is.

In short, the very development of the American city has removed poverty from the living, emotional experience of millions upon millions of middle-class Americans. Living out in the suburbs, it is easy to assume that ours is, indeed, an affluent society.

This new segregation of poverty is compounded by a well-meaning ignorance. A good many concerned and sympathetic Americans are aware that there is much discussion of urban renewal. Suddenly, driving through the city, they notice that a familiar slum has been torn down and that there are towering, modern buildings where once there had been tenements or hovels. There is a warm feeling of satisfaction, of pride in the way things are working out: the poor, it is obvious, are being taken care of.

The irony in this is that the truth is nearly the exact opposite to the impression. The total impact of the various housing programs in postwar America has been to squeeze more and more people into existing slums. More often than not, the modern apartment in a towering building rents at $40 a room or more. For, during the past decade and a half, there has been more subsidization of middle- and upper-income housing than there has been of housing for the poor.

Clothes make the poor invisible too: America has the best-dressed poverty the world has ever known. For a variety of reasons, the benefits of mass production have been spread much more evenly in this area than in many others. It is much easier in the United States to be decently dressed than it is to be decently housed, fed, or doctored. Even people with terribly depressed incomes can look prosperous.

This is an extremely important factor in defining our emotional and existential ignorance of poverty. In Detroit the existence of social classes became much more difficult to discern the day the companies put lockers in the plants. From that moment on, one did not see men in work clothes on the way to the factory, but citizens in slacks and white shirts. This process has been magnified with the poor throughout the country. There are tens of thousands of Americans in the big cities who are wearing shoes, perhaps even a stylishly cut suit or dress, and yet are hungry. It is not a matter of planning, though it almost seems as if the affluent society had given out costumes to the poor so that they would not offend the rest of society with the sight of rags.

Then, many of the poor are the wrong age to be seen. A good number of them (over 8,000,000) are sixty-five years of age or better; an even larger number are under eighteen. The aged members of the other America are often sick, and they cannot move. Another group of them live out their lives in loneliness and frustration: they sit in rented rooms, or else they stay close to a house in a neighborhood that has completely changed from the old days. Indeed, one of the worst aspects of poverty among the aged is that these people are out of sight and out of mind, and alone.

• • • • •

And finally, the poor are politically invisible. It is one of the cruelest ironies of social life in advanced countries that the dispossessed at the bottom of society are unable to speak for themselves. The people of the other America do not, by and large, belong to unions, to fraternal organizations, or to political parties. They are without lobbies of their own; they put forward no legislative program. As a group, they are atomized. They have no face; they have no voice.

Thus, there is not even a cynical political motive for caring about the poor, as in the old days. Because the slums are no longer centers of powerful political organizations, the politicians need not really care about their inhabitants. The slums are no longer visible to the middle class, so much of the idealistic urge to fight for those who need help is gone. Only the social agencies have a really direct involvement with the other America, and they are without any great political power.

• • • • •

Forty to 50,000,000 people are becoming increasingly invisible. That is a shocking fact. But there is a second basic irony of poverty that is equally important: if one is to make the mistake of being born poor, he should choose a time when the majority of the people are miserable too.

J. K. Galbraith develops this idea in *The Affluent Society*, and in doing so defines the "newness" of the kind of poverty in contemporary America. The old poverty, Galbraith notes, was general. It was the condition of life of an entire society, or at least of that huge majority who were without special skills or the luck of birth. When the entire economy advanced, a good many of these people gained higher standards of living. Unlike the poor today, the majority poor of a generation ago were an immediate (if cynical) concern of political leaders. The old slums of the immigrants had the votes; they provided the basis for labor organizations; their very numbers could be a powerful force in political conflict. At the same time the new technology required higher skills, more education, and stimulated an upward movement for millions.

Perhaps the most dramatic case of the power of the majority poor took place in the 1930's. The Congress of Industrial Organizations literally organized millions in a matter of years. A labor movement that had been declining and confined to a thin stratum of the highly skilled suddenly embraced masses of men and women in basic industry. At the same time this acted as a pressure upon the Government, and the New Deal codified some of the social gains in laws like the Wagner Act. The result was not a basic transformation of the American system, but it did transform the lives of an entire section of the population.

• • • • •

Out of the thirties came the welfare state. Its creation had been stimulated by mass impoverishment and misery, yet it helped the poor least of all. Laws like unemployment compensation, the Wagner Act, the various farm programs, all these were designed for the middle third in the cities, for the organized workers, and for the upper third in the country, for the big market farmers. If a man works in an extremely low-paying job, he may not even be covered by social security or other welfare programs. If he receives unemployment compensation, the payment is scaled down according to his low earnings.

One of the major laws that was designed to cover everyone, rich and poor, was social security. But even here the other Americans suffered discrimination. Over the years social security payments have not even provided a subsistence level of life. The middle third have been able to supplement the Federal pension through private plans negotiated by unions, through joining medical insurance schemes like Blue Cross, and so on. The poor have not been able to do so. They lead a bitter life, and then have to pay for that fact in old age.

Indeed, the paradox that the welfare state benefits those least who need help most is but a single instance of a persistent irony in the other America. Even when the money finally trickles down, even when a school is built in a poor neighborhood, for instance, the poor are still deprived. Their entire environment, their life, their values, do not prepare them to take advantage of the new opportunity. The parents are anxious for the children to go to work; the pupils are pent up, waiting for the moment when their education has complied with the law.

Today's poor, in short, missed the political and social gains of the thirties. They are, as Galbraith rightly points out, the first minority poor in history, the first poor not to be seen, the first poor whom the politicians could leave alone.

The first step toward the new poverty was taken when millions of people proved immune to progress. When that happened, the failure was not individual and personal, but a social product. But once the historic accident takes place, it begins to become a personal fate.

The new poor of the other America saw the rest of society move ahead. They went on living in depressed areas, and often they tended to become depressed human beings. In some of the West Virginia towns, for instance, an entire community will become shabby and defeated. The young and the adventurous go to the city, leaving behind those who cannot move and those who lack the will to do so. The entire area becomes permeated with failure, and that is one more reason the big corporations shy away.

Indeed, one of the most important things about the new poverty is that it cannot be defined in simple, statistical terms. . . . If a group has internal vitality, a will—if it has aspiration—it may live in dilapidated housing, it may eat an inadequate diet, and it may suffer poverty, but it is not impoverished. So it was in those ethnic slums of the immigrants that played such a dramatic role in the unfolding of the American dream. The people found themselves in slums, but they were not slum dwellers.

But the new poverty is constructed so as to destroy aspiration; it is a system designed to be impervious to hope. The other America does not contain the adventurous seeking a new life and land. It is populated by the failures, by those driven from the land and bewildered by the city, by old people suddenly confronted with the torments of loneliness and poverty, and by minorities facing a wall of prejudice.

In the past, when poverty was general in the unskilled and semi-skilled work force, the poor were all mixed together. The bright and the dull, those who were going to escape into the great society and those who were to stay behind, all of them lived on the same street. When the middle third rose, this community was destroyed. And the entire invisible land of the other Americans became a ghetto, a modern poor farm for the rejects of society and of the economy.

It is a blow to reform and the political hopes of the poor that the middle class no longer understands that poverty exists. But, perhaps more important, the poor are losing their links with the great world. . . . They are no longer participants in an ethnic culture from the old country; they are less and less religious; they do not belong to unions or clubs. They are not seen, and because of that they themselves cannot see. Their horizon has become more and more restricted; they see one another, and that means they see little reason to hope.

• • • • •

II

There are mighty historical and economic forces that keep the poor down; and there are human beings who help out in this grim business, many of them unwittingly. There are sociological and political reasons why poverty is not seen; and there are misconceptions and prejudices that literally blind the eyes. The latter must be understood if anyone is to make the necessary act of intellect and will so that the poor can be noticed.

Here is the most familiar version of social blindness: "The poor are that way because they are afraid of work. And anyway they all have big cars. If they were like me (or my father or my grandfather), they could pay their own way. But they prefer to live on the dole and cheat the taxpayers."

This theory, usually thought of as a virtuous and moral statement, is one of the means of making it impossible for the poor ever to pay their way. There are, one must assume, citizens of the other America who choose impoverishment out of fear of work (though, writing it down, I really do not believe it). But the real explanation of why the poor are where they are is that they made the mistake of being born to the wrong parents, in the wrong section of the country, in the wrong industry, or in the wrong racial or ethnic group. Once that mistake has been made, they could have been paragons of will and morality, but most of them would never even have had a chance to get out of the other America.

There are two important ways of saying this: The poor are caught in a vicious circle; or, The poor live in a culture of poverty.

In a sense, one might define the contemporary poor in the United States as those who, for reasons beyond their control, cannot help themselves. All the most decisive factors making for opportunity and advance are against them. They are born going downward, and most of them stay down. They are victims whose lives are endlessly blown round and round the other America.

Here is one of the most familiar forms of the vicious circle of poverty. The poor get sick more than anyone else in the society. That is because they live in slums, jammed together under unhygienic conditions; they have inadequate diets, and cannot get decent medical care. When they become sick, they are sick longer than any other group in the society. Because they are sick more often and longer than anyone else, they lose wages and work, and find it difficult to hold a steady job. And because of this, they cannot pay for good housing, for a nutritious diet, for doctors. At any given point in the circle, particularly when there is a major illness, their prospect is to move to an even lower level and to begin the cycle, round and round, toward even more suffering.

This is only one example of the vicious circle. Each group in the other America has its own particular version of the experience. . . . But the pattern, whatever its variations, is basic to the other America.

The individual cannot usually break out of this vicious circle. Neither can the group, for it lacks the social energy and political strength to turn its misery into a cause. Only the larger society, with its help and resources, can really make it possible for these people to help themselves. Yet those who could make the difference too often refuse to act because of their ignorant, smug moralisms. They view the effects of poverty—above all, the warping of the will and spirit that is a consequence of being poor—as choices. Understanding the vicious circle is an important step in breaking down this prejudice.

There is an even richer way of describing this same, general idea: Poverty in the United States is a culture, an institution, a way of life.

There is a famous anecdote about Ernest Hemingway and F. Scott Fitzgerald. Fitzgerald is reported to have remarked to Hemingway, "The rich are different." And Hemingway replied, "Yes, they have money." Fitzgerald had much the better of the exchange. He understood that being rich was not a simple fact, like a large bank account, but a way of looking at reality, a series of attitudes, a special type of life. If this is true of the rich, it is ten times truer of the poor. Everything about them, from the condition of their teeth to the way in which they love, is suffused and permeated by the fact of their poverty. And this is sometimes a hard idea for a Hemingway-like middle-class America to comprehend.

The family structure of the poor, for instance, is different from that of the rest of the society. There are more homes without a father, there is less marriage, more early pregnancy and, if Kinsey's statistical findings can be used, markedly different attitudes toward sex. As a result of this, to take but one consequence of the fact, hundreds of thousands, and perhaps millions, of children in the other America never know stability and "normal" affection.

Or perhaps the policeman is an even better example. For the middle class, the police protect property, give directions, and help old ladies. For the urban poor, the police are those who arrest you. In almost any slum there is a vast conspiracy against the forces of law and order. If someone approaches asking for a person, no one there will have heard of him, even if he lives next door. The outsider is "cop," bill collector, investigator (and, in the Negro ghetto, most dramatically, he is "the Man").

45 The White Man's Theory of Color Caste

GUNNAR MYRDAL

Americans tend to pride themselves on the conviction that this country permits social and economic advancement by able and energetic persons. A society which provides for such mobility is said to have an "open-class" system: one in which persons may move freely up, or down, within the socioeconomic hierarchy. At the other extreme is a "closed-class," or "caste," system. The essence of the caste system is that a person's status is completely determined by biological inheritance, or family identification, and that he is prevented from crossing caste lines through marriage. In his famous study of the Negro in America, Myrdal shows that some aspects of caste are characteristic of our society, despite popular beliefs to the contrary. In this excerpt, based on data collected about 1940, Myrdal presents the white man's attitudes concerning antiamalgamation—attitudes which have helped to maintain separate Negro and white social systems in America. These separate systems and the attitudes on which they are based, some observers maintain, persist to this day.

Every widening of the writer's experience of white Americans has only driven home to him more strongly that the opinion that the Negro is unassimilable, or, rather, that his amalgamation into the American nation is undesirable, is held more commonly, absolutely, and intensely than would be assumed from a general knowledge of American thought-ways. Except for a handful of rational intellectual liberals—who also, in many cases, add to their acceptance in principle of amalgamation an admission that they personally feel an irrational emotional inhibition against it—it is a rare case to meet a white American who will confess that, if it were not for public opinion and social sanctions not removable by private choice, he would have no strong objection to intermarriage.

The intensity of the attitude seems to be markedly stronger in the South than in the North. Its strength seems generally to be inversely related to the economic and social status of the informant and his educational level. It is usually strong even in most of the non-colored minority groups, if they are above the lowest plane of indifference. To the poor and socially insecure, but struggling, white individual, a fixed opinion on this point seems an important matter of prestige and distinction.

But even a liberal-minded Northerner of cosmopolitan culture and with a minimum of conventional blinds will, in nine cases out of ten, express a definite feeling against amalgamation. He will not be willing usually to hinder intermarriage by

SOURCE: Gunnar Myrdal, *An American Dilemma*, pp. 57–67. • The author is professor of international economy at the University of Stockholm, Sweden, and a former member of the Swedish senate. He was executive secretary of the United Nations Economic Commission in Europe from 1947 to 1957. Prior to that, from 1938 to 1942, he had studied the American Negro for the Carnegie Corporation of New York, which resulted in the book *An American Dilemma*. Among his other books are *Population: A Problem for Democracy*, *Economic Theory and Under-Developed Regions*, *Challenge to Affluence*, and *Asian Drama*.

law. Individual liberty is to him a higher principle and, what is more important, he actually invokes it. But he will regret the exceptional cases that occur. He may sometimes hold a philosophical view that in centuries to come amalgamation is bound to happen and might become the solution. But he will be inclined to look on it as an inevitable deterioration.[1]

This attitude of refusing to consider amalgamation—felt and expressed in the entire country—constitutes the center in the complex of attitudes which can be described as the "common denominator" in the problem. It defines the Negro group in contradistinction to all the non-colored minority groups in America and all other lower class groups. The boundary between Negro and white is not simply a class line which can be successfully crossed by education, integration into the national culture, and individual economic advancement. The boundary is fixed. It is not a temporary expedience during an apprenticeship in the national culture. It is a bar erected with the intention of permanency. It is directed against the whole group. Actually, however, "passing" as a white person is possible when a Negro is white enough to conceal his Negro heritage. But the difference between "passing" and ordinary social climbing reveals the distinction between a class line, in the ordinary sense, and a caste line.

This brings us to the point where we shall attempt to sketch, only in an abstract and preliminary form, the social mechanism by which the anti-amalgamation maxim determines race relations. This mechanism is perceived by nearly everybody in America, but most clearly in the South. Almost unanimously white Americans have communicated to the author the following logic of the caste situation which we shall call the *"white man's theory of color caste."*

1. The concern for "race purity" is basic in the whole issue; the primary and essential command is to prevent amalgamation; the whites are determined to utilize every means to this end.
2. Rejection of "social equality" is to be understood as a precaution to hinder miscegenation and particularly intermarriage.
3. The danger of miscegenation is so tremendous that the segregation and discrimination inherent in the refusal of "social equality" must be extended to nearly all spheres of life. There must be segregation and discrimination in recreation, in religious service, in education, before the law, in politics, in housing, in stores and in breadwinning.

This popular theory of the American caste mechanism is, of course, open to criticism. It can be criticized from a valuational point of view by maintaining that hindering miscegenation is not a worthwhile end, or that as an end it is not sufficiently worthwhile to counterbalance the sufferings inflicted upon the suppressed caste and the general depression of productive efficiency, standards of living and human culture in the American society at large—costs appreciated by all parties concerned. This criticism does

[1] The response is likely to be anything but pleasant if one jestingly argues that possibly a small fraction of Negro blood in the American people, if it were blended well with all the other good stuff brought over to the new continent, might create a race of unsurpassed excellence: a people with just a little sunburn without extra trouble and even through the winter; with some curl in the hair without the cost of a permanent wave; with, perhaps, a little more emotional warmth in their souls; and a little more religion, music, laughter, and carefreeness in their lives. Amalgamation is, to the ordinary American, not a proper subject for jokes at all, unless it can be pulled down to the level of dirty stories, where, however, it enjoys a favored place. Referred to society as a whole and viewed as a principle, the anti-amalgamation maxim is held holy; it is a consecrated taboo. The maxim might, indeed, be a remnant of something really in the "mores." It is kept unproblematic, which is certainly not the case with all the rest of etiquette and segregation and discrimination patterns, for which this quality is sometimes erroneously claimed.

not, however, endanger the theory which assumes that white people actually are following another valuation of means and ends and are prepared to pay the costs for attaining the ends. A second criticism would point out that, assuming the desirability of the end, this end could be reached without the complicated and, in all respects, socially expensive caste apparatus now employed. This criticism, however adequate though it be on the practical or political plane of discussion, does not disprove that people believe otherwise, and that the popular theory is a true representation of their beliefs and actions.

To undermine the popular theory of the caste mechanism, as based on the anti-amalgamation maxim, it would, of course, be necessary to prove that people really are influenced by other motives than the ones pronounced. Much material has, as we shall find, been brought together indicating that, among other things, competitive economic interests, which do not figure at all in the popular rationalization referred to, play a decisive role. The announced concern about racial purity is, when this economic motive is taken into account, no longer awarded the exclusive role as the *basic* cause in the psychology of the race problem.

Though the popular theory of color caste turns out to be a rationalization, this does not destroy it. For among the forces in the minds of the white people are certainly not only economic interests (if these were the only ones, the popular theory would be utterly demolished), but also sexual urges, inhibitions, and jealousies, and social fears and cravings for prestige and security. When they come under the scrutiny of scientific research, both the sexual and the social complexes take on unexpected designs. We shall then also get a clue to understanding the remarkable tendency of this presumably biological doctrine, that it refers only to legal marriage and to relations between Negro men and white women, but not to extra-marital sex relations between white men and Negro women.

However these sexual and social complexes might turn out when analyzed, they will reveal the psychological nature of the anti-amalgamation doctrine and show its "meaning." They will also explain the compressed emotion attached to the Negro problem. It is inherent in our type of modern Western civilization that sex and social status are for most individuals the danger points, the directions whence he fears the sinister onslaughts on his personal security. These two factors are more likely than anything else to push a life problem deep down into the subconscious and load it with emotions. There is some probability that in America both complexes are particularly laden with emotions. The American puritan tradition gives everything connected with sex a higher emotional charge. The roads for social climbing have been kept more open in America than perhaps anywhere else in the world, but in this upward struggle the competition for social status has also become more absorbing. In a manner and to a degree most uncomfortable for the Negro people in America, both the sexual and the social complexes have become related to the Negro problem.

These complexes are most of the time kept concealed. In occasional groups of persons and situations they break into the open. Even when not consciously perceived or expressed, they ordinarily determine interracial behavior on the white side.

. . . . .

It has . . . always been a primary requirement upon every Negro leader—

who aspires to get any hearing at all from the white majority group, and who does not want to appear dangerously radical to the Negro group and at the same time hurt the "race pride" it has built up as a defense—that he shall explicitly condone the anti-amalgamation maxim, which is the keystone in the white man's structure of race prejudice, and forbear to express any desire on the part of the Negro people to aspire to intermarriage with the whites. The request for intermarriage is easy for the Negro leader to give up. Intermarriage cannot possibly be a practical object of Negro public policy. Independent of the Negroes' wishes, the opportunity for intermarriage is not favorable as long as the great majority of the white population dislikes the very idea. As a defense reaction a strong attitude against intermarriage has developed in the Negro people itself. And the Negro people have no interest in defending the exploitative illicit relations between white men and Negro women. This race mingling is, on the contrary, commonly felt among Negroes to be disgraceful. And it often arouses the jealousy of Negro men.

The required soothing gesture toward the anti-amalgamation doctrine is, therefore, readily delivered. It is iterated at every convenient opportunity and belongs to the established routine of Negro leadership. For example, Robert R. Moton writes:

> As for amalgamation, very few expect it; still fewer want it; no one advocates it; and only a constantly diminishing minority practise it, and that surreptitiously. It is generally accepted on both sides of the colour line that it is best for the two races to remain ethnologically distinct.

There seems thus to be unanimity among Negro leaders on the point deemed crucial by white Americans. If we attend carefully, we shall, however, detect some important differences in formulation. The Negro spokesman will never, to begin with, accept the common white premise of racial inferiority of the Negro stock. To quote Moton again:

> . . . even in the matter of the mingling of racial strains, however undesirable it might seem to be from a social point of view, he [the Negro] would never admit that his blood carries any taint of physiological, mental, or spiritual inferiority.

A doctrine of equal natural endowments—a doctrine contrary to the white man's assumption of Negro inferiority, which is at the basis of the anti-amalgamation theory—has been consistently upheld. If a Negro leader publicly even hinted at the possibility of inherent racial inferiority, he would immediately lose his following. The entire Negro press watches the Negro leaders on this point.

Even Booker T. Washington, the supreme diplomat of the Negro people through a generation filled with severe trials, who was able by studied unobtrusiveness to wring so many favors from the white majority, never dared to allude to such a possibility, though he sometimes criticized most severely his own people for lack of thrift, skill, perseverance and general culture. In fact, there is no reason to think that he did not firmly believe in the fundamental equality of inherent capacities. Privately, local Negro leaders might find it advisable to admit Negro inferiority and, particularly earlier, many individual Negroes might have shared the white man's view. But it will not be expressed by national leaders and, in fact, never when they are under public scrutiny. An emphatic assertion of equal endowments is article number one in the growing Negro "race pride."

Another deviation of the Negro faith in the anti-amalgamation doctrine is the stress that they, for natural reasons, lay on condemning exploitative illicit amalgamation. They turn the tables and accuse white men of debasing Negro womanhood, and the entire white culture for not rising up against this practice as their expressed antagonism against miscegenation should demand. Here they have a strong point, and they know how to press it.

A third qualification in the Negro's acceptance of the anti-amalgamation doctrine, expressed not only by the more "radical" and outspoken Negro leaders, is the assertion that intermarriage should not be barred by law. The respect for individual liberty is invoked as an argument. But, in addition, it is pointed out that this barrier, by releasing the white man from the consequences of intimacy with a Negro woman, actually has the effect of inducing such intimacy and thus tends to increase miscegenation. Moton makes this point:

> The Negro woman suffers not only from the handicap of economic and social discriminations imposed upon the race as a whole, but is in addition the victim of unfavourable legislation incorporated in the marriage laws of twenty-nine states, which forbid the intermarriage of black and white. The disadvantage of these statutes lies, not as is generally represented, in the legal obstacle they present to social equality, but rather in the fact that such laws specifically deny to the Negro woman and her offspring that safeguard from abuse and exploitation with which the women of the white race are abundantly surrounded. On the other side, the effect of such legislation leaves the white man, who is so inclined, free of any responsibility attending his amatory excursions across the colour line and leaves the coloured woman without redress for any of the consequences of her defencelessness; whereas white women have every protection, from fine and imprisonment under the law to enforced marriage and lynching outside the law.

But even with all these qualifications, the anti-amalgamation doctrine, the necessity of assenting to which is understood by nearly everybody, obviously encounters some difficulties in the minds of intellectual Negroes. They can hardly be expected to accept it as a just rule of conduct. They tend to accept it merely as a temporary expedient necessitated by human weakness. Kelly Miller thus wrote:

> . . . you would hardly expect the Negro, in derogation of his common human qualities, to proclaim that he is so diverse from God's other human creatures as to make the blending of the races contrary to the law of nature. The Negro refuses to become excited or share in your frenzy on this subject. The amalgamation of the races is an ultimate possibility, though not an immediate probability. But what have you and I to do with ultimate questions, anyway?

And a few years later, he said:

> It must be taken for granted in the final outcome of things that the colour line will be wholly obliterated. While blood may be thicker than water, it does not possess the spissitude or inherency of everlasting principle. The brotherhood of man is more fundamental than the fellowship of race. A physical and spiritual identity of all peoples occupying common territory is a logical necessity of thought. The clear seeing mind refuses to yield or give its assent to any other ultimate conclusion. This consummation, however, is far too removed from the sphere of present probability to have decisive influence upon practical procedure.

This problem is, of course, tied up with the freedom of the individual. "Theoretically Negroes would all subscribe to the right of freedom of choice in marriage even between the two races," wrote Moton. And Du Bois formulates it in stronger terms:

> . . . a woman may say, I do not want to marry this black man, or this red man, or this white man. . . . But the impudent and vicious demand that all colored folk shall write themselves down as brutes by a general assertation of their unfitness to marry other decent folk is a nightmare.

Negroes have always pointed out that the white man must not be very certain of his woman's lack of interest when he rises to such frenzy on behalf of the danger to her and feels compelled to build up such formidable fences to prevent her from marrying a Negro.

With these reservations both Negro leadership and the Negro masses acquiesce in the white anti-amalgamation doctrine. This attitude is noted with satisfaction in the white camp. The writer has observed, however, that the average white man, particularly in the South, does not feel quite convinced of the Negro's acquiescence. In several conversations, the same white person, in the same breath, has assured me, on the one hand, that the Negroes are perfectly satisfied in their position and would not like to be treated as equals, and on the other hand, that the only thing these Negroes long for is to be like white people and to marry their daughters.

Whereas the Negro spokesman finds it possible to assent to the first rank of discrimination, namely, that involving miscegenation, it is more difficult for him to give his approval to the second rank of discrimination, namely, that involving "etiquette" and consisting in the white man's refusal to extend the ordinary courtesies to Negroes in daily life and his expectation of receiving certain symbolic signs of submissiveness from the Negro. The Negro leader could not do so without serious risk of censorship by his own people and rebuke by the Negro press. In all articulate groups of Negroes there is a demand to have white men call them by their titles of Mr., Mrs., and Miss; to have white men take off their hats on entering a Negro's house; to be able to enter a white man's house through the front door rather than the back door, and so on. But on the whole, and in spite of the rule that they stand up for "social equality" in this sense, most Negroes in the South obey the white man's rules.

Booker T. Washington went a long way, it is true, in his Atlanta speech in 1895 where he explained that: "In all things that are purely social we [the two races] can be as separate as the fingers, yet one as the hand in all things essential to mutual progress." He there seemed to condone not only these rules of "etiquette" but also the denial of "social equality" in a broader sense, including some of the further categories in the white man's rank order of discrimination. He himself was always most eager to observe the rules. But Washington was bitterly rebuked for this capitulation, particularly by Negroes in the North. And a long time has passed since then; the whole spirit in the Negro world has changed considerably in three decades.

The modern Negro leader will try to solve this dilemma by iterating that no Negroes want to intrude upon white people's private lives. But this is not what Southern white opinion asks for. It is not satisfied with the natural rules of polite conduct that no individual, of whatever race, shall push his presence on a society where he is not wanted. It asks for a general order according to which *all* Negroes are placed under *all* white people and excluded from not only the white man's society but also from the ordinary symbols of respect. No Negro shall ever aspire to them, and no white shall be allowed to offer them.

Thus, on this second rank of discrimination there is a wide gap between the ideologies of the two groups. As we then continue downward in our rank order and arrive at the ordinary Jim Crow practices, the segregation in schools, the disfranchisement, and the discrimination in employment, we find, on the one hand, that increasingly larger groups of white people are prepared to take a stand against these discriminations. Many a liberal white professor in the South who, for his own welfare, would not dare to entertain a Negro in his home and perhaps not even speak to him in a friendly manner on the street, will be found prepared publicly to condemn disfranchisement, lynching, and the forcing of the Negro out of employment. Also, on the other hand, Negro spokesmen are becoming increasingly firm in their opposition to discrimination on these lower levels. It is principally on these lower levels of the white man's rank order of discrimination that the race struggle goes on. The struggle will widen to embrace all the thousand problems of education, politics, economic standards, and so forth, and the frontier will shift from day to day according to varying events.

Even a superficial view of discrimination in America will reveal to the observer: first, that there are great differences, not only between larger regions, but between neighboring communities; and, second, that even in the same community, changes occur from one time to another. There is also, contrary to the rule that all Negroes are to be treated alike, a certain amount of discretion depending upon the class and social status of the Negro in question. A white person, especially if he has high status in the community, is, furthermore, supposed to be free, within limits, to overstep the rules. The rules are primarily to govern the Negro's behavior.

Some of these differences and changes can be explained. But the need for their interpretation is perhaps less than has sometimes been assumed. The variations in discrimination between local communities or from one time to another are often not of primary consequence. All of these thousand and one precepts, etiquettes, taboos, and disabilities inflicted upon the Negro have a common purpose: to express the subordinate status of the Negro people and the exalted position of the whites. They have their meaning and chief function as symbols. As symbols they are, however, interchangeable to an extent: one can serve in place of another without causing material difference in the essential social relations in the community.

The differences in patterns of discrimination between the larger regions of the country and the temporal changes of patterns within one region, which reveal a definite trend, have, on the contrary, more material import. These differences and changes imply, in fact, a considerable margin of variation within the very notion of American caste, which is not true of all the other minor differences between the changes in localities within a single region—hence the reason for a clear distinction. For exemplification it may suffice here to refer only to the differentials in space. As one moves from the Deep South through the Upper South and the Border states to the North, the manifestations of discrimination decrease in extent and intensity; at the same time the rules become more uncertain and capricious. The "color line" becomes a broad ribbon of arbitrariness. The old New England states stand, on the whole, as the antipode to the Deep South. This generalization requires important qualifications, and the relations are in process of change.

The decreasing discrimination as we go from South to North in the United States is apparently related to a weaker basic prejudice. In the North the Negroes have fair justice and are not disfranchised; they are not Jim-Crowed in public means of conveyance; educational institutions are less segregated. The interesting thing is that the decrease of discrimination does *not* regularly follow the white man's rank order. Thus intermarriage, placed on the top of the rank order, is legally permitted in all but one of the Northern states east of the Mississippi. The racial etiquette, being the most conspicuous element in the second rank, is, practically speaking, absent from the North. On the other hand, employment discriminations, placed at the bottom of the rank order, at times are equally severe, or more so, in some Northern communities than in the South, even if it is true that Negroes have been able to press themselves into many more new avenues of employment during the last generation in the North than in the South.

There is plenty of discrimination in the North. But it is—or rather its rationalization is—kept hidden. We can, in the North, witness the legislators' obedience to the American Creed when they solemnly pass laws and regulations to condemn and punish such acts of discrimination which, as a matter of routine, are committed daily by the great majority of the white citizens and by the legislators themselves. In the North, as indeed often in the South, public speakers frequently pronounce principles of human and civic equality. We see here revealed in relief the Negro problem as an American Dilemma.

46 The Negro's Middle-Class Dream

C. ERIC LINCOLN

This selection complements the previous one by describing the middle-class society developed among American blacks as a result of color-caste barriers. Although some light-skinned Negroes have passed into white society, the author indicates here that "lightness" is no longer a primary status factor in the Negro class system. Lightness may now actually have negative value among blacks. The same desires for status, respectability, and economic security motivates blacks as well as whites, but the symbols and behavior that characterize the Negro middle class are in some respects unique. It is these unique features that are dealt with here.

A famous professor at a large university used to begin one of his lectures in social psychology with a description of the characteristics of a typical American family. After he had described the family's income, address, religion, the kind of car they drove, organizations to which they belonged and the occupation of the father, he would then demand to know what social class the family belonged to. But before the students could answer, the professor would add as an apparent afterthought: "Oh, yes, I forgot to mention that this is a *Negro* family!" Inevitably, the students were stymied. What had begun as a simple problem became insolubly complex by the addition of the word "Negro."

Where do Negroes fit into the prevailing American class structure? Most sociologists say they don't. Negroes have a *parallel* social structure, somewhat—but not entirely—analogous to that of whites. This social parallelism, or two-caste society, is created by the color barrier which, with the rarest exceptions, prevents lateral movement from class to class

SOURCE: *The New York Times Magazine*, October 25, 1964. • The author is professor of sociology and religion, Union Theology Seminary, New York City. Among his books are *My Face Is Black*, *The Negro Pilgrimage in America*, *Sounds of Struggle*, and *Is Anybody Listening to Black America?*

between Negroes and whites. As a prominent Negro matron said in Detroit, "We Negroes and whites visit each other at times, and frequently we belong to the same civic organizations and attend the same functions, but the lines are there, and no one has to say where they are."

The Negro class structure had its roots in the institution of American slavery, which, in ignoring the African's cultural presumptions, leveled all classes, and force-fused highly disparate individuals and groups into one conglomerate mass —"the Negro slave," or simply, "the Negro," a word which, in America, became synonymous with "slave" or the "descendant of slaves." Prince and servant, Eboe and Mandingo, Moslem and spirit-worshipper were all the same to the slave master, who saw them only as commodities to be bought and sold, or as a labor supply for his vast plantations.

Whatever the basis of past distinctions, the Negro social structure in America had to evolve out of conditions connected with plantation life, and within a context which recognized the absolute superiority of the white slave owner (although not necessarily that of the small, non-slaveholding white farmers, who supplied the "overseer" class, and who were looked upon by house servants and slave owners alike as "poor white trash").

The Negro's "society," then, had four more or less distinct social classes. In ascending order, they were: (1) field hands (who had least contact with the socializing influences of the white environment); (2) mechanics and artisans (bricklayers, carpenters, iron workers, bakers, etc., who were frequently hired by the month or the year to merchants or builders in the cities); (3) valets, butlers, maids, cooks and other household servants (whose frequent personal contact with whites made them the most "acculturated" class); and (4) free Negroes (who had bought their freedom or had become free by manumission—often because of faithfulness or some heroic exploit).

As slaves, the house-servant class had by far the highest proportion of mulattoes. While this did not by any means exempt them from the normal rigors incident to being slaves, including sale, the light-skinned mistresses of the slave masters were often granted petty privileges and their children were more frequently given their freedom than those of any other class.

At the end of the slave period, the mulattoes sought to establish themselves as a distinct occupational and social class within the Negro subculture. For the most part, they continued as servants and retainers to their erstwhile masters—as dressmakers, barbers, coachmen and the like. For more than a generation they clung tenuously to a certain degree of status derived from catering exclusively to the "quality" folk (as they had done in slavery) under the then current slogan of (serving) "mighty few white folks and no niggers a'tall!"

By the turn of the century, however, as the economy of the South began to revive, the mulatto "retainers" were progressively displaced by European immigrants and poor whites who were suddenly willing to do "Negro work." From that date neither occupation nor color has been a reliable index of social standing among Negroes.

Today, a light skin is not an automatic key to social status. In this day of the Negro's increasing race pride and his subtle impulse to nationalism, a light skin *can* be a handicap, especially if it is associated with "recent" miscegenation. Mass education and the discriminate rise of power and money of significant numbers of Negroes irrespective of their grandparents' station in the slave society have all but destroyed the effectiveness of the Negro's private color bar. Leadership in civil rights as well as in the professions has long since passed from the mulatto class. As a matter of fact, the number of mulattoes in the general Negro population seems to be declining steadily, and there is no evidence that legal integration will soon replace clandestine miscegenation in restoring the ratio of light color.

There is no unanimity of opinion as to what proportion of today's Negroes fall into the traditional "lower," "middle" and "upper" classes of the Negro social structure. Prof. Tillman Cothran, head of the graduate department of sociology at Atlanta University, estimates that "not more than 21 per cent of the Negro population can be called middle class by any reasonable standards. And not more than 5 per cent can be called upper class."

Other sociologists have argued that if one applies the full spectrum of criteria by which the white social structure is measured—ranging from income to education, affiliation, residence, etc.—the Negro middle class is reduced to 4 per cent or 5 per cent of the Negro population, and the Negro upper class vanishes altogether.

Such an estimate is, I think, too drastic. If the theory of parallel social structure is valid (and there seems to be no other way to measure "class" in an essentially segregated society), certainly it can be shown that Negroes and whites of similar education and income exhibit many of the same desires, restraints, conformities and general patterns of behavior.

America's self-image is that of an essentially equalitarian society best represented by the middle class. Most Americans concede that there are a few snobs and millionaires at the top, and a few poor people in Appalachia, or somewhere, at the bottom, but America is middle class, and most Americans identify themselves as belonging to the middle class.

Implicit in this identification is a belief in "democracy" and "fair play," and also the expectation of "the good life"—a home, a car, a regular vacation, an education for the children, regular promotions, and maybe even extras like a boat or a summer place. Despite the pessimism of the sociologists, more and more Negroes share this dream, and to an increasing degree they are making it come true for themselves and their children.

The Negro middle class is made up primarily of Negro professionals, with school teachers probably constituting the largest single bloc. Teachers, along with doctors, lawyers, college professors, small businessmen, ministers, and postal workers have traditionally made up the bulk of the Negro middle class.

However, the recent availability of new kinds of jobs not previously held by Negroes has begun to modify the character of this group. Technicians, politicians, clerical and sales personnel, social workers, labor-union officials, minor government bureaucrats, and an increasing managerial class in such agencies as Federal housing and local units of national corporations have helped broaden the occupational range of the Negro middle class.

Under the Kennedy-Johnson Administration a few Negroes have been appointed to the upper echelons of Government officialdom, and within the past two or three years a few Negroes have reached executive status in white corporations. A dinner in New York honored seven Negroes who were vice presidents or held managerial positions in major firms. In Washington, Dr. James Nabrit, president of Howard University, and Dr.

Frank Jones have been elected to the board of directors of a major bank. And in that city, several Negroes have been elected to the Board of Trade.

It is difficult to set a salary range for a given social class because social status does not depend upon money alone. Some upper-class whites are impoverished, but their families have once held fortunes and they have traditions of culture and attainment. Since the American Negro's family traditions seldom antedate the Civil War, Negro society puts an undue emphasis on money and material acquisitions. It is often said by Negro critics themselves that "anybody with a dollar, no matter where he stole it, can belong to Negro society."

Most Negroes, like most other Americans earn their living legitimately, of course, but because of job discrimination and lack of skills the total income of the typical middle-class Negro family will be substantially lower than that of a typical white family of the middle class. An arbitrary figure of $7,500 a year as the average income of a middle-class family would severely limit the number of Negroes who could be called middle-class.

Some Negro families do exceed a $7,500 income, but the vast majority of those who do are families in which both husband and wife work full time. Very frequently among home-buying Negroes, the head of the family works at two jobs, and occasionally at three. Such supplementary work or "moonlighting"—often driving a taxi, waiting on tables, tending bar or bellhopping—is known as "a hustle," a term quite familiar to the Negro middle class.

In many of the large cities of the North such as New York or Boston where undeveloped land is nonexistent, the middle-class Negro, who has the means and the desire to live elsewhere, is locked in the black ghetto. Only with difficulty can he find a house or apartment outside the ghetto in a white community. As a consequence, many Negroes despair of ever leaving the slums, no matter what their education or income.

Money that would normally go for a new house is spent in the hopeless task of refurbishing antiquated apartments, or in conspicuous consumption which somehow helps them to forget the horror of living in the nation's Harlems. (In the South, the housing problem is not nearly so acute. Space for building can be had in most Southern cities, although it is likely to be in a segregated community.)

The style of living of the Negro middle class does not differ radically from that of its white counterpart. Bridge is a favorite pastime among both men and women. Those who have the leisure belong to innumerable social clubs. An increasing number of Negro men play golf and participate in water sports where facilities are available. In the South, fishing and hunting are favorite pastimes, but only if one has the full regalia of dress, and all the latest equipment shown in the sports magazines.

To a far greater degree than whites, Negroes maintain affiliation in the graduate chapters of their college fraternities and sororities, and these organizations are important indexes of social stratification. Women of a given sorority tend to marry men of its fraternal opposite number. Together, the eight major Negro sororities and fraternities constitute the nucleus of any imaginary "blue book" of Negro society.

The children of the Negro middle class are taught to aspire to middle-class standards. They take lessons in piano and creative dancing on Saturday mornings and attend carefully planned parties on Saturday night. A few are sent East to private schools.

Sometimes the interpretation of middle-class values takes an unusual twist. A Negro matron in a Memphis department store, for example, refused to corral her two children who were busily chasing through the store and littering the aisles with merchandise. She explained: "The white kids do it and the salesclerks think it's cute. I don't want my children inhibited by feeling that they can't do anything any other kids can do."

In Washington, among those aspiring to the middle class, or those who are recently "in," status is measured by the quantity and the cost of whisky served one's guests. The most conspicuous feature in such a home will be the bar appointments, and it is considered equally insulting for a guest to refuse a drink as it is for the host to offer his guests "cheap whisky." One Washingtonian gained prominence in his set by consistently being first to serve rare and expensive imports before they were well known in the Negro community. He learned what was "in" by frequenting an exclusive liquor store patronized by high Government officials.

It used to be said that the difference between a Negro making $50 a week and driving a Cadillac and a white man making $100 a week and driving a Chevrolet was that the Negro, having nowhere to live, needed the bigger car to sleep in! On Atlanta's West Side, where the Cadillac (or Lincoln) frequently comes with a split-level ranch house, it is popular to have the main (or "status") car match the house in color and appointments.

A second car for the Negro professional family is not unusual. Unlike most white middle-class families having two cars, the Negro's second car is likely to be as big and expensive as his first. An expensive automobile to drive to work is often as much a matter of personal prestige for the working Negro woman as for her husband. Hence, it is common to see large numbers of Pontiacs, Oldsmobiles and Mercurys parked near the schools where Negro women are employed as teachers.

A cottage at Oak Bluffs, on Martha's Vineyard, or in Maine or Upper Michigan can be claimed by a few. A very small number of Negroes go to Europe and to the Caribbean or Mexico on vacation. A sort of pilgrimage to Africa has high status value for those seeking to "understand their pre-Western heritage."

Some Negroes are in the middle class because there is nowhere else for them to go. These few might be considered "upper class" but there is a certain incongruity in talking about a Negro "upper class" so long as the color barrier operates to bar Negroes who are otherwise qualified from full participation in American social life. "There may not be an upper class," says Clarence Coleman, southeastern director of the National Urban League, "but there is a 'power élite' which abstracted itself from the rank and file of the middle class and participates to an important extent in the decision-making of the white power structure where Negroes are concerned."

Certainly this power élite does exist. But where it was not created by the white establishment, its power derives from white recognition and respect. Militant civil-rights leaders have discovered this again and again when the white establishment has refused to negotiate with the Negro community except through "recognized channels."

The Negro middle class, like any middle class, is preoccupied with making secure its hard-won social position. This is a characteristic of middle-class aspirations.

Because of this preoccupation the Negro middle class has been criticized frequently for not being more deeply and realistically involved in the struggle for civil rights. The criticism is well placed, for given more manpower, more money and more dedication, it is obvious that more walls could be breached. But this is not the whole story, and the lack of total involvement may not be an accurate index of middle-class feelings and intentions.

Much of the criticism has come from within the ranks of the middle class itself. Clarence Coleman sees the middle class as the buffer between the militants, whose aspirations are frequently unrealistic in terms of present possibilities, and the power élite which seems concerned to protect itself and its privileged positions from too rapid social change.

James A. Tillman, Jr., executive director of the Greater Minneapolis Fair Housing Program and a frequent writer on problems of social change, describes the Negro middle class as "that class of Negroes who have bought the inane, invalid and self-defeating notion that the black man can be integrated into a hostile white society without conflict."

Tillman denounces the power élite as "the fixers and go-betweens who cover up rather than expose the violent nature of racism. They are," he declares, "the most dangerous clique in America."

Tillman's sentiments are echoed by Cecil Moore, militant civil-rights attorney and head of the Philadelphia N.A.A.C.P. Moore, who himself came from an accomplished West Virginia family, insists that "the Negro middle class, and all those who consider themselves above the middle class, 'subsist on the blood of the brother down under,' the brother they are supposed to be leading. Who do these Negroes think they're kidding?" he asks, and then answers his own question. "They're kidding nobody but the white folks who are willing to pay 'philanthropy' to keep from having to come to grips with the central problem, which is 'full and complete citizenship for all Americans, *right now!*' "

Despite all such criticism, however, the Negro middle class has borne the brunt of the civil-rights protest. Critics of the so-called "Black Bourgeoisie" have not always given them credit for the maturity and social responsibility upon which the Negro's fight for first-class citizenship has finally depended. The civil-rights fight, at least insofar as it visualizes an integrated society, is a middle-class fight. The N.A.A.C.P., CORE, the Urban League and the followers of Dr. Martin Luther King are all middle-class. (Indeed, the lower-class Negro has yet to be stirred by the promise of integration. He is more concerned with such immediate needs as jobs and housing than with abstract values like integration. He looks neither to Martin Luther King nor to Roy Wilkins; in fact, the leader of the black masses, has yet to appear.)

In Atlanta and other Southern cities during the massive sit-ins of 1962–63, housewives baked pies, made sandwiches and provided transportation for the students. Negro businessmen donated food, gasoline and other supplies. Then doctors, nurses, professors and businessmen walked the picket lines. Similar middle-class support has assisted the activities of CORE in New York, Cleveland and other cities in the North. Voter registration is essentially a middle-class project.

Middle-class leadership and support of the civil-rights movement has not been without ambivalence. Desegregated schools frequently mean that Negro teachers will lose their jobs. Negro businessmen often lose their most competent clerical help to recently desegregated industries. Negro restaurants, drug stores, real-estate firms and the like may be adversely affected by desegregation. Some Negro churches have lost members to white churches. In a fully integrated society, the Negro middle class would lose its identity. Indeed, it would cease to exist.

Some Negroes recognize all this, of course, and fight against it. Nor can it be said that the majority of the middle class is active in the rights struggle. What can be said is that the struggle is for the most part led, financed and supported by the Negro middle class and, of course, its white allies.

Certainly, Negro leadership has become a "profession," and in some cases a lucrative one. Yet most Negroes trying to help improve things are in search of neither fame nor fortune and may be themselves disadvantaged by the race issue. A. Maceo Walker and Jesse Turner of Memphis, for example, both executive officers of a sensitive banking business that has important white as well as Negro depositors, come to mind. These men and others like them have little to gain for themselves personally, yet they have given leadership to the civil-rights movement in their city for years. Other cases could be cited across the country.

In Washington, I talked with the distinguished Negro attorney, Belford Lawson, and his wife, Marjorie McKenzie, who, as associate judge of the Juvenile Court there, is no less distinguished. The Lawsons were undisturbed about the "black backlash" against the Negro middle class, although they felt that the middle class was just beginning to realize its responsibilities to the Negro masses. Nor did they recognize a middle-class backlash against the lower class (which has been roundly criticized by some Negroes for rioting in the streets and undoing the patient and painful accomplishments of middle-class leaders).

"We must press on to the next phase," Lawson said. "And it would be foolish to wait until all of us have reached the place a few of us have reached today. Negroes, like other people, move at different rates of speed. Our circumstances vary. Now we have a handful of civil rights and no money. Our next front is economic. We want to buy stocks in banks and corporations and sit on their boards. Every time a Negro reaches an executive position in a major corporation, he is in a better position to help that Negro in the streets without a job."

Mr. Lawson believes that it is time to stop complaining and to move on into the American mainstream. "Breaking into the white man's economy" he believes to be essential to any further progress on the part of Negroes. "In Washington," he says, "where many social and cultural affairs are integrated, many doors would open if the Negro would only push on them."

Negroes are pushing—for status and respectability and economic security. They are less concerned with integration for integration's sake than they are with being comfortable—middle-class—and unhindered in enjoying all that America has to offer. The riots in the city streets are not the work of sinister Communist agents, except where such agents move in to exploit an already festering social situation. Nor are they the work of hopheads and hoodlums bent on the destruction of the fruits of years of patient interracial effort.

They are the social expressions of pent-up anxiety and frustration which derive from the hopelessness of the conditions under which those people live. *They* cannot hope for "the good life." *They* cannot appropriate the "middle-class image," the American norm for democratic living.

I sat recently in a comfortable middle-class home in northwest Washington talking with Jerry Coward and his wife, both school teachers in the District of Columbia school system. "You know, when we moved into this neighborhood five years ago," Jerry said, "the whites all threatened to move out. A few stayed. And since that time, two brand-new white families have moved in, right down the block. Professional people, too. When white people start moving into, instead of away from, a Negro neighborhood, I guess we've got it made."

I guess they have.

47 School Integration in Current Perspective

THOMAS F. PETTIGREW

Both this selection and the following one deal with the questions of integration and decentralization of the American public schools. In this article, Thomas Pettigrew reviews the research concerning the effects of integration. Present evidence indicates that black students achieve more in integrated schools than in segregated schools, and that white students do as well in integrated schools as they would in segregated white schools. Pettigrew examines the current arguments by both black and white groups for segregated schools in light of the evidence and the goals of an integrated society. The reader should consider the consequences of these alternatives for stratification and mobility.

I am a racial integrationist. I believe that to the extent that we delay or obstruct racial integration, we are in fact endangering the existence of our democratic society. Therefore, I have specialized in the desegregation of schools and, hopefully, their integration. Actually, I am more a student of race relations than of education; but I have chosen to specialize in education because it is through education that the vicious circle described by Myrdal a generation ago can most effectively be broken.

I do not have to cite in any detail how far we are away from that ideal. In fact, our schools are growing more racially segregated, not less, with time. There is more racial segregation of schools today in the entire United States than there was in 1954 at the time of the Supreme Court decision.

In the South, the figure that 18 percent or so of Negro children are now in schools with white children (according to Office of Education estimates), is inflated of course, because 400 Negro children get counted as desegregated when one white child troops into the school. If you use a more realistic criterion—Negroes in predominantly white schools in the South—it is more like 9 or 10 percent. So progress in the South has been slow and painful since 1954. But in the West and North we have actually regressed; we are in a worse situation than we were at the time of the court ruling.

The Coleman data are probably the

SOURCE: *The Urban Review,* vol. 3, no. 2 (January 1969), 4–8. Reprinted by permission of the author and *The Urban Review,* a publication of the Center for Urban Education. • The author is professor of social psychology at Harvard University. His major interests include race and ethnic relations and social psychology. He is author of *A Profile of the Negro American* and *Social Evaluation Theory: Convergencies and Applications.*

best overall data we have on the standard of segregation in our public schools, though I am sure that they underestimate the segregation, since the most segregationist systems tended to refuse to cooperate with the Coleman survey: Boston, Cleveland, Columbus, Cincinnati, Chicago, Los Angeles, Houston, Wichita, etc. If you choose as an extreme definition of segregation, schools that are 90 to 100 percent Negro, two-thirds of all Negro students in the first grade are in such schools and one-half of all Negro students in the 12th grade are in such schools. In most of our systems in the United States, the number of predominantly Negro schools is perhaps the most reasonable index of segregation. Seven out of eight of all Negro children in the first grade in the United States attend a predominantly Negro school, while two-thirds in the 12th grade attend a predominantly Negro school.

White children are even more segregated than Negro children: four-fifths of the white children in public schools—whether in first grade or 12th grade—are in schools that are 90 to 100 percent white. So I believe that the conclusion of the U.S. Commission on Civil Rights in their 1967 report on racial isolation in the public schools is more than justified: "Racial isolation in the schools is intense whether the cities are large or small, whether the proportionate Negro enrollment is large or small, whether they are located North or South. As far as we can determine through research, segregation effects are most damaging to both Negro and white children in the early grades, so present segregation is greatest at that point at which it does the most damage.

Doing research to determine the effects of isolation in schools is extremely difficult, since so much of the rest of American life is also isolated by race and class and religion. But to the extent that we can do it—not just in the Coleman data, but in other data adapted by the Commission on Civil Rights report—it seems definitely true that segregated schools are damaging to both white and Negro children in much the way that many people thought without such evidence. As a matter of fact, the data surprised me by supporting earlier hypotheses as well as they did because data are usually somewhat dirty and never come out quite like you expect: very clear in *any* direction. These data were, by my standards, beautiful data—they really fell in line much the same way we had thought they would on the basis of observation in the schools.

Race, as it turns out, is not the primary variable. Social class is. The Coleman report and other researches make this clear. The Coleman report shows that while the physical quality of the schools varies, it does not vary nearly as much as we had thought, and that physical facilities do not have an appreciable effect on the achievement of the children in these schools. Some people have misinterpreted this, almost making it sound as if you don't have to have four walls around the school—the wind could come blowing through and it would not make any difference to the children's achievement. This is not what Coleman is saying. He could only measure what exists now, not what might be done, potentially, with the aid of new and innovative educational facilities. Still, he did find that now the social class of the students who go to a given school is the chief *school* variable of a child's achievement score. This can be measured crudely by tabulating the educational level of all of the parents of all of the children in a given school. The higher that is, the higher the achievement is likely to be of children of *all* backgrounds—white and black, rich and poor, urban and rural.

Social class milieu, therefore, turns out to be more important for educational achievement than racial integration. But only one Negro in four is middle class (whether defined by income, white collar occupation, or high school graduation) while more than 60 percent of white Americans are middle class. Now, the Negro middle class has expanded very rapidly since 1940 when it was only 5 percent of the total Negro population. It has expanded five times, even relative to the growing sizes of Negro-American communities. But in spite of that rapid increase, we need racial desegregation to provide a predominantly middle class milieu, simply because there are not enough middle class Negroes; even if they all went to public schools and lived in the right places, there still would not be enough to provide a middle-class milieu in the schools.

The commission report attempted to go one step further than the Coleman data and find out if there is a racial composition effect over and above the very powerful social class effect. We believe there is, but it by no means is as large as the social class effect. We believe that there are important positive effects for the achievement of Negro children in predominantly white classrooms—*classrooms* not schools, since of course we can have segregated classrooms within integrated schools, and such classrooms are often the result of so-called ability grouping. We also can show that white children do not suffer in terms of achievement scores as long as they are in the majority. Even more striking than the positive achievement effects—true for both white and Negro children and adults in the commission study—was the effect on racial attitudes and behavior: white and Negro children who had been to school with each other prefer interracial friends and prefer interracial schools.

This, incidentally, is one of the troubles with the freedom of choice plan in the South, and in many places in the North. That is, we have had nothing but segregation of the children for so long that when we leave them the freedom of choice they will choose what they have had. We are now seeing this in the separatist movement, for there has always been separatism in the Negro community. Similarly, the whites who have only known homogeneous white schools will continue to prefer that. This is a route that the Kerner Commission rightly shows we have been traveling for some time, producing not one nation indivisible but two nations divisible by race, separate and unequal. The way to continue on this route is to continue segregated schools, to make them even more segregated. The way to begin to turn a corner is to have more desegregation of schools.

You can say: "Well, that's all very nice, but the kids lose this, they go back to their all-black or all-white neighborhoods, they live their lives later in separate situations, and any effects you may have had in those interracial schools are washed out." That has been a common hypothesis; it is usually stated as fact although as with most things in the area of race these days, it is unsupported by any data. So we tested this hypothesis with adults throughout the United States. We could only work in the North and West because there had not been enough desegregation in the South for long enough to find results. We simply asked people what kind of schooling they had had. Then, controlling for social class origins, we compared where they started as children; we compared Negro adults who had known interracial schooling with those who had not, and we compared whites who had known interracial schooling with those who had not. The two comparisons differ in the same way: those who had known interracial experience as children were very different adults. The early effects did *not* wash out. These people had very different attitudes toward each other in many different ways. But in addition to attitudes, their overt *behavior* was different. The Negro and white American adults who had known interracial education as children were much more likely than the other Negroes and whites to live on an interracial block, to work with a member of the other race of equal status in their job situation and—the biggest difference of all—*much* more likely to send *their* children to an interracial school. This is the best endorsement of interracial schooling that you could have: these people, the products of integration, strive to provide an interracial education for their children—often at some sacrifice, particularly for the Negro parents—such as the one *they* had. The other side of the coin is that Negroes and whites who have not had interracial schooling do everything to maintain segregation and segregated schooling for their children—sometimes, in the case of some whites, at considerable financial sacrifice. Given the fact I have already mentioned, that we are seeing more segregation, not less, this can only mean that we are producing yet another generation of white and black bigots—people who will not accept each other when they are adults; and we are producing them in our schools.

I might also add that Negroes who had known interracial schools are making more money today than Negroes who had not known interracial schools. And, significantly, they are much more likely to be in a white collar job. . . . Our problems are less the machinations of evil men—not that we don't have them—than structural problems. . . . The basic cause is structural: the way we organize our school districts, especially the way we organize them in the main metropolitan areas. We have over 75 school districts in metropolitan Boston alone and 96 in metropolitan Detroit, and so forth. There are more than 26,000 school districts in the United States, and not even the richest country in the world can afford that many.

Now this implies to me that one of the basic needs of many of our urban areas is consolidation, not decentralization of schools, and particularly cooperation *before* consolidation. Think of yourself as a visitor from someplace, preferably a non-Western country, coming in to look at our school system. You're told that there are 26,000 such systems, and so, having read books lauding on American know-how, you assume that efficiency and sound management must be going on in the schools. But is this the case? For example, how many schools in the same metropolitan area even buy common supplies together? The answer is, very few. In other words, we run a very inefficient system, and there is a limit to how long we can continue to operate that way. New York is a special case to which I will turn in a moment.

But from the race relations point of view, the way we district our schools guarantees that, for the most part, we will segregate the races, as well as class and religion, because the central cities are rapidly becoming more Negro while the suburbs are rapidly becoming more white. Even if you had not segregation within districts at all, you would still have a rather intense pattern of segregation across districts.

But of course we have segregation *within* districts as well, and this leads me to the second major cause of segregation of schools in big central cities: the existence of private schools—parochial schools in particular. Again, this is not the work of evil men. As parochial schools have grown in our central cities, they have tended more and more to draw out whites from the pool of school-age children, making the public school system more and more Negro, by definition. Only 6 to 7 percent of all Negro-Americans are Roman Catholic, and they are not spread evenly over the Negro population of the United States; they are concentrated in such cities as Chicago, St. Louis, and New Orleans. Take away those cities, then you'll have an even smaller percentage than the 6 to 7 percent. What this means is that *de facto* parochial systems will tend to be white and will tend to exacerbate the problem of segregation in the public schools that much more.

The third basic cause of segregation in our central cities is the careful misplacement of schools, the zone drawing, and all the imagination we applied for 50 years on how to segregate schools. We are all familiar with it, even if we do not always do much about it. But I do not believe it is the most fundamental factor—the other two are.

Now what does all this imply about decentralization? Looked at from the perspective of race relations, decentralization, à la Bundy report, is hardly a technique for integration. It is clear that supporters of decentralization do not give integration a very high priority. This is clear from what they write and from what they say publicly and privately. From my perspective, nothing could be more dangerous or erroneous.

Of course, decentralization, like black power, has almost as many meanings as there are people who use the term. I want to define it in its special New York variety.

New York is unique in its bigness. There is a concept in a particular sociological study of large organizations called "effective organizational span of control," and I am convinced, with many of the critics of New York schools, that the New York school system long ago passed the point of effective organizational span of control. If you are not convinced you ought to take a visit to Livingston Street and see what ineffective span of control really means. In most American school systems the span of control is not an issue as it is in New York.

Decentralization's second real issue is parental involvement. I want to stress both words, *parental* and *involvement.* Parental—not organized leaders who are not parents of the children in the schools. In the three so-called local control school districts in New York City in what I consider to be the Ford Foundation's abortive experiment, many of the parents have no more say about what is going on than they ever had. But leaders interested in power—though not too interested in education—have a great deal to say; this is not necessarily bad, but I think the real issue is *parental* involvement more than the political power issue which has, up to now, always been with us.

And *involvement* is not synonymous with control. I believe that full control, as its advocates talk about it, is possible only if the local board has control of and full access to the tax base. To the extent that it does not, if does not really have control. I am afraid that his false sense of control is being perpetrated on some of the parents in some of the areas in and out of New York. In any case, involvement means decision power, it does not mean total control.

These are real issues, and they cannot be overlooked or swept under the rug. But the question I would pose is: can they not be faced effectively without some of the damaging consequences that I am sure would flow from the plan's major proposal, the creation of 30 to 60 little districts—homogeneous districts, not only in terms of race but also in terms of class (which would be more damaging than the race, if you accept the Coleman findings) and religion? In other words, 60 ghettos, sealed in structurally, where local people have a vested interest in keeping the structure that way, even if the education is inferior. I think this is a regressive step. Floyd McKissick, in a letter to *The New Republic,* used the Coleman report data on fate control to show that Negroes who had fate control did better, much better, on achievement scores, controlling for other variables; and he argued that this was an argument for separatism, black schools, black teachers, black control. He omitted one fact of the Coleman report: fate control was much more likely to be found in Negro children who are in *desegregated* schools, not within all-black schools.

Now the critical concept that should underlie the effort toward decentralization, it seems to me, is the concept of the community. We speak of the community, community control, community school board, but how are we going to define *community?* If you define it in terms of a heterogeneous area, then decentralization is not in conflict with integration but, on the contrary, is one way of helping to achieve integration in a large city. Decentralization and integration are not *necessarily* in conflict; but they do conflict in the way they have been presented in New York by the Bundy plan.

Dan Dodson of NYU has shown it *is* possible to draw district lines in New York City which would aid public school desegregation. He showed that it can be done; but it can be done only if you define community in heterogeneous terms, and not in homogeneous terms. It seems to me that up to now in New York—following the Bundy plan—we have been loosely defining it in homogeneous terms. Consequently, I greatly favor the more sophisticated Regents plan of desegregation, which envisages fewer districts and makes more possible the Dodson approach.

How should we think about improving our schools and the conditions of racial isolation that now exist in most of them? What are our possible strategies? Let me use two words that do not yet have ideological meanings but soon will, I am sure: "enrichment" and "dispersal." Varying these in different patterns, you come out with four possible strategies. There is one strategy—the "enrichment alone" strategy—that I think would be supported by Mr. Nixon, as well as by the black power separatists. (I always say separatists because many black power *advocates* are not separatists at all. Our polls still show that roughly 85 percent of Negro adults favor integration. That percentage has not gone down at all in the last couple of years. So you cannot judge what the so-called black community is thinking by reading the front page of the newspaper.) Now the "enrichment alone" strategy—and I believe decentralization, as conceptualized in the Bundy plan, is an enrichment alone strategy—is to simply pour funds into the ghetto. You do what you can to make life more habitable there, but you do not disperse the ghetto population; you try to make it self-contained. So you do not upen up jobs in the suburbs, you build factories *in* the ghetto; you do not spread your public housing, you build it in the ghetto, etc. I think this, alone, is a very dangerous strategy, because to use Kenneth Clark's word, it threatens to "embalm" the ghetto, to institutionalize it further, deepen its roots, build further vested interests. Bundy decentralization is a special case of this; the Regents decentralization would not be.

The second strategy is "dispersal alone," paying no attention whatsoever to the ghetto other than attempting to disperse those who live there. This would have been a difficult strategy even 15 years ago; by now it is clearly too late for the "dispersal alone" strategy. Let me cite some figures to point out what I mean. From 1950 to 1960 the 212 central cities in metropolitan areas in the United States grew annually by 320,000 Negroes. During that same period there was an annual suburban increase of 60,000 Negroes. But since 1960 the central city figure has grown from 320,000 to 400,000 Negroes annually, while in suburban areas—this is the disgraceful part—it is actually decreasing from 60,000 to 33,000 a year. We are going backwards, then, in residence patterns just as in schools. Of course the two are tied together. But the point is, simply to hold the line—not make the ghettos smaller, but keep Harlem, Bedford-Stuyvesant, Watts, and all the rest from growing larger—would require the annual movement of almost half a million Negroes into the suburbs. Obviously this is not to happen any time soon. So the "dispersal alone" strategy hasn't much more chance of succeeding than the "enrichment alone" strategy.

That leaves us, then, with some form of mix of the two. One form would be enrichment primarily, with some form of modest dispersal. For example, we pass a housing law, but we make sure it doesn't really have enforcement procedures that will work. Well, we have done this already. We have worked at it a little, and the suburban block now has two Negro families. That would be the modest dispersal. But the overwhelming effort and expenditure would be going into enrichment programs like that in Bedford-Stuyvesant. Build new and bigger schools and public housing smack in the middle of the ghetto.

The other mix—which I've saved for last because it is the one I favor—would stress dispersal, while recognizing that dispersal alone cannot do the trick, although if we do not at least start working at it we will never get there. It does not mean abolishing ghettos; even if you could get rid of them, you would not want to. The object is to change the nature of ghettos, not eliminate them. Look at the difference between North Boston and the Negro ghetto in Roxbury. North Boston is an Italian area: the people who live there do not have to, they live there by choice. Their sons and daughters tend to live there; they live in Winchester like, say, the Governor. Now it just so happens that Governor Volpe lives in a suburb where Negroes aren't allowed. So the fact is, Roxbury *cannot* be like North Boston because, in addition to the Negroes who live in Roxbury because they want to (like Italians in North Boston), there are Negroes who live there because they *have* to. As long as they live there because they have to, it is not in an ethnic area of choice like North Boston, it is a racial ghetto, a prison. Changing the *prison* quality of ghettos is what we are after, not abolishing the areas as such—which you could not do if you wanted to.

Dispersal, by the way, does not mean salt and pepper residential areas. It can mean "mini-ghettos." Three out of four Negroes who live in suburbs live in ghettos, but they are small ghettos. They beat Bedford-Stuyvesant any day because they can be integrated, their schools can be integrated, and their facilities are much superior to big ghettos. We know *how* to disperse. It is not lack of know-how that is holding us back. It is a lack of political push, along with hostility toward desegregation of housing on the part of many white citizens. Nevertheless, we could make real strides by combining the dispersal techniques already at our command *with* enrichment of the ghetto. But what kind of enrichment? Not all types. The criterion I favor is to *check always to see if the enrichment is productive or counter-productive for later dispersal.* For example, I applied this test to Bundy decentralization and it appears to be counter-productive, while Regents decentralization could be productive.

The test can also be applied to new schools. Do you build fine, spanking-new schools in the middle of the ghetto? I would say no. It is counter-productive to dispersal. What about encouraging co-ops and job training in the ghetto? Yes, because they are productive for dispersal, and so forth. I admit there are some marginal cases where this test may not apply, but I think I have illustrated the point.

Again let me stress that I believe an interracial America to be the only viable America, in a democratic sense, that we have open to us. Some now say that separatism today is the prelude to integration. That strikes me as a classic instance of doublethink. We have to start achieving with integration now, someplace, just as the Kerner Commission indicated.

. . . . .

48 The War for City Schools

IRA MOTHNER

The question of control of school systems has become a most complex and compelling problem in New York City as well as in other large cities throughout the country. Black communities within the cities have lost faith in the possibility of obtaining high-quality schools through integration and have demanded the opportunity to run their own schools. This idea has frequently been encouraged by whites who wish to maintain segregated school systems. Many educators and others who are trying to improve the quality of urban schools, like Thomas Pettigrew in the previous article, maintain that the most effective way to achieve high-quality education is through integration. This conflict over school control has many other social implications. Large-scale bureaucracies such as big-city school systems may *be more effective in producing high-quality education with control centered in local units than with the current centralized control. The implications of this for the maintenance of a segregated, stratified society in contrast to the development of a single, integrated society is of major significance for the nation.*

New York was just the beginning. "It was inevitable here," groans the city's top schoolman, Bernard Donovan, who got caught in the cross fire between union teachers and the "community control" crowd. "All the cities are facing this thing. Only we're the biggest, and we were first."

Why the schools? Why does this revolution start with the schoolhouse and not the Bastille? "Because Americans ask education to do all the things they used to pray to God for," says Charles E. Wilson, who runs the Harlem schools where it all began.

SOURCE: *Look*, vol. 33 (May 13, 1969), 46–49. • Ira Mothner is a senior editor for *Look* magazine.

Generations of mothers beat their kids over the head with that faith. "Keep your nose clean and do good in school, and you can be President of the U.S. or AT&T or GE or GM." Education is the key to America's great goody box, and our parents or their parents or someone along the line came here not to be free but to get rich and respectable.

In Roxbury and North Philadelphia, Watts, Harlem and Hough, in the black cores of all the big cities, mothers still buy the dream. Only their kids aren't learning, not as much as other youngsters, not as fast and not as well. It doesn't much matter to the mother of an illiterate eighth grader that Northern city schools are miles better than Southern and rural schools. Her son can't read. Whitey has let her down once again, and if he can't or won't do the job, she figures somebody black better take a crack at it.

Angry mothers are loud in the chorus sounding out in the ghetto, demanding community control, the right to run schools on their own turf. The move is to carve neighborhood-size chunks out of super-systems in Chicago, Detroit, Boston, Philadelphia, Washington and Los Angeles, as well as New York.

The development of "Parent Power," as spelled out by Preston Wilcox, a down-to-pavement social theorist of community control, "will force schools to put onto their agendas the usually overlooked concerns—poor housing, inadequate heat, low welfare allowances, ineffective police protection, etc." Wilcox wants schools open seven days a week, a meeting place with space for parties, funerals and weddings, "rather than an island in a colony that is open only when the outsiders are present."

Schools are the biggest public buildings in anybody's neighborhood. Plenty of public money flows into them; little flows out. To street-corner activists cultivating the grass roots, schools are a tempting power base. First the classrooms, next the precinct house, fire station and hospital.

The big school systems are ripe for plucking. Fat and sloppy, they just about choked on the latest glob of immigration from the rural South. The need to "decentralize," to parcel out decision-making to smaller units within the systems, was clear long before community control popped up. Break down the big machines before they break up.

Experts, critics and sundry quizzical "educationists" crawled all over the systems a few years back, when ghetto schools suddenly became a national embarrassment (three out of four black city students read below grade). They found what most of them always knew—lower-class kids don't do well in school. They never have. But the biggest chunk of the urban under class was now black, and ghetto redhots were beginning to cry "educational genocide."

"When schools failed before," argues Wilson, "kids went out and got jobs. They dug subways. But if the subways were redug today, they'd be dug by machines, and the unions have the machines, and we can't get into the unions."

The cure for ghetto education seemed simple—integration. Then there would be no more ghetto schools. But while Berkeley, Calif., was able to tear apart its system and put it back together again all racially balanced, integration of the big cities never happened.

New York came up with a scheme to move fifth-grade children into intermediate schools, cutting their time in the highly segregated primary schools. In late summer, 1966, the war for city schools began at Harlem's new Intermediate School 201, which the Board of Education had promised would be integrated. Parents complained that the site was unlikely to draw white students, and were put off by the starkly modern and windowless design. "That's when *they* explained to us what they meant by integration," recalls David Spencer, the fierce-faced chairman of 201's governing board. "They meant 50 percent Puerto Rican and 50 percent black," which is roughly how the neighborhood shapes up. "So that's what moved us to say, 'If we're going to have a segregated school, we'll have to have it segregated all the way.'" The parents threatened a boycott unless they were allowed to name a black principal and have some say about what was going to be taught.

Parents do not decide suddenly to start bucking the city's mighty Board of Education. There was organization. Harlem has plenty—block associations, tenant groups and anti-poverty agencies. This is what they're all about, to organize the community for action. But they didn't create the bitterness that brought on the clash. Parents had stopped trusting schools. They knew their children were not stupid and could not believe that failure was something natural and normal, a function of "cultural deprivation" or "family breakdown." Not that these weren't factors. But so were the sloth and down-turned noses of many ghetto teachers, their meager expectations predictably matched by meager results. Too many parents thought teachers were arrogant; too many teachers thought parents were ignorant.

Suddenly parents were saying, "If that many children can't make it, then something must be wrong with your schools," and a terrifying new idea surfaced—accountability. Why shouldn't teachers and schools be responsible for what they do to children? "So what is so hard about teaching kids?" asks Spencer. "I don't want to hear the excuse about how they come from bad homes. If you are a professional, it is your job to handle that."

When 201 opened, there were boycotts, a brief teacher walkout, but mostly a kind of siege, with pickets and parents harassing teachers outside the school and tuned-in youngsters giving them a hard time inside. What eventually came out of this was a plan to set up three experimental districts with some self-government. Unruly IS 201, with its primary schools, was one of the three, and the parents had learned that walking and talking softly never bought them half as much as a ruckus in front of the schoolhouse.

Bernard Donovan, a sharp superintendent who looks, talks and comes on like Pat O'Brien, was wary of the scheme. He knew what was bugging the parents. "But," he explains, "the only real advantage in decentralization and community involvement is the creation of a new atmosphere. People in the district who *feel* they have more to say will have more confidence in the schools."

The United Federation of Teachers (UFT) was more optimistic. Albert Shanker, its tall, rumpled president, was a frontline civil rights man, as concerned about education as about pay. His union was then pushing MES (More Effective Schools), a program that cuts class size and beefs up the teaching staff. It is a costly package, available to only a few schools, and many critics feel its educational bang is not worth all those bucks. But the promise of MES or something like it in the experimental districts sweetened the pot for the union, which had already seen the chance to gang up with parents to get more money for the schools.

While the union was willing to work with the IS 201 group, it preferred a less prickly bunch and found one in Brooklyn. Out in Ocean Hill-Brownsville, an area wedged between Bedford-Stuyvesant and

Brownsville proper, union teachers were working closely with some parents organized by Father John Powis, a Catholic street-worker priest. At the UFT's suggestion, Ocean Hill-Brownsville was added to the list of experimental districts.

The agreement to set up the experimental districts was casually made. The Board of Education, the union, the 201 parents and the Ford Foundation, which paid the bill to put the districts in business are not a slipshod bunch. There was just little upon which they all agreed. It was, after all, an experiment, and the point of an experiment is to see what happens.

The board and the union didn't want to know what powers the communities were after. Nor did they realize how parents might want to tinker with schools. The foundation, however, was on to most of this. Dr. Mario Fantini, Ford's emissary to the IS 201 parents, figured the communities were a better bet to make real changes than the board or the union, both of which wanted, first off, smaller classes, plus "compensation and remediation" for those culturally out of step with the system. This was more of the same old strategy—redesigning children to fit the schools.

Before the 1966–67 school year ended, relations between the union and the local planning groups turned sour. The planners started talking about screening teachers. The MES proposals were dropped, and a wave of student violence shook teachers enough for the union to demand a heavy-handed "disruptive child" policy. Even union leaders allow, "The way we put that forward was pretty stupid," and the local boards read it as racism. When the UFT started off the fall of '67 with a strike, matters didn't improve. The union was holding out for a brand of educational improvements not all that popular in the new districts.

Meanwhile, the Ocean Hill parents had held an election, chosen a governing board and picked a unit administrator, Rhody McCoy. Eighteen years in the system and an acting principal although he had never taken any promotion exams ("I didn't figure it was worth the time"), McCoy proved out a solid leader whose chief concern was getting something new going in the schools.

But the 1967–68 school year in Ocean Hill-Brownsville was a disaster. Union teachers expected a white principal who had worked closely with Father Powis to get the unit administrator's job. They had hoped the district board would support their strike. They felt betrayed. Experienced teachers and assistant principals fled the district. The principals had already left and were replaced by nominees of the local board not on the civil service list. This brought fearful screams and a lawsuit from the Council of Supervisory Associations (CSA), representing the city schools' brass.

The city then got news that full-scale decentralization was on the way. Mayor John V. Lindsay had asked a panel headed by McGeorge Bundy, president of the Ford Foundation, to come up with a plan to tap added state aid available under decentralization. The Bundy team, with Dr. Fantini as staff director, found the Board of Education so tied in procedural knots that "these constraints bid fair to strangle the system in its own checks and balances. . . ." It proposed 20 to 60 separate districts run by community boards with something less than complete control. "Meaningful participation," the Bundy staff called it.

Before the state legislature could consider several decentralization plans that followed the Bundy proposal to Albany, all hell broke loose in Ocean Hill-Brownsville. The crisis came in May, when the governing board ordered 19 teachers and supervisors out of the district. It was a move McCoy had resisted for months, for the very good reason that neither he nor his board had authority to make the transfers. Since two union chapter chairmen and two teachers from the district's original planning group were among the 19, the UFT was bound to squawk. The Ocean Hill board claims Donovan had offered to move two or three, but not the lot. Donovan insists he never heard a word about the 19. It's unlikely he would have transferred the union's strong men in the district, and these were the teachers the governing board most wanted out, the ones they insisted were sabotaging the experiment.

When the Ocean Hill refugees were ordered back to their schools by Donovan, the battle was on. Returning teachers were barred, police escorted them inside, parents kept the kids out, and finally, 350 teachers (more than half the staff) joined their rejected colleagues in a district-wide strike that lasted, with one interruption, until the school year ended.

In Albany, decentralization plans went onto the shelf. But the legislature let the Mayor enlarge the Board of Education. One of the first appointments was the Rev. Milton Galamison, chief black critic of the city board and strong for community control.

Ten of the ousted teachers were ready to go back to Ocean Hill last fall, along with another 73 who'd struck the previous spring. The local board wanted none of them. The Mayor pushed and the governing board seemed to yield. Still, the union struck for two days and won added job guarantees.

When 83 union teachers showed up at Ocean Hill, they were threatened and harassed by furious parents and crowds of militant outsiders. None of the teachers was given a classroom assignment. Governing-board chairman the Rev. C. Herbert Oliver claimed the community had risen spontaneously, and said he hoped it would do so again. The union went back on strike. That left Ocean Hill running smoothly but shut down most of the city's other schools.

Two weeks later, the union teachers were back. After a shaky start, they were put into classrooms. Then Oliver and the governing board ordered McCoy to yank them out. When push came to shove, McCoy figured he worked for Ocean Hill and he obeyed. The city board then suspended the local board, McCoy and the principals. (Suspending the principals was the only tactic that ever really worked against Ocean Hill.) Three days later, Junior High School 271, the critical school in the district, exploded. An invasion of angry parents, protesters and plain troublemakers tore the school apart, and Donovan closed it.

After a round of dickering, the city board decided to reopen JHS 271 and reinstate the district's principals. Shanker balked, and the Mayor's office pressured the board to hold off. But the school was reopened, and the union walked out for the third time.

Although union leaders had insisted the first two strikes were for "due process" and job security, during strike number three they were holding out for the death of the Ocean Hill district. The Board of Education, led by its new president, John Doar, was not about to pay that stiff a price. When Shanker couldn't get the state legislature to step in, he had to settle.

On November 18, the union agreed to state supervision of Ocean Hill, and the teachers went back. By now, nobody trusted anybody. The Ocean Hill people felt the Board of Education had sold them out. The union had no faith in the city board, and neither side trusted the Mayor, who'd alternately pressured and promised all sides to get it settled and make it go away.

Ocean Hill used to be called "No Man's Land." No one is likely to overlook the district now. Since the strike ended, students have been raging in many of the city's high schools. Black protests over makeup classes gave way to black-white fights and some general hell-raising, and it doesn't take many students to set a school on end.

At the Bedford-Stuyvesant Development and Services Corp., John Doar leans his long frame way back and tilts his chair when asked about the strikes. "This is a tough town," he begins ruefully, and seems for that moment like a wistful Jimmy Stewart come from the sticks. "The crisis occurred," he says, in a harder voice, "when the union was willing to use its ultimate weapon to coerce public officials to act the way the union wanted them to act—to close a school, fire a principal, fire a unit administrator. And when the Board of Education didn't do it, they went out on a city-wide strike. Well, that's unacceptable behavior in this country."

Most New Yorkers didn't see it that way. The unions were solidly behind Shanker, even the black unions. Bayard Rustin backed him, and Rustin had organized the first school boycott Milton Galamison sprang on the city back when they both were on the glory road to integration. But Rustin is dead against the separatism he sees in community control.

Better than 90 percent of the teachers were out. Yet most ghetto schools were open, and many white teachers came in. Parents and teachers, white and black, opened schools that had been closed and locked by principals, for the CSA loved the UFT. But among that variegated clutch of New Yorkers who think of themselves as "liberals," surprisingly few stood up for the folks out in Ocean Hill.

Most occupants of New York's liberal camp have a common faith in integration (from when it used to be called brotherhood—and came cheap), trade unionism and the civil service system. It's easy to forget what the unions meant to the generation that was turned on by *Solidarity Forever,* when "fink" and "scab" had real meaning.

Civil service was a battlement against political payoffs, graft and boss rule. New York's examination system was how all those bright young Jewish teachers got their foot in the school system and took away a good many top jobs from the Irish, who had politically muscled out the WASP's. But the exams have helped create a system where less than ten percent of the teachers and five percent of the administrators are black or Puerto Rican while more than half the students are one or the other.

No one who has studied the New York schools has much good to say for the promotion exams. Such subjective guides as "speaking the language" and "knowing your way around the system" have plenty to do with passing, according to one university study. If it takes community control to give black teachers and supervisors their piece of the action, this doesn't disturb critics like Dr. Marilyn Gittell, of Queens College, who first suggested decentralization.

But what really put off many New York liberals was the smell of anti-Semitism. The ten ousted teachers who returned were Jewish, while the governing board was close to all black. Most New York teachers are Jewish, as are most UFT members. Some bitterly anti-Semitic material got tossed around, not necessarily by Ocean Hill people. The big pusher was the union, which gave far wider circulation to this muck than was ever imagined by its authors.

If the Ocean Hill confrontation had happened in Boston, then the fight would have been between black parents and Irish-Catholic teachers. In Washington, the community would have tangled with middle-class Negro administrators. But in New York, the Jews were it, and the timing was right for discord. Some Jews resent being pushed out of the civil rights mainstream, many distrust the new militancy. To Negroes, there is no question where Jews line up when it gets down to black and white. If the white man is the oppressor in the ghetto, the Jew is often the most visible white on the scene—the shopkeeper or landlord.

Now that the Ocean Hill governing board has been reinstated, the UFT seems to be backing off the issue of anti-Semitism, never a strong point when half of the new teachers who took over in the district were Jewish. "I'm impressed by young Jewish teachers," says Father Powis. "I wish I could say the same for Catholic teachers. They're really vicious." To some historians of the conflict, Father Powis is the Rasputin of Ocean Hill, the cunning manipulator in turn-about collar. He looks like Bing Crosby right out of *Going My Way,* jug ears and all. Outspoken, sometimes rash, Father Powis has been on the streets of Ocean Hill for seven years and is trusted there. Now, he worries that all the fuss in the schools has killed concern for housing and safety in the area: "Lindsay said he'd make Ocean Hill a model district—police, sanitation, rigid housing-code enforcement." Father Powis is still certain the offending 19 had to be plucked out: "We were forced to do it. We tried to talk to them." Yet, he ingenuously insists, "I don't think we caused the confrontation."

Father Powis may be naïve; Rhody McCoy is not. While the local board took what Doar calls "a revolutionary course," the unit administrator was trying vainly to tack, figuring the Mayor, Donovan or someone would help head off the collision. Nobody did. The wielders of real power in the city (Albert Shanker is one) have no patience with people like Ocean Hill's board who don't understand that the best bargain you can get is better than no bargain at all.

McCoy is now a political heavyweight, the rock of Ocean Hill who sat stubbornly and puffed one of his big-bellied pipes while the union raged. He's still sitting and puffing in his narrow office at Ocean Hill headquarters, sounding bitter and feeling poorly used. "Obviously, the Establishment has a vested interest in seeing this thing fail. If it worked, they'd have to give us more." He talks tough as he moves about the city and the country now, preaching community control: "Revolution is nothing to be afraid of. This country has a history of revolution, none of it without bloodshed. I'm not an advocate of violence, but if that's the only way to change, I have to support it."

The Ocean Hill schools are now mostly filled with young new teachers who just don't know what the old pros know, like how to keep a lesson alive for a whole period or hold a class together without resorting to discipline. But they try so hard they often make it. The most obvious change is the para-professionals, the 180 parents and other neighborhood folks in the classrooms not as aides but as assistant teachers. The parents trust them and they understand the children. Over at 110 Livingston Street, the Board of Education's office, administration types complain, "Money doesn't go into the kids' programs but into hiring people. That keeps the district quiet and gives people jobs. It creates an organization."

Yet there are plenty of new programs in Ocean Hill—preschool classes, one run along Montessori lines, and an experimental kindergarten. Project READ, the programmed reading instruction put out by Behavioral Research Laboratories, is in five of the six primary schools, while the sixth has Project LEARN, a more ambitious BRL innovation that programs instructions for all subjects. "Programmed" sounds rigid, but the systems allow youngsters to move through the material at their own speed and provide a script for beginning teachers to follow.

Meanwhile, New York legislators sat on reams of decentralization schemes this spring, and the UFT got into a "due process" scrap with IS 201. Both the city board and state regents pushed local power. "You don't need a superintendent," Donovan told his bosses when he read their plan, "you need a chief clerk," and turned in his resignation soon after.

But the city board proposed nowhere near enough for Galamison, who wants freedom now—control over money, construction, teachers, supervisors; everything. In Harlem, leaders of CORE are demanding a separate school district free from the city. Since few ghetto districts can support their own schools, Galamison doesn't cotton to the plan. He wants all the autonomy Harlem is after, but without the bill. And he doesn't expect to get it easily. "There is no progress without actual confrontation," he insists. "The history of the school crisis bears that out."

Confrontation is a costly way to get ahead, and Ocean Hill was hardly a victory. Still, the idea of community control is not about to go away.

• • • • •

No matter how they decide to do it, the architects of community control are out to run their own affairs. Anything less, they claim, is "colonialism," and they compare their neighborhoods to small suburbs and towns where local boards oversee small districts. Such boards don't really run their schools very much. They make political and money decisions, and leave schooling to the superintendent. This works because the systems are small and the superintendents are trusted. If they aren't, they get bounced. That isn't too different from the way a neighborhood-run city district would work. Politics and money are community business, education is for a pro just so long as he's willing to try to break the old molds and make schools that suit the community kids.

None of the decentralized schools has tried anything wild or hairy. They have pitched plenty of black history, pushed black pride, brought mothers into the schools and worked on teacher attitudes. Some new material is devised in the schools, most bought outside, like BRL programs in Ocean Hill and a General Learning reading project for Anacostia.

Black educators now running these schools say, "Come back in five years." They don't want a series of models and experiments, to be "evaluated" after one year or two. The big systems are always trying something out, evaluating and killing it.

There are neighborhoods within the big cities content with the old systems. Few white communities are demanding control, and the Bundy plan would let the New York districts run as much or as little of their own show as they wished. Nor is separatism a universal goal. New York's Joan of Arc district, now out for independence, will be integrated, as will many other districts within the decentralized city. Still, the first wave of community control is all black, and that is scary to many whites. In the ghetto these fears come off as racism. "What they are saying is that we can't be trusted to run our own schools."

There are no plans to drive out white teachers willing to teach in black-run schools. White principals and assistant principals will find it harder to stay, for the idea of a "black male" as "authority figure" carries much weight with those who want black schools. Some teachers will be frightened off and will be hard to replace. Teaching is no soft deal. To be educator, psychiatrist, nurse, nanny and priest to as many as 30 kids (more in junior and senior highs) is worth better than the average $6,830 teachers get. With the community demanding an accounting for each child, there will be jobs for all who want to stay. And many will, glad to get off *Up the Down Staircase* and on with the business of teaching.

Community control in some form is on the way to happening in just about every big city. Ocean Hill is likely to be fought again somewhere else. But when battle is joined, extremists appear, kids get the message, and schools fall apart.

Black educators themselves are not exactly a band of tame tabbies. They are ready to fight if that's what it takes. At a Harvard educational conference last year, a black caucus declared: "We can battle with whatever weapons and through whatever means necessary to wrest control of these basic institutions from the hands of those in power. . . ."

Chairman of that group was Rhody McCoy, and he wasn't just woofing.

CHAPTER VII

SOCIAL ORGANIZATION

INSTITUTIONS AND ASSOCIATIONS

49 Parkinson's Law

C. NORTHCOTE PARKINSON

Although written with tongue in cheek, Parkinson's "Law" clearly describes one of the most fundamental facts about human society. Human groups, he says, tend to devise increasingly complicated organized ways of doing things (a process that is often termed "institutionalization"), and then frequently keep on doing these things in the established way even when it would appear, from the standpoint of efficiency, not to make sense to do so. Vested interests resist because they might suffer if some change were introduced. The consequences of this tendency are legion: social change is impeded, valuable time and energy are unnecessarily expended, people become more concerned with the procedures and techniques than with goals, and more people are assigned to carry out more specialized tasks.

I. PARKINSON'S LAW OR THE RISING PYRAMID

Work expands so as to fill the time available for its completion. General recognition of this fact is shown in the proverbial phrase "It is the busiest man who has time to spare." Thus, an elderly lady of leisure can spend the entire day in writing and dispatching a postcard to her niece at Bognor Regis. An hour will be spent in finding the postcard, another in hunting for spectacles, half an hour in a search for the address, an hour and a quarter in composition, and twenty minutes in deciding whether or not to take an umbrella when going to the mailbox in the next street. The total effort that would occupy a busy man for three minutes all told may in this fashion leave another person prostrate after a day of doubt, anxiety, and toil.

Granted that work (and especially paperwork) is thus elastic in its demands on time, it is manifest that there need be little or no relationship between the work to be done and the size of the staff to which it may be assigned. A lack of real activity does not, of necessity, result in leisure. A lack of occupation is not necessarily revealed by a manifest idleness. The thing to be done swells in im-

SOURCE: C. Northcote Parkinson, *Parkinson's Law and Other Studies in Administration,* 2–13, 59–69 passim. • C. Northcote Parkinson is an author, historian, and journalist. He is the president of the Parkinson Institute, a business consultants organization, Amsterdam. He has taught at several universities and was the Raffles Professor of History at the University of Malaya from 1950 to 1958. Among his many published works are *Trade in the Eastern Seas, Parkinson's Law: The Pursuit of Progress, The Evolution of Political Thought,* and *East and West.*

portance and complexity in a direct ratio with the time spent. This fact is widely recognized, but less attention has been paid to its wider implications, more especially in the field of public administration. Politicians and taxpayers have assumed (with occasional phases of doubt) that a rising total in the number of civil servants must reflect a growing volume of work to be done. Cynics, in questioning this belief, have imagined that the multiplication of officials must have left some of them idle or all of them able to work shorter hours. But this is a matter in which faith and doubt seem equally misplaced. The fact is that the number of the officials and the quanity of the work are not related to each other at all. The rise in the total of those employed is governed by Parkinson's Law and would be much the same whether the volume of the work were to increase, diminish, or even disappear. The importance of Parkinson's Law lies in the fact that it is a law of growth based upon an analysis of the factors by which that growth is controlled.

The validity of this recently discovered law must rest mainly on statistical proofs, which will follow. Of more interest to the general reader is the explanation of the factors underlying the general tendency to which this law gives definition. Omitting technicalities (which are numerous) we may distinguish at the outset two motive forces. They can be represented for the present purpose by two almost axiomatic statements, thus: (1) "An official wants to multiply subordinates, not rivals" and (2) "Officials make work for each other."

To comprehend Factor 1, we must picture a civil servant, called A, who finds himself overworked. Whether this overwork is real or imaginary is immaterial, but we should observe, in passing, that A's sensation (or illusion) might easily result from his own decreasing energy: a normal symptom of middle age. For this real or imagined overwork there are, broadly speaking, three possible remedies. He may resign; he may ask to halve the work with a colleague called B; he may demand the assistance of two subordinates, to be called C and D. There is probably no instance in history, however, of A choosing any but the third alternative. By resignation he would lose his pension rights. By having B appointed, on his own level in the hierarchy, he would merely bring in a rival for promotion to W's vacancy when W (at long last) retires. So A would rather have C and D, junior men, below him. They will add to his consequence and, by dividing the work into two categories, as between C and D, he will have the merit of being the only man who comprehends them both. It is essential to realize at this point that C and D are, as it were, inseparable. To appoint C alone would have been impossible. Why? Because C, if by himself, would divide the work with A and so assume almost the equal status that has been refused in the first instance to B; a status the more emphasized if C is A's only possible successor. Subordinates must thus number two or more, each being thus kept in order by fear of the other's promotion. When C complains in turn of being overworked (as he certainly will) A will, with the concurrence of C, advise the appointment of two assistants to help C. But he can then avert internal friction only by advising the appointment of two more assistants to help D, whose position is much the same. With this recruitment of E, F, G, and H the promotion of A is now practically certain.

Seven officials are now doing what one did before. This is where Factor 2 comes into operation. For these seven make so much work for each other that all are fully occupied and A is actually working harder than ever. An incoming document may well come before each of them in turn. Official E decides that it falls within the province of F, who places a draft reply before C, who amends it drastically before consulting D, who asks G to deal with it. But G goes on leave at this point, handing the file over to H, who drafts a minute that is signed by D and returned to C, who revises his draft accordingly and lays the new version before A.

What does A do? He would have every excuse for signing the thing unread, for he has many other matters on his mind. Knowing now that he is to succeed W next year, he has to decide whether C or D should succeed to his own office. He had to agree to G's going on leave even if not yet strictly entitled to it. He is worried whether H should not have gone instead, for reasons of health. He has looked pale recently—partly but not solely because of his domestic troubles. Then there is the business of F's special increment of salary for the period of the conference and E's application for transfer to the Ministry of Pensions. A has heard that D is in love with a married typist and that G and F are no longer on speaking terms—no one seems to know why. So A might be tempted to sign C's draft and have done with it. But A is a conscientious man. Beset as he is with problems created by his colleagues for themselves and for him—created by the mere fact of these officials' existence—he is not the man to shirk his duty. He reads through the draft with care, deletes the fussy paragraphs added by C and H, and restores the thing back to the form preferred in the first instance by the able (if quarrelsome) F. He corrects the English—none of these young men can write grammatically—and finally produces the same reply he would have written if officials C to H had never been born. Far more people have taken far longer to produce the same result. No one has been idle. All have done their best. And it is late in the evening before A finally quits his office and begins the return journey to Ealing. The last of the office lights are being turned off in the gathering dusk that marks the end of another day's administrative toil. Among the last to leave, A reflects with bowed shoulders and a wry smile that late hours, like gray hairs, are among the penalties of success.

• • • • •

II. PLANS AND PLANTS OR THE ADMINISTRATIVE BLOCK

Every student of human institutions is familiar with the standard test by which the importance of the individual may be assessed. The number of doors to be passed, the number of his personal assistants, the number of his telephone receivers—these three figures, taken with the depth of his carpet in centimeters, have given us a simple formula that is reliable for most parts of the world. It is less widely known that the same sort of measurement is applicable, *but in reverse*, to the institution itself.

Take, for example, a publishing organization. Publishers have a strong tendency, as we know, to live in a state of chaotic squalor. The visitor who applies at the obvious entrance is led outside and around the block, down an alley and up three flights of stairs. A research establishment is similarly housed, as a rule, on the ground floor of what was once a private house, a crazy wooden corridor leading thence to a corrugated iron hut in what was once the garden. Are we not all familiar, moreover, with the layout of an international airport? As we emerge from the aircraft, we see (over to our right or left) a lofty structure wrapped in scaffolding. Then the air hostess leads us into a hut with an asbestos roof. Nor do we suppose for a moment that it will ever be otherwise. By the time the permanent building is complete the airfield will have been moved to another site.

The institutions already mentioned—lively and productive as they may be—flourish in such shabby and makeshift surroundings that we might turn with relief to an institution clothed from the outset with convenience and dignity. The outer door, in bronze and glass, is placed centrally in a symmetrical facade. Polished shoes glide quietly over shining rubber to the glittering and silent elevator. The overpoweringly cultured receptionist will murmur with carmine lips into an ice-blue receiver. She will wave you into a chromium armchair, consoling you with a dazzling smile for any slight but inevitable delay. Looking up from a glossy magazine, you will observe how the wide corridors radiate toward departments A, B, and C. From behind closed doors will come the subdued noise of an ordered activity. A minute later and you are ankle deep in the director's carpet, ploddng sturdily toward his distant, tidy desk. Hypnotized by the chief's unwavering stare, cowed by the Matisse hung upon his wall, you will feel that you have found real efficiency at last.

In point of fact you will have discovered nothing of the kind. It is now known that a perfection of planned layout is achieved only by institutions on the point of collapse. This apparently paradoxical conclusion is based upon a wealth of archaeological and historical research, with the more esoteric details of which we need not concern ourselves. In general principle, however, the method pursued has been to select and date the buildings which appear to have been perfectly designed for their purpose. A study and comparison of these has tended to prove that perfection of planning is a symptom of decay. During a period of exciting discovery or progress there is no time to plan the perfect headquarters. The time for that comes later, when all the important work has been done. Perfection, we know, is finality; and finality is death.

. . . . .

It is natural . . . to ask at this point whether the Palace of Westminster, where the House of Commons meets, is itself a true expression of parliamentary rule. It represents beyond question a magnificent piece of planning, aptly designed for debate and yet provided with ample space for everything else—for committee meetings, for quiet study, for refreshment, and (on its terrace) for tea. It has everything a legislator could possibly desire, all incorporated in a building of immense dignity and comfort. It should date—but this we now hardly dare assume—from a period when parliamentary rule was at its height. But once again the dates refuse to fit into this pattern. The original House, where Pitt and Fox were matched in oratory, was accidentally destroyed by fire in 1843. It would appear to have been as famed for its inconveniences as for its lofty standard of debate. The present structure was begun in 1840, partly occupied in 1852, but incomplete when its architect died in 1860. It finally assumed its present appearance in about 1868. Now, by what we can no longer regard as coincidence, the decline of Parliament can be traced, without much dispute, to the Reform Act of 1867. It was in the following year that all initiative in legislation passed from Parliament to be vested in the Cabinet. The prestige attached to the letters "M.P." began sharply to decline and thenceforward the most that could be said is that "a role, though a humble one, was left for private members." The great days were over.

• • • • •

But no other British example can now match in significance the story of New Delhi. Nowhere else have British architects been given the task of planning so great a capital city as the seat of government for so vast a population. The intention to found New Delhi was announced at the Imperial Durbar of 1911, King George V being at that time the Mogul's successor on what had been the Peacock Throne. Sir Edwin Lutyens then proceeded to draw up plans for a British Versailles, splendid in conception, comprehensive in detail, masterly in design, and overpowering in scale. But the stages of its progress toward completion correspond with so many steps in political collapse. The Government of India Act of 1909 had been the prelude to all that followed—the attempt on the Viceroy's life in 1912, the Declaration of 1917, the Montagu-Chelmsford Report of 1918 and its implementation in 1920. Lord Irwin actually moved into his new palace in 1929, the year in which the Indian Congress demanded independence, the year in which the Round Table Conference opened, the year before the Civil Disobedience campaign began. It would be possible, though tedious, to trace the whole story down to the day when the British finally withdrew, showing how each phase of the retreat was exactly paralleled with the completion of another triumph in civic design. What was finally achieved was no more and no less than a mausoleum. . . .

The elaborate layout of the Pentagon at Arlington, Virginia, provides another significant lesson for planners. It was not completed until the later stages of World War II and, of course, the architecture of the great victory was not constructed here. but in the crowded and untidy Munitions Building on Constitution Avenue.

Even today, as the least observant visitor to Washington can see, the most monumental edifices are found to house such derelict organizations as the Departments of Commerce and Labor, while the more active agencies occupy half-completed quarters. Indeed, much of the more urgent business of government goes forward in "temporary" structures erected during World War I, and shrewdly preserved for their stimulating effect on administration. Hard by the Capitol, the visitor will also observe the imposing marble-and-glass headquarters of the Teamsters' Union, completed not a moment too soon before the heavy hand of Congressional investigation descended on its occupants.

It is by no means certain that an influential reader of this chapter could prolong the life of a dying institution merely by depriving it of its streamlined headquarters. What he can do, however, with more confidence, is to prevent any organization strangling itself at birth. Examples abound of new institutions coming into existence with a full establishment of deputy directors, consultants, and executives; all these coming together in a building specially designed for their purpose. And experience proves that such an institution will die. It is choked by its own perfection. It cannot take root for lack of soil. It cannot grow naturally for it is already grown. Fruitless by its very nature, it cannot even flower. When we see an example of such planning—when we are confronted for example by the building designed for the United Nations—the experts among us shake their heads sadly, draw a sheet over the corpse, and tiptoe quietly into the open air.

50 Bureaucracy

MAX WEBER

Contemporary American and other Western societies are characterized by highly bureaucratic organizations. This type of structure is common in business and other private social institutions as well as governmental agencies. Here Max Weber has systematically analyzed the nature of bureaucracies and demonstrated their necessity. Although this analysis was written over a half-century ago and is based largely on observations of German and other European organizations, no more thorough or sociologically significant statement on the subject has ever appeared.

CHARACTERISTICS OF BUREAUCRACY

Modern officialdom functions in the following specific manner:

I. There is the principle of fixed and official jurisdictional areas, which are generally ordered by rules, that is, by laws or administrative regulations.

1. The regular activities required for the purposes of the bureaucratically governed structure are distributed in a fixed way as official duties.

2. The authority to give the commands required for the discharge of these duties is distributed in a stable way and is strictly delimited by rules concerning the coercive means, physical, sacerdotal, or otherwise, which may be placed at the disposal of officials.

SOURCE: Max Weber, *Essays in Sociology*, edited and translated by H. H. Gerth and C. Wright Mills, 196–244. Copyright 1946 by Oxford University Press, Inc. Reprinted by permission. • The author (1846–1920) was a German sociologist and political economist. He held the Chair of Political Economy at Freiburg. Weber's sociology is based on his extensive knowledge in economic, political, social, legal, military, and religious fields. He is especially well known for his typological studies of charismatic authority, feudalism, and bureaucracy. He was also a pioneer in the sociology of religion. Among his translated works are *General Economic History, The Protestant Ethic and the Spirit of Capitalism,* and *The Theory of Economic and Social Organization.*

3. Methodical provision is made for the regular and continuous fulfilment of these duties and for the execution of the corresponding rights; only persons who have the generally regulated qualifications to serve are employed.

In public and lawful government these three elements constitute "bureaucratic authority." In private economic domination, they constitute bureaucratic "management." Bureaucracy, thus understood, is fully developed in political and ecclesiastical communities only in the modern state, and, in the private economy, only in the most advanced institutions of capitalism. Permanent and public office authority, with fixed jurisdiction, is not the historical rule but rather the exception. This is so even in large political structures such as those of the ancient Orient, the Germanic and Mongolian empires of conquest, or of many feudal structures of state. In all these cases, the ruler executes the most important measures through personal trustees, table-companions, or court-servants. Their commissions and authority are not precisely delimited and are temporarily called into being for each case.

II. The principles of office hierarchy and of levels of graded authority mean a firmly ordered system of super- and subordination in which there is a supervision of the lower offices by the higher ones.

Such a system offers the governed the possibility of appealing the decision of a lower office to its higher authority, in a definitely regulated manner. With the full development of the bureaucratic type, the office hierarchy is monocratically organized. The principle of hierarchical office authority is found in all bureaucratic structures: in state and ecclesiastical structures as well as in large party organizations and private enterprises. It does not matter for the character of bureaucracy whether its authority is called "private" or "public."

When the principle of jurisdictional "competency" is fully carried through, hierarchical subordination—at least in public office—does not mean that the "higher" authority is simply authorized to take over the business of the "lower." Indeed, the opposite is the rule. Once established and having fulfilled its task, an office tends to continue in existence and be held by another incumbent.

III. The management of the modern office is based upon written documents ("the files"), which are preserved in their original or draught form. There is, therefore, a staff of subaltern officials and scribes of all sorts. The body of officials actively engaged in a "public" office, along with the respective apparatus of material implements and the files, make up a "bureau." In private enterprise, "the bureau" is often called "the office."

In principle, the modern organization of the civil service separates the bureau from the private domicile of the official, and, in general, bureaucracy segregates official activity as something distinct from the sphere of private life. Public monies and equipment are divorced from the private property of the official. This condition is everywhere the product of a long development. Nowadays, it is found in public as well as in private enterprises; in the latter, the principle extends even to the leading entrepreneur. In principle, the executive office is separated from the household, business from private correspondence, and business assets from private fortunes. The more consistently the modern type of business management has been carried through the more are these separations the case. The beginnings of this process are to be found as early as the Middle Ages.

It is the peculiarity of the modern entrepreneur that he conducts himself as the "first official" of his enterprise, in the very same way in which the ruler of a specifically modern bureaucratic state spoke of himself as "the first servant" of the state. The idea that the bureau activities of the state are intrinsically different in character from the management of private economic offices is a continental European notion and, by way of contrast, is totally foreign to the American way.

IV. Office management, at least all specialized office management—and such management is distinctly modern—usually presupposes thorough and expert training. This increasingly holds for the modern executive and employee of private enterprises, in the same manner as it holds for the state official.

V. When the office is fully developed, official activity demands the full working capacity of the official, irrespective of the fact that his obligatory time in the bureau may be firmly delimited. In the normal case, this is only the product of a long development, in the public as well as in the private office. Formerly, in all cases, the normal state of affairs was reversed: official business was discharged as a secondary activity.

VI. The management of the office follows general rules, which are more or less stable, more or less exhaustive, and which can be learned. Knowledge of these rules represents a special technical learning which the officials possess. It involves jurisprudence, or administrative or business management.

The reduction of modern office management to rules is deeply embedded in its very nature. The theory of modern public administration, for instance, assumes that the authority to order certain matters by decree—which has been legally granted to public authorities—does not entitle the bureau to regulate the matter by commands given for each case, but only to regulate the matter abstractly. This stands in extreme contrast to the regulation of all relationships through individual privileges and bestowals of favor, which is absolutely dominant in patrimonialism, at least in so far as such relationships are not fixed by sacred tradition.

THE POSITION OF THE OFFICIAL

All this results in the following for the internal and external position of the official:

I. Office holding is a "vocation." This is shown, first, in the requirement of a firmly prescribed course of training, which demands the entire capacity for work for a long period of time, and in the generally prescribed and special examinations which are prerequisites of employment. Furthermore, the position of the official is in the nature of a duty. This determines the internal structure of his relations, in the following manner: Legally and actually, office holding is not considered a source to be exploited for rents or emoluments, as was normally the case during the Middle Ages and frequently up to the threshold of recent times. Nor is office holding considered a usual exchange of services for equivalents, as is the case with free labor contracts. Entrance into an office, including one in the private economy, is considered an acceptance of a specific obligation of faithful management in return for a secure existence. It is decisive for the specific nature of modern loyalty to an office that, in the pure type, it does not establish a relationship to a *person*, like the vassal's or disciple's faith in feudal or in patrimonial relations of authority. Modern loyalty is devoted to impersonal and functional purposes. Behind the functional purposes, of course, "ideas of culture-values" usually stand. These are *ersatz* for the earthly or supra-mundane personal master: ideas such as "state," "church," "community," "party," or "enterprise" are thought of as being realized in a community; they provide an idealogical halo for the master.

The political official—at least in the fully developed modern state—is not considered the personal servant of a ruler. Today, the bishop, the priest, and the preacher are in fact no longer, as in early Christian times, holders of purely personal charisma. The supra-mundane and sacred values which they offer are given to everybody who seems to be worthy of them and who asks for them. In former times, such leaders acted upon the personal command of their master; in principle, they were responsible only to him. Nowadays, in spite of the partial survival of the old theory, such religious leaders are officials in the service of a functional purpose, which in the present-day "church" has become routinized and, in turn, ideologically hallowed.

II. The personal position of the official is patterned in the following way:

1. Whether he is in a private office or a public bureau, the modern official always strives and usually enjoys a distinct *social esteem* as compared with the governed. His social position is guaranteed by the prescriptive rules of rank order and, for the political official, by special definitions of the criminal code against "insults of officials" and "contempt" of state and church authorities.

The actual social position of the official is normally highest where, as in old civilized countries, the following conditions prevail: a strong demand for administration by trained experts; a strong and stable social differentiation, where the official predominantly derives from socially and economically privileged strata because of the social distribution of power; or where the costliness of the required training and status conventions are binding upon him. The possession of educational certificates—to be discussed elsewhere—are usually linked with qualification for office. Naturally, such certificates or patents enhance the "status element" in the social position of the official. For the rest this status factor in individual cases is explicitly and impassively acknowledged, for example, in the prescription that the acceptance or rejection of an aspirant to an official career depends upon the consent ("election") of the members of the official body. This is the case in the German army with the officer corps. Similar phenomena, which promote this guild-like closure of officialdom, are typically found in patrimonial and, particularly, in prebendal officialdoms of the past. The desire to resurrect such phenomena in changed forms is by no means infrequent among modern bureaucrats. For instance, they have played a role among the demands of the quite proletarian and expert officials (the *tretyj* element) during the Russian revolution.

Usually the social esteem of the officials as such is especially low where the demand for expert administration and the dominance of status conventions are weak. This is especially the case in the United States; it is often the case in new settlements by virtue of their wide fields for profit-making and the great instability of their social stratification.

2. The pure type of bureaucratic official is *appointed* by a superior authority. An official elected by the governed is not a purely bureaucratic figure. Of course, the formal existence of an election does not by itself mean that no appointment hides behind the election—in the state, especially, appointment by party chiefs. Whether or not this is the case does not depend upon legal statutes but upon the way in which the party mechanism functions. Once firmly organized, the parties can turn a formally free election into the mere acclamation of a candidate designated by the party chief. As a rule, however, a formally free election is turned into a fight, conducted according to definite rules, for votes in favor of one of two designated candidates.

In all circumstances, the designation of officials by means of an election among the governed modifies the strictness of hierarchical subordination. In principle, an official who is so elected has an autonomous position opposite the superordinate official. The elected official does not derive his position "from above" but "from below," or at least not from a superior authority of the official hierarchy but from powerful party men ("bosses"), who also determine his further career. The career of the elected official is not, or at least not primarily, dependent upon his chief in the administration. The official who is not elected but appointed by a chief normally functions more exactly, from a technical point of view, because, all other circumstances being equal, it is more likely that purely functional points of consideration and qualities will determine his selection and career. As laymen, the governed can become acquainted with the extent to which a candidate is expertly qualified for office only in terms of experience, and hence only after his service. Moreover, in every sort of selection of officials by election, parties quite naturally give decisive weight not to expert considerations but to the services a follower renders to the party boss. This holds for all kinds of procurement of officials by elections, for the designation of formally free, elected officials by party bosses when they determine the slate of candidates, or the free appointment by a chief who has himself been elected. The contrast, however, is relative: substantially similar conditions hold where legitimate monarchs and their subordinates appoint officials, except that the influence of the followings are then less controllable.

When the demand for administration by trained experts is considerable, and the party followings have to recognize an intellectually developed, educated, and freely moving "public opinion," the use of unqualified officials falls back upon the party in power at the next election. Naturally, this is more likely to happen when the officials are appointed by the chief. The demand for a trained administration now exists in the United States, but in the large cities, where immigrant votes are "corraled," there is, of course, no educated public opinion. Therefore, popular elections of the administrative chief and also of his subordinate officials usually endanger the expert qualification of the official as well as the precise functioning of the bureaucratic mechanism. It also weakens the dependence of the officials upon the hierarchy. This holds at least for the large administrative bodies that are difficult to supervise. The superior qualification and integrity of federal judges, appointed by the President, as over against elected judges in the United States is well known, although both types of officials have been selected primarily in terms of party considerations. The great changes in American metropolitan administrations demanded by reformers have proceeded essentially from elected mayors working with an apparatus of officials who were appointed by them. These reforms have thus come about in a "Caesarist" fashion. Viewed technically, as an organized form of authority, the efficiency of "Caesarism," which often grows out of democracy, rests in general upon the position of the "Caesar" as a free trustee of the masses (of the army or of the citizenry), who is unfettered by tradition. The "Caesar" is thus the unrestrained master of a body of highly qualified military officers and officials whom he selects freely and personally without regard to tradition or to any other considerations. This, "rule of the personal genius," however, stands in contradiction to the formally "democratic" principle of a universally elected officialdom.

3. Normally, the position of the official is held for life, at least in public bureaucracies; and this is increasingly the case for all similar structures. As a factual rule, *tenure for life* is presupposed, even where the giving of notice or periodic reappointment occurs. In contrast to the worker in a private enterprise, the official normally holds tenure. Legal or actual life-tenure, however, is not recognized as the official's right to the possession of office, as was the case with many structures of authority in the past. Where legal guarantees against arbitrary dismissal or transfer are developed, they merely serve to guarantee a strictly objective discharge of specific office duties free from all personal considerations. In Germany, this is the case for all juridical and, increasingly, for all administrative officials.

Within the bureaucracy, therefore, the measure of "independence," legally guaranteed by tenure, is not always a source of increased status for the official whose position is thus secured. Indeed, often the reverse holds, especially in old cultures and communities that are highly differentiated. In such communities, the stricter the subordination under the arbitrary rule of the master, the more it guarantees the maintenance of the conventional seigneurial style of living for the official. Because of the very absence of these legal guarantees of tenure, the conventional esteem for the official may rise in the same way as, during the Middle Ages, the esteem of the nobility of office rose at the expense of esteem for the freemen, and as the king's judge surpassed that of the people's judge. In Germany, the military officer or the administrative official can be removed from office at any time, or at least far more readily than the "independent judge," who never pays with loss of his office for even the grossest offense against the "code of honor" or against social conventions of the salon. For this very reason, if other things are equal, in the eyes of the master stratum the judge is considered less qualified for social intercourse than are officers and administrative officials, whose greater dependence on the master is a greater guarantee of their conformity with status conventions. Of course, the average official strives for a civil-service law, which would materially secure his old age and provide increased guarantees against his arbitrary removal from office. This striving, however, has its limits. A very strong development of the "right to the office" naturally makes it more difficult to staff them with regard to technical efficiency, for such a development decreases the career-opportunities of ambitious candidates for office. This makes for the fact that officials, on the whole, do not feel their dependency upon those at the top. This lack of feeling of dependency, however, rests primarily upon the inclination to depend upon one's equals rather than upon the socially inferior and governed strata. The present conservative movement among the Badenia clergy, occasioned by the anxiety of a presumably threatening separation of church and state, has been expressly determined by the desire not to be turned "from a master into a servant of the parish."

4. The official receives the regular *pecuniary* compensation of a normally fixed *salary* and the old age security provided by a pension. The salary is not measured like a wage in terms of work done, but according to "status," that is, according to the kind of function (the "rank") and, in addition, possibly, according to the length of service. The relatively great security of the official's income, as well as the rewards of social esteem, make the office a sought-after position, especially in countries which no longer provide opportunities for colonial profits. In such countries, this situation permits relatively low salaries for officials.

5. The official is set for a "*career*" within the hierarchical order of the public service. He moves from the lower, less important, and lower paid to the higher positions. The average official naturally desires a mechanical fixing of the conditions of promotion: if not of the offices, at least of the salary levels. He wants these conditions fixed in terms of "seniority," or possibly according to grades achieved in a developed system of expert examinations. Here and there, such examinations actually form a character *indelebilis* of the official and have lifelong effects on his career. To this is joined the desire to qualify the right to office and the increasing tendency toward status group closure and economic security. All of this makes for a tendency to consider the offices as "prebends" of those who are qualified by educational certificates. The necessity of taking general personal and intellectual qualifications into consideration, irrespective of the often subaltern character of the educational certificate, has led to a condition in which the highest political offices, especially the positions of "ministers," are principally filled without reference to such certificates.

• • • • •

TECHNICAL ADVANTAGES OF BUREAUCRATIC ORGANIZATION

The decisive reason for the advance of bureaucratic organization has always been its purely technical superiority over any other form of organization. The fully developed bureaucratic mechanism compares with other organizations exactly as does the machine with the non-mechanical modes of production.

Precision, speed, unambiguity, knowledge of the files, continuity, discretion, unity, strict subordination, reduction of friction and of material and personal costs —these are raised to the optimum point in the strictly bureaucratic administration, and especially in its monocratic form. As compared with all collegiate, honorific, and avocational forms of administration, trained bureaucracy is superior on all these points. And as far as complicated tasks are concerned, paid bureaucratic work is not only more precise but, in the last analysis, it is often cheaper than even formally unremunerated honorific service.

Honorific arrangements make administrative work an avocation and, for this reason alone, honorific service normally functions more slowly; being less bound to schemata and being more formless. Hence it is less precise and less unified than bureaucratic work because it is less dependent upon superiors and because the establishment and exploitation of the apparatus of subordinate officials and filing services are almost unavoidably less economical. Honorific service is less continuous than bureaucratic and frequently quite expensive. This is especially the case if one thinks not only of the money costs to the public treasury—costs which bureaucratic administration, in comparison with administration by notables, usually substantially increases—but also of the frequent economic losses of the governed caused by delays and lack of precision. The possibility of administration by notables normally and permanently exists only where official management can be satisfactorily discharged as an avocation. With the qualitative increase of tasks the administration has to face, administration by notables reaches its limits—today, even in England. Work organized by collegiate bodies causes friction and delay and requires compromises between colliding interests and views. The administration, therefore, runs less precisely and is more independent of superiors; hence, it is less unified and slower. All advances of the Prussian administrative organization have been and will in the future be advances of the bureaucratic, and especially of the monocratic, principle.

Today, it is primarily the capitalist market economy which demands that the official business of the administration be discharged precisely, unambiguously, continuously, and with as much speed as possible. Normally, the very large, modern capitalist enterprises are themselves unequalled models of strict bureaucratic organization. Business management throughout rests on increasing precision, steadiness, and, above all, the speed of operations. This, in turn, is determined by the peculiar nature of the modern means of communication, including, among other things, the news service of the press. The extraordinary increase in the speed by which public announcements, as well as economic and political facts, are transmitted exerts a steady and sharp pressure in the direction of speeding up the tempo of administrative reaction towards various situations. The optimum of such reaction time is normally attained only by a strictly bureaucratic organization.[1]

Bureaucratization offers above all the optimum possibility for carrying through the principle of specializing administrative functions according to purely objective considerations. Individual performances are allocated to functionaries who

[1] Here we cannot discuss in detail how the bureaucratic apparatus may, and actually does, produce definite obstacles to the discharge of business in a manner suitable for the single case.

have specialized training and who by constant practice learn more and more. The "objective" discharge of business primarily means a discharge of business according to *calculable rules* and "without regard for persons."

"Without regard for persons" is also the watchword of the "market" and, in general, of all pursuits of naked economic interests. A consistent execution of bureaucratic domination means the leveling of status "honor." Hence, if the principle of the free-market is not at the same time restricted, it means the universal domination of the "class situation." That this consequence of bureaucratic domination has not set in everywhere, parallel to the extent of bureaucratization, is due to the differences among possible principles by which polities may meet their demands.

The second element mentioned, "calculable rules," also is of paramount importance for modern bureaucracy. The peculiarity of modern culture, and specifically of its technical and economic basis, demands this very "calculability" of results. When fully developed, bureaucracy also stands, in a specific sense, under the principle of *sine ira ac studio.* Its specific nature, which is welcomed by capitalism, develops the more perfectly the more the bureaucracy is "dehumanized," the more completely it succeeds in eliminating from official business love, hatred, and all purely personal, irrational, and emotional elements which escape calculation. This is the specific nature of bureaucracy and it is appraised as its special virtue.

The more complicated and specialized modern culture becomes, the more its external supporting apparatus demands the personally detached and strictly "objective" *expert,* in lieu of the master of older social structures, who was moved by personal sympathy and favor, by grace and gratitude. Bureaucracy offers the attitudes demanded by the external apparatus of modern culture in the most favorable combination.

51 The Outskirts of Hope

MARY W. WRIGHT

The preceding selection shows the sociologist at his purely rational and dispassionate best. The selection that follows illustrates the social worker's unique blend of reason and compassion; his persistence in dealing with bureaucratic complexities and realistic helpfulness to his troubled clients. Weber's classic analysis stresses the virtues of bureaucracy. Mary W. Wright's case report shows the human suffering it produces when it functions badly. A telling phrase of Lyndon B. Johnson about the people who live on "the outskirts of hope" gave the title to "this factual account of one day in and out of a welfare office" in the southern mountains.

. . . I know a man, I'll call him Buddy Banks. He lives in a ravine in a little one-room pole-and-cardboard house he built himself, with his wife, their six children, and baby granddaughter. Mr. Banks, 45 years old, is a sober man, a kindly man, and a passive man. He can read and write a little, has worked in the coal mines and on farms, but over the years he's been pretty badly battered up and today is "none too stout." Last fall, when he could no longer pay the rent where he was staying, his mother-in-law gave him a small piece of ground, and he hastened to put up this little shack in the woods before the snow came. If, as you ride by, you happened to glance down and see where he lives, and see his children playing among the stones, you would say, "White trash." You would say, "Welfare bums."

When the newspaper announced the new ADC program for unemployed fathers, I thought of Buddy Banks. There is not much farm work to be done in the wintertime, and Mr. Banks has been without a job since summer. Here in their ravine they can dig their coal from a hole in the hill, and dip their water from the creek, and each month he scratches together $2 for his food stamps by doing odd jobs for his neighbors, who are very nearly as poor as he is. Other than that there is nothing coming in. I thought, maybe here is some help for Buddy Banks.

Mr. Banks does not get a newspaper, nor does he have a radio, and so he had not heard about the new program. He said, yes, he would be interested. I offered to take him to town right then, but he said no, he would have to clean up first, he couldn't go to town looking like this. So I agreed to come back Friday.

On Friday he told me he'd heard today was the last day for signing up. We were lucky, eh? It wasn't true, but it's what he had heard and I wondered, suppose he'd been told last Tuesday was the last day for signing up, and I hadn't been there to say, well, let's go find out anyway.

Buddy Banks was all fixed up and looked nice as he stepped out of his cabin. His jacket was clean, and he had big rubber boots on and a cap on his head. I felt proud walking along with him, and he walked proud. (Later, in town, I noticed how the hair curled over

SOURCE: *Mountain Life and Work*, vol. 40, no. 1 (Spring 1964), 10–15. • Mary W. Wright was trained as a social worker and was employed at a Presbyterian school and orphanage located at Buckhorn, Kentucky, when this article was written. More recently she has lived in Castries, on the island of St. Lucia, West Indies, where her husband, W. Manson Toynbee, is head of the St. Lucia Teachers College.

his collar, and the gray look about him, and the stoop of his shoulders. If you saw him you'd have said, "Country boy, come to get his check.")

When we reached the Welfare Office it was full of people, a crowd of slouchy, shuffly men, standing around and looking vaguely in different directions. I followed Buddy Banks and his brother-in-law, who had asked to come with us, into the lobby, and they too stood in the middle of the floor. Just stood. It was not the momentary hesitation that comes before decision. It was the paralysis of strangeness, of lostness, of not knowing what to do. A girl was sitting at a table, and after a number of minutes of nothing, I quietly suggested they ask her. No, they told me, that was the food stamp girl. But there was no other. So finally, when I suggested, well, ask her anyway, they nodded their heads, moved over, and asked her. I wondered how long they might have gone on standing there, if I'd kept my mouth shut. I wondered how long the others all around us had been standing there. I had an idea that if I hadn't been right in the way, Buddy Banks just might have turned around and gone out the door when he saw the crowd, the lines, and that smartly-dressed food stamp girl bending over her desk.

Yes, he was told, and after waiting a few minutes, he was shown behind the rail to a chair beside a desk, and a man with a necktie and a big typewriter began to talk with him. They talked a long time, while the brother-in-law and I waited in the lobby. (They had asked the brother-in-law if he had brought the birth certificates. No, he hadn't, and so they said there wasn't anything they could do, to come back next Tuesday. He said nothing, stared at them a moment, then walked away. He stood around waiting for us all day long and never asked them another question. He said he would tend to it some other time. Fortunately, they got Mr. Banks sitting down before they inquired about the birth certificates.)

I knew what they were talking about: I have talked long times with Mr. Banks myself, and they were going over it again, and again, and I could imagine Mr. Banks nodding his head to the question he didn't quite understand, because he wanted to make a good impression, and it would be a little while before the worker realized that he hadn't understood, and so they would go back and try again, and then Mr. Banks would explain as best he could, but he would leave something out, and then the worker wouldn't understand, so that, in all, their heads were bent together for almost an hour and a half. It seemed a long time to take to discover Buddy Bank's need—a visit to his home would have revealed it in a very few minutes, but of course twelve miles out and twelve miles back takes time too, and there are all those eligibility rules to be checked out, lest somebody slip them a lie and the editorials start hollering "Fraud! Fraud!" Actually, I was impressed that the worker would give him that much time. It *takes* time to be sympathetic, to listen, to hear —to understand a human condition.

At last he came out, and with an apologetic grin he said he must return on Tuesday, he must go home and get the birth certificates. Then they would let him apply. (How will you come back, Mr. Banks? Where will you get the $3 for taxi fare by next Tuesday? Perhaps you could scrape it up by Monday week, but suppose you come on Monday week and your worker isn't here? Then perhaps you won't come back at all. . . .)

While Mr. Banks was busy talking, I was chatting with one of the other workers. Because I am a social worker too, I can come and go through the little iron gate, and they smile at me and say, "Well, *hello* there!" We talked about all the work she has to do, and one of the things she told me was how, often, to save time, they send people down to the Health Department to get their own birth records. Then they can come back and apply the same day. I wondered why Mr. Bank's worker never suggested this. Maybe he never thought of it. (Maybe he doesn't live twelve miles out with no car, and the nearest bus eight miles from home. And no bus fare at that.) Or perhaps he *did* mention it, and Mr. Banks never heard him, because his head was already filled up with the words that went before: "Im sorry, there's nothing we can do until you bring us the birth certificates," and he was trying to think in which box, under which bed, had the children been into them . . . ?

So I tried to suggest to him that we go now to the Health Department, but he didn't hear me either. He said, and he persisted, I'm going to the Court House, I'll be right back, will you wait for me? I tried to stop him: let's plan something, what we're going to do next, it's almost lunchtime and things will close up—until suddenly I realized that after the time and the tension of the morning, this was no doubt a call of nature that could not wait for reasonable planning, nor could a proud man come out and ask if there might not be a more accessible solution. And so, as he headed quickly away for the one sure place he knew, I stood mute and waited while he walked the three blocks there and the three blocks back. I wonder if that's something anybody ever thinks about when they're interviewing clients.

Mr. Banks and I had talked earlier about the Manpower Redevelopment Vocational Training Programs, and he had seemed interested. "I'd sure rather work and look after my family than mess with all this stuff, but what can I do? I have no education." I told him about the courses and he said, yes, I'd like that. And so we planned to look into this too, while we were in town. But by now Mr. Banks was ready to go home. "I hate all this standing around. I'd work two days rather than stand around like this." It wasn't really the standing around he minded. It was the circumstances of the standing around. It took some persuading to get him back into the building, only to be told—at 11:30—to come back at ten to one. (Suppose his ride, I thought, had been with somebody busier than I. Suppose they couldn't wait till ten to one and kept badgering him, "Come on, Buddy, hurry up, will you? We ain't got all day!")

I tried to suggest some lunch while we waited, but they didn't want lunch. "We had breakfast late; I'm not hungry, really." So instead, I took him around to the Health Department and the Circuit Court and the County Court, and we verified everything, although he needed some help to figure which years the children were born in.

At ten to one he was again outside the Welfare Office, and he drew me aside and said that he'd been thinking: maybe he should go home and talk this whole thing over a little more. He felt that before jumping into something, he should know better what it was all about. This startled me, for I wondered what that hour and a half had been for, if now, after everything, he felt he must return to his cronies up the creek to find out what it all meant. So we stood aside, and I interpreted the program as best I could, whom it was for and what it required, and what it would do for him and his family, while he stood, nodding his head and staring at the sidewalk. Finally, cautiously, almost grimly, he once again pushed his way into that crowded, smoke-filled lobby.

"Those who are to report at one o'clock, stand in this line. Others in that line." Mr. Banks stood in the one o'clock line. At 1:15 he reached the counter. I don't know what he asked, but I saw the man behind the desk point over toward the other side of the building, the Public Assistance side, where Mr. Banks had already spent all morning. Mr. Banks nodded his head and turned away as he was told to do. At that point I butted in. "Assistance for the unemployed is over there," the man said and pointed again. So I mentioned training. "He wants training? Why didn't he say so? He's in the wrong line." I don't know what Mr. Banks had said, but what *does* a person say when he's anxious, and tired and confused, and a crowd of others, equally anxious, are pushing from behind and the man at the counter says, "Yes?" I butted in and Mr. Banks went to stand in the right line, but I wondered what the man behind us did, who didn't have anybody to butt in for him.

While Mr. Banks was waiting, to save time, I took the birth certificates to his worker on the other side. I walked right in, because I was a social worker and could do that, and he talked to me right away and said, "Yes, yes, this is good. This will save time. No, he won't have to come back on Tuesday. Yes, he can apply today. Just have him come back over here when he is through over there. Very good."

At 1:30 Buddy Banks reached the counter again, was given a card and told to go sit on a chair until his name was called. I had business at 2:00 and returned at 3:00, and there he was, sitting on the same chair. But I learned as I sat beside him that things had been happening. He had talked with the training counsellor, returned to his welfare worker, and was sent back to the unemployment counsellor, after which he was to return once more to his welfare worker. I asked what he had learned about the training. "There's nothing right now, maybe later." Auto mechanics? Bench work? Need too much education. There may be something about washing cars, changing oil, things like that. Later on. Did you sign up for anything? No. Did they say they'd let you know? No. How will you know? I don't know.

At last his ADC (Unemployed) application was signed, his cards were registered, his name was in the file. Come back in two weeks and we'll see if you're eligible. (How will you get back, Buddy? I'll find a way.)

It was four o'clock. "Well, that's over." And he said, "I suppose a fellow's got to go through all that, but I'd sure rather be a-working than a-fooling around with all that mess." We went out to the car, and I took him home. "I sure do thank you, though," he said.

While I'd been waiting there in the lobby, I saw another man come up to the counter. He was small and middle-aged, with a wedding band on his finger, and his face was creased with lines of care. I saw him speak quietly to the man across the desk. I don't know what he said or what the problem was, but they talked a moment and the official told him, "Well, if you're disabled for work, then there's no use asking about training," and he put up his hands and turned away to the papers on his desk. The man waited there a moment, then slowly turned around and stood in the middle of the floor. He lifted his head to stare up at the wall, the blank wall, and his blue eyes were held wide open to keep the tears from coming. I couldn't help watching him, and when suddenly he looked at me, his eyes straight into mine, I couldn't help asking him—across the wide distance of the crowd that for just an instant vanished into the intimacy of human communion—I asked, "Trouble?" Almost as if he were reaching out his hands, he answered me and said, "I just got the news from Washington and come to sign up, and . . ." but then, embarrassed to be talking to a stranger, he mumbled something else I couldn't understand, turned his back to me, stood another long moment in the middle of the crowd, and then walked out the door.

Disabled or not disabled. Employed or not employed. In need or not in need. Yes or no. Black or white. Answer the question. Stand in line.

It is not the program's fault. You have to have questionnaires, and questionnaires require a yes or no. There is no space for a maybe, but . . .

Nor is it the people-who-work-there's fault, for who can see—or take time to see—the whole constellation of people and pressures, needs and perplexities, desires and dreads that walk into an office in the person of one shuffling, bedraggled man—especially when there are a hundred other bedraggled men waiting behind him? You ask the questions and await the answers. What else can you do?

Then perhaps it is the fault of the man himself, the man who asks—or doesn't quite know how to ask—for help. Indeed, he's called a lazy cheat if he does, and an unmotivated ignorant fool if he doesn't. It must be his own fault.

Or maybe it's nobody's fault. It's just the way things are. . . .

52 Roles and Marital Adjustment

LEONARD S. COTTRELL, JR.

Institutions develop around the necessity for humans to fulfill basic and persistent social needs. Sometimes institutional experience is unsatisfying, however, and the effective operation of the institution is jeopardized, because the roles persons have learned to play and which they bring to the institution are not suited to the institutional situation in which they find themselves. Or, equally disruptive to individual and group, the expectations of persons regarding the behavior of others in the institution are unfulfilled. In this selection L. S. Cottrell, Jr., discusses the importance of an understanding of role-behavior and role-expectation in studying the adjustment of husbands and wives to the institutions of marriage and the family.

There are certain points concerning the concept of the rôle which, though recognized by those who developed and refined the concept, need for our purposes added emphasis.

First, in our use of the concept rôle we are prone to think of certain characteristic responses or tendencies to respond which the person makes or tends to make to persons or situations. Frequently we fail to recognize clearly enough what might be called expectations entertained by the subject as to actions or responses which are to come from other persons. The writer recognizes that it is impossible to separate these two things since in reality they are aspects of the same thing. There is no conception of one's rôle, conscious or unconscious, without reference to what action is expected of the situation of which the rôle is a part. It is well, however, to emphasize the expectancy aspect, particularly in using the notion in the study of marriage situations. A number of our cases of marital difficulty seem capable of analysis in terms of the inability of one mate to fit into the expected response pattern called for by the other.

A second point to be called to mind is that in marriage the partners do not play single rôles with respect to one another, although a single rôle may be most characteristic of a given person in his marriage relations. Cases seem to indicate a multiplicity of rôles. For example, a wife may play a much depended upon mother-rôle, a hated sister-rôle, and a loved brother-rôle at different times for her husband. The husband may in turn be for his wife her distantly respected father, her hated younger brother, and her loved older sister. The startling ambivalence frequently displayed by married persons for one another may not be true ambivalence in the strict Freudian sense. It may actually be the result of corresponding attitudes for different rôle patterns derived from early family relations. Thus a husband may call out affectionate as well as hostile responses from

SOURCE: Publication of the American Sociological Society, vol. 27, no. 2, *Papers* (May 1933), 108–15, University of Chicago Press. Reprinted by permission of the author and the publisher.
• Leonard S. Cottrell, Jr., is professor of social psychology at the University of North Carolina. He is a former president of the American Sociological Association and is a consultant to Scott, Foresman, and Company. Among his books are *Delinquency Areas* and *Developments in Social Psychology.* He is the coauthor of *Identity and Interpersonal Competence: New Directions in Family Research* and the coeditor of *Sociology Today.*

his wife by playing rôles of members of her family who earlier called out the different responses. Of course it is not at all necessary nor even likely that either husband or wife will be aware that he is playing such rôles.

A third point to be mentioned is that rôles may be stereotyped and unique. The stereotyped rôles, for example, of husband and father, wife and mother, are defined in the folkways and mores of society. But within these definitions by a given culture there are individual patterns or rôles that are determined by the peculiar social experience of the individual. Thus an adult may continue to play an infantile rôle as a result, let us say, of his having been the youngest child in a family that has coddled him a great deal.

A fourth point which needs emphasis is that, frequently, we might say usually, many of the rôles that persons play are unconscious. If all of the rôles a married pair play for one another are not unconscious, the most significant ones are frequently so.

We shall not here attempt an exegesis of the conception of the unconscious. It is sufficient for our purposes to realize that, if we analyze any act or series of actions, we find that there are phases of the act which can be said to be unknown to the actor, and are, moreover, not subject to his unaided conscious scrutiny and reflection. The conscious phase of the act in which the individual has defined for himself or has defined for him his objects and purposes and motives is one phase only. There are preliminary to and concomitant with his acts, goals, motives, etc., of which he is unconscious. Examples might be taken from the cases cited by Mr. H. D. Lasswell in his *Psychopathology and Politics* in which the conscious political activity directed against a present order turns out to be a displacement of drives and hostilities of the child with respect to its parent or sibling. Of these more primary and elementary motives the person is not aware and accepts his own definitions of goals and reasons as the only ones present in the action. Our contention here is that the same kind of unconscious character can be attributed to much of marital activity.

There may be some objection to thinking of rôles as unconscious. We do not hold that all rôles are unconscious. Some seem to be completely unconscious; some only partially so. We are not wedded to a word. If the term "rôle" is to be used only for conscious action patterns and relationships, then we must give another name to these unconscious patterns and relationships that exist in fact.

The narrowed angle of approach represented in this paper, namely, the study of marriage as an adjustment of rôles, may be indicated by laying down certain propositions.

First, marriage adjustment may be regarded as a process in which marriage partners attempt to re-enact certain relational systems or situations which obtained in their own earlier family groups. Or, in other words, marriage partners tend to play the habitual rôles they evolved in their childhood and adolescence.

Second, the kinds of rôles that marriage partners bring to the marriage will determine the nature of their marriage relationship and the degree of adjustment that they will achieve.

Third, that maladjusted marriages may be regarded as results of the failure of the marriage situation to provide the system of relationships called for by the rôles which the marriage partners bring to the marriage.

Now the writer is quite aware that these propositions leave out of account a great many important factors—cultural, economic, etc.—and there is no effort to deny that such factors are of importance. Let it be emphatically affirmed that these propositions are laid down in an effort to make a logical delimitation of the problem. However, there is considerable justification for the opinion that the unique rôle patterns are the chief determinants of the success or failure of marriages in which the persons come from similar cultural backgrounds. And it should not be forgotten that the greater number of marriages are contracted by persons of reasonably similar cultural backgrounds.

Let us consider the case of Mr. and Mrs. A. who have been married about a year.

Mr. A. (aged 24) is the youngest of a family of seven. When asked to tell about his childhood, he launches into a rather enthusiastic account of his happy and satisfactory family life. From his story one gathers that his mother was a powerful and aggressive personality, the chief center, drive, and control factor in the family. She ran the father's affairs, planned the children's vocational and social activities, maneuvered the daughters' marriages, and tried to maneuver the sons' marriages. Mr. A. boasts of her iron will. He is proud of her determined look, and tells how her spirit never sagged. He tells how she faced death with the same unshaken will and determination never to admit defeat.

The father is described as a pleasant, reliable, steady, quiet, and meek person who seemed to figure merely as an unimportant though kindly fixture in the household. He worked steadily, turned his earnings over to his wife, never seriously opposed her, and after her death, agreeably allowed his daughters to place him in an old people's home.

The three sisters are described as being very much like the mother, particularly the two older ones. These two have married husbands to whom they play pretty much the same rôle which their mother played toward her husband. The youngest sister, whom we shall call Martha, is two years older than Mr. A. Although not quite so Amazonian as her sisters, she is fairly aggressive, active, and adequate in meeting situations. She has played a decidedly mothering rôle to Mr. A., especially since the death of their mother when Mr. A. was about fifteen years old. He says of Martha in an interview, "We have always been very close together. She has comforted me and consoled me in my troubles. I have confided in her and she has shielded me. She used to advise me and tell me what to do." He used to sleep with his sister, and he tells of his surprise on discovering recently that people thought such an arrangement strange. He says: "Even after I was 16 or 17 if I was blue or worried about my future she would take me to bed with her and comfort me." This occurred more frequently after the mother's death. Soon after his marriage he felt he *had* to leave his wife, to get away and think things out. He went home for a visit. The first few days he was very worried and upset. He couldn't sleep at night and one night fell to weeping. Martha took him to bed with her and consoled him. He says: "I felt a motherly warmth and felt released from my troubles and went to sleep. After that I slept in her room every night and felt much better." Mr. A. denies ever having sexual impulses or ideas about Martha at any time, although they have discussed sex quite freely.

In speaking of all the sisters he says: "I was always proud to go places with my sisters. They were lively and popular and I was proud of them. I could walk around and enjoy myself and they could take care of themselves." (This was said in comparing his sisters with his wife, who depends too much on him, he says, for pleasant times at social gatherings.)

Mr. A. does not feel that there was much conflict in his home. Things seemed to be secure and to run smoothly under the orderly supervision of the mother. He feels that the home life was happy. He says: "There was always something going on at my home. My mother and sisters were always doing interesting things, having people over and having jolly times that I like to remember. They didn't sit around like she does (alluding to his wife) and wait for something to happen. My father is quiet and never participated much in what was going on, but he enjoyed watching and listening to other people. I am like my father. I liked to watch and listen, and, if I felt like it, put in a word or do something. I hate to feel I have to talk or take the initiative." (This remark also was made with reference to his wife's irritating dependence upon him.)

Mr. A.'s two brothers are interesting. The older brother, who is also the oldest child, is called the black sheep. His relations with the mother and with the sister next to him were particularly hostile. He rebelled and left home early. The next brother is the middle child. He was the mother's favorite. He was and still is a dependable, quiet, kindly, nonaggressive person. The children say he is the mainstay of the family. Mr. A. describes him as a kind of parent to the younger children.

Mr. A. says that his parents and siblings were always kind to him. "They always took care of me, and my brother told me he would send me to school. My sisters like to have me come to their homes, and they enjoy giving me the comforts of a home. They say, 'You need the comforts of a home'; and I believe they are right, because I often wish I could feel that I had a father and mother and a home I could go back to."

He was punished very little. A typical instance is revealing. His mother and brother scolded him and threatened to punish him for not practicing his music. They told him he should be willing to practice for them if they paid for his lessons. Mr. A.'s comment is interesting: "I remember I was very angry that they should expect anything from me just because they paid for the lessons. I hated to feel obligated." (This represents an attitude characteristic of Mr. A.—that of expecting the environment to minister unto him with no obligation or responsibilities on his part.)

One gets the impression from Mr. A.'s conversation that he was an extremely dependent, much indulged, and coddled child; that he resented any responsibility or expectation or demand from him on the part of the environment; and that he felt insecure in situations where he was thrown on his own initiative. He tended to assume a passive rôle, expecting the environment to furnish aggressive support, backing, and leadership. On several occasions he made what he describes as attempts to win his independency by leaving home. He usually went under the tutelage of a decisive and aggressive boy friend who told him he ought to learn to stand on his own feet. On each occasion when he faced a shortage of jobs or money he felt forced to retreat home. After a few attempts he was ashamed to go home and would retreat to the family of the girl he finally married. He said: "I just can't bear feeling all alone in a strange place with no money and no home I can go to."

Mr. A. met his wife shortly before his mother's death. He says: "I was timid and bashful, but she was pleasant and talked to me and I felt comfortable with her." Soon after Mr. A.'s mother died the girl's family moved to another city. A. wept the night before her departure and said: "First I lose my mother; then I lose you." (The girl had the same first name as Mr. A.'s mother.) He told her he loved her at that time, but felt that he had said more than he meant; and the next day he contrived to arrive at the railroad station too late to see her off. Largely through the girl's efforts, a correspondence was kept up between the two. Later, after some of his unsuccessful forays into the world of affairs, he would seek the shelter of the girl's home. She would be very sympathetic about his trials and tribulations and she readily accepted his alibis for failure and excused him to himself. When she consoled him on his retreats from unsuccessful attempts to make good in the world (which, by the way, he expected to do in short order) he would tell her that she was just like his sister. As he was forced to repeat his returns to the girl's family, he became more and more uncomfortable; for he felt himself more and more obligated to assume responsibilities with respect to the girl. He seemed unable to do without a good deal of sympathetic reassurance; but he became increasingly panicky as it grew more evident that marriage was expected of him.

Before we discuss further the relations between Mr. A. and his wife, it is necessary to describe briefly Mrs. A's family. The families of both Mr. and Mrs. A. represent the same cultural and economic levels; if there is any difference, it is slight and in favor of Mr. A.'s family.

Mrs. A. (aged 23) describes her father as a successful merchant until a few years ago, when he developed an interest in gambling and taking extended vacations. He had never saved money but his business kept the family in good circumstances. For some time now, however, he had been very improvident and irresponsible. He has obtained good positions, but has given them up for very trivial reasons. Mrs. A. says she used to admire and respect her father, but since he has allowed the family to come upon evil days she has lost respect for him and feels very resentful toward him. The father accuses the mother of being responsible for the condition of the family. He says: "You should have taken the money from me and not allowed me to gamble." And "You should have made me attend to our business." Mrs. A. feels her father has acted as something of a spoiled child toward his wife.

The mother is described as patient, long suffering, submissive. Mrs. A. feels that she is close to her mother because, as she says, "I am very much like my mother and can understand her." She has always taken sides with her mother in family arguments, which seems to align the father and older brother against the mother and Mrs. A. These arguments turn out to be tongue lashings from the father and older brother, with the mother and daughter passively resisting.

The oldest brother is very harsh toward the mother, but she submits to his dominating and overbearing treatment. She appears to resent it somewhat, but she excuses him. When he flies into rages and leaves home to avoid paying room and board, the mother will feel sorry for him and will cook up cakes and other dainties, which she carries to his abode and lays at his feet. She treats the father in much the same way, patiently accepting his occasional beratings. When some of the children complain of their father's incompetence the mother will make excuses for him. She will say, "Your father has worked hard all his life and now just look at him. It isn't fair."

There are three children in the family, an oldest son, Mrs. A, and her younger brother. Mrs. A. speaks bitterly of the intense hatred she bears her older brother, who appears from her description to be a very domineering, overbearing, egocentric person. But she follows her statements of hostility toward him with the admission that she secretly admires his aggressiveness and capabilities and envies his assertiveness. She has wished all her life that he would love her. When on rare occasions he would be kind to her or give her a birthday gift, she would feel much encouraged and hope for better relations. She would experience great disappointment when he would resume his usual tactics.

The son's hostilities toward his mother and sister seem to date from early childhood. Mrs. A. has fought back somewhat, but she usually cries, feels blue, and suffers inwardly. She still dreams of having bitter fights with him, but in these dreams her rôle is one of defending herself against his attacks. Occasionally she will dream of a more aggressive rôle in which she vehemently commands her brother to get out of the house. She says that one reason she liked Mr. A. was that he seemed to be the opposite of her brother in every way.

Mrs. A. is fond of her younger brother and feels that they were quite close as children, though their relationship is not so close now.

Mrs. A.'s conversation gives one the impression of a person with some hostile drives, who, nevertheless, tends to assume a passive rôle in all situations. She tends to wait for something to happen, for others to make suggestions and to take the initiative. Her lack of decisive self-assertion is a characteristic which drives her husband, so he says, to distraction.

With this all too meager account of the backgrounds of our subjects, let us turn again to their relationship with one another.

Mr. A. became more and more frightened and restless as it became clearer to him that the natural and expected result of his relationship to Mrs. A. was marriage. He made some attempts to extricate himself by protesting to her that they were in no position to marry and by leaving her home. Quoting from an interview with him: "I wanted to be free to work out my problems alone, but I felt myself dragged deeper and deeper." Early attempts to leave and get a job resulted in failure and an inevitable return to the girl, who was always ready with her sympathy and mothering solicitude. Her family was hospitable; but what worried Mr. A. was that they assumed his frequent returnings for prolonged visits to mean that he was intent on marriage. The father finally became more urgent and tried to encourage the diffident young man by letting him know that what he needed to settle him down was marriage.

These urgings and expectations on the part of the family plus the pleadings of the girl, plus his own inability to do without some sympathetic reassuring, proved too much for him. Finally, he says, he shut his eyes and jumped. We do not have time to give his description of his mental anguish as he walked the streets for two days trying to make up his mind. "Then," he says, "with super-human effort I forced myself to go the the courthouse and say 'I want a marriage license.' "

After the marriage Mr. A. began to

have many fears and forebodings. He was afraid Mrs. A.'s mother or father would die and he would have to help take care of Mrs. A.'s younger brother. He feared that he had wrecked his chances to realize his best self and should get out of the marriage. He began to find Mrs. A. ugly; and this, he said, outraged his aesthetic sensibilities. But the main theme throughout his interviews is: "My wife is a drag on me. She depends too much on me. Instead of feeling myself being pulled forward, I feel like she is pulling me backward. Why can't she be like my sisters? She is weak and casts a gloom over my spirit that I can't shake off. I must go away so I can feel free again and be on my own."

He did break away once to go to his sister for comfort and solace. He said: "While I was there I was happy again unless I thought of my plight. My sister said 'all you need is the comfort of your home' and she was right. While I was with her I felt all right."

The wife complained that she didn't feel secure with her husband. She wished that he could be like other men who seem to know what they want to do and how to go about it, who seem to take charge of things and forge ahead and not appear so helpless. She resented the fact that, although her husband was out of work and she was supporting him, he seemed to take that for granted as his due. Moreover, he showed great irritation toward her if she came home tired and, as he puts it, "sagging and weak looking." He says: "I simply can't stand that sagging, droopy look."

Their sexual adjustment is interesting when seen on this background. Neither knew how to proceed and their first attempts at intercourse were clumsy and unsuccessful. The husband's history shows considerable curiosity during childhood, and avoidance and fear in adolescent encounters. Even after receiving coaching from a physician and becoming somewhat adept in sexual technique, he is still described by his wife as clumsy and diffident in his approaches. He himself reveals a certain resentment and resistance to assuming the rôle of aggressor in relation with his wife. He has to assume a rôle in the sexual situtation that runs contrary to his desires.

In both husband and wife there are evidences of strong repressions of sexual drives. These specifically sexual attitudes are undoubtedly a part of the situation, but they may also be thought of as parts of the basic rôle patterns, particularly in the case of the husband.

This represents the barest outline of some of the high spots in the case, but if we could present all of our materials they would hardly do more than amplify the picture which must be evident from even such a scant description.

The central problem in this case is a problem of basic rôles, which are apparently the result of the early family relationships.

The husband is looking for a solicitous, protecting, aggressive, decisive, parent environment which the wife, who expects something of the same sort of environment, cannot supply. She was able to furnish sympathy and to that extent supplied the rôle of mother and sister in the husband's family. But she is not equipped to supply the more positive and aggressive part of the rôles that these people represented in Mr. A.'s personality development.

Neither of them is quite fully aware of what the basis for their trouble is. The husband thinks his marriage is a mistake, that he is not cut out for marriage, that his artistic temperament needs complete freedom to realize itself. The wife thinks the husband is sulky, inconsiderate, selfish, and jealous of her interest in her family. They both think that relief of the financial tension would be a partial solution.

Those who take the psychoanalytic approach would probably classify the man as a homosexual type, and interpret the difficulties on that basis. If we recognize that for the male the category "homosexual" applies to general psycho-sexual traits of passivity rather than to certain specific sexual attitudes merely, then the classification is probably valid. But it should be pointed out that the classification is not fully descriptive of the rôle pattern Mr. A. represents. He is not only passive but has an infantile dependent attitude or rôle which is not necessarily characteristic of the homosexual.

The case might also be interpreted as a result of guilt feelings which arise when Mr. A. engages in sexual activity with a person who stands as a substitute for his sister Martha. Sexual impulses with reference to his sister must have been heavily repressed and, when they are allowed expression on a love object that stands for her, they give rise to strong guilt feelings from which Mr. A. seeks to escape by terminating the marriage. Even here, however, we get into a usage of the notion of rôles. But it is apparent that this specifically sexual explanation leaves out of account too much of Mr. A.'s general pattern of response to all types of situations.

The writer would suggest that, at the present stage of the game, it seems preferable to use concretetly descriptive categories of rôle types. It may turn out later that some such set of master categories as those now used in the psychonanalytic field will apply. But their application should be made when empirical evidence justifies such usage.

Turning to a different approach, it should be pointed out that analysis of marital problems in terms of the usual categories of economic, cultural, response, temperamental, health, and other tensions is rather sterile unless such analysis is done with the insight that rôle analysis supplies. Any and all of the usual tensions may and do appear in a given case, but frequently they are meaningless unless seen in reference to the basic problem of rôles.

53 The Swedes Do It Better

RICHARD F. TOMASSON

The family as a social institution is today undergoing change because of scientific and technological developments in the society in general. One feature which has been altered markedly is the opportunity for, and orientation toward, employment of married women. The problems raised by working wives have been handled differently in different cultures. In this selection Tomasson contends that Swedish women, as compared with American women, face fewer role conflicts between work and marriage and between a job and bearing children. Numerous arrangements are designed to make the two roles compatible in their industrialized society. And the result, says Tomasson, is a less child-centered society but one with more stable marriages.

Some rational answers to questions that trouble many American women today—and perhaps some illuminating guidelines for the future—can be found in the experience of Sweden. Our countries, to be sure, are different in many respects: Sweden is a small nation with a homogeneous population. But both nations are attached to a democratic political philosophy, and Sweden comes closer to matching our high standard of living than any other European country. While there are many resemblances between our two societies, the Swedes have come closer to resolving issues which are still being uneasily debated in the United States.

Why, for instance, is the familiar conflict between work and marriage so much less of a problem in Sweden? One reason—though by no means the only one—is the fact that Swedish women devote less time and energy to child bearing.

Sweden has, in fact, one of the lowest birth rates in the world, fourteen per thousand population in 1960 compared with twenty-four per thousand in the United States. This is not due to any great difference in ability to control family size. . . . Nor are economic factors the heart of the matter. In fact the relative cost of rearing a child is greater in America than in Sweden, where an expanding system of welfare legislation has provided increasing financial benefits to mothers and children. This aid began in the 1930s to spur the low birth rate which was below replacement level for several years.

All Swedish mothers, married or not, now receive a grant of $180 when a child is born, as well as free delivery and confinement, grants for postnatal health care for mother and child, and an allowance of $180 a year for each child up to the age of sixteen. (Unmarried mothers receive additional cash compensation in recognition of their greater need when a father does not contribute to the support

SOURCE: *Harper's Magazine*, vol. 225, no. 1349 (October 1962), 178–80. Reprinted by permission of the author and the publisher. • Richard F. Tomasson is chairman of the Department of Sociology at the University of New Mexico, Albuquerque. His areas of interest include social and cultural aspects of human fertility, differential mortality, social stratification, sociological theory, and Scandinavian societies. He is the author of *Patterns in Negro-White Differential Mortality, 1930–1957* and *Swedish Society*. He is the coauthor of *Disparities in Visualizing Social Norms, Identifiability of Jews,* and *Student Politics and Higher Education in Scandinavia.*

of the child.) Comprehensive national health insurance makes the child's medical bills negligible and complete dental care is available to all children in the schools. Nor need Swedish parents worry about paying for their children's education. Through the university level, tuition is virtually free and there are generous scholarship and loan programs to help meet students' living costs.

Employers are forbidden by law to discharge a woman employee who gets married or becomes pregnant. She is entitled to a substantial proportion of her pay for a maternity leave of up to six months. With all these inducements one would expect Swedish fertility to exceed ours.

There are, however, important differences in Swedish and American culture which explains the significant disparity in family size. (The Swedish population will probably increase by only 10 per cent between 1960 and 1975 while ours will take a 25 or 30 per cent leap.)

Of prime importance is the simple fact that Swedes marry about four years later than Americans—the median age for Swedish men in the 1950s was twenty-seven; for women, twenty-four. Americans, in fact, marry earlier than the people of any other industrialized nation. This is, of course, one reason for our population explosion. Very young couples have a longer period of fecundity, more energy to deal with the rigors of child-rearing, and a less realistic picture of the burdens of parenthood than those who marry later. It is also true that a girl who goes to marriage directly from her parents' home or the college dormitory adjusts more easily to the confining role of motherhood than one who has had several years of bachelor freedom. And early marriage tends to narrow a woman's horizon to the traditional roles of wife and mother before competing interests have a chance to develop.

Most American wives have worked outside their homes before marriage, a majority do so again some time after marriage, but few—even among college graduates—can be said to have careers. In Sweden, on the other hand, a high proportion of middle-class wives have relatively uninterrupted working lives and there are far more women in the traditionally male occupations than in America.

In Swedish universities, for example, women are now a quarter of the students of medicine, dentistry, and the natural sciences, and 15 per cent of those in law school; a majority of the pharmacy students are women. In all these fields in the United States the proportion of women is small or negligible. Few Swedish wives give up careers when they marry; few American wives have careers to give up.

A SHACK IN THE COUNTRY

Family size and behavior are affected too by a difference in attitudes toward city living. Smaller quarters and the distractions and opportunities of the city discourage large families. In all industrial societies urban families have fewer children than those who live in the country. Statistically, Americans are as urbanized as the Swedes but—as William F. Whyte and Jane Jacobs have eloquently charged—we are essentially anti-city; if we can afford it we prefer to live in the suburbs despite the difficulties and deprivations that go with commuting.

The Swedes, on the other hand, do not share our feeling that we are not doing right by our children if we bring them up in the city. Families are generally content to live in apartments in Stockholm or Gothenburg, though many wish they were larger and easier to get. A vacation shack in the country satisfies their bucolic longings.

An even more striking difference is in the permissive single standard of sexual behavior which prevails in Sweden. . . . There are social pressures against promiscuity, but on the whole unmarried young women have about the same latitude as young men. Thus there is little of the guilt and moral ambiguity about sex relations among the unmarried which act as such a powerful inducement to early marriage in the United States.

Interestingly, Sweden has a divorce rate lower by a third than ours. Considering how far Sweden has moved along the road to full equality for women, it is perhaps paradoxical that the roles of husband and wife are more specifically defined than in the United States. This is, in fact, generally true of Europeans who feel that American husbands do much "woman's work." Swedish (or Dutch, French, or Austrian) fathers will seldom be found diapering, feeding, or bathing their children; nor are they dish driers, grocery shoppers, or baby-sitters. (But this is changing among younger Swedes.) Only in America is it not surprising for a university professor to feel that he must be home by five o'clock in order to help his wife with the children. And it may be that the amiable co-operation of their husbands in some of the onerous duties of child care is an extra inducement to American mothers to have more babies.

More probably, however, the decision to have a third or fourth child results from the mother's feeling that she is on full-time duty at home anyhow and has no compelling outside involvements. It takes an exceptionally well organized woman with great vitality to flout convention and play the mother and career roles simultaneously against all the obstacles American middle-class culture puts in her way. Certainly the conventional wisdom makes it clear that home is the only place for the mother of small—and even not so small—children. Family, neighbors, and friends urge her to stay there as do such diverse instructors as Dr. Spock, Ann Landers, and Russell Kirk. Even the government conspires by allowing only slight tax exemption for the child-care expenses of working mothers.

Swedish women too are under some pressure to stay home with their babies, and most of them take more than just a few months out to have them. But a relatively high proportion of middle-class wives with small children work outside their homes. Facilities for the daytime care of small children are more readily available than in the United States and so are competent domestic helpers. But the crucial difference is the fact that it is not generally considered strange, antisocial, or immoral for the Swedish mother of young children to work outside her home.

Recent evidence accumulated in the United States suggests that we too may have reason to reverse our stand on these questions. . . . Three diverse studies all came to the conclusion that maternal employment *per se* does not have the adverse effects on children's lives attributed to it. One study which covered more than a thousand children in the public schools of Cedar Rapids, Iowa, indicated that the academic performance and social adjustment of children—from nursery school through high school—had no perceptible connection with their mother's employment. Similarly, a study of some six hundred Michigan high-school girls demonstrated that while an employed mother may be under increased physical strain, her dual role does not affect the mother-daughter relationship adversely. The same conclusions were corroborated by interviews conducted in Spokane with 104 nonemployed mothers, 104 who were employed, and 82 mother substitutes. Nothing was found to support the widely held hypothesis that the separation of children from their mothers "has 'bad' psychological, physical, and social effects on children. . . ."

AMERICA'S FERTILITY CHAMPS

Findings of this sort have not yet gained much currency. But as the facts become more widely known, they are bound to contribute to a more rational and less child-centered way of life for American women. There are indeed already signs that our birth rate is declining and that families will be smaller in the years ahead. I have asked hundreds of college students over the past couple of years how many children they wanted. As might be expected they overwhelmingly want two, three, or four. But the interesting fact is that more want two than four. Compared to the 1940s and 1950s, this is a significant change. The uninterrupted decline in the American birth rate between 1957 and 1963 from 25.3 to 21.6 births per 1,000 population may well reflect a real decline in average family size.

It may well be, in fact, that American women born in the early 'thirties will turn out to be the fertility champions of the twentieth century. On the other hand, wives of the 1970s and 1980s may find themselves as free as Swedish women are today from the conflict between the traditional woman's role and the opportunities which an affluent industrial society provides.

The distance still to be bridged is epitomized in two sociological studies. Writing about "Student Culture at Vassar," John H. Bushnell observed. . . :

"The Vassar student's future identity is largely encompassed by the projected role of wife-mother. . . . For these young women the 'togetherness' vogue is definitely an integral theme of future family life with any opportunities for independent action attaching to an Ivy League degree being willfully passed over in favor of the anticipated rewards of close-knit companionship within the home that-is-to-be."

In sharp contrast, . . . a Danish sociologist . . . notes:

"But even if she excels in all these respects [being a good housekeeper and hostess, a loving mother, and an attractive spouse], she will reap slight social esteem, because dominant middle-class opinion will insist on the superior value of choosing a career outside the home and of cultivating literary and artistic interests."

54 Technology, Biology, and the Changing Family

MEYER F. NIMKOFF

Though social institutions tend to be stable, they sometimes change in both form and function. According to this article by Nimkoff, written in 1951, our scientific and technological developments had appeared to have brought us to a point where even the child-bearing function of the family, assumed to be so permanent and fundamental, might become altered beyond recognition. However, persistence of the institutionalized behavior patterns of the family is demonstrated by the fact that relatively little of the change predicted has occurred in the years since this article appeared.

. . . We may experience in the near future a revolution in the biological functions of the family comparable to the revolution which has occurred in the economic functions during the last two hundred years. This new impact on the family derives from discoveries in the rapidly developing field of the biology of sex and reproduction. . . . As a first example, consider the progress that has been made in determining the sex of the child before conception. This is not to be confused with the prediction of the child's sex before birth, which can now be made in certain cases on the basis of various tests, although with less than 100 per cent accuracy.

For some time we have known that the child's sex is determined by the type of sperm cell contributed by the father. There are two types of sperm cell, the male-producing Y-sperm and the female producing X-sperm, whereas in the ova there is only one type of sex cell, the X-type. Each parent contributes one sex chromosome to the child; if two X's combine, the child is female; an X and a Y produce a male. So it is the father, or at least his sex chromosomes, that determines the sex of his children, and the mother has nothing to do with it. Yet many a wife in ignorance of this fact has felt guilty because *she* did not present her husband with a son. King Farouk of Egypt divorced his queen, according to press accounts, because she bore him no son.

The X-chromosome is slightly larger than the Y-chromosome, and the female-producing sperm contains slightly more chromosomal material, making it slightly more dense. Harvey has calculated that the Y-sperm should have a density of 1.07132 and the X-sperm a density of 1.1705. By means of a special centrifuge apparatus (the vacuum type turbine centrifuge) and the use of proper medium for the density gradient (a 20 per cent dextrin in Ringer's solution), Harvey thinks it possible to separate these two kinds of cells. The refinement of technique re-

SOURCE: Reprinted from "Technology, Biology, and the Changing Family," by M. F. Nimkoff, *The American Journal of Sociology*, vol. 57, no. 1 (July 1951), 20–26, by permission of The University of Chicago Press. • Meyer F. Nimkoff (1904–1965) was chairman of the Department of Sociology, Florida State University. He was the author of *The Child* and *Marriage and the Family*, and the coauthor of *Technology and the Changing Family* and *Sociology*.

quired for success is comparable, Harvey points out, to that which separated Uranium 235 and 238. For this reason, says Harvey, "we may designate any process of sorting the two kinds of sperm for control of sex as essentially a separation of biological isotopes."

It should be emphasized that the separation of male-producing and female-producing sperm has not yet been accomplished, but one would be bold indeed who would argue that it will not be done in the future. If and when the two cells are separated, use of them for purposes of reproduction would involve artificial insemination. There is, however, at the present time no important objection to this procedure when the donor is the woman's husband.

• • • • •

Even if scientific research should give us the knowledge of how to control the sex of the child, the question remains: Would we use the knowledge? And, if so, how? Do we have a preference for boys or girls? It may be observed at once that, even if there is no general preference for one sex over the other in society, individual parents may still prefer one sex to the other, or a certain ordering of their families according to sex, in which case the ability to achieve this end may be deemed to contribute to the happiness of the couple. Margaret Mead in *Male and Female* has stated that there are no social reasons why parents in the United States should prefer boys to girls or vice versa, but there is at least the reason that boys preserve the family name, in which there may be pride. Mead thinks most American parents would like to have a balanced family of boys and girls, but the preference is probably that the firstborn be a boy, which means that a son would be the more common choice of one-child families, if there were control.

This discussion assumes that the mores would be favorable to the new knowledge and that prospective parents would be permitted to utilize it. But we have no assurance that the control, if achieved, would be socially sanctioned, especially if it resulted in an appreciable imbalance in the sex ratio. There seems to be no great demand for control of the sex of the child at the present time. At least such a demand, if it exists, is not evident in any considerable application by scientists to the task of solving the technical problems involved. But if a differential in the size of the male population establishes the superiority of one nation over another in war, then it is conceivable that sex control may be encouraged in the future even as a high birth rate, without reference to the sex of the children, is now encouraged in nearly every Western nation by means of subsidies for babies. Dictatorial governments in particular may find sex control appealing and may derive an advantage from the reluctance of democratic states to adopt the practice and/or to favor male births.

We may consider briefly the implications of an unbalanced sex ratio as it relates to the marriage system. The evidence from primitive peoples indicates that an appreciable surplus of women in a society, resulting mainly from the high mortality of male hunters in late adolescence and early manhood, is a condition disposing to polygyny, whereas a surplus of men, usually resulting from female infanticide and/or religious cloistering, disposes toward polyandry. War in modern times in many Western nations has led to a large surplus of women of marriageable ages, but, barring another war, the imbalance in the sex ratio has been temporary, correcting itself in the next generation. If the sex of the child were controlled by science, and a continuing preference for males were to be expressed by a society, it would seem that the bases would exist for a trend toward polyandry. Considerable changes might be expected in the status of the sexes, their social roles, and their attitudes toward each other.

We may speculate further on what effect, if any, controlling the sex of the child would have on the relations of husbands and wives. If sex control is utilized, then procreation must occur by artificial insemination. During the past century or so, the trend has been to emphasize the psychological rather than the procreative function of coitus, as the reduction in the size of the family bears witness. Sex control would presumably further this trend; indeed, procreation and coitus might be rendered entirely separate functions. The fertile period would be emphasized more, and there would be more birth control. In the latter connection we may note in passing another probable biological development in the near future, namely, a long-term contraceptive. Knowledge of how to inhibit ovulation already exists, but such regulation disturbs the balance of the endocrine system.

A further significant discovery in the biology of sex has to do with the preservation of human germ plasm. Success has been reported in preserving human sperm 125 days in dry ice after vitrification in liquid nitrogen, with no appreciable decline in mortality in this period beyond the decline of the first two hours. As much as 60 per cent of the human sperm survived the treatment so far as motility is concerned. The limit was 125 days, because an assistant failed to resupply the dry ice after that time, and the sperm warmed up. The experiment was not resumed, but the experimenter believes that vitrified sperm will keep indefinitely at the temperature of dry ice. But whether they would be able to fertilize, he, of course, does not know. He reports that he was unable to get an adequate yield of sperm other than human to survive at very low temperatures and was therefore unable to perform fertilization experiments.

The doctors object to using preserved semen in human subjects, since they do not know how it will work. Experience with animal insemination has been limited to using semen that has been kept only a relatively short time, a maximum of about 168 hours. If it could be demonstrated that no harmful effects result from the use of vitrified human sperm, the opposition might disappear. The objection would persist if donor semen were used, but where the male is the woman's husband there probably would be no organized religious objection, to judge by the present position of the churches on artificial insemination. If there is no objection, many new possibilities are opened up. For instance, a woman who is married a short time before a war and who bears no children before being separated from her husband may still bear her husband's child even if the husband is killed in action, if his semen is preserved beforehand. Widowhood under the circumstances may become a somewhat different experience from what it now is. Semen banks are a possibility in such a situation.

• • • • •

. . . Reference has been made to the use of the sex hormones. This is another brilliant chapter in the book of recent advance in the biochemistry of reproduction, to which we can here refer only briefly. The literature deals mainly with the lower animals, with whom experimentation is permissible. In one experiment a prepubertal castrated chimpanzee was paired with an intact male. The administration of male sex hormones led to the social dominance by the castrated animal, whereas female sex therapy resulted in its subordination. Following injection of a female rat with estrogen and progesterone, mating responses were induced despite the congenital absence of gonadal tissue. Hormone therapy has also succeeded in reversing sex roles. Thus a single-comb Brown Leghorn hen displayed male mating behavior following successive implants of testosterone propionate pellets, in contrast with the earlier negative findings following single daily injections of the hormone. Some experiments on human subjects have also been made. When 101 women under treatment for endocrine disorders were given androgen administered intramuscularly, subcutaneously, or orally, all but 13 reported some increase in libido. In another experiment progesterone depressed excessive libido and androgen decidedly increased both libido and general well-being, with best results obtained by implantations of pellets of testosterone propionate. On the basis of such experiments, it has been conjectured that the amount of androgens greatly affects the vigor of the sex drive and that the absolute or proportionate amount of estrogens affects its direction. It is, of course, not implied that learning and experience are not also important factors affecting the sex drive but only that constitutional factors are important, especially the hormones of the glands of internal secretion.

The foregoing are only a few of the remarkable developments in the biology and chemistry of reproduction, sufficient perhaps to indicate to us what promise for the future this infant science holds. Time does not permit more than the briefest mention of important developments in other areas, notably the biochemistry of nutrition. For instance, aging in rats has been greatly postponed by heavy doses of vitamin A in the early years. If a comparable result were to be achieved in man, this one fact alone could have a significant effect on the relationship between the sexes and on the relations of parents and children.

Confronting these discoveries, sociologists must consider what social implications they may have. An important consideration is the mores: if they are hostile, the new knowledge will not be widely utilized. Hostile mores are also an obstacle to scientific discovery itself. But, as we have seen, many of the changes which would be effected by the new discoveries are possible within the limits of the existing sex mores. There seems to be no objection to new scientific procedures if they are employed exclusively within marriage. For instance, the Roman Catholic church sanctions artificial insemination if the husband is the donor and if insemination by the physician follows normal coitus. Some of the innovations mentioned above can be confined to the marital pair, and presumably on this account there would be no objection. Such would be the case as regards the control of the sex of the child. But this would involve artificial means in separating the two types of sperm, and to this there might be objection from certain groups, though not all, just as there is objection at present to obtaining the husband's semen by methods other than normal marital coitus, for purposes of assisting in the insemination of the wife. So we conclude that certain of the procedures will meet with acceptance and that other procedures may meet with opposition.

We cannot be certain as to what the public practice will be with regard to man of the biological innovations, since they create new situations for which the old definitions are not adequate. Such is the case, for instance, with artificial insemination at the present time. Artificial insemination has been introduced into our culture by the doctors, and thousands of inseminations have been performed. There is as yet no body of law or clearly defined public opinion regarding the practice. Certain church bodies have taken a stand against it when the donor is not the woman's husband, and there are a few contradictory court decisions. In due course public policy may be formulated on the issue, but it may not be the same in all societies, just as public policy on abortion and birth control varies in different cultures at the present time. Moreover, even if at first there is opposition to the practice, the opposition may eventually moderate, for the mores change.

It may also be observed that the systematic opposition of the group to a practice does not necessarily mean that the practice will not exist. There are many thousands of abortions each year despite the taboo against them. Where a need exists, and the knowledge of how to fill it, it is difficult to suppress the practice in a complex, heterogeneous, rapidly changing society. What the doctors and their patients do in our complex society is not generally known: the statement that thousands of persons have been artificially inseminated is probably news to most citizens.

So we conclude that, even if there is opposition to new biological practices and knowledge, there may still be not a little diffusion of the innovations, with considerable effects on family practices. But it is too soon yet to say whether there will be opposition to many of the discoveries that are in process of being made in the field of biology and chemistry of reproduction. It may, furthermore, be noted that not all scientific discoveries are put to use. For one reason and another, the death rate of inventions and discoveries is high. But if the innovation has great human significance and there is a demand for it, there is considerable probability that it will be developed and diffused.

To sum up, the family in the past has been shaped by changes in the social system of which it is a part, and particularly by changes in technology and economic organization, which are among the most dynamic elements of the social system. These changes in technology have during the past century and a half been revolutionary and have forced radical readjustments in the correlated parts of culture, including the family. These technological changes have been exterior to man the animal and have required changes in adaptation without any radical change in the constitution of man. But now the revolution in science has extended to the sciences of man, and the probabilities are great that discoveries in human biology will revolutionize the constitutional bases of human behavior. There are great discoveries also in the psychological realm of which this paper has taken no account; family behavior may be greatly affected in the years ahead by new knowledge regarding the learning process and the way personality is shaped by group and culture. Sociologists seem to be more mindful of the possibilities in the psychological realm and they have given some attention to the correlations of technology and the rest of the social order. But there does not seem as yet to be much awareness of the social influences that the biological discoveries may exert . . . .

55 Illegitimacy and Value Dilemmas

CLARK E. VINCENT

American family norms place great emphasis on limiting sex relations to marriage partners. Illegitimate births are considered a threat to the marriage institution, and though they are few in number, we constantly express concern about them. In this selection Vincent indicates that the problem of illegitimacy arises from our social structure and the values attached to the family social system in the United States. Hence illegitimacy can be eliminated only by altering both structure and values. Vincent explores several factors involved in reducing the frequency of illegitimacy and concludes that any effective measures "will entail changes in some social attitudes and practices which some people prefer not to change." He makes clear that those who would solve such social problems by merely "passing a law" are deluding themselves. This same principle is applicable to other complex problems of society.

If people engaged in efforts to ameliorate the age-old social problem of illegitimacy are to get results, they should begin with an awareness that most if not all social problems persist because of value dilemmas, and that their solution may require changes in social attitudes and practices most of us would prefer not to change.

Illegitimacy could, of course, be eradicated by abolishing marriage. Without marriage as the recognized legitimation of coition and parturition, all births would be licit. But people who espouse the traditional values of our society rate the maintenance of marriage more highly than elimination of illegitimacy. Similarly, legalized abortions and wider dissemination of contraceptive information are solutions rejected by most people. In fact, such means of reducing illegitimacy tend to be discarded so readily that rarely are they considered as alternatives. And our failure to consider alternatives hinders us from realizing that choices are made that may actually jeopardize the values we profess to cherish.

One area in which an implicit choice has been made is represented by the highly selective and distorted emphases of public information about illegitimacy. The publicity given to illicit births among the nation's very young females might lead one to believe that American young people have completely discarded traditional sex norms. A closer look at the data, however, suggests that the perennial and vociferous censure of youthful misbehavior diverts attention from adult misbehavior and ignores the 90–95 per cent of our young people whose sexual behavior very likely is more exemplary than that of the adults whom they are continually admonished to "grow up and act like." Such censure of course reflects

SOURCE: Copyright 1963 Christian Century Foundation. Reprinted by permission from the June 19, 1963 issue of *The Christian Century*. • The author is professor of sociology and director of the Behavioral Science Center at the Bowman Gray School of Medicine and was formerly chief of the Social Science Section, Training Branch, National Institute of Mental Health. His main interests include medical sociology, sociology of child development, marriage counseling, social problems, and social psychology. He has written *Unmarried Mothers* and edited *Readings in Marriage Counseling* and *Human Sexuality in Medical Education and Practice.*

our idealization of youth and our perennial hope of a better world if only young people would follow the teachings—but not necessarily the deeds—of adults.

It is well known that the number of teen-age females in the United States has increased markedly in recent years, but few people are aware that females aged 10–19 accounted for a smaller proportion of illicit births in 1960 (41 per cent) than in 1938 (48 per cent). In fact, the illegitimacy rate, which is the number of illicit births per 1,000 unmarried females, has risen far less among teen-agers than among older females. Why do popular information and prevention programs ignore the fact that rate increases in illegitimacy since 1940 have been far greater among 20–44 year olds than among teen-agers? For one thing, it is the very young unwed mothers who are the most dependent on parents and taxpayers; their illicit sexual behavior offends our sense of morality far more than does similar behavior among older, more independent females. The point, however, is that concentration of attention on very young unwed mothers serves preventive efforts when it obscures the fact that about 78 per cent of all unwed mothers are 18 or older. Even this figure is probably an underestimate; very likely the percentage is closer to 80 or 85, since many older, white, middle- and upper-class unwed mothers-to-be move temporarily to one of the 15 states that do not record illegitimacy on birth certificates.

In the next few years an adequate statistical perspective on illegitimacy will become more and more important. The *number* of 15- to 19-year-old unwed mothers during the 1960s may be almost twice what it was during the 1950s even if there are no rate or percentage increases, since almost twice as many girls were born between 1945 and 1954 than between 1935 and 1944. Continuation of the popular emphasis on young, teen-age illegitimacy may inadvertently influence some young people to accept illicit sexual behavior as normative, and may further postpone the needed scrutiny of illegitimacy among the many unwed mothers who are 18 and older—old enough to know what they are doing, old enough to be emulated by younger girls.

THE "BAD CAUSES BAD" FALLACY

In terms of the intricate network of norms by which we live it is apparent that some unwed mothers are regarded as "more equal" than others. Evoking the strongest censure are those who are young, poor, nonwhite, and dependent on taxpayers' support. The explicit condemnation and frequent exaggeration of illicit births among females possessing these characteristics contrasts sharply with the playing down of such births among older, white, middle- and upper-class females. This contrast derives in part from the fact that censure of white unwed mothers was tempered in the 1940s and 1950s; at that time they represented the largest single source of adoptable infants and served a useful social function by enabling childless couples to have a family. As physicians, lawyers, and social caseworkers can testify, many of the estimated 1 million involuntarily childless white couples in this country a decade ago would have been highly displeased had this major source of adoptable white infants disappeared. This choice—continued illegitimacy or a reduced supply of adoptable infants—of course was not openly acknowledged. We simply failed to publicize illicit births among white females who had sufficient means and maturity discreetly to leave home during their pregnancy, returning only after they had released their offspring for adoption.

Another area in which alternative

means of reducing illegitimacy are obscured is represented by the explanations of what causes illegitimacy. Most explanations of illegitimacy—indeed, of any social problem—are deeply imbedded in the assumption that "bad causes bad." Between the 1920s and the middle 1950s the bourgeois-oriented theories concerning illegitimacy fostered the belief that "bad illegitimacy" is the result of such "bad causes" as poverty, mental deficiency, broken homes, minority group membership and psychological disturbances. This belief was conveniently supported by descriptions of unwed mothers from domestic court files, charity institutions, "wayside homes" and out-patient psychiatric clinics.

To assume that only bad causes bad and selectively to censure some groups of unwed mothers more than others is to obscure the fact that a number of highly valued social practices are relevant to illegitimacy. This relevance can be illustrated by citing certain practices in education, child-rearing and personnel ideology which accompanied the "philosophy of fun morality" of the 1940s and '50s. In education this philosophy found expression in the notion that a child would learn more and faster if he were "having fun" and "enjoying life," if he were "happy" and "popular." The emergence of fun morality in child-rearing was particularly evident during the '40s, when it was assumed that whatever the child enjoyed had to be good for him. Less and less frequently was a distinction made between what the child *needed* and what he *wanted*. As wants came to be regarded as needs, many parents found themselves dominated by their children. This period of permissiveness in child-rearing began to subside with maternal exhaustion and the subsequent reassertion of parental knowledge in the mid-'50s. By then, however, a generation of youngsters had in varying degrees been implanted with a fusion—not to say confusion—of needs and wants.

This implantation, whether occurring through educational procedures at school or child-rearing patterns at home, is currently flowering in adolescents who are predisposed to believing that what is fun is good. And they read, hear and see few denials of the notion that "sex is fun."

The significance of the philosophy of fun morality in the personnel ideology of industry and business has been discussed by C. Wright Mills, William H. Whyte, Jr., Leo Lowenthal and others. The loss of motivation for work in our technological, assembly-line society and the decrease in the inherent rewards of work have necessitated an increasing emphasis on ways to make work "fun" and working conditions enjoyable. Thus employee parties and other instances of "togetherness" help maintain production quotas by keeping workers happy with their on-the-job relationships—if not with their work. Within such a context employees frequently know more about each other's current problems than do members of their own families.

Then there is the expense account, which often permits the young executive to live a kind of life away from home that makes his home life and a vacation with his family seem dull—and expensive—by comparison. Sometimes the lush away-from-home life includes the services of "escort bureaus," provided at out-of-town conventions and sanctioned as promotional means to the "good" goal of future conventions and consequent city revenue. While this promotional spirit gives respectability to the female escorts of visiting businessmen, it also inadvertently lowers the barriers to heterosexual intimacy.

A WEB THAT ENSNARES

What does all this have to do with understanding illegitimacy? When viewed separately, such social practices as I have noted may appear to have only enough relevance to illegitimacy to attract the attention of "blue-nosed do-gooders." But when viewed collectively, such practices seem to constitute a source of permissive attitudes toward pre- and extra-marital sexual relationships—a web that ensnares many an unsuspecting victim as well as many an invited and knowing guest. The fun-morality notion that a person has a *right* to fun and enjoyment makes it easier for the male who is unhappy in marriage to justify, at least to himself, finding his fun outside the home. His selection of a fun partner is simplified, the risk of an initial rebuff minimized, when the emphasis on close-knit relationships in the occupational setting provides a socially sanctioned context for familiarity. A male-female pair of office employees can share coffee breaks and lunch periods much more frequently and with less chance of censure than can a male-female pair of neighbors.

To suggest that illegitimacy can be an inadvertent by-product of a combination of means to conventional goals is to look outside the evil-causes-evil circle. This approach, however, is not popular, nor is it easily brought into focus. Any one social practice reflects a variety of vested interests and conflicting values, and one man's means are sometimes another man's goals. Moreover, strongly to deplore the means used to increase advertising returns, production quotas and box-office successes is to risk being labeled a "busybody," a "do-gooder," an "infringer on freedom of expression." Such labels—particularly the latter—tend to blur the issue; it becomes lost in a polemical discussion on "freedom vs. restriction of expression," in which the questions "freedom for what?" and "freedom for whom?" are never adequately explored.

But the failure to examine the relevance of accepted social practices is not to be attributed solely to the power of vested-interest groups. The bad-causes-bad assumption is frequently welcomed as a protective device against our own fears, struggles and temptations concerning illicit sexual behavior, and is a way of reaffirming our conviction that "it can't happen to me." For to contend that "bad girls" are the result of poverty, ignorance or minority-group membership is to reaffirm that "good girls" are the result of material blessings, a good education and majority-group membership.

LONG-STANDING DOUBLE STANDARD

The failure to conduct research on unmarried fathers provides another illustration of how value dilemmas impeded our understanding of illegitimacy. Only about one study of unmarried fathers exists for every 30 studies of unmarried mothers. Obviously, illegitimacy cannot be understood, much less remedied, by studying only the female factor. But to observe unwed fathers to the same degree we do their female counterparts requires changes in the conventional double standard by which we judge the sexual behavior of males and females. Semantically, we have no male equivalent of "the fallen woman."

That we generally resist changes in the double standard is evidenced by the following facts: (1) We condemn and stigmatize unmarried mothers far more harshly than unmarried fathers. (2) We tend to express greater indignation over wives involved in extramarital affairs than over husbands. (3) We blame wives more frequently than husbands for unwanted pregnancies occurring within marriage. (4) State legislators frequently consider requiring tubal ligations for recidivist unmarried mothers, but never vasectomies for unmarried fathers.

We inadvertently condone the unmarried father by ignoring him. The unwed mother poses tangible problems, the unmarried father does not. It is she for whom prenatal care, maternity homes and possible child support must be financed; it is her noticeably altering appearance which openly threatens traditional sex mores. The male represents no obvious expense to taxpayers and bears no evidence of unconventional sex behavior. Moreover, the female's need for care during pregnancy and delivery makes her available for study and identifiable for censure; the male's biological role ends at conception, and society's protection of him through disinterest enables him to remain anonymous and unavailable for study.

COMPARING MARRIED AND UNMARRIED MOTHERS

A better understanding of illegitimacy is also hampered by the value dilemma posed by the need to consider similarities in the attitudes of married and unmarried mothers, as well as similarities in the motivations for licit and illicit births. The pregnancies of some married women signify attempts to strengthen a faltering marriage, just as those of some unmarried women signify attempts to obtain a husband. There are those among both married and unmarried females who use pregnancy as a means to resolve emotional problems, just as there are those in both groups who have sexual relations for personal enjoyment with no intent or desire to become pregnant. Moreover, unwanted pregnancies evoke as much indignation, disappointment and emotional upset among some married as among some unmarried women. Conversely, the discovery of pregnancy is welcomed by some women in both groups as the achievement of a much-desired goal and the realization of self-fulfillment.

Open consideration of such similarities could further our understanding of illegitimacy by focusing attention on the more germane problem of unwanted pregnancies. Such pregnancies occurring within marriage may represent a far greater problem, numerically and in terms of abortions and marital strife, than does illegitimacy. However, such a possibility is usually resisted because it poses a dilemma—a choice between either using a more effective approach to understanding illegitimacy or changing some of our cherished assumptions about the relative purity of married mothers' motivations and feelings concerning coition and pregnancy as opposed to those of unmarried mothers.

TOWARD A MORE CONSTRUCTIVE APPROACH

In summary, then, there is no simple explanation of illegitimacy, and every effective measure or method for reducing its occurrence will entail changes in some social attitudes and practices which some people prefer not to change. Thus far, those engaged in preventive efforts have generally played it safe by stressing the conventional scapegoats of youth, poverty, ignorance, psychological disturbance; by prescribing tubal ligations for females but not vasectomies for males; by publicizing the number of unwed Negro mothers on Aid to Dependent Children rolls but ignoring the older white females who supply adoptable infants.

Hopefully, an awareness of the contrarieties in attitudes and practices concerning illicit sexual behavior might result in more constructive approaches to illegitimacy. Surely it is inconsistent for a society on the one hand to condone and even to produce and consume in prodigious quantity sex enticements which foster attitudes favorable to permissive sexual behavior, and on the other to become outraged when the protruding anatomy of the unmarried female reveals an out-of-wedlock pregnancy. What would the Martian visitor say about a society that inundates young people with sexual stimuli and then not only castigates them for responding to such stimuli but also denies them the contraceptive means and knowledge whereby they could at least exercise caution?

To interpret what I have just said as an argument in favor of making contraceptives freely available to youth is again to obscure the issue and to deny the dilemma by avoiding the alternative of withdrawing the stimuli. It may be that as a society we prefer to continue piecemeal and largely ineffective approaches to the understanding and diminution of illegitimacy, rather than to deal with basic value dilemmas and seriously to consider making changes in attitudes and practices we prefer not to change. If such is the case, then we might at least stop pretending that we really want to do away with illegitimacy and devote our funds and research efforts to social problems about which we are less ambivalent.

To continue to support a matrix of social practices which serve to instill permissive attitudes toward illicit sexual behavior and at the same time to intensify efforts to decrease illicit pregnancies is, to say the least, highly illogical.

56 The Division of Labor in Society

EMILE DURKHEIM

One of the recurring basic criticisms of modern society is that the "whole man"—the personality—has been weakened because of specialization, or "division of labor." Said one philosopher, "It is a sad commentary that we have come to the state where we never do anything more than make the eighteenth part of a pin." Said another, "In so far as the principle of the division of labor receives a more complete application, the art progresses, the artisan retrogresses." Many, comparing the life of the modern workman with the "free, bold life of the 'noble' savage," have found the second much preferable to the first. Adoption of such a philosophy, carried to its logical conclusion, would lead to drastic changes in all of social life. (Young people of both sexes wearing beaded headbands, fringed leather jackets, and Indian mocassins, prove that this idea is still very much alive today.) One result of these conflicting philosophies is that young people may be given contradictory vocational recommendations: Specialize. Do not specialize. The result of specialization, in the thinking of Rousseau and others, is the "splintering" of personalities. Emile Durkheim, however, in this conclusion to his The Division of Labor in Society *argued that specialization was the chief source of social solidarity and was becoming the foundation of the moral order.*

I

If there is one rule of conduct which is incontestable, it is that which orders us to realize in ourselves the essential traits of the collective type. Among lower peoples, this reaches its greatest rigor. There, one's first duty is to resemble everybody else, not to have anything personal about one's beliefs or actions. In more advanced societies, required likenesses are less numerous; the absence of some likenesses, however, is still a sign of moral failure. Of course, crime falls into fewer different categories; but today, as heretofore, if a criminal is the object of reprobation, it is because he is unlike us. Likewise, in lesser degree, acts simply immoral and prohibited as such are those which evince dissemblances less profound but nevertheless considered serious. Is this not the case with the rule which common morality expresses when it orders a man to be a man in every sense of the word, which is to say, to have all the ideas and sentiments which go to make up a human conscience? No doubt, if this formula is taken literally, the man prescribed would be man in general and not one of some particular social species. But, in reality, this human conscience that we must integrally realize is nothing else than the collective conscience of the group of which we are a part. For what can it be composed of, if not the ideas and sentiments to which we are most attached? Where can we find the traits of our model, if not within us and around us? If we believe that this collective ideal is that

SOURCE: Reprinted from *The Division of Labor in Society,* 396–409, by permission of The Free Press, Glencoe, Illinois. Copyright 1947. • The author (1858–1917) was a French sociologist and philosopher. He taught at the University of Bordeaux and at the Sorbonne, succeeding Auguste Comte. Besides his doctoral dissertation from which this selection is taken, Durkheim's main works are *The Rules of Sociological Method, The Elementary Forms of the Religious Life,* and *Suicide: A Study in Sociology.*

of all humanity, that is because it has become so abstract and general that it appears fitting for all men indiscriminately. But, really, every people makes for itself some particular conception of this type which pertains to its personal temperament. Each represents it in its own image. Even the moralist who thinks he can, through thought, overcome the influence of transient ideas, cannot do so, for he is impregnated with them, and no matter what he does, he finds these precepts in the body of his deductions. That is why each nation has its own school of moral philosophy conforming to its character.

On the other hand, we have shown that this rule had as its function the prevention of all agitation of the common conscience, and, consequently, of social solidarity, and that it could accomplish this role only by having a moral character. It is impossible for offenses against the most fundamental collective sentiments to be tolerated without the disintegration of society, and it is necessary to combat them with the aid of the particularly energetic reaction which attaches to moral rules.

But the contrary rule, which orders us to specialize, has exactly the same function. It also is necessary for the cohesion of societies, at least at a certain period in their evolution. Of course, its solidarity is different from the preceding, but though it is different, it is no less indispensable. Higher societies can maintain themselves in equilibrium only if labor is divided; the attraction of like for like less and less suffices to produce this result. If, then, the moral character of the first of these rules is necessary to the playing of its role, it is no less necessary to the second. They both correspond to the same social need, but satisfy the need differently, because the conditions of existence in the societies themselves differ. Consequently, without speculating concerning the first principle of ethics, we can induce the moral value of one from the moral value of the other. If, from certain points of view, there is a real antagonism between them, that is not because they serve different ends. On the contrary, it is because they lead to the same end, but through opposed means. Accordingly, there is no necessity for choosing between them once for all nor of condemning one in the name of the other. What is necessary is to give each, at each moment in history, the place that is fitting to it.

Perhaps we can even generalize further in this matter.

The requirements of our subject have obliged us to classify moral rules and to review the principal types. We are thus in a better position than we were in the beginning to see, or at least to conjecture, not only upon the external sign, but also upon the internal character which is common to all of them and which can serve to define them. We have put them into two groups: rules with repressive sanctions, which may be diffuse or organized, and rules with restitutive sanctions. We have seen that the first of these express the conditions of the solidarity, *sui generis,* which comes from resemblances, and to which we have given the name mechanical; the second, the conditions of negative solidarity and organic solidarity. We can thus say that, in general, the characteristic or moral rules is that they enunciate the fundamental conditions of social solidarity. Law and morality are the totality of ties which bind each of us to society, which make a unitary, coherent aggregate of the mass of individuals. Everything which is a source of solidarity is moral, everything which forces man to take account of other men is moral, everything which forces him to regulate his conduct through something other than the striving of his ego is moral, and morality is as solid as these ties are numerous and strong. We can see how inexact it is to define it, as is often done, through liberty. It rather consists in a state of dependence. Far from serving to emancipate the individual, or disengaging him from the environment which surrounds him, it has, on the contrary the function of making him an integral part of a whole, and, consequently, of depriving him of some liberty of movement. We sometimes, it is true, come across people not without nobility who find the idea of such dependence intolerable. But that is because they do not perceive the source from which their own morality flows, since these sources are very deep. Conscience is a bad judge of what goes on in the depths of a person, because it does not penetrate to them.

Society is not, then, as has often been thought, a stranger to the moral world, or something which has only secondary repercussions upon it. It is, on the contrary, the necessary condition of its existence. It is not a simple juxtaposition of individuals who bring an intrinsic morality with them, but rather man is a moral being only because he lives in society, since morality consists in being solidary with a group and varying with this solidarity. Let all social life disappear, and moral life will disappear with it, since it would no longer have any objective. The state of nature of the philosophers of the eighteenth century, if not immoral, is, at least, *amoral.* Rousseau himself recognized this. Through this, however, we do not come upon the formula which expresses morality as a function of social interest. To be sure, society cannot exist if its parts are not solidary, but solidarity is only one of its conditions of existence. There are many others which are no less necessary and which are not moral. Moreover, it can happen that, in the system of ties which make up morality, there are some which are not used in themselves or which have power without any relation to their degree of utility. The idea of utility does not enter as an essential element in our definition.

As for what is called individual morality, if we understand by that a totality of duties of which the individual would, at the same time, be subject and object, and which would link him only to himself, and which would, consequently, exist even if he were solitary,—that is an abstract conception which has no relation to reality. Morality, in all its forms, is never met with except in society. It never varies except in relation to social conditions. To ask what it would be if societies did not exist is thus to depart from facts and enter the domain of gratuitous hypotheses and unverifiable flights of the imagination. The duties of the individual towards himself are, in reality, duties towards society. They correspond to certain collective sentiments which he cannot offend, whether the offended and the offender are one and the same person, or whether they are distinct. Today, for example, there is in all healthy consciences a very lively sense of respect for human dignity, to which we are supposed to conform as much in our relations with ourselves as in our relations with others, and this constitutes the essential quality of what is called individual morality. Every act which contravenes this is censured, even when the agent and the sufferer are the same person. That is why, according to the Kantian formula, we ought to respect human personality wherever we find it, which is to say, in ourselves as in those like us. The sentiment of which it is the object is not less offended in one case than in the other.

But not only does the division of labor present the character by which we have defined morality; it more and more tends to become the essential condition of social solidarity. As we advance in the evolutionary scale, the ties which bind the individual to his family, to his native soil, to traditions which the past has given to him, to collective group usages, become loose. More mobile, he changes his environment more easily, leaves his people to go elsewhere to live a more autonomous existence, to a greater extent forms his own ideas and sentiments. Of course, the whole common conscience does not, on this account, pass out of existence. At least there will always remain this cult of personality, of individual dignity of which we have just been speaking, and which, today, is the rallying-point of so many people. But how little a thing it is when one contemplates the ever increasing extent of social life, and, consequently, of individual consciences! For, as they become more voluminous, as intelligence becomes richer, activity more varied, in order for morality to remain constant, that is to say, in order for the individual to remain attached to the group with a force equal to that of yesterday, the ties which bind him to it must become stronger and more numerous. If, then, he formed no others than those which come from resemblances, the effacement of the segmental type would be accompanied by a systematic debasement of morality. Man would no longer be sufficiently obligated; he would no longer feel about and above him this salutary pressure of society which moderates his egoism and makes him a moral being. This is what gives moral value to the division of labor. Through it, the individual becomes cognizant of his dependence upon society; from it come the forces which keep him in check and restrain him. In short, since the division of labor becomes the chief source of social solidarity, it becomes, at the same time, the foundation of the moral order.

We can then say that, in higher societies, our duty is not to spread our activity over a large surface, but to concentrate and specialize it. We must contract our horizon, choose a definite task and immerse ourselves in it completely, instead of trying to make ourselves a sort of creative masterpiece, quite complete, which contains its worth in itself and not in the services that it renders. Finally, this specialization ought to be pushed as far as the elevation of the social type, without assigning any other limit to it. No doubt, we ought so to work as to realize in ourselves the collective type as it exists. There are common sentiments, common ideas, without which, as has been said, one is not a man. The rule which orders us to specialize remains limited by the contrary rule. Our conclusion is not that it is good to press specialization as far as possible, but as far as necessary. As for the part that is to be played by these two opposing necessities, that is determined by experience and cannot be calculated *a priori*. It is enough for us to have shown that the second is not of a different nature from the first, but that it also is moral, and that, moreover, this duty becomes ever more important and pressing, because the general qualities which are in question suffice less and less to socialize the individual.

It is not without reason that public sentiment reproves an ever more pronounced tendency on the part of dilettantes and even others to be taken up with an exclusively general culture and refuse to take any part in occupational organization. That is because they are not sufficiently attached to society, or, if one wishes, society is not sufficiently attached to them, and they escape it. Precisely because they feel its effect neither with vivacity nor with the continuity that is necessary, they have no cognizance of all the obligations their positions as social beings demand of them. The general ideal to which they are attached being, for the reasons we have spoken of, formal and shifting, it cannot take them out of themselves. We do not cling to very much when we have no very determined objective, and, consequently, we cannot very well elevate ourselves beyond a more or less refined egotism. On the contrary, he who gives himself over to a definite task is, at every moment, struck by the sentiment of common solidarity in the thousand duties of occupational morality.

II

But does not the division of labor by making each of us an incomplete being bring on a diminution of individual personality? That is a reproach which has often been levelled at it.

Let us first of all remark that it is difficult to see why it would be more in keeping with the logic of human nature to develop superficially rather than profoundly. Why would a more extensive activity, but more dispersed, be superior to a more concentrated, but circumscribed, activity? Why would there be more dignity in being complete and mediocre, rather than in living a more specialized, but more intense life, particularly if it is thus possible for us to find what we have lost in this specialization, through our association with other beings who have what we lack and who complete us? We take off from the principle that man ought to realize his nature as man, to accomplish his *οικεῖον ἔργον* as Aristotle said. But this nature does not remain constant throughout history; it is modified with societies. Among lower peoples, the proper duty of man is to resemble his companions, to realize in himself all the traits of the collective type which are then confounded, much more than today, with the human type. But, in more advanced societies, his nature is, in large part, to be an organ of society, and his proper duty, consequently, is to play his role as an organ.

Moreover, far from being trammelled by the progress of specialization, individual personality develops with the division of labor.

To be a person is to be an autonomous source of action. Man acquires this quality only in so far as there is something in him which is his alone and which individualizes him, as he is something more than a simple incarnation of the generic type of his race and his group. It will be said that he is endowed with free will and that is enough to establish his personality. But although there may be some of this liberty in him, an object of so many discussions, it is not this metaphysical, impersonal, invariable attribute which can serve as the unique basis for concrete personality, which is empirical and variable with individuals. That could not be constituted by the wholly abstract power of choice between two opposites, but it is still necessary for this faculty to be exercised towards ends and aims which are proper to the agent. In other words, the very materials of conscience must have a personal character. But we have seen that this result is progressively produced as the division of labor progresses. The effacement of the segmental type, at the same time that it necessitates a very great specialization, partially lifts the individual conscience from the organic environment which supports it, as from the social environment which envelops it, and, accordingly because of this double emancipation, the individual becomes more of an independent factor in his own conduct. The division of labor itself contributes to this enfranchisement, for individual natures, while specializing, become more complex, and by that are in part freed from collective action and hereditary influences which can only enforce themselves upon simple, general things.

It is, accordingly, a real illusion which makes us believe that personality was so much more complete when the division of labor had penetrated less. No doubt, in looking from without at the diversity of occupations which the individual then embraces, it may seem that he is developing in a very free and complete manner. But, in reality, this activity which he manifests is not really his. It is society, it is the race acting in and through him; he is only the intermediary through which they realize themselves. His liberty is only apparent and his personality borrowed. Because the life of these societies is, in certain respects, less regular, we imagine that original talents have more opportunity for free play, that it is easier for each one to pursue his own tastes, that a very large place is left to free fantasy. But this is to forget that personal sentiments are then very rare. If the motives which govern conduct do not appear as periodically as they do today, they do not leave off being collective, and, consequently, impersonal, and it is the same with the actions that they inspire. Moreover, we have shown above how activity becomes richer and more intense as it becomes more specialized.

Thus, the progress of individual personality and that of the division of labor depend upon one and the same cause. It is thus impossible to desire one without desiring the other. But no one today contests the obligatory character of the rule which orders us to be more and more of a person.

One last consideration will make us see to what extent the division of labor is linked with our whole moral life.

Men have long dreamt of finally realizing in fact the ideal of human fraternity. People pray for a state where war will no longer be the law of international relations, where relations between societies will be pacifically regulated, as those between individuals already are, where all men will collaborate in the same work and live the same life. Although these aspirations are in part neutralized by those which have as their object the particular society of which we are a part, they have not left off being active and are even gaining in force. But they can be satisfied only if all men form one society, subject to the same laws. For, just as private conflicts can be regulated only by the action of the society in which the individuals live, so intersocial conflicts can be regulated only by a society which comprises in its scope all others. The only power which can serve to moderate individual egotism is the power of the group; the only power which can serve to moderate the egotism of groups is that of some other group which embraces them.

Truly, when the problem has been posed in these terms, we must recognize that this ideal is not on the verge of being integrally realized, for there are too many intellectual and moral diversities between different social types existing together on the earth to admit of fraternalization in the same society. But what is possible is that societies of the same type may come together, and it is, indeed, in this direction that evolution appears to move. We have already seen that among European peoples there is a tendency to form, by spontaneous movement, a European society which has, at present, some idea of itself and the beginning of organization. If the formation of a single human society is forever impossible, a fact which has not been proved, at least the formation of continually larger societies brings us vaguely near the goal. These facts, moreover, in no wise contradict the definition of morality that we have given, for if we cling to humanity and if we ought to cling to it, it is because it is a society which is in process of realizing itself in this way, and with which we are solidary.

But we know the greater societies cannot be formed except through the development of the division of labor, for not only could they not maintain themselves in equilibrium without a greater specialization of functions, but even the increase in the number of those competing would suffice to produce this result mechanically; and that, so much the more, since the growth of volume is generally accompanied by a growth in density. We can then formulate the following proposition: the ideal of human fraternity can be realized only in proportion to the progress of the division of labor. We must choose: either to renounce our dream, if we refuse further to circumscribe our activity, or else to push forward its accomplishment under the condition we have just set forth.

III

But if the division of labor produces solidarity, it is not only because it makes each individual an *exchangist,* as the economists say; it is because it creates among men an entire system of rights and duties which link them together in a durable way. Just as social similitudes give rise to a law and a morality which protect them, so the division of labor gives rise to rules which assure pacific and regular concourse of divided functions. If economists have believed that it would bring forth an abiding solidarity, in some manner of its own making, and if, accordingly, they have held that human societies could and would resolve themselves into purely economic associations, that is because they believed that it affected only individual, temporary interests. Consequently, to estimate the interests in conflict and the way in which they ought to equilibrate, that is to say, to determine the conditions under which exchange ought to take place, is solely a matter of individual competence; and, since these interests are in a perpetual state of becoming, there is no place for any permanent regulation. But such a conception is, in all ways, inadequate for the facts. The division of labor does not present individuals to one another, but social functions. And society is interested in the play of the latter; in so far as they regularly concur, or do not concur, it will be healthy or ill. Its existence thus depends upon them, and the more they are divided the greater its dependence. That is why it cannot leave them in a state of indetermination. In addition to this, they are determined by themselves. Thus are formed those rules whose number grows as labor is divided, and whose absence makes organic solidarity either impossible or imperfect.

But it is not enough that there be rules; they must be just, and for that it is necessary for the external conditions of competition to be equal. If, moreover, we remember that the collective conscience is becoming more and more a cult of the individual, we shall see that what characterizes the morality of organized societies, compared to that of segmental societies, is that there is something more human, therefore more rational, about them. It does not direct our activities to ends which do not immediately concern us; it does not make us servants of ideal powers of a nature other than our own, which follow their directions without occupying themselves with the interests of men. It only asks that we be thoughtful of our fellows and that we be just, that we fulfill our duty, that we work at the function we can best execute, and receive that just reward for our services. The rules which constitute it do not have a constraining force which snuffs out free thought; but, because they are rather made for us and, in a certain sense, by us, we are free. We wish to understand them; we do not fear to change them. We must, however, guard against finding such an ideal inadequate on the pretext that it is too earthly and too much to our liking. An ideal is not more elevated because more transcendent, but because it leads us to vaster perspectives. What is important is not that it tower high above us, until it becomes a stranger to our lives, but that it open to our activity a large enough field. This is far from being on the verge of realization. We know only too well what a laborious work it is to erect this society where each individual will have the place he merits, will be rewarded as he deserves, where everybody, accordingly, will spontaneously work for the good of all and of each. Indeed, a moral code is not above another because it commands in a drier and more authoritarian manner, or because it is more sheltered from reflection. Of course, it must attach us to something besides ourselves but it is not necessary for it to chain us to it with impregnable bonds.

It has been said with justice that morality—and by that must be understood, not only moral doctrines, but customs—is going through a real crisis. What precedes can help us to understand the nature and causes of this sick condition. Profound changes have been produced in the structure of our societies in a very short time; they have been freed from the segmental type with a rapidity and in proportions such as have never before been seen in history. Accordingly, the morality which corresponds to this social type has regressed, but without another developing quickly enough to fill the ground that the first left vacant in our consciences. Our faith has been troubled; tradition has lost its sway; individual judgment has been freed from collective judgment. But, on the other hand, the functions which have been disrupted in the course of the upheaval have not had the time to adjust themselves to one another; the new life which has emerged so suddenly has not been able to be completely organized, and above all, it has not been organized in a way to satisfy the need for justice which has grown more ardent in our hearts. If this be so, the remedy for the evil is not to seek to resuscitate traditions and practices which, no longer responding to present conditions of society, can only live an artificial, false existence. What we must do to relieve this anomy is to discover the means for making the organs which are still wasting themselves in discordant movements harmoniously concur by introducing into their relations more justice by more and more extenuating the external inequalities which are the source of the evil. Our illness is not, then, as has often been believed, of an intellectual sort; it has more profound causes. We shall not suffer because we no longer know on what theoretical notion to base the morality we have been practicing, but because, in certain of its parts, this morality is irremediably shattered, and that which is necessary to us is only in process of formation. Our anxiety does not arise because the criticism of scholars has broken down the traditional explanation we used to give to our duties; consequently, it is not a new philosophical system which will relieve the situation. Because certain of our duties are no longer founded in the reality of things, a breakdown has resulted which will be repaired only in so far as a new discipline is established and consolidated. In short, our first duty is to make a moral code for ourselves. Such a work cannot be improvised in the silence of the study; it can arise only through itself, little by little, under the pressure of internal causes which make it necessary. But the service that thought can and must render is in fixing the goal that we must attain. That is what we have tried to do.

57 Pharmaceuticals: Valley of the Lies

HENRY GEWIRTZ AND
SAXON GRAHAM

The development of economic institutions to serve particular human needs sometimes becomes distorted. In the following selection we note how the pharmaceutical industry, which has produced a wide range of drugs for the alleviation of illness and suffering, comes to serve its own interests as well as those of the consumers. Although competition presumably maintains reasonable prices, the concentration of economic power and cooperative arrangements within the pharmaceutical industry sometimes serve to control the effect of competition on the market. The following article also illustrates the complex relationship between the pharmaceutical manufacturers and the various health professions in the delivery of medical services to the public.

The Pharmaceutical Manufacturer's Association (PMA) is the organized expression of the 135 drug companies which produce 95 percent of all the prescription drugs sold in the United States today. It represents the 35 leading companies in the field including: Squibb, Searle, Smith, Kline & French, Upjohn, Parke Davis, Merck, Pfizer, Lilly, Abbott and Schering. The major function of this organization is perhaps best described by C. Joseph Stetler, who stated in his presidential address to the Tenth Annual Convention of the PMA in April 1968, that:

> We are to be called on to prove that our industry is an institution in the service of mankind; that we are dedicated to producing the best, the purest, the most effective drugs in the world; and that we cannot fulfill this aim if our operations and our progress are to be stifled by excess of government control.

Thus the PMA exists to demonstrate to all concerned that the drug companies it represents are seeking the betterment of humanity and the advancement of science and that furthermore, they could achieve these ends more easily if the gov-

SOURCE: *Trans-action,* vol. 7, no. 4 (February 1970), 5, 8–10. • Henry Gewirtz is at the State University of New York at Buffalo. • Saxon Graham is professor of sociology and preventive medicine at the State University of New York at Buffalo. His major interests include medical and social change. He is associate research scientist at the Roswell Park Memorial Institute. He has published *American Culture; Sociometric Distribution of Cancer at Various Sites, Buffalo, New York, 1948–1952;* and *Class and Conservation in the Adoption of Innovations.*

ernment would cease its "legislative and regulatory attack" upon the industry.

However, if one considers the costs of drugs today, the nature of the so-called research conducted by the industry, and its position on such legislation as the Kefauver bill (S.1552) and the Long amendment (S.2299) to the Medicare law, it becomes clear that the PMA and the industry it represents present a clear and persistent danger to the health of the people of this nation. This is due to the fact that the cost of prescription drugs borders on the exorbitant, and as a result people are either unable to afford them or else are obliged to sacrifice other necessities to secure the medicine they require. This is especially true of the elderly and the poor. The Task Force on Prescription Drugs, a study group consisting of members of the U.S. Department of Health, Education and Welfare (HEW) noted in August 1968:

> . . . the requirements for appropriate prescription drug therapy by the elderly are very great . . . and that many elderly men and women are now unable to meet these needs with their limited incomes, savings or present insurance coverage. Their inability to afford the drugs they require may well be reflected in needless sickness and disability, unemployability and costly hospitalization which could have been prevented by adequate out-of-hospital treatment.

It is also important to note that the per capita cost of prescription drugs has risen from $6.85 in 1950 to $16.05 in 1966. (During the same period the cost-of-living rose only 31 percent.) This rise is due to both an increase in the number of prescriptions made per person as well as to an increase in the cost per prescription.

PROFITS FROM DISEASE

One of the major reasons for the increased cost per prescription is the amount of profit made by the drug companies. Between 1955 and 1966 the profits of the drug industry (based on after-tax income as a percent of net worth) were never ranked lower than third of the 41 major U.S. industries and in six of those years the industry was ranked first. Furthermore, the drug industry earns an average return of 18.1 percent on its capital whereas 31 other major industries (including defense, autos and trucks, oil, steel, chemicals, airlines, and telephone and telegraph) earn an average of 9.7 percent on capital. It is clear, therefore, that one of the major reasons for high drug prices is the extremely high profits earned by the pharmaceutical industry.

It should be noted at this point that Stetler admits that the "profitability of the drug industry is above average." He argues further that such high profits are necessary in order to maintain the research and development conducted by the industry and also because it is a high risk industry. It is claimed that competition within the industry is extremely great and that the need to attract investment capital for future growth makes it necessary for the industry to make high profits. Furthermore, the industry claims that it spends about $450 million annually for research and development and that the average cost of developing a single new drug amounts to almost $7 million. Since not all drugs developed turn out to be useful, there are losses which must be made up if the industry is to survive and grow. In addition the industry claims that even if a drug does prove to be useful it still takes several years to recoup the initial investment before a profit can be realized from the sale of the drug.

The facts, however, are somewhat different. Willard F. Mueller, the chief economist of the Federal Trade Commission, has testified that "there is no reason to conclude, on the basis of advice being given by investment analysis, that the drug industry is a uniquely risky industry." He points out further that "... their profits are so large that drug companies seldom need go to the capital market for equity capital." Finally, he points out that even if the drug industry had profit rates comparable to most other American industries, it would still have little difficulty in obtaining the capital it requires. Furthermore, the major drug companies have in the past and continue to diversify their operations into other areas so as to minimize their risks. Also it must be noted that none of the major drug companies sells only one drug and thus a loss on one is readily compensated for by high profits on another.

RESEARCH FOR REDUNDANCY

The matter of research and development is equally deceiving unless one is aware of certain facts. In the period 1957–1968, 2,131 new prescription drugs were produced. Of these, the HEW Task Force estimates that 311 or 15 percent were medically important and significant additions. Charles D. May, clinical professor of pediatrics, College of Physicians and Surgeons, Columbia University, has argued that only six new drugs are produced every year which fall into this category. According to his estimates only 66 (3 percent) important drugs would have been produced during this period. The remainder represent either combinations of old drugs or minor molecular modifications of drugs already in existence. The HEW Task Force reports:

> ... expert physicians have served on pharmacy and therapeutics committees to select the drugs needed for both inpatient and outpatient therapy, they have generally found many if not most of these duplicative and combination drugs to be unnecessary.

The *New England Journal of Medicine* has gone so far as to comment editorially that many of these drugs "have no good reason for being on the market except to help their promoters recover some of the investment that went into their production." Since, therefore, anywhere from 85 to 95 percent of the "new" drugs produced every year are at best unnecessary, it is clear that a major proportion of the money spent on research and development of "new" drugs is wasted money. This serves only to increase needlessly the cost of drugs without benefiting the consumer.

The problem of generic versus trade name prescribing of drugs is also intimately related to the high cost of drugs in the United States today. Every drug on the market today has at least three different names. It has a chemical name which is usually extremely long and which accurately describes its chemical structure. A drug also has a generic name which is its official name. This name provides some information as to the chemical composition of the drug but it is also unfortunately long and often difficult to remember and pronounce. Lastly, a drug has a patented trade name which has been chosen for it by its manufacturer. This name rarely provides any clue as to the chemical structure of the drug but has the distinct advantage of being short and simple and easy to remember. This then is one of the major reasons why the vast majority of physicians use trade names when prescribing drugs. The law requires that the pharmacist dispense to the patient exactly what the physician writes for. Thus, if a doctor prescribes Serpasil for his patient, that is what the druggist must dispense even though reserpine, which is the same chemical, costs but a fraction of the price. It should be emphasized that this price differential is not an isolated case but in fact part of a general pattern. The average cost of 379 drugs on the HEW Task Force Master Drug List which were prescribed by trade name was $4.11 per prescription, whereas the average cost of 30 drugs on the list prescribed by generic name was $2.02 per prescription.

The result of this is that the consumer is confronted with a system that encourages the prescription of drugs by their trade name and thus significantly increases the cost of these drugs.

Needless to say, the PMA has fought any legislation that would encourage the prescription of drugs on a generic basis. The most recent example came in its opposition to the Long amendment. This legislation would have allowed elderly people (over 65) to pay an extra premium on the voluntary part of their Medicare insurance to cover out-of-hospital drug expenses. Drugs for which such people would have been reimbursed would have been listed by both trade and generic name. In addition the maximum amount of compensation for each drug would have been determined by a three-man commission. The intent was to set maximum amounts which would have encouraged prescribing on a generic basis. Senator Russell Long claimed that the opposition of the PMA was responsible for the bill's defeat. Stetler in his presidential address to the 1968 PMA convention claimed the same thing.

In defense of the stand taken by the PMA, Stetler claimed that prescribing by trade name assured the physician that he was ordering dependable, reliable, quality drugs for his patient. Furthermore, he suggested that to encourage generic prescribing was to favor price over quality and to put unknown drugs on a par with the known high quality drugs put out by the members of the PMA. In effect he argues that with drugs one gets what one pays for.

This is untrue. All drugs sold in the United States must meet the chemical standards of the U.S. Pharmacopeia and National Formulatory as well as the Food and Drug Administration (FDA) rules and regulations. Thus all drugs sold in this country must pass the same government tests before they can be marketed. Furthermore, generic drugs have long been used by such large organizations as the Department of Defense without any harmful consequences. Indeed the HEW Task Force reports that:

> . . . lack of clinical equivalency among chemical equivalents meeting all official standards has been grossly exaggerated as a major hazard to public health. Where low cost chemical equivalents have been employed in foreign drug programs, in leading American hospitals, in State welfare programs, in Veterans Administration and Public Health hospitals, and in American military operations, instances of clinical non-equivalency have seldom been reported, and few of these have had significant therapeutic consequences.

The situation is perhaps best summarized by the former commissioner of the FDA, James L. Goddard, who said that ". . . on the basis of available evidence it can reasonably be said that two drugs, which contain the same active ingredients and meet the same chemical standards. . . , will act the same way in the human body."

DANGEROUS ANTIBODIES

Furthermore, buying drugs from the PMA member companies is no guarantee of either quality or dependability. The best and most recent evidence concerns the combination antibiotic drugs. On June 12, 1969 the FDA ordered 49 commonly used penicillin-streptomycin and penicillin-sulfa combination drugs off the market. The reason given was that the drugs were either ineffective or dangerous. Upjohn, one of the leaders in the field, figured prominently in this particular incident. Its drug, Panalba, with annual sales as high as $20 million, was one of the drugs ordered off the market.

The Cost of Drugs: Trade or Generic? Take Your Pick

TRADE NAME	PRICE	GENERIC NAME	PRICE
Equanil (Wyeth)	$4.68/100 (200 mg tabs)	Meprobamate	$2.60/100
Lanooxin (Burroughs-Wellcome)	$1.03/100 (.25 mg tabs)	Digoxin	$0.55/100
Empirin w/ Codeine (Burroughs-Wellcome)	$2.34/100 (¼ gr. tabs)	Aspirin, Phenacetin, Caffeine, Codeine	$2.10/100
Raudixin (Squibb)	$3.00/100 (50 mg tabs)	Rauwolfa Serpentina	$0.30/100
Purodigin (Wyeth)	$1.06/100 (.1 mg tabs)	Digitoxin	$0.45/100
Seconal (Lilly)	$1.35/100 (¾ gr. tabs)	Secobarbital	$0.65/100
Nembutal (Abbott)	$2.16/100 (100 mg tabs)	Pentobarbital	$0.70/100
Butisol (McNeil)	$2.05/100 (30 mg tabs)	Butabarbital	$0.80/100
Isopto Carpine (Alcon)	$21.00/30cc–1% sol	Pilocarpine	$1.30/30cc
Peritrate (Warner-Chilcott)	$2.50/100 (10 mg tabs)	Pentaerythritoltetranitrate	$0.25/100
Premarin (Ayerst)	$6.29/100 (125 mg tabs)	Conjugated estrogen equine	$3.00/100
Chlor-Trimeton (Schering)	$33.48/1000 (8 mg tabs)	Chlorpheniramine	$5.75/1000
Achromycin (Lederle)	$11.22/100 (250 mg tabs)	Tetracycline	$2.25/100
Noctec (Squibb)	$2.50/100 (250 mg tabs)	Chloral hydrate	$0.90/100
Gantrisin (Roche)	$25.30/1000 (500 mg tabs)	Sulfisoxazole	$15.00/1000

All prices have been obtained from the *American Druggist-1969-Blue Book.*

Moreover, the chairman of the FDA testified before the monopoly subcommittee of the Senate Select Committee on Small Business that Upjohn has had evidence in its files since 1960 which indicates that Panalba is not as effective as it claims it to be. Yet Upjohn did not make this evidence available until this year. Senator Gaylord Nelson has claimed that this was done deliberately by Upjohn in order to keep the information from the public. It should also be noted that as early as January 1961, Charles D. May had already criticized the way this drug was being promoted. He pointed out at that time that Upjohn's advertisements for the drug showed the results of in vitro (not in vivo) sensitivity tests against organisms known to cause pneumonia. Yet Upjohn claimed that these results were proof of the clinical efficacy of the drug. No references to clinical trials were given in the advertisement to support these claims. May also pointed out that Upjohn used its own brand name to describe the components of this combination drug which further obscured its true nature. Finally, as early as February 1960, the *New England Journal of Medicine* criticized the use of combination antibiotics in general and in addition declared that "the worst of the antibiotic combinations is the mixture of penicillin and streptomycin. . . ." These statements were based on research as well as theoretical knowledge available at that time. Thus almost a decade before the FDA got around to removing these drugs from the market there was good evidence available to show that they shouldn't be used. Nevertheless the drug companies producing these drugs continued to promote them heavily. In light of such disclosures, the claims of quality, dependability and reliability made by the major drug companies are open to serious question.

The patent system in the United States is another important factor that helps to keep the price of prescription drugs high. Under this system the inventor of a new drug is entitled to exclusive rights to that drug for 17 years. Yet it takes only an average of three years to recover the cost of research and development that went into the drug. This system tends to induce fierce production competition within the industry but does nothing about insuring price competition. Companies X, Y and Z may compete vigorously to develop a new drug. However, once one of them comes up with the drug the other two are prohibited from producing it and thus the discoverer is free to charge what the traffic will bear. The result is that the patent system as it now exists works to the benefit of the major drug companies and to the detriment of the patient who must pay for the drug.

High cost is not the only instance of drug-company abuse of the health professions and their clients. There is also the growing problem of iatrogenic illnesses, those caused by the irrational use of drugs. It is estimated that the incidence of drug sickness in hospitals throughout the country runs to 3.5 million cases per year. In 1966 Seidl et al. found that 5 percent of admissions to the public medical service over a three-month period at Johns Hopkins University were due to drug-induced illness. In the same study these investigators also found that "drug reactions following hospitalization were observed in 13.6 percent of patients" admitted to this service. Moreover, it was found that the average patient receives 14 different drugs during an average hospital stay (14 days) and that the incidence of adverse drug reactions increased with the number of drugs taken. It was also found that the average hospital stay of those suffering from drug reactions was almost a full week longer (20.8 days) than the average. It is clear, therefore, that the irrational use of drugs is responsible for increasing the incidence of morbidity and mortality in the population. It is also responsible for increasing the cost of medical care as well.

IGNORANCE DOCTORS

The HEW Task Force has placed the primary responsibility for this situation on the medical schools. It points out that most medical schools fail to offer a course in clinical pharmacology which would offer practical information concerning the actual use and evaluation of drugs. Such information is offered in minimal amounts, if at all, in most basic courses in pharmacology. The result is physicians who are poorly trained in the clinical use and evaluation of drugs.

Taking advantage of this ignorance of physicians, the drug companies conduct an $800 million per year ($3,000 per physician and 35 percent of sales revenue) advertising campaign to convince the medical profession of the wonders of their products. We have already pointed out that the vast majority of the so-called new drugs put out by the industry each year represent either minor molecular modifications of existent drugs or combinations of old drugs. It has also been pointed out that such drugs are either no better than already existent drugs or are even worse. And such "new" drugs are often more expensive than older proven drugs. Yet the major drug companies continue to produce and promote such products and thereby contribute to the growing problem of iatrogenic drug illness.

ADVERTISING POWER

The American Medical Association (AMA), which has had very cordial relations with the PMA, has done little to protect its members and the public from such blandishments and in fact, has even co-operated with the PMA. Prior to 1953 the AMA engaged in several activities which were in the public interest and which were often detrimental to the interests of the drug industry. These activities included: 1) support for laboratory work to test new drugs, 2) a seal of approval program which insured that no drug could be advertised in the *AMA Journal* without this seal, 3) inspection of drug plants, and 4) a campaign for the prescription of drugs on a *generic* basis. But in 1953 the AMA commissioned a study to discover why its advertising revenue had increased only 3 percent since 1946 while that of other journals had increased 50 percent in the same period. The study indicated that the drug industry was unhappy with the AMA's seal of approval program. As a result, after 1953 the AMA discontinued these programs. By 1960 its advertising revenue had jumped from $3.5 to $8.0 million, which accounted for more than half its annual income. The annual number of advertising pages had increased from 470 to 1,402 in the same period. At the present time the AMA earns more than $10.5 million per year from drug advertisements. As a result the AMA has been and continues to be reluctant to antagonize the major drug companies. Rather, the AMA by eliminating its drug evaluation programs constitutes a powerful and important ally of the PMA.

It seems clear that any solution to these problems must concentrate on at least two areas. The first concerns the cost of drugs and the second concerns the prescribers of drugs. Various methods have been proposed to lower drug prices. These include 1) the abolition of patent protection for new drugs, 2) reduction in the life of drug patents, 3) compulsory licensing arrangements where the discoverer is compelled to license other manufacturers to make the new drug, 4) the abolition of trade names with the stipulation that a drug be identified by generic name and its manufacturer, and 5) the regulation of the prices charged by the industry by the federal government in the same way that public utilities are regulated.

The following proposal embodies some of the above. We begin with the assumption that the nature of the product of this industry requires that it be regulated as a public utility. If the airlines and the telephone and telegraph industries are subject to price regulation, it seems absurd that an industry which is supposed to serve the health of the people should set their own prices at levels insuring huge profits to the companies and deprivation of drugs for many patients. The FDA should be empowered to regulate drug prices just as the Federal Communications Commission is empowered to regulate the rates charged by the telephone and telegraph industry.

In addition, the patent system as it applies to the drug industry should be revised. The law should provide that any company that develops a new drug should be compensated for the cost of research and development that went into the drug by any other company which chooses to produce and market that drug. This would promote price competition and in addition would compensate the discoverer of the drug. An expert panel of scientists and clinicians should be established to determine areas of priority for drug research. Any company discovering a new and important drug would be given a tax credit as a reward. The effect of this proposal would be to provide incentives for research deemed worthwhile by a panel of recognized experts. Finally, the use of trade names to identify drugs should be outlawed and a law passed that would require that all drugs be identified by generic name and manufacturer. Generic names could be and should be simplified. This would eventually insure that all physicians spoke, for example, of prednisone instead of calling the same drug by one of its many trade names: Deltra, Deltrasone, Meticorten, Paracort. Identifying the manufacturer would serve as an added check in quality control in the event that a particular company were to turn out a defective product.

It seems clear that the solution to the second part of this problem (i.e. the drug prescribers) is to be found in a revised medical school curriculum. A course in clinical pharmacology should be required of all medical school graduates. Such a course should stress the evaluation of drugs under clinical conditions. It should also stress the principles of predicting drug interactions and of diagnosing adverse drug reactions. Specific information should be given concerning the indications for and dosages of the more commonly used drugs. For the postgraduate physician the medical schools should provide similar courses in order to enable him to keep up with developments in the field. Finally, every practicing physician in the nation should receive a monthly publication which would provide information concerning recent advances made in clinical pharmacology, the latest evidence as to effectiveness of drugs and dangerous side-effects.

These proposals taken together could insure that quality drugs would be available at realistic prices, that new drugs could be developed without the current duplications of effort, that prescription of drugs would be on a more rational basis, and that patients would not be deprived of the medications they need.

58 Letter from Birmingham Jail

MARTIN LUTHER KING, JR.

The power necessary to maintain the social control function of government often encourages those in control to perpetuate special privileges to serve their own ends. In these circumstances the disadvantaged may resort to revolution or civil disobedience to overcome the inequities. Using passive resistance, Mahatma Gandhi led a weaponless mass of South Asians in their struggle to end British rule. The nonviolent action phase of the black revolution, led for over a decade (1956–68) by the late Martin Luther King, Jr., followed the same tradition. In this selection King states his case for nonviolence, the "powerful and just weapon" which he called the Sword That Heals.

April 16, 1963

MY DEAR FELLOW CLERGYMEN:

While confined here in the Birmingham city jail, I came across your recent statement calling my present activities "unwise and untimely." Seldom do I pause to answer criticism of my work and ideas. If I sought to answer all the criticisms that cross my desk, my secretaries would have little time for anything other than such correspondence in the course of the day, and I would have no time for constructive work. But since I feel that you are men of genuine good will and that your criticisms are sincerely set forth, I want to try to answer your statement in what I hope will be patient and reasonable terms.

I think I should indicate why I am here in Birmingham, since you have been influenced by the view which argues against "outsiders coming in." I have the honor of serving as president of the Southern Christian Leadership Conference, an organization operating in every southern state, with headquarters at Atlanta, Georgia. We have some eighty-five affiliated organizations across the South, and one of them is the Alabama Christian Movement for Human Rights. Frequently we share staff, educational and financial resources with our affiliates. Several months ago the affiliate here in Birmingham asked us to be on call to engage in a nonviolent direct-action program if such were deemed necessary. We readily consented, and when the hour came we lived up to our promise. So I, along with several members of my staff, am here because I was invited here. I am here because I have organizational ties here.

SOURCE: "Letter from Birmingham Jail" (April 16, 1963) in *Why We Can't Wait* by Martin Luther King, Jr. • Martin Luther King, Jr. (1929–1968) was president of the Southern Christian Leadership Conference and vice-president of the National Sunday School and Baptist Training Union, Congress of National Baptist Convention. He was awarded the Nobel Peace Prize in 1964 and was the author of *Stride Toward Freedom* and *Where Do We Go From Here: Chaos or Community?* • AUTHOR'S NOTE: This response to a published statement by eight fellow clergymen from Alabama . . . was composed under somewhat constricting circumstances. Begun on the margins of the newspaper in which the statement appeared while I was in jail, the letter was continued on scraps of writing paper supplied by a friendly Negro trusty, and concluded on a pad my attorneys were eventually permitted to leave me. Although the text remains in substance unaltered, I have indulged in the author's prerogative of polishing it for publication.

But more basically, I am in Birmingham because injustice is here. . . . Moreover, I am cognizant of the interrelatedness of all communities and states. I cannot sit idly by in Atlanta and not be concerned about what happens in Birmingham. Injustice anywhere is a threat to justice everywhere. We are caught in an inescapable network of mutuality, tied in a single garment of destiny. Whatever affects one directly, affects all indirectly. Never again can we afford to live with the narrow, provincial "outside agitator" idea. Anyone who lives inside the United States can never be considered an outsider anywhere within its bounds.

You deplore the demonstrations taking place in Birmingham. But your statement, I am sorry to say, fails to express a similar concern for the conditions that brought about the demonstrations. I am sure that none of you would want to rest content with the superficial kind of social analysis that deals merely with effects and does not grapple with underlying causes. It is unfortunate that demonstrations are taking place in Birmingham, but it is even more unfortunate that the city's white power structure left the Negro community with no alternative.

In any nonviolent campaign there are four basic steps: collection of the facts to determine whether injustices exist; negotiation; self-purification; and direct action. We have gone through all these steps in Birmingham. There can be no gainsaying the fact that racial injustice engulfs this community. Birmingham is probably the most thoroughly segregated city in the United States. Its ugly record of brutality is widely known. Negroes have experienced grossly unjust treatment in the courts. There have been more unsolved bombings of Negro homes and churches in Birmingham than in any other city in the nation. These are the hard, brutal facts of the case. On the basis of these conditions, Negro leaders sought to negotiate with the city fathers. But the latter consistently refused to engage in good-faith negotiation.

Then, last September, came the opportunity to talk with leaders of Birmingham's economic community. In the course of the negotiations, certain promises were made by the merchants—for example, to remove the stores' humiliating racial signs. On the basis of these promises, the Reverend Fred Shuttlesworth and the leaders of the Alabama Christian Movement for Human Rights agreed to a moratorium on all demonstrations. As the weeks and months went by, we realized that we were the victims of a broken promise. A few signs, briefly removed, returned; the others remained.

As in so many past experiences, our hopes had been blasted, and the shadow of deep disappointment settled upon us. We had no alternative except to prepare for direct action, whereby we would present our very bodies as a means of laying our case before the conscience of the local and the national community. Mindful of the difficulties involved, we decided to undertake a process of self-purification. We began a series of workshops on nonviolence, and we repeatedly asked ourselves: "Are you able to accept blows without retaliating?" "Are you able to endure the ordeal of jail?" We decided to schedule our direct-action program for the Easter season, realizing that except for Christmas, this is the main shopping period of the year. Knowing that a strong economic-withdrawal program would be the by-product of direct action, we felt that this would be the best time to bring pressure to bear on the merchants for the needed change.

Then it occurred to us that Birmingham's mayoral election was coming up in March, and we speedily decided to postpone action until after election day.

When we discovered that the Commissioner of Public Safety, Eugene "Bull" Connor, had piled up enough votes to be in the run-off, we decided again to postpone action until the day after the run-off so that the demonstrations could not be used to cloud the issues. Like many others, we waited to see Mr. Connor defeated, and to this end we endured postponement after postponement. Having aided in this community need, we felt that our direct-action program could be delayed no longer.

You may well ask: "Why direct action? Why sit-ins, marches and so forth? Isn't negotiation a better path?" You are quite right in calling for negotiation. Indeed, this is the very purpose of direct action. Nonviolent direct action seeks to create such a crisis and foster such a tension that a community which has constantly refused to negotiate is forced to confront the issue. It seeks so to dramatize the issue that it can no longer be ignored. My citing the creation of tension as part of the work of the nonviolent-resister may sound rather shocking. But I must confess that I am not afraid of the word "tension." I have earnestly opposed violent tension, but there is a type of constructive, nonviolent tension which is necessary for growth. Just as Socrates felt that it was necessary to create a tension in the mind so that individuals could rise from the bondage of myths and half-truths to the unfettered realm of creative analysis and objective appraisal, so must we see the need for nonviolent gadflies to create the kind of tension in society that will help men rise from the dark depths of prejudice and racism to the majestic heights of understanding and brotherhood.

The purpose of our direct-action program is to create a situation so crisis-packed that it will eventually open the door to negotiation. I therefore concur with you in your call for negotiation. Too long has our beloved Southland been bogged down in a tragic effort to live in monologue rather than dialogue.

One of the basic points in your statement is that the action that I and my associates have taken in Birmingham is untimely. Some have asked: "Why didn't you give the new city administration time to act?" The only answer that I can give to this query is that the new Birmingham administration must be prodded about as much as the outgoing one, before it will act.

. . . My friends, I must say to you that we have not made a single gain in civil rights without determined legal and nonviolent pressure. Lamentably, it is an historical fact that privileged groups seldom give up their privileges voluntarily. Individuals may see the moral light and voluntarily give up their unjust posture; but, as Reinhold Niebuhr has reminded us, groups tend to be more immoral than individuals.

We know through painful experience that freedom is never voluntarily given by the oppressor; it must be demanded by the oppressed. Frankly, I have yet to engage in a direct-action campaign that was "well timed" in the view of those who have not suffered unduly from the disease of segregation. For years now I have heard the word "Wait!" It rings in the ear of every Negro with piercing familiarity. This "Wait" has almost always meant "Never." We must come to see, with one of our distinguished jurists, that "justice too long delayed is justice denied."

We have waited for more than 340 years for our constitutional and God-given rights. The nations of Asia and Africa are moving with jetlike speed toward gaining political independence, but we still creep at horse-and-buggy pace toward gaining a cup of coffee at a lunch counter. Perhaps it is easy for those who have never felt the stinging darts of segregation to say, "Wait." But when you have seen vicious mobs lynch your mothers and fathers at will and drown your sisters and brothers at whim; when you have seen hate-filled policemen curse, kick and even kill your black brothers and sisters; when you see the vast majority of your twenty million Negro brothers smothering in an airtight cage of poverty in the midst of an affluent society; when you suddenly find your tongue twisted and your speech stammering as you seek to explain to your six-year-old daughter why she can't go to the public amusement park that has just been advertised on television, and see tears welling up in her eyes when she is told that Funtown is closed to colored children, and see ominous clouds of inferiority beginning to form in her little mental sky, and see her beginning to distort her personality by developing an unconscious bitterness toward white people; when you have to concoct an answer for a five-year-old son who is asking: "Daddy, why do white people treat colored people so mean?"; when you take a cross-country drive and find it necessary to sleep night after night in the uncomfortable corners of your automobile because no motel will accept you; when you are humiliated day in and day out by nagging signs reading "white" and "colored"; when your first name becomes "nigger," your middle name becomes "boy" (however old you are) and your last name becomes "John," and your wife and mother are never given the respected title "Mrs."; when you are harried by day and haunted by night by the fact that you are a Negro, living constantly at tiptoe stance, never quite knowing what to expect next, and are plagued with inner fears and outer resentments; when you are forever fighting a degenerating sense of "nobodiness"--then you will understand why we find it difficult to wait. There comes a time when the cup of endurance runs over, and men are no longer willing to be plunged into the abyss of despair. I hope, sirs, you can understand our legitimate and unavoidable impatience.

You express a great deal of anxiety over our willingness to break laws. This is certainly a legitimate concern. Since we so diligently urge people to obey the Supreme Court's decision of 1954 outlawing segregation in the public schools, at first glance it may seem rather paradoxical for us consciously to break laws. One may well ask: "How can you advocate breaking some laws and obeying others?" The answer lies in the fact that there are two types of laws: just and unjust. I would be the first to advocate obeying just laws. One has not only a legal but a moral responsibility to obey just laws. Conversely, one has a moral responsibility to disobey unjust laws. I would agree with St. Augustine that "an unjust law is no law at all."

Now, what is the difference between the two? . . . Any law that uplifts human personality is just. Any law that degrades human personality is unjust. All segregation statutes are unjust because segregation distorts the soul and damages the personality. It gives the segregator a false sense of superiority and the segregated a false sense of inferiority. Segregation, to use the terminology of the Jewish philosopher Martin Buber, substitutes an "I–it" relationship for an "I–thou" relationship and ends up relegating persons to the status of things. Hence segregation is not only politically, economically and sociologically unsound, it is morally wrong and sinful. Paul Tillich has said that sin is separation. Is not segregation an existential expression of man's tragic separation, his awful estrangement, his terrible sinfulness? Thus it is that I can urge men to obey the 1954 decision of the Supreme Court, for it is morally right; and I can urge them to disobey segregation ordinances, for they are morally wrong.

Let us consider a more concrete example of just and unjust laws. An unjust law is a code that a numerical or powei majority group compels a minority group to obey but does not make binding on itself. This is *difference* made legal. By the same token, a just law is a code that a majority compels a minority to follow and that it is willing to follow itself. This is *sameness* made legal.

Let me give another explanation. A law is unjust if it is inflicted on a minority that, as a result of being denied the right to vote, had no part in enacting or devising the law. Who can say that the legislature of Alabama which set up that state's segregation laws was democratically elected? Throughout Alabama all sorts of devious methods are used to prevent Negroes from becoming registered voters, and there are some counties in which, even though Negroes constitute a majority of the population, not a single Negro is registered. Can any law enacted under such circumstances be considered democratically structured?

Sometimes a law is just on its face and unjust in its application. For instance, I have been arrested on a charge of parading without a permit. Now, there is nothing wrong in having an ordinance which requires a permit for a parade. But such an ordinance becomes unjust when it is used to maintain segregation and to deny citizens the First-Amendment privilege of peaceful assembly and protest.

I hope you are able to see the distinction I am trying to point out. In no sense do I advocate evading or defying the law, as would the rabid segregationist. That would lead to anarchy. One who breaks an unjust law must do so openly, lovingly, and with a willingness to accept the penalty. I submit that an individual who breaks a law that conscience tells him is unjust, and who willingly accepts the penalty of imprisonment in order to arouse the conscience of the community over its injustice, is in reality expressing the highest respect for law.

Of course, there is nothing new about this kind of civil disobedience. It was evidenced sublimely in the refusal of Shadrach, Meshach and Abednego to obey the laws of Nebuchadnezzar, on the ground that a higher moral law was at stake. It was practiced superbly by the early Christians, who were willing to face hungry lions and the excruciating pain of chopping blocks rather than submit to certain unjust laws of the Roman Empire. To a degree, academic freedom is a reality today because Socrates practiced civil disobedience. In our own nation, the Boston Tea Party represented a massive act of civil disobedience.

We should never forget that everything Adolf Hitler did in Germany was "legal" and everything the Hungarian freedom fighters did in Hungary was "illegal." It was "illegal" to aid and comfort a Jew in Hitler's Germany. Even so, I am sure that, had I lived in Germany at the time, I would have aided and comforted my Jewish brothers. If today I lived in a Communist country where certain principles dear to the Christian faith are suppressed, I would openly advocate disobeying that country's antireligious laws.

I must make two honest confessions to you, my Christian and Jewish brothers. First, I must confess that over the past few years I have been gravely disappointed with the white moderate. I have almost reached the regrettable conclusion that the Negro's great stumbling block in his stride toward freedom is not the White Citizen's Councilor or the Ku Klux Klanner, but the white moderate, who is more devoted to "order" than to justice; who prefers a negative peace which is the absence of tension to a positive peace which is the presence of justice; who constantly says: "I agree with you in the goal you seek, but I cannot agree with your methods of direct action"; who paternalistically believes he can set the timetable for another man's freedom; who lives by a mythical concept of time and who constantly advises the Negro to wait for a "more convenient season." Shallow understanding from people of good will is more frustrating than absolute misunderstanding from people of ill will. Lukewarm acceptance is much more bewildering than outright rejection.

I had hoped that the white moderate would understand that law and order exist for the purpose of establishing justice and that when they fail in this purpose they become the dangerously structured dams that block the flow of social progress. I had hoped that the white moderate would understand that the present tension in the South is a necessary phase of the transition from an obnoxious negative peace, in which the Negro passively accepted his unjust plight, to a substantive and positive peace, in which all men will respect the dignity and worth of human personality. Actually, we who engage in nonviolent direct action are not the creators of tension. We merely bring to the surface the hidden tension that is already alive. We bring it out in the open, where it can be seen and dealt with. Like a boil that can never be cured so long as it is covered up but must be opened with all its ugliness to the natural medicines of air and light, injustice must be exposed, with all the tension its exposure creates, to the light of human conscience and the air of national opinion before it can be cured.

In your statement you assert that our actions, even though peaceful, must be condemned because they precipitate violence. But is this a logical assertion? Isn't this like condemning a robbed man because his possession of money precipitated the evil act of robbery? Isn't this like condemning Socrates because his unswerving commitment to truth and his philosophical inquiries precipitated the act by the misguided populace in which they made him drink hemlock? Isn't this like condemning Jesus because his unique God-consciousness and never-ceasing devotion to God's will precipitated the evil act of crucifixion? We must come to see that, as the federal courts have consistently affirmed, it is wrong to urge an individual to cease his efforts to gain his basic constitutional rights because the quest may precipitate violence. Society must protect the robbed and punish the robber.

I had also hoped that the white moderate would reject the myth concerning time in relation to the struggle for freedom. I have just received a letter from a white brother in Texas. He writes: "All Christians know that the colored people will receive equal rights eventually, but it is possible that you are in too great a religious hurry. It has taken Christianity almost two thousand years to accomplish what it has. The teachings of Christ take time to come to earth." Such an attitude stems from a tragic misconception of time, from the strangely irrational notion that there is something in the very flow of time that will inevitably cure all ills. Actually, time itself is neutral; it can be used either destructively or constructively. More and more I feel that the people of ill will have used time much more effectively than have the people of good will. We will have to repent in this generation not merely for the hateful words and actions of the bad people but for the appalling silence of the good people. Human progress never rolls in on wheels of inevitability; it comes through the tireless efforts of men willing to be co-workers with God, and without this hard work, time itself becomes an ally of the forces of social stagnation. We must use time creatively, in the knowledge that the time is always ripe to do right. Now is the time to make real the promise of democracy and transform our pending national elegy into a creative psalm of brotherhood. Now is the time to lift our national policy from the quicksand of racial injustice to the solid rock of human dignity.

You speak of our activity in Birmingham as extreme. At first I was rather disappointed that fellow clergymen would see my nonviolent efforts as those of an extremist. I began thinking about the fact that I stand in the middle of two opposing forces in the Negro community. One is a force of complacency, made up in part of Negroes who, as a result of long years of oppression, are so drained of self-respect and a sense of "somebodiness" that they have adjusted to segregation; and in part of a few middle-class Negroes who, because of a degree of academic and economic security and because in some ways they profit by segregation have become insensitive to the problems of the masses. The other force is one of bitterness and hatred, and it comes perilously close to advocating violence. It is expressed in the various black nationalist groups that are springing up across the nation, the largest and best-known being Elijah Muhammad's Muslim movement. Nourished by the Negro's frustration over the continued existence of racial discrimination, this movement is made up of people who have lost faith in America, who have absolutely repudiated Christianity, and who have concluded that the white man is an incorrigible "devil."

I have tried to stand between these two forces, saying that we need emulate neither the "do-nothingism" of the complacent nor the hatred and despair of the black nationalist. For there is the more excellent way of love and nonviolent protest. I am grateful to God that, through the influence of the Negro church, the way of nonviolence became an integral part of our struggle.

If this philosophy had not emerged, by now many streets of the South, would, I am convinced, be flowing with blood. And I am further convinced that if our white brothers dismiss as "rabble-rousers" and "outside agitators" those of us who employ nonviolent direct action, and if they refuse to support our nonviolent efforts, millions of Negroes will, out of frustration and despair, seek solace and security in black-nationalist ideologies—a development that would inevitably lead to a frightening racial nightmare.

Oppressed people cannot remain oppressed forever. The yearning for freedom eventually manifests itself, and that is what has happened to the American Negro. Something within has reminded him of his birthright of freedom, and something without has reminded him that it can be gained. Consciously or unconsciously, he has been caught up by the *Zeitgeist*, and with his black brothers of Africa and his brown and yellow brothers of Asia, South America and the Caribbean, the United States Negro is moving with a sense of great urgency toward the promised land of racial justice. If one recognizes this vital urge that has engulfed the Negro community, one should readily understand why public demonstrations are taking place. The Negro has many pent-up resentments and latent frustrations, and he must release them. So let him march; let him make prayer pilgrimages to the city hall; let him go on freedom rides—and try to understand why he must do so. If his repressed emotions are not released in nonviolent ways, they will seek expression through violence; this is not a threat but a fact of history. So I have not said to my people: "Get rid of your discontent." Rather, I have tried to say that this normal and healthy discontent can be channeled into the creative outlet of nonviolent direct action. And now this approach is being termed extremist.

• • • • •

. . . The question is not whether we will be extremists, but what kind of extremists we will be. Will we be extremists for hate or for love? Will we be extremists for the preservation of injustice or for the extension of justice?

• • • • •

. . . Perhaps the South, the nation and the world are in dire need of creative extremists.

• • • • •

Yours for the cause of
Peace and Brotherhood,
MARTIN LUTHER KING, JR.

59 The Ombudsman Concept in the United States

WALTER GELLHORN

As population within countries increases and as technology becomes ever more complex, the necessity for more services from, and regulations by, government also increases. Such expansion of the functions of the basic institution of government often requires the establishment of more complex bureaucratic structures. Though these new bureaucracies may be necessary and may in general operate effectively, they can easily become dysfunctional for the individual citizen who must cope with them, either because he cannot work his way through their complexities, or because an overzealous bureaucrat is interpreting the rules too rigorously, or because their implementation creates an injustice never intended by their framers. In an attempt to deal with this problem, more and more governments are instituting the Swedish-developed functionary called the Ombudsman—"that high level, independent, legally constituted, greatly respected officer to look into citizens' dissatisfactions with government." In this selection Walter Gellhorn examines the status of the idea and assesses its practicality for the United States.

A Norwegian scholar has recently traced the origins of the Ombudsman institution to a Norse edict of the 13th century: "With the law the land shall be built, not by the lawlessness laid waste. And he who will not grant justice to others shall not himself enjoy the benefit of the law." That sounds to me like good doctrine for the 20th century as well as for the 13th.

Among the forces that have thus far prevented Ombudsmanship from being warmly embraced in the United States is that greatest of all forces in human affairs, the force of inertia. I have to put that aside because inertia affects almost any discussion of any possible change in things as they are.

The first big blockade that has had special pertinence to the particular topic we are discussing today is, to be blunt about it, some legislators' perceptions of self-interest. Many members of legislative bodies—not all of them, by any means, but a substantial number of them—have persuaded themselves that being their constituents' errand boys and helpers is the best route to political survival. They take the view that handling constituents' case-work is a necessary step toward being effective as a legislator, the first step toward effectiveness obviously being reelection. One of my former students who is now a well regarded Representative in the Congress recently said to me: "The first time I ran for Congress I was defeated. After one of my campaign speeches a man in the audience came up

SOURCE: L. Harold Levinson, ed., *Our Kind of Ombudsman,* Studies in Public Administration no. 32 (Gainesville, Fla.: University of Florida Public Administration Clearing Service, 1970), pp. 9–18. Reprinted by permission of the publisher. • Walter Gellhorn is Betts Professor of Law at the Columbia University School of Law, and is a past president of the Association of American Law Schools. Among the many books he has authored are *When Americans Complain* and *Ombudsmen and Others* and he has co-authored *Civil Liberties Under Attack.* • EDITORS' NOTE: This article is an address by Walter Gellhorn to the Southeastern Assembly on the Ombudsman, March 13–15, 1969.

to me and shook me by the hand and said, 'I certainly hope you'll be elected because everything you've said exactly reflects my view of how things should be—I just wish I could vote for you.'" My friend asked, "Well, why can't you?" The gentleman answered: "Because one time I went down to Washington when it was very crowded, and I didn't have hotel reservations. I couldn't find accommodations anywhere. So I called up Mr. X, the then incumbent Congressman, and Representative X got me a hotel room. I've felt obligated to him ever since." My friend, the present Representative who subsequently was elected, said: "Then and there I made up my mind that if I were ever elected to Congress, I'd be the best roomclerk in Washington." And apparently that has been the main plank in his legislative platform ever since. He has now been elected five or six times and seems to be quite secure. I believe he would resist adoption of the Ombudsman idea because he would fear a reduction in the volume of his "business."

You already know that Hawaii has enacted an Ombudsman law. The County of Maui in Hawaii has also adopted an Ombudsman law. And King County in the State of Washington, the county in which Seattle is located, has recently voted favorably on a new county charter that provides for an Ombudsman. Three Canadian provinces have Ombudsmen in being. We know that a large number of American cities have grievance handling mechanisms of various types. The State of Pennsylvania has introduced a system of Governor's Branch Offices, which, scattered throughout the state, provide points of contact between the individual citizen and any branch of the state government about which questions may arise or as to which complaints may relate. The new Pennsylvania program, I have been told, has had a very successful beginning and shows much promise for the future. That just about ends the roll-call. Though it is a perfectly good roll-call so far as it goes, it pretty clearly does not go very far.

Why hasn't the concept of the Ombudsman—that high level, independent, legally constituted, greatly respected officer to look into citizens' dissatisfactions with government—why hasn't that concept made greater progress in our country? I don't think it's because everybody has tremendous confidence in our government and its institutions. I don't suggest that we Americans are as nervous as people in some other parts of the world. A high Polish official has told me with amusement a story that makes the rounds in Warsaw. At the end of a visit to Moscow by Polish Prime Minister Cyrankiewicz, Mr. Brezhnev said to him, "You're not like the other visitors we've been having from Eastern Europe; you haven't asked me a single time what's happened to Khrushchev." Prime Minister Cyrankiewicz, taking no chances, answered blandly, "Khrushchev, Khrushchev, who's Khrushchev?" Then you've probably heard about the two Czechs who were approaching one another from opposite directions on a street in Prague. Both men stopped to look admiringly at a parked motor car. One of them said to the other: "Look at those beautiful clean lines and that fine bodywork and that wonderfully glistening paint and those rugged tires. You certainly can see just by looking at that car that it was made in one of the People's Democracies." The other passer-by looked at the speaker wonderingly and said, "Why, you idiot, don't you know that's a Rolls Royce made in Britain?" The first one said, "Well, just possibly, I do know that this motor car is a Rolls Royce, but I don't know what you are."

I don't suggest at all that we Americans are in the same league as that when it comes to being nervous. But we would be kidding ourselves if we were to explain the absence of Ombudsmen in America by saying that no Americans feel the need for having some sort of spokesman who can be a buffer between them and the government.

Nor can we ascribe Ombudsmanship's slow progress to journalistic opposition. On the contrary, the idea has had a uniformly good press. No informed commentary about experience with Ombudsmanship has suggested animosity toward it or disillusion with it. In saying this I do not mean to suggest that in the countries which have an Ombudsman every citizen believes that all good things come from the Ombudsman. Of course, that is not the case. But it is true that every Ombudsman who is now in existence has scored a resounding popular and journalistic triumph. For example, in New Zealand, which resembles our own country in a great many respects, one of the major conservation organizations has been pushing most strenuously, and apparently now with political success, to have the Ombudsman system extended from the national level all the way down to local government. Moreover, a very strong move is afoot in Scotland to extend the Ombudsman system to that highly individualistic country because England's experiment with Ombudsmanship (which is a very limited experiment as compared with the pure unadulterated strain of Scandinavia) has thus far produced such promising results that the Scots want a system of their own. I repeat, then, that our slow movement in this country is not because we have received any reports of bad experience elsewhere.

In any event, one can now sense the beginning of another current that may accelerate the movement. In many parts of the United States serious legislators are taking serious note of the fact that most legislative bodies are made up of part-time personnel, without adequate professional or clerical staff aides. They are noting, too, that fifty percent of all American state legislators are freshmen. That figure surprised me, but it seems to be statistically the fact. It means that, in any state legislative assembly, experienced legislators are only a part of the whole. They simply do not have the time or the supporting staff they must have if they are to do a very good job of case-work. Increasingly they recognize that being freed from some of the burdens of constituents' case-work would enable them to undertake more significantly important activity—activity which might not only give a sense of considerable personal accomplishment, but might indeed be a means of achieving true political distinction.

In California, where the Ombudsman plan is being seriously considered by the legislature, two of the chief pushers are, very significantly, the senator who represents the Watts district and is politically visible all over the state, and the former Speaker of the Assembly. Both these prominent men are supporting Ombudsmanship so that they can be freed for more significant legislative activity than is involved in constituents' case-work. In Illinois, where also a very strong movement is afoot, the chief sponsor of Ombudsmanship is the majority leader of the Senate, a rather conservative Republican. Like the California Democrats just mentioned, he believes that he and his colleagues can be more importantly useful if they can slough off some of the nonlegislative burdens that now rest upon them. These gentlemen, I might add, are just about as practical politicians as practical politicians can possibly be. So I don't despair. I think the legislative tide is going to turn. It must turn if the instinct of self-preservation is still alive in legislative breasts.

The second big stumbling block in the path of Ombudsmanship has been the fear on the part of some officials that an Ombudsman might strip away their insulation, if I may put it so—their freedom from effective criticism by the public at large. This fear has been especially marked among policemen, some of whom have at times acted as though being immunized against outside inquiry was a perquisite of office, like coffee breaks or pension rights or something of that sort. In Nassau County, which is a suburban county outside New York City with a population of about a million and a half, a proposed charter revision which included provision of an Ombudsman was defeated very largely because the local police organized a campaign against its adoption. The cries of alarm that charter opponents emitted during that campaign were so extreme, so unrelated to reality, that they shocked the reason, though no doubt they were sincerely felt by the alarmists.

Official resistance to the Ombudsman idea is, as a matter of fact, very shortsighted. Maybe those of us who like Ombudsmanship have been a bit careless in presenting it as though we thought that the citizen—the customer, so to speak—is always right. Perhaps we have implied that the Ombudsman is always going to side with the citizen against officials. Of course that isn't the way things have worked out in any degree. Wherever an Ombudsman has functioned, he has been purely and plainly an advocate of sound administration, not an advocate of the position of the complainant. In this respect he has differed from many legislators who tend, when a constituent complains, to become an advocate of the complainant's case without much consideration of its merit; they push the matter because of the source from which it comes, not because of its worth. The Ombudsman, on the other hand, is not a built-in critic of officials, whether elected or not. He is simply stationed at the margin, as it were, between the citizen and the official, and he must be concerned with seeing that justice is done to public servants as well as to the public whom they serve. Believe me, he does protect both groups. I have not the slightest doubt that if a free vote were taken among the police and other officials in any country in which the Ombudsman has functioned, a truly overwhelming majority of the participants in the election would favor the continuation of Ombudsmanship.

Three great advantages can be mentioned in connection with the creation of an Ombudsman. The first one is that he wouldn't displace anything, he wouldn't take away a single shred of jurisdiction or power from anybody who now has jurisdiction or power to deal with citizens' problems—no judicial power would be limited, no legislative power would be limited, officials' power to run their own affairs wouldn't in any sense be limited, even the newspaper's Action Line column wouldn't be limited. The Ombudsman would simply be an addition to, and not a subtractor from, existing mechanisms for dealing with individual citizens' problems.

Secondly, the Ombudsman is a very cheap addition to governmental resources. He would function, I am quite confident, with a very small staff indeed, not a vast bureaucratic machine. If, in fact, he did not prove to be as useful as had been hoped, the Ombudsman's office could be liquidated without any really major bloodletting and certainly without any economic collapse consequent upon the unemployment of a giant staff. In short, creating the office of Ombudsman would not at all mean making an inevitably long-term commitment to a governmental structure for the future.

Third—and this seems to me to be a factor we can't afford to ignore in these troubled times—he might help eliminate at least one big cause of disorder and violence in America, namely, the belief, right or wrong, that orderly mechanisms for the redress of grievances do not now exist or are insufficiently available to those who need them. That belief is undoubtedly one of the conditions underlying the sometimes out-of-hand demonstrations and riotous assemblages that have caused grave concern in recent times. Plainly enough, no Ombudsman can himself create or maintain a civilized society. Undoubtedly that responsibility is one all of us must bear; we cannot transfer it to the shoulders of some great father figure to whom we give the name of Ombudsman. But an Ombudsman can be an adornment of a civilized society. We Americans have moved far—and we continue, day by day, to move—toward a civilized society. We can now afford the luxury of considering how best to adorn the society we seek to foster.

Many right-minded citizens nowadays are engaged in a quest, a probably fruitless quest, for some emotionally satisfying reform that, at one stroke, will end poverty, bring peace to Vietnam, beautify our cities, stamp out narcotics addiction, and even bring civility back to college campuses (though that perhaps is too much to hope for.) No Ombudsman is going to be able to achieve any one of these large social reforms, let alone all of them; and even as to the things that he can do, he is not going to achieve dramatic results overnight. A great many people who are looking for instant gratification lack enthusiasm for something that will not have great sweeping consequences and will not make the night suddenly become day.

Within this past week I attended a conference that dealt not with Ombudsmanship, but with problems related to civil rights. Some of the so-called activists and militants in that conference group were strikingly impatient about continuing to fight issues through the courts. They pointed to past decisions concerning the unconstitutionality of this or that racial malpractice, and then remarked bitterly that racial malpractices still exist. The continuation of improprieties was proof, they contended, that the courts are impotent and that future efforts to achieve justice should not be geared to the judicial process. When this attack upon the utility of the courts was voiced, I recalled a remark made in a different setting by a very great constitutional lawyer, Paul Freund of Harvard, who declared, "The question is not whether the courts can do everything, but whether they can do something." That question is precisely the right one to ask about the Ombudsman, too. Can he do something? Clearly he cannot do everything.

The question about whether the Ombudsman can do something deserves a very strongly affirmative response. He can do a lot. By perceiving implications of the single instance, he can accomplish great good for public administration as well as for persons who are externally affected by public administration.

A Seattle lawyer wrote me not long ago about an unfortunately acute bitterness that had developed in local high schools after a police officer had gone into a classroom to arrest a boy against whom a criminal charge had been made. The parents of the boy (who, incidentally, was completely cleared of the charge) sued the policeman because they thought that he had acted improperly in exposing their son to needless embarrassment. Quite correctly, the local courts disposed of the case summarily; the arrest was made pursuant to a lawful warrant, and that was the end of the matter so far as the judges were concerned. It was far from the end of indignation, however, because though the policeman had acted permissibly, he had not acted wisely. Nothing necessitated making the arrest in a school classroom instead of in the boy's home or elsewhere.

If an Ombudsman had been in existence and if he instead of the court had been appealed to, I doubt that he would have said, "The policeman acted legally, or acted illegally," or, "I'm going to scold the policeman or I'm not going to scold the policeman." The Ombudsman, I believe, would have been little concerned with the particular policeman who arrested the boy. Instead, I think, he would have had a conference with the police chief, saying, "Wouldn't it be better in the future, if it's necessary to arrest a high school student who is living at home, to make the arrest in some other circumstances than those that marked this particular occurrence?" In that way, as it seems to me, the particular instance would have had generative force beyond the episode in itself. This is the way progress in the quality of our public administration is going to be made—not by censuring, not by condemning, not even always by some sort of public criticism, but by seeking to use good judgment, by taking a critical view from the outside—to see if a better job can be done in the future than has been done in the past.

The same type of possibility occurs in social welfare administration. One of my graduate students at Columbia who has been studying social welfare administration in New York City has come upon a really dramatic and significant statistic. In New York the initial decision about an applicant's eligibility for welfare benefit is made in a very decentralized manner. Many persons in a large establishment have power to make the pertinent determinations. A dissatisfied applicant has a right to ask for a hearing, an appellate process. Until recently few appeals have been sought, but now, with the growth of legal services units to assist the needy, more requests for hearings are being made by lawyers in behalf of applicants. A unit has been set up within the welfare administration to hear those cases in which an appeal has been sought. In seventy percent of these cases, the review unit has, on its own motion, acknowledged that a mistake was made in the initial decision and has granted the relief sought without the necessity of further hearing. Seventy percent, mind you—an extraordinarily high percentage of error. Even today, however, appeals are sought by only a tiny fraction of the whole of the necessitous population whose initial requests for help have been rejected.

One might suppose that an administration which had found so large a percentage of error in the cases that were officially reviewed when an appeal was filed would set up some mechanism for reviewing cases generally, or at any rate for doing some retraining of the people who make the original decisions. But according to my graduate student who has just been looking into this situation, not a thing has happened in the administration of social welfare in New York City. Many thousands of decisions continue to be made, most of them are never looked at afterwards, and presumably a high percentage of all those decisions must be marked by undetected errors of the kind discovered in the small sampling of cases appealed. This is public administration of a kind that would arouse an Ombudsman's active concern, in my opinion. He would probably not rest content until steps were taken to improve a branch of law administration that touches so very many humble lives.

The two examples just given have dealt with rather lowly members of society, a youth who is accused of a criminal act and applicants for home relief, the economically destitute. The lowly are not, however, the only people who have problems that would be suitable for an Ombudsman's attention. The great bulk of complaints to Ombudsmen in all of the countries that do have them come from what would loosely be called the great middle class. On the whole, the complainants have not been elements of highly organized parts of society. They have not typically been members of a powerful trade association, for example, or even a powerful labor union. They have been rather, the detached, the unaffiliated sort of person that constitutes the bulk of society at any given time—people who are somewhat baffled by the society in which they live, a society they didn't make, a system they didn't design, but one that in any event does closely bear upon the sort of life they have. The economically depressed people have not provided the Ombudsman's main clientele. Perhaps the poor do not see the newspaper accounts of what the Ombudsman has been doing; word-of-mouth advertising takes more time than the written word to reach all who might be impressed. Nevertheless poor people as well as middle class do manage to learn about and to use the Ombudsman where he does exist.

. . . . .

60 Pygmalion in the Classroom

ROBERT ROSENTHAL AND LENORE JACOBSON

61 The Teacher as Pygmalion: Comments on the Psychology of Expectation

PETER AND CAROL GUMPERT

The next two selections are provided as a single unit. The first summarizes the major findings of the study on the effect of teachers being told that some children in their classroom had high ability and were likely to spurt in their intelligence and achievement. Rosenthal and Jacobson maintain that students are more likely to perform well if teachers believe that they can and expect them to do so. The implications of this for American education are revolutionary. Though critical reviews of the Rosenthal and Jacobson study have identified various weaknesses in the experiment, the Gumperts, in the second selection, indicate that the general findings in the Pygmalion study are supported by different analyses and other research.

Under the present system of education the schools play a major role in allocating students to different strata and positions in society, on the basis of presumed limited abilities to learn. If the theory of expectation discussed in these two selections were combined with an assumption of sufficient ability to perform well, as indicated in selection 9 by Boyer and Walsh, the nature of American education would be drastically changed and the allocation function would probably be removed from American schools.

MR. ROSENTHAL AND MRS. JACOBSON

The central idea of this [research is] that one person's expectation for another's behavior could come to serve as a self-fulfilling prophecy. This is not a new idea, and anecdotes and theories can be found that support its tenability. Much of the experimental evidence for the operation of interpersonal self-fulfilling prophecies comes from a research program in which prophecies or expectancies were experimentally generated in psychological experimenters in order to learn whether these prophecies would become self-fulfilling.

The general plan of past studies has been to establish two groups of "data collectors" and give to the experimenters of each group a different hypothesis as to the data their research subjects would give them. In many such experiments, though not in all, experimenters obtained

SOURCE: Robert Rosenthal and Lenore Jacobson, *Pygmalion in the Classroom: Teacher Expectation and Pupils' Intellectual Development* (New York: Holt, Rinehart and Winston, 1968), excerpts from Chapter 12, "Summary and Implications," pp. 174–79. • Robert Rosenthal is professor of social psychology at Harvard University. He received the Social Psychology Prize of the American Association for the Advancement of Science in 1960 and the Cattell fund award of the Psychological Association in 1967. He is the author of *Experimenter Effects in Behavioral Research*. • Lenore Jacobson was principal of the elementary school in the South San Francisco Unified School District where the research reported here was carried out.

data from their subjects in accordance with the expectancy they held regarding their subjects' responses. Quite naturally, some of the experiments involved expectations held by the experimenters of the intellectual performance of their subjects.

In addition to those experiments in which the subjects were humans, there were studies in which the subjects were animals. When experimenters were led to believe that their animal subjects were genetically inferior, these animals performed more poorly. When experimenters were led to believe that their animal subjects were more favorably endowed genetically, their animals' performance was superior. In reality, of course, there were no genetic differences between the animals that had been alleged to be dull or bright.

If animal subjects believed to be brighter by their trainers actually became brighter because of their trainers' beliefs, then it might also be true that school children believed by their teachers to be brighter would become brighter because of their teachers' beliefs. Oak School became the laboratory in which an experimental test of that proposition was carried out.

Oak School is a public elementary school in a lower-class community of a medium-size city. The school has a minority group of Mexican children who comprise about one-sixth of the school's population. Every year about 200 of its 650 children leave Oak School, and every year about 200 new children are enrolled.

Oak School follows an ability-tracking plan whereby each of the six grades is divided into one fast, one medium, and one slow classroom. Reading ability is the primary basis for assignment to track. The Mexican children are heavily overrepresented in the slow track.

On theoretical grounds it would have been desirable to learn whether teachers' favorable or unfavorable expectations could result in a corresponding increase or decrease in pupils' intellectual competence. On ethical grounds, however, it was decided to test only the proposition that favorable expectations by teachers could lead to an increase in intellectual competence.

All the children of Oak School were pretested with a standard nonverbal test of intelligence. This test was represented to the teachers as one that would predict intellectual "blooming" or "spurting." The IQ test employed yielded three IQ scores: total IQ, verbal IQ, and reasoning IQ. The "verbal" items required the child to match pictured items with verbal descriptions given by the teacher. The reasoning items required the child to indicate which of five designs differed from the remaining four. Total IQ was based on the sum of verbal and reasoning items.

At the very beginning of the school year following the schoolwide pretesting, each of the eighteen teachers of grades one through six was given the names of those children in her classroom who, in the academic year ahead, would show dramatic intellectual growth. These predictions were allegedly made on the basis of these special children's scores on the test of academic blooming. About 20 percent of Oak School's children were alleged to be potential spurters. For each classroom the names of the special children had actually been chosen by means of a table of random numbers. The difference between the special children and the ordinary children, then, was only in the mind of the teacher.

All the children of Oak School were retested with the same IQ test after one semester, after a full academic year, and after two full academic years. For the first two retests, children were in the classroom of the teacher who had been given favorable expectations for the intellectual growth of some of her pupils.

For the final retesting all children had been promoted to the classes of teachers who had not been given any special expectations for the intellectual growth of any of the children. That follow-up testing had been included so that we could learn whether any expectancy advantages that might be found would be dependent on a continuing contact with the teacher who held the especially favorable expectation.

For the children of the experimental group and for the children of the control group, gains in IQ from pretest to retest were computed. Expectancy advantage was defined by the degree to which IQ gains by the "special" children exceeded gains by the control-group children. After the first year of the experiment a significant expectancy advantage was found, and it was especially great among children of the first and second grades. The advantage of having been expected to bloom was evident for these younger children in total IQ, verbal IQ, and reasoning IQ. The control-group children of these grades gained well in IQ, 19 percent of them gaining twenty or more total IQ points. The "special" children, however, showed 47 percent of their number gaining twenty or more total IQ points.

During the subsequent follow-up year the younger children of the first two years lost their expectancy advantage. The children of the upper grades, however, showed an increasing expectancy advantage during the follow-up year. The younger children who seemed easier to influence may have required more continued contact with their influencer in order to maintain their behavior change. The older children, who were harder to influence initially, may have been better able to maintain their behavior change autonomously once it had occurred.

Differences between boys and girls in the extent to which they were helped by favorable expectations were not dramatic when gains in total IQ were considered. After one year, and after two years as well, boys who were expected to bloom intellectually bloomed more in verbal IQ; girls who were expected to bloom intellectually bloomed more in reasoning IQ. Favorable teacher expectations seemed to help each sex more in that sphere of intellectual functioning in which they had excelled on the pretest. At Oak School boys normally show the higher verbal IQ while girls show the higher reasoning IQ.

It will be recalled that Oak School was organized into a fast, a medium, and a slow track system. We had thought that favorable expectations on the part of teachers would be of greatest benefit to the children of the slow track. That was not the case. After one year, it was the children of the medium track who showed the greatest expectancy advantage, though children of the other tracks were close behind. After two years, however, the children of the medium track very clearly showed the greatest benefits from having had favorable expectations held of their intellectual performance. It seems surprising that it should be the more average child of a lower-class school who stands to benefit more from his teacher's improved expectation.

After the first year of the experiment and also after the second year, the Mexican children showed greater expectancy advantages than did the non-Mexican children, though the difference was not significant statistically. One interesting minority-group effect did reach significance, however, even with just a small sample size. For each of the Mexican children, magnitude of expectancy advantage was computed by subtracting from his or her gain in IQ from pretest to retest, the IQ gain made by the children of the control group in his or her classroom. These magnitudes of expectancy advantage were then correlated with the "Mexican-ness" of the children's faces. After one year, and after two years, those boys who looked more Mexican benefited more from their teachers' positive prophecies. Teachers' pre-experimental expectancies for these boys' intellectual performance were probably lowest of all. Their turning up on a list of probable bloomers must have surprised their teachers. Interest may have followed surprise and, in some way, increased watching for signs of increased brightness may have led to increased brightness.

In addition to the comparison of the "special" and the ordinary children on their gains in IQ it was possible to compare their gains after the first year of the experiment on school achievement as defined by report-card grades. Only for the school subject of reading was there a significant difference in gains in report-card grades. The children expected to bloom intellectually were judged by their teachers to show greater advances in their reading ability. Just as in the case of IQ gains, it was the younger children who showed the greater expectancy advantage in reading scores. The more a given grade level had benefited in over-all IQ gains, the more that same grade level benefited in reading scores.

It was the children of the medium track who showed the greatest expectancy advantage in terms of reading ability just as they had been the children to benefit most in terms of IQ from their teachers' favorable expectations.

Report-card reading grades were assigned by teachers, and teachers' judgments of reading performance may have been affected by their expectations. It is possible, therefore, that there was no real benefit to the earmarked children of having been expected to bloom. The effect could very well have been in the mind of the teacher rather than in the reading performance of the child. Some evidence was available to suggest that such halo effects did not occur. For a number of grade levels, objective achievement tests had been administered. Greater expectancy advantages were found when the assessment was by these objective tests than when it was by the more subjective evaluation made by the teacher. If anything, teachers' grading seemed to show a negative halo effect. It seemed that the special children were graded more severely by the teachers than were the ordinary children. It is even possible that it is just this sort of standard-setting behavior that is responsible in part for the effects of favorable expectations.

The fear has often been expressed that the disadvantaged child is further disadvantaged by his teacher's setting standards that are inappropriately low. Wilson has presented compelling evidence that teachers do, in fact, hold up lower standards of achievement for children of more deprived areas. It is a possibility to be further investigated that when a teacher's expectation for a pupil's intellectual performance is raised, she may set higher standards for him to meet (that is, grade him tougher). There may be here the makings of a benign cycle. Teachers may not only get more when they expect more; they may also come to expect more when they get more.

All teachers had been asked to rate each of their pupils on variables related to intellectual curiosity, personal and social adjustment, and need for social approval. In general, children who had been expected to bloom intellectually were rated as more intellectually curious, as happier, and, especially in the lower grades, as less in need of social approval. Just as had been the case with IQ and reading ability, it was the younger children who showed the greater expectancy advantage in terms of their teachers' perceptions of their classroom behavior. Once again, children of the medium track were most advantaged by having been expected to bloom, this time in terms of their perceived greater intellectual curiosity and lessened need for social approval.

When we consider expectancy advantages in terms of perceived intellectual curiosity, we find that the Mexican children did not share in the advantages of having been expected to bloom. Teachers did not see the Mexican children as more intellectually curious when they had been expected to bloom. There was even a slight tendency, stronger for Mexican boys, to see the special Mexican children as less curious intellectually. That seems surprising, particularly since the Mexican children showed the greatest expectancy advantages in IQ, in reading scores, and for Mexican boys, in overall school achievement. It seemed almost as though, for these minority-group children, intellectual competence may have been easier for teachers to bring about than to believe.

Children's gains in IQ during the basic year of the experiment were correlated with teachers' perceptions of their classroom behavior. This was done separately for the upper- and lower-track children of the experimental and control groups. The more the upper-track children of the experimental group gained in IQ, the more favorably they were rated by their teachers. The more the lower-track children of the control group gained in IQ, the more unfavorably they were viewed by their teachers. No special expectation had been created about these children, and their slow-track status made it unlikely in their teachers' eyes that they would behave in an intellectually competent manner. The more intellectually competent these children became, the more negatively they were viewed by their teachers. Future research should address itself to the possibility that there may be hazards to "unwarranted," unpredicted intellectual growth. Teachers may require a certain amount of preparation to be able to accept the unexpected classroom behavior of the intellectually upwardly mobile child.

• • • • •

MR. AND MRS. GUMPERT

Pygmalion in the Classroom is an important and thought-provoking book; anyone concerned with the problems and practices of education should certainly take the trouble to read it. The study provides a perfectly satisfactory demonstration that the teacher expectation effects hypothesized do indeed take place. Though the Oak School experiment is not as sophisticated as it might be, it was done in a "natural" setting (which, incidentally, usually makes it difficult to do elegant research) rather than under the more artificial circumstances of the laboratory. The fact that the effect can be demonstrated in the actual classroom under very ordinary conditions is convincing. That the effect appears to be quite strong and stable in spite of the subtlety and simplicity of the experimental induction is especially dramatic. The results of the experiment fairly demand that much serious attention, thought, and research be devoted to the effect on children of the beliefs and attitudes held about them by school administrators, supervisors, and teachers. It also points

SOURCE: *The Urban Review*, vol. 3, no. 1 (September 1968), 21–25. Reprinted by permission of *The Urban Review*, a publication of the Center for Urban Education. • Peter Gumpert is an assistant professor in the Doctoral Program in Social Psychology at Teacher's College, Columbia University. • Carol Gumpert is a clinical psychologist in the Department of Psychiatry of the Albert Einstein College of Medicine.

up the crucial importance of conducting research on just *how* people's expectations of children become realities. It is possible that we will learn to change teachers' behavior toward children before we learn how to change their attitudes toward them, and thus their expectations of them. It is on this last general consideration—how the expectation of the teacher might have led to modifications of her pupils' performance and classroom behavior—that Rosenthal and Jacobson are weakest in their analysis. Though they do speculate about some aspects of the problem, the heart of the matter remains untouched. In short, they have shown us that teachers' expectations of their students' performances have definite consequences for these (subsequent) performances. But they have not shown us how this process works.

In the remainder of our article, we propose to do some more or less systematic speculating about how the Oak School teachers may have fulfilled the researchers' prophecies. We shall begin by arguing that expectation leads to selectivity of attention, perception, and response, and end by discussing just how increases in interpersonal "warmth" and encouragement might actually lead to superior learning and performance.

SOME PSYCHOLOGICAL EFFECTS OF EXPECTATION

The study of the influence of expectation upon thinking and behavior has been of interest to psychologists for many years in a variety of contexts. There are literally hundreds of studies that are relevant to the notion that a person's attitude, set, or expectation will affect his perceptions and responses. One tentative conclusion that can be drawn from these studies—of particular interest in thinking about expectancy in the classroom—is the following: a person is more likely to perceive a barely perceptible stimulus if he expects it than if he does not. For example, if an experimental subject is given a list from which words are to be presented tachistoscopically, the recognition threshold for words on the list (i.e., the words he is expecting) will be lower than for those not on the list. When shown an ambiguous stimulus which resembled both a letter and a number, for example *B* and *13*, subjects who were told to expect letters saw *B* and those who were told to expect numbers reported seeing *13*. Neither of these results is surprising, possibly because they both confirm what we often observe in our everyday activities—that we are likely to see what we expect to see, and that we tend to interpret ambiguous events in such a way as to confirm our own predictions. Similarly, if a teacher expects to see something, she is likely to find evidence of its occurrence sooner or later.

Further, that a person's expectations exert a powerful influence on the behavior of the people with whom he interacts is a well-documented phenomenon. In the laboratory, for example, if a group of experimenters is told to expect that their subjects will most likely perform well on a particular task, and another group is told to expect their subjects to perform poorly, the subjects in the former group will tend to have significantly higher scores than those in the latter. Expectation effects have even been demonstrated when the experimental subjects were animals. Strupp and Luborsky make the point that a therapist's expectations about the prognosis of treatment may have much to do with its actual outcome. The teacher, similarly, may have a personal stake in seeing what she expects to see in the classroom.

• • • • •

It appears that a person who is in a position to exercise over another the subtle interpersonal influence we have been talking about may do so without being aware either of the content of the message he transmits or the ways he transmits it. The recipient of influence may be equally unaware that any transaction other than the obvious overt one is taking place; he may well do what is expected of him without even realizing that a demand on him is being made. It also appears likely that some people are more effective "covert persuaders" than others. Such things as the physical appearance, confidence, warmth, friendliness, amount of experience or competence, interest, and status of the persuader seem to affect the extent to which expectancies are influential. Some of these personal characteristics are also related to a person's effectiveness as an overt persuader. So it seems plausible that some teachers may be better covert persuaders in the classroom than others. It is also possible that the teacher who is warm, friendly, and sure of herself is a better covert persuader than her less friendly and less competent colleagues, and that the highly skilled and successful teacher is also good at helping make her prophecies come true.

The manner in which one person influences another is not determined entirely in advance by previously existing attitudes and beliefs. Expectation may change, vary, increase, or decrease, depending on the nature of an ongoing social interaction and the reciprocal influence that two people have upon one another. In the classroom, for example, it is likely that a teacher's behavior toward a particular child will not depend consistently on previously existing beliefs about what he can or will do, but may be modified by what occurs between them.

In order to imagine how such variables might affect an interaction, let us construct an oversimplified situation. Imagine that one of Rosenthal and Jacobson's teachers is told that Johnny Second-Grader, an unremarkable-appearing boy, is about to experience a period of intellectual blossoming. Given a situation in which the teacher is trying to communicate a difficult bit of information to Johnny, she is now more likely to expect an indication of comprehension than if she had been told nothing about potential academic progress. (In fact, she might not otherwise have attempted the communication in the first place.) A minor change in Johnny's behavior at this point, say a nod or smile, may be interpreted as a glimmer of understanding so that, encouraged, the teacher intensifies her efforts to reach him. Consequent subtle changes in the teacher's behavior and attitude, such as alterations in her body posture, tone of voice, perceived interest, facial expression, or verbal praise, may similarly interest and encourage Johnny, leading to his increased motivation and attention, and finally to the reward of mastering something new—as well as the fulfillment of his teacher's expectation. The point is that psychological expectation may have a catalytic effect, evoking interactions and leading to events that depend upon much more than the effects of expectation alone, but which might not, and indeed probably would not, have occurred without the belief that such events were possible.

We have discussed something about the effects that a person's expectations may have on his own behavior and thinking and on the behavior and thinking of others. It seems very clear also that the nature of the social structure itself often has similar effects. One of the findings of a study of the British school system reported by Hilde Himmelweit and Judy Wright involved a comparison of two schools with different policies regarding assignment to tracks (or streams, as they are referred to in England). In one school, assignment to a stream was based on ability. In the other, assignment was based on criteria other than intellectual ability. Yet the effect of stream placement on further academic advancement and final performance was identical for the two schools. Thus, the effect of streaming seemed to be a more powerful determinant of performance than were the attributes that led to the pupils' initial placement in streams; streaming turns out to be a potent "leveler" in Britain. This result can be interpreted as indicating that the meaning for an individual of being allocated to a particular stream, and the influence exerted by the experience of stream membership, can be major determinants of his progress. The expectation for a person's behavior that is implicit by virtue of his place in the social structure may exert a powerful influence over what he does, in that he will not only respond to the expectation but may also help to create an environment within which it will be fulfilled.

. . . . .

Let us return now to the teacher who expects to see startling improvement in the performance of a particular pupil. As we have argued above, if she expects a pupil to begin to improve, she may be avidly watching for signs of improvement while ignoring the pupil's usual inadequacies or failures. If she should see something that indicates improvement, she might be especially quick to reward it by her special attention and by her excitement at seeing her expectations begin to be fulfilled. This in turn might give the child new interest in this kind of performance, and might spur him on to new attempts to fulfill an expectation that he might now begin to perceive. Since the teacher is no longer paying as much attention to the child's failures, the child may now feel new room to grow, and indeed might grow with his burgeoning confidence about new learning and new power over his environment. As the child's performance improves, his teacher's standards for his performance may become higher; thus, what Rosenthal and Jacobson term the "benign circle" might develop. And here is an added dividend: a teacher who spends relatively more time rewarding success in the classroom, and therefore relatively less time punishing failure, may be improving the learning environment not only for the few children of whom she expects new things, but for all the children in the room—as is suggested by the results in Rosenthal and Jacobson described above.

Our discussion in this section has been very speculative; certainly, many links are missing in the chain that connects what the teacher expects the student to be able to do and what the student becomes able to do. And, surely, there is not just one thing happening in the entire process, but many things. The phenomenon of subtle interpersonal influence guiding progress in the classroom is as complex as it is fascinating.

. . . . .

62 Like It Is in the Alley

ROBERT COLES

Peter, a remarkably mature, intelligent, and articulate nine-year-old Boston ghetto black boy proved to be a "very good teacher" for Robert Coles, a Harvard University faculty member and psychiatrist doing research in the College of Medicine. If the reader is like Coles—not black and not living in the ghetto—he can likewise learn much that is crucially important about the costs of survival in the hostile northern urban world where many American blacks exist today. They suffer with frighteningly hazardous living conditions, unmet health care needs that are almost endless, school teachers who do not care about the children, municipal government bureaucrats who are neither friendly nor helpful, and token programs for blacks that are ineffective, inappropriate, or inadequate. Such conditions therefore reinforce the hostility and distrust of whites by blacks, especially those blacks who are able, young, poor, and ambitious for a better life. White people who do not understand why there are groups like the Black Panthers will do well to consider, and then do what they can to improve life, on the basis of insights they may gain from "Like It Is in the Alley."

In the alley it's mostly dark, even if the sun is out. But if you look around, you can find things. I know how to get into every building, except that it's like night once you're inside them, because they don't have lights. So, I stay here. You're better off. It's no good on the street. You can get hurt all the time, one way or the other. And in buildings, like I told you, it's bad in them, too. But here it's o.k. You can find your own corner, and if someone tries to move in you fight him off. We meet here all the time, and figure out what we'll do next. It might be a game, or over for some pool, or a coke or something. You need to have a place to start out from, and that's like it is in the alley; you can always know your buddy will be there, provided it's the right time. So you go there, and you're on your way, man.

SOURCE: *Dædalus*, vol. 97, no. 4 (Fall 1968), 1315–30. Reprinted by permission of *Dædalus*, Journal of the American Academy of Arts and Sciences. • Robert Coles is research psychiatrist at the Harvard University Health Services and Lecturer in General Education at Harvard. His chief interests are Negro and white children and their parents and situations of abnormal stress. In 1968 he received the *Parents' Magazine* award for Outstanding Service to Children. He is author of *Children of Crisis: A Study of Courage and Fear*, *Dead-End Street*, and *Erik H. Erikson: The Growth of His Work*.

Like all children of nine, Peter is always on his way—to a person, a place, a "thing" he wants to do. "There's this here thing we thought we'd try tomorrow," he'll say; and eventually I'll find out that he means there's to be a race. He and his friends will compete with another gang to see who can wash a car faster and better. The cars belong to four youths who make their money taking bets, and selling liquor that I don't believe was ever purchased, and pushing a few of those pills that "go classy with beer." I am not completely sure, but I think they also have something to do with other drugs; and again, I can't quite be sure what their connection is with a "residence" I've seen not too far from the alley Peter describes so possessively. The women come and go—from that residence and along the street Peter's alley leaves.

Peter lives in the heart of what we in contemporary America have chosen (ironically, so far as history goes) to call an "urban ghetto." The area was a slum before it became a ghetto, and there still are some very poor white people on its edges and increasing numbers of Puerto Ricans in several of its blocks. Peter was not born in the ghetto, nor was his family told to go there. They are Americans and have been here "since way back before anyone can remember." That is the way Peter's mother talks about Alabama, about the length of time she and her ancestors have lived there. She and Peter's father came north "for freedom." They did not seek out a ghetto, an old quarter of Boston where they were expected to live and where they would be confined, yet at least some of the time solidly at rest, with kin, and reasonably safe.

No, they sought freedom. Americans, they moved on when the going got "real bad," and Americans, they expected something better someplace, some other place. They left Alabama on impulse. They found Peter's alley by accident. And they do not fear pogroms. They are Americans, and in Peter's words: "There's likely to be another riot here soon. That's what I heard today. You hear it a lot, but one day you know it'll happen."

Peter's mother fears riots too—among other things. The Jews of Eastern Europe huddled together in their ghettos, afraid of the barbarians, afraid of the *Goyim*, but always sure of one thing, their God-given destiny. Peter's mother has no such faith. She believes that "something will work out one of these days." She believes that "you have to keep on going, and things can get better, but don't ask me how." She believes that "God wants us to have a bad spell here, and so maybe it'll get better the next time—you know in Heaven, and I hope that's where we'll be going." Peter's mother, in other words, is a pragmatist, an optimist, and a Christian. Above all she is American: "Yes, I hear them talk about Africa, but it don't mean anything to us. All I know is Alabama and now it's in Massachusetts that we are. It was a long trip coming up here, and sometimes I wish we were back there, and sometimes I'd just as soon be here, for all that's no good about it. But I'm not going to take any more trips, no sir. And like Peter said, this is the only country we've got. If you come from a country, you come from it, and we're from it, I'd say, and there isn't much we can do but try to live as best we can. I mean, live here."

What is "life" like for her over there, where she lives, in the neighborhood she refers to as "here"? A question like that cannot be answered by the likes of me, and even her answer provides only the beginning of a reply:

> Well, we does o.k., I guess. Peter here, he has it better than I did, or his daddy. I can say that. I tell myself that a lot. He can turn on the faucet over there, and a lot of the time, he just gets the water, right away. And when I tell him what it was like for us, to go fetch that water—we'd walk three miles, yes sir, and we'd be lucky it wasn't ten—well, Peter, it doesn't register on him. He thinks I'm trying to fool him, and the more serious I get, the more he laughs, so I've stopped.
>
> Of course it's not all so good, I have to admit. We're still where we were, so far as knowing where your next meal is coming from. When I go to bed at night I tell myself I've done good, to stay alive and keep the kids alive, and if they'll just wake up in the morning, and me too, well then, we can worry about that, all the rest, come tomorrow. So there you go. We do our best, and that's all you can do.

She may sound fatalistic, but she appears to be a nervous, hardworking, even hard-driven woman—thin, short, constantly on the move. I may not know what she "really" thinks and believes, because like the rest of us she has her contradictions and her mixed feelings. I think it is fair to say that there are some things that she can't say to me—or to herself. She is a Negro, and I am white. She is poor, and I am fairly well off. She is very near to illiterate, and I put in a lot of time worrying about how to say things. But she and I are both human beings, and we both have trouble—to use that word—"communicating," not only with each other, but with ourselves. Sometimes she doesn't tell me something she really wants me to know. She has forgotten, pure and simple. More is on her mind than information I might want. And sometimes I forget too:

Remember you asked the other day about Peter, if he was ever real sick. And I told you he was a weak child, and I feared for his life, and I've lost five children, three that was born and two that wasn't. Well, I forgot to tell you that he got real sick up here, just after we came. He was three, and I didn't know what to do. You see, I didn't have my mother to help out. She always knew what to do. She could hold a child and get him to stop crying, no matter how sick he was, and no matter how much he wanted food, and we didn't have it. But she was gone—and that's when we left to come up here, and I never would have left her, not for anything in the world. But suddenly she took a seizure of something and went in a half hour, I'd say. And Peter, he was so hot and sick, I thought he had the same thing his grandmother did and he was going to die. I thought maybe she's calling him. She always liked Peter. She helped him be born, she and my cousin, they did.

Actually, Peter's mother remembers quite a lot of things. She remembers the "old days" back South, sometimes with a shudder, but sometimes with the same nostalgia that the region is famous for generating in its white exiles. She also notices a lot of things. She notices, and from time to time will remark upon, the various changes in her life. She has moved from the country to the city. Her father was a sharecropper and her son wants to be a pilot (sometimes), a policeman (sometimes), a racing-car driver (sometimes), and a baseball player (most of the time). Her husband is not alive. He died one year after they all came to Boston. He woke up vomiting in the middle of the night—vomiting blood. He bled and bled and vomited and vomited and then he died. The doctor does not have to press very hard for "the facts." Whatever is known gets spoken vividly and (still) emotionally:

I didn't know what to do. I was beside myself. I prayed and I prayed, and in between I held his head and wiped his forehead. It was the middle of the night. I woke up my oldest girl and I told her to go knocking on the doors. But no one would answer. They must have been scared, or have suspected something bad. I thought if only he'd be able to last into the morning, then we could get some help. I was caught between things. I couldn't leave him to go get a policeman. And my girl, she was afraid to go out. And besides, there was no one outside, and I thought we'd just stay at his side, and somehow he'd be o.k., because he was a strong man, you know. His muscles, they were big all his life. Even with the blood coming up, he looked too big and strong to die, I thought. But I knew he was sick. He was real bad sick. There wasn't anything else, no sir, to do. We didn't have no phone and even if there was a car, I never could have used it. Nor my daughter. And then he took a big breath and that was his last one.

When I first met Peter and his mother, I wanted to know how they lived, what they did with their time, what they liked to do or disliked doing, what they believed. In the back of my mind were large subjects like "the connection between a person's moods and the environment in which he lives." Once I was told I was studying "the psychology of the ghetto," and another time the subject of "urban poverty and mental health."

It is hoped that at some point large issues like those submit themselves to lives; and when that is done, when particular but not unrepresentative or unusual human beings are called in witness, their concrete medical history becomes extremely revealing. I cannot think of a better way to begin knowing what life is like for Peter and his mother than to hear the following and hear it again and think about its implications:

No sir, Peter has never been to a doctor, not unless you count the one at school, and she's a nurse I believe. He was his sickest back home before we came here, and you know there was no doctor for us in the county. In Alabama you have to pay a white doctor first, before he ll go near you. And we don't have but a few colored ones. (I've never seen a one.) There was this woman we'd go to, and she had gotten some nursing education in Mobile. (No, I don't know if she was a nurse or not, or a helper to the nurses, maybe.) Well, she would come to help us. With the convulsions, she'd show you how to hold the child, and make sure he doesn't hurt himself. They can bite their tongues real, real bad.

Here, I don't know what to do. There's the city hospital, but it's no good for us. I went there with my husband, no sooner than a month or so after we came up here. We waited and waited, and finally the day was almost over. We left the kids with a neighbor, and we barely knew her. I said it would take the morning, but I never thought we'd get home near suppertime. And they wanted us to come back and come back, because it was something they couldn't do all at once—though for most of the time we just sat there and did nothing. And my husband, he said his stomach was the worse for going there, and he'd take care of himself from now on, rather than go there.

Maybe they could have saved him. But they're far away, and I didn't have money to get a cab, even if there was one around here, and I thought to myself it'll make him worse, to take him there.

My kids, they get sick. The welfare worker, she sends a nurse here, and she tells me we should be on vitamins and the kids need all kinds of check-ups. Once she took my daughter and told her she had to have her teeth looked at, and the same with Peter. So, I went with my daughter, and they didn't see me that day, but said they could in a couple of weeks. And I had to pay the woman next door to mind the little ones, and there was the carfare, and we sat and sat, like before. So, I figured, it would take more than we've got to see that dentist. And when the nurse told us we'd have to come back a few times—that's how many, a few—I thought that no one ever looked at my teeth, and they're not good, I'll admit, but you can't have everything, that's what I say, and that's what my kids have to know, I guess.

What *does* she have? And what belongs to Peter? For one thing there is the apartment, three rooms for six people, a mother and five children. Peter is a middle child with two older girls on one side and a younger sister and still younger brother on the other side. The smallest child was born in Boston:

It's the only time I ever spent time in a hospital. He's the only one to be born there. My neighbor got the police. I was in the hall, crying I guess. We almost didn't make it. They told me I had bad blood pressure, and I should have been on pills, and I should come back, but I didn't. It was the worst time I've ever had, because I was alone. My husband had to stay with the kids, and no one was there to visit me.

Peter sleeps with his brother in one bedroom. The three girls sleep in the living room, which is a bedroom. And, of course, there is a small kitchen. There is not very much furniture about. The kitchen has a table with four chairs, only two of which are sturdy. The girls sleep in one big bed. Peter shares his bed with his brother. The mother sleeps on a couch. There is one more chair and a table in the living room. Jesus looks down from the living room wall, and an undertaker's calendar hangs on the kitchen wall. The apartment has no books, no records. There is a television set in the living room, and I have never seen it off.

Peter in many respects is his father's

successor. His mother talks things over with him. She even defers to him at times. She will say something; he will disagree; she will nod and let him have the last word. He knows the city. She still feels a stranger to the city. "If you want to know about anything around here, just ask Peter," she once said to me. That was three years ago, when Peter was six. Peter continues to do very poorly at school, but I find him a very good teacher. He notices a lot, makes a lot of sense when he talks, and has a shrewd eye for the ironic detail. He is very intelligent, for all the trouble he gives his teachers. He recently summed up a lot of American history for me: "I wasn't made for that school, and that school wasn't made for me." It is an old school, filled with memories. The name of the school evokes Boston's Puritan past. Pictures and statues adorn the corridors—reminders of the soldiers and statesmen and writers who made New England so influential in the nineteenth century. And naturally one finds slogans on the walls, about freedom and democracy and the rights of the people. Peter can be surly and cynical when he points all that out to the visitor. If he is asked what kind of school he would *like,* he laughs incredulously.

Are you kidding? No school would be my first choice. They should leave us alone, and let us help out at home, and maybe let some of our own people teach us. The other day the teacher admitted she was no good. She said maybe a Negro should come in and give us the discipline, because she was scared. She said all she wanted from us was that we keep quiet and stop wearing her nerves down, and she'd be grateful, because she would retire soon. She said we were becoming too much for her, and she didn't understand why. But when one kid wanted to say something, tell her why, she told us to keep still, and write something. You know what? She whipped out a book and told us to copy a whole page from it, so we'd learn it. A stupid waste of time. I didn't even try; and she didn't care. She just wanted an excuse not to talk with us. They're all alike.

Actually, they're all *not* alike, and Peter knows it. He has met up with two fine teachers, and in mellow moments he can say so:

They're trying hard, but me and my friends, I don't think we're cut out for school. To tell the truth, that's what I think. My mother says we should try, anyway, but it doesn't seem to help, trying. The teacher can't understand a lot of us, but he does all these new things, and you can see he's excited. Some kids are really with him, and I am, too. But I can't take all his stuff very serious. He's a nice man, and he says he wants to come and visit every one of our homes; but my mother says no, she wouldn't know what to do with him, when he came here. We'd just stand and have nothing to talk about. So she said tell him not to come; and I don't think he will, anyway. I think he's getting to know.

What is that teacher getting to know? What *is* there to know about Peter and all the others like him in our American cities? Of course Peter and his friends who play in the alley need better schools, schools they can feel to be theirs, and better teachers, like the ones they *have* in fact met on occasion. But I do not feel that a reasonably good teacher in the finest school building in America would reach and affect Peter in quite the way, I suppose, people like me would expect and desire. At nine Peter is both young and quite old. At nine he is much wiser about many things than my sons will be at nine, and maybe nineteen. Peter has in fact taught me a lot about his neighborhood, about life on the streets, about survival:

I get up when I get up, no special time. My mother has Alabama in her. She gets up with the sun, and she wants to go to bed when it gets dark. I try to tell her that up here things just get started in the night. But she gets mad. She wakes me up. If it weren't for her shaking me, I might sleep until noon. Sometimes we have a good breakfast, when the check comes. Later on, though, *before* it comes, it might just be some coffee and a slice of bread. She worries about food. She says we should eat what she gives us, but sometimes I'd rather go hungry. I was sick a long time ago, my stomach or something—maybe like my father, she says. So I don't like all the potatoes she pushes on us and cereal, all the time cereal. We're supposed to be lucky, because we get some food every day. Down South they can't be sure. That's what she says, and I guess she's right.

Then I go to school. I eat what I can, and leave. I have two changes of clothes, one for everyday and one for Sunday. I wait on my friend Billy, and we're off by 8:15. He's from around here, and he's a year older. He knows everything. He can tell you if a woman is high on some stuff, or if she's been drinking, or she's off her mind about something. He knows. His brother has a convertible, a Buick. He pays off the police, but Billy won't say no more than that.

In school we waste time until it's over. I do what I have to. I don't like the place. I feel like falling off all day, just putting my head down and saying good-bye to everyone until three. We're out then, and we sure wake up. I don't have to stop home first, not now. I go with Billy. We'll be in the alley, or we'll go to see them play pool. Then you know when it's time to go home. You hear someone say six o'clock, and you go in. I eat and I watch television. It must be around ten or eleven I'm in bed.

Peter sees rats all the time. He has been bitten by them. He has a big stick by his bed to use against them. They also claim the alley, even in the daytime. They are not large enough to be compared with cats, as some observers have insisted; they are simply large, confident, well-fed, unafraid rats. The garbage is theirs; the land is theirs; the tenement is theirs; human flesh is theirs. When I first started visiting Peter's family, I wondered why they didn't do something to rid themselves of those rats, and the cockroaches, and the mosquitoes, and the flies, and the maggots, and the ants, and especially the garbage in the alley which attracts so much of all that "lower life." Eventually I began to see some of the reasons why. A large apartment building with many families has exactly two barrels in its basement. The halls of the building go unlighted. Many windows have no screens, and some windows are broken and boarded up. The stairs are dangerous; some of them have missing timber. ("We just jump over them," says Peter cheerfully.) And the landowner is no one in particular. Rent is collected by an agent, in the name of a "realty trust." Somewhere in City Hall there is a bureaucrat who unquestionably might be persuaded to prod someone in the "trust"; and one day I went with three of the tenants, including Peter's mother, to try that "approach." We waited and waited at City Hall. (I drove us there, clear across town, naturally.) Finally we met up with a man, a not very encouraging or inspiring or generous or friendly man. He told us we would have to try yet another department and swear out a complaint; and that the "case" would have to be "studied," and that we would then be "notified of a decision." We went to the department down the hall, and waited some more, another hour and ten minutes. By then it was three o'clock, and the mothers wanted to go home. They weren't thinking of rats anymore, or poorly heated apartments, or garbage that had nowhere to go and often went uncollected for two weeks, not one. They were thinking of their children, who would be home from school and, in the case of two women, their husbands who would also soon be home. "Maybe we should come back some other day," Peter's mother said. I noted she didn't say *tomorrow*, and I realized that I had read someplace that people like her aren't precisely "future-oriented."

Actually, both Peter and his mother have a very clear idea of what is ahead.

For the mother it is "more of the same." One evening she was tired but unusually talkative, perhaps because a daughter of hers was sick: "I'm glad to be speaking about all these things tonight. My little girl has a bad fever. I've been trying to cool her off all day. Maybe if there was a place near here, that we could go to, maybe I would have gone. But like it is, I have to do the best I can and pray she'll be o.k."

I asked whether she thought her children would find things different, and that's when she said it would be "more of the same" for them. Then she added a long afterthought:

Maybe it'll be a little better for them. A mother has to have hope for her children, I guess. But I'm not too sure, I'll admit. Up here you know there's a lot more jobs around than in Alabama. We don't get them, but you know they're someplace near, and they tell you that if you go train for them, then you'll be eligible. So maybe Peter might someday have some real good steady work, and that would be something, yes sir it would. I keep telling him he should pay more attention to school, and put more of himself into the lessons they give there. But he says no, it's no good; it's a waste of time; they don't care what happens there, only if the kids don't keep quiet and mind themselves. Well, Peter has got to learn to mind himself, and not be fresh. He speaks back to me, these days. There'll be a time he won't even speak to me at all, I suppose. I used to blame it all on the city up here, city living. Back home we were always together, and there wasn't no place you could go, unless to Birmingham, and you couldn't do much for yourself there, we all knew. Of course, my momma, she knew how to make us behave. But I was thinking the other night, it wasn't so good back there either. Colored people, they'd beat on one another, and we had lot of people that liquor was eating away at them; they'd use wine by the gallon. All they'd do was work on the land, and then go back and kill themselves with wine. And then there'd be the next day—until they'd one evening go to sleep and never wake up. And we'd get the Bossman and he'd see to it they got buried.

Up here I think it's better, but don't ask me to tell you why. There's the welfare, that's for sure. And we get our water and if there isn't good heat, at least there's some. Yes, it's cold up here, but we had cold down there, too, only then we didn't have *any* heat, and we'd just die, some of us would, every winter with one of those freezing spells.

And I do believe things are changing. On the television they talk to you, the colored man and all the others who aren't doing so good. My boy Peter, he says they're putting you on. That's all he sees, people "putting on" other people. But I think they all mean it, the white people. I never see them, except on television, when they say the white man wants good for the colored people. I think Peter could go and do better for himself later on, when he gets older, except for the fact that he just doesn't *believe*. He don't believe what they say, the teacher, or the man who says it's getting better for us—on television. I guess it's my fault. I never taught my children, any of them, to believe that kind of thing; because I never thought we'd ever have it any different, not in this life. So maybe I've failed Peter. I told him the other day, he should work hard, because of all the "opportunity" they say is coming for us, and he said I was talking good, but where was my proof. So I went next door with him, to my neighbor's, and we asked her husband, and you know he sided with Peter. He said they were taking in a few here and a few there, and putting them in the front windows of all the big companies, but that all you have to do is look around at our block and you'd see all the young men, and they just haven't got a thing to do. Nothing.

Her son also looks to the future. Sometimes he talks—in his own words—"big." He'll one day be a bombardier or "something like that." At other times he is less sure of things: "I don't know what I'll be. Maybe nothing. I see the men sitting around, hiding from the welfare lady. They fool her. Maybe I'll fool her, too. I don't know what you can do. The teacher the other day said that if just one of us turned out o.k. she'd congratulate herself and call herself lucky."

A while back a riot excited Peter and his mother, excited them and frightened them. The spectacle of the police being fought, of white-owned property being assaulted, stirred the boy a great deal: "I figured the whole world might get changed around. I figured people would treat us better from now on. Only I don't think they will." As for his mother, she was less hopeful, but even more apocalyptic: "I told Peter we were going to pay for this good. I told him they wouldn't let us get away with it, not later on." And in the midst of the trouble she was frightened as she had never before been:

> I saw them running around on the streets, the men and women, and they were talking about burning things down, and how there'd be nothing left when they got through. I sat there with my children and I thought we might die the way things are going, die right here. I didn't know what to do: if I should leave, in case they burn down the building, or if I should stay, so that the police don't arrest us, or we get mixed up with the crowd of people. I've never seen so many people, going in so many different directions. They were running and shouting and they didn't know what to do. They were so excited. My neighbor, she said they'd burn us all up, and then the white man would have himself one less of a headache. The colored man is a worse enemy to himself than the white. I mean, it's hard to know which is the worst.

I find it as hard as she does to sort things out. When I think of her and the mothers like her I have worked with for years, when I think of Peter and his friends, I find myself caught between the contradictory observations I have made. Peter already seems a grim and unhappy child. He trusts no one white, not his white teacher, not the white policeman he sees, not the white welfare worker, not the white storekeeper, and not, I might add, me. There we are, the five of us from the 180,000,000 Americans who surround him and of course 20,000,000 others. Yet, Peter doesn't really trust his friends and neighbors, either. At nine he has learned to be careful, wary, guarded, doubtful, and calculating. His teacher may not know it, but Peter is a good sociologist, and a good political scientist, a good student of urban affairs. With devastating accuracy he can reveal how much of the "score" he knows; yes, and how fearful and sad and angry he is: "This here city isn't for us. It's for the people downtown. We're here because, like my mother said, we had to come. If they could lock us up or sweep us away, they would. That's why I figure the only way you can stay ahead is get some kind of deal for yourself. If I had a choice I'd live someplace else, but I don't know where. It would be a place where they treated you right, and they didn't think you were some nuisance. But the only thing you can do is be careful of yourself; if not, you'll get killed somehow, like it happened to my father."

His father died prematurely, and most probably, unnecessarily. Among the poor of our cities the grim medical statistics we all know about become terrible daily experiences. Among the black and white families I work with—in nearby but separate slums—disease and the pain that goes with it are taken for granted. When my children complain of an earache or demonstrate a skin rash I rush them to the doctor. When I have a headache, I take an aspirin; and if the headache is persistent, I can always get a medical check-up. Not so with Peter's mother and Peter; they have learned to live with sores and infections and poorly mended fractures and bad teeth and eyes that need but don't have the help of glasses. Yes, they can go to a city hospital and get free care; but again and again they don't. They come to the city without any previous experience as patients. They have never had the money to purchase a doctor's time. They have never had free medical care available. (I am speaking now of Appalachian whites as well as southern blacks.) It may comfort me to know that every American city provides some free medical services for its "indigent," but Peter's mother and thousands like her have quite a different view of things:

> I said to you the other time, I've tried there. It's like at City Hall, you wait and wait, and they pushes you and shove you and call your name, only to tell you to wait some more, and if you tell them you can't stay there all day, they'll say "lady, go home, then." You get sick just trying to get there. You have to give your children over to people or take them all with you; and the carfare is expensive. Why if we had a doctor around here, I could almost pay him with the carfare it takes to get there and back for all of us. And you know, they keep on having you come back and back, and they don't know what each other says. Each time they starts from scratch.

It so happens that recently I took Peter to a children's hospital and arranged for a series of evaluations which led to the following: a pair of glasses; a prolonged bout of dental work; antibiotic treatment for skin lesions; a thorough cardiac work-up, with the subsequent diagnosis of rheumatic heart disease; a conference between Peter's mother and a nutritionist, because the boy has been on a high-starch, low-protein, and low-vitamin diet all his life. He suffers from one attack of sinus trouble after another, from a succession of sore throats and earaches, from cold upon cold, even in the summer. A running nose is unsurprising to him—and so is chest pain and shortness of breath, due to a heart ailment, we now know.

At the same time Peter is tough. I have to emphasize again *how* tough and, yes, how "politic, cautious and meticulous," not in Prufrock's way, but in another way and for other reasons. Peter has learned to be wary as well as angry; tentative as well as extravagant; at times controlled and only under certain circumstances defiant: "Most of the time, I think you have to watch your step. That's what I think. That's the difference between up here and down in the South. That's what my mother says, and she's right. I don't remember it down there, but I know she must be right. Here, you measure the next guy first and then make your move when you think it's a good time to."

He was talking about "how you get along" when you leave school and go "mix with the guys" and start "getting your deal." He was telling me what an outrageous and unsafe world he has inherited and how very carefully he has made his appraisal of the future. Were I afflicted with some of his physical complaints, I would be fretful, annoyed, petulant, angry—and moved to do something, see someone, get a remedy, a pill, a promise of help. He has made his "adjustment" to the body's pain, and he has also learned to contend with the alley and the neighborhood and *us*, the world beyond: "The cops come by here all the time. They drive up and down the street. They want to make sure everything is o.k. to look at. They don't bother you, so long as you don't get in their way."

So, it is live and let live—except that families like Peter's have a tough time living, and of late have been troubling those cops, among others. Our cities have become not only battlegrounds, but places where all sorts of American problems and historical ironies have converged. Ailing, poorly fed, and proud Appalachian families have reluctantly left the hollows of eastern Kentucky and West Virginia for Chicago and Dayton and Cincinnati and Cleveland and Detroit, and even, I have found, Boston. They stick close together in all-white neighborhoods—or enclaves or sections or slums or ghettos or whatever. They wish to go back home but can't, unless they are willing to be idle and hungry all the time. They confuse social workers and public officials of all kinds because they both want and reject the city. Black families also have sought out cities and learned to feel frightened and disappointed.

I am a physician, and over the past ten years I have been asking myself how people like Peter and his mother survive in mind and body and spirit. And I have wanted to know what a twentieth-century American city "means" to them or "does" to them. People cannot be handed questionnaires and asked to answer such questions. They cannot be "interviewed" a few times and told to come across with a statement, a reply. But inside Peter and his brother and his sisters and his mother, and inside a number of Appalachian mothers and fathers and children I know, are feelings and thoughts and ideas—which, in my experience, come out casually or suddenly, by accident almost. After a year or two of talking, after experiences such as I have briefly described in a city hall, in a children's hospital, a lifetime of pent-up tensions and observation comes to blunt expression:

> Down in Alabama we had to be careful about ourselves with the white man, but we had plenty of things we could do by ourselves. There was our side of town, and you could walk and run all over, and we had a garden you know. Up here they have you in a cage. There's no place to go, and all I do is stay in the building all day long and the night, too. I don't use my legs no more, hardly at all. I never see those trees, and my oldest girl, she misses planting time. It was bad down there. We had to leave. But it's no good here, too, I'll tell you. Once I woke up and I thought all the buildings on the block were falling down on me. And I was trying to climb out, but I couldn't. And then the next thing I knew, we were all back South, and I was standing near some sunflowers—you know, the tall ones that can shade you if you sit down. No, I don't dream much. I fall into a heavy sleep as soon as I touch the bed. The next thing I know I'm stirring myself to start in all over in the morning. It used to be the sun would wake me up, but now it's up in my head, I guess. I know I've got to get the house going and off to school.

Her wistful, conscientious, law-abiding, devoutly Christian spirit hasn't completely escaped the notice of Peter, for all his hard-headed, cynical protestations: "If I had a chance, I'd like to get enough money to bring us all back to Alabama for a visit. Then I could prove it that it may be good down there, a little bit, even if it's no good, either. Like she says, we had to get out of there or we'd be dead by now. I hear say we all may get killed soon, it's so bad here; but I think we did right to get up here, and if we make them listen to us, the white man, maybe he will."

To which Peter's mother adds: "We've carried a lot of trouble in us, from way back in the beginning. I have these pains, and so does everyone around here. But you can't just die until you're ready to. And I do believe something is happening. I do believe I see that."

To which Peter adds: "Maybe it won't be that we'll win, but if we get killed, everyone will hear about it. Like the minister said, before we used to die real quiet, and no one stopped to pay notice."

Two years before Peter spoke those words he drew a picture for me, one of many he has done. When he was younger, and when I didn't know him so well as I think I do now, it was easier for us to have something tangible to do and then talk about. I used to visit the alley with him, as I still do, and one day I asked him to draw the alley. That was a good idea, he thought. (Not all of my suggestions were, however.) He started in, then stopped, and finally worked rather longer and harder than usual at the job. I busied myself with my own sketches, which from the start he insisted I do. Suddenly from across the table I heard him say he was through. Ordinarily he would slowly turn the drawing around for me to see; and I would get up and walk over to his side of the table, to see even better. But he didn't move his paper, and I didn't move myself. I saw what he had drawn, and he saw me looking. I was surprised and a bit stunned and more than a bit upset, and surely he saw my face and heard my utter silence. Often I would break the awkward moments when neither of us seemed to have anything to say, but this time it was his turn to do so: "You know what it is?" He knew that I liked us to talk about our work. I said no, I didn't—though in fact the vivid power of his black crayon had come right across to me. "It's that hole we dug in the alley. I made it bigger here. If you fall into it, you can't get out. You die."

He had drawn circles within circles, all of them black, and then a center, also black. He had imposed an X on the center. Nearby, strewn across the circles, were fragments of the human body—two faces, an arm, five legs. And after I had taken the scene in, I could only think to myself that I had been shown "like it is in the alley"—by an intelligent boy who knew what he saw around him, could give it expression, and, I am convinced, would respond to a different city, a city that is alive and breathing, one that is not for many of its citizens a virtual morgue.

63 Technology, Change, and Continuing Education

EMMANUEL G. MESTHENE

We are now, says Mesthene, in the midst of a technological revolution which calls for us to become more change-oriented than stability-worshiping. But if we are to develop this capacity we must recognize the need to be flexible and adaptable and to be creative in altering our basic institutions of education, especially our colleges and universities, so that they can provide leadership in coming to terms with the age in which we live. Moreover, we must recognize, says Mesthene, that the kind of education we need today can no longer terminate at age eighteen or twenty-two. Our changing world will require that we keep learning and relearning and that we recognize the critical importance of continuing education.

• • • • •

I don't think there has ever been a time, in the whole history of the world, when people haven't asked: What are the implications—for education, for society, for man—of this, that, or the other new development or new trend? So that when we are now asked, "What are the implications of the age of technology?", we sometimes react with a bit of irritation, and wonder what's so new about now. Technology has become a little bit like Mark Twain's weather: it is on everybody's lips, but little seems to be done about it. The French, I suppose, would react with their old saying that the more things change, the more they remain the same.

I think, rather, that the converse is

SOURCE: Emmanuel G. Mesthene, "The University, Adult Education, and the Age of Technology," *Adult Leadership,* vol. 15, no. 4 (October 1966), 113–45, passim. Reprinted by permission of the author and the publisher. • The author is a lecturer and member of the faculty of Business Administration and Director of the Program on Technology and Sociology at Harvard University. His major interests are science and public policy, metaphysics, and aesthetics. He is the author of *How Technology Will Shape the Future* and has published *Science and the Policies of Governments* and *Ministers Talk about Science.*

true. Things continue to appear the same when they have changed in fact. This should not be surprising. The substance of the world will change, normally, before its forms do, so that we tend to use the same formulas, the same mental attitudes and approaches to events, when the events themselves, the contents of the formulas, have changed.

While the form of our question, then, may be familiar, its substance, I think, is new. It is new in two respects. First, there is change; there is novelty. Our time *is* different from past times. It is not just ritual to say this is a time of transition. All times are times of transition, and ours is no exception. If our economic and other measures don't show it, then there is something wrong with the measures. Second, the emphasis on technology is meaningful—it is not just can't—because science and technology are at the root of change and novelty. I should like to dwell on that for a minute.

I think it is possible to support the proposition that science and technology are the principal sources of change and novelty in the world—not just among the sources, but the principal sources. I remind you that Karl Marx attempted to analyze his time by coming up with a model according to which any society or civilization has what he called a "substructure" made up of the relations of the production and distribution of goods, of economic goods. Over and above that, he saw social, cultural, and political "superstructures," whose form was determined, in an essentially one-way relationship, by the economic substructure. The facts of economics were thus, for Marx, somehow more fundamental, more causative, than any other social fact.

In the last hundred years, Marx's analysis has proved inadequate to the wealth and complexity of economic fact. In addition, it suffers from a philosophical weakness: that one factor—the economic—is fundamental, and that all other factors—the social, cultural, and political—are derivative. This is a fallacy known to students of philosophy as the fallacy of reductionism: it reduces the total wealth of reality to one of its elements, and offers that one as sufficient reason for the whole. Yet reductionism would not be so popular as it is, if it didn't have a use. It is valuable for putting emphasis on a particular element or truth that needs illumination. That is why I have reminded you of Marx. With all due caution about the validity of his approach, I want nevertheless to use it to propose that science and technology are better candidates than Marx's for the job of determinants of the shape of society and of the world.

Why? Because science and technology change the *physical* world. Social events, political events, cultural or educational events, economic events, do not of themselves generate literal physical change. Science and technology do, and they thereby affect the rest of the world in a manner reminiscent of Marx's economic substructure. I illustrate with an example that a writer for the current issue of *Fortune* magazine picked up—I am sorry to say, or glad to say, I can't decide which—from an unpublished paper of mine.

There was a time—most of time up to now—when the arena of political action was limited by the physical state of the world at any given time. The political game was played in the context of weapons of a certain kind and power, of oceans and mountains of a certain width and height, of communication and transportation networks of a certain speed and capacity, of economic realities determined by a certain technology. Of course, weapons, and speeds, and technologies—and even mountains—changed. But they *were seen to have* changed—*post facto*, as effects—rather than *being* changed by deliberate employment of available means. And the time unit of change was, moreover, histories or civilizations, rather than years, or maybe even months.

For all practical political purposes, these physical constraints were fixed and certain. They were the ground rules of the game—the rules imposed, literally, by the physical shape of the playing field. The alternative of changing them was not open to the political decision-maker, any more than moving the short left-field ference farther out to counter the opposing team's star right-hand hitter is an alternative available to the baseball manager. The decision-maker therefore, like the baseball manager, confined his consideration to legal feasibility, to interpretation of the rules. As Robert Wood of MIT has put it, the persistent political question, "Can we do this?" meant "Do the rules allow it?" That is a question that lawyers answer, which is why so many of our political decision-makers and political advisers have tended to be lawyers.

The question today is much more often, "Can we change the rules?" The physical conditions of political action are no longer fixed. New weapons can now be developed in no more time than it takes to negotiate an international agreement. Oceans can be spanned in an hour, and mountains moved in a day. Communications are at the speed of light, and transportation way past that of sound. Technological innovation can set the stage for economic revolution in far less time than people are prepared to accept it. The single most pervasive impact of science and technology on politics is perhaps that they have shortened the time span of physical change to the same order as that of social change and political action. It is now, for the first time ever, possible to move the left-field fence *during* the game.

And as with politics, so with law, economics, culture, and society: man's ability derived from his technical prowess, to change the physical world at will and massively removes the only heretofore inviolable constraint on the shape and development of his social systems and institutions. That is why I see science and technology as something like a new determining substructure of the whole of society, and why I find that to ask about the implications of the age of technology—for the university, for education, or for anything else—is meaningful despite its overly familiar ring.

The challenge of technology, in other words, derives from the dawning realization that man is on the point of being able to do anything he wants. Can we transplant human hearts, control personality, order the weather that suits us, travel to Mars or Venus? I do not think there are many of us who doubt that we can, if not now or in five or ten years, then certainly in twenty-five or in fifty or a hundred. But if the answer to the question "What can we do?" is "Anything," then the accent shifts to the questions, "What should we do?", "What, in the end, do we really want?" We take up again, in other words, the task of the ancient Greeks: How to be wise. I might add that it is an infinitely more difficult task now than it was for the Greeks, because we have infinitely more power than the Greeks had.

Wisdom is a matter of values, and values, whatever else they may be, are constants, stabilities, truths. Culture, civilization, has traditionally been a matter of verities, of permanencies, and society in the end has had the job of codifying and storing those accumulated values of the past.

But that is not all. In the past, the stability of values has by and large been based on social stabilities: on eternal institutions, like the church; on a presumed unchanging human nature; on progress toward some ideal state or political system. Wisdom, therefore, has traditionally been construed, not merely as the search for values, but as the pursuit of particular values, the time-tested values on which existing societies were built. Education aimed, not only at teaching, but at indoctrination, and the two functions were for a long time indistinguishable. It is no accident that the medieval church was the first great organized school.

A glance at the natural philosophy of this same medieval time reveals an astronomy centered on the earth, a physics based on four sensible elements, and a biology of hierarchical kinds. The physical world too, thus, was ordered, stable, and known. It had been so, moreover, since Aristotle's time, and it does not require much browsing among the medieval texts to appreciate the degree to which the stability of the social system, and therefore also the stability of values, were dependent, in this time, on the presumed permanent structure of nature.

The evidence is in the long so-called war between religion and science. During the Renaissance and seventeenth century, men began to discover that the physical world was not at all like what Aristotle had thought and Aquinas had taught. The priests, who were also the educators, fought the spread of this new knowledge, because they saw it, rightly, as subversive of the spiritual and social values that had for centuries been based on older natural philosophies. They lost the battle—inevitably—and by the eighteenth century, theology, economy, polity, and society were all transformed. The medieval verities and permanencies yielded, in other words, when the natural verities and permanencies were discovered to be other than believed. Wisdom, which had been retrospective, now became contemporary. The spiritual and eternal were replaced by the scientific and experimental, as men strove for more of the new and liberating knowledge. Education, following suit, gave its attention to method. It moved from inculcation of the known to exploration of the unknown, and from the production of preachers to the training of probers.

The first great scientific revolution thus arose from discovery that the natural world was not as it was believed to be. The present revolution—most accurately called "technological," I think—is in turn the result of awareness that the natural world need not be as it is. We can change it. We *are* changing it. Wisdom, thus, once retrospective and recently contemporary, must now become prospective. And education must complete the road from inculcation, to exploration, to anticipation.

The temper of the time, in other words, is future-oriented. This is the root of many of our discomforts. There are those who say that thus to turn from the past to the future means to abandon all value, since value is anchored in the past. This plaint achieves, sometimes the eminence of a philosophical movement—as in Existentialism—and sometimes the kind of social dislocation that we currently identify by such names as alienation, or anomie: the feeling of negation of identity. But these are the symptoms, I would argue, not of the impossibility of values in a world that must be increasingly future-oriented, but of the wrenching of the moral enterprise away from its traditional anchors in the social and physical stabilities of the past. Those stabilities are going, but that does not mean that all possibility of stability is gone. The stabilities, and permanencies, the verities of value remain, but they must henceforth be forged out of the continuum of human experience with constant change, rather than derived from the illusion of permanence. Values, in short, now reveal themselves as what only they can be—principles, concepts, understandings, plans of action—not static imitations of social habit.

The effect on man of his newfound technical power, therefore, is nothing if it is not potentially liberating. The possibility of enslavement that some worry about inheres, not in the fact of power, but in the uses of it. For more power offers more choices, and more choices mean more freedom. But more freedom requires more wisdom if it is to add up to more humanity. The malaise of our age, as many have noted, is that our power increases faster than our wisdom in dealing with it. Wisdom remains a matter of values, but the values must henceforth be sought, created, reshaped, made over and over again as needed. The permanencies we live by will henceforth have continuously to be hewed out of the impermanencies that we live in. It is no wonder it is so much more difficult now, than ever, to be wise.

Another way to put the challenge of modern technology is that it offers late twentieth-century man the opportunity to create a new Athens. I do not speak of recapturing an ancient golden age. Nostalgia is an enemy of wisdom. The true technological age will embody in relevant form the values we associate with ancient Athens without incurring the costs in slavery and war that we also associate with ancient Athens.

I find strange the number of our contemporaries who do not see the human possibilities in the new technology—the possibilities, to use their ancient Greek names, for justice, citizenship, and human dignity. What is to be done with the slaves of industrial society, they ask, when there is no longer any slave labor for them to do because production will be done by machines? That must surely be the wrong question. Rather should we be asking, "What will people do when they might now for the first time no longer need to be slaves?" The evolution is not inevitably from slaves to vegetables. A question arises, of course, about whether there is not a large proportion of people who are natural slaves, who have little of value to contribute to themselves or to society except their mechanical ability. It would seem so from historical experience, but the case is not proved. The demand on people for the purpose of producing goods has always been so great that few but the most obviously talented have been exempted. With more opportunity to develop, and with an educational system geared to exploring and exploiting different human potentialities, the sociological image might change. Genius is not the only alternative to the slave functioning as a machine.

Another proposition that is frequently heard is that leisure will soon be in oversupply, and that it is the responsibility of society to manufacture respectable cultural pursuits to fill it and to keep it from becoming burdensome. Much of adult education has too often been justified on the same ground. There is some evidence that leisure, defined as cessation of work, increases in inverse proportion to the interest-content of work. In recent years, the society has enjoyed a proportion of its productivity increases in the form of leisure, mainly among its blue collar workers, i.e., among those engaged in essentially routine and mechanical work. Those engaged in more creative work seem, if anything, to work even longer hours than before. It is a reasonable hypothesis, therefore, that rewarding and useful work tends to be preferred to leisure in the negative or passive sense of the term. The implication of the hypothesis is that policies for education and cultural development should aim rather at equipping more human beings to perform more human work, than at entertainment or purposeless self-improvement programs to fill idle hours and keep people out of trouble.

• • • • •

The need for thought is perhaps never greater than before, and the opportunity for it never better. What the society lacks—and needs most—at the present time is the vision of the wisdom that rationality can lead to, and that the society must have before it can be moved to deliberate and self-conscious pursuit of rationality in search of the vision. To hold up that vision is the most glorious and most difficult challenge facing the university and the whole enterprise of education.

The difficulty is imposed by the need of education to cope with the passage of the ancient stabilities—physical and social—that I was talking about a few moments ago. How does the problem break down? Academic subject matter is behind actual knowledge at the moment it is being taught. Job skills are out-of-date on the day of graduation. Specialization, once a haven of stability, withers in the middle of a productive life. The rapid introduction of novelty increases the sheer amount of subject matter that has to be taught and learned.

What is the reaction? My daughter—and probably yours—phrases it this way: "There's so much to learn, and it won't be any good after I learn it anyway, so why should I bother?" It does no good, in answer, to say that education is good. For the premises are right: there *is* too much to learn, and most of it *is not* much good after it is learned. It's the conclusion—"Why bother?"—that we must go after. That conclusion I see as a relic of what I have been talking about, of the traditional worship of the stable—of the feeling that what is and is lasting is good, and that change is uncomfortable, bad, and to be either avoided, or dealt with as quickly as possible to get back to the stable and the good.

I have touched this theme of our predilection for the stable in another place. I tried there to point out that the fundamental job of education—apart from the teaching of particular skills to particular people for particular purposes—is to change the inherited attitude that worships stability. If we can educate a generation that understands change, feels comfortable with it, even expects and looks forward to it, then the two premises slightly rephrased, "There is much to learn" and "It dates quickly," might yield a conclusion different from "Why bother?" They might lead instead to the question, "What steps, in addition to formal education, must I take to stay flexible and adaptable and selective in the face of the volcano of fact and fluidity?"

One of those steps surely is what we are currently falling into the habit of calling continuing education. It is a better term than "adult education" for two reasons. First, adult education implies that *real* education somehow ends at 18 or 22, and that what comes after is, at best, more amusement than education. Second, since real education ends at 18 or 22, the term "adult education" has too often carried the connotation that the adults who engaged in it somehow did not profit fully from their earlier real education, and must therefore now try to make up for it all.

The term "continuing education" does not carry those connotations, because it is entirely clear that from now on everyone will have to be educated continuously. If there is very much to learn and it dates quickly, people will have to keep learning and relearning, if they are to keep up with the world. The big implication of the technological age is that careers, stocks-in-trade, will henceforth be shorterlived than people. Another, I suspect, is that no one will from now on be able to make a career out of a speciality. He may start on one, but he'll have to move to another, and still another, before his working time is done.

There are evident implications for the university. The institution of the university was created, pretty much as we know it today, in another age to meet other intellectual needs than ours. It is characterized, especially in Europe, by an organization according to separate academic chairs or departments that discourages interaction among disciplines, by an aggressive guardianship of ancient values that borders on cultural provincialism, by discouragement of its own growth and development that often forces the promising young man into another country or another business, by a blindness to forms of excellence other than those few that are responsive to traditional academic measures, by a deliberate and cherished isolation from the other sectors and institutions of society that rob it, ultimately, of all influence upon and from them.

The situation of the university in the United States is better in the matter of mobility of personnel among institutions and into and out of government and industry, of the opportunity for individual variety within academic departments, of the greater opportunity it offers youth as a consequence at least of its broader base, of—a somewhat negative virtue—the absence of a weighty cultural tradition requiring a major effort of reinterpretation to adapt it to current concerns, and of the development of increasing numbers of cross-disciplinary centers, programs, and projects whose independent financing and task orientation force something of an intellectual commerce among the more traditional, discipline-oriented academic departments.

Yet even in the United States, the universities remain a conservative influence. Unfortunately, they tend to conserve one of the conditions that inhibit the needed flexibility to meet the demands of a lifelong process of education, i.e., disciplinary provincialism. The social consciousness is present much more than it is in the European university, with the curious further consequence that the specialist is sometimes deluded into thinking that the particular knowledge that he is expert in is all that is needed to solve the problems of the world. The economist is a good contemporary example. To the door of departments of philosophy, in addition may perhaps be laid the further charge that over-concern with the technical has led them to forget their responsibility of bringing to the education of their charges the philosophic breadth of attitude that alone can temper the lack of understanding that comes of exclusive concentration on the small.

Yet the university remains the birthplace of wisdom, and it is the university that we must seek to reform. The need to make it adequate to the radically new educational requirements implied by modern technology calls for serious thought to the reorganization of the university so that it can pull, in the process, the full weight that only it can pull. It is in the universities that lies, still, the best potential for learning to come to terms with our age. They will realize that potential fully when they succeed in bridging the current dichotomy between "schooling" and "adult education" with a concept of continuing education that is alive and sensitive to what will from now on in certainly be a world that will stand still no longer.

64 The Church Trap

ARTHUR HERZOG

Sociologists study the structure and function of religion as one of the basic institutions that is a part of every culture. Religion, especially as practiced in the United States, has both "individual" and "societal" functions. In the former function, it provides security, comfort, and a sense of certainty to the believer. In its latter function, it attempts to provide guidance and leadership regarding social issues about which a logical extension of the church's moral precepts seem to require that it take a stand. It is this societal function that is producing the "church trap" discussed in this article. After examining the failure of church membership and participation to keep pace with our population growth, the author turns to an analysis of the cross-pressures upon religious institutions and their consequences for church organization and operation—especially for the role of the church's chief functionaries—the clergy.

What on earth is happening out there, in those 320,000 churches across the land? Instead of rejoicing at the altars of the richest, most powerful religious organizations in history, they come to a funeral. Hurry! Change the neon from

J
SAVES
S
U
S

to

G
O
D

GOD IS DEAD
D
E
A
D

SOURCE: Arthur Herzog, *The Church Trap* (New York: Macmillan, 1968), pp. 3–22. • Arthur Herzog is a free-lance writer and former magazine editor. He covered the Angolan revolution and has served as a consultant to the Peace Corps. He has contributed articles to the *New York Times Magazine, Harper's, Esquire, The Catholic Digest,* and *True;* and is the author of *The War-Peace Establishment.*

"All the Church is in ferment," said Pope Paul VI, who might have been speaking for any major American denomination or creed. But there is no agreement on the nature of the brew. Some people declare that the churches are poised on the brink of a New Reformation, even in a world which has been called post-Christian, post-ideological, post-just-about-everything. Others think the churches will muddle through; but within the churches themselves today also flourish small, highly vocal bands of latter-day Jeremiahs who predict for organized religion that ultimate of tragedies, decay and death with no hope for an after-life.

The debate is strange, for on paper at least, the churches appear to be marching confidently toward the third millennium. The familiar statistics have often been held up to the world as talismans of American rectitude. Two out of three Americans claim church membership, and 44 per cent of the population is said to comply with the promptings of the public service ads to "worship at the church of your choice" by showing up there once a week (a figure which must be viewed with skepticism, since some religious leaders do not believe the churches can hold that many people on Sundays, sitting or standing). "We are a religious people whose institutions presuppose a divine being," wrote Supreme Court Justice William O. Douglas, and so, in theory at least, religion, if not established, is sanctified by the state and is to be found on our coins, in our oaths, on cornerstones, in short almost everywhere. Evidently, too, Americans like the idea of big, strong churches, seeing them as an anchor against too much and too rapid change, a deterrent to crime in the streets, emblems of our souls. So the conventional portrait is that of a churchy America, as the Protestant theologian Gibson Winter puts it, "pious, pure, holy and noble in a wicked world."

Nonetheless, for organized religion in America not all the News is Good. Religious leaders today can be thought of increasingly as ecclesiastical executives who, in spreading the Lord's word, use computers and PERT (Program Evaluation Review Technique) and flow charts and talk about inputs, outputs and cost-effectiveness. (". . . the almost frantic propagation of modern methods," thought the famous German Protestant, Dietrich Bonhoeffer, who looked with alarm at the American religious scene, "betrays the dwindling of content.") The churches do not pay cash dividends but they are clearly interested in the management techniques of modern corporations. The Roman Catholic Church employs management consultants, and a leading Protestant denomination plans to hire a long-range planner who, "hopefully," would be a Christian, while a Southern Protestant denomination employed a Jew to make a study of its membership because it wanted objective answers. The information arriving at the major religious administration centers—like the National Conference of Catholic Bishops, in Washington, D.C., or the limited partnership of thirty-four Protestant denominations known as the National Council of the Churches of Christ in the U.S.A., in New York City, which occupies a large, glittering structure irreverently called by its occupants "the God-box"—indicates that serious trouble may lie ahead.

Within church circles religious statistics are well-known for their inaccuracy, but some credence, it's thought, can be given to trends. The famous "religious revival" of the 1950's—to which the churches attached great hopes, and which prompted serious scholars to predict a genuinely religious America—now appears to have ended before the decade was out; ended, in fact, just as it was receiving maximum publicity. Since then the trends seem to be running against the churches, and for this reason, perhaps, the yearly releases on church membership are no longer headline news. Membership has been leveling off until it has fallen behind the growth of the general population. In 1965 church membership increased 1.3 per cent while the population rose 1.5 per cent. The Jews considered themselves lucky to hold their own against death, and the "bluechip" Protestant denominations, studying the figures, have begun to wonder if the WASP has lost his sting. "There is," says R. H. Edwin Espy, General Secretary of the National Council of Churches, "the probability of membership leveling off. There is an identifiable trend. It is a critical issue."

"We feel the tide started to flow out in 1958," says John F. Anderson, Executive Secretary of the Board of National Ministries of the Presbyterian Church in the U.S. The denomination has its roots in the South, where the churches are stronger than anywhere else in the country. Evidently the figures were engraved in his mind, for Anderson, a big man in two-toned shoes, was able to rattle off from memory, without hesitation, the statistical course of his million-member denomination. In 1958 the U.S. Presbyterians could show a net increase in membership of 20,000, which went down to 13,000 in 1960; 7,000 in 1964; 4,000 by 1965. In 1966 the increase was up to 5,000, hardly enough for a denominational sigh of relief.

This "decrease in the rate of increase," as it's called, has lasted long enough to be established as an ecclesiastical fact of life. It appears to be affecting almost all churches, regardless of race, color or creed. The possible exceptions to the rule are fundamentalist churches which still claim to be growing faster than the general population, and indeed there might be solid reasons for thinking that conservative religions will grow for the precise reasons that liberal churches will shrink—the former appealing to both the traditionally minded and those afraid of change; the latter, in tailoring themselves to secular society, gradually losing their separate identity and reason for being. Just the same, the less ebullient Northern churchmen don't believe the fundamentalists apply the same rigor to statistics as evangelism. To them, Southern Baptist figures, for instance, are loaded with non-members, and it's true, according to one study, that in several largely Southern Baptist counties in Mississippi the reported church membership actually managed to exceed the *total* number of people who lived there.

But it's not simply membership that has the churches concerned. The Roman Catholic magazine *Commonweal*, pointing out that the church in 1967 had fewer educational institutions, parish elementary pupils, converts, nuns, seminarians, infant baptisms (down 84,096, for Catholics a significant statistic) and a very slow growth rate, went on to say, "U.S. Catholics are deep in their reassessment of traditional Catholicism. The Church has only begun to glimpse the consequences." One might expect to find the Protestants of the future in Sunday School, and yet Protestant figures show sharp declines in Sunday School attendance, to the point where some churchmen would like to write off Sunday School altogether. College church programs attract only a miniscule proportion of students, and while once everybody could be depended on to tell the pollsters dutifully that he believed in God, a large and growing number of high school and college students describe themselves with the dread word "agnostic" or even "atheist." The disenchantment is evident even among Catholics, despite their emphasis on the centrality of the church and its teachings. Catholic leaders are said to be seriously worried by polls like one at a Jesuit high school showing that 84 per cent of the students disagreed with the church's position on birth control, 39 per cent did not pray and 45 per cent did not believe in churches.

On the one hand, then, the churches have fewer replacements in sight, while on the other the present church membership contains a high concentration of old people. This realization has led many churchmen to expect that before very long the decrease in the rate of increase will turn into an absolute decline, bottoming no one knows where. "At meetings of ministers in New York," says a well-informed Lutheran pastor, "there is the unspoken fear that the parishes are going under. One minister vies with the next for members. The result is deep suspicion." "It wouldn't surprise me if, by the year 2000, this parish is down to five per cent of its present membership," I was told by a gloomy young Episcopal clergyman in the West. "The Episcopal church will shrink and shrink. The church is like a fat woman, with too much water in the tissues."

So far the seepage has been slow, almost imperceptible, and one might think the elimination of excess fluid would be healthy. But the churches are committed to gaining adherents, not losing them, and for institutional as well as evangelical reasons. The twin breasts of American religion are membership and money, and if one sags so does the other. For a decade or more the churches have been embarked on an ambitious, billion-dollar-a-year building crusade. They now have an enormous physical plant to maintain and hopefully fill with parishioners on Sundays. There are steeples to paint, electric organs to repair, ministers to feed.

• • • • •

Were you, say, a high church leader surveying the religious scene, observing a whittling away of your membership, a loss of your power to influence people, and a goodly amount of discontent and leaving among your clergy and intellectuals, you would be bound to think that something was wrong. You might well decide that religion should be more attractive, exciting, meaningful to peoples' lives—in a word, "relevant." You would be perfectly honest in feeling this, but at your back would be the needs, the institutional imperatives, of the church organization.

In fact, relevance—meaning not only such things as masses in English but a churchly participation in large public issues like peace, civil rights and poverty—is the battle cry of the churches today, except for the extremely conservative denominations. But relevance takes money and this is one substance the churchgoers have proved reluctant to give for the purposes of social action. Not only is the contribution of the average churchgoer less, in terms of his income and the value of the dollar, than it was thirty years ago, but almost all of what he does give is retained by the local parishes, in the building fund or for a new Hammond organ or electronic chimes. When a denomination must cut back on its social programs, as the United Presbyterian Church in the U.S.A. has warned its flock it would have to do unless greater generosity was forthcoming, the implications, for the theologians of relevance, are serious.

The specter that haunts an increasing number of ecclesiasts is the realization that, faced with penurious parishioners on the one hand and a strong desire to prove themselves relevant on the other, the churches can only make their brave march into the world with government funds. And this on top of what is potentially the most explosive issue confronting religion today—the surprising extent to which churches, parishes, ministers, colleges, hospitals and almost all the charities on which religion prides itself for "good works," are already heavily underwritten or subsidized by the state, meaning church-members and non-church-members alike.

Religion in America is caught in a sociological trap. One jaw represents the fixed expectations of the parishioners who want a solid church organization with all the trimmings, church-as-usual on Sundays, the same old rules by which they've always lived. "I've had ten children," an angry woman told her priest. "If they change the rules on birth control I'm quitting the church." The other jaw is the pressure of a society whose slackening interest in religion brings great pressure on the churches to modernize, to arouse public interest, to get "where the action is," to be vital, to prove that they do have a useful and honest social function. To change in this direction risks alienating the great bulk of church members, while not to change risks becoming ever more isolated from the secular society. Leadership and laity, then, have different ideas about church. The leaders want a platform, a place from which to be heard on social issues. It may well be that the churchly stress on the woes of secular society betrays an inability to talk to their own members in terms meaningful to them. For the laity does not appear to be deeply involved in the pronouncements and judgments the leadership makes to the world. Church members in America look to religion for guidance, support, direction, and help in personal problems, but to individuals churches have less and less to say.

The man in the middle, a principal victim of the church trap, religion's unlucky Pierre, is the minister. As a profession the clergy is at a gravely low ebb. Protestant seminaries report trouble attracting candidates, and those they do get are likely to be at the bottom of the academic pile. A leading Catholic educator, Kenneth M. Reed, S.V.D., calls the decline in Catholic seminarians a "cliff-drop," and, he says, "It is going to continue down and stay down for a long time." Fewer candidates plus more dropouts add up to a decimated clergy. "For us, the problems of the 1970's won't merely be staffing schools and hospitals," says a leading priest-psychologist, "but in finding priests to run the parishes." As it is, even with the free labor of priests and nuns, Catholic schools and hospitals are imploring more and more government support. If the Catholics, with only one priest per eight hundred churchgoers in the U.S., redouble their "prayers for more priests"—it may be an indication of how serious and worldwide a Catholic difficulty this is that the Diocese of Rome, heartland of Catholicism, is presently producing between one and five vocations *per year*—and wonder where the next generation's clergymen are coming from, so must the Jews wonder, with only about a hundred rabbis annually graduating in the U.S., and the Protestants, whose personnel problems are intensified by the desire of new ministers to serve in education, the "inner city," the poverty program, the church bureaucracy, anywhere but in the local parishes.

Word may have filtered down to them that all is not well with the parish minister. "I think between ten and twenty per cent of our clergy would quit tomorrow if they had a job option," I was told by a ranking Episcopal bureaucrat, "and many others are dissatisfied." A Presbyterian official, Rev. Edward S. Golden, a sort of minister to ministers, believes that at least 20 per cent of Presbyterian clergymen *ought* to quit. "Many ministers," he says, "when they face the reality of church life, rankle at it and may lose their faith, although they go on mechanically, that is as part of the church machine."

In the halcyon days of Protestantism sons of ministers often emulated their fathers and became ministers themselves, but this is less and less the case. "You were the first minister in our family and you will be the last," the son of a successful suburban minister in Detroit told his father. The son had watched his father perform, year after year, a delicate balancing act between what the minister thought was right and what his parishioners expected of him. It is no accident that most Protestant faiths today have begun to provide psychological services for disturbed ministers, where they can discuss their troubles and try to sort out their lives. In the opinion of those who provide psychological counsel for the clergy the pulpit today is an anxious seat, a place where potential neuroses are brought out in the open. And it is a sad commentary on the rigidity of American Protestantism that troubled ministers are often reluctant to look for help, because a minister, both by popular expectation and his own, isn't supposed to be *sick*, because of his connection with the divine.

The new openness of the Catholic Church has not extended to revealing the number of "fallen priests," but those close to the problem agree on its scope. "We sense," says Msgr. George Higgins, "that priests and nuns don't leave for the reasons they always did—authority and sex. There is something new in the air. I would call it a problem in Catholic identity." An abbot refers to the "mass exodus from the religious life," and nuns appear to be defecting in striking numbers—dropouts of 30 or 40 per cent in some orders seem to be occurring. Estimates on the number of fallen priests begin at five thousand and go on up—as compared to a priestly population of sixty thousand—but round numbers are only part of the problem. Also important is the shock to the Catholic nervous system —reflected in the interest displayed by the public in the fallen priests themselves, and in the rumors about defections flooding the priestly grapevines—that priests would actually choose to depart the sacred and high terrain of the church. The defectors, moreover, invariably say that they intend to remain Catholic, and to some Catholic authorities the real danger is that ex-priests, loosely banded together, will form a sort of anti-party within the church, undermining official authority and further confusing an already confused laity.

The Roman Catholic problem is always presented as unique, related to the great internal stresses that have wracked the church since the Second Vatican Council. And yet is Vatican II entirely the cause? Not according to John Cogley, former religion editor of *The New York Times* and now a resident intellect at the Center for the Study of Democratic Institutions at Santa Barbara. "The Council cannot be blamed for all this unrest. . . . The hour for revolutionary change had struck. . . . In other words, with or without the Council, we would have had the present headlines," Cogley, a Catholic himself, told a group of Catholic educators. He went on to predict, "Without rapid and drastic change there is, I think, little hope for the Church."

One finds gloomily parallel prophecies from the other faiths, from Jews who ask if anything will survive of Judaism but Jewish jokes and chicken soup, from Protestants who contributed to an angry symposium entitled *Who's Killing the Church?* (The churches are, they cry.) The church, declares an Episcopal minister named Malcolm Boyd, who tried to show precisely how hip and relevant a preacher can be by performing at a San Francisco nightclub, "is to be found somewhere in the position of the *Titanic* heading toward an iceberg."

Such judgments can be heard from high in the church structures, off-the-record or conveyed elliptically, but occasionally stated in black and white. "I always tell young ministers," explains an outspoken Episcopal bishop, Daniel Corrigan, "that before they get to the end of the road, this new church, that new rectory just won't be there. But if they know this ahead of time, if they know that other Christians without big, rich churches have lived effectively, they'll be all right." "We're in the rapids right now," says J. L. Sullivan, Executive Secretary of the powerful Southern Baptist Sunday School Board. "Some are upset by the turbulence and lose their sense of direction." "I compare the Church to a pilot running out of gas over the ocean," says John Wright, Bishop of Pittsburgh, a highly influential Catholic. "Either he slows down in the hope of conserving his fuel or speeds up in hope of getting there before it runs out. Both ways, the hope is probably in vain."

Usually each faith is treated parochially, examined under its own lights, so that Catholics are said to stumble over sex, freedom and authority, Protestants over the Death of God and accusations that they are "weak, tardy, equivocal and irrelevant," Jews over the issue of separatism and the survival of Jewish culture. But though we try to individuate the faiths, it appears that each is undergoing a similar crisis, that the malaise of one is common to all, and that such distinctions in symptomatology as do appear on the surface are really gauges of how far the illness has progressed.

The church crisis is deeply bound up with the myths and aspirations of those who make up the bulk of church membership in America, the white middle class, with its position in the country and the world, with its philosophy, and with its perception of the sacred, meaning reality and power which it wants to locate as close as possible to itself, to its communities and to its country. As Mircea Eliade points out, the feeling of I-am-at-the-center is integral to primitive religion and there is every reason to think it is carried over in church organizations today. But if such beliefs were insecurely held, if the person, community or country had begun to doubt that it was indeed at the center, if it had begun to question its own myths and aspirations, a certain confusion in identity would have to result. In fact, religion in America displays the symptoms of a serious crisis in identity, and it is not too much to say that the churches, though still possessed of large resources and reservoirs of good will, are at the moment holding operations, searching for something to do, something for which to live, some clearer conception of just why they are here and what they are here *for.*

• • • • •

"Founded by Jesus Christ, A.D. 33," asserts an early 1900's legend on a church wall in Nashville, Tennessee, and from this simple faith and rocklike certainty one spans half a century to arrive at "WORSHIP GOD IN YOUR CAR, Casually Dressed, Comfortably Seated—Valley Forge Drive-In Theater" (which probably also showed *The Bible* and charged admission). Over this space of time, as the sociologist Daniel Bell puts it, "The old primary group ties of family and local community have been shattered; ancient parochial faiths are questioned; few unifying standards have taken their place." An oleaginous glow may continue to illuminate the altarpieces, but for practical wisdom people look elsewhere, to scientists, psychiatrists, those with professional credentials. Contrary to the hopeful predictions of religious scholars, there is no sign that any large number of secular intellectuals have become "fellow-travelers of faith." It is not because the churches, eternally optimistic that everyone will come to see the light, haven't tried. The United Presbyterian Church in the U.S.A., for instance, started an experimental ministry at Cape Kennedy, with the idea of lending its spiritual insights to the scientists in the space program, but the scientists apparently felt they could aim for the stars—or Peking—without the aid of organized religion. The secular intellectuals not only determine public policy but they give legitimacy to it, replacing the clergy as standard-setters. The churches, denominational leaders and preachers, take positions on war, nuclear weapons, race and the like —indeed, they are *expected* to—but their predictable pronunciamentos on public matters are conveniently ignored, not just by the men in power but by their own constituents. On one issue where organized religion spoke with considerable unity—against the war in Vietnam—there is no indication that churchly protests had any effect on public policy.

A reason the churches are ignored is that, like ladies of high virtue, they can be counted upon to say, "No." "Thou shalt *not*," thunder the churches—make war, fornicate, covet, commit adultery, or as in the actual case of an order of cloistered nuns, die without the Mother Superior's permission. My own memory of church consists mostly of a pink-cheeked gentleman shaking a verbal finger, and what positives he accentuated sounded suspiciously like platitudes even to young ears. The churchly identity thus fostered is almost entirely negative. The Catholic theologian, Gabriel Moran, speaks of the "negations inherent to Protestantism and incorporated into Catholicism. By seeing God's function as the forgiver of sin, by exalting faith at the expense of reason, post-Reformation Christianity could not find God by going beyond man because it could not accept man." The churches have not only defined man in their own terms, but they have rigidly clung to their definitions even when man, as the new society of abundance has made possible, has insisted on defining himself in new ways. By remaining essentially nay-sayers and conservers—in matters, say, of sex—the churches have paid an enormous price in believability.

All might be well for the churches had they been able to stay with religion as expressed in the local parishes, but change has been pressing hard. Half the population moves every five years and the migration from town to city has hacked away at religion's rural roots. Vice-President Hubert Humphrey once predicted that within not too many years rural America, from the Appalachians to the Rockies, would be virtually deserted except for the cities, occupied only by a few farmers and caretakers. In this atmosphere of dislocation the churches' private vision of the ideal society is still that of a rural communality, in which services are arranged so as not to interfere with milking time and where people had common backgrounds and interests.

"Churches are by definition communal," says the sociologist Norman Birnbaum, "whereas society tends toward privatization. The churches assume there is a sort of unified public which wants guidance, when in fact there is none." The ladies' groups, the church suppers, the bazaars and prize cakes, the socials, the picnics, the inevitable photos of plain people in rimless spectacles singing—although the denominational magazines show that such events still comprise church life, they are clearly images of days past. The newer, more sophisticated parishes in the suburbs are under heavy fire from within the churches for being parochial, inward-looking, a mere social club, selfish and a spiritual luxury. "The attempt," says Gibson Winter, "to perpetuate the local parish or congregation as a basic unit of the Christian church is doomed to failure."

It's not at all surprising, in view of the circumstances in which organized religion finds itself, that the churches should long to attract new people, to appeal to the urbanites and the young, to reclaim their centrality and importance. So we find, presided over by slightly anxious but always smiling "get-with-it" ministers (crammed with Harvey Cox's guidebook to religious urbanity, *The Secular City*), the jazz vespers and beat services, the guitars, the lonely-hearts socials and showings of what looks to the more strait-laced like prurient art—to bring in the customers. But religion's modernity smacks of borrowed gear, as though change does not spring from genuine inner impulse but is imposed from the outside, by external necessity. Walter Kaufmann speaks of the churches' attempts "to balance the imposing archaism of most of their thought with some of the latest jargon," and indeed the churches want so hard to swing. They would like to be "relevant," "where the action is," "at the cutting edge," to "come alive in a church of dialogue" in the "inner city." The goal for themselves and for others is to become "truly human," to all but religious ears a tautology. Repeated endlessly by writer after writer in religious journals, catchwords like these reveal religion's inability to come up with fresh ideas of its own.

One of the brightest aspects of the current church scene is the sincere attempt by most branches of organized religion to take a forthright position on the issue of race. Here, as nowhere else, the churches have been able to exert some leverage, and there are countless examples of heroism among the clergy. And yet, even on the race question, there are signs that the churches are not precisely comfortable as crusaders. For the churches, not believing that civil rights activism was proper for them, were late in joining the fray. The Roman Catholic bishops did not take a stand until 1958, almost a hundred years after the Civil War, the Protestants not much earlier and in some cases later. Many of the famous priests and nuns who marched at Selma, Alabama, would not have gotten there if orders from a certain bishop rescinding permission had arrived on time. In many cities rabbis are still conspicuously absent from civil rights organizations, and the role of many clerics in the history of civil rights could easily be called "profiles in cowardice." Some churches today are badly divided on the race issue, with parishes withholding funds from denominations that move too far, too fast, and acting as a brake on the religious commitment. Particularly depressing for those who want religion to take a passionate stand on race is the fact that Negro clerics within the white denominations are leaving. For them, the churches' progress has been too slow, and the position of the Negro in a white church structure remains ambiguous.

There is, too, a larger issue here. For if, as Reinhold Niebuhr has said, "The race crisis saved the churches from irrelevance," then what can be thought of their relevance beyond it? If the Negro is Christ today, who will He be tomorrow? If the race issue is solved, what else will make religion relevant? Is it true, then, that Christianity has no intrinsic relevance? If as one Christian radical puts it, "Christian faith equals public involvement," then, strictly speaking, there can be no Christian faith outside of public involvement, and what can be said about the panoply of religious liturgies, prayers and services, of religious belief itself? For one can easily have public involvement without the Christian or any other faith, and if good deeds define the Christian then we have no need of churches to define Christians for us.

The evidence suggests that organized religion is moving on exceedingly treacherous waters and whether it can circumnavigate is by no means sure. Caught in a crisis of identity, lacking a clear relationship with society, confronting unrest in its clergy and declines in its growth, the church has three possible futures:

First, churches can respond actively to the gnawing discontent within the religious organizations and a growing disconcern without. To advocates of this way, it means violently wrenching the churches out of their old frames, committing them entirely to social action, progress and the realities of urban life. It means taking churchly eyes off otherworldly horizons and fastening them securely on this one. It means putting church money where its mouth is, and that implies an end to church building funds, probably the abandonment of the local parishes for a geographic, ecumenic, city-wide one. But this, the secularization of religion, carries grave risks. The doctrinal side of religion might hardly exist at all. Already the Episcopal Church has abandoned the notion of heresy, which would seem to indicate that there is little to be heretical about. If it comes to pass that the Pope is not infallible, even in matters of faith and morals, if bishops are elected by popular vote, if priests can marry and nuns serve only a few years before departing to raise families, how will one define the Roman Catholic Church? How will a Catholic be different from a Protestant? How will the Protestant Church, having jettisoned the supernatural, prayer, authority in moral matters, and so on, having committed itself to liberal social causes, differ, say, from Americans for Democratic Action? Why should the individual join one rather than the other? And what *would* a Jew be?

Such developments in the churches, moreover, would alienate the conservative parishioners who populate and largely finance the parishes, confuse the faithful and pious who find in religion a refuge from change, and risk a sharp decline in membership, a serious split between liberals and conservatives, or both. It is a possibility no red-blooded organization could lightly take, and those who threaten the church structure will almost surely be branded as enemies. Indeed, as Patrick Cardinal O'Boyle of Washington, D.C., has already said, "Today the enemies of religion, and of the Catholic Church in particular, are more likely to come from within."

The second possibility, equally repugnant to religion's organization men, is a conscious retreat from denominations back to sects. The sects might (though probably would not) teach a social gospel, but they certainly would put high-minded emphasis on religious doctrine, their separate identity, and would follow their own beliefs and practices, no matter how odd-ball they seem to the outside world. The general society would hear them in their own genuine and perhaps remote tongue (how significantly aloof and other-wordly the Papal language still sounds). But the sects could not have their holy wafers and eat them too. They would be forced to assent to the proposition that Protestants and Catholics, like Jews, are minority cultures in an irreligious state. Secular man would be recognized for what he is, the dominant social force, and the notion that our institutions are underwritten by an Almighty, in the sense that Fort Knox guarantees our currency, would be abandoned. The churches, standing on their own feet, would be taxed. The sects would have the virtue of being honest, to themselves and others, and on their own example, not overblown religious publicity or attempts to manipulate power, they would rest their case. At least the churches would have a chance to show the validity (or irrelevance) of the religious ideal, and the vague and unpleasant odor of spurious sanctity which still hangs over the United States would be dispelled.

Here, too, risks abound for religion, for the Jews, who have tried to preserve a sect-religion, also face absorption into the American blotter. But the third possibility, to hang, or try to hang, motionless in the tides of change, is the greatest risk. Changelessness, after all, is death.

65 The Problems and Promise of Leisure

SEBASTIAN DE GRAZIA

For years writers have been pointing to the shorter work week and the extensive development of mechanical devices as making possible much more opportunity for free-time activities. For those accustomed to such a traditional generalization, this selection by de Grazia may come as a shock. He asserts that "Any primitive tribe enjoys more free time than a resident of the United States today."He also maintains that what free time we have will be considered a burden rather than an opportunity unless we can replace our present "work ethic" and "consumer ethic" with a widely-accepted "leisure ethic." It is especially useful to examine the distinction the author makes between "free time," "recreation," and "leisure" and the conditions and consequences surrounding each.

The otter is playful,
the beaver industrious.
Which leads the better life?
TI-TZU

INTRODUCTION

Over the past fifty or one hundred years the "idleness problem" has been supplanted by the "leisure problem." Though people once excoriated idleness and today laud leisure, the problem is one and the same—the problem of free time. Moreover the problem is not the existence of too little free time but the threat of too much. Medically speaking, in Karl Marx's day a problem of too little free time did exist. Today no labor union would claim that its workers needed more free time for their health's sake. If anything, the thing they, but more particularly ministers, physicians, and psychiatrists fear, is the effect on their health of free time in too large a dose, the effect, that is, on people's mental health or on the social health of the community.

Most Americans when they use the word *leisure* have free time in mind. The confusion in usage is of recent origin. It dates from the rise of the commodity mentality. In selling products for use in free time, advertisers have wished to associate their goods with the ethical connotations of leisure. More recently others, like social workers, psychiatrists, priests, and ministers, worried about free time spent solely along commercial guidelines, have tried to add a self- or social-improvement twist to free time, again by calling it *leisure.* Now it has reached a new stage where, as the whole economy trembles at the slightest threat of unemployment, the word leisure is being groomed for impending, forced free time.

There is another question, the question of real leisure. Here the difficulty is not of too much but of too little. And the penalty for lack of leisure is not the unhealthy, individual or a disturbed community, but an uncreative, unlovely country.

FREE TIME: MORE, LESS, OR THE SAME

To begin, will there be more free time for Americans in the future? Theoreti-

SOURCE: William R. Ewald, Jr., ed., *Environment and Policy: The Next Fifty Years* (Bloomington, Ind.: Indiana University Press, 1968), pp. 114–26. • The author is a free-lance writer and professor of politics at Rutgers University. He is the author of *The Political Community, Errors of Psychotherapy,* and *Of Time, Work and Leisure.*

cally, yes. Projections have been made of how much free time there will be in coming decades. Similarly, calculations can be made as to whom the increase will go and as to whether some classes of the population will be favored above others. The work week is to get shorter by about an hour and a half each decade. By the year 2000, the overall average of hours worked is to be 31 per week or 1600 hours per year. It may go down as far as 21 per week (1100 per year). In the year 2020, on-the-job hours are to average about 26 per week, or 1370 per year, or (as above) as low as 16 hours per week, or 870 hours per year. With such figures at hand, it is not surprising that many wonder what people are going to do with their time.

Regarding who will have this free time, it seems that workers in all industries, be they manufacturing, trade, mining, construction, will benefit equally. Since the population will be both aging and growing younger, those over 65 will not benefit (presumably they are today already out of the labor force), while those at work under 25 will reap the harvest of shorter work weeks. Women, though, are to have less free time, since many more of them are to take jobs in 2000 (43 percent as against a participation rate of 37 percent in 1964), unless one calculates by the usual labor statistics, in which case women have no free time at home but acquire it, paradoxically, when they are counted as working women.

Breakdowns on amounts of free time for the managerial and official classes have received less attention from these projectors for 2000 and 2020, but by the logic of extrapolation alone they will still be working the longest hours. In 1960 they put in on the job an average of ten or twelve hours more than other categories of workers and an on-and-off the job total of over sixty business hours per week.

Studies have also been made of the impact that future expanses of time will have on the physical environment, focusing on how much money and acreage should be set aside for parks, woods and wilds, for roads leading to them, and for saving them all from congestion. Generally, the conclusion a reader might easily draw from them is that the demand for recreational space is as inexhaustible as the money and acreage are not; and that all roads lead to congestion.

• • • • •

TODAY'S TIME

One must bear in mind that readings into the future of free time, which have been tried ever since the industrial revolution, have been scandalously wrong. The problems of more time, how and by whom it will be enjoyed, cannot be separated from people's thoughts, hopes, fears, and goals. Recent forecasting has generally credited Americans with a simplistic psychology in which they appear as craving more free time, no matter what. A scrutiny of the available evidence reveals that they have not taken more free time, do not appear to wish more (though it be available to them), and do not seem likely to change in this respect over the next decade or two. The American full-time male worker puts in an average of nearly eight hours a day, six days a week. Contrary to what is widely believed, he has taken his gains in productivity not in the coin of free time but in coin of the realm. He has no more time free of work than men have had elsewhere when not caught in times of crisis or rough transition.

Technology and free time have sides to them that oppose each other. An age that breeds technology must be one that is beguiled by and desirous of material things and therefore must buy or somehow acquire them, to do which it must use up the time any one machine or device may save. Any primitive tribe enjoys more free time than a resident of the United States today. It is doubtful that any civilization ever had as little free time as we do. The commodity mentality, fascinated by the made and purchasable thing, holds the American worker in a vise of working overtime to buy timesaving devices and "leisure goods."

THE FUTURE: FORCED FREE TIME

Perhaps, independent of what people desire, there are forces coming into being that will propel them toward more time off the job. We have indicated already that increased time and distance between home and job have influenced the demand for more time off the job. In the future, automation, a larger population among which to spread available work, and a rising GNP with which to buy time may lead to increased free time. This may not be the case, however, so long as consumption continues to spiral upward.

An upward and onward spiral is just what the forecasters forecast. I shall not assemble another little table here but merely recall that forecasters see automation marching through business, government, and industry, population mounting lustily, and the graphic peak of the GNP at 2020 disappearing in a roseate cloud. If income doubles, let us say, and expenditures double too, it is hard to see how free time can increase. The worker will be working full-time and overtime as today to spend on what he wants to have. But statistics show that he has more free time today than ever before in history, do they not? No, they do not. They show that the American worker cannot be working any harder than he is now. He has in effect no time for free time.

. . . . .

If consumption keeps pace with production, then, there should be no increase in free time or general unemployment. Yet some of the factors just mentioned may lead to unemployment. Apparently automation, many fear, cannot spread jobs as widely as industrial economy has hitherto been able to do, because the skills it requires demand an above-average intelligence. If this be true (and much of the rest of this paper is based on this possibility) unemployment may be in the offing. But will it necessarily? Instead of calling it unemployment, why not call it free time? Workers may not be asking for more free time, but let us cut down their work year without cutting down their pay, let us call this time off the job, "leisure," and, lo!, unemployment has disappeared.

Politically this is a triumph. Where before the economic system could be charged with failure, now it can be and is already heralded as the great provider of undreamed of leisure. "Undreamed of" is correct. The kinship of unemployment and free time, when both have elements of unwillingness in them, deserves close attention. Workers will take this "leisure," but today they do not ask for it. On the other hand they did not ask to be caught in the swamp of commodities either; yet today they find themselves there, waist-deep. It may all be a question of the proper psychological preparation.

PREPARING FOR THE FUTURE

From one view the future is being adequately anticipated. Business, government, and industry are selling the future as an age of riches and leisure for everyone. There are some, however, who sense that all is not right, that workers are being faced with more time off the job while having no desire to take it. If workers had a desire for more free time, would they not have some idea of what they want to do with it? This is where the stubborn thought reaches in: "the problem of leisure" is not the problem of not enough but of too much free time. On reviewing the arguments pro and con made by various groups—labor and business in their more thoughtful moments, the medical profession and clergy, welfare workers and educators—one can hardly come away without feeling that free time is a threat and a problem rather than the gateway to an exciting age of leisure.

The doubts these voices raise demand a reconsideration of the impact of more time on the individual. By and large the solution they talk most about is not to cut free time down—for that seems to them impossible—but to provide the worker with ways of filling his future empty time. The foreseers of riches and leisure promise the worker all sorts of intriguing new equipment and facilities for sports, travel, comfort and entertainment—at a flick of the finger.

Personally I am weary of reading such predictions of the future. Their fascination with devices and products is incredibly naive. Can they really believe the stuff they put out? Yes, they can. They are testimony to the strength of the technological religion, which in the midst of so much disillusion, conserves its grand illusion, that a great industrial-scientific day is still a-borning. In 2020, reads one projection, our standard of living will be three to seven times higher than that of 1965 and in tune with this increase will be the increase in leisure time. I ask, will we be able to stand it?

The more apprehensive writers do not look to the cornucopia of commodities to fill men's time. For this reason they place more of their faith in government and non-profit institutions. They recommend programs for churches and synagogues, universities, housing authorities, settlement houses, clubs and neighborhood circles. The lion's share goes to the government, but not merely to the central government. A state government should have a Department of Leisure with architects, planners, statisticians, engineers, demographers, and social scientists, while subordinate leisure agencies should include psychologists, sportsmen, naturalists, and hobbyists. Also, each city of, say, 75,000 or more inhabitants, should boast a municipal Department of Leisure. Preparation for leisure would begin no later than high school.

These writers are right to be concerned, but the institutions they propose lack underpinnings. The preparation they would give are in things like aesthetic appreciation, social ease, prowess in games, sightseeing, outdoor life, nature study, skill in hobbies. They may also include preparation in "intellectual growth," but here they reveal a most serious weakness. The only philosophy they have to bank on is that exalting the fullest development of the individual's potentialities. What kind of clue does this give them except to let the individual be an individual, to let him develop his potentialities by himself? If you are going to tell him how to fill his empty time, you will be pushing him along the old road of self-betterment dearly loved by the nineteenth century. On the whole, however, that century kept the government off to one side. The present proposals may end by recommending that state legislatures enforce local standards, that departments of leisure should never try to give people what they want, for most people do not know what they want and should be encouraged or compelled to learn to like things they dislike.

The difficulty is even greater than such writers believe. They think it involves complexity and the possibility of undemocratic compulsion. This would be true were it a simple task like sewage disposal or air pollution, both of which are problems amenable to a rational plan, an organized attack, and an efficient system of execution. Free time cannot easily be handled this way. The word "free" in free time refers to uncommitted or unobligated time. If there is any constraint at all, the freeness vanishes.

The specter is that of an economic system constraining workers not to work. To solve the problem of filling the time then emptied, the system applies the same method it applied successfully to work—rationality, organization, and efficiency. Except that this time the method will not work. Preparing for the future in this way will bring trouble.

For all the fun that is poked at the gospel of work today, it has been a crucial part of American belief. As such it served and still serves to make sense and give meaning to existence. But it is weakening. All the nice talk itself of free time and leisure is a detraction. Writers jeer at the conformity and methodicalness work requires. Their painting a future workless world as a utopia is almost the last straw.

If the economic system is producing unemployment that it must justify as free time, it must yet produce a substitute for the work ethic. What is there to substitute for it? It is useless simply to recommend that men get the same satisfaction from leisure that they get from work. A hard worker used to be an object of esteem. Is he today? Work used to be, and still is, good for you, a remedy for pain, loneliness, the death of a dear one, a disappointment in love, doubts about the purpose of life. Steady methodical work built a great and powerful and prosperous nation. Can leisure do the same?

Religiously, politically, economically, militarily, and mentally it is still thought better to work than to do what you please. The men who go to work in the morning and come home at night are still the pillars of the nation. If these pillars tumble, the country has lost an important part of its cohesion.

To sum up, free time today does not exist in any great quantity. Projections based on the conviction that an extraordinary amount is being enjoyed are in error. Yet free time can be had in the future and in large quantities. It has already been available for a long time but few wished to take it or felt they could afford to. To get them to take it or wish for it, the worker-consumer pattern has to be broken. The "consumer" part of the dualism is not deep. It is a recently acquired belief, post-Depression, to be exact. The "worker" part of the pattern is a longer, ingrained tradition. It may take decades yet to break. Certainly it will not go at the speed projected, but the process may have already begun.

What may shatter the work ethic like Humpty Dumpty will be the need to conceal latent unemployment. One way already in evidence is to call it free time. But since it is not wanted, it is not free but forced free time. The constraint is hidden.

DISAFFECTION

There is another place in which unemployment even today may be inaccurately assessed—in universal college education. Here the young are removed from the labor force for four or five years. When accompanied by a military draft prospect for those not making the grade at school, college becomes for many not a choice but an extension of compulsory education. This may be hidden unemployment too, and not all the young are taken in by it. Possibly for this reason disaffection with the work ethic is appearing most dramatically today among youth.

Among the young there is a vocal minority whose antipathy to work is more ideological than the bum's or the philosophic hobo's once was. Their doctrines include an antipathy to technology and science as well, and to what is sometimes called the Establishment, namely all those in positions of influence in the political, military, industrial, and scientific world. To talk to these persons of a higher standard of living, mounting GNP, the American way of life, larger incomes, more free time, and the cornucopia of commodities reaps nothing but scorn. They no longer worship these gods. What they want in exchange is not clear but what they reject is easy to see—the world prophesied by the projections we have been studying.

Disaffection will not remain restricted to youth. Deprived of a sense of purpose, with the old gods gone and without new ones, other people will fall into a hedonistic attitude toward life, wherein all they can justify is to get what they can out of pleasure. Historically this is at times accompanied but typically followed by some form of religious revival. Until then there is reason to fear, as some do, that more free time, forced free time, will bring on the restless tick of boredom, idleness, immorality, and increased personal violence.

As more and more free time is forced on adults, disaffection will spread. If the cause is identified as automation and its preference for higher intelligence, nonautomated jobs may increase, as it is thought, in the categories of trade and services but they will carry the stigma of stupidity. Men will prefer not to work rather than to accept them. Those who do accept will increasingly come to be a politically inferior class composed of women, immigrants, imported aliens, and humanoids.

There may then be three classes: (1) an elite that works on top policy, administrative or manufacturing tasks with automated accoutrements, or in the arts and communication—writing, filming, designing, etc.; (2) a free time citizenry accepting its dole status but disenchanted and even rebellious; and (3) those of inferior political status who will perform the unpopular trades and services.

There are other alternatives of course, but this one reveals that a whole future world is possible on which today's statistical projections have little bearing.

Should it continue, the process of disaffection will spread most rapidly in the cities. Projections for free time in the future indicate that regional fluctuation in the length of the work week or work year will be small. This may be so but its significance will have a regional difference nonetheless.

One may look on the capital area of the United States as a megalopolis, the urbanized region extending from Boston to Washington. Eventually it may arc over to Chicago. The rest of the country, including climatic resorts like Florida and California, can be regarded as the provinces. From these areas, for decades to come, there will appear in the cities of the capital persons as yet relatively untouched by the disillusion of forced free time. The flow of provincials may provide a breathing spell of stability for the rest of the country, a time in which solutions to the problem of hidden unemployment, forced free time, and disaffection will have to be found.

There should be lots of time free for thinking up a solution, but a problem of such magnitude requires a creative solution. Free time can bring more recreation and an appetite for spectacles, but genius or creativity—that is doubtful. Free time leads to recreation; it is leisure that bears directly on creation.

THE RHETORIC OF LEISURE

For those concerned with the sanity of the individual or the integration of the country, it is natural to worry about too much free time. As we have seen, the problem does not exist at present but well may in the future. Furthermore, it is more serious than anyone thought. Advertisers sell wares within the worker-and-his-job pattern. Social workers may feel that other leadership is necessary besides that of commercialism, but at least it is some guidance. The threat to come is that the worker model which up to now has supported the industrial system will bite the grime and grease, leaving no heirs. In the ideological vacuum, there will be those who will look back on advertising and think nostalgically of the good old days. The advertiser was bound by some standards, slight reeds though they may then have seemed.

Now leisure is a state of being, of being free of everyday necessity. Distinct from free time, it requires freedom from time and work—not hourly, daily, or monthly freedom, but freedom from the necessity to work, preferably over a lifetime. By contrast the present American free time is one-half of a pendulum—jobtime/free time. First you work, then you rest and recreate yourself.

Leisure has no particular activities. Men in a leisure condition may do anything; much of what they do may seem to an outsider suspiciously like work. It is modern usage to refer to such activity as work. Creative work ought not to be called work at all. Not having anything to do, these men do something. Often they may turn to religious ritual, music, wining and dining, friends and poetry, and notably to the play of ideas and theory; in short, to the theoretical life, to contemplation.

With the lack in America of a strong tradition of leisure, it is not surprising that we must ask, "What can leisure do for us?" The benefits are the benefits of cultivating the free mind. If persons have been brought up with a liberal education and have no need to work at anything except what they choose, they enjoy a freedom that lays the conditions for the greatest objectivity (for example in science), the greatest beauty (for example in art), and the greatest creativeness (for example in politics). Leisure is the mother of philosophy, said Hobbes. If such are its benefits, and we need them sorely, can we increase leisure?

To increase leisure is difficult. It is not contained, as is free time, by time (off work) and space (for recreation). To increase free time it is usually enough to send a man, any man, home early from work. For his recreation it is usually enough to give him some space to play in. How to provide leisure?

All steps that can be taken by the government through legislation and institutions, by business organizations, schools, and churches, steps that have a limited value even for free time have much less value for leisure. There are traces of the leisure ideal in some recent attempts by government and universities to provide in centers and institutes a creative setting, for scientists in particular. These efforts and others can help only inasmuch as they diffuse an appreciative climate, through teaching and example. Much more than this cannot be done directly.

There are two important limits to face. First, not everyone has the temperament for leisure. According to the Encyclical *Rerum Novarum,* all mankind would be capable of enjoying leisure were it not for the Fall. For most people, leisure lacks sufficient guidance and sense of purpose; the leisure life is too hard. Those who have the toughness or psychological security for it are not many. Second, since leisure will have nothing to do with work (except that freely chosen, which then by definition should not be called work), it involves having means of support. In modern terms this means that whoever is to lead a life of leisure should have some form of economic independence.

The objectives in creating more leisure should be these: to allow the greatest number of those who have the temperament for it to develop to their fullest extent; to allow them to secure the means of existence without work; and to create an atmosphere more friendly than hostile in which they may live their kind of life.

A number of the developments we have been discussing do affect these objectives. A liberal education is almost a sine qua non for the growth of the leisure temperament. Universal education today may soon see to it that all will have a college education. On the negative side, however, the education is not being freely chosen; military service is the alternative. Education, moreover, has declined in quality and will continue to because of the great numbers of students in compulsory attendance and the nursery school climate of the college as a place to put grown-up children while the adults go to work.

Also, forced free time will not have to expand much to reach a net separation of income from work. Recent proposals for a guaranteed annual wage or salary intimate the separation already. Should this happen, the wherewithal for a life of leisure will be there for all who think they have the temperament. Many will try; many will drop out; among the survivors the right few will be found.

The last-mentioned prerequisite, an atmosphere friendly to leisure, may be brought about by the increase in free time whether forced or not. If both parts of the worker-consumer model break down, if more free time is not only forced upon men but in time also sought and taken, the accompanying change in attitude may well be receptive to true leisure. A more relaxed pace to life may bring about a more favorable view of the whole ideal, as well as more reflection, more refinement, and less ambitious political, military, and economic projects. Play in man's free time is a taste of leisure. In turn the ideal and practice of leisure create standards for the enjoyment of free time. Indeed without leisure the outlook for the resolution of the problems of hidden unemployment and forced free time seems desperate: hedonism, disintegration of social and political ties, crises of law and order, a cynical and callous foreign policy.

There are other developments that may influence the future attitude toward leisure, such as population growth, urbanization, increased prosperity and commercialism, and military events. Population growth and metropolitan concentration do not in themselves prohibit leisure. Traditions related to the leisure ideal in China, India, and England amply support this proposition. As for urban versus rural environment, the stimulus for the very ideals of civility and leisure has come from cities. Prosperity and the business and commercial spirit (to be distinguished from the work gospel and industrial materialism) are not inimical to leisure, as instances from ancient Greece and the Renaissance indicate. Instead the martial or expansionist temper or the desperate defensive position of a nation may be the most harmful influence, for it pits leisure against patriotism. Yet even this hypothesis needs qualification.

The use of professional forces or of mercenaries poses less of a problem than does the drafting of militia. Minor or border wars combined with imperialism, accompanying high spending, climate of experimentation, lack of fear of real danger to the nation, devil-may-care mood of soldiery on leave—these may be compatible with, possibly even conducive to, a favorable view of leisure. Costly, desperate wars, last-ditch defensive wars, though, may stamp out its slightest expression.

Leisure for the few, free time for the many: that is what appears to be coming. A not unpleasant prospect spoiled only by the introduction in free time of the adjective "forced."

THE UNITED STATES AND THE WORLD

All over the globe one encounters the modern attitude to free time. A worldwide change in vocabulary has occurred. The word *leisure* is in the air. Governments now have to promise it, or write it into their constitutions. The United States is partly responsible for furthering this development, especially of late, through its serving as the model for many other of the world's countries. The usual invidious statistical comparisons are made, as misleading as ever, to show how the United States is far advanced in the shorter work week, which then is automatically equated with leisure. Now, although even in Europe as in the United States itself this linguistic change is as recent as the twentieth century, it is important. By turning things upside-down, turning idleness with its contrast to work into leisure, it reveals itself as a revolution.

As long as the United States is militarily dominant, other countries and peoples will measure the success of their economy and government by the length of the work week. Their goal will be to compare with the United States, to acquire and use the technology that brings on such riches and leisure. Migration to the United States will continue, the service occupations will be open for foreigners, and many will come for these relatively well paid but lowly esteemed jobs. There may also be opportunity for the managerial and professional classes; they will come to this country for the riches or prestige they hope to command; of leisure or free time they will have little. Migration of these latter groups has recently been brought to official attention and unofficially dubbed "the brain drain."

Policy and planning must be forearmed. The crisis, if it is to come, will occur before these next fifty years are up. It will be the crisis of disbanding a labor force that is no longer needed, of changing men's faith in work to a faith in what we can see today only dimly as a life of non-work. By 2020—the date is just remote enough—a path may be cut toward the leisurely life. The concern thereafter may merely be to keep the path well trodden.

• • • • •

CHAPTER VIII

SOCIAL ORGANIZATION

COMMUNITY AND ECOLOGY

66 The Urban Unease: Community vs. City

JAMES Q. WILSON

The concept of "community" as defined by sociologists involves elements of geographical space, interdependent interaction, a sense of "belonging," and the capacity to serve most, if not all, of an individual's life needs. This selection introduces an additional element as crucial to the concept of community—consensus as to the "standards of right and seemly conduct in the public places in which one lives and moves." The author explores the relevance of this dimension to the maintenance of community and concludes that this aspect of community is not only critical but is becoming increasingly difficult to establish and maintain, especially within our major urban areas.

One of the benefits (if that is the word) of the mounting concern over "the urban crisis" has been the emergence, for perhaps the first time since the subject became popular, of a conception of what this crisis really means, from the point of view of the urban citizen. After a decade or more of being told by various leaders that what's wrong with our large cities is inadequate transportation, or declining retail sales, or poor housing, the resident of the big city, black and white alike, is beginning to assert his own definition of that problem—and this definition has very little relationship to the conventional wisdom on the urban crisis.

This common man's view of "the urban problem," as opposed to the elite view, has several interesting properties. Whereas scholars are interested in poverty, this is a national rather than a specifically urban problem; the common man's concern is with what is unique to cities and especially to large cities. Racial discrimination deeply concerns blacks, but only peripherally concerns whites; the problem that is the subject of this article concerns blacks and whites alike, and intensely so. And unlike tax inequities or air pollution, for which government solutions are in principle available, it is far

SOURCE: *The Public Interest,* no. 12 (Summer 1968), 25–39. • James Q. Wilson is professor of government at Harvard University. He has served as Director of the Joint Center of Urban Studies at Massachusetts Institute of Technology and Harvard. His major interests include city government and politics, public administration and bureaucracy, and theories of organization. He is coauthor of *City Politics, The Metropolitan Enigma, Negro Politics: The Search for Leadership, Urban Renewal: The Record of Controversy,* and *Varieties of Police Behavior.*

from clear just what, if anything, government can do about the problem that actually concerns the ordinary citizen.

This concern has been indicated in a number of public opinion surveys, but, thus far at least, the larger implications of the findings have been ignored. In a poll of over one thousand Boston homeowners that I recently conducted in conjunction with a colleague, we asked what the respondent thought was the biggest problem facing the city. The "conventional" urban problems—housing, transportation, pollution, urban renewal, and the like—were a major concern of only 18 per cent of those questioned, and these were expressed disproportionately by the wealthier, better-educated respondents. Only 9 per cent mentioned jobs and employment, even though many of those interviewed had incomes at or even below what is often regarded as the poverty level. *The issue which concerned more respondents than any other was variously stated—crime, violence, rebellious youth, racial tension, public immorality, delinquency. However stated, the common theme seemed to be a concern for improper behavior in public places.*

For some white respondents this was no doubt a covert way of indicating anti-Negro feelings. But it was not primarily that, for these same forms of impropriety were mentioned more often than other problems by Negro respondents as well. And among the whites, those who indicated, in answer to another question, that they felt the government ought to do *more* to help Negroes were just as likely to mention impropriety as those who felt the government had already done too much.

Nor is this pattern peculiar to Boston. A survey done for *Fortune* magazine in which over three hundred Negro males were questioned in thirteen major cities showed similar results. In this study, people were not asked what was the biggest problem in their city, but rather what was the biggest problem they faced as individuals. When stated this generally, it was not surprising that the jobs and education were given the highest priority. What is striking is that close behind came the same "urban" problems found in Boston—a concern for crime, violence, the need for more police protection, and the like. Indeed, these issues ranked *ahead* of the expressed desire for a higher income. Surveys reported by the President's Commission on Law Enforcement and Administration of Justice showed crime and violence ranking high as major problems among both Negro and white respondents.

THE FAILURE OF COMMUNITY

In reading the responses to the Boston survey, I was struck by how various and general were the ways of expressing public concern in this area. "Crime in the streets" was *not* the stock answer, though that came up often enough. Indeed, many of the forms of impropriety mentioned involved little that was criminal in any serious sense—rowdy teenagers, for example, or various indecencies (lurid advertisements in front of neighborhood movies and racy paperbacks in the local drugstore).

What these concerns have in common, and thus what constitutes the "urban problem" for a large percentage (perhaps a majority) of urban citizens, is *a sense of the failure of community*. By "community" I do not mean, as some do, a metaphysical entity or abstract collectivity with which people "need" to affiliate. There may be an "instinct" for "togetherness" arising out of ancient or tribal longings for identification, but different people gratify it in different ways, and for most the gratification has little to do with neighborhood or urban conditions. When I speak of the concern for "community," I refer to a desire for the observance of standards of right and seemly conduct in the public places in which one lives and moves, those standards to be consistent with—and supportive of—the values and life styles of the particular individual. Around one's home, the places where one shops, and the corridors through which one walks there is for each of us a public space wherein our sense of security, self-esteem, and propriety is either reassured or jeopardized by the people and events we encounter. Viewed this way, the concern for community is less the "need" for "belonging" (or in equally vague language, the "need" to overcome feelings of "alienation" or "anomie") than the concerns of any rationally self-interested person with a normal but not compulsive interest in the environment of himself and his family.

A rationally self-interested person would, I argue, take seriously those things which affect him most directly and importantly and over which he feels he can exercise the greatest influence. Next to one's immediate and particular needs for shelter, income, education, and the like, one's social and physical surroundings have perhaps the greatest consequence for oneself and one's family. Furthermore, unlike those city-wide or national forces which influence a person, what happens to him at the neighborhood level is most easily affected by his own actions. The way he behaves will, ideally, alter the behavior of others; the remarks he makes, and the way he presents himself and his home will shape, at least marginally, the common expectations by which the appropriate standards of public conduct in that area are determined. How he dresses, how loudly or politely he speaks, how well he trims his lawn or paints his house, the liberties he permits his children to enjoy—all these not only express what the individual thinks is appropriate conduct, but in some degree influence what his neighbors take to be appropriate conduct.

These relationships at the neighborhood level are to be contrasted with other ways in which a person might perform the duties of an urban citizen. Voting, as a Harvard University colleague delights in pointing out, is strictly speaking an irrational act for anyone who does not derive any personal benefit from it. Lacking any inducement of money or esteem, and ignoring for a moment the sense of duty, there is for most voters no rational reason for casting a ballot. The only way such an act would be reasonable to such a voter is if he can affect (or has a good chance to affect) the outcome of the election—that is, to make or break a tie. Such a possibility is so remote as to be almost nonexistent. Of course, most of us do vote, but primarily out of a sense of duty, or because it is fun or makes us feel good. As a way of influencing those forces which in turn influence us, however, voting is of practically no value.

Similarly with the membership one might have in a civic or voluntary association; unless one happens to command important resources of wealth, power, or status, joining such an organization (provided it is reasonably large) is not likely to affect the ability of that organization to achieve its objectives. And if the organization *does* achieve its objectives (if, for example, it succeeds in getting taxes lowered or an open occupancy law passed or a nuisance abated), nonmembers will benefit equally with members. This problem has been carefully analyzed by Mancur Olson in *The Logic of Collective Action* in a way that calls into serious question the ability of any organization to enlist a mass following when it acts for the common good and gives to its members no individual rewards. Some people will join, but because they will get some personal benefit (the status or influence that goes with being an officer, for example), or out of a sense of duty or, again, because it is "fun." As a way of shaping the urban citizen's environment, however, joining a large civic association is not much more rational than voting.

CONTROLLING THE IMMEDIATE ENVIRONMENT

It is primarily at the neighborhood level that meaningful (i.e., potentially rewarding) opportunities for the exercise of urban citizenship exist. And it is the breakdown of neighborhood controls (neighborhood self-government, if you will) that accounts for the principal concerns of urban citizens. When they can neither take for granted nor influence by their actions and those of their neighbors the standards of conduct within their own neighborhood community, they experience what to them are "urban problems" —problems that arise directly out of the unmanageable consequences of living in close proximity.

I suspect that it is this concern for the maintenance of the neighborhood community that explains in part the overwhelming preference Americans have for small cities and towns. According to a Gallup Poll taken in 1963, only 22 per cent of those interviewed wanted to live in cities, 49 per cent preferred small towns, and 28 per cent preferred suburbs. (Only among Negroes, interestingly enough, did a majority prefer large cities —perhaps because the costs of rural or small town life, in terms of poverty and discrimination, are greater for the Negro than the costs, in terms of disorder and insecurity, of big-city life.) Small towns and suburbs, because they are socially more homogeneous than large cities and because local self-government can be used to reinforce informal neighborhood sanctions, apparently make the creation and maintenance of a proper sense of community easier. At any rate, Americans are acting on this preference for small places, whatever its basis. As Daniel Elazar has pointed out, the smaller cities are those which are claiming a growing share of the population; the largest cities are not increasing in size at all and some, indeed, are getting smaller.

A rational concern for community implies a tendency to behave in certain ways which some popular writers have mistakenly thought to be the result of conformity, prejudice, or an excessive concern for appearances. No doubt all of these factors play some role in the behavior of many people and a dominant role in the behavior of a few, but one need not make any such assumptions to explain the nature of most neighborhood conduct. In dealing with one's immediate environment under circumstances that make individual actions efficacious in constraining the actions of others, one will develop a range of sanctions to employ against others and one will, in turn, respond to the sanctions that others use. Such sanctions are typically informal, even casual, and may consist of little more than a gesture, word, or expression. Occasionally direct action is taken—a complaint, or even making a scene, but resort to these measures is rare because they invite counterattacks ("If that's the way he feels about it, I'll just show him!") and because if used frequently they lose their effectiveness. The purpose of the sanctions is to regulate the external consequences of private behavior—to handle, in the language of economists, "third-party effects," "externalities," and "the production of collective goods." I may wish to let my lawn go to pot, but one ugly lawn affects the appearance of the whole neighborhood, just as one sooty incinerator smudges clothes that others have hung out to dry. Rowdy children raise the noise level and tramp down the flowers for everyone, not just for their parents.

Because the sanctions employed are subtle, informal, and delicate, not everyone is equally vulnerable to everyone else's discipline. Furthermore, if there is not a generally shared agreement as to appropriate standards of conduct, these sanctions will be inadequate to correct such deviations as occur. A slight departure from a norm is set right by a casual remark; a commitment to a different norm is very hard to alter, unless of course the deviant party is "eager to fit in," in which case he is not committed to the different norm at all but simply looking for signs as to what the preferred norms may be. Because of these considerations, the members of a community have a general preference for social homogeneity and a suspicion of heterogeneity—a person different in one respect (e.g., income, or race, or speech) may be different in other respects as well (e.g., how much noise or trash he is likely to produce).

PREJUDICE AND DIVERSITY

This reasoning sometimes leads to error—people observed to be outwardly different may not in fact behave differently, or such differences in behavior as exist may be irrelevant to the interests of the community. Viewed one way, these errors are exceptions to rule-of-thumb guides or empirical generalizations; viewed another way, they are manifestations of prejudice. And in fact one of the unhappiest complexities of the logic of neighborhood is that it can so often lead one wrongly to impute to another person some behavioral problem on the basis of the latter's membership in a racial or economic group. Even worse, under cover of acting in the interests of the neighborhood, some people may give vent to the most unjustified and neurotic prejudices.

However much we may regret such expressions of prejudice, it does little good to imagine that the occasion for their expression can be wished away. We may even pass laws (as I think we should) making it illegal to use certain outward characteristics (like race) as grounds for excluding people from a neighborhood. But the core problem will remain—owing to the importance of community to most people, and given the process whereby new arrivals are inducted into and constrained by the sanctions of the neighborhood, the suspicion of heterogeneity will remain and will only be overcome when a person proves by his actions that his distinctive characteristic is not a sign of any disposition to violate the community's norms.

Such a view seems to be at odds with the notion that the big city is the center of cosmopolitanism—by which is meant, among other things, diversity. And so it is. A small fraction of the population (in my judgment, a *very* small fraction) may want diversity so much that it will seek out the most cosmopolitan sections of the cities as places to live. Some of these people are intellectuals, others are young, unmarried persons with a taste for excitement before assuming the responsibilities of a family, and still others are "misfits" who have dropped out of society for a variety of reasons. Since one element of this group—the intellectuals—writes the books which define the "urban problem," we are likely to be confused by their preferences and assume that the problem is in part to maintain the heterogeneity and cosmopolitanism of the central city—to attract and hold a neat balance among middle-class families, young culture-lovers, lower-income Negroes, "colorful" Italians, and big businessmen. *To assume this is to mistake the preferences of the few for the needs of the many.* And even the few probably exaggerate just how much diversity they wish. Manhattan intellectuals are often as worried about crime in the streets as their cousins in Queens. The desired diversity is "safe" diversity—a harmless variety of specialty stores, esoteric bookshops, "ethnic" restaurants, and highbrow cultural enterprises.

ON "MIDDLE-CLASS VALUES"

At this point I had better take up explicitly the dark thoughts forming in the minds of some readers that this analysis is little more than an elaborate justification for prejudice, philistinism, conformity, and (worst of all) "middle-class values." The number of satirical books on suburbs seem to suggest that the creation of a sense of community is at best little more than enforcing the lowest common denominator of social behavior by means of *kaffee klatsches* and the exchange of garden tools; at worst, it is the end of privacy and individuality and the beginning of discrimination in its uglier forms.

I have tried to deal with the prejudice argument above, though no doubt inadequately. Prejudice exists; so does the desire for community; both often overlap. There is no "solution" to the problem, though stigmatizing certain kinds of prejudgments (such as those based on race) is helpful. Since (in my opinion) social class is the primary basis (with age and religion not far behind) on which community-maintaining judgments are made, and since social class (again, in my opinion) is a much better predictor of behavior than race, I foresee the time when racial distinctions will be much less salient (though never absent) in handling community problems. Indeed, much of what passes for "race prejudice" today may be little more than class prejudice with race used as a rough indicator of approximate social class.

With respect to the charge of defending "middle-class values," let me stress that the analysis of "neighborhood" offered here makes no assumptions about the substantive values enforced by the communal process. On the contrary, the emphasis is on the process itself; in principle, it could be used to enforce any set of values. To be sure, we most often observe it enforcing the injunctions against noisy children and lawns infested with crabgrass, but I suppose it could also be used to enforce injunctions against turning children into "sissies" and being enslaved by lawn-maintenance chores. In fact, if we turn our attention to the city and end our preoccupation with suburbia, we will find many kinds of neighborhoods with a great variety of substantive values being enforced. Jane Jacobs described how and to what ends informal community controls operate in working-class Italian sections of New York and elsewhere. Middle-class Negro neighborhoods tend also to develop a distinctive code. And Bohemian or "hippie" sections (despite their loud disclaimers of any interest in either restraint or constraint) establish and sustain a characteristic ethos.

PEOPLE WITHOUT COMMUNITIES

Viewed historically, the process whereby neighborhoods, in the sense intended in this article, have been formed in the large cities might be thought of as one in which order arose out of chaos to return in time to a new form of disorder.

Immigrants, thrust together in squalid central-city ghettos, gradually worked their way out to establish, first with the aid of streetcar lines and then with the aid of automobiles, more or less homogeneous and ethnically distinct neighborhoods of single-family and two-family houses. In the Boston survey, the *average* respondent had lived in his present neighborhood for *about twenty years.* When asked what his neighborhood had been like when he was growing up, the vast majority of those questioned said that it was "composed of people pretty much like myself"—similar, that is, in income, ethnicity, religion, and so forth. In time, of course, families—especially those of childrearing age—began spilling out over the city limits into the suburbs, and were replaced in the central city by persons lower in income than themselves.

Increasingly, the central city is coming to be made up of persons who face special disabilities in creating and maintaining a sense of community. There are several such groups, each with a particular problem and each with varying degrees of ability to cope with that problem. One is composed of affluent whites without children (young couples, single persons, elderly couples whose children have left home) who either (as with the "young swingers") lack an interest in community or (as with the elderly couples) lack the ability to participate meaningfully in the maintenance of community. But for such persons, there are alternatives to community—principally, the occupancy of a special physical environment that in effect insulates the occupant from such threats as it is the function of community to control. They move into high-rise buildings in which their apartment is connected by an elevator to either a basement garage (where they can step directly into their car) or to a lobby guarded by a doorman and perhaps even a private police force. Thick walls and high fences protect such open spaces as exist from the intrusion of outsiders. The apartments may even be air conditioned, so that the windows need never be opened to admit street noises. Interestingly, a common complaint of such apartment-dwellers is that, in the newer buildings at least, the walls are too thin to ensure privacy—in short, the one failure of the physical substitute for community occasions the major community-oriented complaint.

A second group of noncommunal city residents are the poor whites, often elderly, who financially or for other reasons are unable to leave the old central city neighborhood when it changes character. For many, that change is the result of the entry of Negroes or Puerto Ricans into the block, and this gives rise to the number of anti-Negro or anti-Puerto Rican remarks which an interviewer encounters. But sometimes the neighborhood is taken over by young college students, or by artists, or by derelicts; then the remarks are anti-youth, anti-student, anti-artists, or anti-drunk. The fact that the change has instituted a new (and to the older resident) less seemly standard of conduct is more important than the attributes of the persons responsible for the change. Elderly persons, because they lack physical vigor and the access to neighbors which having children facilitates, are especially vulnerable to neighborhood changes and find it especially difficult to develop substitutes for community—except, of course, to withdraw behind locked doors and drawn curtains. They cannot afford the high-rise buildings and private security guards that for the wealthier city-dweller are the functional equivalent of communal sanctions.

In the Boston survey, the fear of impropriety and violence was highest for those respondents who were the oldest and the poorest. Preoccupation with such issues as the major urban problem was greater among women than among men, among those over sixty-five years of age than among those under, among Catholics more than among Jews, and among those earning less than $5,000 a year more than among those earning higher incomes. (Incidentally, these were *not* the same persons most explicitly concerned about and hostile to Negroes—anti-Negro sentiment was more common among middle-aged married couples who had children and modestly good incomes.)

The third group of persons afflicted by the perceived breakdown of community are the Negroes. For them, residential segregation as well as other factors have led to a condition in which there is relatively little spatial differentiation among Negroes of various class levels. Lower-class, working-class, and middle-class Negroes are squeezed into close proximity, one on top of the other, in such a way as to inhibit or prevent the territorial separation necessary for the creation and maintenance of different communal life styles. Segregation in the housing market may be (I suspect it is) much more intense with respect to lower-cost housing than with middle-cost housing, suggesting that middle-class Negroes may find it easier to move into previously all-white neighborhoods. But the constricted supply of low-cost housing means that a successful invasion of a new area by middle-class Negroes often leads to that break being followed rather quickly by working- and lower-class Negroes. As a result, unless middle-class Negroes can leapfrog out to distant white (or new) communities, they will find themselves struggling to assert hegemony over a territory threatened on several sides by Negroes with quite different life styles.

This weakness of community in black areas may be the most serious price we will pay for residential segregation. It is often said that the greatest price is the perpetuation of a divided society, one black and the other white. While there is some merit in this view, it overlooks the fact that most ethnic groups, when reasonably free to choose a place to live, have chosen to live among people similar to themselves. (I am thinking especially of the predominantly Jewish suburbs.) *The real price of segregation, in my opinion, is not that it forces blacks and whites apart but that it forces blacks of different class positions together.*

WHAT CITY GOVERNMENT CANNOT DO

Communal social controls tend to break down either when persons with an interest in, and the competence for, maintaining a community no longer live in the area or when they remain but their neighborhood is not sufficiently distinct, territorially, from areas with different or threatening life styles. In the latter case especially, the collapse of informal social controls leads to demands for the imposition of formal or institutional controls—demands for "more police protection," for more or better public services, and the like. The difficulty, however, is that there is relatively little government can do directly to maintain a neighborhood community. It can, of course, assign more police officers to it, but there are real limits to the value of this response. For one thing, a city only has so many officers and those assigned to one neighborhood must often be taken away from another. And perhaps more important, the police can rarely manage all relevant aspects of conduct in public places whatever may be their success in handling serious crime (such as muggings or the like). Juvenile rowdiness, quarrels among neighbors, landlord-tenant disputes, the unpleasant side effects of a well-patronized tavern—all these are matters which may be annoying enough to warrant police intervention but not to warrant arrests. Managing these kinds of public disorder is a common task for the police, but one that they can rarely manage to everyone's satisfaction—precisely because the disorder arises out of a dispute among residents over what *ought* be the standard of proper conduct.

In any case, city governments have, over the last few decades, become increasingly remote from neighborhood concerns. Partly this has been the consequence of the growing centralization of local government—mayors are getting stronger at the expense of city councils, city-wide organizations (such as newspapers and civic associations) are getting stronger at the expense of neighborhood-based political parties, and new "super-agencies" are being created in city hall to handle such matters as urban renewal, public welfare, and anti-poverty programs. Mayors and citizens alike in many cities have begun to react against this trend and to search for ways of reinvolving government in neighborhood concerns: mayors are setting up "little city halls," going on walking tours of their cities, and meeting with neighborhood and block clubs. But there is a limit to how effective such responses can be, because whatever the institutional structure, the issues that most concern a neighborhood are typically those about which politicians can do relatively little.

For one thing, the issues involve disputes among the residents of a neighborhood, or between the residents of two adjoining neighborhoods, and the mayor takes sides in these matters only at his peril. For another, many of the issues involve no tangible stake—they concern more the *quality* of life and competing standards of propriety and less the dollars-and-cents value of particular services or programs. Officials with experience in organizing little city halls or police-community relations programs often report that a substantial portion (perhaps a majority) of the complaints they receive concern people who "don't keep up their houses," or who "let their children run wild," or who "have noisy parties." Sometimes the city can do something (by, for example, sending around the building inspectors to look over a house that appears to be a firetrap or by having the health department require someone to clean up a lot he has littered), but just as often the city can do little except offer its sympathy.

POVERTY AND COMMUNITY

Indirectly, and especially over the long run, government can do much more. First and foremost, it can help persons enter into those social classes wherein the creation and maintenance of community is easiest. Lower-class persons are (by definition, I would argue) those who attach little importance to the opinions of others, are preoccupied with the daily struggle for survival and the immediate gratifications that may be attendant on survival, and inclined to uninhibited, expressive conduct. (A lower-*income* person, of course, is not necessarily lower *class;* the former condition reflects how much money he has, while the latter indicates the attitudes he possesses.) Programs designed to increase prosperity and end poverty (defined as having too little money) will enable lower-income persons who do care about the opinions of others to leave areas populated by lower-income persons who don't care (that is, areas populated by lower-class persons).

Whether efforts to eliminate poverty by raising incomes will substantially reduce the size of the lower class is a difficult question. The progress we make will be much slower than is implied by those who are currently demanding an "immediate" and "massive" "commitment" to "end poverty." I favor many of these programs, but I am skeptical that we really know as much about how to end our social problems as those persons who blame our failure simply on a lack of "will" seem to think. I suspect that know-how is in as short supply as will power. But what is clear to me is that *programs that seek to eliminate poverty in the cities will surely fail,* for every improvement in the income and employment situation in the large cities will induce an increased migration of more poor people from rural and small-town areas to those cities. The gains are likely to be wiped out as fast as they are registered. To end urban poverty it is necessary to end rural poverty; thus, programs aimed specifically at the big cities will not succeed, while programs aimed at the nation as a whole may.

The need to consider poverty as a national rather than an urban problem, which has been stated most persuasively by John Kain and others, is directly relevant to the problem of community. *Programs that try to end poverty in the cities, to the extent they succeed, will probably worsen, in the short run, the problems of maintaining a sense of community in those cities—and these communal problems are, for most persons, the fundamental urban problems.* People migrate to the cities now because cities are, on the whole, more prosperous than other places. Increasing the advantage the city now enjoys, without simultaneously improving matters elsewhere, will increase the magnitude of that advantage, increase the flow of poor migrants, and thus make more difficult the creation and maintenance of communal order, especially in those working-class areas most vulnerable to an influx of lower-income newcomers. This will be true whether the migrants are white or black, though it will be especially serious for blacks because of the compression effects of segregation in the housing market.

THE DIFFERENCES AMONG PEOPLE

It is, of course, rather misleading to speak in global terms of "classes" as if all middle-class (or all working-class) persons were alike. Nothing could be further from the truth; indeed, the failure to recognize intraclass differences in life style has been a major defect of those social commentaries on "middle-class values" and "conformity." The book by Herbert J. Gans on Levittown is a refreshing exception to this pattern, in that it calls attention to fundamental cleavages in life style in what to the outside observer appears to be an entirely homogeneous, "middle-class" suburb. Partly the confusion arises out of mistaking economic position with life style—some persons may be economically working-class but expressively middle-class, or vice versa.

To what extent can persons with low incomes display and act upon middle-class values? To what extent is there a substitute for affluence as a resource permitting the creation and maintenance of a strong neighborhood community? Apparently some Italian neighborhoods with relatively low incomes nonetheless develop strong communal controls. The North End of Boston comes to mind. Though economically disadvantaged, and though the conventional signs of "middle-class values" (neat lawns, quiet streets, single-family homes) are almost wholly absent, the regulation of conduct in public places is nonetheless quite strong. The incidence of street crime is low, "outsiders" are carefully watched, and an agreed-on standard of conduct seems to prevail.

Perhaps a strong and stable family

structure (as among Italians) permits even persons of limited incomes to maintain a sense of community. If so, taking seriously the reported weakness in the Negro family structure becomes important, not simply because of its connection with employment and other individual problems, but because of its implications for communal order. Indeed, substantial gains in income in areas with weak family and communal systems may produce little or no comparable gain in public order (and I mean here order as judged by the residents of the affected area, not order as judged by some outside observer). What most individuals may want in their public places they may not be able to obtain owing to an inability to take collective action or to make effective their informal sanctions.

"BLACK POWER" AND COMMUNITY

It is possible that "Black Power" will contribute to the ability of some neighborhoods to achieve communal order. I say "possible"—it is far from certain, because I am far from certain as to what Black Power implies or as to how dominant an ethos it will become. As I understand it, Black Power is not a set of substantive objectives, much less a clearly worked-out ideology, but rather an attitude, a posture, a communal code that attaches high value to pride, self-respect, and the desire for autonomy. Though it has programmatic implications ("neighborhood self-control," "elect black mayors," and so forth), the attitude is (to me) more significant than the program. Or stated another way, the cultural implications of Black Power may in the long run prove to be more important than its political implications.

In the short run, of course, Black Power—like any movement among persons who are becoming politically self-conscious, whether here or in "developing" nations—will produce its full measure of confusion, disorder, and demagoguery. Indeed, it sometimes appears to be little more than a license to shout slogans, insult "whitey," and make ever more extravagant bids for power and leadership in black organizations. But these may be only the short-term consequences, and I for one am inclined to discount them somewhat. The long-term implications seem to be a growing pride in self and in the community, and these are prerequisites for the creation and maintenance of communal order.

Historians may someday conclude that while Negroes were given emancipation in the nineteenth century, they had to win it in the twentieth. The most important legacy of slavery and segregation was less, perhaps, the inferior economic position that Negroes enjoyed than the inferior cultural position that was inflicted on them. To the extent it is possible for a group to assert communal values even though economically disadvantaged, Negroes were denied that opportunity because the prerequisite of self-improvement—self-respect—was not generally available to them. The present assertion of self-respect is an event of the greatest significance and, in my view, contributes more to explaining the civil disorders and riots of our larger cities than all the theories of "relative deprivation," "economic disadvantage," and the like. The riots, from this perspective, are expressive acts of self-assertion, not instrumental acts designed to achieve particular objectives. And programs of economic improvement and laws to guarantee civil rights, while desirable in themselves, are not likely to end the disorder.

The fact that these forms of self-expression cause such damage to the black areas of a city may in itself contribute to the development of communal order; the people who are paying the price are the Negroes themselves. The destruction they have suffered may lead to an increased sense of stake in the community and a more intense concern about the maintenance of community self-control. Of course, no amount of either self-respect or commitment to community can overcome a serious lack of resources—money, jobs, and business establishments.

NO INSIDE WITHOUT AN OUTSIDE

Because the disorders are partly the result of growing pride and assertiveness does not mean, as some have suggested, that we "let them riot" because it is "therapeutic." For one thing, whites who control the police and military forces have no right to ignore the interests of the nonrioting black majority in favor of the instincts of the rioting black minority. Most Negroes want *more* protection and security, not less, regardless of what certain white radicals might say. Furthermore, the cultural value of Black Power or race pride *depends in part on it being resisted by whites.* The existence of a "white enemy" may be as necessary for the growth of Negro self-respect as the presumed existence of the "capitalist encirclement" was for the growth of socialism in the Soviet Union. As James Stephens once said, there cannot be an inside without an outside.

Nor does Black Power require that control over all political and economic institutions be turned over forthwith to any black organization that happens to demand it. Neighborhoods, black or white, should have control over some functions and not over others, the decision in each case requiring a rather careful analysis of the likely outcomes of alternative distributions of authority. Cultures may be invigorated and even changed by slogans and expressive acts, but constitutions ought to be the result of deliberation and careful choices. The reassertion of neighborhood values, by blacks and whites alike, strikes me as a wholly desirable reaction against the drift to overly bureaucratized central city governments, but there are no simple formulas or rhetorical "principles" on the basis of which some general and all-embracing reallocation of power can take place. Those who find this reservation too timid should bear in mind that functions given to black neighborhoods will also have to be given to white neighborhoods—it is not politically feasible (or perhaps even legally possible) to decentralize power over black communities but centralize it over white ones. Are those radicals eager to have Negro neighborhoods control their own police force equally eager to have adjoining working-class Polish or Italian neighborhoods control theirs?

In any case, no one should be optimistic that progress in creating meaningful communities within central cities will be rapid or easy. The fundamental urban problems, though partly economic and political, are at root questions of values, and these change or assert themselves only slowly, if at all. And whatever gains might accrue from the social functions of Black Power might easily be outweighed by a strong white reaction against it and thus against blacks. The competing demands for territory within our cities is intense and not easily managed, and for some time to come the situation will remain desperately precarious.

67 The Talk in Vandalia

JOSEPH P. LYFORD

The preceding selection attempted to explore salient dimensions of the concept of "community" in an urban setting. This selection examines the elements of this concept in a relatively simple setting—a small city in south central Illinois. For many readers this description of Vandalia may seem like a visit to the nineteenth century—to a world that no longer exists. Such persons should be reminded that millions of people still live in the "Vandalias" of this country, and the description provided here is rather typical of the kind and quality of interaction found in smaller communities today. A careful reading of Lyford's description of this one town should provide a lively "feeling" for the meaning of community.

I

Judged by the map, the city of Vandalia (population 5,500) has a fine location. It lies across a junction of the Pennsylvania and the Illinois Central Railroads, appears to be the center of a criss-cross of highways, and is on the edge of the Kaskaskia River, which winds its way diagonally downstate to the Mississippi. But the map reader will be deceived. The Kaskaskia, swollen and icy in winter, subsides by summertime into a winding trail of mud and snags; the new super-highways—Routes 40 and 70—pass by to the north, and the only concession by the Pennsylvania's "Spirit of St. Louis" is a raucous bellow as it hurtles through a cut in the center of town an hour before noon. The Illinois Central is more considerate. Occasionally a freight engine shunts back and forth a few blocks outside of town to pick up some crates from one of the small factories along the tracks. "No trains stop here," the stationmaster says. The indifference of the railroads to Vandalia is paid back in full by the town's oldest practicing Democrat, eighty-eight-year-old Judge James G. Burnside. "We don't pay any attention to the railroads any more," he remarks. "They're just passing acquaintances."

A train traveler from the East can alight at Effingham, thirty miles away, trudge through the snow to the Greyhound Post House, and take the 1:30 p.m. bus, which is always overdue. The driver does not smile when along with a St. Louis ticket he gets a request for a stopover in Vandalia, which means that the express bus has to make a ten-minute detour off the main highway. Route 40 runs straight and flat as a tight ribbon through wide umber plains sheeted with winter rain, past farmhouses four or five to the mile. For a few hundred feet at a time the road will stagger and pitch slightly as the land wrinkles into prairie, creek, and brushwood; then it subsides again to a level as monotonous as the roar of the bus. The see-sawing pump of

SOURCE: Joseph P. Lyford, *The Talk in Vandalia,* A Report to the Center for the Study of Democratic Institutions (Santa Barbara, Calif: The Center for the Study of Democratic Institutions, 1962). Reprinted by permission of the publisher. • The author is a free-lance writer and has served as assistant editor of *The New Republic.* He was also staff director for the Public Education Association of New York City and is now a staff member of the Fund for the Republic. He is the author of *Candidate, The Agreeable Autocracies,* and is a contributing author to *Saturday Review, The New Republic,* and *America.*

an occasional oil well is the only motion in the fields on a rainy day. There are a few crossroads villages, then the town of St. Elmo, and, finally, a few miles along Alternate Route 40, the city of Vandalia, once the western terminus of the Cumberland Road, capital of Illinois from 1819 to 1839, seat of Fayette County, and country of Abraham Lincoln of the House of Representatives of the State of Illinois.

The Evans is the taller, hotter, and more impressive of the town's two hotels. A fourth-story room offers a view of the magnificent old state house on the common, a tall-windowed white building, now a museum, where Stephen A. Douglas and Lincoln met with their fellow-legislators more than a century ago. The first-floor windows are not too far from the ground to have prevented a long-legged politician from swinging his leg over the sill when he wanted to make a quick exit. The town's second most noticeable monument is a huge, sand-colored statue of a pioneer woman who gazes down Gallatin Street's rows of two-story buildings, parking meters, vertical signs over a Rexall Drug Store and the Evans Hotel, past a pair of banks standing face to face at the main intersection, and, finally, across the tracks to the Eakin Hotel, the County Courthouse on the hill, and one of Vandalia's many churches.

Robert O. Hasler points out that the town has thirteen churches and ten lawyers. It is his business to know odd statistics because he is president of the Chamber of Commerce. He is handy to the main source of such information because his office is in the Town Hall just above the city clerk. Some time ago Hasler prepared a typewritten economic profile which begins, "Vandalia, centrally located in the heart of the Midwest, is seventy miles from St. Louis, ninety-five miles west of Terre Haute, 245 miles southwest of Chicago . . . total labor force of county, 7,778, unemployed 276, self-employed 738, oil production 536. . . ." Under the heading of "Resources of Transportation" appears the information that on the Pennsylvania and IC railroads goods are "in transition" from Chicago, St. Louis, and Indianapolis—a politic way of saying that Vandalia is a way station. The figures on the sheets are from 1959, but Hasler says this is not a serious matter. "Things around here don't change very much from one year to another."

The township of Vandalia is grouped in three economic units. On its outer ring are the farms, the town's main support, ranging from sixty or eighty acres to several hundred, the average being somewhere in the middle. The chief crops are corn, soybeans, and livestock—mainly hogs and cattle. The land is worked with modern machinery by farmers who combine their own land with leased acreage —as much as they can get.

On the western edge of town are four factories, which employ altogether about 850 people. They are the Princess Peggy dress factory; United Wood Heel, manufacturers of heels for women's shoes; the Johnson, Stephens and Shinkle shoe factory (the largest single employer with a work force of 475), and the Crane Packing Company, which turns out mechanical seals for automobiles, machines, appliances, etc.

At the core is the town itself—the stores, the banks, professional offices, churches, schools, filling stations, garages, plus the Elk, Mason, Moose, Odd-Fellow and Legion Halls, the Town Hall and County Courthouse, one movie theatre, restaurants, and nine of the only taverns in a county noted for its religion and its aridity. Vandalia's supermarkets are big and modern; its dry-goods stores range from the antique-looking Fidelity Clothiers to the Hub Department Store which has quality merchandise at New York prices. Only one commercial establishment—Radliff's Pool Parlor—remains open for business seven days a week. The local newspaper plant is built of yellow brick and houses the editorial staff of two weekly papers, the *Union* and the *Leader*. Most of the business district lies south of the Pennsylvania tracks except some hardware and feed stores, the Farm Bureau offices, and a cleaning establishment. On the north side of town the streets are lined with small frame houses, and a few large and attractive Victorian homes. Some blocks further out are the new County Hospital, the million-dollar Vandalia High School which is the community's pride, and a new development of luxurious, ranch-type homes. Beyond the high school is the intersection of Route 51 out of town and Route 40, which has given rise to a cluster of motels, restaurants, and filling stations. To the west lie the factories and on the far side of Shoe Factory Hill, along the Pennsylvania Railroad, are patches of dilapidated wooden dwellings which make up the hopeless part of town. To the east is the Kaskaskia River. The southern part of town peters out rather quickly a few blocks below the Post Office and the white frame house which is the home of Charlie Evans.

When he is not in the front parlor of his home, which he uses as his office, Mr. Evans is in the lobby of the Evans Hotel. He built the hotel in 1924, and, along with a hardware business and various real estate dealings, it made him probably the richest man in Vandalia. Last year, his eighty-first, the $106,000 library he gave to the town opened its doors. "We were a money-saving family, all of us," he says. "We're Welsh by descent. I was never a man to sell, I always bought and added to it. When I sold the hotel I'd been saving all the time. I guess I'd saved too much. I didn't have any use for the money, so I built the library. When I built it, I didn't try to cut corners. I didn't try to save as if I was building for myself."

Mr. Evans leans back, and crosses his arms when he talks about his town. "This is a historic city. When they moved the capital from here to Springfield in 1839, our population was only 400. We've gained a little bit all the time. Population-wise we've never had a setback. We've never had a boom. We held our ground. A big percentage of people own their own homes, including a lot who work at the factory. This makes us a good town for a factory. The companies know our workers are not fly-by-nighters. Their employees are here to stay. They have money invested in our town. Homes today build from $12,000 to $18,000, and we have a good building and loan program. Banks will lend money to anybody here who wants to build a building. We have good, sound, sincere bankers. Back in the late 20's, when people were trying to buy more and more land for their farms, the bankers warned them against it. When the crash came, we weren't so badly off as some. We had hard times in 1932, oh mercy.

"I think the town is going to develop pretty well. Rental housing is pretty scarce. The homes here are good ones, and people have made substantial payments on them. I don't know what we're going to have to do to keep our young people here, though. When they go to the city, they don't come back. They want new people to get acquainted with. Industry might be the answer. We should have more opportunities for skilled workers. The Crane Packing Company has been very good. They have a training program for employees and they are expanding. The shoe factory is a shoe factory. Their idea is how much work you can get out of your help. It's as good a shoe factory as there is. It's a good town, but we have one bad problem. It's the farmers. The farmers are in trouble."

Evans is not the only person who worries about the Fayette County farmers. The townspeople think and talk a great deal about them these days. They have always depended on them in the past, and they are no longer sure of them. The uncertainty may explain why the business of farming, traditionally honored in the State of Illinois as an independent way of life, is undergoing rapid sanctification. Probably more speeches are delivered at Kiwanis and Rotary clubs on the virtues and contributions of the tillers of the soil than on any other single subject; it is also the favorite topic of the county's political circuit-riders during campaign season. The community's businessmen prepare banquets in honor of local agriculture; the Junior Chamber of Commerce's first big dinner of 1962 was held to proclaim Siebert Hoover the "Outstanding Young Farmer of the Year" and present him with tickets to a Miami or New York vacation. Agricultural experts from the University of Illinois and the Department of Agriculture, armed with pamphlets on fowl disease and hog pest, criss-cross the territory with advice on all phases of scientific farming. Secretary of Agriculture Freeman's emissaries from Washington are available to discuss the farm program at the smallest gatherings. The Farm Bureau offices have special classrooms where experts lecture local farmers and their wives on the economics of farm management. And, in contrast to the days of the Great Depression in other parts of the nation, the banker and the farmer maintain friendly, interdependent relations throughout Southern Illinois. The two bank presidents in Vandalia talk about farmers as if they were business partners and mutual allies under attack by the rest of the nation's economic interests.

The popularity of the farmer in the abstract has not always thawed out farmers in particular, some of whom still harbor ancient resentments against the town. (One farmer says he wants his children to stay in the rural schools because Vandalians think that "farm kids still piss on stumps and never heard of inside plumbing.") But many of the farmers seem to feel closer to the town than before the war, partly because of the knowledge that a lot of other people besides farmers are involved in their economic troubles, and partly because the farmers' own social life has become more and more interlaced with the life of the town. As the one-room rural schoolhouses have dwindled, over the farmers' opposition, from three dozen in the school district to a half dozen, farm mothers have become members of the PTA's of the Washington, Lincoln, and Central elementary schools. There is more talk in the homes of educational problems jointly shared with the townspeople.

Those farmers who work in the factories—"Saturday farmers," J. B. Turner, the county farm agent, calls them—have a growing association with non-farmers, and some even join labor union locals in the shoe and heel factories. Also, the growing cost of running a farm because of the new machinery required and the rising prices of land have increased the extent of the farmer's dependence on local financial institutions. The farmers buy more and more of their food locally—most of them have disposed of their dairy cows and buy their milk at the Tri-City Supermarket and the A&P. The farmer's machinery is repaired by local mechanics. Feed-dealer Norman Michel, who carries as many as 21,000 people on his credit rolls, is a farmer's banker in his own way. Vandalia shapes its commercial activities to suit the farmers' tastes, and the farmer, his wife and children, and his trucks are a regular part of the scenery on Gallatin Street. This is not to say that the town has been taken over by the farmers: in one sense it is the farmers who have changed their habits and tastes—even in dress—to fit the town.

The farmer has responded in other ways to the town. He participates more in local events. He comes more to the city's churches. One outstanding farmer is chairman of the school district's Board of Education. Many of the more prosperous farm families contribute their women's time to fund drives. The high school's football and basketball teams are getting a little more help from the farm youngsters who used to shy away from extracurricular activities after the last school bell. One still hears complaints from the townspeople that the farmer is hard to reach, but he is less and less remote.

• • • • •

II

It would be misleading to say that Vandalia takes everything in its stride, because "stride" implies a measured forward movement which has never been a community characteristic. It is also inaccurate to take the community's easygoing manner at face value. Its calm demeanor is sometimes achieved at the cost of suppressing grave internal discontents. Nevertheless, the atmosphere is rarely charged with the type of emotional storms that test the tempers of New York or Chicago suburbanites. The political fracases that periodically rock a Westport, Connecticut, to its foundations, setting commuter against ancient inhabitant, are unknown. Public controversies usually do not get past the stage of fairly low-pressure arguments over personalities or such transient irritations as disintegrating sidewalks and sheriffs. Candidates do not run for municipal office, they file for it, on ballots that do not mention party affiliations. The only lively competition recently was for the job of county sheriff, but the plenitude of aspirants was attributed to a rise in the unemployment rate, adding considerable glamour to the sheriff's $5,000 yearly stipend. The community blood pressure is unaffected by animosities between Republican and Democrat. County administrations alternate between the two with regularity, and the towns do not even have local political organizations.

The campaign for mayor is not usually one of Vandalia's most exciting events. Last year's canvass was enlivened somewhat when one candidate promised that, if elected, he would fire the police chief. The reformer was elected, but the police chief is still police chief, and there have been no outraged cries from the electorate about broken campaign promises. It is understood that it is pretty hard for a mayor of Vandalia to fire anybody. It is also generally known that Norman Michel didn't really have his heart set on being mayor, anyway. Although he refrains, out of civic pride, from saying so publicly, there is reason to believe that he considers the mayor's job a trivial and unremunerative demand on time that could have been better spent handling the complicated affairs of a successful feed and grain business. In return for enduring the burdens of the town's highest administrative office, Michel receives $1,200 yearly, considerably less than the earnings of each member of the two-man squad that issues from the Town Hall each day to empty nickels from the parking meters. The mayor's perquisites include neither a black limousine nor office space in the Town Hall.

A discussion with Michel in the back office of his feed store is not highly productive of information relating to any riddles and emergencies that may afflict the community. A heavy-set, agreeable man, he frankly states that the main function of the mayor seems to be to sign checks. In addition to this activity, Mr. Michel "works with the Chamber of Commerce and other civic organizations when they want my help." Recently he played an important part in the town's successful effort to induce the Ralston Purina Company, feed manufacturers, to set up a new plant in Vandalia to replace one that had burned down in East St. Louis. The mayor also feels that he ought to "check complaints that come in," but this is a full-time job, certainly not one to be discharged by someone whose feed business has a gross income larger than the town's entire annual general budget. The mayor also runs meetings of the City Council (he has never been an alderman himself, or held political office of any sort), attended by aldermen who are paid $20 per meeting. One such meeting recently authorized an aviation photography outfit in St. Louis to photograph land on Bear Creek, where Vandalia hopes to create a lake for a new water supply. The Kaskaskia River has become so polluted with factory-discharged chemicals that treatment by the town waterworks is becoming prohibitively expensive. Another problem that has agitated the City Council was a degree of local indignation over stray dogs. In the absence of a definite policy on this matter, Marie Bennett, the city clerk, told irate telephoners that the best way to handle the mess was to lock up all dogs, homeless or not, until things blew over.

Michel admits that he ran for mayor because "they couldn't get anybody else." Such a basis of selection has been fairly traditional for many years. Nominations for political leadership are bestowed somewhat as they were in certain primitive societies, on persons who are the least skillful at evading the designation. Even lawyers have to be dragooned into running for court positions. An elective post in Vandalia is barren of power, of financial return, and of prospects for subsequent improvement. Given such a situation, the townspeople regard the biennial struggle to seize control of the Town Hall with only a faint display of emotion.

The columns of the *Leader* and the *Union* mirror the general unconcern with politics. Some of this editorial anaemia comes from a slightly stuffy sense of responsibility which dates back to when the Democratic *Leader* acquired the Republican opposition, the *Union*. Charles Mills, the tall, white-haired editor of the two papers, and one of the most overworked men in town, says that "ever since the opposition was bought out, we have had to realize that when we say something unpleasant about someone, he has no other place to go. We have to present both sides of everything. We think we've got an obligation to promote good activities and criticize bad ones regardless of the politics."

• • • • •

III

Lawyer Martin Corbell's comments about the lack of culture in Vandalia are comparatively mild. A school teacher, repeating the views of most of her associates, says, "Let's face it, the place is a desert." The teacher is not exactly exaggerating. The local entertainment palace, the Liberty Theatre, exhibits only the most excruciatingly fourth-rate films, although distribution syndicates, rather than the Liberty's owner, Herman Tanner, may be the real culprit. The town does not have any concert series, theatrical groups, or local FM radio. Vandalians like Corbell can find the theatre, music, or a passable night club only in St. Louis, seventy miles away. The situation is, if anything, much worse for the teen-agers who have little chance to attend concerts or plays and a rather uneventful social life. High school athletic contests are one occasion on which the young people get together, although the usual Midwestern custom of dances after a basketball game does not seem to have caught on. The chief amusement spots are Nevinger's roller-skating rink and a bowling alley across from the high school. Those who want to dance have to go as far afield as Effingham to do it.

Some time ago, a group of high school seniors, frustrated at the lack of a social center, found themselves a small hall and proceeded to decorate it, with ideas of installing a juke box, coke machine, and ping-pong table. But "Teen Town" collapsed when the minister of the First Baptist Church told the young people in his congregation to stay away. For the most part, the common substitute for something to do is for a gang to pile into a car and drive a traditional circuit in and about town, down Gallatin Street, around in the Kroger Parking lot, back up Gallatin, then out Route 51 to Route 40 to stop for a hamburger, then back on the raceway. Saturday night on Vandalia's main thoroughfare is a steady stream of flap-fendered vehicles, hot rods, and family sedans traveling in both directions and honking at familiar cars going in the opposite direction. The effect is weird in a town where, except for the taverns and a couple of coffee shops, everything closes up tight early in the evening. "Where are they going?" one wonders. A young driver might answer, "Nowhere. But we're under way."

Some persistent souls have attempted to invigorate the town, not without resistance, but then again not without success. Many years ago, Anna Ruth Kains, an English and voice teacher at Vandalia High School, undertook a crusade on behalf of good music. She assembled a choral group. "We got together some nice high school girls—Catholics, Methodists, Pentecostals, and a Jewish girl, among others. We thought we'd offer our voices for Lent." The idea worked well for a while. Several congregations heard some well-trained singers, and the girls discovered something about the insides of churches other then their own. Before long, however, Mrs. Kains's effort foundered on the objections of a Lutheran pastor who wanted young Lutheran ladies in his own church if they were going to be in any church on Sunday.

Mrs. Kains had another go, this time at the formation of a group to sing the Messiah during the Christmas season. She was told by almost everyone that the town wouldn't care much for that sort of thing, but she persisted. A place to practice was not easy to find. One Methodist church turned Mrs. Kains down because the elders had just installed a new red carpet and "they didn't want the singers tracking it all up." But finally the Messiah was presented at the Presbyterian Church and was a tremendous success. Later Messiahs drew so many listeners that the audience spilled out into the street and onto the railroad bridge a few yards from the main entrance of the church. So the Messiah moved to bigger quarters. It is now presented on an improvised stage in the gymnasium of the high school, which has no auditorium. The Messiah has become a Christmas institution.

Mrs. Kains also created a musical disturbance in the high school. She asked the superintendent if the glee club, then a rather sickly organization compared to the band, could sing at graduation exercises. Previously graduation had always been held in church, with choral offerings presented by a church group. "After all, if we were going to have a glee club, we had to have something to get ready for." Permission was granted and the glee club has prospered. Mrs. Kains related that in the beginning the band had sixty-five members and the glee club seventeen, while now glee club membership is up to 100 and the band has shriveled to thirty or thirty-five. "Everybody in school who can carry a tune has a chance to sing."

Significant cultural stirrings are also noticeable in the public library donated last year by Charles Evans. A Friends of the Library group has opened an art gallery in what had originally been designed as the Historical Society Room. The shows have been well attended, featuring the work of high and elementary school students, and some of the more practiced adults. This summer the library scheduled a traveling exhibit from New York City's Museum of Modern Art. Vandalians were well accustomed to abstractions by the time the show arrived, since a sizable percentage of local art work leans to the non-objective. Some credit for this tendency should go to a young art teacher, Bob Barker, who teaches drawing and painting to nearly forty adults in evening classes at the high school.

The library itself has a store of 15,000 volumes, larger than most collections in many bigger and wealthier communities. The library compensates in part for the fact that Vandalia has no bookstore at all. The only local establishment that sells anything above the cheap paper-back level is a local photographic supply house. In defense of Vandalia's reading habits, Mrs. Kitty Kelley, the librarian, reports that Vandalia's average circulation of six books a year per person is four or five times the national average.

. . . . .

Despite the energetic efforts of such people as Mrs. Kains, the Friends of the Library, the town's two librarians, some local teachers, and a few others, it is doubtful if anything but a major upheaval is going to improve the generally doleful character of Vandalia culture. There are some citizens who think a community college might do the trick, and that its establishment is a practical possibility. The college would play many roles. It would bring some higher education within reach of many high school graduates who, for academic or financial reasons, cannot go away to college but who could attend school and work part time while living at home. If, as has been suggested, the college provided training in vocational skills it might become a source of skilled labor that would attract industrial plants considering location in the Fayette County area. In addition, a college adult education program could stimulate whatever latent intellectual resources the town may have. The entry of a new teaching group into community life could make things more attractive to the town's professional people. The high school principal, William Wells, feels that the daily demonstration of a college program would not be lost upon high school students making their own plans for the future. Important people are interested. One, not surprisingly, is Harry Rogier. Others are members of the Board of Education, John Hegg, superintendent of the Crane plant, local ministers like Ralph Smith and Archie Brown. Charles Evans says he would "like to help." The nearby towns of Centralia and Effingham are talking about the community college idea, too. Vandalians don't like to take a back seat to anybody else, so they may just decide to do something about it. After all, Wells says, the town built three factories, why can't it build a college?

. . . . .

IV

Even such a caustic commentator as Father Gribbin agrees that Vandalia's school system, despite some drawbacks, is a good one. The townspeople are particularly proud of the yellow, two-story high school on the edge of town, built in 1950. For the 500 students there are twenty-seven teachers, and the average class size is eighteen to twenty pupils, considerably less than the averages for the town's less modern elementary schools. With its gleaming corridors, bright, well-equipped classrooms, vast gymnasium, the high school is the most impressive building in the community. In the back of the high school a new one-story shop addition, built with a recent bond issue of $175,000, is nearing completion.

One might expect to find that the principal of the high school was an expansive, cheery man inclined to mellow comments about "what we are trying to do here." No such description would fit Bill Wells. He is slender, dark, bespectacled. He speaks quickly, with an air of preoccupation, and sometimes rubs his forehead in perplexity. He has been principal of the high school for eleven out of his twenty-one years in the Vandalia school system. Whatever satisfactions he may feel about his establishment are buried under his immediate concerns about the future of his students. It takes him little time to get across his points.

"Many pupils in the high school come from families with only a ninth or tenth grade education. Many of these are farm families. It's surprising how many of the parents never graduated from high school. The understanding of what an education means and what an educational system needs isn't something that comes easily to the people of our community. We have been lucky to have good leadership to help bring this about. We have to do things one at a time. We have to vote an addition to a school, then an appropriation for another school, then an appropriation for a shop.

"So far we have come along fairly well. But, believe me, we have problems. Our college-bound group is facing a much tougher life in college than they have in the past. Colleges are getting more difficult, the competition to get in is much greater. This means that at one end we have to give our students better preparation all the time. Yet we are not able to hold on to our best teachers. Good new teachers get a little training here and then they leave when they get an offer to go some place else where they can make from $500 to $2,500 more a year. We lose two or three of our best teachers every year to the northern communities, the Chicago suburbs for instance.

"There is a great problem of how to finance our educational system here and it is getting worse. It is going to be tough in the next ten years. I think federal aid is so important. We've got to face the fact that in order to keep our teachers we've got to raise their salaries so that we don't have this great disparity with northern Illinois. And if we don't have these teachers, God help our college-bound kids. Can we keep getting another boost of money from the community? We're near the upper limit of our tax rate, which is fixed by law, and I don't know what we are going to do if we have to jump the tax rate—raise that tax limitation.

"Our kids do keep going on to college. We've been able to put about 30 per cent of each class, even as high as 40 per cent last year, into higher education. This is a good record, particularly when so many families don't have a college background. The parents do encourage them, much of the time. We have real problems with the students who don't go to college, the ones who are going through the vocational program. We know what automation is doing. There are fewer and fewer jobs for ditch-diggers, farmers, and factory workers, people who do semi-skilled work. What happens to the children who drop out of our schools and who take the kind of vocational training that prepares them for jobs that are not going to exist much longer?"

. . . . .

V

Although Vandalia may be suffering from other shortages, it is well supplied with churches. A process of simple division reveals that there is one church to every 400 people in town. The townspeople not only join the town's thirteen churches but attend them regularly and support them generously. Like other towns in the "Bible Belt" of Southern Illinois, the churches have always been at the center of the community's life. Therefore, it is not surprising that Vandalia's clergymen should, as a group, be articulate and informed commentators about their community. More than any other group they have accepted the responsibility to be part of almost every phase of community life, and should they ever lose sight of this fact, their parishioners are quick to remind them. On their part, the ministers do not hesitate to lay about them with a sharp tongue whenever they feel a little castigation is appropriate.

Perhaps the most colorful minister in town is the Reverend Henry Allwardt, pastor of the Holy Cross Lutheran Church, with a membership of 300. He lives in a one-story white frame house at some distance from his church, which is north of town near the high school. A tall, bespectacled man with a very thick shock of shining white hair, he works at a big oak desk covered with books and papers. After preaching in Ohio, Wisconsin, and Michigan and serving as a Navy chaplain in World War II, he came to Vandalia three years ago.

Mr. Allwardt begins with what is almost a standard opening to a Vandalian's conversation:

"There are several classes of people in the community. There are quite a few of the self-satisfied old-timers, a lot of them have good businesses and so forth, then there is a certain element, not as big as it is in some communities, of what I would call the decent, driven cattle. There is a kind of nice social life here, it's the best I've seen in a lot of ways. There is a certain amount of scandal, but on the whole things are pretty decent. I would rate it as a relatively pretty churchly town, not untypical of the communities in this area, and I've been around quite a bit. I haven't lived exactly in a locked trunk. I've been a pastor in the dead of the country, also in a big city like Detroit. A lot of people who behave very well in a small town like this fall away from the church when they get to the big city. It's not an entirely unprogressive community. The Chamber of Commerce has done good work getting plants here, for instance the heel factory. Vandalia is a lot better than the last place I was in, which was Arenzville. I also had a church in Marysville, Ohio. We had a 100-year-old church, and it seemed like most of the people in it must have been charter members."

What was wrong with Arenzville? "Why, everybody up there was so envious of everybody else. There was so darned much hatred. The stores would stay open even on Christmas for fear somebody else would sell something. The population was about 500. It was predominantly a German community. When you get into a German community you should understand the history of Germany if you want to understand the people; for instance, whether they come from north or south Germany. Then you have to understand why their ancestors came to America. The people in Arenzville came here because they thought they were going to get rich. Their standards were quite materialistic. For instance, they didn't know a thing about baking cookies on Christmas. You'd never find that going on in Arenzville.

• • • • •

"I have a lot of Germans in my congregation. They came to Vandalia for quite a different reason from the Arenzville people. They came because the churches of Germany did not allow decent Lutheran preaching. Our Lutherans were in constant trouble over there because the State was trying to foist all manner of practices on the church that they didn't agree with. The Germans in this area came for what the Pilgrims claim they came for. And, by the way, the Pilgrims came because they wanted to be the dominant church. They are the most intolerant people who ever came here. It's too bad the Plymouth rock didn't land on them instead of the other way around. Our people wanted separation of church and state. They wanted a church that could operate unhampered. One of the troubles with our synod, however, was that our people were rather timid. They came in here with a church that was relatively unknown west of the Alleghenies. They were also a foreign-language church, and they felt that they had to feel defensive about this. But in a hundred years, since we organized our synod, which was in 1847, we've gone from twenty to 4,000 congregations in this area. St. Louis has the largest seminary in the world. We're busy in other countries too. We have eighty-three radio stations in Japan.

"What's that about the social activities of the church? I've got you, I'm a jump ahead. You mean, what does the average layman expect of church and what does he do in church? Well, that gets me into one thing. Theology is getting to be sociology these days, which means that a lot of people when they get in the pulpit feel they should never say anything that could be understood. The only trouble with most churches is their pastors. The pulpit has departed so far from what it is here for it isn't even funny. Why do I want to go to church to listen to lectures on prohibition and world affairs? What business has a minister got talking about matters that 30 per cent of his congregation know a lot more about than he does? My responsibility to my congregation is to teach the word of God, and if I happen to have some screwball opinions I'll keep them to myself. That's why we have pastoral conferences, to get ourselves unscrewed, we pastors. Another responsibility I have is to live like a Christian gentleman, and I also have the responsibility to bring children into the church with some understanding of it. The church is not a social club.

"The trouble with a lot of churches is that the Catholic Church is good for people who want soul insurance and the Protestant Church spends most of its time adding a mellifluous odor to the prevailing winds. Pastors ought to mind their own business and stick to their own responsibilities. Another job of the minister is to comfort and help the sick. This is his duty. You go to such a person when you're needed. You may have an opening with a sick person that you may never have again to bring him into the church and an understanding of God.

"I try to instill in the young people the desire to 'seek ye the Kingdom of God in his righteousness.' In these unsettled times this is the job of the church. I think my young people have pretty good moral character. You can't know too easily what they're striving for. The boys especially, though, seem to be serious-minded. The girls don't seem to have anything to talk about but boys when they get into high school.

"You ask about material gain, whether that's what people want instead of helping the community. I'll give you a thousand dollars if you can find three people in any community who aren't looking for material gain. Everybody is after it. Everybody all the way up to the President. Everybody is after what he can get."

• • • • •

The corporation of Vandalia is an aggregate of people and properties, but as a community it is nothing more or less than a single idea, very personal and private, in the mind of each of its citizens. Perhaps someone could draw a composite face of all of them if he were to tailor his questions carefully, but there would be no features in the face. Vandalia is not a place to find a "community attitude," which is probably what Judge Burnside means when he makes the remark, "We're not any special sort of a town. People come here from all over," silently adding that this is where their ideas come from, too.

If the people of Vandalia are not entirely unlike other Americans, there may be some importance in the conclusion that they do not have established sets of ideas, even though they may observe fairly rigid rules of social conduct and share a common vocabulary of stock phrases. It can be argued that this is not a discovery, that it is obvious, and that the people of no community—not even in Puritan New England—ever really had a set of standard thoughts, no matter how total the conformity was on the surface. Even if this argument is granted, the people of Vandalia hardly fit into the Main Street folklore which has been built up around the rural Midwestern town. At least when they are pressed they express self-criticism and lively dissent, and anyone who expects to hear them talk like the people of Sinclair Lewis's Sauk Center will either have to ignore half of what he hears or take charge of the conversations and drive them in the direction he believes they ought to take.

The talks in Vandalia do not support the American myth that a rural town today is a land-locked island inhabited by people who share an abiding complacency with each other. There are the surface appearances of unity and its concomitant sterility in Vandalia, and the appearances are sometimes overwhelming. But they do not persist in the face of its own citizens' conflicting testimony. Vandalians today are in some ways in a better position to observe and to feel, sometimes most painfully, the consequences of a changing society than the suburbanite who lives in a bedroom town or the city dweller who hears about the world mainly from his newspaper and who enjoys the protective layers afforded him by his corporation, his union, and his various other institutional affiliations. There is also a special urgency in the air of Vandalia. A town on the edge of Chicago, Los Angeles, or New York City is forced to deal with the problems of sudden and uncontrolled growth, but Vandalia is beset by the much more desperate problem of how to hold on to what it has in order to survive.

Security is not one of the values the townspeople attach to living in their community. Vandalia families cannot be certain about the future of their community or even of their ability to remain in it. The favorable employment statistics in the Chamber of Commerce's brochure do not veil the fact that jobs now held are in constant danger of disappearing, whether they are in the factory, farm, or local store, and that a great percentage of them cannot support a family or offer any hope for advancement. The family that wants to remain in Vandalia, far from being insulated from the tensions and threats of the outer world, is resisting economic, social, and technological forces that could break the community apart and send the pieces flying in all directions.

Whereas many Americans live in or around the great cities unwillingly because that is where the jobs are, Vandalians live in their town because they want to. Their reasons are not new, but they have an added poignancy because the things these people value are becoming harder to hold on to. They like the freedom of association and personal trust they do not believe can be found in a large city. They hope to maintain a school system in which their children receive a common educational experience in small classes with good teachers. Perhaps, as William Deems says, there is something unhealthy about the way Vandalians meet each local problem with a fund drive; nevertheless, they esteem the relationships with each other that make such solutions practicable.

There are many reasons why a man stays in Vandalia when, as Joe Dees puts it, "he could get the paid vacations and fringe benefits in the city," and most of them recur over and over in the talks. Underlying them all seems to be a desire to be able to know the whole of one's town, to be "some kind of a somebody" in it, to be able to circulate in it freely, and to be part of a social arrangement where there are certain justified assumptions about how people will deal with each other. On a freezing day, Mrs. Mark Miller is operating under one of these assumptions when she asks the postmaster who has just sold her some stamps to call a taxi for her. There is nothing trivial about the transaction.

Vandalia's lawyers and doctors and farmers and teachers and businessmen have their difficulties in talking about what they believe themselves and their community to be. Some of their trouble comes from an unconscious absorption of many of the standard myths about small-town complacency, neighborliness, Godliness, stupidity, provincialism, loyalties, unity, freshness. A tale heard often enough sometimes becomes part of the conversation, and a Vandalian does not usually speak of his community without himself introducing some of the stereotyped criticisms. The view that talks with people in their own environment will dispel the myth of their environment can be misleading.

Despite all their advertised contact with their fellow human beings, many Vandalians seem to do much of their thinking in isolation. Perhaps it is because their problems are so closely bound up with personal relationships that many of them are less inclined to speak openly about them. In a community where almost everyone knows everyone else by name and face, and converses with ease and frequency, the citizens for the most part exchange commonplaces. Dan Hockman, a high school history teacher, describes the situation when he says, "People here are interested in what other people are up to, not in what they think." With all their togetherness—the word is not used with disdain—there are many, many isolated people in the community. Sometimes the isolation is by choice. Alenia McCord says apologetically, "We have our standards and we tend to be a little intolerant of other people if they don't agree with us, but we don't try to railroad our standards on others. If somebody doesn't come up to our standards that's all right just as long as they keep a long distance away from us." More often, however, the isolation is neither sought nor enjoyed. Conversations on the most affecting personal and intellectual matters are given freely—to the outsider who asks for them—but when the conversations end, sometimes after many hours of intense exchange, the conclusion is very often a wish that it might happen again and a remark that it almost never happened before.

Perhaps the absence of serious talk with others in their community explains why so many of the townspeople combine their own inner guesses with mixtures of the prevalent myths, and thereby supplement the myths. There are many remarks about the curse of complacency in the town and, taken together, the people who are disturbed about it make up a sizable portion of the population. But, like the Reverend Ralph Smith, they are really annoyed at the nature of the peace, not the peace itself, at the inertia that seems to be responsible for the lack of conflict and motion in the community. If the inertia proceeds from smugness and total satisfaction with the past, anything Mr. Smith has to say in criticism of "Peaceful Valley" seems relatively mild. But if the inertia grows out of confusion and bewilderment, and the clinging to tradition is done in desperation, then Mr. Smith is being harsh, because the peace in the valley is a troubled one.

It is strange to discover that an assembly of people who live together with a decency unheard of in a large city, and whose community efforts have been astonishingly successful, should at the same time lack the sort of serious communication with each other that would seem to be the basis of democratic life. The potential exists. Vandalia has an unusual assortment of sensitive and informed people. They have opinions, ideas, tempers. They would like to make their town better. But, given this, there is a reticence on important matters that is forbidding, and a lack of a forum—a new England-style town meeting, for instance—in which regular discussions could proceed.

In some ways, Vandalians leave the impression that they are members of a family in which the main strength of the past has become a problem for the future. They have had the advantage of similar origins and close kinship, but perhaps so close that, as the family grows and disperses, too much of the dependency remains. And, like a family, they have lived and talked with each other steadily over the years but have kept their real thoughts and worries about each other inside. The old bonds that held Vandalia in a sort of perpetual stability are breaking. There are many departures from the family and few arrivals.

If there is to be a new way for the town, it has many assets which do not appear in Robert Hasler's typewritten town biography. Vandalia is not condemned to become a suburb of anything just yet, and it still has transportation facilities that can serve whatever new industrial establishments it may attract. One advantage of its unhurried history is that no huge defense plants have dropped down on the town to crush its character forever and then move on in a few years. Vandalia has natural beauties that make it a place apart. Few towns to the north have spreading elms and maples of such beauty, and in May there is the wild spring blaze of lilac and dogwood. The Kaskaskia is a navigator's nightmare now, but in a few years flood-control dams below and above Vandalia will reclaim much valuable farm land, and, not incidentally, provide fishing and boating for local boys and girls and out-of-state tourists.

Obviously, what happens in Vandalia depends on the people who will have to manage these assets, and what improvements they make in their present arrangements of organizing themselves and communicating with each other. One cannot really tell how they will do, even after talking to them for a long, long time. Affairs move slowly. But there are stirrings and there are contradictions. Judge Burnside says nobody pays any attention to the railroads. On the other hand, in his church by the railroad, Mr. Smith has to stop in the middle of his Sunday sermon when he hears the "Spirit of St. Louis" coming down the tracks.

68 Haight-Ashbury in Transition

DAVID E. SMITH, JOHN LUCE,
AND ERNEST A. DERNBURG

Although the Haight-Ashbury district in San Francisco has not been a typical community for a long time, its recent development and change as a hippie settlement demonstrates some of the characteristics of communities in transition. The changes in this area have been associated with the patterns of drug usage and the attendant health problems. Many young people have illusions that such havens as Haight-Ashbury are free of all of the forces affecting human communities. Although unique in many respects, Haight-Ashbury is also similar to many other areas that are in transition.

. . . . .

Three years ago *Time* magazine called San Francisco's Haight-Ashbury "the vibrant epicenter of America's hippie movement." Today the Haight-Ashbury District looks like a disaster area. Some of the frame Victorian houses, flats and apartment buildings lying between the Panhandle of Golden Gate Park and the slope of Mount Sutro have deteriorated beyond repair, and many property-owners have boarded over their windows or blocked their doorways with heavy iron bars. Hiding in their self-imposed internment, the original residents of the area seem emotionally exhausted and too terrified to leave their homes. "We're all frightened," says one 60-year-old member of the Haight-Ashbury Neighborhood Council. "The Haight has become a drug ghetto, a teen-age slum. The streets aren't safe; rats romp in the Panhandle; the neighborhood gets more run down every day. The only thing that'll save this place now is a massive dose of federal aid."

Nowhere is the aid more needed than

SOURCE: David E. Smith, John Luce, and Ernest A. Dernburg, "The Health of Haight-Ashbury," *Trans-action*, vol. 7, no. 6 (April 1970), 35–45. • David E. Smith is assistant clinical professor of toxicology at the San Francisco Medical Center and medical director at the Haight-Ashbury Free Medical Clinic. He has coauthored with John Luce and Ernest A. Dernberg, *Love Needs Care: A History of the Haight-Ashbury Free Medical Clinic, An Analysis of Its Patients and An Examination of Their Drug and Health Problems.* • John Luce is associate editor of *San Francisco Magazine* and public affairs director of the Haight-Ashbury Free Medical Clinic. • Ernest A. Dernburg is a psychiatrist in private practice in San Francisco and former psychiatric director of the Haight-Ashbury Free Medical Clinic.

on Haight Street, the strip of stores that runs east to west through the Flatlands. Once a prosperous shopping area, Haight Street has so degenerated by this time that the storefronts are covered with steel grates and sheets of plywood, while the sidewalks are littered with dog droppings, cigarette butts, garbage and broken glass. According to Henry Sands, the owner of a small realty agency on the corner of Haight and Stanyan streets, over 50 grocers, florists, druggists, haberdashers and other merchants have moved off the street since the 1967 Summer of Love; property values have fallen 20 percent in the same period, but none of the remaining businessmen can find buyers for their stores. The Safeway Supermarket at Haight and Schrader streets has closed, Sands reports, after being shoplifted out of $10,000 worth of merchandise in three months. The one shopowner to open since, stocks padlocks and shatterproof window glass. "The only people making money on Haight Street now sell dope or cheap wine," the realtor claims. "Our former customers are all gone. There's nothing left of the old community anymore."

Nothing is left of the Haight-Ashbury's new hippie community today either. There are no paisley-painted buses on Haight Street, no "flower children" parading the sidewalks, no tribal gatherings, no H.I.P. (Haight Independent Proprietor) stores. Almost all the long-haired proprietors have followed the original merchants out of the district; the Psychedelic Shop at Haight and Clayton stands vacant; the Print Mint across the street and the Straight Theatre down the block are both closed. Allen Ginsberg, Timothy Leary, Ken Kesey and their contemporaries no longer visit the communal mecca they helped establish here in the mid-1960s. Nor do the rock musicians, poster artists and spiritual gurus who brought it international fame. And although a few young people calling themselves Diggers still operate a free bakery and housing office out of the basement of All Saints' Episcopal Church on Waller Street, Father Leon Harris there considers them a small and insignificant minority. "For all intents and purposes," he says, "the peaceful hippies we once knew have disappeared."

They started disappearing almost three years ago, when worldwide publicity brought a different and more disturbed population to the Haight and the city escalated its undeclared war on the new community. Today, most of the long-haired adolescents the public considers hip have left Haight Street to hang out on Telegraph Avenue in Berkeley or on Grant Avenue in San Francisco's North Beach District. Some of the "active" or "summer" hippies who once played in the Haight-Ashbury have either returned home or reenrolled in school. Others have moved to the Mission District and other parts of the city, to Sausalito and Mill Valley in Marin County, to Berkeley and Big Sur or to the rural communes operating throughout northern California.

A few are still trapped in the Haight, but they take mescaline, LSD and other hallucinogenic drugs indoors and stay as far away from Haight Street as possible. When they must go there, to cash welfare checks or to shop at the one remaining supermarket, they never go at night or walk alone. "It's too dangerous for me," says one 19-year-old unwed mother who ran away from a middle-class home in Detroit during the summer of 1967. "Haight Street used to be so groovy I could get high just being there. But I don't know anybody on the street today. Since I've been here, it's become the roughest part of town."

A new population has moved into the district and taken over Haight Street like an occupying army. Transient and diverse, its members now number several thousand persons. Included are a few tourists, weekend visitors and young runaways who still regard the Haight-Ashbury as a refuge for the alienated. There are also older white, Negro and Indian alcoholics from the city's Skid Row; black delinquents who live in the Flatlands or the Fillmore ghetto; Hell's Angels and other "bikers" who roar through the area on their Harley Davidsons. Finally there are the overtly psychotic young people who abuse any and all kinds of drugs, and psychopathic white adolescents with criminal records in San Francisco and other cities who come from lower-class homes or no homes at all.

Uneducated and lacking any mystical or spiritual interest, many of these young people have traveled from across the country to find money, stimulation and easy sex in the Haight and to exploit the flower children they assume are still living here. Some have grown long hair and assimilated the hip jargon in the process, but they resemble true hippies in no real way. "Street wise" and relatively aggressive in spite of the passive longings which prompt their drug abuse, they have little love for one another and no respect for the law or for themselves. Instead of beads and bright costumes they wear leather jackets and coarse, heavy clothes. Instead of ornate buses they drive beat-up motorcycles and hot rods. Although they smoke marijuana incessantly and drop acid on occasion, they generally dismiss these chemicals as child's play and prefer to intoxicate themselves with opiates, barbiturates and amphetamines.

Their individual tastes may vary, but most of the adolescents share a dreary, drug-based life-style. Few have any legal means of support, and since many are addicted to heroin, they must peddle chemicals, steal groceries and hustle spare change to stay alive. Even this is difficult, for there is very little money on Haight Street and a great deal of fear. Indeed, the possibility of being "burned," raped or "ripped off" is so omnipresent that most of the young people stay by themselves and try to numb their anxiety and depression under a toxic fog. By day they sit and slouch separately against the boarded-up storefronts in a drug-induced somnolescence. At night they lock themselves indoors, inject heroin and plan what houses in the district they will subsequently rob.

Although the results of this living pattern are amply reflected in the statistics available from Park Police Station at Stanyan and Waller streets, the 106 patrolmen there are apparently unable to curb the Haight-Ashbury's crime. Their job has been made easier by the relative decrease in amphetamine consumption and the disappearance of many speed freaks from the district over the past few months, but the rate of robbery and other acts associated with heroin continues to rise. Making regular sweeps of Haight Street in patrol cars and paddy wagons, the police also threaten to plant drugs on known dealers if they will not voluntarily leave town. Yet these and other extreme measures seem only to act like a negative filter in the Haight, screening out the more cunning abusers and leaving their inept counterparts behind.

• • • • •

PUBLIC HEALTH: A SUICIDE LICENSE

They have also created one of the most serious health problems in all of San Francisco. Many of the young people who hang out on Haight Street are not only overtly or potentially psychotic, but also physically ravaged by one another as well. Although murder is not particularly popular with the new population, some of its members seem to spend their lives in plaster casts. Others frequently exhibit suppurating abrasions, knife and razor slashes, damaged genitalia and other types of traumatic injuries—injuries all caused by violence.

Even more visible is the violence they do to themselves. Continually stoned on drugs, the adolescents often overexert and fail to notice as they infect and mangle their feet by wading through the droppings and broken glass. Furthermore, although some of the heroin addicts lead a comparatively stabilized existence, others overlook the physiological deterioration which results from their self-destructive lives. The eating habits of these young people are so poor that they are often malnourished and inordinately susceptible to infectious disease. In fact, a few of them suffer from protein and vitamin deficiencies that are usually found only in chronic alcoholics three times their age.

With gums bleeding from pyorrhea and rotting teeth, some also have abscesses and a diffuse tissue infection called cellulitis, both caused by using dirty needles. Others miss their veins while shooting up or rupture them by injecting impure and undissolvable chemicals. And since most sleep, take drugs and have sex in unsanitary environments, they constantly expose themselves to upper respiratory tract infections, skin rashes, bronchitis, tonsillitis, influenza, dysentery, urinary and genital tract infections, hepatitis and venereal disease.

In addition to these and other chronic illnesses, the young people also suffer from a wide range of drug problems. Some have acute difficulties, such as those individuals who oversedate themselves with barbiturates or "overamp" with amphetamines. Others have chronic complaints, long-term "speed" precipitated psychoses and paranoid, schizophrenic reactions. Many require physiological and psychological withdrawal from barbiturates and heroin. In fact, heroin addiction and its attendant symptoms have reached epidemic proportions in the Haight-Ashbury, and the few doctors at Park Emergency Hospital cannot check the spread of disease and drug abuse through the district any better than the police can control its crime.

To make matters worse, these physicians appear unwilling to attempt to solve the local health problems. Like many policemen, the public health representatives seem to look on young drug-abusers as subhuman. When adolescents come to Park Emergency for help the doctors frequently assault them with sermons, report them to the police or submit them to complicated and drawn-out referral procedures that only intensify their agony. The nurses sometimes tell prospective patients to take their problems elsewhere. The ambulance drivers simply "forget" calls for emergency assistance. They and the other staff members apparently believe that the best way to stamp out sickness in the Haight is to let its younger residents destroy themselves.

Given this attitude, it is hardly surprising that the adolescents are as frightened of public health officials as they are of policemen. Some would sooner risk death than seek aid at Park Emergency and are equally unwilling to go to San Francisco General Hospital, the city's central receiving unit, two miles away. Many merely live with their symptoms, doctor themselves with home remedies or narcotize themselves to relieve their pain. These young people do not trust "straight" private physicians, who they assume will overcharge them and hand them over to the law. Uneducated about medical matters, they too often listen only to the "witch doctors" and drug-dealers who prowl the Haight-Ashbury, prescribing their own products for practically every physiological and psychological ill.

• • • • •

HAIGHT-ASHBURY HISTORY

It is necessary to visualize the Haight in 1960, before its present population arrived. In that year, rising rents, police harassment and the throngs of tourists and thrill-seekers on Grant Avenue squeezed many beatniks out of the North Beach District three miles away. They started looking for space in the Haight-Ashbury, and landlords here saw they could make more money renting their property to young people willing to put up with poor conditions than to black families. For this reason, a small, beat subculture took root in the Flatlands and spread slowly up the slope of Mount Sutro. By 1962 the Haight was the center of a significant but relatively unpublicized bohemian colony.

Although fed by beats and students from San Francisco State, this colony remained unnoticed for several years. One reason was its members' preference for sedating themselves with alcohol and marijuana instead of using drugs that attract more attention. Another was their preoccupation with art and their habit of living as couples or alone. This living pattern was drastically altered in 1964, however, with the popular acceptance of mescaline, LSD and other hallucinogens and the advent of the Ginsberg-Leary-Kesey nomadic, passive, communal electric and acid-oriented life-style. The beats were particularly vulnerable to psychoactive chemicals that they thought enhanced their aesthetic powers and alleviated their isolation. Because of this, hallucinogenic drugs swept the Haight-Ashbury, as rock groups began preparing in the Flatlands what would soon be known as the "San Francisco Sound." On 1 January 1966 the world's first Psychedelic Shop was opened on Haight Street. Two weeks later, Ken Kesey hosted a Trips Festival at Longshoreman's Hall. Fifteen thousand individuals attended, and the word "hippie" was born. A year later, after Diggers and HIP had come to the Haight, the new community held a tribal gathering for 20,000 white Indians on the polo fields of Golden Gate Park. At this first Human Be-In, it showed its collective strength to the world.

The community grew immeasurably in size and stature as a result of this venture, but the ensuing publicity brought it problems for which its founders were ill prepared. In particular, the immigration of more young people to the Haight-Ashbury after the Be-In caused a shortage in sleeping space and precipitated the emergence of a new living unit, the crash pad. Adolescents forced to reside in these temporary and overcrowded structures started to experience adverse hallucinogenic drug reactions and psychological problems. The new community began to resemble a gypsy encampment, whose members were exposing themselves to an extreme amount of infectious disease.

Theoretically, the San Francisco Public Health Department should have responded positively to the situation. But instead of trying to educate and treat the hippies, it attempted to isolate and thereby destroy their community. Still convinced that theirs was a therapeutic alternative, the young people packed together in the Haight grew suicidally self-reliant, bought their medications on the black market and stocked cases of the antipsychotic agent Thorazine in their crash pads. Meanwhile, the Diggers announced that 100,000 adolescents dropping acid in Des Moines and Sioux Falls would flock to the Haight-Ashbury when school was out. They then tried to blackmail the city into giving them the food, shelter and medical supplies necessary to care for the summer invasion.

Although the Public Health Department remained unmoved by the Diggers' forecast, a number of physicians and other persons associated with the University of California Psychopharmacology Study Group did react to the grisly promise of the Summer of Love. Among them were Robert Conrich, a former private investigator-turned-bohemian; Charles Fischer, a dental student; Dr. Frederick Meyers, internationally respected professor of pharmacology at the Medical Center; and Dr. David Smith, a toxicologist who was then serving as chief of the Alcohol and Drug Abuse Screening Unit at General Hospital. Several of these men lived in or were loyal to the Haight-Ashbury. Many had experience in treating bad LSD trips and felt that a rash of them would soon occur in the district. All had contacts among the new community and were impressed by the hippies' dreams of new social forms. But they also knew that the hippies did not number health among their primary concerns, although they might if they were afforded a free and accepting facility. In April then they decided to organize a volunteer-staffed crisis center which might answer the growing medical emergency in the area.

• • • • •

Although the organizers anticipated the need for a regional health center in the Haight, they never dreamed that so many adolescents would seek help at the Medical Section. Nor did they suspect that the Diggers would be so close in their estimate of the number of individuals coming to the district that summer. Not all 100,000 showed up at once, but at least that many visitors did pass through the Haight-Ashbury during the next three months, over 20,000 of them stopping off at 558 Clayton Street along the way. A quarter of these persons were found to be beats, hippies and other early residents of the area. A half were "active" or "summer" hippies, comparatively healthy young people who experimented with drugs and might have done so at Fort Lauderdale and other locations had not the media told them to go West. The final quarter were bikers, psychotics and psychopaths of all ages who came to exploit the psychedelic scene.

Most of these individuals differed psychologically, but sickness and drugs were two things they all had in common. Some picked up measles, influenza, streptococcal pharyngitis, hepatitis, urinary and genital tract infections and venereal disease over the summer. Uncontrolled drug experimentation was rampant so others had bad trips from the black-market acid flooding the area. Many also suffered adverse reactions from other drugs, for the presence of psychopaths and multiple abusers brought changes in psychoactive chemical consumption on the street. This first became obvious at the Summer Solstice Festival, where 5,000 tablets were distributed containing the psychomimetic amphetamine STP. Over 150 adolescents were treated for STP intoxication at the clinic, and after an educational program was launched, the substance waned in popularity in the district. But many of its younger residents had sampled intensive central nervous system stimulation for the first time during the STP episode. As a result, many were tempted to experiment next with "speed."

Such experimentation increased over the summer, until the Haight became the home of two separate subcultures, the first made up of "acid heads" who preferred hallucinogens, the second consisting of "speed freaks" partial to amphetamines. At the same time, the district saw the emergence of two different milder adolescent illnesses, the second marked by malnutrition, cellulitis, tachycardia, overstimulation and the paranoid-schizophrenic reactions associated with "speed."

. . . . .

This question could be easily answered, for by the end of the Summer of Love almost all of the original hippies had moved to urban and rural communes outside of the Haight. Many summer hippies had also left the district, and those who remained either fended for themselves or were assimilated into the new population. Staying in the Haight-Ashbury, they quickly changed from experimental drug-users into multiple abusers and needed even more help. For this reason, the clinic organizers were determined to open the Medical Section again.

At the same time, they had another good reason to renew their efforts in the Haight. With the hippie movement spread across the United States by this point, other cities—Seattle, Boston, Berkeley, Cambridge, even Honolulu—were being swept by drug problems. New clinics were being created in the face of this onslaught, all of them looking to the Haight-Ashbury for guidance. Although always a confused and crisis-oriented center, the Haight-Ashbury Free Medical Clinic had become the national symbol of a new and successful approach in reaching a deviant population of alienated adolescents. Thus, its organizers had not only their medical practice but also their position of leadership to resume.

. . . . .

The amphetamines gradually ran their course in the district, and many of the multiple drug-abusers here switched to opiates, barbiturates and other "downers" after becoming too "strung out" on "speed." This change in chemical consumption naturally affected treatment practices, as heroin addicts increased tenfold and young people suffered even more types of chronic illness as a result of their drug abuse. Yet, in spite of the new population's problems, the year was a productive one for the clinic. Over 20,000 patients were treated at the Medical and Psychiatric Sections; research programs were initiated; efforts were made to reach the hippies in their communes; the volunteers became more experienced, although fewer in number; and several ex-staff members became involved in treatment programs of their own.

. . . . .

Whether these conditions continue depends, as always, on the Haight-Ashbury. This is particularly true today because its resident population seems to be changing once again. As some of the drug-abusers drift out of the area, their places are apparently being taken by adventurous college students. More black delinquents from the Fillmore ghetto are also frequenting the district, contributing to its heroin problem, though participating in the Drug Treatment Program for the first time. The Neighborhood Council and Merchants' Association still function, but both are demoralized and at a political impasse. In addition, the area is seeing an increased influx of older Negro families. Because of this, some staff members are urging changes at Medical and Psychiatric Sections. One faction sees the clinic evolving into a health center for the entire neighborhood and wants to purchase one of the abandoned buildings on Haight Street so that all future programs can be consolidated under one roof. Another argues for more decentralization, de-emphasis of certain activities and/or increased expansion within and without the Haight.

. . . . .

69 Effects of the Move to the Suburbs

HERBERT J. GANS

One aspect of the urbanization process in America, especially since World War II, has been an extensive migration from the central city to the suburbs. For some time this suburban life was subjected to scathing criticism, especially by essayists and journalists who claimed the move to the suburbs created many social and social-psychological problems. Most of this writing, however, was impressionistic and was not based on careful, empirical study of those who had moved from city to suburbs. In this selection Gans analyzes data from several systematic studies and concludes that suburban pathology was more myth than fact.

Of the many changes that have taken place in America since World War II, one of the most important, and certainly the most visible, has been the migration of the white middle class from the city to the suburbs. Every American city, large and small, is now ringed by suburban subdivisions of varying sizes and price levels, and where once farmers raised fruits and vegetables for city tables, young families are now raising children.

Much has been written about the suburban exodus, and much of that has been critical. Journalists, essayists, social workers, psychologists, and psychiatrists have argued that the departure from the city, and suburban life itself, have had undesirable effects on the people involved and on the larger society. The critics have suggested that suburbia is one of the slayers of traditional American individualism, that it has made people more conforming and other-directed. They have argued that there is too much socializing, useless hyperactivity in voluntary associations, competition, and conspicuous consumption. Many of these evils are thought to be the result of boredom produced by the demographic homogeneity of suburban life, and by the loss of the stimulation associated with city life. The critics have also described a matriarchy and child-dominated society, resulting from the lack of job opportunities within the average suburb and the husband's consequent absence from the home during the children's waking hours. More recently, a psychiatrist has argued that the suburban way of life is a product of excessive social mobility and is so full of stress that it increases psychosomatic illness, divorce, alcoholism, suicide attempts, and mental illness generally. In short, suburbia is thought to be a source of negative effects in American life.

Although the concept of suburban pathology has entered our folklore, empirical studies of people who have moved from city to suburb suggest that the concept is false, that it is a myth rather than a fact. This paper attempts to describe the actual effects of the move, and to consider the implications these create for city planners, social planners, and the pro-

SOURCE: "Effects of the Move from City to Suburb," from *The Urban Condition*, chap. 14, edited by Leonard J. Duhl with the assistance of John Powell, © 1963 by Basic Books, Inc., Publishers. • The author is professor and Senior Research Associate, Department of Urban Studies and Planning, Massachusetts Institute of Technology. His interests include community studies, stratification, mass media of communication, popular culture, and city planning. He has written *Urban Villagers: Group and Class in the Life of Italian-Americans, The Levittowners,* and *People and Plans.* He has also been a contributing author to *Human Behavior and Social Processes.*

fessions which Erich Lindemann has aptly described as caretakers.

EFFECTS OF THE MOVE FROM CITY TO SUBURB

The effects of suburban life can best be determined through an investigation of behavior changes which people undergo after the move. A number of sociological studies have now been made of this topic. My own analysis will be based primarily on preliminary conclusions from my own research among people who moved from Philadelphia and other nearby cities to a new suburban community of low-priced single-family homes. My findings are similar to those of Berger's study of factory workers who moved from Richmond, California, to a suburban tract in Milpitas; and to Willmott's study of London slum dwellers who moved to Dagenham, a quasi-suburban municipal housing estate. These studies suggest the following conclusions:

1. For the vast majority of city dwellers the move to the suburb results in relatively few, and for the most part, minor changes in the way of life. As one respondent explained: "I don't know how a new house changes your life. You have a pattern you go by, and that stays the same no matter where you live."

2. The most frequently reported changes that do take place are not caused by the move to the suburb, but are reasons for moving there in the first place. These reasons are based on aspirations for ownership of a single-family house that are today satisfied only in suburbia. These aspirations have not been created by the suburbs, however, and are therefore not effects of the move.

3. A few changes in behavior can be traced to life in the suburb itself, independent from aspirations people held before they moved. Some of these can therefore be designated as effects of the move. Most of the changes are positive in nature, but a few result in problems that require solutions.

4. Most of the effects described by the myth of suburbia either can be traced to factors other than the move to suburbia, or do not take place at all.

Each of these conclusions will now be discussed in further detail. The studies I have cited are in agreement that people's lives are not changed drastically by the move to the suburb. Berger found, for example, that factory workers continued to maintain their working-class styles when they became homeowners, and showed no interest in adopting the patterns of social life, religious activity, voting behavior, status-striving, or class mobility predicted by the suburban myth. My own study reached the same conclusions about a more middle-class population. These two studies are based on interviews with people about two years after the move to the suburbs. The same results have been obtained by Willmott's study, however, which indicated that after twenty to forty years of life in Dagenham the residents maintained most of the working-class ways of life that they had pursued in the slums from which they came.

My own research asked people specifically what changes they had experienced as a result of the move. Although the analysis of these interviews is still in process, a preliminary review of the data suggests the following changes as most important: the satisfactions of a new home and of home ownership, the availability of more living space, increased social life, somewhat greater organizational participation, and the development of family and community financial problems. Adolescents and culturally deviant people experience some social isolation, and adaptation problems.

Most of these changes fall into the

second category mentioned above: they are the results of pre-occupancy aspirations, rather than the effects of the suburb. Thus, the changes reported most often derive from owning a home, and having more space inside and outside the house. Home ownership gives people the feeling of having an equity—or sharing it with the bank—more privacy from neighbors than they had either in apartments or Philadelphia row-houses, and an opportunity to improve the house and yard in their own individual way. This not only satisfies desires for self-expression and creativity, but for joint family activity around the house that brings the family closer together. The house is also a locale for the relaxation that many working- and lower middle-class Americans derive from "puttering" and "tinkering." The increased living space which people have obtained as a result of their move permits adults and children to get out of each other's way more easily than before, and this in turn reduces family conflict.

The crucial change here is that of house type, rather than community: from the rented apartment or row-house to the single-family house. Since the opportunity for home ownership is by and large available only in the suburb, at least for new houses in the low and medium price ranges, this is primarily why young families move from the city to the suburb. Even so, I suspect similar changes would be reported by people who move from an apartment to a house within the city limits, or within the suburbs.

Other frequently mentioned changes are an increase in social life and in organizational activity. These have been reported in many new suburbs, and can be traced to the newness of the communities, rather than to the fact that they are suburban. Moving into a new community creates an initial feeling of cohesion and universal friendliness, especially if there are shared problems. These feelings may disappear as people settle down, the novelty of the community wears off, and class and other cultural differences make themselves felt. Even so, there is probably more social life among suburbanites than among city dwellers of equal age and socio-economic level. There are several reasons for this difference. First, many people move to the suburbs with the hope of making new friends, and those that come with this purpose are able to do so. For example, the interviews I conducted six to nine months after the move show that 23 out of 55 couples wanted to do more visiting with other couples and 83 per cent achieved their wish. (These interviews were conducted among a random sample of *all* residents, not just ex-city dwellers, but among the 13 ex-city dwellers in this sample, the 5 who wanted to do more visiting in their new home all achieved their aim.) Also, there are many people of similar age and with similar interests, and many opportunities to meet them. And finally, a new house encourages entertaining, while the absence of movies and restaurants in a new community discourages other forms of diversion.

The increase in community activity can also be attributed to the newness of the community. A new suburb usually lacks the basic church and voluntary organizations which residents need. Consequently, even people who have never been active before and had no intention of becoming so find themselves helping to start organizations in their new community. Once the organization is safely under way, they drop out, and eventually the typical pattern develops, in which a small number of people are active in many organizations and the large majority are inactive.

The remaining changes listed earlier can be attributed to the move itself, and are thus an effect of suburban life. Probably the most important one—at least in a low price suburb—is the development of family and community financial problems. Since a house is more expensive to keep up than the apartments from which most people come, suburban life adds new expenditures to the family budget. Many of them are unavoidable ones. If they coincide with the increasing expenditures of a growing family, as they usually do, the household budget is often under considerable strain. Since the preponderance of young families also creates new needs for classrooms and teachers, the tax rate is likely to rise at the same time, thus increasing the financial burden even further.

This in turn has a number of other effects, most of them undesirable. Financial problems are a prime cause of marital conflicts, or a new source of discord for couples already saddled with marital difficulties. Moreover, these problems have consequences for the entire community. In American society, private expenditures have traditionally had higher priority than public ones. As the former rise, people try to reduce their financial problems by demanding reductions in public expenditures. This hampers the provision of needed community services, and especially so in a new community. Moreover, political conflicts develop between those who want additional services, and can pay the taxes, and those who want services cut to the bone because they are unwilling or unable to pay for them. Since school expenditures constitute about three-fourths of the local public expenditures, this conflict often focuses around the school and may extend to curriculum questions as well. This problem is typically found in the low and medium price suburbs, especially those which lack industrial taxpayers.

The move to the suburbs also creates behavior changes of a largely negative type for the adolescents and for those who deviate culturally from the majority of their neighbors. Adolescents are perhaps the most enthusiastic city dwellers in our society, since they are frequent users of urban entertainment facilities. Many of them suffer in the move to the low density suburb. Unless they have cars, they cannot easily get to the nearby shopping centers; and if they do go there, the proprietors object because high shopping center rents make adolescent trade unprofitable. As a result, the teenagers become bored, and may turn to vandalism and miscellaneous mischief to get even with the adults who have inflicted suburbia—or what some teenagers have called "endsville"—on them. Nevertheless, the actual delinquency rate remains low, mainly because the large majority of adolescents are middle-class ones whose life is taken up with school work and friends.

In the community I studied, the cultural minorities were not ethnic or religious groups, but cosmopolite middle- and upper middle-class families, and working-class people. The cosmopolites may move to suburbia because it is easier to raise their children there, but they miss the city's cultural facilities, as well as people with interests similar to their own. Although they become unhappy, their discontent has positive functions for the community. Quite often, they take more part in community activities than they would have in the city or in a more cosmopolite suburb because, like other minorities, they stream to organizations to find friends. Also, they set up civic groups which try to persuade the community to accept their ideas and high standards for education and municipal government. While the cosmopolites generally lack the votes to implement their standards, they are more influential than their numbers, and contribute organizational skill and knowledge to the community. Moreover, their ability to express themselves in the larger community adds to the total set of alternative policies under public discussion, thus improving the quality of the policy-making process.

A second group of cultural deviants is the working-class population from the city. Not only do they feel the economic pinch most severely, but some report that the distance from the city, and the lack of public transportation have cut them off from relatives and old friends. The ones who suffer most are the people who have come directly from neighborhoods in which they grew up, and especially those who cannot make friends in the new community. Since they may lack the social skills and the geographical mobility of the cosmopolites, they cannot defend themselves as easily against social isolation.

It should be noted that the problems of both the cosmopolites and the working-class people result from being in a numerical minority, rather than from suburban residence. They do not suffer from pressures to conform, but from a shortage of like-minded people in their surroundings. Were they to live in communities with more compatible people, many of their problems would disappear.

Most of the changes attributed to suburban life by the myth of suburbia are either insignificant, or not supported by the available evidence. For example, the increase in commuting time seemed, in my study, to be lower than is often thought. Fifty per cent of 400 people responding to a mail questionnaire indicated their journey to work was longer; 37 per cent, that it was now shorter. For the entire sample, the median journey was only thirty-three minutes each way. Among those interviewed, only about 10 per cent reported spending less time with their family, but about 40 per cent reported spending more time than they did in their previous residence. Moreover, 39 per cent of the respondents reported that the family did more things together than in their previous residence. Fifty-nine per cent reported no change, and only one person reported fewer joint activities.

As I noted earlier, most of the joint family activity is stimulated by the new house, and is likely to decrease as its novelty wears off. Nevertheless, two years of observation revealed no evidence that suburban life had any unilaterally harmful effect on either the quality or quantity of family life. The myth-makers' claim that suburbia is creating a new matriarchy in America is not justified either. Women may have greater equality and more influence in the home than their-mothers and grandmothers, but this is a universal trend in American society, especially among working-class and lower middle-class people.

Maladies such as status-striving, competition, and conformity, which are prominent in the suburban myth, are less so in the actual suburb. My observations suggested that much of what is called competition or status-seeking is really an expression of normal class differences, as seen by those of lower status. Thus, lower income respondents described the way of life of their more affluent neighbors as "showing off," or "trying to keep up with the Joneses," an interpretation that minimized their resentment over income inequalities. Higher income people had similarly deprecating comments about those behavior patterns of lower income people which differed from their own. At the same time, they ascribed similarities in the ways of life of lower income neighbors to a desire for conformity.

Enforced conformity has often been described as the scourge of suburban life; yet in the community I studied, instances of this were rare. Most people are willing to tolerate differences of behavior that do not affect them personally. The vast majority of suburbanites are therefore free to live as they please, and their frequent reports of having more privacy in the suburbs than they had in the city is one illustration of this freedom. People do conform in such matters as lawn care—and demand it from their neighbors—largely because they share personally in the appearance of the entire street front. Suburbanites also conform by copying each other's ideas in home improvements, but only those which they consider desirable or useful. People who deliberately strive to maximize their prestige, show off status symbols, or resort to conspicuous consumption are usually socially marginal types who have difficulty in relating to other people. Their neighbors feel sorry for them even while they criticize them. Such strivers are few in number.

Finally, there is no reason to believe that the move from the city to suburb, or suburban life itself, has any effect on mental health, other than a positive one. Most interview respondents report improvements in health and disposition. The number of crimes, suicide attempts, serious delinquent acts, and cases of mental illness, as noticed by doctors and ministers, are comparatively few in the community I studied; and if translated into rates, far below those reported for city inhabitants. Since the suburbs lack the lower-class populations which account for the majority of such pathologies, this is not surprising. I was able to get information about many of the people whose behavior suggested serious mental illness; and in almost every case, they had histories of similar disturbance in previous residences. Some of them moved to the suburb I studied in the false hope that the newness of the community and the change of environment would solve their problems.

Nor does the move to the suburbs lead to increased boredom and loneliness. Most people find that the house, the yard, and the increased social life leave them less time to be bored—in fact, less spare time generally—than life in a city apartment. For example, 40 per cent of fifty-five ex-Philadelphians interviewed on this question said they had never been bored, either in the city or in the suburb. Of the twenty-three who said they were sometimes bored, 9 reported no change, 8 were less bored in the suburb, and 6, more. These were mainly women, but the reasons for their boredom have little to do with the community. It was the result of the children growing up and needing them less, of husbands whose work kept them away from home too much, or of anxieties brought on by economic and marital problems.

This analysis may be summarized as follows. The move from city to suburb creates relatively few changes in behavior. Most of these, representing the achievement of aspirations held prior to the move, can be described as *intended* changes. They are effects not of suburban life, but of the larger cultural milieu in which people form their aspirations. This milieu has traditionally stressed the desirability of home ownership, and life in a single-family house. Since most of the intended changes stem from the change in house type, rather than the change in settlement type, the move to the suburb may be considered as the most recent form of a traditional aspiration.

A number of behavior changes which took place after people moved to the suburbs had nothing to do with pre-occupancy aspirations or contradicted them. They may be described as *unintended* changes. Some of them result from the newness of the community, but others can be traced to one or another aspect of suburban life. Economic problems, and the difficulties of the adolescents, are two examples. These, then, can be considered as effects of suburban life, although even they are not entirely caused by suburbia. But most of the effects which have been attributed to the suburb by the myth of suburbia are not supported by empirical evidence.

Why then, does the myth exist? By far the most important reason for its existence is the fact that, since World War II, many people have been able to raise their standards of living, and adopt styles of consumption previously available to the upper middle class only. One part of this change has been the move to the suburbs. Since the post-war subdivisions are a new phenomenon and a highly visible one, the ways of life which have been observed there have been attributed to the community, rather than to the age and class position of the people involved.

Most of the people who have written about suburbia come—like other writers—from the cosmopolite upper middle class. Their criticism of suburban life is actually directed at working- and lower middle-class, non-cosmopolite ways, which can be found in most city neighborhoods as well, but are not as visible there as they are in suburbia. For example, the suburbanites are criticized for turning their back on the city's cultural facilities, but what little evidence exists on the use of such facilities suggested that they are avoided by working- and lower middle-class people who live in the city as well. In short, the myth of suburbia is an implicit criticism of the non-cosmopolite nature of the working class and lower middle class, and is only a contemporary variation of a theme that has been prominent in American critical writing for many decades. The major innovation—and one that must be considered undesirable—is for the critic to invoke concepts of mental health and illness, and thus to identify as pathological what is in reality mainly a difference of class cultures between him and those he criticizes.

IMPLICATIONS FOR PHYSICAL AND SOCIAL PLANNING

My analysis of the alleged and real effects of suburbia has a number of implications for social theory, for city or physical planning, for social planning, and for the caretaking professions.

With respect to social theory, the fact that people's lives are not changed drastically by the move from city to suburb suggests that the differences between these settlement types are either fewer, or, more likely, less relevant to the way people live than has been traditionally believed. In short, the community itself does not shape people's ways of life as significantly as has been proposed by ecological and planning theory. The major behavior patterns are determined, rather, by the period of the life-cycle, and the opportunities and aspirations associated with class position.

At one time in American history, the local community did shape the processes that determine ways of life. When the country was rural, income, education, and occupational opportunity were determined within a small area. Today, however, many patterns of life are determined by national economic and social structures, and given the ease of geographical mobility, the community has become less important.

Physical planners, especially those with architectural training, believe that the physical characteristics of the community have important influences on people's ways of living, and that changes in housing and site design, density of structures and amount of open space can change their behavior. The findings I have reported here, and other studies of the impact of physical features on behavior, suggest that this belief is open to serious question. It fails to recognize some of the more important, but non-physical, causes of human behavior. For example, the planners who aim to eliminate urban sprawl—the discontinuous spreading of suburban subdivisions over the rural landscape—and who also wish people to make greater use of the city's downtown districts, have usually proposed that suburbanites move into urban elevator apartments, or into row-house neighborhoods closer to the edge of the city. It is not at all certain that this will solve the problem. Most of the suburbanites I interviewed have little interest in using downtown facilities, and would not move into the city or closer to it for the sake of shortening the journey to work and the wife's monthly or semi-monthly trip to the department store. Urban sprawl and the decline of the downtown can be halted only if more people want to make greater use of the city. These goals cannot be achieved solely by physical design, or even by mass transportation schemes; they require the development of cosmopolite interests among people. This in turn requires—among other things—changes in the education offered in public high schools and most colleges.

Ways of life are determined principally by economic and social conditions, not by architectural schemes. This means that future suburban planning must place greater emphasis on the problems of the suburban population, and this in turn requires the use of social planning methods that involve changes in the social, economic and political structure of our society, and in the programming of public services and caretaking functions.

Despite the generally positive effect of the suburban move, suburban residents have their share of problems. These problems are neither as sensational nor as distinctive to suburbia as the mythmakers have suggested, however. They are old and familiar ones that exist in the city as well, and have not yet been solved there—or wherever people may live.

Perhaps the most important problems are located in the family, both in the marital relationship and among the children. As I have already suggested, ex-city residents find family life improved after the move to the suburbs, but couples who had marital problems in the city have them in the suburbs too. These are familiar difficulties, brought about by sexual or cultural incompatibility, personality clashes, and emotional disturbances in one or both of the spouses. The children's problems are also familiar ones; for example, learning difficulties, serious emotional disturbances, conflicts over discipline with parents and teachers, as well as organic impairment and retardation.

One of the major causes of marital problems, in the suburbs as elsewhere, is economic. In many cases, it is not the lack of money per se which causes problems, since there is usually enough for the basic needs. The conflicts result from disagreement about the allocation of money for items other than food and shelter, and often reflect cultural differences and blocked communication between the spouses. Even so, there are also people for whom the problem is first and foremost financial; who could not really afford to move to the suburbs but have done so nevertheless. It would be arrogant—and useless—to recommend that they go back to the aging apartment buildings or crowded city neighborhoods from which they came. The only real solution is an economic one. Our society may be wealthy compared to others, but families who try to raise three children on $6000 a year are hardly affluent. In the short run, housing subsidies will help, but in the long run, further increases in real income are necessary. These—as well as changes in the tax structure—will subsequently reduce the financial difficulties of suburban municipalities.

My study supports previous findings that unhappy suburbanites are more likely to be women than men. For the latter, the suburb is a peaceful retreat from the city and the job. Most of the women are also content there. The wives of traveling salesmen, airplane pilots, and of other men whose work takes them out of the house for days or weeks on end are probably most unhappy. Many of the marital problems in the community I studied were found among such families. Their problem is not a suburban one, and indeed, the women seem to feel less isolated in the suburb than they did in their previous residence.

A less serious but numerically more important problem is that of the women who want to be more than housekeepers and mothers, especially among those who have gone to college. Some have solved this problem by taking part-time jobs, or be finding satisfying unpaid work in voluntary organizations and community service, meanwhile sending their children to nursery schools or day-care centers. Their problem is not unique to suburbia, and it is likely to become more widespread as larger numbers of women obtain college educations.

Adolescents, as I have already noted, face problems in suburbia, because they lack the after-school facilities that are available to them in the city. If these cannot be supplied commercially, they will have to be made available from public resources, with care being taken that they are programmed on the basis of adolescent needs, rather than by adult desires. This is more easily said than done. Adults have reacted quite negatively to the development of the adolescent youth culture that has developed in America, as elsewhere, over the past two decades. Many adults, especially in the working and lower middle classes, stereotype all teen-agers as delinquents. As a result, community leaders are hesitant about providing them with recreational facilities for fear that gang fights, sexual episodes, and other forms of misbehavior will upset the voters and cause them to blame the public officials.

The problems of bored middle-class adolescents are much less serious than those of working-class and lower-class ones. As Paul Goodman and others have noted, our society provides no function for the teen-ager who does not want to remain in school. This problem, which has nothing to do with the suburbs, is exacerbated in middle-class suburbs by the fact that such teen-agers are a hostile and unhappy minority in a predominantly middle-class environment.

Finally, another group who suffer in the suburbs—as they do everywhere—are people who differ too greatly from their neighbors and other residents, and are therefore socially isolated. As I noted earlier, in the community I studied, this affected primarily the cosmopolite minority, and working-class women. The former can fend for themselves, and eventually move to a community of more compatible people. In this process, however, the original community loses their participation in civic problem-solving activities. I am frankly uncertain whether or not this is a serious loss in a working-class or lower middle-class community. While upper middle-class people have the intellectual and administrative skills I described earlier, they also tend to see community problems—and their solutions—from an upper middle-class perspective, and they are often blind to the problems faced by the other classes. This question urgently requires empirical research.

Working-class women—as well as their families—who are in a minority in the neighborhood cannot solve their isolation problem as easily as others, especially those who have difficulty in entering into new roles. They might be better off if they remained in their old neighborhoods in the city, or if they moved into the modern dwellings being made available there by urban renewal projects in their price range.

I have tried to describe what appear to be the major problems of suburban residents, especially in low and medium priced communities. Few are distinctive to suburbia, and they bear little resemblance to those described in the myth of suburbia. The problems aired by the myth-makers are principally those of their suburban cosmopolite friends, and of the upper middle class generally.

Needless to say, most suburbanites are not cosmopolites; they are people who lived in the city more from necessity than from choice. Thanks to the FHA, the suburbs have made it possible for them to achieve much of what they want out of life, although the suburban exodus has in turn raised yet unsolved problems in metropolitan government, such as the financing of public services, which I have not discussed here.

Because suburbanites are above average in education, income, and many other characteristics—even in a lower middle-class suburb—their life is comparatively problem-free, and the problems I have listed are much less serious than those of less fortunate Americans. Indeed, the most critical problems in American society are to be found among the people who cannot move to the suburbs, who are doomed to a deprived existence in urban and rural slums because of low income, lack of occupational skill, and racial discrimination. Their needs take precedence over all of the problems I have described here.

70 Individual and Group Values

ROBIN M. WILLIAMS, JR.

Though it is difficult to analyze an entire sociocultural system as a single entity, it is useful in comparative studies to attempt to describe the basic values of an entire society. In this selection, Williams not only specifies the fifteen major value-belief clusterings that he feels characterize American culture but also attempts to indicate the direction of change in these values in the twentieth century. Moreover, he provides an insightful exploration of the ways and means by which values can change—a useful analysis providing sharp contrast to a commonly held position that values are stable and constant.

• • • • •

It is striking that the social diagnoses of our times that have attracted the widest popular attention and acclaim are interpretations only loosely connected with any systematic analysis of "hard" data. Are Americans today more "other-directed" than in the 1890's? Where is the unequivocal evidence? Is our society being deadened by overconformity—or is it disintegrating through lack of consensus and commitment? Is the Organization Man of the 1960's more stereotyped than the businessmen of the 1920's? Are the urban middle classes today more preoccupied with "status-seeking" than the newly rich of the Gilded Age or the respectable small-town citizens of the age of Babbitt? Have the contemporary American people lost humane sensitivity in an urban world hurrying on under the awareness of genocide, hydrogen bombs, and technologically advanced surveillance and brutality in a thousand forms? Where is the evidence? Yet confident assertions abound.

Many observers of the national society suggest that the intensity of commitment to particular values and beliefs has diminished. It is said that exposure to a vast variety of experiences reduces exclusive beliefs, and absolute commitments. Is there systematic evidence of changes in commitment? If change in this respect has taken place, does it really mean an important change in such behavior as paying taxes, answering the call of the military draft, abiding by marriage and familial norms, defending political principles, and so on? In our view, the presently available data on the alleged value changes are very far from satisfactory—yet the allegations in question bear on the very foundations of societal survival.

"Ethnocentric" values are not all of one piece, and it is essential to make distinctions concerning both content and "formal" properties (intensity, rigidity, differentiation, explicitness). If succes-

SOURCE: *The Annals of the American Academy of Political and Social Science,* vol. 371 (May 1967), 20–37. Reprinted by permission of the author and the publisher. • The author is Henry Scarborough Professor of Social Science, Cornell University. He has served with the Research Branch of the United States War Department. He has been a member of the Scientific Advisory Board and a consultant to the Welfare Administration and is currently a member of the National Advisory Mental Health Council. He is past president of the American Sociological Association. His major interests include social organization and race and ethnic relations. He is the author of *The Reduction of Intergroup Tensions, American Society,* and *Strangers Next Door;* and coauthor of *Schools In Transition.*

sive studies, using a large battery of comparable indicators, show a reduction in conventionalized, simple, rigid, dogmatic evaluations and stereotypes of racial, ethnic, and religious groupings, it will be important to know the extent to which the apparent reduction in "prejudice" is paralleled by growth in more complex and intellectualized invidious evaluations.

Knowledge, beliefs, and values evolved out of psychiatric and social science research and experience have been influential to an appreciable degree in a limited shift away from punishment and custody toward treatment and rehabilitation. Periodic sample studies of values relevant to this area would be highly useful in evaluating national and state and local policies and practices.

Currently it is difficult to gauge the extent to which an "apprehensive concern" with leisure extends outside a few limited circles of intellectuals and publicists. Certainly, however, the complex and changing evaluations of work and leisure in different strata and segments of the nation will be highly relelvant to many future policies.

Great debate has centered upon alleged changes in expressive or aesthetic values supposed to have occurred with the extension of literacy and the rise of "mass" media. The criticisms against "popular culture" are sufficiently repetitive to bear the appearance of "an established ideology or critique." The critique asserts that popular taste is low and is being further lowered by commercialized popular culture—a process which in turn debases high culture, adversely affects values and emotional processes of consumers, and corrodes the social structure. What are the value facts? Does anyone know? If not, why not?

Many critics of American society today seem to concentrate upon two alleged characteristics—*shapelessness* and *meaninglessness.* Under the first, we find recitals of loss of sense of belonging, absence of standards, loss of norms, uprootedness, destruction of traditions, disintegration of multibonded groups and "organic" communities, loss of cultural continuity and sense of history, and blurring of qualitative distinctions in experience. Under the second indictment we encounter references to "existential nausea," emptiness, loss of interest in work, alienation, diffusion of identity, total relativism, "failure of nerve." Are these foreboding diagnoses incorrect? If there is serious truth in them, where and how and to whom do they apply?

The listing of "needed" information on values easily could be extended. We are under no illusions, however, that anything like "full coverage" is to be expected. The suggestions here advanced are intended only to illustrate a range of promising possibilities.

In any case, we do believe that—whatever else is done or not done in this field —we should work toward a comprehensive system of social data-reporting and analysis in which information concerning values would contribute to a diagnosis of the main emphases of the national societal system. In the past, heavy emphasis in American policy has been upon the *goal-attainment* sector, with secondary effort toward maintaining and strengthening generalized *adaptative* capacities (capital formation, some technological development, some—instrumental—education). Conspicuously neglected have been the other two main functional aspects of social systems—the *integration* of components and *pattern-maintenance.* In our national drive to "get things done," we have generated vast internal social cleavages and frictions—dislocations and disintegrations that represent enormous societal "overhead costs" of a peculiarly serious kind. Similarly, the intense concentration upon political, military, technological, and economic attainments probably has severely strained the maintenance of some parts of the central systems of beliefs and value criteria; this might be thought of as a kind of depletion of cultural capital. It would be conceivable that inadequate sensitivity to such, largely unintended, consequences could set off such sequences of maldistribution of the flow of societal energies as to eventually interfere in a major way with the system's generalized capacities to survive in its environment, for example, through poisoning and pollution of the biosphere, through disabling internal social conflicts, or through excessive dissipation of human and material resources in exhausting national-political enterprises.

• • • • •

MODES OF CHANGE IN VALUES AND BELIEFS

Among the ways in which values and beliefs can change, the following are noteworthy:

1. *Creation:* A new evaluative criterion or belief is developed out of new experience and becomes effective, at some level, in regulating behavior.
2. *Relatively sudden destruction:* Although extremely rare, there are some instances in which there is a quick extinction of a previously accepted value.
3. *Attenuation:* Slow diminution of the intensity of affect and commitment; decrease in interest and attention, as fewer and fewer persons promote, support, teach, or defend the belief or value orientation.
4. *Extension:* Application to objects and events in addition to those included in the original sphere of relevance.
5. *Elaboration:* The value or belief is progressively rationalized, symbolized, dramatized, documented and otherwise made more complex or more embedded in its sociocultural context.
6. *Specification:* A generalized orientation increasingly is defined in terms of a variety of particular contexts, resulting in modifications and restrictions. In the United States it seems that "freedom" is not now felt to be violated by compulsory school attendance, or peacetime military conscription.
7. *Limitation:* It would be a limiting case if any given value—in confronting other values—were not altered at all; generally there is some change even if only in the direction of absolution. A frequent outcome, however, is that a particular value comes to be bounded or limited by the recognized claims of other values. Thus, in American democratic creeds and practices, it has always been necessary to accommodate a persisting strain between *freedom* and *equality:* each is necessary for the democratic position, but neither can be pushed to extremes without negating the other.
8. *Explication:* In the form of folk virtues, values are typically implicit—indeed, often altogether inaccessible to explicit formulation by their bearers. At the opposite extreme, highly systematic explications of values are formulated in creedal or philosophical systems. In American society there is a vast accumulation of explicit value statements. Scattered evidence suggests increasingly explicit affirmation of major values. Such explication seems to be favored by rapid changes in specific social conditions and norms as well as by direct challenges to the standards themselves, for example, the attacks of totalitarian political movements.
9. *Consistency:* A concern with consistency itself represents a distinctive value position. Greater systematic explicitness at the level of national political assertions and mass-media creeds almost certainly increases a sense of "contradiction," "inconsistency," and "hypocrisy" when viewed against some of the daily realities of behavior.
10. *Intensity (absolution, centrality):* A value initially accepted as one among many standards may become so intensely held

and promoted as to become the center of life. A value formerly the focus of many other criteria may lose its central intellectual and emotional *raison d'être*, become relativized, and recede into the ranks of the ordinary criteria of daily life.

A society in which the store of knowledge concerning the consequences of action is large and is rapidly increasing is a society in which received norms and their "justifying" values will be increasingly subjected to questioning and reformulation. As our knowledge concerning the consequences of racial segregation has exposed effects upon education, employment, income, family life, crime, and intergroup hostility and conflict, value conflicts have been revealed, and some appear to have been sharpened. As we learn more about the consequences of different kinds of childhood discipline upon personality development, pressures are generated to re-evaluate punitive measures, permissiveness, and so on.

It is likely that in the United States over the last three decades there has developed an increase in the positive evaluation of *cognitive* criteria for judging both individual conduct and collective policy and practice. As levels of formal education rise—both on the average and in terms of the proportion of persons mastering really high levels of knowledge and conceptual skills—and as societal processes inexorably call attention to interdependence of consequences of social actions, the disregard of facts and causal reasoning is likely to be increasingly regarded as a *moral* fault. This tentative prediction is not intended to be an expression of wish-fulfillment. Rather we believe that the indicated direction of value movement already is objectively present, as suggested by the increased part played in legislative, administrative, and even judicial decisions by relatively systematic attention to cognitive considerations as to both "the facts of the case" and to "causes and consequences"—with regard to military strategy and tactics, welfare policies, penal and correctional practices (rehabilitation, the death penalty), effectiveness of educational and therapeutic practices, economic policies, transportation, urban development, environmental pollution, and many other areas. Obviously, this is not to say that "rationality" (however conceived) is necessarily increasing, nor that attempted solutions to problems are necessarily increasingly "adequate," whatever that might mean. It is only to suggest as worthy of further definition and study the proposition that a "knowledgeable society" will increasingly give a positive evaluation of knowledge—up to some limit not yet closely approached.

. . . . .

PRESENT KNOWLEDGE OF VALUES IN AMERICAN SOCIETY

It is not possible here, of course, to present the massive materials required to support synthesizing descriptions of values in the total social system of the United States. On the basis of an earlier extended analysis we have distinguished some fifteen major value-belief clusterings that are salient in American culture, as follows: (1) activity and work; (2) achievement and success; (3) moral orientation; (4) humanitarianism; (5) efficiency and practicality; (6) science and secular rationality; (7) material comfort; (8) progress; (9) equality; (10) freedom; (11) democracy; (12) external conformity; (13) nationalism and patriotism; (14) individual personality; (15) racism and related group superiority.

Running through these complex orientations, as still more highly generalized themes, is an emphasis on the worth of active mastery rather than passive acceptance of events; an external rather than an inward view of the world; an outlook that perceives society and history as open-ended, not static; an inclination to prefer or put trust in rationalism as opposed to traditionalism; an interest in orderliness; a universalistic rather than a particularistic social ethic; horizontal or equalitarian rather than hierarchical social relationships; and a high evaluation of individual personality rather than collective identity and responsibility.

A highly useful synthesis of data on public opinion by V. O. Key, Jr., has added specificity to several of the above characterizations and contains important analyses of the structures and processes that intervene between the orientations of the populace and the decisions and actions of legislators and administrators and executives. One of the clearest findings is that political and governmental decisions in the short-run often are not closely connected with the diffusely held values of the unorganized electorate.

The most important evidence on values comes from records of actual behavior in all areas of American life. Supplemental data from research on records of expressive culture have only recently begun to accumulate. The following example may suggest how this type of new information is being generated.

That the possibilities of value-analysis through studies of mass-readership fiction goes beyond any simple "counting" procedure is illustrated by an ingenious and fine-grained study of magazine fiction. Comparing 1890, 1925, and 1955, the analysis shows that major characters in more recent times have been depicted more often in terms of "fun morality" (rather than "puritanism"), technological progress (rather than technological conservatism), and lessened familism. Positive orientations to sexual freedom and rejection of marriage reached a peak in 1925, declining somewhat by the mid-1950's. For most of the values studied, the magazine fiction seems to have appealed to an urban and well-educated readership that was considerably more "liberal" than the general population. Thus, the fictional accounts did not simply "reflect reality" in some average or total way, but showed quite specific kinds of transformation directed toward the readership population. Allowing for this selectivity, the stories seem to reveal important directions of change in values. Major omissions of certain ideological values, for example, concerning religion, divorce, sexual promiscuity, capitalism, or overtly political issues, suggests "veto" or "censoring" mechanisms intervening between prevailing values and published content.

A number of works have relied heavily upon a variety of historical documents and commentaries; although many of the conclusions thus derived are necessarily impressionistic, they do provide usual points of departure for establishing base lines of change.

Increasingly, the assertions of such studies are being tested by more detailed and systematic approaches. Thus, the general impression that recent decades have witnessed a decline in achievement values has been examined by several specific analyses of cultural products. For instance, classification of a random sample of editorials in the *National 4-H Club News* from 1924 to 1958 showed a significant decline in emphasis on the value of achievement (and no significant change in *affiliation* or *co-operation* values). Similar results were found in an analysis of advertising in the *Ladies' Home Journal* from 1890 to 1956. Magazine fiction and mass heroes (for example, entertainers) also show indications of lessened stress on excellence of achievement and more on the "rewards"

Value-Belief Complexes	Directions of Change—Period (Approximate)	
	1900–1945	1945–1966
Activity	Indeterminate	–*
Work	–	–
Achievement	–	+ (post-Sputnik I)
Success	+	+
Material Comfort	+	+
Humanitarianism (Domestic)	+	+
Humanitarianism (War)	+	–
"Absolute" Moral Orientation	–	Indeterminate
Practicality	+	–
Efficiency	+	–
Science and Secular Rationality	+	+
Progress	+	–
Freedom	Indeterminate	–
Equality	+	+
Democracy	+	Indeterminate
Conformity (to Social Pressure)	+	+
Individual Personality	+	Indeterminate
Nationalism	+	– to +
Racism–Group Superiority	–	–
Totals		
Increase	13	8
No Change or Indeterminate	2	3
Decrease	4	8

* (–) is decrease; (+) is increase.

of being successful. McClellan shows that frequency of achievement imagery in stories in widely used children's readers rose to a peak about 1890 and then declined to a point in 1950 at about the level of 1850. (An index of innovation patents issued per million population rose also to a peak in 1890 and then declined.) Several other studies have pointed in the same direction. Our own impression from the assorted available information is that "achievement" has indeed receded in salience and intensity in relation to "success," but that the change is a shift in emphasis rather than a reversal of values and that achievement remains an outstanding value orientation.

In an ingenious study, Greenstein was able to fit together a number of studies of children's heroes and exemplars ("What person you would most like to resemble?"), dating from the 1890's down to very recent years. The data indicated declining interest in "serious" as over against "popular" entertainers, consistent with Lowenthal's finding concerning magazine biographies. But there is no clear evidence of any trend in identification or aspiration with regard to business and political leaders—such figures always have been chosen as objects of avowed emulation by only a very small percentage of the children studied at any particular period. We suggest the hypothesis that *achievement* values will be stressed in a society that has both a strong consensus on moral standards and relatively good objective opportunity for goal-achievement. On the other hand, *affective* values, stressing "enjoyment," tend to come to the forefront in two different types of situations: (a) in prosperous and secure societies, or (b) in societies in which rewards for sustained achievement are low and risks high. *Collective-integrative* values, yet again, will be stressed in societies severely and persistently threatened by other societies. War and the threat of war are major stimuli to collectivism, both as a condition and as a value orientation.

Space forbids similar documentation of change and continuity for the other fourteen themes in our list. In another place the writer has tried to summarize tentative impressions of change, based on a fuller review of existing studies, in the table above.

In terms of these broad estimates, during the period from around 1900 up to the end of World War II, the major thrust was in the direction of further positive development of the themes analyzed. Since 1945, however, there is a suggestion of lessened emphasis on activity and achievement, some disillusionment concerning "progress," and some loss in humanitarianism under the exigencies of war. The available information is highly imprecise, and these changes should not be overemphasized; on net balance, during the last half-century the conclusion probably has to be "the same main values—only more so." The changes that have occurred are clearly important, but for the most part they grow directly out of elements already present at the beginning of the period of review.

• • • • •

71 Toward the National Urban Society: The Japanese Experience

CHARLES F. GALLAGHER

The pace of urbanization has become so rapid in many of the developed nations of the world that it seems possible to conceive of a "national urban society"—one in which industrialization and urban attitudes pervade an entire nation. Though no such nation yet exists, it appears that Japan is well on the way to reaching that level of industrialization. This selection, then, gives us some idea of what life might be like in a society that is completely urbanized.

In the domain of urbanization, as well as in the entire area of social modernization of which it is a vital part, Japan has offered in this century overlapping and at times almost coexisting views of a process operating in three kinds of societies: the traditional pre-industrial; the classical industrial urban; and the post-industrial national urban. The particular advantage of the Japanese case is that it reveals, more closely and intricately bound together and more clearly than elsewhere, the immediate past, the present, and the shadow of many things to come. In the standard terminology of urban studies, this is to say that Japan has been transformed in the past century from a largely agrarian country with a considerable number of traditional mercantile and administrative centers forming a solid urban nucleus, to a predominantly (74 percent at the end of 1968) urban industrial society, which in turn is now on its way to becoming the world's first *de facto* large-scale, information-oriented, national urban society, in which distinctions of class, status, education, culture, place of origin and residence have already been or are rapidly being eliminated. A study of the process or urbanization in contemporary Japan underlines the direction in which its universalist meritocracy is moving to create a society in which virtually everything is available to everybody everywhere, in accordance with his aspirations and his achievements.

. . . . .

A macroscopic view of urbanization within the framework of national development requires an understanding of what is happening in rural areas and of the relationship of those areas to the modern cities. In Japan for the past

SOURCE: Charles F. Gallagher, "Urbanization, Integration, and National Society: The Japanese Experience," in *Man, City, and Nature,* tentative title (Hanover, N.H.: American Universities Field Staff, in press). The selection is from the proceedings of a conference on "Urbanization: Freedom and Diversity in the Modern City," sponsored by the American Universities Field Staff, Hanover, N.H. Reprinted by permission of the author and the publisher. • Charles F. Gallagher is a member of the American University Field Staff, a nonprofit educational organization working with a number of universities in the United States. He served as a Japanese Language Officer in World War II and later served as Cultural Property Advisor during the occupation of Japan. His major interests include the study of Japan and the countries of North Africa. He is the author of *The United States and North Africa* and is contributing author to *Foreign Affairs, The Virginia Quarterly Review,* and *The Middle East Forum.*

twenty years or so, there has been a steady physical drainoff from the countryside together with a pronounced material, and to a degree cultural, upgrading of life. The average Japanese farmer today is comparatively more privileged in the ownership of major consumer durables than his rural counterpart in France or than the population of West Germany as a whole, both urban and rural, five years ago. Within his own society, the rural Japanese is virtually abreast of his city cousin in ownership of television sets, electric washing machines, sewing machines, and a number of minor electric appliances (such as the electric rice cooker which has transformed domestic life everywhere in the nation). Moreover, rural areas are more than fully participating in national economic growth and prosperity. Consumption-expenditure level studies of the Japanese government indicate that with 1960 as a base (=100), consumption in urban households reached 138.6 in 1967, while that of rural households rose to 156.7.

To affluence of rural Japan is easily visible to the observer. To a certain extent it is linked, as in several other industrial states, with the residual political influence of a bloc that became aware of its power at a time when it was being exhorted, just after the war, to see the nation through difficult times by increasing its productivity. But affluence is only part of the rural scene; even more important is the technological innovation and progress that has in part brought about the affluence, and equally worthy of underlining is the receptivity to innovation on the part of the rural population, without which the transformation would have been impossible. The Japanese farmer has always been a skilled and industrious cultivator, but today he has become a technician using improved cultivation methods, mechanical and chemical aids, and modernized farm management procedures, all of which have made him into an agro-businessman.

Nevertheless,—partly because of the call of the city to younger people and partly because modern farming requires many fewer hands—the countryside continues to empty at a regular rate. Twenty-three of Japan's 46 prefectures lost population between 1960–65. The farm household population declined by almost 6,000,000 persons between early 1960 and the end of 1966, and the number of persons engaged in farming within each household also declined. At the same time, the number of households engaged only in farming decreased in the same period from 2,078,000 to 1,151,000, while the number of those engaged in part-time nonfarming activity increased from 1,942,000 to 2,514,000. Because of the accessibility of Japanese towns, such secondary nonfarming activity often involves part-time or periodic work in nearby medium-sized cities. In this way, too, the division between urban and rural life has recently been much narrowed.

The outstanding result of what has been described above—the extreme concentration of population and the urban sprawl now extending beyond and between the largest cities and metropolitan regions—has been the gradual formation of a metropolitan corridor analogous to those in the northeastern United States and the Benelux-Ruhr area. However, population density along the national urban axis stretching through ten prefectures from the Tokyo-Yokohama region to the Osaka-Kobe region is greater than in similar regions of America and Europe. About 46,000,000 persons inhabit an area of 46,648 sq. km., roughly the size of Maryland and Delaware together. Slightly more than half the Japanese population (54 million of 101 million)—a figure almost equal to the entire population of West Germany or the United Kingdom—is found in 14 contiguous prefectures along the Pacific coast from Fukuoka in the southwest to Chiba in the northeast. This comprises an area of 73,140 sq. km., less than one-third the area of West Germany or the United Kingdom. Of these about 22 million live in the Keihin (Tokyo-Yokohama) Metropolitan Region, 12 million in the Keihanshin (Kyoto-Osaka-Kobe) Metropolitan Region, and 6 million in the Nagoya Metropolitan Region. By 1975 these figures will be even more disconcerting; it is estimated that about 54–55 million persons will then be living in the ten-prefecture national urban axis.

• • • • •

The emergence of a national urban culture naturally involves the generalizing of urban attitudes, values, and behavior patterns throughout the society. This feedout touches several crucial areas: participancy (the feeling that all nationals are effectively taking part in the construction of the society); equality (of all citizens vis-a-vis national institutions—which, when the time-space dimensions of the society are reduced, are no longer so remote and abstract); contract relations and impersonality in public dealings; and a much-widened area of freedom of choice and opportunity for diversity (in this respect, one has only to look at groups of Japanese with obviously large rural or neo-urban components—the Dodsworths of their time—touring Hong King, Honolulu, or Rome, to see the widened area as a reality).

Japan today is on the edge of the knife with regard to the emergence of a national urban society; it will probably be so for another decade at least. But the drift is clear. Feedout can be seen in the many small- and medium-sized towns (there are 120 cities with more than 100,000 inhabitants) which, with their multi-storied *hyakkaten* or *depato* (variety and department stores), a number of sometimes simple but sometimes elegant specialty shops, self-styled "supermarkets," *pachinko* parlors, cinemas, bars, and restaurants, are taking on metropolitan consumption and behavior patterns at a galloping rate. Hitherto Japanese sociologists have regarded a population figure of 200,000 as necessary for urban patterns to take and in turn spread their influence. Now that figure is coming down, and there are increasing numbers of towns with 50,000–100,000 inhabitants that are evolving into small-scale metropolitan centers. Even with a higher figure, however, there is not one prefecture in Japan which does not have a city of at least 150,000.

Feedout is also seen today in the changed psychological relations of the city dweller and the countryman. It is harder and harder to find a "genuine" peasant. Locally-produced specialties (*meibutsu*) which travelers to distant areas once brought back as gifts, are today for sale everywhere in the nation, usually made, packed, and distributed by cooperatives who have multiple shop outlets in the large cities. Lingering rural feelings of inadequacy are counterbalanced by the growing urban nostalgia for the peace and quiet of the countryside, as well as often for a resurgence of the old, "more solid" rural values. If suburbanization has not taken hold in Japan as it has in other advanced countries, in contrast, the idea of a second home seems to be becoming popular: a mountain chalet, a small beach house, a vacation home in Hokkaido, are all part of the urban dream that now begins to view the country with new eyes. As, in the recent past, the sometime village-like character of large Japanese cities provided a link with tradition for migrants to the city, so now the increased sophistication of the country has an equally important role. Both have worked in the national interest: the first helped Japan pass through the crucible of industrialization; the second is smoothing the transition to a post-industrial national urban society.

It needs stressing that the groundwork for this process was carefully laid out some time back in the domains of information, education, and communications. The relevance of transportation has already been insisted upon. And wherever one turns in the study of the modernization of Japan the role played by information-diffusion stands out. With regard to urban-rural relations, the blanketing of the nation by national newspaper chains publishing simultaneous regional editions with the highest circulations in the world have been of importance since the beginning of the century. Certainly the most vital factor for rural integration is the ubiquitousness of television, the unusually high quality of mass programming, and the instructional (as opposed to the informational and discussive) bent of educational TV—generally considered by those in the field to be the best in the world—mainly directed at secondary and primary school students with the aim of making instruction everywhere of equal excellence. Beyond that, though, national educational TV in Japan is beginning to put across the idea of continuous technical and intellectual retraining, a nation constantly at school—a concept furthered by the extensive use of TV training and control in all large Japanese enterprises today. The rapid growth of advertising, in which field expenditures have risen almost 700 percent in the last ten years, and the semi-subliminal use of slogan lines during regular TV programming, bring together communications and consumption in a package which, while it may be regretted by some, has done more than any other single item to make rural Japan urban-equivalent.

Finally, though, it is not merely the existence of communications facilities but their use that is significant. Nothing is more indicative of the Japanese transformation than this: that with approximately as many telephones per capita as West Germany or France, the call frequency rate per telephone is about 2,600 a year in Japan compared to 700 in West Germany and 400 in France. In the same way, the Japanese take more train trips per capita, in the classical period of the cinema (until 1960) they saw more movies per capita, and they now spend more hours watching television per capita than anyone else.

• • • • •

A word of caution should perhaps be inserted here so that it be clearly understood that it is a macrocosmic, medium-range, and dominant trend that is being described. Of course, the urban-equivalent national society in Japan is still incomplete. Of course, rural existence in southern Kyushu or the Tohoku cannot be compared in variety, quality, or income to urban life. More excitement and more money are still more easily to be had in the cities, and considerable variations exist in average earnings according to region. These are, by and large however fewer than in France and many fewer than in Italy. Moreover, they are diminishing rapidly. In the summer of 1968 agricultural workers were being offered the equivalent of $10 a day in vain; they were not available and their place was being taken by newly-developed, automated rice-planters and harvesters.

Equally, the quality of urban life in Japan leaves much to be desired with respect to housing, sanitation facilities, air pollution, lack of green spaces, etc. Some observers of the Japanese scene may choose to emphasize the negative elements in modern urban life, and many Japanese researchers themselves tend to underscore them—often because they passionately wish to better things via exposure, and sometimes for ideological reasons.

It is true that, more often than not, city life in Japan is harried, exhausting, hectic, claustrophobic, grimy, and at times vulgar and tasteless. But is is also electric in concentrated excitement, intellectually stimulating, culturally rich and varied in the capital, more civil than in most countries, and above all in a state of constant ferment and change. It is distinctly not a mere struggle to exist, and when one wonders how the Japanese stand the pace, the answer may lie in their understanding that the process at work is, like that of modernization as a whole, one of a ceaseless upgrading of responses to situations of ever-increasing complexity and variety. Given their penchant for determined response to intellectual challenges, the Japanese ability to maintain the pace becomes more comprehensible.

In the end, what is of much greater importance than these static descriptions, is the *tempo* of socio-psychological change and, in its most recent speedup, the broad diffusion of attitudinal change among all strata of the population. *The intellectual framework for a national urban society appears to have been laid as solidly as has the physical infrastructure, and both are equally vital.* When questions of habitat, sanitary facilities, and social services are more fully taken up within a few years—the next Medium Term Economic Plan now renamed the Economic and Social Development Program (April 1967–March 1972) begins to treat them with new emphasis—it seems likely that they will be tackled with the massive gusto that has marked the Japanese approach to all other matters of modernization.

The importance of tempo and trend in socio-psychological change can best be shown by comparing Japan to highly urbanized societies in Europe, especially Latin Europe. There, where a strong sense of individualism had previously existed, the citizen today often feels constrained by the pressure of city life on his individualism, and the public level of frustration is high. In Japan, however, urbanization for the past generation and the beginnings of a national urban society today are associated with the removal of social restraints and a new flowering of individualism. This has happened in so short a time that the memory of past restraint is still strong, so that both tempo and trend reinforce a crosslinkage of urbanism, modernity, and freedom. Thus, even when complaining about the worst problems of city life, the Japanese have in this important respect been more prepared psychologically to understand what modern urbanism might offer at its best potential, and to see that it is the intellectual, social, and physical mobility in their society today that gave birth to their present "urban condition," is an essential ingredient of it, and is, in the last analysis, the watchdog for it.

But just as mobility brings opportunities for freedom, so does freedom carry with it the threat of loneliness inspired by autonomy, and the dangers of the unlimited possibilities for change, longed for yet feared as unknown. The nervousness so often remarked in contemporary urban society in Japan is in part linked to the tensions of the day, clearly, but it also derives from an excitement of the spirit that realizes that this present is keyed into the awesome opportunities of the future.

Thus, the national urban society comes to the thresholds of spatial freedom and chronological freedom at the same time. For it can flourish everywhere with equal facility, and the seemingly unbearable tensions of the present lead to the almost unimaginable accomplishments of the future. And these thresholds are in fact horizons which are completed by what might be called the ultimates of freedom that are implicit in the entire process of modernization: constant self-renewal through the rational reexamination of all pertinent information and the continuous search for objective truth.

Only the past then remains to be integrated into the all-embracing, timeless freedom of a modern society. As it transcends its present with its future, how can it reconcile itself with its past? The concept of constant self-renewal suggests one answer, and this takes us back, at the end, to the Ise Shrines—ritually and periodically dismantled every twenty years and then replaced by an identical set of structures. Here, where every Japanese wishes to make a pilgrimage at least once in his lifetime, at the wellsprings of Japanese culture and history, can be seen better than anywhere else the subtle relationship between changing and remaining, adapting and becoming, the past and the future.

• • • • •

72 What Makes Mao a Maoist?

STUART R. SCHRAM

73 Report on an Investigation of the Peasant Movement in Hunan, March, 1927

MAO TSE-TUNG

Americans know relatively little about the political institutions of most non-Western nations and probably less about the People's Republic of China than the others. The limited communication between the United States and mainland China perpetuates our ignorance and breeds misinformation and misunderstanding. The following two selections provide some insight into the development of the contemporary Maoist government. In the first of the two selections Stuart Schram, a British student of China, analyzes some of the factors that led to the Communist revolution, and the development of the People's Republic under Mao Tse-tung's leadership. This provides a background for the second selection by Mao himself. The latter, from one of Mao's early (1927) reports, is his reply to critics of the peasants' revolutionary activities. It illustrates the revolutionary process of destroying the old and creating new political institutions. In a letter to one of this book's editors, Edgar Snow characterized the report from which this selection by Mao is taken as follows:

> *. . . the whole content of the Report is so down to earth, so full of the flavor of rural life and toil, and the deeps of murderous passions of the landlord-peasant class struggle, which Mao understood and succeeded in articulating and mobilizing, that it helps us to comprehend the revolution better than "mature" theorizing of a later period.*

MR. SCHRAM

In May, 1853, a correspondent for The New York Tribune by the name of Karl Marx, who regularly wrote for that newspaper on the European workers' movement, contributed an article called "Revolution in China and in Europe." In it he discussed the possible impact of "rebellion" in China on England—then the leading world power—and through England on the European order as a whole, venturing the "very paradoxical assertion" that events in China might well prove to be the most important single cause of revolutionary change in Europe. He found in this a striking illustration of the views of that "most profound yet fantastic speculator," Georg Friedrich Hegel, who was "wont to extol as one of the ruling secrets of nature what he called the law of the contact of extremes."

"It would," wrote Marx, "be a curious spectacle, that of China sending dis-

SOURCE: *The New York Times Magazine* (March 8, 1970), pp. 32–82, passim. • Stuart R. Schram is professor of politics and head of the Contemporary China Institute of the School of Oriental and African Studies at The University of London. He is author of *Protestantism and Politics in France, The Political Thought of Mao Tse-Tung,* and *Mao Tse-Tung.*

order into the Western world while the Western powers, by English, French and American war-steamers, are conveying 'order' to Shanghai, Nanking and the mouths of the Great Canal." Of such a curious spectacle we are today the witnesses—but the details of the picture diverge substantially from those foretold by Marx. America now comes first rather than last in the list of the "European" powers intervening in the Far East, weapons more modern than "war-steamers" are employed, and the action takes place well to the south of Shanghai. But these are merely external and superficial differences compared to the change in the nature of the Chinese "disorder," and the way it is transmitted to the West. If there was one thing Marx thought Asians were incapable of producing, it was ideas relevant to the modern world. In his view, China would contribute to revolution in Europe only by disrupting British commerce. And yet today the Little Red Book, containing the words of a peasant from Hunan Province, is read and quoted by students from Berkeley to the Sorbonne. What is the explanation for this "contact of extremes"?

The response that Mao's ideas have found in the West must be understood in the context of developments within our own society, but the ideas themselves have been shaped by half a century's experience of the Chinese revolution. It would be exceedingly rash to assert that Mao's contribution to the theory and practice of revolution has now been finally and definitively spelled out, and that he has no more surprises in store for us. Nevertheless, the Ninth Congress of the Chinese Communist party in April, 1969, marked, if not the end of the cultural revolution, at least the end of one major phase, and in the intervening months the broad contours of the pattern that Mao is endeavoring to establish have become increasingly clear. It is therefore an appropriate moment to sum up his life's work.

The inhabitants of Mao's native province have long been renowned in China for their military and political talents. When Mao was born in 1893, Hunan was already in the forefront of the strivings toward intellectual and political renewal that were to lead to the Reform Movement of 1898. This attempt to modernize the political system was soon crushed by the reactionary Empress Dowager, but the problems it had raised remained. China was in danger, not merely from the incursions of the foreigners, Western and Japanese, who had been trampling on the country and carving out spheres of influence ever since the Opium War of 1840, but above all from her own weakness and failure to adapt to the modern world. Only if a remedy could be found for the lack of political and economic dynamism that lay at the root of Chinese military inferiority would there be a future for Mao Tse-tung's generation at all, or in any case a future worthy of their ambitions for their country and themselves.

Mao has recounted that he first began to have "a certain amount of political consciousness" when, as an adolescent, he read a pamphlet beginning: "Alas, China will be subjugated." He has spent a lifetime endeavoring to transform the Chinese people in such a way as to defeat this prophecy—and in his own eyes the task is not yet done.

Mao Tse-tung grew to manhood in the first and second decades of the 20th century, at a time when the most progressive Chinese revolutionaries or reformists were seeking in the West the secrets of the strength which would make it possible to resist the West. It was characteristic of Hunan, however, that the older generation of scholars, who were Mao's teachers and models, did not restrict themselves to the "new learning" from abroad, but at the same time promoted the study of China's own tradition, and especially of the philosophers who, at the time of the Manchu conquest three centuries earlier, had exhorted the Chinese to revive the pragmatism and martial spirit of their ancestors. Such ideas were more immediately accessible to Mao than those of foreign origin. His first published article, written in 1917 when he was 23, is filled with references to the "heroes, martyrs and warriors" of old, and quotes admiringly from a poem attributed to the unsuccessful rival of the founder of the Han Dynasty: "My strength uprooted mountains, my energy dominated the world." Thus, while preaching the need to influence people's "subjective attitudes" in order to promote "self-awareness," Mao was still concerned at this time above all with the self-discipline and strength of will that should be cultivated by an élite.

Already Mao had been exposed, both through reading and the instruction of his teachers, to the basic ideas of Western liberalism, and for two or three fleeting years he came to share its ideals. "Wherever there is repression of the individual," he wrote in 1918, "there can be no greater crime." The traditional social order, with its ingrained respect for authority, both political and parental, must therefore be destroyed, together with the Confucian philosophy that buttressed it, in order that individual freedom might prevail.

By 1920 Mao had been converted to Communism, under the impact of the Russian revolution. Henceforth, he was persuaded that the liberation of every Chinese could only be a collective liberation resulting from victory over the foreign oppressors and the domestic reactionaries. Nevertheless, he retained the conviction that men themselves and their attitudes had to be transformed if society was effectively to be changed. A genuine revolutionary movement had to be made up of individuals consciously carrying out tasks accepted of their own free will. This enterprise could only appear to skeptics like squaring the circle, but the cultural revolution demonstrates that Mao has still not given up trying.

Mao Tse-tung and his comrades now regarded themselves as Marxists, and they did their best to learn how to be "Marxist-Leninists" as well (though the term had not yet been coined). In other words, they set about assimilating the modifications in Marxist theory that Lenin had made in order to adapt it to conditions in Asiatic Russia and in the even more backward lands to the east. There, Lenin had proclaimed, the patriotic capitalists were not necessarily (at least in the first instance) the enemies of the Communist revolutionaries, but could even be their allies for a time in the struggle for national liberation and independent economic development. Moreover, the peasants and not the workers would provide the main strength of the revolutionary movement, though they would, of course, require the leadership of the workers' party—i.e. of the Communists—not to mention the "international proletariat," as incarnate in the representatives of the Comintern.

Even with these modifications, Marxism (or Marxism-Leninism) remained a fundamentally urban-centered philosophy. Progress and enlightenment would radiate outward from the cities to the backward countryside. Mao Tse-tung himself had become thoroughly impregnated during his student days with the traditional contempt of the Chinese intellectuals for physical labor. And though as a Communist he could no longer retain an attitude of superiority toward manual workers in general, his early experience as a trade-union organizer fostered in him the snobbish disdain for the dirty and ignorant peasants that has characterized Marxist thinking since Marx himself first stigmatized "the class that represents barbarism in the midst of civilization."

Then, almost accidentally, while resting in his native village, Mao suddenly found himself confronted with an extremely militant peasant movement which had sprung up in the Chinese countryside in the wake of the nationalist outburst provoked by the massacre of a number of Chinese by the foreign police in Shanghai on May 30, 1925. At one stroke, the urban intellectual turned back to the countryside, and grasped that there China's fate would be decided. The peasants were (as he put it in early 1927) "like a tornado or tempest—a force so extraordinarily swift and violent that no power, however great, will be able to suppress it." Mao set out to organize that power. He was forced to desist momentarily in the spring of 1927, when Stalin ordered the Chinese Communists to refrain from actions that might jeopardize the alliance with the Kuomintang, and thereby menace the security of his Siberian frontier. But soon this policy led to bloody catastrophe and the utter destruction of the urban workers' movement in China. Mao took refuge in the mountain range known as the Chingkangshan, and there began a long search for revolutionary methods better adapted to the realities of the Chinese countryside.

In these gropings Mao endeavored to take as a guide the principles of Marxism as he understood them, including the dogma of working-class leadership; but inevitably, being thus plunged once more into the peasant world of his youth, he thought again of the legends that had been the companions of his youth. The organ of the Chinese Communist party was soon accusing him of emulating the Robin Hood-like bandit heroes of "Water Margin" (translated by Pearl Buck under the title "All Men are Brothers"), and a few years later he was ridiculed for deriving his military tactics from the famous novel of war and statecraft, "The Romance of the Three Kingdoms."

It would, of course, be absurd to suggest that Mao had simply fallen back into the intellectual universe of his adolescence. He already had, when he went to the Chingkangshan, some knowledge of Marxist theory, and considerable experience with and mastery of the organizational principle of Leninism. A decade later, when more Soviet books had been translated into Chinese, and he had the leisure in his headquarters in Yenan to engage in reading and study, he greatly deepened and extended his knowledge of Marxism. Nevertheless, both Mao and the revolution he led remained most profoundly marked by the rural environment in which the revolutionary process was taking place.

Much has been written about the originality (or lack of originality) of the Chinese revolution, and the crucial points have long since been identified: a revolution from the bottom up rather than from the top down; protracted warfare in the countryside rather than a rapidly victorious urban insurrection; the Red Army rather than the armed workers as the spearhead. In all of these respects, the Soviet pattern, with its stress on the workers and the cities, was far more in conformity with the basic precepts of Marxism than was the Chinese pattern. But perhaps the most un-Marxist thing that Mao did was to reject the need for Soviet guidance. Marx regarded Asia as hopelessly backward and stagnant until prodded into action by the impact of the West. Such backward societies and cultures were quite incapable, in his view, of modernizing in their own way; the only salvation for them lay in "Europeanization." Moreover, they would require the Europeans to tell them "how it is done." Soviet insistence that the revolution in the agrarian lands of the East, where there was hardly any indigenous working class, must be carried out under the guidance of a "proletarian" International dominated by the Europeans, was thus solidly rooted in Marx's own thinking about Asia. (The fact that the most influential of these Europeans turned out to be Russians would have been less satisfying to Marx, since he regarded Russia herself as an Oriental despotism.)

Mao had seen in 1927 the fruits of such guidance—and therefore, while endeavoring to keep in the good graces of Stalin in order to forestall Russian intervention on the side of his rivals, he progressively asserted the right and the ability of the Chinese to solve their own problems without European tutelage. Asked by Edgar Snow in 1936 whether, if the Chinese revolution were victorious, there would be "some kind of actual merger of governments" with the Soviet Union, Mao replied abruptly, "We are certainly not fighting for an emancipated China in order to turn the country over to Moscow!" And in 1943, hailing the dissolution of the Comintern, he declared that, although the International had not meddled in the affairs of the Chinese Communist party since 1935, that party had "done its work very well, throughout the whole anti-Japanese war of national liberation."

Mao himself recognized, in 1949, that his road to power was an unorthodox one, but he declared that henceforth these tendencies would be reversed:

"From 1927 to the present the center of gravity of our work has been in the villages—gathering strength in the villages, using the villages in order to surround the cities and then taking the cities. The period for this method of work has now ended. The period of 'from the city to the village' and of the city leading the village has now begun. The center of gravity of the party's work has shifted from the village to the city."

In the first few years of the existence of the Chinese People's Republic, an effort was indeed made to follow the Soviet pattern. Large numbers of urban workers were recruited into the Chinese Communist party—which had functioned for two decades primarily as a soul or parasite in the body of Mao's peasant army in the countryside—in order to make of it a "proletarian" party not only in theory but in fact. Simultaneously, a beginning was made toward planned economic development on the Soviet model, with the active participation of Soviet advisers. But these attempts at following the orthodox path soon clashed head-on with Mao's conception of what revolution was all about.

Chinese society in 1949 was overwhelmingly rural. Perhaps the most important single question presenting itself to Mao as he assumed control of the nation's destiny was whether the key to the transformation of the Chinese countryside lay within the villages themselves or without. The answers to this question dictated by Marxist theory and Soviet practice were diametrically opposed to those drawn from his own experience.

Marx had regarded the peasants as totally incapable of independent political action, and this view had dictated the approach of his Soviet disciples to collectivization and agricultural development.

Stalin had dispatched élite workers

from Moscow and Leningrad at the beginning of the collectivization drive of 1929–30 to provide the political consciousness, organizing capacity and technical knowledge that the peasants were, in his view, incapable of generating themselves. And today, 40 years later, a patronizing attitude toward people in the countryside still prevails in the Soviet Union.

Mao's experience, on the other hand, was that of a revolution which not only took place in the countryside, but which (despite the lip service paid to Marxist slogans about "proletarian hegemony") derived its leadership largely from the countryside, and its strength from the fact that it genuinely reflected the aspirations of the peasantry. To be sure, Mao and his comrades cherished ultimate goals, such as collectivization and the introduction of modern technology, which did *not* correspond to what the peasants themselves spontaneously wanted. But the 20 years of symbiosis between Mao's guerrilla forces in the countryside and the peasants who provided the "ocean" in which the "fish" of the revolutionary army could swim, had laid the basis for a relationship between the Communists and the peasants totally different from that in the Soviet Union.

Instead of ordering the rural people—from without and from above—to accept a complete upheaval in their way of life, the Chinese Communists were in a position to communicate with them through men within the villages enjoying their confidence, and to obtain their adhesion to a much greater degree than had been possible in Russia. This was, of course, partly the result of the unbelievable degree of exploitation to which the Chinese peasantry had been exposed at the hands of the landlords—exploitation which for centuries had lent to their revolts, whenever they finally burst out, the "violence of a hurricane" noted by Mao in 1927. But the ability of the Chinese Communists to communicate with the peasants and to channel their bitterness to revolutionary ends was greatly increased by their political methods, and by their physical and moral presence in the countryside over a long period.

Although Mao and his comrades have, on the whole, been closer to the peasants than Lenin or his successors ever were, there have been significant fluctuations in this respect. In the early nineteen-fifties, when the Chinese were making a conscious effort to learn from the Soviet example (the more so as the Russians considered such conformity to be only the normal price of continued economic aid), Mao himself appeared to accept the principle that the really fundamental developments were taking place in the cities, where the heavy industry necessary to further economic growth was being created. But such an emphasis in fact contradicted his most cherished beliefs: that revolution was above all a matter of changing the patterns of thought and behavior of human beings, and that ideological indoctrination and social mobilization were more important than technical factors in bringing about such changes.

Mao's speech of July, 1955, advocating a speed-up in the formation of rural cooperatives marked the first decisive step toward reversing the order of priorities that characterized not only the Soviet model, but the logic of Marxism itself. Discussing the relationship between collectivization and mechanization, Mao declared: "The country's economic conditions being what they are, the technical transformation will take somewhat longer than the social." In other words, the potential for reshaping the Chinese peasantry was to be found in the revolutionary virtue of the peasants themselves, and not in mere material instruments produced by a minority of technical specialists and skilled workers.

These tendencies had their culmination in the Great Leap Forward of 1958. The foundations of Socialism, and even of Communism, were to be laid in the countryside, where the "people's communes" provided the best form for the transition to the future ideal society. Progress toward social and moral transformation would be somewhat slower in the cities, where "bourgeois ideology" was still prevalent.

Not surprisingly, the Great Leap Forward, with its emphasis on the revolutionary capacity of the "poor and blank" Chinese people, was accompanied by a growing skepticism regarding the utility either of the Soviet example or of Soviet assistance. In a speech of June, 1958, Mao declared that, while it was necessary to obtain Soviet aid, the main thing was for China to develop her economy by her own efforts. Nor should the Chinese blindly copy Soviet methods, either economic or military.

"Some people have suggested that if our comrades, the Soviet advisers, see we are not copying from them, they will complain or be discontented. Well, I might ask these [Soviet] comrades, 'Are you copying from China?' If they say they are not copying from us, then I could say, 'If you don't copy from us, we won't copy from you either.' "

Summing up the problem of learning from the Soviet Union, Mao declared that the slogan for internal use should be "Study critically," while the slogan for public consumption put it somewhat more tactfully as "Study selectively."

The Great Leap policies led to grave economic difficulties, not only because Mao had overestimated the technical capacity of the rural population at that particular stage, but also because he deliberately flouted the need for effective coordination of the economy. This much Mao admitted himself in a speech delivered in July, 1959, in which he assumed responsibility for the failure of the planners to attend to the plans:

"What I mean by saying that they didn't attend to planning is that they rejected comprehensive balances—they completely failed to calculate the amounts of coal, iron and transport required. Coal and iron cannot walk by themselves. They must be transported in carriages. This point I had not foreseen. . . . Prior to August of last year I devoted most of my energy to the revolutionary side of things. I am fundamentally incompetent on economic construction, and I do not understand industrial planning."

The pendulum therefore swung back toward an emphasis on technical factors and the role of the manager and the expert. This was clearly most distasteful to Mao, but he was forced to bow to circumstances and to the opinions of the "capitalist roaders" in the Chinese Communist party. At the same time, he had learned from the experience of the Great Leap. Therefore, when, beginning in 1963, he made a new attempt to change the temper of society, he did not limit himself, as in 1955–58, primarily to the rural sector. This time, on the contrary, he attached greater importance to remolding urban intellectuals, as well as the party and state bureaucrats in the cities, so as to make use of them in modernizing the countryside.

The cultural revolution has been, as everyone now knows, to a very considerable extent a struggle for power between Mao and his partisans on the one hand, and the proponents of a more orthodox brand of Communism, such as Liu Shao-ch'i and Teng Hsiao-p'ing, on the other. But it has also been a great and wide-ranging debate about the nature of revolution, and at the center of this debate has been the problem of the role to be played by "intellectuals" in society.

The Chinese, like the Soviets, use this term in a far wider sense than is commonly imparted to it in the West, to designate any literate person with a modicum of specialized knowledge who makes use of this training in his work. In China, however, the word has resonances quite different from those in Russia, because of the traditionally high social status of the intellectuals and the fact that in the past many of them actually exercised political power as scholar-officials. This offered a unique opportunity for the Chinese Communists to fill the void left by the collapse of the old imperial bureaucracy (as the Kuomintang had tried and failed to do), but it also concealed a most dangerous snare in the temptation to imitate the arrogance and contempt for the common people that often characterized the old imperial officials.

It is because he had become convinced, by 1964 at the latest, that party cadres in general (and not merely a corrupt minority) were all too prone to succumb to this temptation, that Mao proceeded to discipline the party from without, with the support of the army, rather then undertaking another "rectification" campaign within the party, as he had done in the past.

Such campaigns had long been a characteristic feature of Mao's leadership style. The greatest and most memorable of them had taken place during World War II, in 1942 and 1943. When the United States Army mission came to Yenan in August, 1944, Mao described rectification as a manifestation of the democratic spirit of the Chinese Communists, declaring to John S. Service:

"Of course, we do not pretend that we are perfect. We still face problems of bureaucracy and corruption. But we do face them. We welcome observation and criticism—by the Americans, by the K.M.T. or by anyone else. We are constantly criticizing ourselves and revising our policies toward greater efficiency and effectiveness."

The results of these and other policies, Mao continued, were visible in the areas then ruled by the Communists: "You can see the difference in our areas—the people are alive, interested, friendly. They have a human outlet. They are free from deadening repression."

Even at the time this was something of an idealization—though the reports of many visitors to Yenan during the war years attest that there was much truth in it. But Mao did express in simple language, in these remarks to an American diplomat, the two basic aims of this and all subsequent rectification movements: to combat the bureaucratic tendencies of the party cadres by subjecting them to mass criticism, thus developing at the same time a sentiment of participation and therefore of freedom among the people.

Similar campaigns were conducted in the early nineteen-fifties, and again in 1957, after the outcome of the "Hundred Flowers" experiment, in which all citizens were invited freely to criticize the party and the Government, had revealed to Mao that the Chinese had not yet been as thoroughly re-educated as he imagined. Although they involved mass criticism sessions that were often highly traumatic for the individuals concerned, all such campaigns prior to the cultural revolution remained clearly under the control of the Chinese Communist party, which was expected to reform itself from within, under the stimulus of outside criticism.

Although the bureaucratic tendencies of those enjoying even a small parcel of authority are a particular source of concern to Mao, the problem with which he has been grappling in recent years is, as already suggested, much broader, involving not merely that small fraction of "intellectuals" who constitute the party apparatus, but the relation between all those who possess modern skills and the other members of society.

In the long run, of course, Mao is persuaded that the gulf between the educated and the uneducated will disappear, with the progressive effacement of differences between town and countryside and between mental and manual labor. But for the time being it persists, and nourishes attitudes on the part of those who do have some "book learning" of which Mao is all the more wary, since he once entertained them himself. "I began as a student and acquired the habits of a student," he declared in 1942. "Surrounded by students who could neither fetch nor carry for themselves, I used to consider it undignified to do any manual labor, such as shouldering my own luggage. At that time it seemed to me that the intellectuals were the only clean persons in the world; next to them the workers and peasants seemed rather dirty." It was only after becoming a revolutionary, Mao continued, and living together with the workers and peasants of the revolutionary army, that he divested himself of the "bourgeois and *petit bourgeois* feelings" implanted in him by the bourgeois schools, and came to feel that "it was those unreconstructed intellectuals who were unclean. . . , while the workers and peasants were after all the cleanest persons. . . , even though their hands were soiled and their feet smeared with cow dung."

No doubt it is a mixture of guilt resulting from his own past feelings, and resentment by a man partly self-taught who never took a proper university degree (though he has an excellent grounding in traditional Chinese history and philosophy) that has led Mao to adopt an increasingly hostile and patronizing attitude toward the intellectuals. "Throughout history," he declared in 1964, "no highest graduate of the Hanlin Academy has been outstanding. . . . The reading of too many books is harmful, and one with too much education cannot be a good emperor. . . . We must read Marxist books, but we should not read too many of them either. It will be enough to read a few dozen of them."

The culmination of Mao's suspicions regarding both the uselessness and the inherently narrow and selfish outlook of the intellectuals was first of all the assault by the young students constituting the Red Guards on the "reactionary bourgeois academic authorities," who had hitherto regarded themselves as indispensable, and ruled the universities according to their own pleasure. Mao himself, though he had launched the movement, was startled by the violence of the first outburst in the autumn of 1966. At the end of October he declared, "I did not foresee that as soon as the big-character poster from Peking University was broadcast [on Mao's orders], the whole country would be in an uproar. . . . Red Guards in the whole country were mobilized, and charged with such force as to throw you into dismay. I myself had stirred up this big trouble, and I can hardly blame you if you have complaints against me."

But if he had not realized that events would take quite this turn, Mao set out deliberately to accomplish the end which was in fact accomplished, namely to make sure that henceforth no one in China (except himself) would dare to demand unquestioning obedience by virtue of either official status or specialized knowledge. His chosen instrument for this purpose was a highly ambiguous one. Seen in relation to the party, the Red Guards appeared as "masses," attacking the ruling élite from outside. But at the same time, in relation to the real masses of the Chinese people, they themselves were very much élite. And so, once the students had accomplished their function of humiliating the "authorities" in the cities, they were packed off to the countryside, there to learn humility by listening to the tales of the peasants about the hardships and oppression of former days, and to discover thus how little they knew of real life.

The ambiguous role of the Red Guards is, of course, only one facet of the ambiguous and contradictory nature of the cultural revolution as a whole. On the one hand, it has involved opening wide the floodgates of criticism, and turning what was, four years ago, a tightly organized political system entirely in the hands of party leaders into the world's biggest experiment in direct democracy, where at any moment those theoretically in charge of a certain sector—be it a school, a factory, or a government department—might find things taken out of their hands by a mass meeting or a group of Red Guards or "revolutionary rebels." On the other hand, the whole movement originated not spontaneously, but at Mao's command, and under the guidance of the army—even though, as Mao later said, the results surprised even him. Subsequently, these anarchistic tendencies were brought under control by the network of "Revolutionary Committees" which are (despite the lip service paid to party leadership since the Ninth Congress) effectively dominated by the army. And above the whole scene towers the figure of the Great Leader, Chairman Mao, who decides in accordance with his infallible historical vision which groups, movements and ideas are genuinely proletarian and revolutionary.

This ambiguity of Mao's own personality and of the revolution he leads explains the singularly disparate nature of the groups that have rallied around his name in today's "contact of extremes" between China and the West. The first phase of the cultural revolution, when young people shouting the slogan "To rebel is justified!" attacked all received opinions and all established authority, called forth a profound echo among students of Europe and America in search of new political and social forms whereby small groups can shape their own lives. At the same time, Mao's defense of Stalin against "modern revisionism," and his vigilance in unmasking one after the other as counter-revolutionaries all those who venture to oppose his "correct proletarian line," have drawn to the pro-Chinese splinter parties in the West a number of unrepentant and unregenerate Stalinist bureaucrats and hacks filled with nostalgia for the reassuring certainties of a world dominated by the "Father of the Peoples."

The picture just sketched—two halves of Mao's personality, corresponding to two categories among his supporters—is of course an oversimplified one, for anarchist and authoritarian tendencies are linked, both in Mao and in his disciples. The thirst for absolute purity that characterizes much of the New Left today inclines one to view all those who differ as evil men who must be prevented from leading others astray. And the denial of the collective authority of the party, on the grounds that any organization whose members automatically enjoy power over others is by definition a bureaucracy, leads necessarily to the exaltation of the personal authority of chairman Mao as the only instrument for deciding who is evil and must be suppressed.

In a speech of January, 1958, Mao claimed that one day China would teach the West the true meaning of democracy:

"If we are to exert our utmost efforts, if we are to leave the West behind us, must we not rectify and get rid of bourgeois thinking? No one knows how long it will take the West to get rid of bourgeois thinking. If Dulles wanted to get rid of his bourgeois style, he too would have to ask us to be his teacher."

It would be all too easy to dismiss these pretensions, in the light of Mao's doubtful success in rooting out selfishness and creating a new humanity in China herself. But there may be something to be learned from the experience of the cultural revolution, precisely because it has taken place in a pre-industrial society. In the last analysis, Mao's aim is to prevent the emergence in China of tendencies that he calls "capitalist," and which characterize, in fact, advanced industrial societies: the progressive alienation of the individual in an economic system that has become a vast impersonal machine, and in which it is hard to find out who is responsible for the decisions affecting people's lives; increasing functional specialization and economic inequality; and, as a result of all this, the tendency for people to bury themselves in the pursuit of self-interest and personal satisfaction.

Mao's declared aim is to prevent such a society from taking shape in China (as, in his view, it has already done in the Soviet Union—hence the term "capitalist restoration"). Read literally, such fears are groundless, or at least premature, for China has not yet reached the economic and technological level where she could begin to be threatened by phenomena of this kind. There is servitude enough in China, but it is of a different type, rooted less in technology and more in the arbitrariness of human beings. But Mao, who has always shown the strongest interest in laying the economic foundations for China's status as a great power, is, as he has repeatedly stated, looking to the future—to the fate of the Chinese revolution in the decades and centuries to come. He sees his fellow countrymen, from the highly paid bureaucrats and technicians to the moderately well-off peasants, all too preoccupied with their own material well-being, and asks himself whether things would not become much worse if there were more wealth to covet.

However inadequate are Mao's answers to these questions (as already pointed out, his utopia is in fact run by the army), he is the first major political leader to have raised them with such urgency. This in itself is enough to explain the sympathy he has aroused among many students in the West, who find in his statements and policies an echo of their own most fundamental conviction: that the principal concern of men should be with the equality of human life, rather than with the accumulation of things as an end in itself. On the other hand, though the experience of a nation on the verge of large-scale industrialization can provide a stimulus to self-examination, the real solution to the problem of the human use of technology and of the material wealth it produces can only be devised by those who are themselves the victims of technology.

Marx would, of course, have found outrageous the suggestion that Europeans could learn anything from Asians at all. In any case, he was persuaded that detachment from material possessions could flourish only in highly industrialized societies where an abundance of products was available to all. The experience of the U.S.S.R. and of other "Socialist" countries in Europe does not provide evidence of any such tendency, but this does not mean that salvation must come from the East. Mao's project for regenerating the West by the example of Chinese virtue is no more viable in the 20th century than was Marx's project for the Europeanization of Asia in the 19th. The "contact of extremes" must remain a two-way street. street.

CHAIRMAN MAO TSE-TUNG

During my recent visit to Hunan I made a first-hand investigation of conditions in the five counties of Hsiangtan, Hsianghsiang, Hengshan, Liling and Changsha. In the thirty-two days from January 4 to February 5, I called together fact-finding conferences in villages and county towns, which were attended by experienced peasants and by comrades working in the peasant movement, and I listened attentively to their reports and collected a great deal of material. Many of the hows and whys of the peasant movement were the exact opposite of what the gentry in Hankow and Changsha are saying. I saw and heard of many strange things of which I had hitherto been unaware. I believe the same is true of many other places, too. All talk directed against the peasant movement must be speedily set right. All the wrong measures taken by the revolutionary authorities concerning the peasant movement must be speedily changed. Only thus can the future of the revolution be benefited. For the present upsurge of the peasant movement is a colossal event. In a very short time, in China's central, southern and northern provinces, several hundred million peasants will rise like a mighty storm, like a hurricane, a force so swift and violent that no power, however great, will be able to hold it back. They will smash all the trammels that bind them and rush forward along the road to liberation. They will sweep all the imperialists, warlords, corrupt officials, local tyrants and evil gentry into their graves. Every revolutionary party and every revolutionary comrade will be put to the test, to be accepted or rejected as they decide. There are three alternatives. To march at their head and lead them? To trail behind them, gesticulating and criticizing? Or to stand in their way and oppose them? Every Chinese is free to choose, but events will force you to make the choice quickly.

SOURCE: *Selected Works of Mao Tse-tung,* vol. 1 (Peking: Foreign Language Press, 1944), pp. 23–34, passim. • Mao Tse-Tung is a Chinese Communist political leader and Chairman of The People's Republic of China. He was chairman of the first All-China Congress of Soviets, which formed the Soviet Republic of China in 1931. He was also chairman of the Central People's Government. He is author of *Selected Works of Mao Tse-Tung* (four volumes).

GET ORGANIZED!

The development of the peasant movement in Hunan may be divided roughly into two periods with respect to the counties in the province's central and southern parts where the movement has already made much headway. The first, from January to September of last year, was one of organization. In this period, January to June was a time of underground activity, and July to September, when the revolutionary army was driving out Chao Heng-ti, one of open activity. During this period, the membership of the peasant associations did not exceed 300,000–400,000, the masses directly under their leadership numbered little more than a million, there was as yet hardly any struggle in the rural areas, and consequently there was very little criticism of the associations in other circles. Since its members served as guides, scouts and carriers of the Northern Expeditionary Army, even some of the officers had a good word to say for the peasant associations. The second period, from last October to January of this year, was one of revolutionary action. The membership of the associations jumped to two million and the masses directly under their leadership increased to ten million. Since the peasants generally enter only one name for the whole family on joining a peasant association, a membership of two million means a mass following of about ten million. Almost half the peasants in Hunan are now organized. In counties like Hsiangtan, Hsianghsiang, Liuyang, Changsha, Liling, Ninghsiang, Pingkiang, Hsiangyin, Hengshan, Hengyang, Leiyang, Chenhsien and Anhua, nearly all the peasants have combined in the peasant associations or have come under their leadership. It was on the strength of their extensive organization that the peasants went into action and within four months brought about a great revolution in the countryside, a revolution without parallel in history.

DOWN WITH THE LOCAL TYRANTS AND EVIL GENTRY! ALL POWER TO THE PEASANT ASSOCIATIONS!

The main targets of attack by the peasants are the local tyrants, the evil gentry and the lawless landlords, but in passing they also hit out against patriarchal ideas and institutions, against the corrupt officials in the cities and against bad practices and customs in the rural areas. In force and momentum the attack is tempestuous; those who bow before it survive and those who resist perish. As a result, the privileges which the feudal landlords enjoyed for thousands of years are being shattered to pieces. Every bit of the dignity and prestige built up by the landlords is being swept into the dust. With the collapse of the power of the landlords, the peasant associations have now become the sole organs of authority and the popular slogan "All power to the peasant associations" has become a reality. Even trifles such as a quarrel between husband and wife are brought to the peasant association. Nothing can be settled unless someone from the peasant association is present. The association actually dictates all rural affairs, and, quite literally, "whatever it says, goes." Those who are outside the associations can only speak well of them and cannot say anything against them. The local tyrants, evil gentry and lawless landlords have been deprived of all right to speak, and none of them dares even mutter dissent. In the face of the peasant associations' power and pressure, the top local tyrants and evil gentry, have fled to Shanghai, those of the second rank to Hankow, those of the third to Changsha and those of the fourth to the county towns, while the fifth rank and the still lesser fry surrender to the peasant associations in the villages.

"Here's ten yuan. Please let me join the peasant association," one of the smaller of the evil gentry will say.

"Ugh! Who wants your filthy money?" the peasants reply.

Many middle and small landlords and rich peasants and even some middle peasants, who were all formerly opposed to the peasant associations, are now vainly seeking admission. Visiting various places, I often came across such people who pleaded with me, "Mr. Committeeman from the provincial capital, please be my sponsor!"

In the Ching Dynasty, the household census compiled by the local authorities consisted of a regular register and "the other" register, the former for honest people and the latter for burglars, bandits and similar undesirables. In some places the peasants now use this method to scare those who formerly opposed the associations. They say, "Put their names down in the other register!"

Afraid of being entered in the other register, such people try various devices to gain admission into the peasant associations, on which their minds are so set that they do not feel safe until their names are entered. But more often than not they are turned down flat, and so they are always on tenterhooks; with the doors of the association barred to them, they are like tramps without a home or, in rural parlance, "mere trash." In short, what was looked down upon four months ago as a "gang of peasants" has now become a most honourable institution. Those who formerly prostrated themselves before the power of the gentry now bow before the power of the peasants. No matter what their identity, all admit that the world since last October is a different one.

"IT'S TERRIBLE!" OR "IT'S FINE!"

The peasants' revolt disturbed the gentry's sweet dreams. When the news from the countryside reached the cities, it caused immediate uproar among the gentry. Soon after my arrival in Changsha, I met all sorts of people and picked up a good deal of gossip. From the middle social strata upwards to the Kuomintang right-wingers, there was not a single person who did not sum up the whole business in the phrase, "It's terrible!" Under the impact of the views of the "It's terrible!" school then flooding the city, even quite revolutionary-minded people became down-hearted as they pictured the events in the countryside in their mind's eye; and they were unable to deny the word "terrible." Even quite progressive people said, "Though terrible, it is inevitable in a revolution." In short, nobody could altogether deny the word "terrible." But, as already mentioned, the fact is that the great peasant masses have risen to fulfil their historic mission and that the forces of rural democracy have risen to overthrow the forces of rural feudalism. The patriarchal-feudal class of local tyrants, evil gentry and lawless landlords has formed the basis of autocratic government for thousands of years and is the cornerstone of imperialism, warlordism and corrupt officialdom. To overthrow these feudal forces is the real objective of the national revolution. In a few months the peasants have accomplished what Dr. Sun Yat-sen wanted, but failed, to accomplish in the forty years he devoted to the national revolution. This is a marvellous feat never before achieved, not just in forty, but in thousands of years. It's fine. It is not "terrible" at all. It is anything but "terrible." "It's terrible" is obviously a theory for combating the rise of the peasants in the interests of the landlords; it is obviously a theory of the landlord class for preserving the old order of feudalism and obstructing the establishment of the new order of democracy, it is obviously a counter-revolutionary theory. No revolutionary comrade should echo this nonsense. If your revolutionary viewpoint is firmly established and if you have been to the villages and looked around, you will undoubtedly feel thrilled as never before. Countless thousands of the enslaved—the peasants—are striking down the enemies who battened on their flesh. What the peasants are doing is absolutely right; what they are doing is fine! "It's fine!" is the theory of the peasants and of all other revolutionaries. Every revolutionary comrade should know that the national revolution requires a great change in the countryside. The Revolution of 1911 did not bring about this change, hence its failure. This change is now taking place, and it is an important factor for the completion of the revolution. Every revolutionary comrade must support it, or he will be taking the stand of counter-revolution.

THE QUESTION OF "GOING TOO FAR"

Then there is another section of people who say, "Yes, peasant associations are necessary, but they are going rather too far." This is the opinion of the middle-of-the-roaders. But what is the actual situation? True, the peasants are in a sense "unruly" in the countryside. Supreme in authority, the peasant association allows the landlord no say and sweeps away his prestige. This amounts to striking the landlord down to the dust and keeping him there. The peasants threaten, "We will put you in the other register!" They fine the local tyrants and evil gentry, they demand contributions from them, and they smash their sedan-chairs. People swarm into the houses of local tyrants and evil gentry who are against the peasant association, slaughter their pigs and consume their grain. They even loll for a minute or two on the ivory-inlaid beds belonging to the young ladies in the households of the local tyrants and evil gentry. At the slightest provocation they make arrests, crown the arrested with tall paper-hats, and parade them through the villages, saying "You dirty landlords, now you know who we are!" Doing whatever they like and turning everything upside down, they have created a kind of terror in the countryside. This is what some people call "going too far," or "going beyond the proper limits in righting a wrong," or "really too much." Such talk may seem plausible, but in fact it is wrong. First, the local tyrants, evil gentry and lawless landlords have themselves driven the peasants to this. For ages they have used their power to tyrannize over the peasants and trample them underfoot; that is why the peasants have reacted so strongly. The most violent revolts and the most serious disorders have invariably occurred in places where the local tyrants, evil gentry and lawless landlords perpetrated the worst outrages. The peasants are clear-sighted. Who is bad and who is not, who is the worst and who is not quite so vicious, who deserves severe punishment and who deserves to be let off lightly—the peasants keep clear accounts, and very seldom has the punishment exceeded the cirme. Secondly, a revolution is not a dinner party, or writing an essay, or painting a picture, or doing embroidery; it cannot be so refined, so leisurely and gentle, so temperate, kind, courteous, restrained and magnanimous. A revolution is an insurrection, an act of violence by which one class overthrows another. A rural revolution is a revolution by which the peasantry overthrows the power of the feudal landlord class. Without using the greatest force, the peasants cannot possibly overthrow the deep-rooted authority of the landlords which has lasted for thousands of years. The rural areas need a mighty revolutionary upsurge, for it alone can rouse the people in their millions to become a powerful force. All the actions mentioned here which have been labelled as "going too far" flow from the power of the peasants, which has been called forth by the mighty revolutionary upsurge in the countryside. It was highly necessary for such things to be done in the second period of the peasant movement, the period of revolutionary action. In this period it was necessary to establish the absolute authority of the peasants. It was necessary to forbid malicious criticism of the peasant associations. It was necessary to overthrow the whole authority of the gentry, to strike them to the ground and keep them there. There is revolutionary significance in all the actions which were labelled as "going too far" in this period. To put it bluntly, it is necessary to create terror for a while in every rural area, or otherwise it would be impossible to suppress the activities of the counter-revolutionaries in the countryside or overthrow the authority of the gentry. Proper limits have to be exceeded in order to right a wrong, or else the wrong cannot be righted. Those who talk about the peasants "going too far" seem at first sight to be different from those who say "It's terrible!" as mentioned earlier, but in essence they proceed from the same standpoint and likewise voice a landlord theory that upholds the interests of the privileged classes. Since this theory impedes the rise of the peasant movement and so disrupts the revolution, we must firmly oppose it.

THE "MOVEMENT OF THE RIFFRAFF"

The right-wing of the Kuomintang says, "The peasant movement is a movement of the riffraff, of the lazy peasants." This view is current in Changsha. When I was in the countryside, I heard the gentry say, "It is all right to set up peasant associations, but the people now running them are no good. They ought to be replaced!" This opinion comes to the same thing as what the right-wingers are saying; according to both it is all right to have a peasant movement (the movement is already in being and no one dare say otherwise), but they say that the people running it are no good and they particularly hate those in charge of the associations at the lower levels, calling them "riffraff." In short, all those whom the gentry had despised, those whom they had trodden into the dirt, people with no place in society, people with no right to speak, have now audaciously lifted up their heads. They have not only lifted up their heads but taken power into their hands. They are now running the township peasant associations (at the lowest level), which they have turned into something fierce and formidable. They have raised their rough, work-soiled hands and laid them on the gentry. They tether the evil gentry with ropes, crown them with tall paper-hats and parade them through the villages. (In Hsiangtan and Hsianghsiang they call this "parading through the township" and in Liling "parading through the fields.") Not a day passes but they drum some harsh, pitiless words of denunciation into gentry's ears. They are issuing orders and are running everything. Those who used to rank lowest now rank above everybody else; and so this is called "turning things upside down."

VANGUARDS OF THE REVOLUTION

Where there are two opposite approaches to things and people, two opposite views emerge. "It's terrible!" and "It's fine!" "riffraff" and "vanguards of the revolution"—here are apt examples.

We said above that the peasants have accomplished a revolutionary task which had been left unaccomplished for many years and have done an important job for the national revolution. But has this great revolutionary task, this important revolutionary work, been performed by all the peasants? No. There are three kinds of peasants, the rich, the middle and the poor peasants. The three live in different circumstances and so have different views about the revolution.

. . . . .

The poor peasants have always been the main force in the bitter fight in the countryside. They have fought militantly through the two periods of underground work and of open activity. They are the most responsive to Communist Party leadership. They are deadly enemies of the camp of the local tyrants and evil gentry and attack it without the slightest hesitation. "We joined the peasant association long ago," they say to the rich peasants, "why are you still hesitating?" The rich peasants answer mockingly, "What is there to keep you from joining? You people have neither a tile over your heads nor a speck of land under your feet!" It is true the poor peasants are not afraid of losing anything. Many of them really have "neither a tile over their heads nor a speck of land under their feet." What, indeed, is there to keep them from joining the associations? According to the survey of Changsha County, the poor peasants comprise 70 per cent, the middle peasants 20 per cent, and the landlords and the rich peasants 10 per cent of the population in the rural areas. The 70 per cent, the poor peasants, may be sub-divided into two categories, the utterly destitute and the less destitute. The utterly destitute, comprising 20 per cent, are the completely dispossessed, that is, people who have neither land nor money, are without any means of livelihood, and are forced to leave home and become mercenaries or hired labourers or wandering beggars. The less destitute, the other 50 per cent, are the partially dispossessed, that is, people with just a little land or a little money who eat up more than they earn and live in toil and distress the year round, such as the handicraftsmen, the tenant-peasants (not including the rich tenant-peasants) and the semi-tenant-peasants. This great mass of poor peasants, or altogether 70 per cent of the rural population, are the backbone of the peasant associations, the vanguard in the overthrow of the feudal forces and the heroes who have performed the great revolutionary task which for long years was left undone. Without the poor peasant class (the riff-raff," as the gentry call them), it would have been impossible to bring about the present revolutionary situation in the countryside, or to overthrow the local tyrants and evil gentry and complete the democratic revolution. The poor peasants, being the most revolutionary group, have gained the leadership of the peasant associations. In both the first and second periods almost all the chairmen and committee members in the peasant associations at the lowest level were poor peasants (of the officials in the township associations in Hengshan County the utterly destitute comprise 50 per cent, the less destitute 40 per cent, and poverty-stricken intellectuals 10 per cent). Leadership by the poor peasants is absolutely necessary. Without the poor peasants there would be no revolution. To deny their role is to deny the revolution. To attack them is to attack the revolution. They have never been wrong on the general direction of the revolution. They have discredited the local tyrants and evil gentry. They have beaten down the local tyrants and evil gentry, big and small, and kept them underfoot. Many of their deeds in the period of revolutionary action, which were labelled as "going too far," were in fact the very things the revolution required. Some county governments, county headquarters of the Kuomintang and county peasant associations in Hunan have already made a number of mistakes; some have even sent soldiers to arrest officials of the lower-level associations at the landlords' request. A good many chairmen and committee members of township associations in Hengshan and Hsianghsiang Counties have been thrown in jail. This mistake is very serious and feeds the arrogance of the reactionaries. To judge whether or not it is a mistake, you have only to see how joyful the lawless landlords become and how reactionary sentiments grow, wherever the chairmen or committee members of local peasant associations are arrested. We must combat the counter-revolutionary talk of a "movement of riffraff" and a "movement of lazy peasants" and must be especially careful not to commit the error of helping the local tyrants and evil gentry in their attacks on the poor peasant class. Though a few of the poor peasant leaders undoubtedly did have shortcomings, most of them have changed by now. They themselves are energetically prohibiting gambling and suppressing banditry. Where the peasant association is powerful, gambling has stopped altogether and banditry has vanished. In some places it is literally true that people do not take any articles left by the wayside and that doors are not bolted at night. According to the Hengshan survey, 85 per cent of the poor peasant leaders have made great progress and have proved themselves capable and hard-working. Only 15 per cent retain some bad habits. The most one can call these is "an unhealthy minority," and we must not echo the local tyrants and evil gentry in indiscriminatingly condemning them as riffraff." This problem of the "unhealthy minority" can be tackled only under the peasant associations' own slogan of "strengthen discipline," by carrying on propaganda among the masses, by educating the "unhealthy minority," and by tightening the associations' discipline; in no circumstances should soldiers be arbitrarily sent to make such arrests as would damage the prestige of the poor peasants and feed the arrogance of the local tyrants and evil gentry. This point requires particular attention.

. . . . .

CHAPTER IX

SOCIAL PROCESSES

74 Life, Liberty and the Pursuit of Privacy

ALAN F. WESTIN

It seemed fitting to the editors to begin a chapter on the "social processes" with an examination of the function for man of the avoidance *of social interaction—the values of "nonsocial process," if you will. In this selection Alan Westin perceptively reviews the various ways in which privacy is treated in many societies. He then analyzes the major functions privacy performs for individuals and groups in Western democratic nations. The reader will find here a thorough and detached assessment of the need for balance between respect for privacy and the necessity for some mechanism to oversee conduct in order to maintain social order.*

To its profound distress, the American public has recently learned of a revolution in the techniques by which public and private authorities can conduct scientific surveillance over the individual. In chilled fascination, the press, television programs and popular books have described new means of telephone tapping, electronic eavesdropping, hidden television-eye monitoring, "truth measurement" by polygraph devices, personality testing for personnel selection, and growing dossiers of personal data about millions of citizens. As the late 1960s arrived, it was clear that American society had developed a deep concern over the preservation of privacy under the new pressures from surveillance technology.

In my view, the modern claim to privacy derives first from man's animal origins and is shared, in quite real terms, by men and women living in primitive societies.

One basic finding of animal studies is that virtually all animals seek periods of individual seclusion or small-group intimacy. This is usually described as the tendency toward territoriality, in which an organism lays private claim to an area of land, water or air and defends it against intrusion by members of its own species. A meadow pipit chases fellow pipits away from a private space of 6 feet around him. Except during nesting time, there is only one robin on a bush or branch. Antelopes in African fields and

SOURCE: *Think,* vol. 35, no. 3 (May–June 1969), 12–21. Reprinted by permission of the author and The Association of the Bar of the City of New York. • Alan F. Westin is professor of public law and government and Director of the Center for Research and Education in American Liberties at Columbia University. He is also director of a National Academy of Sciences nationwide study of the problems computerized data banks pose for individual privacy and due process of law. He is a member of The District of Columbia Bar and the National Board of Directors of The American Civil Liberties Union. He is the author of *Privacy and Freedom* and a forthcoming biography of Martin Luther King, Jr.

dairy cattle in an American farmyard space themselves to establish individual territory. For species in which the female cannot raise the young unaided, nature has created the "pair bond," linking temporarily or permanently a male and a female who demand private territory for the unit during breeding time. Studies of territoriality have even shattered the romantic notions that when robins sing or monkeys shriek, it is solely for the "animal joy of life." Actually, it is often a defiant cry for privacy, given within the borders of the animal's private territory.

Ecological studies have demonstrated that animals also have minimum needs for private space without which the animal's survival will be jeopardized. Since overpopulation can impede the animal's ability to smell, court or be free from constant defense reactions, such a condition upsets the social organization of the animal group. The animals may then kill each other to reduce the crowding, or they may engage in mass suicidal reductions of the population, as lemmings do. Experiments with spacing rats in cages showed that even rats need time and space to be alone. When they were deliberately crowded in cages, patterns of courting, nest building, rearing the young, social hierarchies and territorial taboos were disrupted. Studies of crowding in many animals other than rats indicate that disruption of social relationships through overlapping personal distances aggravates all forms of pathology within a group and causes the same diseases in animals that over-crowding does in man—high blood pressure, circulatory diseases and heart disease.

THE VEIL OF THE TUAREG

Anthropological studies have shown that the individual in virtually every society engages in a continuing personal process by which he seeks privacy at some times and disclosure or companionship at other times.

A sensitive discussion of this distance-setting process has been contributed recently by Robert F. Murphy of Columbia University. Murphy noted that the use of "reserve and restraint" to provide "an area of privacy" for the individual in his relations with others represents a "common, though not constant" factor in all social relationships. The reason for the universality of this process is that individuals have conflicting roles to play in any society; to play these different roles with different persons, the individual must present a different "self" at various times. Restricting information about himself and his emotions is a crucial way of protecting the individual in the stresses and strains of this social interaction. Murphy also notes that creating social distance is especially important in the individual's intimate relations, perhaps even more so than in his casual ones.

Murphy's work among the Tuareg tribes of North Africa, where men veil their faces and constantly adjust the veil to changing interpersonal relations, provides a visual example of the distance-setting process. Murphy concluded that the Tuareg veil is a symbolic realization of the need for privacy in every society.

Another element of privacy that seems universal is a tendency on the part of individuals to invade the privacy of others, and of society to engage in surveillance to guard against anti-social conduct. At the individual level, this is based upon the propensity for curiosity that lies in each individual, from the time that as a child he seeks to explore his environment to his later conduct as an adult in wanting to know more than he learns casually about what is "really" happening to others. Gossip, which is only a particular way of obtaining private information to satisfy curiosity, seems to be found in all societies.

Curiosity is only half of the privacy-invading phenomenon, the "individual" half. There is also the universal process of surveillance by authorities to enforce the rules and taboos of the society. Any social system that creates norms—as all human societies do—must have mechanisms for enforcing those norms. Since those who break the rules and taboos must be detected, every society has mechanisms of watching conduct, investigating transgressions and determining "guilt."

The importance of recognizing this "social" half of the universal privacy-invading process is similar to the recognition of the individual curiosity—it reminds us that every society which wants to protect its rules and taboos against deviant behavior must have enforcement machinery.

PRIVACY IN DEMOCRACIES

It is important to realize that different historical and political traditions among contemporary democratic nations have created different types of overall social balances of privacy. Britain has what might be called a "deferential democratic balance," based on England's situation as a small country with a relatively homogeneous population, strong family structure, surviving class systems, positive public attitude toward government, and elite systems of education and government services. This combination has produced a democracy in which there is a great personal reserve between Englishmen, high personal privacy in home and private associations, and a faith in government that bestows major areas of privacy for government operations. There is also a tradition of tolerating nonconformism which treats much deviant political and social conduct as permissible private action.

West Germany today has what might be called an authoritarian democratic balance. The Bonn Republic defines privacy in a nation where the traditions of democratic self-government came late; authoritarian patterns are deeply rooted in German family structure and social life; both law and government are permeated by high public respect for officialdom and experts; and neither German law nor government showed high capacity, until the post-World War II period, to enforce a meaningful system of civil liberties restraints on government surveillance practices or harassment of dissent. The result is a democratic state in which privileged elements having the authority of family, wealth and official position often enjoy substantial privacy and government enjoys great rights of secrecy; but the privacy of the critic and the nonconformist is still not secure in West German life.

Where does the United States fall in this spectrum?

American individualism—with its stress on unique personality in religion, politics and law—provides a major force for privacy in the United States. This attitude is derived from such factors in American national experience as frontier life, freedom from the feudal heritage of fixed class lines, the Protestant religious base of the nation, its private property system, and the English legal heritage. Along with the individualist stress has gone a complementary trait of associational life—the formation of numerous voluntary groups to pursue private and public goals. An outcome partly of our heterogeneous immigrant base and partly of the American's search for group warmth in a highly mobile, flexible-status society, associations have long been a distinctive aspect of our culture, with well-established rights of privacy against government surveillance or compulsory public disclosure. A final value supporting privacy is the American principle of civil liberty, with its belief in limits on government and private power, freedom of expression and dissent, and institutionalized mechanisms, particularly the legal system and independent courts, for enforcing these rights.

Were these the dominant values of the American sociopolitical tradition, the privacy balance in the United States might be called wholly libertarian. But, from colonial days down to the present, foreign and native analysts have observed other powerful tendencies in American life that press against privacy and support restrictive rules of disclosure and surveillance. The classic American belief in egalitarianism and "frontier democracy" gives rise to several trends: a denial of various "status rights" to privacy that once were attached to European aristocratic classes and are now claimed by elite groups of culture, intellect and science; a propensity toward "leveling curiosity" in social and political life that supports inquisitive interpersonal relationships; and a demand for external conformity of a high order, in the name of a middle-class system in which the blessings of equality and opportunity carry with them a heavy burden of ideological and social conformity.

The United States is thus a democracy whose balance of privacy is continually threatened by egalitarian tendencies demanding greater disclosure and surveillance than a libertarian society should permit.

PRIVACY AND THE SENSES

Privacy also differs from nation to nation in terms of the impact of culture on interpersonal relations. The most extensive recent work, on this theme comes from the cultural anthropologist Edward Hall, who states that people in different cultures experience the world differently not only in terms of language, but also with their senses. They "inhabit different sensory worlds," affecting the way they relate to one another in space, in matters ranging from their concepts of architecture and furniture arrangement to their setting of social distance and interpersonal contact.

To compare these differences, Hall studied a number of contemporary cultures to see how their notions of sensory pleasure and displeasure affected their definitions of interpersonal space. First, he compared the dominant norms of American society, as set by the white middle and upper classes, with three European cultures with which the American middle and upper classes are most closely linked historically and culturally—Germany, England and France.

Germans, Hall found, demand individual and enclosed places to achieve a sense of privacy. This need is expressed in closed doors to business and government offices, fenced yards and separate closed rooms in the home, discomfort at having to share facilities with others, and strict "trespass" rules regulating the person-to-person distance on social, business and ceremonial occasions.

In contrast, Americans are happy with open doors in offices, do not require fencing or screening of their homes to feel comfortable, and are far more informal in their rules of approach, order and distance. An American does not feel that a person walking close to a group or a home has "intruded" on privacy; Germans, on the other hand, will feel this a trespass.

English norms of privacy, Hall found, lie between the American and the German. The English accomplish with reserve what Germans do with doors, walls and trespass rules. Because English children in the middle and upper classes do not usually have separate rooms but share in the nursery with brothers and sisters until they go away to boarding school and live in dormitories, the Englishman grows up with a concept of preserving his individual privacy within shared space rather than by solitary quarters. He learns to rely on reserve, on cues to others to leave him alone. This habit is illustrated in later life by the fact that many English political and business figures do not have private offices; members of Parliament, for example, do not occupy individual offices, and they often meet their constituents on the terrace or in the lobbies of the House of Commons. Englishmen speak more softly and direct the voice more carefully so that it can be heard, only by the person being spoken to, and the eyes are focused directly during conversation. Where an American seeking privacy goes to a private room and shuts the door, an Englishman stops talking, and this signal for privacy is respected by family, friends and associates. By contrast, when an American stops talking, it is usually a sign that something is wrong among the persons present.

Hall found that the influence of Mediterranean culture set the French apart from the American, English and German patterns. Mediterranean peoples pack more closely together in public, enjoy physical contact in public places, and are more involved with each other in sensory terms than more northern peoples. On the other hand, while the American brings friends and acquaintances into his home readily, the French home is reserved for family privacy and is rarely opened to outsiders, even co-workers of long standing or social acquaintances.

INDIVIDUAL PRIVACY

Recognizing the differences that political and sensory cultures make in setting norms of privacy among modern societies, it is still possible to describe the general functions that privacy performs for individuals and groups in Western democratic nations. These functions can be grouped conveniently under four headings: personal autonomy, emotional release, self-evaluation, and limited and protected communication. Since every human being is a whole organism, these four functions constantly flow into one another, but their separation for analytical purposes helps to clarify the important choices about individual privacy that American law may have to make in the coming decade.

Personal Autonomy Each person is aware of the gap between what he wants to be and what he actually is, between what the world sees of him and what he knows to be his much more complex reality. In addition, there are aspects of himself that the individual does not fully understand but is slowly exploring and shaping as he develops. Every individual lives behind a mask in this manner; indeed, the first etymological meaning of the word "person" was "mask," indicating both the conscious and expressive presentation of the self to a social audience. If this mask is torn off and the individual's real self bared to a world in which everyone else still wears his mask and believes in masked performances, the individual can be seared by the hot light of selective, forced exposure. The numerous instances of suicides and nervous breakdowns resulting from such exposures by government investigation, press stories, and even published research constantly remind a free society that only grave social need can ever justify destruction of the privacy which guards the individual's ultimate autonomy.

The autonomy that privacy protects is also vital to the development of individuality and consciousness of individual choice in life. Leontine Young has noted that "without privacy there is no individuality. There are only types. Who can know what he thinks and feels if he never has the opportunity to be alone with his thoughts and feelings?" This development of individuality is particularly important in democratic societies, since qualities of independent thought, diversity of views, and nonconformity are considered desirable traits for individuals. Such independence requires time for sheltered experimentation and testing of ideas, for preparation and practice in thought and conduct, without fear of ridicule or penalty, and for the opportunity to alter opinions before making them public. The individual's sense that it is he who decides to "go public" is a crucial aspect of his feeling of autonomy.

Emotional Release Life in society generates such tensions for the individual that both physical and psychological health demands periods of privacy for various types of emotional release. At one level, such relaxation is required from the pressure of playing social roles. Social scientists agree that each person constantly plays a series of varied and multiple roles, depending on his audience and behavior situation. On any given day, a man may move through the roles of stern father, loving husband, car-pool comedian, skilled lathe operator, union steward, water cooler flirt, and American Legion committee chairman. Like actors on the dramatic stage, individuals can sustain roles only for reasonable periods of time, and no individual can play indefinitely, without relief, the variety of roles that life demands. There have to be moments "off stage" when the individual can be "himself": tender, angry, irritable or dream-filled. Such moments may come in solitude; in the intimacy of family, peers or woman-to-woman and man-to-man relaxation; in the anonymity of park or street; or in a state of reserve while in a group. Privacy in this aspect gives individuals, from plant workers to presidents, a chance to lay their masks aside for a rest. To be always "on" would destroy the human organism.

Self-Evaluation Every individual needs to integrate his experiences into a meaningful pattern and to exert his individuality on events. For such self-evaluation, privacy is essential.

At the intellectual level, individuals need to process the information that is constantly bombarding them, information that cannot be processed while they are still "on the go."

The evaluation function of privacy also has a major moral dimension. While people often consider the moral consequences of their acts during the course of daily affairs, it is primarily in periods of privacy that they take a moral inventory of on-going conduct and measure current performance against personal ideals. For many persons this process is a religious exercise. Even for an individual who is not a religious believer, privacy serves to bring the conscience into play, for, when alone, he must find a way to continue living with himself.

A final contribution of privacy to evaluation is its role in the proper timing of the decision to move from private reflection or intimate conversation to a more general publication of acts and thoughts. This is the process by which one tests his own evaluations against the responses of his peers. Given the delicacy of a person's relaxations with intimates and associates, deciding when and to what extent to disclose facts about himself—and to put others in the position of receiving such confidences is a matter of enormous concern in personal interaction, almost as important as whether to disclose at all.

MENTAL DISTANCE

Limited and Protected Communication The greatest threat to civilized social life would be a situation in which each individual was utterly candid in his communications with others, saying exactly what he knew or felt at all times.

In real life, among mature persons, all communication is partial and limited, based on the complementary relation between reserve and discretion that has already been discussed. Limited communication is particularly vital in urban life, with its heightened stimulation, crowded environment, and continuous physical and psychological confrontations between individuals who do not know one another in the extended, softening fashion of small-town life. Reserved communication is the means of psychic self-preservation for men in the metropolis.

Privacy for limited and protected communication has two general aspects. First, it provides the individual with the opportunities he needs for sharing confidence, and intimacies with those he trusts—spouse, the family, personal friends and close associates at work. The individual discloses because he knows that breach of confidence violates social norms.

In its second general aspect, privacy through limited communication serves to set necessary boundaries of mental distance in interpersonal situations ranging from the most intimate to the most formal and public. In marriage, for example, husbands and wives need to retain islands of privacy in the midst of their intimacy if they are to preserve a saving respect and mystery in the relation. Successful marriages usually depend on the discovery of the ideal line between privacy and revelation and on the respect of both partners for that line. In work situations, mental distance is necessary so that the relations of superior and subordinate do not slip into an intimacy which would create a lack of respect and an impediment to directions and correction. Thus, physical arrangements shield superiors from constant observation by subordinates, and social etiquette forbids conversations or off-duty contacts that are "too close" for the work relationship.

The balance of privacy and disclosure will be powerfully influenced, of course, by both the society's cultural norms and the particular individual's status and life situation. In American society, for example, which prefers "activism" over contemplation, people tend to use their leisure time to "do things" rather than to rest, read and think in privacy. And, in any society, differences in occupation, socioeconomic level and religious commitment are broad conditioning factors in the way each person allots his time and tunes his emotional wavelength for privacy.

In general, however, all individuals are constantly engaged in an attempt to find sufficient privacy to serve their general social roles as well as their individual needs of the moment. Either too much or too little privacy can create imbalances which seriously jeopardize the individual's well-being.

• • • • •

IDEALIZED PORTRAITS

Just as individuals need privacy to obtain release from playing social roles and to engage in permissible deviations from social norms, so organizations need internal privacy to conduct their affairs without having to keep up a "public face." This involves, in particular, the gap between public myth and organizational reality.

For the same basic reasons that standards of moral expectation are set for individuals, churches, labor unions, corporations and government agencies ought to operate. These idealized portraits are usually based on notions of rational decision-making, fair-minded discussion, direct representation of membership viewpoints by the leadership, dedication to public over personal interest, and orderly control of the problems assigned to the organization's care. In fact, much of the behavior of both private and public organizations involves irrational decision-making procedures, harsh and/or comic discussion of "outside," people and causes, personal motivations for decisions, and highly disorderly procedures to cope with problems seen by the organizations as intractable or insoluble. Despite press and social-science exposures of the true workings of organizations, society at large persists in believing that these are departures from a norm and that properly led and dedicated organizations will adhere to the ideal procedures.

Given this penchant of society for idealized models and the far different realities of organizational life, privacy is necessary so that organizations may do the divergent part of their work out of public view. The adage that one should not visit the kitchen of a restaurant if one wants to enjoy the food is applied daily in the grant of privacy to organizations for their staging processes. Privacy affords the relaxation which enables those who are part of a common venture, public or private, to communicate freely with one another and to accomplish their tasks with minimum of social dissembling for "outside" purposes. Without such privacy the operations of law firms, businesses, hospitals, welfare agencies, civic groups, and a host of other organizations would be seriously impaired.

Of course, society decides that certain phases of activity by some organizations are so charged with public interest that they must be carried out in the open. This is illustrated by rules requiring public agencies or private organizations to conduct certain proceedings in public (such as regulatory-agency hearings or union elections), to publish certain facts about their internal procedures (such as corporate accounting reports and other public-record requirements for private groups), and to open their premises to representatives of the public for periodic inspections of procedures (such as visiting committees of universities and government inspectors checking safety practices or the existence of discrimination in personnel policies).

• • • • •

The other aspect for organizational decision-making is the issue of timing—when and how to release the decision—which corresponds to the individual's determination whether and when to communicate about himself to others. Groups obviously have a harder time keeping decisions secret. The large number of persons involved increases the possibility of leaks, and the press, competitors and opponents often seek energetically to discover the decision before the organization is ready to release it. Since most organizational decisions will become known eventually, privacy is a temporary claim—a claim of foundations, university administrations, political parties and government agencies to retain the power of deciding for themselves when to break the seal of privacy and "go public."

While the timing problem is not unique to government (advance news of a corporate decision is worth a great deal in the stock market and may harm the company's plans), its scope is greatest in governmental life. A major need is to prevent outsiders from taking unfair advantage of a government decision revealed through secret surveillance, careless leaks, or deliberate disclosure by a corrupted employee.

The basic point is obvious; privacy in

governmental decision-making is a functional necessity for the formulation of responsible policy, especially in a democratic system concerned with finding formulas for reconciling differences and adjusting majority-minority interests. Nevertheless, drawing the line between what is proper privacy and what becomes dangerous "government secrecy" is a difficult task. Critics have complained that the public often has a right to know what policies are being considered and, after a decision is taken, to know who influenced the result and what considerations moved the government leaders.

THE PEOPLE WATCHERS

Surveillance is obviously a fundamental means of social control. Parents watch their children, teachers watch students, supervisors watch employees, religious leaders watch the acts of their congregants, policemen watch the streets and other public places, and government agencies watch the citizen's performance of various legal obligations and prohibitions. Records are kept by authorities to organize the task of indirect surveillance and to identify trends that may call for direct surveillance. Without such surveillance, society could not enforce its norms or protect its citizens, and an era of ever-increasing speed of communication, mobility of persons, and coordination of conspiracies requires that the means of protecting society keep pace with the technology of crime. Yet one of the central elements of the history of liberty in Western societies has been the struggle to instill limits on the power of economic, political and religious authorities to place individuals and private groups under surveillance against their will. The whole network of American constitutional rights—especially those of free speech, press, assembly and religion; forbidding the quartering of troops in private homes; securing "persons, houses papers and effects" from unreasonable search and seizure; and assuring the privilege against self-incrimination—was established to curtail the ancient surveillance claims of governmental authorities. Similar rules have evolved by statute, common law and judicial decision to limit the surveillance powers of corporations and other private agencies.

WHY WORRY?

Though this general principle of civil liberty is clear, many governmental and private authorities seem puzzled by the protest against current or proposed uses of new surveillance techniques. Why should persons who have not committed criminal acts worry whether their conversations might be accidentally overheard by police officers eavesdropping on public telephone booths or at public places used by suspected criminals? Why should truthful persons resist verifying their testimony through polygraph examination? Shouldn't anyone who appreciates the need for effective personnel placement accept personality testing? And aren't fears about subliminal suggestion or increased data collection simply nervous response to the new and the unknown? In all these instances, authorities point to the fact that beyond the benefits of the surveillance for the organization or the community, the individual himself can now prove his innocence, virtue or talents by "science" and avoid the unjust assumptions frequently produced by "fallible" conventional methods.

The answer, of course, lies in the impact of surveillance on human behavior.

· · · · ·

SOMETHING IS TAKEN AWAY

The right of individuals and organizations to decide when, to whom, and in what way they will "go public" has been taken away from them. It is almost as if we were witnessing an achievement through technology of a risk to modern man comparable to that primitive men felt when they had their photographs taken by visiting anthropologists: a part of them had been taken and might be used to harm them in the future.

American society now seems ready to face the impact of science on privacy. Failure to do so would be to leave the foundations of our free society in peril.

75 Experiments in Group Conflict

MUZAFER SHERIF

This selection by Sherif not only explores the concept of "conflict" but also illustrates one of the methods used by social scientists in their research. By providing a relatively natural setting in which interaction can take place, while at the same time introducing inconspicuous but effective controls over certain crucial elements or variables, Sherif has been able to obtain new evidence about the behavior of individuals and groups in conflict situations. The reader should be cautioned, of course, not to assume that the conclusions drawn from such an experimental setting are applicable to all kinds of groups under all circumstances without further testing.

Conflict between groups—whether between boys' gangs, social classes, "races" or nations—has no simple cause, nor is mankind yet in sight of a cure. It is often rooted deep in personal, social, economic, religious and historical forces. Nevertheless it is possible to identify certain general factors which have a crucial influence on the attitude of any group toward others. Social scientists have long sought to bring these factors to light by studying what might be called the "natural history" of groups and group relations. Intergroup conflict and harmony is not a subject that leads itself easily to laboratory experiments. But in recent years there has been a beginning of attempts to investigate the problem under controlled yet lifelike conditions, and I shall report here the results of a program of experimental studies of groups which I started in 1948. Among the persons working with me were Marvin B. Sussman, Robert Huntington, O. J. Harvey, B. Jack White, William R. Hood and Carolyn W. Sherif. The experiments were conducted in 1949, 1953 and 1954; this article gives a composite of the findings.

We wanted to conduct our study with groups of the informal type, where group organization and attitudes would evolve naturally and spontaneously, without formal direction or external pressures. For this purpose we conceived that an isolated summer camp would make a good experimental setting, and that decision led us to choose as subjects boys about 11 or 12 years old, who would find camping natural and fascinating. Since our aim was to study the development of group relations among these boys under carefully controlled conditions, with as little interference as possible from personal neuroses, background influences or prior experiences, we selected normal boys of

SOURCE: *Scientific American,* vol. 195, no. 5 (November 1956), 54–58. By permission of the author and the publisher. • Muzafer Sherif is professor of social psychology and Director of the Psychological-Social Studies Program at Pennsylvania State University. Born in Turkey, he was educated in his native country and in the United States. He is the author of *The Psychology of Social Norms* and the coauthor of *An Outline of Social Psychology* and *Groups in Harmony and Tension.*

homogeneous background who did not know one another before they came to the camp.

They were picked by a long and thorough procedure. We interviewed each boy's family, teachers and school officials, studied his school and medical records, obtained his scores on personality tests and observed him in his classes and at play with his schoolmates. With all this information we were able to assure ourselves that the boys chosen were of like kind and background: all were healthy, socially well-adjusted, somewhat above average in intelligence, and from stable, white, Protestant, middle-class homes.

None of the boys was aware that he was part of an experiment on group relations. The investigators appeared as a regular camp staff—camp director, counselors and so on. The boys met one another for the first time in buses that took them to the camp, and so far as they knew it was a normal summer of camping. To keep the situation as lifelike as possible, we conducted all our experiments within the framework of regular camp activities and games. We set up projects which were so interesting and attractive that the boys plunged into them enthusiastically without suspecting that they might be test situations. Unobtrusively we made records of their behavior, even using "candid" cameras and microphones when feasible.

We began by observing how the boys became a coherent group. The first of our camps was conducted in the hills of northern Connecticut in the summer of 1949. When the boys arrived, they were all housed at first in one large bunkhouse. As was to be expected, they quickly formed particular friendships and chose buddies. We had deliberately put all the boys together in this expectation because we wanted to see what would happen later after the boys were separated into different groups. Our object was to reduce the factor of personal attraction in the formation of groups. In a few days we divided the boys into two groups and put them in different cabins. Before doing so, we asked each boy informally who his best friends were, and then took pains to place the "best friends" in different groups so far as possible. (The pain of separation was assuaged by allowing each group to go at once on a hike and camp-out.)

As everyone knows, a group of strangers brought together in some common activity soon acquires an informal and spontaneous kind of organization. It comes to look upon some members as leaders, divides up duties, adopts unwritten norms of behavior, develops an *esprit de corps*. Our boys followed this pattern as they shared a series of experiences. In each group the boys pooled their efforts, organized duties and divided up tasks in work and play. Different individuals assumed different responsibilities. One boy excelled in cooking. Another led in athletics. Others, though not outstanding in any one skill, could be counted on to pitch in and do their level best in anything the group attempted. One or two seemed to disrupt activities, to start teasing at the wrong moment or offer useless suggestions. A few boys consistently had good suggestions and showed ability to coordinate the efforts of others in carrying them through. Within a few days one person had proved himself more resourceful and skillful than the rest. Thus, rather quickly, a leader and lieutenants emerged. Some boys sifted toward the bottom of the heap, while others jockeyed for higher positions.

We watched these developments closely and rated the boys' relative positions in the group, not only on the basis of our own observations but also by informal sounding of the boys' opinions as to who got things started, who got things done, who could be counted on to support group activities.

As the group became an organization, the boys coined nicknames. The big, blond, hardy leader of one group was dubbed "Baby Face" by his admiring followers. A boy with a rather long head became "Lemon Head." Each group developed its own jargon, special jokes, secrets and special ways of performing tasks. One group, after killing a snake near a place where it had gone to swim, named the place "Moccasin Creek" and thereafter preferred this swimming hole to any other, though there were better ones nearby.

Wayward members who failed to do things "right" or who did not contribute their bit to the common effort found themselves receiving the "silent treatment," ridicule or even threats. Each group selected symbols and a name, and they had these put on their caps and T-shirts. The 1954 camp was conducted in Oklahoma, near a famous hideaway of Jesse James called Robber's Cave. The two groups of boys at this camp named themselves the Rattlers and the Eagles.

Our conclusions on every phase of the study were based on a variety of observations, rather than on any single method. For example, we devised a game to test the boys' evaluations of one another. Before an important baseball game, we set up a target board for the boys to throw at, on the pretense of making practice for the game more interesting. There were no marks on the front of the board for the boys to judge objectively how close the ball came to a bull's-eye, but, unknown to them, the board was wired to flashing lights behind so that an observer could see exactly where the ball hit. We found that the boys consistently overestimated the performances by the most highly regarded members of their group and underestimated the scores of those of low social standing.

The attitudes of group members were even more dramatically illustrated during a cook-out in the woods. The staff supplied the boys with unprepared food and let them cook it themselves. One boy promptly started to build a fire, asking for help in getting wood. Another attacked the raw hamburger to make patties. Others prepared a place to put buns, relishes and the like. Two mixed soft drinks from flavoring and sugar. One boy who stood around without helping was told by the others to "get to it." Shortly the fire was blazing and the cook had hamburgers sizzling. Two boys distributed them as rapidly as they became edible. Soon it was time for the watermelon. A low-ranking member of the group took a knife and started toward the melon. Some of the boys protested. The most highly regarded boy in the group took over the knife, saying, "You guys who yell the loudest get yours last."

When the two groups in the camp had developed group organization and spirit, we proceeded to the experimental studies of intergroup relations. The groups had had no previous encounters; indeed, in the 1954 camp at Robber's Cave the two groups came in separate buses and were kept apart while each acquired a group feeling.

Our working hypothesis was that when two groups have conflicting aims—i.e., when one can achieve its ends only at the expense of the other—their members will become hostile to each other even though the groups are composed of normal well-adjusted individuals. There is a corollary to this assumption which we shall consider later. To produce friction between the groups of boys we arranged a tournament of games: baseball, touch football, a tug-of-war, a treasure hunt and so on. The tournament started in a spirit of good sportsmanship. But as it progressed good feeling soon evaporated. The members of each group began to call their rivals "stinkers," "sneaks" and "cheaters." They refused to have anything more to do with individuals in the opposing group. The boys in the 1949 camp turned against buddies whom they had chosen as "best friends" when they first arrived at the camp. A large proportion of the boys in each group gave negative ratings to all the boys in the other. The rival groups made threatening posters and planned raids, collecting secret hoards of green apples for ammunition. In the Robber's Cave camp the Eagles, after a defeat in a tournament game, burned a banner left behind by the Rattlers; the next morning the Rattlers seized the Eagles' flag when they arrived on the athletic field. From that time on name-calling, scuffles and raids were the rule of the day.

Within each group, of course, solidarity increased. There were changes: one group deposed its leader because he could not "take it" in the contests with the adversary; another group overnight made something of a hero of a big boy who had previously been regarded as a bully. But morale and cooperativeness within the group became stronger. It is noteworthy that this heightening of cooperativeness and generally democratic behavior did not carry over to the group's relations with other groups.

We now turned to the other side of the problem: How can two groups in conflict be brought into harmony? We first undertook to test the theory that pleasant social contacts between members of conflicting groups will reduce friction between them. In the 1954 camp we brought the hostile Rattlers and Eagles together for social events: going to the movies, eating in the same dining room and so on. But far from reducing conflict, these situations only served as opportunities for the rival groups to berate and attack each other. In the dining-hall line they shoved each other aside, and the group that lost the contest for the head of the line shouted "Ladies first!" at the winner. They threw paper, food and vile names at each other at the tables. An Eagle bumped by a Rattler was admonished by his fellow Eagles to brush "the dirt" off his clothes.

We then returned to the corollary of our assumption about the creation of conflict. Just as competition generates friction, working in a common endeavor should promote harmony. It seemed to us, considering group relations in the everyday world, that where harmony between groups is established, the most decisive factor is the existence of "superordinate" goals which have a compelling appeal for both but which neither could achieve without the other. To test this hypothesis experimentally, we created a series of urgent, and natural, situations which challenged our boys.

One was a breakdown in the water supply. Water came to our camp in pipes from a tank about a mile away. We arranged to interrupt it and then called the boys together to inform them of the crisis. Both groups promptly volunteered to search the water line for the trouble. They worked together harmoniously, and before the end of the afternoon they had located and corrected the difficulty.

A similar opportunity offered itself when the boys requested a movie. We told them that the camp could not afford to rent one. The two groups then got together, figured out how much each group would have to contribute, chose the film by a vote and enjoyed the showing together.

One day the two groups went on an outing at a lake some distance away. A large truck was to go to town for food.

But when everyone was hungry and ready to eat, it developed that the truck would not start (we had taken care of that). The boys got a rope—the same rope they had used in their acrimonious tug-of-war—and all pulled together to start the truck.

These joint efforts did not immediately dispel hostility. At first the groups returned to the old bickering and name-calling as soon as the job in hand was finished. But gradually the series of cooperative acts reduced friction and conflict. The members of the two groups began to feel more friendly to each other. For example, a Rattler whom the Eagles disliked for his sharp tongue and skill in defeating them became a "good egg." The boys stopped shoving in the meal line. They no longer called each other names, and sat together at the table. New friendships developed between individuals in the two groups.

In the end the groups were actively seeking opportunities to mingle, to entertain and "treat" each other. They decided to hold a joint campfire. They took turns presenting skits and songs. Members of both groups requested that they go home together on the same bus, rather than on the separate buses in which they had come. On the way the bus stopped for refreshments. One group still had five dollars which they had won as a prize in a contest. They decided to spend this sum on refreshments. On their own initiative they invited their former rivals to be their guests for malted milks.

Our interviews with the boys confirmed this change. From choosing their "best friends" almost exclusively in their own group, many of them shifted to listing boys in the other group as best friends. They were glad to have a second chance to rate boys in the other group, some of them remarking that they had changed their minds since the first rating made after the tournament. Indeed they had. The new ratings were largely favorable.

Efforts to reduce friction and prejudice between groups in our society have usually followed rather different methods. Much attention has been given to bringing members of hostile groups together socially, to communicating accurate and favorable information about one group to the other, and to bringing the leaders of groups together to enlist their influence. But as everyone knows, such measures sometimes reduce intergroup tensions and sometimes do not. Social contacts, as our experiments demonstrated, may only serve as occasions for intensifying conflict. Favorable information about a disliked group may be ignored or reinterpreted to fit stereotyped notions about the group. Leaders cannot act without regard for the prevailing temper in their own groups.

What our limited experiments have shown is that the possibilities for achieving harmony are greatly enhanced when groups are brought together to work toward common ends. Then favorable information about a disliked group is seen in a new light, and leaders are in a position to take bolder steps toward cooperation. In short, hostility gives way when groups pull together to achieve overriding goals which are real and compelling to all concerned.

76 The Student Revolution

KENNETH KENISTON

One of the pervasive social movements in contemporary society is the student demand for change in the educational institutions as well as in many other aspects of society. In this selection Keniston provides an analysis of the causes of the widespread student revolt. Other scholars have proposed alternate explanations but Keniston's analysis of the causes and their targets provides a useful basis for discussion of this movement.

. . . . .

We have learned to expect students in underdeveloped countries to lead unruly demonstrations against the status quo, but what is new, unexpected and upsetting to many is that an apparently similar mood is sweeping across America, France, Germany, Italy and even Eastern European nations like Czechoslovakia and Poland. Furthermore, the revolts occur, not at the most backward universities, but at the most distinguished, liberal and enlightened—Berkeley, the Sorbonne, Tokyo, Columbia, the Free University of Berlin, Rome and now Harvard.

This development has taken almost everyone by surprise. The American public is clearly puzzled, frightened and often outraged by the behavior of its most privileged youth. The scholarly world, including many who have devoted their lives to the study of student protest, has been caught off guard as well. For many years, American analysts of student movements have been busy demonstrating that "it can't happen here." Student political activity abroad has been seen as a reaction to modernization, industrialization and the demise of traditional or tribal societies. In an already modern, industrialized, detribalized and "stable" nation like America, it was argued, student protests are naturally absent.

Another explanation has tied student protests abroad to bad living conditions in some universities and to the unemployability of their graduates. Student revolts, it was argued, spring partly from the misery of student life in countries like India and Indonesia. Students who must live in penury and squalor naturally turn against their universities and societies. And if, as in many developing nations, hundreds of thousands of university graduates can find no work commensurate with their skills, the chances for student militancy are further increased.

These arguments helped explain the "silent generation" of the nineteen-fifties and the absence of protest, during that period, in American universities, where students are often "indulged" with good living conditions, close student-faculty contact and considerable freedom of speech. And they helped explain why "super-employable" American college graduates, especially the much-sought-

SOURCE: Kenneth Keniston, "You Have to Grow Up in Scarsdale to Know How Bad Things Really Are," The *New York Times Magazine* (April 27, 1969), pp. 27–28, 122–30. • The author is associate professor of psychology at the Yale Medical School and associate director of the social and community psychiatry training program. He is the author of *Young Radicals: Notes on Committed Youth* and *The Uncommitted: Alienated Youth in American Society.*

after ones from colleges like Columbia and Harvard, seemed so contented with their lot.

But such arguments do not help us understand today's noisy, angry and militant students in the advanced countries. Nor do they explain why students who enjoy the greatest advantages—those at the leading universities—are often found in the revolts. As a result, several new interpretations of student protest are currently being put forward, interpretations that ultimately form part of what Richard Poirier has termed "the war against the young."

Many reactions to student unrest, of course, spring primarily from fear, anger, confusion or envy, rather than from theoretical analysis. Governor Wallace's attacks on student "anarchists" and other "pin-headed intellectuals," for example, were hardly coherent explanations of protest. Many of the bills aimed at punishing student protesters being proposed in Congress and state legislatures reflect similar feelings of anger and outrage. Similarly, the presumption that student unrest *must* be part of an international conspiracy is based on emotion rather than fact. Even George F. Kennan's recent discussion of the American student left is essentially a moral condemnation of "revolting students," rather than an effort to explain their behavior.

If we turn to more thoughtful analyses of the current student mood we find two general theories gaining widespread acceptance. The first, articulately expressed by Lewis S. Feuer in his recent book on student movements, "The Conflict of Generations," might be termed the "Oedipal Rebellion" interpretation. The second, cogently stated by Zbigniew Brzezinski and Daniel Bell, can be called the theory of "Historical Irrelevance."

The explanation of Oedipal Rebellion sees the underlying force in all student revolts as blind, unconscious Oedipal hatred of fathers and the older generation. Feuer, for example, finds in all student movements an inevitable tendency toward violence and a combination of "regicide, parricide and suicide." A decline in respect for the authority of the older generation is needed to trigger a student movement, but the force behind it comes from "obscure" and "unconscious" forces in the child's early life, including both intense death wishes against his father and the enormous guilt and self-hatred that such wishes inspire in the child.

The idealism of student movements is thus, in many respects, only a "front" for the latent unconscious destructiveness and self-destructiveness of underlying motivations. Even the expressed desire of these movements to help the poor and exploited is explained psychoanalytically by Feuer. Empathy for the disadvantaged is traced to "traumatic" encounters with parental bigotry in the students' childhoods when their parents forbade them to play with children of other races or lower social classes. The identification of today's new left with blacks is thus interpreted as an unconscious effort to "abreact and undo this original trauma."

There are two basic problems with the Oedipal Rebellion theory, however. First, although it uses psychoanalytic terms, it is bad psychoanalysis. The real psychoanalytic account insists that the Oedipus complex is universal in all normally developing children. To point to this complex in explaining student rebellion is, therefore, like pointing to the fact that all children learn to walk. Since both characteristics are said to be universal, neither helps us understand why, at some historical moments, students are restive and rebellious, while at others they are not. Second, the theory does not help us explain why some students (especially those from middle-class, affluent and idealistic families) are most inclined to rebel, while others (especially those from working-class and deprived families) are less so.

In order really to explain anything, the Oedipal Rebellion hypothesis would have to be modified to point to an unusually *severe* Oedipus complex, involving especially *intense* and unresolved unconscious feelings of father-hatred in student rebels. But much is now known about the lives and backgrounds of these rebels—at least those in the United States—and this evidence does not support even the modified theory. On the contrary, it indicates that most student protesters are relatively *close* to their parents, that the values they profess are usually the ones they learned at the family dinner table, and that their parents tend to be highly educated, liberal or left-wing and politically active.

Furthermore, psychological studies of student radicals indicate that they are no more neurotic, suicidal, enraged or disturbed than are nonradicals. Indeed, most studies find them to be rather more integrated, self-accepting and "advanced," in a psychological sense, than their politically inactive contemporaries. In general, research on American student rebels supports a "Generational Solidarity" (or chip-off-the-old-block) theory, rather than one of Oedipal Rebellion.

The second theory of student revolts now being advanced asserts that they are a reaction against "historical irrelevance." Rebellion springs from the unconscious awareness of some students that society has left them and their values behind. According to this view, the ultimate causes of student dissent are sociological rather than psychological. They lie in fundamental changes in the nature of the advanced societies—especially, in the change from industrial to post-industrial society. The student revolution is seen not as a true revolution, but as a counter-revolution—what Daniel Bell has called "the guttering last gasp of a romanticism sourced by rancor and impotence."

This theory assumes that we are moving rapidly into a new age in which technology will dominate, an age whose real rulers will be men like computer experts, systems analysts and technobureaucrats. Students who are attached to outmoded and obsolescent values like humanism and romanticism unconsciously feel they have no place in this post-industrial world. When they rebel they are like the Luddites of the past—workers who smashed machines to protest the inevitable industrial revolution. Today's student revolt reflects what Brzezinski terms "an unconscious realization that they [the rebels] are themselves becoming historically obsolete"; it is nothing but the "death rattle of the historical irrelevants."

This theory is also inadequate. It assumes that the shape of the future is already technologically determined, and that protesting students unconsciously "know" that it will offer them no real reward, honor or power. But the idea that the future can be accurately predicted is open to fundamental objection. Every past attempt at prophecy has turned out to be grievously incorrect. Extrapolations from the past, while sometimes useful in the short run, are usually fundamentally wrong in the long run, especially when they attempt to predict the quality of human life, the nature of political and social organization, international relations or the shape of future culture.

The future is, of course, made by men. Technology is not an inevitable master of man and history, but merely provides the possibility of applying scientific knowledge to specific problems. Men may identify with it or refuse to, use it or be used by it for good or evil, apply it humanely or destructively. Thus, there is no real evidence that student protest will emerge as the "death rattle of the historical irrelevants." It could equally well be the "first spark of a new historical era." No one today can be sure of the outcome, and people who feel certain that the future will bring the obsolescence and death of those whom they dislike are often merely expressing their fond hope.

The fact that today's students invoke "old" humanistic and romantic ideas in no way proves that student protests are a "last gasp" of a dying order. Quite the contrary: *All* revolutions draw upon older values and visions. Many of the ideals of the French Revolution, for example, originated in Periclean Athens. Revolutions do not occur because new ideas suddenly develop, but because a new generation begins to take *old* ideas seriously—not merely as interesting theoretical views, but as the basis for political action and social change. Until recently, the humanistic vision of human fulfillment and the romantic vision of an expressive, imaginative and passionate life were taken seriously only by small aristocratic or Bohemian groups. The fact that they are today taken as real goals by millions of students in many nations does not mean that these students are "counterrevolutionaries," but merely that their ideas follow the pattern of every major revolution.

Indeed, today's student rebels are rarely opposed to technology *per se*. On the contrary, they take the high technology of their societies completely for granted, and concern themselves with it very little. What they *are* opposed to is, in essence, the worship of Technology, the tendency to treat people as "inputs" or "outputs" of a technological system, the subordination of human needs to technological programs. The essential conflict between the minority of students who make up the student revolt and the existing order is a conflict over the future direction of technological society, not a counter-revolutionary protest against technology.

In short, both the Oedipal Rebellion and the Historical Irrelevance theories are what students would call "put-downs." If we accept either, we are encouraged not to listen to protests, or to explain them away or reject them as either the "acting out" of destructive Oedipal feelings or the blind reaction of an obsolescent group to the awareness of its obsolescence. But if, as I have argued, neither of these theories is adequate to explain the current "wave" of student protest here and abroad, how can we understand it?

• • • • •

One factor often cited to explain student unrest is the large number of people in the world under 30—today the critical dividing line between generations. But this explanation alone, like the theories just discussed, is not adequate, for in all historical eras the vast portion of the population has always been under 30. Indeed, in primitive societies most people die before they reach that age. If chronological youth alone was enough to insure rebellion, the advanced societies—where a greater proportion of the population reaches old age than ever before in history—should be the *least* revolutionary, and primitive societies the *most.* This is not the case.

More relevant factors are the relationship of those under 30 to the established institutions of society (that is, whether they are engaged in them or not); and the opportunities that society provides for their continuing intellectual, ethical and emotional development. In both cases the present situation in the advanced nations is without precedent.

. . . . .

Only as industrial societies became prosperous enough to defer adult work until after puberty could they create institutions—like widespread secondary-school education—that would extend adolescence to virtually all young people. Recognition of adolescence also arose from the vocational and psychological requirements of these societies, which needed much higher levels of training and psychological development than could be guaranteed through primary education alone. There is, in general, an intimate relationship between the way a society defines the stages of life and its economic, political and social characteristics.

Today, in more developed nations, we are beginning to witness the recognition of still another stage of life. Like childhood and adolescence, it was initially granted only to a small minority, but is now being rapidly extended to an ever-larger group. I will call this the stage of "youth," and by that I mean both a further phase of disengagement from society and the period of psychological development that intervenes between adolescence and adulthood. This stage, which continues into the 20's and sometimes into the 30's, provides opportunities for intellectual, emotional and moral development that were never afforded to any other large group in history. In the student revolts we are seeing one result of this advance.

I call the extension of youth an advance advisedly. Attendance at a college or university is a major part of this extension, and there is growing evidence that this is, other things being equal, a good thing for the student. Put in an oversimplified phrase, it tends to free him—to free him from swallowing unexamined the assumptions of the past, to free him from the superstitions of his childhood, to free him to express his feelings more openly and to free him from irrational bondage to authority.

I do not mean to suggest, of course, that all college graduates are free and liberated spirits, unencumbered by irrationality, superstition, authoritarianism or blind adherence to tradition. But these findings do indicate that our colleges, far from cranking out only machinelike robots who will provide skilled manpower for the economy, are also producing an increasing number of highly critical citizens—young men and women who have the opportunity, the leisure, the affluence and the educational resources to continue their development beyond the point where most people in the past were required to stop it.

So, one part of what we are seeing on campuses throughout the world is not a reflection of how bad higher education is, but rather of its extraordinary accomplishments. Even the moral righteousness of the student rebels, a quality both endearing and infuriating to their elders, must be judged at least partially a consequence of the privilege of an extended youth; for a prolonged development, we know, encourages the individual to elaborate a more personal, less purely conventional sense of ethics.

What the advanced nations have done is to create their own critics on a mass basis—that is, to create an ever-larger group of young people who take the highest values of their societies as their own, who internalize these values and identify them with their own best selves, and who are willing to struggle to implement them. At the same time, the extension of youth has lessened the personal risks of dissent: These young people have been freed from the requirements of work, gainful employment and even marriage, which permits them to criticize their society from a protected position of disengagement.

But the mere prolongation of development need not automatically lead to unrest. To be sure, we have granted to millions the opportunity to examine their societies, to compare them with their values and to come to a reasoned judgment of the existing order. But why should their judgment today be so unenthusiastic?

What protesting students throughout the world share is a mood more than an ideology or a program, a mood that says the existing system—the power structure—is hypocritical, unworthy of respect, outmoded and in urgent need of reform. In addition, students everywhere speak of repression, manipulation and authoritarianism. (This is paradoxical, considering the apparently great freedoms given them in many nations. In America, for example, those who complain most loudly about being suffocated by the subtle tyranny of the Establishment usually attend the institutions where student freedom is greatest.) Around this general mood, specific complaints arrange themselves as symptoms of what students often call the "exhaustion of the existing society."

To understand this phenomenon we must recognize that, since the Second World War, some societies have indeed begun to move past the industrial era into a new world that is post-industrial, technological, post-modern, post-historic or, in Brzezinski's term, "technectronic." In Western Europe, the United States, Canada and Japan, the first contours of this new society are already apparent. And, in many other less-developed countries, middle-class professionals (whose children become activists) often live in post-industrial enclaves within pre-industrial societies. Whatever we call the post-industrial world, it has demonstrated that, for the first time, man can produce more than enough to meet his material needs.

This accomplishment is admittedly blemished by enormous problems of economic distribution in the advanced nations, and it is in terrifying contrast to the overwhelming poverty of the Third World. Nevertheless, it is clear that what might be called "the problem of production" *can,* in principle, be solved. If all members of American society, for example, do not have enough material goods, it is because the system of distribution is flawed. The same is true, or will soon be true, in many other nations that are approaching advanced states of industrialization. Characteristically, these nations, along with the most technological, are those where student unrest has recently been most prominent.

The transition from industrial to post-industrial society brings with it a major shift in social emphases and values. Industrializing and industrial societies tend to be oriented toward solving the problem of production. An industrial ethic—sometimes Protestant, sometimes Socialist, sometimes Communist—tends to emphasize psychological qualities like self-discipline, delay of gratification, achievement-orientation and a strong emphasis on economic success and productivity. The social, political and economic institutions of these societies tend to be organized in a way that is consistent with the goal of increasing production. And industrial societies tend to apply relatively uniform standards, to reward achievement rather than status acquired by birth, to emphasize emotional neutrality ("coolness") and rationality in work and public life.

The emergence of post-industrial societies, however, means that growing numbers of the young are brought up in family environments where abundance, relative economic security, political freedom and affluence are simply facts of life, not goals to be striven for. To such people the psychological imperatives, social institutions and cultural values of the industrial ethic seem largely outdated and irrelevant to their own lives.

Once it has been demonstrated that a society *can* produce enough for all of its members, at least some of the young turn to other goals: for example, trying to make sure that society *does* produce enough and distributes it fairly, or searching for ways to live meaningfully with the goods and the leisure they *already* have. The problem is that our society has, in some realms, exceeded its earlier targets. Lacking new ones, it has become exhausted by its success.

When the values of industrial society become devitalized, the élite sectors of youth—the most affluent, intelligent, privileged and so on—come to feel that they live in institutions whose demands lack moral authority or, in the current jargon, "credibility." Today, the moral imperative and urgency behind production, acquisition, materialism and abundance has been lost.

Furthermore, with the lack of moral legitimacy felt in "the System," the least request for loyalty, restraint or conformity by its representatives—for example, by college presidents and deans—can easily be seen as a moral outrage, an authoritarian repression, a manipulative effort to "co-opt" students into joining the Establishment and an exercise in 'illegitimate authority" that must be resisted. From this conception springs at least part of the students vague sense of oppression. And, indeed, perhaps their peculiar feeling of suffocation arises ultimately from living in societies without vital ethical claims.

Given such a situation, it does not take a clear-cut issue to trigger a major protest. I doubt, for example, that college and university administrators are in fact *more* hypocritical and dishonest than they were in the past. . . . The conditions for students in America have never been as good, especially, as I have noted, at those élite colleges where student protests are most common.

But this is *precisely* the point: It is *because* so many of the *other* problems of American society seem to have been resolved, or to be resolvable in principle, that students now react with new indignation to old problems, turn to new goals and propose radical reforms.

So far I have emphasized the moral exhaustion of the old order and the fact that, for the children of post-industrial affluence, the once-revolutionary claims of the industrial society have lost much of their validity. I now want to argue that we are witnessing on the campuses of the world a fusion of *two revolutions* with distinct historical origins. One is a continuation of the old and familiar revolution of the industrial society, the liberal-democratic-egalitarian revolution that started in America and France at the turn of the 18th century and spread to virtually every nation in the world. (Not completed in any of them, its contemporary American form is, above all, to be found in the increased militancy of blacks.) The other is the new revolution, the post-industrial one, which seeks to define new goals relevant to the 20th and 21st centuries.

In its social and political aspects, the first revolution has been one of universalization, to use the sociologist's awkward term. It has involved the progressive extension to more and more people of economic, political and social rights, privileges and opportunities originally available only to the aristocracy, then to the middle class, and now in America to the relatively affluent white working class. It is, in many respects, a *quantitative* revolution. That is, it concerns itself less with the quality of life than with the amount of political freedom, the quantity and distribution of goods or the amount and level of injustice.

As the United States approaches the targets of the first revolution, on which this society was built, to be poor shifts from being an unfortunate fact of life to being an outrage. And, for the many who have never experienced poverty, discrimination, exploitation or oppression, even to *witness* the existence of these evils in the lives of others suddenly becomes intolerable. In our own time the impatience to complete the first revolution has grown apace, and we find less willingness to compromise, wait and forgive among the young, especially among those who now take the values of the old revolution for granted—seeing them not as goals, but as *rights.*

A subtle change has thus occurred. What used to be utopian ideals—like equality, abundance and freedom from discrimination—have now become demands, inalienable rights upon which one can insist without brooking any compromise. It is noteworthy that, in today's student confrontations, no one requests anything. Students present their "demands."

So, on the one hand, we see a growing impatience to complete the first revolution. But, on the other, there is a newer revolution concerned with newer issues, a revolution that is less social, economic or political than psychological, historical and cultural. It is less concerned with the quantities of things than with their qualities, and it judges the virtually complete liberal revolution and finds it still wanting.

"You have to have grown up in Scarsdale to know how bad things really are," said one radical student. This comment would probably sound arrogant, heartless and insensitive to a poor black, much less to a citizen of the Third World. But he meant something important by it. He meant that *even* in the Scarsdales of America, with their affluence, their upper-middle-class security and abundance, their well-fed, well-heeled children and their excellent schools, something is wrong. Economic affluence does not guarantee a feeling of personal fulfillment; political freedom does not always yield an inner sense of liberation and cultural freedom; social justice and equality may leave one with a feeling that something else is missing in life. "No to the consumer society!" shouted the bourgeois students of the Sorbonne during May and June of 1968—a cry that understandably alienated French workers, for whom affluence and the consumer society are still central goals.

What, then, are the targets of the new revolution? As is often noted, students themselves don't know. They speak vaguely of "a society that has never existed," of "new values," of a "more humane world," of "liberation" in some psychological, cultural and historical sense. Their rhetoric is largely negative; they are stronger in opposition than in proposals for reform; their diagnoses often seem accurate, but their prescriptions are vague; and they are far more articulate in urging the immediate completion of the first revolution than in defining the goals of the second. Thus, we can only indirectly discern trends that point to the still-undefined targets of the new revolution.

What are these trends and targets?

First, there is a revulsion against the notion of quantity, particularly economic quantity and materialism, and a turn toward concepts of quality. One of the most delightful slogans of the French student revolt was, "Long live the passionate revolution of creative intelligence!" In a sense, the achievement of abundance may allow millions of contemporary men and women to examine, as only a few artists and madmen have examined in the past, the quality, joyfulness and zestfulness of experience. The "expansion of consciousness"; the stress on the expressive, the aesthetic and the creative; the emphasis on imagination, direct perception and fantasy—all are part of the effort to enhance the quality of this experience.

Another goal of the new revolution involves a revolt against uniformity, equalization, standardization and homogenization—not against technology itself, but against the "technologization of man." At times, this revolt approaches anarchic quaintness, but it has a positive core as well—the demand that individuals be appreciated, not because of their similarities or despite their differences, but because they *are* different, diverse, unique and noninterchangeable. This attitude is evident in many areas: for example, the insistence upon a cultivation of personal idiosyncrasy, mannerism and unique aptitude. Intellectually, it is expressed in the rejection of the melting-pot and consensus-politics view of American life in favor of a post-homogeneous America in which cultural diversity and conflict are underlined rather than denied.

The new revolution also involves a continuing struggle against psychological or institutional closure or rigidity in any form, even the rigidity of a definite adult role. Positively, it extols the virtues of openness, motion and continuing human development. What Robert J. Lifton has termed the protein style is clearly in evidence. There is emerging a concept of a lifetime of personal change, of an adulthood of continuing self-transformation, of an adaptability and an openness to the revolutionary modern world that will enable the individual to remain "with it"—psychologically youthful and on top of the present.

Another characteristic is the revolt against centralized power and the complementary demand for participation. What is demanded is not merely the consent of the governed, but the involvement of the governed. "Participatory democracy" summarizes this aspiration, but it extends far beyond the phrase and the rudimentary social forms that have sprung up around it. It extends to the demand for relevance in education—that is, for a chance for the student to participate in his own educational experience in a way that involves all of his faculties, emotional and moral as well as intellectual. The demand for "student power" (or, in Europe, "co-determination") is an aspect of the same theme: At Nanterre, Columbia, Frankfurt and Harvard, students increasingly seek to participate in making the policies of their universities.

This demand for participation is also embodied in the new ethic of "meaningful human relationships," in which individuals confront each other without masks, pretenses and games. They "relate" to each other as unique and irreplaceable human beings, and develop new forms of relationships from which all participants will grow.

In distinguishing between the old and the new revolutions, and in attempting to define the targets of the new, I am, of course, making distinctions that students themselves rarely make. In any one situation the two revolutions are joined and fused, if not confused. For example, the Harvard students' demand for "restructuring the university" is essentially the second revolution's demand for participation; but their demand for an end to university "exploitation" of the surrounding community is tied to the more traditional goals of the first revolution. In most radical groups there is a range of opinion that starts with the issues of the first (racism, imperialism, exploitation, war) and runs to the concerns of the second (experimental education, new life styles, meaningful participation, consciousness-expansion, relatedness, encounter and community). The first revolution is personified by Maoist-oriented Progressive Labor party factions within the student left, while the second is represented by hippies, the "acid left," and the Yippies. In any individual, and in all student movements, these revolutions coexist in uneasy and often abrasive tension.

Furthermore, one of the central problems for student movements today is the absence of any theory of society that does justice to the new world in which we of the most industrialized nations live. In their search for rational critiques of present societies, students turn to theories like Marxism that are intricately bound up with the old revolution.

Such theories make the ending of economic exploitation, the achievement of social justice, the abolition of racial discrimination and the development of political participation and freedom central, but they rarely deal adequately with the issues of the second revolution. Students inevitably try to adapt the rhetoric of the first to the problems of the second, using concepts that are often blatantly inadequate to today's world.

Even the concept of "revolution" itself is so heavily laden with images of political, economic and social upheaval that it hardly seems to characterize the equally radical but more social-psychological and cultural transformations involved in the new revolution. One student, recognizing this, called the changes occurring in his California student group, "too radical to be called a revolution." Students are thus often misled by their borrowed vocabulary, but most adults are even more confused, and many are quickly led to the mistaken conclusion that today's student revolt is nothing more than a repetition of Communism's in the past.

Failure to distinguish between the old and new revolutions also makes it impossible to consider the critical question of how compatible they are with each other. Does it make sense—or is it morally right—for today's affluent American students to seek imagination, self-actualization, individuality, openness and relevance when most of the world and many in America live in deprivation, oppression and misery?

The fact that the first revolution is "completed" in Scarsdale does not mean that it is (or soon will be) in Harlem or Appalachia—to say nothing of Bogotá or Calcutta. For many children of the second revolution, the meaning of life may be found in completing the first—that is, in extending to others the "rights" they have always taken for granted.

For others the second revolution will not wait; the question, "What lies beyond affluence?" demands an answer now. Thus, although we may deem it self-indulgent to pursue the goals of the new revolution in a world where so much misery exists, the fact is that in the advanced nations it is upon us, and we must at least learn to recognize it.

Finally, beneath my analysis lies an assumption I had best make explicit. Many student critics argue that their societies have failed miserably. My argument, a more historical one perhaps, suggests that our problem is not only that industrial societies have failed to keep all their promises, but that they have succeeded in some ways beyond all expectations. Abundance was once a distant dream, to be postponed to a hereafter of milk and honey; today, most Americans are affluent. Universal mass education was once a Utopian goal; today in America almost the entire population completes high school and almost half enters colleges and universities.

The notion that individuals might be free, en masse, to continue their psychological, intellectual, moral and cognitive development through their teens and into their 20's would have been laughed out of court in any century other than our own; today, that opportunity is open to millions of young Americans. Student unrest is a reflection not only of the failures, but also of the extraordinary successes of the liberal-industrial revolution. It therefore occurs in the nations and in the colleges where, according to traditional standards, conditions are best.

But for many of today's students who have never experienced anything but affluence, political freedom and social equality, the old vision is dead or dying. It may inspire bitterness and outrage when it is not achieved, but it no longer animates or guides. In place of it, students (and many who are not students) are searching for a new vision, a new set of values, a new set of targets appropriate to the post-industrial era—a myth, an ideology or a set of goals that will concern itself with the quality of life and answer the question, "Beyond freedom and affluence, what?"

What characterizes student unrest in the developed nations is this peculiar mixture of the old and the new, the urgent need to fulfill the promises of the past and, at the same time, to define the possibilities of the future.

77 On Keeping Our Cool in the Halls of Ivy

THOMAS FORD HOULT,
JOHN W. HUDSON, AND
ALBERT J. MAYER

The preceding selection focused on the causes of one special form of social conflict—the student revolt. This selection addresses itself to institutional response to questions about, and threats to, an institution's organization and methods of operation, and illustrates these ideas by analyzing the university scene within which the student revolt is focused. The authors, recognizing the potential for destruction of academic freedom in the university, then propose ways in which they feel universities should respond to these conflict situations. It should be noted that two generations ago these concepts could have been best illustrated by examining labor-management relations; today the university seems to be the significant setting within which to illumine these questions that are so much in debate—"Who shall control?" "How shall this control be obtained?" and "How shall this control be exercised without demolishing the university as society's primary arena for the free exchange of ideas?"

Current student protest movements have raised the question—"Who should control the university?" Answers to the question vary with the values of those answering it. *Our* values are such that we answer thus:

> Any university should be controlled by those persons and groups, and in such a way, that the university's function is most expeditiously fulfilled.

SOURCE: *AAUP Bulletin*, vol. 55, no. 2 (Summer 1969), 186–91. Reprinted by permission of the authors and the publisher. • Thomas Hoult is professor and chairman of the Department of Sociology at Arizona State University. His major interests include social problems and political sociology. He is the author of *Sociology of Religion* and the *Dictionary of Modern Sociology*. • John Hudson is professor of sociology at Arizona State University. His major interests include marriage and family and social psychology. He is the author of "Value Issues in Marital Counseling." • Albert Mayer is professor of sociology at Arizona State University. His interests include urban sociology and demography. He is coauthor of *Medical Public Relations*.

Since we base our answer on the function of the university, the obvious next question is: "What is the basic function of the university?" Our answer, gleaned from a wide range of historical experience, is that the university exists to preserve, extend, and disseminate accurate knowledge. This idealistic conception of the university's function is, of course, not acceptable to those who would like the university to be a handmaiden to the establishment or become (as one observer put it) an "all-purpose brothel." But when a university is thus made to serve specific interests, it is diverted from the task of helping to meet society's critical need for knowledge. This need is met systematically and adequately in the university setting alone, and only to the degree that the university is permeated with a sense of freedom from partisan ideological control, whether such control emanates from left or right, black or white, business or labor. This means, in turn, that we disagree with Christian Bay's view that the university should be politically active. He has asserted:

> We want . . . to extricate the university from its present stance of indifference and passive or active support to ugly government policies like the war in Viet Nam.

We agree that the U.S. Viet Nam policy is unwarranted and, *as individuals*, we have strongly opposed it. But we have not asked the university, as such, to join us in this protest because we know that the politically committed university almost always degenerates so that it becomes little more than a tool for whoever is in power at any given time. It is unfortunate that the politically neutral university unavoidably lends indirect support to an existing regime, but the consequences of active commitment appear to be worse, as illustrated by the sad state of schools which have proscribed all but "Aryan science," "free enterprise economics," or "Marxian dialectic."

Those accepting the foregoing point of view—the view that the university's purpose is cultivation of the life of the mind and that control of the university should be such as to facilitate its purpose—have, in effect, a general guide for making appropriate responses when various individuals or groups make demands on the university. The guide can be summarized as a question to be asked and answered when a demand is made: "If this demand is acceded to, will the functioning of the university be enhanced?"

We are convinced that much of the chaos now gripping so many campuses can be alleviated or avoided only to the degree that those concerned adopt, and firmly and consistently adhere to, a guide such as that suggested above. To clarify the important implications of this point, we have formulated a number of relevant assertions, ranging from pure value judgments to factual observations; we list these assertions below, together with conclusions that appear to follow logically. By "relevant assertions" we mean those particularly applicable to the university," the latter phrase being used here to designate universities and liberal arts colleges in general. A few of the conclusions will, at first glance, seem to contradict others; but further thought will indicate that this is only superficially so, since a rational approach to a subject as complex as the campus crisis calls for an attitudinal set that is a unique blend of realism and idealism.

I. ***Assertion*** Aside from the restrictions imposed by relevant aspects of the requirements of academic freedom and the democratic process, ultimate control over the university should logically be exercised by the most knowledgeable members of the university community.

Conclusion Faculty members and administrative officials should strenuously resist the various moves to implement total student control over the university. If, in comparison to students generally, faculty members and other senior participants in the university community do not have a better grasp of the educational process and of historical perspective, then the faculty are being paid under false pretenses. Students who do not agree with this point of view are wasting their time, energy, and money, since the basic premise of almost every school is that the faculty has special know-how which can be acquired by students who apply themselves adequately.

The knowledge and campus privilege differential between faculty and students does not, of course, imply that faculty are "better" than students; it implies only that members of the two groups temporarily have different tasks in the division of labor. Thus, there is no master-slave relationship between students and faculty, as claimed in Jerry Farber's "The Student as Nigger." Students become teachers, but slaves never become masters.

Varying time-involvement is another justification for faculty-administration control of academic affairs. Unlike faculty members in general, students do not have to live with the results of various changes that can be made. Furthermore, youthful students typically have transitory interests that alter before they can be implemented. "Hurry up and grant my non-negotiable demands before I forget what they are," shouts the protester in a recent Hugo cartoon.

Faculty-administrative control over academia need not, however, be arbitrary or absolute. Students quite properly want and should have control over their own day-to-day concerns—the activity funds they subsidize, the student news media, their own private lives, and so on. In addition, the student point of view should be well-represented on all appropriate university committees, in the formulation of new programs, and even—along with that of faculty—on controlling boards of regents or trustees.

But the student views represented should obviously be those of genuine students in general, not the pseudo-students whose aim is destruction rather than growth. "Student power will take over the universities; we will wreck them or we will burn them down," the 1968–69 president of the 365,000 member Canadian Union of Students has declared publicly. Giving such a person an official voice on campus is equivalent to choosing Nasser as spokesman for the Israelis. Modern society is, after all, the accumulated wisdom of the ages, and this wisdom is stored in the facilities and professional personnel of the university community. Destroying the university, thus, promises nothing but a return to the conditions prevailing during the dark ages.

II. ***Assertion*** When more than a relatively small number of participants in a social system become seriously alienated from the system, the latter will usually not survive unless the extent of the alienation is sufficiently reduced by appropriate and timely reforms.

Conclusion On any given university campus, responsible administrative officials must carefully ascertain the real nature of local student protest movements and activity. If such study indicates that particular difficulties are almost solely due to a few noisy nihilists, then it is reasonable to conclude that the trouble-makers can be handled without undue complication—although, in the interests of justice, some reforms may be appropriate.

On the other hand, if a proper survey indicates that readily visible protest activities are outward symbols of widespread unrest, then suitable fundamental changes are necessary and should be instituted immediately—a conclusion which is prompted by the obvious fact that the basically undermined social organization can hardly accomplish its purpose. This point has been illustrated all too graphically at San Francisco State College. Presently available information suggests that months before serious difficulty surfaced at San Francisco State, various student groups were given the classic run-around when they made legitimate requests such as that more students be included on appropriate committees, that courses dealing realistically with black Americans be innaugurated, etc. Finally, repeated frustration resulted in the various explosions and absurd demands about which we now know more than we really want to know.

For those willing to learn, the San Francisco State story has two important lessons: one is that orderly dissent, ignored, readily becomes disorderly; the other is that in the modern Western world, any social system will function effectively and peaceably only to the degree that a large majority of those expected to abide by the system's norms are convinced that they have both a say and a stake in the norms. These principles can be given meaningful expression in the campus setting by involving students in various appropriate decision-making processes. Putting the point more bluntly, senior members of the university community need to share some of the power that has always been exclusively theirs. This will pain a number of those who feel nothing should ever be done the first time, but realists will see that the alternative to such sharing can easily become a breakdown of the whole system followed by a power reshuffle that is unlikely to leave any prerogatives in the hands of those representing the old establishment.

So—faculty members and administrative officials, awake! You have nothing to lose but your livelihoods if you continue in a blissful unawareness that students will no longer tolerate the sense of being used. As one student wrote in a recent letter to the editor: "We are angry because we are powerless. We have no voice in the forces which so completely control our lives."

III. ***Assertion*** A university's limited funds and energies are needlessly depleted when university officials, performing as such, engage in activities that are not reasonably related to the creation and dissemination of knowledge.

Conclusion Universities should publicly disavow the doctrine of *in loco parentis* and should therefore cease the attempt to regulate the personal life of students. If students violate the law, they can pay the attendant penalties; but it is no direct concern of the university that its students, when off campus, smoke marijuana, engage in legally prohibited sexual behavior, consume alcoholic beverages, etc. When the university's basic function is kept in mind, it becomes clear that the university's concern with non-academic behavior is properly confined to doing research on, and teaching about, the likely consequences of any given kind of action.

IV. ***Assertion*** Arbitrary categorization of men, such as on the basis of race, is one of the root causes of human misery.

Conclusion Demands for Jim Crow dormitories, student unions, and curriculums should be resisted vigorously. Racism on the part of whites has always been reprehensible; it does not achieve respectability when it is manifested by blacks. University officials should not be misled by irrational guilt feelings arising from the customary treatment of blacks by whites. This treatment has obviously been almost totally deplorable, but it is not mitigated in any meaningful way by new forms of the very evil underlying the treatment.

For these same reasons, proposals for courses teaching "race pride" should be opposed. It is particularly unfortunate that black Americans have, in effect, accepted the prevailing general value that "black is bad"—but the answer to this sad result is cultivation of self-acceptance, not racism in a new form. If race pride on the part of blacks is acceptable—e.g., black is beautiful *because* it is black—then the logical grounds for opposing white racism are removed.

A related matter is the current cry on the part of some militants that a separate black world would somehow lead to a better life for the average black man. But this is a misleading idea and, if historical experience is any guide, quite inaccurate. It is therefore obligatory for knowledgeable members of the university community—in line with the university's function of disseminating *accurate* information—to tell it like it really is when it comes to the question of black separatism. And this is the way it really is: It would be a violation of constitutional principles to block those who wish to withdraw from participation in society at large, but the present distribution of power, knowledge, and resources is such that creation of separate black and white worlds would very likely condemn the vast majority of blacks to a state of permanent inferiority. The black world would almost certainly become a case of *Emperor Jones* writ large. According to Roy Wilkins, NAACP head:

> Racial separatism is but a comforting delusion for those who impose it. It is a hell in a thousand different big and little ways for those upon whom it is imposed.

The American Indian reservation experience is relevant—there we can see the consequences of separatism for those who have long and sadly been dominated: an illiteracy rate of 75 per cent, alcoholism as a way of life, and, for many participants, a degraded and hopeless existence that makes a mockery of the separatist claim, "At least we'll have dignity." It would be telling it like it is to assert, "If that is dignity, then the word has lost all meaning."

The foregoing does not mean that a black studies curriculum—as distinguished from "autonomous" Jim Crow schooling—is inappropriate. Surely there is as much justification for black studies as for the Latin American and Asian studies that already exist in so many schools. In addition, a well-run black studies curriculum can serve the dual purpose of providing a more familiar academic home-away-from-home for particular students, and it can help to compensate for the devastating sense of having no place-in-the-sun that underlies the self-rejection so common among black Americans.

V. ***Assertion*** Students are misled when they are not taught that in the United States today one can become occupationally successful in the best jobs only to the extent that one manifests what may roughly be termed middle-class behavior (willingness to postpone reward, diligent and systematic attention to tasks, clock orientation, etc.—in short, the Puritan work ethic).

Conclusion We should resist the pressure to apply lower standards to students who, because of their membership in a disadvantaged minority group, are ill-prepared for traditional college life. Students so treated inadvertently learn something that is erroneous and potentially damaging to them—namely, that moaning about the past gets the same results as hard work in the present, or that one can make it in American life simply by pleading one is a victim of historical injustice. This may work with softhearted instructors, but it gains nothing but tokenism in the harsh world of business.

However, the university helps to perpetuate injustice if it does not have well-staffed and financed remedial programs designed to aid the culturally disadvantaged meet normal requirements. A university which does not have such programs is contributing to the conditions that spark revolution since it is saying, in effect, "Successful participation in the general social system now requires a university education, but numerous people must be denied such education because they unfortunately chose the wrong kind of forebears." Such a statement is equivalent to saying, "Let them eat cake," and promises the same type of consequences.

Programs set up to help system outsiders become insiders do not, of course, insure positive results. Indeed, it is only realistic to observe that a distressingly large number of persons reared in ghetto circumstances probably cannot be trained to meet ordinary academic standards. This observation applies particularly to those persons who have been doubly damned—i.e., those who not only face the usual disadvantages arising from segregation and discrimination, but who have also become long-term victims of the stultifying effects of deficient health conditions.

The logical answer for such life-time victims of a social system that has deprived them of chances for normal development is an appropriate social-welfare-and-technical-training program that is accompanied by related massive social changes designed to eliminate the factors presently dooming whole categories of people to become second-class citizens. But since logic does not always prevail, harassed college officials—fearing censure for the continued racial imbalance in the student body—often admit to conventional programs some persons who clearly cannot become qualified for traditional academic work. Such a response to the problem subverts the university's function and is no help to those who can't possibly make the regular grade, academically speaking. The latter typically become drop-outs, thus giving false substance to prevailing negative stereotypes; and they quite understandably become more frustrated and bitter than ever since they have been given a taste of a sweet life that they know is forever barred to them. Who can reasonably blame them for then listening sympathetically to extremists that vow to wreck the system that has wrecked them?

The technical-training program referred to above could well be a college-sponsored and degree-granting parallel to the vocational high school. This would accommodate to the reality that a four-year college degree is now the social equivalent to the high school diploma of yesteryear—and, just as public high schools had to find ways to admit and graduate virtually all students, so must tax-supported undergraduate colleges.

VI. ***Assertion*** Education is not, strictly, speaking, something that is done to people; it is something they do to themselves.

Conclusion Many of the protests about "poor teaching," "irrelevant classes," and lack of meaningful courses are based on the false premise that education is something that is injected into people if teachers are clever enough to know how to wield the appropriate type of instrument. Actually, however, education that is truly significant for any given individual is the information he seeks out and integrates into a personal philosophy. In the words of Arizona State University's first president ("Territorial Normal School" then), "Self-effort educates." The best universities are those which provide a setting such that they attract the type of student who is most inclined to dig out the facts and work out the relationships for himself. Even in the lesser universities, the enterprising student can, with an assiduous reading and library program, compensate for all manner of poor teaching, irrelevant subject matter, or non-existent curriculums dealing with this and that. Such self-help programs will, of course, not seem attractive to the complainers whose demands suggest that they think there must be a gimmick making it possible to get a degree without serious effort, or alternatively, that education is something which can somehow be silver-plattered to the passive.

VII. ***Assertion*** The essence of the university is that it is a place for the conduct of various forms of *reasoned* debate, but such debate cannot take place when there is serious physical interference with the usual academic activities of members of the university community.

Conclusion Those responsible for the operation of the university must use all necessary measures to block any who wish to impede the regular functioning of the university. If, in some rare instances, "all necessary measures" must include twenty-four hour guards and a closed campus protected much like a restricted-access air base, then so be it. The even less savory alternative may be another kind of closed campus—the one that is completely ruined by shouting nihilists who proclaim that the whole social system must be overturned because only thus can adequate reforms be instituted.

The use of physical force is understandably repugnant to scholars whose commitment is to the life of the mind. But timid academicians should keep two interrelated points in mind: First—If, in any local situation, the use of illegitimate force is not adequately countered, then the chances are great that social control will gravitate to the most unscrupulous persons in the community. Second—At most colleges today there are a few campus hangers-on whose primary interest is not to get an education, but to foment a revolution that will give them total power. They focus on universities because it is there that they find their most implacable enemy *and* their fundamental tool.

The deadly enemy of the . . . extremist—whether from the far left or far right—is the university tradition of free thought which throws the cold light of scholarship on the extravagant claims of self-proclaimed messiahs. Such scholarship has repeatedly found something that [extremists] must, at all costs, keep from their followers—namely, that reforms carried out by wildly impatient true-believers always end as exploitation of the many by the unprincipled few. In the words of George Kennan:

> I have seen more harm done in this world by those who tried to storm the bastions of society in the name of utopian beliefs, who were determined to achieve the elimination of all evil and the realization of the millennium within their own time, than by all the humble efforts of those who have tried to create a little order and civility and affection within their own intimate entourage, even at the cost of tolerating a great deal of evil in the public domain.

The basic tool of the campus revolutionist is the mass of students whose general innocence, youth, and sincere interest in building a better world, make many of them so easy to excite into a thoughtless frenzy of destructive behavior. In addition, every campus has a large number of adolescent types who, seeking any excuse not to attend class, will gleefully join in the forcible occupation of buildings—especially since experience suggests that good old mother university, so often staffed by the timid and the uncertain, will not really reject her errant children no matter what they do. With such help, a few arrogant anarchists have been able to bring particular schools to a complete halt. Halts of this sort could probably be eliminated, or at least sharply curtailed, if university administrators and faculty members would make it clear, in advance, that teaching of various classes will go on even if classes must meet off campus, and that students not meeting the normal requirements of attendance and scholarship will be graded as appropriate. Meanwhile, back at the ranch so-to-speak, building invaders can be left to stew in an isolation that will soon be as satisfying as is the temper tantrum to the child who is ignored but who knows he will somehow have to compensate for any damage he does.

The other side of the coin which has just been examined is that the views of an unchallenged establishment too easily become unchallengeable dogma; and, "law and order" based on anything other than a widespread sense of justice is, at best, only a temporary respite from chaos. Therefore, to the end that justice and orderly change shall prevail, the university must encourage and support constitutionally protected methods of dissent and protest. This support and encouragement, to be meaningful, must be systematized so there is little chance it can be stifled. Indeed, the wise administrator will officially sponsor forums for the expression of dissent. Such forums have the double merit of releasing pressure and providing information that can contribute to the making of wise decisions. As Bay has written, ". . . radical intellectual and political inquiry . . . are more essential than ever in a world that changes so fast. . . . Only sheltered societies can depend on the unchallenged wisdom of their elders." Communication lines should be kept open, even to youths so disaffected we cannot reach them— ". . . we should give them the opportunity to reach us," Bertram Davis has observed, "for by attending carefully we may see some flashes of insight which will shed some light upon our institutions and ourselves."

VIII. ***Assertion*** Despite all their admitted limitations, the American social system generally, and the university social system particularly, have produced some very admirable results.

Conclusion Little consideration need be given to the few irrational students and faculty who cry that nothing good has been produced by American society and universities, and therefore both must be destroyed. Faculty members who speak thus, obviously exempt themselves; and students testify to their own irrationality if they continue to go to class, yet genuinely believe a modern university education is unalterably trivial or irrelevant. That such a belief is often not genuine is suggested by the number of youths who decry the workaday world in favor of meditating with their favorite guru, but —when afflicted with a gut ache—are eager to partake of the benefits of the work and research done in university laboratories or by university-trained medical personnel.

As for the social system at large, the United States has one of the highest standards of living known to man, and a governmental organization that is democratic enough and flexible enough to weather constant loud-spoken New Left charges that there is no free speech and that totalitarianism abounds—which, if true, would of course preclude making such charges more than once. But on the other hand, it is equally true that the government is often insensitive and that the benefits of American life are maldistributed in the sense that some large categories of citizens enjoy almost no privileges—two realities which, it bears repeating, can undermine the entire social system if adequate reforms are not quickly instituted.

Those who claim that current difficulties on the campus are a temporary aberration which can best be handled by simple repression alone unwittingly confess to the narrowness of their vision. It seems more realistic to view many aspects of the campus revolt as part of a world-wide revulsion against all that is implied by the term "colonialism." Everywhere, people who have been thoughtlessly exploited, and who have accepted such exploitation virtually without protest, are now saying *Enough!*

In Viet Nam, in Algeria, in black ghettos, in India, South America, and Africa —and on those campuses where students have long been treated in a cavalier fashion—the downtrodden have indicated they will no longer tolerate arbitrary control by outsiders who clearly want to *use* people rather than help them develop. This is no temporary movement! It is the shape and cry of the future, and it will be joined by all who have a sense of justice or a grasp of the direction of historical forces. It was these same forces that produced the American revolution, the Magna Charta, and the Bill of Rights. But the rights secured by these magnificent instruments have largely been restricted to the privileged few. They can now be extended to the many, thus creating widespread commitment to social order—if we take the proper steps. Taking the proper steps, however, is dependent upon having accurate information which it is the function of the university to provide, hence the critical need to protect the university from those who would alter its fundamental nature.

Defense against attackers from the far right has always been necessary; now the direction of attack is more often from the extreme left. But the essential battle remains precisely the same—namely, to keep the university free of partisan control so it can increasingly serve mankind in general rather than particular men. It is not easy to counter the activities of the modern Robespierres who stalk the campuses of the land and mouth slogans such as "Freedom! Brotherhood! Peace!" while they shout down opponents and destroy laboratories and libraries. Coping with such tactics is difficult, but by no means impossible. As Bertram Davis has pointed out—

> . . . colleges and universities have strong sustaining powers. For all their faults, they are the freest of American institutions and a bulwark of freedom and progress in society. They are at once the preservers of an old culture and the outposts of a new, the very root and vine of our growth.

78 Gossip in the Small Town

ALBERT BLUMENTHAL

Social control—the technique by which society induces conformity to group norms—is actually one of the social processes, although it is not ordinarily included with them in introductory texts. Social control can be of the informal type, for example praise or blame, or the formal as by laws and codes. This selection by Albert Blumenthal well illustrates informal social control by gossip, a method that is effective in any situation where people live close together, are dependent upon each other, and have commonly agreed upon standards of behavior. It is, therefore, especially effective in small towns. Says E. W. Burgess of the book from which this selection is taken, "The main characteristics of small town life stand out in clear perspective: close acquaintanceship of everyone with everyone else, the dominance of personal relations, and the subjection of the individual to continuous observation and control by the community."

One of the favorite themes of novels, stage plays, and jokes has long been the petty gossiping in small towns. Even the small-town residents themselves poke some fun at the inevitable and perennial gossiping in their midst, and are contiually crying out against it and grumbling about it. For all that is so traditional about the small and isolated community is woven about the far-reaching power of gossip—of communication by word of mouth.

In Mineville, "gossip" is a term much used, especially by women and in description of them. It has two general meanings. Sometimes it includes all local news which is transmitted by word of mouth; and at other times it means only that information involving a fellow-resident which any particular resident would not want told of himself, or which people feel they must whisper stealthily lest they incur the displeasure of someone. Whether or not the resident wishes the word to carry a derogatory stigma is told by the intonation of his voice or by other gestures. In the following discussion it will be used in both senses under the assumption that the context will indicate to what extent a distinction is meant to be made between mere talk, and that sort of talk which anyone thinks should be whispered or not told.

SOURCE: *Small-Town Stuff* (Chicago: The University of Chicago Press, 1932), 128–43. Reprinted by permission of the author and the publisher. • The author is associate professor of sociology, Wisconsin State University, Eau Claire. *Small-Town Stuff* was his Ph.D. dissertation, University of Chicago, under the title "A Sociological Study of a Small Town." His interests include criminology, juvenile delinquency, the family, and sociological theory. He is a contributing author to *American Anthropologist* and *Social Forces.*

WHO ARE THE GOSSIPERS?

Over the telephone a Mineville woman may quite frankly say, "I thought I would call up and see if you have heard the latest gossip." But while she is herself in the midst of spreading a scandal she is not unlikely to cast discredit upon another woman by calling her a "terrible old gossip." This illustrates the tendency of the people to make light of their own gossiping and that of their friends and to condemn it in others. For whether or not a person is rated as a gossip in the discrediting sense of the term depends not upon what he actually says but upon the attitude toward him held by the person making the rating.

Violent outbursts of anger and disgust at the "damned gossipers" are characteristic of most Minevillers when some of their own private affairs are aired in public. The part they themselves play in airing the affairs of others they seem to overlook. While it is true that most of them pretend to refrain from circulating information which will be harmful to the other fellow, all townsfolk (excepting infants and very small children) are dispensers of gossip, be it harmful or not. Those persons who might locally be known as non-gossipers are merely persons who are comparatively little interested in collecting whispered information and who, when they secure it, impart it more tactfully and considerately than the people as a whole. But even they have a few strong dislikes which cause them to show little consideration for some people.

In classifying the gossiping proclivities of the people the first criterion to suggest itself is that of sex, because from time immemorial men have jested about woman's tendency toward personal gossip. The explanation is clear. She merely talks of that about which her life is centered. She spends comparatively little time discussing the stock market, sports, politics, and impersonal problems of workaday life such as do the men. Her preoccupation is with local events—particularly those local events which have a strong tinge of the personal such as bridge parties and moral scandals. She frankly admits that when she goes calling she "talks about everything in town." She touches at great length upon the care of babies, children, and husbands; illnesses, childbirth, cooking, clothing, and other subjects closely related to the home—always illustrating her theory in terms of Mineville personalities. Unlike her husband, she never tires of talking shop, and when she talks shop, persons are generally involved. Also, she can gossip for an hour over the telephone at will while he works with a lone partner in a dark recess far below the surface of the earth. In this way she may act as a gossip collector for him during the day and detail her findings to him when he returns from work. He may tell her what he has heard "at the mine," but this usually is much less than she has to tell him, and less personal.

A usual remark about those in the community who are known as "gossips" is: "Tell Mrs. So-and-So anything as a secret if you want it advertised all over town in a hurry." But Mineville has so many proficient gossipers that to select only those who are reputed to be gossips and to ignore the rest would be to produce an erroneous picture. A few typical examples will serve to bring out this point.

First we may note some factors which cause Mrs. Dunwell to be rated as the community's leading female "gossip." Mrs. Dunwell occupies a position of social prominence which normally places her somewhat in the public eye aside from publicity which she might derive from her gossiping. She is frank and quick to "jump to conclusions"; she spares no one, not even herself, when she decides to give her opinion. This impulsive frankness causes her to reveal passing flurries of envy and jealousy which would remain undisclosed in the case of the ordinary woman. Consequently, she is readily accused of having a tendency to exaggerate and distort, and is feared and disliked by many. But there is no doubt that were she less prominent and less frank to all persons anywhere, she might gossip equally as much without being renowned as a community gossip, in the derogatory sense of the term.

The leading gossips tend to be persons with unusual ability to remember "everything about everybody." One of these is Ed Slade, who is known more as a "talker" than as a "gossip" because he is not a woman. Another was Mrs. Drake, who was not known as a gossip mainly because she was a recluse. Both Mr. Slade and Mrs. Drake were recognized as vocal social historians of the community, as can be seen from the following advice given when certain inside information was sought:

> Miss X: You should see Ed Slade. He can tell you everything you want to know.
>
> Mr. X [*her father—interrupting*]: Yes, see Ed Slade. He knows all about everything in town. I came in 1889 and he was tending bar before he worked for me at that time. He can tell you lots and more too.
>
> Mrs. X: And he will be glad to tell you things. It's odd how some people can remember things. There was Mrs. Drake. Whenever I wanted to know anything I used to go over to her. She seemed to know everything about everybody and everything in town. It's too bad she died. She could have helped you.
>
> She was not a gossip. She never told unless you asked but when you asked she sure knew.
>
> Mr. X: Sid Marshall is quite a talker. He came here after I did but he sure could tell you about everything since he came.

It is interesting that the men are especially prone to speak of the talkative members of their sex as "talkers" while females with the same propensities are classified as "gossips." In reply, the women contend, and perhaps not without justification, that the men are the "worst gossipers." Whatever the truth may be, Mineville has some very talkative males who are much better situated to secure and spread the news than are the women. Among these is Sid Marshall.

"Sid" is the proprietor of a tailor shop in which an almost perpetual talk-fest is in progress throughout the day and often until late at night. Man after man "drops into Sid's place" for a sociable chat and leaves such news as he has in return for a large supply from Sid and others who may have been present. Everything is discussed: from the habitual debtors of Mineville to the debtor nations of the World War; from the scandal of a Mineviller who just passed by the window to that involving presidents and kings. Religion, politics, psychology, economics, milady's styles, fishing trips, smutty stories, the weather, and the merits of one anothers chewing tobacco—nothing is barred. But it would be a mistake to conceive of this visiting center as those of small towns are so often caricatured, that is, as made up of men of naïve intelligence who presume great wisdom. Their ideas and attitudes on problems of larger import are not provincialisms, but rather are the same as those had by city people, because of being derived from the same immediate sources: editors of leading periodicals, the radio, and the movies. On the other hand, on local matters the individuals force one another to keep close to facts by the ruthlessness by which they pounce upon him who errs.

There is no better place in Mineville to sense shifts in public opinion than Sid's tailor shop. For news generally is not "out" long before someone brings it to Sid's, whose position is much like that of the editor of a paper in that he tends to hear all sides of questions more rapidly than people in general. From these diverse points of view he tries to arrive at the true statement of a situation. He becomes one of the best-informed men in town on local affairs, and his shop is one of Mineville's best substitutes for a daily newspaper and scandal sheet—a function pleasant to him and in no sense to his discredit, even though he is subjected to criticism by women who imagine that they are the particular objects under discussion in his shop.

• • • • •

There are, of course, other outstanding agents of gossip and other gossiping centers on Main Street. Not only are there several businessmen who are very proficient gossips, but most of the business establishments have particular persons who "hang around and talk." In fact, wherever the people assemble informally a gossiping center tends to arise.

Those traditional gossip-dispensing bureaus, the barber shops, where the barber tries to talk about as many interesting things as possible to his customers, have changed somewhat since the war. One of the barbers observes:

> Do you remember how there always used to be a gang of men hanging around the barber shops? I try to discourage them from hanging around my place nowadays since women and girls are an important part of my trade. Boy, how the guys used to talk in the old days! I'll bet there were more dirty jokes and more dirty remarks passed in the barber shops than anywhere in town. And how they gossiped! But things have changed. If the fellows do hang around now they have to be careful what they say in the presence of women and girls and so there isn't much to encourage them to loiter in a shop. Besides, women don't like to come into a shop if a lot of men are sitting around. There is plenty of talk now, but the subjects are different—as long as women are in the shop, at least.

Away from Main Street and from home the men do most of their gossiping in the mines and mills. Each group of workers tends to have certain members who stand out for their general talking abilities. Of forty-six men on one shift at the Salmon Mine two of these entertainers are in the limelight. To quote a fellow-workman:

> Talk about gossip! On our shift we have Fred Hare and Charlie Ratner in the center of the bunch before we go down the mine and at eating time, and I'll bet there ain't a woman in town who can equal those fellows. They never run out of gossip. You ought to see how they monopolize the conversation. It seems almost impossible that they can possibly know so much. Month after month their supply of gossip holds out.

Even among children there are prominent agents of gossip. They function much as do their elders, and when they are indiscreet they are subjected to the same disrepute. Breta Gaynor (age eleven) is a good example in the grade school. She talks incessantly and keeps widely informed upon the affairs of the school children, and upon those of adults as well. At a tender age Mineville children commence to take a naïve interest in the events of community gossip because they are likely to have had some acquaintance with a large share of persons and things of which they hear adults talk. The more intelligent five-year-old kindergarten children, for instance, have already reached a stage at which they are able to impart surprising bits of information to their teacher.

Influenced by small-town conditions, as are mature residents, Mineville children have leisure time, frankness, curiosity, and close contacts with large numbers at school to facilitate their gossiping. Through the grade school and through the high school waves of gossip of all sorts surge. Indeed, the schools are the largest gossiping centers in town although townsfolk, as a rule, are not aware of the fact.

GOSSIP AND THE FORMATION OF PUBLIC OPINION

Talking of things in general appears to be the favorite indoor and outdoor sport in Mineville. This is due in part to the neighborliness and community of interest among the people, and in part to the deficiency of other leisure-time activities in which there is an element of sociability. An interesting sidelight upon the effect of a community of interest was observed by a candidate for a county office:

> I'll tell you something that surprised me. Because I was never much of a mixer, I thought I would have a hard time when I ran for office. I thought I wouldn't be able to find anything to talk about to people I didn't know. It sure surprised me how easy it is to find something to talk about. We have so much in common with one another in this town, and even in the county, that we know a lot about people we've never talked to. For that reason I found that I could predict pretty well what would be an interesting topic of conversation to nearly everyone. I always knew some of their friends, where they worked, something about their children, and so forth. In a jiffy I could bridge the gap between not knowing people and becoming intimate with them. The trouble was not in finding something to talk about but rather that I had to be careful not to talk too much about intimate things for fear someone would start talk going around that the people shouldn't vote for me because I'm just an old gossiper anyhow. And then, I was pretty sure that some of the people were trying to get me to feel intimate with them so that I would confide things in them which they could use against me politically.

With such community of interest, and a general desire to tell the other fellow the latest news, it is not surprising that an exceptionally live bit of news, such as the death of a prominent citizen, attains almost complete circulation in the community in about two hours. Most of the people are likely to have the news in an hour. In a few minutes it reaches all of the business establishments on Main Street. "Too bad about Mr. So-and-So," the merchant characteristically says to his customers one by one. And wherever a group is congregated along the street the death becomes a topic of conversation. Meanwhile, with half of the people in town having telephones and by the age-old practice of "running in" to tell a neighbor, the news soon reaches those who perchance have not visited Main Street or otherwise encountered someone who might tell them. Community expectation of rapidity of circulation is attested by the fact that should such a death occur at nine o'clock in the morning and the information not reach a resident until late in the afternoon, his usual expression is, "I can't understand why I didn't hear about that sooner," and others say to him, "Where have you been? Everybody knew that by noon."

For several days such a topic is likely to be focal in the community. The man, his last illness, his family, etc., are discussed and rediscussed. A multitude of diverse bits of information and points of view have been brought into play before the subject drops out of the limelight.

Because as a social unit it is small and isolated, Mineville offers a most interesting laboratory for the study of public opinion. The participant-observer can witness the crystallizing of opinion in detail from its initial gropings to the final product in which more or less uniform attitudes and ideas in respect to a matter are characteristic over the whole community or in large factions. He will be struck with the rapid and varied shifts of opinion from one side of a question to another. He will see occasional cases when opinion becomes so fixed that there is a community-wide tendency for the people to become emotional if they are asked to consider the merits of the minority side of a matter. But he will find that such cases of callousness are usually temporary periods of high resistance, and that in the long run the "truth" is acknowledged by the people as a whole, if an item of gossip is sufficiently alive to keep it before them long enough. The people are so persistently confronted with untruths or partial truths in local rumor that they have a wholesome skepticism regarding it which naturally results in a rigorous, although often unconscious, piecing-together of evidence before a final conclusion is reached.

When news "gets out," one of the first steps of a resident is to trace it, and, as a rule, he is quite keen in tracing the origins and course of gossip because of his insight into the relations of Minevillers to one another. Resolutely he sets about to build his theory as to the channels through which an item of gossip has passed, through certain outstanding gossipers, and through a network of relatives, friends, and others who have frequent and intimate contact with one another. He knows much of the probable motives of these people and of the reliability of what they might say. In questioning the truth of a bit of news, for instance, he will say, "She got it from Mrs. Jacobs and it's a cinch Mrs. Jacobs got it from Mrs. Black and you know what a liar Mrs. Black is."

HOW GOSSIP DESTROYS PRIVACY

We have already indicated how gossip brings together odds and ends of one's private life which he reveals about himself to numerous persons over a long period of time. We have not yet discussed the factor which accounts for the feeding of most of the very intimate personal information into the streams of gossip, that is, betrayed confidences.

Everyone trusts that certain persons in possession of intimate facts of his personal life will not betray him. He would feel most wretched if he actually believed that no one is to be trusted to hold such knowledge in due respect. His father, mother, wife, brother, and several good friends he assumes will shield parts of his life from the public gaze. And while we have no evidence upon which to assert that his faith is not justified for the most part, bit by bit details of his private affairs sift out by way of betrayed confidences. This happens everywhere, but the consequences are especially serious in a small town such as Mineville where people seize with alacrity upon such information and shortly insure its perpetuation by making it a public acquisition. Husbands, for instance, little know what information of their private affairs their wives may have told "in confidence" to women friends who in turn have broadcast it to the community "in confidence." It is by means of just such a network of interlocking confidences that the "whole town" secures the most whispered of information almost as readily as it does ordinary news, despite the strong inhibitions the people have regarding "talking about" others because of being afraid that their words will "get back" to the person "talked about." Fortunately, however, most Minevillers do not seem to realize how well others know them, and so the human longing for someone in whom to confide, to whom to unburden the weight of troubles, still finds extensive expression in the town.

By way of illustration, the following phenomena attending broken confidences may be noted as commonplace in Mineville, as elsewhere:

a) There are irresponsible information purveyors—persons who must tell.

b) While people are on intimate terms they normally confide in and otherwise learn a great deal about one another. When their relations are temporarily or permanently broken, the situation is ripe for the wholesale breaking of confidences.

c) The desire to appear interesting to others often causes indiscretion to the point of violation of confidences.

d) Persons are led into disclosing confidential information in order to prove points in arguments.

e) There are "accidental slips" which are not realized as broken confidences until after they have occurred.
f) Many confidences are broken because as time passes people are likely to forget that they received the information concerned in confidence.
g) Some people care less about privacy than others and so they easily disregard what are to them the excessive requests of others for secrecy. The leading female gossip of the town, as has been indicated, secures her disrepute largely because of telling about others that which she does not care if others tell about her.

SCANDALS

Novelists have painted vivid pictures of small-town life which have captured the popular imagination and have made small-town people appear to be a peculiar species of scandal-hungry creatures. Somehow the lurid exposés featured by city daily papers have been considered to be more worthy of sophisticated people than rural gossip, and there has been a tendency to minimize the fact that city folks do a great deal of gossiping among their more intimate associates.

If Minevillers have a greater interest in scandal then urbanites, it is because of a difference in situation, not in people. It so happens that besides sensational news derived from city dailies, the residents of the town are living under conditions conducive to the ferreting-out, spreading, and perpetuation of an extensive fund of local scandal. And this news is the more interesting because it affects the status of persons with whom they are obliged to have close social relationships. Certainly it would be more interesting if one were to know that the only iceman in town has tendencies to be a paramour than it is to read in a city paper of the same proclivities on the part of some strange iceman one has never seen.

There is a fund of whispered gossip about every resident of a small town. Actually but an infinitesimal part of this is communicated directly to the person concerned, although the people say, "Everything gets back sooner or later in this town." Such news characteristically travels in channels which avoid him. It frequently buzzes among his closest friends and yet escapes him. This is particularly true of scandal. . . .

FEAR OF GOSSIP

In Mineville, individual variation in respect to fear of gossip is very wide. There is to be found the whole gamut of degrees from persons who are excessively fearsome lest their affairs become matter of gossip to those who defy, ignore, or are not well cognizant of the relentlessness with which news travels and the thorough circulation which it attains.

In the main, however, Minevillers wittingly and unwittingly are affected by a strong fear of gossip. Long experience has shown them that information tends to become distorted in passing from person to person, and so, even though the public in question is small enough that the truth is likely to become generally known in time if it is known to a few persons, the people do not wish to have their affairs thrown into the gristmill of conversation and argument through which so much news must pass before it is accurately consumed. This reluctance to be "talked about" does much to inhibit the circulation not only of reprehensible gossip but of permissible news. A warning voice is ever ready to whisper into the resident's ear, "Be careful! It will get all over town," or "What will people say?" And even in formal meetings someone may arise to say, "We'd better watch our step or the whole town will be on our necks before we adjourn."

No resident of Mineville supposes that he is not "talked about." Even obscure townsfolk complain that they live under the spotlight of the public eye and hence must become hardened to the inevitable gossip, if they are to have peace of mind. But withal, there is so much open defiance to gossip as to suggest that many residents do not realize the harm which their acts may bring upon their reputations at present, and even twenty years in the future.

79 Social Control and Non-Conformity in a Southern Town

EDGAR A. SCHULER AND
ROBERT L. GREEN

In the previous selection we have seen how gossip functions as a means of social control in a small community. In this selection Schuler and Green have edited an extended interview that the senior author had with a prominent educator in a southern town. In the interview Dean Gordon Moss relates how shunning and other processes of social control operated in efforts to force his compliance with the local norms regarding segregated schools. This case study also illustrates how belief in educational opportunity for all, and other values acquired in the larger society, produced the nonconformity of a respected community leader. The analysis of the conflicting social forces with his resolution of them and the stages of non-conformity and ostracism in the community is an insightful documentation of these social processes.

Prince Edward County, located in south-central Virginia, is a predominantly rural area containing approximately 8,000 whites and 5,000 Negroes. Both the County and the town of Farmville, its County seat, manifest the cultural, social, economic, and interracial situations typical of many southern counties and towns. The children of both Negro and white families come primarily from lower and lower-middle class socio-economic backgrounds, and the same social and racial barriers exist as are normally found in comparable southern communities.

For the past thirteen years Prince Edward County has exhibited a pattern of growing interracial conflict, emerging openly in 1951 in a strike engineered by Negro high school students to obtain more adequate educational facilities.

During this period the Negro citizens of Prince Edward County began to perceive the issue of equal school facilities and education as being integrally related to the more basic problem of school desegregation. After a number of lawsuits had been initiated by local Negro citizens, the County Board of Supervisors in 1959 closed both the white and Negro public schools rather than comply with court-ordered desegregation. Shortly thereafter certain members of the white community established a privately financed segregated school for their children.

SOURCE: Interview with Dean Gordon Moss, Dean of Longwood College, Farmville, Va. (May 23, 1963). Conducted and recorded by Edgar A. Schuler in connection with a study directed by Professor Green, which was financed by the U.S. Office of Education, Grant 2321. The interview was reprinted substantially without change in *Phylon*, vol. XXVIII, no. 1, pp. 28–40, under the title "A Southern Educator and School Integration: An Interview." • Edgar A. Schuler is professor of education and sociology and a staff member of the Social Science Teaching Institute, Michigan State University. From 1959 to 1962 he was senior advisor of the Pakistan Academy for Village Development at Comilla. • Robert L. Green is professor of educational psychology and Director of the Center for Urban Affairs at Michigan State University. He was the administrator of the Citizenship Education Program for the Southern Christian Leadership Conference during 1965–66. He wrote *The Educational Status of Children in a District without Public Schools*, in which he reported the study of Negro children in Prince Edward County, Virginia, and edited *Racial Crisis in American Education*.

Since 1959 approximately 1,300 of the 1,700 Negro children of school age who live in Prince Edward County have had almost no formal, and very little informal, education. In the summer of 1963 and continuing through September of 1965 a team of social scientists under the direction of Robert L. Green of Michigan State University has been involved in a research project in Prince Edward County, Virginia, supported by the U.S. Office of Education. The major objective of the project is to assess what effect four years of non-schooling has had upon the achievement and aptitude levels of the Negro school-age children in this county. Furthermore, an analysis is being made of the social impact of the schools' closing upon the community.

As the school issue developed and gained in momentum a number of prominent Prince Edward County residents became involved in the school controversy. Outstanding among these individuals has been C. G. Gordon Moss, Dean of Longwood College, a State-supported institution of higher education located in Farmville, which enrolled only white students up to the time of the interview. In connection with initiation of the field activities of the research team the senior author of this paper, a faculty member in the Colleges of Education and Social Science at Michigan State University and sociological consultant to the research project, interviewed Dean Moss at Farmville, Virginia, in May of 1963 in an attempt to gather information pertinent to the research project. Except for the italicized paragraphs and the topical subheadings, the following is an edited version of the transcribed recording of what Dean Moss had to say.

PERSONAL BACKGROUND

We are getting to a sort of impasse here in Farmville, insofar as our local situation is concerned. We have been in such an impasse for some months now, since we are really awaiting court decisions and neither side can do anything one way or the other until the legal situation is clarified.

With regard to my own background, I should begin with the fact that I am just fifty miles away from my birthplace. I was born in Lynchburg, Virginia, at the end of the 19th century, and I have lived in Virginia all my life except some three years of residence in New Haven when I did my graduate work at Yale and the one year that I taught in North Carolina. Other than those four years, I have spent my entire life in Virginia: in Lynchburg, in Fredericksburg to the north, in Alexandria for three years back at the beginning of my teaching career, and here in Farmville. I certainly grew up in the normal, the average, and the traditional southern atmosphere. I can remember, as a child, having several Negro friends—one, in particular, was a close friend. But, of course, as I grew up, I was unconsciously subjected to the normal 19th century southern attitudes regarding the Negro. I can remember having jumped right over a seat in a streetcar in Washington when a Negro sat down beside me. That must have been around 1912 or 1913—when I was a very young boy.

I can remember avoiding eating with Negroes at various public meetings and conferences into my adult life. But I can also remember that in my home there was never any hatred or fear of Negroes, and that we maintained an attitude that was normal in the era—the kindliest possible relationship with the Negro servants. I did not become aware, and certainly not intensely aware, of any major issue in regard to Negroes until this situation developed here in Prince Edward County.

I have no recollection of even being

aware of the difficulties Negroes were having with regard to education until at least the 1940's. The only thing I do remember was my relief when my mother-in-law sold some Negro residential property that she had inherited down in the slum areas of the town. I felt relieved because it was perfectly obvious that the property was being used for economic exploitation. By "economic exploitation" I mean that it was the cheapest, slummiest, scummiest type of property on which she had spent nothing in the way of improvement and consequently all of the rent was pure profit to her. She spent nothing on physical improvements, neither as an investment nor in improving her inheritance, and I couldn't have been a normal rational human being if I hadn't realized that such disinterest was not the best way to behave.

PATERNALISM AS A SALVE FOR THE TROUBLED WHITE CONSCIENCE

If I may attempt to summarize as briefly as possible, first the developments in Prince Edward County, but more particularly, my reaction and relationship to the developments, it would have to begin with the fact that as a normally sensitive person, I have been aware at least subconsciously for as long as I have known anything about Farmville in Prince Edward County—and that would go back to 1926—of the most paternalistic attitude maintained by the ruling white majority toward the Negro in this community. This was and is an attitude of love for the Negro, if the Negro will accept everything from the white rulers—if he will, to use common southern language, "stay in his place." But I would say that this paternalistic attitude toward the Negro is probably stronger in this particular locality than generally throughout Virginia.

I believe this attitude represents an unconscious salving of the conscience of the white man in this community. The white men have known that the Negroes who made up almost 50 per cent of the population were uneducated, patient, and willing to remain in its low situation. They wanted that Negro population for the dirty work of raising tobacco on farms or laboring in the local tobacco processing plants. The housewives of the County wanted the Negro population for household servant work. And, whether they were able to consciously admit it to themselves or not, I believe that they have known that by keeping the Negro uneducated, poor, available for what they wanted from him was unjust to the Negro, and as a result they had to in some manner protect their own consciences against what they were doing. Consequently, they have developed the feeling that they were the benefactors of the Negro. They treated Negroes personally and individually in a friendly and kindly way, and were helpful to them in their personal problems—give or lend the Negro who is becoming a drunkard money when he needs to buy another bottle of cheap wine, pay his fine so he can get out of jail in order that he can work your garden for you again. This protective position or attitude was both beneficial to the Negro and to the white man in easing the latter's conscience with regard to what he was doing to the Negro. This preserves the kind of image that we like to hold of ourselves . . . that we are kindly masters concerned with the personal life of our servants (no longer our slaves but now our servants) and that we want to make them as happy as possible, always assuming that they can be entirely happy in this totally subservient status.

INFERIOR EDUCATION FOR NEGROES

The paternalistic attitude as a slave for the white man's conscience had its most specific social reaction and implication in terms of the educational system maintained by the County for the Negroes. All through the 1930's and into the 1940's an admittedly inferior school system for the Negroes was manifested in the buildings, in the teachers, and in the school administration, and as a result, in inferior educational content. But the white man eased his conscience by thinking and by assuming that this very modicum of education was all that the Negro wanted, and that he was entirely satisfied with it. When, in the 1930's and on into the 1940's, the schools for the Negroes—particularly in the town of Farmville in contrast to the surrounding County community—became severely overcrowded, the white people were not willing to spend the necessary money to relieve the crowded condition in any reasonable and effective manner. They were only willing to do this inch by inch, as they were forced to do so, and to do it in the cheapest way possible, such as putting up temporary buildings—tar paper shacks.

I recall now that around 1945 a friend of mine from Longwood College was asked to give a science lecture at the Negro high school. When he came back, he told me how impossibly crowded the high school building was, that he could barely get to the platform to deliver the lecture because every square inch of space was taken up by the students. I believe that this was my first concrete, specific realization of the crowded conditions.

NEGRO EFFORTS TO IMPROVE NEGRO EDUCATION

I am aware that throughout the 1940's the Negroes through their Parent-Teachers Association were persistently and continuously urging the School Board to build adequate structures for the education of their children. There was no effort then to build for integration. It was merely an effort to increase the physical facilities for the admittedly "Negro" schools. The whites resisted any such obligations to provide such needed facilities. As a result, if I recall correctly, the Negro children by 1951 had become utterly disillusioned and thought that there would never be any schools.

So in the spring of 1951, the Negro children initiated on their own, without any adult help or even knowledge, a strike in the Negro high school. They went out on strike and declared that they were going to stay out on strike until the School Board agreed to build a structure. The strike brought in the N.A.A.C.P. led by Reverend L. Francis Griffin who is the local Baptist Negro minister and now President of the local and state N.A.A.C.P. This group sought to help the Negro children in their endeavors and led to the initiation of a legal suit originally designed, I believe, to promote more adequate physical facilities for the Negro children, but eventually demanding that segregation in the school system be abandoned. I am quite certain that suit was in the Federal Courts in 1952, and it was the beginning of the combination of suits which reached the Supreme Court in 1954.

With the above threat hanging over the heads of the ruling whites of the County they *did* go ahead and find the money they had previously said they were unable to find. They found the money, and borrowed to build an entirely adequate high school for the Negro children of the town and the County. This new school, the Moton High School located on the southern outskirts of the town, is far and away the best school building in the entire County, white or Negro. The white people were trying to "buy the Negroes off" by giving them more than they had asked for in the way of physical facilities and thus hoped to stop the desegregation suit. The new school was in use when the Supreme Court decision of May 1954 was handed down.

POPULAR REACTIONS TO THE SUPREME COURT DECISION

The next milestone to be considered is the reaction of the people of the County to the Supreme Court decision of 1954. I believe the white community's reaction was originally one of utter confusion and dismay, and then, very rapidly, of anger and determination to resist to the utmost the decision and all of its implications. This feeling resulted in the formation of the so-called Defenders of State Sovereignty—a southside Virginia organization, not merely a Prince Edward County organization—an organization that was determined to resist by all possible legal means, as they said, any end of segregation whatsoever.

My reaction to the decision was one that I did not have to make publicly for a while. However, when the occasion arose, I did make it known whenever possible—that the County should open the white schools immediately to the Negro children and abandon segregation at once. The schools would be crowded with Negroes for the first week or two or for a brief interval of time, and then it would become difficult to find even a single Negro—certainly not more than a bare sprinkling—who would be able to persist in the white schools with the latter's higher standards and the difficult social situation for the Negro children. No consideration was given to my proposal by anybody in authority whatsoever.

Then, after the second Supreme Court decision of 1955, with it implementation of the 1954 decision, there was the immediate local reaction—a public county-wide meeting to consider action. Undoubtedly careful preparation was made for that meeting in terms of speakers and proposals. The attendance was just about as large as one could expect—it overflowed the 1,200 seat auditorium of Longwood College. There was essentially no opposition voice raised in the meeting at all, and it was at that meeting that they organized their Prince Edward Educational Foundation Corporation to conduct private schools for the white children if and when that became necessary. That was in the spring of 1955. I had no opportunity to participate at that time since I was in the hospital with coronary thrombosis and under doctor's orders not to become involved in the local controversy until well into 1956.

I believe that my first public statement was at a meeting of the high school Parent-Teachers Association when I was the only person who voted "No" on a resolution that the P.T.A. would resist integration of schools by all possible means. I had to ask specifically for the opportunity to cast my negative vote—the chairman did not think it was necessary even to ask for the negative vote. From that time, which was probably somewhere in the spring of 1956, until 1959, there has been really no opportunity for public protest whatsoever. I became known throughout the community as a proponent for public schools and for whatever integration was necessary to maintain the public schools. I doubt that I had developed my own thinking to any appreciable point beyond merely believing that the Negroes should be allowed to continue to have the right to education, and for those Negroes who wanted it, integrated education.

REFUSAL TO COMPROMISE LEADS TO PRIVATE SCHOOL FOR WHITES, 1959

Finally in May 1959 the Board of Supervisors refused to adopt a budget providing for the continuance of public schools because the Federal District Court decision had been rendered, demanding that such schools would have to be integrated in the fall of 1959. In June of 1959 the Board of Supervisors decided to hold a public hearing on that action of May 1959. The public hearing was the occasion of my first real public expression of opinion. At that time I protested against the closing of schools and insisted that there was no necessity for such closing even to preserve segregation (if they wanted to preserve segregation) because not a single Negro had applied for admission to the white schools in June of 1959 for the subsequent September opening of the schools. There were several white citizens that did make such protests in that public meeting, but it was an entirely futile action because the Board of Supervisors merely went through the motions but not the reality of listening to us. I recall definitely that Henry Bittenger, a colleague of mine on the Longwood College faculty, also spoke. Possibly, he and I were the only two white people at the first to protest.

After the public hearing, upon realizing that there was no possible local way of preventing the closure of the schools, Bittenger and I, wondering if there was anything else we could do, began to meet from time to time. By September 1959 we succeeded in finding two Negro leaders who were willing to meet with us to explore the possibilities of maintaining free public education. We proposed that they, speaking for the Negroes, accept voluntary segregation for three years with the possibility of continued voluntary segregation beyond that point as the only possible way to having schools in the County in the year 1959-1960. They agreed to this proposal, but admitted that their agreement did not necessarily mean that all of the Negroes of the County would go along with them. We carried that agreement to the State Government, as well as to . . . , the outstanding spokesman of the white supremacists in the County. [He] . . . refused to consider it at all. He said that he would not discuss anything with the two Negro leaders and that he would only discuss private education with Negroes of his own choice, but that he would not discuss resumption of public education with anyone.

I consider it highly significant to call attention to this situation in the fall of 1959—that the white supremacists were determined to have no public schools at all, segregated or integrated. They rejected the opportunity to have segregated schools, as I have indicated. It was only after their Prince Edward Foundation had begun to operate the white private schools that they organized a separate group, claiming that this would assist the Negroes in establishing a private school for the Negro children in the County. They attempted to get an academic friend of mine, a sort of "academic son" of mine of the Longwood College faculty, to head the organization for private schools for Negroes—a move, I assume, to undercut any opposition on my part. I did succeed in persuading that young man not to accept the position. Late in the fall of 1959—it was possibly as late as December 1, I am not certain—they issued what in a sense was an ultimatum to the Negroes: they would give them until the first of January to accept the idea of these private schools, and if the Negroes did nothing about it, the project would be dropped. This ultimatum was delivered, and if I recall correctly, in the form of a circular letter to every parent requesting their replies as to whether or not they would send their children to the private school system if established. January 1, 1960, arrived with only one Negro family having indicated that it would place its children in such a school—and within two weeks time the white Foundation had made an official request to the School Board to rent the white public school buildings for the private school system. I do not think there is a mere coincidence involved in those dates. It is definitely known that during the fall of 1959 they had found the lack of adequate buildings to be the greatest difficulty in running the white private school system. They realized their desperate need for the public white schools, and saw that if they could get the Negroes to accept the token of a private school system and the use of Negro public schools, then they would have no difficulty whatsoever in obtaining the use of the white schools for the white private school system.

I am stressing the above point at considerable length because ever since the winter of 1959–1960, recurrently until it has become virtually a monotonous sing-song, they keep on repeating that they offered the Negroes a private school system, that they offered it honestly, that the Negroes refused it, and therefore the whites were absolved from any guilt caused by the Negro children not having an education. The offer was a mere paper offer and nothing was done in any sense to actually organize the private schools such as obtaining school teachers or determining the location of the buildings or of acquiring money to operate them. It was a paper offer made by and for the white people in an effort to be able to use the white schools.

I personally did not sense any real criticism, or hatred by the white people of the County, until I spoke in strong opposition at a public meeting of the School Board in late January or early February of 1960 held to consider whether or not to grant the request for the use of the white school buildings by the private school system. The School Board members turned down the request. I believe they had decided to do so before they even held the public meeting. They simply wanted to show at least some support from the public for such an action.

EMERGENCE OF THE NEW VIEW: NEGROES ARE FELLOW HUMAN BEINGS

My next personal crisis in the conflict came in January and February of 1961 when I attended the national annual meeting at Williamsburg of the Episcopal Society for Cultural and Racial Unity. The incidents and details of the matter are not of any public concern, but the local people used them in an attempt to pin on me the label of a total integrationist—even to the extent of believing in intermarriage of the two races. This resulted in a turmoil in my own church and in strained relations for me there ever since.

I have talked every time, every year —1959, 1960, 1961, 1962—when the Board of Supervisors held their annual public meeting with regard to a budget to include schools. I have, I think, gone through a very definite progression in my own thinking. I believe I have already referred to the fact that in 1959, at that first Board of Supervisors meeting at which I spoke, I was initially simply a proponent for public education for Negroes and whites regardless of whether it involved integration or not. But during the four years of the non-school system, as a result of my continuous private biracial conferences that had begun in 1959 between the two Negro leaders and Bittenger and myself, my thinking regarding the issue has changed. The conferences have become more frequent, with meetings approximately once a month from 1959 to the present, the spring of 1963. As a result, I have had to reexamine my own thoughts on the racial situation, and I think I have grown.

To me, the question of integrated schools is a very minor part of the problem in even so peaceful a county as Prince Edward. The real issue has grown beyond the mere question of integration to nothing more nor less than whether or not the white people are going to accept the Negroes as fellow human beings. And I doubt very much if even 10 per cent of the white population of the County would consider looking at the issue in so fundamental a form as that. And among the 10 per cent, one would be more likely to find the better educated (for example, members of the faculties of the two colleges in the County).

I do not believe that religion, however, would be a factor in determining whether one would look at Negroes as fellow human beings. Essentially all of the white churches and the white ministers of the County have refused to look at what has happened as a moral issue. One Presbyterian preacher was driven away at the beginning of the controversy in 1956 or 1957 because he insisted upon recognizing the problem as a moral issue. There is one Presbyterian minister out in the County now—has been there since 1962—who accepts it as such. But with the exception of those two men, I do not know of any white minister anywhere in the town or County who, in the last ten or twelve years, has ever been brave enough to accept it as such.

We have also had one physician who from the first has been very sympathetic to the Negroes, but who has not been willing to take a public and open stand, although he has allowed his wife to do so with moderation. Another physician was originally sympathetic and started out admitting that the Negroes had been grossly mistreated. However, he had now succeeded in rationalizing his withdrawal from the issue and his acceptance of the status quo. A third physician did accept the chairmanship of the County School Board in 1961, at the time the previous chairman and most of the School Board resigned. He was a very beloved physician who unfortunately has since died, and I never had the opportunity to discuss the matter with him. I believe he accepted the position with the hope that he could do something constructive by working from within with those who controlled the situation. He certainly never made any public statement advocating integration or advocating that we ought to do something for the Negroes in the County.

As to those who controlled the situation, I have already mentioned one person.

The open, entirely known, active leaders of the movement are, however, few in number but without them I don't believe the situation would have developed, and I doubt very much if, without them, there would have been any controversy and concrete issue here at all.

Whether or not it is true that one man, or several men, are behind these recognized leaders has always been a question in my own mind. I have very strong reasons to believe that there is one person, but I have no proof of it and so I will not even name that person. But it is altogether likely that in the final analysis the County's actions have resulted from one person's beliefs and ideas.

The local bar has not supported the cause of the Negroes. One member of that bar was legal counsel for the School Board at the beginning of the case. That was W. Cabell Fitzpatrick. He was gravely mistreated at the time when the lease or sale of the school buildings was an active issue. But he has never taken any open stand. Only one other person, who was trained for the law (but did not actively practice it) for a time took an active stand in favor of the Negro.

SOCIAL MECHANISMS TO MAINTAIN CONFORMITY

Though Dean Moss has not himself referred to this, Reverend L. Francis Griffin, the local Negro minister, has described the kind of ostracism to which Dean Moss has been exposed. This is a kind of punishment the community has imposed on him because he spoke out and purportedly advocated not only integrated education but also intermarriage.

The senior author notes, in passing, that this kind of social control, i.e., ostracism, operates in much the same manner in the East Pakistani villages he had occasion to visit. There the mechanism was called "outcasting." The ruling group of old men led by the headman would investigate a case and tell the individual what he must do if he would accept their control. If the individual refused to conform to the traditional ideals of this local leader and the others compromising the village power group, there was a formal outcasting procedure after the completion of which he was cut off from any communication and all social contacts within the village. This process of social action is known as "Ek ghore," i.e., "keeping the person in solitary confinement." In rural East Pakistan, where everyone depends on others for almost all types of daily services, this is the most severe type of punishment which the village community can impose. No one will speak to him. The grocer will not sell his merchandise to him. The banker will not offer his services. Teachers will not instruct his children. The religious leader will not give his blessings. The rickshaw puller will not transport him. In other words, all types of specialized skills and services available in the villages are denied to him. At the same time, no one will buy his services, thus imposing on him an economic boycott. In addition, a type of social stigma is attached to his personality. If any villager sees him in the morning before breakfast that villager will refrain from taking breakfast himself as evidence of protest at his non-conformity. According to Dean Moss, in general terms, his experience and that of other people in the Farmville community could be used as illustrations of the mechanism presented above.

Here I am, a native of Virginia, born in Lynchburg, only 50 miles to the west of Prince Edward County. My ancestors on both sides of my family have been in Virginia since the 17th century. I came to Farmville interpretation of the racial college teaching. I married a native of Farmville in 1929. I returned to Farmville to teach in 1929 and 1930 and left only because the substitute position I took in 1929 and 1930 did not develop into the permanent position I had hoped it would. I was continuously visiting in the town from 1930 until my return to the faculty of Longwood College in 1944. I have been associated with various civic organizations, such as the Rotary Club and so forth.

However, because I do not accept the Farmville interpretation of the racial issue, I am a foreigner, as much of a foreigner as if I had come from Iowa or even East Pakistan I expect. On the contrary, one of the principal spokesmen for the white supremacists is a native of Pennsylvania and is the mouthpiece of the publisher of the *Farmville Herald* and is a member of the Board of Supervisors. He married, not a native of Prince Edward County, but the widow of a native of

Prince Edward County. But because he goes along with the ruling clique, he is a native and not a foreigner.

My sin, really, is that I am a scalawag: a native but a non-conformist. The Foundation people have continuously argued that this matter should be settled by natives of Farmville, but look at this situation: When they needed legal counsel, they took a lawyer from Blackstone, Virginia, as their principal legal counsel. Blackstone is 35 miles to the east, which is almost as far as Lunchburg, 50 miles to the west; however, I suppose the eastward direction is all-important! And furthermore, when they needed additional legal counsel, they took another outsider, a lawyer from Richmond, Virginia, and became very much incensed when, in the public hearing on school leases, I insisted upon establishing the fact that their principal counsel was not a native. I was accused of being most impolite to a person who had been invited into the County. It is not who you are or where you are from; it is whether or not you go along with the rules that determines your nativity.

I do not think that I have particularly suffered, personally, because of my criticism of the local situation. I have been snubbed on Main Street by virtually lifetime friends. I sit in a pew by myself every Sunday. I am not allowed to serve on the vestry although they are quite willing to accept my work as treasurer of the church.

On the positive side, let me add this. When the schools were closed in 1959, I had one remaining child in public school. He was ready for the eighth grade and I publically refused to allow him to go to the Prince Edward County school even though it was going to have the same faculty it had had for years as a public school, for the County school was, according to my views, based upon evil principles. So I refused to allow my son to go to that school and sent him away at the age of 13 to a boarding school much against his personal wishes, and he has been away from the local schools throughout the four years. Nevertheless, that boy has retained all of his friends in the Prince Edward Academy and his principal desire throughout these four years has been to get home as frequently as possible in order to be with his friends. So far as I know, he has never been snubbed in any way by any of his age peers.

I would therefore like to think that the attitudes of the adolescents differ from their parents and thus make the future look more hopeful, and that is what I thought for a good while—possibly for the first two years of the school system.

It would be a bit difficult to prove, but I have increasingly gotten the impression for the past two years that the white children in the private school systems are beginning to inherit and adopt their elders' ideas and that they are beginning to develop in themselves positive attitudes of hatred toward the Negroes. That is difficult to prove, and I would not attempt to do so now.

FOUNDATIONS OF A PHILOSOPHY OF TOTAL INTEGRATION

Actually, I have prevented any too strong personal attack being launched upon myself since I have always insisted that my opposition was based upon, first, my belief that public education was an absolutely necessary foundation stone for America if America was going to be a leading world nation.

Second, I have insisted that my opposition was based upon my belief in democracy, and that in democracy you cannot have second-class citizens.

And, finally, I based my opposition, and insisted that it be so recognized, on Christianity—on the principle that Christianity forbade the mistreatment of any subordinate group in the society.

Accordingly, I have virtually defied people and insisted that if they wanted to criticize me, they would have to admit that they did not believe in public education, that they did not believe in democracy, and that they did not believe in Christian principles. Even so, it has threatened my life professionally and economically. Within a matter of days after my first public speech for public schools, a delegation was in the office of the president of Longwood College demanding that I be fired.

In the winter of 1961, an attempt was made to circulate a petition to the State Board of Education to fire me. They could not get enough signatures on the petition to make it of any weight, but they did carry it privately to the State Board of Education. An effort was made at that time to shut me up with the threat that if I did not stay quiet, I might lose my job. I guess what rankles the leaders of the opposition most is that in 1956–1959, when I began my opposition, I was merely Chairman of the History Department of Longwood College, but since then I have been promoted to Associate Dean and finally to the position of Academic Dean of the College, which is a rather bitter pill for most people in the community to take.

PRESENT STATUS OF PUBLIC SCHOOLS

A private foundation known as the Prince Edward Free School Association was organized in September 1963. It made available elementary and secondary education to all Prince Edward County children on a desegregated basis. The Free School Association was financed by grants and contributions from foundations and private citizens. Although approximately 1,500 Negro youngsters attended the Free Schools, only four out of approximately 2,000 white school-age children were enrolled. Among the four white children was a 17-year-old senior named Richard Moss, the son of Dean Gordon Moss.

A court order which directed the reopening of public schools in the county on an integrated basis in the Fall of 1964 rendered unnecessary continuation of the Free School Association's educational operation. Most white children of school age in Prince Edward County, however, are still attending—in 1967—the segregated private academy.

80 Pictures in Our Heads

OTTO KLINEBERG

Several years ago Walter Lippmann made a classic analysis of what he referred to as the stereotypes that people hold of other persons and groups. He termed those stereotypes "pictures in our heads" and indicated how these images, often based on inadequate knowledge and overgeneralized ideas, provide the basis for our behavior in relation to others. Here Otto Klineberg examines some of the stereotypes commonly held of several national groups and discusses the consequences of spuriously based images.

About a year ago I was in London at the invitation of British psychologists and sociologists in order to lecture on "National Stereotypes." Throughout the preceding day, during which I was undoubtedly made more sensitive by my preoccupation with this topic, I kept running into examples of such stereotyped thinking.

In my hotel, I heard someone say, "Oh, she has that Scottish stubbornness, you know." A book review in a newspaper used the phrase, "With true Gallic wit." At the theatre that evening, during the interval, I caught part of a conversation in which a pretty girl said to her escort, "I know that all Americans have a 'line' "; and in a mystery story that I read before retiring, there was a reference to "typical German thoroughness."

These are all instances of those "pictures in our heads" to which Walter Lippmann gave the name of stereotypes. They are typical of the ease with which most of us generalize about national or ethnic groups, usually without even stopping to think where such "information" comes from, and whether it represents the truth, the whole truth, or anything like the truth.

There are certainly very few, if any, among us who have not succumbed to the temptation to stereotype nations. One might almost describe the tendency as inevitable, or at least very nearly so. We *know* that Englishmen are reserved, and Irishmen pugnacious; we have heard it all our lives; besides most people agree with us. If we are asked, however, *how* we know, we would not easily find a suitable answer.

One of the earliest careful studies of this tendency was made by Katz and Braly, in 1932, in connexion with the stereotypes held by Princeton University students. The technique was simple.

Each student was given a list of traits, and a list of nationalities; from the first list he chose the five traits which he regarded as characteristic of each national or racial group.

The results showed a fair degree of unanimity, e.g. out of 100 students, 78 described the Germans as "scientifically minded," and 65 described them as "industrious"; 53 students used the adjective "artistic" for the Italians; the same percentage described the English as "sports-

SOURCE: UNESCO *Courier,* vol. 8, no. 4 (September 1955), 5–9. Reprinted by permission. • The author is professor of psychology, Columbia University and visiting professor, Sorbonne, University of Paris. He was formerly Director of Research for the "Tensions Project," UNESCO. His chief interests are race differences, national differences, and attitudes. He has written *Race Differences, Social Psychology,* and *Tensions Affecting International Understanding.*

manlike"; 79 agreed that the Jews were "shrewd" and 54 stated that the Turks were "cruel"; 84 regarded Negroes as "superstitious," and 75 described them as "lazy."

We may summarize the results in a slightly different manner by indicating the three or four characteristics most commonly ascribed to each nationality. These included, for the Germans, scientifically-minded, industrious, stolid; the Italians, impulsive, artistic, passionate; Negroes, superstitious, lazy, happy-go-lucky, ignorant; the Irish, pugnacious, quick-tempered, witty; the English, sportsmanlike, intelligent, conventional; the Jews, shrewd, mercenary, industrious; the Americans, industrious, intelligent, materialistic, ambitious; the Chinese, superstitious, sly, conservative; the Japanese, intelligent, industrious, progressive; the Turks, cruel, religious, treacherous.

A recent study of the stereotypes of German students at the Free University of Berlin by Sodhi and Bergius showed a similar willingness to stereotype nations and, on the whole, comparable results. Americans, for example, were described as sportsmanlike, democratic, materialistic; the Italians as warmblooded, musical light-hearted; the Chinese as poor, inscrutable, modest; the German as conscious of duty, loving their homeland, intelligent; the English as proud of their nation, bound by traditions, sportsmanlike. There were some variations between the German and the American stereotypes, but on the whole the overlapping is considerable.

On a more extensive scale, a study conducted in 9 countries under the auspices of UNESCO in 1948 and 1949, showed that such stereotyped thinking could easily be elicited almost anywhere. In each country approximately 1,000 respondents, representing a cross-section of the population, were given a list of 12 traits, and asked to choose those which they thought were most applicable to themselves, to Americans, to Russians, and in some cases, to two or three other national groups as well. They could choose as many of the traits as they wished.

The British, for example, thought of Americans as primarily progressive, conceited, generous, peace-loving, intelligent, practical. The Americans regarded the British as intelligent, hard-working, brave, peace-loving, conceited and self-controlled. The Norwegians described the Russians as hard-working, domineering, backward, brave, cruel and practical. The full results can be found in the volume by Buchanan and Cantril, "How Nations See Each Other."

The "self-image" is also revealing. The British saw themselves as peace-loving, brave, hard-working, intelligent; the French saw themselves as intelligent, peace-loving, generous, and brave; the Americans saw themselves as peace-loving, generous, intelligent and progressive. All the groups agreed on one item: their own nation was the most peace-loving of all!

Few people realize how much the existence of stereotypes may colour our relations with other people, even to the extent of seeing them differently as a result. Psychologists have long known that our perceptions of the external world, and particularly of human beings, are determined not only by what is *out there,* but also by what is *in ourselves.* What we see is determined in part by what we expect to see. If we believe, for example, that Italians are noisy, we will have a tendency to notice those Italians who are indeed noisy; if we are in the presence of some who do not fit the stereotype, we may not even realize that they, too, are Italian. If someone points that fact out to us and says:

"Look, those people are Italians, and they are not noisy," we can always dismiss them as exceptions.

Since there is no limit to the number of cases that can be so dismissed, we may continue to cling to the pictures in our heads, in spite of all the facts to the contrary. This does not always happen. Stereotypes do sometimes change in the light of new experiences, and evidence for this is presented later. If we have had them for a long time, however, we surrender them with great reluctance.

A number of significant investigations have shown in a very dramatic manner how our stereotypes may determine our perceptions. Some years ago Allport and Postman, psychologists at Harvard University (Cambridge, U.S.A.) studied some of the phenomena associated with the spread of rumours, making use of a technique known as "serial reproduction," a very simple device which anyone can use with a group of friends in his own home. They showed a picture to one student, and he described to a second student what he saw in the picture. The second then told a third what the first had told him; the third told the fourth, and so on, through a series of 8 to 10 reproductions. Then a comparison was made between the final result and the original presentation.

One of the pictures used in this investigation showed a scene in a subway in which, in addition to a number of people seated, there were two men standing, one a white man, the other a Negro. The white man was dressed in working clothes, with an open razor stuck in his belt. It so happens that the stereotype of the Negro held by some people in the USA includes the notion that Negroes carry with them an open razor, of which they make ready use in an argument.

The psychologists were able to demonstrate that in half of the groups who served as subjects in these experiments, before the end of the series of reproductions had been reached, the razor had "moved" from the white man to the Negro. In some instances, the Negro was even represented as brandishing the razor violently in the face of the white man. This does not mean that half of the subjects in the experiment saw the Negro with the razor, since if only one person in the chain made this error, it would be repeated by those that followed. Interestingly enough, this did not occur when the subjects were Negroes (who rejected the stereotype), or young children (who had not yet "learned" it).

Another study conducted by Razran in New York points in the same direction. A group of college students in the USA were shown photographs of 30 girls, and asked to judge each photograph on a 5-point scale, indicating their general liking of the girl, her beauty, her intelligence, her character, her ambition, and her "entertainingness." Two months later, the same students were again shown the same photographs, but with surnames added. For some of the photographs Jewish surnames were given, such as Rabinowitz, Finkelstein, etc.; a second group received Italian names, such as Scarano, Grisolia, etc.; a third group Irish surnames, such as McGillicuddy, O'Shaughnessy, etc.; a fourth, "old American" names like Adams and Clark.

The investigator was able to demonstrate that the mere labeling of these photographs with such surnames definitely affected the manner in which the girls were perceived. The addition of Jewish and Italian names, for example, resulted in a substantial drop in general liking, and a similar drop for judgments of beauty and character. The addition of the same names resulted in a rise in the ratings for ambition, particularly marked in the case of the Jewish surnames. It seems clear that the same photographs *looked different* just because they could now be associated with the stereotype held by these students.

If a great many people agree that a particular trait is associated with a particular nation, does that make it true? There is a fairly widespread theory to the effect that "where there's smoke there's fire"; or, in other words, that the very existence of a stereotype is, to some extent at least, an argument in favour of its truth. Otherwise, the argument runs, where does the stereotype come from? How would it come into existence?

There is, however, a good deal of evidence as to the possibility that stereotypes may develop without any kernel of truth whatsoever. We all know how widespread is the notion that intelligent people have high foreheads, yet scientific investigation in this field has failed to reveal any such relationship. The stereotype of the criminal as bearing in his features the mark of his criminality is widely accepted, but it is equally without foundation; the famous British criminologist, Sir Charles Goring, was able to demonstrate that a composite photograph, representing criminals in British gaols, bore no resemblance to the accepted stereotype of the criminal.

Stereotypes frequently change. In some cases it may be argued that this corresponds to a real change in the characteristics of the people; in others, however, it seems much more likely to be due to external circumstances which have little or nothing to do with the group concerned. The Dutch sociologist, Shrieke, has, for example, made a collection of some of the descriptive phrases applied to the Chinese during the course of their residence in the state of California, U.S.A.

When the Chinese were needed in California, in order to carry on certain types of occupation, they were welcome there; during that period, newspapers and journals referred to them as among "the most worthy of our newly adopted citizens"; "the best immigrants in California"; they were spoken of as thrifty, sober, tractable, inoffensive, law-abiding. This flattering picture prevailed over a considerable period of time, but around 1860, presumably because economic competition had grown much more severe, there was a marked change in the stereotype of the Chinese. The phrases now applied to them included: "a distinct people," "unassimilable," "their presence lowered the plane of living," etc. They were spoken of as clannish, criminal, debased, servile, deceitful, and vicious.

This startling change can hardly be accounted for by any real modification of the characteristics of the Chinese population of California. The most acceptable explanation is that when it became advantageous to reduce the competition from the Chinese, the stereotype was altered in a direction which would help to justify such action. In this historical case it seems reasonable to conclude that the change in the characteristics ascribed to the Chinese throws doubt on the notion that stereotypes must necessarily contain some truth.

Another Dutch sociologist, Den Hollander, has studied the historical changes in the stereotype of the Hungarians in Europe. He points out that for centuries after the migration of Hungarians to Central Europe, they had a bad reputation, and were regarded as culturally different, and therefore inferior, to Europeans generally. During the 15th and 16th centuries, however, when they joined in the war against the Turks, they were pictured as a brave, devout, and chivalrous people.

By the second half of the 18th century their popularity had again declined, and they were described as savage, lazy, egotistical, unreliable, and tyrannous. This picture changed again a little later, when the Hungarians became romanticized and idealized. Den Hollander believes that the image followed the pattern of political interrelationships; it seems unlikely that there was sufficient transformation in the character of the people to justify the change in the national image.

One of the most amusing examples of a stereotype which has apparently developed without any kernel of truth emerges from an investigation by Schoenfeld on stereotypes associated with proper names. Here again the technique used was a simple one. The American students who served as subjects in this study were given a list of eight proper names and a list of eight adjectives; their task was to "match" or pair each name with the adjective regarded as most appropriate.

Since there were 120 students, and eight names, the results to be expected by chance alone, that is to say, if no stereotype existed, would be 120 divided by eight, or 15 for each name. The actual results showed that 63 out of the 120 judges matched Richard with "good looking"; 58 judged Herman to be "stupid"; 59 judged Rex as "athletic"; 71 associated Adrian with "artistic"; and 104 agreed that Cuthbert was "a sissy." In a similar experiment with American girls judging feminine names, 54 regarded Minnie as stupid; 60 saw Linda as sophisticated; 69 said that Mary was religious; 58 that Maisie was talkative; and 73 that Agatha was middle-aged.

Although this study was done with American students, it seems quite certain that comparable stereotypes would be found in languages other than English.

In any case, it can hardly be argued that Richard is really better looking than John, or Herman more stupid than Cuthbert. To return to ethnic stereotypes, one significant study may be cited which demonstrates the manner in which stereotypes may develop without any basis in truth. The American sociologist, La Piere, studied the attitudes of residents of California towards first and second generation Armenian immigrants in Fresno County in that State. There was almost complete agreement that these Armenians had more than their share of faults, and the general attitude toward them was relatively unfriendly.

La Piere proceeded to question non-Armenians as to the reasons for their antipathies, and he was able to classify the answers into three stereotypes. In the first place, it was stated that Armenians were treacherous, lying, deceitful. In actual fact, when measured by the criterion of business integrity, the Armenian merchants turned out to be equal and frequently superior to others. In the second place, they were alleged to be parasites, making excessive demands upon charitable organizations, free clinics, etc. Actually, such demands by them were less than half of what would be expected in terms of their proportion of the population.

Finally, it was said that they had an inferior code of morality, and they were always getting into trouble with the law. In fact, police records showed that they appeared in only 1.5% of Police Court cases, although they constituted approximately 6% of the population. La Piere concludes that all of these stereotypes have one factor in common, viz. that they are definitely false. This does not mean that stereotypes *never* contain any truth. It does mean that they *can* develop without any truth whatsoever.

There is, however, the possibility that a little truth may enter into a stereotype through the back door, so to speak. A Frenchman, with considerable experience of international meetings, once said that when he had occasion to address such a meeting he usually did so in a rather oratorical, flowery, "Latin" style. He said that otherwise his Anglo-Saxon colleagues would be disappointed! When he was with other Frenchmen, he reverted to a quieter, more matter-of-fact, "un-Latin" manner, which really suited him personally much better.

In this case, the stereotype itself determined his behavior under certain circumstances, and undoubtedly reinforced the conviction of the Anglo-Saxons that they really knew what Frenchmen were like. More rarely, the stereotype may operate in reverse. A member of a group with the reputation for frugality may go out of his way to spend freely, and tip lavishly; if the stereotype calls for lack of punctuality, he may make it a point to arrive at his destination well before the hour specified. Since, in that case, as was indicated above, he will probably be regarded as an exception, the stereotype will still prevail.

Stereotyped thinking may be *almost* inevitable, but there is good evidence that it can at least be reduced, if not eliminated. Eighteen years after the Katz and Braly study, another psychologist (Gilbert) applied the same technique to a new generation of Princeton students. He found that there was some persistence of stereotypes, but also a very important change which he describes as "a fading effect."

There is much less agreement among the students in 1950 than in 1932; any specific trait is usually checked by a much smaller proportion of students in the later study. In 1932, for example, 84% of the students described the Negroes as lazy; in 1950 the percentage had dropped to 31. The description of Italians as artistic drops from 83 to 28.

In London, a UNESCO study conducted by H. E. O. James and Cora Tenen showed how specific personal experiences might affect the nature and content of stereotypes. What they did was to obtain from schoolchildren their opinions of other ethnic groups, particularly of African Negroes, and then bring them into contact with two able African women teachers who spent a few weeks in the schools.

The "before and after" picture is very striking. As an example, a child before the experience stated that "I do not like black people; it's the colour; it makes me nervous; they might be savage . . . they are different in nature to us, more savage and cruel sometimes, so you don't trust them ever." The same child after the experience said: "Miss V. and Miss W. were nice people . . . there does not seem any difference between them and us except the colour. I think that Negroes are like that—just like us, except for the colour. I like them. They are nice people."

The authors give many examples of similar changes that occurred. Stereotypes cannot always be modified so strikingly nor so fast, but the fact that they can be changed at all as a result of experience is itself encouraging.

Sometimes just growing older helps. In a study sponsored by UNESCO, Piaget and Weil report the results of a series of interviews with Swiss children of different ages. One interview with a little girl aged eight years ran as follows:

> "Have you heard of foreigners?—Yes, there are Germans and French.—Are there any differences between these foreigners?—Yes, the Germans are bad, they are always making war. The French are poor and everything is dirty there. Then I have heard of Russians, but they are not at all nice.—Do you have any personal knowledge of the French, Germans, or Russians, or have you read something about them?—No.—Then how do you know?—Everyone says so."

On the other hand, a boy aged thirteen years, after having mentioned a large number of foreign countries of which he had heard, was asked, "Are there any differences between all those countries?", and his answer was, in part, *"you find all types of people everywhere."* We are not all as "mature" as this 13-year-old boy, but perhaps we can move in that direction. Or is it possible that the Swiss are . . . ? Oh no! No stereotypes!

The understanding of national characteristics represents an important task for all of us. . . . The difficulties in the way are great: nations are made up of many different kinds of individuals, and generalizations are dangerous if they do not give adequate consideration to the range of individual variations.

An important first step will be taken if we treat "the pictures in our heads" with a strong dose of scepticism, and if we keep our minds closed to stereotypes and open only to facts. No one is denying the existence of national characteristics.

A knowledge of them can aid our understanding of people, as well as our enjoyment of the varieties of behaviour and personality that are found in different parts of the world. We need to make sure, however, that the "pictures in our heads" correspond as closely as possible to reality.

81 Tea and Sympathy: Liberals and Other White Hopes

LERONE BENNETT, JR.

The processes by which societies change vary from drastic revolutionary changes on the one hand to maintenance of a relatively stable society with little or no change on the other. Advocates of various types of change have often been classified as radicals, liberals, and conservatives. This selection by Lerone Bennett and the following one by Harry Ashmore focus on the position of liberals in contemporary society. Bennett analyzes the liberal position on contemporary changes in the status of blacks in American society, and identifies the limitations of this position in the present situation that demands more rapid and more drastic change than liberals are likely to accept. This perception of the liberal from the point of view of those who have long been oppressed is a striking contrast to the position of Ashmore in the next selection.

• • • • •

Who is *our*, who is man's, who is freedom's friend?

The white liberal answers; let us begin with him. The white liberal is a man who finds himself defined as a white man, as an oppressor, in short, and retreats in horror from that *designation.* But—and this is essential—he retreats only halfway, disavowing the title without giving up the privileges, tearing out, as it were, the table of contents and keeping the book. The fundamental trait of the white liberal is his desire to differentiate himself psychologically from white Americans on the issue of race. He wants to think and he wants others to think he is a man of brotherhood.

The white liberal talks brotherhood;

SOURCE: Lerone Bennett, Jr., *The Negro Mood* (Chicago: The Johnson Publishing Company, 1964). • The author is senior editor of *Ebony* Magazine. He received the Book of the Year Award from the Capital Press Club in 1963 and the Patron Saints award in 1965. Among his many books are *Confrontation: Black and White, The Negro Mood,* and *Before the Mayflower: A History of the Negro in America, 1619–1964.*

he writes about it, prays for it, and honors it. But:

Between the idea
And the reality
Between the motion
And the act
Falls the shadow.

The white liberal is Augustine praying before his conversion, "Give me chastity and continency, but not yet."

He is Andrew Johnson saying to Negroes in 1864, "I will be your Moses," and taking, in 1865, the posture of Pharaoh.

He is Abraham Lincoln biting his lip, as he put it, and keeping silent.

The white liberal is the man who was not there in Montgomery and Little Rock and Birmingham; the white liberal is the man who is never there. The liberal, as Saul Alinsky, the brilliant white radical said, is the man who leaves the meeting when the fight begins.

It was of the white liberal, or someone like him, that men were thinking when they invented the phrase: he wants to have his cake and to eat it, too. The essential point here is that the white liberal is of no color or race or creed. He is Everyman. "For the good that I would I do not; but the evil which I would not, that I do."

That is it, precisely:

Between the desire
And the spasm
Between the potency
And the existence
Between the essence
And the descent
Falls the Shadow.

The Shadow of safety, the Shadow of comfort, the Shadow of greed, the Shadow of status. This is the white liberal: a man of Shadows, a friend of freedom who pauses, calculates, hesitates.

The dancing waves of revolt and rebellion have exposed with pitiless clarity the dark shadows of the white liberal soul. As a result, the reputation of white liberals in the Negro community is at an all-time low. This is not, as some claim, a perverse spasm of a frustrated folk. The Negro senses dimly that white liberals, despite their failings, are the best America has to offer. And he clings to the white liberal, as a drowning man clings to a plank in a raging sea, not because the plank offers hope of salvation but because it is the very best he has.

The plank is rotten; the sea is choppy —the plank must be made better or we shall all drown.

Let us look closer at the white liberal.

What characterizes the liberal, above all, is his inability to live the words he mouths. The white liberal cannot bear the great white whale of guilt that rises from the sea of Negro degradation and he joins groups and assumes postures that permit him and others to believe something is being done. The key word here is *believe.* The white liberal believes something should be done, but not too soon and not here. He is all negation, the white liberal: now is not the time, this is not the place, the weapon you have is too large or too small. He is all ceremony, all ritual. He pretends, he postures, he resolves. Always, everywhere, in every age, the white liberal flees the principle made black flesh. He wants results without risks, freedom without danger, love without hate. He affirms tomorrow, denies yesterday, and evades today. He is all form, all means, all words —and no substance.

The white liberal is *sui generis.* Men of similar tone and texture exist in South Africa and other countries. But the breed, white liberal, is peculiar to America. No other country has felt called upon to create this office, for it is an office, if not a profession. Lévi-Strauss reminds us that "in any society it is inevitable that a percentage . . . of individuals find themselves placed, as it were, outside of any system or between two or more irreducible systems. The group asks and even requires that these individuals represent certain forms of compromise which cannot be achieved on the collective level, that they stimulate imaginary transitions and embody incompatible syntheses."

To "simulate imaginary transitions," to embody incompatible syntheses: this is the function of white liberals. They are ordained to stand in the middle, to sustain hope, to personify an "impossible ideal," and to suffer. They serve the same purpose in the Negro community as token Negroes serve in the white community: they are public monuments of racial progress. In a period of real crisis, white liberals are shoved into the breach between the contending groups to perform four key functions: 1) symbolic flames (tokens of white interest and white good faith); 2) flagellants (whipping boys and deflectors of Negro discontent); 3) channels of communications between separate communities; and 4) expendable platoon leaders of the most advanced positions of the white camp. White liberals are charged, above all, with preventing the coagulation of a massive black clot of Negro discontent. In the March on Washington, it was considered significant that white people participated, thereby preventing an all-Negro demonstration against all white people. In all crises, at all times, white liberals have two basic aims, to prevent polarization and to prevent racial conflict.

Because their aims are so narrow, white liberals are of limited value to Negro leadership. The basic postulates of the white liberal are that bigotry is caused by ignorance and that changes must be carried out quietly, surreptitiously, as it were, so white people will not notice. These assumptions ignore basic considerations of interest and power and permit white liberals to nibble at the edges of the problem without mounting basic assaults on structures of influence and affluence. As Ralph J. Bunche pointed out in the forties, white liberals "are attempting to work within a system which is opposed to any basic change, and they do not try nor do they desire to change that system in any of its fundamentals."

By word and by deed, white liberals insist that Negroes subordinate their claims to the emotions of racists. In the liberal rhetoric, it is considered a provocative act to irritate white racists. It never seems to occur to white liberals that irritated or not they are still the same old racists.

The modern version of this paternalistic theory is that demonstrations enrage white people and imperil the advance of democracy. This statement contains two wholly unacceptable premises. It assumes, first, that white people have some freedom to give and, secondly, that they can dole it out based on the smiles or lack of smiles of the victims. This is a nursery rhyme approach to the historical process and it explains, in part, the continuing distrust of liberals and other white hopes.

White liberals are much given to victim analysis. Nothing pleases the average liberal more than a long and leisurely contemplation of the defects of the victim. The liberal sees quite clearly that the Negro has been robbed, but in violation of all logic and all law he insists that the robbed instead of the robber make restitution. It is not a pretty picture, this, to see the robber lecturing his victims on the virtues of thrift. Silence were better.

But silence is not the liberal's strong point. Refusing, like practically all other white Americans, to accept Negroes as serious social actors, liberals lecture Negroes on cleanliness, godliness and the duty of obeying laws which white Americans, with white liberal help, have violated for more than one hundred years. Liberals, like practically all other Americans, are paternalistic, patronizing, condescending; they think they can tell Negroes how to frame their posture of protest, how to scream and how to cry or, indeed, whether they should cry at all.

The word *masses* separates Negro activists from Negro militants; the word *conflict* separates white liberals and Negroes. Liberals want orderly change; Negroes want change, orderly if possible, disorderly if necessary. Above all else, the liberal recoils from the shock of conflict. He tends to study much and to pray much. He accepts the goals, but disagrees on the method. The liberal is an aesthete, much preoccupied with form and means and techniques. He looks out on a raging battlefield and sees error everywhere, and he thinks he can find the truth by avoiding error. He is reasonable, the liberal; he preaches and surveys while men are burning churches and rats are biting children.

Prejudice is irrational to its core, but liberals insist that the Negro fight rationally. The Negro is fighting a barroom brawler who knees in the clinches and gouges between rounds; but liberals, standing on the edge of the ring, hold the Negro to *Robert's Rules of Order.*

Moderation: that is the dominant liberal value. Liberals are moderately for the Fourteenth Amendment; they are moderately for Negro freedom, and they think Negroes ought to be moderate. This means almost always that Negroes must dilute their demands, that they must wait, that they must not rock the boat. On every question involving Negro rights, the liberal is moderate—on every question except two: Negro hate and Negro violence. This man, so moderate, so reasonable, so content, becomes an extremist when Negroes hate and hit back. Why? From whence comes this obsession with Negro violence? It stems from an unconscious perception of the ambiguity of the liberal position. Liberals fear Negro violence more than anything else because Negro violence, more than anything else, illuminates the precarious ledge of their posture. White violence, though deplorable, is endurable, and white liberals endure it amazingly well. But Negro violence creates or threatens to create a situation which forces white liberals to choose sides; it exposes their essential support of things as they are.

• • • • •

In order for Negroes and white liberals to communicate they must break out of the glass cage of caste and hate that contains them. Negroes have a duty to assimilate their situation, to accept it and transmute it so they can view white liberal approaches with greater objectivity. But the power and the glory are the white man's; and so is the responsibility. An act to the end is a minimum requirement. Anything else is silence, evasion, and untruth. The Negro hates his role in America and he hates white liberals who approach him in the aspect of *white* liberals and remind him, however obliquely, of his situation. For white people to pretend surprise at this fact is not only naive but downright cynical. And to pretend, as many do, that Negro hate is of the same tone and texture as white hate is ludicrous. As Arnold Rose pointed out—and I use Rose because he is a perceptive non-Negro—"[Negro] hatred of white people is not pathological—far from it. It is a healthy human reaction to oppression, insult, and terror. White people are often surprised at the Negro's hatred of them, but it should not be surprising.

"The whole world knows that the Nazis

murdered millions of Jews and can suspect that the remaining Jews are having some emotional reaction to that fact. Negroes, on the other hand, are either ignored or thought to be so subhuman that they have no feelings when one of their number is killed because he was a Negro. Probably no week goes by in the United States that some Negro is not severely beaten, and the news is reported in the Negro press. Every week or maybe twice a week almost the entire Negro population of the United States suffers an emotional recoil from some insult coming from the voice or pen of a leading white man. The surviving Jews had one, big, soul-wracking 'incident' that wrenched them back to group identification. The surviving Negroes experience constant jolts that almost never let them forget for even an hour that they are Negroes. In this situation, hatred of whites and group identification are natural reactions."

There are hundreds of ways of hating the white man in America, including imitating him. But the harsh fact is that the choice for most Negroes is not between hating or loving but between hating and hating, between hating themselves or hating their oppressors.

This should surprise no literate man. You cannot deny people the basic emotions of rage, resentment and, yes, hate. Only slaves or saints or masochists love their oppressors. If you humiliate a man, if you degrade him, if you do this over and over for hundreds of years, he will either hate you or hate himself. This is a basic fact of humanity, and Negroes are human. At best, you will get that strange kind of love Camus spoke of—the love of Jesus and Gandhi, a love that expresses itself in creative resentment, in the cursing of fig trees and the driving of money changers from temples.

A strange kind of love or a strange kind of hate.

Martin Luther King, Jr., or Malcolm X. Either/or.

It would help enormously in America if there were a ten-year moratorium on the use of the word love. Love and hate are not mutually exclusive phenomena; they are two sides of the same coin and they are found almost always in different degrees in the same relation. The Negro loves white Americans but he also hates white Americans and there is nothing that can be done about it until the white liberal addresses himself to conditions that breed love, hate, and desperation. It is not required, finally, that we love each other. What is required is something infinitely more difficult, for us to confront each other.

But this is what the white liberal refuses to do. The white liberal is fleeing the truth of his, of *our* situation. He is seeking personal salvation not justice. He is moved not only by a vision of the future but by a horror of the past, not by the Negro, but by himself. What moves him is guilt. What the liberal seeks is his lost innocence. What the liberal wants, paradoxically, is for the Negro to tell him that he is not as white and as cold as snow.

82 Where Have All the Liberals Gone?

HARRY S. ASHMORE

In this selection Ashmore defines the liberal creed and commitment to freedom as an organizing principle and policy in human society. He recognizes the problems of the liberal in crisis situations but maintains that liberals do know what not to do. This thesis should be examined in contrast to Bennett's charge in the previous article that liberals do not know what to do during such crises in human relations.

. . . . .

Encyclopaedia Britannica defines liberalism as "the creed, philosophy, and movement which is committed to freedom as a method and policy in government, as an organizing principle in society, and as a way of life for the individual and community." So it was, in its seventeenth-century beginnings, in its eighteenth-century revolutionary triumphs, and in its nineteenth-century consolidation as the dominant political order of the West. But by the turn of our own century it was clear that Adam Smith's invisible hand, which was presumed to set human affairs aright if all were guaranteed freedom of thought and economic action, had disappeared in the smoke of the urbanizing Industrial Revolution. In an increasingly complex society free men could starve, and properly endowed democrats could founder in political impotence. In 1911 one of the high priests of the order, L. T. Hobhouse, of Oxford, wrote: "Liberty without equality is a name of noble sound and squalid meaning." Summarizing the condition of liberalism in the second half of the twentieth century, Britannica notes: "It might certainly be said that the classical and largely negative phases of liberalism had gone with the winds of history. What was not clear was whether this applied also to the democratic and welfare phases of the affirmative liberal state."

The surviving liberalism can best be described as a cast of mind and a code of personal conduct. The commitment is to the maintenance of an open society which accords all its members social justice. The liberal recognizes that, in his own time at least, the ideal is impossible to attain, and that his primary task may be to see that the necessary compromises are not fatal. While his own history has made him skeptical of the short-range results of democracy, he sees no substitute for self-government as the only feasible check on the managerial and scientific/technological elites required for the functioning of an advanced society. He acknowledges the existence of power, and distrusts it; he accepts the use of force only when it is allied with constituted authority and the rule of law; he puts his ultimate trust in the capacity of men to reconcile their differences without coercion if society can be made to ap-

SOURCE: *The Center Magazine,* vol. 2, no. 4 (July 1969), 33–35. Reprinted by permission of *The Center Magazine,* a publication of The Center for the Study of Democratic Institutions in Santa Barbara, California. • Harry S. Ashmore is Director of Research and Development, Editorial Projects for The Encyclopaedia Britannica, and served as past editor in chief. In 1958 he received the Pulitzer Prize for editorial writing, the Sidney Hillman award, and the Freedom House award. He is the author of *The Negro and the Schools, An Epitaph for Dixie, The Other Side of Jordan,* and *The Man in the Middle.*

proximate Thomas Jefferson's free marketplace of ideas. There can be no community without consensus, he holds, and an enduring consensus can only grow out of dialogue. Hence tolerance is the liberal's cardinal virtue, and he cherishes civility as the literal and essential derivation of civilization.

The stance, of course, is not satisfactory to moralists. In his concern with the parts of society, and his acceptance of imperfection, the liberal offends classical philosophers, who condemn him as a pragmatist addicted to an untidy pluralism. Holding that if there is ever to be a new man he will be no less the product of evolution than the current model, he cuts himself off from the radical utopians. The vision of the apocalypse is alien to the liberal not only because of the gratuitous cruelty of its mass indictment but because he can find no rational basis for locating all of mankind's moral guilt among those who do not profess the innocence of self-alienation. He would agree with Stringfellow Barr that "it's very hard to think when you are top dog," but he would insist that coherent thought is hardly easier for the underdog, beset as he is by real and fancied persecutions and the debilitating necessities of survival. Thinking, in his view, requires a degree of detachment, of self-doubt, even of self-irony, all of which are conspicuous elements in the liberal style and are conspicuously absent in that of the radical.

The liberal's habit of skepticism, and his concession that his own human limitations embody the possibility of error, apply even in the most weighty considerations of life and death. Thus in the great days of religious influence, and now in its period of decline, he might find himself inside the institutional church criticizing its professions and practices, or outside attacking the whole system of theological thought. In either position he respects the other. Conceding that he was incapable of sharing the moment of truth of a Tolstoy or a Simone Weil, Sir Herbert Read wrote: "To those who have not received it, the grace of God seems an arbitrary gift, and I resent the suggestion of the initiates that we who live in outer darkness do so because of our intellectual pride. I am completely humble in my attitude toward the mystery of life, and accept gratefully such intuitions as come to me from the writings of the mystics, and from works of art."

The liberal is properly accused of having difficulty in deciding what to do in the face of crisis. However, he knows what not to do—what, indeed, he cannot do without abandoning the values he lives by. When Marxist theory emerged in the last century to challenge the economic and social precepts of Western liberal democracy, he could find merit in its scathing analysis and in some of its prescriptions. He could become a socialist, and many liberals did. But he could not become a Communist, or at least could not remain one after he faced up to the inhuman physical and spiritual repressions the Marxist revolution would require on the road to utopia. Irving Howe, in a more or less autobiographical essay in *Commentary*, has recounted the shattering experience of the group of influential New York intellectuals who lived through the unmasking of Joseph Stalin: "During the nineteen-thirties and -forties their radicalism was anxious, problematic, and beginning to decay at the very moment it was adopted. They had no choice: the crisis of socialism was worldwide, profound, with no end in sight, and the only way to avoid that crisis was to bury oneself, as a few did, in the left-wing sects. Some of the New York writers had gone through the 'political school' of Stalinism, a training in coarseness from which not all recovered; some even spent a short time in the organizational coils of the Communist Party . . . [but] no version of orthodox Marxism could retain a hold on intellectuals who had gone through the trauma of abandoning the Leninist *Weltanschauung* and had experienced the depth to which the politics of this century, most notably the rise of totalitarianism, called into question the once-sacred Marxist categories. From now on, the comforts of the system would have to be relinquished."

In what Seymour Krim has described as "the over-cerebral, Europeanish, sterilely citified, pretentiously alienated" world of New York's radical intellectuals, where endless polemics provide much of the mental exercise, the old anguish of the nineteen-thirties has continued, in one way or another, down to the present day. Here is Professor Howe's reflection on the inevitable aftermath of the great Stalinist cleavage: "Like anti-capitalism, anti-Communism was a tricky politics, all too open to easy distortion. Like anti-capitalism, anti-Communism could be put to the service of ideological racketeering and reaction. Just as ideologues of the fanatic Right insisted that by some ineluctable logic anti-capitalism led to a Stalinist terror, so ideologues of the authoritarian Left, commandeering the same logic, declared that anti-Communism led to the politics of Dulles and Rusk. There is, of course, no 'anti-capitalism' or 'anti-Communism' in the abstract; these take on political flesh only when linked with a larger body of programs and values, so that it becomes clear what *kind* of 'anti-capitalism' or 'anti-Communism' we are dealing with."

To young revolutionaries who consider all history ancient, the foregoing is also consigned to the wonderfully capacious category of irrelevance. Yet two of the most durable gurus of the movement, the two who have earned acceptance across the age barrier by attempting to endow the revolution with some coherent theoretical structure, are conspicuous products of the period. Professor Howe places Paul Goodman in the political spectrum by describing him as "a very courageous writer, who stuck to his anarchist beliefs through years in which he was mocked and all but excluded from the New York journals." The elusive doctrine of Herbert Marcuse, he finds, is based on "contempt for tolerance on the ground that it is a veil for subjection, a rationale for maintaining the status quo, and his consequent readiness to suppress 'regressive' elements in the population lest they impede social 'liberation.' About these theories, which succeed in salvaging the worst of Leninism, Henry David Aiken has neatly remarked: 'Whether garden-variety liberties can survive the ministrations of such "liberating tolerance" is not a question that greatly interests Marcuse.' "

The question does, of course, greatly interest liberals, who find the most striking contradiction of the new movement in its nihilistic devotion to the personal desires of its members and its calculated dismissal of the rights of others. If for no other reason, the legitimacy of the revolution would be questioned by conventional Marxists because of its rejection of the stern, puritan self-discipline the master demanded of all his followers, high and low. If even the mild dissidence of the Czechs proved anathema to the mellowing Soviet commissars, it is easy to imagine what would happen to a cadre of pot-smoking, free-loving, gut-communicating rebels in Mao's China, where the real, 100-proof doctrine is still in vogue.

• • • • •

83 We Have Marched, We Have Cried, We Have Prayed

ERNEST W. CHAMBERS

In this selection Chambers, a black civil rights advocate, dramatically evaluates the civil rights revolution in the United States and the processes designed to prevent such changes. The parallels drawn with the American revolution, which was highly valued in American society, suggest the similarity in revolutionary processes. Chambers boldly demonstrates how the perception of events by a suppressed black differs from the perception commonly held by dominant whites in American society. The failure of whites to comprehend the conditions and processes in the same manner as do blacks is a major force in creating the conditions from which violence stems.

We have marched, we have cried, we have prayed . . . we have voted, we have petitioned, we have been good little boys and girls. We have gone out to Vietnam as doves and come back as hawks. We have done every possible thing to make this white man recognize us as human beings. And he refuses.

He teaches us in school about the American Revolution. Do you know that those people who you teach me in school are patriots, around Rhode Island, burned a British frigate because it was too active in cutting off what they felt were their "legitimate" smuggling activities? 1771 . . . The Gaspee was the name of the British ship. And do you know that those people in Virginia—who you teach me were patriots—did not condemn it? They praised this "patriotic" action, this blow struck for freedom.

George III was the King. The 13 American colonies were British Territories. They were extensions of the Mother Country, there for the purpose of Britain. A colony provides raw materials and then markets for the Mother Country. You all know what colonialism is. We know what it is in *fact*, in America as black people.

You teach us that these colonies were not wrong when they spoke against George III and when Patrick Henry came out specifically against him and compared him to Caesar with his Brutus, somebody said, "Treason!" And he said, "If this is treason, make the most of it."

Then I look at what you're trying to do to Rap Brown and Stokely Carmichael —calling it sedition and treason. And saying if there isn't a law against them, there should be. Then you want to turn around and tell the world that these men couldn't speak like this if they didn't have freedom of speech . . . if they lived in Russia what would happen to them. Yet what

SOURCE: National Advisory Committee on Civil Disorders, as quoted in *Ebony*, vol. 23, no. 6 (April 1968), 29–32, 36–38. • Ernest Chambers is a member of the Nebraska State Senate and has served as a consultant to the United States Office of Education. He gained national recognition for his role in a television documentary, "A Time for Burning," produced under the sponsorship of the Lutheran Council in the United States of America and dealing with the attempted racial integration of an Omaha church.

you are saying, when you say a law should be passed against these men, is that Russia, in fact, has the right idea—and you'd better catch up with Russia and pass a law against these men so they cannot tell the truth.

Then there is a Freedom School in Tennessee which you want to say is teaching hatred because it tells black people that your ancestors brought us over on the Good Ship Jesus. You raped our women; you mutilated our men. You took away our dignity and our manhood. Any vestige of a culture, religion or language, you took away from us.

You can understand why Jews who were burned by the Nazis hate Germans, but you can't understand why black people who have been systematically murdered by the government and its agents—by private citizens, by the police department—you can't understand why they hate white people.

And you know what you want to do? And again we are learning all this in school, about how you reacted to the way people have done you—because in your background and history you have a Revolution, of which you are very proud. You celebrate July 4th as Independence Day because you stood up against the British Empire and told them to go to hell. Your ancestors committed treason, and you celebrate it now; and you were not treated nearly as badly as black people in this country.

As Malcolm X said, we're catching more hell than Patrick Henry ever saw or thought of. Patrick Henry wouldn't have been able to take it. You can understand Patrick Henry and make a hero out of him to me in school, but then you're going to turn around and condemn us when we use peaceable methods, like Father Groppi and other individuals, to get the rights that your Constitution promised us.

I didn't say being born or naturalized in this country was enough to make me a citizen. You said it. The Bill of Rights is yours. The civil rights bills are your bills. When the government itself violates the law, it brings the whole law into contempt.

A policeman is an object of contempt. A policeman is a paid and hired murderer. And you never find the policeman guilty of a crime, no matter what violence he commits against a black person. In Detroit, you were shooting "snipers." So you mounted a .50 caliber machine gun on a tank and shot into an apartment and killed a four-year-old "sniper." . . .

Yet you have the Mafia setting up headquarters outside of Cicero, Illinois—where the black people are not good enough to live—and taking out a charter of incorporation in Delaware; and you don't bring tanks and machine guns against the Mafia.

The Justice Department leases some of its offices from the Mafia.

And you want to talk about "respect for the law."

In history, they teach me how great Teddy Roosevelt was. Yet when he wanted a certain canal built—and he didn't have the authority, based on the way the laws are constructed in this country—you know what Teddy Roosevelt said? "Damn the law! Build the canal."

They taught me that in a white school.

And they taught me that Thomas Jefferson was a hero and a patriot because he wrote, "all men are created equal." And Thomas Jefferson was a slaveholder. And you want to teach my child that this man who would have enslaved him had he been alive in those days, is a hero to him?

Patrick Henry, who talked about freedom being so great that he would rather take death than enslavement, was a slaveholder himself.

Then George Washington—the President—"first in war, first in peace, first in the hearts of his countrymen," was a slaveholder.

And you want to teach my child that these are great men.

Then Abraham Lincoln, one of the most pious hypocrites of all time—and you can read from his own words where he said he had doubts whether black men were as well endowed as white people. Here is the only thing he would grant the black man: the right to eat the food that his hands produced. He was against slavery *morally;* but he said since he was the President, *officially* there was nothing he could do except what would benefit the Union. And his wanting to do what benefited the Union prevented him from carrying out what he, many stated, felt was his moral responsibility. Then you want to tell me about morality operating in this country—the "last stronghold of freedom."

The "free world"—the Statue of Liberty, "give me your tired, your poor, your hungry, those yearning to be free." And a black man who fought in every conflict that this country ever had—*that this country ever had*—the first blood spilled from the body of Crispus Attucks during the American Revolution.

Now I want to draw a parallel between what happened at the so-called Boston Massacre on Boston Common and what we do now. Here was Captain Preston with a detachment of British soldiers. And they had a right to be there because this was a colony. But the colonists felt oppressed because Boston was being occupied by a "foreign" force. So some of the citizens got together.

They didn't just sing *We Shall Overcome*. They didn't ask the soldiers: "Can we sit down here and pray to our God?" They got slabs of stone and snowballs and clubs and attacked the soldiers. When the soldiers fired into the crowd and killed seven people, the Americans called it a "massacre," and they say that was a great patriotic action by those people.

Yet black people doing ordinary, reasonable, peaceful things in this country are attacked by the police; and the police are praised for it. And you talk about giving the police more money and more power. You have got them as walking arsenals now—pistols, guns, clubs, saps; some of them carry knives, cattle prods, the new tear gas canister, high-powered rifles. They will be giving them hand grenades next. They can call in tanks with .50 caliber machine guns—in the United States of America in 1967.

When you are raising hell in Vietnam killing people and can't straighten out what's happening in this country, don't wonder why I would tell a black boy: "Don't fight for this racist country"—and it is a racist country.

They use the term "nigger" on the floor of Congress. And look at Senator Dodd—good old Christian Senator Dodd; and then old black Adam Clayton Powell. Dodd had more charges against him than you can shake a stick at, and in black and white from his own documents what he had done. And you people sat around debating "whether we are going to censure him or whether we are to reprimand him." You didn't talk about taking away his seniority. You didn't talk about unseating him. None of these things.

Then here is Adam Clayton Powell where the charges are very nebulous and uncertain. But the problem is that he was a black man with too much power. And he was uppity. And he acted just like you have always acted. He arrogantly smoked his cigar, which you couldn't stand. So you kick him out and say he is a bad man for us.

Then we look at Senator Dodd. And you know what Dodd said? "I'm sorry I'm the first one. But the reason I am is they haven't checked all your files." Then

Long, in the Senate, stood and said: "He is here, and we're not because they exposed what is in his files"—implying that every senator is a thief. Every senator misuses public funds. Then the same scoundrels are going to get up and talk to me about lawlessness in the streets. And far more lawlessness is perpetrated in the halls of Congress than anywhere else.

And do you know why I think they voted against the rat control bill? It fits right in with what Senator Long said. The first victims may have been sitting in the Senate chambers. That is where the rats are.

But then let's make it literal rats. They fear black people more than they do the bubonic plague and other diseases that rats carry, because they wouldn't appropriate $40 million to control rats. But you will appropriate all kinds of money to give the National Guard increased training in how to wipe us out. And it's a funny thing that in all these so-called "riots," the police and National Guard kill far more people than the so-called "rioters."

And as for the "sniping," don't you believe that. If all of you were sitting in this room, I could just shoot at random, and I would hit somebody. Why are no cops killed? They ought to be killed. I think the cops should be killed. I believe the National Guard should be fought like they are telling us we should fight in Vietnam.

When a man comes into my community and he is going to endanger the life of my wife and my children, he should die. And if it is within my power, I will kill him. We are tired of sitting around with white people saying we have to *die* for what we believe. We have been dying ever since we have been in this country for what *you* believe and what you have taught us.

You know what you're going to tell *your* kid? George Washington, Patrick Henry, the great patriots—Benjamin Franklin discovered that lightning and electricity are synonymous. Everybody who ever did anything is white.

Here is what you are going to give my child. I am going to send him to school and teach him to respect authority. So here is a cracker teacher standing in front of my child making him listen to *Little Black Sambo*. See, that's the image the school gives him when he's young to teach him his "place." A caricature, wearing outlandish clothing that even the animals in the forest don't want to wear. His name is "Sambo." His mother's name is "Mumbo." And his father's name is "Jumbo." What are you telling him about family ties in America? That child does not have the same last name as either one of his parents. Since his parents have different last names, they are not even married.

All right. So he goes through the caricature like I did when I was a small child in grade school. And I don't forget these things. I wasn't born from the womb with the attitudes I have now. They were put in me by crackers. I sat through *Little Black Sambo*. And since I was the only black face in the room, I became Little Black Sambo. If my parents had taught me bad names to call the little cracker kids—and I use that term on purpose to try to get a message across to you—you don't like it. Well, how do you think we feel when an adult is going to take our child (we teach our child to respect that adult) and that adult gives these little white kids bad names to call him? Why don't you have Little Cracker Bohunk? Little Cracker Dago? Little Cracker Kike? You can't stand that. But yet you're going to take our little black children and expose them to this kind of ridicule, then not understand why we don't like it.

All right. He gets a little older, so he can't be Little Black Sambo because he's too old for that. So you turn to good old Mark Twain, one of your great writers. And the black child grows from Little Black Sambo into Nigger Jim. And the white kids read this stuff and they laugh at the black child; and he's got to sit there and take it. He is required to attend these schools by law, and this is what he gets.

All right. After he is Nigger Jim, he goes to high school and reads *Emperor Jones* written by Eugene O'Neill, who they are taught is a great playwright. And not only do they have to read it silently and master it, they've got to come to school and discuss orally about the "bush niggers." But still nothing about kikes. And nothing about dagos and spiks and wetbacks and bohunks and wops.

And then after he has passed through these degrading ages of the black man, and they have whipped the spirit out of him—after they have made him feel he's not fit to walk the earth and he always has to apologize to you for being here, then they crown him. They say, "I'm going to tell you what your granddaddy had been; what your daddy had been; what you are going to be: Old Black Joe. And you know how Old Black Joe comes? With his head hanging low."

You tell us what you want to do to us and make of us. And this is the "educational process" which our children go through. And you wonder why they don't want to sit up in school.

And there is brutality in Omaha schools. A junior high school teacher had beaten, kicked and cut little black children. We took these children with their parents to the mayor's office. He would take no action. So in conjunction with his Human Relations Board director—a man named Homer Floyd who I think is one of the sharpest human relations men in the country; he's now in Topeka heading the Kansas Human Relations Commission—we went to the office of the city attorney with these parents who wanted to bring an action on behalf of their children. He was shown the injuries. There was a doctor named Johnson who photographed the injuries and was willing to testify in court as to the extent of them and the treatment he gave. And do you know the city attorney refused to accept the complaint and would not allow the parents to file charges against the teacher?

We contacted two lawyers, one's name is John Miller, the other Leo Eisenstatt—I mention the names because they are influential in Omaha—they contacted various members of the Omaha Board of Education and we sent written copies of the complaints to each individual member of the Board, to each individual member of the City Council, the mayor, the safety director, the chief of police and all of the cracker agencies which are so interested in teaching us about law and order and decency and democracy and respect—and not a bit of action was taken. This man was promoted from junior high to high school. And he now teaches in South High School. What do you think of that?

A teacher wrote "f—k" on a piece of paper and showed it to my little sister who was in the fifth grade. When she told me, I went straight over there. And I stood in his room. And I told him if he even looked wrong I'd beat his brains out. And I meant it.

I went to the principal and told him the same thing—that if he did not do something about moving that man I was going to move him out of that classroom physically myself. The man is gone. But do you know what the principal wanted to do first? Put my little sister in a different fifth grade room. I said, "How about those other children, man? You miss the point. This monkey shouldn't be in the schools at all." So the principal said, "Then we'll move the teacher into a different fifth grade room." I said, "You'd better get him out of the school altogether." So he's gone.

At Horace Mann, a Negro junior high, about two months ago, my nephew—the teacher didn't know he was my nephew. They don't bother my nephews or other little children who are friends of mine. She didn't know he was my nephew because my sister's last name is different from mine, naturally because she's married. . . . The teacher hit him on the side of the head with a wooden paddle and broke the skin and left a swelling. I went to Horace Mann and said, "You're going to get rid of her or I'm going to do the same thing to her which she did to my nephew." And they tried to defend her action. But she's gone.

Why should we have to take each individual case of brutality and handle it personally like this? The school system is terrible. It's rotten. They have incompetent teachers. There is discrimination in the placement of teachers and pupils. The School Board just spent $5,000,000 to complete a white high school. An argument developed over whether they should put a planetarium in it; yet at Technical High, where most of the Negroes go, they can't even get blackboards. Again I had to go personally to the Board of Education and tell them they had better put some blackboards in there or some of the other schools that have them are not going to have them. But Tech is going to have everything it needs. Then the blackboards found their way there.

Some textbooks that my little boy didn't have in his classroom this semester came there only after I made a personal visit to Lothrop School where he attends. And there was water leaking through the roof, buckets all over—and I have pictures of it with me—water running through the light fixtures, dripping in the cafeteria on to the table where sandwiches were being made. Then when I went over to Lothrop School where all this was happening, the principal, instead of wanting to correct this, wanted to know "why in the hell" they didn't come to get him and let him know I was there. So I told them, "You ask him why in the hell he doesn't come to see me." He knows where I am. And by the way, I don't pick on people smaller than me. He's about 6′4″ and weighs about 260 pounds. I call him the Jolly White Giant. And I told him and the superintendent of schools he had better muzzle this white ox or he would be slaughtered.

You know why I don't mind telling you this stuff? Because you put us in jail for nothing. This man told you what trivial and pretended causes you use to put black people in jail. If I go to jail, its going to be for something; not like the last time about a year ago when I was standing on the steps of the barber shop where I work. I looked at a cracker cop and went to jail for "interfering with an officer" and "disturbing the peace." I have a transcript of the trial with me because you don't like to believe what we tell you. Then you want us to respect the police. "Help your police fight crime." To do that, we would have to fight the police because they, with Congress, are the greatest perpetrators of crime in this country.

You know what the police are mad about relative to Supreme Court decisions? They're upset because the Court says they have to respect the Fourth Amendment to the Constitution and other Constitutional guarantees of the people's freedom in a so-called democratic society.

We are being forced by police misconduct to get together to fight the police. You know when I'll believe that saying "We Shall Overcome" is an effective way to fight the police? When I see you send your Marines, your Airmen and your Infantrymen into Vietnam led by the Mormon Tabernacle choir—then making a landing on the beach singing *We Shall Overcome* and fighting them with prayer books.

You know that kind of action is not going to work over there. It hasn't worked anywhere. It won't work here. We are going to fight you people like you fight us.

And don't say I'm revealing too much, because if something happens to me there are other people who will come up. They killed Malcolm X and produced Stokely and Rap. You kill Rap, he will multiply. You kill Stokely, he will multiply.

Now you don't know me, so maybe you don't want to kill me. You might just want me in jail. But you get me off the scene, and I'll multiply, because each time you handle one of us in this way, you show what you are. And you show the way you have to be dealt with.

There are a couple of specific things I want to mention, then I'm going to stop because I don't want to take up the time.

But there is discrimination in housing in Omaha. The mayor likes to say a Negro can purchase property wherever he can afford to, anywhere he wants to. Bob Boozer plays professional basketball—I don't know if any of you know him. I think he plays with the Chicago Bulls. He wanted to buy a house. They refused to sell him a lot on which he can build himself a house. And he makes more money than any cracker in that neighborhood. So the mayor was caught here in a vise. On the one hand, he talks about Negroes being able to buy a house anywhere he chooses in the city, then he goes to the Nebraska legislature to support an open housing law. Why is this necessary if we can buy anywhere we want to? By the way, before the legislature killed open housing, they authorized the governor to use $500,000 to put down "riots," as they call them in our area.

We can't buy a house.

They refused to pass legislation necessary to help relieve these tensions, but they will pass—they will authorize this man $500,000. And he made some threats about his little 1800-man National Guard—how they are going to come into our community and do something to us. When they come, something is going to be waiting for them. And it's not singing *We Shall Overcome.* And its not playing these little footsy games we have been playing all these years.

Let me tell you one other thing about the police setup in Omaha. It flows right from this open housing situation I mentioned in the legislature. The paid representative of the Police Union is also in the Legislature. He voted against open housing. And yet he is still paid by the Omaha Police Union. When he did this and the officials (Union, City, AFL-CIO) refused to take corrective action, 17 Negro officers withdrew from the Police Union. And they brought forth other complaints which we had also had brought against the Police Department years ago, when I was co-chairman of the Police-Community Relations Council.

We have exhausted every means of getting redress, and it has not come. The police murdered a black boy named Eugene Nesbitt a year ago. He was against a fence. The cop was supposed to have been chasing him. His car—the tires had been shot off—hit a fence. A cop came up behind him, and from a distance of about nine feet, shot him in the back with a shotgun. Before the boy's body was cold, the safety director came out with a public statement and said the shooting was "regrettable" but "justified." There was no inquest. There was no autopsy. The cop was not relieved of duty pending an investigation. Nothing.

In March of this year, a 5′2″ Negro youth was detained in the county jail. Five-foot-two. The following morning—there was a door frame six and a half feet high from which he was found hanging—with his belt, supposedly. There was nothing in the cell for him to stand on. Yet a 5′2″ youth "committed suicide" in county jail. And again there was no investigation, but a whitewash. We are getting tired of having our people killed.

You have a National Teachers Corps in Omaha. Some interns were dropped from it because the director claimed there was not enough money in the local program to keep them. You know which interns were dropped? Two Negroes. And the program is designed to function in the Negro neighborhood. If those Negroes don't get back in the Teacher Corps, you are not going to have a Teacher Corps operational in Omaha. And I'm telling you that, too. And I'm going to do everything in my power to keep that Teacher Corps out of our area. And if they send them in anyway, they send those young whites in at their own peril.

I have taken a long time, and I guess that is just about everything I'll say for now.

One thing more. We have a mayor who is being consulted by Mr. Robert Weaver, Secretary of HUD, on a lot of things because this mayor talked in behalf of some legislation Mr. Weaver wanted in Housing and Urban Development. Now this mayor is on the board of Directors of what is known as Good Neighbor Homes. There is a Negro church with an Uncle Tom chicken-eatin' preacher for the pastor, who is fronting for the mayor's corporation; they are the sponsoring agency. Yet the mayor is on the board of Directors. The mayor's personal lawyer, Shafton, represents this group; and he is making that federal money which is put up for lawyer's fees. It is 221 (d) (3) housing. And this project was built in an area that is already overcrowded. And it is supposed to be for low-income people. Yet the rent starts at $115 a month. That is one of the mayor's interests.

He is also in charge of what is known as the Omaha Redevelopment Corporation (ORC)—and I have newspaper clippings on these things if you want to see them afterwards. They have about 45 houses in the ghetto which they have been buying up, his corporation. Now they have got some money under a federal program which is designed to help code enforcement and bring those houses up to standard.

Now at first they were tricky. They went into South Omaha and used some of this federal money. Then they went into the fringe of the Negro area to use some of this money. And then, the third time, it is called Project Pride, they went right into the area where between 30 and 33 of the mayor's corporation houses are located, and $40,000 in federal funds is being used there.

This same mayor asked me to review his Model City proposal because he needed what he called a "grass-roots" analysis. What he really needed was somebody who could make a hodgepodge look legitimate. But I am going to give him just what that thing deserves. It is justification for violent revolution in Omaha by black people.

We are late. If you read the admissions of the City of Omaha's application, you'll wonder why we Uncle Tom, handkerchief-head Negroes in Omaha haven't burned that city to the ground. This includes City Hall and everything else.

They admit that they don't give us the social services. We don't get the welfare attention. The buses don't give adequate service. The city itself doesn't clean the streets. There is inadequate garbage disposal. The police are poorly trained. They have bad, anti-Negro attitudes. All of this is presented. And you know why he did it? Because of the promise of the possibilities of getting some federal dollars. This made him admit crimes and flaws and shortcomings in the city which other considerations of morality never could.

We have been trying to bring these things to their attention for years, but they wouldn't acknowledge anything before. Then the federal government said "If you can show you have the imagination and you understand the causes of problems of the core cities, you can get some money." The mayor laid it all out, and there it is. And this is what I come from in Omaha, Nebraska.

You had better be glad—you see, some people there call me "militant." How can you call me "militant" when, in view of all these things I have mentioned to you, I haven't started a riot. I haven't burned a building. I haven't killed a cop.

You are looking at somebody who is more rational than any of you—or some of you—because some of you support the war in Vietnam, but you wouldn't support us if we burned down Omaha.

CHAPTER X

SOCIAL AND CULTURAL CHANGE

DISORGANIZATION, PLANNING, AND VALUES

84 Death by Dieselization: A Case Study in the Reaction to Technological Change

W. FRED COTTRELL

We in America tend to value "change." We seem to welcome all kinds of miracles of modern scientific technology: spacecraft carrying men to the moon, communication satellites that link the nations of the world in instantaneous video and audio contact, and the atom-splitting technology of nuclear physics providing new sources of power (for good or ill). When a new development is considered to be "good," the public commonly takes the position that any side effects in the way of "costs" to small segments of the population are more than offset by the benefits to "society as a whole." We may even consider it unpatriotic or immoral for groups unfavorably affected by technological changes to call for reparations for the losses they suffer. This selection dramatizes the widespread side effects of an invention and helps us to understand something of the position of those on whom the social costs of that invention fell most directly.

In the following instance it is proposed that we examine a community confronted with radical change in its basic economic institution and to trace the effects of this change throughout the social structure. From these facts it may be possible in some degree to anticipate the resultant changing attitudes and values of the people in the community, particularly as they reveal whether or not there is a demand for modification of the social structure or a shift in function from one institution to another. Some of the implications of the facts discovered may be valuable in anticipating future social change.

The community chosen for examination has been disrupted by the dieselization of the railroads. Since the railroad is among the oldest of those industries organized around steam, and since therefore the social structure of railroad communities is a product of long-continued processes of adaptation to the technology

SOURCE: *American Sociological Review*, vol. 16, no. 3 (June 1951), 358–65. Reprinted by permission of the author and The American Sociological Association. • The author is director of the Scripps Foundation and professor of sociology and political science at Miami University, Oxford, Ohio. He is interested in the effects of technology upon society and has written *The Railroader, Men Cry Peace,* and *Energy and Society.*

of steam, the sharp contrast between the technological requirements of the steam engine and those of the diesel should clearly reveal the changes in social structure required. Any one of a great many railroad towns might have been chosen for examination. However, many railroad towns are only partly dependent upon the railroad for their existence. In them many of the effects which take place are blurred and not easily distinguishable by the observer. Thus, the "normal" railroad town may not be the best place to see the consequences of dieselization. For this reason a one-industry town was chosen for examination.

In a sense it is an "ideal type" railroad town, and hence not complicated by other extraneous economic factors. It lies in the desert and is here given the name "Caliente" which is the Spanish adjective for "hot." Caliente was built in a break in an eighty-mile canyon traversing the desert. Its reason for existence was to service the steam locomotive. There are few resources in the area to support it on any other basis, and such as they are they would contribute more to the growth and maintenance of other little settlements in the vicinity than to that of Caliente. So long as the steam locomotive was in use, Caliente was a necessity. With the adoption of the diesel it became obsolescent.

This stark fact was not, however, part of the expectations of the residents of Caliente. Based upon the "certainty" of the railroad's need for Caliente, men built their homes there, frequently of concrete and brick, at the cost, in many cases, of their life savings. The water system was laid in cast iron which will last for centuries. Business men erected substantial buildings which could be paid for only by profits gained through many years of business. Four churches evidence the faith of Caliente people in the future of their community. A twenty-seven bed hospital serves the town. Those who built it thought that their investment was as well warranted as the fact of birth, sickness, accident and death. They believed in education. Their school buildings represent the investment of savings guaranteed by bonds and future taxes. There is a combined park and play field which, together with a recently modernized theatre, has been serving recreational needs. All these physical structures are material evidence of the expectations, morally and legally sanctioned and financially funded, of the people of Caliente. This is a normal and rational aspect of the culture of all "solid" and "sound" communities.

Similarly normal are the social organizations. These include Rotary, Chamber of Commerce, Masons, Odd Fellows, American Legion and the Veterans of Foreign Wars. There are the usual unions, churches, and myriad little clubs to which the women belong. In short, here is the average American community with normal social life, subscribing to normal American codes. Nothing its members had been taught would indicate that the whole pattern of this normal existence depended completely upon a few elements of technology which were themselves in flux. For them the continued use of the steam engine was as "natural" a phenomenon as any other element in their physical environment. Yet suddenly their life pattern was destroyed by the announcement that the railroad was moving its division point, and with it destroying the economic basis of Caliente's existence.

Turning from this specific community for a moment, let us examine the technical changes which took place and the reasons for the change. Division points on a railroad are established by the frequency with which the rolling stock must be serviced and the operating crews changed. At the turn of the century when this particular road was built, the engines produced wet steam at low temperatures. The steel in the boilers was of comparatively low tensile strength and could not withstand the high temperatures and pressures required for the efficient use of coal and water. At intervals of roughly a hundred miles the engine had to be disconnected from the train for service. At these points the cars also were inspected and if they were found to be defective they were either removed from the train or repaired while it was standing and the new engine being coupled on. Thus the location of Caliente, as far as the railroad was concerned, was a function of boiler temperature and pressure and the resultant service requirements of the locomotive.

Following World War II, the high tensile steels developed to create superior artillery and armor were used for locomotives. As a consequence it was possible to utilize steam at higher temperatures and pressure. Speed, power, and efficiency were increased and the distance between service intervals was increased.

The "ideal distance" between freight divisions became approximately 150 to 200 miles whereas it had formerly been 100 to 150. Wherever possible, freight divisions were increased in length to that formerly used by passenger trains, and passenger divisions were lengthened from two old freight divisions to three. Thus towns located at 100 miles from a terminal became obsolescent, those at 200 became freight points only, and those at 300 miles became passenger division points.

The increase in speed permitted the train crews to make the greater distance in the time previously required for the lesser trip, and roughly a third of the train and engine crews, car inspectors, boilermakers and machinists and other service men were dropped. The towns thus abandoned were crossed off the social record of the nation in the adjustment to these technological changes in the use of the steam locomotive. Caliente, located midway between terminals about six hundred miles apart, survived. In fact it gained, since the less frequent stops caused an increase in the service required of the maintenance crews at those points where it took place. However, the introduction of the change to diesel engines projected a very different future.

In its demands for service the diesel engine differs almost completely from a steam locomotive. It requires infrequent, highly skilled service, carried on within very close limits, in contrast to the frequent, crude adjustments required by the steam locomotive. Diesels operate at about 35 per cent efficiency, in contrast to the approximately 4 per cent efficiency of the steam locomotives in use after World War II in the United States. Hence diesels require much less frequent stops for fuel and water. These facts reduce their operating cost sufficiently to compensate for their much higher initial cost.

In spite of these reductions in operating costs the introduction of diesels ordinarily would have taken a good deal of time. The change-over would have been slowed by the high capital costs of retooling the locomotive works, the long period required to recapture the costs of existing steam locomotives, and the effective resistance of the workers. World War II altered each of these factors. The locomotive works were required to make the change in order to provide marine engines, and the costs of the change were assumed by the government. Steam engines were used up by the tremendous demand placed upon the railroads by war traffic. The costs were recaptured by shipping charges. Labor shortages were such that labor resistance was less formidable and much less acceptable to the public than it would have been in peace time. Hence the shift to diesels was greatly facilitated by the war. In consequence, every third and sometimes every second division point suddenly became technologically obsolescent.

Caliente, like all other towns in similar plight, is supposed to accept its fate in the name of "progress." The general public, as shippers and consumers of shipped goods, reaps the harvest in better, faster service and eventually perhaps in lower charges. A few of the workers in Caliente will also share the gains, as they move to other division points, through higher wages. They will share in the higher pay, though whether this will be adequate to compensate for the costs of moving no one can say. Certain it is that their pay will not be adjusted to compensate for their specific losses. They will gain only as their seniority gives them the opportunity to work. These are those who gain. What are the losses, and who bears them?

The railroad company can figure its losses at Caliente fairly accurately. It owns 39 private dwellings, a modern clubhouse with 116 single rooms, and a twelve-room hotel with dining-room and lunch-counter facilities. These now become useless, as does much of the fixed physical equipment used for servicing trains. Some of the machinery can be used elsewhere. Some part of the roundhouse can be used to store unused locomotives and standby equipment. The rest will be torn down to save taxes. All of these costs can be entered as capital losses on the statement which the company draws up for its stockholders and for the government. Presumably they will be recovered by the use of the more efficient engines.

What are the losses that may not be entered on the company books? The total tax assessment in Caliente was $9,946.80 for the year 1948, of which $6,103.39 represented taxes assessed on the railroad. Thus the railroad valuation was about three-fifths that of the town. This does not take into account tax-free property belonging to the churches, the schools, the hospital, or the municipality itself which included all the public utilities. Some ideas of the losses sustained by the railroad in comparison with the losses of others can be surmised by reflecting on these figures for real estate alone. The story is an old one and often repeated in the economic history of America. It represents the "loss" side of a profit and loss system of adjusting to technological change. Perhaps for sociological purposes we need an answer to the question "just who pays?"

Probably the greatest losses are suffered by the older "non-operating" employees. Seniority among these men extends only within the local shop and craft. A man with twenty-five years' seniority at Caliente has no claim on the job of a similar craftsman at another point who has only twenty-five days' seniority. Moreover, some of the skills formerly valuable are no longer needed. The boilermaker, for example, knows that jobs for his kind are disappearing and he must enter the ranks of the unskilled. The protection and status offered by the union while he was employed have become meaningless now that he is no longer needed. The cost of this is high both in loss of income and in personal demoralization.

Operating employees also pay. Their seniority extends over a division, which in this case includes three division points. The older members can move from Caliente and claim another job at another point, but in many cases they move leaving a good portion of their life savings behind. The younger men must abandon their stake in railroad employment. The loss may mean a new apprenticeship in another occupation, at a time in life when apprenticeship wages are not adequate to meet the obligations of mature men with families. A steam engine hauled 2,000 tons up the hill out of Caliente with the aid of two helpers. The four-unit diesel in command of one crew handles a train of 5,000 tons alone. Thus, to handle the same amount of tonnage required only about a fourth the man-power it formerly took. Three out of four men must start out anew at something else.

The local merchants pay. The boarded windows, half-empty shelves, and abandoned store buildings bear mute evidence of these costs. The older merchants stay, and pay; the younger ones, and those with no stake in the community will move; but the value of their property will in both cases largely be gone.

The bondholders will pay. They can't foreclose on a dead town. If the town were wiped out altogether, that which would remain for salvage would be too little to satisfy their claims. Should the town continue there is little hope that taxes adequate to carry the overhead of bonds and day-to-day expenses could be secured by taxing the diminished number of property owners or employed persons.

The church will pay. The smaller congregations cannot support services as in the past. As the church men leave, the buildings will be abandoned.

Homeowners will pay. A hundred and thirty-five men owned homes in Caliente. They must accept the available means of support or rent to those who do. In either case the income available will be far less than that on which the houses were built. The least desirable homes will stand unoccupied, their value completely lost. The others must be revalued at a figure far below that at which they were formerly held.

In a word, those pay who are, by traditional American standards, *most moral.* Those who have raised children see friendships broken and neighborhoods disintegrated. The childless more freely shake the dust of Caliente from their feet. Those who built their personalities into the structure of the community watch their work destroyed. Those too wise or too selfish to have entangled themselves in community affairs suffer no such qualms. The chain store can pull down its sign, move its equipment and charge the costs off against more profitable and better located units, and against taxes. The local owner has no such alternatives. In short, "good citizens" who assumed family and community responsibility are the greatest losers. Nomads suffer least.

The people of Caliente are asked to accept as "normal" this strange inversion of their expectations. It is assumed that they will, without protest or change in sentiment, accept the dictum of the "law of supply and demand." Certainly they must comply in part with this dictum. While their behavior in part reflects this compliance, there are also other changes perhaps equally important in their attitudes and values.

The first reaction took the form of an effort at community self-preservation. Caliente became visible to its inhabitants as a real entity, as meaningful as the individual personalities which they had hitherto been taught to see as atomistic or nomadic elements. Community survival was seen as prerequisite to many of the individual values that had been given precedence in the past. The organized community made a search for new industry, citing elements of community organization themselves as reasons why industry should move to Caliente. But the conditions that led the railroad to abandon the point made the place even less attractive to new industry than it had hitherto been. Yet the effort to keep the community a going concern persisted.

There was also a change in sentiment. In the past the glib assertion that progress spelled sacrifice could be offered when some distant group was a victim of technological change. There was no such reaction when the event struck home. The change can probably be as well revealed as in any other way by quoting from the Caliente *Herald*:

. . . [over the] years . . . [this] . . . railroad and its affiliates . . . became to this writer his ideal of a railroad empire. The [company] . . . appeared to take much more than the ordinary interest of big railroads in the development of areas adjacent to its lines, all the while doing a great deal for the communities large and small through which the lines passed.

Those were the days creative of [its] enviable reputation as one of the finest, most progressive—and most human—of American railroads, enjoying the confidence and respect of employees, investors, and communities alike!

One of the factors bringing about this confidence and respect was the consideration shown communities which otherwise would have suffered serious blows when division and other changes were effected. A notable example was . . . [a town] . . . where the shock of division change was made almost unnoticed by installation of a rolling stock reclamation point, which gave [that town] an opportunity to hold its community intact until tourist traffic and other industries could get better established—with the result that . . . [it] . . . is now on a firm foundation. And through this display of consideration for a community, the railroad gained friends—not only among the people of . . . [that town] . . . who were perhaps more vocal than others, but also among thousands of others throughout the country on whom this action made an indelible impression.

But things seem to have changed materially during the last few years, the . . . [company] . . . seems to this writer to have gone all out for glamor and the dollars which glamorous people have to spend, sadly neglecting one of the principal factors which helped to make . . . [it] . . . great: that fine consideration of communities and individuals, as well as employees, who have been happy in cooperating steadfastly with the railroad in times of stress as well as prosperity. The loyalty of these people and communities seems to count for little with the . . . [company] . . . of this day, though other "Big Business" corporations do not hesitate to expend huge sums to encourage the loyalty of community and people which old friends of . . . [the company] . . . have been happy to give voluntarily.

Ever since the . . . railroad was constructed . . . Caliente has been a key town on the railroad. It is true, the town owed its inception to the railroad, but it has paid this back in becoming one of the most attractive communities on the system. With nice homes, streets and parks, good school . . . good city government . . . Caliente offers advantages that most big corporations would be gratified to have for their employees—a homey spot where they could live their lives of contentment, happiness and security.

Caliente's strategic location, midway of some of the toughest road on the entire system has been a lifesaver for the road several times when floods have wreaked havoc on the roadbed in the canyon above and below Caliente. This has been possible through storage in Caliente of large stocks of repair material and equipment—and not overlooking manpower—which has thus become available on short notice.

. . . But [the railroad] or at least one of its big officials appearing to be almost completely divorced from policies which made this railroad great, has ordered changes which are about as inconsiderate as anything of which "Big Business" has ever been accused! Employees who have given the best years of their lives to this railroad are cut off without anything to which they can turn, many of them with homes in which they have taken much pride; while others, similarly with nice homes, are told to move elsewhere and are given runs that only a few will be able to endure from a physical standpoint, according to common opinion.

Smart big corporations the country over encourage their employees to own their own homes—and loud are their boasts when the percentage of such employees is favorable! But in contrast, a high [company] official is reported to have said only recently that "a railroad man has no business owning a home!" Quite a departure from what has appeared to be [company] tradition.

It is difficult for the *Herald* to believe that this official however "big" he is, speaks for the . . . [company] . . . when he enunciates a policy that, carried to the letter, would make tramps of [company] employees and their families!

No thinking person wants to stand in the way of progress, but true progress is not made when it is overshadowed by cold-blooded disregard for the loyalty of employees, their families, and the communities which have developed in the good American way through the decades of loyal service and good citizenship.

This editorial, written by a member of all the service clubs, approved by Caliente business men, and quoted with approbation by the most conservative members of the community, is significant of changing sentiment.

The people of Caliente continually profess their belief in "The American Way," but like the editor of the *Herald* they criticize decisions made solely in pursuit of profit, even though these decisions grow out of a clear-cut case of technological "progress." They feel that the company should have based its decision upon consideration for loyalty, citizenship, and community morale. They assume that the company should regard the seniority rights of workers as important considerations, and that it should consider significant the effect of permanent unemployment upon old and faithful employees. They look upon community integrity as an important community asset. Caught between the support of a "rational" system of "economic" forces and laws, and sentiments which they accept as significant values, they seek a solution to their dilemma which will at once permit them to retain their expected rewards for continued adherence to past norms and to defend the social system which they have been taught to revere but which now offers them a stone instead of bread.

IMPLICATIONS

We have shown that those in Caliente whose behavior most nearly approached the ideal taught are hardest hit by change. On the other hand, those seemingly farthest removed in conduct from that ideal are either rewarded or pay less of the costs of change than do those who follow the ideal more closely. Absentee owners, completely anonymous, and consumers who are not expected to cooperate to make the gains possible are rewarded most highly, while the local people who must cooperate to raise productivity pay dearly for having contributed.

In a society run through sacred mysteries whose rationale it is not man's privilege to criticize, such incongruities may be explained away. Such a society may even provide some "explanation" which makes them seem rational. In a secular society, supposedly defended rationally upon scientific facts, in which the pragmatic test "Does it work?" is continually applied, such discrepancy between expectation and realization is difficult to reconcile.

Defense of our traditional system of assessing the cost of technological change is made on the theory that the costs of such change are more than offset by the benefits to "society as a whole." However, it is difficult to show the people of Calient just why *they* should pay for advances made to benefit others whom they have never known and who, in their judgment, have done nothing to justify such rewards. Any action that will permit the people of Caliente to levy the costs of change upon those who will benefit from them will be morally justifiable to the people of Caliente. Appeals to the general welfare leave them cold and the compulsions of the price system are not felt to be self-justifying "natural laws" but are regarded as being the specific consequence of specific bookkeeping decisions as to what should be included in the costs of change. They seek to change these decisions through social action. They do not consider that the "American Way" consists primarily of acceptance of the market as the final arbiter of their destiny. Rather they conceive that the system as a whole exists to render "justice," and if the consequences of the price system are such as to produce what they consider to be "injustice" they proceed to use some other institution as a means to reverse or offset the effects of the price system. Like other groups faced with the same situation, those in Caliente seize upon the means available to them. The operating employees had in their unions a device to secure what they consider to be their rights. Union practices developed over the years make it possible for the organized workers to avoid some of the costs of change which they would otherwise have had to bear. Feather-bed rules, make-work practices, restricted work weeks, train length legislation and other similar devices were designed to permit union members to continue work even when "efficiency" dictated that they be disemployed. Members of the "Big Four" in Caliente joined with their fellows in demanding not only the retention of previously existing rules, but the imposition of new ones such as that requiring the presence of a third man in the diesel cab. For other groups there was available only the appeal to the company that it establish some other facility at Caliente, or alternatively a demand that "government" do something. One such demand took the form of a request to the Interstate Commerce Commission that it require inspection of rolling stock at Caliente. This request was denied.

It rapidly became apparent to the people of Caliente that they could not gain their objectives by organized community action nor individual endeavor but there was hope that by adding their voices to those of others similarly injured there might be hope of solution. They began to look to the activities of the whole labor movement for succor. Union strategy which forced the transfer of control from the market to government mediation or to legislation and operation was widely approved on all sides. This was not confined to those only who were currently seeking rule changes but was equally approved by the great bulk of those in the community who had been hit by the change. Cries of public outrage at their demands for make-work rules were looked upon as coming from those at best ignorant, ill-informed or stupid, and at worst as being the hypocritical efforts of others to gain at the workers' expense. When the union threat of a national strike for rule changes was met by government seizure, Caliente workers like most of their compatriots across the country welcomed this shift in control, secure in their belief that if "justice" were done they could only be gainers by government intervention. These attitudes are not "class" phenomena purely nor are they merely occupational sentiments. They result from the fact that modern life, with the interdependence that it creates, particularly in one-industry communities, imposes penalties far beyond the membership of the groups presumably involved in industry. When make-work rules contributed to the livelihood of the community, the support of the churches, and the taxes which maintain the schools; when feather-bed practices determine the standard of living, the profits of the business man and the circulation of the press; when they contribute to the salary of the teacher and the preacher; they can no longer be treated as accidental, immoral, deviant or temporary. Rather they are elevated into the position of emergent morality and law. Such practices generate a morality which serves them just as the practices in turn nourish those who participate in and preserve them. They are as firmly a part of what one "has a right to expect" from industry as are parity payments to the farmer, bonuses and pensions to the veterans, assistance to the aged, tariffs to the industrialist, or the sanctity of property to those who inherit. On the other hand, all these practices conceivably help create a structure that is particularly vulnerable to changes such as that described here.

Practices which force the company to spend in Caliente part of what has been saved through technological change, or failing that, to reward those who are forced to move by increased income for the same service, are not, by the people of Caliente, considered to be unjustifiable. Confronted by a choice between the old means and resultant "injustice" which their use entails, and the acceptance of new means which they believe will secure them the "justice" they hold to be their right, they are willing to abandon (in so far as this particular area is concerned) the liberal state and the omnicompetent market in favor of something that works to provide "justice."

The study of the politics of pressure groups will show how widely the reactions of Caliente people are paralleled by those of other groups. Amongst them it is in politics that the decisions as to who will pay and who will profit are made. Through organized political force railroaders maintain the continuance of rules which operate to their benefit rather than for "the public good" or "the general welfare." Their defense of these practices is found in the argument that only so can their rights be protected against the power of other groups who hope to gain at their expense by functioning through the corporation and the market.

We should expect that where there are other groups similarly affected by technological change, there will be similar efforts to change the operation of our institutions. The case cited is not unique. Not only is it duplicated in hundreds of railroad division points but also in other towns abandoned by management for similar reasons. Changes in the location of markets or in the method of calculating transportation costs, changes in technology making necessary the use of new materials, changes due to the exhaustion of old sources of materials, changes to avoid labor costs such as the shift of the textile industry from New England to the South, changes to expedite decentralization to avoid the consequences of bombing, or those of congested living, all give rise to the question, "Who benefits, and at whose expense?"

The accounting practices of the corporation permit the entry only of those costs which have become "legitimate" claims upon the company. But the tremendous risks borne by the workers and frequently all the members of the community in an era of technological change are real phenomena. Rapid shifts in technology which destroy the "legitimate" expectations derived from past experience force the recognition of new obligations. Such recognition may be made voluntarily as management foresees the necessity, or it may be thrust upon it by political or other action. Rigidity of property concepts, the legal structure controlling directors in what they may admit to be costs, and the stereotyped nature of the "economics" used by management make rapid change within the corporation itself difficult even in a "free democratic society." Hence while management is likely to be permitted or required to initiate technological change in the interest of profits, it may and probably will be barred from compensating for the social consequences certain to arise from those changes. Management thus shuts out the rising flood of demands in its cost-accounting only to have them reappear in its tax accounts, in legal regulations or in new insistent union demands. If economics fails to provide an answer to social demands then politics will be tried.

It is clear that while traditional morality provides a means of protecting some groups from the consequences of technological change, or some method of meliorating the effects of change upon them, other large segments of the population are left unprotected. It should be equally clear that rather than a quiet acquiescence in the finality and justice of such arrangements, there is an active effort to force new devices into being which will extend protection to those hitherto expected to bear the brunt of these costs. A good proportion of these inventions increasingly call for the intervention of the state. To call such arrangements immoral, unpatriotic, socialistic or to hurl other epithets at them is not to deal effectively with them. They are as "natural" as are the "normal" reactions for which we have "rational" explanations based upon some pre-scientific generalization about human nature such as "the law of supply and demand" or "the inevitability of progress." To be dealt with effectively they will have to be understood and treated as such.

85 Steel Axes for Stone Age Australians

LAURISTON SHARP

The preceding selection describes the seriously disruptive effects of the introduction of a new invention on an American community. This selection deals with a similar problem, but in a primitive setting where the introduction of the new culture trait is almost completely destructive rather than merely disruptive. The destructive results—demoralization of the individual, disintegration of the culture, and perhaps even dissolution of the society as a viable, distinct entity—appear to have been unavoidable once the trait was widely adopted. One writer has referred to this particular article as the story of "The Steel Axe That Destroyed a Tribe." It is important to note that a similar story could hardly be written about a complex and less integrated society such as ours. But problems that are only quantitatively (not qualitatively) different from those faced by the Yir Yoront appear in every society that undergoes change.

THE PROBLEM

Like other Australian aboriginals, the Yir Yoront group at the mouth of the Coleman River on the west coast of tropical Cape York Peninsula originally had no knowledge of metals. Technologically their culture was of the old stone age or paleolithic type; they supported themselves by hunting and fishing, obtaining vegetable foods and needed materials from the bush by simple gathering techniques. Their only domesticated animal was the dog, and they had no domesticated plants of any kind. Unlike some other aboriginal groups, however, the Yir Yoront did have polished stone axes hafted in short handles, and these imple-

SOURCE: Edward H. Spicer, ed., *Human Problems in Technological Change* (New York: Russell Sage Foundation, 1952), Case 5, pp. 69–90. • The author is professor of anthropology and director of Cornell University Studies in Culture and Applied Science. His chief interests are in the study of Oceania and Southeast Asia. He has written *Siamese Rice Village, Bibliography of Thailand, Some Principles of Cultural Change,* and has edited *Handbook on Thailand.*

ments were most important in their economy.

Toward the end of the nineteenth century metal tools and other European artifacts began to filter into the Yir Yoront territory. The flow increased with the gradual expansion of the white frontier outward from southern and eastern Queensland. Of all the items of western technology thus made available, none was more acceptable, none more highly valued by aboriginals of all conditions than the hatchet or short-handled steel axe. . . .

RELEVANT FACTORS

If we concentrate our attention on Yir Yoront behavior centering about the original stone axe, rather than on the axe—the thing—we should get some conception of the role this implement played in aboriginal culture. This conception, in turn, should permit us to foresee with considerable accuracy some of the results of the displacement of stone axes by steel axes acquired directly or indirectly from Europeans by the Yir Yoront.

The production of a stone axe required a number of simple skills. With the idea of the axe in its various details well in mind, the adult men—and only the adult men—could set about producing it, a task not considered appropriate for women or children. . . .

The use of the stone axe as a piece of capital equipment for the production of other goods indicates its very great importance in the subsistence economy of the aboriginal. Anyone—man, woman, or child—could use the axe; indeed, it was used more by women, for theirs was the onerous, daily task of obtaining sufficient wood to keep the campfire of each family burning all day for cooking or other purposes and all night against mosquitoes and cold (in July, winter temperature might drop below forty degrees). In a normal lifetime any woman would use the axe to cut or knock down literally tons of firewood. Men and women, and sometimes children, needed the axe to make other tools, or weapons, or a variety of material equipment required by the aboriginal in his daily life. . . .

While the stone axe helped relate men and women and often children to nature in technological behavior, in the transformation of natural into cultural equipment, it also was prominent in that aspect of behavior which may be called conduct, primarily directed toward persons. Yir Yoront men were dependent upon interpersonal relations for their stone axe heads, since the flat, geologically recent alluvial country over which they range, provides no stone from which axe heads can be made. The stone they used comes from known quarries four hundred miles to the south. It reached the Yir Yoront through long lines of male trading partners, some of these chains terminating with the Yir Yoront men, while others extended on farther north to other groups, having utilized Yir Yoront men as links. Almost every older adult man had one or more regular trading partners, some to the north and some to the south. His partner or partners in the south he provided with surplus spears, and particularly fighting spears tipped with the barbed spines of sting ray which snap into vicious fragments when they penetrate human flesh. For a dozen spears, some of which he may have obtained from a partner to the north, he would receive from a southern partner one stone axe head. . . . Thus trading relations, which may extend the individual's personal relationships out beyond the boundaries of his own group, are associated with two of the most important items in a man's equipment, spears and axes, whether the latter are of stone or steel. Finally, most of the exchanges between partners take place during the dry season at times when the great aboriginal fiestas occur, which center about initiation rites or other totemic ceremonials that attract hundreds and are the occasion for much exciting activity besides trading.

Returning to the Yir Yoront, we find that not only was it adult men alone who obtained axe heads and produced finished axes, but it was adult males who retained the axes, keeping them with other parts of their equipment in camp, or carrying them at the back slipped through a human hair belt when traveling. Thus, every woman or child who wanted to use an axe—and this might be frequently during the day—must get one from some man, use it promptly, and return it to the man in good condition. While a man might speak of "my axe," a woman or child could not; for them it was always "your axe," addressing a male, or "his axe."

This necessary and constant borrowing of axes from older men by women and children was done according to regular patterns of kinship behavior. A woman on good terms with her husband would expect to use his axe unless he were using it; a husband on good terms with his wives would let any one of them use his axe without question. If a woman was unmarried or her husband was absent, she would go first to her older brother or to her father for an axe. Only in extraordinary circumstances would she seek a stone axe from a mother's brother or certain other male kin with whom she had to be most circumspect. A girl, a boy, or a young man would look to a father or an older brother to provide an axe for her or his use, but would never approach a mother's brother, who would be at the sa[illegible] potential father-in-law, with such a request. Older men, too, would follow similar rules if they had to borrow an axe.

It will be noted that these social relationships in which the stone axe had a place are all pair relationships and that the use of the axe helped define and maintain the character of the relationships and the roles of the two individual participants. Every active relationship among the Yir Yoront involved a definite and accepted status of superordination or subordination. A person could have no dealings with any other on exactly equal terms. Women and children were dependent on, or subordinate to, older males in every action in which the axe entered. Among the men, the younger was dependent on the older or on certain kinds of kin. The nearest approach to equality was between brothers, although the older was always superordinate to the younger. Since the exchange of goods in a trading relationship involved a mutual reciprocity, trading partners were usually a kind of brother to each other or stood in a brotherly type of relationship, although one was always classified as older than the other and would have some advantage in case of dispute. It can be seen that repeated and widespread conduct centering on the axe helped to generalize and standardize throughout the society these sex, age, and kinship roles, both in their normal benevolent and in exceptional malevolent aspects, and helped to build up expectancies regarding the conduct of others defined as having a particular status.

The status of any individual Yir Yoront was determined not only by sex, age, and extended kin relationships, but also by membership in one of two dozen patrilineal totemic clans into which the entire community was divided. A person's names, rights in particular areas of land, and, in the case of a man, his roles in the totemic ceremonies (from which women are excluded) were all a function of belonging to one clan rather than another. Each clan had literally hundreds of totems, one or two of which gave the clan its name, and from any of which the personal names of clan members were derived. These totems included not only natural species or phenomena like the sun, stars, and daybreak, but also cultural "species": imagined ghosts, rainbow serpents, heroic ancestors; such eternal cultural verities as fires, spears, huts; and such human activities, conditions, or attributes as eating, vomiting, swimming, fighting, babies and corpses, milk and blood, lips and loins. While individual members of such totemic classes or species might disappear or be destroyed, the class itself was obviously ever present and indestructible. The totems therefore lent permanence and stability to the clans, to the groupings of human individuals who generation after generation were each associated with one set of totems that distinguished one clan from another.

Among the many totems of the Sunlit Cloud Iguana clan, and important among them, was the stone axe. The names of many members of this clan referred to the axe itself, or to activities like trading or wild honey gathering in which the axe played a vital part, or to the clan's mythical ancestors with whom the axe was prominently associated. When it was necessary to represent the stone axe in totemic ceremonies, it was only men of this clan who exhibited it or pantomimed its use. In secular life the axe could be made by any man and used by all; but in the sacred realm of the totems it belonged exclusively to the Sunlit Cloud Iguana people.

Supporting those aspects of cultural behavior which we have called technology and conduct is a third area of culture, including ideas, sentiments, and values. These are most difficult to deal with, for they are latent and covert or even unconscious and must be deduced from overt actions and language or other communicating behavior. In this aspect of the culture lies the "meaning" of the stone axe, its significance to the Yir Yoront and to their cultural way of life. The ideal conception of the axe, the knowledge of how to produce it (apart from the purely muscular habits used in its production) are part of the Yir Yoront adult masculine role, just as ideas regarding its technical use are included in the feminine role. These technical ideas constitute a kind of "science" regarding the axe which may be more important in relation to behavioral change than are the neurophysiological patterns drilled into the body by years of practice. Similarly there are normative ideas regarding the part played by the axe in conduct which constitute a kind of "morality" of the axe, and which again may be more important than the overt habits of social interaction in determining the role of the axe in social relationships. More than ideas regarding technology, ideas regarding conduct are likely to be closely associated, or "charged," with sentiment or value. Ideas and sentiments help guide and inform overt behavior; in turn, overt behavior helps support and validate ideas and sentiments. . . .

Important for an understanding of the Yir Yoront culture is a system of ideas, which may be called their totemic ideology. A fundamental belief of the aboriginal divided time into two great epochs, a distant and sacred period at the beginning of the world, when the earth was peopled by mildly marvelous ancestral sense are the forebears of the clans; and a beings or culture heroes who in a special second period, when the old was succeeded by a new order that includes the present. Originally there was no anticipation of another era supplanting the present; the future would simply be an eternal continuation and reproduction of the present, which itself had remained unchanged since the epochal revolution of ancestral times.

The mythical sacred world of the ancestors with which time began turns out on investigation to be a detailed reproduction of the present aboriginal world of nature, man, and culture altered by phantasy. In short, the idea system expressed in the mythology regarding the ancestral epoch was directly derived from Yir Yoront behavior patterns—normal and abnormal, actual and ideal, conscious and unconscious. The important thing to note, however, is that the native believed it was just the other way around, that the present world, as a natural and cultural environment, was and should be simply a detailed reproduction of the world of the ancestors. He believed that the entire universe "is now as it was in the beginning" when it was established and left by the ancestors. The ordinary cultural life of the ancestors became the daily life of the Yir Yoront camps, and the extraordinary life of the ancestors remained extant in the recurring symbolic pantomimes and paraphernalia found only in the most sacred atmosphere of the totemic rites.

• • • • •

ANALYSIS

The introduction of the steel axe indiscriminately and in large numbers into the Yir Yoront technology was only one of many changes occurring at the same time. It is therefore impossible to factor out all the results of this single innovation alone. Nevertheless, a number of specific effects of the change from stone axes to steel axes may be noted; and the steel axe may be used as an epitome of the European goods and implements received by the aboriginals in increasing quantity and of their general influence on the native culture. The use of the steel axe to illustrate such influences would seem to be justified, for it was one of the first European artifacts to be adopted for regular use by the Yir Yoront; and the axe, whether of stone or steel, was clearly one of the most important items of cultural equipment they possessed.

The shift from stone to steel axes provided no major technological difficulties. While the aboriginals themselves could not manufacture steel axe heads, a steady supply from outside continued; and broken wooden axe handles could easily be replaced from bush timbers with aboriginal tools. Among the Yir Yoront the new axe never acquired all the uses it had on mission or cattle stations (carpentry work, pounding tent pegs, use as a hammer, and so on); and indeed, it was used for little more than the stone axe had been, so that it had no practical effect in improving the native standard of living. It did some jobs better, and could be used longer without breakage; and these factors were sufficient to make it of value to the native. But the assumption of the white man (based in part on a realization that a shift from steel to stone axe in his case would be a definite regression) that his axe was much more efficient, that its use would save time, and that it therefore represented technical "progress" toward goals which he had set for the native was hardly borne out in aboriginal practice. Any leisure time the Yir Yoront might gain by using steel axes or other western tools was invested, not in "improving the conditions of life," and certainly not in developing aesthetic activities, but in sleep, an art they had thoroughly mastered.

Having acquired an axe head through regular trading partners of whom he knew what to expect, a man wanting a stone axe was then dependent solely upon a known and an adequate nature and upon his own skills or easily acquired techniques. A man wanting a steel axe, however, was in no such self-reliant position. While he might acquire one through trade, he now had the new alternative of dispensing with technological behavior in relation with a predictable nature and conduct in relation with a predictable trading partner and of turning instead to conduct alone in relation with a highly erratic missionary. If he attended one of the mission festivals when steel axes were handed out as gifts, he might receive one simply by chance or if he had happened somehow to impress the mission staff that he was one of the "better" bush aboriginals (their definition of "better" being quite different from that of his bush fellows). Or he might—but again almost by pure chance—be given some brief job in connection with the mission which would enable him to earn a steel axe. In either case, for older men a preference for the steel axe helped create a situation of dependence in place of a situation of self-reliance and a behavior shift from situations in technology or conduct which were well structured or defined to situations in conduct alone which were ill defined. It was particularly the older ones among the men, whose earlier experience or knowledge of the white man's harshness in any event made them suspicious, who would avoid having any relations with the mission at all, and who thus excluded themselves from acquiring steel axes directly from that source.

The steel axe was the root of psychological stress among the Yir Yoront even more significantly in other aspects of social relations. This was the result of new factors which the missionary considered all to the good: the simple numerical increase in axes per capita as a result of mission distribution; and distribution from the mission directly to younger men, women, and even children. By winning the favor of the mission staff, a woman might be given a steel axe. This was clearly intended to be hers. The situation was quite different from that involved in borrowing an axe from a male relative, with the result that a woman called such an axe "my" steel axe, a possessive form she never used for a stone axe. (Lexically, the steel axe was differentiated from the stone by an adjectival suffix signifying "metal" the element "axe" remaining identical.) Furthermore, young men or even boys might also obtain steel axes directly from the mission. A result was that older men no longer had a complete monopoly of all the axes in the bush community. Indeed, an old man might have only a stone axe, while his wives and sons had steel axes which they considered their own and which he might even desire to borrow. All this led to a revolutionary confusion of sex, age, and kinship roles, with a major gain in independence and loss of subordination on the part of those able now to acquire steel axes when they had been unable to possess stone axes before.

The trading partner relationship was also affected by the new situation. A Yir Yoront might have a trading partner, in a tribe to the south whom he defined as a younger brother, and on whom as an older brother he would therefore have an edge. But if the partner were in contact with the mission or had other easier access to steel axes, his subordination to his bush colleague was obviously decreased. Indeed, under the new dispensation he might prefer to give his axe to a bush "sweetheart" in return for favors or otherwise dispose of it outside regular trade channels, since many steel axes were so distributed between natives in new ways. Among other things, this took some of the excitement away from the fiesta-like tribal gatherings centering around initiations during the dry season. These had traditionally been the climactic annual occasions for exchanges between trading partners, when a man might seek to acquire a whole year's supply of stone axe heads. Now he might find himself prostituting his wife to almost total strangers in return for steel axes or other white men's goods. With trading partnerships weakened, there was less reason to attend the fiestas, and less fun for those who did. A decline in one of the important social activities which had symbolized these great gatherings created a lessening of interest in the other social aspects of these events.

Not only did an increase in steel axes and their distribution to women change the character of the relations between individual and individual, the paired relationships that have been noted, but a new type of relationship, hitherto practically unknown among the Yir Yoront, was created in their axe-acquiring conduct with whites. In the aboriginal society there were almost no occasions outside the immediate family when one individual would initiate action to several other people at once. For in any average group, while a person in accordance with the kinship system might be superordinate to several people to whom he could suggest or command action, at the same time he was also subordinate to several others, in relation with whom such behavior would be tabu. There was thus no over-all chieftainship or authoritarian leadership of any kind. Such complicated operations as grass-burning, animal drives, or totemic ceremonies could be carried out smoothly because each person knew his roles both in technology and conduct.

On both mission and cattle stations, however, the whites imposed upon the aboriginals their conception of leadership roles, with one person in a controlling relationship with a subordinate group. Aboriginals called together to receive gifts, including axes, at a mission Christmas party found themselves facing one or two whites who sought to control their behavior for the occasion, who disregarded the age, sex, and kinship variables among them of which they were so conscious, and who considered them all at one subordinate level. Or the white might impose similar patterns on a working party. (But if he placed an aboriginal in charge of a mixed group of post hole diggers, for example, half of the group, those subordinate to the "boss," would work while the other half, who were superordinate to him, would sleep.) The steel axe, together, of course, with other European goods, came to symbolize for the aboriginal this new and uncomfortable form of social organization, the leader-group relationship.

The most disturbing effects of the steel axe, operating in conjunction with other elements also being introduced from the white man's several subcultures, developed in the realm of traditional ideas, sentiments, and values. These were undermined at a rapidly mounting rate, without new conceptions being defined to replace them. The result was a mental and moral void which foreshadowed the collapse and destruction of all Yir Yoront culture, if not, indeed, the extinction of the biological group itself.

From what has been said it should be clear how changes in overt behavior, in technology and conduct, weakened the values inherent in a reliance on nature, in androcentrism or the prestige of masculinity, in age prestige, and in the various kinship relations. A scene was set in which a wife or young son, his initiation perhaps not even yet completed, need no longer bow to the husband or father, who was left confused and insecure as he asked to borrow a steel axe from them. For the woman and boy the steel axe helped establish a new degree of freedom which was accepted readily as an escape from the unconscious stress of the old patterns, but which left them also confused and insecure. Ownership became less well defined, so that stealing and trespass were introduced into technology and conduct. Some of the excitement surrounding the great ceremonies evaporated, so that the only fiestas the people had became less festive, less interesting. Indeed, life itself became less interesting, although this did not lead the Yir Yoront to invent suicide, a concept foreign to them.

The whole process may be most specifically illustrated in terms of the totemic system, and this will also illustrate the significant role which a system of ideas, in this case a totemic ideology, may play in the breakdown of a culture.

In the first place, under pre-European aboriginal conditions in which the native culture has become adjusted to a relatively stable environment in which there can occur few, if any, unheard of or catastrophic crises, it is clear that the totemic system must serve very effectively to inhibit radical cultural changes. The closed system of totemic ideas, explaining and categorizing a well-known universe as it was fixed at the beginning of time, presents a considerable obstacle to the adoption of new or the dropping of old culture traits. The obstacle is not insurmountable and the system allows for the minor variations which occur about the norms of daily life, but the inception of major changes cannot easily take place.

Among the bush Yir Yoront the only means of water transport is a light wood log, to which they cling in their constant swimming of rivers, salt creeks, and tidal inlets. These natives know that forty-five miles north of them are tribes who have a bark canoe. They know these northern tribes can thus fish from midstream or out at sea, instead of clinging to the river banks and beaches, and can cross coastal waters infested with crocodiles, sharks, sting rays, and Portuguese-men-of-war without the recurring mortality, pain, or anxiety to which they themselves are constantly subjected. They know they lack any magic to do for them what the canoe could do. They know the materials of which the canoe is made are present in their own environment. But they also know, as they say, that their own mythical ancestors lacked the canoe, and therefore they lack it, while they assume that the canoe was part of the ancestral universe of the northern tribes. For them, then, the adoption of the canoe would not be simply a matter of learning a number of new behavioral skills for its manufacture and use. The adoption would require at the same time a much more difficult procedure, the acceptance by the entire society of a myth, either locally developed or borrowed, which would explain the presence of the canoe, associate it with some one or more of the several hundred mythical ancestors (and how decide which?), and thus establish it as an accepted totem of one of the clans ready to be used by the whole community. The Yir Yoront have not made this adjustment, and in this case we can only say that ideas have for the time being at least won out over very real pressures for technological change. In the elaborateness and explicitness of the totemic ideologies we seem to have one explanation for the notorious stability of Australian cultures under aboriginal conditions, an explanation which gives due weight to the importance of ideas in determining human behavior.

At a later stage of the contact situation, as has been indicated, phenomena unaccounted for by the totemic ideological system begin to appear with regularity and frequency and remain within the range of native experience. Accordingly, they cannot be ignored (as the "Battle of the Mitchell River" was apparently ignored), and an attempt is made to assimilate them and account for them along the lines of principles inherent in the ideology. The bush Yir Yoront of the mid-1930's represent this stage of the acculturation process. Still trying to maintain their aboriginal definition of the situation, they accept European artifacts and behavior patterns, but fit them into their totemic system, assigning them as totems to various clans on a par with original totems. There is an attempt to have the mythmaking process keep up with these cultural changes so that the idea system can continue to support the rest of the culture. But analysis of overt behavior, of dreams, and of some of the new myths indicates that this arrangement is not entirely satisfactory; that the native clings to his totemic system with intellectual loyalty, lacking any substitute ideology; but that associated sentiments and values are weakened. His attitudes toward his own and toward European culture are found to be highly ambivalent.

All ghosts are totems of the Head-to-the-East Corpse clan. They are thought of as white, and are, of course, closely associated with death. The white man, too, is white and was closely associated with death, so that he and all things pertaining to him are naturally assigned to the Corpse clan as totems. The steel axe, as a totem, was thus associated with the Corpse clan. But it is an "axe," and is clearly linked with the stone axe, which is a totem of the Sunlit Cloud Iguana clan. Moreover, the steel axe, like most European goods, has no distinctive origin myth, nor are mythical ancestors associated with it. Can anyone, sitting of an afternoon in the shade of a ti tree, create a myth to resolve this confusion? No one has, and the horrid suspicion arises that perhaps the origin myths are wrong, which took into account so little of this vast new universe of the white man. The steel axe, shifting hopelessly between one clan and the other, is not only replacing the stone axe physically, but is hacking at the supports of the entire cultural system.

The aboriginals to the south of the Yir Yoront have clearly passed beyond this stage. They are engulfed by European culture, in this area by either the mission or cattle station subcultures, or for some natives a baffling, paradoxical combination of both incongruent varieties. The totemic ideology can no longer support the inrushing mass of foreign culture traits and the myth-making process in its native form breaks down completely. Both intellectually and emotionally a saturation point is reached, so that the myriad new traits which can neither be ignored nor any longer assimilated simply force the aboriginal to abandon his totemic system. With the collapse of this system of ideas, which is so closely related with so many other aspects of the native culture, there follows an appallingly sudden and complete cultural disintegration and a demoralization of the individual such as has seldom been recorded for areas other than Australia. Without the support of a system of ideas well devised to provide cultural stability in a stable environment but admittedly too rigid for the new realities pressing in from outside, native behavior and native sentiments and values are simply dead. Apathy reigns. The aboriginal has passed beyond the reach of any outsider who might wish to do him well or ill. . . .

86 The Principle of the Hiding Hand

ALBERT O. HIRSCHMAN

Efforts at planned social change, if they are to be successful, require thorough consideration in advance. Is the idea feasible? What investments of energy and dollars will be required? What will be the "side effects"? As to the last question, the two preceding selections have been illustrative. This selection addresses itself to aspects of the first two questions, for the author points out that we are often too inclined to overemphasize the difficulties involved in instituting a program and too likely to underestimate the potential for creativity that seems often, almost miraculously, to surface when problems arise. Hirschman analyzes this feature of planned social change—which he calls "The Hiding Hand"—and illustrates it with projects in underdeveloped countries, where the principle can usually be seen in its most dramatic form.

After two decades of intensive work by social scientists, the processes of economic, social, and political development of the so-called underdeveloped countries—in Latin America, Asia, and Africa—remain poorly understood. Theories that were attractive because of their simplicity and because they had clearcut and hopeful policy implications have been badly battered by academic critics; worse, they have been faulted by events. Nevertheless, it is not true to say that we have learned nothing from the experience of the past twenty years. It's just that what we have learned is not quite what we expected to learn. . . .

SOURCE: *The Public Interest*, no. 6 (Winter 1967), 10–16. This material was also published as Chapter 1 of Albert O. Hirschman, *Development Projects Observed* (Washington, D.C.: Brookings Institution, 1967). • Albert O. Hirschman is Littauer Professor of political economy at Harvard University. He is former financial advisor of the National Planning Board, Bogotá, Colombia, and former Chief of West European and British Commonwealth Section, Federal Research Board, Washington. He is the author of *National Power and the Structure of Foreign Trade, The Strategy of Economic Development,* and *Journeys toward Progress: Studies of Economic Policy-Making in Latin America.*

I

The Karnaphuli pulp and paper mill is one of the earliest large-scale industrial enterprises to have been set up in Pakistan after partition and independence. Planned by the official Industrial Development Corporation to utilize the vast resources of the bamboo forests of the Chittagong Hill Tracts along the upper reaches of the Karnaphuli river in East Pakistan, the mill started to operate in 1953. It had perhaps more than its share of technical and managerial teething troubles, but considerable progress had been achieved in these respects by 1959 when management of the mill passed into private hands. Soon thereafter, a major upset endangered the very life of the mill: the bamboo began to flower, an event entirely unforeseen and probably unforeseeable in the present state of our knowledge, since it occurs only once every 50 to 70 years: given the resulting paucity of observations, the life cycle of the many varieties of bamboo is by no means fully known. In any event, the variety which supplied the Karnaphuli mill with some 85% of its raw material, flowered and then, poetically but quite uneconomically, died.

It was known that flowering of the bamboo results in death of the whole plant and in regeneration from the seeds, rather than, as normally, from the rhizomes; but it was *not* known that the bamboo that dies upon flowering would be unusable for pulping since it would disintegrate upon being transported and floated down the river. Another unpleasant surprise was the discovery that, once flowering was over, a number of years would have to pass before the new bamboo shoots would grow up to the normal size fit for commercial exploitation. In its seventh year of operation, the mill therefore faced the extraordinary task of having to find itself another raw material base.

In a temporary and costly way, the problem was solved by importing pulp, but other, more creative responses were not long in coming: an organization to collect bamboo in villages throughout East Pakistan was set up (the waterways crisscrossing the country make for cheap transportation of bulky cargo), sundry lumber was cut in the Tracts, and, most important, a research program got underway to identify other fast growing species which might to some extent replace the unreliable bamboo as the principal raw material base for the mill. Permission was obtained to plant an experimental area of six square miles with several of the more promising species and plans to cover eventually a much larger area are underway. Thus, the crisis of the flowering bamboo may in the end lead to a diversification of the raw material base for the mill.

Looking backward it may be said that the Karnaphuli mill was "lucky": its planners had badly overestimated the permanent availability of bamboo, but the mill escaped the possibly disastrous consequences of this error by an offsetting underestimate or, more correctly, by the unsuspected availability of alternative raw materials.

The question which I wish to explore is whether this really is a matter of pure luck or whether there are reasons to expect some systematic association of such providentially offsetting errors. A phenomenon very similar to the one just noted can be observed in successful irrigation and irrigation-hydroelectric projects: the river that is being tapped is frequently found not to have enough water for all the agricultural, industrial, and urban uses which had been planned or which are staking claims, but the resulting shortage can then often be remedied by drawing on other sources which had not been within the horizon of the planners: ground water can be lifted by tubewells, the river flow can be better regulated through upstream dams, or the water of more distant rivers can be diverted. At present such plans are afoot for the San Lorenzo irrigation scheme in Peru, and for the Damodor Valley in India.

It would obviously be silly to expect that any overestimate of the availability of a given material resource is always going to be offset by an underestimate of alternative or substitute resources; but if we generalize a little more, we obtain a statement which no longer sounds wholly absurd: on the contrary, it is quite plausible and almost trite to state that each project comes into the world accompanied by two sets of partially or wholly offsetting potential developments: (1) a set of possible and unsuspected threats to its profitability and existence, and (2) a set of unsuspected remedial actions which can be taken whenever any of these threats materializes.

We have much experience of development projects that fit this very broad proposition. For example, the San Lorenzo irrigation project in Northern Peru suffered serious and at times exasperating delays caused by political change and second thoughts on the kind of irrigation farming which the project should promote; but the economic losses implied by these delays were at least in part offset by the fact that, as a result of these second thoughts, San Lorenzo irrigation eventually became a pilot project for the subdivision of land into small but viable family farms, with credit and technical assistance being given to previously landless farmers; the project thus set an entirely new pattern for Peruvian agriculture and turned into a breeding ground for administrators who would be ready to apply elsewhere in Peru the lessons learnt in San Lorenzo.

A Uruguayan livestock and pasture improvement project also experienced extraordinary delays, first because of slowness in political and administrative decision-making and then because the key technical task of improving the natural grasslands by introduction of legumes into the soil turned out to be unexpectedly complex; yet the solutions that were gradually found, through scientific research and practical experimentation, and which were then applied over an expanding area, have now started to make this program into a particularly successful operation and have served to spread the spirit of innovation among a large group of Uruguay's farmers.

The common structure of the Pakistani, Peruvian, Uruguayan projects can now be recapitulated as follows:

1) If the project planners had known in advance all the difficulties and troubles that were lying in store for the project, they probably would never have touched it, because a gloomy view would have been taken of the country's ability to overcome these difficulties by calling into play political, administrative, or technical creativity.

2) In some, though not all, of these cases advance knowledge of these difficulties would therefore have been unfortunate, for the difficulties and the ensuing search for solutions set in motion a train of events which not only rescued the project, but often made it particularly valuable.

II

We may be dealing here with a general principle of action. *Creativity always comes as a surprise to us; therefore we can never count on it and we dare not believe in it until it has happened. In other words, we would not consciously engage upon tasks whose success clearly requires that creativity be forthcoming. Hence, the only way in which we can bring our creative resources fully into play is by misjudging the nature of the task, by presenting it to ourselves as more routine, simple, undemanding of genuine creativity than it will turn out to be.*

Or, put differently: since we necessarily underestimate our creativity it is desirable that we underestimate to a roughly similar extent the difficulties of the tasks we face, so as to be tricked by these two offsetting underestimates into undertaking tasks which we can, but otherwise would not dare, tackle. The principle is important enough to deserve a name: since we are apparently on the trail here of some sort of Invisible or Hidden Hand that beneficially hides difficulties from us, I propose "The Hiding Hand."

What this principle suggests is that, far from seeking out and taking up challenges, people are apt to take on and plunge into new tasks because of the erroneously presumed *absence* of a challenge—because the task looks easier and more manageable than it will turn out to be. As a result, the Hiding Hand can help accelerate the rate at which men engage successfully in problem-solving: they take up problems *they think* they can solve, find them more difficult than expected, but then, being stuck with them, attack willy-nilly the unsuspected difficulties—and sometimes even succeed. People who have stumbled through the experience just described will of course tend to retell it as though they had known the difficulties all along and have bravely gone to meet them—*fare bella figura* is a strong human propensity. While we are rather willing and even eager and relieved to agree with a historian's finding that we stumbled into the more shameful events of history, such as war, we are correspondingly unwilling to concede—in fact we find it intolerable to imagine—that our more lofty achievements, such as economic, social or political progress, could have come about by stumbling rather than through careful planning, rational behavior, and the successful response to a clearly perceived challenge. Language itself conspires toward this sort of asymmetry: we fall into error, but do not usually speak of falling into truth.

III

While some presence of the Hiding Hand may be helpful or required in eliciting action under all latitudes, it is no doubt specially needed where the tradition of problem-solving is weak and where invention and innovation have not yet been institutionalized or routinized. In other words, in developed countries less hiding of the uncertainties and likely difficulties of a prospective task is required than in underdeveloped countries where confidence in one's creativity is lacking, and where new tasks harboring many unknowns must be presented as though they were all "cut and dried" in order to be undertaken.

The Hiding Hand principle is in effect a close relative, or perhaps a generalization, of an idea proposed several years ago by an economic historian, John Sawyer. Having looked at development projects that were undertaken in the first half of the 19th century in the United States, he noted that underestimates of cost resulting from "miscalculation or sheer ignorance" were, in a number of great and ultimately successful economic undertakings, "crucial to getting an enterprise launched at all." "Had the total investment required been accurately and objectively known at the beginning, the project would not have been begun." The eventual success of these ventures, in spite of the large initial miscalculation and the consequent financial trouble at various stages, derived from the fact that, once the necessary funds were secured and the project was brought to completion, "the error in estimating costs was at least offset by a corresponding error in the estimation of demand."

This has a close resemblance to the Hiding Hand principle. The difference is that in Sawyer's model the underestimate of the benefit is unexplained and acts rather as a *deus ex machina* to save selected projects from becoming failures, once they turn out to cost so much more than expected. In our Hiding Hand principle, Sawyer's unexplained underestimate of benefits becomes the easily intelligible underestimate, on the part of the project planner, of his own problem-solving ability. The principle then simply goes on to state that, in view of this underestimate, a similar underestimate of the difficulties themselves is required so that projects which in the end turn out to be perfectly feasible and productive will actually be undertaken.

Which are the projects that are chosen because their difficulties tend to be underestimated? And which ones tend to be systematically neglected because their difficulties are too obvious? By asking these questions we realize that the Hiding Hand principle, while permitting an increase in the rate at which projects are taken up, also leads to a bias in project selection whose nature must now be briefly explored.

First of all, it becomes clear that projects derive a crucial advantage from being based on a technique that *looks* transferable even though it may not actually be nearly as transferable as it looks. This is perhaps a principal reason which gives industrial projects so large an edge over others. Time and again, industrial projects, particularly those that are not limited to administering "last touches" to a host of imported semi-finished products, run into very considerable technical and managerial difficulties when they are transplanted to a different environment. But factories *look* as though they could be picked up and dropped anywhere—whereas in other activities, such as agriculture and education, the need for adaptation and the concomitant problems are immediately obvious. Industry thus lends itself eminently to the operations of the Hiding Hand, whereas agricultural projects suffer in comparison from the sincerity with which they flaunt their prospective difficulties.

This conclusion is reinforced when the principle of the Hiding Hand is viewed in the perspective of time. For its mechanism to work it is necessary that the operators be thoroughly "caught" by the time the unsuspected difficulties appear; caught in the sense that having spent considerable money, time, and energy and having committed their prestige, they will be anxious to generate all the problem-solving energy of which they are capable.

Just as the Hiding Hand principle states that the to-be-experienced difficulties should be hidden at the moment of the decision to go ahead with the project, so it *implies* that these difficulties should not appear *too early* after the execution of the project has started—for, within a certain range, the propensity to tackle the difficulties will be roughly proportional to the effort, financial and otherwise, already furnished. Therefore, a given level of difficulties may be wholly discouraging for the prosecution of the project if it turns up early, while it would be tackled with alacrity and perhaps solved if it arose at a later stage.

In spite of the somewhat paradoxical ring of this assertion—paradoxical only because medical science has thoroughly impregnated us with the notion that the sooner a malady is recognized and diagnosed the better—it appears to be confirmed by experience with development projects, and it again underlines the disadvantageous position of agricultural as compared with industrial and public-work projects. With the (important) exceptions of irrigation and of tree crop projects, agricultural projects have a short gestation period, and therefore production or marketing difficulties unfold rather soon after the projects have been started; hence, attempts to rescue them are often half-hearted and they are readily pronounced failures and abandoned. This is the story of many colonization projects in Latin America and Africa.

In the case of projects with longer gestation periods and more permanent structures, similar difficulties tend to appear much later and then lead to far more serious efforts to overcome them. This difference between projects with short and long gestation periods is well exemplified by the contrasting fates of the East African Groundnut Scheme and the Owen Falls Hydroelectric Station in Uganda. Undertaken at the same time, in the same region, by the same kind of colonial administrators wishing to turn over a new progressive leaf and harboring similar illusions about the nature of the development process, both schemes met with similar financial difficulties during their early years. After a very few years, the Groundnut scheme was abandoned and nothing remains of it; the Owen Falls Hydro station, on the other hand, has had many lean years, but it has endured and finally come into its own and will soon have to be supplemented by new generating capacity. For once it had become clear that the originally anticipated industrial boom in the Owen Falls area was not going to materialize, the Uganda Electricity Board made an effort to tap, through the building of transmission lines, new markets for its power to neighboring Kenya at first, and then to a host of smaller industries and towns of Uganda.

By itself, the mere ability of the Owen Falls Station to survive cannot of course be taken as a vindication of the original investment decision. While later administrators were right in considering as bygone the heavy costs which had been sunk into the project in its early years, the project as a whole may still have to be given a poor mark in any ex-post appraisal. It is well known that, with long-gestation projects, one runs the risk that good money will be thrown after bad. We are here pointing out that short-gestation projects are subject to the opposite risk: the failure to throw good money after what looks bad, but could be turned into good, if only the requisite rescue effort were forthcoming.

The foregoing remarks permit a policy conclusion: projects whose potential difficulties and disappointments are apt to manifest themselves at an early stage should be administered by agencies having a long-term commitment to the success of the projects; also such projects should be developed as much as possible in an experimental spirit, in the style of a pilot project gathering strength and experience gradually, for in that case they will be able to escape being classed and closed down as failures when they are still in their infancy. The Uruguayan livestock and pasture improvement project followed both these precepts and has thus been able to survive and to achieve maturity and success.

87 The Role of Universities

JULIUS K. NYERERE

In recent years several social scientists have examined the contribution of various types of education to social change. Most of this work involves the analysis of education in non-Western societies by Western scholars. In the following selection President Nyerere of Tanzania, a former teacher, examines the role of the university in a developing society.

. . . . .

Every time I myself come to this campus—which is fairly frequently—I think again about our decision to build here, and our decision about the type of buildings. Sometimes I wonder whether we made the right decision, although really I know it is too early for an answer to be given to that question. For the answer depends upon what the graduates of this University College do in the future, and to what extent their actions have been influenced by the expenditure of more than Shs. 50/- million. In other words, the answer depends upon the future—and includes an immeasurable factor anyway!

Yet the question itself is an important one; it involves the whole problem of what a university could, and should, do in a developing society. For I believe that the pursuit of pure learning can be a luxury in society; whether it is or not depends upon the conditions in which that society lives. Perhaps I am being foolhardy in making such a statement at a university gathering, but I am going to repeat it; when people are dying because existing knowledge is not applied, when the very basic social and public services are not available to all members of a society, then that society is misusing its resources if it pursues pure learning for its own sake.

If there are philosophy students among this gathering I suspect that they are already making mental demands that I define my terms: what do I mean by "pure learning," and "for its own sake." And if I hold these reservations about the function of a university in this developing society, why is it that I myself am proud to be Chancellor of the University of East Africa, and Visitor of this University College?

These are valid responses to my rather provocative statement, because one of the very important traditional functions of a university has been this pursuit of pure knowledge—knowledge about things which exist, or happen, just for the sake of finding out more about them. Indeed very many of the advances in the human condition rest upon the foundation of work done at universities which had no apparent relevance to man's life on the

SOURCE: Julius K. Nyerere, *Freedom and Socialism* (Nairobi, London, New York: Oxford University Press, 1968), pp. 179–86. Reprinted by permission of the author. • Julius Nyerere is president of the United Republic of Tanzania. He formed the Tanganyika African National Union and served as its president and campaigned for the Nationalist Movement in 1954. He addressed the United Nations Trusteeship Council in 1955 and was a member of the United Nations General Assembly in 1956 and the Legislative Council in 1957. He was elected a member for Eastern Province in 1958, and was president of the Republic of Tanganyika from 1962–64 when it merged with Zanzibar in 1965 to form the United Republic of Tanzania.

earth. I believe that scientists divide their research into two categories—pure and applied—and it is the former which is normally carried out in universities while the latter may also be undertaken in industrial or agricultural complexes. Economists do not—as far as I know—make this same formal distinction, but reading some economists' research papers about theoretical measurements of immeasurable factors it appears that in practice the same division exists! The men and women who seek to solve particular problems of science and society then sometimes use and develop these apparently useless pieces of knowledge, and as a result huge advances are made in dealing with very pressing problems of individuals and communities.

I have no doubt in my mind, therefore, but that the university function of extending the frontiers of knowledge is very important for humanity. I will go further, and say that in the course of time universities in developing countries must also make their contribution to the world of knowledge in this direction. We must not establish in our new young countries institutions of higher learning which simply receive. They must give as well.

But in all things there are priorities, and we have to look at the immediate future, and the immediate present, and decide what it is that universities in our kind of society can at present most usefully give to the world of which we are a part. And it is my conviction that universities in countries like Tanzania have other urgent tasks to fulfil which will test their resources—human and material—to the utmost. I do not believe that they can at this stage pursue "pure research" and "knowledge for its own sake" without neglecting other functions which are for the time being more important.

Before I explain what I believe these other functions to be let me make one thing clear. At any good university some of the best brains of the day should be living together. And good brains cannot be turned on and off; a man who thinks about his work will not stop thinking at the end of his day, or when the students are on vacation. If he then finds it relaxing—or exciting, depending upon temperament—to investigate an apparently irrelevant matter, he should certainly be encouraged to do so, and given use of such facilities as are available. And if this means that later he is able to produce a paper explaining, let us say, why certain fish change colour when taken out of water, then he deserves congratulation. My original statement was not that pure learning is useless; it was that it is a luxury under certain conditions. And a man who spends his spare time on this luxury is certainly entitled to our gratitude more than a man who spends his spare time on other equally luxurious, but less constructive, pastimes.

Neither should my assessment of priorities be taken to imply that we expect from our university merely the dissemination of established facts. Whether in a developing country or elsewhere, a university does not deserve the name if it does not promote thinking. But our particular and urgent problems must influence the subjects to which thought is given, and they must influence, too, the approach. Both in university-promoted research, and in the content of degree syllabuses, the needs of our country should be the determining factor.

What are the problems we face in the discipline concerned? What are the obstacles which might prevent the achievement of a particular national goal, and how can they be overcome? Is a particular policy conducive to the attainment of the basic objectives of the society? These are the type of questions to which the university can and should be giving attention. In these fields university staff and students should be co-operating with Government and the people.

There are some people who would undoubtedly challenge this assumption that university should co-operate with Government. They would say that the task of a university is to seek for truth, and to ignore all other responsibilities, leaving it to those outside the university to accept or reject the result in their practical politics. Yet this is to say that a university could, and should, live divorced from its society. It implies, too, that there is an automatic conflict with Government—that Government is not concerned with truth! It is my conviction that this attitude is based on a half-truth, and has within it great dangers, both for society as a whole and for the university itself.

I fully accept that the task of a university is to seek for truth, and that its members should speak the truth as they see it regardless of consequences to themselves. But you will notice the words "to themselves"; I do not believe they should do this regardless of the society. A university which tries to put its professors and its students into blinkers will neither serve the cause of knowledge, nor the interests of the society in which it exists. But to try and deal objectively with a particular problem, and in a scientific manner to analyse and describe it—that is one thing. To move from that to an assumption that the consequences are irrelevant is entirely different. What we expect from our university is both a complete objectivity in the search for truth, and also commitment to our society—a desire to serve it. We expect the two things equally. And I do not believe this dual responsibility—to objectivity and to service—is impossible of fulfilment. In this I find support in the speech of the first Principal of the Dar es Salaam University College, Professor R. C. Pratt, who said when the campus was opened:

> We must strive consciously and deliberately to assure that the life and work of the College is in harmony with the central positive objectives that underlie the national policies of our Governments . . . The University of East Africa must be a committed institution, actively relating our work to the communities it seeks to serve. This is in no sense in contrast to, or in contradiction of, the intellectual objectivity and respect for truth which must also be an essential feature of a University. Commitment and objectivity are not opposites, are not in contradiction to each other. Rather the best scholarship is often a product of deep commitment . . .

To question that is, I believe, to pretend that a society can progress if it is based on falsity, or that the truth is so unimportant that it can be buried in intellectual tomes which have no relevance to the work of a people who are trying to revolutionize their conditions of life.

In fact, a university in a developing society must put the emphasis of its work on subjects of immediate moment to the nation in which it exists, and it must be committed to the people of that nation and their humanistic goals. This is central to its existence; and it is this fact which justifies the heavy expenditure of resources on this one aspect of national life and development. Its research, and the energies of its staff in particular, must be freely offered to the community, and they must be relevant.

Applied research, however, is only one aspect of university work. The dissemination of knowledge to undergraduates and other members of society is equally important. But it is not simply facts which must be taught. Students must be helped to think scientifically; they must be taught to analyse problems objectively, and to apply the facts they have learned—or which they know exist—to the problems which they will face in the future. For when a society is in the process of rapid change—which is a definition of a developing society—it is no use giving students the answers to today's problems. These are useful mainly as a training ground; the real worth of the university education will show itself much later when these same men and women have to cope with problems which are as yet unseen.

Yet once again, the real problem in our societies is a different one. For universities all over the world have this task of trying to educate and expand the minds of their students. Universities in developing countries have also another, and in some ways a more difficult problem. It is this same problem of commitment and it brings me back to the question I started with—the question of whether these fine buildings are really the right environment for our new university.

The library, the hostels, the lecture rooms and so on which make up this campus were all designed to enable the students here to work well—to concentrate their energies on learning and thinking. It is because we need young people to do this that we started the University College and devote a considerable proportion of our recurrent revenue to its upkeep. But anyone who walks off this campus into the nearby villages, or who travels up country—perhaps to Dodoma or into the Pare Hills—will observe the contrast in conditions here and the conditions in which the mass of our people live. And the purpose of establishing the university is to make it possible for us to change these poverty-stricken lives. We do not build sky-scrapers here so that a few very fortunate individuals can develop their own minds and then live in comfort, with intellectual stimulus making their work and their leisure interesting to themselves. We tax the people to build these places only so that young men and women may become efficient servants to them. There is no other justification for this heavy call being made on poor peasants.

How can the reality of this responsibility be maintained all the time for students who live here? How can we ensure that they remain—or become—constructively concerned about the task of transforming our national poverty, so that they regard the conditions here as an interim in their lives and not as something to which they are entitled?

What all this really amounts to is not a question about buildings; these are the physical surroundings designed to assist efficiency. The real problem is that of promoting, strengthening, and channelling social attitudes which are conducive to the progress of our society. For, as I have already said, we in poor societies can only justify expenditure on a university—of any type—if it promotes real development of our people. And the buildings become relevant only because they could introduce one further factor dividing university students from the masses who sent them here. But they do not necessarily have this effect. The factors which really determine whether university students shall remain an integral part of a classless society or become members of an alien elite, are much more subtle—and much more difficult to deal with.

In our traditional societies every member was fully aware of his membership of the society—his responsibility to his fellows as well as their responsibility to him. All individuals lived the same sort of life; it was a hard one in which the need for co-operation was an obvious fact. The social institutions themselves encouraged this psychology of interdependence, and it was part of the environment in which every child grew up. Yet now we take certain of our children and separate them from others by giving them opportunities for secondary schooling which are not available to everyone. Later we choose a still more limited number and send them to universities. And throughout this process we have been taking the individual out of his community, and only too often at the same time encouraging him to work hard by promises of individual advancement if he does so. It is he, as an individual, who is stressed; it is he who alone reads and learns and gets the opportunity for advance. This is inevitable; all of us have different brains, and the complexities of a modern society demand very many different kinds of skills—which require different individual training.

But with all this stress on his individual responsibility how can we at the same time safeguard the individual against the arrogance of looking upon himself as someone special, someone who has the right to make very heavy demands upon society, in return for which he will deign to make available the skills which that society has enabled him to acquire? In particular, what can a university do to ensure that its students regard themselves as "servants-in-training"?

This is one of the most vital, and most difficult, of the functions of a university in a developing country. For some students this "lesson" is almost unnecessary. They take for granted the fact that they should work with their fellow citizens in National Service, in lonely up-country posts, and so on. But unfortunately this is not true of all; and certainly as a body there is always a temptation for students to regard themselves as a group which has rights without responsibilities. We have seen how many groups of students demand ever better conditions of study, ever larger allowances. They demand that they should be treated separately from others when questions of National Service arise—not in order to give more, but in order to give less. And most difficult of all they compare themselves as a group, and themselves as graduates individually, with students and graduates of universities in the wealthy countries of the world. Then they feel resentful if their conditions are worse, or their pay lower. And all the time the masses continue to live on an annual income of about £20 per head per year.

A university in a country like Tanzania has to deal with this problem. It has to meet the challenge—"Physician, heal thyself." For if it is acknowledged that only united effort for development will enable the transformation of the underdeveloped nations of the world, then it must also be acknowledged that the universities of those nations, their staffs and students, must also be united with the rest of those societies in that task. And this can only happen if the university men and women themselves feel their identity with their fellows—including those who never went to school at all. It can only happen if the university graduates merge themselves back into the communities from which they came, and transform them from within.

Many different techniques are used to strengthen and rebuild the relationship between university students and the other members of their society. Work camps, vacation work, National Service, voluntary nation-building and so on are all valuable methods for helping with this problem. Yet it can remain a problem unless the whole atmosphere of the university is one of giving service, and expecting service, from all its members and students; unless, in other words, the prevailing attitude is one of social responsibility. And this must not be the idea of "giving aid to the poor." That arrogance has no place in Tanzania at any rate. It must be an attitude of wanting to work, in whatever work there is to do, alongside and within the rest of the community, until finally there is no more distinction between a graduate and an illiterate than there is between a man who works as a carpenter and his fellow who works as a brickmaker. Graduates and illiterates would then accept their tasks as distinctive, and as making different demands on them, but as being in both cases but a part of a single whole.

. . . . .

For this is really what I have been saying. The role of a university in a developing country is to contribute; to give ideas, manpower, and service for the furtherance of human equality, human dignity, and human development.

88 Agrarian Revolution and Economic Progress

RAINER SCHICKELE

The major social changes in contemporary societies are occurring in the non-Western world. The emergence of independent nations in Asia and Africa and the modernization of their economic and social systems are parallel aspects of this movement. In the following selection Rainer Schickele, who has assisted several countries in the modernization process, examines the motivation for and processes of change in these societies. He places his analysis in an historical perspective through a comparison with the Western industrial revolution.

We are witnessing a drama of breathtaking sweep throughout the newly developing world.

We are in the second act on which the curtain rose after World War II. The first act started in the wake of the French and American revolutions, around the year 1800. The center of the stage in the first act was Europe and North America. In the second act, it has shifted from the West to the East and South, to Asia, Africa and Latin America.

The central protagonist is the worker, the peasant, the small craftsman, the clerk, the poor man working in the factory, field, workshop, and office. The plot of the drama deals with his frustrations and triumphs as he struggles along his way from subservience to human dignity and citizenship, from poverty to wealth, under the guiding spirit of humanist ideology, of democracy and the equality of man.

THE INDUSTRIAL REVOLUTION OF THE WEST

In the first act, during the Industrial Revolution up to World War II, technol-

SOURCE: Rainer Schickele, *Agrarian Revolution and Economic Progress: A Primer for Development* (New York: Praeger Publishers, 1968), pp. 1–9. Reprinted by permission of the publisher. • The author is visiting professor of agricultural economics at Michigan State University. He formerly served with the United Nations Food and Agriculture Organization in Rome, as an associate of the Agricultural Development Council, Inc., New York, and as visiting professor at the University of Ceylon. His interests have focused upon processes of economic development in newly developing regions of the world. Among his many publications are *Agricultural Policy*, and *Farm Management Research for Planning Agricultural Development*.

ogy brought about a tremendous increase in productivity. Application of science to the production processes increased the capacity of people to produce so much that, for the first time in the history of mankind, it became possible to wipe out hunger and poverty. The humanist ideology taught people that the purpose of an economic system is the creation of wealth for the satisfaction of human wants, and that men are created equal. This means that men of all races and creeds have a basic human right to equality of opportunity and civic dignity, that the satisfaction of the human wants of the poor is as important as that of the rich, and that degrading poverty is incompatible with the principle of human rights in a modern democracy.

The economic system during the Industrial Revolution was based mainly upon private entrepreneurs. Although producers were always subject to various public policies and regulations, these were in the beginning formulated in the interest of industrial producers and of commerce with no regard for expanding also the opportunities for the millions of poor workers employed at starvation wages and working under most horrible sweatshop conditions. During the nineteenth century, many people became rich, but many, many more people remained extremely poor. As late as the middle of the twentieth century, the richest of the Western industrial countries still had far too many families living in poverty, in the midst of plenty.

This weakness of the private enterprise system in distributing its rising output to also meet the needs of the poor became apparent as early as the middle of the nineteenth century. Our drama's hero, the worker, farmer and small craftsman, with the help of philosophers and economists, came forth with the proposal of an alternative economic system, that of state enterprise, whose purpose was to create wealth for the satisfaction of human wants according to physical and social need rather than ability to pay. It was, however, only as late as the 1920's, and only in one country, Russia, that a centralized state enterprise system was actually put into practice during the first act of our drama. It performed well in reducing abject poverty among the masses of the people, but was much less successful in the task of increasing productivity, particularly in agriculture.

The hero, when he saw more than half a century go by without any Western country adopting the state enterprise system, began struggling for a fundamental reform, for a reorientation of the private enterprise system which would strengthen its performance in satisfying the human wants of the poor, without weakening its performance in producing wealth. In their political ascendancy, people assigned to the state the responsibility for guiding the private enterprise economy with social and economic welfare policies so as to reduce poverty and give equal opportunities to the poor for education, health and bargaining power in the market. These policies compensated, at least in part, for the lack of the market system's response to the needs of the poor, and still preserved the incentives and initiatives of private enterprise in production.

This "mixed economy" where private enterprise produces and trades within a framework of public policies and controls designed to promote the economic welfare of people as a whole, and particularly of the poor and disadvantaged, achieved a dramatic breakthrough in most of the Western industrialized countries during the 1920's and 30's. In the Scandinavian countries, poverty has almost been wiped out, private enterprise is producing efficiently and profitably, and living standards are among the highest in Europe. Also, in many of the other Western industrialized countries, the extent of poverty has been reduced more or less depending on the scope and efficiency of the public policies for equalizing opportunities and reducing poverty. There remains no economic or moral justification for poverty in an industrially developed affluent society where excess production capacity and surpluses are more troublesome than shortages. So our drama's hero continues his struggle in the West, but with a strong stance which promises to bring him soon within reach of his economic goal—the abolition of poverty.

This is the state of affairs, the scenery and the stage of the plot at the end of the drama's Act I, the Industrial Revolution of the West.

THE AGRARIAN REVOLUTION OF THE NEWLY DEVELOPING WORLD

As the curtain rises on Act II around the year 1950, the Agrarian Revolution of the East and South has started. The scene is the vast region of Asia, Africa, and South America, a rural region where most people live on farms and in villages and derive their livelihood from agriculture. Here, 800 to 900 million people achieved political independence from colonial rule in recent years, and another 400 million people are bringing about fundamental changes in their old traditional governments. Of the 1.25 billion people in this newly developing part of the world, 90 per cent live in countries with an average per capita income of less than $200 per year. This simply means that the vast majority of the people are very poor indeed.

The people want to consummate their newly won political independence and strive toward their new aspirations of human dignity, freedom as responsible citizens, and equality of opportunity. This means they must raise their production and do so for the main purpose of reducing poverty.

The hero finds himself in a state of deep and widespread poverty. His trials deal with finding ways of harnessing the wealth-creating drive of private enterprise within a framework of governmental policies that satisfy the human wants of the poor, in order to unleash the pent-up capacities and energies of the people which are now stunted, suppressed by lack of education, health, food, and other bare necessities of life.

The drama's hero is not a heroic character. He takes on the shape of many different persons in all walks of life. He appears as an Indian farmer, overlooking his fields parched by the drought of the failing monsoon, with his wife, children and grandparents. Where will the food come from to keep his family alive? He appears as an office clerk in Nigeria who was fired by the manager to make room for a cousin, and who cannot find another job because he comes from the wrong tribe. He appears as a woman in a textile factory in Malaysia, a fisherman in Haiti, a blacksmith in the Northeast of Brazil—and whenever some little thing goes wrong he is down and out. There are so many little things over which he has no control and which can go wrong for him, because he has no influence over his environment, no influence with his employer, landlord or creditor in the conduct of public and community affairs. But he knows that if he is given a chance, if he can get education, food, and other prime necessities of life, he can do well, and he has proven it again and again on the rare occasions when he did get a chance. He is determined to get this chance for the multitude of poor people everywhere.

There are leaders emerging who articulate the aspirations of the people, who educate them in political and economic matters, who organize them into cooperative groups and political parties, who are rapidly learning the art and science of modern politics and government. Some of these leaders come from poor families, from peasant farms and shantytowns; but many come from well-to-do families, from educated classes, from professional and civil service ranks and landed aristocracies. Gandhi, whose father and grandfather were chief ministers of several Indian states, shared the life of the poor voluntarily in the service to their cause. Nyerere was a teacher, Senghor a philosopher and poet, Cardenas a general, before they became great leaders of their people. They identified themselves with them, they came to political power with their support and held their confidence. This emergence of progressive leaders of the common people is proceeding everywhere, slowly in some places, faster in others. There is today no government, no group of rulers and wealthy merchants and landowners who do not sense the political ascendancy of the poor.

This pervasive spirit of the times is our drama's hero. This spirit is energized by the vision of man coming into his own, as an individual on equal terms with his brethren of all races, creeds and nations, with equal opportunities to develop his talents, to apply his productive efforts, and to be treated with respect by other persons and by his government. This is the freedom aspect of this ideology; its counterpart, fully as indispensable, is the responsibility aspect—the vision of man as a member of the community, who accepts the obligation to serve the needs of society, who participates in public affairs as a responsible citizen with the community's interest at heart.

The practical meaning of this ideology, this spiritual credo of our time, is that the individual has the right to choose and act freely within the limits of compatibility with community welfare; and that the government, in its promotion and safeguarding of the community's welfare, exercises its power with the consent of the people at large, and within the limits of compatibility with individual freedom and dignity.

Who is the villain in our drama? The plantation owner with a whip? The feudal prince in his palace with wives in silk brocades and thousands of peasants in rags and abject servitude? The colonial administrator backed by mercenaries?

These characters are disappearing rapidly with the demise of colonial empires, the achievement of political independence and the creation of representative democratic governments, although there are still areas where they are fighting covertly, but ruthlessly, for their power and social status.

The real antagonist is the old traditional spirit of privilege and power of the few over the many, of the elite over the "innately inferior," of the born aristocrat over the plebs, of the wealthy over the poor. This antagonist still has great strength which is rooted in past traditions of thousands of years. He also takes on the shape of many different persons in all walks of life. He appears as a peasant who has no respect for the dignity of his wife and mistreats her as a slave. How can his children grasp the belief in human dignity when they see their own mother mistreated? He appears as a government official who abuses the power of his office, who intimidates people and demands bribes. He appears as a landowner who keeps his tenants and laborers ignorant and poor and in debt to him, or as a foreman in a factory who bars his workers from advancement and keeps them in constant fear of dismissal.

This metaphoric prologue symbolizes the essence of the forces underlying modern economic development problems. For the first time in mankind's history, technology offers the possibility of producing enough for every man, woman, and child to live in decency, free from hunger and stultifying want. This constitutes the material base upon which a democratic society can be built embracing all the people rather than only a small elite.

GENERATORS OF PROGRESS

These are two powerful generators of economic development: the humanist ideology, and science and technology.

The great moral force which ushered in the American and French revolutions of the late eighteenth century and shaped the concept of a modern democratic social system was rooted in the belief that men are created equal before God, or in worldly terms, that men are equal before the law and have equal rights for opportunities to develop their capacities, to reap the fruits of their productive efforts, and to participate in the shaping of their communities, in the molding of their institutions and governments. This idea is still an infant in world history's perspective, and is very new indeed to the traditional cultures of two thirds of the world population. But this humanist idea is on the march everywhere, is stirring in the minds and hearts of people throughout the world, and will continue to shape the history of mankind throughout the current and the coming centuries.

In the West, this humanist ideology transformed a feudal elite society into a democratic society of citizens in which universal suffrage, one-man, one-vote, became the revolutionary invention for making government responsible to the people. It transformed a highly restrictive and esoteric educational system for the privileged few into a universal, largely free educational system for everyone. It abolished slavery and established a code of law and a system of courts before which every man was considered equal in his rights and responsibilities. It created the goal of people's economic welfare, of equitable sharing of the nation's wealth and opportunities, of abolition of hunger and poverty—a logical sequel to the abolition of slavery. These were tremendously powerful innovations which triggered a revolution of rising aspirations and unleashed pent-up energies of people for building a new society, new institutions and standards of behavior, new laws and forms of government. Even after 150 years of political potency in the Western industrial world, no one claims that this humanist ideology has found its full realization in modern Western society; it is still far from it. But since the middle of the current century, it has become the dominant world spirit and driving force. It is giving the direction, the orientation for progress throughout the world, in the industrial West and newly developing agrarian countries alike.

Science and technology transformed the traditional production processes in industry, agriculture, and trade into instruments of amazing power for making the natural resources of the earth the servants of the material needs of man. In the industrial West, during the last hundred years, output per worker increased manyfold in every line of production. It created a large variety of new goods and services which were not even conceivable a hundred years ago. This application of a rapidly expanding science to practical production processes is now beginning to spread throughout the developing world, and is bringing about new attitudes of people toward their work, new forms of organization and group activities in production techniques, in market structures and government functions. Science and technology has given man the power to abolish poverty, for the first time in history—but also to destroy himself by instantaneous mass-murder. The greatest challenge to mankind in the coming centuries is to uphold the mastership of the humanist ideology, of the spiritual and moral values of modern society, over the application of technology, over the use of science in human affairs. This applies to the use of atomic energy as well as to the use of mechanization and automation.

These two great generators of progress, the humanist ideology and the scientific technology, are the West's constructive legacy to the newly developing regions of the world; they have to adapt them to their own peculiar conditions, but they need not invent them anew. Herein lies the hope for a victorious outcome of the race against time.

If progress lags too much, there is real danger of mankind losing control over technology. A serious disintegration of the spiritual power which the idea of the equality and dignity of man holds over our hearts and minds may readily lead to an atomic holocaust, or to a technocratic society of robots along the alpha-beta-gamma lines of Huxley's *Brave New World* or the nightmare of Orwell's *1984*.

The *material aspect* of the race against time is that between food and population, between production and poverty. Will we succeed in abolishing hunger and poverty fast enough to prevent a world-wide breakdown of interhuman and international relations, of national and world peace?

The *ideological aspect* is the question: Will people's faith in the humanist idea of the respect for our fellowman's and neighbor-nation's dignity and right of self-government withstand the frustrations and trials on the road to progress, or will this faith falter in us before a modicum of realization is reached?

These are the two basic disturbing aspects of the race against time which leaders must ponder honestly, at all levels, in all walks of life, in all countries throughout the world.

89 Descent to Anomy

ROBERT M. MacIVER

Our social ties, the values by which we live, and our sense of "belonging" are so much a part of most of our lives that we have little conception of their deep significance to us and to our society. Hence, we are inclined to take social cohesion for granted. But this social cohesion through which the unity of our personalities is secured and maintained always rests in delicate balance. In a complex society, even under the most favorable conditions, there are individuals who fall into anomy (now usually spelled anomie)—a condition where the sense of "belonging" to the group is lost and the norms or values of society are ignored or rejected. In times of crisis "whole groups are exposed to the malady." In this selection MacIver describes three types of anomic persons and examines the problems faced by democracies if they are to deal with anomy "as a disease and not as a sin."

Let us look next at *anomy*, the other malady of democratic man that becomes most virulent in times of crisis and turbulent change, the breakdown of the individual's sense of attachment to society, to all society. Anomy is not simply lawlessness. A gangster or a pirate or a mere law-evading rogue is not as such, indeed is not likely to be, anomic. He has his own code of law against law and is under strong sanctions to obey it. He need not be the victim of that inner detachment, of that cleavage between the real self and the projected self, of that total rejection of indoctrinated values that characterizes the anomic person. Anomy signifies the state of mind of one who has been pulled up from his moral roots, who has no longer any standards but only disconnected urges, who has no longer any sense of continuity, of folk, of obligation. The anomic man has become spiritually sterile, responsive only to himself, responsible to no one. He derides the values of other men. His only faith is the philosophy of denial. He lives on the thin line of sensation between no future and no past.

In any times particular individuals may fall into anomy. It happens when sensitive temperaments suffer without respite a succession of shocks that disrupt their faith. And not a few men have temporary moods that resemble anomy, periods when the spirit of denial rules them, after they have experienced some grave bafflement. But there are times of profound disturbance when whole groups are exposed to the malady. The soldiers in Mailer's novel, *The Naked and the Dead*, talk the language of anomy. They have been torn in youth from their environments, their careers, their dreams, their hopes, to face laborious tedium and the ugliest forms of death. They have been bereft of the sustaining ways of their culture. They are thrust back on the immediate needs and demands of each perilous hour. The present offers nothing but sensations; there are periods of boredom and

SOURCE: *The Ramparts We Guard*, chap. 10 (New York: Macmillan Co., 1950), 84–92. Reprinted by permission. • Robert M. MacIver (1882–1970) was Lieber Professor Emeritus of Political Philosophy and Sociology, Columbia University. He was former chancellor of the New School for Social Research and founder of the New School's Center for New York City Affairs. He was also a former president of the American Sociological Association. Among his many books are *Society: Its Structure and Changes, The Web of Government, Life: Its Dimensions and Its Bounds,* and *As a Tale That Is Told.*

drudgery, and then they are alone with nature and sudden death. So they use the language of sensation—there is nothing else to express. It means little but there is nothing else to mean. The livid, gory, sexy words they utter soon convey precisely nothing, nothing but the denudation they feel. For them, however, for those who survive, there is a return to nearly all the things they have lost. For most of them anomy wears away in their restoration to their society. But there are others, the hopelessly displaced, the totally uprooted, the permanently insecure, those who need the support of authority and have lost it without hope of recovery, the over-sophisticated who find that the challenges of life cannot be met by sophistication—among such people anomy takes full command.

Anomy is a state of mind in which the individual's sense of social cohesion—the mainspring of his morale—is broken or fatally weakened. In this detachment of the anomic person from social obligation his whole personality is injured. He has lost the *dynamic unity* of personality. The anomic fall into various types, though we do not have so far the psychological researches necessary for the adequate classification of these types. We can, however, broadly distinguish the following.

First, there are those who, having lost altogether, or in great measure, any system of values that might give purpose or direction to their lives, having lost the compass that points their course into the future, abandon themselves to the present, but a present emptied of significance. They resort, in other words, to a sophisticated cynicism, by aid of which they rationalize their loss. They live by the hour, seeking immediate gratification on whatever level it is available. They tend to be sensationalists and materialists. It is their defense against the ghosts of perished values.

Second, there are those who, having lost their ethical goals, having no longer any intrinsic and socialized values to which they can harness their drive to action, transfer this drive to extrinsic values instead, to the pursuit of means instead of to the pursuit of ends beyond them, and particularly to the pursuit of power, so far as that lies within their reach. It has been claimed that there is a "strain toward anomy" in modern capitalistic society, with its emphasis on competitive success measured by the purely extrinsic standard of money-making. There can be little doubt that engrossment in the competitive struggle, especially when it is carried on under the aegis of the "soul-less body-less" corporation, diverts men from the search for intrinsic satisfactions and erodes their recognition of the common interests of their society, the inclusive more abiding interests that bind men in the responsible fellowship of their community. At the same time, the experience of the past two generations suggests that it requires the violence of change, the deeper perturbations that disorient and displace men from their former ways, their former goals, their former faiths, to bring anomy to its full being, and in particular this second type of anomy. Those who exhibit it tend to be domineering, sadistic, ruthless, irascible, vain, inherently destructive. Unlike the first type, they live for a future, they have objectives that bind today to the further tomorrow, but these objectives are self-centered, ego-glorifying, bereft of social obligation. Often they profess adherence to some intrinsic faith or value, but primarily because that profession enhances their private designs. They are then like Machiavelli's prince, who must appear to be religious and high-minded if he is to retain his prestige and power. Moreover, they make the creeds of other men the instruments of their own aggrandisement, the utilitarian myths of their authority. On another level they are racketeers, buccaneers of industry or finance, unprincipled exploiters of whatever position, privilege, or power they acquire. All men or nearly all men cherish their private interest and frequently enough they allow it to overcome their public obligation. But they are restrained within certain limits set by loyalties of one kind or another, and when they transgress they are conscious of dereliction. But the truly anomic man has no limit short of necessity and no conscience that is more than expediency.

Third, we may distinguish a type of anomy that is characterized above all by a fundamental and tragic insecurity, something that cuts deeper than the anxieties and dreads that beset other men. It is the insecurity of the hopelessly disoriented. They have lost the ground on which they stood, the ground of their former values. Usually it happens when they have lost also their former environment, their former connections, their social place, their economic support. In the profoundest sense they are "displaced persons." The displacement, however, may not be physical. There is, for example, the social alienation of those who feel themselves rejected and become the victims of a persecution complex. This is perhaps the bitterest of all forms of anomy. There is a crushing sense of indignity, of exclusion, of injustice, of defeat, arousing feelings of intense hate, counter-aggressiveness, total revulsion from things as they are, sometimes accompanied by unquiet introspection and self-torture.

This cursory review is intended to suggest types, not to classify them. In any event there is a considerable overlapping of attributes between our types. We should also remember that many people approach the full bent of anomy in various degrees. As we have already suggested, the conditions of our civilization create some predisposition to it and when our kind of civilization is racked by abrupt and violent change anomy grows rampant. Anomy is a disease of the civilized, not of the simpler peoples. As Durkheim pointed out, one index of anomy is the number of suicides, and suicide is much more frequent among the civilized.

It is noteworthy that modern doctrines of violent social change are initiated by those who have at least a tendency to anomy. Let us take for example the case of Karl Marx. He was from his early youth subjected to some of the conditions that breed anomy. His family belonged to the rabbinical elite in Germany. While he was still an infant his father, to the general surprise, announced his conversion to the Protestant Evangelical Church. This was the cause of a bitter dispute between his father and his mother. In the end, when Karl was six years old, his father had his way, and Karl, along with the six other children of the family, was baptized into the new faith. We know from modern studies how deeply disturbing it is to the mind of a child to have his first indoctrinations shattered by a "culture clash" on the hearth. The secret churning of the young boy's mind was the first preparation of the revolutionist-to-be, greatly heightening that sense of aloofness and disorientation that is the lot of many a Jewish boy in a society that stupidly clings to its hoary prejudices. The first obvious effect on Karl Marx was his loathing of all religions.

He grew into an impetuous, irascible, opinionated, and still idealistic youth. Then his ambitions suffered a series of reverses and frustrations. At this stage he fell in with the "communist rabbi," Moses Hess. He was ripe for the new gospel. He embraced it avidly, inclining at first toward the French socialists but soon repudiating and scorning them to assert his own truly scientific brand. It was the culmination of a process that began in the disorientation of childhood. Marx had become completely alienated from the society in which he lived, not its economic order particularly but its whole being and all the culture it nourished. In the background of his mind there flickered visions of an ideal society. But his love of the ideal was pale and distant compared with his hatred of the actual. He turned early to dreams of power, of lonely mastery. He was at enmity with the world. He denounced with incredible bitterness his own best friends the moment they ventured to question in any way his authority.

A man may condemn the society in which he lives without being himself anomic. But only if he is sustained by the engrossing vision of a better society, only if he is working to hasten the coming of some "new Jerusalem," only if he lives in fellowship with some brotherhood of the faithful who share his vision, only, in the last resort, if he is already, prophetically, a member of the society for which he yearns. There are those who believe the main inspiration of Marx was just some such redemption of mankind, that he was filled with the vision of a world in which men would be liberated from exploitation and injustice, from the gross oppression of every form of power. To the present writer that seems a mistaken interpretation. In the voluminous writings of Marx there are only one or two most fleeting references to "the good society." There is no evidence that he really cared for his fellowmen. He never uses kindly language except for those who looked upon him as their infallible leader. He hated those of his own party who showed any independence of thought. He was venomous toward all whom he could not dominate.

Marx focused his sharp intelligence on the worst sore of the society he hated. A new industrial system had been growing up. It was being exploited with callous disregard for the welfare of the workers. In the "dark Satanic mills," as the poet Blake called them, men, women, and young children labored endlessly long days, under the worst conditions, for subsistence wages or less. There were riots and threats of revolution. The French Revolution had shown how a class system could be overthrown. Here Marx found his opportunity. With immense vigor and remarkable propagandistic skill he proclaimed the inevitable victory of the proletariat. Marx had never mixed with any proletarians. He was himself a bourgeois. He never showed any interest in proletarians as human beings—only as a class. As he himself said, he found in the proletariat the "material weapon of philosophy," of his philosophy, of his revenge on society, of his triumph. He was the wrathful divider. The "bourgeoisie" became the fixed objective of his hate, the source of all evil. He identified it with the society that had rejected him. It was anathema. He devoted his being to its destruction.

The presence of anomy in modern society is evidenced by the spread of violently divisive doctrines, doctrines of all-or-nothing, doctrines that loudly preach a reactionary or a revolutionary authoritarianism, doctrines that appeal to men not as human beings but as de-individualized masses in motion. The anomic and near-anomic persons of the second and third types are particularly prone to such doctrines. For they offer a congenial release from anomy, a drastic remedy for its bitterness and frustration, a refuge from its insecurity, a means of reconciling its destructive tendencies with its secret need for social reintegration.

All these doctrines are enemies of democracy. They reject its tolerance, its acceptance of difference, its respect for the individual, its faith in the healing processes of free opinion. The anomic man has lost the balance of social health, mostly through no fault of his own. In his alienation he seeks a quick and false prescription. The anomic who cannot be masters are often ready to be slaves. They cry out for the superman to save them, for some equivalent of a Providence, a God, the ineluctable authority who will end their alienation by saying, "I command you to follow," making his command ring with the magic of a lost obligation.

What then can democracy do to meet these two perils that threaten it in this age of violent change—group anarchy and individual anomy? We remarked in passing that we should not blame the anomic for their plight; they are suffering from a disease incident to our civilization. The remark may seem at best a truism—of what other social ailment might not the same be said? But it was said to call attention to the proper ways in which democracy can safeguard itself against these dangers. When we seek to heal a social ailment—or a physical one—we should always treat it as a disease and not as a sin. Unfortunately we often proceed on the latter assumption, as we have been doing, for example, in our "denazification" policies, with mostly unhappy consequences. To protect democracy against anomy or against group anarchy we must endeavor to get at and to remove their causes.

In the first place we should realise that all our efforts to protect democracy against these and other dangers are wholly futile unless we can protect it first against the catastrophe of war. For war has now become so immeasurably ruinous that the shaken and impoverished survivors would be driven to desperate measures that might be fatal to the very existence of democracy. Therefore while we still possess the inestimable spiritual heritage of democracy we must assure it against the very possibility of war, showing an alertness and a forethought that in the past two generations the democratic world most deplorably failed to show.

To achieve this end democracy must be strong in its quality as democracy, not only in its arms. The spiritual weakness of democracy is the strength of its enemies. In some respects we still make only a pretence at democracy. Ask the Mexican-Americans within our borders, whom we do not permit to sit at the same table with our noble Nordics. Ask the Negroes, whom we segregate as pariahs, so that we may not be contaminated by the social presence of a lower caste. Ask the Jewish people, who cannot live in the same hotels, sometimes cannot even be treated in the same hospitals as their democracy-loving fellow-Americans. Ask the Eastern Europeans, who are still frequently treated as second-class citizens, especially if their names have a Slavic sound. Ask the Chinese among us, the Japanese, the Filipinos, the Hindus—and remember that by our treatment of these people we are betraying our democracy before the greater part of the human race; remember also that the Orient is now stirring to new political life and that its decision between democracy and dictatorship will profoundly affect our future and the future of all mankind. Ask these questions, remember these things, and you must see that *our* failure to be true to *our* democracy is in the last resort the main reason why democracy is in danger.

The diseases of group anarchy and of personal anomy are peculiarly incident to modern democracies. The unfree systems are authoritarian; by authority and by sheer compulsion they suppress such manifestations. Democracy places responsibility in the individual and in the group—it asks their free allegiance, their free cooperation. But it must on that account assure its citizens the conditions in which they can exercise their freedom. It must guard them from haunting economic insecurity or their civic freedom becomes a mockery. It must guard them against the rank prejudice that cuts them off from the equal partnership of democratic society. Otherwise democracy will breed the seeds of its own destruction.

Lastly, it must make its own meaning, its own philosophy, its own spirit, positive and vital. It cannot rest in the outworn liberalism that never rose above the negative of non-intervention. No vague negative faith can meet men's needs in this age where dogmatic authoritarian creeds deride the democratic ideal, and promise men, however falsely, a greater security and a greater reward. Democracy must become self-conscious of its own worth. Here we reach a theme that needs our most earnest attention.

90 The People versus the Pentagon

GEORGE S. McGOVERN, GAYLORD A. NELSON, GEORGE BROWN, JR., PHILLIP BURTON, JOHN CONYERS, JR., DON EDWARDS, DONALD M. FRASER, ROBERT W. KASTENMEIER, BENJAMIN S. ROSENTHAL, AND WILLIAM F. RYAN

This selection addresses itself to the question of our national priorities and to the question of who *is determining them. The authors, all United States senators or representatives at the time the article was written, contend that our national priorities are being excessively influenced by a loosely interrelated "national security bureaucracy" that has resulted in our investing excessive resources in the defense establishment rather than in programs which will promote our national well-being. They do not consider it a "conspiracy" but rather "an enormous, self-perpetuating institutional organism" and call for a broad public debate which will "reverse our present priorities."*

On March 28, 1969, two separate but ironically related events occurred which insistently pointed to the most urgent public issue of our time: the role of the military-industrial establishment in the United States.

The first event of that day was the death of Dwight David Eisenhower, himself a hero of the American military heritage. As a departing President he had startled the nation with his Farewell Address, in which he warned of a military establishment supported by an immense arms industry which "has the potential for a disastrous rise of misplaced power." Eight years later his words take on new import—after at least $500 billion dollars sunk in military expenditures, a disastrous war in Vietnam, a senseless intervention in the Dominican Republic, more than forty-two treaty commitments to as many countries to intervene "in case of aggression"—all this while acute poverty and distress persist within the United States itself.

SOURCE: *The Progressive* (June 1969), pp. 5–8. Reprinted by permission of the publisher. • The ten authors of this article are a group of United States senators and representatives who initiated a Congressional Conference on the Military Budget and National Priorities.

These misplaced priorities were the setting for the other event of March 28, the Congressional Conference on the Military Budget and National Priorities, which brought together former Government leaders, foreign policy scholars, experts on weapons technology, economists, Senators and Representatives to investigate the actual enormity of that "misplaced power" of which President Eisenhower warned.

We initiated the Conference in the conviction that Congressional control of military policy must be reasserted and that the level of Congressional analysis of these critical issues can be raised through a greater intimacy between the legislative branch and the intellectual community. Our purpose was to articulate the basic issues of the militarization of American society for the general public as well as for Congress, and to examine concrete proposals for restoring democratic control over the military budget. Two principal themes should be underscored.

The first is the nature of the national security bureaucracy itself. It is composed of the Armed Services, the Central Intelligence Agency, the National Security Agency, the Atomic Energy Commission, and other bodies provided for in the National Security Act of 1947, and it is closely linked to the aerospace and armaments industry, segments of the labor movement, and a new middle class of scientists, engineers, businessmen, and universities with defense research contracts. This complex is not a conspiracy; it is an enormous, self-perpetuating institutional organism. It receives such a disproportionate amount of Federal funds that there is no effective counterbalance to it, and such decisions as those on Vietnam and ABM are generated from institutional momentum rather than conscious policy decisions.

Second, to reassert control over this enormous bureaucracy we must undertake a new look at our own role in the world, assess the nature of our own social, economic, and political institutions, and redetermine our national priorities. Without such a public debate, we will be unable to translate public anxieties into political realities and forge a new political will to reverse our present priorities.

We hope this Conference will be a forerunner of a debate that will be taken up by local organizations, political clubs, university groups, and every individual man and woman who cares about the society in which he lives. There is a fundamental decision to be made by all of us, and that is how we want our tax dollar to be spent. We are heavily taxed by Federal, state, and local levies. Even with added sales taxes, gasoline taxes, surtaxes, not enough money is generated to provide for such necessary services as schools, public transportation, parks, pollution control. The pattern is nationwide.

The urgency of our concern is underscored by the critical juncture at which we stand in the development of nuclear weapons. The reason we called for the postponement of ABM deployment, a moratorium on testing of MIRV (multiple individually-targetable re-entry vehicle), and immediate commencement of strategic arms talks with the Soviet Union is that the time for such talks may soon pass the point of no return. Because of the impossibility of detecting the number of warheads inside the deployed missiles we will reach a stage in a few months when neither nation will be able to accept a limitation on its strategic force. The Soviet Union has been pressing for such talks, and we have been putting them off while we complete testing.

A profound indication of the acceleration of the arms race is the fact that our own military strategists are presently engaged in a debate to shift the basic question of defense policy from preventing nuclear war to surviving it.

Unless we act decisively within the next few months, the opportunities for maintaining any kind of security in the next decade may be almost non-existent. The bureaucratic momentum of the defense establishment, with its parochial view of the world, is projecting decisions that are contrary to the needs of the nation and to the well-being of mankind.

The staggering costs of this proposed arms spiral cannot be measured accurately in dollars or in percentage of Gross National Product. The proper measures are in "opportunities foregone": funding the Manned Orbiting Laboratories, or providing Upward Bound summer courses for 600,000 ghetto students who have college potential; permitting excessive contractor costs to go unchecked, or providing Head Start education for 2,250,000 additional children plus enough school lunches to feed twenty million children for a whole year; spending this year's Safeguard funds, or training 510,000 more hard-core unemployed.

In the decade from 1959 to 1968, direct defense outlays of the United States came to more than $551 billion. This is twice the amount spent for new private and public housing in the same decade, and nearly twice as much as Federal, state, and local governments allocated to education. In 1967 alone, a conservative estimate of military-related spending was $100 billion. This was more than all Federal, state, and local expenditures on health, hospitals, education, old age benefits, welfare, unemployment, and agriculture.

This order of priorities prevails at a time when twenty million Americans live in dilapidated, rat-infested housing while the building industry cannot even keep up with the population increase and is in fact declining in productivity; when there are at least ten million victims of malnutrition and untold thousands of children with permanent brain damage because of insufficient food; when there are close to forty million people living in poverty with little access to medical or welfare care; while millions of children are doomed to lives of misery and poverty because of inadequate or non-existent school facilities.

The degree of economic damage done each year by the massive allocation of resources to military spending has been noted by such economists as Kenneth Boulding, who points out that by reducing "domestic consumption by about fifteen per cent and by diverting the growth resource into the rat hole of competitive weapons systems, or even space technology, it unquestionably diminishes the rate of growth by as much as two per cent per annum."

Unlike investments in education or in new factories, expenditures for missiles add nothing to the nation's productive capacity, although they do generate income for a certain segment of the population. Other costs are just as great, although less easily quantified. Civilian businesses suffer because they cannot match the salaries offered by subsidized defense firms; scientists and engineers are trapped into doing research that is contrary to life-serving causes; a new class of business executive arises—men who know little about marketing or cost controls, but who know how to negotiate effectively with Government officials.

The most striking evidence of the decay of our society is that we have sought to meet the local crises of race and poverty by increasing militarization—by training more than 400,000 National Guardsmen and police in local riot control. The pervasive use of military means to solve our social and political problems is the most alarming indication of the emptiness of other conflict-resolving institutions.

In many other subtle ways individual values and ideals have been eroded. We are slowly becoming conditioned to the acceptance of regimentation, wiretapping, snooping, and spying by large national and internal-security related agencies. In many communities the existence of large defense installations has retarded necessary social reform by reinforcing prevailing patterns of segregation and economic rigidity. In industry the military have taken over fundamental business decisions, even necessitating security clearances for business executives.

Eventually we must recognize that the factors which determine our massive military budget are to be found less abroad than they are here at home. The reason we are able to move a wounded Marine from the jungles of Vietnam to the finest medical care in minutes, yet cannot do the same for a sick child on the Mississippi delta or on an Indian reservation, is very much bound up in our image of ourselves.

Being the greatest power in the world carries not only political and economic implications, but psychological elements which many of us have not yet truthfully faced. We do a great deal to buttress that image of power. Other sacrifices we find harder to make. We are six per cent of the world's population using more than sixty per cent of its goods and developed resources. We are convinced that the American way of life is the best in the world, that American management and enterprise are the best in the world, and that capitalism is the best tool for development. The result is that our foreign policy is not dictated as much by external threats, as we would like to think, but is an extension of our own economic, political, and social institutions.

The questions we must ask ourselves are not who are the Russians, or what are the Chinese or Vietnamese about, but who and what are Americans? If anti-Communism is all we can agree on as a national credo, we will never be able to break the psychosis of force and destruction which is the American tragedy.

Our national priorities were set out in the Constitution. Somehow we have forgotten them. The priorities of our forefathers were "to form a more perfect union, establish justice, ensure domestic tranquillity, and to provide for the common defense." Our first task is to reinterpret these great goals in light of the realities of the Twentieth Century and the dawn of the Twenty-first Century.

"*To form a more perfect union*" is to end the racism and discrimination that have long permeated American life. "Our society is moving toward two societies, one white, one black—separate and unequal." The extraordinary Kerner Commission Report on Civil Disorders outlines the decisive deepening of the racial division of our country. To continue on our present course can only lead to the fragmentation of America into increasingly violent and repressive factions and to the ultimate destruction of basic democratic values. Despite all our talk of strength and wealth and power, we are a weak and divided society.

To form a more perfect union is surely our first task.

"*To establish justice*" is to end the exploitation of the poor and the weak and to make our legal system one that will insure we are governed by laws and not by men.

At a time when we have equated justice with law and order, it is important that we take a look at the "crime" in our society. The crime we talk about in

America is crime in the streets. What about the crime of a society which would shoot a sixteen-year-old for looting a television set but think nothing of hungry children in a land of surplus food? What is not talked about is the crime of a society with dual standards of justice, where property is protected at any price while the costs of extortion, price-fixing, rake-offs, restraint of trade through duress or threat, blackmail, and consumer frauds are either ignored or passed on to the citizen in the form of higher prices. Organized crime drains the body politic of an estimated $22 billion per year. This crime does not appear in the statistics, but it underlies the moral fabric of our society and gives a hypocritical ring to cries for law and order. The real issue is justice.

"To ensure domestic tranquillity" is to redefine the difficult yet essential role of the police in contemporary society; to assist them in becoming more effective and creative servants of a pluralistic society; and to make sure that their role is not reduced to that of mere agents of a local power structure. The continued training of police and National Guardsmen in military techniques will not eliminate the economic and social failures which generate discord and disruption.

In the next five years twenty million Americans will leave the rural poverty in which they no longer can eke out a livelihood and migrate to cities which cannot house, feed, educate, or employ them. Massive disorder will be the inevitable result.

In the next few years millions of students will rebel against institutions which allow them no real responsibility, offer them careers they find abhorrent, and send them off to die for wars in which they cannot believe. They will disrupt the only segment of society over which they have any control—schools and universities.

The police and National Guard can quell riots. They cannot bring tranquillity. "There is no more urgent task than to break down the walls of isolation which surround our local police," warned the President's Commission on Law Enforcement. Our police are isolated from the society they serve, and the redefining and reorganization of our entire system of law enforcement—police, courts, and correctional apparatus—are essential to ensuring domestic stability and tranquillity.

"To provide for the common defense" means in the nuclear age to find new ways of leading in international cooperation, of building international institutions which can provide effective arms control and disarmament. The common defense does not require maintaining an American force for every conceivable contingency, however remote, nor does it require an endless arms race of nuclear and thermonuclear weapons which, if used, would destroy exactly what we are trying to protect.

One nuclear exchange between the United States and the Soviet Union would claim at least 120 million American lives. To offer up a percentage of our population as a human sacrifice is not to provide for the common defense.

The current strategic plans of our armed forces do not meet their Constitutional obligations as historically defined. To provide for defense in the nuclear age is to formulate and carry through a policy aimed at a stable peace. It means, at this point in time, a moratorium on further testing, no further ABM deployment, and successful arms limitation and disarmament agreements with the Soviet Union and other nations. A policy consciously directed towards creation of a stable peace which allows for profound change in the third world must now be fashioned to provide for the common defense of the United States.

How can we reassert the realities of our national priorities? It is clear that President Nixon will be no more able to control military spending than were Presidents Johnson or Kennedy. The size of our national security institutions precludes any partisan responsibility. The most urgent challenge confronting the Congress today is to reassert control of the military bureaucracy and the policy decisions it has preempted.

This can be accomplished only by effective Congressional leadership backed by a broadly-based, informed, and concerned public constituency. In recent years the military budget and weapons policies have been determined by the Pentagon and the Armed Services Committees without critical evaluation by the Congress or the public. Last year the House Armed Services Committee held months of hearings on the military budget, but of hundreds of witnesses only two were not employees of the Pentagon.

The size and complexity of the military budget make effective review almost impossible once the appropriations measures reach the floor of either House.

. . . . .

If we are asked, for example, to vote millions of dollars for high speed troop transport, we should ask whether or not we want to be able to move troops around the world to various trouble spots at a moment's notice, and if we do, why? Our policies should determine our weapons and not vice versa.

. . . . .

91 How I Got Radicalized

JOHN FISCHER

In this article, a long-time member of the "establishment," John Fischer, publicly testifies that he has given up his belief in three fundamental aspects of American life—the virtue of growth, technology can fix anything, and faith in private property. Fischer joins forces with many modern youth who are attempting to bring about a nonviolent revolution in our culture. The ultimate goal of this revolution for Fischer is a comprehensive re-ordering of our beliefs and priorities so that a "Survivable Society" can be created. Such a society, he says, can be "brought about only by radical political action—radical enough to change the whole structure of government, the economy and our national goals."

To my astonishment, the political convictions that I had cherished for most of my life have suddenly deserted me. Like my children, these were convictions I loved dearly and had nurtured at considerable expense. When last seen they were—like all of us—somewhat battered by the events of the last decade, but they looked durable enough to last out my time. So I was disconcerted when I found that somehow, during the past winter, they sort of melted away, without my consent and while I was looking somewhere else.

Their place has been usurped by a new set of convictions so radical that they alarm me. If the opposite kind of thing had happened, I would have felt a little melancholy but not surprised, since people traditionally grow more conservative as they get older. But to discover that one has suddenly turned into a militant subversive is downright embarrassing; at times I wonder whether it signals the onset of second childhood.

Except that I seem to be a lot more radical than the children. Those SDS youngsters who go around breaking windows and clubbing policemen now merely depress me with their frivolous irrelevance. So do most other varieties of New Leftists, such as the Women's Liberation movement; if some dire accident should, God forbid, throw one of those ladies into my clutches, she can be sure of instant liberation. I am equally out of tune with those old fogies, the Communists. The differences between capitalism and Communism no longer seem to me worth fighting about, or even arguing, since they are both wrong and beside the point. Or so it seems to me, since the New Vision hit me on my own small road to Damascus.

Let me make it plain that none of this was my doing. I feel as Charles Darwin must have felt during the last leg of his voyage on the *Beagle*. When he embarked he had been a conventional (if slightly lackadaisical) Christian, who took the literal truth of Genesis for granted. He had been raised in that faith, as I was raised a Brass Collar Democrat,

SOURCE: *Harper's Magazine,* vol. 240, no. 1439 (April 1970), 18–30 passim. Copyright © 1970, by *Harper's Magazine,* Inc. Reprinted by permission of the author. • John Fischer is a contributing editor on the staff of *Harper's Magazine* and author of its "Easy Chair" column. Among his books are *Why They Behave Like Russians, Master Plan USA,* and *The Stupidity Problem.*

and had no thought of forsaking it. Only gradually, while he examined fossil shellfish high in the Andes and measured the growth of coral deposits and the bills of Galapagos finches, did he begin to doubt that the earth and all its inhabitants had been created in six days of October, 4004 B.C., according to the pious calculations of Archbishop James Ussher. By the time he got back to England, he found himself a reluctant evolutionist, soon to be damned as a heretic and underminer of the Established Church. This was not his fault. It was the fault of those damned finches.

Recently I too have been looking at finches, so to speak, although mine are mostly statistical and not nearly as pretty as Darwin's. His gave him a hint about the way the earth's creatures came into being; mine, to my terror, seem to hint at the way they may go out. While I am by no means an uncritical admirer of the human race, I have become rather fond of it, and would hate to see it disappear. Finding ways to save it—if we are not too late already—now strikes me as the political issue which takes precedence over all others.

One of the events which led to my conversion was my unexpected appointment to a committee set up by Governor John Dempsey of Connecticut to work out an environmental policy for our state. Now I had been fretting for quite a while about what is happening to our environment—who hasn't?—but until the work of the committee forced me into systematic study, I had not realized that my political convictions were in danger. Then after looking at certain hairy facts for a few months, I found myself convinced that the Democratic party, and most of our institutions of government, and even the American Way of Life are no damned good. In their present forms, at least, they will have to go. Either that, or everybody goes—and sooner than we think.

To begin with, look at the American Way of Life. Its essence is a belief in growth. Every Chamber of Commerce is bent on making its Podunk grow into the Biggest Little City in the country. Wall Street is dedicated to its search for growth stocks, so that Xerox has become the American ideal—superseding George Washington, who expressed *his* faith in growth by speculating in land. Each year Detroit prays for a bigger car market. Businessmen spend their lives in pursuit of an annual increase in sales, assets, and net profits. All housewives—except for a few slatterns without ambition—yearn for bigger houses, bigger cars, and bigger salary checks. The one national goal that everybody agrees on is an ever-growing Gross National Product. Our modern priesthood—the economists who reassure us that our mystic impulses are moral and holy—recently announced that the GNP would reach a trillion dollars early in this decade. I don't really understand what a trillion is, but when I read the news I rejoiced, along with everybody else. Surely that means that we were in sight of ending poverty, for the first time in human history, so that nobody would ever again need to go hungry or live in a slum.

Now I know better. In these past months I have come to understand that a zooming Gross National Product leads not to salvation, but to suicide. So does a continuing growth in population, highway mileage, kilowatts, plane travel, steel tonnage, or anything else you care to name.

The most important lesson of my life—learned shamefully late—was that nonstop growth just isn't possible, for Americans or anybody else. For we live in what I've learned to recognize as a tight ecological system: a smallish planet with a strictly limited supply of everything, including air, water, and places to dump sewage. There is no conceivable way in which it can be made bigger. If Homo sapiens insists on constant growth, within this system's inelastic walls, something has to pop, or smother. Already the United States is an overpopulated country: not so hopelessly overcrowded as Japan or India, of course, but well beyond the limits which would make a good life attainable for everybody. Stewart Udall, former Secretary of Interior and now a practicing ecologist, has estimated that the optimum population for America would be about 100 million, or half of our present numbers. And unless we do something, drastic and fast, we can expect another 100 million within the next thirty years.

So our prime national goal, I am now convinced, should be to reach Zero Growth Rate as soon as possible. Zero growth in people, in GNP, and in our consumption of everything. That is the only hope of attaining a stable ecology: that is, of halting the deterioration of the environment on which our lives depend.

This of course is a profoundly subversive notion. It runs squarely against the grain of both capitalism and the American dream. It is equally subversive of Communism, since the Communists are just as hooked on the idea of perpetual growth as any American businessman. Indeed, when Khrushchev was top man in the Kremlin, he proclaimed that 1970 would be the year in which the Russians would surpass the United States in output of goods. They didn't make it: a fact for which their future generations may be grateful, because their environment is just as fragile as ours, and as easily damaged by headlong expansion. If you think the Hudson River and Lake Erie are unique examples of pollution, take a look at the Volga and Lake Baikal.

No political party, here or abroad, has yet even considered adopting Zero Growth Rate as the chief plank in its platform. Neither has any politician dared to speak out loud about what "protection of the environment" really means —although practically all of them seem to have realized, all of a sudden, that it is becoming an issue they can't ignore. So far, most of them have tried to handle it with gingerly platitudes, while keeping their eyes tightly closed to the implications of what they say. In his January State of the Union message, for instance, President Nixon made the customary noises about pollution; but he never even mentioned the population explosion, and he specifically denied that there is any "fundamental contradiction between economic growth and the quality of life." He sounded about as convincing as a doctor telling a cancer patient not to worry about the growth of his tumor.

The Democrats are no better. I have not heard any of them demanding a halt to all immigration, or a steeply progressive income tax on each child beyond two, or an annual bounty to every woman between the ages of fifteen and forty-five who gets through the year without becoming pregnant. Neither Ted Sorensen nor any of the other Kennedy henchmen has yet suggested that a politician with a big family is a spacehog and a hypocrite, unworthy of public trust. No Democrat, to my knowledge, has ever endorsed the views of Dr. René Dubos of Rockefeller University, one of the truly wise men of our time. In an editorial in the November 14, 1969, issue of *Science* he predicted that in order to survive, "mankind will have to develop what might be called a steady state . . . a nearly closed system" in which most materials from tin cans to sewage would be "recycled instead of discarded." His conclusion—that a viable future depends on the creation of "social and economic systems different from the ones in which we live today"—apparently is too radical for any politician I know.

Consequently I feel a little lonesome in my newfound political convictions. The only organization which seems to share them is a tiny one.

. . . . .

Yet I have a hunch that I may not be lonesome for long. Among college students a concern with ecology has become, almost overnight, nearly as popular as sideburns. On many campuses it seems to be succeeding civil rights and Vietnam as The Movement. For example, when the University of Oregon announced last January a new course, "Can Man Survive?", it drew six thousand students, the biggest class in the university's history. They had to meet in the basketball court because no classroom would hold them.

Who knows? Maybe we agitators for Zero may yet turn out to be the wave of the future.

At the same time I was losing my faith in the virtues of growth, I began to doubt two other articles of the American credo.

One of them is the belief that technology can fix anything. Like most of us, I had always taken it for granted that any problem could be solved if we just applied enough science, money, and good old American know-how. Is the world's population outrunning its food supply? Well, then, let's put the laboratories to work inventing high-yield strains of rice and wheat, better fertilizers, ways to harvest seaweed, hydroponic methods for growing food without soil. If the air is becoming unbreathable, surely the technologists can find ways to clean it up. If our transportation system is a national disgrace, all we have to do is call in the miracle men who built a shuttle service to the moon; certainly they should be able to figure out some way to get a train from New York to New Haven on time.

I was in East Haddam, Connecticut, looking at an atomic power plant, when I began to suspect that technology might not be the answer after all. While I can't go along with the young Luddites who have decided that science is evil and that all inventions since the wheel ought to be destroyed, I am persuaded that technology is a servant of only limited usefulness, and highly unreliable. When it does solve a problem, it often creates two new ones—and their side effects are usually hard to foresee.

One of the things that brought me to East Haddam was curiosity about the automobile. Since the gasoline engine is the main polluter of the air, maybe it should be replaced with some kind of electric motor? That of course would require an immense increase in our production of electric power, in order to recharge ten million batteries every night. Where would it come from? Virtually all waterpower sites already are in use. More coal- and oil-fired power stations don't sound like a good idea, since they too pour smoke into the atmosphere —and coal mining already has ruined countless streams and hundreds of thousands of acres of irreplaceable land. Atomic power, then?

At first glance, the East Haddam plant, which is fairly typical of the new technology, looked encouraging. It is not as painful an eyesore as coal-burning stations, and not a wisp of smoke was in sight. When I began to ask questions, however, the company's public-relations man admitted that there are a few little problems. For one thing, the plant's innards are cooled with water pumped out of the Connecticut River. When it flows back in, this water raises the river's temperature by about twenty degrees, for a considerable distance. Apparently this has not yet done any serious damage to the shad, the only fish kept under careful surveillance: but its effect on other fish and algae, fish eggs, microorganisms, and the general ecology of the river is substantial though still unmeasured.

It would be possible, though expensive, for the company to build cooling towers, where the water would trickle over a series of baffles before returning to the river. In the process it would lose its heat to the atmosphere. But this, in turn, threatens climatic changes, such as banks of artificial fog rolling eastward over Long Island Sound, and serious wastage of water through evaporation from a river system where water already is in precarious supply. Moreover, neither this process nor any other now known would eliminate the slight, but not negligible, radiation which every atomic plant throws off, nor the remote but still omnipresent chance of a nuclear accident which could take thousands of lives. The building of an additional twenty plants along the banks of the Connecticut—which some estimates call for, in order to meet future demand for electricity—would be a clear invitation to an ecological disaster.

In the end I began to suspect that there is no harmless way to meet the demands for power of a rising population, with rising living standards—much less for a new herd of millions of electric cars. Every additional kilowatt levies some tax upon the environment, in one form or another. The Fourth Law of Thermodynamics seems to be: "There is no free lunch."

Every time you look at one of the marvels of modern technology, you find a by-product—unintended, unpredictable, and often lethal. Since World War II American agriculture has performed miracles in increasing production. One result was that we were able for years to send a shipload of free wheat every day to India, saving millions from starvation. The by-products were: (1) a steady rise in India's population; (2) the poisoning of our streams and lakes with insecticides and chemical fertilizers; (3) the forced migration of some ten million people from the countryside to city slums, as agriculture became so efficient it no longer needed their labor.

Again, the jet plane is an unquestionable convenience, capable of whisking a New Yorker, say, to either the French Riviera or Southern California in a tenth of the time he could travel by ship or car, and at lower cost. But when he reaches his destination, the passenger finds the beaches coated with oil (intended to fuel planes, if it hadn't spilled) and the air thick with smog (thanks in good part to the jets, each of which spews out as much hydrocarbon as ten thousand automobiles).

Moreover, technology works best on things nobody really needs, such as collecting moon rocks or building supersonic transport planes. Whenever we try to apply it to something serious, it usually falls on its face.

An obvious case in point is the railroads. We already have the technology to build fast, comfortable passenger trains. Such trains are, in fact, already in operation in Japan, Italy, and a few other countries. Experimental samples—the Metroliners and Turbotrains—also are running with spectacular success between Washington and Boston. If we had enough of them to handle commuter and middle-distance traffic throughout the country, we could stop building the highways and airports which disfigure our countryside, reduce the number of automobiles contaminating the air, and solve many problems of urban congestion. But so far we have not been able to apply the relatively simple technology needed to accomplish these aims, because some tough political decisions have to be made before we can unleash the scientists and engineers. We would have to divert to the railroads many of the billions in subsidy which we now lavish on highways and air routes. We would have to get rid of our present railway management—in general, the most incompetent in American industry—and retire the doddering old codgers of the Railway Brotherhoods who make such a mess out of running our trains. This might mean public ownership of a good many rail lines. It certainly would mean all-out war with the unions, the auto and aviation industries, and the highway lobby. It would mean ruthless application of the No Growth principle to roads, cars, and planes, while we make sensible use instead of something we already have: some 20,000 miles of railways.

All this requires political action, of the most radical kind. Until our Great Slob Society is willing to take it, technology is helpless.

My final apostasy from the American Creed was loss of faith in private property. I am now persuaded that there no longer is such a thing as truly private property, at least in land. That was a luxury we could afford only when the continent was sparsely settled. Today the use a man makes of his land cannot be left to his private decision alone, since eventually it is bound to affect everybody else. This conclusion I reached in anguish, since I own a tiny patch of land and value its privacy above anything money can buy.

What radicalized me on this score was the Department of Agriculture and Dr. Ian McHarg. From those dull volumes of statistics which the Department publishes from time to time, I discovered that usable land is fast becoming a scarce resource—and that we are wasting it with an almost criminal lack of foresight. Every year, more than a million acres of farm and forest land is being eaten up by highways, airports, reservoirs, and real-estate developments. The best, too, in most cases, since the rich, flat bottom lands are the most tempting to developers.

Since America is, for the moment, producing a surplus of many crops, this destruction of farmland has not yet caused much public alarm. But some day, not too far off, the rising curve of population and the falling curve of food-growing land inevitably are going to intersect. That is the day when we may begin to understand what hunger means.

Long before that, however, we may be gasping for breath. For green plants are our only source of oxygen. They also are the great purifiers of the atmosphere, since in the process of photosynthesis they absorb carbon dioxide—an assignment which gets harder every day, as our chimneys and exhaust pipes spew out ever-bigger tonnage of carbon gases. This is a function not only of trees and grass, but also of the tiny microorganisms in the sea. Indeed, its phytoplankton produces some 70 percent of all the oxygen on which life depends. These are delicate little creatures, easily killed by the sewage, chemicals, and oil wastes which already are contaminating every ocean in the world. Nobody knows when the scale will tip: when there are no longer enough green growing things to preserve the finely balanced mixture of gases in the atmosphere, by absorbing carbon dioxide and generating oxygen. All we know is that man is pressing down hard on the lethal end of the scale.

The Survivable Society, if we are able to construct it, will no longer permit a farmer to convert his meadow into a parking lot any time he likes. He will have to understand that his quick profit may, quite literally, take the bread out of his grandchildren's mouths, and the oxygen from their lungs. For the same reasons, housing developments will not be located where they suit the whim of a real-estate speculator or even the convenience of the residents. They will have to go on those few carefully chosen sites where they will do the least damage to the landscape, and to the life-giving greenery which it supports.

• • • • •

The current excitement about the environment will not come to much, I am afraid, unless it radicalizes millions of Americans. The conservative ideas put forth by President Nixon—spending a few billion for sewage-treatment plants and abatement of air pollution—will not even begin to create the Survivable Society. That can be brought about only by radical political action—radical enough to change the whole structure of government, the economy, and our national goals.

How the Survivable State will work is something I cannot guess: its design is a job for the coming generation of political scientists. The radical vision can, however, give us a glimpse of what it might look like. It will measure every new law, every dollar of investment by a cardinal yardstick: Will this help us accomplish a zero rate of growth and a stabilized environment? It will be skeptical of technology, including those inventions which purport to help clean up our earthly mess. Accordingly it will have an Anti-Patent Office, which will forbid the use of any technological discovery until the Office figures out fairly precisely what its side effects might be. (If they can't be foreseen, then the invention goes into deep freeze.) The use of land, water, and air will not be left to private decision, since their preservation will be recognized as a public trust. The landlord whose incinerator smokes will be pilloried: the tanker skipper who flushes his oil tanks at sea will be hanged at the nearest yardarm for the capital crime of oxygen destruction. On the other hand, the gardener will stand at the top of the social hierarchy, and the citizen who razes a supermarket and plants its acreage in trees will be proclaimed a Hero of the Republic. I won't live to see the day, of course; but I hope somebody will.

92 Ignorance Is Strength

GEORGE ORWELL

Lightened in part though it is by a boy-meets-girl theme, the novel 1984 *from which this selection is taken is a deadly serious, satirical exposition of life as it might become in a totalitarian society. Its author, George Orwell, develops to their logical limits the characteristics of the institutions in modern authoritarian cultures. In this excerpt, Orwell sets forth the rationale and method of operation of his 1984 society. He begins with the contention that modern science and mass production have made it technically possible to eliminate the great class differences in material and mental well-being that have heretofore characterized the major societies of the world. Orwell then describes how, in the face of this possibility, a ruling class can still maintain itself in power through carefully calculated strategies such as the use of "doublethink" and the firm guidance of "Big Brother."*

Throughout recorded time, and probably since the end of the Neolithic Age, there have been three kinds of people in the world, the High, the Middle, and the Low. They have been subdivided in many ways, they have borne countless different names, and their relative numbers, as well as their attitude toward one another, have varied from age to age; but the essential structure of society has never altered. Even after enormous upheavals and seemingly irrevocable changes, the same pattern has always reasserted itself, just as a gyroscope will always return to equilibrium, however far it is pushed one way or the other. . . .

The aims of these groups are entirely irreconcilable. The aim of the High is to remain where they are. The aim of the Middle is to change places with the High. The aim of the Low, when they have an aim—for it is an abiding characteristic of the Low that they are too much crushed by drudgery to be more than intermittently conscious of anything outside their daily lives—is to abolish all distinctions and create a society in which all men shall be equal. Thus throughout history a struggle which is the same in its main outlines recurs over and over again. For long periods the High seem to be securely in power, but sooner or later there always comes a moment when they lose either their belief in themselves, or their capacity to govern efficiently, or both. They are then overthrown by the Middle, who enlist the Low on their side by pretending to them that they are fighting for liberty and justice. As soon as they have reached their objective, the Middle thrust the Low back into their old position of servitude, and themselves become the High. Presently a new Middle group splits off from one of the other groups, or from both of them, and the struggle begins over again. Of the three groups, only the Low are never even temporarily successful in achieving their aims. It would

SOURCE: *1984* by George Orwell. Copyright, 1949, by Harcourt, Brace and World, Inc. Reprinted by permission of Brandt & Brandt. • George Orwell (1903–1950), a nom de plume for Eric Arthur Blair, was a British novelist and essayist. He was born in Motihari, India, of Anglo-Indian parents. He served on the Republican side in the Spanish Civil War, and one result of his time as a soldier was his book *Homage to Catalonia.* He wrote many other books, including *Down and Out in Paris and London, Burmese Days,* and *Animal Farm.*

be an exaggeration to say that throughout history there had been no progress of a material kind. Even today, in a period of decline, the average human being is physically better off than he was a few centuries ago. But no advance in wealth, no softening of manners, no reform or revolution has ever brought human equality a millimeter nearer. From the point of view of the Low, no historic change has ever meant much more than a change in the name of their masters.

By the late nineteenth century the recurrences of this pattern had become obvious to many observers. There then arose schools of thinkers who interpreted history as a cyclical process and claimed to show that inequality was the unalterable law of human life. This doctrine, of course, had always had its adherents, but in the manner in which it was now put forward there was a significant change. In the past the need for a hierarchical form of society had been the doctrine specifically of the High. It had been preached by kings and aristocrats and by the priests, lawyers, and the like who were parasitical upon them, and it had generally been softened by promises of compensation in an imaginary world beyond the grave. The Middle, so long as it was struggling for power, had always made use of such terms as freedom, justice, and fraternity. Now, however, the concept of human brotherhood began to be assailed by people who were not yet in positions of command, but merely hoped to be so before long. In the past the Middle had made revolutions under the banner of equality, and then had established a fresh tyranny as soon as the old one was overthrown. The new Middle groups in effect proclaimed their tyranny beforehand. Socialism, a theory which appeared in the early nineteenth century and was the last link in a chain of thought stretching back to the slave rebellions of antiquity, was still deeply infected by the Utopianism of past ages. But in each variant of Socialism that appeared from about 1900 onwards the aim of establishing liberty and equality was more and more openly abandoned. The new movements which appeared in the middle years of the century, Ingsoc in Oceania, Neo-Bolshevism in Eurasia, Death-worship, as it is commonly called, in Eastasia, had the conscious aim of perpetuating *un*freedom and *in*equality. These new movements, of course, grew out of the old ones and tended to keep their names and pay lip-service to their ideology. But the purpose of all of them was to arrest progress and freeze history at a chosen moment. The familiar pendulum swing was to happen once more, and then stop. As usual, the High were to be turned out by the Middle, who would then become the High; but this time, by conscious strategy, the High would be able to maintain their position permanently.

The new doctrines arose partly because of the accumulation of historical knowledge, and the growth of the historical sense, which had hardly existed before the nineteenth century. The cyclical movement of history was now intelligible, or appeared to be so; and if it was intelligible, then it was alterable. But the principal, underlying cause was that, as early as the beginning of the twentieth century, human equality had become technically possible. It was still true that men were not equal in their native talents and that functions had to be specialized in ways that favored some individuals against others; but there was no longer any real need for class distinctions or for large differences of wealth. In earlier ages, class distinctions had been not only inevitable but desirable. Inequality was the price of civilization. With the development of machine production, however, the case was altered. Even if it was still necessary for human beings to do different kinds of work, it was no longer necessary for them to live at different social or economic levels. Therefore, from the point of view of the new groups who were on the point of seizing power, human equality was no longer an ideal to be striven after, but a danger to be averted. In more primitive ages, when a just and peaceful society was in fact not possible, it had been fairly easy to believe in it. The idea of an earthly paradise in which men should live together in a state of brotherhood, without laws and without brute labor, had haunted the human imagination for thousands of years. And this vision had had a certain hold even on the groups who actually profited by each historic change. The heirs of the French, English, and American revolutions had partly believed in their own phrases about the rights of man, freedom of speech, equality before the law, and the like, and had even allowed their conduct to be influenced by them to some extent. But by the fourth decade of the twentieth century all the main currents of political thought were authoritarian. The earthly paradise had been discredited at exactly the moment when it became realizable. Every new political theory, by whatever name it called itself, led back to hierarchy and regimentation. And in the general hardening of outlook that set in round about 1930, practices which had been long abandoned, in some cases for hundreds of years—imprisonment without trial, the use of war prisoners as slaves, public executions, torture to extract confessions, the use of hostages and the deportation of whole populations—not only became common again, but were tolerated and even defended by people who considered themselves enlightened and progressive.

It was only after a decade of national wars, civil wars, revolutions and counter-revolutions in all parts of the world that Ingsoc and its rivals emerged as fully worked-out political theories. But they had been foreshadowed by the various systems, generally called totalitarian, which had appeared earlier in the century, and the main outlines of the world which would emerge from the prevailing chaos had long been obvious. What kind of people would control this world had been equally obvious. The new aristocracy was made up for the most part of bureaucrats, scientists, technicians, trade-union organizers, publicity experts, sociologists, teachers, journalists, and professional politicians. These people, whose origins lay in the salaried middle class and the upper grades of the working class, had been shaped and brought together by the barren world of monopoly industry and centralized government. As compared with their opposite numbers in past ages, they were less avaricious, less tempted by luxury, hungrier for pure power, and, above all, more conscious of what they were doing and more intent on crushing opposition. This last difference was cardinal. By comparison with that existing today, all the tyrannies of the past were half-hearted and inefficient. The ruling groups were always infected to some extent by liberal ideas, and were content to leave loose ends everywhere, to regard only the overt act, and to be uninterested in what their subjects were thinking. Even the Catholic Church of the Middle Ages was tolerant by modern standards. Part of the reason for this was that in the past no government had the power to keep its citizens under constant surveillance. The invention of print, however, made it easier to manipulate public opinion, and the film and the radio carried the process further. With the development of television, and the technical advance which made it possible to receive and transmit simultaneously on the same instrument, private life came to an end. Every citizen, or at least every citizen important enough to be worth watching, could be kept for twenty-four hours a day under the eyes of the police and in the sound of official propaganda, with all other channels of communication closed. The possibility of enforcing not only complete obedience to the will of the State, but complete uniformity of opinion on all subjects, now existed for the first time.

After the revolutionary period of the Fifties and Sixties, society regrouped itself, as always, into High, Middle, and Low. But the new High group, unlike all its forerunners, did not act upon instinct but knew what was needed to safeguard its position. It had long been realized that the only secure basis for oligarchy is collectivism. Wealth and privilege are most easily defended when they are possessed jointly. The so-called "abolition of private property" which took place in the middle years of the century meant, in effect, the concentration of property in far fewer hands than before; but with this difference, that the new owners were a group instead of a mass of individuals. Individually, no member of the Party owns anything, except petty personal belongings. Collectively, the Party owns everything in Oceania, because it controls everything and disposes of the products as it thinks fit. In the years following the Revolution it was able to step into this commanding position almost unopposed, because the whole process was represented as an act of collectivization. It had always been assumed that if the capitalist class were expropriated, Socialism must follow; and unquestionably the capitalists had been expropriated. Factories, mines, land, houses, transport—everything had been taken away from them; and since these things were no longer private property, it followed that they must be public property. Ingsoc, which grew out of the earlier Socialist movement and inherited its phraseology, has in fact carried out the main item in the Socialist program, with the result, foreseen and intended beforehand, that economic inequality has been made permanent.

But the problems of perpetuating a hierarchical society go deeper than this. There are only four ways in which a ruling group can fall from power. Either it is conquered from without, or it governs so inefficiently that the masses are stirred to revolt, or it allows a strong and discontented Middle Group to come into being, or it loses its own self-confidence and willingness to govern. These causes do not operate singly, and as a rule all four of them are present in some degree. A ruling class which could guard against all of them would remain in power permanently. Ultimately the determining factor is the mental attitude of the ruling class itself.

After the middle of the present century, the first danger had in reality disappeared. Each of the three powers which now divide the world is in fact unconquerable, and could only become conquerable through slow demographic changes which a government with wide powers can easily avert. The second danger, also, is only a theoretical one. The masses never revolt of their own accord, and they never revolt merely because they are oppressed. Indeed, so long as they are not permitted to have standards of comparison they never even become aware that they are oppressed. The recurrent economic crises of past times were totally unnecessary and are not now permitted to happen, but other and equally large dislocations can and do happen without having political results, because there is no way in which discontent can become articulate. As for the problem of overproduction, which has been latent in our society since the development of machine technique, it is solved by the device of continuous warfare, which is also useful in keying up public morale to the necessary pitch. From the point of view of our present rulers, therefore, the only genuine dangers are the splitting-off of a new group of able, underemployed, power-hungry people, and the growth of liberalism and skepticism in their own ranks. The problem, that is to say, is educational. It is a problem of continuously molding the consciousness both of the directing group and of the larger executive group that lies immediately below it. The consciousness of the masses needs only to be influenced in a negative way.

Given this background, one could infer, if one did not know it already, the general structure of Oceanic society. At the apex of the pyramid comes Big Brother. Big Brother is infallible and all-powerful. Every success, every achievement, every victory, every scientific discovery, all knowledge, all wisdom, all happiness, all virtue, are held to issue directly from his leadership and inspiration. Nobody has ever seen Big Brother. He is a face on the hoardings, a voice on the telescreen. We may be reasonably sure that he will never die, and there is already considerable uncertainty as to when he was born. Big Brother is the guise in which the Party chooses to exhibit itself to the world. His function is to act as a focusing point for love, fear, and reverence, emotions which are more easily felt toward an individual than toward an organization. Below Big Brother comes the Inner Party, its numbers limited to six million, or something less than two per cent of the population of Oceania. Below the Inner Party comes the Outer Party, which, if the Inner Party is described as the brain of the State, may be justly likened to the hands. Below that come the dumb masses whom we habitually refer to as "the proles," numbering perhaps eighty-five per cent of the population. In the terms of our earlier classification, the proles are the Low, for the slave populations of the equatorial lands, who pass constantly from conqueror to conqueror, are not a permanent or necessary part of the structure.

In principle, membership in these three groups is not hereditary. The child of Inner Party parents is in theory not born into the Inner Party. Admission to either branch of the Party is by examination, taken at the age of sixteen. Nor is there any racial discrimination, or any marked domination of one province by another. Jews, Negroes, South Americans of pure Indian blood are to be found in the highest ranks of the Party, and the administrators of any area are always drawn from the inhabitants of that area. In no part of Oceania do the inhabitants have the feeling that they are a colonial population ruled from a distant capital. Oceania has no capital, and its titular head is a person whose whereabouts nobody knows. Except that English is its chief lingua franca and Newspeak its official language, it is not centralized in any way. Its rulers are not held together by blood ties but by adherence to a common doctrine. It is true that our society is stratified, and very rigidly stratified, on what at first sight appear to be hereditary lines. There is far less to-and-fro movement between the different groups than happened under capitalism or even in the pre-industrial ages. Between the two branches of the Party there is a certain amount of interchange, but only so much as will ensure that weaklings are excluded from the Inner Party and that ambitious members of the Outer Party are made harmless by allowing them to rise. Proletarians, in practice, are not allowed to graduate into the Party. The most gifted among them, who might possibly become nuclei of discontent, are simply marked down by the Thought Police and eliminated. But this state of affairs is not necessarily permanent, nor is it a matter of principle. The Party is not a class in the old sense of the word. It does not aim at transmitting power to its own children, as such; and if there were no other way of keeping the ablest people at the top, it would be perfectly prepared to recruit an entire new generation from the ranks of the proletariat. In the crucial years, the fact that the Party was not a hereditary body did a great deal to neutralize opposition. The older kind of Socialist, who had been trained to fight against something called "class privilege," assumed that what is not hereditary cannot be permanent. He did not see that the continuity of an oligarchy need not be physical, nor did he pause to reflect that hereditary aristocracies have always been shortlived, whereas adoptive organizations such as the Catholic Church have sometimes lasted for hundreds or thousands of years. The essence of oligarchical rule is not father-to-son inheritance, but the persistence of a certain world-view and a certain way of life, imposed by the dead upon the living. A ruling group is a ruling group so long as it can nominate its successors. The Party is not concerned with perpetuating its blood but with perpetuating itself. *Who* wields power is not important, provided that the hierarchical structure remains always the same.

All the beliefs, habits, tastes, emotions, mental attitudes that characterize our time are really designed to sustain the mystique of the Party and prevent the true nature of present-day society from being perceived. Physical rebellion, or any preliminary move toward rebellion, is at present not possible. From the proletarians nothing is to be feared. Left to themselves, they will continue from generation to generation and from century to century, working, breeding, and dying, not only without any impulse to rebel, but without the power of grasping that the world could be other than it is. They could only become dangerous if the advance of industrial technique made it necessary to educate them more highly; but, since military and commercial rivalry are no longer important, the level of popular education is actually declining. What opinions the masses hold, or do not hold, is looked on as a matter of indifference. They can be granted intellectual liberty because they have no intellect. In a Party member, on the other hand, not even the smallest deviation of opinion on the most unimportant subject can be tolerated.

A Party member lives from birth to death under the eye of the Thought Police. Even when he is alone he can never be sure that he is alone. Wherever he may be, asleep or awake, working or resting, in his bath or in bed, he can be inspected without warning and without knowing that he is being inspected. Nothing that he does is indifferent. His friendships, his relaxations, his behavior toward his wife and children, the expression of his face when he is alone, the words he mutters in sleep, even the characteristic movements of his body, are all jealously scrutinized. Not only any actual disdemeanor, but any eccentricity, however small, any change of habits, any nervous mannerism that could possibly be the symptom of an inner struggle, is certain to be detected. He has no freedom of choice in any direction whatever. On the other hand, his actions are not regulated by law or by any clearly formulated code of behavior. In Oceania there is no law. Thoughts and actions which, when detected, mean certain death are not formally forbidden, and the endless purges, arrests, tortures, imprisonments, and vaporizations are not inflicted as punishment for crimes which have actually been committed, but are merely the wiping-out of persons who might perhaps commit a crime at some time in the future. A Party member is required to have not only the right opinions, but the right instincts. Many of the beliefs and attitudes demanded of him are never plainly stated, and could not be stated without laying bare the contradictions inherent in Ingsoc. If he is a person naturally orthodox (in Newspeak, a *goodthinker*), he will in all circumstances know, without taking thought, what is the true belief or the desirable emotion. But in any case an elaborate mental training, undergone in childhood and grouping itself round the Newspeak words *crimestop*, *blackwhite*, and *doublethink*, makes him unwilling and unable to think too deeply on any subject whatever.

A Party member is expected to have no private emotions and no respites from enthusiasm. He is supposed to live in a continuous frenzy of hatred of foreign enemies and internal traitors, triumph over victories, and self-abasement before the power and wisdom of the Party. The discontents produced by his bare, unsatisfying life are deliberately turned outwards and dissipated by such devices as the Two Minutes Hate, and the speculations which might possibly induce a skeptical or rebellious attitude are killed in advance by his early acquired inner discipline. The first and simplest stage in the discipline, which can be taught even to young children, is called, in Newspeak, *crimestop*. *Crimestop* means the faculty of stopping short, as though by instinct, at the threshold of any dangerous thought. It includes the power of not grasping analogies, of failing to perceive logical errors, of misunderstanding the simplest arguments if they are inimical to Ingsoc, and of being bored or repelled by any train of thought which is capable of leading in a heretical direction. *Crimestop*, in short, means protective stupidity. But stupidity is not enough. On the contrary, orthodoxy in the full sense demands a control over one's own mental processes as complete as that of a contortionist over his body. Oceanic society rests ultimately on the belief that Big Brother is omnipotent and that the Party is infallible. But since in reality Big Brother is not omnipotent and the Party is not infallible, there is need for an unwearying, moment-to-moment flexibility in the treatment of facts. The key word here is *blackwhite*. Like so many Newspeak words, this word has two mutually contradictory meanings. Applied to an opponent, it means the habit of impudently claiming that black is white, in contradiction of the plain facts. Applied to a Party member, it means a loyal willingness to say that black is white when Party discipline demands this. But it means also the ability to *believe* that black is white and more, to *know* that black is white, and to forget that one has ever believed the contrary. This demands a continuous alteration of the past, made possible by the system of thought which really embraces all the rest, and which is known in Newspeak as *doublethink*.

The alteration of the past is necessary for two reasons, one of which is subsidiary and, so to speak, precautionary. The subsidiary reason is that the Party member, like the proletarian, tolerates present-day conditions partly because he has no standards of comparison. He must be cut off from the past, just as he must be cut off from foreign countries, because it is necessary for him to believe that he is better off than his ancestors and that the average level of material comfort is constantly rising. But by far the more important reason for the readjustment of the past is the need to safeguard the infallibility of the Party. It is not merely that speeches, statistics, and records of every kind must be constantly brought up to date in order to show that the predictions of the Party were in all cases right. It is also that no change of doctrine or in political alignment can ever be admitted. For to change one's mind, or even one's policy, is a confession of weakness. If, for example, Eurasia or Eastasia (whichever it may be) is the enemy today, then that country must always have been the enemy. And if the facts say otherwise, then the facts must be altered. Thus history is continuously rewritten. This day-to-day falsification of the past, carried out by the Ministry of Truth, is as necessary to the stability of the regime as the work of repression and espionage carried out by the Ministry of Love.

The mutability of the past is the central tenet of Ingsoc. Past events, it is argued, have no objective existence, but survive only in written records and in human memories. The past is whatever the records and the memories agree upon. And since the Party is in full control of all records, and in equally full control of the minds of its members, it follows that the past is whatever the Party chooses to make it. It also follows that though the past is alterable, it never has been altered in any specific instance. For when it has been recreated in whatever shape is needed at the moment, then this new version *is* the past, and no different past can ever have existed. This holds good even when, as often happens, the same event has to be altered out of recognition several times in the course of a year. At all times the Party is in possession of absolute truth, and clearly the absolute can never have been different from what it is now. It will be seen that the control of the past depends above all on the training of memory. To make sure that all written records agree with the orthodoxy of the moment is merely a mechanical act. But it is also necessary to *remember* that events happened in the desired manner. And if it is necessary to rearrange one's memories or to tamper with written records, then it is necessary to *forget* that one has done so. The trick of doing this can be learned like any other mental technique. It *is* learned by the majority of Party members, and certainly by all who are intelligent as well as orthodox. In Oldspeak it is called, quite frankly, "reality control." In Newspeak it is called *doublethink*, although *doublethink* comprises much else as well.

Doublethink means the power of holding two contradictory beliefs in one's mind simultaneously, and accepting both of them. The Party intellectual knows in which direction his memories must be altered; he therefore knows that he is playing tricks with reality; but by the exercise of *doublethink* he also satisfies himself that reality is not violated. The process has to be conscious, or it would not be carried out with sufficient precision, but it also has to be unconscious, or it would bring with it a feeling of falsity and hence of guilt. *Doublethink* lies at the very heart of Ingsoc, since the essential act of the Party is to use conscious deception while retaining the firmness of purpose that goes with complete honesty. To tell deliberate lies while genuinely believing in them, to forget any fact that has become inconvenient, and then, when it becomes necesssary again, to draw it back from oblivion for just so long as it is needed, to deny the existence of objective reality and all the while to take account of the reality which one denies—all this is indispensably necessary. Even in using the word *doublethink* it is necessary to exercise *doublethink*. For by using the word one admits that one is tampering with reality; by a fresh act of *doublethink* one erases this knowledge;

and so on indefinitely, with the lie always one leap ahead of the truth. Ultimately it is by means of *doublethink* that the Party has been able—and may, for all we know, continue to be able for thousands of years—to arrest the course of history.

All past oligarchies have fallen from power either because they ossified or because they grew soft. Either they became stupid and arrogant, failed to adjust themselves to changing circumstances, and were overthrown, or they became liberal and cowardly, made concessions when they should have used force, and once again were overthrown. They fell, that is to say, either through consciousness or through unconsciousness. It is the achievement of the Party to have produced a system of thought in which both conditions can exist simultaneously. And upon no other intellectual basis could the dominion of the Party be made permanent. If one is to rule, and to continue ruling, one must be able to dislocate the sense of reality. For the secret of rulership is to combine a belief in one's own infallibility with the power to learn from past mistakes.

It need hardly be said that the subtlest practitioners of *doublethink* are those who invented *doublethink* and know that it is a vast system of mental cheating. In our society, those who have the best knowledge of what is happening are also those who are furthest from seeing the world as it is. In general, the greater the understanding, the greater the delusion: the more intelligent, the less sane. One clear illustration of this is the fact that war hysteria increases in intensity as one rises in the social scale. Those whose attitude toward the war is most nearly rational are the subject peoples of the disputed territories. To these people the war is simply a continuous calamity which sweeps to and fro over their bodies like a tidal wave. Which side is winning is a matter of complete indifference to them. They are aware that a change of overlordship means simply that they will be doing the same work as before for new masters who treat them in the same manner as the old ones. The slightly more favored workers whom we call "the proles" are only intermittently conscious of the war. When it is necessary they can be prodded into frenzies of fear and hatred, but when left to themselves they are capable of forgetting for long periods that the war is happening. It is in the ranks of the Party, and above all of the Inner Party, that the true war enthusiasm is found. World-conquest is believed in most firmly by those who know it to be impossible. This peculiar linking-together of opposites—knowledge with ignorance, cynicism with fanaticism—is one of the chief distinguishing marks of Oceanic society. The official ideology abounds with contradictions even where there is no practical reason for them. Thus, the Party rejects and vilifies every principle for which the Socialist movement originally stood, and it chooses to do this in the name of Socialism. It preaches a contempt for the working class unexampled for centuries past, and it dresses its members in a uniform which was at one time peculiar to manual workers and was adopted for that reason. It systematically undermines the solidarity of the family, and it calls its leader by a name which is a direct appeal to the sentiments of family loyalty. Even the names of the four Ministries by which we are governed exhibit a sort of impudence in their deliberate reversal of the facts. The Ministry of Peace concerns itself with war, the Ministry of Truth with lies, the Ministry of Love with torture, and the Ministry of Plenty with starvation. These contradictions are not accidental, nor do they result from ordinary hypocrisy: they are deliberate exercises in *doublethink*. For it is only by reconciling contradictions that power can be retained indefinitely. In no other way could the ancient cycle be broken. If human equality is to be forever averted—if the High, as we have called them, are to keep their places permanently—then the prevailing mental condition must be controlled insanity.

But there is one question which until this moment we have almost ignored: It is: *why* should human equality be averted? Supposing that the mechanics of the process have been rightly described, what is the motive for this huge, accurately planned effort to freeze history at a particular moment of time?

Here we reach the central secret. As we have seen, the mystique of the Party, and above all of the Inner Party, depends upon *doublethink*. But deeper than this lies the original motive, the never-questioned instinct that first led to the seizure of power and brought *doublethink*, the Thought Police, continuous warfare, and all the other necessary paraphernalia into existence afterwards. This motive really consists. . . .

93 Inaugural Address, January 20, 1961

JOHN FITZGERALD KENNEDY

The Inaugural Address of John F. Kennedy will long be remembered as one of the most eloquent and inspiring statements of modern American values. It was delivered at a time when there was doubt, uncertainty, confusion, and skepticism concerning the values in which Americans really believe. Within this forbidding context President Kennedy won a worldwide following of enthusiastic admirers, among both young and old, for the idealism expressed here.

We observe today not a victory of party, but a celebration of freedom—symbolizing an end, as well as a beginning—signifying renewal, as well as change. For I have sworn before you and Almighty God the same solemn oath our forebears prescribed nearly a century and three quarters ago.

The world is very different now. For man holds in his mortal hands the power to abolish all forms of human poverty and all forms of human life. And yet the same revolutionary beliefs for which our forebears fought are still at issue around the globe—the belief that the rights of man come not from the generosity of the state, but from the hand of God.

We dare not forget today that we are the heirs of that first revolution. Let the word go forth from this time and place, to friend and foe alike, that the torch has been passed to a new generation of Americans—born in this century, tempered by war, disciplined by a hard and bitter peace, proud of our ancient heritage—and unwilling to witness or permit the slow undoing of those human rights to which this Nation has always been committed, and to which we are committed today at home and around the world.

Let every nation know, whether it

SOURCE: *Inaugural Address of President John Fitzgerald Kennedy, January 20, 1961,* Doc. No. 9, 87th Cong., 1st Sess. • John Fitzgerald Kennedy (1917–1963) was president of the United States from 1961 to 1963. He had served in both houses of Congress between 1947 and 1961. He was the author of *Why England Slept, Strategy of Peace, To Turn the Tide,* and *Profiles in Courage,* which was awarded the Pulitzer Prize for biography in 1957.

wishes us well or ill, that we shall pay any price, bear any burden, meet any hardship, support any friend, oppose any foe, in order to assure the survival and the success of liberty.

This much we pledge—and more.

To those old allies whose cultural and spiritual origins we share, we pledge the loyalty of faithful friends. United, there is little we cannot do in a host of cooperative ventures. Divided, there is little we can do—for we dare not meet a powerful challenge at odds and split asunder.

To those new States whom we welcome to the ranks of the free, we pledge our words that one form of colonial control shall not have passed away merely to be replaced by a far greater iron tyranny. We shall not always expect to find them supporting our view. But we shall always hope to find them strongly supporting their own freedom—and to remember that, in the past, those who foolishly sought power by riding the back of the tiger ended up inside.

To those peoples in the huts and villages across the globe struggling to break the bonds of mass misery, we pledge our best efforts to help them help themselves, for whatever period is required—not because the Communists may be doing it, not because we seek their votes, but because it is right. If a free society cannot help the many who are poor, it cannot save the few who are rich.

To our sister republics south of our border, we offer a special pledge—to convert our good words into good deeds, in a new alliance for progress, to assist free men and free governments in casting off the chains of poverty. But this peaceful revolution of hope cannot become the prey of hostile powers. Let all our neighbors know that we shall join with them to oppose aggression or subversion anywhere in the Americas. And let every other power know that this hemisphere intends to remain the master of its own house.

To that world assembly of sovereign states, the United Nations, our last best hope in an age where the instruments of war have far outpaced the instruments of peace, we renew our pledge of support—to prevent it from becoming merely a forum for invective—to strengthen its shield of the new and the weak—and to enlarge the area in which its writ may run.

Finally, to those nations who would make themselves our adversary, we offer not a pledge but a request: that both sides begin anew the quest for peace, before the dark powers of destruction unleashed by science engulf all humanity in planned or accidental self-destruction.

We dare not tempt them with weakness. For only when our arms are sufficient beyond doubt can we be certain beyond doubt that they will never be employed.

But neither can two great and powerful groups of nations take comfort from our present course—both sides overburdened by the cost of modern weapons, both rightly alarmed by the steady spread of the deadly atom, yet both racing to alter that uncertain balance of terror that stays the hand of mankind's final war.

So let us begin anew—remembering on both sides that civility is not a sign of weakness, and sincerity is always subject to proof. *Let us never negotiate out of fear. But let us never fear to negotiate.*

Let both sides explore what problems unite us instead of laboring those problems which divide us.

Let both sides, for the first time, formulate serious and precise proposals for the inspection and control of arms—and bring the absolute power to destroy other nations under the absolute control of all nations.

Let both sides seek to invoke the wonders of science instead of its terrors. Together let us explore the stars, conquer the deserts, eradicate disease, tap the ocean depths, and encourage the arts and commerce.

Let both sides unite to heed in all corners of the earth the command of Isaiah—to "undo the heavy burdens and to let the oppressed go free."

And if a beachhead of cooperation may push back the jungle of suspicion, let both sides join in creating a new endeavor, not a new balance of power, but a new world of law, where the strong are just and the weak secure and the peace preserved.

All this will not be finished in the first 100 days. Nor will it be finished in the first 1,000 days, nor in the life of this administration, nor even perhaps in our lifetime on this planet. But let us begin.

In your hands, my fellow citizens, more than in mine, will rest the final success or failure of our course. Since this country was founded, each generation of Americans has been summoned to give testimony to its national loyalty. The graves of young Americans who answered the call to service are found around the globe.

Now the trumpet summons us again—not as a call to bear arms, though arms we need; not as a call to battle, though embattled we are; but a call to bear the burden of a long twilight struggle, year in, and year out, "rejoicing in hope, patient in tribulation"—a struggle against the common enemies of man: tyranny, poverty, disease, and war itself.

Can we forge against these enemies a grand and global alliance, North and South, East and West, that can assure a more fruitful life for all mankind? Will you join in that historic effort?

In the long history of the world, only a few generations have been granted the role of defending freedom in its hour of maximum danger. I do not shrink from this responsibility—I welcome it. I do not believe that any of us would exchange places with any other people or any other generation. The energy, the faith, the devotion which we bring to this endeavor will light our country and all who serve it—and the glow from that fire can truly light the world.

And so, my fellow Americans, ask not what your country can do for you: Ask what you can do for your country.

My fellow citizens of the world: Ask not what America will do for you, but what together we can do for the freedom of man.

Finally, whether you are citizens of America or citizens of the world, ask of us the same high standards of strength and sacrifice which we ask of you. With a good conscience our only sure reward, with history the final judge of our deeds, let us go forth to lead the land we love, asking His blessing and His help, but knowing that here on earth God's work must truly be our own.

EPILOGUE

SOCIOLOGY AND EDUCATION FOR ACTION

PERSPECTIVES OF JAMES W. NEWTON, GEORGE WALD, KENNETH E. BOULDING, AND JOHN PLATT

This book opened with a "prologue," in which emphasis was given to the fact that the study of sociology is not only useful for earning a living but also deserves to be recognized as a humanistic study. We end the book with an "epilogue," focusing on some of the current social issues about which sociology should have something to say. For it is our belief that sociology should not only play a part in producing the occupationally proficient man and the broadly knowledgeable and contemplative man but also should help to produce the concerned and "active" man—one who sees injustice and attempts to rectify it, one who recognizes errors in judgment made by his society and has the intelligence and fortitude to apply the appropriate corrections; one who has the capacity to distinguish the "truly important" from the "merely urgent" and has the skill to act on this distinction. It is with the specific intent of arousing a sense of these matters and the role that sociology does and could play in connection with them that these last four selections have been included.

We early realized, of course, that we could make up an entire book of articles dealing with significant social concerns of which we were cognizant and on which we felt intelligent and rigorous stands should be taken. After lengthy and sometimes heated discussions, however, we settled on the four that follow. There was, however, one aspect of our current human dilemma which we especially would have wished to include if we could have but found exactly what we sought. Missing here, because of our failure to find what we desired, is a vivid illustration of a too-seldom recognized aspect of the price we pay for engaging in such a war as that in Southeast Asia—a price not only in bodies broken and lives lost, not only in natural resources wasted and lands devastated, not these alone but a price in a socialization to violence that can permanently brutalize and train the mind to view whole peoples as less than human and therefore as "objects" to be destroyed. Failing to find exactly what we wanted as an illustration of this point, even after repeated efforts, we can only state the idea here and hope that our point is clear and our assessment of its tragedy unmistakable.*

*See Richard Hammer, *One Morning in the War: The Tragedy at Son My* (New York: Coward-McCann, 1970). See also Neil Sheehan, "Should We Have War Crime Trials?" *New York Times Book Review*, March 28, 1971, pp. 1–3, 30–34.

SOURCE: James W. Newton, "Valedictory Address for the Class of 1968." This paper is published in this volume for the first time by permission of James W. Newton. • James Newton is Assistant Peace Education Secretary for the American Friends Service Committee's Pacific Southwest region. In 1964 he was awarded the George Washington Honor Medal Award from the Freedoms Foundation at Valley Forge for "helping to bring about a better understanding of the American way of life." He was instrumental in forming the Dartmouth Peace Committee and in establishing a draft information center and a college sponsored draft counseling service. His major interests include attitude change, nonverbal communication, and the social structuring of individual reality.

MR. NEWTON (A)

We of the Class of 1968 are gathered here today in order that we may properly take leave of Dartmouth College.

Dressed in the gowns of tradition, we will cross the platform to collect our certificates of success. Then, having completed the rites of passage, we will go our many separate ways. What has been Dartmouth College will be for us memories of road trips and snowball fights, Winter Carnivals and term papers, visits from George Wallace and Stokely Carmichael. These and other memories will stay with us, as we live and act in a larger society.

But it seems to me that there is a paradoxical element in the education we have received at Dartmouth. Through our highly qualified faculty and our fine facilities, we have been given the opportunity to develop our minds and stock them with funds of knowledge. Yet our location in the wilderness, for all its virtues, may have shielded us from some of the main currents of life in our society. I would suggest that our liberal education, in the absence of a prolonged confrontation with social reality, may suffer from a serious inadequacy; it may obscure a vital link between our knowledge and its relevance to the world beyond Dartmouth College. . . .

It is traditional for a valedictory speaker to talk of the mingled nostalgia, exhilaration and apprehension he and his fellow graduates experience as they anticipate crossing the threshold into the larger society. A Dartmouth man should look forward to a full life in his post-college years. He should expect to do graduate work or get a promising job, see lots of women and, maybe, travel abroad for a while. Then he may raise a family and settle down in a comfortable suburban home with a three-car garage and a little place out back where he can protect his motor boat from the snows of winter. Such expectations may have been realistic once, but for most of us in the Class of 1968 they are daydreams.

They are daydreams because the larger society we will enter is in turmoil. For us, the act of commencement is tainted with a nightmare vision of smoking cities policed by soldiers, of silent factories, and of empty stores. These are our own American cities we envision, and they are the cities of the people whom we have made the victims of our "protection" abroad. Our powerful, complex American society trembles before the threat that the cancerous injustices it has tolerated so long may now destroy it from within. We who graduate today are the citizens who must resolve the injustices of the nation we shall inherit. We shall also be called to wear the khaki of the soldier who puts his airborne torch to foreign cities; cities he is told to destroy in order that they may be saved. We fool ourselves if we think we can build our own society and destroy a foreign nation at the same time.

Of the many pressing domestic needs we face, I believe it is most crucial that we respond to the needs of our oppressed black, tan and red minorities. Having suffered intolerably under the burden of discrimination, they are now prepared to thrust it from their shoulders. We white elite may make that difficult for them, or we may lend our shoulders to the burden and help to cast it away—but with us or in spite of us, it *will* be gotten rid of.

Let us be clear that we must either promote or oppose this process, but we cannot be neutral. There is no option of noninvolvement today. All of us, regardless of the colors of our skins, are constituent elements of the established society that has institutionalized oppression. Those of you who are nonwhites know this with the certainty of experience, and you are acting accordingly. We who are white must also realize that to evade the responsibility of reform is to passively aggravate the conditions that must be transformed if this society is to be worth living in. In the words of the National Advisory Commission on Civil Disorders:

> "Segregation and poverty have created in the racial ghetto a destructive environment totally unknown to most white Americans.
>
> What white Americans have never fully understood—but what the Negro can never forget—is that white society is deeply implicated in the ghetto. White institutions created it, white institutions maintain it, and white society condones it."

Surely it must be apparent to us, as highly educated people, that the domestic problems we face today are of compelling urgency. They are radically different from the problems faced by past generations of Americans, and so they demand radically new solutions—solutions that aim at their roots. Had our nation adopted the programs urged by students of minority group relations forty years ago—and those programs were radical in their day—we might now be graduating into a very different society. I quote again from the report of the National Advisory Commission on Civil Disorders:

> "This is our basic conclusion: Our nation is moving toward two societies, one black, one white—separate and unequal.
>
> To pursue our present course will involve the continuing polarization of the American community and, ultimately, the destruction of basic democratic values.
>
> The alternative . . . is the realization of common opportunities for all within a single society.
>
> This alternative will require a commitment to national action—compassionate, massive and sustained, backed by the resources of the most powerful and the richest nation on this earth. From every American it will require new attitudes, new understanding, and above all, new will."

There is no question but that America has at her disposal the material and financial resources that a national commitment to the goals of social justice would require. We here can bring our educated minds, our youthful energy, and our determined wills to the endeavor. We can transform our society, but we can do so only if we are able to stop the present destructive mischanneling of our talents, our resources, and ourselves. The national effort for which we and others of our age are manipulated makes "niggers" of us all, regardless of the colors of our skins. I refer, of course, to the Asian war that has begun in Vietnam.

Most of us who graduate today will find that our career plans, our graduate educations, and our attempts to respond to the needs of this nation will be interrupted by a notice to report for induction into the Armed Forces of this country. Many of those drafted will be ordered to join in the military effort in Asia. I urge you to make the fullest use of the academic skills you have gained at Dartmouth College before you accept that governmental imperative. Study the history of the Vietnam war, and study its conduct. Study the impact it is having on Asian societies, on Asian attitudes toward America, and on America's conception of herself. Men of the Class of 1968, educated men, Dartmouth men, before you set off to participate in the devastation of that small country, Vietnam, and to risk your lives into the bargain, consider what you are about.

As you study this war I believe you will become convinced, as I am convinced, that it is more than an accident, or a freak accumulation of mistakes. It is the inevitable fruit of an international policy aimed at maintaining an oppressive status quo. It is my conclusion that the Vietnam war is a colossal stupidity, a vast international atrocity, and an expensive lesson in the futility of modern aggressive imperialism—for, thank God, we are losing that war. The battles we claim to be winning have moved from the countryside to Saigon itself, where we feel forced to "protect" the people by firing rockets and cannons at their homes.

These are sad, shocking things to say, and I do not say them lightly. I say them in the spirit of President John Sloan Dickey's 1961 Convocation Address. The President said on that occasion that "we must reckon with the fact that it will not profit America to 'win' any struggle if thereby as a nation we lost our character, or as the Bible would put it, our soul," and he expressed his conviction that an American "success" in the Bay of Pigs invasion would have been a great tragedy for this nation.

Before you answer the call to fight, think well of what this war means for America. It underscores the words our honored alumnus, Daniel Webster, spoke in 1811: ". . . a free government, with an uncontrolled power of military conscription, is a solecism, at once the most ridiculous and abominable that ever entered into the head of man." Begun and maintained on a platform of official falsehood, the war has taught us to speak cynically of a "credibility gap" between ourselves and the men who by tradition and by law should represent us honestly and honestly inform us of their actions. It drains from our land the wealth that should provide hospitals, schools and homes, making a farce of progressive domestic legislation. In truth, the short-range profits that derive from a war-time economy are deceptively attractive, for in the long run a society pays dearly for its investments in wars.

Men of the Class of 1968, educated men, Dartmouth men, use the skills that you have gained here as you plan your courses of action. We must find our places in an on-going universal struggle for freedom and human dignity. I urge you to refuse to fight in Vietnam when that call comes to you. Take the path that seems appropriate for you. It may be conscientious objection, draft resistance, or escape to a country of greater freedom in the north. Those of you in ROTC and those of you who believe we must maintain a standing army for defense may face the much more difficult path of refusing to comply with an order to go to Vietnam. But whatever you do, I pray that you will not sacrifice your minds and your bodies in the service of this ignoble cause.

My friends, we cannot win hearts and minds through brutal coercion, nor can we hide the ugly sight of social injustice beneath a wave of uniforms. The society we seek at home and the cooperative world we must have can come only through the commitment of our talents and our resources to the tasks of peaceful, constructive change. We must make that commitment our own.

MR. WALD (B)

All of you know that in the last couple of years there has been student unrest breaking at times into violence in many parts of the world: in England, Germany, Italy, Spain, Mexico and needless to say, in many parts of this country. There has been a great deal of discussion as to what it all means. Perfectly clearly it means something different in Mexico from what it does in France, and something different in France from what it does in Tokyo, and something different in Tokyo from what it does in this country. Yet unless

SOURCE: George Wald, "A Generation in Search of a Future," *The Boston Globe* (March 8, 1969). Reprinted by permission of the author and publisher. • George Wald is professor of biology at Harvard University and in 1967 received the Nobel Prize for Medicine. His major interests include the chemistry and physiology of vision and biochemical evolution. He is coauthor of *General Education in a Free Society* and *Twenty-Six Afternoons of Biology*.

we are to assume that students have gone crazy all over the world, or that they have just decided that it's the thing to do, there must be some common meaning.

I don't need to go so far afield to look for that meaning. I am a teacher, and at Harvard, I have a class of about 350 students—men and women—most of them freshmen and sophomores. Over these past few years I have felt increasingly that something is terribly wrong—and this year ever so much more than last. Something has gone sour, in teaching and in learning. It's almost as though there were a widespread feeling that education has become irrelevant.

A lecture is much more of a dialogue than many of you probably appreciate. As you lecture, you keep watching the faces; and information keeps coming back to you all the time. I began to feel, particularly this year, that I was missing much of what was coming back. I tried asking the students, but they didn't or couldn't help me very much.

But I think I know what's the matter, even a little better than they do. I think that this whole generation of students is beset with a profound uneasiness. I don't think that they have yet quite defined its source. I think I understand the reasons for their uneasiness even better than they do. What is more, I share their uneasiness.

What's bothering those students? Some of them tell you it's the Vietnam War. I think the Vietnam War is the most shameful episode in the whole of American history. The concept of War Crimes is an American invention. We've committed many War Crimes in Vietnam; but I'll tell you something interesting about that. We were committing War Crimes in World War II, even before the Nuremberg trials were held and the principle of war crimes stated. The saturation bombing of German cities was a War Crime. Dropping atom bombs on Hiroshima and Nagasaki was a War Crime. If we had lost the war, some of our leaders might have had to answer for those actions.

I've gone through all of that history lately, and I find that there's a gimmick in it. It isn't written out, but I think we established it by precedent. That gimmick is that if one can allege that one is repelling or retaliating for an *aggression*—after that everything goes. And you see we are living in a world in which all wars are wars of defense. All War Departments are now Defense Departments. This is all part of the double talk of our time. The aggressor is always on the other side. And I suppose this is why our ex-Secretary of State, Dean Rusk—a man in whom repetition takes the place of reason, and stubbornness takes the place of character—went to such pains to insist, as he still insists, that in Vietnam we are repelling an aggression. And if that's what we are doing—so runs the doctrine—anything goes. If the concept of war crimes is ever to mean anything, they will have to be defined as categories of acts, regardless of alleged provocation. But that isn't so now.

I think we've lost that war, as a lot of other people think, too. The Vietnamese have a secret weapon. It's their willingness to die, beyond our willingness to kill. In effect they've been saying, you can kill us, but you'll have to kill a lot of us, you may have to kill all of us. And thank heavens, we are not yet ready to do that.

Yet we have come a long way—far enough to sicken many Americans, far enough even to sicken our fighting men. Far enough so that our national symbols have gone sour. How many of you can sing about "the rockets' red glare, bombs bursting in air" without thinking, those are *our* bombs and *our* rockets bursting over South Vietnamese villages? When those words were written, we were a people struggling for freedom against oppression. Now we are supporting real or thinly disguised military dictatorships all over the world, helping them to control and repress peoples struggling for their freedom.

But that Vietnam War, shameful and terrible as it is, seems to me only an immediate incident in a much larger and more stubborn situation.

Part of my trouble with students is that almost all the students I teach were born since World War II. Just after World War II, a series of new and abnormal procedures came into American life. We regarded them at the time as temporary aberrations. We thought we would get back to normal American life some day. But those procedures have stayed with us now for more than 20 years, and those students of mine have never known anything else. They think those things are normal. Students think we've always had a Pentagon, that we have always had a big army, and that we always had a draft. But those are all new things in American life; and I think that they are incompatible with what America meant before.

How many of you realize that just before World War II the entire American army including the Air Force numbered 139,000 men? Then World War II started, but we weren't yet in it; and seeing that there was great trouble in the world, we doubled this army to 268,000 men. Then in World War II it got to be 8 million. And then World War II came to an end, and we prepared to go back to a peacetime army somewhat as the American army had always been before. And indeed in 1950—you think about 1950, our international commitments, the Cold War, the Truman Doctrine, and all the rest of it—in 1950 we got down to 600,000 men.

Now we have 3.5 million men under arms: about 600,000 in Vietnam, about 300,000 more in "support areas" elsewhere in the Pacific, about 250,000 in Germany. And there are a lot at home. Some months ago we were told that 300,000 National Guardsmen and 200,000 reservists—some half a million men—had been specially trained for riot duty in the cities.

I say the Vietnam War is just an immediate incident, because so long as we keep that big an army, it will always find things to do. If the Vietnam War stopped tomorrow, with that big a military establishment, the chances are that we would be in another such adventure abroad or at home before you knew it.

As for the draft: Don't reform the draft —get rid of it.

A peacetime draft is the most un-American thing I know. All the time I was growing up I was told about oppressive Central European countries and Russia, where young men were forced into the army; and I was told what they did about it. They chopped off a finger, or shot off a couple of toes; or better still, if they could manage it, they came to this country. And we understood that, and sympathized, and were glad to welcome them.

Now by present estimates four to six thousand Americans of draft age have left this country for Canada, another two or three thousand have gone to Europe, and it looks as though many more are preparing to emigrate.

A few months ago I received a letter from the Harvard Alumni Bulletin posing a series of questions that students might ask a professor involving what to do about the draft. I was asked to write what I would tell those students. All I had to say to those students was this: If any of them had decided to evade the draft and asked my help, I would help him in any way I could. I would feel as

I suppose members of the underground railway felt in pre-Civil War days, helping runaway slaves to get to Canada. It wasn't altogether a popular position then; but what do you think of it now?

A bill to stop the draft was recently introduced in the Senate (S. 503), sponsored by a group of senators that ran the gamut from McGovern and Hatfield to Barry Goldwater. I hope it goes through; but any time I find that Barry Goldwater and I are in agreement, that makes me take another look.

And indeed there are choices in getting rid of the draft. I think that when we get rid of the draft, we must also cut back the size of the armed forces. It seems to me that in peacetime a total of one million men is surely enough. If there is an argument for American military forces of more than one million men in peacetime, I should like to hear that argument debated.

There is another thing being said closely connected with this: that to keep an adequate volunteer army, one would have to raise the pay considerably. That's said so positively and often that people believe it. I don't think it is true.

The great bulk of our present armed forces are genuine volunteers. Among first-term enlistments, 49 percent are true volunteers. Another 30 percent are so-called "reluctant volunteers," persons who volunteer under pressure of the draft. Only 21 percent are draftees. All re-enlistments, of course are true volunteers.

So the great majority of our present armed forces are true volunteers. Whole services are composed entirely of volunteers: the Air Force for example, the Navy, almost all the Marines. That seems like proof to me that present pay rates are adequate. One must add that an Act of Congress in 1967 raised the base pay throughout the services in three installments, the third installment still to come, on April 1, 1969. So it is hard to understand why we are being told that to maintain adequate armed services on a volunteer basis will require large increases in pay; that they will cost an extra $17 billion per year. It seems plain to me that we can get all the armed forces we need as volunteers, and at present rates of pay.

But there is something ever so much bigger and more important than the draft. That bigger thing, of course, is the militarization of our country. Ex-President Eisenhower warned us of what he called the military-industrial complex. I am sad to say that we must begin to think of it now as the military-industrial-labor union complex. What happened under the plea of the Cold War was not alone that we built up the first big peace time army in our history, but we institutionalized it. We built, I suppose, the biggest government building in our history to run it, and we institutionalized it.

I don't think we can live with the present military establishment and its $80 billion a year budget, and keep America anything like we have known it in the past. It is corrupting the life of the whole country. It is buying up everything in sight: industries, banks, investors, universities; and lately it seems also to have bought up the labor unions.

The Defense Department is always broke; but some of the things they do with that $80 billion a year would make Buck Rogers envious. For example: the Rocky Mountain Arsenal on the outskirts of Denver was manufacturing a deadly nerve poison on such a scale that there was a problem of waste disposal. Nothing daunted, they dug a tunnel two miles deep under Denver, into which they have injected so much poisoned water that beginning a couple of years ago Denver began to experience a series of earth tremors of increasing severity. Now there is a grave fear of a major earthquake. An interesting debate is in progress as to whether Denver will be safer if that lake of poisoned water is removed or left in place. (*New York Times*, July 4, 1968; *Science*, Sept. 27, 1968.)

Perhaps you have read also of those 6000 sheep that suddenly died in Skull Valley, Utah, killed by another nerve poison—a strange and, I believe, still unexplained accident, since the nearest testing seems to have been 30 miles away.

As for Vietnam, the expenditure of fire power has been frightening. Some of you may still remember Khe Sanh, a hamlet just south of the Demilitarized Zone, where a force of U.S. Marines was beleaguered for a time. During that period we dropped on the perimeter of Khe Sanh more explosives than fell on Japan throughout World War II, and more than fell on the whole of Europe during the years 1942 and 1943.

One of the officers there was quoted as having said afterward, "It looks like the world caught smallpox and died." *New York Times*, Mar. 28, 1968.)

The only point of government is to safeguard and foster life. Our government has become preoccupied with death, with the business of killing and being killed. So-called Defense now absorbs 60 percent of the national budget, and about 12 percent of the Gross National Product.

A lively debate is beginning again on whether or not we should deploy antiballistic missiles, the ABM. I don't have to talk about them, everyone else here is doing that. But I should like to mention a curious circumstance. In September, 1967, or about 1½ years ago, we had a meeting of M.I.T. and Harvard people, including experts on these matters, to talk about whether anything could be done to block the Sentinel system, the deployment of ABM's. Everyone present thought them undesirable; but a few of the most knowledgeable persons took what seemed to be the practical view, "Why fight about a dead issue? It has been decided, the funds have been appropriated. Let's go on from there."

Well, fortunately, it's not a dead issue.

An ABM is a nuclear weapon. It takes a nuclear weapon to stop a nuclear weapon. And our concern must be with the whole issue of nuclear weapons.

There is an entire semantics ready to deal with the sort of thing I am about to say. It involves such phrases as "those are the facts of life." No—they are the facts of death. I don't accept them, and I advise you not to accept them. We are under repeated pressure to accept things that are presented to us as settled—decisions that have been made. Always there is the thought: let's go on from there! But this time we don't see how to go on. We will have to stick with those issues.

We are told that the United States and Russia between them have by now stockpiled in nuclear weapons approximately the explosive power of 15 tons of TNT for every man, woman and child on earth. And now it is suggested that we must make more. All very regrettable, of course; but those are "the facts of life." We really would like to disarm; but our new Secretary of Defense has made the ingenious proposal that now is the time to greatly increase our nuclear armaments so that we can disarm from a position of strength.

I think all of you know there is no adequate defense against massive nuclear attack. It is both easier and cheaper to circumvent any known nuclear defense system than to provide it. It's all pretty crazy. At the very moment we talk of deploying ABM's, we are also building the MIRV, the weapon to circumvent ABM's.

So far as I know, the most conservative estimates of Americans killed in a major nuclear attack, with everything working as well as can be hoped and all foreseeable precautions taken, run to about 50 millions. We have become callous to gruesome statistics, and this seems at first to be only another gruesome statistic. You think, Bang!—and next morning, if you're still there, you read in the newspapers that 50 million people were killed.

But that isn't the way it happens. When we killed close to 200,000 people with those first little, old-fashioned uranium bombs that we dropped on Hiroshima and Nagasaki, about the same number of persons was maimed, blinded, burned, poisoned and otherwise doomed. A lot of them took a long time to die.

That's the way it would be. Not a bang, and a certain number of corpses to bury; but a nation filled with millions of helpless, maimed, tortured and doomed persons, and the survivors of a nuclear holocaust will be huddled with their families in shelters, with guns ready to fight off their neighbors, trying to get some uncontaminated food and water.

A few months ago Sen. Richard Russell of Georgia ended a speech in the Senate with the words: "If we have to start over again with another Adam and Eve, I want them to be Americans; and I want them on this continent and not in Europe." That was a United States senator holding a patriotic speech. Well, here is a Nobel Laureate who thinks that those words are criminally insane. (Prolonged applause.)

How real is the threat of full-scale nuclear war? I have my own very inexpert idea, but realizing how little I know and fearful that I may be a little paranoid on this subject, I take every opportunity to ask reputed experts. I asked that question of a very distinguished professor of government at Harvard about a month ago. I asked him what sort of odds he would lay on the possibility of full-scale nuclear war within the foreseeable future. "Oh," he said comfortably, "I think I can give you a pretty good answer to that question. I estimate the probability of full-scale nuclear war, provided that the situation remains about as it is now, at 2 percent per year." Anybody can do the simple calculation that shows that 2 percent per year means that the chance of having that full-scale nuclear war by 1990 is about one in three, and by 2000 it is about 50-50.

I think I know what is bothering the students. I think that what we are up against is a generation that is by no means sure that it has a future.

I am growing old, and my future so to speak is already behind me. But there are those students of mine who are in my mind always; and there are my children, two of them now 7 and 9, whose future is infinitely more precious to me than my own. So it isn't just their generation; it's mine too. We're all in it together.

Are we to have a chance to live? We don't ask for prosperity, or security; only for a reasonable chance to live, to work out our destiny in peace and decency. Not to go down in history as the apocalyptic generation.

And it isn't only nuclear war. Another overwhelming threat is the population explosion. That has not yet even begun to come under control. There is every indication that the world population will double before the year 2000; and there is a widespread expectation of famine on an unprecedented scale in many parts of the world. The experts tend to differ only in the estimates of when those famines will begin. Some think by 1980, others think they can be staved off until 1990, very few expect that they will not occur by the year 2000.

That is the problem. Unless we can be surer than we now are that this generation has a future, nothing else matters. It's not good enough to give it tender loving care, to supply it with breakfast foods, to buy it expensive educations. Those things don't mean anything unless this generation has a future. And we're not sure that it does.

I don't think that there are problems of youth, or student problems. All the real problems I know are grown-up problems.

Perhaps you will think me altogether absurd, or "academic," or hopelessly innocent—that is, until you think of the alternatives—if I say as I do to you now: we have to get rid of those nuclear weapons. There is nothing worth having that can be obtained by nuclear war: nothing material or ideological, no tradition that it can defend. It is utterly self-defeating. Those atom bombs represent an unusable weapon. The only use for an atom bomb is to keep somebody else from using one. It can give us no protection, but only the doubtful satisfaction of retaliation. Nuclear weapons offer us nothing but a balance of terror; and a balance of terror is still terror.

We have to get rid of those atomic weapons, here and everywhere. We cannot live with them.

I think we've reached a point of great decision, not just for our nation, not only for all humanity, but for life upon the Earth. I tell my students, with a feeling of pride that I hope they will share, that the carbon, nitrogen and oxygen that make up 99 percent of our living substance, were cooked in the deep interiors of earlier generations of dying stars. Gathered up from the ends of the universe, over billions of years, eventually they came to form in part the substance of our sun, its planets and ourselves. Three billion years ago life arose upon the Earth. It seems to be the only life in the solar system. Many a star has since been born and died.

About two million years ago, man appeared. He has become the dominant species on the Earth. All other living things, animal and plant, live by his sufferance. He is the custodian of life on Earth. It's a big responsibility.

The thought that we're in competition with Russians or with Chinese is all a mistake, and trivial. Only mutual destruction lies that way. We are one species, with a world to win. There's life all over this universe, but in all the universe we are the only men.

Our business is with life, not death. Our challenge is to give what account we can of what becomes of life in the solar system, this corner of the universe that is our home and, most of all, what becomes of men—all men of all nations, colors and creeds. It has become one world, a world for all men. It is only such a world that now can offer us life and the chance to go on.

MR. BOULDING (C)

When we talk about preventing something we imply two things. We imply, first, that there is a dynamic system which is now proceeding that, if allowed to proceed unchanged, will result in an event which is regarded as undesirable and which, therefore, we want to prevent. We imply also that it is possible to

SOURCE: Kenneth E. Boulding, "The Prevention of World War III," *The Virginia Quarterly Review*, vol. 38, no. 1 (Winter 1962), 1–12. Reprinted by permission of the author and the publisher. • The author is professor of economics at the University of Colorado. He has served as Research Director of The Center for Research in Conflict Resolution and as past president of the American Economic Association. His major interests include general economic theory, economic development, and agricultural economics. Among his many published works are *Economics of Peace, Disarmament and the Economy, The Meaning of the 20th Century,* and *The Impact of the Social Sciences.*

change the dynamic system in question and replace it by another dynamic system in which the unwanted event does not occur. Thus, suppose we find ourselves driving towards a railroad crossing and suddenly we see the red lights flashing and a train approaching. Our dynamic system at the moment consists simply of velocity and direction. We are proceeding, say at 50 miles per hour, towards the crossing. The distant early warning system of our eyes informs us the crossing is dangerous. The knowledge which we have of our existing dynamic system informs us that if it continues we will arrive at the crossing at the precise moment when the train is there. The combination of a distant information system coupled with the simple dynamics of automobiles enables us, however, to prevent the disaster. We do this by putting on the brakes long before we get to the crossing. This in effect changes the dynamic system under which we have been operating. It introduces a new variable into it, indeed a new dimension, deceleration. Because of this, we are able to prevent the disaster, as we are able to avoid simultaneous occupancy of the crossing by ourselves and the train.

We must be careful, of course, in applying the analogy of a simple psychomechanical system like a man driving a car to the enormous complexities and uncertainties of the international system. However, the international system is still a system, even though it has important random elements in it. Because it is not entirely random, it has elements of predictability. One of the greatest difficulties lies precisely in the stochastic nature of the system. We are driving a car, as it were, that may or may not respond to brakes according to whether dice held by the driver indicate "respond" or "fail." The situation is made all the more difficult by the fact that we face here a stochastic system with a very small universe, that is, a very small number of cases. Stochastic systems with a large number of cases can be treated by the theory of probability. We have a pretty fair idea, for instance, how many people are going to die in automobile accidents next year, although we do not know exactly who they are.

The problem of reducing the total number of automobile accidents is a very different kind of problem from the one that faces the driver of the preceding paragraph. Nevertheless, even with our present knowledge it would not be difficult to design an automobile and a road system which would kill, let us say, 20,000 people a year instead of 40,000. What we would be doing here would be to reduce the probability of disaster on the part of a single individual. It is by no means impossible to think of the international system in a rather similar way, and to talk about the things we can do to reduce the probability of disaster. What we mean by this is that if we had a very large number of planets roughly identical with our own we could postulate changes in the system which would reduce the number of cases in which disaster occurred. This would be the analogue of treating road deaths as a public health problem and seeking to reduce their probability. As far as we know, however, we do not have a large number of planets like ours and for our purposes at least there is only one. Hence, reducing the probability of disaster does us very little good if the disaster actually occurs. The problem of stochastic systems with a small number of cases has received insufficient attention in the theoretical literature. It is precisely this kind of system, however, with which we have to deal in international affairs.

I believe the present international system to be one which has a significant probability built into it of irretrievable disaster for the human race. The longer the number of years we contemplate such a system operating, the larger this probability becomes. I do not know whether in any one year it is one per cent, ten per cent, or even fifty per cent. I feel pretty sure, however, that it is of this order of magnitude, not, shall we say, of the order of magnitude of .01 per cent. The problem of system change, therefore, is urgent and desperate, and we are all in terrible danger. This is largely because of a quantitative change in the parameters of the international system under which we now live. This is still essentially the system of unilateral national defense in spite of the development of the United Nations and certain international organizations. Unilateral national defense is workable only if each nation can be stronger than its potential enemies in its home territory. This is possible under two circumstances. The first is that the nations must be far enough away from each other, and the extent to which their power declines as they operate further away from their own home bases must be sufficiently great. Then each nation can be stronger than the other *at home* with on-the-spot forces because of the fact that in a nation's home territory the enemy operates at a certain disadvantage. There is a second condition, however, which is that each nation must be able to dominate an area around its home base equal in depth to the range of the deadly missile. Because of quantitative changes in these conditions even in the last few years the system of unilateral national defense has become infeasible on a world scale. No nation is now far enough away from potential enemies to be sure that it can dominate even its own territory. Furthermore, the range of the deadly missile is rapidly reaching 12,500 miles, which means that the second condition cannot possibly be fulfilled. The condition which unilateral national defense attempts to establish, therefore, which I call *unconditional viability,* is now no longer possible.

The urgent and desperate nature of the present situation is created by the universality of the disaster with which we are threatened. The system of unilateral national defense has never given permanent security. The rise and fall of nations and empires is a testament to this fact. Indeed, looking with a large historical eye, one may say that unconditional viability has never existed except perhaps for brief periods and the best that unilateral national defense could do for any society was to postpone disaster. The situation of the individual society, that is, is rather analogous to that of the individual, whose life, on this earth at any rate, must also end in irretrievable disaster, that is, in death. Where we have a large number of individuals, however, death for the individual is not death for the race. In fact death for the individual is necessary if the race is to survive. Where the number of individuals becomes smaller and smaller, however, there comes to be a critical point where death for the individual is also death for the race and the irretrievable disaster which the individual suffers is likewise irretrievable disaster for the species. The unilaterally defended national state now seems to me to have got to this state in its development. It is no longer appropriate as a form of organization for the kind of technical society in which we live. Its death throes, however, may destroy the whole human race. The age of civilization out of which we are passing was characterized by a large number of nation-states or independent political organizations practicing unilateral national defense. Because of the large number of these organizations there were always some being born and always some ready to rise into the places of those which suffered disaster. With the number of effectively independent nation-states now reduced to two or perhaps at most three, the possibilities of irretrievable disaster become much greater.

The problem which we face, therefore, is how to effect a system change in the international order, or perhaps we should say the world political order, sufficient to lower the probability of disaster to a tolerable level. The critical problem here might be described as that of "system perception." To revert again to the analogy of the car and the railroad crossing, if the driver of the car does not see that he is approaching the crossing, if the warning lights are not working, and if he cannot see the train approaching, he will naturally not take any steps to avert the disaster. The world problem here is perhaps psychological rather than mechanical. There is a fairly widespread sense abroad of impending doom. The doom, however, is so large that we do not really believe it and we go about our daily actions as if it did not exist. This is the mechanism, as Jerome Frank has pointed out, known to the psychologists as "denial." Up to a point this is actually healthy. We all know that we are going to die sometime and we may die tomorrow; but we act pretty much as if we are going to live forever. We do not spend much time in taking tearful farewells and in writing our last wills and testaments. We plan ahead for months and even for years, in spite of the fact that these plans may never come to fruition. This perfectly legitimate response to uncertainty becomes pathological when it prevents us from taking steps which would postpone disaster or make it less likely. The man who is afraid that he has a cancer but who will not go to a doctor because he might find out that he has one is a good example. Where the prospect of disaster, therefore, is so vague or so uncertain that it merely results in pathological denial, it is necessary to bring the actor to a more realistic appraisal of the system within which he is acting.

If the problem of "denial" is to be overcome, it is necessary to do more than merely scare people with horrendous pictures of the possible future. Indeed, the more horrendous the picture which is drawn, the more it is likely to result in denial and pathological inactivity. The future which faced our driver at the railroad crossing was also horrendous, but instead of denying this and continuing on his way he presumably applied the brakes, that is, initiated a system change. The problem in the international system is that we seem to have no brakes. That is, it is hard for people to visualize the nature of the system change which is necessary for survival. This, then, is one of the major tasks today of the political scientist, the philosopher, the journalist, and the prophet: to give the people an image of changes in the international system which seems small enough to be feasible yet large enough to be successful. It is not useful to picture Utopias which seem utterly unattainable—this perhaps is the main difficulty with the World Federationists—even though the function of Utopias in providing a constant driving force in social dynamics should not be underestimated. The present situation, however, calls not for Utopia, but for political solutions. Indeed, one of our great difficulties today is that we have too many Utopias. We need to think, therefore, in terms of a world social contract: that is, a minimum bargain between the contending parties which will give the world a sufficient system change to relieve it from the intolerable burden which it now bears. This social contract does not even have to be explicit or contractual.

It can begin by being tacit; indeed, one can argue that a world social contract already exists in a tacit embryo form. We can visualize perhaps the following five stages of development.

I. The stage of tacit contract. In systems which have an inherent instability, such as duopoly in the relations of firms, or a bipolar system of mutual deterrence in the relations of states, it is often possible to maintain a quasi-stable position for a long time through tacit contract: that is, through mutually consistent unilateral behavior on the part of each party. A quasi-stable position is like that of an egg on a golf-tee—it is stable for small disturbances but not for large. For considerable periods of time, however, the disturbances may be small enough so that Humpty-Dumpty does not fall. Comes a slightly larger disturbance, however, and all the King's horses and men cannot put him together again. The international system under the Eisenhower administration exhibited this kind of quasi-stability. An important element in that stability was a tacit agreement between the United States and the Soviet Union to do nothing effective about civil defense. We agreed, in effect, that our civilian populations should be mutually exchanged as hostages, for we each had the power to destroy large numbers—at least half—of each other's civilians. This meant that the chance of deliberate nuclear war was very small, though the chance of accidental war was appreciable; indeed, the missiles almost went off on at least two occasions. A natural accident, such as a large meteor, or an electronic breakdown, or a social accident, such as a mad pilot, or a political accident, such as an unwise commitment to an irresponsible third party, could under these circumstances easily set off a mutual exchange of nuclear weapons, so that the system could not be regarded as more than a temporary expedient.

Another example of tacit contract was the mutual suspension of nuclear tests, recently broken by the Soviet Union. Here the fear, perhaps, of world opinion, and the fear also of the technical consequences of an uncontrolled race for technical development of weapons, created a temporary tacit agreement. We have had similar tacit agreements in regard to spheres of influence and intervention in third-party quarrels. The United States did not interfere in Hungary, nor the Soviet Union in Egypt during the Suez crisis. The Russians allowed themselves to be thrown out of the Congo, and are not threatening to be more than a nuisance in Cuba. The conflicts in Korea and Viet Nam were temporarily settled by latitudinal partitions. The Arab-Israeli conflict does not become an arena of the cold war. All these represent systems of mutuality of conduct which might be classified as tacit agreement.

II. The fate of the tacit agreement on nuclear testing, and what looks like the impending fate of the tacit agreement on civil defense, is a testimony to the inherent instability of the tacit agreement in the long run. It is something like the gentleman's agreement in economic competition, which suffers from the defect that not all people are gentlemen. The danger is that in the absence of organization between contending parties their only means of communication is by a "threat system." A threat system, which is characteristic of unilateral national defense, is based on the proposition, "If you do something bad to me I will do something bad to you," by contrast with an exchange system, which is based on "If you do something good to me I will do something good to you." Both systems tend to lead to consummation, but whereas the consummation of exchange is an increase of goods, the consummation of threats is an increase of "bads." War is mainly the result of the depreciation in the credibility of threats in the absence of their consummation; and hence a threat system has a basic instability built into it, which tacit contract may postpone but cannot ultimately avoid. The great problem, therefore, is how to get rid of threat systems. This, I suspect, happens historically mainly by their being overlaid with other systems of relationship—trade, communication, organization—until they fall so much to the bottom of the pile that they are no longer significant.

The essential instability of threat systems and the weakness of tacit agreements, therefore, make it highly desirable to pass into the second stage of formalized agreement, and the building of what might be called "peace-defending" organizational structures. The first of these obviously is an arms control organization designed at first perhaps only to limit the present arms race but capable of the ultimate hope of policing genuine disarmament. We could begin, perhaps, with an organization for the prevention of accidental war. This will be a joint organization of the major armed forces of the world. Once this has been accomplished, a major system change is under way. It is the organizational disunity of the armed forces of the world which constitutes the real threat to humanity. If they were united they might threaten us with a great many disagreeable consequences but they would not threaten us with extinction. An arms control organization, therefore, would be the beginning of a very powerful social change. It would constitute the formal recognition of the fact that unilateral national defense is no longer possible. Once this initial break is made, system change may be expected to take place quite rapidly. It may be that we shall have to look forward to a substantial separation of the armed forces organization from the states which they are supposed to defend, and which they can no longer defend. Just as we solved the problem of religious wars by the separation of church and state, so we may be able to solve the problem of nuclear war by the separation of the armed forces from the state. The plain fact is that today the threat which the armed forces of the world present to their own civilian populations is much greater than any conflict among the nations. Arms control will be the beginning of the recognition of this social fact.

III. Arms control must move fairly rapidly into disarmament; otherwise it will be unstable. The organization of the world armed forces will be a loose and unstable one at first, and it will always threaten to break up. It may be, of course, that the major pressure towards disarmament will come from the economic side. Once the threat of war is removed by arms control and by organizational unity of the world armed forces, the economic burden of maintaining these monstrous establishments will seem intolerable, especially in view of the fact that it is the arms burden (equal to the total income of the poorest half of the human race!) which perhaps prevents the world from really tackling the problem of economic development and which condemns hundreds of millions of people and their descendants to live in misery. One looks forward, therefore, to the third stage of rapid and total disarmament, under the arms control organization. There are many difficult problems involved in this which have not been worked out and on which research desperately needs to be done. These problems, however, are difficult rather than insoluble.

IV. Even universal total disarmament, however, is not enough, for this too is likely to be unstable even though disarmament itself will reduce many of the sources of conflict, especially those which arise out of strategic considerations. It will not eliminate all conflicts by any means. In a world as divided as this, ideologically and economically, we may expect serious conflicts continually to arise. These conflicts will constantly present the temptation to the losing side to resort to violence and to redevelop organized armed forces. If disarmament is to be stable, therefore, there must be a system of conflict control. Conflict control is one of the essential functions of government. It is not, however, the only function. In thinking of world government, this is probably where we ought to begin. In the early stages it is more important to establish conflict control than to establish justice or to solve all social problems. Conflict control as a function of government has been inadequately studied and identified. This is perhaps because the study of conflict systems themselves is still in its infancy. However, this is a rapidly developing body of social science and one hopes that it may be possible in the not-too-distant future to develop a substantial body of knowledge on the identification and control of conflict systems. The problem, of course, is the identification of conflict processes in early stages before they become pathological. There are very difficult problems here in the definition of the pathology of conflict, as this, of course, goes very deep into our value systems. Conflict which is regarded as pathological by one person may not be so regarded by another. If, however, we regard violence as generally a sign of pathological conflict, we may be able to identify the processes of social dynamics which lead towards it, and we may therefore be able to interpose counterweights which will correct these processes. We may revert once more to the analogy of the car at the crossing. We need to develop both perception of dangers ahead and also organizations which can act as brakes. These processes have been fairly well worked out in industrial relations, where a whole profession of mediators and conciliators and personnel experts has come to being. There is no reason why these principles should not be applied in other fields of social life and especially to the conflict of states.

V. The last stage, of course, is true world government, capable not only of controlling conflict but of expressing and developing the common concerns and aims of mankind. At the moment this seems to be a long way off. Fortunately, the prevention of war does not depend, I think, on the establishment of full world government. If the stages of development which I have outlined can be pursued rapidly enough, war may be postponed for longer and longer periods until the postponement becomes indefinite by the establishment of a true world government. We must therefore find halfway houses and quarter-way houses which are moderately habitable. We must not allow Utopian longings to deprive us of political bargains. The actual negotiation of the world social contract is going to be a long and arduous business. We need to put many more resources into this than we are now doing. Nevertheless, there is something here which can be done. There is a road which leads somewhere. If we are to break out of the apathy, irrationality, and despair which beset us, we must gain a vision of that road of escape and make at least one step along it. This is the great significance of the growing movement for peace research. Just as we no longer accept depressions as "acts of God," wholly unpredictable and uncontrollable, so we need no longer accept mass violence as unpredictable and uncontrollable. The fact that we cannot yet predict or control it should stir us to a great intellectual effort in this direction, for this way lies hope. The only unforgivable sin in the present crisis of mankind is despair.

MR. PLATT (D)

Within just the last 25 years, the Western world has moved into an age of jet planes, missiles and satellites, nuclear power and nuclear terror. We have acquired computers and automation, a service and leisure economy, superhighways, super-agriculture, supermedicine, mass higher education, universal TV, oral contraceptives, environmental pollution and urban crises. The rest of the world is also moving rapidly and may catch up with all these powers and problems within a very short time. It is hardly surprising that young people under 30, who have grown up familiar with these things from childhood, have developed very different expectations and concerns from the older generation that grew up in another world.

What many people do not realize is that many of these technological changes are now approaching certain natural limits. The "S-curve" is beginning to level off. We may never have faster communications or more TV or larger weapons or a higher level of danger than we have now. This means that if we could learn how to manage these new powers and problems in the next few years without killing ourselves by our obsolete structures and behavior, we might be able to create new and more effective social structures that would last for many generations. We might be able to move into that new world of abundance and diversity and well-being for all mankind which technology has now made possible.

The trouble is that we may not survive these next few years. The human race today is like a rocket on a launching pad. We have been building up to this moment of take-off for a long time, and if we can get safely through the take-off period, we may fly on a new and exciting course for a long time to come. But at this moment, as the powerful new engines are fired, their thrust and roar shakes and stresses every part of the ship and may cause the whole thing to blow up before we can steer it on its way. Our problem today is to harness and direct these tremendous new forces through this dangerous transition period to the new world instead of to destruction. But unless we can do this, the rapidly increasing strains and crises of the next decade may kill us all. They will make the last 20 years look like a peaceful interlude.

THE NEXT TEN YEARS

Several types of crisis may reach explosion-point in the next 10 years: nuclear escalation, famine, participatory crises, race crises, and what have been called the crises of "administrative legitimacy." It is worth singling out two or three of these to see how imminent and dangerous they are, so that we can fully realize how very little time we have for preventing or controlling them.

Take the problem of nuclear war, for example. A few years ago, Leo Szilard estimated the "half-life" of the human race with respect to nuclear escalation as

SOURCE: John Platt, "What We Must Do: A Mobilization of Scientists as in Wartime May Be the Only Way to Solve Our Crisis Problems," *Ekistics*, vol. 28, no. 169 (December 1969), 447–51. Reprinted by permission of the author and the publisher. • John Platt is a research biophysicist and Associate Director of the Mental Health Research Institute at The University of Michigan. His main interests include theory of chemical spectra, physics of perception and creativity in science.

being between 10 and 20 years. His reasoning then is still valid now. As long as we continue to have no adequate stabilizing peace-keeping structures for the world, we continue to live under the daily threat not only of local wars but of nuclear escalation with overkill and megatonnage enough to destroy all life on earth. Every year or two there is a confrontation between nuclear powers —Korea, Laos, Berlin, Suez, Quemoy, Cuba, Vietnam, and the rest.

It is easy to see that five or ten more such confrontations in this game of "nuclear roulette" might indeed give us only a 50-50 chance of living until 1980 or 1990. This is a shorter life expectancy than people have ever had in the world before. All our medical increases in length of life are meaningless, as long as our nuclear lifetime is so short.

Many agricultural experts also think that within this next decade the great famines will begin, with deaths that may reach 100 million people in densely populated countries like India and China. Some contradict this, claiming that the remarkable new grains and new agricultural methods introduced in the last three years in Southeast Asia may now be able to keep the food supply ahead of population growth. But others think that the reeducation of farmers and consumers to use the new grains cannot proceed fast enough to make a difference.

But if famine does come, it is clear that it will be catastrophic. Besides the direct human suffering it will further increase our international instabilities, with food riots, troops called out, governments falling, and international interventions that will change the whole political map of the world.

In addition, the next decade is likely to see continued crises of legitimacy of all our overloaded administrations, from Universities and unions to cities and national governments. The problem is not peculiar to America or to capitalist countries, as we can tell by looking at student revolutions around the globe! It is not a matter of rich or poor, or of Left or Right, in the old sense. We find the suburbs marching against school busing at the same instant that the ghettos are marching against slum clearance plans.

This may seem like a trivial problem compared to war or famine until we realize the dangerous effects of these instabilities on the stability of the whole system. A high-information society now insists on being consulted and not commanded. This is reasonable enough, but it puts a further burden on administrations already faced with mounting responsibilities and new puzzles that no one yet knows how to handle. Traditional methods of election and management do not give them the speed, capacity and knowledge needed for these new problems. Too often they become swollen, incompetent, unresponsive—and vulnerable. Every day now some distinguished leader is pressured out of office by protesting constituents.

This in turn makes the nuclear crisis and all the other crises more dangerous—because administrators or mediators today may often work out a basis of agreement between conflicting groups or nations, only to find themselves repudiated by their people on one or both sides, who are then left with no mechanism except to escalate their battles.

THE CRISIS OF CRISES

What finally makes all of our crises still more dangerous is that they are now coming on top of each other. Most administrations are able to endure or even enjoy an occasional crisis, with everyone working late together and getting a new sense of importance and unity. What they are not prepared to deal with is multiple crises, a crisis of crises all at one time. Every problem may escalate because those involved no longer have time to think straight. What would have happened in the Cuban missile crisis if the East Coast power blackout had occurred by accident that same day? Or if the "hot line" between Washington and Moscow had gone dead? There might have been hours of misinterpretation, and some fatally different decisions.

I think this multiplication of domestic and international crises today will shorten that short half-life. In the continued absence of better ways of heading off these multiple crises, our half-life may no longer be 10 or 20 years, but more like 5 to 10 years, or less. We may have even less than a 50-50 chance of living until 1980.

Anyone who feels more hopeful about getting past the demons of the 1970's has only to look beyond them to the giants of pollution and population rising up in the 1980's and 1990's. Whether we have 10 years or more like 20 or 30, unless we systematically find new large-scale solutions, we are in the gravest danger of destroying our society, our world, and ourselves in any of a number of different ways well before the end of the century. Our futurologists who predict what the world will be like in the year 2000 have neglected to tell us that.

But the real reason for trying to make a rational estimate of these deadlines is not because of their shock value but because they give us a rough idea of how much time we may have for finding and mounting some large-scale solutions. The time is short but, as we shall see, it is not too short to give us a chance that something can be done, if we begin immediately.

Today we are like men in a dark tunnel in a coal mine who can hear the rock rumbling already, but who can also see a little square of light at the end of the tunnel. Against this background, I am an optimist—in that I want to insist that there is a square of light and that it is worth trying to get to. For the light at the end of the tunnel is very bright indeed. If we can only devise new mechanisms to help us survive this round of terrible crises, we have a chance of moving into a new world of incredible potentialities for all mankind. But if we cannot get through this next decade, we may never reach it.

TASK FORCES FOR SOCIAL RESEARCH AND DEVELOPMENT

What can we do? I think the problem before us requires something very similar to the mobilization of scientists for solving crisis problems in wartime. Nothing less than the application of the full intelligence of our society is likely to be adequate. I think we are going to need large numbers of scientists forming something like research teams, or Task Forces, for Social Research and Development. We need full-time interdisciplinary teams, including natural scientists, social scientists, doctors, engineers, teachers, lawyers, and many other trained and inventive minds, who will put together our stores of knowledge and powerful new ideas into action-oriented, "social inventions" that will have a chance of being adopted soon enough and widely enough to be effective.

Technology did not create human conflicts and inequities, but it has made them unendurable. And where science and technology have expanded the problems in this way, it may only be more scientific understanding and better technology that can carry us past them. The cure for the pollution of the rivers by detergents is nonpolluting detergents. The cure for bad management designs is better management designs.

The time-scale that such Task Forces would have to work on is very different from what is usual in science. In the past, most scientists have tended to work on something like a 30-year time-scale, hoping that their careful studies would fit into some great intellectual synthesis that might be years away. But we need to think rather in terms of a 3-year time-scale—or more broadly, a 1-to-5 year time-scale. In World War II, the ten thousand scientists who were mobilized for war research knew they did not have 30 years, or even 10 years, to come up with answers. But they did have time for the new research, design and construction that brought sonar and radar and atomic energy to operational effectiveness within 1 to 4 years. Today we need the same large-scale mobilization for innovation and action and the same sense of constructive urgency.

PRIORITIES: A CRISIS INTENSITY CHART

It is most important to be clear about which problems are the real priority problems in such an enterprise. To get

Classification of Problems and Crises by Estimated Time and Intensity

GRADE	*Estimated Crisis Intensity* (number affected times degree of effect)	*Estimated Time to Crisis* (if no major effort at anticipatory solution) 1–5 YEARS	5–20 YEARS	20–50 YEARS
1. 10^{10}	*Total Annihilation*	*Nuclear or RCBW Escalation*	*Nuclear or RCBW Escalation*	*(solved or dead)*
2. 10^{9}	*Great Destruction or Change (Physical, Biological,* or *Political)*	(too soon)	Famines Eco-balance Development Failures Local Wars Rich-Poor Gap	Economic Structure and Political Theory Population and Eco-balance Patterns of Living Universal Education Communications-Integration Management of World Integrative Philosophy
3. 10^{8}	*Widespread Almost Unbearable Tension*	Administrative Management Need for Participation Group and Race Conflict Poverty-Rising Expectations Environmental Degradation	Poverty Pollution Race Wars Political Rigidity Strong Dictatorships	?

Classification of Problems and Crises by Estimated Time and Intensity (*cont.*)

GRADE	*Estimated Crisis Intensity* (number affected times degree of effect)	*Estimated Time to Crisis* (if no major effort at anticipatory solution) 1–5 YEARS	5–20 YEARS	20–50 YEARS
4. 10^7	*Large-Scale Distress*	Transportation Diseases Loss of Old Cultures	Housing Education Independence of Big Powers Communications Gap	?
5. 10^6	*Tension Producing Responsive Change*	Regional Organization Water Supplies	?	?
6.	*Other Problems—Important, but Adequately Researched*	Technical Development Design Intelligent Monetary Design		
7.	*Exaggerated Dangers and Hopes*	Mind Control * Heart Transplants * Definition of Death *	Sperm Banks * Freezing Bodies * Unemployment * from Automation	Eugenics Melting of Ice Caps
8.	*Non-Crisis Problems Being "Overstudied"*	Man in Space *Most Basic Science*		

* Mainly U.S.A.

this straight, it is valuable to try to separate the different problems according to some measures of their scale and urgency. A possible classification of this kind is shown in the Table in which I have tried to rank a number of present or potential problems or crises, vertically, according to an estimate of their order of intensity or "seriousness"; and horizontally, by a rough estimate of their time to reach climactic importance.

The successive rows indicate something like order-of-magnitude differences in crisis intensity, as estimated by a rough product of the size of population that might be hurt or affected, times some estimated average effect in the disruption of their lives. Thus the top row corresponds to total or near-total annihilation, the second row to great destruction or change affecting everybody, the third row to a lower tension affecting a smaller part of the population or a smaller part of everyone's life, and so on.

Informed men might easily disagree about one row up or down in intensity, or one column left or right in the time-scales, but these order-of-magnitude differences are already so great that it would be surprising to find much larger disagreements.

Clearly an important initial step in any serious problem study would be to refine such estimates.

The one crisis that must be ranked at the top in total danger and imminence is, of course, the danger of large-scale or total annihilation by nuclear escalation or by radiological-chemical-biological-warfare (RCBW). The crisis continues through the 1–5 year period and the 5–20 year period as Crisis Number 1, unless and until we get a safer peacekeeping arrangement. But in the 20–50 year column, I think we must simply put a big "X" at this level, on the grounds that this problem will either be solved by that time or we will probably be dead.

At the second level, the 1–5 year period may not be a period of great destruction (except nuclear). But the problems at this level are building up. Many scientists fear the destruction of our ecological balance in the U.S. by mismanagement or pollution in the 5–20 year period; others now fear great political damage from participatory confrontations, or by backlash or by dictatorship, if these problems are not solved before that time.

On a world scale in this period, famine and ecological catastrophe head the list of destructive problems. We will come back later to the items in the 20–50 year column.

The third level of crisis problems includes the problems that are already upon us: administrative management of communities and cities, slums, participatory democracy, and race conflict. In the 5–20 year period, the problems of pollution and poverty or major failures of law and justice could escalate to this level of tension if they are not solved. The last column is left blank because secondary events and second-order effects will interfere seriously with any attempt to make longer-range predictions at these lower levels.

The rest of the items need not be discussed here in detail. Some are common headline problems which are included to show how they might rank quantitatively in this kind of comparison. Anyone concerned with any of them will find it a useful exercise to estimate for himself their order of seriousness, in terms of the number of people they actually affect and the average distress they cause.

WHERE THE SCIENTISTS ARE

Below Grade 5, three less quantitative categories are listed, where the scientists begin to outnumber the problems. Grade 6 consists of problems that are important but are "adequately researched" at the present time. Military R and D belongs in this category. It is certainly important in our present world of nation-states, but it engrosses hundreds of thousands of scientists and engineers, and it is being taken care of generously. Likewise fusion power, interesting as it may be, is being studied at the hundred-million-dollar level, but if we had it tomorrow, it would scarcely change our rates of application of nuclear energy to the power problem of the world.

Grade 7 contains the "exaggerated problems" which are being talked about to worked on out of all proportion to their true importance, such as heart transplants, which can never affect more than a few thousand people out of the billions in the world. It is sad to note that the symposia on "social implications of science" at many national scientific meetings are often on the problems of Grade 7.

In the last category, Grade 8, are two subjects which I am sorry to say I must call "overstudied." By this I mean that they are overstudied with respect to the real crisis problems today. The Man in Space flights to the moon and back are the most beautiful technical achievements of man, but they are not urgent except for national display, and they absorb tens of thousands of our most ingenious technical brains.

And in the "overstudied" list I think I must also put most basic science. There are some studies that are immediately relevant to our human problems further up the scale, but for every one of these I think there may be a dozen others exploring tinier and tinier corners of knowledge or repeating the same kind of studies over and over again on the next thousand molecules.

. . . . .

Probably no human institution will survive unchanged for another 50 years, because they will all be changed by the crises if they are not changed in advance to prevent them. There will surely be widespread rearrangements in all our ways of life everywhere, from our political theory and economic structure and patterns of living to our whole philosophy of man. But whether the world will resemble an open humanist democracy based on technical abundance with coexistence of numerous diverse forms, or something more like Orwell's 1984, or a crippled society in a post-nuclear desert with its scientists hanged—is something that our acts of leadership or accidents in the next few years will decide.

MOBILIZING SCIENTISTS

Perhaps the anti-submarine warfare work in 1940 or the Manhattan Project on atomic energy may be the closest parallels to what we must do in terms of novelty, scale and urgency, and in terms of the methods of mobilization and the success to be achieved. In the anti-submarine campaign, Blackett assembled miscellaneous scientists and other clever minds in his "back room," and within a few months they had worked out the "operations analysis" that made an order-of-magnitude difference in the success of the campaign. In the atomic energy work, scientists started out by spending nights and weekends on the new problem. They formed a central committee to channel their secret communications and then, after they had begun to see the dimensions of the problem, they went to the government for large-scale support which led to the setting up of the great laboratories and production plants.

Fortunately, work on our crisis problems today would not require secrecy. Scientists from many countries would have an interest in the work because they know that these problems are already beginning to be their problems as well as ours, and they might contribute very different viewpoints and ideas.

Probably the first step today should be the organization of intense technical discussion and education groups in every laboratory. When it is clearer what lines are promising and interesting to a given group, they might begin systematic part-time studies, hopefully with the permission or active assistance of administrators.

SOCIAL INVENTIONS AND THEIR EFFECTIVENESS

The thing that discourages many scientists—even social scientists—from thinking in these research-and-development terms is their failure to realize that there are such things as social inventions and that they can have large-scale effects in a surprisingly short time. A recent study with Karl Deutsch has examined some 40 of the great achievements in social science in this century, to see where they were made and by whom and how long they took to become effective. They include developments such as the following:

Keynesian economics
Opinion polls and statistical sampling
Input-output economics

Operations analysis
Information theory and feedback theory
Theory of games and economic behavior
Operant conditioning and programmed learning
Planned programming and budgeting (PPB)
Non-zero-sum game theory

Many of these have made remarkable differences within just a few years in our ability to handle social problems or management problems. The opinion poll became a national necessity within a single election period. The theory of games, published in 1946, had become an important component of American strategic thinking by RAND and the Defense Department by 1953, in spite of the limitation of the theory at that time to zero-sum-games, with their dangerous bluffing and "brinksmanship." Today, within less than a decade, the PPB management technique is sweeping through every large organization.

This list is particularly interesting because it shows how much can be done outside official government agencies by inventive men putting their brains together. Most of the achievements were the work of teams of two or more men, almost all of them located in intellectual centers such as Princeton or the two Cambridges.

APPENDIXES

SOCIOLOGISTS AT WORK

Appendix A
Careers in Sociology

DEPARTMENT OF SOCIOLOGY,
UNIVERSITY OF KENTUCKY

In the preparation of this volume the editors have sought to facilitate the efforts of all students who seek a better understanding of society. This and other experiences may lead some to pursue further work in the field and consider careers in sociology. Sociologists at the University of Kentucky have prepared the following statement on careers for undergraduates who wish to know what opportunities are available to them at various levels of preparation. Students in other colleges and universities should also find it helpful in making decisions about work in sociology.

Young men and women starting careers as sociologists face almost unlimited opportunity in the sense that a vast, almost totally unexplored, field of endeavor is before them. Of course, leading thinkers in all ages have been concerned about society, human conduct, and the creation of a social order that would bring forth the best that man is capable of. But, the study of these problems with the techniques and approaches of science is only a little more than a century old.

It was only about 125 years ago that Auguste Comte published his *Cours de philosophie positive* which first included sociology as one of the scientific disciplines. No course in sociology was available in an American University until 1876 at Yale, and not until after 1890 at the University of Chicago could students in the United States obtain an undergraduate major in social science. Before 1900 all the men who identified themselves as professional sociologists were trained originally in other fields such as history, politics, economics, law, and religion. Today, undergraduate students can obtain training in sociology in almost all American four-year liberal arts colleges and in many agricultural colleges and specialized schools; more than 70 schools offer a doctoral program in sociology and many additional schools offer Masters' degree programs. Opportunities and rewards to those trained in the field have expanded with equal, almost explosive rapidity.

SOURCE: *Should You Be a Sociologist?* Prepared by the Department of Sociology, University of Kentucky, Lexington, Ky. Reprinted by permission.

Before World War I the opportunities for employment of men and women with professional training in sociology were largely limited to college teaching and research. Besides teaching and research, sociologists today are engaged in more than 25 different kinds of work in professional schools, in local, state, federal, and private agencies, and in business. They work in the fields of education, medicine, law, theology, corrections, agricultural extension, welfare, population study, community development, health, technological change, and the like. In short, sociologists are working on almost all the problems that concern man in relation to his fellow man and the consequences of this relationship for himself and others.

WHAT DOES A SOCIOLOGIST DO?

You are familiar with what a teacher of sociology in a college or university does, but let's see what some other persons who are professional sociologists or who have had training in sociology are doing.

Here is a *research sociologist* in a social research institute interviewing a cross-section of people in a community which has been struck by a hurricane. His purpose is the systematic collection of information on the different responses people make in potential and actual disaster situations. Why are some people more successful than others in their attempts to protect themselves and their property? From his careful study and those of other researchers he develops a theory of human behavior in disaster situations. His insights and the facts he has collected enable public and private agencies to develop more effective programs in preparation for such emergencies—to plan ways of minimizing damage and speeding recovery.

In another locale a *community development specialist* is meeting with the Industrial Development Committee of a local Chamber of Commerce. He is advising the Committee on needed information and educational programs, techniques of community organization, and ways of gaining local support for the development program. A year or so later the same community development man may be found in India, Pakistan, or some other underdeveloped country, working with local officials there in planning self-help development programs.

In a firm designing and producing electrical equipment, gradual changes in the company organization over a period of time have reduced the status of the design engineers and affected their enthusiasm, spontaneity, and cooperativeness, with consequent effects on production. The *personnel director,* whose college training included courses in sociology, recognizes the importance of job-status to satisfaction with work and persuades the company to modify its organization, thereby alleviating their dissatisfaction.

An *urban planning specialist,* employed by a local planning and zoning commission, is assembling information on the probable social consequences of a proposed zoning change for the schools, churches, and families in the affected area and for the larger community. On the basis of this information and that from other sources the Commission must decide whether or not the proposed change is likely to result in net benefits to most of the people in the community.

Here is a *minister* who finds that people in the community in which his new church is located are troubled because their teen-age young people patronize undesirable establishments outside the community for their recreation. Owing to his earlier studies in sociology he recognizes the need to provide more opportunity locally for recreation appealing to today's youth. Under his leadership youth programs in the church and community are being expanded, thereby enriching the lives of the young people, the church, and the community.

Here is an *inter-group relations specialist* meeting with a local Board of Education. They are trying to work out a plan for compliance with the 1954 Supreme Court decision on school desegregation in a way that is most satisfactory to Negroes and white persons in the community. He is helping the School Board understand how the feelings of all people can be considered and what must be done to minimize misunderstanding and to guard against groups of people thinking that they must take matters into their own hands. On the wisdom and carefulness of their planning hinges the possibility of peaceful integration with a minimum of dissatisfaction—or the possibility of mutual distrust and possible violence.

In an industrialized community an *industrial relations specialist* is preparing a written report to the Board of Directors of a manufacturing company. They are concerned with worker absenteeism and low morale. His report includes findings as to the basis of this problem and his recommendations on how the management might work more closely with the workers to reduce worker dissatisfaction, to increase production, and to improve the firm's competitive position.

Here is a sociologist who is a member of a therapeutic team in a mental hospital. Should the relationships of aides and nurses to patients be close and informal or reserved and authoritarian? Should patients be given responsibilities and freedom of movement or should they be carefully watched and guarded? Progress in therapy hinges on making correct assessments of the impact of the hospital environment on the patient at each stage in his treatment, and of what changes must be made at each stage in order to insure continued progress.

A young *housewife,* who majored in sociology in college, recognizes that the future consequences of failure to establish a full-time planning commission in the local government will be real estate deterioration, increasing crime rates, loss of community pride, and the like. Being concerned with the growth and development of the community in which she lives she is working energetically with civic groups helping to organize a planning committee and develop citizen support for its activities.

An *extension rural sociologist,* employed in the Cooperative Extension Service in Agriculture and Home Economics, is conducting a leadership training course for 4-H Club workers in X County. He is demonstrating how the skilled leader can help young people to analyze a social situation and make intelligent choices. Tomorrow he may be working with an Extension Committee in another county, helping to set up a study to evaluate the effectiveness of a new health program.

A *research sociologist* in a university is studying the characteristics of the manpower available for industrial employment in a region. Other sociologists are studying the decision-making processes of doctors, of farmers, of industrial plant managers, and of community groups. Still others are studying factors in the development of a delinquent career, a medical career, the decision to go to college, and many more problems having theoretical and practical significance.

From this list, you can see that the sociologist may teach, he may do research in the advancement of scientific knowledge or in the solution of a practical problem, he may serve as a consultant to agencies and organizations which have international, national, state, and local community programs, or he may possibly combine several of these activities . . . all providing opportunities to find satisfaction in a lifetime of activity. In almost any field the person who has had college work in sociology finds daily uses for his knowledge in his work, civic, familial, and leisure activities.

HOW DOES A YOUNG MAN OR WOMAN BECOME A SOCIOLOGIST?

The kinds of jobs and activities that are open to you as a sociologically trained person greatly depend on your interests and the kind and the extent of your training. The more professional training you get the more qualified you become to work as a professional sociologist. In some respects the training requirements and job opportunities can be represented by a tree at different stages of its growth.

By fulfilling the requirements for an undergraduate major in sociology or rural sociology, your career tree has gained the proportions, perhaps, of a sapling. If you terminate your academic education at this point a variety of job opportunities await you. Actually the number of different jobs which may be attractive to you is probably greater than it will be if you continue your education. The reason is that, while having majored in sociology, your primary qualification is your liberal arts training which enables you to enter a broad range of nontechnical occupations. Your professional identification in this case is primarily with the job that you get (e.g., recreation worker, agency representative, personnel assistant, or salesman) rather than with the sociological training that you have had and will use in the performance of your duties.

To be sure, however, there are a number of jobs for which an undergraduate major in sociology is especially appropriate. Personnel officers considering applicants for jobs in health programs, social and welfare work, community planning and zoning, farm organization work, and the like, give special consideration to graduates who have had a major in sociology.

The value of an undergraduate major in sociology is not limited to persons who plan to take a job on graduating or to continue on to graduate work in sociology. An undergraduate major or minor in sociology will provide an especially valuable background if you plan eventually to become a clergyman, attorney, economist, psychologist, political scientist, or historian, or to enter many other professional fields.

It is with graduate training in sociology that you begin especially to be identified by the particular type of professional training that you have had and this tendency increases the further you go in your training. By the end of the first or second year of your graduate study you should obtain your Master's degree. At this time you qualify as a sub-professional specialist for jobs in planning and zoning, extension education, social services, community development, research, small college teaching, and the like. Since you are to some extent identified as a sociologist, your opportunity is greater to obtain a job in which a degree of competence in sociology is expected and desired.

If you plan for a career as a full-fledged professional sociologist your academic goal is the Doctor of Philosophy degree in sociology. The occupational fruit of this tree is usually harvested in the third to fifth year of graduate work. Depending on your interests you may accept a job as a teacher or researcher, or join agencies concerned with a variety of human problems in public affairs that require sociological knowledge for their solutions.

If you plan to end your education with an A.B. or B.S. degree, you may want to develop the trunk of your career tree somewhat differently than if you plan to continue academic work beyond that point. If you do not plan to continue your academic training you may emphasize "practical" courses in sociology; but courses in philosophy, mathematics, scientific methods, and in the principles of different scientific disciplines should be your fare if you are looking forward to graduate work. Your major advisor can help you make wise selections from among approved courses.

The academic "trees" of persons who pursue graduate studies in sociology differ in other respects from those who stop with the bachelor's degree. If your undergraduate studies have included a broad range of basic science, philosophy, history, mathematics, and English, a major in sociology will enable you to move directly into professional sociology courses in graduate school. But many graft a sociological career tree on other roots; you may decide to begin graduate studies in sociology after having majored as an undergraduate in history, psychology, political science, engineering, animal husbandry, mathematics, and the like. While in the beginning you may have to take some of the basic courses that a sociology major already will have had, your background in another field is likely to be an asset as you continue your professional training and later work.

Graduate education is not as expensive as it seems at first. Most students are able to obtain financial support while they are in graduate school. This may come from a fellowship or scholarship which does not have a work commitment, or an assistantship which is usually for half-time work in a Department of Sociology. Increasingly, there are opportunities for able students to engage in part-time semi-professional work outside the university while pursuing their advanced studies.

WHAT ARE THE REWARDS AND DRAWBACKS?

One of the most tempting aspects of professional work in sociology is its broad and expanding horizon. It is exciting to be a part of something with ever enlarging opportunities and rewards.

Thirty years ago few people made their living as professional sociologists. Today, there are more than 4,300 Fellows, Active members and Associate members of the American Sociological Association. In ten years the number of student members—about 2,000 in 1960—has increased by 60 per cent, indicating that young men and women increasingly recognize the opportunities to have satisfying careers as sociologists. The many occupations that professional sociologists have now mean that ambitious young men and women can move readily from one interesting job to another in search of variety of experience and opportunities for promotion.

The starting salaries for sociology majors with a bachelor's degree compare favorably with those of other liberal arts and agriculture graduates. Because of the demand for trained people, advancement within a company or agency can be quite rapid. In college teaching and research, starting salaries for young men and women with a Ph.D. degree in sociology range between $7,500 and $10,000. . . . (For those who go into the civil service or private industry, as more and more are doing, starting salaries average somewhat higher.) Nationally, these figures are increasing at the rate of 2 to 3 per cent a year. The annual salaries of a few top sociologists are now in excess of $20,000. Such salaries are exceptional today, but so were salaries of $12,000 a few years ago, and the record amply indicates that becoming a professional sociologist does not demand a vow of poverty as many people mistakenly believe.

However, a high order of social, emotional, and intellectual maturity is required to earn a Master's and a Doctor's degree. To take these as your academic goals you must find satisfaction in working *toward* answers to human problems rather than in *having* the "right" answer beforehand. You must be willing to view people and their behavior objectively—to suspend judgment of whether their behavior is "good" or "bad" in terms of conventional morality. You must be willing to develop competence in mathematics and written and oral communications, and to pursue intellectual interests in the broad range of the humanities and sciences. It isn't easy to understand the significance of so intangible a thing as society to the attainment of individual and group purposes. But, if you are intellectually curious, and especially if you are interested in people—in understanding and helping them, in discovering why they behave as they do, and how human needs are satisfied in society—you will find a career as a sociologist exciting, rewarding, and satisfying.

"More important than any amount of money or medals to me," writes one research sociologist, "is the thrill in suddenly discovering that in deciding between alternative courses of action for which the precise consequences are unknown a person needs the emotional support of a friend and confidant. On the basis of this insight a number of puzzling and apparently inconsistent facts about the process of human decision-making are given coherence and meaning." An extension sociologist felt forever rewarded, even though he obtained no tangible benefit, on being told that what he had said and done in a crisis faced by a local community recreation committee had led not merely to saving the recreation program and the Recreation Director's job but to the expansion of the program to embrace all groups in the entire community.

We would be less than candid, however, if we left the impression that the job of the sociologist is all fun and satisfaction. First, the task of gaining a graduate degree requires hard, unremitting labor. It requires personal dedication and intellectual endeavor of the highest order; but only in this manner can one gain the confidence and competence necessary to perform one's professional responsibilities with credit to oneself, one's profession, and one's society.

As a sociologist you frequently will find that the people and groups whom you are able to help are unaware of what you can do or sometimes even disparage your abilities. Often it is necessary to sell yourself and your field before you can begin work on the problem needing your attention. But this difficulty confronts the pathmaker in all new fields of endeavor, and herein lies much of the challenge and opportunity awaiting professional sociologists.

Hard to take, sometimes, is the feeling that your job is never done, no matter how much you do; and your failures as a human relations specialist or as a researcher can keep you awake nights wondering, "What should I have said to that committee to enable them to see the significance of approaching the problem in this way?" "What have I failed to take into account in attempting to explain the behavior of that organization paralyzed by conflict and poor morale?"

The fact that the rewards far outweigh the drawbacks, however, is indicated each year by the increasing number of young people like yourself who become professional sociologists. In 1940 only 155 men and women were awarded Master's degrees in sociology in the United States and only 50 were awarded the Doctor of Philosophy degree in sociology. In 1963, however, 684 received a Master's degree and 208 the Doctor's degree.

. . . . . .

If you think you might be interested in becoming a sociology or rural sociology major, or in taking several courses in sociology, you will want to find out more about the opportunities, rewards and requirements than is provided here. The undergraduate and graduate advisors in Sociology can supply additional helpful information and help you plan an interesting and rewarding program of study. They will welcome the opportunity to meet you and to discuss with you what courses would be most helpful to you in preparing for your career. You can arrange a meeting with an advisor through an instructor in one of your sociology courses. . . .

Appendix B
Toward a Code of Ethics for Sociologists

AMERICAN SOCIOLOGICAL ASSOCIATION

In his 1968 introduction to the proposed Code of Ethics the American Sociological Association Executive Officer, Edmund H. Volkart, said: "Most important, Council believes that ASA must begin to take steps to meet its social responsibilities and, with the active assistance of the membership, Council expects to support an evolving Code of Ethics that will enable our profession to meet the highest standards of professional and scientific conduct." A Standing Committee on Professional Ethics was authorized and first steps were taken by the ASA toward performance of its task, as stated by Volkart, "to provide more explicit guidelines covering ethical issues in all activities of sociologists." Below is reproduced the Committee Preamble forwarded to the Council for its action, and the Council Preamble and Code of Ethics as adopted by the Association's voting members in February 1970.

COMMITTEE PREAMBLE

Sociology as a Human Enterprise

Although sociology can, within limits, exist within the context of any highly developed social structure, it is a significant fact that as a human enterprise it has grown up and prospered within democratic or democratizing societies. Among the central characteristics of such societies have been the trends toward maximizing the opportunity for people to participate in the making of decisions by which their lives are vitally affected and toward maximizing the range of significant choice. This opening of the social structure into institutional patterns of shared decision making and into patterns of choice within the institutional framework has been based on the assumption of the essential freedom of the human person. From this assumption of essential freedom and from the pressure for maximizing its institutional forms stem the other values which cluster around the person of modern man: dignity, privacy, and the positive assessment of reason. Therefore, as sociology attempts to relate itself to its ethical responsibilities toward the society of which it is a part and as it defines its own internal ethic, these standards of essential and institutional freedom are central. Ultimately, sociological research and knowledge must always be related to the task of creating and maintaining human freedom. Such research and knowledge are, of course, part of the universal human quest for knowledge and freedom and are not the monopoly, either in their making or in their application, of any special nation or people.

In pursuing its task of creating and maintaining human freedom, sociological research, to command proper support from a society, must in the long run justify such support by contributing its fair share of the social science knowledge needed and realistically attainable for the rational solution or amelioration of that society's major social problems. Further-

SOURCE: *The American Sociologist* (November 1968), pp. 316–18. Reprinted by permission of the publisher.

more, as these problems develop increasingly vital and international dimensions, sociological research must enlarge the scope of the subject matter it considers relevant until ultimately it undertakes to study and understand sociological phenomena throughout mankind.

The Assumption of Complementary Rights and Obligations, Freedoms and Responsibilities

Sociology, like other forms of specialized research and knowledge, cannot be created by one group alone. Its development depends upon a complementary and reciprocal set of rights and obligations, freedoms and responsibilities, shared among sociologists as a specialized profession, other professional and political groups, and the public at large. Everyone, in sum, has a measure of responsibility to contribute to social research just because it is one essential form of expression of the basic social value and need for rational knowledge in every democratizing society. The presumption of an obligation of others besides sociologists to contribute to research through providing services, funds, and other resources does not mean that this obligation can be taken for granted by sociologists in all cases, nor is it unqualified by the necessity for continual attention by sociologists to essential safeguards for the various "weak" groups whose collaboration they require. Sociologists believe in reciprocal freedoms among different social groups and they believe that these reciprocal freedoms, guarded by reciprocal responsibilities, will create more freedom for themselves and others.

The Research, Teaching, and Practice Complex

Sociological research is inherently part of a larger complex which includes teaching and practice. There are differences among these three components of the complex, but there are also common principles, overlaps, and interpenetrations among them. As sociologists seek to achieve ethical responsibility, they must take both these differences and interpenetrations into account.

Institutionalized Innovation and Strain

Sociological research involves innovation, and even institutionalized innovation such as this inevitably causes social strain as well as social benefit in the situation of reciprocal freedoms and responsibilities which sociology seeks to maintain and enlarge. This likelihood of strain for various groups should be directly faced and the problem of dealing with it should be taken as a continuing moral and intellectual enterprise. In considerable measure, this continuing moral and intellectual enterprise is itself a sociological task.

The Ethical Responsibilities of the Profession, the Corporate Professional Association, and the Individual Sociologist

As sociology seeks to define its ethical responsibilities, it distinguishes among ethical freedoms and responsibilities at three levels: the profession as a whole, the corporate professional association, and the individual sociologist. What sociology expects of itself, and what other groups expect of sociology, will differ as one considers the profession as a whole, the corporate professional association, and individual sociologists. The profession may have larger freedoms and responsibilities than the corporate professional association. And no individual sociologist, as an individual, is charged with quite the same responsibilities or granted the same freedoms as the profession as a whole or the corporate professional association.

Intellectual Debates and Ethical Issues

Sociology as a profession has a basic ethical commitment to the pursuit of knowledge. This inevitably involves technical intellectual differences among individuals or groups of sociologists. Given the historical facts that, in all the sciences, there have been many paths to knowledge and that there have been important cases of resistance by scientists themselves to fundamental scientific innovation, it is an ethical obligation for sociologists to try to avoid turning intellectual debates into ethical issues. Defaults in regard to this obligation tend to destroy the moral consensus which is essential for the large sociological obligation to pursue knowledge.

A Constitution, Not a Statute Book

In the situation which sociology presently faces, one in which there is a lack of consensus among sociologists about not only the substance of, but even the need for, a code of ethics, we must start with a constitution, not a statute book, a set of general premises and principles, not the set of specific norms toward which we hope slowly to move. For the moment, sociology rests content with a statement of ethical principles that is nearly as general as the Mosaic Tablets. But it recognizes the need to move on, as soon as possible, to more specific normative expressions of these general ethical principles. In recognizing this need to move on, sociology considers its eventual, more specific code as an homology to the Common Law. The specific code for sociology, like the specific code for all professional associations, should be built up as the Common Law has been built up, on the slow accumulation and testing of case law. The concrete cases which confront sociology with ethical problems involve the interpenetration of many different, high-level values. To accommodate these different and very general values in concrete cases requires the deliberate and careful consideration of multiple cases. Such has been the experience of the Common Law and such also will be the requirement for sociology.

COUNCIL PREAMBLE

Sociological inquiry is often disturbing to many persons and groups. Its results may challenge long-established beliefs and lead to change in old taboos. In consequence such findings may create demands for the suppression or control of this inquiry or for a dilution of the findings. Similarly, the results of sociological investigation may be of significant use to individuals in power—whether in government, in the private sphere, or in the universities—because such findings, suitably manipulated, may facilitate the misuse of power. Knowledge is a form of power, and in a society increasingly dependent on knowledge, the control of information creates the potential for political manipulation.

For these reasons, we affirm the autonomy of sociological inquiry. The sociologist must be responsive, first and foremost, to the truth of his investigation. Sociology must not be an instrument of any person or group which seeks to suppress or misuse knowledge. The fate of sociology as a science is dependent upon the fate of free inquiry in an open society.

At the same time this search for social truths must itself operate within constraints. Its limits arise when inquiry infringes on the rights of individuals to be treated as persons, to be considered—in the renewable phrase of Kant—as ends and not as means. Just as sociologists must not distort or manipulate truth to serve untruthful ends, so too they must not manipulate persons to serve their quest for truth. The study of society, being the study of human beings, imposes the responsibility of respecting the integrity, promoting the dignity, and maintaining the autonomy of these persons.

To fulfill these responsibilities, we, the members of the American Sociological Association, affirm the following Code of Ethics:

CODE OF ETHICS

1. *Objectivity in Research*

In his research the sociologist must maintain scientific objectivity.

2. *Integrity in Research*

The sociologist should recognize his own limitations and, when appropriate, seek more expert assistance or decline to undertake research beyond his competence. He must not misrepresent his own abilities, or the competence of his staff to conduct a particular research project.

3. *Respect of the Research Subject's Rights to Privacy and Dignity*

Every person is entitled to the right of privacy and dignity of treatment. The sociologist must respect these rights.

4. *Protection of Subjects from Personal Harm*

All research should avoid causing personal harm to subjects used in research.

5. *Preservation of Confidentiality of Research Data*

Confidential information provided by a research subject must be treated as such by the sociologist. Even though research information is not a privileged communication under the law, the sociologist must, as far as possible, protect subjects and informants. Any promises made to such persons must be honored. However, provided that he respects the assurances he has given his subjects, the sociologist has no obligation to withhold information of misconduct of individuals or organizations.

If an informant or other subject should wish, however, he can formally release the researcher of a promise of confidentiality. The provisions of this section apply to all members of research organizations (i.e., interviewers, coders, clerical staff, etc.), and it is the responsibility of the chief investigators to see that they are instructed in the necessity and importance of maintaining the confidentiality of the data. The obligation of the sociologist includes the use and storage of original data to which a subject's name is attached. When requested, the identity of an organization or subject must be adequately disguised in publication.

6. *Presentation of Research Findings*

The sociologist must present his findings honestly and without distortion. There should be no omission of data from a research report which might significantly modify the interpretation of findings.

7. *Misuse of Research Role*

The sociologist must not use his role as a cover to obtain information for other than professional purposes.

8. *Acknowledgment of Research Collaboration and Assistance*

The sociologist must acknowledge the professional contributions or assistance of all persons who collaborated in the research.

9. *Disclosure of the Sources of Financial Support*

The sociologist must report fully all sources of financial support in his research publications and any special relations to the sponsor that might affect the interpretation of the findings.

10. *Distortion of Findings by Sponsor*

The sociologist is obliged to clarify publicly any distortion by a sponsor or client of the findings of a research project in which he has participated.

11. *Disassociation from Unethical Research Arrangements*

The sociologist must not accept such grants, contracts, or research assignments as appear likely to require violation of the principles above, and must publicly terminate the work or formally disassociate himself from the research if he discovers such a violation and is unable to achieve its correction.

12. *Interpretation of Ethical Principles*

When the meaning and application of these principles are unclear, the sociologist should seek the judgment of the relevant agency or committee designated by the American Sociological Association. Such consultation, however, does not free the sociologist from his individual responsibility for decisions or from his accountability to the profession.

13. *Applicability of Principles*

In the conduct of research the principles enunciated above should apply to research in any area either within or outside the United States of America.

Appendix C
Sociological Snoopers and Journalistic Moralizers

NICHOLAS VON HOFFMAN,
IRVING LOUIS HOROWITZ,
AND LEE RAINWATER

The previous selection states the code of ethics adopted by the American Sociological Association to guide the behavior of sociologists in their research and professional activities. The following selection presents both sides of a case in which a sociologist is charged with being a snoop and therefore being unethical in conducting his research. This illustrates an area in which the definitions of ethical behavior in sociological research are not universally acclaimed. The first part is from a column by Von Hoffman in the Washington Post, *and the second part is a reply by Horowitz and Rainwater in* Trans-action.

MR. VON HOFFMAN

We're so preoccupied with defending our privacy against insurance investigators, dope sleuths, counterespionage men, divorce detectives and credit checkers, that we overlook the social scientists behind the hunting blinds who're also peeping into what we thought were our most private and secret lives. But they are there, studying us, taking notes, getting to know us, as indifferent as everybody else to the feeling that to be a complete human involves having an aspect of ourselves that's unknown.

If there was any doubt about there being somebody who wants to know about anything any other human being might be doing it is cancelled out in the latest issue of *Trans-action,* a popular but respected sociological monthly. The lead article, entitled "Impersonal Sex in Public Places," is a resume of a study done about the nature and pattern of homosexual activities in men's rooms. Laud Humphreys, the author, is an Episcopal priest, a duly pee-aich-deed sociologist, holding the rank of assistant professor at Southern Illinois University. The article is taken from a forthcoming book called *Tearoom Trade: Impersonal Sex in Public Places* (Aldine Publishing Company, Chicago, March 1970).

Tearoom is the homosexual slang for men's rooms that are used for purposes other than those for which they were designed. However, if a straight male were to hang around a tearoom he wouldn't see anything out of the ordinary so that if you're going to find out what's happening you must give the impression that you're one of the gang.

"I had to become a participant ob-

SOURCE: *Trans-action,* vol. 7, no. 7 (May 1970), 4–8. • Nicholas Von Hoffman is a staff writer for *The Washington Post.* He has served as Associate Director of the Industrial Areas Foundation, Chicago, and as a staff member of the *Chicago Daily News.* He is the author of *Mississippi Notebook, Multiversity,* and *We Are the People Our Parents Warned Us Against.*

server of the furtive felonious acts," Humphreys writes in explaining his methodology. "Fortunately, the very fear or suspicion of tearoom participants produces a mechanism that makes such observation possible; a third man—generally one who obtains voyeuristic pleasure from his duties—serves as a lookout, moving back and forth from door to windows. Such a 'watchqueen,' as he is labeled in the homosexual argot, coughs when a police car stops nearby or when a stranger approaches. He nods affirmatively when he recognizes a man entering as being a 'regular.' Having been taught the watchqueen role by a cooperating respondent, I played that part faithfully while observing hundreds of acts of fellatio."

Most of the people Humphreys observed and took notes on had no idea what he was doing or that they, in disguised form, would be showing up in print at some time in the future. Of all the men he studied only a dozen were ever told what his real purpose was, yet as a sociologist he had to learn about the backgrounds and vital facts of the other tearoom visitors he'd seen. To do this Humphreys noted their license numbers and by tracing their cars learned their identities. He then allowed time to pass, disguised himself and visited these men under the color of doing a different, more innocuous door-to-door survey.

He describes what he did this way: "By passing as a deviant, I had observed their sexual behavior without disturbing it. Now I was faced with interviewing these men—often in the presence of their wives—without destroying them. . . . To overcome the danger of having a subject recognize me as a watchqueen, I changed my hair style, attire and automobile. At the risk of losing the more transient respondents, I waited a year between the sample gathering (in the tearoom) and the interviews, during which time I took notes on their homes and neighborhoods and acquired data on them from the city and county directories."

Humphreys said that he did everything possible to make sure the names of the men whose secrets he knew would never get out: "I kept only one copy of the master list of names and that was in a safe deposit box. I did all the transcribing of taped interviews myself and changed all identifying marks and signs. In one instance, I allowed myself to be arrested rather than let the police know what I was doing and the kind of information I had."

Even so, it remains true that he collected information that could be used for blackmail, extortion, and the worst kind of mischief without the knowledge of the people involved. *Trans-action* defends the ethics of Humphreys' methodology on the basis of purity of motive and the argument that he was doing it for a good cause, that is getting needed, reliable information about a difficult and painful social problem.

Everybody who goes snooping around and spying on people can be said to have good motives. The people whom Sen. Sam Ervin is fighting, the ones who want to give the police the right to smash down your door without announcing who they are if they think you have pot in your house, believe they are well-motivated. They think they are preventing young people from destroying themselves. J. Edgar Hoover unquestionably believes he's protecting the country against subversion when he orders your telephone tapped. Those who may want to overthrow the government are just as well motivated by their lights. Since everybody can be said to be equally well motivated, it's impossible to form a judgment on what people do by assessing their intentions.

To this Laud Humphreys replies that his methods were less objectionable than getting his data by working through the police: "You do walk a really perilous tightrope in regard to ethical matters in studies like this, but, unless someone will walk it, the only source of information will be the police department, and that's dangerous for a society. The methods I used were the least intrusive possible. Oh, I could have hidden in the ceiling as the police do, but then I would have been an accomplice in what they were doing."

Humphreys believes that the police in many cities extort bribes from homosexuals they catch in tearooms. He also thinks that "what's more common is putting an investigation report on file. Often when they catch somebody, they don't arrest him but they get his name, address and employer. There's no defense against this and no way of knowing when the information will be used in the future. I agree there may be a dangerous precedent in studying deviant behavior this way but in some places vice squads use closed circuit TV to look into tearooms and in many cities they use decoys. To my mind *these* are the people who're the dangerous observers."

Some people may answer that by saying a study on such a topic constitutes deviant sociological behavior, a giving-in to the discipline's sometimes peculiar taste for nosing around oddballs. But in the study of man anything men do should be permissible to observe and try to understand. Furthermore, Humphreys has evidence and arguments to show that, far from being a rare and nutty aberration, tearoom activity is quite common.

He cites a UCLA law review study showing that in a four-year period in Los Angeles 274 of a total of 493 men arrested for homosexual activities were picked up in tearooms. He has another study in Mansfield, Ohio, that rural fleshpot, saying that police operating with a camera behind a one-way mirror caught 65 men in the course of only two weeks. FBI national crime figures don't have a special category for tearoom arrests, but Humphreys has enough indicative evidence to allow him to say it's a big problem. Even if it weren't, so many parents are worried about their sons being approached by homosexuals that we believe it's a big problem.

Humphreys' study suggests that tearoom habitues stay clear of teen-agers. "I never saw an instance of a teen-ager being approached. The men in the tearoom are scared to death of teen-agers. When a teen-ager comes in the action breaks off and everybody gets out. You have to give a definite sign before you'll be approached (in his book he goes into detail) so they never approach anyone who hasn't done so. Anyway, there's no problem of recruiting teen-agers because teen-agers are too busy trying to join."

Incontestably such information is useful to parents, teen-agers themselves, to policemen, legislators and many others, but it was done by invading some people's privacy. This newspaper could probably learn a lot of things that the public has a right and need to know if its reporters were to use disguises and the gimmickry of modern, transistorized, domestic espionage, but there is a policy against it. No information is valuable enough to obtain by nipping away at personal liberty, and that is true no matter who's doing the gnawing, John Mitchell and the conservatives over at the Justice Department or Laud

Humphreys and the liberals over at the Sociology Department.

MR. HOROWITZ AND MR. RAINWATER

Columnist Nicholas Von Hoffman's quarrel with Laud Humphreys' "Impersonal Sex in Public Places" starkly raises an issue that has grown almost imperceptibly over the last few years, and now threatens to create in the next decade a tame sociology to replace the fairly robust one that developed during the sixties. For most of their history, the disciplines of sociology and social psychology were considered a kind of joke, an oddball activity pursued by academic types who cultivated an arcane jargon that either concealed ivory tower views about human reality, or simply said things that everyone knew already.

Somehow, during the 1960s, that image began to shift quite dramatically. People suddenly began to look to sociologists and social psychologists for explanations of what was going on, of why the society was plagued with so many problems. Sociological jargon, perspectives and findings began to enter people's conversation and thinking in a way that no one would have imagined a few years before. All during the sixties enrollment in sociology classes in colleges and universities increased at an accelerating rate. What sociologists had to say about international relations, or race problems, or deviant behavior, or health care or the crisis of the city became standard parts of the ways Americans explained themselves to themselves.

SOURCE: Irving Louis Horowitz is professor and Chairman of the Department of Sociology at Rutgers University. His chief interests include politics and theory, political sociology and history and theory of sociology. He is the editor-in-chief of *Trans-action* and the author of *Three Worlds of Development: The Theory and Practice of International Stratification* and *Professing Sociology: Studies in the Life Cycle of Social Science.* • Lee Rainwater is professor and Faculty Associate at the Joint Center for Urban Studies of the Massachusetts Institute of Technology and Harvard University and is a member of the Department of Social Relations at Harvard University. His major interests include urban sociology and behavioral development. He is Senior Editor of *Trans-action* and author of *Workingman's Wife: Her Personality, World and Life Style, Family Design,* and is coauthor of the *Moynihan Report and the Politics of Controversy.*

. . . . .

Sociologists have tended to assume that well-intentioned people fully accept the desirability of demystification of human life and culture. In the age of Aquarius, however, perhaps such a view will be recognized as naive.

"They are there, studying us, taking notes, getting to know us, as indifferent as everybody else to the feeling that to be a complete human involves having an aspect of ourselves that's unknown." Von Hoffman seems to mean this to be a statement about the right to privacy in a legal sense, but it really represents a denial of the ability of people to understand themselves and each other in an existential sense. This denial masks a fear, not that intimate details of our lives will be revealed to *others,* but rather that we may get to know *ourselves* better and have to confront what up to now we did not know about ourselves. Just as psychoanalysis was a scientific revolution as threatening to traditional conceptions as those of Galileo and Kepler had been, it may well be that the sociologist's budding ability to say something about the how's and why's of men's relationships to each other is deeply threatening not only to the established institutions in society, but also in a more personal way to all members of society.

Von Hoffman says he is talking about the invasion of privacy, but his celebration of the "aspect of ourselves that's unknown" shows a deeper worry about making rational and open what he conceives to be properly closed and dark in human reality. Von Hoffman concentrates his outrage on the methods Humphreys used to learn what he did, but we believe that at bottom he is not much different from other critics of behavioral science who make exactly the same points that von Hoffman makes with respect to research, even when it involves people who freely give their opinions, attitudes and autobiographical data to interviewers. This, too, is regarded as a threat because eventually it will remove some of the mystery from human life.

But von Hoffman recognizes that his most appealing charge has to do with privacy, and so he makes much of the fact that Humphreys collected information that could be used for "blackmail, extortion, and the worst kind of mischief without the knowledge of the people involved."

Here his double standard is most glaringly apparent. Journalists routinely, day in, day out, collect information that could be used for "blackmail, extortion, and the worst kind of mischief without the knowledge of the people involved." But von Hoffman knows that the purpose of their work is none of those things, and so long as their information is collected from public sources, I assume he wouldn't attack them. Yet he nowhere compares the things sociologists do with the things his fellow journalists do. Instead, he couples Humphreys' "snooping around," "spying on people" with similarly "well-motivated" invaders of privacy as J. Edgar Hoover and John Mitchell.

To say the least, the comparison is invidious; the two kinds of enterprises are fundamentally different. No police group seeks to acquire information about people with any other goal than that of, in some way, prosecuting them. Policemen collect data, openly or under cover, in order to put someone in jail. Whatever it is, the sociological enterprise is not that. Sociologists are not interested in directly affecting the lives of the particular people they study. They are interested in those individuals only as representatives of some larger aggregate—in Humphreys' case, all participants in the tearoom action. Therefore, in almost all sociological research, the necessity to preserve the anonymity of the respondent is not an onerous one, because no purpose at all would be served by identifying the respondents.

In this respect, journalists are in fact much closer to policemen than sociologists are. Journalists often feel that their function is to point the finger at particular malefactors. Indeed their effort to acquire information about individuals is somewhat like that of the police, in the sense that both seek to affect importantly the lives of the particular individuals who are the object of their attention. Perhaps this kind of misconception of what the sociologist is about, and the total absence of any comment on the role of the journalist, leads von Hoffman to persistently misinterpret Humphreys' research as "invading some people's privacy." Yet everything Humphreys knew about the deviant behavior of the people he studied was acquired in a public context (indeed, on public land).

We believe in the work Humphreys has done, in its principled humaneness, in its courage to learn the truth and in the constructive contribution that it makes toward our understanding of all the issues, including the moral, raised by deviant behavior in our society. *Trans-action* has always been supportive of and open to the sort of enterprise he has so ably performed; we only wish there were more of it. Furthermore, a vigorous defense of Laud Humphreys' research (and that of others before and after him) is eminently possible and glaringly needed.

Sociologists uphold the right to know in a context of the surest protection for the integrity of the subject matter and the private rights of the people studied. Other groups in society may turn on different pivots: the right of law, the protection of individuals against invasion of privacy and so forth. But whoever is "right" in the abstract, there is a shared obligation for all parties to a controversy to step forth with fullness and fairness to present their cases before the interested public—and to permit that public to enter discussions which affect them so directly. Without this, a right higher than public disclosure or private self will be denied—the right to full public discourse.

Von Hoffman's points are: that in studying the sexual behavior of men in restrooms, Humphreys violated their rights to intimacy and privacy; that the homosexuals were and remain unaware of the true purpose of Humphreys' presence as a lookout; and that in the follow-up questionnaire the researcher further disguised himself and the true nature of his inquiry. For von Hoffman the point of principle is this: that although Humphreys' intent may have been above reproach and that in point of fact his purposes are antithetical to those of the police and other public officials, he nonetheless in his own way chipped away at the essential rights of individuals in conducting his investigations. Therefore, the ends, the goals, however noble and favorable to the plight of sexual deviants, do not justify the use of any means that further undermine personal liberties. Let us respond to these propositions as directly as possible.

COPS AND KNOWLEDGE

First, the question of the invasion of privacy has several dimensions. We have already noted the public rather than the private nature of park restrooms. It further has to be appreciated that all participants in sexual activities in restrooms run the constant risk that they have among them people who have ulterior purposes. The vocabulary of motives is surely not limited or circumscribed by one man doing research but is as rich and as varied as the number of participants themselves. The fact that in this instance there was a scientific rather than a sexual or criminal "ulterior motive" does not necessarily make it more hideous or more subject to criticism, but perhaps less so.

Second, the question of disguising "the true nature" and purpose of this piece of research has to be put into some perspective. To begin with, let us assume that the research was worth doing in the first place. We know almost nothing about impersonal sex in public places, and the fact that we know so little has in no small way contributed to the fact that the cops feel that *they* know all that needs to be known about the matter. Who, then, is going to gather this countervailing knowledge? Von Hoffman implies that the research enterprise would be ethically pure if Humphreys were himself a full participant, like John Rechey. But to be able to conduct investigations of the type Humphreys performed requires a sociological imagination rare enough among his professional peers, much less homosexuals in public places. Moreover, to assume that the investigator must share all of his knowledge with those being investigated also assumes a common universe of discourse very rarely found in any kind of research, much less the kind involving sexual deviance. Furthermore, the conduct of Humphreys' follow-up inquiries had to be performed with tact and with skill precisely because he discovered that so many of the people in his survey were married men and family men. Indeed, one of the great merits of Humphreys' research is that it reveals clearly etched class, ethnic, political and occupational characteristics of sexual participants never before properly understood. Had he not conducted the follow-up interviews, we would once again be thrown back on simpleminded, psychological explanations that are truly more voyeuristic than analytic, or on the policeman's kind of knowledge. It is the sociological dimensions of sexuality in public places that make this a truly scientific breakthrough.

To take on the ethic of full disclosure at the point of follow-up interviews was impossible given the purposes of the research. If Humphreys had told his respondents that he knew they were tearoom participants, most of them would have cooperated. But in gaining their cooperation in this way he would have had to reveal that he knew of their behavior. This he could not responsibly do, because he could not control the potentially destructive impact of that knowledge. Folding the participants into a larger sample for a different survey allowed for the collection of the data without posing such a threat. And the purpose of the research was not, after all, destruction, as von Hoffman concedes. Therefore, the posture of Humphreys toward those interviewed must be viewed as humane and considerate.

But what von Hoffman is arguing is that this research ought not to have been done, that Humphreys should have laid aside his obligation to society as a sociologist and taken more seriously his obligation to society as a citizen. Von Hoffman maintains that the researcher's intentions—the pursuit of truth, the creation of countervailing knowledge, the demystification of shadowy areas of human experience—are immaterial. "Everybody who goes snooping around and spying on people can be said to have good motives," von Hoffman writes, going on to compare Humphreys' work with policemen armed with a "no-knock" statute.

This is offensive, but it is also stupid. We have called von Hoffman a moralizer, and his moralizing consists precisely in his imputing a moral equivalence to police action, under probably unconstitutional law, and the work of a scholar. Of course the road to hell is paved with good intentions, but good intentions sometimes lead to other places as well. The great achievement of Humphreys' research has been in laying bare the conditions of the tearoom trade, the social classes who engage in such activities and the appalling idiocy and brutality of society's (police) efforts to cope with the situation. Moreover, he has, relative to some of his professional colleagues, answered the question Which side are you on? with uncharacteristic candor, while at the same time he has conducted himself in the best tradition of professional sociology.

The only interesting issue raised by von Hoffman is one that he cannot, being a moralizer, do justice to. It is whether the work one does is good, and whether the good it does outweighs the bad. "No information," he writes, "is valuable enough to obtain by nipping away at personal liberty. . . ." It remains to be proven that Humphreys did in fact nip away at anyone's liberty; so far we have only von Hoffman's assertion that he did and Humphreys' assurance that he did not. But no amount of self-righteous dogmatizing can still the uneasy and troublesome thought that what we have here is not a conflict between nasty snoopers and the right to privacy, but a conflict between two goods: the right to privacy and the right to know.

What is required is a distinction between the responsibilities of social scientists to seek and to obtain greater knowledge and the responsibilities of the legal system to seek and obtain maximum security for the private rights of private citizens. Nothing is more insidious or dangerous than the overprofessionalization of a trade. But for social scientists to play at being lawyers, at settling what the law is only now beginning to give attention to, is clearly not a sound way of solving the problems raised.

LIBERAL CONTRADICTIONS

It is certainly not that sociologists should deliberately violate any laws of the land, only that they should leave to the courtrooms and to the legislatures just what interpretation of these laws governing the protection of private citizens is to be made. Would the refusal of a family to disclose information to the Census Bureau on the grounds of the right to privacy take precedence over the United States government's right to knowledge in order to make budgetary allocations and legislation concerning these people? The really tough moral problem is that the idea of an inviolable right of privacy may move counter to the belief that society is obligated to secure the other rights and welfare of its citizenry. Indeed one might say that this is a key contradiction in the contemporary position of the liberal: he wants to protect the rights of private citizens, but at the same time he wants to develop a welfare system that could hardly function without at least some knowledge about these citizens. Von Hoffman's strident defense of the right to privacy is laudable; we are all behind him. What is inexcusable in someone of his intelligence is that he will not see that the issues he raises pose a moral dilemma that cannot be resolved in the abstract, only in the particular case. He may think that Humphreys' research is the moral equivalent of John Mitchell's FBI. We don't, and we have tried to explain why.

Several other minor points in the von Hoffman article require at least brief recollection. First, *Trans-action* has made no statement until this time on the ethics of the kind of research conducted by Laud Humphreys. Indeed, our editorial statements have always emphasized the right to privacy of the researcher over and against the wishes of established authority. To say that *Trans-action* has defended this piece in terms of "priority of motive" is an error of fact. The intent of *Trans-action* is to present the best available social science research, and we believe Humphreys' work admirably fits that description.

PUBLIC RIGHTS AND PRIVATE AGONY

Finally, von Hoffman's gratuitous linkage of the "conservatives over at the Justice Department" and the "liberals over at the Sociology Department" makes for a pleasant balance of syntax, but it makes no sense in real life terms. The political ideology of Laud Humphreys is first of all not an issue. At no point in the article or outside the article is the question of the political preference of the researcher raised.

We would suggest that von Hoffman is the real "liberal" in this argument, for it is he who is assuming the correctness of the classical liberal argument for the supremacy of the private person over and against the public commonweal. This assumption makes it appear that he is willing to suffer the consequences of the abuse of homosexuals by blackmailers, policemen or would-be participants, but that he is not willing to suffer the consequences of a research design or to try to change the situation by a factual understanding of the social sources of these problems.

Laud Humphreys has gone beyond the existing literature in sexual behavior and has proven once again, if indeed proof were ever needed, that ethnographic research is a powerful tool for social understanding and policymaking. And these are the criteria by which the research should finally be evaluated professionally. If the nonprofessional has other measurements of this type of research, let him present these objections in legal brief and do so explicitly. No such attempt to intimidate Humphreys for wrongdoing in any legal sense has been made, and none is forthcoming. The only indictment seems to be among those who are less concerned with the right to know than they are with the sublime desire to remain in ignorance. In other words, the issue is not liberalism vs. conservatism or privacy vs. publicity, but much more simply and to the point, the right of scientists to conduct their work as against the right of journalists to defend social mystery and private agony.

try to change the situation by a "factual" [illegible] and do so explicitly. [illegible] such attempt to understanding of [illegible] social sources [illegible] for [illegible] in the problem.

[illegible] beyond the [illegible] The only indic[illegible] sexual behavior [illegible] those who are [illegible] to know [illegible] words [illegible] conserva[illegible] but which should [illegible] the [illegible] night [illegible] to [illegible] work, as [illegible] defend [illegible] and [illegible].

Correlation of READINGS IN SOCIOLOGY with Sociology Texts

Text Chs.	Abrahamson SOCIOLOGY American Book, 1969	Aubert ELEMENTS OF SOCIOLOGY Charles Scribner's Sons, 1967
	Related articles in READINGS IN SOCIOLOGY, 4th ed.	
1	**Prologue, 1–5, 7, 8**	**1, 3**
2	**Prologue, 1–5, 7, 8, Appendix C**	**7–9, 13–15, 18–20, 24–26, 60, 61, 89**
3	**4, 10, 12, 14, 18, 27, 28, 32, 35, 42, 50, 52–57, 59, 62–64, 66, 67, 69, 71–73, 86, 91**	**7–9, 13, 18–20, 22–26, 52, 60, 61**
4	**2, 6, 23, 36, 54, 63, 64, 72, 73, 76, 83–88, 93, Epilogue B**	**2, 4, 6–11, 13–15, 18–21, 24–27, 55, 60–62, 67, 68, 77–79, 92, Epilogue A, Appendixes B, C**
5	**10, 18, 27–29, 32, 35, 42, 50, 59, 62, 66, 67, 69, 71–73, 86, 91, Epilogue D**	**40, 41, 43–46, 66, 72, 81, 92**
6	**40, 41, 43–46, 66, 81**	**6, 7, 19, 20, 34, 55, 68, 75, 76, 79, 81, 90, Epilogues A–C, Appendix C**
7	**7–9, 13, 18–20, 24–26, 60, 61**	**6–9, 13–15, 18–20, 24–26, 34, 40, 41, 43–46, 55, 60, 61, 66, 68, 75, 76, 79, 81, 89, 90, Epilogues A–C, Appendix C**
8	**13–15, 52–55, 89**	
9	**38, 41, 47, 48, 60–63, 76, 77, 82, 87**	
10	**2, 4, 6, 7, 10, 11, 14, 15, 20, 21, 24, 26, 27, 55, 60–62, 67, 68, 77–79, 89, 92, Epilogues A, C, Appendixes B, C**	

Text Chs.	Bell and Sirjamaki SOCIAL FOUNDATIONS OF HUMAN BEHAVIOR, 2d ed. Harper and Row, 1965	Bertrand BASIC SOCIOLOGY Meredith Publishing, 1967
	Related articles in READINGS IN SOCIOLOGY, 4th ed.	
1	**Prologue, 1–5, 7, 8, Appendix C**	**Prologue, 1–5, 7, 8**
2	**7–9, 13, 18–20, 24–26, 60, 61**	**26, 28, 32, 42, 50, 59, Epilogue C**
3	**5, 10–15, 18, 43, 55, 70**	**Prologue, 1–5, 7, 8, Appendix C**
4	**5, 10–15, 18, 43, 55, 70**	**7–9, 13, 18–20, 24–26, 60, 61**
5	**5, 10–15, 18, 43, 55, 70**	**7–10, 13, 18–20, 24–26, 55, 60, 61**
6	**5, 10–15, 18, 43, 55, 70**	**5, 10–15, 18, 43, 55, 70**
7	**10, 12, 14, Appendix C**	**5, 10–15, 18, 43, 55, 70**
8	**7, 18–20**	**2, 6, 23, 36, 54, 63, 64, 72, 73, 76, 83–88, 93, Epilogue B**
9	**7, 18–20**	**29–32, 56**
10	**21, 35, 37, 45–48, 58, 62, 66, 80–83**	**40, 41, 43–46, 66, 81**
11	**7, 18–20**	**72, 92**
12	**2, 16, 17**	**19, 29–32, 34, 36, 56, 75, 76, 81, 82, 90, Epilogues A–C**
13	**21, 24**	**6, 7, 20, 55, 68, 79, Epilogue A, Appendix C**
14	**29–32**	**6, 7, 20, 55, 68, 79, Epilogue A, Appendix C**
15	**29–32, 56**	**3, 6, 23, 33–39, 57, 58, 72–74, 76, 81, 83, 88, 90, 92, Epilogues A–C**
16	**26–30**	**2, 4, 10, 11, 14, 15, 21, 24, 26, 27, 60–62, 67, 77–79, 92, Epilogue C, Appendixes B, C**
17	**20, 21**	**14, 52–55**
18	**7, Appendix C**	**12, 38, 47, 48, 60, 61, 63, 64, 76, 77, 82, 87**
19	**7–9, 13–15, 18–20, 22–26, 29–32, 52, 56, 60, 61, 81, 89**	**4, 6, 10, 56, 57, 59, 62, 63, 69, 72, 74, 82, 83, 86, 88, 90–93, Epilogue A**
20	**29–32, 56**	**2, 16, 17**
21	**19, 34, 36, 75, 76, 81, 82, 90, Epilogue A, B**	**10, 18, 35, 62, 66, 67, 69, 71–73, 86, 91, Epilogue D**
22	**2, 4, 10, 11, 14, 15, 21, 24, 26, 27, 60–62, 67, 77–79, 92, Epilogue C, Appendix B**	**10, 18, 35, 62, 66, 67, 69, 71–73, 86, 91, Epilogue D**
23	**27, 28, 32, 42, 50, 59, Epilogue D**	
24	**40, 41, 43–46, 66, 81**	
25	**49, 50**	
26	**2, 6, 23, 36, 54, 63, 64, 72, 73, 76, 83–88, 93, Epilogue B**	
27	**2, 6, 23, 36, 54, 63, 64, 72, 73, 76, 83–88, 93, Epilogue B**	
28	**23–32, 56**	
29	**10, 18, 35, 62, 66, 67, 69, 71–73, 86, 91, 92, Epilogue D**	

Text Chs.	Bierstedt THE SOCIAL ORDER, 3d ed. McGraw-Hill, 1970	Biesanz and Biesanz INTRODUCTION TO SOCIOLOGY Prentice-Hall, 1969
	Related articles in READINGS IN SOCIOLOGY, 4th ed.	
1	**Prologue, 1–5, 7, 8, Appendixes A–C**	**Prologue, 1–5, 7, 8, Appendixes A–C**
2	**18, 19**	**5, 10–15, 18, 43, 55, 70**
3	**18–20**	**5, 10–15, 18, 21, 43, 55, 79**
4	**2, 16, 17**	**10–15, 18, 43, 55, 70**
5	**5, 11**	**5, 10–15, 18, 43, 55, 80**
6	**12, 13, 15**	**29–32, 40, 41, 43–46, 56, 66, 81**
7	**7, 9, 20, 21**	**27, 28, 32, 42, 50, 59, Epilogue C**
8	**11, 15, 21**	**40, 41, 43-46, 66, 81**
9	**22, 23, 81**	**40, 41, 43-46, 66, 81**
10	**29–32, 56**	**21, 35, 37, 45–48, 58, 62, 66, 79, 80–83**
11	**29–32, 49, 50, 56**	**8, 10, 12, 21, 29–32, 35, 37, 45–48, 55, 56, 58, 62, 64, 66, 80–83**
12	**26, 27**	**7–9, 13, 18–20, 24–26, 60, 61**
13	**26–30**	**7–9, 13, 18–20, 24–26, 29–32, 56, 60, 61**
14	**10, 13, 14, 23**	**13–15, 89**
15	**14, 15, 52–55**	**6, 7, 13–15, 20, 55, 68, 79, 89, Epilogue A, Appendix C**
16	**10, 18, 35, 62, 66, 67, 69, 71–73, 86, 91**	**2, 6, 23, 36, 54, 63, 64, 72, 73, 76, 83–88, 93, Epilogue B**
17	**40, 41, 43–46, 66, 81**	**2, 6, 10, 23, 36, 54, 56, 57, 62–64, 72, 73, 76, 83–88, 91, 93, Epilogue B**
18	**21, 35, 37, 45–48, 58, 62, 66, 80–83**	**2, 16, 17**
19	**7–9, 13, 18–20, 25, 26, 60, 61**	**14, 52–55**
20	**2, 6, 23, 36, 54, 63, 64, 72, 73, 76, 83–88, 93, Epilogue B**	**10, 56, 57, 62, 63, 72, 86, 88, 91**
21		**4, 6, 59, 69, 72, 73, 74, 82, 83, 90–93, Epilogue A**

Text Chs.	Broom and Selznick SOCIOLOGY, 4th ed. Harper and Row, 1968	Chinoy SOCIETY, 2d ed. Random House, 1967
	Related articles in READINGS IN SOCIOLOGY, 4th ed.	
1	**Prologue, 1–5, 7, 8, Appendix C**	**Prologue, 1–5, 7, 8, Appendixes A–C**
2	**27, 28, 32, 42, 50, 59, Epilogue D**	**5, 10–15, 18, 29–32, 43, 55, 56, 70**
3	**5–7, 10–15, 18, 20, 23, 26, 36, 43, 54–57, 63, 64, 68, 70, 72, 73, 76, 79, 83–88, 91, 93, Epilogues A, B Appendix C**	**9, 11, 18, 19, 23, 80**
4	**7–9, 13, 18–20, 24–26, 60, 61**	**7–9, 13, 18–20, 24–26, 60, 61**
5	**29–32, 56**	**1–5, 7, 8, Appendix C**
6	**40, 41, 43–46, 66, 81**	**29–31**
7	**6, 27–32, 42, 49, 50, 56, 59**	**14, 52–55**
8	**3, 6, 23, 33–39, 57, 58, 72–74, 81, 83, 88, 90, 92, Epilogues A, B, C**	**22, 23, 40, 41, 43–46, 66, 81**
9	**2, 16–18, 35, 62, 66, 67, 69, 71–73, 86, 91, Epilogue D**	**21, 35, 37, 45–48, 58, 62, 66, 79, 80–83**
10	**2, 3, 5–20, 23–39, 41–46, 50, 55–61, 66, 70, 72–74, 76, 81, 83, 88, 90, 92, Epilogues A, B, D**	**27, 28, 32, 42, 50, 59**
11	**2, 3, 5–20, 23–48, 50, 55–61, 63, 66, 70, 72–74, 76, 77, 81–83, 86, 87, 90, 92, Epilogues A, B, D**	**10, 18, 35, 62, 66, 67, 69, 71–73, 86, 91, Epilogue D**
12	**2, 3, 6–10, 13, 16–20, 23–46, 50, 56–62, 66, 67, 69, 71–74, 76, 81, 83, 86, 88, 90–92, Epilogues A, B, D**	**10, 56, 57, 62, 63, 72, 86, 88, 89**
13	**10, 18, 35, 62, 66, 67, 69, 71–73, 86, 91, Epilogue D**	**4, 6, 59, 69, 72, 82, 83, 90–93, Epilogue A**
14	**10, 56, 57, 62, 63, 72, 86, 88, 91**	**12, 64**
15	**4, 6, 19, 34, 59, 69, 72–76, 81–83, 90–93, Epilogues A, B, C**	**38, 47, 48, 60, 61, 63, 76, 77, 82, 87**
16		**54, 63, 87, Epilogue D**
17		**2, 16, 17**
18		**2, 4, 10, 11, 14, 15, 21, 24, 26, 27, 60–62, 67, 77–79, 92, Epilogue C, Appendix B**
19		**6, 7, 20, 22, 23, 55, 68, 79, Epilogue A, Appendix C**
20		**2, 6, 23, 36, 38, 54, 58, 63, 64, 72, 73, 76, 82–88, 93, Epilogue B**
21		**2, 3, 8**

Text Chs.	Cuber SOCIOLOGY, 6th ed. Meredith Corporation, 1968	DeFleur, D'Antonio, DeFleur SOCIOLOGY: MAN IN SOCIETY Scott, Foresman, 1971
	Related articles in READINGS IN SOCIOLOGY, 4th ed.	
Prologue		**Prologue, 1–5, 7, 8, Appendix C**
1	**Prologue, Appendix A**	**19, 27–32, 34, 42, 50, 56, 59, 75, 76, 81, 90, Epilogues A–D**
2	**1–4**	**2, 4, 10, 11, 14, 15, 21, 26, 27, 29–32, 40, 43–46, 50, 52, 56, 59, 60–62, 66, 67, 77–79, 81, 92 Epilogue C, Appendix B**
3	**Prologue, 5, Appendixes, B, C**	**5, 10–15, 18, 43, 55, 70**
4	**27, 28, 74, 89, 92**	**7–9, 13, 18–20, 24–26, 29–32, 56, 60, 61,**
5	**5, 10–15, 18, 43, 55, 70**	**7–9, 13, 18–20, 24–26, 60, 61**
6	**5, 10–15, 18, 43, 55, 70**	**2, 6, 23, 36, 54, 63, 64, 72, 73, 76, 83–88, 93, Epilogue B**
7	**10, 55, 70**	**4, 6, 14, 22, 23, 38, 40, 41, 43–48, 52–55, 59–61, 63, 66, 69, 74, 76, 77, 81–83, 86, 90–93, Epilogue A**
8	**2, 6, 23, 36, 54, 63, 64, 72, 73, 76, 83–88, 93, Epilogue B**	**2, 16, 17, 72, 73**
9	**7, 8, 19, 20**	**10, 18, 35, 62, 66, 67, 69, 71–73, 86, 91, Epilogue D**
10	**7–9, 13, 18–20, 24–26, 60, 61**	**21, 34, 35, 37, 45–48, 52, 62, 66, 75, 76, 79, 80–83, 90**
11	**7–9, 13, 18–20, 24–26, 60, 61**	**3, 6, 23, 33–39, 57, 58, 72–74, 76 81, 83, 88, 90, 92, Epilogues A, B, D**
12	**13–15, 89**	**2, 4, 6, 7, 10, 11, 14, 15, 20, 21, 24, 26, 27, 55, 60–62, 67, 68, 77–79, 92, Appendix C**
13	**6, 7, 20, 55, 68, 79, Epilogue A, Appendix C**	**3, 6, 23, 33–39, 57, 58, 72–74, 76, 81, 83, 88, 90, 92, Epilogues A, B, D**
14	**21, 24, 60, 61, 80**	**4, 6–9, 13, 18–20, 24–26, 34, 59–61, 69, 72, 74–76, 81–83, 90–93, Epilogues A–C**
15	**7–9, 13, 18–20, 22–26, 52, 60, 61**	**10, 18, 27, 28, 32, 35, 42, 50, 56, 57, 59, 62, 63, 66, 67, 69, 71–73, 86, 88, 91, Epilogue D**
16	**29–32, 56**	**2, 6, 14, 23, 36, 52–55, 63, 64, 72, 73, 76, 83–88, 93, Epilogue B**
17	**27, 42, 50**	**12, 40, 41, 43–46, 64, 66, 81**
18	**21, 35, 37, 45–48, 50, 62, 66, 79, 80–83**	**27, 38, 40–48, 50, 60, 61, 63, 66, 76, 77, 81, 82, 87**
19	**2, 16, 17**	
20	**10, 18, 35, 62, 66, 67, 69, 71–73, 86, 91, Epilogue C**	
21	**10, 18, 35, 62, 66, 67, 69, 71–73, 86, 91, Epilogue C**	
22	**40, 41, 43–46, 66, 81**	
23	**49, 50**	
24	**14, 52–55**	
25	**10, 56, 57, 62, 63, 72, 86, 88, 91**	
26	**4, 6, 59, 69, 74, 82, 83, 90–93, Epilogue A**	
27	**38, 47, 48, 60, 61, 63, 76, 77, 82, 87**	
28	**12, 64**	
29	**27, 28, 32, 42, 50, 59, Epilogue C**	
30	**72, 92**	
31	**29–32, 56**	
32	**6, 16, 17, 37, 43, 44, 51, 55, 66, 68, 74, 82, 84, 85, 88–90, Epilogue D**	
Epilogue		**Prologue, Epilogue B, D, Appendix A, B**

Text Chs.	Dressler SOCIOLOGY: THE STUDY OF HUMAN INTERACTION Alfred A. Knopf, 1969	Green SOCIOLOGY, 5th ed. McGraw-Hill, 1968
	Related articles in READINGS IN SOCIOLOGY, 4th ed.	
1	**Prologue, 1–5, Appendix A**	**Prologue, 1–5, 7, 8, Appendixes A–C**
2	**7, 8, Appendixes B, C**	
3	**5, 10–15, 18, 43, 55, 70**	**22, 23, 29–32, 40, 41, 43–46, 52, 56, 66, 81**
4	**10, 55, 70**	**29–32, 56**
5	**6, 7, 13–15, 20, 55, 68, 79, 89, Epilogue A, Appendix C**	**5, 10–15, 18, 43, 55, 70**
6	**15, 49, 50**	**5, 10–15, 18, 43, 55, 70**
7	**2, 6, 23, 36, 54, 63, 64, 72, 73, 76, 83–88, 93, Eilogue B**	**7–9, 13, 18–20, 24–26, 60, 61**
8	**9, 20, 21**	**7–9, 13, 18–20, 24–26, 60, 61**
9	**7–9, 13, 18–20, 24–26, 60, 61**	**2, 16, 17**
10	**6, 7, 20, 55, 68, 79, Epilogue A, Appendix C**	**40, 41, 43–46, 66, 81**
11	**29–32, 56**	**41, 46**
12	**27, 28, 32, 42, 50, 59, Epilogue D**	**21, 35, 37, 45–48, 58, 62, 66, 80–83**
13	**27, 28, 33, 34, 74, 89, 92**	**10, 18, 35, 62, 66, 67, 69, 71–73, 86, 91, Epilogue D**
14	**22, 23, 52, 81**	**27, 40–46, 50, 66, 81**
15	**40, 41, 43–46, 66, 81**	**14, 52–55**
16	**10, 18, 35, 62, 66, 67, 69, 71–73, 86, 91, Epilogue D**	**14, 52–55**
17	**29, 30–32, 56**	**8, 10, 12, 55, 64**
18	**4, 16, 17, 37, 43, 44, 51, 55, 56, 66, 68, 74, 82, 84, 85, 88–90, Epilogue D**	**8, 10, 12, 55, 64**
19	**2, 16, 17**	**10, 56, 57, 62, 63, 72, 86, 88, 91**
20	**21, 35, 37, 45–48, 58, 62, 66, 79, 80–83**	**4, 6, 59, 69, 74, 82, 83, 90–93, Epilogue A**
21	**31, 43, 44, 51, 62**	**2, 4, 10, 11, 14, 15, 21, 24, 26, 27, 60–62, 67, 77–79, 92, Epilogue C, Appendix B**
22	**68, 89**	**2, 4, 10, 11, 14, 15, 21, 24, 26, 27, 60–62, 67, 77–79, 92, Epilogue C, Appendix B**
23	**49, 50**	**63, 65**
24	**14, 52–55**	**23, 26, 36, 54, 63, 64, 72, 73, 76, 83–88, 93, Epilogue B**
25	**12, 64**	**6, 74, 84, 85, 88–92, Epilogues A–D**
26	**38, 47, 48, 60, 61, 63, 76, 77, 82, 87**	
27	**4, 6, 10, 56, 57, 59, 62, 63, 69, 72, 74, 82, 83, 86, 88, 90–93, Epilogue A**	
28	**Prologue**	

Text Chs.	Himes THE STUDY OF SOCIOLOGY Scott, Foresman, 1968	Horton and Hunt SOCIOLOGY, 2d ed. McGraw-Hill, 1968
	Related articles in READINGS IN SOCIOLOGY, 4th ed.	
1	**Prologue, 1–5, 7, 8, Appendix C**	**1–5, 7, 8, 54, 63, 87, Epilogue D, Appendixes A–C**
2	**Appendixes A, B**	**Prologue, 1–5, 7, 8, Appendixes A–C**
3	**27, 28, 32, 42, 50, 59, Epilogue D**	**5, 10–15, 18, 43, 55, 70**
4	**5, 10–15, 18, 43, 55, 70, 89**	**5, 10–15, 18, 43, 55, 70**
5	**29–32, 56, 79**	**7–9, 13, 18–20, 24–26, 60, 61**
6	**27, 28, 32, 42, 50, 59**	**22–24, 34, 52, 81**
7	**10, 18, 35, 62, 66, 67, 69, 71–73, 86, 91**	**2, 4, 6, 7, 10, 11, 14, 15, 20, 21, 24, 26, 27, 55, 60–62, 67, 68, 77–79, 92, Epilogue C, Appendixes B, C**
8	**4, 6, 10, 57, 59, 62, 63, 69, 72, 74, 82, 83, 86, 88, 90–93, Epilogue A**	**29–32, 56**
9	**8, 10, 12, 14, 38, 47, 48, 52–55, 60, 61, 63, 64, 76, 77, 82, 87**	**27, 28, 32, 42, 49, 50, 59, Epilogue D**
10	**2, 16, 17**	**14, 52–55**
11	**40, 41, 43–46, 66, 81**	**40, 41, 43–46, 66, 81**
12	**7–9, 13, 18–20, 24–26, 60, 61**	**41, 46**
13	**6–9, 13, 18–20, 24–26, 55, 60, 61, 68, 79, Epilogue A, Appendix C**	**19, 34, 36, 75, 76, 81, 82, 90, Epilogues A–C**
14	**27, 28, 74, 89, 92**	**34, 38, 72, 77, 92**
15	**3, 6, 23, 33–39, 57, 58, 72–74, 76, 81, 83, 88, 90, 92, Epilogues A, B, D**	**21, 35, 37, 45–48, 58, 62, 66, 79, 80–83**
16	**6, 16, 17, 23, 26, 36, 37, 43, 44, 51, 54, 55, 63, 64, 66, 68, 72–74, 76, 82, 83, 88–90, 93, Epilogues B, D**	**3, 6, 23, 33–39, 57, 58, 72–76, 81, 83, 88, 90, 92, Epilogues A, B, D**
17		**2, 16, 17**
18		**10, 18, 35, 62, 66, 67, 69, 71–73, 86, 91, Epilogue D**
19		**23, 26, 36, 54, 63, 64, 72, 73, 76, 83–88, 93, Epilogue B**
20		**3, 6, 23, 33–39, 57, 58, 72–74, 76, 81, 83, 88, 90, 92, Epilogues A, B, D**

Text Chs.	Lenski HUMAN SOCIETIES McGraw-Hill, 1970	Lowry and Rankin SOCIOLOGY: THE SCIENCE OF SOCIETY Charles Scribner's Sons, 1969
	Related articles in READINGS IN SOCIOLOGY, 4th ed.	
1	**Prologue, 18, 19**	**Prologue, 1–5, 7, 8, Appendixes A–C**
2	**7–9, 18–21**	**7–9, 13, 18–20, 24–28, 32, 42, 50, 59–61, Epilogue D**
3	**8, 18, 19**	**5, 10–15, 18, 43, 55, 70**
4	**8, 21, 24, 85, Epilogues B–D**	**19, 30–32, 34, 36, 56, 75, 76, 79, 81, 82, 90, Epilogues A–C**
5	**2, 6, 8, 23, 36, 54, 63, 64, 72, 73, 76, 83–88, 93**	**3, 6, 23, 27, 28, 33–39, 57, 72–74, 76, 81, 83, 88–90, 92, Epilogues A, B, D**
6	**27, 28, 32, 42, 50, 59, Epilogue D**	**40, 41, 43–46, 66, 81**
7	**10, 18, 19, 85**	**27–32, 42, 50, 56, 59, Epilogue D**
8	**10, 12, 18, 19**	**10, 18, 35, 55, 62, 66, 67, 69, 70–73, 86, 91, Epilogue D**
9	**10, 12, 18, 19, 73, 88**	**49, 50**
10	**29, 63**	**2, 4, 6, 7, 10, 11, 14, 15, 20, 21, 24, 26, 27, 55, 60–62, 67, 68, 77–79, 92, Epilogues A, C, Appendixes B, C**
11	**56, 63, 71, 84, 88**	**2, 6, 16, 17, 23, 36, 54, 63, 64, 72, 73, 76, 83–88, 93, Epilogue B**
12	**2, 4, 6, 16–18, 27, 28, 32, 35, 42, 50, 59, 62, 66, 67, 69, 71–74, 82, 83, 86, 90–93, Epilogues A, D**	
13	**10, 40, 41, 43–46, 56, 57, 62, 63, 66, 72, 81, 86, 88, 91**	
14	**8, 10, 12, 14, 52–55, 64**	
15	**2, 6, 23, 36, 54, 63, 64, 72, 73, 76, 83–88, 93, Epilogue B**	
16	**6, 91, 92, Epilogues A–D**	

Text Chs.	Lundberg, Schrag, Larsen, and Catton SOCIOLOGY, 4th ed. Harper and Row, 1968	McKee INTRODUCTION TO SOCIOLOGY Holt, Rinehart and Winston, 1969
	Related articles in READINGS IN SOCIOLOGY, 4th ed.	
1	**Prologue, 1–5, 7, 8, Appendix C**	**Prologue, 1–5, 7, 8, Appendix C**
2		**Prologue, 5, Epilogues B, D**
3	**29–32, 56**	**Prologue, 1–5, 7, 8, Appendix C**
4	**16, 62, 91**	**29–32, 56**
5	**22, 23, 52**	**2, 4, 5, 7–15, 18–21, 24–27, 29–32, 55, 56, 60–62, 67, 70, 77–79, 89, 92**
6	**5, 10–15, 18, 43, 55, 70**	**7–9, 13, 18–20, 24–26, 60, 61**
7	**4, 6, 8, 10, 12, 55, 59, 64, 69, 74, 82, 83, 90–93, Epilogue A**	**29–32, 56**
8	**7, 9, 21, 33, 74, 78, 79**	**27, 28, 32, 42, 50, 59, Epilogue D**
9	**9, 15, 18–20, 25**	**10, 18, 35, 62, 66, 67, 69, 71–73, 86, 91, Epilogue D**
10	**21, 24, 60, 61**	**22, 23, 40, 41, 43–46, 66, 81**
11	**21, 56, 80**	**21, 35, 37, 45–48, 58, 62, 66, 79, 80–83**
12	**40–46, 66, 81**	**31, 40, 41, 43–46, 51, 62, 66, 81**
13	**22, 23, 27, 29–32, 42, 50, 52, 56**	**14, 52–55**
14	**38, 47, 48, 60, 61, 63, 76, 77, 82, 87**	**38, 47, 48, 60, 61, 63, 76, 77, 82, 87**
15	**33, 57, 90, 92**	**10, 56, 57, 62, 63, 72, 86, 88, 91**
16	**3, 6, 23, 33–39, 57, 72–74, 76, 81, 83, 88, 90, 92, Epilogues A, B, D**	**4, 6, 59, 69, 72–74, 82, 83, 90–93, Epilogue A**
17	**6, 37–39, 43, 44, 48, 54, 55, 62, 66, 68, 84, 85**	**54, 63, 87, Epilogue D**
18	**6, 7, 20, 55, 68, 79, Epilogue A, Appendix C**	**12, 64**
19	**2, 6, 23, 36, 54, 63, 64, 72, 73, 76, 83–88, 93, Epilogue B**	**3, 6, 23, 33–39, 57, 58, 72–74, 76, 81, 83, 88, 90, 92, Epilogues A, B, D**
20	**31, 36–38, 58, 81–83**	**3, 6, 23, 33–39, 57, 58, 72–74, 76, 81, 83, 88, 90, 92, Epilogues A, B, D**
21	**10, 56, 57, 62, 63, 72, 86, 88, 91**	**2, 16, 17**
22	**2, 16, 17**	**6, 7, 16, 17, 20, 37, 43, 44, 51, 66, 68, 74, 79, 82, 84, 85, 88–90, Epilogues A, D, Appendix C**
23	**49, 50**	**6, Appendixes A, B**
24	**Prologue, 5, Epilogues B, D**	

	McNall THE SOCIOLOGICAL EXPERIENCE, rev. ed. Little, Brown, 1971	Mack and Young SOCIOLOGY AND SOCIAL LIFE, 4th ed. American Book Company, 1968
Text Chs.	**Related articles in READINGS IN SOCIOLOGY, 4th ed.**	
1	**Prologue, 1–5, 7, 8**	**Prologue, 1–5, 7, 8, 54, 63, 87, Epilogue D, Appendix C**
2	**Prologue, 7, 18, 19**	**29–32, 56**
3	**Prologue, 1–5, 7, 8**	**5, 10–15, 18, 43, 55, 70**
4	**5, 10–15, 18, 43, 55, 70**	**10, 13–15, 55, 70, 89**
5	**29–32, 56**	**7–9, 13, 18–20, 24–26, 60, 61**
6	**7–9, 13, 18–20, 24–26, 60, 61**	**53, 61, 64, 72**
7	**27, 29–32, 42, 50, 56**	**19, 34, 36, 75, 76, 81, 82, 90, Epilogues A–C**
8	**2, 16, 17**	**22, 23, 52, 81**
9	**10, 18, 35, 62, 66, 67, 69, 71–73, 86, 91, Epilogue D**	**40, 41, 43–46, 66, 81**
10	**40, 41, 43–46, 66, 81**	**41, 46**
11	**6, 7, 20, 55, 68, 79, Epilogue A, Appendix C**	**21, 35, 37, 41, 45–48, 58, 62, 66, 79, 80–83**
12	**3, 6, 23, 33–39, 57, 58, 72–74, 76, 81, 83, 88, 90, 92, Epilogues A, B, D**	**2, 16, 17**
13	**3, 6, 23, 33–39, 57, 58, 72–74, 76, 77, 81, 83, 88, 90, 92, Epilogues A, B, D**	**10, 18, 35, 62, 66, 67, 69, 71–73, 86, 91, Epilogue D**
14	**21, 35, 37, 45–48, 58, 62, 66, 79, 80–83**	**10, 18, 35, 62, 66, 67, 69, 71–73, 86, 91, Epilogue D**
15	**14, 52–55**	**10, 18, 35, 62, 66, 67, 69, 71–73, 86, 91, Epilogue D**
16	**4, 6, 59, 69, 72–74, 82, 83, 90–93, Epilogue A**	**49, 50**
17	**12, 64**	**14, 52–55**
18		**38, 47, 48, 60, 61, 63, 76, 77, 82, 87**
19		**12, 64**
20		**10, 56, 57, 62, 63, 72, 86, 88, 91**
21		**4, 6, 59, 69, 74, 82, 83, 90–93, Epilogue A**
22		**6, 7, 20, 55, 68, 79, Epilogue A, Appendix C**
23		**2, 6, 23, 36, 54, 63, 64, 72, 73, 76, 83–88, 93, Epilogue B**
24		**16, 17, 93, Epilogues B, D**

	Mercer and Wanderer THE STUDY OF SOCIETY Wadsworth Publishing Company, 1970	Merrill SOCIETY AND CULTURE, 4th ed. Prentice-Hall, 1969
Text Chs.	**Related articles in READINGS IN SOCIOLOGY, 4th ed.**	
Introduction		**Prologue, 1–5, 7, 8**
1	**Prologue, 1–5, 7, 8, Appendix C**	**29–32, 56**
2	**5, 7–15, 18–20, 24–26, 43, 55, 60, 61, 70**	**29–32, 56**
3	**7–9, 13, 18–20, 24–26, 60, 61**	**29–32, 56**
4	**19, 22, 23, 29–32, 34, 36, 56, 75, 76, 81, 82, 90, Epilogues A–C**	**13–15, 89**
5	**6, 7, 16, 17, 20, 37, 43, 44, 51, 55, 66, 68, 74, 79, 82, 84, 85, 88–90, Epilogues A, D, Appendix C**	**5, 10–15, 18, 43, 55, 70**
6	**3, 6, 23, 29–39, 56, 57, 72–74, 76, 81, 83, 88, 90, 92**	**7–9, 13, 18–20, 24–26, 60, 61**
7	**22, 23, 40, 41, 43–46, 66, 81**	**22, 23, 52**
8	**21, 35, 37, 45–48, 58, 62, 66, 79, 80–83**	**6, 7, 20, 55, 68, 79, Epilogue A, Appendix C**
9	**14, 49, 50, 52–55**	**21, 35, 37, 45–48, 58, 62, 66, 79, 80–83**
10	**12, 27, 28, 32, 34, 50, 64**	**40, 41, 43–46, 66, 81**
11	**38, 47, 48, 50, 59–61, 63, 76, 77, 82, 87**	**40, 41, 43–46, 66, 81**
12	**4, 6, 27, 28, 32, 42, 50, 59, 69, 72–74, 82, 83, 90–93, Epilogue A**	**41, 46**
13	**10, 27, 28, 32, 42, 50, 56, 57, 59, 62, 63, 72, 86, 88, 91**	**49, 50**
14	**2, 16, 17**	**14, 52–55**
15	**10, 18, 35, 62, 66, 67, 69, 71–73, 86, 91**	**27, 42, 50**
16	**2, 6, 23, 36, 54, 63, 64, 72, 73, 76, 83–88, 93, Epilogue D**	**10, 18, 35, 62, 66, 67, 69, 71–73, 91**
17		**2, 6, 23, 36, 54, 63, 64, 72, 73, 76, 83–88, 93, Epilogue B**
18		**3, 6, 23, 33–39, 57, 58, 72–74, 76, 81, 83, 88, 90, 92, Epilogues A, B, D**
19		**3, 6, 23, 33–39, 57, 58, 72–74, 76, 81, 83, 88, 90, 92, Epilogues A, B, D**
20		**27, 28, 74, 89, 92**
21		**6, 16, 17, 37, 43, 44, 51, 55, 66, 68, 74, 82, 84, 85, 88–90, Epilogues C, D**

Text Chs.	Nisbet THE SOCIAL BOND Alfred A. Knopf, 1970	Phillips SOCIOLOGY: SOCIAL STRUCTURE AND CHANGE Macmillan, 1969
	Related articles in READINGS IN SOCIOLOGY, 4th ed.	
1	**Prologue, 1–5, 7, 8, Appendix C**	**Prologue, 1–5, 7, 8, Appendix C**
2	**Prologue**	**18–20**
3	**13–15, 22, 23, 29–32, 52, 56, 89**	**29–32, 49, 56**
4	**29–32, 56**	**7–9, 13, 18–20, 24–26, 60, 61**
5	**29–32, 56**	**7–9, 13, 14, 18–20, 24–26, 52–55, 60, 61**
6	**72, 92**	**27–32, 42, 50, 56, 59, Epilogue C**
7	**22, 23, 52**	**14, 22, 23, 52**
8	**22, 23, 81**	**40, 41, 43–46, 66**
9	**2, 12, 13–17, 64, 89, Epilogue B**	**21, 35, 37, 45–48, 58, 62, 66, 80–83**
10	**6, 7, 20. 55, 68, 79, 89, Epilogue A, Appendix C**	**2, 16–18, 35, 62, 66, 67, 69, 71–73, 86, 91, Epilogue D**
11	**2, 6, 23, 36, 54, 63, 64, 72, 73, 76, 83–88, 93, Epilogue B**	**10, 56, 57, 62, 63, 72, 86, 88, 91**
12	**6, 83–88, 91, 92, Epilogue D**	**8, 10, 12, 55, 64**
13	**Prologue, Epilogues A–D**	**38, 47, 48, 54, 60, 61, 63, 76, 77, 82, 87, 88, Epilogue D**
14	**5, 42, 53, 63, 64, 93**	**4, 6, 59, 69, 72–74, 82, 83, 90–93, Epilogue A**
15		**10, 18, 35, 62, 66, 67, 69, 71–73, 86, 91, Epilogue D**
16		**3, 6, 23, 33–39, 57, 58, 72–74, 76, 81, 83, 88, 90, 92, Epilogues A, B, D**
17		**2, 6, 23, 36, 54, 63, 64, 72, 73, 76, 83–88, 93, Epilogue B**
Epilogue	**Prologue, 5, 6**	

Text Chs.	Remmling and Campbell BASIC SOCIOLOGY Littlefield, Adams, 1970	Rose and Rose SOCIOLOGY: THE STUDY OF HUMAN RELATIONS, 3d ed. Alfred A. Knopf, 1969
	Related articles in READINGS IN SOCIOLOGY, 4th ed.	
1	**Prologue**	**Prologue, 1–5, 7, 8, 18, 19, Appendix C**
2	**Prologue**	**5, 7–15, 18–20, 24–26, 43, 55, 60, 61, 70**
3	**1–5, 7, 8, Appendix C**	**7–9, 13, 18–20, 24–26, 60, 61**
4	**5, 10–15, 18, 43, 55, 70**	**2, 4, 10, 11, 14, 15, 21, 24, 26, 27, 60–62, 67, 77–79, 92, Epilogue C, Appendix B**
5	**5, 10–15, 18, 43, 55, 70**	**49, 50**
6	**2, 4, 10, 11, 14, 15, 21, 24, 26, 27, 60–62, 67, 77–79, 92, Appendix B**	**14, 52–55**
7	**14, 52–55**	**29–32, 56**
8	**14, 52–55**	**4, 6, 10, 12, 38, 47–50, 56, 57, 59–64, 69, 72, 74, 82, 83, 87, 90–93, Epilogue A**
9	**12, 38, 47, 48, 60, 61, 63, 64, 76, 77, 82, 87**	**29–32, 56**
10	**4, 6, 10, 56, 57, 59, 62, 63, 69, 72, 74, 82, 83, 86, 88, 90–93, Epilogue A**	**40, 41, 43–46, 66, 81**
11	**63, 65**	**3, 6, 23, 33–39, 57, 58, 72–74, 76, 81, 83, 88, 90, 92, Epilogues A, B, D**
12		**2, 16, 17**
13	**21, 35, 37, 40, 41–48, 58, 62, 66, 80–93**	**10, 18, 35, 62, 66, 67, 69, 71–73, 86, 91, Epilogue D**
14	**27, 28, 32, 42, 50, 59, Epilogue C**	**2, 6, 23, 36, 54, 63, 64, 72, 73, 76, 83–88, 93, Epilogues B, D**
15	**3, 6, 19, 23, 34–39, 57, 58, 72–76, 81–83, 88, 90, 92, Epilogues A–D**	**19, 34, 75, 76, 79, 81, 90, Epilogues A–C**
16	**2, 6, 16, 17, 23, 36, 37, 43, 44, 51, 54, 55, 63, 64, 66, 68, 72–74, 76, 82–90, 93, Epilogues B, D**	
17	**7–9, 13, 18–20, 24–26, 60, 61**	
18	**Prologue, 1–5, 7, 8, Appendix C**	
19	**Prologue, 1–5, 7, 8, Appendixes A–C**	

	Smelser, ed. SOCIOLOGY: AN INTRODUCTION John Wiley & Sons, 1967	SOCIETY TODAY CRM Books, 1971
Text Chs.	**Related articles in READINGS IN SOCIOLOGY, 4th ed.**	
Introduction	**Prologue, 1–5, Appendix A**	
1	**22, 23, 29–32, 36, 56, 72, 81, 82, 92**	**3, Appendix A**
2	**10, 18, 35, 62, 66, 67, 69, 71–73, 86, 91**	**5, 10–15, 18, 43, 55, 70**
3	**27, 28, 32, 42, 50, 59**	**7, 9, 18–20, 60, 61**
4	**40, 41, 43–46, 66, 81**	**7–9, 13, 18–20, 24–26, 60, 61**
5	**10, 49, 50, 56, 57, 62, 63, 72, 86, 88, 91**	**2, 16, 17**
6	**12, 49, 50, 64**	**10, 18, 35, 62, 66, 67, 69, 71–73, 86, 91, Epilogue C**
7	**38, 47–50, 60, 61, 63, 76, 77, 82, 87**	**35, 37, 48, 62, 66, 67, 71**
8	**4, 6, 49, 50, 69, 74, 82, 83, 90–93, Epilogue A**	**23, 25, 52, 53**
9	**7–9, 13, 14, 18–20, 24–26, 52–55, 60, 61**	**25, 29, 30–32, 56**
10	**7–9, 13, 18–20, 24–26, 60, 61**	**14, 21, 24, 60–62, 65**
11	**6–9, 13, 18–20, 24–26, 55, 60, 61, 68, 79, Epilogue A, Appendix C**	**27, 32, 42, 49, 50**
12	**2, 6, 23, 36, 54, 63, 64, 72, 73, 76, 83–88, 93, Epilogue B**	**27, 32, 41, 46, 56, 65**
13		**40–46, 66, 81**
14		**41, 43, 44, 46, 51**
15		**41, 43, 44, 51**
16		**40, 41, 46, 62, 69**
17		**21, 35, 36, 45–48, 58, 62, 66, 79, 80–83**
18		**14, 52–55**
19		**10, 56, 57, 62, 63, 72, 86, 88, 91**
20		**4, 6, 59, 69, 72–74, 82, 83, 90–93, Epilogue A**
21		**38, 47, 48, 60, 61, 63, 76, 77, 82, 87**
22		**8, 10, 12, 55, 64**
23		**6, 47, 56**
24		**6, 7, 20, 55, 68, 79, Epilogue A, Appendix C**
25		**6, 59, 74**
26		**57**
27		**7, 9, 21, 23, 74, 78, 79**
28		**Prologue, 54, 63, 87, Epilogue D**
29		**65**
30		**2, 6, 23, 36, 54, 63, 64, 72, 73, 76, 83–88, 93, Epilogue B**
31		**3, 6, 23, 33–39, 57, 72–74, 76, 81, 83, 88, 90, 92, Epilogues A, B, D**
32		**33, 34, 37, 77**
33		**34, 90, Epilogues A, B, C**
34		**27, 28, 89**
35		**63, 84–88**
36		**Prologue, 2, Epilogues A–D, Appendix C**

Text Chs.	Toby CONTEMPORARY SOCIETY, 2d ed. John Wiley & Sons, 1971	Vander Zanden SOCIOLOGY: A SYSTEMATIC APPROACH, 2d ed. The Ronald Press, 1970
	Related articles in READINGS IN SOCIOLOGY, 4th ed.	
1	**Prologue, 1–5, 7, 8, 13–15, 22, 23, 29–32, 52, 56, 89**	**Prologue 1–5, 7, 8, Appendix C**
2	**Prologue, 1–5, 7, 8, Appendix C**	**5, 10–15, 18, 43, 55, 70**
3	**5, 10–15, 18, 43, 55, 70**	**7–9, 13, 18–20, 24–26, 60, 61**
4	**7–9, 13, 18–21, 25, 26, 60, 61**	**6, 7, 20, 55, 68, 79, Epilogue A, Appendix C**
5	**7–9, 13, 18–20, 24–26, 60, 61, Appendix C**	**7–9, 13, 18–20, 22–26, 52, 60, 61**
6	**10, 56, 57, 62, 63, 65, 72, 86, 88, 91**	**29–32, 56**
7	**10, 18, 35, 62, 66, 67, 69, 71–73, 86, 91, Epilogue D**	**40, 41, 43–46, 66, 81**
8	**12, 64**	**21, 35, 37, 45–48, 58, 62, 66, 79, 80–83**
9	**4, 6, 59, 69, 72, 74, 82, 83, 90–93, Epilogues A, B**	**3, 6, 23, 33–39, 57, 58, 72–74, 76, 81, 88, 90, 92, Epilogues A, B, D**
10	**27, 28, 32, 42, 50, 59, Epilogue D**	**2, 6, 23, 36, 49, 50, 54, 63, 64, 72, 73, 76, 83–88, 93, Epilogue B**
11	**21, 38, 47, 48, 60, 61, 63, 76, 77, 82, 87**	**2, 6, 14, 23, 36, 52–55, 63, 64, 72, 73, 76, 83–88, 93**
12	**40, 41, 43–46, 66, 81**	**12, 64**
13	**2, 4, 6, 7, 10, 11, 14, 15, 20, 21, 24, 26, 27, 55, 60–62, 67, 68, 77–79, 92, Epilogues A, C, Appendix C**	**10, 56, 57, 62, 63, 72, 86, 88, 91**
14	**2, 6, 23, 35–37, 45–48, 64, 72, 73, 76, 83–88, 93, Epilogue B**	**4, 6, 59, 69, 72–74, 82, 83, 90–93, Epilogue A**
15	**2, 4, 10, 11, 14, 15, 21, 24, 26, 27, 34, 60–62, 67, 77, 78, 92, Epilogue C**	**38, 47, 48, 60, 61, 63, 76, 77, 82, 87**
16		**2, 16, 17**
17		**10, 18, 35, 62, 66, 67, 69, 71–73, 86, 91, Epilogue D**

Text Chs.	Vernon HUMAN INTERACTION The Ronald Press, 1965	Wilson SOCIOLOGY, RULES, ROLES, AND RELATIONSHIPS, rev. ed. The Dorsey Press, 1971
	Related articles in READINGS IN SOCIOLOGY, 4th ed.	
1	**Prologue, 1–5, 7, 8, Appendixes A–C**	**1–5, 7, 8, Appendix C**
2	**1, 3, 5**	**2, 16, 17**
3	**7, 9, 18, 19**	**5, 10–15, 18, 43, 55, 70**
4	**20, 24**	**7–9, 13, 18–20, 24–26, 60, 61**
5	**9, 18, 19**	**14, 29–32, 38, 47, 48, 52–56, 60, 61, 63, 76, 77, 82, 87**
6	**5, 10–15, 18, 43, 55, 70**	**22, 23, 52, 81**
7	**10, 55, 70**	**2, 10, 16–18, 35, 62, 66, 67, 69, 71–73, 86, 91, Epilogue D**
8	**13–15, 89**	**40, 41, 43–46, 66, 81**
9	**22, 23, 52**	**14, 38, 47, 48, 52–55, 60, 61, 63, 76, 77, 82, 87**
10	**7–9, 13, 18–20, 24–26, 60, 61**	**27, 32, 41, 42, 46, 49, 50, 56, 65**
11	**15, 22, 23, 25, 52**	**4, 6, 8, 10, 12, 55, 59, 64, 69, 72–74, 82, 83, 90–93, Epilogue A**
12	**7–9, 13, 18–20, 24–26, 60, 61**	**3, 6, 7, 20, 23, 33–39, 55, 57, 68, 73, 74, 76, 79, 81, 83, 88, 90, 92, Epilogue A, Appendix C**
13	**22, 23, 52**	**41, 69, 84, 85**
14	**3, 6, 23, 33–39, 57, 58, 72–74, 76, 81, 83, 88, 90, 92, Epilogues A, B, D**	**2, 79, Epilogues A–D**
15	**22, 23, 52**	**Prologue, Appendixes A, B, C**
16	**40, 41, 43–46, 66, 81**	
17	**29–32, 56**	
18	**21, 29–32, 35, 37, 45–48, 56, 58, 62, 66, 79, 80–83**	
19	**27, 28, 32, 42, 50, 59, Epilogue D**	
20	**2, 16, 17, 91**	
21	**29–32, 56**	
22	**14, 52–55**	
23	**27, 42, 50**	
24	**8, 10, 12, 55, 64**	
25	**2, 6, 23, 36, 42, 54, 63, 64, 72, 73, 76, 83–88, 93, Epilogue B**	

Text Chs.	Woods INTRODUCTORY SOCIOLOGY Harper and Row, 1966	Worsley INTRODUCING SOCIOLOGY Penguin Books, 1970
	Related articles in READINGS IN SOCIOLOGY, 4th ed.	
1	**Prologue, 1–5, 7, 8, Appendixes A–C**	**Prologue, 1–5, 7, 8, Epilogues A–C**
2	**Prologue, Epilogue D, Appendixes A, B**	**1–3**
3	**Prologue, 1–5, 7, 8, 54, 63, 87, Epilogue D, Appendix C**	**14, 52–55**
4	**7, 9, 18–20**	**7–9, 13, 18–20, 24–26, 38, 47, 48, 60–63, 76, 77, 82, 87**
5	**7–9, 13, 18–20, 24–26, 60, 61**	**27, 32, 41, 46, 49, 50, 56, 65**
6	**2, 5, 6, 10–15, 18, 23, 36, 43, 54, 55, 63, 64, 70, 72, 73, 76, 83–88, 93, Epilogue B**	**62, 63, 66, 68, 69, 71, 84, 85, 89**
7	**29–32, 56**	**40–46, 68, 81**
8	**19, 29–32, 34, 36, 56, 75, 76, 81, 82, 90, Epilogues A–C**	**6, 15, 21, 24, 74, 77–79, 92, 93**
9	**5, 7–15, 18–20, 24–26, 43, 55, 60, 61, 70**	
10	**6, 7, 10, 13–15, 20, 55, 68, 70, 79, 89, Epilogue A, Appendix C**	
11	**22, 23, 52, 81**	
12	**3, 6, 23, 33–39, 57, 58, 72–74, 76, 81, 83, 88, 90, 92, Epilogues A, B, D**	
13	**2, 16, 17**	
14	**40, 41, 43–46, 66, 81**	
15	**21, 35, 37, 45–48, 58, 62, 66, 79, 80–83**	
16	**10, 18, 35, 62, 66, 67, 69, 71–73, 86, 91, Epilogue D**	
17	**4, 6, 12, 14, 27, 28, 32, 42, 49, 50, 52–55, 59, 64, 69, 74, 82, 83, 90–93, Epilogues A, D**	
18	**22, 23, 27–32, 42, 49, 50, 56, 59, 81, Epilogue D**	

INDEX